W9-ABH-542

Praise for The Rough Guide to World Music

"Utterly essential … combines detail with sheer readability.
There is one better way to get a complete planetary
overview, but it involves becoming an astronaut."
Mojo

"A great reference book, put together with care and huge amounts of
detailed knowledge, while simultaneously managing to be a good read.
There are loads of fascinating photos, the connections are well made, and
reading the book feels at times like a treasure hunt for good grooves."
Straight No Chaser

"If you thought the first edition was remarkable, be prepared to have gob firmly
smacked by this one … hard to imagine the job could realistically be done
better by other mere humans … as desert island choices go, you can dispense
with the Shakespeare. They just improved the bible out of recognition."
Folk Roots

"Topnotch."
Q

"Truly comprehensive … authoritative, entertaining and scholarly
without being pedantic. It belongs on every music lover's bookshelf."
Cincinatti Enquirer

"Valuable reference and, at this price, a steal."
Rolling Stone, Australia

"A wealth of information, fun, and a bargain. The challenge, once you've
bought it, will be to control that insatiable urge to acquire exotic new sounds."
Rhythm Magazine

"The bible for World Music writers, musicians and fans … heavily illustrated
and smartly laid out … right up to date. You simply cannot go wrong."
Seattle Times

"Our hotline to cultures under threat from capitalist mass entertainment …
The first edition came like manna from heaven … now we're twice as happy."
Independent

"You may be used to the Rough Guide series being comprehensive, but nothing will prepare you for the exhaustive *Rough Guide to World Music*. We spent an afternoon trying to catch it out in omission and failed miserably ... one of our books of the year."
Sunday Times

"Much vaunted and pretty indispensable."
Time Out

"Very few books on any subject can be truly called indispensable; this is one of the few."
St Petersburg Times, Florida

"One of the best books on music I have seen. It must rank as one of the ten music books one would take to a desert island ... absolutely a must have – the music book of the year."
Passion

"The only reference book world music lovers will ever need."
Berkeley Express

"Heaven on a stick ... the chapter titles seduce you into wanting to read more and more."
dB Magazine

"Truly excellent ... easily the most accessible publication in its field, it's an essential book for anyone with an enquiring ear to the world."
New Internationalist

"A great book ... excels in that it covers a plethora of music scenes and the cultural differences between them."
The Voice

"The most comprehensive survey yet undertaken, and as complete a reference work as you'll find, with the added bonus that it's written by knowledgeable enthusiasts, which keeps the scholarly elements easily digestible."
Tower Records Magazine

"It seems like every page of this amazing resource, *The Rough Guide to World Music*, sends me out to yet another record store trying to find something new that was described so interestingly."
David Harrington, Kronos Quartet

THE ROUGH GUIDE to
World Music
Europe and Asia

compiled and edited by
Simon Broughton, Mark Ellingham
and Jon Lusk

www.roughguides.com

Credits

In-house editors: Kate Berens, Peter Buckley, Duncan Clark,
Tracy Hopkins, Matthew Milton, Neil Foxlee, Joe Staines, Ruth Tidball
Layout: Nikhil Agarwal, Ankur Guha, Jessica Subramanian, Anita Singh
Picture research: Nathaniel Handy
Proofreading: Amanda Jones and Anita Sach
Production: Rebecca Short and Vicky Baldwin
Reference Director: Andrew Lockett

Publishing Information

This third edition published December 2009 by
Rough Guides Ltd, 80 Strand, London WC2R 0RL
375 Hudson St, New York 10014, USA
Email: mail@roughguides.com

Distributed by the Penguin Group:
Penguin Books Ltd, 80 Strand, London WC2R 0RL
Penguin Putnam, Inc., 375 Hudson Street, NY 10014, USA
Penguin Group (Australia), 250 Camberwell Road, Camberwell, Victoria 3124, Australia
Penguin Books Canada Ltd, 90 Eglinton Avenue East, Toronto, Ontario, Canada M4P 2YE
Penguin Group (New Zealand), Cnr Rosedale and Airborne Roads, Albany, Auckland, New Zealand

Printed in Singapore by SNP Security Printing Pte Ltd

Typeset in Minion and Myriad to an original design by Duncan Clark

A catalogue record for this book is available from the British Library

ISBN: 978-1-84353-866-0

1 3 5 7 9 8 6 4 2

Contents

Part 1: Europe

Part 2: Asia

Introduction

Since **The Rough Guide to World Music** first appeared in 1994, the world music scene has grown dramatically. Vast numbers of CDs are released each month, artists from across the world perform regularly in major concert halls in the "West", while festivals of local music have sprung up across the globe. In addition, ease of travel makes it feasible for those in Europe and America to go and experience the music of the world, in person, in situ. Now world music enthusiasts can easily find albums online – sometimes directly from the artist – and attend an ever-increasing number of eclectic festivals. Music can be a window on and a passport to the world.

This third edition of *The Rough Guide to World Music* reflects the music's burgeoning popularity – most obviously in its size. Following on from **Africa & Middle East**, this book, **Europe, Asia & Pacific**, covers a comparably vast territory, and these two volumes together already comprise over one thousand four hundred pages. But then the *Rough Guide* has earned the tag of being the "World Music Bible".

We have strived in this new edition to chart the changing scene, including coverage, for instance, of numerous revivals, which have swept across Europe in recent years. Also represented are the club and DJ scenes, which have been energized by global sounds, with dynamic fusions based on everything from Bhangra beat to Sufi music. We have also addressed omissions in the last edition, with brand new chapters on Sardinia, Slovenia, Bangladesh, Burma and others – as well as musical styles that have become particularly dynamic in the last few years, such as Balkan brass and Gypsy music.

In this volume, our (impossible) aim is to cover European and Asian music of every style – popular and classical, religious and secular, new and traditional. It's music you can buy on CD, see performed at festivals and concerts, and hear in villages, in clubs, at celebrations and on the radio around the world. The book attempts to represent all of these contexts, with nods to key venues, festivals, producers and record labels, as well as singers and instrumentalists.

How the book works

This second volume of *The Rough Guide to World Music* is divided into two sections: **Europe** and **Asia**. Within each section the chapters are arranged alphabetically by country or sometimes by ethnic group – for instance with the music of the Sámi. There are running heads and an index to help you find your way.

Each chapter consists of an article, discography and playlist. The **articles** are designed to provide the background to each country's musical styles, explaining the history, social background, politics and cultural identity, as well as highlighting the lives and sounds of each country's musicians. The **discographies** begin with reviews of compilation albums and then move on to individual artists, each of whom gets a brief biography and a list of recommended recordings. Please note these are selective and not comprehensive discographies, which we hope will lead you into an artist's best work. The ⊙ symbol denotes CDs, ▭ cassettes (which are still prevalent in some regions), ▱ DVDs and ● LPs. Our top recommendations for each country or genre are highlighted with a ★ symbol.

A new feature of this edition are the **playlist** boxes at the end of each discography. These are intended as an alternative way into the music, giving a representative cross-section of the very best tracks that you might want to load onto an iPod or other MP3 player. They are not necessarily available on iTunes yet, but a trawl around the Web (on sites such as *www.mondomix.com*) will often unearth downloadable files.

Enjoy…

About the editors

Simon Broughton was born in London in 1958 and is a writer and filmmaker who has been involved in the world music scene for many years. He is editor of the world music magazine *Songlines*, the leader in its field. Recent TV documentaries for the BBC and Channel 4 include *Sufi Soul: The Mystic Music of Islam* and *Mariza and the Story of Fado*. Broughton was one of the editorial team that produced the first edition of *The Rough Guide to World Music* in 1994 – and remains part of the team today.

Mark Ellingham was a founder of Rough Guides where he worked in many capacities as author or editor on numerous titles including all three editions of *The Rough Guide to World Music*. He left the company in 2007 and currently is a contributing editor at *Songlines* world music magazine, and runs a green and ethical publishing list for Profile Books. He is also a director of the travel magazine *Wanderlust* and co-publisher of Sort Of Books.

Jon Lusk is a New Zealand-born freelance writer and photographer, based in London. He specializes in popular and unpopular music from around the world. His work has appeared in *The Guardian, The Times, The Sunday Times, The Independent*, the *Financial Times, fRoots* and BBC online, among others.

Part 1

Europe

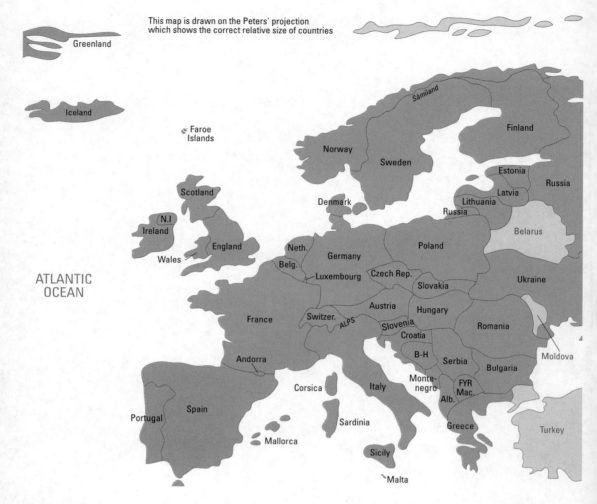

This map is drawn on the Peters' projection which shows the correct relative size of countries

Greenland

Iceland

Faroe Islands

Sámiland

Finland

Norway

Sweden

Estonia

Russia

Latvia

Lithuania

Scotland

Denmark

Russia

Belarus

N.I Ireland

England

Neth.

Poland

Wales

Belg.

Germany

Ukraine

Luxembourg

Czech Rep.

ATLANTIC OCEAN

Slovakia

France

Switzer.

Austria

Hungary

ALPS

Slovenia

Romania

Andorra

Croatia

Moldova

B-H

Serbia

Corsica

Italy

Monte-negro

Bulgaria

FYR Mac.

Spain

Alb.

Portugal

Sardinia

Greece

Mallorca

Turkey

Sicily

Malta

Europe

Albania

wings of song

La Famille Lela de Permet
Indigo

Albania, popularly known as "land of the eagles", came out of isolation after the fall of Communism to meet just about every problem the modern world could throw at it – corruption, economic collapse, crazed pyramid schemes, social disorder, and in 1999 an influx of "ethnically cleansed" refugees fleeing Kosovo. Despite all this, it remains a land of great natural beauty with a fascinating culture and an astonishingly rich, varied and powerful musical tradition. And Albanians are no slouches at picking up modern musical trends, either, claims **Kim Burton**.

The Albanians in the Balkans are divided between the Republic of Albania (3.2 million) on the Adriatic/Ionian Sea, the republics of former Yugoslavia (about 2 million), and Greece. The Albanians of Kosovo in Serbia, where they make up around ninety per cent of the population, together with their cousins in western Macedonia, became separated from those in Albania itself in the early twentieth century when the final collapse of Ottoman imperial power in the Balkans led to the creation of new states and the drawing up of new maps. In the jostling for land and influence that accompanied the formation of these new states, independent Albania ended up as a small strip on the sea, bordered for the most part by forbidding mountains. During the years following World War II, its natural isolation became still more pronounced as the hardline Stalinist regime of Enver Hoxha drew in upon itself, resisting influence from abroad and attempting to enforce unquestioning obedience upon its citizens. With the fall of the Communist government in late 1990, the Albanians found themselves at last able to travel (within immigration constraints), to follow the Western media and to make contact with foreign individuals and ideas without fear of imprisonment, forced labour or internal exile. Yet at the same time, waves of economic and political disasters added to their burdens.

In a sense, the deepest, most secret soul of a people lies in their music, and Albanian music is as rich, complex and beautiful as any. It falls into three major and very different stylistic groups; the contrast between the two cultures of the northern **Ghegs** and the southern **Tosks** and **Labs** is reflected in their music, while the style of the capital **Tirana** and its surrounding area shows the strong **Turkish influence** common to urban music throughout the Balkan region. In a small and separate category, the songs of the northern city of **Shkodër**, which is generally regarded as the most cosmopolitan and sophisticated community in the country, express a romantic and inward character all of their own.

What unites all these styles is the intensity that both performers and listeners give to their music as a medium for patriotic expression and as a vehicle carrying the narrative of **oral history**. Although everybody puts the purely musical content first, composers and performers are always aware of extra-musical meaning. In the days of Hoxha this aspect was forced into service to build support for the Party – even lullabies expressed the wish that the infant would grow up to be a strong worker for Enver.

The collapse of Communism led to a surge of songs dealing either whole-heartedly, or slyly, with the new circumstances: support for political parties, the revival of the custom of *gurbet* (seeking seasonal work abroad), or other changes

Alb Pop

As well as out-and-out Europop, Albania has a wide range of popular music – *muzikë argëtuese* – styles. In the capital, **Tirana**, and central Albania in general, much of the pop has a noticeable Gypsy flavour, exemplified in the hot clarinet-led band of the gravel-voiced **Myslim Leli**, whose tapes and CDs are sold on every street corner. Mixed with influences from the eastern Mediterranean (Turkish music, particularly the oriental and sentimental type known as Arabesk, is very popular in Albania), this forms the basis of the style heard in the work of **Merita Halili** and glamour queen **Parashqvili Simaku**, both of whom are presently living outside Albania and performing for the large emigrant audience in the US and Western Europe.

Much Albanian pop – such as the music of Kosovar megastars **Adelina Ismajli**, **Leonora Jakupi** and the Korçë-born **Bleona Qereti** – borrows heavily from traditional styles. In Kosovo, especially, the folk-pop amalgam has led to an Albanian version to Serbia's **turbofolk** (see p.375). The two strains sound so similar that the number one turbofolk song in Serbia prior to NATO's 1999 bombing was, ironically, a cover of an Albanian one! The biggest stars in this genre include **Ramadan Krasniqi**, **Ilir Shaqiri** and **Afrim Muçiqi**. Distinct from turbofolk is *tallava*, a rougher style popular in cafés around Kosovo. Amongst its leading stars are **Gazmend Rama**, **Mazllum Shaqiri** (**Lumi**) and **Misini**.

Amongst the large army of disenchanted Albanian youth, however, the music of choice is local hip-hop. **Ritmi i Rrugës** from Prishtina sing about issues such as unemployment and the only option open to many young men – organized crime. **West Side Family**, meanwhile, gained prominence by releasing a track featuring the rapping of Edi Rama, the colourful mayor of Tirana. Rama used their joint hit, "Tirona", as his election campaign song.

Nick Nasev

in everyday life. Popular sentiments are greeted with an outbreak of applause even at the most formal of concerts, with the downside being that in the early 1990s there were cases of those found listening to older songs, in praise of the Party, suffering physical assault despite their protestations that they were listening for the music and not the words.

In both Albania itself and Kosovo the **new pop** (see box opposite) continues to fulfil this extra-musical role, while since 1999 in Kosovo more traditional styles continue to celebrate both historical heroes and the Kosovo Liberation Army and its successor, the civilian Kosovo Protection Corps, including songs which in earlier days could lead to arrest or ill-treatment by the authorities and which were sung only in private or circulated clandestinely on cassette.

Epics of the North

Albania itself can be divided roughly into two cultural areas, with the river Shkumbin separating the two. The **Ghegs** of the north also make up the population of Kosovo and the vast majority of the ethnic Albanian population of Macedonia, and much of their music shares a rugged and heroic quality.

The most serious and uncompromising musical form of north Albania is the **sung epic poem**. The oldest type, known as *Rapsodi Kreshnikë* (Poems of Heroes) and accompanied by the singer himself on the one-stringed fiddle, the *lahuta*, sounds very similar to the music of the Montenegrin and Serbian guslars (see p.378), with a set of melodic cells that produce a structure on which poems of immense length can be sung. This music is the province of old men, and when Albanians talk about it they will sweep their fingers across their upper lip with a flourish to express the luxuriant growth of moustache thought necessary for the singer.

Recently, Kosovo has seen a revival of this style, with a number of songs on the subject of the fighting in 1998 and 1999 on releases with such titles as "With Our Boys on the Roads of Freedom", often complete with sound effects of automatic weapons fire and bursting shells and a melodramatic synthesizer backdrop. This tradition is particularly identified with the inhabitants of the remote northern highlands, but another, more accessible ballad tradition is found throughout the Gheg area, with particularly important schools in Dibër (Debar) and Kerçovë (Kičevo) in Macedonia, as well as districts of northern

Albania. Here the singer is accompanied by the *çifteli*, a deceptively simple two-stringed instrument related to the Turkish *saz*; one string carries the melody while the other is used mainly as a drone.

The tales tell of heroes such as the fifteenth-century warrior Skanderbeg, leader of the struggle against the Turks, and they portray semi-historical, semi-mythical events that are bound up with the constant Albanian themes of honour, hospitality, treachery and revenge. The performances can be highly emotional with compelling shifts of rhythm and tempo quite unlike the epics of their Slav neighbours. Up until recently the performers were always men, but women have started to make inroads into the field of epic balladry. In the past the only women performing a traditionally male repertoire were the **Vajze të betuar**, genetic women who lived as men either for reasons of conviction or to ensure that family inheritances were not alienated from the line of descent.

Both epic traditions serve as a medium for oral history in what was until quite recently a pre-literate society (there was not even a generally agreed alphabet until 1909) and also preserve and inculcate moral codes and social values. In a culture that retained the blood-feud as its primary means of law enforcement until well into the twentieth century such codes were literally matters of life and death. Song was one of the most efficient ways of making sure that each member of the tribe was aware of what obligations he or she was bound to.

The çifteli is also used, together with its big brother, the *sharki*, the violin and the tambourine-like *def*, to accompany dances and lyric songs, whose imagery is generally drawn from country life ("You are the flower of the mountain … the morning dew"). Since World War II, bands of massed **çifteli and sharki** have become popular with Albanians both inside and outside Albania. The same repertoire of songs, given an ad hoc harmonization, is performed by small bands based round clarinet and accordion at weddings and feasts.

In the countryside, **shepherds** play for their own amusement using various home-made wind instruments of the type common to shepherds and cowherds throughout the Balkan area. More unusual is the *zumarë*, a double "clarinet" made from two tubes of cane or the hollow bones of a bird tied side-by-side and provided with a simple reed at one end, and with a flaring bell of cow or goat horn at the other. Its tone is piercing and rousing, yet most of its tunes are melancholic and contemplative. The player uses circular breathing, a technique that children learn by blowing through

Hilary Hazzard

A group of singers from Laberia in full polyphonic flow

a straw into a glass of water, trying to keep a continuous stream of bubbles.

The songs of the northern city of **Shkodër** – always the most cosmopolitan of Albanian towns and the centre of intellectual life – are very different to the rural music. Lyrical, romantic and sophisticated, with oriental-sounding scales and a constant interplay of major and minor, they bear an affinity with the *sevdalinke* of Bosnia (see p.42) and the neighbouring Sandžak to the north, but differ from them in their extreme and typically Albanian restraint and the exceptional fluidity of rhythm and tempo. Early descriptions of groups performing such songs, dating from the end of the nineteenth century, suggest a remarkable sound: violin, clarinet, saz, def, sometimes an Indian-style harmonium and percussion provided by rattling a stick between two bottles. These days the accordion and guitar have replaced the more exotic instruments, but the intimate approach of the singers remains the same. Among the great names of the recent past are **Bik Ndoja**, **Florinda Gjergji**, **Shyqyri Alushi** and **Naile Hoxha**, while relatively younger names to watch out for include **Violeta Zefi**, **Bujar Qamili**, **Valdete Hoxha**, **Myfarete Laze**, **Adnan Bala** and **Sabahet Vishnja**.

Roses of the South

The music of the southern Albanians – Tosk and Lab alike – is profoundly different to the determined and heroic northerly traditions. This music, both vocal and instrumental, is relaxed, gentle and exceptionally beautiful. It has a highly developed polyphonic structure, with up to four independent parts, depending on the area from which it comes. The **Labs** have a saying that "one traveller is alone, two will quarrel, but three will sing".

The most complex and strangest of the **vocal styles** – some fine examples of which are to be heard on the Chant du Monde recording *Albanie: Polyphonies Vocales et Instrumentales,* among others – stems from around the port of **Vlorë** in the southwest. Each singer has his or her own title – taker, thrower, turner or drone – and a separate part to play in the rich web of independent lines and sustained notes, decorated with falsetto and vibrato, and sometimes interrupted by wild and mournful cries. Much of the power of this music stems from the tension between the immense emotional weight it carries, rooted in centuries of pride, poverty and oppression, and the strictly formal, almost ritualistic nature of its structure. The force of the songs is extraordinary – unparalleled in any other Balkan music – and the tradition remains vibrantly alive. It's heard and sung with great pleasure, including comic and erotic songs that evoke bursts of laughter and sly looks.

A number of groups – professionals such as **Ensemble Tirana** as well as amateurs or semi-professionals like the groups of shifting and shared membership from Vranisht and Vlorë – have now recorded for Western labels, and make the occasional tour. The reach of this tradition is further extended by singers, notably **Ardit Gjebrea**, who make a point of using such songs in their more popular-flavoured material, albeit as a backdrop rather than an integral part of the music. The last few years have seen the rise of a flourishing sub-genre, with mostly female singers such as **Poni**, **Nertila Vreto** and **Mariola** singing simple melodies over a throbbing groove with copious use of fragments of traditional polyphony, looped and layered.

Tosk music, although it also has a complex polyphonic structure, is gentler, and in small towns the predominant ensemble is one which mixes instruments – violin, clarinet, *llautë* (lute), def and these days often accordion and guitar – with two or three singers. The most important centres are the city of **Korçë**, home of **Eli Fara**, now yet another emigrant but still one of southern Albania's most loved female singers, and the remote mountain town of **Përmet**, one of the great musical centres of Albania and birthplace of two of the country's most important musicians: clarinettists **Laver Bariu**, who still lives there, and the late **Remzi Lela**, founder of an important musical dynasty whose members are now represented in every aspect of musical life in Tirana, from wedding band to symphony orchestra. The group Lela led has been one of the few to have toured and recorded in the West under the title of **La Famille Lela de Përmet**. Albanians say that the most beautiful of Përmet's songs are those sung for the bride at weddings. "The bride stands in the middle of the room, arrayed like the Morning Star", they sing. "The many-petalled rose passes down the lane, the boys and girls follow after her." The **Vëllezërit Curri** (The Curri Brothers) from Përmet and the **Grupi Tepelenës** (from Tepelenë) both have excellent CDs on Albanian labels.

Instrumental music in the south obeys more or less the same rules as the vocal music. Southern Albanians use many string instruments of the lute family related to the Turkish saz and Greek *bouzouki* to perform dance melodies and rhapsodic meditations on slow airs, but the glory of their instrumental music is the **kaba**. A kaba (the word is Turkish meaning "low" or "deep") is a half-improvised melancholy form led by a clarinet or violin supported by a drone from accordion or llautë and usually followed by a dance tune to release the tension. The melodies, ornamented with swoops, glides and growls of an almost vocal quality, sound both fresh and ancient at the same time, and exemplify the combination of passion with restraint that is the hallmark of Albanian culture.

The district of **Dropuli**, south of Gjirokastër, has a sizeable ethnic Greek population, and their music is related to the music of Epirus, south of the border. Using the same scales and rhythmic patterns as their Albanian neighbours, but without the same polyphonic complexity and with a rougher and more aggressive tone, their music is well worth seeking out.

Ben Mandelson

Laver Bariu

Live on Stage...

Unless you are lucky enough to happen across a wedding celebration or other festivity, or to make the acquaintance of a musician, it can be difficult to hear live music in Albania. In previous years the Communist government, besides organizing large orchestras of traditional instruments "in the spirit of collective labour", supported local amateur groups in a network of festivals that culminated in the huge quinquennial event at **Gjirokastër** (on the understanding that every group included a song in praise of Enver Hoxha and the Party). There is little money available now for such festivals (although Gjirokastër looks set to continue while Korçë, Vlorë and Elbasan have their own smaller events, which showcase local styles and performers).

Furthermore, traditional music is out of favour with the younger generation. It still retains its attraction for many young people in the diaspora, as a plethora of websites bears witness. At home however, the only organisation actively involved in promoting such music is **Albanian Radio**

Albanian music in Kosovo and Macedonia

A large number of Albanians, predominantly Ghegs, live outside Albanian's borders in Kosovo and Macedonia, and they make up a significant minority in part of southern Serbia. All these areas have suffered from conflict to a greater or lesser degree. Kosovo in particular is in a troubled situation, independent in name but unrecognized as such by many countries, with a defiant Serbian minority, politically divided and still largely dependent on foreign sponsorship. Albanian music in all these areas is much like that of northern Albania, and ranges from basic violin, çifteli and sharki groups to more urbanized sounds with clarinet, accordion, synthesizer and beat-box. Both Macedonia and Kosovo are home to an extensive recording industry, which pushes out a flood of mostly disposable product. Many singers, including some of the out-and-out pop artists, are equally at home with the most traditional of styles; even the electro-pop hits of the glamorous **Adelina Ismajli** hark back to traditional sounds in one way or another. And the iconic çifteli, especially, is widely played, even by non-professionals.

Singers worth keeping an eye and ear out for include **Violetë Kukaj** (who has also experimented very successfully with songs from Korça), **Shkurte Fejza**, **Mahmut Ferati**, the **Vëllezërit Aliu** (Aliu Brothers), the **Motrat Mustafa** (Mustafa Sisters), and from an earlier generation **Nexhmije Pagarusha** (the "Nightingale of Kosovo", whose rather lush style now seems rather dated) and **Qamili i Vogël**, who died quite recently but retains a large following. There are many other promising names, however, and they can often be found performing abroad in countries with a significant Kosovar Albanian presence.

Television (RTSh), which is hoping to revive the festival network with the aid of private sponsors.

The recording sector is also in a low. In the mid-1990s there was a rush to record all manner of styles (by Vefa-Holding, for instance, part of the pyramid network), but at the moment privately owned labels seem to concentrate on reissues of archive recordings. Piracy presents an enormous problem, and there is little appetite on the part of either musicians or producers to throw good money after bad.

If the pattern of neighbouring countries is repeated, the generation of Albanians following this one will begin to rediscover their traditional music. In the mean time, there are still sporadic concerts at the Opera (the one-time Palace of Culture in central Tirana) but otherwise few opportunities for players or listeners. The poverty of the country means that those usual Balkan venues for bands – cafés and restaurants – either can't afford to employ musicians or, if they can, cater for well-to-do foreigners, the occasional ambitious tourist or the temporary visitor on business. The bands in these restaurants rarely play local music.

Many of the best-known singers are now living abroad, performing for the exile community, and they provide the best opportunity to hear the hard-driving, popular style of Tirana and other large towns. Germany, Switzerland and Austria, in particular, have a wide network of venues where visiting stars play, but they can be difficult to locate.

The more ancient layers of folk music may sometimes be heard at world music festivals abroad, but the best place to catch them is in situ – at a wedding or around the family table. With luck, time and a little persistence, the traveller should be able to make the acquaintance of one of Europe's richest and most beautiful musical traditions.

DISCOGRAPHY Albania

⊙ **Albanian Village Music**
Heritage, UK
An interesting collection of cuts made in Tirana and Shkodër by HMV in 1930, this CD (despite its title) features music from the urban south and north. Very full-throated singing and playing, with very good sound quality considering the date of the recording, make this a very recommendable disc.

★ **Albania: Vocal and Instrumental Polyphony**
Le Chant du Monde, France
More music from the southern Albanian treasure-house, beginning with an astonishing song from Vlorë and ending with a heart-rending piece from Përmet. Most of this is acapella, with a couple of instrumental kabas. Very well recorded.

★ Anthology of World Music
Rounder, USA

A truly excellent selection of recordings made in 1993, concentrating on a few main vocal and instrumental groups, most of which get the chance to perform several numbers, giving a far better in-depth view of the music than most anthologies.

⊙ Dil Moj Dil: Perlat e Jugut
EuroStar, Albania

Pearls from the South, featuring young guns Poni, Ylli Baka and Silva Gunbardha, plus veteran star Hysni Zela, in a startling liaison of the unaccompanied polyphony of the Vlorë district and techno beats. A sunny reminder that Albania is, after all, a Mediterranean country.

⊙ Folk Music of Albania
Topic, UK

The first commercial Western recording of music from Albania, this dates from 1966 but is a good introduction to the music of the country. Unusually, A.L. Lloyd, the compiler, seems to have been able to make some original field recordings instead of relying on "approved" material, and the rough and ready nature of some of the performances is very appealing. It also includes some top-notch çifteli playing.

⊙ Kënga Magjike 2007
Super Sonic Records, Albania

Albania's Magical Songs Festival has been running since 1999, and it celebrates the out-and-out pop singers. This double CD covers the entries for 2007, and features the winning entry by Aurela Gaçe, as well as a host of dance-based or sentimental entries by newcomers and established stars such as Leonora Jakupi.

⊙ Kosovo Gypsies
Archifon, Slovenia

Field recordings from the 1980s and early 1990s, with a content which is by no means exclusively Albanian, but reflects the one-time multi-ethnic nature of the province, and featuring music from a number of the various Rom, Ashkali and other Gypsy groups, some of which is almost impossible to get outside the area. Video clips and fascinating notes are another attraction.

⊙ Marcel Cellier presents Mysterious Albania
ARC, UK/USA

Old-school state-sponsored archive recordings by the man who unleashed the *Bulgarian Mystère* on an unsuspecting world. Well-worth revisiting – although this is not actually particularly mysterious it's very, very good.

⊙ Pays Labe – Plaintes et chants d'amour
Ocora, France

Not actually "various artists" but another nameless group from the villages of Vranisht and Lapardha near Vlorë, covering a number of different styles (each village normally has its own patterns which the singers stick to), this stands out through the well-structured sequencing of very varied tracks. Exceptionally informative notes.

★ Vocal Traditions of Albania
Saydisc, UK

Don't be put off by the rather academic title – this might as easily be called 29 All-time Albanian Greats. Recorded in front of an enthusiastic audience at the 1995 festival in Berat, the music comes from all over the country and includes a couple of examples of the urban songs tremendously popular inside Albania but rarely heard outside. Informative notes are a plus.

Laver Bariu

Përmet's great clarinettist Laver Bariu was a bandleader for over forty years and exerted a tremendous influence on younger generations.

★ Songs from the City of Roses
GlobeStyle, UK

Recorded in Përmet itself, this collection of favourite songs (including a couple of classics by Laver's father) and instrumentals by a group spanning three generations is a great introduction to the southern repertoire. As a bonus it includes a couple of songs and dances learned from musicians in Tirana.

Naxhije Bytyqi

Female performers on the çifteli are not unknown, but they are rare. Bytyqi's singing and playing are outstanding, and as a result she is afforded male privilege in Kosovo's highly patriarchal society.

⊙ Deshmoreve të Pamvarsis
Shqiponja, Kosovo

A compelling performance of a terrific collection of ballads for the Martyrs of Independence. Evidence that traditional singing has not been eclipsed by the popularity of Albanian pop and rap.

Vëllezërit Curri

Elder statesmen from Përmet, and formidable singers.

⊙ Këngë të zgjedhura Përmetare
Super Sonic Records, Albania

To tell the truth, this appears to be a release of older recordings by various artists, but it features Laver Bariu and some of his musicians, and the atmosphere and ensemble playing are immaculate. There are some great songs here.

Eli Fara

Korçë's best known singer, possibly of Vlach origin, living abroad and with a gentle but penetrating voice.

⊙ Më thotë zemra
Vizioni, Kosovo

This is perhaps not the best of her work, but it's recent and easily available, the electronic drums are not as obtrusive as they have been, and the singing and real musicians are marvellous. A nice mix of traditional music and sentimental rock ballads, too.

Mahmut Ferati

This highly regarded singer, born in Macedonia, has lived and worked in Kosovo for many years. He is known for his performances of traditional material with çifteli and sharki, and as a specialist in the Gheg two-voice polyphonic style, which he introduces even in his more modern-styled recordings.

⊙ O, a e di?
L & I, Kosovo

A relatively recent recording, and a good example of the transformation of older styles into a more poppy guitar- and synth-based affair. It mostly features love songs, with a lament for a fallen fighter at the end. Some of the arrangements are by the masterful "Wirusi", whose name on an album generally means it's worth a listen.

Adelina Ismajli

An extremely popular singer with the younger generation, only rivalled by Leonora Jakupi.

⊙ Prej fillimit
Zico Company, Kosovo, Serbia and Montenegro

A solid pop CD but very varied, with a surprising amount of influences and instruments from folk and traditional music.

It's mostly slanted towards the clubbing experience, though admittedly most club hits do not contain quite so much patriotic cheerleading.

Violetë Kukaj – Retkoceri

A fine Kosovar singer from Retkoc village, now living in Prishtina.

⊙ Manushaqe
Arboni, Kosovo
This CD grew out of Kukaj's project to record some songs from the southern Albanian repertoire, and she succeeds extremely well in capturing the spirit of Korçë, with contemporary arrangements that show more sensitivity and restraint than those of some better-known singers from Albania itself. Her more purely Kosovar recordings (for example, *Kёngё tё zgjedhura*) are also well worth hearing.

Famille Lela de Përmet

Based in Tirana, and led by the late Remzi Lela, one of the finest Albanian clarinettists, this ensemble was introduced to the wider world by the much-missed ethnomusicologist Benjamin Kruta. The rest of the family are still active, having colonized the capital's symphony orchestra and opera as well as carrying on with their own traditions.

★ Polyphonies Vocales et Instrumentales d'Albanie
Label Bleu/Indigo, France
A very beautiful and approachable collection of songs from the Përmet and Korçë regions of southern Albania, with clarinet, lute, accordion and violin creating an enchantingly mournful sound. The album showcases the more thoughtful side of the Lela repertoire, and is wonderfully calming.

Grupi Tepelenës

This group from Tepelenë, with many of the musicians hailing from a single family, have a more straightforward style than the Përmet musicians, but with the same subtle weave of voices and instruments.

⊙ Ali Pashai
Shqipja 2000, Albania
Forceful singing and good solid support from the band of clarinet, accordion, def and llautë make this CD very rewarding.

Ensemble Tirana

This Ensemble Tirana (there are more than one) is a group of experienced professional singers, some of them members of the Opera, who tour frequently in Europe.

⊙ Chants polyphoniques d'Albanie
Arco Iris, France
Extremely varied repertoire, solidly sung and with a better representation of Tosk material than usual – though these professional performers are a little less off-the-wall than more locally identified groups.

Hekuran Xhamballi

A Gypsy musician from the south, with a superb sound and a wide repertoire.

⊙ Kaba & Valle d'Albanie
Al Sur, France
The notes to this recording are in English, French, Rromanes and Albanian, which must be a first. It begins with some magnificent renditions of kaba and dance music, and moves on to rather less deep material – and it's none the worse for that.

PLAYLIST
Albania

1 ZENEL KADRIA Mark Pashku from *Folk Music of Albania*
A remarkable ballad with çifteli accompaniment about a CIA-backed coup attempt in the 1950s. "While snow falls, while rain falls, the rifle cracks."

2 VALLE E TIRANËS Laver Bariu from *Songs from the City of Roses*
A slow introduction gives way to a darkly insistent dance, with fine clarinet playing from the master.

3 FUCKERS Adelina Ismajli from *Prej fillimit*
The Diva of Kosovo gets in your face with a peppy little number.

4 MË E MIRA JE Eli Fara from *Më thotë zemra*
Violin and clarinet entwine around Fara's wonderful voice. Sequenced drums push the song forward.

5 ASAMAN MOJ GJËTHEZA Unnamed group from Përmet from *Kёngё tё zgjedhura Përmetare*
A beautiful song from Përmet with a strangely lurching rhythm and gorgeous singing.

6 KARAJFILI KUQ SI GJAKU Pjeter Bushati & Shoqnija Vjerdha from *Albanian Village Music*
A song from one of Shkodёr's finest singers, recorded in 1930 by an HMV expedition, and backed up by a very good band.

7 PO VJEN LUMI TRUBULL-O Vocal group from Labёria region from *Pays Labё: Plaintes et chants d'amour*
The eerie, haunting sound fits the subject of the song – the murky river washes up a drowned boy…

8 DIL MOJ DIL Poni from *Dil moj Dil*
Headlong surfing beats with a good helping of wailing clarinet complementing Poni's compelling vocals, combined with the buzzing, discordant harmonies of the Lab country.

9 SHQIPTARIA BASHKË GJITHMONË Unidentified group from Tropojë district from *Vocal Traditions of Albania*
A ubiquitous melody from north Albania, which can be endlessly repeated to carry heroic and patriotic lyrics for hours at a time. This version, applauding Albanian unity, lasts just over three and a half minutes.

10 MORA RRUGËN PËR JANINË Ensemble Tirana from *Chants Polyphoniques d'Albanie*
A song of emigration receives a heartfelt performance from seven unaccompanied singers.

Alpine Music

traditions and beyond

Stimmhorn
C.H. Buhter

Fifteen years ago the phenomenon of the "Alpine New Wave" was heard for the first time, rocking the beer tents and yodel festivals in the mountains of Switzerland, Austria and southern Germany with Alpine punk and hardcore yodelling. Young musicians had started to do something different with their musical heritage and were stretching the boundaries of the traditions by mixing them with pop, rock and jazz. Today the genre is well established and its main exponent, Hubert von Goisern, has even become a household name. But the search for new forms of expression continues and surprising hybrids and fusions are arriving all the time, as **Christoph Wagner** reports.

Alpine traditionals, of course, remain in place. There are authentic, old-style Alpine musics, sometimes differing from one valley to the next – as well as a variety packaged into a predictable thump by commercial bands who play in the hotels and restaurants. But of late, beneath the snowline, things are moving as young musicians reshape the traditional folk music. It's this music that most demands your attention.

Bavaria

The best-known alternative Bavarian group and the pioneers of the whole genre are **Biermosl Blosn**, founded in 1976 by three brothers from the Well family who play trumpet, horn and accordion and irritate local right-wing politicians by writing satirical lyrics to traditional tunes and producing records with titles like *The Yodelling Horror Monster Show*. Their most notorious performance was on Bavarian TV in 1980, just before Bavarian president Franz Josef Strauss made his New Year speech, when they played the Bavarian anthem with new words which directly attacked his politics, resulting in a long-term ban from Bavarian radio and TV. They still do political cabarets, often with satirist Gerhart Polt. Leaving politics aside, they exist in another incarnation as **Well-Buam** (Well Boys), specializing in stomping dance music on clarinets and brass.

Hundsbuam

In a gentler mood are **Fraunhofer Saitenmusik**, who play traditional music from Bavaria and related countries using only string instruments such as the harp and a variety of zithers – an instrument which was introduced to the south of Germany by vagrant musicians in the eighteenth century. The **hammered dulcimer** was an even earlier arrival. Today the best-known virtuoso of this instrument is **Rudi Zapf**, who plays a huge range of styles from classical music to jazz and avant garde.

His trio **Grenzenlos** ("Borderless"), with Martina Eisenreich (violin) and Harry Scharf (double bass), takes listeners on a musical journey from Bavaria to Greece, Argentina and Ireland and back again. His other band is **Zapf'nstreich**. With his wife Ingrid on double bass, her sister Evelyn Huber on harp, and Andreas Seifinger on guitar, he mixes acoustic textures with electric guitar sounds.

During the 1990s the revival of alpine folk became a fashionable trend under the banner of *Neue Volksmusik*, and new faces were brought into the public eye. One of the bands which emerged at the time and are still around are **Hundsbuam**, formerly known as **Hundsbuam Miserablige**. Founded in 1994, they attempted to penetrate the mainstream rock market by playing heavy metal *ländler* with noisy guitars, heavy drums and wild on-stage antics.

When the trio **Die Interpreten** split in the late 1990s, one of the pioneer ensembles of the Alpine New Wave vanished. From the ashes emerged **Hammerling**, a collaboration between Interpreten percussionist **Erwin Rehling** and singer and multi-instrumentalist **Fritz Mosshammer**. Hammerling continued with Die Interpreten's experimental approach, exploring the soundmaking possibilities of traditional instruments in surprising ways. As improvization is at the heart of their performances, waltzes and ländler feature only rarely. Sometimes they groove like a New Orleans street band, making the alpine horn sound like a tuba, at other times they play dreamlike melodies on a home-made vibraphone built from a set of tuned cow bells or stones.

Unterland is more interested in bringing a new twist to traditional material. A six-piece band from Lower Bavaria, they give a fusion treatment to dance tunes and write new songs in a neo-traditional way. Harp, hammered dulcimer and musical saw keep the music rooted in the old folk tradition while saxophone, drums, keyboards and bass guitar add jazz, pop, funk and latin styles.

Unterland's songs often have a humorous edge, as do those of **4Xang** (pronounced "vierxang"), an acapella quartet who take the old tradition of Viergesang (four-part singing) into new areas. They perform traditional melodies with cheeky new lyrics alongside vocal interpretations of Deep Purple and Beethoven pieces, in a firework show of vocal clowning.

Switzerland

The desire for a new approach is also shared by most of the younger Swiss musicians. When the pioneering ensemble of the Alpine New Wave **Appenzeller Space Schöttl** called it a day, hammered dulcimer player **Töbi Tobler** began several projects of his own. He gave solo recitals, founded a trio with **Matthias Lincke** (violin) and **Ivo Schmid** (double bass) and joined an all-star ensemble called **Das Neue Original Appenzeller Streichmusik Projekt**. Two of the main players in the line-up were ECM recording artist **Paul Giger** (violin) and folk music researcher and avant-garde composer **Fabian Müller** (cello). The band took traditional string music and made it sound as refined as a Schubert string quartet. Unfortunately it didn't last long. The band produced only one album – a gem, full of musical craftsmanship – before splitting up.

A similarly delicate sound is cultivated by the **Oberwalliser Spillit** from western Switzerland. In this slightly larger ensemble, the instruments playing the leading parts – clarinet, melodeon and hammered dulcimer – are doubled up, giving the band a full sound. **HujGroup** are in the same category, keeping close to the traditional path. They dig deep to find long-forgotten polkas, mazurkas, waltzes and *allemandes*, which were heard on rural dance floors before the more recent ländler, in slow 3/4 time, squeezed them out.

Stimmhorn from Basel is a well-established partnership between **Balthasar Streiff** on trumpet, alphorn and *alperidu* (an Alpine horn played like a didgeridoo) and the amazing vocalist **Christian Zahnder** who combines Mongolian overtone singing with archaic yodelling as well as playing self-invented instruments such as the "rockordion" – transformed from an accordion – and the "milking-machine organ" (organ pipes operated by a milking machine). Their general approach is minimalistic and meditative. They paint colourful musical landscapes of jagged sounds like the Alps around them and enrich their performances with theatrical effects. The addition of electronic wizard **Tomek Kolczynski**

(aka "kold") to the line-up has given them an even more avant-garde sound.

Hornroh ("Raw Horn") is a sideline of Balthasar Streiff's. This ensemble of four alpine horns cultivate the raw sounds of the instrument, working with its unadorned harmonics, natural intervals and overtones. They follow in the footsteps of **Hans Kennel**, whose **Contemporary Alphorn Orchestra** was the first ensemble to take the instrument into new territory.

Kennel and saxophonist **Juerg Solothurnmann** were leaders of the **Alpine Jazz Herd**, the first group to begin mixing traditional Swiss music with other styles. They are followed today by ensembles such as the **Rigi Orchestra** of **Roland von Flue**, an original composer and saxophonist fluent in jazz, rock and latin music as well as the folk repertoire.

Aeschbacher x Hägler, a collaboration between traditional melodeon player **Werner Aeschbacher** and avant-garde percussionist **Martin Hägler**, is an oddity, even in the extremely individualistic Swiss folk music scene. Aeschbacher plays straight tunes from his vast repertoire of dance melodies, using a variety of melodeons, accordions and bandoneons, and Martin Hägler adds highly original and imaginative drum beats and percussive sounds to create estrangement effects, which sometimes bemuse the audience. Hägler's speciality is playing on big sheets of brass, the sound enveloping the melodeon waltzes and ländler in a strange whirlpool of noise.

In the Italian-speaking part of Switzerland, to the south of the Alps, is Ticino, a region with a strong musical identity. The area is part of a broader Lombard culture which dominates the north of Italy. In the steep valleys and wooded mountains, songs and singing remain the most important part of the musical heritage which is celebrated at seasonal festivals in the small villages glued to the hillsides.

Musicians here constantly try to reinvent local traditions. **Vent Negru** (meaning "the wind which clears the sky of rain clouds" in the Onsernone valley dialect) is the result of a long collaboration between **Esther Rietschin** (vocals, saxophone) and melodeon player and singer **Mauro Garbani**. They give a new face to vintage songs while keeping their lyrics and message intact. The songs speak of love and loss, and the hopes of the people of this mountainous area, where poverty was once severe and the rate of emigration high. The song "La Luna Sul Poncione" tells the story of villagers who tried to steal gold from the shining moon.

L'orchestrina often plays as a small band. At its core is the long-standing partnership between ethnomusicologist **Pietro Bianchi**, who sings and plays fiddle, hurdy-gurdy and accordion, and singer and guitar player **Roberto Maggini**. L'orchestrina's repertoire is divided into expressively sung ballads and dance tunes such as the long-forgotten *monfrina*, in 6/8 time, which Bianchi dug up during his extensive research into the musical past of the Ticino.

The quintet **Vox Bleni**, from the Bleni valley, excel in multi-harmony singing. **Aurelio Beretta**, who often leads with her vivid voice and strong tremolo, is backed by four male vocalists. They accompany themselves with fiddle, guitar, double bass, accordion and tambourine. Vox Bleni's repertoire is drawn from the region's strong heritage of song, and they make particular use of the style and dialect of their home valley. They can sometimes be seen busking in the streets of Lugano where they draw huge crowds.

Austria

In Austria the scene was dominated for years by **Attwenger**, who triggered the whole new musical avalanche. Starting as alpine punks (some called them the Austrian Pogues), **Markus Binder** and **Hans-Peter Falkner** developed musically with each succeeding record. With the distorted sound of a button accordion from the Steiermark mountain region played through a wah-wah pedal, gunshot drum tracks and electronic hip-hop rhythms, they tried "to find the meeting point between folk music and punk". Binder, drummer and lyric writer, explained: "Old and new styles are contrasted, fresh and strong, by using reduced instrumentation arranged in a dense, expressionistic manner."

Attwenger regard both alternative pop culture and traditional tunes as an expression of rebellion in everyday life. Despite their underground gloss, however, their starting point is the music of their home region where a number of unique dance tunes have survived. In their hands *Schleiniger*, *Innviertler Ländler* and *Aberseer Ländler* become wild songs with aggressive beats. Although they enjoyed tremendous critical acclaim, they folded in 1995 due to musical exhaustion and a refusal to be part of the Alpine New Wave hype. Refreshed, they reunited two years later and took the public by surprise with an even more radical reductionist attitude. The folk elements were so diluted that they only surfaced occasionally over repetitive trip-hop and jungle beats. With *Sun* (2002) they returned to a more balanced mix, supported on a few tracks by Balkan brass band **Boban Marković Orkestar**, and avant-garde guitarist **Fred Frith**.

In the late 1990s **Hans Falkner** started his own label, Fisch Records, to counteract the watering down of traditional music by the commercial Volksmusik which dominates radio and television. He has released half a dozen real gems. They include early recordings from the **Hohla-Biereder Duo** and the **Geschwister Simböck** which give an insight into the wild yodelling of the past. The recordings of the **Unger-Pedarnig Quintet** from Tirol and the **Pernecker Klarinettenmusi** and **Wildenstein Sänger** show that this music is still alive on the dance floors of Upper Austria, well away from the tourists' paths.

Hubert von Goisern, whose music is more mainstream, is an even bigger name. The

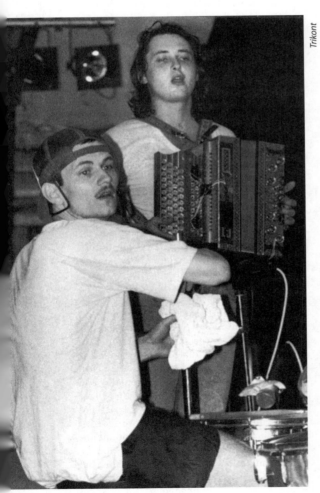

Trikont

Attwenger

melodeon player and singer became a pioneer of the **Alpine New Wave** in the late 1980s as one half of the duo **Alpinkatzen**. He still enjoys huge success today as a solo artist, re-inventing himself again and again. His latest project, *Trad*, goes back to the folk songs of his childhood, remodelling them for the twenty-first century. There is plenty of yodelling and the push and pull of the melodeon, as well as energetic rock, reggae rhythms, jazz double-bass lines, bluesy slide guitar and keyboard chords. On some of these recordings his band is joined by the **Hohtraxlecker Sprungschanznmusi**, a traditional ensemble, which gives the music more roots credibility.

These days, **Aniada a Noar** is one of the most popular folk bands in Austria. The quartet, whose name means "everybody is a fool" in their native Styrian dialect, have played together since 1983 and produced nearly a dozen albums. The line-up is: two violins, melodeon and bagpipes, plus guitar, recorder and mandolin. Deeply rooted in tradition, they present old pieces from Styria and other regions, and also write new songs in the traditional style.

Although these are all highly individual bands, what they have in common is a vision of Alpine folk music which is rooted in tradition, but modern at the same time. It's a successful mix, often leavened with humour and imagination.

DISCOGRAPHY Alpine Music

★ The Alps: Music From The Old World
World Network, Germany

Both the old and new school of alpine folk music – although more old than new. Includes alphorn duets, exuberant yodelling from Austria's Citoller Tanzgeiger and even three rare tracks by the legendary Appenzeller Space Schöttl who haven't made any recordings before or since.

★ Arunda – Musica Alpina vols 1&2, 3&4, 5&6
Frizzey Records, Austria

A fantastic series of three double CDs. For the last thirty years Gerlinde and Hans Haid have recorded music at festivals, in taverns and in living rooms and kitchens, documenting styles as diverse and exciting as it's possible to imagine, from ancient yodels, bell ringing and small dance-music ensembles to massed bands and big choirs. The result is a fascinating sound atlas of a vast area, covering Austria, Switzerland, Slovenia, Italy and France. It gives an insight into a musical culture which exists beneath the surface of the streamlined folklore presented to tourists. All CDs come with a comprehensive booklet containing explanations of the song and text transcriptions in German, Italian and English plus photos. (Distributed by *www.extraplatte.at*.)

⊙ Bergtöne: Sounds from the Mountains
Migros, Switzerland

A very informative overview of contemporary composers working with traditional material, ranging from ethno fusion by the Rigi Orchestra to the yodel songs of chansonette Betty Legler. A traditional ländler written by respected new music composer Heinz Holliger is played by the Oberwalliser Spillit using the Gutteruspil, a xylophone made out of tuned bottles. Perhaps surprisingly, Holliger's more usual atonal style appears only at the end of the track.

⊙ Musical Landscapes – Switzerland
Ocora, France

A colourful tour of Switzerland's mountain music. Leading musicologist Brigitte Bachmann-Geiser has picked the cream from a large pool of brilliant performers. The music ranges from conventional dance music played on violin, hammered dulcimer and melodeon to French-influenced sounds from the west of the country. Utterly delightful.

⊙ The Story of Swiss Music
Hangar 21, Switzerland

Swiss label Hangar 21 offers a history of Swiss folk music on two CDs with 49 tracks, from its ancient beginnings to the digital sounds of the present.

⊙ Urmusig
CSR Records, Switzerland

Wonderful field recordings from the Swiss Alps. This double CD was originally taken from a film soundtrack and includes some of the living legends of traditional music in Switzerland, like the late Rees Gwerder who pumps out some driving dance tunes on his Schwyzer Örgeli, a special melodeon found only in Switzerland.

Aniada a Noar

Hard-gigging band from Styria with a more folksy style in which the influence of the Anglo-American folk revival mixes with the local traditions: Bob Dylan in Lederhosen.

⊙ Heaz & Steaz
Extraplatte, Austria

The best CD by this south-Austrian folk quartet. Contains lots of wild fiddle playing, harmony singing and yodelling and even a version of "I ain't got no home" in Styrian dialect.

Attwenger

Since their arrival in the early 1990s, Attwenger have taken the Austrian music scene by storm, becoming the most influential band and kick-starting a whole new genre.

★ Most
Trikont, Germany

Their first and best album, from 1991, features liberal radical humour and traditional dance tunes played with hip-hop drum rhythms and a head-banging ländler-beat from the wildest of the Alpine groups.

⊙ Sun
Trikont, Germany
Latest album from the inventors of Alpine punk. A departure from the almost totally electronic previous album, it's an interesting soundscape made from drifting melodeon melodies, funky drums and dada poetry.

Pietro Bianchi and Roberto Maggini

Exquisite duo with a large array of instruments. Their repertoire is taken from an enormous pool of material collected by Pietro Bianchi while researching his doctoral thesis.

⊙ Canta pai sass
SRG SSR, Switzerland
The harmony singing on this double CD is superb, with great feeling and expression. Interesting songs about wine, the coming of spring, emigration and various political topics. One tells the story of the anarchists who were thrown out of Switzerland in 1894. As they left they accused the Swiss government of bending to foreign pressures and betraying the memory of William Tell.

Biermosl Blosn

The founders and longest-lasting band of the "Alpine New Wave" are the brothers Christoph, Hans and Michael Well. Growing up in a large family where music was their daily bread, it is no wonder they play such a wide variety of instruments.

⊙ Unter Bayern
Mood Records, Germany
These witty songs, sung in close harmony, take the ridiculous phenomena of modern life – mobile phones, satellite TV and modern agriculture – as their subject. They paint a critical portrait of the "idyllic" life of the Bavarian countryside, and mock their fellow countrymen. Their impressive musical skills can be heard in several instrumental pieces.

Fraunhofer Saitenmusik

The ensemble got its name from the famous Fraunhofer restaurant in Munich where they played as a house band for years. For a long time Richard Kurländer (harp and hammered dulcimer), Heidi Zink (hammered dulcimer and zither) and Gerhard Zink (acoustic bass) played as a trio. With fourth member Michael Klein they added the sounds of guitar and forest zither.

⊙ Dezember
Trikont, Germany
This atmospheric album from Munich's string band catches the mood of the cold season. This chamber-music folk is quiet, tasteful and gentle. Includes rare songs from Moravia, Bavaria and Austria.

Hammerling

Hammerling is the productive partnership between percussionist Erwin Rehling (formerly of Die Interpreten) and Fritz Mosshammer, a virtuoso on alpine horn, Jew's harp and pocket trumpet.

⊙ Lisi
Kulturbuero, Germany
Explorations of the sonorities of traditional alpine instruments are blended into colourful soundscapes.

Hornroh

Alphorn quartet founded by Stimmhorn's Balthasar Streiff.

⊙ Zirp
MGB, Switzerland
The band here explore some pretty archaic sounds.

HujGroup

This band is deeply rooted in the tradition of burenmusi, the dance music of the countryside which is played at the annual festivals of peasant life.

⊙ Nois Alts
MGB, Switzerland
A sensitive exploration of traditional tunes, sometimes stretching their boundaries – but only a little. Colourful instrumentation, original arrangements and a heavy dance groove provided by boogie-woogie style piano. What more do you need?

Hundsbuam

Band leader Streitbichi Michi's inspiration came when he attended an Attwenger concert and was converted to Alpunk. That band's influence on Hundsbuam is still clear today.

⊙ Hoam
BMG
On this 2003 album, the Bavarian quintet prove that rock rhythms work well with folk dance steps, and traditional accordion staccato with heavy metal riffs. They know how to rock the beer tent.

Das Neue Original Appenzeller Streichmusik Projekt

The Kronos Quartet of Swiss folk music.

★ Das Neue Original Appenzeller Streichmusik Projekt
MGB, Switzerland
The band with the longest name in folk history plays old tunes in such a delicate way that they begin to sound like classical music. They also cover new ground, exploring possibilities in a gentle, organic fashion.

Stimmhorn

Christian Zehnder and Balthasar Streiff began collaborating in 1995 and were soon noticed for successfully bridging the gap between the old and the new.

WITH KOLD ELECTRONICS

⊙ Igloo
RecRec, Switzerland
With the addition of electronic specialist Tomek Kolczynski (aka kold), Stimmhorn continue their unique journey into the archaic dimension of sound. Alpine yodelling, shamanistic throat singing, raw melodies of different alpine horns, colourful electronics – all add up to an extraordinary musical experience.

Töbi Tobler

Tobler was once one half of veteran ensemble Appenzeller Space Schöttl. He now plays solo recitals on his hammered dulcimer.

⊙ Solos
Phonag Records, Switzerland
A beautiful album from the Swiss maestro of the hammered dulcimer who plays a version of the instrument only found in the Appenzell region. Original compositions are followed by traditional tunes to create a calm and peaceful atmosphere. A meditation in folk music!

Vent Negru

Vent Negru combines the strong melodies and sweet harmonies of the Ticino area with contemporary arrangements highlighted by jazzy saxophone.

⊙ Leva su ca canta u gall
Vent Negru, Switzerland
Vent Negru's fourth CD. The arrangement and instrumentation of the songs remain true to the tradition, as well as being open to new influences. Great playing, expressive singing, powerful songs!

Vox Bleni

Well-respected ensemble from the Ticino.

⊙ Lavura ti pour'om
Vox Bleni, Switzerland
New arrangements by the band of fifteen traditional songs. Impressive, powerful harmony singing brings the songs alive. A very distinguished sound!

Zapf'nstreich

Hammered dulcimer virtuoso Rudi Zapf has been a key player in the Bavarian revival movement for many years. He is not only an excellent musician but also the organizer of the International Hammered Dulcimer Festival, which takes place every two years in Munich.

⊙ MCMXCVI
Pantaleon Records, Germany
This is the first record by Zapf's latest band. The "hammered dulcimer king" focuses mainly on new adaptations of alpine string music played on harp, hammered dulcimer and electric guitar, but also includes pieces from other parts of the world.

PLAYLIST
Alpine Music

1 FÜRE THOM U SI MANDOLINE Aschbacher x Hägler from *Aschbacher x Hägler*
This wonderful dance tune is a good example of the quirky style of this highly original duo.

2 FIRN Hammerling from *Lisi*
A piece played on stone-xylophone and drums with an expressive alphorn melody.

3 MINIMAL-LÄNDLER/RUGGUSSERLI Das Neue Original Appenzeller Streichmusik Projekt from *Das Neue Original Appenzeller Streichmusik Projekt*
A ländler dance tune turns into a piece of minimal music through the use of constant repetition.

4 MAGGIO DI CASLANO Pietro Bianchi and Roberto Maggini from *Canta pai sass*
A driving piece with a very catchy melody sung by the Swiss duo in a moving way. It hails the arrival of spring while knowing that winter is the real time for love.

5 SON QUI SOTO LE TUE FINESTRE Singing group from Bienno/Valcamonica (North Italy) from *Arunda 2*
A field recording from northern Italy of one of the most intensive performances of group singing in the Alps. The song is about proposed and rejected love.

6 ZÄUERLI Streichmusik Alder from *Musical Landscapes – Switzerland*
The Alder String Ensemble from Urnäsch in the Canton of Appenzell put down their violins and hammered dulcimer and sing a yodel without words – just pure harmony. Accompanied by the humming sounds of a rolling coin in a big bowl. Magic!

Austria

from blue danube to the danube blues

Schrammel band, early twentieth century
Collection Christoph Wagner

Viennese music is not all Strauss waltzes, Mozart arias and Beethoven symphonies. The Austrian capital on the Danube, once one of the world's greatest political and cultural powerhouses, is the home of a particular brand of urban folk music which developed in the nineteenth century and continues today. Instrumental *schrammelmusik* and its close relative *Wienerlied* (Viennese Song) are still alive and kicking, as **Christoph Wagner** explains.

The genre of **Wienerlied** – traditional Viennese songs – is living proof of Vienna's wistful, melancholic heart. In the restaurants of the Viennese suburbs of Ottokring and Simmering, **Kurt Girk** is one of the few old timers left who celebrate the city's folk music heritage in the traditional way. The audience gather round tables, washing down *wiener schnitzel* and dumplings with large glasses of local wine. He signals to his accordion player and they break into a heartbreaking song, Girk underlining the pathos with dramatic gestures. These half-forgotten songs from the past are still in high demand, and for a few euros, Girk will sing any one of them. He has known them all by heart since he was a boy.

Trude Mally is in many ways Girk's female equivalent. Her voice is full of vibrato and has a fragile timbre which adds to the heartfelt poignancy of the songs. When she launches into the wild ornamentation of a *dudler* (yodel), her songs gain pace and power.

Other venerable keepers of the flame are **Karl Hodina** and **Rudi Koschelu**. Hodina, who was seventy in 2005, is one of the old masters of the accordion, which was invented in Vienna in 1829, while Koschelu plays a special kind of Viennese guitar with a double neck. They play dances and waltzes in the old-fashioned way, adding dynamics by slowing down in particular passages before dramatically speeding up again, all to accompany their perfect harmony singing. The music has a jazz swing, which is not due to tradition, but to Hodina's love of bebop.

Schrammel Roots

The tradition of Viennese folk music, which has evolved from a clash of musical styles. It emerged from the industrial age, when tens of thousands of people from rural Austria, the Alps, Hungary, Bohemia, Moravia and Slovenia poured into the slums of the fast-growing capital of the Austro-Hungarian empire, transforming it within a few decades into a multicultural metropolis. It soon developed its own musical language. Polkas, Gypsy melodies, tunes from the Balkans, and rural Alpine yodels and dances mingled with Viennese waltzes, ländlers and string quartets to create an exciting new style.

The key event in Vienna's folk music tradition was in 1878 when **Johann** (1850–93) and **Josef Schrammel** (1852–95) formed a trio with bass guitarist Anton Strohmayer. They called it **D'Nussdorfer** after the suburb where they

performed. The two brothers became so famous that their surname was given to the whole genre. *schrammelmusik* was born

Before long, the style settled into a regular quartet form, with the addition of a small G-clarinet (played by folk-clarinettist **Georg Dänzer** in the Schrammels' original band), sometimes replaced by an accordion. In the 1880s and 90s, schrammel quartets emerged all over Austria and over the border in the Alpine regions of southern Germany.

Neuwirth and the New Wave

The long-haired, bearded, hat-sporting **Roland Neuwirth** is a unique musician on today's traditional Viennese music scene. His acoustic quintet, **Die Extremschrammeln**, with a traditional line-up of accordion, two violins, contra guitar and vocals, stretches the tradition to its limits, adding blues chords and soul grooves.

As a young man Roland Neuwirth wanted to be a blues singer. Then he discovered the "Viennese blues" on his own doorstep – schrammelmusik has strong links with the red-light district of Old

Christian Potzmann

Roland Neuwirth

Vienna, where love songs and murder ballads were sung in taverns and brothels. He added electric guitars and drum, creating the template for the **Danube New Wave**. But in the 1980s he returned to the acoustic format, aiming to sound as authentic as possible, only adding new ingredients which seemed to fit naturally. He rehearsed with two violin players for many weeks to achieve the classic Viennese timbre of slow vibrato, while his accordion player, **Walther Soyka** (who plays one of the famous squeeze boxes built in the workshop of Fritz Budowitz over a century ago) softens his instrument's tone by putting a page of newspaper inside it.

After his departure from Extremschrammeln in 2003 **Soyka** became one of the movers and shakers of a young and lively scene. In his solo recitals Soyka chooses an avant-garde approach to his squeeze box, adding prepared electronic ambient sounds. He has worked to establish the **schrammel quartet** as serious chamber music, using Schoenbergian influences. Soyka guests occasionally with the duo **Die Strottern**, who are one of the more serious contenders in the Wienerlied genre. He also plays with **Familie Pischinger**, a loose workshop ensemble of like-minded musicians, named after composer and violinist **Anton Pischinger** (1801–1905); he performs wild and atonal music with zither player **Karl Stirner**; while the experimental schrammel-electronic band **Des Ano** is another creation of Soyka's versatile creativity. In the late 1990s he started the independent record company **Non Food Factory**, to document the latest trends and to offer a platform for new bands. His reputation has grown steadily and in 2004 he was asked to compose a schrammel opera for the prestigious Austrian new music festival **Steirischer Herbst**.

Only ten years ago it was hard to find a schrammel quartet with a vision beyond the old

coffee house style. Today there are more than a dozen excellent ensembles in Vienna who all have their own particular ideas. **Neue Wiener Concert Schrammel** are led by two violins in perfect harmony. Their concert programme is a bold mix of old classics and pieces from Viennese composers such as Johann Strauss, Richard Strauss and Arnold Schoenberg, played in schrammel style.

The **Attensam Quartett** is similarly ambitious and has a clear direction of its own. The group was formed by members of **Klangforum Wien**, the world class New Music ensemble from Vienna. Alongside precise interpretations of old compositions by Johann Schrammel and **Alois Strohmayer**, the Attensam Quartett plays new works by composers **Oskar Aichinger**, **Christoph Dienz** and **Christian Muthspiel**, which have been specially written for them. These pieces often use poems by H.C. Artmann or Gerhard Rühm as lyrics, and are sung by tenor **Walter Raffeiner**. The bands feeling, timing and sensitivity is superb.

A similar revolution has taken place in **Wienerlied**, which overlaps with the schrammel tradition. A younger generation is reinventing the style for the twenty-first century. They add elements of blues, pop, rock, punk and sharp humour and write new songs dealing with modern life rather than celebrating the past. **Bratfisch**, **Die Strottern** and the duo of **Steinberg & Havlicek** all fall into this category. But the wild men of the scene are the trio **Kollegium Kalksburg**, who invest schrammel with some of the gravel of Tom Waits. Their songs are full of raw vocals. The witty lyrics play with the cynicism, dark humour and sarcasm that is typical of the Viennese character, and the music stops at nothing. Even though purists are appalled, Kollegium Kalksburg bring a younger generation of listeners back to their own roots.

DISCOGRAPHY Austria

See also Alpine music (p.15) and German folk (p.165).

⊙ **Die besten Schrammeln Instrumental**
Trikont, Germany
Compiled by Roland Neuwirth, this is a superb collection of rare instrumentals by the great masters of the genre. In a recording from early this century you can even hear Anton Strohmayer, who was guitarist in the original Schrammel Brothers trio. Real gold dust!

⊙ **Neue Wiener Welle – Wienerlied 2001**
Non Food Factory, Austria
An interesting insight into the new and anarchic singer/songwriter scene which emerged in Vienna in the mid-1990s. It features neo-traditionalists like Die Strottett and Steinberg & Havlicek but also punk bands such as the Dead Nittels and rough blues screamers such as Wiener Mischung singing in Viennese dialect. A wider perspective on the tradition.

⭐ **Wean Hean – Das WienerliedFestival Vols 1–4**
HeiVo, Austria
Here are all the important names – young and old – in a splendid overview: Kurt Girk, Trude Mally, Karl Hodina, Roland Neuwirth & Extremschrammeln, Die Strottern, Neue Wiener Concert Schrammeln, Attensam Quartett and many more. The best quick survey of the scene that's available.

⊙ **Wien: Volksmusik: Rare Schellacks 1906–1937**
Trikont, Germany
A superb historical collection of soulful, passionate songs featuring the main singers and ensembles of Vienna some seventy years ago. This is the Danube blues – the characteristic repertoire of the heurigen (wine bars), which has almost disappeared.

Die Extremschrammeln

Roland Neuwirth, the "Schrammel King" of contemporary Viennese folk music works with his authentic offshoot band Herzton-Schrammeln, but it's the four-piece progressive Die Extremschrammeln for whom he is best known.

⊙ **Essig & Öl**
WEA/Warners, Austria
The band was at the height of their art on this recording from 1994. The expressive harmony singing of Neuwirth and Mizzi Moravec alternates with fine instrumental dances, where the schmaltz of the twin violins mingles perfectly with the colours of the accordion. Not as extreme as the name of the band suggests – just extremely good!

Kollegium Kalksburg

The trio of Heinz Bitsch (accordion, vocals), Paul Skrepek (contra guitar, vocals and percussion) and Vincenz Wizlsperger (vocals, tuba, trombone, musical saw) really revolutionized schrammel.

⊙ **Imma des söwe**
Extraplatte, Austria
Kalksburg often take traditional melodies and write new lyrics for them, dealing with issues of modern life in a darkly cynical and fatalistic way. They use Viennese dialect in their wild anarchic performances and understanding the songs is difficult even for German speakers, who might find it easier to follow the one song in English, "If Jesus is busy".

Neue Wiener Concert Schrammeln

One of the best schrammel quartets around: Peter Uhler and Valmir Ziu (violins), Günter Haumer (accordion) and Peter Havlicek (contra guitar).

⭐ **Auf der Rennbahn**
Preiser Records, Austria
The CD puts together unlikely companions – Schubert, Schoenberg and Johann Schrammel – and points out the secret connections between them. Wonderfully passionate playing with just the right degree of sweetness and fantastic timing.

Steinberg & Havlicek

This duo are one of the best representatives of the Wienerlied scene today. Their sensitive approach to the songs shows excellent craftsmanship and great musicality.

⊙ **Himmel und Hölle**
Non Food Factory, Austria
A colourful set of thirteen songs and one instrumental ranging from old classics such as the "Glasschermtanz" and

PLAYLIST
Austria

1 DER TRAURIGE BUA Trude Mally, Karl Hodina & Rudi Koschelu from *Wean Hean Vol. 1*
A heartbreaking old folk song with a yodelled chorus from the grand old lady of Wienerlied, supported by sensitive backing vocals and instrumental excellence.

2 CERVENÁ SUKYNKA Kurt Girk & Schrammelbaron from *Wean Hean Vol. 3*
This soulful Czech song is based on a waltz melody. Kurt Girk (the Frank Sinatra of Ottakring) and Franz Pressfreund learned it from their Bohemian mothers.

3 PRIMA VISTA Neue Wiener Concert Schrammeln from *Auf der Rennbahn*
A wonderful piece by Josef Mikulas, written in the nineteenth century. The superb Neue Wiener Concert Schrammeln lend it a fresh quality.

4 CAFÉ WESTEND Die Strottern from *Mea ois Gean*
Fantastic, close-harmony male and female singing in this melancholy love song with colourful accompaniment from Walther Soyka's accordion.

5 IF JESUS IS BUSY Kollegium Kalksburg from *Imma des söwe*
An English version of the old classic by the musical destructionists Kollegium Kalksburg; a glimpse into the dark and cynical fatalism of the Viennese soul.

"Ein himmlisches Behagen" (sung first in 1870 by female folk singer legend Anna Ulke) to their own melodies set to the lyrics of poet Peter Ahorner, presented with close-harmony vocals.

Die Strottern

Die Strottern is a joint venture of David Müller (vocals, guitar) and Klemens Lendl (vocals, violin). A third, secret member of the band is the Viennese poet Peter Ahorner, who has written most of their lyrics.

⊙ **Mea Ois Gean**
Preiser Records, Austria
A banquet of songs executed superbly with close-harmony singing and the help of Walther Soyka (accordion) and Doris Windhäger (vocals). They deal with love and life's disasters in a typically philosophical Viennese way. Even if they use an electric Fender Rhodes piano instead of the acoustic guitar and play the violin in a jazzy way, it still sounds 100 percent Vienna.

The Baltic States

revolutions in song

Setu singers
Andrew Cronshaw

Moving from the Soviet Union to the European Union in less than fifteen years, the three Baltic States of Estonia, Latvia and Lithuania have swiftly re-connected themselves with Western Europe. Huge mass song festivals played a significant role in achieving independence in 1991 and, alongside the arrival of global pop and Eurovision successes in 2001 and 2002 (for Estonia and Latvia), Baltic musicians are reinterpreting their musical roots closer to home. **Andrew Cronshaw** assesses the state of play.

ndependence for the three Baltic States was first achieved in the 1920s as they escaped the imperial clutches of Germany and Soviet Russia. Freedom and peace didn't last long, however. In 1940 (1939 in Lithuania) Soviet troops broke the 1920 treaties and invaded, followed a year later by the German army, which was ousted in 1944 by the returning Soviets. In the process, hundreds of thousands of Baltic people were deported to Siberia or killed. Many more fled to the West, depleting the population of these three small countries by up to a third and swelling Baltic exile communities, particularly in North America. Repression continued after the war. On a single day in 1949 nearly 43,000 Latvians were deported to the Gulags. During the Soviet period large numbers of Russians were moved into the Baltic States.

On 6 September 1991, after another traumatic series of events which were variously bizarre, tragic, heroic and musical, the three countries regained independence. For each of them, the **mass singing festivals**, which had taken place since the nineteenth century and regularly involved tens of thousands, were a focus for national consciousness. In 1988, the year when the "**singing revolution**" began, 300,000 singers gathered at the *Eestimaa Laul* (Estonian Song) rally in Tallinn, at which Trivimi Velliste, the head of Eesti Muinsuskaitse Selts (the Estonian Heritage Society), voiced the demand for independence.

Ironically, it was Stalinist policy that had decreed Baltic folk music dead and ordered its replacement by mass song. Even in Soviet days, however, paeans to the merits of collectivization were by no means the only form of song. As Latvian folk musician and ethnomusicologist Valdis Muktupāvels, who was regularly summoned by the KGB to explain his dubious activities with the patently not deceased folk tradition, puts it: "The Russians didn't speak Latvian, so we sang the songs they told us we had to sing and added a whole lot more that we wanted to sing!"

The language issue was crucial for Baltic culture. All three **Baltic languages** use Roman characters, rather than the Russian Cyrillic alphabet. Estonian is closely related to Finnish in the Finno-Ugrian linguistic group while Latvian and Lithuanian languages are related to each other and form a Baltic subgroup of the widespread Indo-European linguistic group.

There are considerable national and regional differences between (and within) the three countries. But they share in the continuity of culture around the Baltic (including Finland and the Russian Baltic areas) which reaches back thousands of years. All have folk song-poetry of the **runo-song** type and they have in common several traditional instruments, notably **Baltic zithers** variously called *kantele*, *kannel*, *kokles* or *kanklės*. As a result of historical domination, however, the Baltic States manifest Germanic and Slavic cultural traits not found in Finland.

Changes in society during and after the Soviet period have meant that the social contexts of much traditional song and dance, as a key part of village life, have virtually disappeared, but the material remains in living memory.

Despite its pronouncement of the death of Baltic folk music, the Soviet government encouraged the formation of (supervised) folklore troupes wearing idealized village costumes, usually classically harmonizing and playing standardized forms of folk instruments. But during the 1960s and 70s there were folklore movements in which young city researchers and musicians made field trips to the villages, and learned and performed the material they found there. Even among these there was a tendency to dress historically, and that still persists for some groups today, but now in all three countries a few musicians and bands are attempting to create something that uses traditional musical forms and textures but connects with the present day.

The full effect of European Union membership on Baltic musics has yet to be seen, but in all three states music that would never have been tolerated in Soviet days is emerging. Some of it has a definite Baltic character, in some cases deeply influenced by traditional music and exploring its possibilities, in others – particularly the popular Baltic brands of dark metal and death metal – borrowing visual and conceptual images from Baltic paganism and seasonal ritual.

Estonia

Until 2000 there were virtually no CDs of Estonian roots music on Estonian labels, and precious few on any others. But recently that has changed, as traditional music has developed an enthusiastic youth following and a growing number of young musicians and bands are emerging.

Runo-Song

Estonian runo-song, *regilaul*, has the same basic form as the Finnish variety to which it is related: the line has eight beats, the melody rarely spans more than the first five notes of a diatonic scale and its short phrases tend to use descending patterns.

A large number of regilaul texts have been collected, largely from women, and thus offering a female point of view. They cover most aspects of life, including work, rituals, spells, ballads and mythical stories, and tend to a stoic sadness, or wry observation of life's realities, rather than extreme expressions of joy or love. The more ornamented **swing-songs** were sung while sitting on the big communal village swing whose movement made its own rhythmic demands.

Estonia's national epic **Kalevipoeg**, by folklorist **F. Reinhold Kreutzwald** (1803–82), was published in the 1860s, paralleling folklorist Elias Lonnröt's creation from runo-song sources of Finland's *Kalevala*, first published in 1835. **Armas Launis**'s collection of melodies from the runo-songs from which Kalevipoeg had been constructed was published in 1930.

By the early twentieth century runo-song was largely overtaken by more European forms of rhyming folksong with wider-spanning tunes and sometimes instrumental accompaniment. But it survived in a few areas – notably in **Setumaa**, which straddles Estonia's Russian border, and also on the island of **Kihnu** and among Estonian-resident members of Ingria's repeatedly displaced population.

Setu Song

The songs of the **Setu people** have considerably influenced contemporary roots singers, both in Estonia and in Finland. There's been a recent revival in Setu culture and the speaking of its dialect. Several villages, such as Värska, Kosselka, Helbi, Obinitsa and Uusvada, have established women's vocal groups that perform songs traditionally sung and danced while working or at social events, particularly the three-day wedding celebration. The eight-syllable runo pattern of these songs is often interrupted by extra syllables and refrains, and unlike other Estonian vocal traditions, they are sung polyphonically, the other singers taking the leader's line (the *torrõ*) and adding a lower part (the second torrõ), and a higher, penetrating single voice (the *killõ*) which often uses just two or three notes.

Kannels and Zithers

The old pastoral wind instruments such as animal horns, wooden birchbark-bound trumpets, willow overtone whistles and bagpipes have lost their traditional herding context but are used to some extent by present-day folk-rooted musicians. The fiddle, the ever-popular accordion and the long-bellowed concertina are used in the playing

of couple-dance tunes, the most prevalent form of which is the polka.

Polkas also feature, together with older music, in the repertoire of the **kannel**, the Estonian version of the Baltic zither, which, though it tends to have six strings rather than five, is of the same basic design as Finland's *kantele* – a carved, wedge-shaped box, with strings passing direct from pegs to a single attaching bar. Players died out during the twentieth century but the instrument itself survived (if only to hang on the wall) amongst the many exiles in North America – where the small kannel has had something of a revival. In Estonia itself, the formation of Soviet-style folkloric ensembles involved the creation of an "orchestral series" of bigger chromatic box-kannels. However, visits from contemporary Finnish kantele-players such as Hannu Saha and Antti Kettunen have helped to stimulate new interest in small kannels.

Setumaa has its own form of kannel, usually with a soundboard extended wing-like beyond the box rather like those found in eastern Latvia and parts of western Russia. This form is increasingly used, for example by Finnish kantele virtuoso Timo Väänänen. Leading Estonian kannel players include **Tuule Kann** and multi-instrumental ethnomusicologist **Igor Tõnurist**.

In Estonia, as in Latvia and Lithuania, folk players of a wide and ingenious range of **board-zither** or **chord-zither** can be found. These aren't true kannels/kanteles but are closer in design to the factory-made zithers, autoharps and other domestic multi-stringed instruments made largely in German factories and sold across northern Europe and North America. The bowed lyre, **hiiu-kannel** (called a **jouhikko** in Finnish) was played until the twentieth century in the Swedish enclaves of Estonian islands (relics of Sweden's fifty-year rule over Estonia from 1660 until 1710), particularly Runö, and is finding a role again today in some of the modern folk bands.

Musicians and Festivals

During the 1960s instructions were sent by Moscow to cultural organizers throughout the Soviet Union that supervised manifestations of genuine, living folk culture were to be encouraged, to demonstrate the government's support for the needs and expressions of the masses. In the Baltics, reluctant members of these "masses" were researching these same living cultures, not in response to Moscow's wishes but in order to explore the distinctiveness of their own culture.

Performing ensembles fell into two groups: "ethnographic" – which came from a particular area and specialized in local forms – and "folkloric" – which drew on the whole country's traditions. The first of the "ethnographic" type to appear in the more liberal climate of the 1960s was the Setu choir **Leiko** from Värska, formed in 1964. Of the "folkloric" type, **Leigarid** (formed in 1969 to entertain tourists at Tallinn open-air museum) soon turned away from the colourful folkloric spectacle approach towards a more authentic style rooted in village traditions. Regional ethnographic performance groups were formed, too, as were young city-based ensembles such as **Leegajus** (led by **Igor Tõnurist**) and **Hellero**.

More fuel for the continuation of traditional music in "post-folklore" circumstances had been provided by the publication between 1956 and 1965 of the five volumes of **Eesti Rahvalaule Viisidega** (Estonian Folk Songs with Notations), edited by **Herbert Tampere**, who had been working on and publishing folk music since the 1930s and who at the end of the 1960s also began a folklore radio programme. In 1969 the first book of the eight-volume anthology of Estonian folk song texts *Eesti Rahvalaulud* appeared. The first anthology of recordings on LP, **Eesti Rahvalaule ja Pillilugusid** (Estonian Folk Songs and Instrumental Music), was released in 1967 and a second followed in 1970.

Estonia's most famous composer internationally, **Arvo Pärt**, doesn't show any obvious borrowings from traditional music, but some others have reflected it as inspiration or by incorporating it in their music. The best known of these is **Veljo Tormis**, most of whose big choral works are interpretations and expansions of folk songs.

The mass singing festivals continue: the All Estonian Song Festival, **Laulupidu**, which started in Tartu in 1869, is held every five years in Tallinn. It's still a huge event: there can be over 20,000 choir members and 100,000 in the audience. The Setu people have their own song festival, **Leelopäev**, a gathering of singing groups for performance and celebration with traditional food and costume, held every three years in the village of Värska.

In 1986 the **Viru Säru** folklore festival began, which riskily connected folk music and customs with contemporary life. The first was "Protest Säru", which was "against promoting national folk culture in socialistic contents and in national form"; 1987's was "Danger Säru", themed on "becoming aware of the crisis in the USSR and awakening people to free spirit; protest against mining phosphorite in Estonia". The **Baltica** festival, which moves each year to a different Baltic state, began in 1987, and Tallinn first hosted it in 1989. These widened performance opportunities and Estonia's move towards independence stimulated developments including the opening of a folk music department at the Cultural College in Viljandi in 1990. **Viljandi Folk Music Festival** in July, which presents the new young Estonian roots bands alongside leading roots bands from abroad, began in 1993, and has gathered a large, predominantly young audience whose enthusiasm is a great encouragement for the new wave of bands and soloists inspired by regilaul and traditional dance music. Most of them are alumni of the Viljandi courses and the new **Estonian Traditional Music Centre** (*www.folk.ee*) that stands in the heart of the festival grounds and hosts teaching and events throughout the year. The same organization runs the small **Maa ja Ilm** indoor festival in March in Tartu.

Latvia

The land of amber has its own forms of Baltic zither, as well as drone-based singing and a large body of traditional song-poetry – **dainas** – with strong pre-Christian symbolism and a lack of heroes.

The Daina

The Latvian **daina** is a short song of just one or two stanzas, one or two lines in length, without rhyme, and largely in the same four-footed trochaic metre as runo-songs. Dainas feature mythological subjects and most aspects of village life, but the stories and heroic exploits described in many countries' folksongs are notably absent.

The sun is a dominant image, often personified as **Saule**, and her daily course across the sky and through the year is linked metaphori-

Andrew Cronshaw

New wave Estonian roots group Ro:toro

cally with human life. While the sun is female, **Mēness**, the moon, is male, and a frequent song theme is courtship between them or other celestial figures such as the twin sons of Dievs (God) and the daughter of the sun. The solstices were traditional occasions for celebration – in particular **Jāni** (midsummer), whose central figure was Jānis, the archetypal vigorous, potent male with strong phallic associations. As the *ligotne* (midsummer song) "Jāna Daudzinajums" describes him:

> Oh Jānis, the son of Dievs,
>   what an erect steed you have
> The spurs are glittering through forests,
>   the hat above trees
> Jānis was riding all the year
>   and has arrived on the Jāni eve;
> Sister, go and open the gate, and let Jānis in
>
> *Translation by Valdis Muktupāvels*

The major collection of dainas was made by **Krišjānis Barons** (1835–1923); the six volumes of his *Latvju Dainas* were published between 1894 and 1915, and contain about 300,000 texts.

In keeping with other regions of the Baltics, newer song-forms spread during the nineteenth century, when chordal, fixed-scale instruments – such as the accordion – arrived. Thus **zinge** is a singing style with a strong German influence. The older forms remained, however: **dziesma** means a song with a definite melody, while **balss** means "voice" or "speech" and has no clearly defined melody, changing with the rhythm of the words. Balss was the style used in calendar celebrations as well as during work. It usually follows a three-voice form: the leader sings a couple of stanzas of a daina, then the others repeat them. In some regions these repetitions are sung over a vocal drone – a distinctive feature not found elsewhere in the Baltics.

Instruments

Traditional Latvian instruments, used in *sadzīves* music – the dances and songs of the villages – include *kokles* (zither), *dūdas* (bagpipe), *taure* (wooden trumpet), *stabule* (whistle), *rata lira* (hurdy-gurdy), *trideksnis* (rattle-stick), *vargas* (Jew's harp), *gīgas* (trough fiddle) and more recently violin and accordion.

Of these, the instrument with the greatest national-symbolic status is the **kokle** or **kokles**, Latvia's version of the Baltic zither. As in the neighbouring Baltic states, the traditional instruments are small and hand-carved, usually from a single piece of wood, but larger, heavier box-built kokles with more strings were developed for use in Soviet-style folkloric ensembles. These, fitted with screw-in legs and often ornamented with a central jewel of the locally abundant amber, are attractive in appearance and ensemble sound, but not very responsive as instruments, with musicians displaying a rather stiff playing style based on a Western classical approach.

Renewed interest in the traditional smaller carved kokles began during the folklore movement of the 1970s. The instrument survived in the living tradition of only a few areas: the Catholic enclaves of Kurzeme in western Latvia and Latgale in the east. The strongest influence in this revival was **Jānis Porikis**, who made a couple of hundred kokles and organized workshops and performances. **Valdis Muktupāvels**, Latvia's leading player, learned the style of the Suiti region from Porikis, and has gone on to champion the instrument.

Muktupāvels normally plays a nine-string kokles of the type found in eastern Latvia – with a "wing" extension of the soundboard beyond the soundbox and pegs. Drones occur in Latvian singing, and it's usual to tune the lowest string of a kokles to a drone a fourth below the key note. There are several regional playing styles involving plucking or strumming and damping, including – as in some Estonian styles – resting the fingers of the left hand on the soundboard between the strings and moving them from side to side, damping sets of strings alternately to leave the rest ringing as chords while strumming with the other hand.

In North America the small kokles has become the main instrument of Latvian-American cultural groups. While in Latvia there's no dominant design – the instruments were home-made and each maker-player put in individual features – most of these American kokles are of a single pattern, wingless and with almost identical soundboard decoration, probably because buyers from the handful of North American makers want an instrument identical to the one they've seen played at Latvian-American gatherings.

A wide variety of interesting designs of **citara** (chord-zither) are found in Latvia. Most have large numbers of strings, some or all of which are tuned as ready-made chords. These are not principally related to Baltic zithers but rather to the mostly German factory-made chord-zithers and autoharps sold since the nineteenth century across Europe and North America. Individual Baltic makers have made ingenious modifications, resulting in some very big instruments and a few that are cylinder-shaped. There are also hybrid forms between citara and kokles, known as **citarkokles**.

In the eastern province of Latgale, hammered dulcimers have been played since the early nineteenth century, a borrowing from nearby Belarus.

Performers

Latvia's national song festival has been taking place, usually at five-year intervals, since 1888. In 1990, the first after the country's return to independence, it reached its largest size with over 35,000 singers, dancers and instrumentalists. Latvia also takes its turn as host of the Baltica festival, and has a range of other folk-music-related festivals of varying regularity, as well as the **Porta** world music festival, which began in 2000 and includes some Latvian roots bands.

Like the other Baltic States, Latvia still has local and regional **folklore groups** and **ethnographic ensembles**, most of them largely vocal rather than instrumental. (The website *www.folklora.lv* has a list of many of them.) While what they do is a preservation, both of songs and of costume, it is nevertheless a community activity – they meet to rehearse, make costumes and so on – and these groups, often established many decades ago and with members of all ages, are in themselves a folk culture.

Then there are the folk bands going deep into traditional music and its instrumentation, but using it in new configurations. Since they don't feel themselves to be folk musicians in the old sense of village culture, they dub their music "post-folklore". There have been a number of formative bands in this development but a couple of names run throughout it: those of ethnomusicologist, kokles player and bagpiper **Valdis Muktupāvels**, and of the band **Iļģi**, which since its formation in 1981 by singer and fiddler **Ilga Reizniece** has developed from a quiet acoustic group to a strong performing and recording unit.

Iļģi's and Muktupāvels' albums, and much of today's other Latvian tradition-rooted music as well as some pop and jazz, are on the **UPE** label, owned and run by **Ainars Mielavs**. Mielavs had considerable pop success in Latvia as leader of the band Jauns Mēness, and is now a songwriter, traditional singer, bandleader and radio DJ. At a time when there were almost no recordings of Latvian traditional or post-folklore music available, and little money around to finance them, Mielavs gathered leading musicians on the post-folklore scene and began a series of elegantly recorded and well-packaged CD projects on UPE including the ongoing *Latvian Folk Music Collection*.

The shores of the gulf of Riga are home to one of Europe's smallest linguistic groups, the Livs, who speak Livonian, a Finno-Ugrian language unrelated to Latvian. There are only a few hundred Livs, and fewer than fifty still speak the language, but songs are a way of keeping it and Livonian culture alive, and there are several Livonian folklore groups, the best known over the past three decades being **Skandinieki**, the vocal ensemble centred on the **Stalts** family. Having sung throughout her childhood in Skandinieki, **Julgi Stalte** moved to Estonia to study traditional music at Viljandi Culture College, and in 1999 she formed, with Estonian musicians, the Livonian-language folk-rock band **Tulli Lum** ("Hot Snow").

Lithuania

The largest Baltic state has a rich variety of folk forms, including layered polyphonic music, sung or played on reed instruments, flutes and, in common with its northern neighbours, Baltic zithers.

Song

Thousands of Lithuanian traditional songs – **dainos** – have been collected. They deal with every aspect of life, and wedding and love songs feature particularly prominently. Some would be passed on as well-known songs, but others, such as lullabies, would be varied or improvised to suit the occasion. In the early twentieth century many women who were predominantly the creators and carriers of songs had repertoires of a hundred or more songs.

Singing can be solo or in a group, in unison or in parallel chords of thirds, fourths or fifths. Aukštaitija, Lithuania's northeastern region, has a distinctive and well-known tradition of polyphonic songs, sutartinės, whose melody and form are also transferred to instrumental music. They are duophonic – two voices, or groups of voices in harmony. In the case of dvejinės (by twos) and keturinės (by fours) two harmonizing lines are sung together, then they stop and are replaced by a second group of singers and two different harmonizations, while in trejinės three parts overlap, two at a time, as in a canon. The word stresses create a syncopating internal rhythm.

Instruments

There is a relatively large range of Lithuanian traditional instruments. The basic form of the Lithuanian version of the Baltic zither, the **kanklės**, differs regionally in playing style and in the number of strings, which can be anywhere between five and twelve. The repertoire of the traditional kanklės consisted of old-style material such as sutartinės and more modern dance tunes such as polkas, waltzes and quadrilles. As with the Estonian kannel and Latvian kokles, a "concert series" of large many-stringed box kanklės was devised for the Soviet-style ensembles.

Whereas the old round dances (*rateliai*) were traditionally accompanied by singing only, during the nineteenth and twentieth centuries instrumental ensembles commonly played the newer dance forms. Instrumental groups playing kanklės and *lamzdeliai* (wooden or bark whistles) existed as far back as the sixteenth century. Later the fiddle and three-stringed bass *basetle* joined them, followed in the nineteenth and early twentieth centuries by accordions, bandoneons, concertinas, Petersburg accordions and harmonicas, mandolins, balalaikas, guitars, modern clarinets and cornets. During the Soviet era, dressed-up ensembles emerged using box kanklės and *birbynés* (folk clarinets – they used the developed form which is a mellow-sounding thick tube with a cowhorn bell). These groups actually made quite a pleasant sound, not so different from a disciplined village band, but they were often used, to the annoyance of those searching out the "real thing", in classically influenced arrangements to accompany choral singing of harmonized and denatured so-called sutartinės with all their dissonances smoothed out.

In the northeast, tunes of the sutartinė type were played on *skudučiai* – rather like dismantled pan-pipes, played by a group of men. The same type of tune was played by five-piece sets of birchbark-bound wooden trumpets (*ragai*), or alternatively, by pairs of the straighter, longer *daudytės*; each of the latter could produce up to five natural harmonics, so only two daudytės were needed for a set.

Other wind instruments include *švilpas* (overtone whistle), goat-horns and *sekminiu ragelis* (a single-drone bagpipe). Percussion instruments include *tabalas* (a flat piece of wood hung and hit like a gong) and drums. A curious instrument, rarely seen today, is the *pūslinė* – a musical bow with an inflated pig's bladder resonator containing a rattling handful of dried peas.

Ensembles to Bands

As the social structure changed, and Sovietization altered Lithuanian society from the outside, the old ways of music lost much of their role. Tradition moved to post-traditional, or "secondary folklore", with material collected from those who remembered the old ways converted to a form considered suitable for performance to an audience.

The first Lithuanian folklore ensembles were formed around the beginning of the twentieth century. One was the **Skriaudžiai Kanklės Ensemble**, formed by maker and player Pranas

Puskunigis in 1906, which is now based at the folk museum in Skriaudžiai, near Kaunas. Subsequently, ethnographic plays – theatrical reconstructions of village life and folk customs – such as "The Kupiskenai Wedding" were staged. While these tried to reflect genuine village life, concert ensembles worked on the premise that the rough old folk songs needed sprucing up.

As in the other Baltic States, a strong choral movement developed, with a repertoire drawing on folk songs but inevitably putting them into arranged forms, and these came together in huge song festivals. Lithuania's is called **Dainu Švente** ("The Feast of Songs") and takes place every five years. The state folk song and dance ensemble **Lietuva** was founded in 1940. "Modernized" folk instruments were created, and traditional dress was formalized into national costume.

While this was the form of national expression acceptable to the Soviet regime, considerably more suspicious was the back-to-the-villages folklore movement that began in the 1960s and was spurred on later that decade by the Prague Spring events in Czechoslovakia. Rasa (the summer solstice) and other Baltic pagan events were publicly celebrated despite persecution by the KGB. **Folklore ensembles** sprang up in towns and cities, and the village musicians from whom they collected formed performing units themselves, usually known as "ethnographic ensembles". There were folklore camps and competitions. The annual **Skamba Skamba Kankliai** festival in Vilnius's Old town began in 1975. The first **Baltica** International Folklore Festival, which moves between the Baltic States each year, took place in 1987 in Vilnius.

The ethnographic and folklore ensembles in Lithuania today, as in the other Baltic States, might appear more as historical-costumed preservers of memories and identity than as distinguished or creative musicians. But it would be a mistake to ignore them in a search for either imagined "authenticity" or creative evolution. In Soviet times they were striving to maintain a sense of Lithuanian identity, a need which continues post-liberation, and the local ensembles reflect community and maintain knowledge of traditional repertoire and instruments, resources that are needed by individuals seeking now to make new developments with traditional roots.

Even performers taking some new steps with folk music, such as the nationally esteemed and very fine traditional singer **Veronika Povilioniené** or the traditional band **Sutaras**, often project their musical genre visually by wearing historical costume or borrowings from it; the CD cover of **Ethnojazz.lt**, Sutaras' collaboration with a jazz quartet, portrays two contrasting dress codes that indicate a meeting of musical styles.

The next generation of tradition-rooted progressive bands, such as folk-rock band **Atalyja**, combine kanklės, bagpipes and other traditional instruments with those of rock for an emphatic, wild expression of sutartinės and other traditional material. Beyond folk-rock stretches a spectrum of post-Soviet, pan-Baltic, pagan-image bands, from "ritual folk" such as that of **Kulgrinda** to "martial-folklore", "folk-metal", "dark-metal" and "dark-ambient". A good spread of such bands appears at the "independent post folk, alternative and contemporary heathen culture festival" **Mėnuo Juodaragis** ("black-horned moon") in August on an island in northeast Lithuania's Zarasai lake.

DISCOGRAPHY The Baltic States

⊙ Voix des pays Baltes: chants traditionnels de Lettonie, Lituanie, Estonie
Inedit, France
Field recordings, mostly made by Lithuanian Radio, from all three Baltic countries going back as far as the 1930s, including calendar songs, work songs and Lithuanian sutartinės.

Estonia

⊙ Eesti Rahvalaule Ja Pillilugusid
Estonian Literary Museum, Estonia
Field recordings, most from 1957–67, of a variety of runo-songs plus a few instrumentals. Assembled largely from the collections of ethnomusicologist Herbert Tampere, it was originally released on vinyl in the 1970s, and has now been re-released as a three-CD set with a 228-page booklet. Featuring mostly solo singers when the material would normally have been call-and-response, it is nevertheless a key collection.

★ Estonia: Olden Tunes
Ocora, France
Twenty-six tracks, mostly recorded by Estonian national radio, of performers, solo and in groups, using traditional instruments – kannel, torupill (bagpipe), karjapasun (herder's horn), roopill (reed pipe) and vilepill (willow whistle) – with some archive recordings from as early as 1912.

⊙ Estonia: Seto Songs
Ocora, France
Recorded in Setumaa, southeast Estonia, between 1936 and 2006, this is an enlightening and well-documented collection of the Seto (or Setu) people's distinctive rhythm-overlapping songs, hypnotically chant-like with solo call and strident polyphonic chorus response. Alongside regilaul, Setu song is a key influence in Estonia's current roots revival.

⊙ Estonian Traditional Music 2006
Estonian Traditional Music Centre, Estonia
It's indicative of the new roots music activity that there are now enough Estonian-released CDs to make seventeen tracks from different albums released since 2001. Not a full Estonian roots sampler, but a useful taster of what's happening now, particularly among the Viljandi-centred young musicians.

Kärt Johanson

Kärt Johanson is a leader in a distinctive new Estonian direction, a quietly personal music that draws on regilaul to make her own expression. She has a variety of performing contexts, including with her three brothers and with her pianist husband, Tõnis Mägi.

⊙ Unistadt
Arm, Estonia
Johanson sings simply and intimately with quirky, unusual acoustic and electronic backdrops from Mägi and others.

Kirile Loo

Born in the northern Estonian village of Varinurme, singer Kirile Loo studied at Tallinn school of music. For a time she moved promisingly into live performance with a band combining electronics and traditional instruments, but she seems to have disappeared from view in recent years.

⊙ Saatus (Fate)
Erdenklang, Germany; Alula, US
Runo-song-based material in sparse, atmospheric settings arranged by Peeter Vähi with traditional instruments – kannels (played by Tuule Kann), bagpipe, reed-pipe, straw whistle, Jew's harp – plus keyboards and guitar.

★ Lullabies for Husbands
Erdenklang, Germany
Her second album (1999) moves to a hefty world-beat sound, in which all the instruments – violin, flutes, guitar, hiiukannel, synths and samples – are played by Tiit Kikas.

Veljo Tormis

Influential composer, born 1930, particularly celebrated for his choral works rooted in the folk songs of Estonian and other Finno-Ugrian and Baltic peoples.

⊙ Forgotten Peoples
ECM, Germany
Critically acclaimed double CD of six Tormis compositions based on the music of Livonian, Votic, Izhorian and Karelian Finno-Ugrian peoples, sung by the Estonian Philharmonic Chamber Choir.

Vägilased

This band, "The Mighties", while still developing, is clearly one of the leaders in the new movement. Singer-fiddler Meelika Hainsoo and Cätlin Jaago on bagpipes, flutes and Jew's harp are joined by Russian diatonic accordion, guitar, bass and drums.

⊙ Ema Õpetus
Eesti Raadio & Vägilased, Estonia
Arranging runo-songs in ways that will turn modern ears isn't easy, but with appealing, inventive unpretentiousness Vägilased weaves textures, harmonies and rhythms around and across them, punctuating with the occasional less ancient

dance tune, and in this shifting instrumental environment the songs' short lines and melodic repetition become a virtue.

Latvia

⊙ Best of Folk Music from Latvia
ARC, UK

Compiled by Riga-based "culture management centre" and increasingly significant record label Lauska, this is a useful overview of recent recordings by a good spread of today's Latvian revival-folk bands, some pioneers from the 1980s or 90s, some from the new crop. Most mix roots research and traditional instrumentation with new developments, largely with a characteristically Latvian gentle approach.

⊙ Ligo
UPE, Latvia

Six singers, including Zane Smite and Ainars Mielavs, focus on the songs associated with the main Latvian calendar celebration, Ligo (Midsummer night). The minimalist instrumentation isn't specifically Latvian traditional, having for example guitar and touches of duduk, but the result – veiled, breathy and grainy, with a prevailing sense of wistfulness – is very distinctively Latvian.

★ Native Music – Latvia: Traditional/Folk/World- Music
Latvian Music Information Centre, Latvia

These well-sequenced multi-label promos from the Latvian Music Information Centre are by far the best samplers available of today's strengthening Latvian traditional and trad-roots scene, showcasing both archive recordings and the emerging range of ways, from silvery kokles to dense, edgy chanting, of interpreting the stark, often limited-compass melodies of Latvian traditional songs to make contemporary music.

Marija Golubova

Despite a hard life, Marija Golubova, born in 1907, was still in amazingly fine, energetic voice when recorded 95 years later.

⊙ Stāsti Un Dziesmas
UPE, Latvia

A recording, made in 2003, of Marija singing folksongs and telling of her life and the natural world in the language of the Latvian region of Latgale and also in Russian. Even for a non-speaker of these languages, her spirit is so strong and the cadences of her voice so clear that somehow one understands.

Iļǵi

It hasn't been easy to bring the insistent, minimalist melodies of Latvian traditional music to a world stage. Iļǵi, led by singer-fiddler Ilga Reizniece and Māris Muktupāvels, player of kokles, bagpipe and other traditional instruments, have been working on it since 1981, including collaboration with Ainars Mielavs' rock band Jauns Mēness, line-up changes and set-toughening US touring.

⊙ Kaza Kāpa Debesīs (A Goat Climbed Up Into the Sky)
★ Ne Uz Vienu Dienu (Not For Just One Day)
UPE, Latvia

With these two albums, released in 2003 and 2006 respectively, the tentativeness of the early work has turned into confident strength and occasional rockiness, in material part traditional, part trad-rooted new composition.

Valdis Muktupāvels

A prime mover in maintaining and reviving Latvian traditional music during the difficult Soviet days and carrying it through to the new Latvia, Muktupāvels is ethnomusicologist, player of kokles and bagpipes, singer, event organizer and teacher.

★ Kokles
UPE, Latvia

A double CD, one of traditional tunes, the other of Muktupāvels' own compositions for kokles.

Biruta Ozoliņa

Once a member of Iļǵi, this singer from the eastern Latvian region of Latgale has an unaffected, clear voice, and is an able kokles player.

⊙ Balta Eimu
UPE, Latvia

Sparse, elegant performances of Latgale traditional material, mainly just Ozoliņa with her kokles.

Ugis Praulins

Programmer, producer, singer and keyboard, kokles and flute player Praulins combines traditional music with current studio technology.

⊙ Paganu Gadagramata
UPE, Latvia

Material from the folk song collections of Emilis Melngailis, in very sympathetic atmospheric settings featuring Jauns Mēness guitarist Gints Sola and the voices and traditional instruments of Ilga Reizniece and Māris Muktupāvels. Released in 1999, it's an impressive start to the "Latvian Folk Music Collection" from Ainars Mielavs' UPE label.

Skandinieki

Formed back in 1976 by Liv folklore movement pioneers Helmī Stalte and Dainis Stalts, and still led by them, the folk vocal group Skandinieki sings the old Latvian and Livonian songs.

⊙ Skandinieki
UPE, Latvia

Thirty songs of rural life, nature, seasons, gods and symbolism in which Saule, the sun, is prominent. With natural female and male vocals, occasionally accompanied on fiddle, accordion or Jew's harp, they have a warm, unaffected, hypnotic folk-chorale sound with a quiet dignity that's very Latvian/ Livonian.

Lithuania

⊙ Lithuanian Folk Dreams
Kuku, Lithuania

A 2003 sampler of progressive, fusion and jazz approaches to traditional music by groups and projects including Atalyja, Veronika Povolioniené and Sutaras.

⊙ Lithuanian Folk Music
33 Records, Lithuania

Forty-six recordings from the 1930s to the 1980s, of work, ritual, wedding, nature, children's, historical and war songs, plus instrumental music – with extensive English notes.

★ Lituanie: le pays des chansons
Ocora, France

Excellent, varied collection of 35 traditional songs and instrumentals, including horn, kanklès and sutartinès, recorded for Lithuanian Radio from 1958 to 1990. Notes in French and English.

⊙ Songs and Music from Suvalkija
Institute of Lithuanian Literature and Folklore, Lithuania
Recordings made in 1935–39 in southwest Lithuania, including reaping, wedding, family and love songs, waltzes, marches, schottisches, krakowiaks and mazurpolkas on fiddle or whistle, and kanklės playing by the founder of the Skriaudžiai Kanklės Ensemble.

⊙ Songs, Sutartinės and Instrumental Music from Aukštaitija
Institute of Lithuanian Literature and Folklore, Lithuania
Two CDs of recordings made in 1935–41 in northeastern Lithuania. Polyphonic vocal sutartinės and some played on kanklės, plus ritual songs, shepherds' songs and wedding songs, tunes on skudučiai, wooden trumpets (ragai), whistles (lamzdelis) and goat horn, polkas, waltzes and suktinis on cimbolai (hammered dulcimer) or fiddle.

★ A String of Sutartinės
Kuku, Lithuania
This gives a strong sense of sutartinės' possibilities. A handful of 1930s recordings are mixed in with a wide range of contemporary approaches. Philip-Glass-like shifting, overlapping patterns from musicians and bands including rockish Atalyja, Pievos and Žalvarinis, ritualistic Kūlgrinda, Lithuanian/North Indian group Lyla, folklore groups Sedula, Dijūta and Sutaras, and vocal group Trys Keturiose in conjunction with the techno fusion of Linas Rimsa and Linas Paulaskis.

Atalyja

Large band with five singers, female and male, plus instruments including kanklės, bagpipes, fiddle, viola, flute, skuduiiai, guitar, tabla and drums.

★ Atalyja
Sutaras/Kuku, Lithuania
Powerful and fresh 2001 debut release of new developments based on seasonal songs and sutartinės. The melodies virtually never stray outside a repeated short sequence made from the first five notes (or fewer) of a minor scale, but they are developed by floating the grainy vocals over bass guitar patterns, and adding the textures of the traditional instruments.

Veronika Povilionienė

Long highly regarded in Lithuania for her serene, rich-toned voice, she sings traditional songs learnt from her family and her subsequent folkloric studies.

★ Vai Ant Kalno
Sutaras/Kuku, Lithuania
Compilation of her recordings between 1986 and 2000, some unaccompanied except for the sounds of the forest where they were recorded, others involving unexpected and wonderfully eccentric collisions with rock, jazz and avant-garde.

Rinkinys

A group with several albums of traditional song and instrumentals, performed straight without added arrangement.

⊙ Sutartinės
Studija, Lithuania
Sutartinės in strong male voices or played on kanklės or wind instruments.

Sutaras

This five-strong group was formed in 1988 by musicians from the Lithuanian Folklore Theatre. They specialize in reviving ancient instruments and repertoire.

⊙ Call of the Ancestors
Lituanus, Lithuania
The 38 tracks include vocal and instrumental sutartinės, the playing of kanklės, horns, whistles and pūsline, and polkas and other dance tunes on fiddle, accordion, harmonica and basetle.

PLAYLIST
The Baltic States

1 LAULA VÕIM Kirile Loo from *Lullabies for Husbands*
Forsaking the big ambient backings, and accompanied just by Tiit Kikas' fiddle, Loo shows her vocal vigour in a song about … the power of song.

2 OZOLIŅŠ SADEGA Iļģi from *Kaza Kāpa Debesīs*
Ilga Reizniece and a grinding deep male voice alternate over Jew's harp and a folk-rock rhythm section.

3 KOPA, KOPA Various from *Ligo*
An archetypal Latvian midsummer song, done as a sound-story of herders gathering for the celebrations.

4 NĀC ĀRĒJU, SAIMENIEKS Skandinieki from *Skandinieki*
A song wishing happiness to the owner of a house: a strong female solo voice calls, a male and female chorus respond in thick parallel harmony.

5 PRŪŠŪ VEDĪBU DZIESMA Valdis Muktupāvels from *Kokles*
A Muktupāvels original, featuring vocals from his wife Rūta accompanied by his kokles and by cello.

6 VIDURY LAUKŲ GRŪŠELĖ AUGA Veronika Povilionienė from *Vai Ant Kalno*
Povilionienė's serene voice in an advent carol, around which weaves Petras Vyšniauskas' equally serene sax.

7 TRYS, KETURIOSE Atalyja from *Atalyja*
Bawled female vocals overlap hypnotically in a sutartinė over backing of kanklės, plucked fiddle, bass guitar figures and shuffling drumkit.

8 GRIEZIKAI 'SALNIU INTAKAS' Rinkinys from *Sutartinės*
The strange, hypnotic sound of a sutartinė played on skudučiai, their flute-notes overlapping just as in vocal sutartinės.

9 LÄHME NURME KÜNDMA! (LET'S GO PLOUGHING, YOU GUYS!) Male Setu singers from *The Folk Music of Estonia*
Most recent recordings of Setu song are of female singers, but here the oscillating call and compressed-harmony response is from muscular males.

10 PATEIK MAN Biruta Ozoliņa from *Sirdsgrieži*
Ozoliņa's clear voice with an elegantly sympathetic accompaniment from piano and her kokles.

31

Belgium

flemish, walloon and global fusion

Jaune Toujours
Jak Kilby

In Belgium, Latin and Germanic cultures converge: the north is Flemish and its 5.5 million inhabitants speak Dutch, while in the south 4.5 million Walloons speak French. The capital, Brussels, is bilingual but predominantly French-speaking, and in the east a minority speak German. These days, more than just Latin and Germanic cultures meet in Belgium; sounds from all continents flow through the increasingly multicultural music scene. As everywhere in Western Europe, the twentieth century has seen local cultures undervalued, but also revived. **Paul Rans** tells the story.

Flanders

As flautist and researcher **Wim Bosmans** has demonstrated, on the recordings of his folk group **Jan Smed** as well as in his book on traditional music in Flanders (published in Dutch), many traditional Belgian tunes have migrated from one part of the country to another and are now shared not only by Flanders and Wallonia but by various European countries, their real origins unknown. Some are even in the classical mainstream, having been adopted by nineteenth-century opera composers. The repertoire, which also has distinct Flemish and Walloon traditions, began to decline early in the twentieth century but much survives due to the efforts of folk-song and dance-tune collectors of the 1900s.

Interest in folk music was rekindled in the 1960s by people such as **Wannes Van de Velde** – a towering figure in Flanders – and **Hubert Boone** who, besides his fieldwork (collecting, for example, from village brass bands or the old guilds' instrumental ensembles), also led the traditional music group **De Vlier**. During the early 1970s **Herman Dewit** and his group **'t Kliekske** (Little Clique/ Small Band) went on a legendary trip around Flanders on horse and cart, performing in villages and towns, and at the same time collecting songs and tunes from older people.

In the late 1960s and early 1970s there was also a movement to modernize traditional music, with Wannes Van de Velde singing his own urban songs in his native Antwerp dialect, as well as traditional ones. Van de Velde's songs are some of the best ever written in Flanders. Musically and lyrically innovative, yet rooted in tradition, they draw on traditional elements from Flanders but also on those of other European countries, especially Greece and Spain, and even on contemporary classical music. Wannes Van de Velde, singer and instrumentalist, playwright, poet and artist, died in 2008, aged 71.

Ghent-born sculptor and singer **Walter de Buck** revived many of the old Ghent broadside ballads and added his own, meanwhile initiating the *Gentse Feesten* – street parties which have since evolved into a two-week summer festival. **Rum** was the first group to take Flemish folk (in a blend of ballads and dance-songs, exciting instrumentals and humorous presentation) across the language border into Wallonia and then around Europe. They toured from 1969 to 1978, when they went their separate ways. The band reformed briefly in 2005 but singer **Dirk Van Esbroeck**, who was equally at home in Flemish songs as in tangos from Argentina where he grew up, died of cancer in 2007, aged sixty.

Hubert Boone's **Brabants Volksorkest** has travelled even more widely, taking its mainly

Marc Masschelein/SOFAM

Wannes Van de Velde

nineteenth-century traditional repertoire to Siberia, Cuba and Africa. The orchestra specializes in dance and serenade music of the Brabant and the Campine region: structured melodies, harmonized in a style which flourished in the nineteenth and early twentieth centuries. His latest group, **Limbrant**, offer a similar repertoire but in a more slender line-up.

The 1980s were a slim time for folk music. Although Wannes Van de Velde, 't Kliekske and the Brabants Volksorkest kept the flame burning, and the folk-rock band **Kadril** continued to widen its own audience, folk music of any kind was considered unfashionable. Herman Dewit didn't worry too much about fashion and continued to perform, making bagpipes, fifes and hurdy-gurdies, while also organizing annual summer courses in Gooik, west of Brussels. The courses were, and still are, very successful events which began to bear fruit in the mid-1990s with young groups emerging such as **Hauman & de Moeite**, **Fluxus**, and especially Ambrozijn and Laïs.

Laïs is the most popular Flemish group in Belgium as well as internationally. **Jorunn Bauweraerts**, **Annelies Brosens** and **Nathalie Delcroix** first surprised audiences in the late 1990s with their acapella renderings of traditional as well as new songs. Laïs sold an amazing number of CDs (their first album over 80,000 copies) and despite taking part in the Gooik workshops Laïs never really aimed to sing in a traditional Flemish way. On their latest albums they sing more French and English than Flemish songs.

Combining a singer of character and style (**Ludo Vandeau**) with three highly skilled and inventive instrumentalists (fiddler Wouter Vandenabeele, guitarist **Tom Theuns** and diatonic accordion/melodeon player **Wim Claeys**), **Ambrozijn** brought new life into traditional and contemporary songs and music.

The band no longer exists but its members all play successfully with other groups. In particular, **Wouter Vandenabeele** is increasingly making his mark in various world music projects. He is the leader of world music big band **Olla Vogala**, formed in the late 1990s when he and a group of friends, who used to improvise to silent films, started playing outside cinemas, with an actor who recited Middle Dutch poetry and medieval recipes. Vandenabeele played the violin, **Tom Theuns** sitar and **Dirk Moelants** bass viol and they mainly improvised on ancient Flemish and Italian themes. Wouter soon introduced many more musicians, including **Ludo Vandeau** and the Algerian rai vocalist **Djamel**, and also started

composing and arranging new material. Olla Vogala absorbs many influences, from Flemish, French and Celtic traditions to African music, jazz and classical, but despite so many ingredients the result is far from chaotic.

Kadril has been the most prominent folk-rock band in Flanders for a good many years. In the 1990s they managed to go beyond the world of the folkies with singer **Patrick Riguelle**. They keep reinventing themselves, and always in good company. Since the Laïs girls went their own way, Kadril have launched a series of new female singers, including **Eva De Roovere**, who sang with Oblomow and has now gone solo. **Oblomow** is a Flemish band with musical roots around the world which demonstrates a poetic awareness of today's social and political problems as well as a sense of humour. Its founder **Gerry De Mol** has also written a book on nine women singers from various parts of the world, now living in Belgium. He not only writes about them, he also plays with them, including **Marlène Dorcéna** from Haiti, **Minyeshu Kifle Tedla** from Ethiopia, **Talike Gellé** from Madagascar (also singing with Tiharea), **Laila Amezian** from Morocco (also with Arabanda) and **Naira Noian** from Armenia.

Wallonia

In Wallonia the folk music revival was initially not as strong as in the north, although old traditions such as fife and drum bands, fanfares (brass bands) and hunting-horn ensembles were maintained. During recent years, however, there has been a surge of new bands, with **Urban Trad** making big waves, not least by coming second in the 2003 Eurovision Song Contest. Their name says it all: acoustic instruments, music inspired by tradition but set in a contemporary urban environment, typified by a solid rhythm section and modern programming, including some cosmic electronic effects. In its first edition the band included quite a few big names in Belgium: **Luc Pilartz**, **Didier Laloy**, **Tom Theuns** and **Perry Rose**. With the latest line-up, a mix of expert Flemish and Walloon instrumentalists, Urban Trad looks at the whole of Europe for its inspiration.

Progressive interpretations of music from the four corners of Europe is the basis for a large number of contemporary bands in Belgium. **Panta Rhei** was the first band to work in this way, with musicians from very different musical backgrounds, from classical and jazz to pop and folk. **Trio Trad** have paid homage to the music of Scandinavia, Hungary, Bulgaria and Ireland, but in a style which remains much closer to the originals. They have also released an excellent album focusing on music from Wallonia itself, titled **Violon Populaire en Wallonie**.

Claude Flagel is a French singer and hurdy-gurdy player whose repertoire spans many centuries of French and Walloon balladry. He has lived in Brussels for several decades and has worked with both Flemish and Walloon musicians. He also runs the **Fonti Musicali** label specializing in ethnic music from Wallonia to the Congo, Rwanda and Burundi, including percussionist **Mamady Keita** and the late **Momo Wandel**.

Didier Laloy is an accordion wizard who has played with Urban Trad, plays in Trio Tref with fellow Flemish accordionist Wim Claeys, and is involved in many other projects, both north and south of the language border. He released a brilliant solo double album in 2004 called *S-tres*, mixing traditions and his own compositions. Other up-and-coming bands include **Dazibao**, **Musaraigne**, **Deux Accords Diront** and **Aurelia**.

Mixing it up

Belgium, as elsewhere in Europe, has become increasingly multicultural. Many bands have

Think Of One

Think Of One's music is hard to define, but has an immediate appeal. They mix brass band elements and a singer who sings mainly in his Antwerp dialect with rock, reggae and other styles from all around the world. Leader David Bovée says their music isn't fusion. It's more like a soup, he claims, with the different ingredients combining to produce one basic taste.

The band used to travel around in their van, performing wherever people would listen, and meanwhile learning a great deal. In Morocco they played with local musicians, absorbing Moroccan trance music. Later they went to northeastern Brazil, where they plunged into *côco, frevo, maracatú* and other local styles which themselves are the result of fusions between Indian, African and European elements. They recorded their *Chuva em Pó* album with some of the local musicians and then toured with them in Europe, showcasing singer **Dona Cila do Côco** and percussionist **Carranca**. In 2005 they worked with Inuit singers. David Bovée had heard their intriguing throat singing for the first time while in Marrakech, and sought them out in northern Quebec. Again the band paid its respects to the original music, while giving it the Think Of One treatment.

They released another Brazilian album, *Trafico*, and their latest is *Camping Shââ-bi*, returning to the rhythms of Morocco. Having received the **BBC Radio 3 World Music Award** for Boundary Crossing in 2004 and also the Belgian **Zamu Award for World Music**, they have decided to take a break in 2009 – and it may well last a little while.

Guy Kokken

Think Of One

Zap Mama

"I feel I can be a bridge between two cultures", Zap Mama's leader **Marie Daulne** has said. True enough. Her group has proved to be a vibrant bridge between many cultures, stunning audiences all round the world.

Daulne's story is extraordinary. She was born in 1964 in what was then the Democratic Republic of the Congo (1960–71), but three weeks after her birth her Belgian father was killed in a rebellion and her mother took her children into the forest for eight months where they were protected by Pygmies. The Belgian Army airlifted the family to Belgium and she grew up in Brussels. There she teamed up with other Belgian-Africans and two white singers with a genuine feel for multi-culturalism. Drawing on Pygmy polyphony and yodel techniques, as well as other African and European vocal styles, they thrust their virtuoso five-strong female acapella group on an unsuspecting world in 1989.

In their first album they explored all sorts of vocal sounds – squeals, grunts, pants, laughs, giggles, vocal percussion as well as warm velvety tones and harmonies. They also put together one hell of an energetic, inventive and polished stage show.

Their second album, *Sabsylma* (1994) took a more global viewpoint. "Before I spoke about the Pygmies and the people around them. Now I want to talk about the people around me. Some of the most rewarding travel I've done was just ringing my neighbours' doors. My Moroccan neighbour shared her Moroccan world. The Pakistani man at the grocery showed me Pakistan. That's what *Sabsylma* is about. I suggest that people dream and travel in their own cities by talking to their neighbours."

Daulne sees herself as a sort of global *griotte* bringing a power from an ancestral world: "A man in Mali told me that there are seven senses. Everyone has five, some can use their sixth, but not everyone has the seventh. It is the power to heal with music, calm with colour, to soothe the sick soul with harmony. He told me that I have this gift, and I know what I have to do with it."

Daulne seemed to turn her back on Zap Mama when she moved to New York to explore nu-soul, R&B and hip-hop on her solo album *A ma zone* (2000). Many fans may not be too thrilled with Daulne's new direction, but Zap Mama has also gained a new audience. Their latest album *Ancestry in Progress* (2004) continues to manifest the new Black American influences, but the Ancestry in the title refers to their African heritage and that is still audibly present.

At a special acapella concert on Women's Day in March 2009, Marie Daulne surprised her audience with the original Zap Mama line-up in a fabulous performance. And that was followed by the release of a new album, *ReCreation*.

Zap Mama

been formed, bringing together "locals" and immigrants. Examples are **Olla Vogala** (Flanders, North Africa), **Melike** (Flanders, Turkey, Iraq, Morocco), **Luthomania** (Belgium, Morocco, China) and **Think Of One** (Belgium, Morocco, Brazil, Inuit… see box on p.35).

Quite a few musicians look further afield to find musical partners. Olla Vogala has worked with singers from various European and African countries. **Zap Mama** has always been a mixed band. Jazz sax player **Pierre Vaiana**, himself of Sicilian origin, has been particularly successful in bringing together musicians from Burkina Faso and Belgium after teaching and studying in Ouagadougou for a number of years. The result can be heard in his band **Foofango**.

Belgium's main link with Africa lies in what is now again called the **Democratic Republic of Congo**, formerly Zaire and before that the Belgian Congo (1884–1960).

During the colonial era – and indeed, up until the 1980s – not much attention was paid to Congolese music, outside ethnomusicological circles. However, immigrants, students and temporary visitors from Congo, Rwanda and Burundi have always performed their music in Brussels for themselves, concentrating in the Matongé quarter. The recent interest in world music has ensured that some of those excellent musicians and singers have been able to reach wider audiences, and in **Zap Mama**, Belgium has one of the most dynamic bands on the world music scene (see box below).

The old Afro-Belgian links first bore fruit in the early 1980s with **Bula Sangoma**, in which Flemish percussionist **Chris Joris** was joined by some brilliant Central African musicians, such as singer/composer **Dieudonné Kabongo** (who finds inspiration in his Luba tradition), Rwandan singer **Cécile Kayirebwa**, and Congolese singer **Princesse Mansia M'Bila**, as well as by jazz musicians such as American sax player **John Ruocco**. Joris, who is also a pianist and composer, was the first in Belgium to show an interest in African music and to play with African musicians, long before anyone had heard of world music. He still continues his explorations with African and other musicians.

Among the various other immigrant communities in Belgium there have been some genuinely interesting fusions. **Luthomania**, for example, brings together three lutes: the Chinese pipa, the Arab oud and the European lute. These are played by Hua Xia, Abid El Bahri and Philippe Malfeyt, often in the company of Chris Joris on percussion. Classical, jazz, folk tunes and innovative compositions melt into their own brand of world music. **Karim Baggili**, a guitarist and 'ud player with Balkan and Jordanian roots, is one of the most exciting musicians around and can be heard solo, with his acoustic quartet, with jazz ensembles and with a world-rock band. **Zahava Seewald** has recorded some fascinating albums of Jewish songs on the Tzadik label. There is **Tri a Tolia** with the melancholy voice of **Melike Tarhan** (Turkey-Belgium), **Osama Abdulrasol** on qanun (Iraq) and the imaginative cello playing of **Lode Vercampt**. And there is also Tunisian-born singer **Ghalia Benali** who has an irresistible stage presence and a great voice. The same can be said of flamenco singer **Amparo Cortés** who has made three albums, two of them with her cousin, guitarist Enrique de Melchor.

DISCOGRAPHY Belgium

Flanders and Wallonia

⊙ **Belgique: Ballades, danses et chansons de Flandre et de Wallonie**
Ocora, France
Reissue of older BRTN/VRT Radio 3 recordings from 1952 to 1980 but still a fine selection of traditional performers representative of both Flanders and Wallonia, juxtaposing old field recordings and revival versions.

 **Folk Music from Belgium**
Auvidis Ethnic, France
Good mix of authentic traditions and revival groups, all recently recorded by Hubert Boone. Old traditional forms on this double CD include fife and tabor bands, hunting-horns from the Ardennes, accordion players, drummer bands from Antwerp and the famous carnival drums of the "Gilles de Binche". The revival groups include the Brabants Volksorkest, 't Kliekske, Polka Galop, Rue du Village and Kadril "unplugged".

⊙ **Traditionele muziek uit Vlaanderen: Mogen wij vreemd gaan?**
Eufoda, Belgium
The last in a series of eight albums surveying the roots of traditional song and music in Flanders, recorded by VRT Klara. The focus is on the music itself, rather than the arrangements or the performers' virtuosity. Most forms of traditional music are covered, rural as well as urban. This CD looks to the future, featuring young and innovative bands in Flanders, including Ambrozijn, Ballroomquartet, Laïs, Tref, Troissoeur, Water en Wijn, Olle Geris, Herlinde Ghekiere and Iep Fourier.

Ambrozijn

Ambrozijn sing and play with great virtuosity and a lot of punch, and have released several excellent CDs featuring traditional Flemish songs alongside their own material.

⊙ Kabonka
Alea Wild Boar Music, Belgium
Ambrozijn are taking a break from performing together as a band, but this is perhaps their best recording. It includes French guest singers Sylvie Berger and Gabriel Yacoub, who also produced the album.

Kadril

The most prominent folk-rock band in Flanders, Kadril has been going for a good many years now, with their unusual combination of electric guitars, bass and drums with fiddle, bagpipes and hurdy-gurdy.

⊙ De Andere Kust
Alea Wild Boar Music, Belgium
This album's theme is European emigration to the US from the 1870s to the 1920s. Kadril introduced three new voices here: Hungarian Szilvia Bognár, British Heather Grabham and Flemish Mariken Boussemaere, who is the lead singer on their latest release, *Mariage*.

Laïs

Laïs' harmony singing has touched audiences from Toronto to Shanghai and South Africa.

⊙ Laïs Lenski
Bang!, Belgium
For this 2009 CD Laïs joined forces with cellist Simon Lenski, member of DAAU (Die Anarchistische AbendUnterhaltung). He has definitely put his stamp on this album. Laïs leave the folkies well behind as Lenski steers them through uncharted territory, supporting their voices on cello and electronics.

Oblomow

Oblomow is a Flemish band with musical roots around the world. Eva De Roovere sings in Dutch, Laila Amezian in Arabic and French. Gerry De Mol (vocals, guitar, oud) is the driving force, providing quite a few lyrics and music. The other members are Mattias Laga (soprano sax and clarinet), Lode Vercampt (cello), Jan Cordemans (E-bow, fretless and fretted bass) and Azzedine Jazouli (percussion).

⊙ Ya Waaw
HA!, Belgium
This second CD fulfills all the promise of the first and goes even further with excellent singing and playing, and a fine balance in bringing together the old and the new, roots from home and from far afield. Two guest musicians on this disc: the Russian duduk player and flautist Serguey Klevensky (Farlanders) and Flemish accordion virtuoso Ivan Smeulders.

Luc Pilartz/Violon Populaire en Wallonie

Having played so much music from all over Europe, Luc Pilartz decided to take a look at his own musical background with a band called Violon Populaire en Wallonie.

⊙ Meslanges
Alea Wild Boar Music, Belgium
Meslanges is old French for mix and these excellent musicians present a programme dating mainly from the eighteenth and nineteenth centuries when a lot of dance tunes travelled around Europe. Sometimes they have a Swedish tinge (a good

number of Walloon people emigrated to Sweden to find work), some sound a bit Hungarian or even Greek, but altogether the musicianship is such that the origin of the music is irrelevant.

Panta Rhei

Panta Rhei perform contemporary interpretations of folk music from around Europe. The name is from Heraclitus, "All things flow, nothing lasts forever".

⊙ Strides
Alea Wild Boar Music, Belgium
Pascal Chardome (guitar) and Steve Houben (saxophone and flute) are both jazz musicians and composers, but they don't jazz up the European folk music which they play on *Strides*. Faithful to the roots, they play with great virtuosity and make it very much music of today.

Wannes Van de Velde

The best-known voice of Flemish folk. He had an encyclopaedic knowledge of tradition but also wrote some of the best songs in Flanders.

⊙ In de maat van de seizoenen
Granota, Belgium
Sadly this is Wannes Van de Velde's ultimate CD, released two years before his death in 2008. A musical Don Quixote, as he calls himself in one of his songs, he could be sharply critical, sometimes deeply poetic and also very funny, while the music is always strong and often surprising.

Fusion

DVD Didier Laloy invites...
Alea Wild Boar Music, Belgium
On CD and DVD, accordion wizard Didier Laloy presents a live concert in which he plays with a plethora of bands, including Urban Trad, Panta Rhei, Tref, Laïs, French singer Gabriel Yacoub, Irish singer Perry Rose and many more. This ranges from acoustic traditional to loud and thumping folk-rock but the quality is always high.

Ghalia Benali

Ghalia Benali was born in Tunisia but lives and works in Brussels. Not only a singer, she is also a dancer with an impressive stage presence. She is an artist as well, and does the impressive artwork for her CDs.

WITH BERT CORNELIS

⊙ Al Palna
Zimbraz, Netherlands
Ghalia Benali has made some fine solo albums, such as *Romeo & Leila*, but here she works with Belgian sitar player Bert Cornelis, fusing North African and Indian music with the help of the excellent Indian tabla player Prabhu Edouard and Moroccan percussionist Azzedine Jazouli. The Iraqi singer and djoze player Anwar Abudragh also joins them on several tracks. From meditative and spiritual improvisations to explosive expressions of joy.

Jaune Toujours

Jaune Toujours still has some links in the folk scene and the old village brass bands, but the musicians have different musical backgrounds, from folk and world to rock, hip-hop, jazz and contemporary chamber music. A very gutsy band.

⊙ Kolektiv
Chou, Belgium

Jaune Toujours is basically a Flemish band but accordion player Piet Maris sings mostly in French, a statement against narrow nationalism. He sings about Brussels, urban life and social and political problems, mixing rock with chanson and world music touched by dub, ska, reggae and Balkan brass.

Chris Joris

In 1976 percussionist and pianist Chris Joris met South African double bass player Johnny Mbizo Dyani and this was the start of his love affair with African music and jazz. He has been fusing the two ever since, creating his own brand of world music.

DVD Live – Into the Light
FAZ, Belgium

Chris Joris live on DVD in the company of Belgian and African musicians providing the now famous Chris Joris Experience. The line-up includes Pierre Vaiana, Chris Mentens, Pieter Thys, Frédéric Malempré, Dieudonné Kabongo, Ken N'Diaye, Ben Ngabo, N'Faly Kouyaté and Jean Bosco Safari.

Luthomania

Abid El Bahri (Morocco) plays the Arab oud, Hua Xia (China) plays the pipa and Philippe Malfeyt (Belgium) plays lutes and theorbo (a long-necked lute, popular in Renaissance and Baroque periods).

⊙ Itinérances
Papyros, Netherlands

Their first CD captivated world music enthusiasts as well as classical music lovers. They continue their original music making on this second CD, in the company of percussionist Chris Joris, jazz saxophonist Steve Houben, harmonica virtuoso Olivier Poumay, French accordion and bandoneon player Gwenaël Micault and cellist Sigrid Vandenbogaerde.

Think Of One

A Flemish band with a difference. Their music shows influences from just about everywhere – and it works.

⊙ Camping Shââbi
Crammed Discs, Belgium

After two Brazilian albums, and before taking a break, David Bovée and his band returned to their love for Moroccan shââbi – popular music derived from Berber traditions and rhythms but urban in character. The music is given the Think Of One treatment, with a little help from their Moroccan friends, Belgian-Tunisian singer Ghalia Benali and even Laïs. There is also a nine-minute bonus DVD track.

Wouter Vandenabeele

Wouter Vandenabeele leads the Olla Vogala big band, was a member of Ambrozijn and is the driving force behind many special projects, including touring Senegal, playing and directing Manos Hadjidakis's music at the Greek cultural Olympiad and recording his first solo album.

⊙ Chansons sans paroles
homerecords.be, Belgium

Wouter's fiddle playing is all-important here, but he's joined by virtuoso diatonic accordion player Anne Niepold, Arne Van Dongen on double bass, Soetkin Baptist on vocals (without lyrics), Osama Abdulrasol on qanun and two Senegalese musicians, percussionist Serigne C.M. Gueye and hoddu-player Malick Pathé Sow. Intimate music making, which improves with repeated listening.

PLAYLIST
Belgium

1 KA'SI Ghalia Benali and Bert Cornelis from *Al Palna*
My glass, the wine and the waiter make three, and I, burning with desire, make four. Traditional Arab lyrics with music by Ghalia and Bert.

2 MARIEKE Laïs from *Douce Victime*
Laïs's gripping acapella singing works not only in Flemish folksongs, but also in other languages. Here they mix Dutch and French in a song by that most Belgian of singers, Jacques Brel.

3 TRANSSIBERIA Luthomania from *Itinérances*
Arab, Chinese and European lutes blend, with a little help from percussionist Chris Joris. They are clearly enjoying themselves.

4 SAMRA Olla Vogala from *Siyabonga*
A song about infidelity and despair by the Algerian rai singer Djamel. His repetitive style blends perfectly with Issa Sow's fiddle.

5 DE MINNEBODE Olle Geris and Willem Schot from *Mogen wij vreemd gaan?*
A very old Flemish traditional love song. Olle Geris's unaffected singing and Willem Schot's accordion accompaniment are both deceptively simple.

6 74/75 Panta Rhei, Trio Trad, Tref from *Didier Laloy invites…*
European-wide music from Didier Laloy performed live by a union of three Belgian bands.

7 PALETÓ Think of One from *Chuva em Pó*
David Bovée singing in his native Antwerp dialect in the company of his Brazilian friends. Perhaps an unlikely mix, but enticingly original and irresistible.

8 VOOR DE DEUR VAN DE TAVERNE Wannes Van de Velde from *In de maat van de seizoenen*
As a boy Wannes heard Greek sailors making music in the port area of Antwerp. To a Greek tune he describes Greek men sitting in front of a taverna, talking with Ulysses on their tongue.

9 CACHE CACHE Zap Mama from *Ancestry in Progress*
New York makes its influence clear in Marie Daulne's latest work but this is still Zap Mama, with a strong African presence behind the modern urban sound.

10 ROSAS NEGRAS (SEVILLANAS) Amparo Cortés and Enrique de Melchor from *Sueños*
Flamenco singer Amparo Cortés singing about how she arrived in Brussels as a young woman without money, a cardboard suitcase in her hand and longing for Seville.

Zap Mama

Still the most famous group from Belgium, although it is now very much Marie Daulne and backing band. From the start Zap Mama mixed every influence going and that is even more true today.

⊙ Zap Mama/Adventures in Afropea
CramWorld, Belgium; Luaka Bop/Warners, US
Zap Mama's first 1991 album is still a world music classic, with its imaginative and virtuosic vocal arrangements.

★ Ancestry in Progress
Luaka Bop, USA
Marie Daulne's American adventures result in music that may not please fans who fell primarily for the Pygmy yodelling and Afropean harmonies. Yet behind all the nu-soul, hip-hop, R&B and electronics the African basis is still clearly present.

Bosnia and Herzegovina

in the rose garden

Mostar Sevdah Reunion

Stunningly beautiful, Bosnia and Herzegovina is a land of flat plains, wooded hills, broad rivers and barren, sunbaked mountains. The breathtaking diversity of this landscape is reflected in its music, which ranges from sophisticated and complex urban melodies to the solid beats of remote country villages. **Kim Burton** samples the Bosnian pot.

Over a decade after the Dayton Accords brought a halt to the war in the Republic of Bosnia and Herzegovina, the country remains formally divided between the Republika Srpska, whose population is predominantly Serb and Orthodox, and the Federation of Bosnia and Herzegovina, a still uneasy union of Catholic Croats and Muslims (many of whom prefer to be known by the less religiously specific term Bosniak). Efforts by the international administration imposed on the country to unite these two entities have met with resistance from local political elites, and recovery from the tremendous economic damage inflicted by the fighting is proving slow and unsteady, a problem exacerbated by widespread corruption and cronyism. Worst of all, perhaps, are the psychological after-effects of the frequently brutal and cruel principle on which the war was fought – the forced displacement of ethnic and religious communities in order to create ethnically "pure" areas. This was previously an area of remarkable ethnic diversity and interpenetration, including an extremely high number of mixed marriages, but the experience of neighbours turning on one another has left deep scars and a legacy of mistrust. Yet the huge propaganda effort required to turn these neighbours against one another demonstrates how deep the links between the peoples were, and even now these bonds are being re-forged on both a personal and an institutional level. One area where this is taking place is, unfortunately, organized crime. Another is music.

The Bosnian Mix

Within the old Yugoslavia, Bosnia had the reputation of being the musical powerhouse of the entire nation, producing singers, composers and instrumentalists. Some gravitated to Sarajevo or Belgrade, where they performed and recorded the popular folk-based **novokomponovana narodna muzika** which developed into Serbia's **turbofolk** (see p.375), while others stayed closer to home, and to more traditional forms of music. Meanwhile, the area's pop and rock bands drew on those same traditions to make hard-hitting, sometimes sarcastic comments on the times.

Turbofolk and its Serbian superstars are wildly popular among the urban youth in Sarajevo and beyond, and with all ethnic groups. This is hardly surprising, since the novokomponovana narodna muzika scene was a joint Serbian and Bosnian production, with many of its stars Bosnians of different ethnicities. Even though the scenes diverged with the outbreak of war, with the Bosnian developments staying closer to the sound of the 1980s and drawing on Turkish and Arab influences more overtly than is done in Belgrade, the traffic goes both ways. Veteran singer **Šemsa Suljaković** recorded her 2005 CD, *Šemsa*, in Serbia, and **Osman Hadžić's** *Ti me ne voliš* was a major hit in the country in 2003. Other Bosniak turbofolk stars include veterans of the novokomponovana scene like **Halid Muslimović**, **Halid Bešlić** and **Kemal Malovčić**, while newer faces include **Selma Bajrami** and **Sejo Kalač**.

Before the process of "ethnic cleansing" redrew the map of Bosnia, although many areas of the country were predominantly Croat, Muslim or Serb, there were everywhere minorities within the majority group. Thus, the mainly Muslim area of eastern Bosnia held a sizeable Serb minority, and Herzegovina in the west, mainly Croat, held many Muslims. This interpenetration of communities meant that rural music styles tended to be geographically based rather than linked to ethnic identity. For instance, in the northeast and in parts of central Bosnia Serbs, Muslims and Croats all played the energetic and compelling *izvorna* (authentic) music on violin and *šargija* (a country cousin of the more sophisticated urban *saz*). Likewise, in the hills above the southern reaches of the River Neretva, both Croat and Muslim villagers sang the ancient and dissonant vocal *gange* of the Dinaric mountains, whose sounds are reminiscent of the unaccompanied polyphonic songs of the Bosnian Krajina. This area is now predominantly populated by Serbs, who sing in the villages the songs they once shared with their former neighbours, now displaced or refugees.

As is often the case, the most important division – in a wider cultural sense and more specifically in the field of music – lay between the village and the town; the village with its rough-and-ready antique harmonies and powerful rhythms, and the town with a more sophisticated, supple and sinuous melody supported by harmonies with a clear Western component.

Sevdalinke

The most typical form of **urban music** in Bosnia is the **sevdalinka** or love song. (The name is derived from the Turkish word *sevda* – love – but in Bosnia it has come to mean a yearning, hopeless and painful love, doomed never to be consummated.) The broad, ornamented melodies often use oriental scales and chromatic inflections, with a free and flexible rhythm and sweeping arches of melody. The lyrics speak of star-crossed lovers, faith or betrayal and breathe an atmosphere of regret and resignation. In essence, it is a very intimate music, technically demanding for the singer. In its original form it was performed unaccompanied, for a small company, and one oft-repeated saying describes it as music that should only be heard by those seated at the same table as the singer, however powerful the singer's voice. For a time it seemed to be the province of elder statesmen, and pre-war attempts to update it foundered on a less than nuanced use of electric instruments and rock or pop rhythms. More recently, the style has been enjoying a new lease of life, with members of the younger generation remaking the songs in a fresh, open and unforced way. However, very many of those who made their names before the war are still on the scene, although the majority of recordings available (often, unfortunately, pirated) are reissues of their older material.

Accordionist Omer Pobrić's **Institute of Sevdah**, based in Visoko, north of Sarajevo, is an ambitious and highly enthusiastic private institution aiming to track down little-known songs, record them, publish them, and teach them to younger singers. Run on something of a shoestring, it has managed to publish a string of CDs, DVDs, books and more-or-less scholarly studies, as well as organizing festival performances in Sarajevo and elsewhere.

The origins of sevdalinke lie in the interaction of the musical forms brought by the fifteenth-century Turkish invaders with the ballads and lyric songs of the local Slav population. The Turkish influence on this music is unmistakable, but many sevdalinke display typically Slav melodic formulas and cadential patterns, and it is generally accepted that the once significant Sephardic Jewish population made their own contribution to the mix, with the Mostar duo Arkul still keeping the flame alight.

Each town has its own sevdalinke tradition, with songs reflecting the town's particular quirks of history or geography. **Zvornik**, for example, on the River Drina between Bosnia and Serbia, was known as the Gate of Bosnia and was, in the time of Turkish rule, the point from which armies were despatched to put down revolts and uprisings in Serbia. Consequently, many of the sevdalinke from Zvornik deal with loss and with lovers who are never to meet again. One famous song says: "The Drina flows from hill to hill, not with rain or white snow, but

Jak Kilby

Amira

with the tears of the maidens from Zvornik." In contrast, **Sarajevo**, the capital of the province, was the home of rich landowners and merchants who carefully guarded the honour and marriage prospects of their daughters by keeping them hidden away from undesirable suitors, so many Sarajevan sevdalinke speak of thwarted love.

Traditionally, when not sung by a single bare voice, sevdalinke were performed to the accompaniment of the **saz**, a stringed instrument of Turkish origin with a pear-shaped body and long neck. Ideally male singers would accompany themselves (women were rarely if ever acquainted with instrumental technique, save for the tambourine-like *daire*, although they were and are frequently valued as singers). The sound of the saz is quiet and contemplative and fits the mood of sevdalinke perfectly, and although at one time it looked set to die out, it is now undergoing a revival. Among the most notable pre-war singers were **Hasim Muhamerović**, **Kadir Kurtagić** and **Muhamed Mesanović-Hamić**. Today, one very distinguished singer is **Emina Zečaj**, with a remarkably pure voice.

The twentieth century saw the arrival of the folk orchestra of accordion, violin, clarinet and guitar, with harmonies influenced by Western models, and less rhythmic subtlety, but retaining the supple and mournful beauty typical of these songs. The older saz players looked on this style as adulterated and less capable of expressing subtle emotions, but the small group performances of **Safet Isović**, **Hanka Paldum**, **Sejo Pitić**, **Zaim Imamović**, **Himzo Polovina** and others, many now dead but well remembered, are part of a long and sophisticated tradition. Many of these are equally noted for their performances of the generally less demanding newly composed folk music, and Imamović was himself a talented and prolific composer. **Silvana Armenulić**, who died tragically young in a car accident in 1976, was in the opinion of many one of the finest singers of both kinds of music. The songs may also be backed by the liquid shimmer of a *tamburica* band (see p.70).

The post-war years have seen increased interest in sevdalinke among younger people, with notable figures being **Mostar Sevdah Reunion** (see box on p.45), the young Sarajevan singer **Amira**, and guitarist and singer **Damir Imamović** (grandson of Zaim), whose small band has a harder-edged approach drawing on Turkish roots and blues.

One tradition which is often claimed to have contributed to the development of sevdalinke is the Ottoman religious music known as **kaside** and **ilahije**. In fact, their often rather plain lines and manner of performance by massed choirs singing in unison, sometimes accompanied by frame drums with notable rhythmic swing, suggest otherwise. Nevertheless, this once rather under-represented genre can now frequently be heard on the television during Ramadan, and there are a number of recordings available. Related to this style are the songs performed during the Mevlud, a gathering to mark the birth of the Prophet Muhammad. The **Ibn Arebi** and **Nešidu-l-Huda** choirs have made a very fine recording of such songs in traditional style, while the indefatigable **Omer Pobrić** has gathered materials for a Bosnian incarnation, giving it a more local sound through a simple melodic scaffolding and restrained use of the accordion to provide drones.

Bosnian Roots

There are many other types of music in Bosnia, including a Muslim tradition of heroic ballads similar to those of the Serbs and Montenegrins, but often accompanied by the strummed tambura (lute) rather than the *gusle*, and celebrating the feats, naturally enough, of Muslim rather than Christian warriors. However, one of the most widespread styles is *Izvorna Bosanska muzika*, which means roughly "roots music".

At one time performed at village celebrations known as *sijela* (sittings), marking the end of harvest time, ploughing or sowing, and on feast days, more recently this music is to be heard at the Saturday-night dance in the local house of culture or bar. It is usually performed by a small group consisting of a couple of singers, two violinists and a šargija player, sometimes joined by accordion or even, on occasion, a rough-and-ready assault on a drum kit. Of course, recent years have seen the introduction of electrification. Although often looked down upon by the urban population, and in general now harder to find than a couple of decades ago, this music is still around, played on local radio stations and recorded in small local studios, as well as occasionally performed at extraordinary bullfights cum funfairs known as *koride*.

The sound of this roots music is quite startling to the stranger, as its ideas of harmony and consonance draw on a tradition totally different from that of western Europe or its descendants in American popular song. Essentially it involves two voices singing together in very close harmony –

Jesus Moreno/vde

Nešidu-l-Huda

Rebuilding Bridges: Mostar Sevdah Reunion

Mostar Sevdah Reunion is one of the finest bands to have emerged in the Balkans in recent years. Not only do they make great music, but their story is also part of the healing process that is the only way forward for the region. The seeds were sown in the darkest days of the Bosnian war (1992–95) when Mostar, one of the jewels of Bosnia and Herzegovina, was split along religious and ethnic lines with Catholic Croats on the western side of the river and Muslim Bosnians on the east. Even while the war was raging, veteran singer **Ilijaz Delić** and the young accordionist **Mustafa Šantić** gave candlelit concerts. "I went to a performance near the mosque where there was room for twenty or thirty people who were crazy enough to risk their lives running between the grenades to listen to a guy singing *sevdah*", remembers **Dragi Šestić** who is now the band's manager. "It was the first time I'd heard this passionate, expressive way of singing sevdah and thought, my God, this is the John Lee Hooker of Bosnian blues."

Mostar has long been the heartland of sevdalinke. It's the musical equivalent of the beautiful sixteenth-century Turkish bridge that was the symbol of the city until it was destroyed by Croat shells in 1993. After the war Dragi married a Dutch photo-journalist and moved to Amsterdam, but returning to Mostar in 1998 he got Delić and Šantić into the newly built Pavarotti Music Centre and a demo was made.

MSR's first CD, released in 1999, showcased a splendid band built around the original duo of Delić and Šantić; it is a magnificent celebration of sevdalinke, performed by a multi-ethnic band representing everything the old Bosnia used to be. On subsequent albums, they have brought some wonderful old Gypsy singers out of retirement – **Šaban Bajramović** and the swarthy-voiced **Ljiljana Buttler** (see p.210). Buttler's recording with MSR, *The Mother of Gypsy Soul*, is their best to date. She recalls her early days singing in Skadarlija, Belgrade's "Bohemian quarter", very close to where much of the city's media are based. "The atmosphere was fantastic. The people laughed and cried during the music. They came from Radio Belgrade to the cafés, listened to the music and if they liked it, asked us back to the studios to record." Sadly, as is the way with many successful bands in the Balkans, MSR have now split into two rival bands, with singer Delić in one and Dragi Šestić working with the other.

Simon Broughton

so close, indeed, that the Western ear perceives a grinding dissonance where the Bosnian hears a satisfying consonance. It is not known how far back this way of singing dates, but it is widespread in southeastern Europe, from Istria to eastern Bulgaria, though the Bosnian bands have developed it in a very interesting way, being remote enough to preserve it but close enough to trade routes and small towns to acquire modern instruments and adapt them to the old music.

It was around the time of World War I that string bands of this type made their first appearance, but in the 1960s and later, as the music's local audience began to travel abroad as *Gastarbeiter* (guest workers) to Germany and other relatively wealthy European countries, they increased their economic power, both in their own lives and by sending money home to their families. This provided the impetus for many local record companies to record the music, giving it an unusually wide distribution for what had been a rather obscure form of village music. Most of these bands, Croat, Muslim and Serb, enjoy local fame only, but among those who have made more of a name for themselves **Kalesijski Zvuci** remain outstanding. The more

traditional groups of **Halid Musić**, the **Mahovski Slavuji**, **Braća Babajić**, **Braća Jelić** and **Braća Geljić** are also worth seeking out. Along with nostalgic songs about parents and memories of home, there's a strand of salty humour, well represented by Derventa's **Mara & Lole**, huge stars with a winningly irreverent and good-humoured charm. Although the average urban Bosnian may look on this scene rather scornfully, it's in rude health.

The past few years have seen the reformation of a number of bands, fundamentally pop- and rock-oriented but drawing on local traditions, who had disbanded in the 1980s or 90s but retained a nostalgic middle-aged following. These include **Zabranjeno Pušenje** (under the name of **Emir Kusturica's No Smoking Orchestra**) and **Bijelo Dugme**. Singer-songwriters **Kemal Monteno** and **Dino Merlin** (the latter given to barbed social comment) still have a high profile, while comedy stars **Nervozni Poštar**, again recently reformed under the leadership of **Fadil Šabović**, have taken a punkish swing at the folk-pop scene. Indeed the country as a whole is beginning to re-exert its former dominance over the post-Yugoslav scene.

▶▶ *See the article on Serbia for discs that cover the whole of former Yugoslavia.*

Compilations

 Antologija BH Sevdalinke
Muzička produkcija javnog servisa BiH, Bosnia and Herzegovina
An ongoing series of releases from the archives of Radio Sarajevo, featuring some of the greatest singers: Zaim Imamović, Safet Isović, Himzo Polovina, Emina Zečaj and many more, mostly accompanied by a small folk band or tamburica orchestra, although one volume is devoted to songs accompanied by saz. These are essentially live recordings, fresh and effective, and what is more, available and legal.

⊙ **Bosnia: Echoes from an Endangered World**
Smithsonian Folkways, US
Issued during the war, and restricted to performers of Muslim origin only, this nevertheless showcases a lot of different musicals styles. There is some wonderful singing of urban and country music, plus songs from a dervish ritual.

⭐ **Sevdalinke: Sarajevo Love Songs**
Piranha, Germany
The perfect introduction to the beauty of sevdalinke, with a 2007 assortment of songs in contemporary arrangements. Artists include Mercan Dede, Emina Zečaj and Jadranka Stojaković, who sang the theme song for the Sarajevo Winter Olympics in 1984. Her performance of "Što te nema" here is a desert island disc.

Artists

Amira

Amira Medunjanin is a young Sarajevan singer, who, coming as she does from outside the mainstream tradition, brings a fresh and original approach to the music of Bosnia and Herzegovina and beyond.

 Rosa
Snail Records, The Netherlands
The combination of Amira's crystalline voice with imaginative arrangements performed by a group which includes members of MSR and this writer, among others, has produced a disc of great subtlety, intimacy and beauty.

Hor Ibn Arebi i hor Nešidu-l-Huda

These two Sarajevo-based male-voice choirs specialize in Islamic sacred music, ilahije and kaside.

⊙ **Mevlud**
Muzička produkcija javnog servisa BiH, Bosnia and Herzegovina
The musical content of a Mevlud performed in full by two notable choirs; austere, plain yet deeply passionate, with moments of piercing beauty.

Damir Imamović

The grandson of legend Zaim Imamović, with a powerful voice and an approach that rethinks sevdalinke, using inflections from the blues, North Africa and beyond.

⊙ **Abrašević Live**
Ekipa, Bosnia and Herzegovina
Imamović, accompanying himself on guitar, is joined by acoustic bass and violin in a live performance, with sparse and bare arrangements that are intensely affecting.

Safet Isović

One of the greats, Isović was a trained singer and a mainstay of Sarajevo Radio's music programmes from the 1960s to the turn of the century, with a voice of intense power and beauty. His death in 2007 left a gap which will be hard to fill.

⊙ **Doajeni bosanskohercegovačke sevdalinke: Safet Isović**
Muzička Produkcija Radio-Televizije BiH, Bosnia and Herzegovina
A double CD of recordings from the early 1960s, with Isović often accompanied by just two accordions. The occasional roughness in sound quality is more than compensated for by his direct, passionate performance.

Flory Jagoda

Of Sarajevan origin, Jagoda left Bosnia shortly after World War II and moved to the United States, where she now lives. She is probably the most prominent performer of songs in Judeo-Spanish from the Sephardic tradition in Bosnia.

⊙ **Memories of Sarajevo: Judeo-Spanish Songs from Bosnia**
Global Village Music, US
Folky guitars and handclaps back a set of sweetly attractive melodies, most of which retain a notably Spanish melodic shape and feeling. Confusingly, the most Slav sounding of all is the only one to refer overtly to a Jewish festivity.

Kalesijski Zvuci

Led by Ramo Salkić and Hasan Požegić, this band hailing from close to the market town of Kalesija remains one of the most inventive in the roots tradition, with violins, šargija, guitar and accordion backing up the jammed-together village voices of the leaders.

⊙ **Bosnian Breakdown**
GlobeStyle, UK
Recorded in 1991, before the outbreak of the war, the title has gained a terrible irony, but this remains about the only example of this music on a Western label. A couple of the tunes are in traditional acoustic style with two violins and a šargija, while the rest are beefed up with modern instruments and drums.

Avdo Lemeš

Sarajevo-based *sazlija* and singer Lemeš has dedicated himself to researching and preserving almost forgotten songs, as well as continuing and enriching the tradition of *pevanje uz saz.*

⊙ Aman Jada od Akšam do Sabaha

Muzička Produkcija Radio-Televizije BiH, Bosnia and Herzegovina

An exceptional CD, combining robust singing and playing from Lemeš himself with sensitive accordion and string arrangements – practically unprecedented, but highly effective.

Mostar Sevdah Reunion

Veteran singer Iljaz Delić from Mostar was the main singer of the band, whose members include musicians of all ages and backgrounds. Their remarkable inventiveness and willingness to introduce new sounds and ideas to the field of sevdalinke has made them one of the very few groups to attain popularity and respect at home and abroad.

⊙ Mostar Sevdah Reunion

World Connection, Netherlands

MSR's eponymous debut album from 1999 includes some dark, intense songs for voice and accordion and some popular sevdah classics like "The Bazaars of Mostar". A strong debut.

★ A Secret Gate

Snail Records, The Netherlands

Mostar Sevdah Reunion attained a new maturity on this 2003 release, a mixture of up-tempo bounce and subtly balanced slow ballads, with a remarkably clean sound and assured playing.

Hanka Paldum and Sejo Pitić

Skilled vocalists Hanka Paldum and Sejo Pitić are both equally at home in local popular and traditional singing.

⊙ Hanka Paldum and Sejo Pitić: Iz Kulturne Baštine 1

Muzička produkcija javnog servisa BiH, Bosnia and Herzegovina

Hanka Paldum and Sejo Pitić's fine voices are displayed to advantage on this set of classic recordings from the radio archives, which feature some of the best-known of all sevdalinke.

Himzo Polovina

The late Himzo Polovina was not a professional singer, but a doctor, yet his subtle, understated and sensitive performances of sevdalinke are some of the finest examples of the art ever recorded.

⊙ Doajeni BH sevdalinke – Himzo Polovina

Muzička produkcija javnog servisa BiH, Bosnia and Herzegovina

Magnificent four-CD set of Polovina singing standards, and some of his own compositions, backed up by groups ranging from an accordion duet to a full tambura orchestra.

Emina Zečaj

Veteran singer Emina Zečaj was one of the very few women to sing with saz accompaniment, although she also recorded with the radio orchestra and other groups. Her once sweet and pure voice has developed into a rich maturity: unfortunately she performs very rarely these days.

⊙ Traditional Bosnian Songs

Gramofon, Bosnia and Herzegovina

Simple but heartfelt performances by Zečaj, sensitively accompanied by saz player Mehmed Gribajčević.

PLAYLIST
Bosnia and Herzegovina

1 DUNJALUČE, GOLEM TI SI Himzo Polovina from *Echoes from an Endangered World*
A hushed and fascinating performance of a mysterious and moving song.

2 SJAJNA ZVIJEZDO Hanka Paldum from *Iz Kulturne Baštine*
An assured version of a beautiful tune, demonstrating fine rhythmic subtleties.

3 MUJO DJOGU PO MEJDANU VODA Amira from *Rosa*
Wonderful singing of a complex arc of melody over the simplest of accompaniments.

4 OKRENI SE NIZ DJUL-BAŠTI Mostar Sevdah Reunion from *A Secret Gate*
A perfect balance of heartfelt vocals and poised instrumental interludes.

5 AKO ŽELIŠ MENE Kalesijski Zvuci from *Bosnian Breakdown*
Somehow the simple grinning triads of the accordion manage to coexist with the complex interrelationship of the vocals and violin in a remarkable song.

6 DVA SE DRAGA Damir Imamović Trio from *Abrašević Live*
With lyrics by an unknown author set to music written by Imamović himself, the song revisits the saz tradition and remakes it in an utterly convincing, intense performance.

7 KRAJ VRBASA Safet Isović from *Doajeni bosanskohercegovačko sevdalinke*
Accompanied by a single accordion, the affecting simplicity of this performance displays the control and emotional depth which was such a feature of Isović's style.

8 IMAL JADA KO KAD AKŠAM PADA Avdo Lemeš from *Aman Jada od Akšam do Sabaha*
The dark, almost despairing mood of the song is reflected in dark, impassioned vocals form Lemeš, backed by ominous strings.

9 STO TE NEMA Jadranka Stojaković from *Sevdalinke: Sarajevo Love Songs*
A typically Bosnian tune that tugs at the heart strings, sung by a striking voice in a gorgeous arrangement.

Bulgaria

orpheus's fairground

Ivo Papasov
Jak Kilby

Direct, soulful and powerful, Bulgarian music is immensely varied. It ranges from a deeply rooted and still vibrant village tradition, through complex and sophisticated arrangements of the same by trained composers and sentimental, comic or patriotic popular music, to breathtaking instrumental virtuosity in the Gypsy or wedding band styles. For so long the favoured (although closely monitored) child of the Communist regime, the country's orchestras of folk instruments and infamous women's choirs are now starved of money and many of their finest musicians have retired or struggle on as best they can, while *popfolk* or *chalga*, which barely existed fifteen years ago, has conquered the airwaves and drives a newly established and lucrative private recording industry. Meanwhile, a loosely connected grouping of musicians, such as the influential *kaval* (end-blown flute) player Teodosii Spassov, are continuing to produce immensely inventive and exciting music, firmly underpinned by tradition but wide open to influences from further afield. **Kim Burton** pays close attention.

Much Bulgarian music, whether sung or played, is traditionally performed without harmony, or at most with a simple drone, like that of the bagpipe. Rhythmically charged songs performed in unison by several singers (often divided into two groups that answer one another antiphonally) are used to accompany dancing, while the slow and richly ornamented solo numbers on mythological, romantic or historical subjects attract the close attention of listeners. Such songs are primarily the remit of women, and used to be sung at the social events called *sedyanki* (evenings when unmarried girls would gather to sew and embroider, gossip and compare fiancés) or performed for the guests on festive occasions. Their ornamentation, although subtly varied with each performance, is perceived as an integral and vital part of the melody. Indeed, it is only the very aged with voices past their best who would even consider omitting them.

Nonetheless, some areas boast an extraordinary system of **polyphonic performance**. In the Shop district, around the capital Sofia, village women sing in two- and three-part harmony, although not a harmony that Western ears are at all familiar with, characterized by dissonance and grinding tone clusters, and decorated with whoops, vibratos, slides and glottal stops. The singers, the best-known of whom come from the village of Bistritsa and thereabouts, say they try to sing "as bells sound", and there is indeed something bell-like in the clash and shimmer of overtones as the dissonances pile up. In the Pirin mountains of the southwest the villagers sometimes sing two different two-voice songs with different texts simultaneously, ending up with a complex and dizzying four-part texture. In general, this style of polyphony is the particular domain of women, and it too was associated with women's gatherings, although in the Pirin district men also sing in harmony, albeit with a different repertoire and a simpler, more robust approach.

The **rhythmic complexity** and speed of Bulgarian music is also striking. A system of building rhythmic units from a series of long and short beats in a ratio of 3:2 is widespread all over the Balkans, where such times as 7/8 and 9/8 are common, but Bulgarians have developed them, and the fleetly intricate dance steps associated with them, to a remarkable pitch of complexity. The commonest of these are probably the *râchenitsa* couple dance, with its three beats of unequal length arranged as 2-2-3, and the *kopanitsa* line dance (2-2-3-2-2), but more complex patterns such as *buchimish* (2-2-2-2-3-2) and the 3-2-2-2-3 *Petrunino horo* are not infrequent. On the other hand, ordinary two-beat patterns of the sort found in a relatively simple 6/8 *Shopsko horo* are also very common – although even here ambitious syncopations ratchet up the rhythmic tension and drive.

Even though Bulgaria is a relatively small country, with a population of around seven-and-a-half million, it boasts several clearly defined regional styles. The earthy, serious dances of the Dobrudzha district in the northwest are utterly different in character to the lightning-fast dances found among the people of Shop, and the long, heart-rending songs from the central Thracian plain contrast with the sweet and pure melodies of the northwest and the banks of the Danube. In the remoter reaches of the Rodopi mountains it's still possible to hear shepherds playing the kaval to their flocks, and in the villages and small towns of their valleys groups of people sing slow unmeasured songs to the accompaniment of the deep-voiced *kaba gaida* bagpipe. These days, and especially in the case of instrumental music, the differences are becoming rubbed away, with the ornate and powerful Thracian style in particular influencing the work of many professional accordionists and clarinettists. Yet distinct styles still persist locally (sometimes very locally, perhaps restricted to a single village), and many of the best-known urban wedding bands such as Thrace's **Orfei**, Ruse's **Orkestâr Horo**, Dobrudzha's **Izvor** and the **Vievska Folk Grupa** from the Rodopi retain a strong local identity.

Ritual Music

Back in the village, the yearly round of peasant life was defined by the rhythm of the seasons – sowing and harvest and the winter lull. Many rituals were intended to ensure good fortune and fertility, and their associated music and dances still survive, although adapted and often kept up more from force of habit than from the conviction that they will have a magical and supernatural effect. In the Christmas-time custom of *Koleduvane*, groups of young men process around the village asking the householders for gifts and singing *koledi*, Christmas songs. This is followed by *Laduvane* at the New Year, and by the springtime *Lazaruvane* – the songs of St Lazarus Day – when it is the turn of the young women to sing and dance through the streets. The numerous songs associated with these customs are often repetitive and relatively straightforward melodically, and each activity – leaving the house, travelling about the village, entering the house – has a song for the occasion. More of a living tradition are the New Year masquerades, with their *kukeri* – dancers dressed as bears or bizarre long-necked monsters. Strangely masked, cross-dressed or clad in animal skins, they can sometimes be genuinely terrifying, all the more so when accompanied by the piercing sound of the *zurna* oboe and the thunderous roar of the *tâpan* barrel-drum, as they are in the villages and small towns of the southwest.

The most startling of all rites is **Nestinarstvo**, once performed in the villages of Bâlgari, Kondolovo and Rezovo in the Strandzha district, when the chosen fell into a trance and danced on glowing coals to the sound of bagpipe and drum to mark the climax of the feast of saints Konstantin and Elena. Still performed at festivals and folklore shows, the ritual still just about hangs on in Bâlgari, where the reckless and not particularly welcome participation of enthusiastic and inexperienced amateurs sometimes ends with them making an unplanned trip to hospital.

Marriage is, of course, the most important of the rites of passage in contemporary Bulgaria, in town and countryside alike, and every moment of the ceremony is marked by music – the arrival of the groom's wedding party, the leading out of the bride to greet it, the procession to the church, and so on. Traditionally, the songs sung at the bride's house the night before the wedding are the saddest of the whole body of Bulgarian music, for the bride is leaving home, never to live in her parents' home again. The wedding meal is also accompanied by music, the slow and intricate melodies called *na trapeza* (at the table), and later on there is music for dancing. The type of band depends on the part of the country, but commonly small groups with accordion, guitar, clarinet and drum kit are found, while over the past 25 years or so the synthesizer has made an entrance, and virtuoso players are in great demand. The whole wedding band phenomenon of the 1980s (discussed later) grew out of these groups, which made their appearance in the first part of the twentieth century.

Many Bulgarians are highly skilled dancers, and everyone knows the basic steps of the *horo* – so much so that in May 2005, during an attempt to form "the longest horo in the world" in the hopes of an entry in *The Guinness Book of Records*, Sofia's Nevski Square was jammed solid with over 11,000 dancers led by no less a figure than the Speaker of the Parliament, as children in folk costume, leather-jacketed young blades, grandmothers clutching their handbags and middle-aged men with beer bottles thrust in their waistbands twined and twisted, firmly clutching one another's hands. Even in the disco, under the mirror balls and in front of huge video screens, a horo is likely to break out to the sound of chalga as the evening wears on.

Folk Instruments

Most of the bands that play at **weddings** and other celebrations use modern factory-made instruments, often amplified with more enthusiasm than subtlety. However, in some areas – notably around the town of Yambol in Strandzha district in the east of the country – many people retain a preference for folk instruments, and, if they can afford it, will hire a professional band of such instruments for the occasion. The usual line-up of such a band is *gaida*, *kaval*, *gâdulka* and *tambura*, sometimes supported by the *tâpan*.

These instruments were sometimes referred to as *bitovi* (popular, national) *instrumenti*, just as the music they play was referred to as *bitova muzika*, though it is now more commonly *avtentichen folklor*, i.e. authentic folklore. They were always common in the countryside, and in the years following World War II, when the state founded its **Folk Song and Dance Ensembles**, they were chosen to make up the new folk music orchestras (*Orkestri ot narodni instrumenti*). The demands of large ensembles (primarily reliable tuning at a standard pitch, and the development of families of instruments to facilitate the formation of large sections) led to technical developments and refinements, while the creation of a class of permanently employed paid professionals and schools where they were trained spurred remarkable increases in virtuosity.

The **gaida** is perhaps the best known of these instruments. It is of simple construction – a bagpipe with a single drone, a chanter capable of playing a partly chromatic scale (unusual among bagpipes) of just over an octave, a mouth tube with a one-way valve, and a goatskin bag which acts as a reservoir for the air. Yet in the hands of such masters as the late **Kostadin Varimezov**, **Petko Stefanov**, **Nikolai Atanasov** or **Georgi Dolchev**, its wild sound has an astonishing turn of speed and rhythmic drive, while a sophisticated system of fingering allows subtle variations in articulation and phrasing. Expert players can use the instrument's potential for rich ornamentation to perform beautiful versions of slow song melodies and other melodies na trapeza. In the Rodopi mountains, far to the south, the musicians use a larger and deeper-pitched version, the kaba gaida, to accompany songs and dances. With a bag large enough to allow the player to accompany his own singing, the instrument is played alone or in groups of two, three, four or even more. One enormous ensemble goes by the title of **Sto kaba gaidi** (one hundred bagpipes), an accurate reflection of its size, and both the sight and sound of one hundred pipers performing intricate ornamentation in immaculate unison is undeniably impressive. There are a number of fine players, but **Georgi Musorliev** is one notable player relatively easy to find on record, and the sound of a ballad performed by singer **Valya Balkanska** to the accompaniment of the instrument is close to spine-chilling.

Like the gaida, the **kaval** was originally a shepherd's instrument, and some of its melodies – or rather freely extemporized meditations on certain specific motifs – go by such names as "Taking the herd to water", "At noon" and "The lost lamb". The modern kaval is made of three wooden tubes fitted together, the topmost of which has a bevelled edge that the player blows against to produce a note. The middle one has a series of seven finger-holes plus one for the thumb, and the foot joint has four more holes, not fingered, which stabilize the tone and the tuning. These last are sometimes referred to as the *Dzhavolski dupki* (the Devil's holes) in reference to a folk tale that tells of how they were made by the Evil One himself, driven to such a pitch of jealousy by the playing of a young shepherd that he stole his instrument while he was sleeping in the shade at midday and bored the extra holes to wreck it. Yet when the shepherd awoke he discovered that his kaval sounded even sweeter than before, and in the best tradition of folktales, the Devil was caught in his own snare.

The school of kaval playing that developed in the second half of the twentieth century, led by **Nikola Ganchev** and **Stoyan Velichkov**, is extremely refined and its adherents are capable of producing nuances of sound from the deceptively innocent-looking instrument. The tone is sweet and clear (the people say "honeyed"), the low (*kaba*) register is rich and buzzy, and more recently **Teodosii Spassov** and his followers have extended the range in both pitch and timbre still further. Both **Matyo Dobrev Milev** and **Nedyalko Nedyalkov** have a thorough knowledge of traditional styles and can also hold their own on the turbo-charged wedding band circuit.

The **gâdulka**, a distant relative of the medieval *rebec*, is a bowed instrument with a pear-shaped body held upright on the knee, tucked into the belt or cradled in a strap passed around the player's neck. It has three or sometimes four bowed strings and as many as nine sympathetic strings which pass below them through the bridge and resonate when the instrument is played, reinforcing the tone and producing a strange shimmering halo of sound behind the melody. There are no frets, not even a fingerboard, and the top string is stopped with the fingernails rather than the fingertips, yet the best players surmount these obstacles with apparent ease. These challenges may, however, go some way towards explaining why of all the folk instruments the gâdulka has undergone the greatest decline in popularity, for few young players appear to be taking it up. The stunningly assured **Darinka Tsekova** is a doubly remarkable exception, since she is one of the very few women to have made their mark in Bulgarian music as an instrumentalist rather than a singer. Among the older generation, **Mihail Marinov**, **Georgi Gardzharov** and **Atanas Vâlchev** are important figures, with **Georgi Petrov** and **Georgi Andreev**

Simon Broughton

Gâdulka player

notable members of the younger generation, not merely as performers but as composers and conductors too.

The **tambura** is a member of the lute family, with a gently curved pear-shaped body and a long fretted neck. In its original form, found in Pirin and the central Rodopi, it had just two courses of strings, one of which usually provided a drone while the melody was played on the other. The **Sestri Biserovi** (**The Bisserov Sisters**), an outstanding vocal trio from Pirin, accompany themselves in this style. The commonest contemporary version, however, designed for the needs of the large folk orchestras, has four double courses tuned like the top four strings of a guitar, and is used to strum chords and provide running counter-melodies, as well as acting as the solo instrument, a fairly recent development. For the purposes of these orchestras, supersized cello and contrabass tamburas and gâdulkas were also designed and built, and play much the same supporting role as do cellos and basses in the normal symphony orchestra. **Mihail Marinov** and **Rumen Sirakov** are widely regarded as two of the finest tambura players. Another notable player is **Stoyan Velichkov**, a member of the influential **Trakiiskata Troika** which found fame outside the country as part of the **Balkana** package in the late 1980s.

The State Ensembles

In the late 1940s and 50s, various local and national **State Ensembles** were set up under the auspices of the new Communist government as part of a cultural drive on the Soviet model, and schools were established specifically to teach folk instruments and train performers, singers and composers. In part, this was a cultural engineering project, intended to channel potentially disruptive national feelings into the service of the one-party state. Some songs were quite blatant in their "educational" aims, with lyrics about, yes, collective farms and tractors, in a carefully observed "authentic" style.

The first and most prominent of these groups was the **State Ensemble for Folk Songs and Dances** under the leadership of **Filip Kutev** (1903–82), an extraordinarily talented composer and arranger and a former teacher and military bandmaster whose stylistic innovations became the model for a whole network of professional and amateur groups throughout the country. His great gift was his ability to take the sounds of village singers – drone-based and full of close dissonances, but essentially harmonically static – and forge from

them a musical language which answered to European concepts of artistic form and harmony. In this way, he was able to create sustained pieces of some length, without losing touch with the atmosphere of the original melodies. If you compare his work with the attempts of earlier composers to force the melodies into a harmonic system that they did not truly fit, the success of his approach is striking. His imitators were many, and for a time there seemed to be nothing around which did not sound like Kutev, leading to the not infrequently expressed view that he was both the best and the worst thing to ever happen to Bulgarian music.

However, a number of arrangers and composers have gone on to develop their own individual voices. Among the best of these are **Kosta Kolev**, also a talented accordionist, **Nikolai Kaufman**, a leading ethnomusicologist who has recently concentrated on exploring the country's rich **Jewish musical tradition**, the much-missed **Stefan Mutafchiev** who worked with the **Ensemble Trakiya**, and **Ivan Spasov**, who experimented with aleatoric techniques, in which the duration and placing of individual notes is left partly to chance, to build up massive sonorities. Many of these also wrote for the **Women's Choir of Radio Television Sofia**, which was one of those to become famous under the generic title of **Le Mystère des Voix Bulgares**. The State Ensemble, now known as the **Filip Kutev Ensemble** (or **Philip Koutev Ensemble**), is still in existence, as are some of the regional ensembles. Nonetheless, the end of large-scale state funding has meant the end of a number of these ensembles, and more importantly created considerable hardship for the musicians themselves, so that buskers with kavals and gaidas are now to be seen on the streets of Sofia. Meanwhile, the struggle to survive in the new harsher conditions led to a plethora of cloned women's choirs touring and recording under the banner of the Mystère, against a backdrop of rivalries and lawsuits. Composer and conductor **Stefan Dragostinov** also embarked on an ambitious project entitled "The Key to the Mystery", aiming to present a series of recordings covering every area of the country. To a great extent groups share a common sound, style and repertoire.

There were smaller instrumental groups too, represented these days by bands such as **Bâlgari**, under the leadership of **Georgi Dolchev**, and **Georgi Petrov and Friends**. Turning to small-scale unaccompanied vocal groups, the **Trio Bâlgarka** – **Yanka Rupkina**, **Stoyanka Boneva** and **Eva Georgieva** (each of whom also has a high reputation as a soloist) – toured in the 1980s and

90s as a part of Balkana. The **Eva Kvartet**, youthful but ambitious and highly experienced, are one of the best of the smaller groups, working with some of the best composers and unafraid to experiment with jazz and even drum'n'bass. One very successful left-field group – now sadly disbanded – was **Folk Scat**, whose acapella arrangements plus simple percussion managed to fuse the Bulgarian sound with jazzy harmonies and a lively sense of rhythm.

Modern Instruments

Parallel to the folk instrumental groups were those using clarinet, accordion, guitar and bass, and sometimes drums. Although these instruments began to appear on the scene towards the end of the nineteenth century, performing dance melodies and accompanying singers, the style only really started to get going in the 1930s. The accordionist **Boris Karlov** (1924–64), an elegant and restrained performer who based his style on folk tunes, and whose ornamentation and phrasing were influenced by bagpipe techniques, became a commanding presence in the 1940s and 50s, and his influence remains strong today. Like many of those who have made enormous contributions to Bulgarian music, he came from a Rom family, as do other important accordionists such as **Traicho Sinapov** and **Ibro Lolov**. Currently the most exciting and imaginative player is Pazardzhik's **Petâr**

Ralchev, who studied in Plovdiv and whose astonishing flights of improvisation with the **Zig-Zag Trio** push further into unexplored territory. Ralchev has also collaborated on a number of other projects, and he is one of the most influential of contemporary accordionists. The clarinet too, in the hands of such masters as **Petko Radev** and **Nikolai Iliev**, plays an extremely important role, especially in the speedy whirl of Thracian music. Other leading clarinettists include **Mladen Malakov**, leader of **Orkestâr Biseri** and yet another Rom virtuoso, and **Ivo Papasov** (see box), one of the most important figures in the wedding band movement, and another to emerge from the bubbling Thracian cauldron.

Artists such as these recorded and broadcast, and were well known and well respected, but many other bands of this sort worked the restaurants and bars or, if they had gained a local reputation, might graduate to the far more lucrative wedding and family celebration circuit. Those stuck in the restaurant treadmill were of course being employed by the state, and so their material and even style of playing was subject to scrutiny and control by the authorities. Even those that were fortunate enough to perform on the radio had to submit their repertoire beforehand for approval. One musician, speaking in the early 1990s, told of having had to submit his pieces to "The Committee of Pensioners" before he was permitted to perform them on the radio. If they were deemed "insufficiently Bul-

Ivo Papasov

Ivo (Ibryama) Papasov is a commanding figure in every sense, and despite stiff competition probably the most important clarinettist to have emerged from Bulgaria. He has come a long way from his beginnings in the Thracian town of Kârdzhali, where he was born into a Turkish-speaking family in 1952. He began to play the accordion at the age of nine, but soon turned to the clarinet. On his earliest recordings he showed himself to be fluent and well-versed in the standard Thracian style, but he rapidly fell under the influence of jazz, working with the fusionists **Plovdiv Folk Jazz Band**, and forming his own group **Trakiya** in the 1970s. He was soon recognized as the foremost musician working the wedding circuit, and became a household name. During the 1980s, when the government mounted an anti-Turkish campaign in a ham-fisted attempt to bolster its waning popularity by playing the nationalist card, Papasov ran into trouble with the authorities, but although briefly detained, he was spared a prison sentence. Even in this period, however, it was possible to obtain clandestine cassettes of him wailing in typically Turkish style above syncopated oriental rhythms.

In the early 1990s a couple of releases on the American Rykodisc label brought his breathtaking sound and hurtling turbojet rhythms to an even wider audience, but over the next ten years he kept a lower profile, occasionally making an appearance on one of the folk jazz projects of which Bulgarians are so fond, before making a triumphant return in 2004 with *Panair*. Whatever he had been experimenting with in the previous decade had brought him a new maturity, and the coherence and force of this recording won him a **Radio 3 World Music Award** in 2005. His wife **Mariya Karafezieva**, who performs with the band, is a splendid singer in her own right.

garian" then permission was refused. Even when it was granted, the manner of performance had to be acceptable too. "Once they told me that I was playing too fast, and that Bulgarian music is not played so fast. This was a tune that I myself had written, I was playing it, and I am a Bulgarian. How could they tell me the way to play my own composition? But they could!"

It was, then, groups working in areas not subject to such stringent controls that were able to follow their own paths, although not without the risk of falling foul of the authorities on occasion. By the mid-1980s, these groups had developed into the so-called *svatbarski orkestri*, the **wedding bands**.

Wedding Bands

These supercharged groups were free to experiment with instrumentation, mixing folk instruments like the gaida and kaval with accordions, clarinets and saxophones, electric guitars, synthesizers and drum kits, rock and jazz rhythms and foreign tunes. Their energetic approach to their music, technically highly accomplished, performed at breakneck speed and with lengthy improvised solos, became immensely popular with the public, and their far-reaching reinvention of their local music eventually became impossible to ignore. Thanks to the far-sighted efforts of some musicologists and other members of the cultural apparatus, in the mid-1980s the authorities eventually caved in and were persuaded to recognize this music as worthy of public support. In 1986 a festival was inaugurated in the town of **Stambolovo**. It presented the music in perhaps slightly bowdlerized form – bands were subjected to the "assistance" of approved musical directors – but nonetheless drew crowds of visitors, and became a biennial event. **Ivo Papasov**'s band was by far the most famous to take part, and deservedly so, but the festival brought national attention to bands such as **Mladost**, **Kanarite**, **Horo**, **Vievska Folk Grupa**, **Orfei**, **Trâstenik** and **Kristal**, who had previously enjoyed a local reputation only. The state-owned record label **Balkanton** – in fact the only record label – began to issue recordings of these bands, and they began to receive attention in the media. They were still restricted to "Bulgarian" music, but they normally included Serbian, Greek and even Turkish material in their sets. And many of these musicians were Roma, bringing their own approach to all of this.

Simultaneously, home-made tapes were beginning to appear on sale at local markets. These so-called *demokaseti*, originally with handwrit-ten covers, and frequently of a technical quality far below that of the music they contained, were widely available and extremely popular. They not only gave musicians an opportunity to develop their ideas, but with the economic liberalization (and resulting economic chaos) that followed the collapse of the monolithic state they eventually led to the rise of privately owned record companies and broadcast media, which laid the foundations for what is now a huge Bulgarian popular music industry. One of the first record companies to appear, in 1990, was **Payner**, and although the majority of companies have fallen by the wayside, Payner and its Planeta brand have grown into a vast empire including shops, clubs, recording studios and a television station showing videos of its artists on heavy rotation. It is now one of the biggest presences in a huge market, hungry for chalga.

The Tough and the Tender

As elsewhere in the Balkans, Bulgaria is now home to a locally produced **high-tech popular music**, complete with stars and their stylists, hit videos, remixes, scandalous gossip and of course massive profits. Although there is a mind-boggling array of sub-styles, they are all covered by the colloquial term **chalga**, or more politely **popfolk** or **etnopop**. Although the original model was predominantly the newly composed folk music and turbofolk of the former Yugoslavia, itself a grab bag of influences, chalga also borrows widely – to put it more bluntly, steals – from Serbian, Turkish, Greek and other sources. This phenomenon is hardly unique to Bulgaria, though, as hits in one country soon make the rounds of the others, little changed except for the lyrics.

At its more tedious extremes chalga shades into imitative **Eurodisco**, but at its best it's a hard-driving groovy music with some great, focused and precisely embellished singing. The vast majority of the big stars are women, many of them Roma, with **Sofi Marinova** being one of the biggest and certainly most noteworthy names. The vivacious star narrowly escaped being chosen to represent Bulgaria in the Eurovision song contest (known locally as Eurosong), in a juicy scandal with accusations and counter-accusations of vote-rigging and threats being flung about. Even more revered is **Gloria**, who is widely known as "primata na popfolka". First names only is the order of the day, with **Ivana**, **Boni** and **Desislava** among the other notable and hugely popular singers, some of whom are very capable performers of folk music as well, while among the men **Azis** is outstanding. His

rather heavy-handed play with gender transgression certainly attracts attention, but unfortunately tends to obscure the fact that he is an extremely fine singer, with very well thought out arrangements. Controversial he certainly is: once a musician I was talking to switched off the television when one of Azis's videos came on, to protect me from the awful sight. An astute businessman, Aziz owns a large club in the centre of Sofia, **O'azis**, which sometimes mounts live concerts. The only chalga singer to have so far made it onto a Western label is **Jony Iliev**, ironically not singing chalga at all, but Gypsy favourites.

Much like its equivalents in the surrounding countries, chalga attracts its fair share of opprobrium for extra-musical reasons, usually its rumoured links with the mafia and its being a poor advertisement for Bulgaria. However, the skill and professionalism of the performers and producers seems a very good advertisement for the advances the country has made in the last fifteen years. In a more folkloric vein, and far more to the taste of chalga's opponents, are the likes of **Iliya Lukov**, a solid but good singer and composer, and Yambol's **Slavka Kalcheva**, who occupies something of a middle ground and is a great favourite. Sentimental Macedonian-style urban songs are especially loved, with the pudgy but appealing **Volodya Stoyanov** one of the most prominent figures – and one of the few to have returned to a more folkloric style after making a name in chalga.

On the Road

Kaval player **Teodosii Spassov** and accordionist **Petâr Ralchev** are two of the leading figures in a quite different trend, hard to define because it spills over so many borders. Ralchev, for instance, came from the conservatory, worked for a time with the group **Orfei**, and has flirted with jazz, Serbian dance music, French musette and more to produce a unique sound with more than a touch of sly humour. Spassov too, who astonished audiences in the 1980s with his blistering technique and stunning range of timbres, sprang from the academy and has gone on to produce avant-garde folk, compose film scores and work with both the **Filip Kutev Ensemble** and his own jazz trio. Spassov is also an enthusiastic collaborator on other musicians' projects, notably the multinational **Balkan Horses** band. Along with Ralchev and Papasov, he made a guest appearance on the debut album by percussionist **Stoyan Yankulov** and singer **Elitsa Todorova**, who use simple acoustic means to build up amazingly complex structures drawing on more

traditions than those of Bulgaria alone. Another important member of this grouping is the quicksilver guitarist **Ateshhan Yuseinov**, whose fleet dry-textured runs and chunky chords grace a startling range of recordings. Papasov himself rarely plays in Bulgaria any more, since economic circumstances prevent most families staging the large-scale weddings that bring the money in for musicians, but he tours extensively abroad, and recently rejoined an old band mate from **Trakiya**, the exceptional saxophonist **Yuri Yunakov** (now resident in the US), to record and to perform concerts.

Once again, these musicians have been able to do what they have done as a consequence of the growth of independent record companies. The most radical of them is **Kuker Records**, which has a small but excellent catalogue. It includes one of the very few available recordings of a Bulgarian Rom brass band, **Karandila** – although brass

Jony Iliev

Roma Chalga

Communist Bulgaria was a nation so grey, so repressed, that the Zhivkov dictatorship seemingly extinguished not only the nation's creative spirit but also any sense of sensuality. Post-1989, things have changed radically: homosexuality is now legal, while the sex industry (pornography, prostitution and lap-dancing clubs) is booming. The soundtrack to Bulgaria's sexual revolution is **chalga**, an electronic music largely, but not entirely, shaped by Gypsy musicians. Derided by Bulgaria's middle classes as "truck driver music" – i.e. mindless, sleazy stuff – chalga is quite simply great, trashy fun. Like many modern pop forms, chalga enjoys a fast turnover of stars, yet two Roma singers, Azis and Sofi Marinova, appear to have won loyal, lasting followings.

Azis is the most famous (and infamous) artist in recent Bulgarian history. When he first arrived on the scene in 1999 he was seen as just another Gypsy chalga singer, albeit one with a beguiling vocal style. But a newly exoticized image and a series of outrageous videos helped him become Bulgaria's most lucrative entertainer. His bleached hair, tattooed torso and wildly camp persona have inspired much moral outrage, fed by live performances in which he arrives on stage on a motorbike and simulates sex with men and women. Appropriately, Madonna is his hero. All of this would, of course, mean little if Azis didn't make good records – but when he lets his eerie, erotic voice soar over a goulash of Balkan, bhangra and pop styles he sounds like no one else and makes the most exciting contemporary music in Eastern Europe.

Sofi Marinova's voice is so strong, her presence so immediate, that she easily overshadows her busty competitors (many chalga videos emulate porn rather than MTV – it's a Thracian thing…). Her albums are horribly overproduced, yet she can wail like a young **Esma Redžepova** on a traditional ballad like "Danyova mama" (Danny's Mama) or tear off a funky chalga duet (with Azis) in "Edin zhivot" (One Life). Nicknamed "Romska Perla" (the Gypsy pearl), Sofi is much loved by Bulgaria's Roma.

Both singers are so popular in Bulgaria – and with growing fan bases in the surrounding Balkan nations – that, so far, they have shown little interest in winning a Western audience. Not that chalga would appeal to many fans of traditional Balkan Gypsy music. Yet one young Bulgarian Gypsy singer who has got some attention abroad is **Jony Iliev**. Iliev is from a musical family in Bulgaria's southwest and grew up singing at weddings. He tried his hand at chalga but only scored fleeting success. Managing to attract the attention of Henry Ernst, the German manager-producer of **Fanfare Ciocărlia**, Iliev cut *Ma Maren Ma*, a tough, rocking album of Bulgarian Gypsy roots music that received wide acclaim. Yet back in Sofia's clubs Iliev and band still pump out the chalga, this being what the dancers demand.

Chalga's popularity is helping combat the prejudice many Bulgarians have, for centuries, directed at the nation's Roma. Just as white America's wholesale racism was crippled when confronted by the talent and beauty of Sam Cooke and Lena Horne, Orthodox Bulgaria can't consider Turks and Roma ignoble peasants when their songs command the clubs and their videos dominate TV screens. One nation under a chalga groove? Hard to believe, sure, but chalga has certainly led Bulgaria's first ever pop culture revolution.

Garth Cartwright

instruments have been around for some time, and Boris Karlov's father, **Karlo Aliev**, was a famous trumpet player. **Gega New** has a wider range, including classical and liturgical music, reissues and new recordings of standard folk ensembles large and small, Jewish music and more.

In its richness, variety and daring, the Bulgarian music scene seems almost unrecognizable in comparison to what it was a mere twenty years ago. If the network of traditional music festivals has diminished, the biggest of them all at **Koprivsh-titsa** (see box) thankfully continues, and private businessmen with an eye to publicity have been sponsoring popfolk festivals such as **Pirinfolk** and the "authentic" music festival **Pirin Pee**, while **Stara Zagora** hosts a festival devoted to Rom culture, the **Romfest**. The end of state funding has meant real hardship for some musicians, but this has been balanced by increased freedom for others. As Bulgaria settles into its new position in the European Union, you would be wise to hold on to your hats.

Koprivshtitsa: The Bulgarian National Folk Art Festival

A visit to the **Bulgarian National Folk Art Festival** at Koprivshtitsa is an unforgettable experience for any folklore enthusiast. Founded by the Communist State to preserve folklore in its traditional forms, the festival marks the climax of village-level competitions, with performances by the winners. It has been held around the first weekend in August roughly every five years since 1965.

The main part of the event takes place in the Voivoda Meadows above the village, where seven specially constructed stages nestle into the hillside, each acoustically separated. Buses arrive from all over Bulgaria bringing thousands of amateur performers of all ages, who first perform in front of the judges on their regional stage. The winners from each region then move to the central stage, and these performances are broadcast on TV to the rest of Bulgaria.

Until 1991 the emphasis was on traditional singers, solo instrumentalists or stage-adapted versions of local customs or rituals. This has changed over the last three festivals, with a steady increase in village dance groups, performing "lightly" choreographed suites of their local dances, fewer solo musicians and less lengthy custom "plays". There is still an ample presence of *koledari* (pagan carol singers), kukeri (masked fur-clad characters with large resounding cowbells round their waists who perform fertility rituals at New Year) and *rusalii* (sword dancers) accompanied by deafeningly loud zurna and tâpan.

Folkroots Archive

The venue is around thirty minutes' walk from the village. On the way you pass locals dressed in colourful, traditional village costumes making their way to the festival site. Once the entrance is reached it can take up to an hour to get to the furthest stage, or even all day, depending on how many performances or impromptu rehearsals you stop to watch on the way. There is so much happening at the same time that choices have to be made. The best variety can be seen on the central stage but the visibility there is not always good. The alternative is to spend a while at each stage depending on what catches your eye.

There are now numerous food and drink stalls on site, unlike in Communist times when the drinks ran out by the last day! The two caravans selling plastic souvenirs and a few records have also been replaced by a plethora of stalls selling Bulgarian handicrafts, handmade folk instru-

Dancing villagers

ments, CDs and cassettes, pieces of old folk costumes and all other types of antiques. It is a real treasure trove for the Balkan enthusiast.

If you tire of the action on the festival site, you can return to the village, where there are even more antique and craft stalls, and yet another stage. On the Saturday evening traditional Thracian **nestinari** (firewalkers) perform in the square, although visibility is limited due to the vast number of spectators.

Each evening, once the stage performances have finished, the action continues at the campsite. Here modern instruments such as accordions appear, to fight for their place beside the incessant but addictive zurna and tâpan, and impromptu dancing continues for most of the night.

By the end of the three days even the most enthusiastic may have reached saturation point, but the relaxed and friendly atmosphere, compulsive music and picturesque location will leave vivid memories in your mind and you will want to return again in five years' time.

Liz Mellish

DISCOGRAPHY Bulgaria

⊙ 15 Vechni Hita: Makedonski Pesni za Dushata
Diapason Records, Bulgaria
The sweet harmonies and gentle swing of these fifteen "eternal hits" from the likes of Volodya Stoyanov, Rumyana Popova and Nadya Evtimova should steal your heart away. Old favourites with up-to-date acoustic arrangements and solid backing.

★ Anthologie de la Musique Bulgare
Le Chant du Monde, France
Between 1977 and 1983, Belgian folklorist Herman Vuylsteke made a series of trips to Bulgaria, where he collected a vast amount of material from village musicians all over the country. Vuylsteke can be a bit sniffy about the state ensembles and their "perversion" of folklore, but given the riches that he uncovered, he can certainly be forgiven. So far five volumes have been issued, with the fifth, from north central Bulgaria, the most varied.

★ Gypsy Summer/Tsigansko Iyato
Kuker, Bulgaria
The highlight of this film soundtrack is the storming Karandila brass band from Sliven, but there is also some fabulous singing from Anita Hristi and some spot-on playing of the rarely heard *tsimbal* (hammered dulcimer) from veteran Milan Alvazov.

⊙ Hitovete na Planeta Payner 3
Payner, Bulgaria
A three-CD or cassette compilation of Payner's biggest stars from 2004. It's the sound of chalga at its best, with tough beats, great playing, remixes and direct full-hearted singing from the likes of Ivana, Gergana, Azis and Extra Nina.

⊙ Musical Instruments of Bulgaria: Gaida
Gega New, Bulgaria
One of an ongoing series from Gega New, this features everything from the fat sound of a kaba gaida ensemble to solos backed by large folk orchestra. It also includes the masterful Kostadin Varimezov accompanied by explosive tâpan, and some extraordinary work on a rare double-chanter and droneless gaida from the Varna region. Wonderful performances from some of the greatest players.

★ Song of the Crooked Dance: Early Bulgarian Traditional Music 1927–42
Yazoo/Shanachie, US
A well-researched collection of pre-World War II recordings, excellently remastered. It's fascinating to hear the lively kaval playing of Tsvyatko Blagoev, so different from today's legato, meditative style. Other highlights include a song about an earthquake in 1928, the striking heroic song "Kapitan", and an appearance by Boris Karlov's dad. The notes by Lauren Brody are both scholarly and accessible.

⊙ Two Girls Started to Sing…
Rounder, US
These real field recordings focus on vocal music made between 1978 and 1988 in village locations around Bulgaria. They provide a fine example of the sort of music that you might be lucky enough to hear sung spontaneously in the field (or in the pub), including work, sedyanka, table, wedding and dance songs sung by non-professional musicians. Good notes.

⊙ Village Music of Bulgaria
Nonesuch Explorer, US
An excellent selection of material (first released in the 1970s), mostly by professionals but with their village roots showing unabashed. It includes a stunning performance of the Rodopi song "Izlel e Delyo Haidutin" by Valya Balkanska, the first Bulgarian song to escape the bonds of gravity when it travelled on the spacecraft Voyager as one of its examples of Earth culture.

⊙ Vocal Traditions of Bulgaria
Saydisc, UK
A splendid selection of songs by amateur and professional performers taken from the radio archives, covering the whole country, and with the emphasis on the village rather than the town. Indispensable.

Azis

With the face of a devil and the voice of an angel, Azis simply cannot be ignored, however much some shocked and conservative Bulgarians would like us to do so. If his recently announced political ambitions take him away from performing he will be sorely missed.

★ Na Golo
Sunny, Bulgaria
Azis plunders the global jukebox to create a true masterpiece of Balkan pop. Bollywood-style arrangements, Pirin-style accordion, blazing zurna and duelling bouzoukis over a massive beat back up his powerful, flexible voice.

The Bisserov Sisters (Sestri Biserovi)

A trio of chunky villagers from the highlands of southwestern Bulgaria, the Bisserov sisters combine their long professional experience as members of the Kutev Ensemble with a deep knowledge of their own village tradition.

⊙ Three Generations of the Bisserov Sisters
PAN, Netherlands
A mixture of songs, some acapella, some accompanied by the sisters themselves on tambura, *darabuka* goblet drum and *daire* tambourine, and others in more elaborate arrangements. In addition, their mums offer drone-based village songs in an untempered scale and their daughters join in now and again as singers and instrumentalists. Every one is a winner.

The Bistritsa Grannies and their Granddaughters

The village of Bistritsa, Shop district, is home to a particularly powerful form of unaccompanied antiphonal polyphonic singing, and the Bistritsa Grannies have been singing together for years. Although like everyone else they received "assistance" from professionals, they are a tough if charming bunch, and one imagines that the assistance was more or less restricted to booking tickets and counting heads at the airport.

⊙ Authentic Bulgarian Folksongs
Gega New, Bulgaria
For once authentic means just what it says (OK, it's a debatable term, but not as debatable as all that). These thirty songs

bear witness to a tradition that may be very ancient, is certainly extremely complex and – if the granddaughters are anything to go by – looks set fair to survive a good few years yet.

The Bulgarian State Television Female Vocal Choir

The most important, and the original, Mystère choir.

⭐ Le Mystère des Voix Bulgares
4AD, UK

This was the disc of thirteen tracks, originally compiled in 1975 by Marcel Cellier, that first turned the world onto Bulgarian singing in the late 1980s. It remains a classic.

⊙ Ritual
Electra Nonesuch, US

Dora Hristova conducts immaculate performances of songs for the Christmas and St Lazarus Day rituals arranged by the cream of Bulgarian arrangers. (More rootsy versions of some of these are to be found on Gega New's *Bulgarian Custom Songs*, which makes an interesting contrast.) There are also some beautiful versions of Sephardic Jewish songs arranged by Nikolai Kaufman.

Bulgarian Voices "Angelite"

Disentangling the web of the roaming rival female choirs is a complex job, but this incarnation, going under the name of "The Angels" and the baton of Vania Moneva, has a strong line-up and a wide repertoire.

⊙ Melody, Rhythm and Harmony
Jaro, Germany

A double live CD, recorded in Norway in 1993, with splendid performances of some classics and strong support from a small band of folk instruments.

Eva Kvartet

Gergana Dimitrova, Sofiya Kovacheva, Evelina Stoilova and Daniela Stoichkova are still relatively young, but vastly experienced, and at home in both village styles and complex arrangements. They are also unafraid to experiment with jazz and more.

⊙ Harmonies
Kuker, Bulgaria

Polished and expert acapella performances of well-chosen material, ranging from thoroughly traditional songs to recent compositions. A highly atmospheric disc.

Jony Iliev

Jony Iliev is the first of Bulgaria's popfolk singers to make it onto a Western label. His voice is a mixture of sweet and harsh, slightly slurred but supremely assured. He's not a major star at home, but he's a solid all-round performer.

⊙ Ma Maren Ma
Asphalt Tango, Germany

In some ways this CD, with its romantic acoustic arrangements and slightly old-fashioned material, seems to take a cautious approach so as not to frighten the Western horses. All the same, it's not so easy to find this material elsewhere, the singing is fine and the swing is tremendous.

Boris Karlov

Whether Karlov is the father, godfather or grandfather of today's Bulgarian accordion style, his influence is pervasive, and his delicate and precise ornamentation still stands as a model. He is such a vital presence that it comes as a shock to find that he died in 1964, at the age of only forty.

⭐ Legend of the Bulgarian Accordion
BMA, Canada

This collection of practically all Karlov's instrumental recordings, from early solos to later versions accompanied by chamber orchestra – plus a couple of songs – is a true labour of love, and absolutely indispensable for anyone interested in Bulgarian music. The notes, too, are a mine of information.

Korova

Four singers/tambura players and a percussionist from the village of Draginovo in the western Rodopi, performing local material in a fresh and unmediated fashion, Korova almost look like the first steps of a folk music revival, something that eventually crops up in any post-peasant society.

⊙ A Distant Echo
Kuker, Bulgaria

Unlike the more polished and highly trained choirs, the members of Korova are happy to leave their occasional cheerful adjustments of pitch and less than perfect synchronization as they are, and this lends their performances an authority and emotional depth that the former sometimes lack. The four male voices drifting in and out of harmony above the strum of the tamburas make a lovely sound, and the slow unmeasured ballads are powerfully moving.

Demko Kurtev

Master zurna player Demko Kurtev comes from a long line of players of this instrument, usually described rather pallidly as a "folk oboe", but in reality one of the shrillest, most piercing instruments it's possible to encounter. Played by Rom musicians, and linked with Turkish culture, this music was banned by the former regime for a period, but is now back and in fine fettle in the far southwest of Bulgaria.

⭐ Musical Instruments in Bulgaria: Demko Kurtev's Zurna Group
Gega New, Bulgaria

Put together by two Bulgarian ethnomusicologists who have spent considerable time and effort exploring and documenting this music from outside the mainstream, this compilation showcases the richness and power of this village Death Metal. On first hearing, this terrifying music can feel rebarbative, but perseverance will be rewarded.

Sofi Marinova

Rom superstar Sofi Marinova's voice, threatening, imploring, sometimes half-shouting and half-weeping, is quite extraordinary. It can transform absolute dross into gold – something that it has to do more often than one would like, unfortunately. An extroverted and good humoured performer, it's no wonder she is one of chalga's biggest names.

⊙ 5 Oktavi Lyubov
Sunny, Bulgaria

This is where you can hear "Edinstveni" (United), a duet with the nowhere near as good singer Slavi Trifunov which would have been Marinova's Eurovision entry, but there is plenty more top-class Bulgarian popfolk to be found here too.

Orkestâr Horo

Horo, from Ruse on the Danube, were first formed in 1962, and have been a fixture on the scene ever since. All acoustic, clarinet and accordion-led, unpretentious, without obvious and flashy virtuosity but with a bouncy swing and unforced charm, they haven't lasted for over forty years for no reason.

⊙ Nai-dobrite ot Horoto
Silvena, Bulgaria

Released to mark the band's fortieth anniversary – some of the current members weren't even born when it was first formed – this is a great collection of dance tunes, with chattering accordion and fluid clarinet. If you can't find this particular recording, you can't go far wrong with anything this reliable bunch of musicians have done.

Orkestâr Kanarite

The Thracian wedding band Kanarite were formed about ten years after Horo, and they have a more modern sound. The voices of their three female singers blend perfectly, and their instrumentalists are masters of the typically Thracian style of spinning one phrase from another to form a seemingly endless chain of sparkling improvisations. One of the country's favourite bands.

⊙ S Ritâma na Vremeto
Payner, Bulgaria

Although this CD is mostly of songs performed with grace and charm by Kanarite's three women singers, it also features some guests from the glamorous world of popfolk, proving that they are no slouches at more traditional styles. There is some fine instrumental playing here too, on accordion, clarinet and kaval. The band's roots and the basis of their style are Thracian, but they are shrewd enough to include songs from all over, appealing to as wide an audience as possible.

Orkestâr Kristal

Kristal are a Rom band with a much heavier synth-based sound, driving bass-lines and techno drums, plus skirling clarinet. Led by Krasimir Hristov, who writes and arranges practically all their material, they are probably the best of a very talented squad of bands patrolling the borderland between hard-core Rom music and chalga.

⊙ Romski Biseri
Payner, Bulgaria

The Turkish element in this music can be heard plainly in the clarinet playing and punchy unison interjections from the synths, while the forceful drumming under throaty vocals pushes the groove forward relentlessly. These "Rom Pearls" are sung in Rromanes, and if some of them sound familiar despite their being ascribed to band members, well, it's all reasonable give and take.

Ivo Papasov

Clarinettist Ivo Papasov is a phenomenon, a virtuoso and an innovator, who runs a very tight ship indeed. Certainly the most remarkable of the wedding band leaders, he is more often to be heard abroad than at home, where he still draws enormous crowds whenever he does appear.

★ Panair/Fairground
Kuker, Bulgaria

Panair marked Papasov's return to the recording studio after an absence of thirteen years. Kicking off with a short duet between a keening clarinet and the shattering sound of the tâpan, following it with a hurtling râchenitsa and culminating in a final, elegiac unaccompanied clarinet solo, this doesn't put a foot wrong. Fine singing too from his wife Mariya Karafezieva.

⊙ Together Again
Traditional Crossroads, US

This 2005 CD sees the former members of Trakiya teaming up again to produce a relatively (although only relatively) traditional and more dance-oriented sound, with a heavy Turkish feel.

The Philip Koutev Ensemble for Folk Songs and Dances

The first of the large-scale ensembles, and largely the model for the rest, with a body of highly skilled and well trained singers, musicians and dancers, this group continues to embody the spirit of Kutev's vision.

⊙ Folk Songs and Dances
Gega New, Bulgaria

Any recording from this group is worth listening to, but this collection of new material and re-recordings of old favourites gives a really good overview of what they can do.

Teodosii Spassov

Spassov is simply the finest kaval player around. His dedication to experimentation and willingness to take risks sometimes lead him astray, but when his ambition pays off there is no one to touch him.

★ Titla
Gega New, Bulgaria

Simply because Spassov's range is so vast, it's hard to pick out a single CD to recommend, but this 2003 recording sees him playing solos, with a vocal quartet, a small group of top folk musicians, a jazz piano trio, the Radio Folk Orchestra… And even then it doesn't cover everything he is capable of. If you like this, try his *Na Trapeza* with clarinettist Nikola Iliev, also on Gega, which is more contemplative and gives both musicians a chance to stretch out and explore.

Vievska Folk Grupa

Led by accordionist Emil Uzunski, and grounded in the music of the Rodopi (most obviously in the approach of the singers), this band is one of the few where you'll find the kaba gaida coupled with the synthesizer.

⊙ Rodopski Zvân 2004
Payner Music, Bulgaria
A collection of traditional songs given deceptively simple but imaginative arrangements, the music trots rather than gallops, but still swings along infectiously.

Stoyan Yankoulov and Elitsa Todorova

Drummer Yankoulov has worked with the best in the business, including Papasov, Ralchev, Spassov – and Bobby McFerrin. Singer Todorova is younger, but still with a wealth of experience. Their fairly recently inaugurated project has so far resulted in only one recording, but is a work in progress.

★ Drumboy
private production, distributed by Kuker, Bulgaria
The "drumboy" of the title is a Jew's harp, and it features heavily on this magical recording, in which the pair sometimes seem to read one another's minds, so breathtaking is their rapport. Yankoulov is master of a wide range of percussion, and Todorova's voice, a combination of fragility and sinewy strength, can be both playful and deeply moving. This music

is firmly rooted in tradition, but is put together in such a way that the over-used term "unprecedented" is unavoidable and fitting. Papasov, Ralchev and Spassov all guest to riveting effect. Absolutely phenomenal.

Zig-Zag Trio

Ralchev and Yankoulov are joined by guitarist Ateshhan Yuseinov in what we can only hope was not a one-off project, because the almost orchestral sound the trio produce is a revelation.

★ Kogato Pchelite Sâbirat Med/When the Bees Are Gathering Honey
Kuker, Bulgaria
The three master musicians push one another to the limit on this extraordinary collaboration, which harnesses virtuosity to imagination. One moment grows organically into the next, phrases are flung back and forth, abrupt changes of texture and tempo succeed one another, and jetstream modalism gives way to chromatic harmonies, while cheeky quotes from folk material leaven the mix.

PLAYLIST
Bulgaria

1 POLEGNALA E TUDORA Philip Koutev Ensemble for Folk Songs and Dances from *Folk Songs and Dances*
One of Kutev's most successful pieces for female choir, and many people's favourite, given a beautiful interpretation under the baton of his daughter Elena.

2 OBÂRNI SE/TURN AROUND Zig-Zag Trio from *When the Bees Are Gathering Honey*
The simplest of bass-lines serves as the springboard for a complex and thrilling weave of drum, guitar and accordion swapping lines, the musicians interacting as though by telepathy.

3 CELESTE Ivo Papazov from *Panair/Fairground*
Papasov and his band zip through one of his trademark complex themes, then sink down onto a grim funky groove with slap bass bearing up wailing solos.

4 MECHMETIO Bulgarian Voices "Angelite" from *Melody, Rhythm and Harmony*
A brilliant avant-garde piece from the pen of Ivan Spasov, piling one line upon another to produce great clashing masses of sound.

5 NA GOLO Azis from *Na Golo*
An absurdly over-dramatic opening gives way to an absurdly infectious groove, with Azis emoting nineteen-to-the-dozen over the top. The melody may be familiar, but what an arrangement!

6 DAIČOVO HORO Boris Karlov from *Legend of the Bulgarian Accordion*
A sweet and clever old-school dance melody in 9/8, displaying Karlov's mastery of subtle ornamentation.

7 RESTORANTI, DISKOTEKI Orkestâr Kristal from *Romski Biseri*
The tune is, once again, familiar, but the phrasing of singers Fila and Kati over a rocking *kyuchek* beat is phenomenal.

8 ZAMURKNAYA PETSTOTIN AIDUKA Turmakchite from *Vocal Traditions of Bulgaria*
A group of women from the village of Plana, Sofia, sing about *haiduti* (bandit guerrillas) in the dissonant style that so influenced Kutev.

9 NASHENSKO HORO/OUR HORO Teodosii Spassov from *Titla*
Spassov is joined by Georgi Petrov on gâdulka, Lyubomir Vladimirov on tambura and the Radio Folk Orchestra in a tune that begins as a standard dance before moving off in unexpected directions.

10 MAKEDONSKO BAVNO ORO/ MACEDONIAN SLOW HORO Demko Kurtev from *Demko Kurtev's Zurna Group*
An eight-minute medley of tunes, with Kurtev giving a masterclass on zurna techniques.

Corsica

passionate polyphony

Cantu U Populu Corsu

Powerful and mysterious, the spiralling harmonies of Corsican polyphony are redolent of both the island's dramatic landscapes and the deep-rooted pride and passion that have always made its inhabitants a people apart. Although virtually extinguished by the end of World War II, the flame of this ancient musical form, kept alive by a handful of elderly villagers in the interior, caught fire during the nationalist resurgence of the 1970s. It now blazes brighter than ever, providing inspiration for a new generation of composers and singers, as well as strengthening the identity on an island whose struggle for greater autonomy from the French state still erupts into periodic violence. David Abram takes a peek behind the white bandanna at Corsica's troubled soul.

"It was like hearing a voice from the depths of the earth; a song from the dawn of time; from a beginning that one never dares believe is accessible." So wrote historian **Dorothy Carrington** in 1948, after her first encounter with Corsican polyphony. Invited to attend Mass on Christmas Eve at a remote mountain village, she was enthralled when, instead of the organ music she expected, otherwordly acapella swelled through the little Baroque chapel. In its counterpoint of familiar cadences with heavily ornamented, improvised harmonies, she discerned traces of Genoan madrigal, Gregorian plainchant, Roman liturgy, the call of an Arab *muzzein* and, just below the surface, something wild and strange resonating from Corsica's pre-Christian past.

Dorothy Carrington's first taste of **polyphony** came at a time when the form was on the verge of extinction, practised only by a scattering of old men in poor granite villages depopulated by two world wars and mass migration. In more prosperous times, when the island's olive groves and chestnut forests fed a thriving export market, polyphony accompanied most aspects of life. Shepherds sang to while away long evenings in lonely *bergeries* (sheepfolds); farmers sang to the rhythms of the threshing circle; and everyone listened to polyphony in church, where Mass was traditionally sung by the men standing together in a tight circle in front of the altar, with their eyes closed and their hands cupped over their ears.

Although Corsica has much in common with other Mediterranean oral-based societies, what really sets the island's singing tradition apart is its unique sound, best exemplified by that most Corsican of forms, the **paghjella**. Death and separation are generally the inspiration for this profane song style, charged with strong emotions of love, loss and lament. Paghjellas are traditionally sung in three parts: the *seconda* leads the melody, joined soon after by the anchor notes of the *bassu*, delivered in a more plain style; over the top of these, the *terza* adds a complex harmony line of fluctuating notes, much embellished and with a slight drag, or *ribuccata*, setting it apart. The staggered entries and overall absence of a strict meter means these elements swirl around each other, occasionally drifting into dissonant overlaps that sound very foreign to the Occidental ear.

Sacred Corsican song, heard in the island's churches and monasteries, tended to be more formal and in Latin, although elements of paghjella style and Corsican lyrics inevitably crept in (generally depending on how far into the mountains the Mass was performed). At major religious festivals – saints' days or processions of hooded penitents to mark Easter – the singing was (and still is) performed by **Lay Brotherhoods**, or *Confraternitia*.

Confraternitia also provided the musical accompaniment for funerals. But at the wake afterwards, a single female relative would sometimes sing a **voceru**, its time marked by the thump of feet or gun butts on the floorboards. If the deceased was a victim of a vendetta murder (all too common in Corsica until well into the twentieth century), the improvised dirge would become a searing incantation which registered not only the pain of bereavement, but also the urgency of revenge, aimed at spurring the surviving men to retribution.

A third type of song, known as **chiami e rispondi** (questions and answers), took the form of a competition in which two male contestants had to improvise a dialogue (usually of ritualized insults) in strictly rhyming verse. They could sing about anything, but often chose to aim abuse at the assembled company or else declaim about political issues. Agricultural fairs, such as **Santa di u Niolu** in the Niolu Valley, remains the main stage for this peculiarly Corsican genre.

The Riacquistu

Long before World War II sounded the death knell for Corsica's rural population, the days of the island's singing traditions were numbered. Realizing this, two musicologists dedicated their careers to recording those polyphony singers and songs that survived in the island's most remote villages. The work of the first, folklorist **Austin de Croze**, went largely unnoticed when it was published around the turn of the century. But thanks to phonographic and radio technology, the field recordings made by **Félix Quilici** between 1948 and 1963 enabled authentic polyphony to reach audiences whose only previous exposure to Corsican music had been the garishly dressed folk troupes in Parisien variety theatres.

At that time, public reaction to Quilici's compilations on 78rpm (and later broadcasts for Radiodiffusion France) was far from positive, veering from scepticism to xenophobia, and eventually – on the island itself – to naked embarrassment. "Ah, nos pauvres oreilles!" (Our poor ears) declared one critic; "Que vont penser de nous les continaux?" (What will the continentals think of us?) wondered another. However, Quilici's archive would prove a musical gospel for later generations.

One of the groups featured most prominently in his archive was a trio from Tagliu village led by seconda **Ghjuliu (Jules) Bernadini**. His sons caused a stir at the Santa di u Niolu singing competitions of the 1970s and, after his death, became Corsica's most commercially successful musical export, **I Muvrini**. But it was the famous broadcast of one of Bernadini's own compositions, "Lettr'a Fritellu" (Letter to my Brother) – written to mark the political imprisonment of a friend in 1974 – that is widely credited with first coupling polyphony with **nationalist politics**.

Throughout the 1970s, resentment at France's economic neglect and the suppression of Corsica's language and culture gradually coalesced into a fully fledged nationalist movement. Rallies were held in Bastia and Ajaccio, at which groups singing patriotic songs and old-style polyphony became an essential feature. None turned in more emotive performances than **Cantu U Populu Corsu** (The Corsican People Sing), a bearded array of young radicals in flared jeans who were eventually banned for their association with the armed struggle being waged by the paramilitary **FLNC** (Fronte di Liberazione Naziunale di a Corsica).

However, others stepped in to take their place, and by the end of the decade, polyphony was not only synonymous with nationalist politics, but also cool again. Whereas the Bernadini boys used to practise secretly in their village to avoid being teased at school, by the early 1980s they were centre stage in a movement to reclaim the island's traditional culture, dubbed the "**Riacquistu**".

Tradition versus Evolution

An unwieldy ensemble of around thirty individuals, Canta U Populu Corsu fragmented after recording nine albums, its key members heading off to pursue their own musical agendas. At the

I Muvrini

root of the split were disagreements between the "traditionalists", who wanted to adhere to the old repertoire and singing styles, and the "evolutionists", who wanted to spread their musical wings. To some extent, this debate has dogged the island's music ever since. Mixing polyphony with other forms or styles – and even using modern instruments – is seen by some hard-liners as a kind of betrayal. It explains why Corsican artists are always at pains to reaffirm the importance of their roots, even while departing radically from them – hence the all but mandatory inclusion of the Corsican national anthem, "Dio vi salvi Regina", on their albums and the recurring visual references to the **Corsican flag**, which shows a black boy wearing a white bandanna.

One of the original Cantu members who has largely followed the traditional path is **Jean-Paul Poletti**. After completing his formal music studies in Florence, he returned to the town of Sartène in the far south to form the **Chœur d'Hommes de Sartène**, and later founded a dedicated polyphony school. The choir's perfectly drilled harmonies provide a beautiful underscore for Poletti's powerful, operatic tenor, and their recordings are considered some of the most polished and pure to date.

At the opposite end of the island in the Balange region, another attempt to research and revive traditional Corsican music is a project called **E Voce di u Commune**, based in the pretty village of Pigna. An association of instrument makers and musicians, the group refined not only regional polyphony, but also the making and playing of local instruments. These include the Corsican lute-like *cetera* (a type of cittern), the *pifana* (an aerophone made from a goat's horn) and *cialamella* (a kind of crude reed instrument), all of which had disappeared long before Quilici's field recordings were made. The results can be heard on the albums of the village ensemble, **A Cumpagnia**, and at the annual **Festivoce** music festival in August.

While many singers and groups stick staunchly to traditional polyphony, most have dabbled with other idioms at some point. Among them is Poletti's erstwhile Cantu partner, **Petru Guelfucci**, a part-time beekeeper from the Venaco valley whom many regard as the other *plus belle voix corse*. One of the founders of the traditional ensemble **Voce di Corsica**, Guelfucci paid his dues to old-school polyphony, but since tended towards more mainstream French *chanson*, recording covers of Brel, Brassens and Ferré classics. Despite some success on the continent (and in Quebec, where he was briefly a top-selling artist), his career has never reached the heights of that other great Corsican *chansonnier*, **Tino Rossi**, whose warblings made him a household name in France in the 1930s.

The other main Cantu spin-off was **Chjami Aghalesi**, a core group of around fifteen singers who started out with the old repertoire, but soon began experimenting with original material and different musical styles (notably South American). They were the first all-male group to record with women, collaborating with **Patrizia Poli** and the Nouvelles Polyphonies Corses. They also recorded the soundtrack to the hit period epic, *La Reine Margot*. However, their greatest hour in the sun was a cover version of Luis Llach's "L'Estacos", renamed "Catena" (Chains), which became a nationalist rallying cry in the elections of 1992.

Another outfit who began life as a conventional polyphony choir but have since evolved into something much more distinctive, is **A Filetta** (The Fern). Under the direction of **Jean-Claude Acquaviva**, they first attracted attention performing at the Easter Passion performances in Calenzana in the 1980s. They then carved out an international career recording ambient movie scores (including Eric Valli's hit *Himalaya*). Their success is due in no small part to the genius of Acquaviva, whose phenomenal, wood-toned voice always seems charged with typically Corsican anguish – perfect for conveying the spiritual torment of sacred polyphony, or the visceral despair of paghjellas. He's also written and arranged new material which, while pushing back the boundaries of modern polyphony, retains a distinctively Corsican sound.

Jean-Paul Poletti et le Chœur d'Hommes de Sartène

Girl Power and Beyond

Corsican polyphony, and more particularly the bleak insistence at its heart, has always been regarded as a male domain. Traditionally, it was acceptable for women to sing at home, and perhaps at funerals, but certainly not in front of the altar. Only in 1992 were such attitudes challenged head on when the all-women polyphony group **Donnisulana** released a traditional album of spine-tingling brilliance, which silenced in an instant the boys-only brigade with its emotional intensity and harmonic precision. Made as a memorial to a mutual friend, *Per Agata* brought together the finest female voices on the island, including the internationally famous mezzo-soprano, **Jacky Micaelli**.

The album's triumph coincided with the arrival on the scene of another (predominantly) female group, **Les Nouvelles Polyphonies Corses**. From the outset, NPC were flamboyantly unconventional. With back-up from traditionalist Jean-Paul Poletti on the one hand, and experimental collaborators Hector Zazou, John Cale and Patti Smith on the other, they took polyphony into hitherto unimagined realms, laying it over electronically generated keyboard washes, Georgian choirs, Moroccan *oud* riffs and flamenco percussion – to great effect. Their eponymous debut notched up huge sales in France as well as at home, and a track from it was chosen for the opening ceremony of the 1992 Winter Olympics at Albertville. Now also performing as the **Trio Soledonna**, the three female vocalists have continued to evolve their sound, with bolder compositions backed by a broad canvas of musical inspiration from across the globe.

In purely commercial terms, however, no Corsican group has hit the big time quite like crossover maestros **I Muvrini**. The two "Little Mountain Sheep" from Tagliu were the first to effectively combine traditional Corsican polyphony with electric guitars, synths, bass and drums. French folk instruments (accordion, hurdy gurdy and bagpipes) also feature in the mix, overlaid by soaring harmonies and Corsican lyrics typically recalling forgotten places and ways of life. It's a sound that's unlikely ever to break into UK or US world music markets, but the Bernadini brothers play sell-out stadium gigs across France and Germany. Moreover, their success is a source of considerable pride on the island, encouraging a new wave of Corsican groups to experiment with their musical inheritance. One group worth singling out is **Isula**, a duo who released an album in 2002 mixing modern dance grooves with traditional polyphony, including material specially recorded by the *grande dame* of Corsican singing, Jacky Micaelli.

Where to hear Corsican polyphony

The summer tourist season, between June and mid-September, is the time you're most likely to catch live performances of Corsican polyphony. The island's foremost groups nearly all stage tours of the main towns and resorts around this time, invariably playing in front of the ramparts of an old Genoan citadel. More sombre recitals, minus the light shows and modern instruments, are also held in ancient Pisan churches and cathedrals, where the acoustics are optimal. The **Casa Musicale** in Pigna hosts regular gigs by A Cumpagnia and guests, in the intimate setting of its dining hall.

In addition, well-established **music festivals** punctuate the Corsican calendar. At the **Santa di u Niolu** fair in Casamoccioli, deep in the mountains of the Niolu Valley, chiami e rispondi and an Eisteddfod-style singing competition form the keystones of an age-old rural get together in early September. Dedicated polyphony festivals include Festivoce (Pigna in early July) and Rencontres de Chants Polyphoniques (Calvi in mid-September), the latter a four-day affair celebrating acapella music from around the world, hosted by A Filetta.

To see Corsican polyphony in its most traditional, sacred context, however, you should aim to catch one of the island's many **religious events**. Easter is the big one, featuring candlelit processions by hooded Confraternitia in Sartène (U Catenacciu), Calvi (La Granitola) and Erablunga (La Cerca). Calvi also hosts a famous re-enactment of the Easter Passion, sung by Jean-Claude Acquaviva and A Filetta.

DISCOGRAPHY Corsica

Compilations

⊙ Corsica/Sardinia
WDR/World Network, Germany
Members of Cantu and A Filetta teamed up in 1995 to record eight well-known hymns and a paghjella for this compilation, which also includes tracks from Donnisulana's benchmark album *Per Agata*. Not the most inspiring of selections, but the only one offering polyphony from both Corsica and Sardinia.

★ L'Âme Corse
Auvidis, France
Songs by Jacky Micaelli, Donnisulana, Tavagna, A Filetta, Cantu and Poletti's Chœur d'Hommes de Sartène are the highlights of this excellent all-rounder from Corsica's main label. A couple of unusual instrumental tracks are also thrown in – all recorded to a high standard.

⊙ Polyphonies Corses
Cité de la Musique/Actes Sud, France
Accompanied by a book outlining the history of Corsican polyphony, this CD features 22 well-chosen tracks. Its focus is squarely on traditional forms, with a mix of sacred and profane songs, including one of Félix Quilici's difficult to find 1960s recordings of the legendary Tagliu Trio. Most of the big names from the 1970s to the 1990s are represented.

Artists

Cantu U Populu Corsu

Cantu played a seminal role in the Riacquistu of the 1970s and 80s. Its output was divided between pure polyphony and folksy political ballads and rally songs. While the latter (accompanied by strummed acoustic guitar, mandolin and fiddle) sound dated these days, Cantu's traditional repertoire has better weathered the test of time.

⊙ C'hè Dinù
Ricordu, Corsica
The definitive Cantu album, this was recorded in 1982 when the group were at the forefront of the nationalist resurgence. Its mix of pure polyphony and stirring protest songs (some of them from the Basque country and Catalunia) perfectly capture the spirit of the times.

Cumpagnia

Formed in 1978, this collective, based in the Balagne village of Pigna under the directorship of Tony Casalonga, has done much to revive traditional polyphony and Corsican instrumental music, making it accessible to a wider audience through the Casa Musicale and Festivoce event.

⊙ In Paghjella
Casa/Melodie, Albania
Sacred and profane songs, with some original compositions (in very traditional style), sung by a top-notch male-voice choir. For once, the cover notes are full and detailed, with English translations and lots of interesting background information on the songs and their lyrics.

⊙ Nanne di Corsica
Casa, Albania
A selection of exquisite lullabies, full of poetry inspired by the landscape and natural world. Although some are tinged with typically Corsican melancholy, most radiate domestic cosiness and optimism. The arrangements make great use of traditional instruments, most of them from Pigna itself.

Filetta

One of only two professional choirs on the island, A Filetta infuse traditional polyphony with a wonderfully dark edge. Collaborations with film score composer Bruno Coulais have brought them international acclaim and enough clout (and budget) to experiment with both radical acapella and lush orchestral arrangements. Recent albums, in particular, have been startlingly original, with Jean-Claude Acquaviva's musical imagination at full stretch.

⊙ Passione
Olivi Music, France
Music from A Filetta's legendary Holy Week recital, recorded in Calvi cathedral and the Convent of Corbara. It's as bleak as you'd expect of a Corsican Passion, for which Acquaviva's tormented, sublime voice could have been purpose-made.

★ Intantu
Olivi Music, France
A state-of-the-art album, in terms of both its vocal performances and its choice of material. The songs cover the full gamut of forms, from an old-style paghjella to gut-wrenching political laments penned during the Riacquistu, plus a handful of the group's trademark modern compositions. Polyphony at its most versatile, lyrical and powerful.

Isula

Isula formed in 2002 when I Muvrini band member and singer Joseph Figarelli teamed up with bassist and synth maestro Jean-Cyril Masson. Their concept was to make contemporary fusion music using dance beats and ambient keyboard sounds under traditional polyphony.

⊙ Isulamea
Crossing Records, France
Despite the presence of quality Corsican voices, polyphony is one of the many musical textures spun through Masson and Figarelli's computer-generated collage. The dance beats are heavy-handed at times, but on some tracks everything comes together brilliantly – not least on Jacky Micaelli's "Misere", which sounds like it was re-mixed by Massive Attack.

Jacky Micaelli

Widely held to be the finest living female voice on the island, mezzo-soprano Jacky Micaelli has always rooted her career in polyphony. Her involvement with Donnisulana lent a gravitas to the group, which helped the female singers break through the gag of insular chauvinism. She has also collaborated with world-grooves project, Isula.

⊙ Corsica Sacra
Auvidis, France
Pure polyphony, accompanied by intimate trios of male and female voices. The arrangements of both the old and original compositions are beautifully stark, allowing the full expressiveness of Micaelli's voice to shine through.

I Muvrini

As I Muvrini, Bernadini brothers Jean-François and Alain have become a national institution. In the early 1990s, their trademark mix of polyphonic vocals with a modern band sound struck a chord both on the island and with expatriates living in metropolitan France, eventually snowballing into a mass popularity that has broken all records and many musical boundaries along the way.

⊙ À Bercy
Columbia, France
This live recording, made at a celebratory concert in Paris in 1996, captures the Bernadini brothers on the crest of a musical wave. Opening with one of Jean-François' poetic laments, it's essentially a greatest hits selection which you'll either love or loathe depending on your tolerance of electronic keyboard chords and slow rock rhythms.

⊙ Pulifunie
Higher Octave, US
Just to prove they can do the old stuff too, this is inspirational polyphony just as their dad and uncles taught them, only slightly marred by overbaked studio reverb.

Les Nouvelles Polyphonies Corses (Trio Soledonna)

Sisters Lydia and Patrizia Poli, and their friend Patrizia Gattaceca, caused a sensation when they teamed up with Jean-Paul Poletti, singers from his Scola di Cantu, producer Hector Zazou and talented musicians from all over the world to record as Les Nouvelles Polyphonies Corses. The result – superimposing expansive paghjella-style vocals over an electro-acoustic backdrop – was a runaway success. They've since tended more towards pure acapella, but as the Trio Soledonna, the original female core of the group has once again started to sing with musicians – predominantly from Spain, Greece and the Maghreb.

★ Le Meilleur des Nouvelles Polyphonies Corses
Philips, France
Their best of album (released before 2001's excellent *Isulanima*) charts Nouvelles Polyphonies Corses' evolution from Hector Zazou to their Trio Soledonna days. Throughout, the harmonies are razor sharp, the singing is warm and seductive, and the arrangements are highly original.

Jean-Paul Poletti et le Chœur d'Hommes de Sartène

Along with A Filetta, Jean-Paul Poletti's choir is Corsica's polyphonic flagship – a prominence it fully merits. Unlike Acquaviva's ensemble, though, this one has stuck resolutely to its roots, singing a traditional repertoire in text-book style. Its one notable innovation was the revival of a lost sacred choral piece called "Transitus", which lay forgotten in a nearby Franciscan monastery for seventy years.

★ Cantu di a Terra
Accord, US
A definitive album in all respects: flawless renditions of sacred and profane songs, led by Jean-Paul Poletti at the peak of his vocal prowess. Moreover, the recording quality is superb.

Tavagna

Tavagna are an old, established quintet with a foot in both the traditionalist and progressive camps, having recorded both pure polyphony and albums of chanson and jazz-fusion, as well as original theatre scores. They're at their best, however, when singing old-fashioned *chants sacrés*.

⊙ A Capella
Silex, France
Superb versions of paghjella and sacred polyphony, plus a few original numbers, beautifully sung in high traditional style, with their trademark slow slides lending plenty of typically Corsican dissonance to proceedings.

Tempus Fugit

An amateur choir from Nebbiu in the northeast of the island, Tempus Fugit formed in the early 2000s to revive the sacred music of their home territory. Though lacking the great voices of better-known ensembles, they conjure a dramatic intensity from their medieval repertoire, much of which hasn't been sung for centuries.

⊙ Chants Sacrés: Nebbiu
Longdistance, France
Plainchants, processional songs, mystical liturgies and hymns from the ninth to the thirteenth centuries provide the *hors d'oeuvre* for this album's main event, a Roman Mass that was banned in Corsica for over a thousand years. The "Vultum Tuum" was believed to hold miraculous properties: when sung in a state of pure, spiritual harmony, it could recall the face of the Virgin Mary. Tempus Fugit's intense rendition brings to mind Dorothy Carrington's remarks about polyphony being like a "voice from the depths of the earth".

Voce di Corsica

Voce di Corsica assembled in 1990 around former Cantu vocalist Petru Guelfucci. Nearly all the members of the group, from the villages of Sermanu and Rusiu in the Venaco region, were the sons or nephew of singers who featured prominently in Félix Quilici's 1960s field recordings – in fact, some of the older members actually appeared in the archives themselves when they were teenagers.

⊙ Polyphonies
Sony, France
With its distinctive black cover and strident graphics, this became a landmark polyphony album in 1990. It features traditional pieces, both secular (paghjella, Tuscan troubador songs and madrigals) and sacred (hymns and death laments), alongside new compositions. It's one of the top pure polyphony recordings ever to come out of the island.

PLAYLIST
Corsica

1 PAGHJELLA Jean-Paul Poletti and the Chœur d'Hommes de Sartène from *Cantu di a Terra*
A fine example of the most Corsican of polyphonic forms, the primordial paghjella, traditionally sung by shepherds.

2 BERNADINU Tavagna from *A Capella*
Sacred polyphony sung in much the same style as it has been in the island's churches for hundreds, and possibly thousands, of years.

3 LAMENTU DI GHJESU Jacky Micaelli from *Corsica Sacra*
A searing Easter lament, charged with emotional intensity, by Corsica's finest living female singer.

4 A PAGHJELLA DI L'IMPICCATI A Filetta from *Intantu*
Written in the 1990s, this political paghjella recalls the massacre by French troops of eleven Corsican rebels in 1774 – it has become a modern classic.

5 U CASTICU A Filetta from *Intantu*
A beautiful Jean-Claude Acquaviva composition, full of rich, innovative vocal textures, and at the cutting edge of modern polyphony.

6 GIRAMONDU Nouvelles Polyphonies Corses from *Le Meilleur des Nouvelles Polyphonies Corses*
Produced by Hector Zazou, this song opened the 1992 Winter Olympics and catapulted Corsican music centre stage in France.

7 CURAGIUI Muvrini from *À Bercy*
Classic anthem from the Bernadinis, with their trademark soaring harmonies and folk-rock sound.

8 QUANDU LU MONTE DI TAGLIU Isula from *Isulamea*
Driving dance remix of an old Félix Quilici-recorded love song by the Tagliu Trio.

Croatia

ringing strings and stirring songs

Darko Rundek and Cargo Orkestar
Piranha Records

The Republic of Croatia stretches in a great crescent from the Mediterranean to the Hungarian plains, and its strikingly varied music reflects long contact with many foreign cultures, as well as a rich native tradition. The country's complex musical mosaic ranges from the mellifluous chromaticism of the Dalmatian coast to jolly Alpine knee-slapping in the north, by way of challenging dissonance in the Istrian peninsula and its surrounding islands. **Kim Burton** uncovers Croatia's beauty.

I f there is one style of music that typifies Croatia in the popular imagination, it is that of the **tamburica band**. These ensembles are found all over the country, but are particularly associated with the area of the Slavonian plain to the north and east of Zagreb, where the first such band was formed in 1847, in the town of Osijek. As the name suggests, the ensembles consist of various versions of the tamburica, a plucked and strummed long-necked lute that comes in a variety of shapes and sizes, from the tiny mandolin-like *prim* to the large *berde*, the size of a double bass. It's actually a small tambura (the Balkan version of the Turkish saz), one of the many musical legacies of the Ottoman presence in the Balkans and a clear demonstration that Croatia's musical links reach east as well as west.

Tamburica Bands

Ensembles range from the enormous, such as the Tamburica Orchestra of Croatian Radio-Television, to smaller groups of five or six, and the instrument may also be played solo or used to accompany a singer. The lively dances (principally variations on the *kolo* round dance) and dance songs are often accompanied by encouraging whistles from the men and high-pitched squealing from the women. The slow songs are sentimental and betray the sticky-sweet influence of Vienna, while the fast ones are extremely lively with scurrying inner parts and interwoven counterpoints.

Tamburica bands form the backbone of the many amateur folklore groups scattered around the country, but there are also many professional ensembles. Among the most prominent and popular are **Najbolji Hrvatski Tamburaši** (The Best Croatian Tamburists, previously known as Zlatni Dukati), who have a colourful history of splits and legal battles, and a sophisticated, poppy approach. The first of the smaller groups to make a living as professionals (excepting the state-supported groups attached to the radio stations) was the Zagreb-based **Ex Pannonia**, formed in the 1970s. Current favourites include **Zdenac, Berde Band**

Tamburica

and **Slavonski Lole**, all of whom perform a mixture of traditional songs and new material. The contemporary-sounding **Gazde** (The Bosses), whose shows owe more to leather-clad rock'n'roll than either village green or romantic restaurant, appeared in the mid-1990s and are still going strong, while in a more traditional vein **Krunoslav ("Kićo") Slabinac** and **Vera Svoboda** are probably still the best-known individual singers. Kićo's collaboration with tamburica player **Antun Nikolić** in the group **Slavonski Bećari** (Slavonian Bachelors) preserved a good deal of traditional material which was in danger of being lost.

The tamburica ensemble is an important symbol of Croatian national identity; during the conflict of the early 1990s there was an upsurge of new patriotic songs in response to the fighting. When in the summer of 1995 Zagreb was hit by rockets launched by Serb separatists, within minutes the airwaves were filled with such songs accompanied by tamburice. This status partly explains the remarkable number of such ensembles, both at home and amongst emigrant communities abroad. It is indeed the tamburica that provides the musical soundtrack to the daily life of the common man and woman. The town of **Požega** in central Slavonia hosts an annual festival of the music, **Zlatne žice Slavonije** (Slavonia's Golden Strings), dedicated to the performance of newly composed songs. Most of these are on the soupy side, but some of the faster examples have startling echoes of bluegrass. There are any number of smaller festivals dotted around the country.

Around the Regions

The usual network of local amateur groups, some of them highly skilled, keep older forms of music alive. The reviving tourist industry can point the visitor towards a wealth of festivals where they perform. The most important is Zagreb's **Medjunarodna Smotra Folklora** (International Folklore Review), a week-long event, usually in July, that hosts musicians from abroad as well as a huge selection of groups from all over Croatia. Some of these groups preserve tradition, some recreate or revive it, either on their own initiative or in collaboration with academics. The tremendous range of sounds that are still thriving can be heard on the Institute of Ethnology and Folklore Research's CD *Hrvatska Tradicionalna Glazba*.

There is a rich tradition of **unaccompanied singing**, all the way from Slavonia to the coast. The range of styles is tremendous, some of it harsh and dissonant, some of it in the outwardly simple two-part harmony style known as *na bas*, but the most highly developed style is that of the *klapa*. Smooth, fluent and sophisticated, klapa music has seen a tremendous growth in popularity over the last few decades. Originally found on the Dalmatian coast and the islands, *klape* are choirs of up to ten members, usually but not exclusively men, with a single lead voice supported by skilfully composed textures and harmonies. Love songs make up the bulk of the repertoire, whether traditional or adapted from popular commercial hits, but there are also religious and patriotic songs, as well as comic and satirical pieces. The biggest festival, showcasing the public and slick version of the style, is at Omiš in central Dalmatia, while smaller festivals and informal get-togethers are developing the style in sometimes unexpected directions. Of the hundreds of groups out there, some, like the **Klapa Trogir**, are long-established and boast a wide range of material, while others, like the Zagreb-based women's group **Dišpet**, are recently formed and quite experimental.

At the northern extreme of the coast, on the Istrian peninsula, the music is utterly different. Here the performers not only sing and play using a distinctive local scale with very small intervals, but also harmonize in parallel seconds. This is probably a very ancient tradition, and it has given rise to an entire body of instruments dedicated to producing such harmonies. The *roženica* or *sopila* is a type of large oboe which is always played in pairs, one large and one small. The much smaller *curla*, two pipes played with a single mouthpiece, allows one player to play two parts at once. The **Istrian bagpipe**, the **diple**, works on the same principle – it has no drone, but instead has a double chanter.

Towards the end of the 1980s, songs from the area of **Medjimurje**, on the Hungarian border, became very popular. The songs are mostly lyrical, with a few more energetic examples; some bear melodic and structural similarities to the music of Hungary, while others feel strongly Croatian. The region also boasts a strong tradition of unaccompanied narrative song, largely sung by women. Octogenarian Elizabeta Toplek, known as **Teta Liza** (Aunt Lizzie), is one of the best-known singers of this music and is still an active performer.

A little further south, in the rolling hills of the **Zagorje** around Zagreb, the music is almost indistinguishable from the polkas and waltzes of Slovenia and Austria, with forceful harmony singing accompanied by accordion and guitar. Although it is highly popular locally, it has not made many inroads outside its home ground.

The Zagreb-based **Lado** is a large professional group of singers, instrumentalists and dancers that has moved on from being the state folklore ensemble to become an important musical force in its own right. While its performances are, naturally enough, tidied up for the stage, its shows and recordings provide an ideal introduction to the country's various musical styles.

Contemporary Developments

The last decade has seen an increasing hybridization of Croatian roots music, with a string of performers attempting to breathe new life into traditional forms. Some have experimented with the techniques of the recording studio, and many have drawn inspiration from the fringe areas of Croatian folk (notably Medjimurje and Istria), thereby offering an alternative to the nationalistic folk-schlager-pop on the airwaves.

First off the mark were **Vještice**, who gained a wide audience by blending Medjimurje folk songs with 1990s rock attitude. The group **Legen** and singers **Dunja Knebl** and **Lidija Bajuk** followed their lead, mining collections of folk melodies. Legen has subsequently moved in a more radical direction, laying out tough and demanding rootsy singing and playing over dark-hued electronic grooves. The grandiloquent Istrian jazz singer **Tamara Obrovac** and her Transhistria Ensemble have been increasingly under the spell of the traditional music of her homeland, although jazz and its improvisatory approach remains the foundation of her style. Singer-songwriter **Darko Rundek** is another figure who repays attention: although traditional influences on his music are minimal, his intelligent take on popular music is very rewarding.

The most prominent figure currently working in this area is **Mojmir Novaković**, a Legen alumnus, whose group **Kries** dispenses a brilliant, authoritative combination of ancient tradition and punchy percussive drive. Guitarist **Miroslav Evačić** mixes the music of the Podravina with slide guitar to startling effect, while his wife and musical collaborator Gordana is an astonishing player of the local hammered dulcimer, the *cimbula*. Taking things even further, ethnopunks **Cinkuši** cluster traditional vocals and instruments around a searing electric guitar to thrilling effect, and on the other end of the scale the all-acoustic **Afion** provide a gentler take on music from the whole of the Slavic Balkans.

Compilations

⊙ XI Bašćinski Glasi
Aquarius Records, Croatia
This recording of a number of well-known klape performing at a festival concert in Rijeka gives a good overview of the polished sound that these groups produce. The songs and feel are fairly standard, as one might expect from the slightly staid surroundings of a municipally sponsored festival, but this is a good introduction to the style nonetheless.

⊙ Croatie: Musiques d'Autrefois
Ocora, France
A survey of traditional songs and instrumental music, taken from Croatian Radio Archives between 1958 and 1993. Divided by region, it begins with some Medjimurje songs and includes plenty of good tamburica bands, Istrian and klapa singing and instruments such as the diple, sopila and *licera*.

★ Croatie: Musiques Traditionelles d'Aujourd'hui
Auvidis/Unesco, France
This excellent record documents practically the whole range of Croatian music, from obscurities that you would be lucky to hear to the sort of commercial and sentimental songs given so much radio play that you would be lucky to avoid them. There is music from Istria, Medjimurje, Slavonia, Dalmatia and more, and the very useful notes are a big plus.

★ Hrvatska Tradicijska Glazba (Croatian Traditional Music)
Institut za Etnologiju i Folkloristiku, Croatia
An absolutely indispensable two-CD collection recorded in the field in the late 1990s by the Institute of Ethnology and Folklore Research. Its extraordinary coverage demonstrates that a massive amount of the music that might have been thought gone for ever is healthily alive.

Artists

Lidija Bajuk
Bajuk is an ethnographer, poet and songwriter with a sweet voice and a wide imagination.

⊙ Kneja
CBS/Croatia Records, Croatia
This 1999 recording, a mix of original material and respectful but not craven arrangements of traditional material, is probably the best introduction to Bajuk's music.

Berde Band
Formed in 1992, Slavonski Brod's eight-strong Berde Band has become one of the most popular contemporary tamburica groups. Their repertoire includes folk tunes, newly composed music in a folk-pop style and religious songs.

⊙ Pred Zoru
own label, Croatia
Old favourites here, with an accent on the more contemplative side of the music and an attractive, homely feel to the recording.

Cinkuši
A six-piece band mixing electric guitar with mandolin, acoustic bass, violin and bagpipes, Cinkuši have a challenging mix of the scholarly and irreverent in their approach to Croatian music.

⊙ Domesticus Vulgaris
Cantus, Croatia
Abundant energy informs the singing and playing on this 2005 release, where, once the shock has worn off, it's easy to hear their deep knowledge of the music that they are so happily deconstructing.

Miroslav Evačić
A former member of the etno-rock band Šćukin Berek, multi-instrumentalist Evačić is a master of slide guitar, which he somehow manages to combine with traditional instruments to great effect.

★ Chardash Blues
Scardona, Croatia
A slightly odd but extremely attractive compilation of self-penned pieces and ever so slightly twisted arrangements of traditional material performed by Evačić and his wife Gordana in the company of traditional musicians. Very atmospheric and with a certain amount of dry humour.

Klapa Dišpet
An all-female group formed in 1998 by students at the University of Zagreb, Klapa Dišpet caused an immediate stir, going on to garner a number of awards and prizes. One of the best there is.

⊙ ...za dišpet
Aquarius Records, Croatia
Dišpet's first recording is a beautiful set of arrangements of traditional material, marvellously sung, with an enviable command of timbre, dynamic and emotional force.

Klapa Trogir
The male Klapa Trogir was formed over forty years ago, and covers a wide range of styles from the standard to the experimental. A very experienced group, it set the standard for the many that followed.

⊙ ...grad sretnog trenutka
Aquarius Records, Croatia
This fortieth-anniversary collection of recordings from the 1970s to the early 1990s is a fine introduction to the group's sound. There are some absolute gems here, from classical-sounding pieces to songs with a strong folkloric component.

Dunja Knebl
Singer and guitarist Knebl from Zagreb discovered indigenous folk traditions relatively late in life and began singing professionally aged 47. She became an important figure in the Croatian folk revival, extending her repertoire to include songs from England and Russia, among others.

⊙ Četiri Frtalji
Dancing Bear, Croatia
Interesting and effective arrangements of Croatian folk material, mostly from Medjimurje.

Lado

Lado is a large-scale enterprise, with its members and associates not merely performing and recording but also conducting field research and working to preserve traditions. The group is on the conservative side, admittedly, but maintains important links with those working in more experimental areas.

⊙ Iz Hrvatske Narodne Glazbene Riznice 2 (From the Treasure of Croatian Folk Music 2)
Aquarius Records, Croatia
This 2005 release contains music from all over the country. With its expert arrangements and polished performances, it makes an interesting contrast to both the unvarnished field recordings and the wilder sounds of the younger generation.

⊙ Teta Liza i Lado
Aquarius Records, Croatia
Veteran singer Elizabeta Toplek teams up with a string band reinforced with cimbula and clarinet, plus a small brass band, for stoutly confident performances of the Medjimurje repertoire.

Legen

Formed in the early 1990s, Legen laid folk instruments over clanging industrial beats to produce a bleak and menacing soundscape far removed from the image of cheery peasant merrymaking.

⊙ The Best of 1992–2002
Kopito Records, Croatia
This compilation contains a good deal from the band's best single CD, *Paunov Ples*, plus music for a theatre show, live performances and other material. It's unrelenting, but rewarding.

Mojmir Novaković

A founder member of Legen, singer Novaković combines a fine voice and a deep knowledge of traditional song with an inventive aural imagination.

WITH KRIES

★ Ivo i Mara
Kopito Records, Croatia
Based on folk materials and melding *lijerica*, bagpipes, violin and African percussion with synthesizer and drum programming to produce a single coherent whole, this colourful and powerful CD is probably the single most successful product of the Croatian etno movement to date.

PLAYLIST
Croatia

1 KONJI VRANI Mojmir Novaković and Kries from *Ivo i Mara*
Loping percussion backs up sinewy lijerica and dramatic vocals in this mosaic of traditional and original materials. The same song in original form is to be found on the *Hrvatska Tradicijska Glazba* CD.

2 MAFRINA Perica Marinovi from *Hrvatska Tradicijska Glazba*
Atypical but wonderful dance music played on button accordion by a young self-taught musician from the island of Korčula, with an almost Madagascan sound and a strangely haunting air.

3 TOVARNIKU, TOVARNIKU, SELO NA VIDIKU KUD Antun Gustav Matoš from *Hrvatska Tradicijska Glazba*
A stately wedding song given a full-throated performance by the members of an amateur Cultural and Artistic Association from the village of Tovarnik. A fine example of the rich harmonies of Slavonia.

4 OTOČE Klapa Dišpet from *...za dišpet*
Proving that they can turn their hands to anything, Dišpet give this good-humoured arrangement of a Croatian rock song, the only non-traditional song on the CD. A beaming performance.

5 DALMATINO, POVIŠĆU PRITRUJENA Klapa Trogir from *...grad sretnog trenutka*
Virtuoso singing of a complex and harmonically rich composition, ranging from the hushed and confidential to dramatic, with echoes of church chants.

6 SVATOSKI TANEC Miroslav Evačić from *Chardash Blues*
A completely off-the-wall and entirely lovable dance with tamburica and cimbule entwining, never quite sure whether they are on the banks of the Drava or the Mississippi.

7 ŠOKAIKI SASTANAK Lado from *Iz Hrvatske Narodne Glazbene Riznice 2*
Lado's musicians demonstrate their considerable prowess in a sequence of Slavonian melodies on double flute, bagpipe, violin and tamburice, ever-increasing in speed and intensity. It's theatre, of course, but it's splendid.

8 PAUNOV PLES Legen from *1992–2002*
Legen's trademark combination of folk instruments and singing with trippy synth and menacing industrial rhythms works here to terrifying effect, creating a grim and comfortless soundscape.

9 SPAVAJ, SPAVAJ, DITIĆU Lado from *Iz Hrvatske Narodne Glazbene Riznice 2*
A hushed lullaby from the women is interrupted by outbursts of joyful strength from the whole choir.

10 JEDAMPOT JE IŠLA MAMA Lidija Bajuk from *Kneja*
A lovely and atmospheric performance of a beautiful folksong from Medjimurje, with crystalline piano and quiet synth harmonies sustaining Bajuk's confiding vocal.

Czech & Slovak Republics

a bridge between east and west

Věra Bílá
Nikola Tačevski

In spite of the political division of Czechoslovakia in 1993, there are strong historical and cultural links between the recently established Czech and Slovak Republics. Bohemia, the western part of the Czech Republic, belongs musically to Western Europe, while Slovakia is a member of the eastern European musical family – together with Ukraine, southeastern Poland, Hungary and Romania. Moravia (the eastern part of the Czech Republic) is a bridge between them – connecting Bohemian folk music on the western bank of the Morava River with the extremely rich and melodic folk music on the eastern bank which reflects Slovak, Hungarian and Balkan influences. Jiří Plocek surveys the situation.

Collections of **folk songs** have been a vital source of traditional music for village ensembles in western Bohemia, south-eastern Moravia and Slovakia. Tens of thousands of songs were written down around the turn of the twentieth century, as the national movement raised interest in local tradition. The region was also fortunate to have the composer **Leoš Janáček** (1854–1928), who helped to lay the foundations for modern ethnomusicology in the Czech lands. Like Hungarian composer Béla Bartók, Janáček made important cylinder recordings in the field and this familiarity with his country's folk music was crucial in forming his own composing style – amongst the most distinctive of the twentieth century. Of course Janáček and the other great Czech composer of the twentieth century, **Bohuslav Martinů** (1890–1959), were themselves following the illustrious nineteenth-century tradition of **Bedřich Smetana** (1824–84) and **Antonín Dvořák** (1841–1904) in drawing on national music.

Folk to Folklorism

By the time Janáček was recording folk music in the 1880s, traditional music was declining in everyday life and migrating to concert and festival performance. Folk music was giving way to "folklorism". Nonetheless, the music was adopted with enthusiasm. At the 1895 National Czecho-Slavonic Ethnographical Exhibition in Prague Janáček prepared a musical programme from Moravia featuring his beloved string band from Velká nad Veličkou. It became apparent that folk music expressed not only an inner need, but also a national identity. The exhibition ushered in an era of folk music gatherings, celebrations and festivals, bolstered by the creation of the Czechoslovak Republic in 1918. Similar feelings of joy at the liberation after World War II gave rise to the foundation of the biggest folklore festival in the country in Strážnice, Moravia, in 1946. There are several similar festivals in Moravia today.

The **Communists**, who ruled the country from 1948, co-opted the folklore movement into the socialist cause. In the 1950s and 60s they started to support ensembles financially and influence them politically, and also set up new professional ensembles. The idea was to create a new sort of popular music removed from the influence of decadent Western pop and jazz. Many young enthusiasts adopted this idea and started to create "neo-folk" songs. But the musical style of these ensembles tended to be conformist, artificial and sanitized

– what Czech writer Milan Kundera described as "fakelore".

Nonetheless, the pan-European strains of the folk revival blew in the sounds of jazz and rock, together with an interest in the genuine forms of traditional music. An important impulse to the folk movement was the two-week visit of US folk singer **Pete Seeger** during his world tour in 1964. He left in his wake a burgeoning movement of Czech singer-songwriters.

Two streams of traditional folk music existed in the 1970s and 80s. One was officially supported, and stressed a professional attitude in composing and arranging. The **National Radio Folk Orchestras** in Brno and Bratislava are good examples. The second stream returned to genuine folk music while encouraging new and individual interpretations. **New and electric folk music** carried an exciting "non-conformist" cachet in a totalitarian state, and the **Porta Festival** (established in 1966) attracted over 30,000 young people at its peak in the late 1980s and was nicknamed the "Czech Woodstock".

Since the Velvet Revolution of 1989, musicians have been able to experiment more freely with the different sorts of music, including traditional and modern folk music, rock and jazz, both local and world.

Bohemia

The most famous Czech dance must be the **polka**, a lively Bohemian couple dance in duple time, which became one of the most popular society dances of the nineteenth century – and has had vast influence on music throughout Europe and even Latin America. Like many Czech songs and dances, it begins with a heavily accented first note. The sort of upbeat common in Anglo-German music, for instance, is virtually unknown in Czech music, as Czech words are stressed on their first syllable.

In Bohemia today, the main living traditional folk music is in the **Chodsko** region in the southwest. This hilly district in the Czech-German borderlands has its own distinctive identity and is famous for its **dudy** (bagpipes). The annual **Chodsky Festival** in Domažlice presents local virtuoso bagpipers such as Zdeněk Bláha, Antonín Konrády and Vladimír Baier. An **International Bagpipers Festival** also takes place in Strakonice every other year. Outstanding local names are **Josef Režný** and his Prácheňský Ensemble (founded 1949), and the Pošumavská Dudácká Muzika. Chodsko boasts a remarkable polyphonic style of instrumental playing by small peasant bands of bagpipes, clarinet and fiddle, a rich repertoire of songs and some distinctive local dances with variable rhythms.

The first cylinder recordings of Chodsko bagpipers were made in 1909. The tradition has survived thanks to the appearance of revival players in the 1910s and 20s – school teachers such as **Stanislav Svačina** from Domažlice and **Karel Michalíček** from Košíře, Prague. The fear that the button accordion (which appeared in the 1860s) and string and brass band music would push traditional bagpipe music out never materialized. In fact, today's revival groups are so strong that they have helped resurrect the vanished tradition of bagpipe music just over the border in Germany and Austria.

Another type of genuine Bohemian folk music (dating from the early nineteenth century) can be found farther east, in the Czech-Moravian Highlands. **Skřipácká** music employs a rough, home-

Jan Kobes: bagpiper from Domažlice

made rectangular violin, viola and double bass. It was a virtually vanished exotic tradition, but has had something of a revival with good bands in Jihlava and Telč.

The contemporary folk boom of the 1960s gave birth to a group called **Minnesengři**, whose sweet harmony vocals gathered around singer-songwriter **Pavel Žalman Lohonka**. The band discovered

many lost folk songs from the south Bohemian lake area in the archives and revived them. During the 1980s and 90s **Dagmar Andrtová** evolved from a ballad singer into a remarkable guitar player and composer, while the folk singer, guitar and lute player **Vladimír Merta** widened his scope from songs directed against the totalitarian regime to music inspired by Jewish, and especially Sephardic, roots. Contemporary folk singer-songwriters still have an important place on the Czech music scene, even if their role is not as political as in the past. Among the names that have stood the test of time are **Jaroslav Hutka**, **Karel Plíhal**, **Jaromír Nohavica** and the late **Zuzana Navarová**. Besides her own excellent songs, Navarová deserves credit for "discovering" the famous Roma singer **Věra Bílá** and helping to raise the profile of a new star on the Czech folk scene, the charismatic girl with an accordion, **Radůza**.

Traditional songs from Moravia (especially those from the nineteenth-century song collections of **František Sušil** and **František Bartoš**) are a great source of inspiration for musicians in Bohemia. Folk singer-songwriter Jaroslav Hutka (born in 1947 in Moravia, resident in Prague) was the first to use old Moravian ballads to address topical issues. He achieved national fame in the 1970s, shortly before he was forced into exile for political reasons. Similarly, in more recent years the band **Čechomor** has built its impressive repertoire on old songs from Moravia. Jiří Hrdina, the co-founder of Čechomor in the late 1980s, does the same in his own band Marcipán, oriented more towards chamber music.

During the 1990s, a world music scene developed in Prague, represented mainly by bands like **Traband**, **Ahmed má hlad** and **Gothart**. Their lively and energetic music combines Czech and other Slavic songs with Balkan grooves and melodies backed by drums, percussion and accordion. The widespread popularity of Celtic music in Bohemia gave rise to bands like **Kukulín** (headed by legendary violinist **Jan Hrubý**) and **Dún an doras**, with its extraordinary Czecho-Spanish singer **Katka García**.

From the mid-nineteenth century, **brass band music**, originating in the military bands of the Habsburg Empire, spread rapidly through Bohemia. It was one of the things that destroyed traditional folk music, and nearly did the same in Moravia in the first half of the twentieth century. Until the arrival of modern bands and taped music, brass bands were used for weddings, dances and even funerals (and still are, to some extent). The repertoire was arranged folk songs, marches

Čechomor

One of the Czech Republic's most successful and culturally pivotal bands, Čechomor have never ceased to experiment, working with the Czech indie rock singer **Lenka Dusilová**, the Japanese *taiko* drummer and *shakuhachi* player **Joji Hirota** and Killing Joke's **Jaz Coleman**. But no matter what guise you hear them in – whether electric or unplugged, with orchestra or one of their musical collaborators – it could only be them. What's more, they have the knack of convincing you that you have known their slippery tunes – such as "Slunécko" (Sunset), "Mezi Horami" (Among the Mountains) or "Neber Sobě" (Don't Marry) – your entire life the first time you hear them.

Čechomor's origins go back to 1988 and the founding of a band with the rather more unwieldy name of **Českomoravská Nezávislá Hudební Společnost** (a mouthful even by Czech standards), meaning the Czech-Moravian Independent Musical Company. They started out performing in Czechoslovakian town markets and the like on an amateur or semi-professional basis. Inevitably, being confined to a small repertoire of "folklore" crowd-pleasers began to wear thin, and they found themselves part of the movement towards professionalizing folk music and dance. They had already grounded themselves in the collections of František Sušil, whose landmark anthology of several thousand Moravian songs had first been published in 1860. Thereafter it was a matter of keeping the songs fresh, even if that meant, as on "Za Gorum, Za Vodum" (Beyond the Hills, Beyond the Waters), singing in a dialect largely impenetrable to speakers of Standard Czech. When they started to become famous, the band shortened their name to the snappier Čechomor.

Čechomor subsequently discovered electricity. There should be no quarrel, as a consequence, with describing them nowadays as a folk-rock band. But they have continually displayed an inability to stick to norms. It is no exaggeration to call them the Czech-Moravian equivalent of Thailand's Carabou (Caravan). And that is not a lightly given panegyric.

Ken Hunt

and dances by brass band composers like František Kmoch (1850–1913).

Pub Songs and Tramps

Prague's celebrated *pivnice* (beer houses) are home to **staropražské písničky** (old Prague songs), performed most notably by **Šlapeto**, a band whose traditions stretch back more than a century. The name roughly translates as "It's going well" and they play old pub songs and love songs, accompanied by accordion, fiddle, guitar and double bass. The style owes something to Viennese *Schrammel* music, thanks to its historical connections with Vienna and mixed Czecho-German culture.

Another sort of urban folk, **trampská hudba** (tramp music), is a favourite amongst Czechs who have hit the road to form emigrant communities all over the world. The music of the *trampové* grew out of the migrations of young workers to industrial areas in the early decades of the twentieth century and it reflects that era's popular music through its use of guitars and mandolins. It's a specifically Czech phenomenon with no equivalent in any other European country, and it is still alive.

Czech tramp music is probably responsible for the fraternal welcome that greeted American **bluegrass and country music** in the early 1960s. The **Annual Banjo Jamboree**, first held in 1972 in Kopidlno (east Bohemia), is the oldest European bluegrass festival. Many bands try to imitate traditional American bluegrass music. However, the national favourites, **Robert Křesťan** and **Druhá tráva**, which evolved from the pioneering band **Poutníci**, enrich bluegrass and newgrass music with Czech lyrics – deeper and more emotional than your average bluegrass song – and a few traditional Czech tunes. They have recently worked with such names as American folk singer Peter Rowan, Irish *uilleann* piper Davy Spillane and American mouth organ player Charlie McCoy.

Moravia

Dozens of festivals and hundreds of musicians champion traditional **Moravian music**. The most vital tradition can be found in southeast Moravia where the lowlands meet the rolling hills. Bands still play for weddings, dances and fairs, and at Shrovetide musicians go from house to house. While Bohemia is beer country, in south Moravia they drink wine or *slivovice* (plum liquor). In the fields near the villages, there are wine cellars

Simon Broughton

Carnival procession in Moravia

where, in the summer or autumn, music and singing drift out through the open doors.

The music is provided by **cimbalom bands**, consisting of a cimbalom (a type of hammered dulcimer), several violins, clarinet and double bass. The original small portable cimbalom has now been replaced by the larger Hungarian-style concert cimbalom with a pedal. Besides the *primáš* (leader – usually the first violin) and other instrumentalists, there are male and female vocalists and sometimes even choirs.

Cimbalom bands are the most widespread type of instrumental group in Moravian folk music. The best known is **Hradišťan**, who have toured Europe, America and Asia. Formed in 1950 and led by violinist **Jiří Pavlica**, Hradišťan perform both traditional music and original compositions. They are particularly known for their fusions of Moravian roots with rock and world music, and have recorded an album with Japanese instrumentalist and composer Yas-Kaz and South African musician Dizu Plaatjies.

While some people disapprove of Hradišťan's contemporary leanings, primáš and singer **Martin Hrbáč** and his **Horňácká** cimbalom band appeal to the most traditional tastes. Hrbáč is a disciple of the legendary primáš Jožka Kubík (1907–78). His music comes from the Horňácko region in the Moravian Highlands, where Janáček did some of the best field collections. Today the best traditional

festival is in **Velká nad Veličkou**. Violin players Jaroslav Staněk (founder of Hradišťan), Slávek Volavý and Jura Petrů were other important band leaders of the post-war era elsewhere in Moravia.

Other small, but distinctive, folk regions in the north include **Valašsko (Valachia)** and **Lašsko (Lachia)**, where Janáček was born in Hukvaldy. Valachia is famous for its pastoral culture and the name comes from a historical or legendary migration of Romanian shepherds (Wallachs) in the Middle Ages, while Lachia has strong Polish influences. Many cultures have met and intermingled in Moravia.

The most typical Moravian dance is the **sedlácká** (peasant dance, from *sedlák* – peasant). This is a fast couple dance, often with disconcerting rhythmic flexibility. There is also the **verbuňk**, a Hungarian-style male recruit dance with distinctive dotted rhythms, and the **táhlá**, a slow song without a regular rhythm, sung or played by the primáš with the accompanying musicians following his solo.

There are two older types of traditional band in Moravia: **gajdošská muzika** (bagpipe music sometimes accompanied by a fiddle) and **hudecká muzika** (string band music with one or twin fiddles, viola, double bass and sometimes a clarinet). These old instrumental set-ups were almost displaced by bigger cimbalom bands, but nowadays seem to be undergoing a revival, especially in the most traditional Moravian region,

Horňácko, with the bands of primášes **Miroslav Minks** and **Petr Mička**.

There's a lively contemporary roots scene based on Moravian traditions. **Vlasta Redl** is a charismatic composer, singer and guitarist. He has worked with the rock groups **Fleret** and **AG Flek**, though all of them exist independently now. New blood in this field is represented by the young band **Docuku** from Valachia, the folkish **Muziga** and the funky-jazzy etnorock band **Benedikta**. Singer and fiddler **Iva Bittová** (see box) has toured abroad extensively, her musical roots and composing talent making her a star of alternative music wherever she appears. Her sister **Ida Kelarová** also brings an ethnic approach to her singing projects, adhering most famously to Roma music.

Emil Viklický is the foremost Czech jazz pianist. Together with Hradišťan violinist Jiří Pavlica and cimbalom player and singer **Zuzana Lapčíková**, he has fused jazz with Moravian traditional music in the trio **Ad Lib Moravia**. He and Lapčíková now often perform as a duo; their collaboration with the famous American jazz bass player of Czech origin, **George Mraz**, ushered in the excellent CD *Morava*.

Brother and sister vocalists **Petr** and **Hana Ulrychovi** brought Moravian melodies into the popular music of the 1970s and now compose their own music accompanied by the **Javory Cimbalom Band**. The excellent cimbalom player **Dalibor Štrunc** has combined traditional and contemporary folk music in his **Cimbal Classic** band. **Teagrass** – with a mandolin instead of a fiddle in the hands of its primáš – mixes Moravian, Balkan, Klezmer and American bluegrass music into a compelling global sound. On the CD *Wide Is the Danube* (2000) the well-known Hungarian singer **Irén Lovász** joined Teagrass to create a multicoloured contemporary East European folk fusion. The duo of **Jiří Plocek** (fiddle, mandolin, folk flutes) and **Jitka Šuranská** (vocals, violin) has evolved out of Teagrass and is oriented more towards the traditional string music of the Carpathian regions.

Iva Bittová

"I've spent so many years with the violin", explains Iva Bittová, "so many years practising that the violin has become one with my body. My speech and the violin are the same. The sound of the violin is so deep within me that my voice can do it too. My body and the instrument are one. For me, it's a matter of vibration. The instrument's body resonates and if you have sung and played together for so many years they resonate and vibrate together."

Trying to compartmentalize Iva Bittová or her art is pointless. She is too many things. That is why communicating a clear sense of her, her status and her importance within contemporary Czech culture to outsiders is tricky, even though she was one of the few Czech acts whose vinyl recordings were licensed on the other side of the Iron Curtain before Czechoslovakia's "De-Reunification" in 1993.

She is a vocalist and classically trained violinist. She still has a violin teacher, **Rudolf Šťastný** – "in many respects a second father to me" – the retired leader of the **Moravské Kvarteto** (Moravian Quartet) at the **Janáček Academy of Music and Dramatic Arts** in Brno. She is also a composer and an acclaimed actress, having appeared, for example, in the 2003 Academy Award-nominated film *Želary* and the 2008 Czech Lion "Best Film" winner *Tajnosti* (Secrets), titled *Little Girl Blue* in English. She grew up steeped in music, absorbing traditional, popular and classical music through every pore in her body. In her performances, she ranges over traditional folk and Roma forms, classical, improvised and avant-garde music, playing and singing with a passion and intensity that can border on the frightening. What's more, she is a one-woman duettist. Talking to the Czech writer and broadcaster **Petr Dorůžka**, the violinist **Dorothea Kellerová** once exclaimed at how Bittová bowed the right-hand part of a Chick Corea piano composition while singing the left-hand part. Take it as a given that she is a true cultural icon in her homeland and one of the planet's greatest performance artists, whether she is forging new music from old, as in her unforgettable solo Roma testimony in the documentary film *Holocaust: A Music Memorial* (2005), or going back to the roots of the Czech composer Janáček.

As she observes, "It's not a plan but I like to go back to the roots, to what is natural. I can feel it better, accept it more that way. I'm not the type to force new directions. I'm someone who goes back to the roots to seek out what is natural. That is, to what I see as real and truthful."

The aptly named DVD *Superchameleon* (Indies) captures the magical visual qualities and vital otherness of her performance, both solo and in collaboration with Mañana, Pavel Fajt and Richard Ferdinand, Miroslav Donutil and Miloš Štědroň, Dunaj, Vladimír Václavek, Bílé Inferno, the Nederlands Blazers Ensemble, the Škampa Quartet and Bang On A Can.

Ken Hunt

Festivals

Czech Republic

Chodské slavnosti Festival of Czech bagpipe music, held in August in the Bohemian town of Domažlice.

Horňácké slavnosti Very traditional festival of the Horňácko region, which takes place in Velká nad Veličkou in northern Moravia in the second half of July.

Strážnice The biggest festival in the Czech and Slovak Republics, with local and international artists. It is held in the small town of Strážnice in southern Moravia, the last weekend in June.

Prázdniny v Telči One of the most popular non-traditional festivals, located in the beautiful medieval town of Telč in southern Moravia. Main performances are held in the courtyard of the castle, with bands like Hradišťan, Teagrass, Cimbal Classic and Vlasta Redl. It lasts two weeks at the turn of July and August.

Colours of Ostrava The biggest and best world music festival in the Czech Republic. It takes place in Ostrava, northern Moravia, in June.

Slovakia

Západoslovenské folklórné slavnosti Traditional festival of western Slovakia, held in the town of Myjava in June.

Detva The traditional folklore festival of central Slovakia, held in July.

Východná A traditional festival that presents folklore of northern and eastern Slovakia, held the last weekend in June.

For more information about festivals, folklore ensembles and musical events visit *folklorweb.cz* (Moravia) or *ppfound.sk* (Slovakia).

Slovakia

Slovakia has the richest living village folk traditions in central Europe. That perhaps explains why world music or urban folk music has not developed as intensively here as in neighbouring countries. Besides genuine traditional music and singing, most contemporary folk activity is happening in the "folkloristic" mode – i.e. "scenic folklore", with professional choreography and costumed dancers and musicians, "sanitized", instrumentally refined cimbalom music, and so on. This is a legacy of the Communist system. However, the Slovaks have an energy and emotion in their blood which adds something special to all their musical expressions. This is most remarkable, of course, among the most authentic folk musicians – be it the folk band of **Július Šuka Bartoš** from Iierny Balog in central Slovakia or village string bands from the mountains of the north.

The beautiful, mountainous landscape of northern and central Slovakia is home to various **shepherds' flutes**, from a small whistle to the *fujara*, between one and two metres long and made from a single piece of wood. The fujara has a unique sound – smoothly soft in the low range, and expressive in its upper registers. These flutes can be played solo – as in the hands of **Pavel Bielčik** – or combined with small bagpipes (*gajdy* in Slovak). Other instruments in the mountain music bands include fiddles, a half-size double bass and a small button accordion.

Slovakia's mountain regions are where the best **folklore festivals** take place, highlighting regional bands and singers like the **Mucha Brothers** from Terchová, **Ján Ámbroz** from Telgárt, **Ďatelinka** from Detva, **Rozsutec** from Žilina and **Šarišan** from Prešov. The instrumental music of the Tatra mountains – with string bands comprised of several violins and a cello – is similar to the *górale* music of Podhale across the border in Poland. As in southern Poland, the popular subject of song texts here is **Jánošík**, a local Robin Hood figure. In Slovakia he occurs in songs and fairy tales, and for poor people he was, and still is, the embodiment of justice – even if in reality such brigands were generally common criminals.

The southern lowlands have absorbed Hungarian and Gypsy influences into their cimbalom bands, resulting in the swinging, virtuoso style that is usually associated with Slovak music. The most popular dance is the fiery **čardáš**. Bandleader and fiddler **Miroslav Dudík**, grandson of the legendary Slovak fiddler **Samko Dudík** (1880–1967) and much admired by Janáček, is an heir to the Slovak cimbalom band tradition, although his recordings favour ensembles that are too big and folkloristic.

Eastern Slovakia is a world apart. It is isolated and culturally very rich, with Slovak, Polish, Ruthenian (Ukrainian), Hungarian and Gypsy influences combining in wild cimbalom band music and a living folk culture. The traditional music is still strongly connected with folk customs and village celebrations and therefore has not really been transformed into contemporary folk music. The folklore ensemble **Železiar** from Košice give folkloristic performances, but also try to record and learn old village musical traditions (especially Ruthenian ones) in remote parts of Eastern Slovakia.

Singer-songwriter **Zuzana Homolová** works with old Slovak ballads and performs them in their most powerful form – acapella – or with violinist **Samo Smetana**, who recently founded the world music group **Banda**. The group **Družina** have been one of the most distinctive representatives of folk-rock-jazz fusion during the last few years, along with singer **Zuzana Mojžišová** and her band. The distinctive vocalist and instrumentalist **Suí Vesan** has brought a new dimension to contemporary folk music with her "punk folk for the twenty-first century"; her debut CD, *Suí* (2001), sold well.

Trio Pacora is one of the latest discoveries on the Slovak world music scene. Its three phenomenal musicians – violin player **Stano Palúch** (dubbed the "Slovak Grappelli"), Moldavian cimbalom player **Marcel Comendant** and bass player **Robert Ragan** – perform ethnojazz of the finest kind. Rooted in swing, they absorb Moravian, Slovak and Romanian folk elements, blending them all with incredible improvisational abilities.

The group **Ghymes** comes from the Hungarian minority in the south of the country. Like many *táncház* groups in Hungary, they have combined local traditions with their own eclectic tastes and imagination to produce some excellent recordings and great gigs.

The village of Dolná Krupá (near Trnava northeast of Bratislava) has an intriguing place in musical history. It was the home of the **Dopyera family** before their emigration to the US in 1908. In 1926 the Dopyera brothers invented the famous **Dobro guitar**, with its circular resonating plate, and since 1992 Trnava has commemorated that with an annual Dobrofest.

Roma – Gypsies

Gypsies have been living in Bohemia, Moravia and Slovakia for centuries – although all but six hundred Czech and Moravian Gypsies were killed in Nazi concentration camps during World War II. The communities revived somewhat in the postwar years but relations today are not easy, and in Slovakia, in particular, Gypsies have been subject to violent harassment from their settled neighbours in the post-Independence nation.

Fortunately, there are several institutions and unions that are working hard to increase respect for Gypsies and their culture. The **Museum of Roma Culture** in Brno (Moravia) organizes fine exhibitions, conducts field research, and has released a CD with a unique collection of Roma vocal music, compiled by the great Roma expert **Eva Davidová**. A festival of Gypsy music (Romfest) was established in 1991, but lasted only a few years.

Gypsies figure prominently in the Moravian and Slovak cimbalom bands. Their music is highly emotional and band leaders such as **Evžen Horváth**, **Josef Griňa** and **Ňudovít Kováč** show great virtuosity and showmanship on violin or cimbalom. One vocalist to watch out for is **Věra Bílá**, who sings with the band **Kale**. Bílá is a descendant of Roma people who came to West Bohemia from Slovakia after the war. Thanks to the support of the famous Prague singer-songwriter Zuzana Navarová, she became popular not only in the Czech Republic, but also abroad. She has a strong personality which has helped to increase respect for contemporary Roma music and Roma people in the Czech Republic.

There is now another band following in the footsteps of Kale – but more jazzy and musically colourful – **Terne Čhave** from Eastern Bohemia. Brno city is the home of the funky Roma band **Gulo čar**, whose 2003 debut CD *Baro Drom* (Long Journey) was highly acclaimed.

See the Gypsy Music article (p.196) for more on the wider context of Gypsy music in Europe.

With thanks to Jan Sobotka, Irena Přibylová and Ken Hunt

DISCOGRAPHY Czech & Slovak Republics

A good online store for Czech and Slovak music can be found at *www.cdmusic.cz*. Alternatively, try the labels directly: Indies Records (*www.indiesrec.cz*), Arta Records (*www.arta.cz*), Lotos (420 2 5721 1478). The other labels mentioned below can be obtained through Gnosis Brno: Rezkova 30, 602 00 Brno; *jplocek@volny.cz*; *www.mujweb.cz/www/gnosis_brno*.

Bohemia

⊙ Cikánský Pláč (Gypsy Lament)
Supraphon, Czech Republic
An excellent anthology of Gypsy songs and cimbalom music in Czechoslovakia, full of emotion and deep feeling.

★ Dudy a Dudácká Muzika 1909 (Bagpipe and Bagpipe Music 1909)
Institute of Ethnology of Czech Academy of Sciences, Czech Republic
The oldest recording of Czech folk music. A unique collection of singing and bagpipe music from southern Bohemia and so-called *malá selská muzika* (little peasant music – bagpipe, violin, clarinet) from the Chodsko region. Extensive booklet notes in Czech, English and German.

⊙ Hrály Dudy: The Hidden Spell of the Czech Bagpipe
Bonton, Czech Republic
Field recordings made between 1974 and 1992 by Josef Režný, the veteran Czech expert on bagpipe music. Includes bagpipes with fiddles and remarkable historical bagpipes.

⊙ Strážnice Folk Festival 1946–95
Supraphon, Czech Republic
This includes many rare and precious recordings of Bohemian, Moravian, Slovak and Gypsy folk music, with an emphasis on the authentic village style. It was compiled by producer Jaromír Nečas, who has made recordings in Strážnice since 1946.

Pošumavská Dudácká Muzika

This is a pretty traditional bagpipe band from the region at the foot of the Šumava mountains, with some 1960s folk revival influences.

⊙ Poslyšte Mládenci: Wedding Songs from Čestice and Pošumaví Region
Musicvars, Czech Republic
Traditional music with some unusual repertoire and instruments. A good example of development within the tradition.

Moravia

★ Proměny v Čase: Traditional Folk Music in Moravia in the Twentieth Century
Gnosis Brno, Czech Republic
This essential two-CD compilation provides a portrait of the folk music of the whole of Moravia – past and present. It features old village music, new regional folk music and folklorism. There are extensive liner notes, in both Czech and English.

⊙ The Oldest Recordings of Folk-singing from Moravia and Slovakia, 1909–1912
Gnosis Brno, Czech Republic
A selection from the wax cylinders originally recorded by Leoš Janáček and his collaborators. Obviously of specialist interest, the CD comes complete with English translations and descriptions of Janáček's ethnomusicological activities.

Children From Uherskobrodsko Region

If there is a future for Moravian traditional music, it is in the children. There are many boys and girls all over southeast Moravia singing in the traditional way – a phenomenon that does not exist in other parts of country. And no one has been able to realize this potential better than teacher Vlastimil Ondra (born 1972) from Nivnice, near the town of Uherský Brod. In a simple, very natural way, he leads children to sing old songs spontaneously – and it sounds absolutely traditional!

★ Mladé Vzpomínky (Young Memories)
Gnosis Brno, Czech Republic
This 2004 collection of songs describes a life from birth to marriage. Young singers from three to eighteen sing traditional songs with the utmost delicacy, mostly with very simple accompaniments of accordion or small string band.

Martin Hrbáč

The charismatic singer and fiddler Martin Hrbáč is one of the legends of Moravian folk music, and his cimbalom band is one of the best around.

⊙ Horňácký Hudec Martin Hrbáč
Gnosis Brno, Czech Republic
A collection of traditional music from the distinctive Horňácko region of northern Moravia. The CD includes examples of string band, cimbalom band and bagpipe music; both slow songs and wild dances are played in an idiomatic style.

František Okénka

Born in 1921 in the Horňácko region, Okénka is a singer, teacher and member of the legendary Jožka Kubík band.

⊙ František Okénka
Gnosis Brno, Czech Republic
A mixture of archive tracks and new recordings made in 1996 when Okénka was 75. The latter represent some of the most authentic Moravian rural music to be recorded in recent years. Okénka is accompanied on most tracks by a four-piece string band led by Martin Hrbáč – considered the purest Horňácko folk sound.

Varmužova Cimbálová Muzika

Probably Moravia's best group of singers and a real family band. Josef Varmuža (bass) is joined by his brother Pavel (cimbalom), his four sons – Pavel (lead violin), Petr (second violin), Josef (viola) and Jiří (viola) – and his wife Hedvika and daughter Kateřina, whose voices provide a gentle contrast to the men's virile sound.

⊙ Na Kyjovsku
Gnosis Brno, Czech Republic

Music from the region of Kyjov in southern Moravia. The songs are often wild and spirited, although some numbers sound more formal.

Slovakia

⊙ Fujara, Fujara
MUSICA, Slovak Republic

This CD showcases several outstanding fujara players from across Slovakia – among them Pavel Bělčík from Kokava nad Rimavicou, Ján Palovič from Poniky and Ján Hanuska from Detva.

⊙ Slovak Csardas: Dance Tunes from the Pennsylvania Coal Mines
Heritage/Interstate, UK

Many Slovaks emigrated to the US to work in the coal mines and refineries of Pennsylvania. These recordings were made for the Victor and Columbia labels between 1928 and 1930. Four bands are included and (apart from the Michael Stiber tracks which are badly distorted) the recordings sound good for their age. The repertoire is Gypsy-style *csardas* and polkas, but what's remarkable is their raw, unsanitized style, which evokes the rowdy village bands of early-twentieth-century Slovakia.

★ Slovakia: Folk Music
Ocora, France

The best compilation of traditional Slovak music, this CD of recordings made by Slovak Radio between 1972 and 1999 provides a good overview of musical styles, avoiding, for the most part, souped-up material. It includes the Mucha brothers from Terchová and Martin Kubinec and his sons playing two-metre-long fujara pipes from the Polana hills – shimmering with overtones.

⊙ Slovakia: Music from Polana
Inedit, France

The Polana hills near Banska Bystrica have a strong pastoral musical culture, including the tall fujara pipes, which are unique in Europe. This CD contains a good selection of music for flutes and bagpipes from this region of central Slovakia, plus Jaroslav Harazin's string band.

⊙ Z Hl'bín Času (From the Depths of Time)
Slovenský Rozhlas (Slovak Radio Bratislava), Slovak Republic

Subtitled "Recordings of authentic Slovak folk music from 1929–1959", this is a great archive selection. It includes the oldest recording of primáš Samko Dudík's band from 1929, plus singing, folk whistles and old mountain string bands from the whole of Slovakia. Highly recommended.

Samko Dudík

Legendary fiddler and bandleader Samko Dudík (1880–1967) was championed by Janáček and influenced many Slovak and Moravian folk musicians.

◉ Samko Dudík
Opus, Slovakia

Rare recordings made by Brno Radio in the late 1950s of the Dudík family band – an eight-piece ensemble of strings and cimbalom. This is wonderful old-style Slovak music which should be reissued on CD.

Mucha Brothers

The four Mucha brothers are an excellent string band from Terchová, a village in the mountains of northern Slovakia.

This is the highland music also heard across the border in Poland. The strings are sometimes joined by shepherds' flutes and a button accordion (*heligónka*) played by Rudolf Patrnčiak.

★ Do Hory, do Lesa Valaši
A.L.I. Records, Slovakia

Some of the best Slovak traditional music, played with incredible energy. This disc is actually a collection of folk carols. Any of their other CDs will be equally good.

Železiar

A folklore ensemble from Košice, established in 1964. From the start, Železiar has been committed to the presentation of the traditional music of eastern Slovakia, both Slovak and Ruthenian. The women of Železiar choir visited old Ruthenian village singers to learn the traditional way of singing. Bass player Milan Rendoš is also a very talented player of folk instruments like the button accordion (heligónka), mouth organ (*harmonika*), folk whistles (*píšt'alky*) and bagpipe (gajdy).

⊙ Moja Mila, Jaka Ši (My darling, what you are about...)
Kultobin, Slovak Republic

This musical profile of the band, released in 2001, features typical songs and dances from the eastern Slovak regions of Zempli, Abov and Šariš, including *kariika* (a round dance for girls), verbuňk, čardaš and eastern polka.

Beyond the Traditional

⊙ Indies Records: 2004 And Best of 15 years
Indies Records, Czech Republic

Indies Records is the most representative label for Czech and Moravian contemporary folk, world and alternative rock music. On this two-CD compilation, you will find the majority of the important performers and bands, including Iva Bittová, Hradišt'an, Zuzana Navarová, Traband, and Jan Hrubý and his band Kukulín.

Věra Bílá

Small, but packing quite a punch, Bílá is the most successful Romany performer to emerge from the former Czechoslovakia. She was born in 1954 into a musical family in eastern Slovakia, but with her band Kale she has broadened her musical reach to embrace Latin sounds performed in an unmistakably Romani manner.

★ Queen of Romany
BMG/GIGA, Austria

A 1999 "best of" disc drawing together tracks from two of her many albums. There are some fizzing up-tempo numbers with Kale's guitars and vocal harmonies and the tragic "When I'm Getting Drunk", one of the greatest Romani vocals on disc.

⊙ Věra Bílá & Kale: C´est Comme Ca
Sony Music Entertainment, Czech Republic

The latest studio CD of the Roma diva and her band, released in 2005 after more than three years of intense concert activities.

Iva Bittová

Born in 1958 in Bruntál, Iva Bittová is indisputably one of the world's most maverick musical originals. She is the second of three daughters born to the multi-instrumentalist Koloman Bitto and teacher and singer Ludmila Bittová (Bittová is the surname's female construction). Her sisters have also entered the arts – they are the singer Ida Kelarová and the actress Regina Bittová.

 Bílé Inferno
Indies Records, Czech Republic
This monument to creativity, co-credited to guitar and bass player Vladimír Václavek, is a milestone in Bittová's career. From two CDs crammed with ideas of extraordinary originality and vigour, music spills out as if from a Czech cornucopia. Ida Kelarová also appears.

⊙ **Béla Bartók's 44 Duets For Two Violins**
Rachot/Behémot, Czech Republic
Bartók's 44 Duets have had a sorry life, all too often consigned to the violinistic kindergarten. Bittová and Dorothea Kellerová's folk re-interpretations realign Bartók's compositions with their original elemental inspiration.

⊙ **j.h.**
Indies, Czech Republic
j.h. is short for "jako host" ("as guest"). This is a family affair and not merely because Ida Kelarová and Bittová's percussionist ex-partner Pavel Fajt take part. It is a sampler that presents many sides of her music, such as her work with the Netherlands Blazers Ensemble (from their magnificent joint album *Ples Upírů* (Night of the Vampires) and a sterling "Gloomy Sunday" from the film *The Man Who Cried* (2000).

Čechomor (Czechomor)

Čechomor is one of the Czech Republic's most long-lived and adaptable bands. Their name signals their commitment to Czech-Moravian music, a commitment undaunted by myriad line-up (and name) changes since they started out in 1988.

⊙ **Mezi Horami (Amidst the Mountains)**
Polygram/Venkow, Czech Republic
This 1996 album blends Bohemian and Moravian songs in a way that satisfies both innovators and purists. There's also a touch of Celtic inspiration.

⊙ **Proměny**
Venkow, Czech Republic
Released in 2001, and co-credited to Killing Joke's Jaz Coleman, *Proměny* (Transformations) reflects the band's evolving quest to make albums with different sound palettes from their standard sound. This one sees their repertoire undergoing an orchestral metamorphosis. The film *Rok Ďábla* from 2002 includes footage from these sessions with Coleman conducting (and acting).

 Co Sa Stalo Nové/What Happened Next
Columbia, Czech Republic
On this 2005 album a classic line-up of the band create their trademark sound based on guitar, fiddle, Czech bagpipes, electric cello, accordion, trumpet and kit drum, but augmented with cimbalom, uilleann pipe, shakuhachi, taiko drum and slide guitar. For newcomers, this should be the first call.

Vladimír Godár

The Slovak composer Vladimír Godár, born in 1956 in Bratislava, was hardly known outside his homeland until the liturgical tour de force *Mater*. His music is typified by extraordinary vibrancy and colour.

 Mater
Pavian Records, Slovakia/ECM New Series, Germany
Godár had worked with Iva Bittová on various film soundtrack and recording projects but this is timeless stuff. Bittová sings in Slovak, Latin and English. "Stálá Matka" (Mother stood) is simply heart-rending.

Zuzana Homolová

Zuzana Homolová is one of Slovakia's strongest and most interesting folk singers.

⊙ **Slovenské Balady (Slovak Ballads)**
Pavian Records, Slovakia
On this 1995 album Homolová's sad and dramatic Slovak ballads are accompanied by multi-instrumentalist Vlasta Redl, who brings great sensitivity to his arrangements and performance.

Hradišt'an

Hradišt'an is probably the most innovative cimbalom band in Moravia. They started in the 1950s as a traditional outfit led by Jaroslav Staněk. Since his death in 1978, under the leadership of Jiří Pavlica, they have become far more eclectic.

⊙ **Ozvěny Duše (Moravian Echoes)**
Lotos, Czech Republic
This 1994 album takes a journey through the history of Moravian music from Old Church Slavonic music to regional and pan-Moravian styles.

Ida Kelarová

Ida Kelarová is a distinctive and original Czech vocalist. After various experiments with voice expression, she has established herself as a charismatic singer of Roma songs.

⊙ **Ida Kelarová & Romano Rat: Staré Slzy (Old Tears)**
Indies Records, Czech Republic
If Věra Bílá and her band's music could be called Roma-pop, the music of Romano Rat is Roma-jazz, soft and soulful. The deep voice of Ida Kelarová brings incredible power.

Zuzana Lapčíková, Emil Viklický and George Mraz

Singer and cimbalom player Zuzana Lapčíková and pianist Emil Viklický are part of the trio Ad Lib Moravia. In 2001, they collaborated with Czech-American jazz bass player George Mraz.

 George Mraz: Morava
Milestone Records, US
Despite the title, this music is not defined only by the excellent bass performance of George Mraz. There is also fine piano playing by Emil Viklický and drums by Billy Hart. Lapčíková's singing of Moravian folk songs is smoothly emotional, and her cimbalom playing shifts the jazzy stuff into more esoteric spaces.

Zuzana Mojžišová

Singer, musicologist and classical music radio producer Zuzana Mojžišová is a rebel of the Slovak folklore scene. Raised in a milieu of folklorism, she decided at last to sing traditional songs according to her own heart. In 2001, she appeared on a CD with the folk-rock band Jej Družina and was derided by orthodox folklorists. Since that time, she has gained some respect for what she is doing and now her music is a fine blend of folk-rock and jazz influences with beautiful Slovak folk songs.

 Zuzana Mojžišová
Slovak Radio, Slovakia
Zuzana Mojžišová's first solo project brings together the best Slovak folk, rock and jazz musicians: Rast'o Andris on folk whistles, fujara and bagpipes; Stano Palúch on violin; Andrej

Šeban on guitars; and Martin Valihora on drums. The album received four nominations at the AUREL awards (the Slovak Grammys), and won two of them. Rather successful for a rebel.

Vlasta Redl and Jiří Pavlica

Folk singer and rock musician Vlasta Redl is one of Moravia's favourite contemporary performers, and Jiří Pavlica, primáš of the Hradišťan ensemble, is an outstanding personality in traditional music.

⊙ **Vlasta Redl, A.G. Flek & Jiří Pavlica: Hradišťan**
BMG/Ariola, Czech Republic
This 1994 album is a tasteful combination of rock and pop with Moravian cimbalom band music. On top there's the deeply emotional voice of Alice Holubová, one of the best young Moravian folk singers.

Tara Fuki

Two charismatic singing cello players from northern Moravia, Andrea Konstakiewicz and Dorota Barova, formed the duo Tara Fuki in 2001. Their debut CD, *Piosenki Do Snu* (The Songs To Dreaming), was highly successful.

⊙ **Kapka**
Indies Records, Czech Republic
The "difficult second album syndrome" did not affect the quality and originality of this CD. The music and singing are softly emotional and full of sensuality, and the arrangements – thanks to guest composer Mario Buzzi – are artful and intimate.

PLAYLIST
Czech & Slovak Republics

1 **KAČENKA (LITTLE KATHY) Children from Uherskobrodsko** from *Mladé Vzpomínky*
Boys from a village in eastern Moravia. If you listen to them, you will believe everything, even lies.

2 **MLYNARE, MLYNARE (OH, MILLER, MILLER!) Zuzana Mojžišová** from *Zuzana Mojžišová*
A beautiful arrangement of a Slovak folk song.

3 **HÁJ, HÁJ, HÁJ, HÁJ, ZELENÉ OŘEŠÍ (GROVE, GROVE, GREEN GROVE) Martin Hrbáč** from *Horňáký Hudec Martin Hrbáč*
A dance song from Horňácko, the most traditional place in Moravia. Men's voices with raw fiddling.

4 **FUJARA SONG Jan Palovič** from *Fujara, Fujara*
The voice of Slovakia. Typical slow, emotional playing and singing.

5 **NARODIL SA KRISTUS PÁN (LORD JESUS CHRIST WAS BORN) Mucha Brothers** from *Do Hory, do Lesa Valasi*
A noble Slovak version of the famous carol which is also sung in Bohemia and Moravia.

6 **ZELENÝ VÍNEČEK (A GREEN GARLAND) Iva Bittová and Vladimír Václavek** from *Bílé Inferno*
A folk tune adapted by Bittová. She sings, Jaromir Honzák plays string bass and Ida Kelarová sings and plays piano. They are joined by the Lelky Chorale.

7 **CO SA STALO NOVÉ (WHAT HAPPENED NEXT) Čechomor** from *Co Sa Stalo Nové*
The tune's title hints at Čechomor's new direction. It features Joji Hirota on taiko drums and Jan Mikušek on cimbalom.

8 **DVOUDOBÉ KOLEČKO (TWO-BEAT CIRCLE) Josef Režný** from *Hrály Dudy: The Hidden Spell of the Czech Bagpipe*
Great bagpipe playing by a legendary player from Strakonice in western Bohemia, in typical polka rhythm.

9 **U MAMĚNKY V DOMĚ Alice Holubová** from *Vlasta Redl, A.G. Flek, Jiří Pavlica: Hradišťan*
An old song arranged in a tasteful folk-rock way, featuring one of the best Moravian folk singers.

10 **BALVAJ PHURDEL (THE WIND IS BLOWING) Ida Kelarová and Romano Rat** from *Staré Slzy*
Deep melancholic emotions. This delicate jazzy music distils Roma soul in a song.

Denmark & the Faroe Islands

a new pulse for the pols

Lars Lilholt
Danish Folk Music Council

The southernmost Nordic country, Denmark has long played genial host to the music of other countries at its numerous festivals and folk venues, while music identifiably Danish in tradition has struggled to survive. Since the turn of the millennium, however, there has been an upsurge in the number of skilled young musicians making ever more impressive – and distinctively Danish – music based on the country's traditional tunes and songs. Meanwhile, far out in the north Atlantic, the tiny Faroe Islands have maintained a remarkable and quite distinct culture of their own, as Andrew Cronshaw explains.

A Nordic country with a Nordic language, Denmark controlled the whole of Scandinavia in the middle ages. But it differs from its neighbours in ways that have affected its music. It is a small, densely populated country that is nowhere more than forty miles or so from the sea. It has none of Norway or Sweden's distant valleys where unique traditions could flourish and remain sheltered from the breezes of musical fashion. Nevertheless, some individual areas and islands did develop distinct musical traditions, and a few of these have continued into the present day, where they have been cultivated by the musicians of the current renaissance.

Dance Fashions

As in other European countries, a large proportion of what is today considered traditional Danish music consists of regional interpretations of the dance fashions of the seventeenth to nineteenth centuries: waltz, polka and other couple dances such as *hopsa*, *rheinlænder*, *schottish*, *trekanter*, and the set dances *firtur* and *tretur*. Since that time, the prevailing instruments have been the **fiddle** and the **accordion**. Other folk instruments used in the past and now occasionally revived are the **humle**, a long-box fretted zither (of the same family as Norway's *langeleik* and the US's Appalachian dulcimer) and the **nyckelharpa**, which was depicted in a church carving as long ago as the fifteenth century.

The oldest surviving folk dance in Denmark is the **pols**, which was popular in the seventeenth century. It has mainly endured in **Sønderho** on the isle of Fanø. The local dance forms there, the *sønderhoning* and *fannik*, are unusual because they alternate between a duple-time march and a triple-time swing while the music stays in duple time. The main tradition bearers of Sønderho music in the twentieth century were the Brinch family, the last musicians being fiddlers **Søren Lassen Brinch** (d.1988) and **Frits Attermann Brinch** (d.1993), and piano player **Erling Brinch** (d.1994). Erling was part of the **Jæ' Sweevers** trio, and since his death the other members have continued to play Fanø music and the rest of the folk-dance repertoire, as do so many other Danish roots musicians.

Another influence on young musicians digging into their dance-music heritage was the lively and emphatic Himmerland fiddler **Evald Thomsen** (d.1993), who was first recorded by pioneering folklorist **Thorkild Knudsen**. Thomsen was employed by the state as a folk music consultant in the 1970s, along with singer **Ingeborg Munch** (d.1978) from Torup.

Looking Outwards and Inwards

While in most other Nordic countries there was a turn towards traditional indigenous music in the 1970s, young Danes became enthusiastic about the folk music and performers of the US, Ireland and Scotland, and many took up their instruments in those styles. However, a handful moved over to Danish music. The **Lang Linken** trio formed in 1970 and concentrated entirely on Danish material, seeking out and learning from the old players and eschewing guitars in favour of the fiddle, diatonic accordion, **hurdy-gurdy** and **Danish bagpipe**. Lang Linken remains a seminal band; its members are still performing together and continue to influence a new wave of younger players.

During the 1970s, enthusiasm for Celtic and American music continued – as it does to the present day – and very few musicians picked up the threads of Danish traditional music, the exception being the members of **Jydsk På Næsen**, a quartet featuring two fiddles, an accordion and bass which formed in 1979. During the 1980s, while many bands still favoured Irish, Scottish and American music, some began to take an interest in their Danish roots. A few revival bands formed, most notably **Jæ' Sweevers**, the bowed-strings quintet **Rasmus** (named after the writer of one of the eighteenth-century tunebooks from which they draw their material), the Danish/Faroese/American band **Spælimenninir** and, a little later, **Baldrian**.

One of the fiddlers in Rasmus, **Lars Lilholt**, is best known in Denmark as a singer-songwriter, guitarist and fiddler with his own pop-rock/folk-rock band. In 1988, the Lars Lilholt Band had a hit with "Kald Det Kærlighed" ("Call It Love"), which is now considered a Danish pop classic. The band remains a big live draw, but Lilholt has maintained his connection with the folk tradition and their songs mix a hefty rock sound with a substantial amount of Danish traditional dance material.

The **Danish Folk Council** (*www.folkemusik.dk*) was set up in 1994 and went on to have a major influence on the visibility of Danish roots music at home and abroad. The council publicized revival groups and any tradition-rooted musical activity, publishing *Folk & Musik* magazine (now succeeded by the online mag *www.Rootzone.dk*) and, from 1995, releasing well-packaged showcase compilations from whichever albums – including demos – were available. The council's confidence in the Danish folk music scene, both traditional roots and songwriting, has since proved well-founded. Funded by a government arts grant, they continue to assist the burgeoning scene in many ways, including co-ordinating the annual folk music awards and helping with CD distribution, publicity and foreign travel for musicians.

During the 1990s tradition-inspired Danish music began to expand and evolve as young musicians formed a string of acoustic bands such as **Baltinget, Kætter Kvartet, Phønix, ULC, Puls** and **Ostinat Expressen**, and the folk-rockier **Danish Dia Delight, Fenja Menja** and **Dug**. A project that had considerable commercial success was **Sorten Muld**. Inspired by the likes of the Swedish and Finnish band Hedningarna and Britain's Massive Attack, it mixed the breathy vocals of **Ulla Bendixen** with electronic rhythms and the sounds of folk instruments such as bagpipe, hurdy-gurdy and Jew's harp in wide-screen treatments of traditional ballads.

Some of the bands founded in the 1990s and earlier are still active and developing, and since 2000 they have been joined by an expanding scene of bands and partnerships, often with criss-crossing membership. Current and recent acoustic instrumental groupings, the majority featuring fiddle, include **Trio Mio, Færd, Trio THG, Habbadám, Basco** and **Hal & Nikolaj**, as well as the Danish-Finnish **Kings of Polka** and Danish-Finnish-British **Baltic Crossing**. Taking a rockier line have been **Serras, Tumult, Instinkt** and **Valravn**, the latter a powerful, visual electric band featuring singer **Anna Katrin Egilstrød**, whose work with Nordic traditional ballads carries forward the sonic approach, largely initiated by Hedningarna, that came to be dubbed "drone-rock".

One of those who has done the most criss-crossing is fiddler **Harald Haugaard**, who played with many of the innovating bands including Dug, Serras, Puls and Sorten Muld, and now has his own solo and band projects. His longest and best-known partnership has been with guitarist **Morten Alfred Høirup**, who founded Danish Dia Delight and played with US and Finnish musicians in the American Café Orchestra. The duo **Haugaard & Høirup**, from 1998 until they went their separate ways in 2009, became Danish roots music ambassadors, always to be found in the thick of a session at festivals and playing far more gigs around the world than any other Danish folk act.

The majority of the revival has been instrumental, drawing on traditional dance music, but recently fine singers have been appearing, largely female and often with experience in other fields of music. They include **Karen Mose Norgaard** (daughter of Lang Linken's Keld Nørgaard) with **Helene Blum** (now singing with Phønix) in the vocal duo **Karen and Helene** and her own solo project, **Sine Lahm**

Lauritsen of Zar, **Louise Støjberg** of **Zenobia** and **Anna Katrin Egilstrød** of **Valravn**.

Surviving Songs

Denmark has a substantial body of folk songs and a share of Europe's **medieval ballads** – great songs of love, magic and violence. While some just about survived into the early twentieth century in the oral tradition, many of the ballads became separated from the music and were regarded as poetry rather than songs to be sung.

Some ballads and topical songs were circulated between the sixteenth and early twentieth centuries by means of the **skillingstryk** or **skillingsviser**, printed ballad sheets that were sold by street vendors. From the mid-nineteenth century, a regular theme on these sheets was emigration; over 300,000 Danes emigrated between 1850 and 1914, mostly to the US. These **emigration songs** covered such subjects as the gold rush, disasters at sea, going to Utah with recruiting Mormons and nostalgia for the homeland, but few of these became part of the oral tradition.

School's Out

The greatest influence on the twenty-first century upturn in Danish roots music has been the creation, in 1998, of a course for folk music teachers at the **Carl Nielsen Academy**. Harald Haugaard studied at the Academy before the course even existed, and was the first student to be allowed to learn from traditional fiddlers as part of his studies. He became the head of the folk music programme, where other teachers include Lang Linken's Carl Erik Lundgaard and **Peter Uhrbrand**, a Fanø fiddler and a member of Jæ' Sweevers and ULC.

The majority of the new young names in Danish folk music are students or graduates of the course. Their rapid progress isn't only the result of dedicating four years to studying and playing traditional music, but also in communicating with musicians on other courses. This exchange of ideas has resulted in a new style of Danish music that combines the forms and skills of traditional music with those of young, fresh-thinking jazz players.

One of the first graduates was fiddler **Kristine Heebøll**, once a member of the band Phønix. She has taken the traditions onwards and outwards with her **Trio Mio**, playing her own shapely tunes with jazz-educated pianist/accordionist **Nikolaj Busk** and Swedish guitar and bouzouki player **Jens Ulvsand**, who teaches at the Academy. Heebøll says of the opening of the course, "It was the beginning of a lot of the things that are happening now, with young folk musicians playing the traditional Danish style but adding something more to it. And even going vocal – that's very new in Denmark – and composing their own music."

As mentioned earlier, fine singers are increasingly emerging, via the Nielsen Academy and from other directions, but the biggest upsurge has been in the number of young fiddlers playing traditional music and reactivating a living tradition by writing their own pieces. Joining Kristine Heebøll and Harald Haugaard, and their elders and mentors, is an ever-expanding cast of sparky, skilful new bowers forming bands and releasing albums, including **Kristian Bugge**, **Henrik Jansberg**, **Michael Graubæk**, **Andreas Tophøj**, **Ivan Damgård**, **Jørgen Dickmeiss**, **Ditte Fromseier Mortensen** and **Klaus Pindstrup**.

Denmark also has its share of singer-songwriters, and they are not all US-orientated guitar-players. The Danish traditions of writing literary ballads and setting poems to music have been exemplified by the songwriter-poet team of **Povl Dissing** and **Benny Andersen**. Other successes include **Erik Grip** and **Niels Hausgaard**, with the latter singing in the dialect of his native Vendsyssel in northern Denmark.

The Faroe Islands

The beautiful, wild Faroes – eighteen islands in the North Atlantic with a total population of 47,000 – are a largely self-governing part of Denmark, roughly equidistant from Norway, Iceland and Shetland. The islands' everyday language is Faroese, but the locals also speak Danish, and many English. Although they have long had fishing contacts with other nations, the islands aren't on a major sea-route, and from 1709 to 1856, a time of great change in Europe, the presence of a monopoly trading station meant that their only official commercial contact was with Denmark. Culturally, the Faroes have remained very distinct.

Circle-dancing

The old Faroese traditional music was vocal. The **fiddle** arrived in the seventeenth century, and by the eighteenth, pan-European dances such as the minuet and polka, and English and Scottish dances had reached the islands. However, such innovations were largely restricted to the smart Danish set in the capital, Tórshavn, and among the wider population they didn't displace the old custom of **circle-dancing ballads**.

Foroya Skulabokagrunnur

Ballad dancing

Throughout northern Europe it was common for groups of people to sing ballads while dancing in a circle. But only in the Faroes has this tradition persisted unrevived to the present day. The group holds hands, facing inwards and the circle moves clockwise. Normally one person leads the singing, and the rest join in at the chorus. The song rhythm, particularly in the oldest **heroic ballads**, is frequently a different number of beats from the unchanging rhythm of the footstamp, giving the music a polyrhythmic, overlapping feel.

There are three main types of danced ballads. The most popular are the heroic type, **kvæði**, which are related to the medieval ballads sung by other Nordic and Germanic peoples. They are usually stories about the Nibelung or Charlemagne, or Nordic myths featuring heroes battling trolls and giants. Kvæði often run to over a hundred stanzas. The second type, **vísur**, are not always clearly distinguishable from kvæði. They're often Danish ballads converted to Faroese form, and they tend to be shorter. The third type are satirical ballads, **tættir**, which mock individuals or politics. Their tunes are more regular rhythmically and structurally than those of the old ballads. Some broadsheet and biblical ballads from Norway and Denmark also found their way into the dance repertoire.

In the nineteenth century people began to write the ballads down, and many were collected and published as *Corpus Carminum Færoensium*. The volume contained 44,000 stanzas – a huge number considering they were collected from a population which then only numbered about 5000 – suggesting the ballads must have been sung very frequently. Their popularity isn't so suprising, however, when considering that they were – and are – sung to winding, rhythmic tunes with long interesting melodic lines. They're also packed with rich imagery and epic stories that have been carried down through the centuries: Charlemagne killing an army with the dead Roland's sword at Roncevaux; Signhild being murdered by the dwarf father of her fifteen children; Nornagestur who couldn't die until a candle inside his harp burnt down; a young man making silver wings to fly to his beloved.

After World War II, it looked as though ballad-dancing might die out, so **dance societies** were formed, and small but determined groups of young Faroese people now continue to dance the ballads. The dances are essentially entertainment for the people in the circle, not performances for an audience – the dancers face inwards, not outwards. There is also a sense of the dance as a Faroese statement.

Another Faroese song tradition that has continued into the present day is that of **skjaldur**. These magic and fairytale songs have irregular beats that follow the rhythm of the words; they were typically sung by adults for children, but are now often sung by the children themselves. The Faroese also had a tradition of singing **hymns** – not only in church, but often also before or after a fishing or egg-collecting trip. The nineteenth-century installation of church organs didn't completely oust the old rhythmically free, pitch-sliding microtonal way of singing hymns, as it did in Iceland, for example. This style of religious singing was known as **kingosálmar** or **kingosangur** after the *Kirke-Psalme-Bog*, a hymn book published in 1699 by Thomas Kingo. The kingosangur tradition disappeared from normal church use during the twentieth century, but recordings of singers who remembered the old ways were made as late as the 1970s.

Faroese Music now

The prevalent live music in the Faroes today is rock and pop, but the islands also have a small, but creative, **roots music scene**. Faroese roots music is characterized by musical sea-faring – the creative linking of traditional forms with ideas and musicians from other cultures. Its major exponent is Danish-born keyboard player, composer, concert promoter and record label-owner **Kristian Blak**.

Blak is a communicator between diverse musical worlds: playing piano in the twin-fiddle-led folk band **Spælimenninir**; creating Nordic jazz-inflected arrangements of traditional Faroese song and hymn tunes; writing his own compositions (including an opera and pieces for concerts performed in boats in a sea-cave); and managing various projects featuring musicians from abroad. His band **Yggdrasil** mixes Faroese and Icelandic folk song material with jazz and Shakespeare sonnets.

The islands' most internationally successful singer, **Eivør Pálsdóttir**, known just as **Eivør**, joined Faroese rock band Clickhaze at sixteen, recorded her first solo album at seventeen, gained multiple Icelandic pop awards for her second album and was voted "Faroese of the Year" in 2004, aged just 21. Active in many musical fields, she has performed with Yggdrasil, Canadian singer-guitarist Bill Bourne, the Danish Radio Big Band and the **Faroese Symphony Orchestra**, but an important feature of her work remains her striking unaccompanied renditions of Faroese ballads and songs.

Others working from Faroese roots include singer **Annika Hoydal** and the band **Enekk**, who draw on jazz and the input of Bulgarian musicians, among others, to create a distinctively Faroese mix. Faroese singer **Anna Katrin Egilstrød** brings a Faroese dimension to Danish roots band Valravn.

Denmark

⊙ Danemark: Chanteurs et Ménétriers
Ocora, France

Recordings from the 1930s to the 1980s (many made by Thorkild Knudsen) of traditional musicians and singers, including Evald Thomsen, Frits and Søren Lassen Brinch, and singer Ingeborg Munch. From the collections of the Danish Folklore Archives, Danmarks Radio and the Folk Music House in Hogager.

★ Folk Music from Denmark
MXP, Denmark

Each year the Danish Folk Council (*www.folkemusik.dk*) releases a well-packaged, informative promo-compilation of tracks from new folk music releases. If you can get hold of one, it's the best overview of the current scene.

Kristian Bugge

A prime exponent of Danish-style fiddling, Bugge is a talented young player who, in 2004, received Danish Radio's first Radium Award for being a promising young musician. He has since become a key musician in the Danish-Finnish-British instrumental band Baltic Crossing and the Danish-Finnish Kings of Polka.

⊙ Kristian Bugge
Danish Radio P2, Denmark

A fresh and varied debut album of finely judged playing and arrangements, featuring leading folk musicians from Denmark, Finland and the UK performing sønderhonings, polkas from Læsø and more. Paradoxically, the inclusion of musicians from other traditions brings out the distinctiveness of the Danish tunes and fiddle styles.

Danish Dia Delight

A seminal Danish roots band that featured guitarist Morten Alfred Høirup, saxophonist Henrik Bredholt and Lang Linken's melodeon player Carl Erik Lundgaard, plus bass and drums.

⊙ Live
CE Musik, Denmark

Traditional and new tunes are thrown around by the players with characteristic energy, charm, wit and a lot of skill.

Haugaard & Høirup

The impeccably tight and mobile duo of fiddler Harald Haugaard and guitarist Morten Alfred Høirup has done more to spread enthusiasm for Danish roots music abroad than any other combo.

⊙ Gæstebud
GO' Danish, Denmark

The duo's fourth album, from 2005, differs from their previous releases by having just a couple of duo tracks. The rest of the album features guests – kindred musician and singer friends from Denmark, Finland, Sweden, North America, the UK and Ireland – recorded in small groups all over the world.

Kristine Heebøll

After a long period with Phønix, Kristine Heebøll emerged as not only a fine, subtle fiddler, but also as a remarkable writer of beautifully structured, memorable tunes.

⊙ Trio Mio
GO' Danish, Denmark

Heebøll's 2004 solo album is full of shapely, highly developed, beautifully played compositions. She has gone on to form a tight gigging and recording band of the same name with pianist and accordionist Nikolaj Busk and Swedish guitar and bouzouki player Jens Ulvsand.

Instinkt

Instinkt, whose farewell gig took place in 2008, were Kætter Kvartet's Søren Korshøj (fiddle, guitar, vox) and Vivi di Bap (drums, vox), plus wind, bowed strings and Jew's harp player Martin Seeberg, fiddler Louise Vangsgaard and bassist Malene Beck

⊙ Hur!
GO' Danish, Denmark

All original tracks, springing out of the roots tradition, in a varied mix of punchy folk-rock, scat, narrative song and atmospherics; vocals include di Bap's surprising, powerful contralto.

Karen and Helene

A fine blend of two voices, those of Karen Mose Nørgaard and Helene Blum. The pair came together, as did much else of the new wave in Danish roots music, in the creative environment of Odense's Carl Nielsen Academy.

★ Solen
GO' Danish, Denmark

A beautiful, subtly arranged and sung CD, produced by Harald Haugaard, that exemplifies the happy meeting between musicians with folk, jazz and classical backgrounds. Released in 2004, *Solen* was a major milestone in turning attention to the revival of a much older repertoire of songs; its fine, melodic spaciousness alerting foreign critics to the fact that something was happening in Danish roots music.

Kætter Kvartet

A vocal and instrumental group – Søren Korshøj (fiddle), John Bæk (mandolin), Svend Seegert (keyboard) and Vivi di Bap (drums) – combining the structures of Nordic tunes with the lift and backbeat of other, hotter parts of the world.

⊙ Den Sidste Schottish
FMS, Denmark

A live recording of the band's triumphant farewell concert at the Tarm Festival in 2000.

Lang Linken

The multi-instrumental and occasionally vocal trio of Poul Lendal, Keld Nørgaard and Carl Erik Lundgaard carried the small glimmering flame of Danish traditional music onto public stages in the 1970s, 80s and 90s, and their wit and wisdom was a keystone in the flare-up of the early 2000s.

Knorifas
GO' Danish, Denmark

Winner of the 2001 Danish Music Award for folk, this shows the trio still finding new life and angles in traditional music, joined by the vocals of two of their daughters, Sofie Aagaard and Karen Mose Nørgaard.

Lars Lilholt

Singer-songwriter, guitarist, fiddler and bagpiper Lilholt has had pop hits with his band, but also maintains contact with Danish traditional roots.

⊙ Next Stop Svabonius
Danish Folk Council, Denmark

Per and Lars Lilholt and a team of leading roots players, including members of Rasmus, use approaches ranging from string quartets to screaming rock to explore the dance music of the late eighteenth century.

Phønix

A key instrumental band in the 1990s revival who wrote their own material and found new approaches to trad, Phønix is now a quartet: reeds player Anja Præst Mikkelsen, piano-accordionist Jesper Vinther Petersen, percussionist Jesper Falch and singer Karen Mose Nørgaard.

⊙ Pigen & Drengen
GO' Danish, Denmark

The band's fourth album – its first with Karen Mose – demonstrates the new focus her traditional ballads and songs bring to Phønix's chunky weave of accordion, fiddle and flutes, underpinned by bass clarinet and percussion.

Rasmus

Michael Sommer, Lars Lilholt, Bent Melvej, Ove Andersen and Benny Simmelsgaard are a quintet of bowed strings – variously fiddles, octave fiddle, viola and bass – who released their first album in 1983.

⊙ Rasmus Storm #2
Nattergal, Denmark

Their second album (2003) is a rich and elegant collection of tunes – march, *polonaise*, *serras*, *engelsk*, minuet – from the late eighteenth-century tunebooks of Rasmus Storm, Jens Christian Svabo, Niels Gottlob, the Bast brothers and others.

Serras

Ubiquitous fiddler Harald Haugaard, saxophonist Hans Mytskov, guitarist Sune Hansbæk, bassist Mads Riishede and drummer Sune Rahbek brought their varied musical backgrounds to bear on Danish trad dance tunes. They were a powerful, audience-galvanizing live band, and their records combine melodious subtlety with all-out rock muscularity.

⊙ Stand Clear of the Closing Door, Please
GO' Danish, Denmark

This 2004 album, produced by Morten Alfred Høirup and featuring guests Lang Linken and Swedish fiddler Magnus Stinnerbom, varies from winding sax and fiddles through reflective pieces to hefty fiddle-led rock.

Sorten Muld

A techno-based trio who made impressive atmospheric grooves around traditional ballads sung by Ulla Bendixen, blended with the sound of roots musicians, such as Harald Haugaard, on fiddles, hurdy-gurdy and bagpipes. They split soon after the release of their well-received second album.

⊙ Mark II
Sony/Pladecompagniet, Denmark

Their 1999 debut of well-varied techno and blended-in instruments went gold in Denmark.

Tumult

Folk-rock band built around the traditional repertoire and compositions of fiddler and singer Jørgen Dickmeiss, with electric guitars, bass and drums.

⊙ Wallegnav
GO' Danish, Denmark

Tumult's 2001 debut comprises stirring but unpompous folk-rock versions of traditional songs and new-made tunes.

ULC

The ULC trio are Fanø fiddler Peter Uhrbrand, diatonic accordionist and harmonica player Sonnich Lydom and guitar and bouzouki player Seamus Cahill.

⊙ Sik og Sejs
ULC, Denmark

An album full of sønderhonings (and one fannik), played with an elegant thoughtfulness and spring that brings out the tunes' shapeliness and variety.

Valravn

Faroese singer Anna Katrin Egilstrød howls, cajoles and spits with a slightly Björk-like breathless gamine character to her voice, fiercely relishing the sounds of her Nordic languages. With her are Instinkt's Martin Seeberg on viola, flutes and Jew's harps, Søren Hammerlund on hurdy-gurdy and mandola, and percussionist Juan Pino, most of whom pitch in with sampled sounds.

★ Valravn
Tutl, Faroes

Based on traditional Danish, Faroese, Icelandic and Swedish material, including the ballads "Svend i Rosengaard" and "Vallevan" as well as less familiar fare, this is an album of wild-dark textures and, even in the more intimate moments, a feeling of relentless, pulsing forward movement.

Zar

After releasing one album as an instrumental trio, Zar leapt to greater prominence after recruiting singer Sine Lahm Lauristen, whose pop background brought a new approach to the singing of folk songs and ballads.

⊙ Tusind Tanker
Tame, Denmark

Outstanding playing and classy arrangements from the band whose elegant instrumentals surround Lauritsen's fine vocals.

Faroe Islands

The main Faroese record company is Tutl (*www.tutl.com*), which was founded in 1977 and boasts a catalogue of more than two hundred jazz, rock, classical and Faroese roots releases.

⊙ Alfagurt Ljóðar Mín Tunga
Tutl, Faroes

Kvæði, vísur, tættir, kingosálmar and skjaldur record-ings made between 1959 and 1990, accompanied by the excellent book *Traditional Music in the Faroe Islands* (*Føroya Skúlabókagrunnur*), which was a useful source in the writing of this chapter.

⊙ Flúgvandi Biðil
Tutl, Faroes

Twenty songs and ballads from 1902 to 1997, mostly from the Faroese University archive, featuring fine voices singing rich old stories to remarkable winding, tripping rhythmic tunes. A revelation that shows the Faroes' importance among north European song traditions.

★ Traditional Music in the Faroe Islands 1950–1999
Frémeaux & Associates, France

A double CD largely taken from field recordings made in 1959 by Swedish Radio of ballads, skjaldur and game-songs in Faroese, and ballads and hymns in Danish. With vocal sounds full of grainy individuality in their wild, wind-blown melodies, this is extraordinary, powerful stuff, a craggy sea-stack of European music.

⊙ Tutl 2000: Folk/Ethnic
Tutl, Faroes

This 2000 selection from the Tutl catalogue could perhaps do with being updated, but it is still a reasonable overview of the tradition-rooted releases of the islands' main label.

Eivør

The Faroes' best-known singer, Eivør Pálsdóttir, works in all musical fields from deep tradition, through big-band jazz and classical to pop and rock.

★ Eivør Pálsdóttir
Tutl, Faroes

Pálsdóttir made this album of traditional songs at the age of seventeen – and it still sounds good. She has an appealing, open voice, which has an alluring fragility as well as a know-ing mature strength. Her vocals are elegantly complemented by a core band of electric and acoustic guitars, double bass and drums, with occasional subtle keyboard touches.

Enekk

A long-established progressive roots band that plays arrangements of traditional and original material draw-ing on jazz, art and world music. Its core line-up includes vocalist and guitarist Kári Sverrisson and pianist Óli Olsen.

⊙ Meðan vit Nærkast Jørðini
Tutl, Faroes

The band's fourth CD has Faroese-language lyrics from a vari-ety of sources, including Federico García Lorca. It also features bassist Mikael Blak, electric guitarist Heðin Ziska Davidsen and Bulgarian guests, who contribute vocals and tambura.

Yggdrasil

This band is led by the prime musical mover in the Faroes, keyboardist Kristian Blak.

⊙ Live in Rudolstadt
Tutl, Faroes

Recorded in 2003 at a German music festival, this album of jazzy, ambient approaches to Blak originals and traditional themes from the Faroes and other parts of the North Atlantic, has Eivør Pálsdóttir's voice as its focus.

PLAYLIST
Denmark & the Faroe Islands

1 LYSTEN VALS Kristine Heebøll from *Trio Mio*
A restless, nervy waltz.

2 BARNEMORDERSKEN Karen and Helene from *Solen*
A child-murder ballad, with a rich string and piano arrangement.

3 RUSSEREN/LEJERDRENGEN Danish Dia Delight from *Live*
Quirky contrapuntal, acapella group vocals alter-nating with a joyous dance tune.

4 LYSETS ENGEL Haugaard & Høirup from *Gæstebud*
Reflective and lyrical treatment of a dance piece.

5 LARS BRINCH'S Kristian Bugge from *Kristian Bugge*
Sønderhoning with a particularly memorable tune.

6 KINGO PEDERSENS VESTENOM / KNORIFAS Lang Linken from *Knorifas*
Melodies learnt from a Læso musician and a Thy dancer played on a quivering accordion, Jew's harp, *seljefløyte* and fiddle.

7 ÒLAVUR RIDDARARÒS Valravn from *Valravn*
A wild, drum-driven dance-impelling approach to a Faroese song.

8 TUSIND TANKER Zar from *Tusind Tanker*
Tender singing and a delicate arrangement on a traditional song of lost love.

9 RUNSIVALS STRIÐIÐ Singer/dancers led by Elmar Pedersen from *Traditional Music in the Faroe Islands*
A ballad about Charlemagne and Roland at the battle of Roncesvalles, sung in the Faroes in 1959.

10 FØROYAR MIN MÓÐIR Eivør Pálsdóttir from *Eivør Pálsdóttir*
Adventurous and beautiful vocals over pulsing drum, chiming vibrato electric guitar and darkly slithering double bass.

England | Folk/Roots

learning to be english

Kathryn Tickell

Not so long ago, it would have been impossible to imagine England's folk-music heritage as playing anything other than a cartoonesque bit-part in the nation's cultural-identity parade, ridiculed and kicked around by a mainstream popular culture seemingly sympathetic to every hybrid known to music-kind except its own traditions. Old clichés of straggly beards, fingers in ears, nasal voices and overweight Morris dancers die hard, but the emergence of a world-music constituency has opened ears to some esoteric riches at home and slowly chipped away at the deeply ingrained disdain for those tired old notions of Englishness. **Colin Irwin** looks at the fast-changing environment of English folk music.

England's cultural horizons started changing dramatically towards the end of the twentieth century and have continued to shift in startling fashion since the start of the twenty-first. The influx of immigrants and the exciting multiculturalism and cross-fertilization they have produced have demanded a radical reassessment of the very nature of Englishness; thrilling blends of everything from bhangra and reggae to hip-hop, Celtic and Eastern European styles have been absorbed into the music to offer a new and very different musical landscape.

Yet far from blowing away the traditional values in which English folk song is rooted, the changing winds have effectively reawakened awareness of and interest in the old folk music and traditions. Many of the musicians who helped usher in the British folk revival through the 1960s and 70s have acquired a decent level of respect, while Mercury Music Prize nominations for **Norma Waterson**, her daughter **Eliza Carthy** (twice) and **Kate Rusby** have helped gain unlikely mainstream attention in spite of the indifference of most national radio and mass media.

The whole reissue market has focused attention back on some of the great names of the post-revival years, from **Anne Briggs** to **Robin and Barry Dransfield**, while the great **Nic Jones** – tragically forced into retirement following a horrific road crash in 1982 – has become an almost iconic figure for many of the newer names on the block. The recordings of some of the great old traditional singers who kept the folk songs alive, like **Harry Cox**, **Sam Larner** and **Walter Pardon**, are now more widely available than they ever were in their lifetimes.

Birth and Rebirth

English folk song, however, might well have died out in the early part of the twentieth century but for the diligent work of various collectors, notably **Cecil Sharp**, who was inspired in his task after chancing upon some Morris dancers at Heading-

Lords of the Dance

Morris dancing is at the very heart of clichéd English imagery and hasn't yet been rescued from ridicule by roots music. Who knows, perhaps it never will be. But for all its apparent absurdity, the dance is amazingly popular, and there is, after all, something spectacular and heart-warming in the sight of the dancers in their whites waving bells and hankies, re-enacting some obscure fertility ritual. Isn't there?

The history of Morris is ancient and cloudy. Nobody's quite sure how it evolved, or indeed if it's a specifically English tradition. Nonetheless, with its related offshoots, it has evolved as an eccentric culture entirely its own. Long-held customs that women are not allowed to dance the Morris have been the subject of fierce debate, with female dance-teams emerging at a frantic pace with variations of Morris, rapper and clog. The "serious" teams, meanwhile, preserve their own territorial traditions with a protective discipline that seems positively archaic, but is rigorously encouraged by the Morris Ring, the movement's unofficial governing body.

Yet while old clichés die hard, there's been enough sea changes in attitudes to Morris to encourage *fRoots* magazine to breathlessly declare in 2004 that Morris dancing is cool, due to an unlikely upsurge in youthful involvement. The group at the forefront of the new dance is **Morris Offspring**, which had its beginnings at the Shooting Roots sessions, a kind of youth wing of Sidmouth Festival, where many new fresh ideas and initiatives have been hatched. One key member of Morris Offspring, **Laurel Swift**, has been a leading light in the regeneration of folk tradition generally with a well-received debut album *Beam* to her name. Drawn from all round the country, Offspring themselves have given a refreshing new face to Morris, constructing their own dances and performing with a vitality that makes Morris seem, well ... sexy.

There are any number of other strange traditions lurking where you least expect to find them. Most exhilarating of all, perhaps, is the annual **May Day Obby Oss** celebration at Padstow in Cornwall – a song and dance ritual of mindboggling colour and alcohol intake. **Rapper** and **long sword dancing** still abound, notably in Yorkshire and the Northeast, and you'll find lots of **clog dancing**. Chance upon the Staffordshire village of Abbots Bromley in September and you might encounter the strange **Horn Dance** ritual that has been a feature of the area since the mid-seventeenth century at least. Still more bizarre is the tradition of the **Britannia Coconut Dancers**, who dance with garlands, frocks, clogs and blackened faces through the streets of Bacup in the Calder Valley of Lancashire on Easter Saturday. They also wear coconuts strapped to their hands and knees which they clap together – providing them with the not altogether inappropriate nickname of "nutters".

ton Quarry, near Oxford, on Boxing Day, 1899. He subsequently set off cycling round the West Country on his bike notating songs and music. Sharp has been criticized for his methods, and he and other collectors are often accused of selectiveness in how they chose to present these songs for polite society, but there would have been scant material for the folk revival to devour without them. He set up the English Folk Dance Society in 1911 as a way of preserving traditional dance forms, and in 1932 it merged with the Folk-Song Society to form the **English Folk Dance and Song Society**.

Sharp was among the first to recognize the importance of the folk club as a basic unit in that revival, a unit without which the movement might never have made a significant impact. In London, he founded (with Alan Lomax, Bert Lloyd, Seamus Ennis and others) the Ballads and Blues Club, later to become the famed **Singers Club**. The club opened in 1953 and closed in 1991.

When **Lonnie Donegan** set off the extraordinary yet short-lived skiffle craze of 1956–57 with makeshift but instantly appealing versions of American folk-blues songs like "Rock Island Line" and "Cumberland Gap", he inspired a host of eager young musicians to take up acoustic guitars, double basses and washboards. Once skiffle had died, however, there was no outlet for their interest in folk song. The result was the emergence of a **network of folk clubs**, and – encouraged by the two most influential figures, **Ewan MacColl** and **A.L. Lloyd** – some frantic research into the British folk tradition.

The heyday of the English folk-club movement was in the 1960s and 70s, when – fuelled by the protest era – the clubs acquired social relevance and an unlikely atmosphere of alternative trendiness. There were interesting developments in contemporary songwriting, from **Ralph McTell**, Roy Harper and Al Stewart onwards; there was a veritable goldmine of guitar stylists from **Davy Graham** to **Bert Jansch** and **John Renbourn**; there were the great folk-rock experiments led by **Fairport Convention** and **Steeleye Span**; there was a formidable array of artists of varying styles providing a solid backbone for a scene whose heartbeat still lay in the great traditional music of English history.

But if you stand still you go backwards, and other styles and movements queued up to kick sand in the face of English folk music. Folk clubs have never regained their fashionable status – and probably never will do – but the music has slowly reaffirmed its dignity, albeit in a dissipated fashion, ironically acquiring respect through patronage from other genres.

Efdss

Cecil Sharp in Aldeburgh, Suffolk, 1923

The rebirth had its beginnings during the mid-1980s when the likes of Billy Bragg, The Pogues and The Men They Couldn't Hang set about English/Irish folk song with an almost manic energy that was as shocking as it was exciting. Outraged letters to the folk mags from diehard folkies, appalled by the irreverence of these new-wave bands, confirmed the necessity of such radicalism. English folk music had carefully constructed its own elitist ghetto in the folk clubs for too long, a blindly independent strand not even paying lip service to the rest of the music industry, and, as a result, it had turned into a museum relic.

The sudden outburst of punk-folkery swiftly lost its appeal as a movement as it became obvious that the artists involved had little in common beyond attitude and a genuine respect for the giants of the preceding generations – the MacColls, Carthys and so on. The long-term ramifications were huge, however, and they remain inspirational. **Billy Bragg** stepped out of his role as contemporary political commentator to reinvent himself as Woody Guthrie's voice on earth with his *Mermaid Avenue* album of newly discovered Guthrie material, and then went on to redefine nationality on the album *England, Half English*.

The folk-rock years are long gone, as is the age of the singer-songwriter. Yet the **Oysterband** have continued to fly the flag for a highly individual rocking folk-music, while the extraordinary **Richard Thompson** remains one of the finest English songwriters, with regular tours, challenging material and intriguing ideas (even covering Britney Spears on one celebrated occasion). Meanwhile artists such as Durham-born **Jez Lowe**, the uncommonly sharp **Thea Gilmore**, West Country songwriter Steve Knightley of **Show Of Hands**, the gruff-voiced social observer **Pete Morton**, state-of-the-nation commentator **Maggie Holland** and the highly politicized **Leon Rosselson** and **Robb Johnson** plough lonely furrows, occasionally dipping into the tradition as an inspiration for their own compositions. Most upcoming English songwriters, however, imagine themselves as the new Coldplay, bypassing the solo route and surrounding themselves with a suitably sensitive band at the first opportunity.

But as England itself has changed dramatically, so multiculturalism has brought about a vastly different musical landscape too. A landscape where cultures collide, resulting – at its best – in entirely new styles and concepts of Englishness. Mostly it hasn't worked, but at what feels like the beginning of a new era, there have already been some striking developments that suggest an exciting future for a different kind of English music. **Blowzabella**, for example, pioneered the integration of English music with Eastern European rhythms and styles, while **3 Mustaphas 3** blazed a trail with their thrilling fusion of global beats.

Inevitably, the techno era has also made its contribution. The varying results include everything from the pounding beats of **Transglobal Underground** to **Asian Dub Foundation**, whose concerted campaign for the release of Satpal Ram offered an alternative view of a new English music. **King Edward the Second and the Red Hot Polkas** – who over the years became Edward II and e2K – perhaps treated the fusion most seriously of all, using a reggae rhythm-section to back their English tunes and songs, and a second-generation Jamaican, Glenn Latouche, as a singer for several years. Yet perhaps the most direct demonstration of how potent the combination of ancient and modern could be came in the unlikely shape of **Chumbawamba**, the Lancashire anarchist band who had an international number one with "Tubthumping" and hit the UK headlines with a water attack on deputy prime minister John Prescott at the Brit Awards. Their 2000 album *Readymades* featured a series of well-chosen samples, notably from Coope, Boyes and Simpson, Lal Waterson and the great traditional Norfolk singer **Harry Cox**, whose looped refrain "And they sent me to the wars to be slain, to be slain..." from "The Pretty Ploughboy" was used to brilliant effect on "Jacob's Ladder", a track made all the more haunting by the onset of the Iraq War.

The pleasing paradox of all this is that it has had the effect of focusing attention on the real traditional music of England – a powerful, relevant and rich tradition that continues to survive the ravages of fashion and cultural abuse, and which, against all the odds, is better represented than it has been for a very long time. **Eliza Carthy** consciously set out her stall to play and raise awareness of a specifically English music and it appears to have worked, with a whole new generation of young musicians taking their inspiration not from the Celtic countries, but the hitherto much-derided and generally neglected traditional dance music and song of England. **Jon Boden** and **John Spiers** – inducted by Carthy as regular members of her own band – have taken on the mantle in commendably original and startlingly energetic style, but there are plenty of others, from the intriguing meanderings of **Jim Moray** to bands like **Dr Faustus**.

Nonetheless, English roots remains the Cinderella music of the British Isles. While its Celtic cousins rose relentlessly, an English *Riverdance* would have been laughed out of sight by a media seemingly intent on burying the beast alive. Only *fRoots* and *Songlines* (and to a lesser degree the Scottish-based *Living Tradition*) offer press coverage of any depth, while national radio coverage lies solely in the hands of the BBC's *Mike Harding Show*. Yet a quick glance across the hundred or so **folk festivals** regularly held all over England throughout the year suggests robust health – you need to get in early to ensure a ticket for Cambridge, the biggest binge of the lot. Oddly, however inventive, exciting and heartfelt the music gets, it still seems forever destined to remain in the shadows of the national consciousness.

Northumbrian Roots

Nowhere is English roots music more alive than in the border lands of Northumbria, the one part of England to rival the counties of the west of Ireland for a rich unbroken tradition. It is a tradition sustained uniquely by the rich splendour of a countryside that has constantly been interwoven with its indigenous music.

Changing times may have dissipated the music's importance to the local communities, but it has never come close to eradicating it. Whether it be sheep-farming in the moorlands or raucous nights in the pubs in the old mining communities, the old music still survives as a backdrop even though the mining industry itself has grimly declined. The work of **Tommy Armstrong**, a unique Tyneside balladeer of the late nineteenth/early twentieth century, remains in popular circulation, and his "Trimdon Grange Explosion" – momentously recorded by Martin Carthy – is still heartbreaking.

Sometimes bleak, sometimes tragic, often wildly happy, Northumbrian music has remained an integral part of the local character, and performers like Jack Armstrong, Joe Hutton, Billy Atkinson, Jimmy Pallister, Tommy Edmondson, Willy Taylor, Tom Clough, Billy Conroy, George Hepple and Billy Pigg are revered locally for their role in perpetuating that tradition.

Much of this proud tradition is due to the proximity of Scotland and its history of country dance bands, and to the influence of Irish migrants. As a result, outstanding accordion players, fiddlers and even mouth-organists have consistently abounded, though the instrument that really gives the area its unique role in English music is the **Northumbrian pipes**. One of the smallest and least intimidating members of the bagpipe family, these pipes are also more versatile than most of their Celtic relatives,

and as a result blend in more easily with other instruments. **Billy Pigg**, who died in 1968, is still regarded as the king of the Northumbrian pipes for the vibrant originality of his playing, his prolific writing of tunes and the high profile he gave the instrument in particular and Northumbrian music in general.

His influence remains strong and there's a clear line between him and the still youthful **Kathryn Tickell**, who at times has appeared to be on a one-woman crusade for the instrument and has done so much to break down musical barriers and take the music to new audiences. Tickell's current influence in the perpetuation of the legend of Northumbrian music is incalculable, and she may even have redefined Northumbrian music with her superb 1999 album *Debatable Lands*, revolving around a suite inspired by the disputed area between England and Scotland that was long a target for border raiders. But it would be wrong to ignore the role of many others, both musicians and enthusiasts, who have promoted the music of the area with fanatical zeal.

Bob Davenport and **Louis Killen** were key figures in the early days of the British folk revival. Davenport did much to align Northumbrian traditional songs with a more modern folk tradition – he'd think nothing of merging an old Geordie favourite like "Cushy Butterfield" with Bob Marley's "Get Up Stand Up"; and Killen was both a superb traditional singer and concertina player, who did much to popularize the music in America. The **High Level Ranters** flew the local flag internationally for many years. Northumbrian culture was served magnificently by their devotion to colourful dialect songs like "The Lambton Worm", "Blaydon Races", "Keep Your Feet Still Geordie Hinnie" and "Dance To Yer Daddie", as well as grittier stories of strife in the collieries.

The Ranters' Colin Ross acted as an ambassador for the Northumbrian pipes at a time when most people looked at the instrument and fled, and his work was admirably continued by **Alistair Anderson**, originally a vigorous concertina player and subsequently a piper and composer of a new Northumbrian tradition. His "Steel Skies" suite, directly inspired by the Northumbrian countryside and its traditions, remains one of the most important original works of recent years. "It was written to be played by musicians steeped in traditional music, and its development from the tradition was evolutionary rather than revolutionary", Anderson said of the work. "I hope it retained the spirit of the music it has grown from, while opening up some new musical ideas on the way."

The Northumbrian Pipers Society has also worked wonders to keep interest in the instrument alive, to the extent of helping to open a pipes museum in Newcastle. A number of border festivals have doggedly and successfully concentrated on local music, even including (somewhat controversially) competitions for various instruments in the manner of the Irish fleadhs.

It's a tradition that has even seeped into the rockier side of the story. Great Geordie folk-rock bands **Lindisfarne**, **Jack The Lad** and **Hedgehog Pie** dug into their own local heritage for inspiration in a way that bands from other areas rarely did.

Plenty of Northumbrians will tell you they don't even see themselves as part of England at all, such is the fierce mood of independence, geographi-

The Copper Legend Continues

In early 2005, the crowds gathered as usual at Lewes Folk Club to celebrate the birthday of English folk song's most revered character – **Bob Copper**. It was his ninetieth birthday and family, friends and admirers all squashed together in the upstairs room of the pub to sing the wonderful old songs that had been synonymous with the family name for centuries and indeed had provided the heart and soul of the British folk revival for five decades. The one person who wasn't there was Bob Copper himself.

Bob had passed away less than a year earlier, just days after travelling to Buckingham Palace to receive a long overdue MBE from Prince Charles for his services to folk song. But the good-humoured, kindly man who had spent his working life as a farmhand, policeman, publican, author and broadcaster had left such an indelible legacy that everyone decided there was plenty to celebrate. They were right, too, for among the tributes and anecdotes offered from friends like Shirley Collins, the most telling performance had been from the youngest people in the room – Bob's grandchildren. The respective offspring of his son John and daughter Jill had secretly practised and sang some of the family songs as a Christmas present for their grandfather a few years earlier, and Bob's most cherished wish – that the family singing tradition would be continued by the new generation – was fulfilled in style as the **Young Coppers** started doing their own gigs.

It continues a family singing tradition that can be traced back over two hundred years, although local parish records date back to the sixteenth century. Copper songs represented a significant source for the British folk revival and as one of the few singers around representing a link with the old traditions, the personable Bob Copper was one of its most deeply loved characters. He even wrote a couple of immensely readable books, *A Song For Every Season* and *Songs And Southern Breezes*, which colourfully described life in a small Sussex farming community and placed the history of the music in its proper context.

Barry Shuel

The Copper Family

Waterson:Carthy – the Dynasty Lives On

The names Waterson and Carthy have been a constant and vital part of the British folk revival virtually since it began. While Yorkshire's **Watersons** were writing the book on earthy harmony singing and introducing a whole range of ritual songs to the scene, **Martin Carthy** was emerging as one of the supreme revival singers and guitar stylists.

A young pioneer of the early post-skiffle folk-club movement, Carthy was a resident at London's famous Troubadour Club in the 1960s folk boom and a role model for such emergent American folk singers as Bob Dylan (who based "Bob Dylan's Dream" on Carthy's version of "Lord Franklin") and Paul Simon (who adopted his arrangement of "Scarborough Fair"). Carthy had a brilliant partnership with Dave Swarbrick, was a pivotal figure in the folk-rock movement of the 1970s during spells with the Albion Band and Steeleye Span, and later helped lead the introduction of brass into folk song with the excellent band Brass Monkey. When Carthy married Norma Waterson and joined the family singers in the 1970s, it re-energized them both, but it's another member of the family, their daughter **Eliza Carthy**, who has been taking the music – and the name – into the 21st century.

Introduced early to the family singing group, Eliza initially set off on her own path in partnership with **Nancy Kerr**. They had a lot in common, both fiddle-playing singers raised on traditional music – Nancy's mother

Jak Kilby

Eliza Carthy

cal isolation and the powerful cultural influence of Scotland and Ireland (although paradoxically the county shunned the chance of its own regional assembly in a referendum in 2004). Yet the best of its musicians portray a strong feel of the beautiful countryside and the warm character of the people, and Northumberland retains a unique sense of its own identity.

Little surprise, then, to find the region pioneering the study of traditional music through the Folkworks initiative, promoting tours, summer camps and classes. This rapidly developed into partnerships with Newcastle University, which in 2001 resulted in the country's first performance-based folk and traditional music degree course, with many of the scene's leading lights like Alistair Anderson, Kathryn Tickell, Karen Tweed and Sandra Kerr as tutors. A further partnership with Gateshead's swanky new Sage Theatre in 2004 built on the initiative to offer incentive and direction to

Sandra Kerr is a highly regarded singer who was once a member of Ewan MacColl's Critics group – and they made one well-received album together. Nancy Kerr has gone on to forge a successful duo with Australian musician James Fagan and, never content merely to recreate the achievements of her family, Eliza Carthy has consistently pushed her own highly individual envelope. In **Kings of Calicutt**, she fronted a young band taking exciting liberties with rhythm and arrangements, and in various incarnations of her own band, she's continually shown a style and attitude that are both daringly original and wholly true to the spirit of the tradition which inspires it.

A vivacious, forceful personality, Eliza's arrival was a refreshing addition to an ageing scene sorely in need of the rejuvenating thunderbolt she provided. The mass media even pricked up its ears and, as savvy as she was musically inventive, Eliza gave good copy with multicoloured hair and the nous to exploit the publicity benefits of the "folk babe" tag ludicrously used to bracket her with Kate Rusby. Her partly experimental double album *Red Rice* (Topic) won a Mercury Music Prize nomination in 1998, and, signed by major label Warner, she recorded an album of her own songs, *Angels and Cigarettes*. It was a temporary diversion and Carthy was never spiritually far from traditional music. As she was at great pains to point out, she was on a mission to promote specifically English music. This flowered to most potent effect on her 2002 album *Anglicana*, which won her a second Mercury Music Prize nomination and set a fresh benchmark for the new generation of English musicians. Her re-emergence in 2005 with *Rough Music* (Topic) saw her fronting a typically ebullient band, the Ratcatchers, presenting English music with both swing and swagger, and featuring two of the leading young guns of the new music, John Spiers and Jon Boden.

Eliza's commitment to and love of tradition have been constantly reaffirmed by her continuing involvement with the family in **Waterson:Carthy**, a musical dynasty dating back to the early 1960s when Norma Waterson, her sister Lal, brother Mike and their cousin John Harrison first started singing together in Hull. After a prolonged absence in the late 1960s, **The Watersons** reformed in spectacular fashion following *Bright Phoebus*, a groundbreaking album of contemporary songs by Mike and Lal Waterson, featuring many leading folk musicians of the day. With Martin Carthy assimilated into the ranks, The Watersons again assumed their rightful place as the country's flagship vocal harmony group.

Carthy continued his own glittering solo career between spells with Steeleye Span, the Albion Band and a revival of one of his earliest musical partnerships, with Dave Swarbrick. A much revered figure, he was awarded an MBE in the 1998 Queen's Birthday Honours. His progressive 2004 album, *Waiting for Angels* (part-produced by Eliza), was widely lauded and included an epic reworking of one of his most famous ballads "The Famous Flower of Serving Men".

The Watersons became Waterson:Carthy when Mike and Lal tired of the road, but the various participants continued to make their mark. In 1996, **Norma Waterson**'s solo debut album came close to beating Pulp's *Different Class* to the Mercury Music Prize. **Lal Waterson**, too, reverted to the songwriting brilliance first revealed on *Bright Phoebus*, with a stunning – if stark – album, *Once in a Blue Moon*, made with her son **Oliver Knight**. Her sudden death from cancer in 1998 cruelly cut short the career of a unique singer and writer, although she had already recorded enough of a new album to enable Knight to complete the almost unbearably poignant posthumous album *A Bed of Roses*.

a whole raft of exuberant, youthful talent, ensuring plentiful session music in the local pubs.

The Rural Tradition

Northumbria isn't the only area where musical traditions have survived unbroken. Indigenous music survives in parts of East Anglia, Sussex, Cornwall, Devon and Humberside, although you may need to hunt it down.

East Anglia might seem an unlikely setting for a roots scene, but scratch around and you will find some surprising riches. Informal pub sessions still abound both in Suffolk and Norfolk. Two of the greatest traditional singers in the entire folk tradition were from this area: farm labourer **Harry Cox** and fisherman **Sam Larner**. Larner was seventy-nine when he made his first record but his subsequent output, and that of Cox, gave the 1960s folk revival a huge source of material and inspiration.

Kate Rusby: a Yorkshire Garland

Immersed since childhood in traditional song, a whole new generation of young singers and musicians emerged to take English folk music into the 21st century. If Eliza Carthy was the most prominent, the tiny winsome-voiced **Kate Rusby** achieved a level of mainstream awareness and acceptance unthinkable a few years earlier. From Barnsley and proud of it, her droll humour and self-effacing stage manner proved an admirable foil for the tragedy-filled "castle-knocking-down songs" she favoured. She was shortlisted for a Mercury Music Prize (for *Sleepless*), seemed to win every BBC Folk Award going and prided herself on winning the hearts and minds of the uninitiated, who invariably introduced themselves with the words "I hate folk music but I love you."

Many of the songs with which Rusby seduced audiences were learned as a child from her parents, though Kate herself trained as an actress and nearly wound up in the soap opera *Emmerdale*. She teamed up with another young Barnsley singer Kathryn Roberts and they swiftly took the UK folk scene by storm before engaging Devon's Lakeman brothers as backing band for a festival. This evolved into the "bratfolk" band Equation, swiftly signed by a major label. Talk of hit singles and lavish videos, however, had Kate fleeing for the hills (the Pennines, anyway) and she tried her luck as a solo artist, setting up the Pure label with her family. Her charm and sensitivity were refreshing, and the early albums *Hourglass*, *Sleepless* and *Little Lights* were major breakthroughs.

Her marriage to Scots fiddler John McCusker reinforced her musical cachet and she assembled a band featuring some of the finest young musicians in the land. She added songwriting to her armoury: among her clutch of awards is one for the 2000 Song of the Year, "Who Will Sing Me Lullabies?" – a deeply affecting tribute to the late Scottish singer Davey Steele. A role in the movie *Heartlands* and extensive mainstream airplay for the romantic "Underneath the Stars" – another original song that ended up as the title track on her 2003 album – added to her credence as a folk icon. She's accused of being one-dimensional, sticking too closely to the melancholy fragility that is her calling card, but even her toughest critics find it hard to quarrel with a voice so rarefied and alluring.

It was given further impetus by Norfolk revivalist Peter Bellamy's mid-1970s discovery of the great traditional singer **Walter Pardon**, who had lived all his life in the same cottage at Knapton, Norfolk without realizing that the fund of long-neglected songs he'd learnt as a child could form such a vital ingredient of England's folk tradition. Pardon went on to make a couple of important albums for Topic and sang locally and nationally for several years until he died in 1996.

Sussex also has a proud folk music tradition. Much of the local traditional repertoire came through the hands of the late great **Scan Tester**, who played dance music in local pubs with his Imperial Band from before World War I right up until his death in 1972. Tester's music is still a delight and can be heard to good effect on the Topic compilation album *I Never Played Too Many Posh Dances*. Sussex is also the base of the **Copper Family** of Rottingdean (see box) and the great revival singer **Shirley Collins**.

There's plenty of folk music to be found, too, in **Lancashire**, where traditional groups such as the **Oldham Tinkers** represent just the tip of the iceberg, while **Yorkshire** is home to another famous roots family, the **Watersons**, still going strong, albeit in different guises (again, see box).

The vocal tradition was a key area in the great British folk revival of the 1960s and 70s. The Coppers' harmonic style was adopted and adapted with fine results by the flamboyant **Young Tradition**, who were immensely influential in the 1970s, and The Watersons have kept the vocal torch burning to wondrous effect in various guises through the last three decades. But there have been many others along the way. Fronted by the ebullient Dave Brady, **Swan Arcade** picked up on Young Tradition's bullish harmonic unaccompanied style and raised it several decibels. And while modern groups like **Coope, Boyes and Simpson** capably continue this proud vocal tradition, the great solo performers like Martin Carthy, June Tabor and Shirley Collins were followed by the likes of Kate Rusby, Kathryn Roberts and Eliza Carthy.

The one record that is still cited as the biggest influence in traditional music circles is *English Country Music*. Compiled in 1965 by Reg Hall and Bob Davenport, it was issued in a limited edition of ninety-nine copies and sold out within a fortnight. Among the primarily Norfolk musicians featured were the fiddler Walter Bulwer, Billy Cooper on dulcimer, Reg Hall on melodeon and fiddle, Daisy Bulwer on piano, Mervyn Plunkett on drums, and Russell Wortley on pipe and tabor. It was, astonishingly, the first-ever recording of English traditional instrumental music and it fired in a variety of young musicians a feel for their own tradition that has led to all manner of development and experimentation.

For serious students of the English tradition, a trip to the **English Folk Dance and Song Society** headquarters in Regents Park Road, Camden, North London, may be essential. The EFDSS has long been criticized for its failure to move with the times and its perception of being greatly more interested in dance than song. Some of the events staged there can be unbearably starchy, but it does house a magnificent library and is a goldmine of history and information. The building itself is named after the great folk song collector Cecil Sharp.

Electric Avenue

It all sounds unbelievably mundane now, but back in 1971 English folkies thought the world had stopped when Martin Carthy plugged in his electric guitar on stage. Dylan thought he'd been given a hard time when he went electric at Newport Folk Festival a few years earlier, but at least he was pillaging his own songs. Martin Carthy, the doyen of English folk musicians, was doing it with a national treasure.

The idea of a band playing traditional English music with all the trappings of a rock band had initially been discussed by Ashley Hutchings and Bob Pegg at Keele Folk Festival at the end of the 1960s. Having coaxed the folk singer Sandy Denny into their ranks, Hutchings propelled **Fairport Convention**, then projecting a Muswell Hill interpretation of Californian soft-rock, full-tilt in an English folk direction. The move was to invest their guitarist Richard Thompson with a unique songwriting style of his own which has served him brilliantly for over two decades, and it turned their *Liege and Lief* album into a momentous bit of musical history.

But Fairport were seen mainly as a rock band playing with folk music, and Hutchings wanted to pursue the idea of an electric folk band to the limits. He quit Fairport Convention specifically to form such a group, engaging the most respected musicians on the folk club circuit to see it through. The result was **Steeleye Span**, initially involving Maddy Prior and Tim Hart and the Irish duo Gay and Terry Woods, whose presence instantly scuppered any purist notions of Englishness. They made one album, *Hark the Village Wait*, before the Irish contingent quit to form their own band

(Terry later re-emerging with The Pogues) and Steeleye really got underway with the induction of Martin Carthy and fiddler Peter Knight on the seminal *Please To See The King* album.

Steeleye went on to a glorious career, exerting a positive influence on the whole genre which had spawned them, even if some of their ideals became blurred in the process. They still tour intermittently, **Maddy Prior** combining the band with a prolific though uneven solo career. Carthy was a relatively early casualty (though he did return briefly in company with John Kirkpatrick for what was generally conceived as their last throw of the dice) and Hutchings himself abandoned ship to launch another new vehicle for his vision, the **Albion Country Band**, when he saw the pressures of success diluting intent. None of Steeleye had ever envisaged that worldwide tours and hit singles would ever become part of the equation for traditional music.

The Albion Country Band were something of a folk supergroup, featuring various ex-Fairports, Richard Thompson and Martin Carthy amid its ever-evolving incarnations. In the early 1980s, Hutchings changed the group's name to the **Albion Dance Band**, and shifted the music accordingly, deciding that the future lay with "English Country Dance", a music rooted in history, yet which didn't have to be rigidly structured and indeed provided scope for development. He turned the Albion Band into an institution, albeit in a radical assort-

Richard Thompson

103

ment of styles and line-ups through the years – it became a standing joke that a spell in the Albions was the musical equivalent of the draft. It's hard to knock Hutchings, though, given that he had been the linchpin of three of the most important folk bands in the country – Fairport, Steeleye and the Albions – as well as playing a crusading role in folk-music theatre and creating a series of imaginative stage projects such as *An Evening With Cecil Sharp* and an ingenious 2002 album *Street Cries*, which attempted to rewrite a series of famous traditional ballads as modern parables.

The annual **Cropredy Festival** in Oxfordshire is like an annual gathering of the clans for the folk-rock fraternity, offering tangible evidence of its enduring spirit. Evidence of the familial togetherness of the whole scene is scarcely better illustrated than by the rallying response to the long-standing respiratory illness suffered by one of its favourite sons, fiddle maestro **Dave Swarbrick**. A regular touring partner of Martin Carthy, long-time focal point of Fairport Convention and front man of his own band **Whippersnapper**, Swarbrick became one of the few people who got to read their own obituaries after a national newspaper mistakenly reported his death as a result of problems which eventually resulted in a lung transplant in 2004.

Many other folk-rock bands emerged in the wake of Steeleye's success. Most of them were awful, although the other half of that original Keele think-tank, Bob Pegg, achieved great critical acclaim if little commercial success alongside

The Oyster Bandits

The Oyster Band have dominated English roots music to such an extent across the last years that it's easy to imagine they have been keeping the flame alive entirely on their own. That may be unfair to others who have made valuable contributions along the way, but the Oysters have nevertheless pioneered a highly individual style of specifically English music and unflinchingly defied the fickle dictates of fashion and commercial pressures, developing their art within the parameters of a hostile rock world. More than that, they have become a major international name, establishing a clear connection to the English oral tradition while evolving an often ferocious instrumental sound coupled with biting political lyrics.

The group started out purely as an informal dance band of flexible personnel and erratic style after meeting at university in Canterbury in the 1970s, with some initial adventures under the name Fiddlers Dram. Interested in exploring the relatively uncharted territory of roots dance music, the Oysters achieved a settled line-up with **Ian Telfer** (actually a Scotsman) on fiddle, **Alan Prosser** (guitar), **John Jones** (melodeon/ vocals) joined by **Ian Kearey** on bass. After several well-received folk albums, things really exploded in the mid-1980s when they added drummer **Russell Lax** and adopted a rock dynamic, dramatically upping the decibel count and the fan base. An explosive version of the old traditional standard "Hal-An-Tow" was their unmistakable statement of intent and their 1986 album *Step Outside* was a notable landmark for roots music.

"Being English can be the kiss of death", John Jones has commented. "You've got to overcome so many things to actually make it feel radical and different and genuinely alternative." They took a huge credibility risk by plunging into full-blooded electric status, but they were rewarded by taking their own unique brand of roots music to an entirely new audience, while staying friends with the old.

Their next two albums, *Wide Blue Yonder* and *Ride* saw them progress into savage songwriters railing against the complacency of 1980s music and the iniquities of the Thatcher government. The arrival of bass/cello/kitchen-sink player **Chopper** in place of Ian Kearey – and later still **Lee** (new members aren't allowed surnames) taking over the drumsticks – seemed to drive them on to even greater fury and innovation, and they've continued to startle, amaze and delight ever since. Their intriguing collaborative *Freedom and Rain* album and subsequent tour with **June Tabor** was hugely successful and they've continued to grow through spectacular albums like *Holy Bandits* and *The Shouting End of Life*.

The Oysters are a band who have included traditional English standards and New Order covers on the same album. In 1998 they even twisted the folk tradition on its head, embarking on an "unplugged" tour, and ended the millennium with another huge leap, forming their own label Running Man to release the Alaric Neville-produced "look back in anger" album *Here I Stand*. They've continued to innovate and encourage the next generation on a series of package tours involving younger musicians such as Cara Dillon, Eliza Carthy and Jim Moray and won many accolades in 2004 for their involving collaborative live album, *The Big Session Volume 1*, including an extraordinary duet between John Jones and June Tabor singing "Love Will Tear Us Apart".

his fiddle-touting, singing wife, Carole Pegg, in the volatile **Mr Fox**. One of their offshoots, **Five Hand Reel**, later took the notion of electric folk to new areas of authenticity with the Scottish traditional singer **Dick Gaughan**; and there was a brief flurry of folk-rock excitement during the 1980s when two respected folk figures, Bill Caddick and John Tams, combined to create **Home Service** from the remains of one of Hutchings' Albion enterprises, merging Steeleyesque ideas with a full-blooded brass section.

But bands like the Home Service were impossibly expensive to sustain, and with the record industry moving on to new toys, the folk-rock movement collapsed amid grumbling about insensitive drummers and going up one-way streets backwards. The one really enduring group were the **Oyster Band** (see box), a wonderful outfit who dipped liberally into folk and pop traditions, and hit on a more rock sound in collaboration with June Tabor.

Folk-rock effectively died as a trailblazing force once the initial energy, excitement and commercial impact of the form had faded in a haze of rigid drum rhythms and mechanical adaptations of traditional styles. Its legacy remains, however, and not merely through the work of the Oyster Band or the occasional nostalgic Fairport and Steeleye tours. Bands like the **Blue Horses**, **Daily Planet** and **Pressgang** have gamely found fresh ways of rejuvenating old styles. Maverick fiddle king Dave Swarbrick proved there was life after Fairport by making further progress with Whippersnapper and various partners, including a nostalgic reunion with Martin Carthy which culminated in a couple of albums.

The ideas and instrumentation first ventured by the original folk-rock pioneers are now scattered routinely across a wide selection of musicians of differing backgrounds and inspirations, borrowing from the English tradition much as others might borrow from reggae or hip-hop, with varying degrees of success.

Wild in the Country

If the 1960s were dominated by protest music and the singer-songwriters, and the 1970s by Steeleye/Fairport folk-rock, then the 1980s were the domain of roots dance music.

The moving spirit behind this new roots scene was one **Rod Stradling**, a long-time iconoclast on the folk scene who had been involved since the early 1970s in a series of hugely influential bands. The first of these, **Oak**, concentrated on English country music, inspired by the seminal 1965 *English Country Music* anthology. They were followed by the **Old Swan Band**, who affected defiant attitudes as an antidote to the Celtic music that obsessed the English folk scene of the time. Then came the **English Country Blues Band**, with bottleneck and slide-guitarist Ian A. Anderson, who laced their dance music with blues, and slowly transmuted into **Tiger Moth** – a raucous electric band who themselves splintered into Orchestre Super Moth, mixing in all manner of world music influences.

In the late 1980s, however, Stradling concentrated his considerable energies on yet another new band, **Edward the Second and the Red Hot Polkas**. This was his most ambitious and defiant idea to date, forging English country dance music, sublimely, with reggae. You can't take such liberties without getting up somebody's nose and the group certainly did that, but their work with reggae dubmaster the Mad Professor at the mixing desk remains possibly the single most significant leap for English country music. You have to like reggae in the first place, of course, but the idea of merging the traditional music of rural England with the sound of the modern cities was a masterstroke, and for all its audacity a logical one. The band's first album, *Let's Polkasteady* in 1987, was a veritable earthquake in roots circles, and in the ensuing decade, most of it without Stradling, Edward II moved on to develop an arresting Caribbean-English fusion, which influenced other free-thinkers from the folk idiom like Irish accordion superstar Sharon Shannon and, even more tellingly, one or two reggae/dance groups too.

Stradling had originally seen Edward II as a dance band, albeit somewhat more visionary than the Ashley Hutchings' Albion incarnations. Subsequently people with ever wilder hair and stranger instruments took up the baton. **Blowzabella**, erratic but never dull, carved out a starring role, introducing English country dance to rhythms from the Balkans and beyond, with Nigel Eaton cranking things out on hurdy gurdy.

Other notables included **Flowers & Frolics**, who played more traditional dance material – jigs, polkas, hornpipes, and the like – in a somewhat Oyster Band mode, and the **Cock & Bull Band**, from the unlikely home of Milton Keynes, who laced an exotic range of instruments with the inspiration of French piper Jean-Pierre Rasle.

Whether it's exasperation with the plastic predictability of mass-market pop music, the blossoming of the seeds scattered by the likes of Eliza Carthy, Nancy Kerr and Kate Rusby, or simply a natural swing of the pendulum directing people back to their own roots, the early years of the 21st century have seen a hugely encouraging upsurge in English music. At least we've seen a horizon full of young musicians intent not only on achieving musical excellence, but doing something positively different with it to take it on to the next level and appeal to a new generation. **Jim Moray** (see box) has perhaps achieved most attention on this score, but don't underestimate the influence of **Jon Boden and John Spiers**, a duo of almost irre-

sistible drive and vitality, backed by a seemingly bottomless well of new ideas. They reached their biggest audiences as members of Eliza Carthy's band The Ratcatchers, but they've done some magnificent work with English music in their own right, particularly on the album *Bellow*. The combination of Boden's vigorous fiddle-playing, slightly eccentric vocals – strongly influenced by the late Peter Bellamy – and Spiers' dynamic melodeon, allied to excitingly original arrangements, lit up the scene.

Jim Moray and the Winds of Change

Something strange happened at the 2001 Young Folk Awards. An unknown Birmingham student called **Jim Moray** sang a selection of traditional English songs and accompanied them not with fiddle, melodeon or the usual tools of the trade, but a computer. You could almost see the sands shift.

He wasn't the first to apply techno to folk music, but he was perhaps the first of a generation who had grown up with modern technology and saw it not as an innovatory device, but as a logical accompaniment, as natural as the acoustic guitar in preceding generations.

Curiously, he didn't win the competition – that honour went to Give Way, three sisters from Scotland playing strict-tempo dance music – but Moray's progress was rapid and spectacular. His first album *Sweet England*, released in 2003 when he was still barely 21, caused a sensation with its ambitious, complex arrangements, rich in thick, computerized layers of sound, boldly inventive counter-melodies and quasi-classical choral undertones, samples and programming on primarily sombre traditional material. One excited reviewer called it the most important folk album since Fairport Convention's folk-rock landmark *Liege and Lief*, a national newspaper compared it to Radiohead and it attracted gushing reviews everywhere.

The sense that this was an important new voice in English folk music was compounded by the enigmatic character of Moray himself. After spending his formative years in Macclesfield and Stafford, Moray embarked

David & David

on a four-year music course at Birmingham Conservatoire and handed in the finished copy of his album as his degree coursework. He studied classical music and became obsessed with avant-garde art music, began writing songs and fronted a rock band, but when they split he found himself playing the folk songs he had absorbed as a child from his family.

Moray is not a product of folk clubs and professes to have no interest in them – "they're irrelevant to me, a tool of the last folk revival", he says. His own sights are firmly on a fresh folk revival emerging organically from his own generation and he has targeted mainstream events and media as his preferred habitat. He fiercely believes a change is gonna come – but not from the usual suspects. "It'll come from people who discover the music for themselves, not because they've been brought up in it … someone who's never heard folk music before and then completely immerses themselves in it and comes up with something that is truly great."

Jim Moray

Even more significant is **Bellowhead**, Boden and Spiers' spectacular big-band offshoot, complete with full-on brass section. Their opening set at the 2005 BBC Folk Awards – where they won the prize for best live act – was sensational. The band reopened ears to the potential of applying brass to folk music, something that's rarely been done outside of the now defunct Home Service and occasional band Brass Monkey. People still talk in awe of Bellowhead's set at the fiftieth Sidmouth Folk Festival, Devon in 2004.

Apart from Spiers and Boden, other exciting young musicians include **Benji Kirkpatrick** (son of the ex-Albion Band and stalwart folk club duo John Kirkpatrick and Sue Harris), **Paul Sartin** and **Rachel McShane**. The aforementioned Sidmouth Festival could almost be classified as a landmark, pointing the way to a brave new future of young English folk musicians. Bands like **Dr Faustus**, **Mawkin** and the **English Acoustic Collective** explored new ways of doing things alongside inventive musicians like the wonderful squeezebox players **Andy Cutting**, **Luke Daniels** and **Simon Ritchie**, whose instrumental interpretations of tunes as diverse as "Move Over Darling" and "Anarchy In The UK" on his *Squeezebox Schizophrenia* album (X-Tradition) are simply delicious. The resurgence of dance music through exciting bands like **Whapweasel**, **Hekety** and **Tickled Pink** is another indication of a music that appears to be on the march.

The increasingly cosmopolitan nature of English roots music also bodes well for the future. Edward II's experiments with reggae were but a drop in the ocean of musical cultures now second nature to most urban areas of the country. The Asian bhangra and ghazal traditions have made their mark, initially explored by the likes of **Najma Akhtar** and **Sheila Chandra** and artists like **Asian Dub Foundation**, **Transglobal Underground** and **Talvin Singh** taking a new kind of English fusion into the strange world of beats and club culture. They are moving the corner flag, the grandstand and the centre circle as well as the goalposts, and that's no bad thing.

The colour and patterns of English roots music have changed dramatically. In musical terms, this offers the thrilling potential of mixing new cultures with the old. A few have experimented, with encouraging results, but the surface of this potential has scarcely been scratched. The upsurge of younger musicians with minds that are open and free from old preconceptions and a misguided loyalty to traditional purity at the exclusion of all else suggests that English music is on the verge of a brave new world.

DISCOGRAPHY England | Folk/Roots

⊙ A Century Of Song
EFDSS, UK
Subtitled *A Celebration Of English Traditional Singers Since 1898*, the traditional treasures on this 25-track CD include cylinder recordings made by the renowned folk-song collector Cecil Sharp dating back to 1907. Among the legendary, but rarely heard, source singers are Harry Cox, the Copper Family, Fred Jordan, Walter Pardon, Phil Tanner and Mary Ann Haynes.

★ The Rough Guide to English Roots Music
World Music Network, UK
This pitches together some of the greatest influences in English music (The Watersons, the Albion Band) with source singers and musicians (Louise Fuller, Harry Cox, Billy Pigg) and modern strands of the revival (the Oyster Band, Edward II, Rory McL eod, Billy Bragg, Hank Dogs). The result is a well-balanced overview that entertains as much as it educates.

⊙ New Electric Muse Vols 1 and 2
Essential, UK
Mid-price CD updates of celebrated 1970s albums telling the story of folk into rock. Include most of the usual suspects, using their subtitle as the vaguest excuse to include everything from the Copper Family and Davey Graham to Richard Thompson, June Tabor and Energy Orchard.

⊙ The Voice Of The People
Topic, UK
A superb twenty-volume anthology of the primarily unaccompanied source singers, fiddlers, accordion players and the like who provided the bulk of the material and inspiration for modern folk song. Virtually every traditional singer of note (bar the Copper Family) is featured and placed in context by Reg Hall's superb notes. The volumes (which are available individually) are ordered by subject, and range from drinking songs through dance music and tragedy ballads to travellers' songs.

3 Mustaphas 3

Combining their traditional roots music with explorations of Balkan, African and Indian beats, the Mustaphas had a whole panoply of imitators. But in the original hands of this floating group of legendary Szegerely musicians, the music was (nearly) always a revelation, the time signatures bafflingly complex, and the wit upfront.

⊙ Heart Of Uncle
GlobeStyle, UK
This 1989 album is the best possible introduction to the Mustapha sound. Indeed, it's the best thing they ever did.

Albion Band

After Fairport Convention and Steeleye Span, bass player and musical visionary Ashley Hutchings turned his formidable talents to a band incorporating even wider aspects of the English tradition. The group changes personnel every couple of years or so, and is sometimes acoustic, sometimes electric, but Hutchings remains the linchpin.

⊙ The BBC Sessions
Strange Fruit, UK
Superb collection of recordings made at the BBC between 1972 and 1978, taking in several incarnations of the band. The paradoxical combination of Shirley Collins' mumsy voice and the band's full-blown folk-rockery still works stirringly, while Graeme Taylor's exuberant guitar and Ric Sanders' jazz-inflected fiddling sound equally impressive.

Peter Bellamy

Flamboyant singer from Norfolk who originally came to fame with the ebullient close-harmony revival group Young Tradition. Bellamy's stylized vocals weren't to everyone's taste, but he was a hugely important figure with a wealth of ideas. Sadly, he fell on hard times and in September 1991 he took his own life.

★ The Transports
Free Reed, UK
This 1977 album, based on the story of the first convicts transported to Australia in 1788, remains Bellamy's most enduring legacy. Involving most of the leading characters on the folk scene at the time, from Martin Carthy to A.L. Lloyd, it was turned into a stage production and on its 25th anniversary was reissued as a 2-CD box set.

Blue Murder

Barry Coope, Norma Waterson, Martin Carthy, Eliza Carthy, Jim Boyes, Lester Simpson and Mike Waterson have all contributed hugely over the years, and when they got together in 2000 to revive a group idea that had originally pitched the Watersons with Swan Arcade in the 1980s, they seemed to inspire each other to ever more inspirational heights.

⊙ No One Stands Alone
Topic, UK
A virtuoso collection of brilliant singing on a well-balanced mix of material, including traditional songs, sacred material and a couple of typically ebullient Mike Waterson songs.

Billy Bragg

The bard of Barking arrived ranting and howling in the mid-1980s to give the genteel English roots scene a punky kick up the backside. Once they had got over their initial shock, fans of traditional music realized that Bragg's sharply drawn social observations were indeed modern folk songs.

⊙ Mermaid Avenue
EastWest, UK
For an artist indelibly associated with East London, it's perhaps strange to be recommending an album dripping with Americana. This pits Bragg with US band Wilco on an important project setting newly discovered Woody Guthrie lyrics to music. It's easily the best thing he's ever done.

Anne Briggs

Nottinghamshire's Anne Briggs was blessed with a beautiful voice, an instinctive feeling for the oral folk tradition and an irrepressible wanderlust. She was young, sexy, talented, wild and mysterious ... and seemed to fall off the face of the earth after a frustrating spell with folk-rock band Ragged Robin in the early 1970s. It transpired she had moved to a remote Scottish island and turned her back on performing.

★ Anne Briggs: A Collection
Topic, UK
A 22-track compilation of early Briggs singing, dating from 1962. It's a good showcase of a singer who seemed to know no fear, tackling hugely demanding ballads like "Willie O'Winsbury" and "Polly Vaugn" without stylization, and with only subtle ornamentation. Earthy and dangerous, the album shows she was indeed the modern embodiment of the source singers who kept the music alive for so many years. An inspiration to a generation of female folk singers, it's instructive to hear her beautiful version of "Blackwaterside", accompanied by *bouzouki*, demonstrating where Bert Jansch and then Jimmy Page found their inspiration.

Eliza Carthy

The singing/fiddle-playing daughter of Norma Waterson and Martin Carthy has emerged as the flag-bearer of the modern generation of folk artists, noisily beating the drum for English music with incessant vitality and an irrepressible sense of adventure.

⊙ Rough Music
Topic, UK
Outstanding 2005 album pitching Carthy with the Ratcatchers (Jon Boden, Ben Ivitsky and John Spiers). Driving rhythms, joyful instrumentals, beautiful singing and telling material, including the self-composed "Mohair", a tribute to her late aunt, Lal Waterson.

Martin Carthy

Guitar stylist, singer and song-researcher Carthy (b. 1941) is the single most influential living figure on the English roots music scene. A pioneer of the post-skiffle folk-club movement, he was a role model for American folk singers such as Bob Dylan and Paul Simon.

⊙ Signs of Life
Topic, UK
Performing inimitably with stark arrangements, Carthy sets out the musical signposts of his long career. Includes radical interpretations of material as varied as "New York Mining Disaster 1941", "Heartbreak Hotel" and "The Lonesome Death Of Hattie Carroll".

Shirley & Dolly Collins

Always strange, always familiar, the music of the Collins sisters is among the world's most unusual. Such is the purity of their vision that their faithful, simple arrangements sound almost avant-garde.

★ Love, Death and the Lady
Fledgling, UK
Dolly Collins anachronistic chamber orchestrations, using portative organ, piano, fiddle and other chamber instruments are wedded to Shirley's deadpan yet spectral voice. Rural folk songs end up sounding like European art music, despite sticking firmly to their roots. No album in the world has ever sounded quite like this one.

The Copper Family

The most cherished name in English traditional song, generations of Coppers have provided an unbroken link with the past. Copper songs predominantly reflect gentler times in rural Sussex, which they have defined with distinctive harmonies and an irrepressible sense of character.

 Come Write Me Down
Topic, UK

A magnificent 28-track compilation released in 2001, with informative notes which not only collate many landmark recordings by different line-ups of the family through the 1950s and 60s, but contextualize them with intriguing reminiscences from Bob Copper's father Jim.

Sandy Denny

A wonderful singer-songwriter whose unmistakable voice was a fixture of the folk revival. After early acclaim with The Strawbs, she provided the catalyst for Fairport Convention's conversion to English roots, subsequently forming her own band Fotheringay before embarking on a solo career. English music lost something precious when she died after a fall in 1978.

⊙ **Who Knows Where The Time Goes**
Island, UK

Ambitious 4-CD box set, displaying the frequent frailties as well as the soaring glories of Denny's work. It mixes her own poppier material with traditional songs, demos and unreleased tracks, and comes complete with a handsome booklet. Through it all runs the almost unbearable sense of pain and melancholy that were to be her epitaph.

Robin and Barry Dransfield

Duo who lit up the scene in the 1970s and 80s with their imaginative and compelling interpretations of traditional songs. Barry's earthy fiddle-playing and rich vocal style contrasted attractively with elder brother Robin's smoother approach, which along with their Yorkshire accents and charismatic stage presence gave them a strong identity.

 Up To Now
Free Reed, UK

Definitive 2-CD compilation, including material from all their albums as a duo and as solo artists, including several previously unreleased tracks. A 32-page booklet accompanies the package.

Fairport Convention

The first of the onrush of late 1960s/early 70s bands who changed the face and dusty image of traditional English song by playing it with electric instruments and the intensive power of a rock band. In durability and versatility they were also the best, repeatedly overcoming adversity to create a distinctive and greatly loved folk-rock style. They still tour regularly and their annual reunion festival in the Oxfordshire village of Cropredy is a real event.

 **Liege and Lief**
Hannibal, UK

The 1969 album commonly cited as the launching pad of the folk-rock revolution, with Sandy Denny and Richard Thompson majestically conspiring to create an explosively dramatic vision. Fairport's body of work includes other exceptional albums (*Unhalfbricking*, *Full House*, *Babbacombe Lee*) but this is the one that made it all possible.

Davy Graham

Graham is the acoustic guitarist most other guitarists point to as the guv'nor from those heady 1960s days. Before you qualified for anything you had to be able to master "Anji" by Davy Graham. An aficionado of blues and modern jazz, Graham fell into the English folk movement by accident. He is equally intrigued by Far Eastern music and is constantly dreaming up new fusion styles that nobody else gets near.

WITH SHIRLEY COLLINS
⊙ **Folk Roots, New Routes**
Topic, UK

The idea of Collins, the princess of English traditional folksong, pairing up with the most eclectic guitarist around sounds bizarre. But linking Anglo-Appalachian ballads to "world music" arrangements (several decades before the term was invented) made sense to a visionary like Graham.

Nic Jones

Nic Jones was one of the great revival performers and a massive influence both as singer and guitar stylist until a horrific road crash effectively ended his working career in 1982. The contemporary feel of his arrangements of traditional songs made his 1970s albums landmarks for revival music.

 **Penguin Eggs**
Topic, UK

A seminal album, marking Jones's sudden transformation from accomplished but more or less straightforward interpreter of folk song to innovative arranger and intricate performer. It remains a classic.

John Kirkpatrick

A constant on the English folk scene for over thirty years, Kirkpatrick is a fine accordion and melodeon player, singer, writer and morris dancer. He and his wife, the singer and oboe player Sue Harris, recorded several outstanding albums together, and John went on to play a significant part in the Albion Band and Steeleye Span. He is still an influential figure, developing as a songwriter over a succession of solo albums.

⊙ **Plain Capers**
Topic, UK

Originally released in 1976 this was a landmark collection of 27 morris dance tunes from a wide range of Cotswold traditions. Far from being an academic exercise, it couched the tunes in folk-rock arrangements with John K's lively accordion imaginatively backed by Sue Harris on oboe and hammered dulcimer, Fi Fraser on fiddle, Martin Brinsford on mouth organ and old sparring partner Martin Carthy keeping rhythm on guitar. A much more credible collection than Ashley Hutchings' better known *Morris On*.

Jim Moray

A genuine original and free-thinker, Moray's insistence on targeting young non-folk audiences has caused controversy and he's ruffled a lot of feathers, but his work on tour with the Oysterband and determination to do things his way suggest he could have lasting influence.

 Sweet England
Niblick is a Giraffe, UK

Moray's 2003 debut album was deluged with ecstatic reviews. His slightly fey voice doesn't always carry off the elaborate techno arrangements, but this was still a sharp gust of fresh air that still bears sustained listening.

Old Swan Band

This Cotswold-based group gave real fire to the re-emergence of English country dance music. Featuring sisters Fi Fraser and Jo Freya, percussionist Martin Brinsford and fiddle player/trombonist John Adams, the band have remained central figures on the scene.

⊙ Swan-Upmanship
Wild Goose
There was a huge upsurge of new English dance music in 2004, but when *Swan-Upmanship* appeared it pretty much blew all other efforts out of the water. It was their first original recording for twenty years and they exploded out of the traps with a rocking collection of tunes.

James Raynard

Blessed with an improbably folky surname and a warm deep voice, Raynard is a singer with a distinctly musty and medieval muse. He released a stunning debut album in 2005, consisting almost entirely of traditional material performed in a impressively deadpan yet paradoxically lively fashion. He then vanished without a trace. When so many new English folk releases today are either twee or middle-of-the-road, his idiosyncratic voice is sorely missed.

⊙ Strange Histories
One Little Indian, UK
Raynard benefited from some lessons with Martin Carthy, and there's a superficial resemblance in the tough, no-nonsense presentation of these antic songs. But Raynard's his own man, and he brings light, shade and a charming sense of rhythm to this reliquary of often bizarre old songs.

Kate Rusby

A terrific young singer from Yorkshire, Rusby has been submerged in traditional music since childhood and is deeply committed to the cause of English roots music. Her solo career took off in a big way in 1997, but she juggled it with regular appearances with the excellent all-female group The Poozies until mid-1999, when pressure of work forced her departure from the band.

⊙ The Girl Who Couldn't Fly
Pure, UK
Despite criticisms that her albums all follow the same cosy format, this 2005 work – including seven original songs – is a beautifully rounded effort. With husband John McCusker, Ian Carr, Andy Cutting, Mike McGoldrick, Kellie While and members of the Grimethorpe Colliery Band also on board, the musical arrangements are immaculate.

Martin Simpson

Simpson first started gigging at fifteen, when his precocious talents as a highly individual guitarist and an unusually aggressive singer came to the fore at his local folk club in Scunthorpe. A celebrated partnership with June Tabor cemented his reputation. His interest in American folk music led to sixteen years in the US, but he returned to England and English music with the award-winning *The Bramble Briar* in 2002.

⊙ Kind Letters
Topic, UK
Featuring many of the songs that originally converted him to folk song as a teenager, this album is an object lesson in passionate performance allied to technical excellence. Nancy Kerr, James Fagan and the superb Irish band Danu offer instrumental back-up.

Steeleye Span

The most commercially successful English electric folk band of them all, Steeleye enjoyed a succession of mid-1970s chart hits. Their greatest attraction was always their twirling front woman Maddy Prior. They still tour occasionally, though Prior more regularly fronts her own gigs and also records in a trio called The Girls.

⊙ Please To See The King
Mooncrest, UK
The crucial 1971 album which gave profound impetus and credibility to folk-rock. Martin Carthy strapped on electric guitar for the first time, Maddy Prior's voice soared gloriously and Peter Knight was full of guile and daring on the fiddle.

June Tabor

The charismatic Tabor has been dividing opinion for 25 years with the starkness and suppressed passion of her singing. She has recorded and toured with The Oyster Band, Maddy Prior, Martin Simpson and Huw Warren, and she's dabbled in jazz, standards and Brecht. Yet her forte remains the traditional ballad, which she invariably delivers with a uniquely telling tension.

★ Always
Topic, UK
Comprehensive 4-CD anthology covering every facet of Tabor's career, from early unaccompanied gems to the complex, atmospheric arrangements of her work with the Creative Jazz Orchestra. There's folk-rock, dark ballads, torch songs and lilting ditties – all united by Tabor's majestic voice.

Linda Thompson

For much of her career, Linda has lived in the shadow of ex-husband Richard, content to sing his words with sumptuous grace and guile. When they split she made one fairly uneventful solo album before dropping out altogether. Coaxed back to sing on the wonderful John Tams album *Unity*, she re-emerged with a superb new album and successful live performances.

★ Fashionably Late
Topic, UK
It took her long enough, but Linda finally proved in 2002 that she was a major songwriter in her own right. She could still sing like a dream, the more weather-beaten quality of her voice lending itself to her sharp, evocative material, including a wonderful little-known Lal Waterson song, "Evona Darling".

Richard Thompson

Arguably the most complete and consistent English performer thrown up in the 1970s folk-rock explosion, Thompson is impressive for his blitzkrieg guitar-playing alone, but the quality and originality of his songwriting put him in a class of his own. After Fairport he formed a wonderful partnership with his wife Linda. When they split up he reverted to a solo career that has survived all the vagaries of fashion and age.

PLAYLIST
England | Folk/Roots

1 GALLANT HUSSAR Eliza Carthy and The Ratcatchers from *Rough Music*
Colourful and involving traditional song given an arrangement that demonstrates the full range of Carthy's excellent band.

2 A BLACKSMITH COURTED ME Martin Simpson from *Kind Letters*
A stunningly tender instrumental version of a famous traditional song, with a tune also used in the hymn "To Be a Pilgrim".

3 THE SEEDS OF LOVE Jim Moray from *Sweet England*
Perhaps Moray's most extreme arrangement: a performance of the first traditional song collected by Cecil Sharp using choral vocals, a trip-hop beat and bizarre orchestral backdrop.

4 THE CLAUDY BANKS The Copper Family from *Come Write Me Down*
One of the loveliest and most famous songs in the Copper treasury, this 1951 recording features Bob Copper and his father Jim.

5 NO ONE STANDS ALONE Blue Murder from *No One Stands Alone*
Ferociously uplifting harmony singing, so rousing it should be sung on the terraces as a football anthem.

6 SOME OLD SALTY Lal Waterson and Oliver Knight from *Once in a Blue Moon*
Lal allows herself some warm reminiscences of youth on this uplifting track from an otherwise dark album. Sampled by Chumbawamba, and something of a classic.

7 COURTING IS A PLEASURE Nic Jones from *Penguin Eggs*
The great Nic Jones at his very best, building the atmosphere almost imperceptibly, with his rhythmic guitar patterns pulling you into the narrative.

8 AQABA June Tabor from *Always*
A dark, mysterious Bill Caddick song based on the Lawrence of Arabia story. Tabor turns it into an epic, brooding *tour de force*.

9 MATTY GROVES Fairport Convention from *Liege and Lief*
Perhaps the track that best defines the folk-rock explosion of 1969, with Sandy Denny inspired to give one of her most impassioned vocal performances. A gripping yarn.

10 THE GREAT VALERIO Richard and Linda Thompson from *Watching the Dark*
One of Richard Thompson's most dramatic – and mysterious – songs, with typically cinematic lyricism and erupting instrumental work.

★ **Watching the Dark**
Hannibal, UK; Ryko, US
Triple-CD compilation charting most aspects of Thompson's celebrated career, ranging from his most traditional excursions to occasional outbursts of pure rock'n'roll. Includes material from his Fairport days, Linda and various backing bands, as well as unreleased cuts.

Kathryn Tickell

The leading Northumbrian piper and fiddle-player, Tickell draws direct lineage from great Northeastern musicians like Billy Pigg and Joe Hutton and has inspired a whole new wave of dedicated young traditional musicians.

★ **The Northumberland Collection**
Park, UK
After various excursions into other territories, Tickell showcases her Northumbrian heritage in blissfully pure form, with a supporting cast including famous fiddle player Willie Taylor and – for the first time on a Tickell album – vocal tracks from Carolyn Robson and Terry Conway.

Lal Waterson

When Lal Waterson suddenly died of cancer in 1998, she had been at the very heartbeat of English music for three decades. Although most people were entirely unaware of her stunning songwriting ability, she wrote much of the Watersons' controversial album *Bright Phoebus* (1971). Self-effacing and publicity-shy, she hated touring and the whole process of being in a group, and was quite happy to hide her light under a bushel.

WITH OLIVER KNIGHT

★ **Once In A Blue Moon**
Topic, UK
You can listen to this intently for a long time and still not get to grips with the subtle nuances and stark truths of Lal's lyricism and spellbinding voice, steeped in a tradition too rich and intense for easy listening. This is a really great album. The posthumously released follow-up, *A Bed Of Roses* (Topic, UK), is equally stark, brooding and magnificent.

England/UK |
Bhangra/Asian Beat
the great british invasian

The Dhol Foundation, fronted by Johnny Kalsi

From bhangra to Bollywood and Bombay Dreams, and from Apache Indian to Asian Underground and the latest East/West fusions, it's taken decades for British Asian music to truly make its mark in the mainstream culture. The musical journey of three generations of UK Asians from the 1950s to the current day is traced by club promoter, BBC Radio broadcaster and co-founder of Outcaste Records **DJ Ritu**.

I n the 1950s Britain became the home of many settlers from its former colonies in the Indian subcontinent and the Caribbean. Taking on menial jobs at the invitation of the British government, they gravitated to cities like London, Manchester and Birmingham. A majority of the Asian incomers were from the Punjab, a region that had been divided and devastated by Indian partition. More arrived in 1972 after Idi Amin's expulsion of 30,000 Ugandan Asians, bringing a predominantly Gujarati business-savvy community who forged new ventures in Leicester and West London. Completing the South Asian kaleidoscope, a sizeable Bangladeshi community emerged in East London, having fled a war-torn and cyclone-shattered former East Pakistan.

Bhangra and Beyond

Outside work, creative juices were fuelled by homesickness for the mother countries and the demand for wedding and temple entertainers grew in proportion with the South Asian population. Bemused by the Beatles, and star-struck by Ravi Shankar collaborating with George Harrison, Pakistanis favoured qawwals and ghazals, Gujaratis had gharbar and bhajans, and Hindi film music largely transcended regional bias. But it was the majority Punjabi community – Indian and Pakistani - that delivered the first popular British Asian music genre: bhangra.

This traditional folk style evolved from India's fertile northwest region, where it was often performed to celebrate occasions like the harvest. Accordingly its dance-moves mimic agricultural activities such as sowing and reaping, while the name derives from *bhang* (hemp), a staple Punjabi crop. Dance is bhangra's chief purpose and drums like the loud, brash, double-sided wooden *dhol* play a central role. Melodic support in the form of the single-stringed *tumbi* is interspersed with (usually) men singing about dancing, drinking, beautiful girls or some nationalistic ruse in Punjabi. Bhangra has its female counterpart in *gidda*.

The foundations of the British Asian music industry were laid in the 1970s. Early bands like Bhujungy and Alaap fused traditional bhangra with Western pop, using electric guitars, synthesizers and conventional drums to entice young Asians who might otherwise be Rolling Stones or Mud fans.

Pioneers

The first generation found that the UK wasn't all that it had been cracked up to be by colonial propaganda. South Asians struggled for survival against a background of "rivers of blood" speeches and National Front marches. With the BBC's national Asian programming limited to the TV show *Naya Zindagi Naya Jeevan* (new way, new life), it was common for film fans to go and watch Hindi films in some rundown cinema armed with reel-to-reel tape-recorders to get the latest songs.

Many yearned for more of a taste of "back home". In London this meant heading to the East End or Southall to find Asian food, clothes and music. Southall gave birth to some of the early bhangra bands and Naya Zindagi snapped them up. PolyGram A&R man **Pran Gohill** had established Multitone Records to import cassettes by Indo-disco stars like Salma Agha and Musserat Nazir. Spotting Alaap on the programme in 1978, he realized the potential for developing UK-based talent.

A decade earlier in Birmingham, **Mohammed Ayub** had created OSA Records, releasing music from Pakistan by artists like Shaukat Ali, Gulam Ali Khan, The Sabri Brothers and, by 1978, Nusrat Fateh Ali Khan. But with an eye on local talent too, Ayub secured a TV appearance for the hugely popular Midlands band Bhujungy, and launched the annual Asian Song Contest at Wembley Conference Centre to showcase British Asians.

It was time for a British bhangra record to be made, and together with Alaap's guitarist, **Deepak Kazanchi**, Gohil released *Terri Chunni Di Sitare* (1980), a concoction of synth sounds, Punjabi rhythms, dhol and tabla, with Channi Singh's soaring vocals uniting the East/West components.

Reassured that British Asians could actually release material, new bands formed rapidly. Deepak Kazanchi launched **Heera**, featuring the vocals of **Dhammi** and **Kumar**, who wowed audiences with their bhangra/disco hybrids and white flares, and featured on BBC TV's children's programme *Blue Peter*. His Arishma label was also home to 1980s supergroups **Holle Holle** and **Azaad**.

Premi joined the Multitone stable, and **Malkit Singh** sang for OSA from 1984. There was a fair degree of variety among the early artists. Midlands band **Apna Sangeet** went for a two-pronged vocal attack with **K.S. Bhamrah** and **Sardara Gill**, who emphasized the traditional elements of bhangra with beaming smiles, colourful silk *lehnghas* and a crazed dhol player called Gurcharan Mall. Conversely, "modern" band **DCS**, formed in 1983, featured **Danny Choranji** and classically-trained singer **Shin** in Western attire, making sounds dominated by electric guitar and keyboards and without any dhol.

Hugely gifted Kuljit Bhamra composed or re-crafted classic Punjabi folk tunes like "Rail Gaddi" and "Nachdi Di Gooth Gulugaye" for all the labels and many groups. He produced the first British bhangra album by a female artist, his mother **Mohinder Kaur Bhamra**, and following the launch of his own late-1980s imprint Keda, provided a springboard for top women like **Sangeeta** and **Baldip Jabble**. Sangeeta caused a stir in this men-only environment partly for gender reasons, but also because her songs were Punjabi in style but unconventionally sung in Hindi, with *dholki* hand-drums and "Hoi Hoi's" punctuating romantic songs like "Pyar Ka Hai Bairi". Nevertheless, there were few women on the UK bhangra scene, in contrast to India where there were many female folk singers, like Punjabi sisters Surinder and Prakash Kaur, and playback siblings Lata Mangeshkar and **Asha Bhosle**, who reigned over the Hindi film industry for half a century.

By the end of the 1980s, the UK bhangra scene had shifted more towards the Midlands, as new labels like Kiss, Roma, and Nachural Records soaked up the explosion of suave and sophisticated bands like **The Sahotas**, suited and booted **Achanak**, and more traditional artists like **The Safri Boys** and **A.S. Kang**. **Amarjit Sidhu**, singer with bhangra-muffin pioneers **Chirag Pehchan**, changed the Asian Song Contest into the Asian Pop Awards, moving them to Birmingham, and went on to create the Kamlee label. In a decade which saw Britain's urban youth rioting in most major cities, and Asian gangs forming to defend their communities against racism, many first and second-generation Asians were at last finding a voice through music they could call their own.

God is a DJ

Clubs and radio DJs are an invaluable tool in the spread of new music. With Asians rendered almost invisible by the media, people who had never heard of **Johnny Zee** or seen **Pardesi** at WOMAD first heard the "Southall Sound" in clubs where DJs would momentarily shelve Michael Jackson and drop Alaap's "Bhabiye Ni Bhabiye" into their set. DJs gave credibility and "cool" to the new sounds. For young British Asians it was a rare positive affirmation of roots and cultural identity.

Specialised "bhangra raves" became commonplace across the UK during the mid-1980s: venue owners reluctant to allow Asian promoters prime night-time slots offered up afternoons instead. Attracting youth who were curfewed at night – particularly girls – Asian youngsters skipped

Nachural

Achanak

school to attend. The British press took interest in this growing trend because for years they had stereotyped Asians as law-abiding citizens, models of good behaviour and academic excellence.

Press coverage had begun in Asian newspapers and new magazines like *Ghazal* and *Beat*. In London there was LBC Radio's weekly show *Geetmala*, while **Danny Choranji** (DCS) took over the *East and West* programme in Birmingham. Away from the bhangra scene, **Biddhu** produced Carl Douglas's number-one hit "Kung-Fu Fighting", but the major surprise came in seeing sixteen-year-old **Sheila Chandra** and her group Monsoon on *Top Of The Pops* in 1982. The Indo-pop classic "Ever So Lonely" launched her lengthy career in world music. A year later, percussionist **Pandit Dinesh** and **Deepak Kazanchi** were on the same show with the group **Blancmange**.

It was the daytime raves that made the news, however, bringing the word "bhangra" into the wider British vocabulary. Early crews like **Calibar Roadshow**, **Entasia** and **Hustlers Convention** spiced up the latest bhangra beats with soul, disco, and hip-hop. **X-Executive Sounds** produced the best-selling "Xtra-Hot" remix LPs through Multitone in the early 1990s, showcasing their multicultural DJ style on vinyl. Fusion of this kind made sense, as the second generation – being Asian and British – were into all kinds of music. In clubs or in remixes, DJs simply reflected this, paralleling similar fusions on the hip-hop scene (Eric B. and Rakim's "Paid In Full" being a prime example). Birmingham DJ Bally Sagoo mixed styles on his titanic 1990 debut EP "Wham Bam", a house-infused bhangra hybrid with reverberating basslines and a dub sensibility. In the mid-1990s **Panjabi MC** travelled to the Punjab to record legendary singers like **Kuldip Manak** and **Gurdas Mann** – and wove their raw vocals into tough hip-hop breaks and beats back in his Coventry studio, crafting a dynamic **desi-fusion** (from the Hindi word *des*, homeland) that earned him cult status on the Asian club scene.

Record labels began to export British Asian music and a few DJs started touring, becoming pivotal in the breakthrough of Asian music worldwide as the UK's Asian music industry became established as the premier trend-setter outside India itself. Aside from one-off large capacity events, however, the only regular hangouts for Asian clubbers were *Shakti* on the gay scene and *Jaclyn's* in London, where **DJ Taz Jay** spun soul tunes for a loyal crowd.

When the *Bombay Jungle* club started in 1993, it arrived with a bang. Opened by three student sound-systems – Hustlers Convention, **Maximum NRG** and **Impact** – this Tuesday night two-floor weekly was staged at the prestigious Wag Club. Swing, soul and hip-hop blended on the downstairs menu, while bhangra, ragga and jungle merged upstairs. Soon there was a plethora of other venues to choose from, and the mainstream press suddenly perked up again for the first time since the mid-1980s, spurred on by the emergence of new Asian popstar **Apache Indian**, who created a huge stir with the Punjabi/patois fusion of his debut single "Movie Over India".

Dubbed "bhangra-muffin", this charismatic Handsworth boy happened to be Indian but loved reggae. Promptly signed by Island Records, Apache's unique sound crossed over, charting at Number Five in the UK Top 40 with "Boom Shak A Lack" in 1992. Signing to Sony Columbia, Bally Sagoo sourced tunes by inimitable film composer **R.D. Burman** for the phat b-line'n'beats on his superb **Bollywood Flashback** album, spawning Hindi-remix fever across the Brit-Asian industry. Chart success also followed with single "Dil Cheez" in 1996. It was still rare to see Asian acts on *Top of The Pops*, so glimpses of these artists whipped up a frenzy. **Taz**, the artist formerly known as Johnny Zee, reinforced optimism with his minor hit "I'm Still Waiting!".

As global interest mounted, exposure for the music grew. Local BBC Radio started to develop a network of Asian programmes across the UK. The 24-hour Asian station Sunrise secured its licence to broadcast legally. Apache Indian became Radio One's first (albeit short-lived) Asian presenter in 1994 and DJ Ritu repeated the coup on Kiss 100 and the BBC World Service. And the arrival of 24-hour programming came via Zee TV.

An infrastructure of distributors, pirate radio stations, magazines and Asian PR companies were now all in place to support British Asian music. But innocence in playing by the rules of the establishment was still apparent. CDs were rarely barcoded and cassettes were sold cheaply in Asian music shops, bypassing the chart return system. Coupled with limited mainstream exposure, music not produced on major labels could not penetrate the mainstream charts. So despite typical individual artist sales exceeding 50,000, bhangra remained confined to the Asian ghetto.

The Asian Underground

Asian youth in Britain have tended to have an affinity with black music. George Benson and Stevie Wonder were heroes in the 1980s, while reggae and hip-hop ruled in working-class areas. A rap/electro scene developed, notably among non-Punjabi Asians, who were largely unimpressed by bhangra – just one Asian genre from one region of the subcontinent. In London's East End, sound systems like **Joi**, **State of Bengal** and **Osmani Sounds** experimented with conscious rap, conveying experiences of poverty and racism, and mixing in traditional Bengali folk lyrics and flutes over breakbeats. Such second-generation stories echoed those of Turkish youth in Kreuzberg and Algerian youngsters in Marseille.

In Bradford, punk drummer **Aki Nawaz** was inspired by a whole host of sounds ranging from dub, techno and bhangra to anything that wasn't pop. In 1990 he formed Nation Records with Cath Canoville as a vehicle for his uncompromising anti-establishment band **Fun-Da-Mental**, which voiced the anger of dispossessed youth and caused controversy with T-shirts depicting women wearing the hijab while armed with rifles. Nation soon became host to more "global-chaos" groups with a political edge, and their first compilation, *Fuse*, included tracks from unsigned acts like **Mahatma T** (Talvin Singh), and **Pulse 8** (Jah Wobble and On-U Sound's David Harrow). **Transglobal Underground** (formerly 1980s pop-outfit Furniture), **Asian Dub Foundation**, **Natasha Atlas**, **Joi**, **T.J. Rehmi**, **Hustlers HC** (the original DJ crew expanded into the world's first Sikh rap outfit), **Loop Guru** and **Recycler** also joined the Nation roster, promoting a world-fusion of tabla loops, African chants, electro beats and powerful defiant lyrics.

The 1990s also saw the emergence of **Kaleef**, all-girl band **The Voodoo Queens** and the **KKKings** who baffled everybody musically but charmed

the media into dubbing the whole scene as "The New Asian Kool". A small but thriving club scene attracted mainly non-Asians and media/trendy folk, and world-music radio presenters like Andy Kershaw, Jo Shinner and John Peel devoted airspace to the nu-Asian rebels.

Under Bubbles Over

With so much activity, the "underground" had to spill overground. In 1994 Outcaste Records was launched by record-plugger Shabs Jobanputra and DJ Ritu to nurture a new East/West sound by artists who didn't conform to the bhangra stereotype but couldn't get a major-label deal either.

After releasing an acclaimed white label combining the talents of Apache Indian and **General Levy**, Outcaste "discovered" Kentish accountant **Nitin Sawhney**, whose *Migration* CD blended drum'n'bass, flamenco, jazz piano, tabla, and English and Asian vocals into the perfect East/West mix. Young junglist **Easy Mo** soon followed. A contemporary of **Sam Zaman** (State of Bengal) and other East End Bengali DJ boys, he eventually teamed up with Shri, the Indian-based IndusCreed bassist, to form **Badmarsh and Shri**. "Original nuttah" UK Apachi would later complete the line-up. Talented producer/DJs like **Gesse**, **Niraj Chag** and **Mo Magic** signed up too. Outcaste had the added bonus of its PR wing, Media Village, to propel these new acts into mainstream consciousness and created a monthly club that generated vast press interest. Top DJs like Gilles Peterson graced the decks while celebrities such as Björk checked the vibe.

Tabla prodigy **Talvin Singh** created his own label and in 1996 launched the legendary weekly *Anokha* club at London's trendy Blue Note. Already an icon in underground and world music circles, the East Londoner had collaborated with acts like Massive Attack. His 1997 *Anokha: Soundz of The Asian Underground* compilation cemented a golden year for the genre, though many of its protagonists weren't happy with the label. Singh's 1998 debut solo CD *OK* combined Indian classical instrumentation, drum'n'bass, techno and trip-hop, winning the Mercury Music Prize in 1999.

The club scene expanded and many one-off events offered a complete "live" showcase with MCs and tabla-players. Drum'n'bass, the most exciting new musical genre to emerge at the time, gave Asian producers a form that synchronized flawlessly with complex Indian beat cycles, and the advent of MIDI keyboards brought an explosion in the number of bedroom studios. Despite being the least popular genre within the Asian commu-

Barbak

Asian Dub Foundation

nity itself, the familiar dance-music references of Asian Underground blended easily into the global club scene and the form has been perpetuated by a steady stream of new artists: **Trickbaby**, **Sonik Gurus**, **The Sona Family**, and **Juttla** in the UK, **Midival Punditz** in India and **Karsh Kale** and **Cheb i Sabbah** in the US.

Jazz/World/other...

Cross-cultural exchanges producing fresh sounds have gone in and out of fashion and in East-West terms the list is endless: Ravi Shankar/George Harrison, John McLaughlin/Zakir Hussein, Boy George/Baluji Srivastava, Bill Laswell, John Meyer, Genetic Drugs, Don Cherry, Trilok Gurtu...

Sheila Chandra went on to form the Indi-pop label, later producing a series of "minimalist" albums focussing on drone and voice for the Real World label. In 1987, **Najma Akhtar** won the Asian Song Contest and released her brilliant ghazal/jazz album *Quareeb* on Triple Earth, featuring the likes of saxophonist Ray Carless (Incognito/Jazz Jamaica) and violinist **Nawazish Ali Khan** (Alaap/Fundamental). Way ahead of her time, Akhtar went on to work with Led Zeppelin's Robert Plant.

Talvin Singh was a tabla-player in Akhtar's original "live" team before his solo career went into orbit. Fast-forward to 2005 and Talvin Singh and ADF were both commissioned to produce projects with English National Opera, following Nitin Sawhney's collaboration with the Britten Sinfonietta in 2004. **Susheela Rahman** is lauded for her ethereal creations with partner Sam Mills. **State of Bengal** has worked extensively with 1970s psychedelic soundtrack-king **Ananda Shankar** and recorded some fine work with **Paban Das Baul** for Real World.

Performance-based groups have also done well on the jazz/world circuit. **The Dhol Foundation**, under the direction of the exuberant **Johnny Kalsi**, has wowed audiences worldwide since 1995 with their dhol extravaganza, while DJ-based **Asian Equation/Sister India** have developed cult status without ever releasing a record. The flamboyantly attired **Bollywood Brass Band** offer a completely unique sound with their covers of Hindi film songs. And whichever genre ADF or Fundamental can be said to belong to, their raw energy, anger and frenetic shows leave fans breathless.

Enter the new Millennium

Exciting progress was made after the mid-1990s. Though Sony disposed of Bally Sagoo, Warners captured no less than six Asian acts in the space of a year, including Island cast-off Apache Indian. It seemed the majors were taking notice at last as State Of Bengal joined One Little Indian and ADF signed to London Records.

And there was more pop chart action. Tejinder Singh's Cornershop scored a 1998 number one with "Brimful Of Asha", complete with a Fatboy Slim remix. Jas Mann's Babylon Zoo reached the top spot with "Spaceman" and Jyoti Misra's "Whitetown" followed suit. Non-Asians were at it too. Kulashaker with their "Govinda" single, Madonna with henna-painted hands... Bally Sagoo supported Michael Jackson on tour while Cornershop did the same for Oasis, ditto ADF with Radiohead, and Nitin Sawhney hooked up with Sting and switched to major label V2.

Several exciting new acts emerged on the bhangra circuit such as **Sukshinder Shinda**, **Jazzy B.**, production-duo **Partners In Rhyme**, **Dr Zeus**, **RDB** (rhythm, dhol and bass) and **B21**. Named after their Birmingham postcode, this "boy-band" trio boasted designer suits, powerful lead vocalist **Jassi Sidhu**, and no instruments but some killer dancefloor tunes. New label **Moviebox** had conceived B21 and thereafter found a legion of artists wanting to sign up, giving them a virtual monopoly. Panjabi MC released his groundbreaking 1998 album *Legalised*, which contained a track called "Mundian To Bach Ke" sampling the *Knight Rider* theme.

The Rise of Bollywood

As 2000 unfolded, Asian entry into mainstream culture was boosted by Hindi-based cinema. The films *Monsoon Wedding* and *The Guru* extended at least some of the sounds and references of Mumbai across the globe. Being "musicals" with CD soundtracks increased their impact on the non-Asian market, introducing novices to the vocals of playback giants Udit Narayan and Jaspinder Narula. Gurinder Chadha's *Bend It Like Beckham* followed suit with a crossover British/bhangra CD compilation, and a host of "Bollywood" clubs sprang up. In 2008 *Slumdog Millionaire* – with an Oscar-winning score by Indian composer **A.R. Rahman** – brought Bollywood yet further into the mainstream.

The launch of the *Bombay Dreams* musical in London's West End in 2001 had an unprecedented impact. Bollywood was given the ultimate sanction through Sir Andrew Lloyd Webber, a score by A.R. Rahman and a script penned by Meera "Goodness Gracious Me" Syal. Selfridges organized "three and a half weeks of Bollywood" and The Victoria and Albert Museum hosted "Bollywood Babylon" and a Bollywood Poster Exhibition.

British Asian music could only benefit from such publicity. To the untrained ear there was no difference between bhangra and Bollywood, but "Asian music" was seeping slowly into the nation's psyche. Yet Warners had dropped all its Asian artists in 2000. Of them, only **Black Star Liner**, **Amar** and **Spellbound** actually released any product, while those of others, like **Deepika** (now Deeyah) and **The Core** never saw the light of day.

Media Rockets

Asians were becoming topical wherever one looked: in dance, literature, fashion, alternative therapies and as a culinary force to be reckoned with. In 2002 the BBC Asian Network – previously ghettoized as a local station in the Midlands – was relaunched as a national digital station. Another BBC digital station, 1XTRA, featured a weekly Asian show. Club Asia, a new voice for young Asians, took over a medium wave licence. Radio One commissioned a weekly Asian music programme, and KISS 100 rapidly followed suit. Suddenly Asian bands had a multitude of significant outlets for their music.

It came as no surprise, then, when the year closed with Panjabi MC entering the pop charts. The aforementioned "Mundian To Bach Ke" was licensed to a Buddha Bar compilation, remixed by Jay-Z. It eventually went to number one in Germany and reached number two in the UK. For the first time ever a "real" bhangra record, i.e. one sung completely in Punjabi, had made it to the top of the charts, not just in the UK, but also abroad.

Ariel Van Straten @ Stella Pye

Panjabi MC

Bhangra and Bling

Asians in the new millennium suddenly found black music playing ball. Missy Elliot stormed the clubs with her tabla-looped, tumbi-twanging "Get Ur Freak On". Dr Dre produced Truth Hurts' "Addictive", illegally sampling Lata Mangeshkar. Hip-hop's hard men The Neptunes and Timbaland had been looking to the East for inspiration for some time, and were now joined by Snoop Doggy Dog, Erik Sermon, Craig David and… err… Shania Twain. Finally, a dialogue between the genres had replaced the longstanding one-way monologue, with R&B heroes bringing more credence and new audiences for Asian sounds.

Some Asian artists were able to take up the baton in this relay with great integrity. Former Fundamental frontman Mushtaq found his production skills in great demand by groups like Misteeq, and his recent collaboration with Terry (Specials) Hall produced the acclaimed *Hour Of Two Lights* album. Rishi Rich began his career at the age of thirteen under the watchful eye of top producer Pankaj Jethwa. Co-producing a string of successful Bollywood remix albums for the 2kool series, Rich's key influence came from Teddy Riley, so he was in his element with the "Urban Asian" trend. Madonna, Britney Spears and Mary J Blige have all called on him for an Asian-edged remix. Rich's reputation magnetized equally capable vocalists Jay Sean and Juggy D., and under "The Rishi Rich Project" banner they secured three top tens in 2004. The style is catchy – black, British and Asian all at once – and the latest hybrid after bhangra-house, bhangra-muffin and bhangra-garage.

The UK remains a mecca for other diasporic Asians. In 2004 young, charismatic **Raghav** jetted in from Calgary in Canada to show the Brits a trick or two, scoring hits with "So Confused" (with 2Play), the solo "Can't Get Enough" and the Sly and Robbie-produced "Angel Eyes". Raghav's Asian references were Hindi-based but phrased around poppy R&B vibes, with rolling riddims and memorable hooklines. When Jay Sean and Raghav appeared on the front cover of publications like *Touch* magazine, there was a renewed sense of achievement in the Brit-Asian music industry.

More women are capitalizing on this Asian/R&B fusion: long-term Rishi Rich collaborator Veronica, Norwegian diva Deeyah (Deepika), MIA, Rouge, Bat For Lashes (Natasha Khan), Ms Scandalous and Hardkaur are some of the names that may enhance the fortunes of bhangra's only current female contenders, Gunjan and Mona. The daughter of Channi Singh, Mona joins a growing number of sons and daughters of bhangra pioneers who are now artists in their own right. Three generations of Asian musicians in Britain have built something from nothing and the big market now is India. The third generation is heading back home for mass recognition and vast sales, so the next chapter remains to be written. But whichever generation British Asians are from, it's clear that they will continue to dictate the global South Asian music agenda.

Bhangra

⭐ **Asian Beat Bazaar**
Virgin, UK

Compiled by Trickbaby and released in 2004, this is a wide selection of straight-up urban fusion and grassroots bhangra, featuring offerings from stalwarts such as Apache Indian and Malkit Singh as well as nu-breed artists like L'il Sach and Dalvinder Singh.

⊙ **The Rough Guide to Bhangra**
World Music Network, UK

A 1999 CD that provides a much-needed historic trawl through the music.

⭐ **The Rough Guide To Bhangra Dance**
World Music Network, UK

This 2005 follow-up is even better: a comprehensive collection of the genre's finest tunes.

⊙ **UrbanFlavas Vols 1 & 2**
Untouchables, UK

From 2002 and 2004 respectively, these two selections showcase top tracks from artists who led the bhangra-garage trend, such as Gubi Sandhu, RDB, Metz and Trix.

Alaap

Formed in Southall, West London in 1977 by Channi Singh to play Punjabi functions, Alaap became the pioneers of modern bhangra.

⭐ **Dance with Alaap**
Multitone, UK

Bhangra-fusion in its infancy (1981). Probably their most successful and accessible album, this features the massive "Bhabiye Ni Bhabiye", which first established Alaap and the "Southall Sound".

Heera

Headed by vocal duo Dhami and Kumar, this ten-piece band enjoyed enormous success in the 1980s.

⭐ **Diamonds From Heera**
Arishma, UK

Taking the "Southall Sound" a few steps further, this 1982 album is a bhangra-house classic.

Mona

The daughter of Channi Singh of Alaap follows in her infamous father's footsteps. After releasing a debut CD in 2000, she has rapidly established herself as the UK's new first lady of bhangra.

⭐ **Kankan De Ohle**
Moviebox, UK

A soft blend of pure vocals and memorable bhangra rhythms from 2003.

Panjabi MC

A much-loved Birmingham producer and hip-hop/bhangra maestro who has produced numerous albums over the last decade – and of course the worldwide hit single "Mundian To Bach Ke".

⭐ **Dhol Jageero Da**
Moviebox, UK

Fans regard this 2000 album as one of his best.

Partners In Rhyme

Little is known about this publicity-shy production duo.

⊙ **Replay**
OSA, UK

Brilliant tunes incorporating bhangra/qawwali/Hindi grooves.

Jay Sean

This former medical student has gone on to develop a very successful career as a solo artist.

⊙ **Me Against Myself**
Relentless, UK

Sean's debut album shows him to be a fine lyricist, vocalist and beatboxer.

Sukshinder Shinda

Midlands-based bhangra hero: a superb vocalist, multi-instrumentalist and in-demand producer.

⊙ **Balle**
Kamlee, UK

His latest album (2005), which gained a great deal of acclaim internationally.

Tigerstyle

Scotland's only working production-outfit mix desi sounds with interesting Western grooves while adhering to hard-core Punjabi musical values.

⊙ **Virsa**
Kismet, UK

This 2002 album includes the dancefloor classic "Truck Jatt Da" – clubbers' delight!

119

Asian Overground

★ Anokha: Soundz of the Asian Underground
OMNI, UK

Talvin Singh's essential selection of classic early sounds from the mid-1990s includes cutting-edge producers like Osmani Soundz and State Of Bengal's "Flight IC 408" – one of the biggest British Asian dancefloor tunes ever. Singh appears on the cover in his parka. Pukka!

⊙ Eastern Drum & Breaks Vols 1 & 2
Nasha Records, UK

Asian drum'n'bass from 2004-5 by East End DJ/producers like Gesse and Osmani Soundz.

⊙ Essential Asian R&B
Outcaste, UK

This 2005 collection includes material from Rishi Rich and Raghav.

⊙ Outcaste Untouchable Beats Vols 1–5
Outcaste, UK

Fine collections spanning five years of the "Asian Underground" scene.

⊙ The Rough Guide To Asian Underground
World Music Network, UK

A trek through the golden age of this genre.

⊙ State Of The Nation
Nation, UK

A fine assortment of classics showing where this dependable label was at in 2004.

★ Untouchable Outcaste Beats – Volume 1
Outcaste Records, UK

A must-have compilation for anyone excited by the Asian "overground", this features classic tracks from forefathers of the genre (the late Amanda Shankar, Dave Pike Set) and upcoming acts such as Badmarsh & Shri and Niraj Chag. Volume 2, *Outcaste Too Untouchable*, is pretty essential too, including Massive Attack's remix of Nusrat Fateh Ali Khan's "Mustt Mustt", tracks from Cornershop, Badmarsh and Shri, and Nitin Sawhney, plus Ananda Shankari's version of "Jumping Jack Flash".

★ Urban Explosion
Sony/Warner

Much-applauded 2003 compilation featuring Asian and black artists such as General Levy, Missy Elliott and Dr Zeus. The first CD to showcase R&B and Asian artists side-by-side.

Tigerstyle

Apache Indian

Handsworth Punjabi star who found international fame in the early 1990s. Still a key player today.

★ Best Of
Spectrum, UK

Bhangra-muffin at its best. His new album, *Time For Change,* is well worth checking too.

James Asher

Brother of actress Jane Asher, this talented Indophile composer has made some exciting albums.

⊙ Tigers Of The Raj
New Earth, UK

Moving melodies including an interesting 1998 reworking of the prayer "Ragu Pathi Ram".

Asian Dub Foundation (ADF)

Radical dub/rap/trip-hop-influenced group of London and Birmingham musicians who back up their message with community educational work. Their unmistakable sound stems partly from guitarist Steve Chandrasonic tuning all his strings to one note, like a sitar, and speed-rapper Master D.

⊙ Rafi's Revenge
Slash, UK

Asian instrumentation meets jungle rhythms on this Mercury Prize-nominated release, with drum'n'bass, sitars, tablas and a ton of attitude backed by heavy breakbeats.

Joi

Brothers Farook and Haroon Shamsher emerged as the Joi Bangla Sound in the 1980s. Tragically, just as mainstream success beckoned, Haroon died suddenly in 1999 at the age of just 34.

★ One and One is One
Real World, UK

Excellent debut CD mixing trance, breakbeats and electro with powerful Asian melodies and chants.

Raghav

Raised in Calgary, Canada, the young Raghav is something of a heartthrob.

⊙ Storyteller
V2, UK

Gliding effortlessly between Hindi and English, Raghav's 2004 debut contains some sparkling hits.

Bally Sagoo

Birmingham-based DJ who turned producer/remixer in 1990 and has caused a huge stir ever since.

⊙ Star Crazy 1
OSA, UK

A 1991 production containing the ragga-bhangra blockbuster "Mera Laung Gawacha".

⊙ Bollywood Flashback
Sony, UK

Gorgeous R.D. Burman classics reworked by Sagoo in 1994.

Sangeeta

Leicester-based BT worker Sangeeta juggled her singing career around her full-time job for years after 1987, becoming one of the very few women to grace bhangra stages.

 Flower In The Wind
Keda, UK

Sangeeta's best CD, produced by Kuljit Bhamra in 1992.

Nitin Sawhney

This former accountant grew up in 1960s Kent. A skilled keyboardist and guitarist, he released his first album *Spirit Dance* on World Circuit Records.

 Migration
Outcaste, UK

Sawhney's critically acclaimed debut remains the prototype for its successors. A dash of flamenco, a touch of drum 'n'bass, and an Indo/jazz canvas.

Talvin Singh

Classically trained tabla-player Singh has forged an amazing reputation, working with Björk and Massive Attack, as well as running his own club and label. A key figure in British music at the end of the 1990s, he was awarded the Mercury Music Prize in 1999.

OK
Island, UK

Singh's award-winning debut solo album describes itself as "Music without boundaries" and proceeds through ambient and drum'n'bass by way of synths, flutes and sitars.

Taz

Starting out in the early 1990s as Johnny Zee, Taz had a massive hit with his debut *Hit The Deck*.

Slave II Fusion
Moviebox, UK

Cutting-edge pop circa 2000 from this timeless singer/songwriter.

Trickbaby

Steve Ager and former Radio One producer Saira Hussein have come up with a contemporary sound that merges their influences, from Led Zeppelin to Asha Bhosle.

⊙ **Hangin' Around**
Chachaman, UK

A kitsch 2003 take on Asian fusion.

PLAYLIST
England/UK | Bhangra/Asian Beat

1 **KORI Panjabi MC** from *Dhol Jageero Da*
Gidda track that intermittently slows down and speeds up, sending clubbers into a frenzy.

2 **MERA LAUNG GAWACHA Bally Sagoo** from *Star Crazy 1*
Bhangra-muffin classic by Rama and rapper Cheshire Cat. The title means "I've lost my nose-ring".

3 **PYAR KE HAI BAIRI Sangeeta** from *Flower In The Wind*
Her most popular song to date, with lyrics by Preet Nihal and music by Kuljit Bhamra. Here, Sangeeta sings in Hindi instead of the Punjabi customary in bhangra music.

4 **FLIGHT IC 408 State Of Bengal** from *Anokha: Soundz Of The Asian Underground*
Massive drum'n'bass tune with swirling sitars and frenetic tabla beats.

5 **NEELA Trickbaby** from *Hangin' Around*
Compelling, hypnotic East-West instrumental.

6 **PRAYER WHEEL James Asher** from *Tigers Of The Raj*
Beautiful reinterpretation of the prayer "ragu Pathi ram" (a favourite of Mahatma Gandhi), with sublime flutes and lilting percussion.

7 **BOR BOR Partners In Rhyme** from *Replay*
Bouncy bhangra at its best.

8 **FINGERS Joi** from *One and One Is One*
Trancey techno with a house vibe featuring vocals from Shusheela Raman and sitar.

9 **NACHANGEH SARI RAATH Taz** from *Slave II Fusion*
Hindi pop-house number with a Latin edge.

Finland

new runes

Kimmo Pohjonen
Milena Strange

In Finland's music, as in its other arts, there is a distinctive mix of tradition, classicism, striking or shy minimalism, bold experiment and self-mocking humour. Interest among young Finns in their traditional musics has burgeoned since the 1980s, and as a result names such as Värttinä, JPP, Maria Kalaniemi and Kimmo Pohjonen have become well known at home and created interest abroad. In recent years they have been followed by an emerging second wave of younger musicians. In addition, alongside Finland's notable contributions to the world's classical, pop, avant-garde and jazz musics, there's self-parodying humppa and the very Finnish adaptation of tango. **Andrew Cronshaw** takes a closer look.

Finland is a big, quiet place of lakes and forests, its flattish terrain only rising to mountains well north of the Arctic Circle. It is divided from all but the extreme north of the Scandinavian peninsula by the Gulf of Bothnia.

Politically and economically the country faces west, but its cultural ties tend to go east and south, towards the Balto-Finnic peoples within Russia and the Baltic states, particularly those in former parts of Finland and in Estonia. Indeed, Estonia is the only other country whose language is close enough in the Finno-Ugrian group to be mutually comprehensible with Finnish.

Finland hasn't existed as a state for long. It was ruled by Sweden until 1809, then by Russia until the Bolshevik revolution, when it painfully emerged after a war of independence and civil war. Part of the region of Karelia, a heartland of traditional culture, remained in the Soviet Union then, and more was lost to Russia between 1939 and 1944. Then the northern third of Finland was devastated by retreating German troops, who had been allowed in to fight Russia.

Peace with the USSR entailed the payment by Finland of huge reparations, but it has emerged as a highly technologized, orderly country with a standard of living in sharp contrast to that of today's Russia just across its forested eastern border.

Song: Runolaulu and Rekilaulu

A good deal of the rhythmic shape of all Finnish song (*laulu*) stems from two factors. First, in Finnish the stress is virtually always on the first syllable of the word – so lines pretty much have to begin with an accented beat, or at least with a verbal stress. Second, the length of a sound can affect the meaning of a word.

Until the seventeenth century, and in some areas much later, virtually all Finnish singing was of the **runolaulu** (literally "poem-song") form, of which close relatives are found throughout the Balto-Finnic area. The rhythm of the words of runolaulu is in most cases four-footed trochaic – four syllables per line are stressed – like this: "Dum-di Dum-di Dum-di Daa-daa". The tunes have a narrow range, usually using just the first five notes of a scale (major, minor or somewhere between). Time signatures are nearly always 4/4 or 5/4 and much of the melodic interest stems from variation of the melodic line. The line-ends don't rhyme, but there's strong alliteration, as there is in other ancient European poetry such as the Icelandic sagas or *Beowulf*.

Among runo-song there is a large body of epic poetry – tales of heroes such as Kullervo, Lemminkäinen and, centrally, Väinämöinen, who could control the forces of nature, sometimes holding all in thrall with his kantele-playing. It was these epics that doctor and folklorist **Elias Lönnrot** linked and organized to make **Kalevala** (sometimes called in English *The Kalevala*, but there's no definite or indefinite article in Finnish). Its first publication in 1835 didn't make much impression, but twenty years after the revised second edition appeared in 1849 it became the focal point for an awakening of Finnishness in a country dominated by Tsarist Russia, whose intellectuals were more likely to speak Swedish or Russian than the language in which it was written. *Kalevala*, and Lönnrot's second volume of runo-song, *Kantele-tar*, were the inspiration for further research and a great deal of monumental and romantic art, and became iconic in the emerging national identity. Karelia, where Lönnrot and others collected many of the *Kalevala* stories, came to represent the artistic soul of Finland.

It isn't all tales of epic deeds, however. There are runo-songs of everyday life, love and misery, many of them made and sung by women, such as the extraordinary sobbing *itku* (crying) songs, and lullabies sometimes even wishing for the merciful death of the infant. There were many songs, both happy and warning of sadness, associated with the biggest ritual occasion – the wedding. The other important ritual – death – was accompanied by singing as well, although laments tended to be more freeform than normal runolaulu.

In common with much of the old layer of song-poem throughout the Nordic countries, runo-songs were often danced. In Ingria (an area of constantly displaced population at the south of the Karelian Isthmus, north of St Petersburg) a more recent layer of **dance-song** is still performed, notably by the Röntyskä group from the village of Rappula.

As the present-day folk revival has progressed, there has been considerable interest among performers in the runo-song repertoire, its melodic and rhythmic character, and the possibilities of making new material on the old foundations. The work of Värttinä, for example, is very strongly shaped by runolaulu.

During the seventeenth century, rhyming in songs began to take over from alliteration; runolaulu evolved into **rekilaulu** (literally sleigh-song, but actually a round-dance song form with no particular sleigh connection). It has a very regular pattern, with four lines per stanza, the second and fourth lines rhyming.

In some areas, notably Karelia, the change was slower, partly because the dominant Christian religion was Orthodox. The Orthodox priests were often not Finnish speakers and showed little disapproval of their flocks' songs, whereas the Lutherans of the western regions shared their parishioners' background and tended to disapprove of "pagan" customs and songs; furthermore their worship involved rhyming hymns in stanzas. Although this worked against runo-song, another tradition evolved of distinctive Finnish hymns, neither runolaulu nor rekilaulu, which still exists and whose melodies have as yet been little heard in the folk music revival except in the work of **Sinikka Järvinen-Kontio**.

Right up to the present day, reki-song is common in popular Finnish songs. A form on which to hang new stories or improvise humour, with ready audience participation because of the tune's familiar structure, it was a prevalent pattern in the old-fashioned rural-comic songs of such singers as **Erkki Rankaviita**, as well as among Finnish-American performers in the early days of recording. It can still be heard in the songs of young bands such as **Tötterssön**, from the Kaustinen area of Central Ostrobothnia.

Kantele, Jouhikko and Other Old Instruments

Kalevala recounts how Väinämöinen made the first **kantele** from the jawbone of a giant pike, stringing it with hair from the Devil's gelding and, when that prototype was lost at sea, making the second from birch and a maiden's hair. The basic form of the actual instrument is a small tapering box, traditionally hollowed out of a single piece of wood. It bears five strings, once of horsehair or iron wire, now normally of steel, tuned to the first five notes of a diatonic scale, the same narrow pitch range as most runo-song tunes.

Unusually among stringed instruments, a kantele has no bridge or other direct contact between string and soundboard; the strings pass directly from a single metal anchoring bar at the narrow end to wooden tuning pegs at the other. Though that makes it comparatively inefficient in terms of volume, less of the strings' energy is absorbed by the soundboard so it produces a distinctive silvery ringing tone that's loud enough to carry in a quiet wooden house, particularly when the instrument rests on a table for added resonance.

Though the kantele is Finland's national instrument, closely related instruments are played in the Baltic states and among some of the peoples of northwest Russia.

The small kantele's role in the past was one of self-expression rather than performance; a player would immerse themselves in the rhythmic possibilities of those five notes. Three fingers of one hand and two of the other would play a string each or, in a style more common in the east and across the Baltic, one hand would damp while the other strummed.

During the last couple of centuries, as Finland absorbed musical styles with wider tonal ranges than runo-song and newer approaches to harmony, larger kanteles with more strings developed. On those with fifteen or more, the box is made not by carving but by gluing several boards together. Metal tuning pegs are used, and the common anchoring bar is replaced by an individual pin for each string.

These larger instruments and the new music called for changes in playing technique; the hands moved apart, and one tended to take the melody while the other played an accompaniment. Around the beginning of the twentieth century some players began to turn the instrument around so that the longer, lower-pitched strings were nearest to them. Turning it round never caught on in Central Ostrobothnia, however, where there is a vigorous style of playing dance music on big kantele. Notable players in this Perho River valley tradition include **Eino Tulikari** (1905–77) and the three **Alaspää brothers**.

In the Saarijärvi area of central Finland a different box-kantele design and playing style evolved, in which the strings are plucked with a pick held in the right hand while the left damps unwanted strings.

During the nineteenth century the big kanteles began to be used for performance to an audience, rather than just in the home, and in this period a Kaustinen woman, **Kreeta Haapasalo** (1815–93), gained national fame as a professional kantele performer. Kantele makers, teachers and tuition books appeared, and soon aspirations arose to play Western classical music on the kantele. That required a chromatic kantele, so in the 1920s Paul Salminen developed the "concert kantele", which has an elegant lever mechanism for lowering and raising the tension on particular strings. The most famous classical concert kantele player of the twentieth century was **Ulla Katajavuori**.

The five-string kantele remained as a cultural icon in the twentieth century, but it was played less and less. The work and recordings of **Martti Pokela**, beginning in the 1950s, were important in reawakening interest in the range of kanteles and their use in traditional music and improvisation.

Falun Folk Festival

Old-time kantele players

His work bridged the gap between classical and folk approaches; in 1975 he became the first teacher of kantele at Finland's national music university, the Sibelius Academy, and instigated the creation of a folk music department there. Assisted by some of the new generations of kantele players who graduated from that department, he continued to evolve his open-minded, innovative and witty compositions until not long before his death in 2007.

Another leading figure in bringing non-concert kanteles back into use is **Hannu Saha**, a fine player of small kanteles and of the large diatonic Perho-style instrument. Director of Finland's National Folk Music Institute, then artistic director of the national Folk Arts Centre, both of them in Kaustinen, he has spent some years as chairman of the Arts Council of Finland (imagine a folk musician being chairman of Arts Council England!) and is now Professor of the Sibelius Academy Folk Music Department. In the 1980s he set up a successful scheme to get kanteles into every school in Finland and to get them played, not just hung on the wall for history lessons. Around that time his appearance at Kaustinen festival with an ostentatiously (and at that time not very effectively) electrified five-string kantele was a mischievous challenge to the instrument's iconic image – a "banish stuffiness, back to the people" gauntlet.

As an instrument for present-day public performance, the kantele has had its problems. The big kanteles, and often the small ones too, are commonly played laid flat on a table, which means that when a player is on stage strings and hands are almost invisible to the audience. There's also the problem of audibility; quietness is a fundamental aspect of the instrument and its music, and it's hard to amplify without brutalizing the sound. But by the beginning of the twenty-first century kantele makers, in particular **Hannu Koistinen**, had begun to make tilted tables and well-electrified, re-engineered concert and small kanteles. New developments in sound and repertoire are gradually being made in the hands of skilled players such as **Timo Väänänen, Matti and Sinikka Kontio, Hannu Saha, Vilma Timonen, Arja Kastinen, Riitta Huttunen, Minna Raskinen, Anna-Karin Korhonen** and **Pauliina Syrjälä**. Each of these musicians tends to concentrate on a particular version of the instrument, from the small kanteles through Perho valley and Saarijärvi box kanteles to the big chromatic concert kantele and the recent electrified versions. Kantele is also increasingly popular as an instrument for accompanying singing.

The **jouhikko** is a bowed lyre, a Finnish variant of an instrument also found in neighbouring regions including Sweden and Estonia. Like the kantele, its exact origins are lost in the mists of Baltic history, but it persisted into the twentieth century in the eastern regions of Savo, Karelia and across the Russian border in Ingria.

Designs vary, but essentially it's a long box bearing usually three strings, made of twisted horse-hair and tuned in fifths. Holding it upright on the knee, the player shortens the sounding length of one (or, depending on the instrument's design and the player's technique, occasionally two) of the strings by

125

touching them with the back of the fingers of their left hand, reaching from the back of the instrument through a slot in its body. The remaining strings act as drones. The short bow is finger-tensioned and usually arched. The jouhikko's tone is whispery and dry, melody against chugging drone. Making and playing of the instrument has been revived recently; **Rauno Nieminen** almost single-handedly returned the jouhikko to use in the 1970s, and continues to research the old instruments and build new ones. In 1916 key Finnish ethnomusicologist A.O. Väisänen made recordings of jouhikko player Feodor Pratšu, from Impilahti on the Karelian Isthmus; these have been a particular influence on today's players, including Nieminen's colleagues in the all-jouhikko quartet **Jouhiorkesteri**.

Another significant category of old Finnish instruments is a variety of wind instrument – trumpets, whistles and clarinets – usually made of wood bound with birch-bark. An important carrier into the modern age of the making and playing of such instruments was Ingrian-born shepherd Feodor Safronoff (1886–1962), known as **Teppo Repo**. Among present-day players, **Etnopojat/The World Mänkeri Orchestra** make new music using the old instruments, such as the *mänkeri* and *liru* clarinets, whose construction they explore in their workshop in Nakkila.

Simon Broughton

Jouhiorkesteri playing in a log hut in Karelia

Pelimanni Music: Fiddling and Harmoniums

Pelimanni (from the Swedish *spelman*) means "folk musician", and the term is particularly applied to players of folk dance music. **Pelimanni music** and

its dances are a much more recent development than the runo-song layer of Finnish music. The first couple dances to become popular, in the seventeenth century, were the minuet and polska. By 1800 the waltz had arrived, followed by the polka, mazurka and *schottische*. All of these developed a Finnish character – on the whole rather restrained. The Finnish polska, for example, has none of the rhythmic complexity of the Swedish version. Later developments and imports included *humppa* and *jenkka*.

Weddings were always the major and most relished social occasions, and presented the biggest opportunity for dance. Special music was associated with the almost theatrical sequence of events in the traditional wedding celebration – both songs and instrumental music, including marches for processions, happy dance tunes and sad ones for the bride's leaving. The **fiddle** (*viulu*), which arrived in the mid-seventeenth century, became the main instrument for dance music. When the **accordion** – first the one- or two-row diatonic (*hanuri*), then the larger chromatic versions (*haitari* or *harmonikka*) – spread throughout Europe in the nineteenth century the fiddle was to some extent drowned out.

In some places, however, the fiddle remained strong. Mixed ensembles developed towards the end of the nineteenth century; in the fiddle-favouring Kaustinen area the standard line-up for wedding bands became one or more fiddles, a double bass and a harmonium. A pedal-powered reed organ that effectively bridges the pitch gap between fiddles and double bass, the harmonium continues to be a key instrument, not just in pelimanni music but in the other musics of today's folk-rooted musicians. It isn't played in a lugubrious churchy way, but is pumped energetically, with the keys stabbed so forcefully that they jump, giving a tune-impelling brisk staccato over chunky chords.

Kaustinen

Inevitably, when talking about pelimanni music, indeed in any discussion of current Finnish roots music, the name of a group of small townships on the Perho River in Keski-Pohjanmaa (Central Ostrobothnia) comes up regularly – **Kaustinen**.

Early in the twentieth century, Santeri Isokangas's coffee-shop in Kaustinen was a place where music was encouraged; there was a harmonium, and a fiddle hung on the wall ready for use. The fiddlers of Kaustinen, Veteli and Halsua, such as **Friiti Ojala** and **Antti Järvelä**, would gather there. **Konsta Jylhä**'s mother worked in the coffee-shop, his family played music; it was natural he would too.

In 1946 the church organist Eero Polas assembled a ten-piece band for weddings, including Konsta. They played the suites of seven to twelve linked dances known as *purppuri* (pot-pourri), and so took the name **Purppuripelimannit**. By the 1950s the line-up had resolved to the typical Ostrobothnian wedding band format of two fiddles, harmonium and double bass, and it made recordings and radio appearances. In 1961 Konsta, who worked as a lorry driver, had a road accident which stopped him playing the fiddle for a while, so he began writing songs and tunes. His first effort, "Konstan Parempi Valssi" (Konsta's better waltz), became popular, and many others followed before his death in 1984.

The 1960s was a boom time for roots discovery and in 1968 Kaustinen staged the first **Kaustinen International Folk Music Festival**. Local music and dance were strongly represented, particularly the now famous Purppuripelimannit, but the festival also brought in guests from abroad. It was clear the Finnish folk revival had begun: twenty thousand people came, and the number doubled a year later. (The Woodstock character in the Finnish version of the *Peanuts* cartoon strip is called Kaustinen.) In a country whose population has moved relatively recently from the countryside to the towns, and whose old family homes have become its summer cottages, Kaustinen Festival gave a focus for celebration of the old ways and the old fun. Striped-waistcoated pelimannit showed up from all over Finland, joined by both the older generation and the newly interested youth. The festival has become a showplace for new projects in Finnish music, spiced by top musicians and dance groups from abroad, but still very much centred on local music and dance.

In 1974 a fine old wooden log house was bought and reconstructed atop a rise on the festival site to become Pelimannitalo, the headquarters of **Kansanmusiikki-instituutti (KMI)**, the national Folk Music Institute, which has a leading role not only in research but also in encouraging and propagating roots music, publishing many recordings and books.

In 1997 the Institute moved to the new national **Folk Arts Centre (Kansantaiteenkeskus)**, a high-tech complex in a cavern blasted through a nearby hillside. It includes a four-hundred-seat concert hall, recording studio, folk instrument museum and workshop, plus rehearsal rooms and the offices of the folk music festival and of the state-salaried folk group **Tallari**. There's also a shop, a restaurant and of course, this being Finland, a sauna. The centre hosts not just folk music but also local concerts, an annual chamber music festival and exhibitions of folk and "outsider" art.

Kaustinen revolves around music. Its high school has a music focus, and there are summer folk music courses and links with folk music courses in colleges across Finland. The local community is extraordinarily musically active. There's a costumed wedding choir and local fiddle bands, including Purppuripelimannit and young high-energy folk bands such as **Tötterssön**. The folk dance group **Ottoset** has its own bands and has now expanded to several age groups, each teaching the one below; it regularly spawns professional dancers and choreographers. **Mauno Järvelä**, a member of the band JPP, teaches fiddle to local children so successfully that a band of over two hundred current and past pupils – **Näppärit** (the nippers) – can be amassed; many of them are or are becoming well-known as folk or classical players themselves.

Music has become Kaustinen's major industry, but it isn't commercial or corporate; it's still a thing of individual musicians and their delight in playing together. And just as Konsta Jylhä grew up in the local music and developed it, so have succeeding generations, bringing remarkable new levels of fiddling and compositional skill while remaining strongly connected to the tradition. The first big new step came with the band JPP.

JPP and Onwards

The parish of Järvelä is within walking distance of Kaustinen, along the Perho River, and there at the beginning of the 1980s young members of the fiddling families Järvelä and Varila were playing with the oldsters in the band **Järvelän Pelimannit**. (It's common in agricultural Ostrobothnia for village names and family names to be the same.) They were joined by harmonium player **Timo Alakotila** from Nurmijärvi, way down south near Helsinki. Gradually the youngsters, who became known as **Järvelän Pikkupelimannit**, "the little musicians of Järvelä", or JPP for short, set out on their own, winning their first award as a group in 1982.

That same year a band from Sweden, the trio **Forsmark Tre**, appeared at Kaustinen Festival. They had a line-up similar to that of JPP, of fiddles and harmonium, but rather than playing straight unison as in the Finnish wedding bands their two fiddlers revelled in harmony. Seeing them spurred JPP to explore something similar with Kaustinen music, and it was a turning point. The band metamorphosed into a swingy string orchestra, still with the wedding-band instrumentation but using twisting key changes and an increasing number of new tunes, written by Alakotila and by fiddlers **Mauno Järvelä** and his nephew **Arto Järvelä**. JPP became, and remains, Finland's flagship fiddle band, and a big influence on the next wave of even more skilled players, many of them graduates of Mauno Järvelä's Näppärit fiddle-education programme. The fourth generation of fiddlers from the Järvelä family are among the most notable: Mauno's son **Esko Järvelä**, daughter **Alina Järvelä** and nephew **Antti Järvelä** all play in the hot fiddle band **Frigg**, which comprises five Finns and two Norwegians. The Kaustinen tradition is open-ended, continuous not only with classical music but with pop, jazz and rock; notable among those exploring these latter paths are fiddlers **Ville Kangas** and **Ville Ojanen**.

Kaustinen doesn't have a monopoly on fiddlers and bands taking pelimanni music far beyond; leading fiddlers of the new generation from elsewhere include **Piia Kleemola**, **Suvi Oskala** and **Emilia Lajunen**, who work together in the beautifully choreographed fiddling-while-dancing group **Silmu** as well as independently in a slew of the most interesting and innovative current bands including **Hyperborea**, the **Auvo Quartet**, **Polka Chicks**, **Avertere**, **Spontaani Viire**, **Kirjava Lintu** and **Suo**.

The Karelian Sound

Meanwhile, on the other side of Finland, in Karelia up against the Russian border, another sound and scene was developing. It was in this area that many of the runo-songs had been collected, but by the end of the twentieth century the old traditions had dwindled. In 1983, in the village of Rääkkylä, teenage sisters **Mari** and **Sari Kaasinen** formed a youth group to sing traditional songs and play kanteles and accordions. Much of the material they sang was found by their mother in books. The group, **Värttinä** (meaning spindle), grew to about twenty members, dressed in local traditional costume. Their singing was enthusiastic and very unsophisticated, but on the Finnish folk revival scene it was a distinctive sound and during that decade they made two albums, the second of which created considerable interest in Finland and abroad.

In 1990 many members left to continue their education, and the group was rebuilt smaller, with five female singers and a six-piece backing band. The first album from the new line-up, *Oi Dai*, reached number three in the Finnish pop charts and Värttinä became a big name, surprising the modern audience with the female strength and earthiness of traditional lyrics. Since then, moving through several more line-up changes, there have been a string of albums and international success, and the band has grown into a stronger and stronger live act. It has also become involved in

Aki Paavola

JPP

such unexpected projects as co-writing with **A.R. Rahman** the music for the lavish stage musical version of *The Lord of the Rings*.

Värttinä have progressed from using traditional material to writing their own. Their early material was mainly in reki-song form, but more recently they have moved on from the very limited rhythmic and rhyming patterns of reki-song, to explore the much older runo-song style. The very distinctive Värttinä vocal sound has also evolved, with Bulgarian vocal influences now showing through. Though it's not obvious, the instrumental accompaniments have been considerably inspired by bluegrass.

Of the original 1983 members, only singer Mari Kaasinen and wind and bouzouki player **Janne Lappalainen** remain among the current three singers and six-piece backing band.

As well as welcoming performers from across Finland, Rääkkylä's **Kihaus Folk Music Festival** in July is a showcase for the latest projects of musicians and bands with roots in the area, including singer, accordionist and fiddler **Pauliina Lerche**, the band **Burlakat** and of course present and former members of Värttinä.

Swedish Finland

Six percent of the Finnish population speak Swedish as their first language, and the masses of islands in the Gulf of Bothnia – Ahvenanmaa/Åland and the Turku/Åbo archipelago – as well as parts of west-coast Finland are mainly Swedish in language and culture. Indeed, well into the twentieth century these areas harboured aspects of old song and tradition that had become rare in Sweden itself. A collection of music, song, dance and custom in many volumes has been published by Svenska Litteratursällskapet i Finland, and the Finnish-Swedish folk music research and propagation institute **Finlands Svenska Folkmusikinstitut** is located in the

Finnish city of Vaasa. The band **Gjallarhorn**, also based in the Vaasa area, has toured internationally with its powerful music rooted in Finlands-Svensk ballad and instrumental tradition. There are also a number of fiddle-led spelman groups, and other notable performing groups include the trio of **Mikael Fröjdö**, **Görel Särs** and **Niklas Nyqvist** and the all-female fiddle band **Jepokryddona**.

Tango and Humppa

Tango reached Finland, as it did the rest of Europe, in the 1920s. But while in other countries its popularity has, like other dance crazes, ebbed and flowed, in Finland it took strong root, particularly during World War II, and has made its way into Finnish tradition to become part of the standard pelimanni repertoire. In doing so it has changed: Finnish tango is usually in a minor key, the *bandoneon* is replaced by an accordion, the dancing is generally unspectacular, often not much more than a slow shuffle, and the lyrics are sentimental, yearningly mournful, often about lost love and the bitter-sweet beauties of the Finnish countryside.

In some ways it's a sort of Finnish country music; the biggest names among tango singers have risen from, or are identified with, tough working-class roots. Its first and most famous star, **Olavi Virta**, had a wartime hit and went on to make over five hundred records and several films, before a tragic alcoholic decline that saw him jailed for drunk driving in 1962. His lifestyle caught up with him in 1972, but his name, rich baritone and most popular songs – some of the first ones Argentinian but later mostly Finnish originals – are still well known by just about every Finn. In the 1960s tango managed to compete with the Beatles and other international pop, with hits such as "Satumaa", sung by **Reijo Taipale**.

These days, many of tango's new names first reach a substantial public at summer outdoor dances, the biggest of which is the huge **Tango-markkinat festival** in the south Ostrobothnian town of Seinäjoki in early July; the crowning there of a new young tango king and queen each year makes the national newspaper front pages.

It is sometimes said, by Finns themselves, that it's in the Finnish national character to champion the underdog, however under that dog might get. The very Finnish downbeat humour in the films of **Aki Kaurismäki** is perhaps a self-deprecatory overstatement, but it's also to be found in the ironic celebration of big suits and drinking that is today's **humppa** scene. Humppa, which, with the slower but very musically similar *jenkka*, features occasionally in the repertoires of pelimanni groups, is a Finnish dance music descended from the German variant of the originally Czech polka. In humppa bands it is a musically unsubtle thing typically played on accordion with an insistent two-beat rhythm pounded out by bass guitar and drums. The lyrics are usually comedic, and the songs often parodies of popular hits; humppa band **Eläkeläiset** (The Pensioners) is admittedly more ironic than some but its song titles give the gist: "Humppa Dancing and Widow Charming", "Hip-Hip Hurry Up to the Liquor Store", "I'm Dancing With the Lower Half of My Body On Fire…"

Accordion and harmonicas

The **accordion**, be it **diatonic** (one or two rows of melody buttons, one note on the push, another on the pull) or **chromatic** (same note either way, with either piano keys or buttons) has been as ubiquitous in Finland as elsewhere, and not necessarily highly regarded. But a couple of Finnish accordionists in particular have become known at home and abroad for their skill and innovation: **Maria Kalaniemi** and **Kimmo Pohjonen**.

Both come from a folk music background, and have facility on other instruments including

"Study familiar culture as if it was exotic"

So said **Heikki Laitinen**, professor of folk music at the **Sibelius Academy**. Kantele master **Martti Pokela**'s presence at the Academy was instrumental in the setting up in 1983 of a folk music degree course there. His influence, and the charismatic, free-thinking approach of Heikki Laitinen, himself a powerful singer and vocal performance artist uniting deep tradition with the avant-garde, have made it a highly creative place in which to carry through Laitinen's mission statement "to learn the old styles of playing and singing and to break through all perceived limits to create the folk music of the future".

It's a testimony to the success of the course that, despite its annual intake being just six students, the majority of the musicians mentioned in this chapter's discography have studied there. Other music colleges around Finland now also have folk music courses, each a focus for ever-increasing skill and creativity.

diatonic accordion, but they are best known for their work on the big five-row chromatic button accordion, in Kalaniemi's case sometimes the so-called "free-bass", where the left-hand buttons play single bass notes rather than chords. Kalaniemi is noted for her extreme subtlety, in material drawing on Finnish tradition, the highly developed tango of Astor Piazzolla, avant-garde music and her own compositions. Pohjonen has developed an extraordinary *son et lumière* approach, using loops and delays to create a massive churning, spinning wall of accordion sounds combined with dramatic lighting, movement and body language. He has expanded that approach to work with other musicians, including a sampling percussionist, jazz saxophonist, rock guitarists and symphony orchestras, and to performance events in the countryside duetting with farm machinery.

Johanna Juhola is now achieving as major a profile as Pohjonen and Kalaniemi with very individual, exciting approaches that take the button-key chromatic to new heights of skill, inventive composition, visual performance and novel uses of electronics.

Button-key chromatic rather than piano-accordion is the instrument of choice of most of Finland's leading players, including **Hannu Kella**

of Tsuumi Sound System. **Markku Lepistö**, who led the influential band Pirnales and now, as well as solo projects, is a member of a string of bands including Värttinä and Progmatics, plays it too, but chooses diatonic accordion (known in the UK as a melodeon) in duos with mandolinist Petri Hakala and bassist Pekka Lehti. **Antti Paalanen** favours the one- and two-row diatonics, too, in his duo work with harmonica player Eero Turkka and in bands including Hyperborea. A rising name to watch, also on diatonic, is **Terhi Puronaho**.

Though the accordion takes up all his time these days, Kimmo Pohjonen plays that other free-reed instrument, the harmonica, and at the Sibelius Academy he taught **Jouko Kyhälä**, for whom the small instrument became a passion. He in turn was teaching **Eero Turkka** when, for an exam, the two of them put together the quartet **Sväng**, which makes a big, complete sound using just harmonicas, in a range from diatonic through chordal down to bass. It has rapidly become very popular in Finland and abroad with its dazzling, witty, largely self-composed material.

Finnish Roma

Particularly striking on city streets are Finnish Roma women in long, hip-padded black velvet skirts and bright, waisted blouses. In much of Europe, aspects of traditional music which have all but disappeared in the country as a whole have been preserved among Roma musicians, and that's true in Finland too, where Roma singing has been an influence on many of the present generation of Finnish revival singers.

The older Roma songs, and many of the new, are in a minor mode with a characteristic Eastern-sounding dip of a semitone or tone onto the last note of the melody. The prevailing singing style is lyrical, slightly swooping – remarkably similar to that of Scotland's traveller singers such as Belle Stewart. Horsemanship, prison, love and remembrance of lost friends are frequent themes in the lyrics, which are mostly in Finnish but occasionally in Romanes. The warm but sad-sounding delivery comes close to that of the older Finnish tango singers, among whom Roma have sometimes figured.

The leading Roma singer today is **Hilja Grönfors**, who, feeling she might be the end of the line, not only sings her own repertoire but adds to it, collecting whatever songs she can find before they disappear. Indeed there seems to be little interest in these songs among the next generation of Finnish Roma, but Hilja is a magnificent role model who might yet find that others follow her example.

Festivals

The easiest way to find live Finnish roots music in quantity, and to get a sense of how it fits into the community, is to go to a festival. The biggest one, with many Finnish traditional and roots-progressive musicians and dance spectacles, plus some major foreign performers, is **Kaustinen**, in west central Finland southwest of Kokkola, which runs for nine days in mid-July. **Haapavesi**, a couple of hundred kilometres northeast of Kaustinen, is at the turn of June into July, while **Kihaus**, at Rääkkylä in Karelia south of Joensuu, is in early July; both of these have a mix of Finnish and foreign performers and run courses and workshops in traditional music. **Tangomarkkinat**, the big tango event, is at Seinäjoki in western Finland, about fifty kilometres southeast of Vaasa, in early July.

Finland has a large number of other music and arts festivals, some of which occasionally feature aspects of the music described in this chapter. They take place mainly during the short summer, when even south of the Arctic Circle the daylight – and hence the music – lasts nearly all night. The summer weather is usually warm, but can be wet.

The Sámi

The **Sámi** are a highly significant group, both culturally and musically. Sámiland runs across the northern parts of Norway, Sweden and Finland and on into northwest Russia, and has its own section in this book, but suffice it here to say that Sámi musicians of Finnish nationality include **Wimme Saari**, **Angelit**, **Ulla Pirttijärvi** and the late **Nils-Aslak Valkeapää**.

Good sources of Finnish CDs include Digelius Music in Helsinki (*www.digelius.com*) and CDRoots in the US (*www.cdroots.com*).

★ Arctic Paradise
Arctic, Finland

The Finnish Music Information Centre has put out a series of more or less annual compilations from recent albums by Finnish roots performers. They're promos, so not in the shops, but they are excellent if you can get hold of them.

★ Finnischer Tango: Tule Tanssimaan
Trikont, Germany

The definitive album to illustrate the strange history of Finnish tango. The choice of its 24 tracks – from a range of labels and sources from 1915 to 1998 – is spot on, and the booklet is rich with human stories.

⊙ The Kalevala Heritage
Ondine, Finland

These field recordings of singers in Finland, Karelia and Ingria, dating from between 1905 (the oldest recordings of Finnish folklore) and 1967, are drawn from the archive of SKS, the Finnish Literature Society. Lönnrot made *Kalevala* from songs such as these, which tell of Väinämöinen, Lemminkäinen, the first kantele, the birth of fire and everyday life in another world which to us is drifting away but which these singers still inhabited.

⊙ Tulikulkku
KMI, Finland

A surprise fiftieth birthday present from many of Finnish new roots' finest to the man who has carried through a vision of the folk music of the future, Heikki Laitinen. In prime form are Me Naiset, Hedningarna, Arja Kastinen, Martti Pokela with Pirnales, Niekku, Virpi Forsberg, Etnopojat, Tuulenkantajat, Väinönputki, Wimme Saari, Hannu Saha ironically setting fire to a kantele (literally) with Primo, and the unsuspecting birthday boy, howling in the street with Suomussalmi-ryhmä.

Nikolai Blad

With his quirky, dryly humorous manner, ingenious original music and unusual and compelling singing of vivid, often surrealist, lyrics, Blad deserves to be recognized as a national treasure.

⊙ Nikolai Blad
EiNo, Finland

In songs whose wit, musical interest and variety of approach transmit even to non-Finnish speakers, Blad is supported by Tapani Varis (double bass and overtone flute), mandolinist Jarmo Romppanen and a team of folk luminaries.

Eläkeläiset

"The Pensioners" – an ironic, and long-established, humppa band. Their website, *www.humppa.com*, says plenty, and has whole-track MP3s.

⊙ Humppa!
Stupido, Finland

If you must go further, here's a compilation of 21 of their songs, including a humppamedia video…

Frigg

The Kaustinen-rooted fiddle band of the next generation, with Norwegian connections too. It comprises Mauno Järvelä's fiddling offspring Esko and Alina, their cousin Antti on bass, guitarist and *dobro* player Tuomas Logrén and player of frets and Estonian bagpipe Petri Prauda, with two of Norway's finest young fiddlers, Gjermund and Einar Olav Larsen.

★ Keidas/Oasis/Oase
Frigg, Finland

Frigg's 2005 second album features impeccable harmonizing by four fiddles, plus bagpipes, dobro, chamber orchestra and church organ, in new and traditional tunes, often zippy but also including the stately Kaustinen classic "Hintrikki Peltoniemi's Funeral March".

Gjallarhorn

This strong Finlands-Svensk band features singer-fiddler Jenny Wilhelms in ringing dance-tunes and epic ballads from the tradition of Finland's Swedish-speaking minority.

★ Sjofn
Vindauga, Finland

The band's second album, released in 2000. Hugely impressive, very well produced, with strong melodies, microtonal singing, interweaving fiddle and viola, rippling, barking didgeridoo and deep drums, it strikes an exquisite balance between beauty and guts.

Hilja Grönfors

For years Finnish Rom Hilja has been ploughing a fairly lonely furrow gathering and performing Finnish Rom songs. Her singing has appealing and unassuming warmth, poise and musicality, and the sliding, song-embracing style that evokes Balkan Roma and Scottish traveller singers.

⊙ Phurane Mirits: Songs of the Finnish Roma
Global Music Centre, Finland

Over the last few years Hilja has been encouraged and awarded by the Finnish folk music scene, whose singers have often covered Roma songs, and from that connection has emerged this band of accordion, violins, guitars, mandolin and bass. Songs of sorrow and longing, foaming wine and poverty, white horses stirring flurries of snow, golden cups, pine forest, happy childhood turning to bitter tears, love cut off by the tolling bells of death. But it's a beautiful sorrow, and the music floats and skips with the vitality and charm of a remarkable and striking woman.

Hedningarna

At core a Swedish band, but with Finnish singers – in its prime they were Sanna Kurki-Suonio and Tellu Turkka (then Tellu Paulasto) – Hedningarna's music of churning drones, bowed strings and gutsy percussion was mightily powerful and popular in the 1990s.

⊙ Karelia Visa
Silence, Sweden/NorthSide, US
Hedningarna's other albums are covered in the Swedish chapter, but for this 1999 album the band took a trip to Finnish Karelia for inspiration and the result is very runo-song-oriented.

Hiien Hivuksista

An assembly of ten of the leading jouhikko players in Finland, including jouhikko revival pioneers Rauno Nieminen and Jouni Arjava, plus Outi Pulkkinen, Tytti Metsä, Piia Kleemola, Eero Turkka and others.

⊙ Hiien Hivuksista
KMI, Finland
The whispery sound of horsehair strings driven by horsehair bow haunts this CD, as the group play their own compositions as well as tunes from Feodor Pratšu and other traditional sources. The performers play both individually and in groups, occasionally joined by Jew's harp, liru, nyckelharpa, *cittern*, harmonium, drum or voice.

Sinikka Järvinen and Matti Kontio

Two key figures in contemporary kantele.

⊙ Kantele Duo: Finnish Folk and Favourites
Ondine Octopus, Finland
Ignore its dull title – this is extremely skilful playing of duets on chromatic concert kanteles. The duo use a range of techniques (including train impersonations) largely on their own compositions.

JPP

JPP is the mother-ship of today's Kaustinen fiddle music, and much-travelled worldwide. Today's line-up is Arto Järvelä, Mauno Järvelä, Matti Mäkelä and Tommy Pyykönen (fiddles), Timo Alakotila (harmonium) and Antti Järvelä (double bass).

★ String Tease
RockAdillo, Finland
This 1998 release comprises largely new compositions – it's a living tradition – by Alakotila and Arto Järvelä.

⊙ Devil's Polska/Pirun Polska
Olarin, Finland/Xenophile, US
JPP's 1992 "greatest hits" album is also recommended for a sense of the evolution of their distinctive twist to Kaustinen tunes. Polkas, polskas, waltzes and more, including of course a tango.

Johanna Juhola

Juhola takes the button-key chromatic to new heights of skill, excitement and inventive composition, projecting the visual aspects of performance and using electronics in novel ways. Her involvements include bands Troka, Spontaani Vire, Tango Orchestra Unto and las Chicas del Tango, duos with violinist Pekka Kuusisto and pianist Milla Viljamaa, and the Johanna Juhola Trio with guitarist Roope Aarnio and sound designer Hannu Oskala.

AS KRAFT

⊙ Max Höjd
Texicalli, Finland
Kraft, the duo of Juhola and classical violinist and folk fiddler Pekka Kuusisto, make wild genre-unrestricted live music, adding electronics and a toy piano to accordion and acoustic or electric violin.

Konsta Jylhä

Konsta Jylhä died in 1984, but his spirit is still strong in Finnish fiddling. Even so, he himself was more composer and band leader than virtuoso.

⊙ Finnish Folk Music Vol. 2 – Kaustisen Purppuripelimannit & Konsta Jylhä
Finlandia, Finland
Recorded between 1970 and 1972, this CD by Konsta and his band Purppuripelimannit includes many of the most well-known Kaustinen tunes, the majority written by Konsta.

Maria Kalaniemi

Maria Kalaniemi is Finland's subtlest accordionist, drawing together threads from runo-song to Astor Piazzolla on five-row button accordion, using both chordal and free-bass techniques. Her fluid playing, extremely skilled but never showy, is far from the brashness often associated with accordions; she radiates a focused intensity.

⊙ Bellow Poetry
Aito, Finland
Probably her most satisfying album to date (and the first of her own on which she sings). Virtually all her own composition, but shaped by the runo-song, pastoral and Roma music of Finland. It's reflective, surging, slow-unfolding. Favouring an attractive, pure tone, she explores the melodic lines with a technical mastery and modesty that says "listen to this music" rather than "see how smart this is".

Arja Kastinen

Kastinen sits hunched on the floor, the fifteen-string kantele propped on one foot, building a web of chiming strings as a single candle measures time until it flickers out and the silvery ringing dies away.

⊙ Kantele Meditation
Finlandia Innovator, Finland
Touching the soul of the old way of kantele music, this consists of a single improvisation. (Previously issued as *Iro*.)

Sanna Kurki-Suonio

A singer of great live presence and subtlety, Kurki-Suonio was one of the two original Finnish singers in Hedningarna, and has since worked on her own projects, as well as guesting with Norwegian Sámi band Transjoik and others.

★ Musta
Zengarden, Finland/Northside, US
This, her 1998 solo album, contains some remarkable singing, from silky to ululating, full of intense energy. These new songs are shaped by the scale-forms, lyrics and inexorable rhythms of the runo-song tradition while moving freely among techno tools.

Pirnales

An excellent, under-exposed band led by another of Finland's leading five-row and diatonic accordionists,

Markku Lepistö, with kantele player Sinikka Järvinen (now Kontio) and fiddler Marianne Maans. Originally a quartet with a strong component of kantele exploration and some vocals, it later reformed as an instrumental septet with greater emphasis on robust dance music.

⊙ **Aquas**
KMI, Finland
Innovative developments of music drawn from tradition and band compositions, with kantele guests Martti Pokela and Hannu Saha.

Kimmo Pohjonen

He's originally a folk player, and still an excellent one, but what began as an experiment – running his five-row accordion through loop-sampling electronics – has taken Pohjonen into uncharted realms for the accordion, of performance art, lighting spectacle and collaborations with samplers, percussionists and orchestras.

⊙ **Kielo**
RockAdillo, Finland
You have to be there to get the full point of a Pohjonen show; solo in particular he's magnetic. This doesn't fully come across on CD, but here's his first, solo, album from 1999. It's not folk music, but it's certainly deeply Finnish. For visuals, try the DVD *Kalmuk*, made of his project with the Tapiola Sinfonietta.

Martti Pokela

The most influential figure, as player, composer and motivator, in modern kantele.

★ **Tuulikumpu**
KMI, Finland
Still-fresh Pokela recordings from the 1950s and 60s, including traditional pieces on the big diatonic kantele of his native Haapavesi, explorations of the sound of old kanteles in the Finnish National Museum (including Elias Lönnrot's own twenty-string kantele), some of his atmospheric kantele and voice music for ballet, and the title opus, which typifies Pokela's approach of combining fine kantele playing with innovation and witty avant-gardism.

⊙ **Snow Kantele: Sámi Suite**
Warner Finlandia Innovator, Finland
A 1997 CD in which younger players Timo Väänänen, Sari Kauranen, Matti and Sinikka Kontio and Pokela himself play his new compositions, mainly on big chromatic concert kanteles, with a touch of five-string, jouhikko and saw, plus occasional wordless vocals from Anna-Kaisa Liedes and Maija Karhinen.

Hannu Saha

A member of several of the formative groups of the Finnish revival, including Mummi Kutoo, Primo and Salamakannel, long-time director of the Folk Music Institute, artistic director of the national Folk Arts Centre, chairman of Finland's Arts Council and now professor of folk music at the Sibelius Academy, Saha is a key, free-thinking innovator and skilful kantele player.

⊙ **Mahla**
KMI, Finland
A wide-ranging collection of Saha compositions, and some trad, played on kanteles from 5- to 36-stringed diatonic, including some strung with carbon-fibre for the dry, horsehair sound. He's joined by singers Sanna Kurki-Suonio, Heikki Laitinen and Aija Puurtinen and instrumentalists including

Kimmo Pohjonen, Arto Järvelä, bassist Timo Myllykangas, a Kaustinen string quartet, Ville Kangas' electric bouzouki and, on Sibelius's "Finlandia Hymn", Hasse Walle's soaring electric guitar.

Suden Aika

A four-member largely unaccompanied female vocal group formed by Tellu Turkka. The line-up has changed since the first album.

⊙ **Suden Aika**
KMI, Finland
Stark and magnificent, this is the story, in resonant runo-song images, of a woman's birth, entrapment and quest for her own life. It unfolds through the intertwining voices, moving between silky and hard-edged, of Tellu, Sanna Kurki-Suonio, Liisa Matveinen and Pia Rask, with Outi Pulkkinen, Anita Lehtola and Swedish percussionist Tina Johansson.

Sväng

This hot harmonica quartet – Jouko Kyhälä, Eero Turkka, Eero Grundström and Pasi Leino – make a big sound. No other instrument is used, but the group employ the full range of harmonicas, from small diatonic and chromatic through keyed chord-harmonica to bass.

⊙ **Sväng**
Aito, Finland
What elevates a neat idea into something with more substance is the quality and variety of the band's material and arrangements. Opening with two Turkka originals – a snappy 7/8 tune in Romanian style and a tango – they move through tunes of Finnish, Russian, Romanian, US and Swedish extraction, finishing with Turkka's cartoonish "Svängtime Rag".

Pauliina Syrjälä

Pauliina plays a Saarijärvi kantele, which looks like one of the older form of box kanteles with a rounded stern but only about twenty strings. The brisk and intricate style of playing, using a pick rather than the fingers, had nearly died out; Syrjälä, who is now head of Kaustinen's folk music college, is one of the very few to specialize in it, and she's taking it to new heights.

⊙ **Monet Nävöt**
Own label, Finland
Six tracks, mostly her own compositions, based on improvisation but strongly structured. Using traditional and innovative techniques, she gets a remarkable range of strong, exciting sounds out of the instrument, rippling clusters, ringing harmonics, abrasive chopping, koto-like bent notes, scratching, clicking and wonderfully deep chiming bass. One of the very few recordings featuring Saarijärvi kantele, and one of the most interesting and impressive kantele recordings available.

Tallari

This state-salaried Kaustinen-based group was formed in 1986 to display the styles and instruments of Finnish folk music. Leading singers and musicians pass through it, joining core members Antti Hosioja, Ritva Talvitie, Timo Valo and Risto Hotakainen.

⊙ **Lunastettava Neito**
KMI, Finland
This 1990 album illustrates the range of Finno-Ugrian musics, and features one of Wimme Saari's most magnificent recorded moments, his soaring *joik* (Sámi song form, see p.350)

accompanied by a magical arrangement of bowed strings over shifting harmonium and bass drones.

Töttersсön

Kaustinen's current top folk-thrash band. Local youth heroes, they're great players, fiddling with mad energy while singing songs in Ostrobothnian dialect. Fronted by Suggs-like singer-fiddler Kyösti Järvelä, with two more fiddles, Frigg's Esko Järvelä on hard-smacked harmonium, and guitar and bass, they're like a manic, shout-singing JPP. Wild and witty, they play brilliantly and tight in the joyful, top-string-celebrating Kaustinen style, unafraid of crass but able to turn on a Euro-cent to the tightest sweet-toned fiddle harmonizing.

 XO
Visio, Finland

Even though as a band they were only aiming for local fun, they've made an album whose energy, wit and tune-making should and could burst out on the wider world. The tunes, mostly written by Kyösti, are varied and memorable, fit perfectly into the tradition and evoke strong echoes of all the Kaustinen music that's brought them this far.

Troka

Another twist in the Kaustinen dance combo tradition came with Troka, a group of top young players with a high-energy sound and a slew of new material: fiddlers Ville Ojanen and JPP's Matti Mäkelä with accordionist Minna Luoma (later Johanna Juhola), JPP's Timo Alakotila on harmonium and piano and the fine and widely experienced bassist generally known as "Monsteri", Timo Myllykangas (later replaced by Antti Järvelä).

⊙ **Smash**
KMI, Finland

Hot playing of winding, twisting, rhythmically complex but memorable melodies, including guest Ville Kangas' surging, lyrical waltz "Kirsin ja Villen Häävalssi". There are occasional Hungarian and Norwegian references.

Tsuumi Sound System

TSS is based down south in Helsinki, but Kaustinen is in much of the shape and sound of its music, partly because its two fiddlers are Tommi Asplund of Frigg and Esko Järvelä of Frigg and Töttersсön.

⊙ **Hotas**
Aito, Finland

TSS began as, and still is, the band for Tsuumi, a pro dance company basing its work on folk dance, but *Hotas* is music by the band for itself. The strong, intricate material, written by Järvelä accordionist Hannu Kella and piano and harmonium player Pilvi Talvitie, uses occasional Balkan rhythms but feels like a muscular extension of the Kaustinen style.

Värttinä

Finland's best-known roots band, Värttinä produce a high-energy runo-song-based sound. A group of energetic women singers are supported by a skilful band.

 Vihma
BMG/Wicklow, US

In this 1998 release, the Värttinä approach comes together triumphantly. The well-developed vocals include touches of throat-singing and pygmy hocketing, while the strong technologized and acoustic instrumental backings pick up ingeniously on the rhythmic shifts and interplays within the narrow-range runolaulu which remains central to the band's music.

PLAYLIST
Finland

1 KRUUNU-MARJAANAN POLSKA Konsta Jylhä and Purppuripelimannit from *Finnish Folk Music Vol. 2*
A perky, twisting tune written by Konsta that has most of the features of classic Kaustinen wedding-band pelimanni music.

2 MAHLA Hannu Saha from *Mahla*
A song – the title means "sap" – written by Saha and sung by Aija Puurtinen with all the deep-toned serene warmth that is so attractive in the Finnish female speaking voice.

3 PELTONIEMEN HINTRIIKIN SURUMARSSI Frigg from *Keidas/Oasis/Oase*
This tune by Kaustinen fiddler Peltoniemi (1854–1936) is played at funerals and other social events. An unusual arrangement, with Petri Prauda's Estonian bagpipes, chamber orchestra and church organ.

4 KIRPOSI TULIKIPUNA Primo from *Tulikulkku*
A five-string kantele burns, the steel strings snapping, while Hannu Saha, Rauno Nieminen, Arto Järvelä and Kurt Lindblad play a hypnotic tune on fifteen-string kantele, jouhikko, fiddle and Jew's harp.

5 KAIPAUSTANGO Sväng from *Sväng*
An instrumental new tango, written by Eero Turkka, from the hot harmonica quartet Sväng.

6 ZOOVAXIBLUES Nikolai Blad from *Nikolai Blad*
Blad's "turtle voice" and guitar, over Jarmo Romppanen's skittering mandolin and Tapani Varis's bass, with hocketing female voices in the background.

7 COLA-OSKA Töttersсön from *XO*
Kaustinen young rascals toss off a set of trad tunes, wittily slithering, sliding and harmonium-pounding with all the carefree abandon of players who've been born and raised with a fiddle in their hands.

8 VIHMA Värttinä from *Vihma*
Big cave-like sounds, breaking into wild abrasive fiddling, surround and compete with the fast-spitting edgy vocals of the three female singers.

9 HALE-BOPP JPP from *String Tease*
One of the signatures of Kaustinen's most famous fiddle, harmonium and bass band, with its leaps of melody and rhythm, slithering and surging bowing and bouts of pizzicato.

10 SUVETAR Gjallarhorn from *Sjofn*
The text of a Karelian runo-song with Jenny Wilhelm's multitracked vocals to her own tune over a driving, abrasive backing of fiddle, viola, grinding, barking didgeridoo and gutty drums.

France

a mosaic of sounds

Manu Chao
Because Music

With millions of second- or third-generation immigrants and more recent newcomers of very diverse ethnic origins, France is a truly multicultural nation. Combined with the revival in regional and traditional culture, this has created a melting pot that makes the French music scene particularly creative and exciting. **Jean-Pierre Bruneau** and **Philippe Krümm** invite us on a very musical Tour de France.

Successive waves of immigrants settled in France throughout the twentieth century: Armenians fleeing Turkish genocide, Italian labourers, Poles working in the coal mines of the north, Russians after the Bolshevik revolution of 1917, Askhenazi Jews during the 1920s, and Spanish Republicans fleeing Franco. After World War II, large numbers of Portuguese, Algerians, Tunisians, Moroccans, West Indians and Black Africans arrived, all in search of a better life. The end of the Algerian War in 1962 saw an influx of *pieds-noirs* (European-Algerians) and Sephardic Jews from North Africa. In the 1970s it was the turn of political refugees from Chile, Brazil and later from Indochina during the Vietnam war. Newcomers are now mostly Chinese, but also Kurds, Serbs, Pakistanis and Tamils, making France a mosaic of people, all having a huge influence on the music being produced.

In rural France, scores of artists, groups and festivals rework regional traditions into contemporary forms. As a reaction against synthesized and machine-produced disco music and dance, the concept of "*bal folk*" was launched in the 1970s and became popular all over France but especially in the northern part of the country. It gave birth to the celebrated "Boombal" in neighbouring Belgium, and "Folkbal" in the Netherlands. The inventor of bal folk may well be the older folk band in France, **Groupe Sans Gain** that started playing in the late 1950s. In a bal folk, all kinds of group or round dances as well as couple dances are being performed, always to the sound of live bands, the steps being explained by dance instructors. Impromptu bal folk may take place everywhere, including in public squares and on streets. Remember the Woody Allen movie *I Love You* and the tango dancers on a bank of the Seine River in front of Notre Dame de Paris? That was not staged. It is still taking place at least three days a week with different styles of trad music. But the strong political motivation of many regionalists and revivalist musicians in the 1980s and 90s has often been eroded and their dreams rarely fulfilled. **Regional languages** are spoken less and less and the ideal of autonomous rural societies reinventing their culture has proved illusory. "The French countryside", wrote noted folklorist **Olivier Durif** from Limousin, "is increasingly becoming the green suburb of the nearest big city and culturally subordinated to it. This 'rurban' territory has now lost its autonomy and its original identity. Often what is left is nostalgia for times gone by." There is, of course, one notable exception to this situation: Brittany.

Brittany

Breton music draws on the common Celtic heritage of the Atlantic seaboard and has been a unifying and inspiring part of the culture of the province for centuries.

Always at the cutting edge of the revival in French roots music, the Breton music craze has reached new heights in the new millennium. Jean-Pierre Pichard, main organizer of the **Festival Interceltique de Lorient** (see box on p.138) claims that this annual two-week extravaganza is attended by 600,000 people, making it the largest roots music festival in Europe. Since 2002, Pichard has also succeeded in filling some of France's largest sports arenas with Breton and Celtic acts – no small achievement.

One of the oldest forms of Breton music is that of the **bagad**, the Breton **pipe band**. It comprises quintessential Breton instruments: the loud and raucous *bombarde* (shawm) and *biniou* (small Breton bagpipe), plus marching drums. Such bands were an essential component of any procession or festival, and they still appear, though usually with the larger *biniou braz* (essentially a copy of Scottish pipes). The older form of bagad has been re-created by **Roland Becker** and his trio **L'Orchestre National Breton** who have also elaborated the music into theatrical shows with nineteenth-century costumes and masks. There are also more modern bagad incarnations of which the **Bagad Kemper** (with jazz musicians) and **Kevrenn Alre Bagad** (with forty musicians and ranks of dancers) are amongst the best known.

The best setting for traditional Breton music is undoubtedly a *festoù-noz* (night feast) – a night of serious eating, drinking and dancing, similar to a *ceilidh*. These are common in the summer months, attracting hoards of revellers from miles around.

Once the evening gets underway, the dancers, often in their hundreds, whirl around in vast dizzying circles, sometimes frenzied and leaping, sometimes slow and graceful with their little fingers intertwined. The oldest dances, the *an-dro*, *hanter-dro*, *rond* and *gavotte* are all **line or circle dances**. It can be a bizarre and exhilarating spectacle.

The traditional **festoù-noz music** is a *couple de sonneurs* – a pair of musicians playing bombarde and biniou. They play the same melody line, with a drone from the biniou, and keep up a fast tempo – one player covering for the other when they pause for breath. This is pure dance music, with no vocals and no titles for the tunes, although there are countless varieties of rhythms.

A purely vocal, and probably older, form of dance music is known as **kan ha diskan**. In its basic form, this is performed by a pair of unaccompanied "call and response" singers. The best singers might also give the dancers the odd break with a **gwerz**, or ballad, again sung unaccompanied.

Over the last thirty years, these festoù-noz accompaniments have been supplanted by four- or five-piece bands like **Carré Manchot**, **Skolvan**, **Bleizi Ruz**, **Sonerien Du** or **Pennou Skoulm**, a Breton "dream team" of sorts, who add fiddle and accordion, and sometimes electric bass and drums, to the bombarde and (less often) the biniou. The tunes have been updated to give more of a rock sound, while the ballads have given way to more of a folk singer-songwriter style, with guitar backing.

It was **Alan Stivell** who started the ball rolling for the modern Breton music scene with one of the first **folk-rock** bands in Europe. Born Alan Cochevelou, he adopted the name Stivell (Breton for "spring" or "source") in the 1960s. The playing of the *telenn* or Breton harp had effectively died out until Stivell's father decided to revive it and his son put it decisively back on the map. His internationally successful album, *Renaissance of the Celtic Harp* (1971) helped introduce Breton – as well as Irish, Welsh and Scottish – traditional music to a worldwide audience.

The album that followed, *Chemins de Terre*, went further, combining – in a similar fashion to that of Fairport Convention or Steeleye Span in Britain – a rock rhythm section with folk instruments. Stivell played harp, bagpipes and Irish flute alongside **Dan Ar Bras** on electric and acoustic guitar. Ar Bras, who played with Fairport Convention in 1976, has produced the very successful *Héritages des Celtes* series of shows, CDs and DVDs, as well as more personal and acoustic solo albums. Other notable harpists include the mystically bearded Merlin-lookalike **Myrdhin** and **Kirjuhel**.

The most famous traditional female singer is now **Annie Ebrel**, who has elevated the acapella Breton tradition to new heights since touring with upright-bass player **Ricardo del Fra**. She often sings solo, but also likes to join other singers such as **Yann Fanch Kemener**, celebrated for his powerful voice and unbelievably long performances of gwerz. Singers **Gilles Servat** (his "La Blanche Hermine" is a Breton hymn of sorts), **Andrea Ar Gouilh**, **Kristen Nikolas** and her daughter, **Nol-**

Disques Dreyfus

Alan Stivell

137

Some Great French Festivals

Brittany

Festival Interceltique de Lorient
International Celtic extravaganza attracting really huge crowds. First fortnight of August.
www.festival-interceltique.com

Festival de Cornouaille, Quimper
A celebration of all things Breton, which started in 1923, making it the oldest festival in France. End of July.
www.festival-cornouaille.com

Fête du Chant de Marin, Paimpol
Sea shanties from all over the world. Beginning of August. *www.paimpol-2009.com*

Central France

Saint Chartier
This three-decades-old "hurdy-gurdy and bagpipe encounters" event held in the Berry region has turned into a model folk music festival. Unbeatable. Mid-July. *www.saintchartier.org*

Festival des Nuits de Nacre, Tulle
Lots of musette, of course, but also accordion music from different backgrounds with a different theme each year. Mid-September. *www.accordeon.org*

Grand Bal de l'Europe, Gennetines
Surfing on the bal folk craze, a unique week long get together of over 3000 dancers and 100 live bands. Mid-July and beginning of August. *www.gennetines.org*

Ile de France

Africolor, Pairs
African communities get together in various venues in the northern and eastern suburbs of Paris. December.
www.africolor.com

Festival Django Reinhardt, Samois sur Seine
Gypsy swing in a "Renoirian" setting near Rambouillet. End of June. *www.django.samois.free.fr*

Provence

Les Suds à Arles
Wonderful acts and great provençal ambience. Mid-July. *www.suds-arles.com*

Fiesta des Suds, Marseille
Marseille-style celebration of Mediterranean music (and way beyond). Second fortnight of October. *www .dock-des-suds.org/fiesta*

Southwest

Estivada, Rodez
Top celebration of Occitan culture. End of July. *www.estivada-rodez.com*

Nuits atypiques de Langon
Atypical festival, with a strong militant emphasis. End of July. *www.nuitsatypiques.org*

Musique Métisses, Angoulême.
One of the oldest world music festivals in continental Europe, whose forte is top African line-ups. Last weekend of May. *www.musiquesmetisses.com*

Tempo Latino, Vic Fezensac
In the local Plaza de Toros; largest salsa and son event held in France. End of July. *www.tiempolatino.com*

wenn Korbell, and the duo **Bastars Hag e Vab** (Bastard and Son) are also stalwarts of the live circuit. Formed in 1972, the most popular Breton band is **Tri Yann** (originally Tri Yann an Naoned, literally "the three Johns from Nantes"), whose brand of progressive Celto-medieval folk-rock still attracts huge crowds.

New Bands and Current Trends

Although it has its fair share of good rock bands like **Red Cardell**, **Matmatah**, **Soldat Louis** or **Wig A Wag**, the Breton scene has become incredibly eclectic. Jazz-oriented artists include the bombarde and saxophone player **Roland Becker**, hailed as "The King of the Breton Music Hall", who re-creates a unique jazz-circus music played in Brittany until the 1950s – either as a duo (as on *Kof a Kof: Café Breton*) or with a hundred musicians, as on his CD *Mr Kerbec et ses Belouzes*. Influenced by Albert Ayler, and both innovative and energizing, the **Niou Bardophones** (niou as in biniou, bard as in bombarde, phone as in saxophone) juxtapose American jazz and Armorican beat, with fiery bagpipes, thundering baritone sax and frenzied bombarde. Classically trained pianist and composer **Didier Squiban** also mixes jazz and Celtic themes, while the spellbinding duo **Bugel Koar**, consisting of singer **Marthe Vassalo** and accordion player **Philippe Ollivier**, shows some connection with surrealistic theatre.

No experiment is too daring for Breton cross-pollination, which has seen **Bagad Men Ha Tan** touring and recording with the Senegalese drum master **Doudou N'Diaye Rose**, the group **Kerhuen** mixing gavotte with Moroccan *gnawa* sounds, the Badume's Band, travelling to Ethiopia to record with their idol, singer Mahmoud Ahmed, the famous **Molard Brothers** performing with Bulgarian singers and **Patrick Molard** starting a bagpipe/fretless guitar duo with **Alain Genty**. But Brittany's leading figure in musical fusion is singer and clarinet player **Erik Marchand**, whose latest album *Pruna* was made with outstanding Romanian and East European musicians.

One of the first Breton musicians to successfully combine traditional and electronic styles is **Denez Prigent**. A *gwerziou* and kan ha diskan specialist (sometimes singing acapella with **Louise Ebrel**), Prigent has introduced elements of breakbeat and drum'n'bass into his music; a track from his *Gortoz a Ran* album was chosen by Ridley Scott for the soundtrack to *Black Hawk Down*. The "kan dub" of **Pascal Lamour** also uses cutting-edge beats in an electro-Celtic style: the title of his *Shamans of Brittany* CD reflects his belief that druids are the Celtic equivalent of shamans.

Long frowned upon by Breton nationalists for being "too French", the **Gallo language** of eastern Brittany has enjoyed a musical revival lately, thanks to two excellent bands: **Obrée Alie**, featuring the remarkable singer **Bertan Obrée**, and **Jolie Vilaine**, led by the equally exceptional singer **Véronique Bourjot** and top accordionist **Yann-Fanch Perroches**. (Jolie Vilaine literally means pretty ugly, but Vilaine is also the river that gives its name to the *département* of Ile et Vilaine where Gallo is spoken.)

Central France

The former provinces of central France – **Berry**, **Bourbonnais**, **Nivernais**, **Morvan**, **Limousin** and **Auvergne** – form one of the strongholds of traditional music. This is the heartland of the **bagpipe** and **hurdy-gurdy** and of a dance called the **bourrée**. The northern version, in 2/4 time, lends itself to virtuosity, while the southern, in 3/8, favours rhythmic improvisation.

Bagpipes and Hurdy-gurdys

France claims a greater variety of **bagpipes** (*cornemuses*) than any other country, the most notable being the *grande cornemuse* and *cabrette* from the old provinces of **Berry** and **Bourbonnais**. The region is also a stronghold of the **hurdy-gurdy** or *vielle-à-roue*; indeed it once had a whole town (Jenzat in Auvergne) involved in hurdy-gurdy manufacture.

Notable hurdy-gurdy players include **Gilles Chabenat** (originally with the Berry group Les Ecoliers de St Genest), **Valentin Clastrier**, **Pascal Lefeuvre**, **Anne-Lise Foy**, **Dominique Regef** and **Patrick Bouffard**. Masters of the *grande bourbonnaise* bagpipes include **Philippe Prieur**, **Eric Montbel**, **Jean Blanchard**, **Willy Soulette**, and musicians of the ensemble **La Chavannée**, especially bagpipe and clarinet player **Frédéric Paris**, who also plays with Gilles Chabenat in the **Duo Chabenat-Paris**. These players explore new melodies based on the old 2/4 bourrée and have also developed mixed polyphonic ensembles like the **Trio Sautivet**. Blanc, Blanchard and Montbel were previously involved in two of the best folk revival groups of the 1970s, **La Bamboche** and **Le Grand Rouge**, whose excellent eponymous albums of Auvergnat and Limousin music were ground-breaking in combining ensemble and solo playing.

Montbel has explored the Limousin repertoire with his group **Ulysse**. He has been particularly instrumental in the revival of the *chabrette*, uncovering older musicians with unusual playing techniques (like the use of the chanter to provide a wah-wah effect). Limousin, and particularly the Corrèze plateau, is also known for its **violin music**, in particular that of the **Trio Violon** and **Françoise Etay**. The tradition has been passed on to a new generation of fiddlers such as **Jean-François Vrod**, **Jean Pierre Champeval**, **François Breugnot** and **Olivier Durif**. Durif's own son, Gabriel, plays chabrette and diatonic accordion and leads **Le Band de Seilhac**, a remarkable ensemble of very young musicians.

In the Morvan, a wooded area east of the centre, the group **Faubourg de Boignard** and its piper **Raphaël Thiery** have revived old melodies, taking them on a more muscular path with the addition of a rhythm section and occasional stream-of-consciousness poetry. Folk songs from this and the neighbouring Nivernais region were collected in the early twentieth century by **Achille Millien**, and this repertoire is being revived by the groups **Les Ménétriers du Morvan**.

The Auvergne: Cabrettes

Further south, the remote Auvergne region is dominated by the mountains of the Massif Central. The cabrette – "little goat" in Auvergnat dialect – is a droneless bagpipe made of goatskin, "blown"

Birth of the Bal Musette

Viens à la Bastille,
Tu verras des filles
Qui tricotent des gambettes,
Viens danser au bal musette…

From a song by Guy Béart

The **musette** reached Paris at the end of the nineteenth century when migrant workers from the **Auvergne** moved en masse to the capital. By 1880 there were some 150 Auvergnat dance halls in the Bastille area and in the eastern suburbs like Montreuil. The cabrette (smallpipes) players leading the dance were often Auvergnat coal merchants, the most famous of whom, **Antoine Bouscatel**, allegedly invented the pairing of cabrettes and Italian accordion. Soon the accordion relegated the cabrette to an accompanying role and finally supplanted it.

The earliest recordings of the genre date from the early 1900s and its truest exponent was **Emile Vacher** (1883–1969), who played a small diatonic accordion in a light rhythmic style with a characteristic tremolo. During the 1920s a few intellectuals dared to mingle with the *apaches* or *mauvais garçons* (bad boys) of the Bastille and soon the **bal musette** and a dance called the **java** became popular among the working class all over the country and especially in the *guinguettes* dotting the banks of the Marne River near Paris. Alongside the accordion, dance bands started to include a drum kit (called jazz), banjo, double bass, clarinet or sax. Alongside **Tony Murena**, Belgian-born **Gus Viseur** was a great stylist and the undisputed king of the accordion players of his time, splendidly mixing musette and jazz beat.

After World War II, musette groups evolved into large accordion-led orchestras who plied the French and Belgian rural circuits. Their grand star was female player **Yvette Horner**, who cut 150 albums (including one with Nashville harmonica player Charlie McCoy) which, combined, sold over thirty million copies. She was also famous for performing during eleven Tours de France between 1952 and 1963, playing in front of the racers perched atop of a 15 CV Citroën driven by her husband. The other accordion stars of the period were **Jo Privat**, **André Verchuren**, **Aimable**, **Marcel Azzola** and **Edouard Duleu**. Today the most gifted young players like **Richard Galliano**, **David Venitucci**, **Daniel Mille** or **Ludovic Beier** show a greater affinity with the jazz idiom, while six-times world champ **Jérome Richard** excels at playing all styles. And some 400,000 young amateurs are learning how to master the squeeze box in accordion schools all over France. Interestingly, the world expert on musette is none other than the famous US cartoonist **Robert Crumb**, an avid 78 collector who lives in southern France and used to play banjo and mandolin with a French revival group called **Les Primitifs du Futur**.

Jean-Pierre Bruneau

by a small pair of bellows pumped by the elbow, like the Northumbrian or Irish *uillean* pipes. The sound is bright and shrill: one of its original players, **Joseph Ruols**, would tell his students: "Make sure that the little goat sings; that's what makes the sound beautiful."

Today, many players are following in Ruols' footsteps, notably **Michel Esbelin**, **Jean Bona** and **Dominique Paris**, all experts in the typical 3/8 dance music of the area, which also has some beautiful, slow and melancholic ritual airs, aptly known as *regrets*. The cabrette was also the humble origin of France's famous bal-musette tradition (see box).

Paris and elsewhere

Known as Ile-de-France, dominating the country in more than one way, the Paris region has ten million inhabitants (a sixth of France's population), many of them of provincial or foreign origin.

The typical Parisian music of yesterday (musette and chanson réaliste) is not much in vogue anymore, though it sometimes inspires rock and folk artists such as accordion player **Gérard Blanchard** (of "Rock Amadour" fame) or **François Hadji Lazaro** (who wrote a great "Parisian" song "Le Bar tabac de la rue des Martyrs" played with his band Pigalle). Ladji Hazaro was also a producer of renown who launched Paris Combo, la Mano Negro and many others in the 1980s on his now defunct Boucherie Productions label. In 2009 he revived Pigalle, the band of his beginnings.

Sometimes referred to as the "capital of world music", Paris is a hotbed for all kinds of music, especially North African. Algerian icons **Rachid Taha** and **Khaled** live and work there and so does **Akli D** (whose album *Ma Yela* was produced by Manu Chao). Youcef Boukella's **Orchestre National de Barbès** took the country by storm in the early 2000s after memorable live concerts, but more or less vanished in 2003, only to reappear in mid-2005. The band is named after its home base, the African neighbourhood of Barbès in Paris, also home to **Karim Albert Kook**, whose heart is in Algeria, soul in Louisiana and feet in Paris. His 2003 album is titled *Barbès City Limits*.

Two other North African icons are the delicate *Kabyle* singer **Idir** (he wrote and sang one of the first world music hits "A Vava Inouva" in 1973) and Algiers-born folk-rock singer **Souad Massi**, often compared to Tracy Chapman. She first came to France in 1999, decided to stay and has never stopped touring since.

The Sephardic Jewish community's best-known artist is the singer **Enrico Macias**, a pied noir icon who made a surprising and welcome splash in the late 1990s by playing the *maalouf* music of his Algerian teenage years. Sadly, the delicious "francarabe" Jewish/Arabic music beautifully performed by **Lili Boniche** (born in Algiers in 1921) seems to be a disappearing genre since the death of Boniche in 2008. The Klezmer music scene, however, is very much alive, with **Yom**, the undisputed king of klezmer clarinet (backed by piano player Denis Cuniot); Yiddish singer/raconteur **Ben Zimet**; and groups such as Klezmer Nova and Les Yeux Noirs. In 2008 emerged Israeli (but Paris-born and -based) **Yael Naim**, whose album, mostly sung in Hebrew, met with considerable success. It contained the hit song "New Soul" (in English), which reached the top ten in the US and was used in a commercial for Apple.

The Black African musical scene is very rich, with hundreds of first- or second-generation musicians from French and other former colonies – Mali, Senegal, Ivory Coast, Congo, Benin, Madagascar and Gabon (Pierre Akendengué), but also Zaïre, Cape Verde (whose two main record labels are Paris-based), Nigeria (Keziah Jones, Tony Allen, and Asa, Ayo and Nneka, three young women singers taking France by storm), Angola (Bonga) and Uganda (Geoffrey Oryema). From Cameroon came the Faussart sisters, better known as Les Nubians.

From Argentina came bandoneon grand master **Juan José Masolini** and Eduardo Makaroff (co-founder of the famous **Gotan Project**) and his friend Juan-Carlos Cacérès (tango roots/*murga*/*milonga* specialist). Among the many South American political refugees that settled in France the most notable were Chilean Juan Cedrón (who leads the Cuarteto Cedrón), singer Angel Parra (son of Violetta Parra) and the band Quilapayún.

Relatively new to France, the Asian scene is best represented by the Vietnamese guitarist **Nguyên Lê**, who also plays jazz and has made outstanding albums with the traditional singer **Huong Than**. Also Paris-based are two of the most renowned Baul singers from Bengal, Paban Das Baul and Senses bandleader Bapi Das Baul, son of Purna Das Baul (who appeared on the cover of Dylan's *John Wesley Harding*!). Rajasthan's singer and dancer Gulabi Sapera long toured and recorded with the world-class guitarist **Thierry Titi Robin**, who, in 2009, started exploring new paths with Pakistani qawwali star Faiz Ali Faiz. In 2008/2009, the swing manouche style invented by

Django Reinhardt (see box on p.207) found a new life. Manouche guitar players are now invited into the fancy jazz clubs of the capital and more and more "gadgé" musicians are tempted to espouse the genre, such as guitar player **Thomas Dutronc**, the son of Ye Ye chanteuse Françoise Hardy and the great singer **San Severino** whose first band was called Les Voleurs de poules (Chicken Stealers!). There is also a new and very successful electronica/swing band of six musicians dressed in zoot suits called **Caravan Palace**.

Very hard to classify are France's biggest world star **Manu Chao** (see box opposite); accordion player Marc Perrone, who has a folk-music background but now covers new ground including film scores; Hendrix- and Indian music-influenced guitarist **Mad Sheer Khan**; and veteran band **Bratsch**, brilliant exponents of everything East and South European from klezmer through Gypsy music to *rebétika*). Another veteran ensemble *extraordinaire* is **Hadouk Trio**, composed of Didier Malherbe, Loy Ehrlich and Steve Shehan. Then there's the warm and very danceable music of **Lo' Jo**, led by the energetic and eccentric Denis Péan, who was very much involved in helping the Tuareg group **Tinariwen** debut and launch their celebrated "Festival au Desert" near Timbuktu (Mali); and finally

the fusion projects initiated by former Malicorne member **Hughes de Courson**: *Lambarena-Bach to Africa*, recorded in Gabon with the help of Pierre Akendengué, *Mozart l'Egyptien*, *O'Stravaganza-Vivaldi l'Irlandais*, and the captivating *Lux Obscura*, his new electro-medieval adventure, which should turn on Gryphon fans.

The South

Occitania

Roughly the southern half of France, also known as "le Midi" and inhabited by 15 million people, this is the linguistic area where the **Occitan language** or Langue d'Oc (derived from the Provençal of twelfth-century troubadours) used to be spoken. It includes Provence, The Riviera, Languedoc-Roussillon, Midi-Pyrénées and Aquitaine. The dying language found new life during the 1970s thanks to folk singers **Rosina de Peira**, **Patric**, **Claude Marti** and **Joan Pau Verdier** and though hardly spoken anymore, it is still carried on by new generations of singers. The typical Provençal sound is that of a duo with **fifre** (fife) and drum, or

Jak Kilby

Thierry "Titi" Robin

Manu Chao

International star **Manu Chao** is the son of exiled Spanish writer **Ramon Chao**, whose politics and philosophy were to have a strong influence on Manu and his trumpet-playing brother Tonio. Before forming Mano Negra, Manu played in **Los Carayos** and in the **Hot Pants**, a now-legendary band that played pure rockabilly. No doubt feeling too constrained playing just one style, he founded **Mano Negra** in 1987 with Tonio and their cousin, ex-Hot Pants drummer Santiago Casariego. Recorded with members of the French alt.rock bands Dirty District and Casse-Pieds, their first album *Patchanka* (1988) established Mano Negra's delightfully eclectic musical style. After the smash hit "Mala Vida", the group left the independent Boucherie Productions label for Virgin.

A year later *Puta's Fever* really sealed their success. This seminal recording is a wonderful mix of rock'n'roll, ska, reggae, doo-wop, calypso, salsa and various other styles that took Mano's fancy, sung in English, French, Spanish and Arabic. Soon Mano Negra were being hailed wherever they played as one of the best stage acts since The Clash. A live album, *In the Hell of Patchinko*, perfectly captured the frenzy and intensity of their stage act, while *King of Bongo* was raw and dark rock'n'roll, with most of the lyrics in English. Their last and best album, *Casa Babylon* (1994), featured swaying Latin and reggae rhythms.

Chao reappeared with his solo debut *Clandestino* in 1998. With its worldwide success, he soon became a sort of anti-globalization Latino Bob Marley in South America, and capitalizing on this, Virgin released a *Best of Mano Negra* compilation. In 2001, he brought out the disappointing *Proxima estacion: Esperanza*, a rehash of *Clandestino*, with more sampling and brass here and there. From 2000 to 2003, he once again toured the world with the explosive **Radio Bemba Sound System**. As borne out by their eponymous live album, they had the same energy as Mano Negra, with a distinct penchant for *ragga*/reggae dub sounds. Freed from his contract with Virgin, Chao brought out a book and CD called *Sibérie Métait Contée*, a collaboration with the illustrator **Wozniak**, which was sold in France in both music shops and bookshops. In 2005, he teamed up with the two blind Malian musicians **Amadou & Mariam** to produce their ravishing *Dimanche à Bamako* album which had Chao's trademark samples, effects, guitar, songwriting and vocal presence stamped all over it. Predictably, it was a huge hit.

François Guibert

from ensembles of **galoubets-tambourins**, three-holed pipes. Both are played with drums and used for street processions. But since the folk revival, virtuosos like **André Gabriel**, **Miqueu Montanaro**, **Patrice Comte** and **Yves Rousguisto** have enlarged the instrumentation and repertoire.

Languedoc-Roussillon

The Languedoc has some strange local instruments: traditional **oboes** like the *graille* and the *aboès*, often played alongside the **bodega**, the local bagpipe. The latter is a very striking instrument, with a huge bag made of an entire goatskin and a single large shoulder drone. It has a bright, low sound.

The bodega and oboes are used in the regional ensembles **Calabrun**, **Trencavel** and **Trioc**. Oboe player **Laurent Audemard** was the inspirational figure behind the group **Une Anche Passe** (a punning title involving a reed, an angel and a pregnant pause), which has combined a love of Languedoc-style oboes with related instruments from elsewhere. The group have produced some amazing albums, notably *Le Grand Troupeau* (the great herd), recorded in Flanders, which pays tribute to the half a million soldiers killed there during World War I.

Local dances are called "baleti" and two favourite bands of that circuit are **Du Sartas** and **Spi et la Gaudriole**, the latter led by former punk rocker Jean Michel Poisson. **La Mal Coiffée** is a refreshing all-women band of six singers from the Minervois wine region. They do "traditional Languedoc songs from the vineyards and the bistros learned from their grandmothers".

Roussillon is French Catalonia, whose capital is Perpignan. On both sides of the border, the national dance is the **sardana**, most commonly played by brass and wind bands or *cobles*, with three sorts of oboe – the *tible*, the *tarota* and the *tenora*. Among the traditional ensembles, look out for **La Cobla de Joglars**, **Els Ministrels del Rossellano** and the **Cobla Mil-Lenaria**.

Five thousand people strong, the largest Gypsy community of Western Europe is to be found in Perpignan, in the historic and decaying St Jacques neighbourhood, a former Jewish ghetto.

Marseille's Musical Bouillabaisse

France's main seaport and its third largest city, **Marseille** has always been a cosmopolitan town, and is home today to over thirty ethnic groups. Here you will find world-music stars such as the Grammy-nominated flamenco guitar player **Juan Carmona**, the Sephardic Andalou singer **Françoise Atlan** and Oran-born Jewish pied noir piano wizard **Maurice El Médioni**, the first to mix Arabic tunes with rumba and boogie, paving the way for rai. Also from Oran are rai singers **Houari Benchenat**, **Cheb Hamid** and **Cheb Bilal**. From Iran come the percussion virtuosi known as the **Chemirani Brothers**. The young Guinean combo **Ba Cissoko** (renowned for its electric *koras* played with wah-wah pedals) was formed here and so was the very popular rap group **IAM** leaded by Akhenaton, aka **Philippe Fragione**, the son of Neapolitan immigrants. There are *chaabi* singers by the dozen as well as *twara* (*chebli*) bands from the Comoros and **Jagdish & Kreol Connexion**, a group that hails from the Indian community of Réunion and mixes *sega* and *raga*. An amazingly eclectic guitar player, **Louis Winsberg**, is involved in many different groups and projects (**Sixun**, **Jaleo**, **Douce France**, **la Danse du Vent** and his last one aptly named **Marseille, Marseille**). Jubilant international musical nomads **Watcha Clan** mix electronica and various Mediterranean grooves (and way beyond). Sometimes compared to Transglobal Underground or Balkan Beat Box, led by Sista K (of mixed Ashkenazi, Sephardic and Berber ancestry), their raga-influenced fusion music epitomizes the true soul of the city.

This musical bouillabaisse is nothing new, as singer **Moussu T** and guitarist **Blu** of the trailblazing Massilia Sound System discovered when they read the Jamaican writer **Claude McKay**'s 1929 novel *Banjo*, based on a year he had spent on the docks among a group of black expatriates, drifters and hoboes from the US, the Caribbean and Africa. In one passage, for instance, an accordion and shaker duo play the *beguine*, which McKay describes as "just a Martinique variant of the 'jelly roll' or the Jamaican '*burru*' or the Senegalese '*bombé*'". As **Moussu T e Lei Jovents** (could translate as Mr T and the Youngsters), Moussu, Blu and Brazilian percussionist Jamilson da Silva recorded *Mademoiselle Marseille*, a re-imagining of this 1920s scene with a unique, raw, acoustic sound mixing blues, Caribbean dance music, African instruments, harbour shanties and a dash of Marcel Pagnol-style ambience for good measure. It was followed in 2008 by a CD in the same vein (albeit less exciting) named *Home Sweet Home*.

Moussu T e Lei Jovents

Created in the mid-1980s by **Joe Corbeau** (a great local figure known as the Armenian Rastaman), **Jali** and **Tatou**, the **Massilia Sound System** were strongly influenced by reggae when they invented their own brand of French or rather Provençal raggamuffin (sometimes described as "troubamuffin") that has been at the forefront of the French scene. They have created several offshoot groups, sometimes touring together under the collective name "**La Comédia Provençala**".

From the neighbourhood called La Plaine comes the intense poet Sam Karpiena (ex-Dupain) and his "dirty folk sound of Massalia", as well as a really marvellous band getting international recognition, **Lo Cor de la Plana**, a feverish handclapping and foot-stomping male-voice choir founded in 2001 by Manu Theron. Influenced by Theron, there is also the all-women brilliant polyphonic ensemble **Original Occitana**.

No story about Marseille's music would be complete without mentioning Algerian born **Hector Zazou**, who died an untimely death in 2008. Alongside Peter Gabriel or David Byrne, he was one of the most innovative composers and producers of his time and worked with, among others, Suzanne Vega, Björk, John Cale, Värttina, Carlos Nunez, Yungchen Lamo and les Nouvelles Polyphonies Corses. He loved melting folk music with contemporary sensibilities, creating albums of subtle beauty such as *Sahara Blue* and *Songs from the Cold Seas*.

Jean-Pierre Bruneau

FRANCE

These *Gitanos* speak Spanish and Calo. They mostly play rumba catalane, a mix of flamenco and Cuban rumba invented in Barcelona. The American writer Fernanda Eberstadt befriended several women of the Baillardos and Espinas clan, founders of the **Tekameli band**, and made waves when her excellent book *Little Money Street: in Search of Gypsies and their Music in the South of France* was published here in 2007. Tekameli (it means "I love you" in the Calo language) play their own version of rumba catalane and so does another outstanding local band called **Kaloomé**. More Gitanos are to be found in Arles, in the river Rhone delta. The most famous of them is the veteran guitarist Ricardo Baliardo, better known as **Manitas de Plata** ("little silver hands"). Born in 1921 and discovered by Picasso, he became one of the first world music stars and is the father of Jacques, Maurice and Tonino Baliardo of the Gipsy Kings (see box on p.206).

The Alps

In the Alpes Maritimes area there is a choral tradition that spills over into the Piedmont and Ligurian regions of Italy, with the group **Corou de Berra** and **La Compagnie Vocale** being the best examples. Further north, **Patrick Mazellier** and the groups **Drailles** and **Rigodon Sauvage** have revived the violin tradition and *rigaudon* dance of the Dauphiné province.

The old province of **Savoie** has strong links with the Italian valleys of Aoste and Piedmont, harking back to the times when they were a single political unit straddling and communicating via the high mountain passes of the Alps. Here a specific repertoire explored by **La Kinkerne** reminds us that the hurdy-gurdy was the principal instrument of this area for centuries.

Grenoble, the main city of the Alps, is home to **MusTraDem** (*Musiques traditionnelles de demain*, tomorrow's trad music), a collective created by brother and sister **Norbert** and **Isabelle Pignol** (he plays accordion and she hurdy-gurdy) and including the groups **Dédale**, **Djal** and **Obsession**.

Toulouse and the Linha Imaginot

There is a linking of sorts between artists from Marseille and Toulouse. Called the Linha Imaginot (a pun on the useless Maginot line erected before World War II to protect France against a new German invasion), the *linha* is a concept invented, after meeting members of Massilia

Sound System, by **Claude Sicre**, a Toulousain cultural activist *extraordinaire* and the second half (the other being human beatbox **Ange B**) of the wisecracking **Fabulous Trobadors**. The Fab Trobs' art is based on the ancient art of *tenson*, which according to Sicre is "a kind of lyric jousting match or poetic verbal exchange played out between two singers/musicians". Another of their sources of inspiration is the Brazilian *embaladores*, tambourine players, singers and poetic vocal improvisers from the Sertão. The result is hard to categorize. Sicre says "we are using rap, but we are not rappers, we play music from Brazil, but we don't do world music, we sing in French, but we don't do *chanson française*. We are total mavericks." Nonetheless this Occitan/Brazilian association really proved popular in Toulouse, where two other local bands, **Bomb 2 Bal** and **Femmouses T** (for Famous Trobaritz), both operate under Sicre's wings.

But the best band to ever come out of the "Pink City" was **Zebda** (a pun on a French slang word for Arab) and its satellite groups **Motivés** and **100% Collègues**. With their superb Toulouse accent they mixed rock, rap, flamenco and reggae beats, occasionally resurrecting proletarian songs from around the world. The collective, a multiracial band, offered a successful mix of cheerfulness, dedicated social activism and enthusiastic stage performances but went their separate ways in 2003. Lead singer **Magyd Cherif** brought out his excellent solo album *Cité des Etoiles* and the brotherly baldheaded duo **Mouss and Hakim Amokrane** released *Mouss et Hakim ou le contraire* and in 2009 the remarkable *Origines Contrôlées*, paying homage to the Algerian immigrant's music of the last fifty years with the help of two excellent accordion players, **Jean-Luc Amestoy** and **Lionel Suarez**, who have always been close to the Zebda collective.

Today's most celebrated Occitan rural band of the area is **La Talvera**, based in the beautiful medieval village of Cordes sur Ciel and founded by **Daniel Loddo**. The ensemble's main asset is its amazing singer, **Céline Ricard**, with a voice out of this world.

Aquitaine (Gascony, Bearn, Basque Country)

The cultural identity of Gascony, in southwest France, was given a boost during the traditional revival of the 1970s by the band **Perlinpinpin Folc** and their seminal album *Musique Traditionnelle de Gascogne*. They evolved into an extraordinary band called **Ténarèze**.

Gascony also has some unusual small pipes in the form of the **boha** or *bouhe*, with a unique rectangular chanter and drone combination. The sheepskin bag with the fleece showing gives it an eerie animal-like appearance and old photographs show shepherds living in the swamps of the area, playing them on stilts! Notable boha players are Ténarèze's **Alain Cadaillan**, **Yan Cozian** and Guillaume Lopez who often plays with accordion player Cyrille Brotto. The **Lopez Brotto Duo** is getting due recognition for its great dance music. Particularly active hurdy-gurdy master **Pascal Lefeuvre** is well known for his Tre Fontane medieval music ensemble, playing songs of the "trobars" (troubadours) and the "joglars" (jugglers) of the area. In 2009 he launched a promising folk-rock band named **ZanzibarCie**. The most popular group from the area is **Nadau**, a folk-rock outfit who sing in Béarnais, as does the internationally known minimalist singer **Marilis Orionaa**. **Familha Artus** (named after King Arthur) is a radical avant-garde band from Béarn whose members mix saturated hurdy-gurdy and energetic drum'n'bass.

Béarn is only half of the *département* of Pyrénées Atlantiques, whose other half is the French Pays Basque, where the Euskara language is still spoken by roughly 70,000 inhabitants. Among the traditional musical instruments are the *txistu* (a high-pitched wooden wind instrument), the *dultzaina* (a conical wind instrument) and the *alboka* (a distant relative of the clarinet made up of two horns). Produced by hitting variously pitched planks of wood with wooden sticks, the *txalaparta* is a rousing rhythmic music and so is the *trikitixa*, played on a tambourine and a diatonic accordion. But the Basque country is essentially famous for its singers, be it polyphonic ensembles like **Oldarra**, **Otxote Aizkota** and **Otxote Lurra**, who favour academic forms, or, on the lighter side, operetta singers such as **André Dassary**, **Rudi Hirigoyen** and **Luis Mariano**, who all became nationally known during and after World War II. Since the 1970s modern Basque music has flourished within a broader cultural (and political) approach, with folk singers **Anne Etchegoyen**, **Benat Achiary** and the rock-oriented **Akelarre** and **Niko Etchart** being the most prominent artists.

DISCOGRAPHY France

If you can't find them on import, most of the CDs listed here can be bought from *www.alapage.com*, *www.amazon.fr* or *www.fnac.fr*. For smaller regional labels, contact the Fédération des Associations de Musiques et Danses Traditionnelles (info@famdt.com).

⊙ **L'Ame de l'Auvergne**
Sony, France
A compilation with a strong 1920s flavour, gathering a wealth of original recordings for piano-accordion, cabrette and hurdy-gurdy, and containing some of the sources for many revival groups.

⊙ **Anthologie de la Chanson Française: La Chanson Traditionnelle**
EPM, France
A monumental fifteen-CD box set of three hundred songs covering every aspect of French song over five centuries. Mostly revival arrangements with a wide range of collaborators, this labour of love was produced by the late Marc Robine with the help of Emmanuel Pariselle and Gabriel Yacoub.

⊙ **Au Coeur de la Musique Bretonne, Vol. 1 & Vol. 2**
Coop Breizh, France
Although you won't find the top Breton stars here, this includes important artists and groups of various styles such as Gwerz, Yann Fanch Kemener, Roland Becker and Annie Ebrel.

⊙ **Fest Vraz, Musiques bretonnes Vol. 1 & Vol. 2**
Keltia, France
Generous compilation from a Quimper-based label, showing a good range of traditional and contemporary music from les Sœurs Goadec to Dan Ar Braz.

⊙ **Occitania Qu'es Aquo**
Daqui, France
A sample of the new Occitan scene, featuring some of its best-known exponents, notably Massilia Sound System, Fabulous Trobadors, Dupain, Michel Macias, Pascal Lefeuvre and Marilis Orionaa.

★ **The Rough Guide to Gypsy Swing**
World Music Network, UK
Fine collection, featuring the master himself, Django Reinhardt, on four tracks and some of his most gifted heirs (Bireli Lagrène, Tchavolo Schmidt, Patrick Saussois). There are even a few oldies (Jo Privat and Matelot Ferré) showing the connection with musette. Beautiful music.

⊙ **The Rough Guide to Paris Café Music**
World Music Network, UK
From Antoine Bouscatel's cabrette to rock-oriented contemporary bands, a great historical musette and accordion collection, including Gus Viseur and Edith Piaf's famous "L'Accordéoniste".

Françoise Atlan

The voice of France's Sephardic Jewish community.

⊙ **Andalussyat**
Buda Musique, France
With the help of Orchestre Arabo-Andalou from Fez (Morocco), this is a touching evocation of the lost mythical multi-ethnic paradise of Andalusia before Isabel the Catholic blew it all away.

Bagad Kemper

The best-known Breton pipe and drum band.

⊙ **Lin Ar Maout**
Keltia, France
A mostly live recording from this formidable ensemble, producing a true "wall of sound", plus a few studio tracks experimenting with softer moods.

Roland Becker

Pioneer of Celtic jazz.

⊙ **Chant dans la nuit**
Oyoun Music, France
Amazing synthesis of traditional Breton sounds, pop music and electronics.

Pierre Bensusan

One of the world's leading acoustic guitar virtuosos, strangely undervalued in his home country.

⊙ **Anthology**
Dagdagmusic, France
Spanning twenty years and eight albums, with two unreleased tracks. Beautifully produced.

La Bergère

The stage name of Sylvie Berger, one of the most beautiful voices on the trad scene.

⊙ **Ouvarosa**
Le Roseau, France
A collection of original and traditional songs, all elegantly produced by Gabriel Yacoub.

Patrick Bouffard

A lyrical, innovative and expressive hurdy-gurdy player from Central France.

⊙ **Transept**
Modal, France
A brilliant and energetic concept album, with Bouffard backed by six musicians.

Les Brayauds

Part of an umbrella organization of the same name, the members of the group have worked in various instrumental combinations to explore the music of the Lower Auvergne and their own compositions.

⊙ **Eau Forte**
Ocora, France
A classic: timeless arrangements of traditional themes with bagpipes, hurdy-gurdies and melodeons.

Manu Chao

Chao's work with post-punk fusion band Mano Negra from 1986–94 is captured at its joyful, crazy best on *Puta's Fever* (Virgin). He now plays solo, drawing on ragga, salsa and Latin styles with punk energy. This global nomad is, without a doubt, Europe's biggest world-music star.

★ **Radio Bemba Sound System**
Virgin Records, UK
This killer 29-track album is the next best thing to seeing Manu Chao live, and exemplifies the work of this modern-day militant and multilingual troubadour. The music comes mostly from *Proxima Estacion: Esperanza* with some from *Clandestino* and his early days with Mano Negra. Essential.

La Chavannée

A great collective of traditional players from central France, revolving around Frédéric Paris.

⊙ **Bateau Doré**
Modal, France
Poetic and sensitive evocation of the life of the *mariniers* or river sailors of the past.

Keyvan Chemirani

An innovative Iranian percussionist who plays a *zarb*, or Persian goblet drum as a melodic solo instrument. He is also a member, with his father and brother, of the zarb-only Trio Chemirani.

⊙ **Le Rythme de la Parole**
Accords Croisés, France
Each track features Chemirani's zarb and a different singer from a different country – Mali, India, Morocco, Pakistan and so on. A *tour de force*, and a superb and unique musical patchwork.

La Compagnie Vocale

Provence-based sixteen-strong mixed choral group (and social club!) performing rootsy acapella music in the local dialects of various regions of southern France.

⊙ **Piada Desliura – Chants Polyphoniques Provençaux**
Iris, France
Music from Provence, Piedmont, Béarn and Auvergne. The Provençal song of a shepherd struggling across the mountains to bring cheese to the baby Jesus is charming.

Lo Cor de la Plana

A male voice choir from Marseille directed by Manu Theron and devoting themselves to medieval dance songs as well as religious themes with a definite contemporary twist.

⊙ **Tant Deman**
Buda Musique, France
Primeval vibes, soaring harmonies, cheerful drones and dissonances.

DCA Trio

Dynamite music for dancing from a band composed of Dominique Paris (cabrette), Hervé Capel (accordion) and Anne-Lise Foy (hurdy-gurdy and vocals).

Trio DCA
Amta, France
The wild and irresistible dance music of Upper Auvergne at its best.

Duo Bertrand en Cie

Exquisite music from the salt marshes known as the Marais Breton Vendéen.

Fleurs de Racines
Cie des Arts d'Hier Pour Aujourd'hui, France
The uncle/nephew duo founded by Thierry and Sébastien Bertrand has grown into a full band of six members, who are not afraid of experimentation and using rare instruments like the Chapman stick.

Fabulous Trobadors

A duo founded by Claude Sicre, one of the main cultural activists of Southern France.

Duels de Tchache et Autres Trucs du Folklore Toulousain
Tôt ou Tard, France
Knowing a little French will certainly help you to enjoy these incredibly witty verbal exchanges.

Gipsy Kings

Spanish-speaking Gypsies from the Arles region in Provence, who became enormously popular in the late 1980s with their "Catalonian rumba" sound.

Roots
Nonesuch, UK
The title says it all. Eschewing their previous pop fusion experiments, the Reyes family members return to the acoustic guitar-driven style of their beginnings. Just what the doctor ordered.

Hadouk Trio

Superior ethno jazz trio comprising Didier Malherbe, Steve Shenan and Loy Ehrlich, all playing unusual instruments.

Baldarmare
Naive, US
Virtuosity and improvisation at its best in this live recording.

Lamour

Truly original electro musician Pascal Lamour is the inventor of Breton trance music.

Shamans of Brittany
BNC Production, France
A fine example of Lamour's successful mixture of electronic wizardry with Breton roots.

Malicorne

The influence of this now-disbanded seminal 1970s European folk-rock band is still felt today.

Légende
Rykodisc, UK
Compilation from Malicorne's most creative years, when Marie Yacoub, Gabriel Yacoub, Hughes de Courson, Olivier Kowalski and Laurent Vercambre led the way. The magic is still here.

Erik Marchand

A great gwerz singer and clarinet player from Brittany, eager to explore all kinds of new paths.

Pruna
Chant du Monde, France
A beautifully successful collaboration with Romanian, Serbian and Gypsy musicians.

Maurice El Médioni

Legendary piano player from Oran, granddad of rai and much more.

Descarga Oriental
Piranha, Germany
A true masterpiece of "pianoriental" with the help of Cuban percussionist Roberto Rodriguez and top-notch salsa artists.

Moussu T e Lei Jovents

The most creative offshoot of the great Massilia Sound System collective, featuring François Ridel (alias Moussu T), guitar- and banjo-player Blu and Brazilian percussionist Jamilson Da Silva.

★ Mademoiselle Marseille
Harmonia Mundi, UK
A delightful acoustic re-creation – with strong African and Caribbean influences – of life on the Marseille docks circa 1920, and much more. Blending old and new, Moussu T proves here that he is an enthralling chansonnier, unmistakably Marseillais but truly universal.

Obrée Alie

Featuring Bertran Obrée, a new Breton talent who is a gifted poet and singer.

Vente Sou Lez Saodd
Coop Breizh, France
Sung in the Breton Gallo patois, French and Spanish, this album contains rich and exciting sounds.

Orchestre National de Barbès

This twelve-piece Paris-based band has taken the North African and French music scenes by storm in recent years with their powerful mix of rai, chaabi, Moroccan gnawa and European rock-funk.

Alik
Wagram, France
Alik means "look" and is ONB's older and wiser but still cooking third album. Great cover of "Sympathy for the Devil".

Titi Robin

Restless virtuoso oud and guitar player under Gypsy influence.

FRANCE

148

⊙ Alezane
Naive, US
A double-CD anthology of 25 years of recordings by Robin.

Spi et la Gaudriole

Former high-energy punk-rocker Spi (aka Jean-Michel Poisson) is now into polkas, mazurkas, bourrées, rondes and gavottes. The French trad sensation of 2005.

⊙ En Avant Baleti
Cinq Planètes, France
A sort of Occitan-style fest noz, with oboe, hurdy-gurdy and catchy vocals to match.

Alan Stivell

The saviour of Breton music. In the early 1960s when Breton and Celtic sounds were forgotten and totally uncool, the young harp player had the foresight to revive them, almost single-handedly.

⊙ Renaissance of the Celtic Harp
Philips, UK
The 1971 album that began it all.

⊙ Again
Keltia III, France
Remastered reissue of his 1994 album, which contains most of his best songs.

La Talvera

Great Occitan dance band.

⊙ Bramadis
Association Cordae, France
Interesting cover of Brazilian Luis Gonzaga's Nordeste anthem "Asa Branca".

Huong Than

A magnificent traditional Vietnamese singer from a family of Saigon opera singers.

⊙ Dragonfly
Act, France
Old Asian melodies with modern instrumentation, including N'Guyen Lê on guitar. Stunning.

Une Anche Passe

A brass- and reed-based group, led by Laurent Audemard on the piercing Languedoc oboe. Year by year, Audemard has integrated new musicians from the Mediterranean into this utterly unique band.

⊙ Le Grand Troupeau
MAP Records/Culture Records, Benelux
A memorable and deeply moving musical suite, recorded live with Belgian musicians in Passchendaele (Flanders), where half a million soldiers were slaughtered in World War I.

Gus Viseur

Legendary accordion player and the first to mix musette with jazz in the 1930s.

⊙ L'As de l'Accordéon: à Bruxelles
Paris Jazz Corner, France
A live recording from 1942 with a great CD cover by Robert Crumb.

Hector Zazou

France's Peter Gabriel, Zazou died too soon in 2008.

⊙ Songs of the Cold Seas
Sony Columbia, US
Featuring Björk and others, an awesome mixture of electronics and ethnic music to illustrate a journey around the Arctic.

Zebda

A multi-ethnic raggamuffin band from Toulouse who took France by storm during the early 2000s.

⊙ La Tawa
Barclay, France
A live "best of" album, recorded just before the group disbanded.

PLAYLIST
France

1 **PRINCE D'ORANGE Malicorne** from *Légende*
Quintessential anti-military song by Europe's best folk-rock band of the 1970s.

2 **YA RAYAH Rachid Taha** from *Diwan*
Beautiful chaabi song about the plight of the Algerian migrant worker.

3 **MADEMOISELLE MARSEILLE Moussu T e lei Jovents** from *Mademoiselle Marseille*
All the spirit of this great Mediterranean port.

4 **ALORS… VOILÀ! Tchavolo Schmitt** from *Django's Legacy*
Star of Tony Gatlif's movie *Swing*, Schmitt is one of today's most gifted manouche guitarists.

5 **TRI MARTOLOD Alan Stivell** from *Again*
About three sailors finding their way to Newfoundland. Stivell's version is still the best.

6 **MI VIDA Manu Chao** from *Proxima Estacion: Esperanza*
A beautifully written melancholic song, in sharp contrast to the rest of the album.

7 **POLKA À ALFRED MOURET DCA Trio** from *Musique de Haute Auvergne*
Energetic cabrette-accordion-hurdy-gurdy combination.

8 **KOUNKOURÉ Ba Cissoko** from *Sabolan*
Before Ba Cissoko, nobody could dream of taking the kora to such Hendrix-like climaxes.

9 **QUAND LA CHANSON EST BONNE Spi & la Gaudriole** from *En Avant, Baleti*
This Schottische composed by Marc Perrone is as good as its title promises.

10 **TOMBER LA CHEMISE Zebda** from *La Tawa*
One of the great successes of the celebrated southern French raggamuffin scene.

France | Chanson

a world in three couplets

Jacques Brel
Jean Pierre Leloir

In addition to its folk, France possesses a rich heritage of popular music, centred loosely around the art of *chanson*. An urban form born of the twentieth-century Parisian milieu, with international stars like Brel and Piaf, chanson communicates a sense of place – and style – like few other genres, and has proved remarkably adaptable to changing fashions, as **Philip Sweeney** observes.

Defining modern chanson so as to filter out Anglo-American influence is a contentious task, involving what one might term the Johnny Hallyday Dilemma – deciding which French stars to exclude to satisfy the roots sensibilities of the Anglophone world music listener. It's clear, however, that the character of French song is due to the musicality of the French language, the emphasis placed on poetry – and thus on intelligibility – of lyrics, and the fact that it can easily incorporate international trends in instrumentation without disfiguration.

Cabarets and Bals-Musette

Two historic musical movements feed into modern chanson, both of them Parisian. The first was the art of the eighteenth-century **satiric chansonniers**, who performed in forerunners of basement clubs known as *caveaux*. By the end of the nineteenth century, this had given birth to the earliest **realist chansons**, songs about the lives, dreams and tragedies of ordinary people, with a strong side interest in those on the fringes of legality, as performed by **Aristide Bruant** in the Montmartre cabaret Le Chat Noir. By the 1920s, *chanson réaliste* had its first stars, two charismatic women, **Damia** and **Fréhel**, who set the mode for theatrical performance later raised to its greatest heights by **Édith Piaf** and **Jacques Brel**. Damia, known as "la tragedienne de la chanson", combined sophisticated presentation – she was the first to make major use of the spotlight – with a penchant for setting the lyrics of serious poets such as Verlaine, anticipating Brel and **Brassens** by half a century. Her rival Fréhel not only sang of tragedy, but lived it, beginning as a poor, star-struck child street singer and rising through the music-halls to become a great star, with her Parisian accent, hardship- and alcohol-etched looks and raw emotional delivery.

The second important style was primarily an instrumental dance genre, but its success stamped on mid-twentieth-century French popular song the characteristic sound of the **accordion**. This was the domain of the **bal musette**, and couples dancing close to the *java* and the waltz in districts such as the Bastille, where pimps and *apaches* rubbed shoulders with shop-girls and slumming aristos (see previous chapter).

Although the musette stars were not themselves chanson performers, nor from Paris, accordionists played critical roles as accompanists to chanson stars, and later as mentors to the new generation which re-embraced the instrument in the 1990s.

A prime example is **Jean Corti**, Brel's chief accompanist, sought out thirty years later to work with the **Têtes Raides**, stars of the *chanson neo-réaliste*.

The Jazz Age

During the 1920s and 30s, the showbusiness side of chanson flourished. The old café-concerts – early cabarets where all Paris came to eat, drink and be entertained – had given way to the new music halls, showy concert palaces with big revues of variety acts and star singers such as **Mistinguett**. The songs they performed were still rooted in traditional vernacular melodies and refrains, but London and New York loomed large on the horizon, and the French soon had their first international star, **Maurice Chevalier**, a gangling young man from the working-class suburb of Ménilmontant, made his mark as a member of Mistinguett's chorus, then as her lover, and the couple were for a decade the toast of Paris. Chevalier's cleverly constructed stage persona – a mixture of Parisian wide-boy and suave toff – and his smooth, expressive voice, made him a huge star.

At the same time, a wave of musical influence from across the Atlantic washed through chanson's ranks. The way was opened by **Mireille** – a Conservatoire-trained pianist who worked in Noël Coward musicals in London and New York. With the lyricist **Jean Nohain**, Mireille began to compose light, rhythmic songs, with tongue-in-cheek lyrics. Their "Couchés dans le foin" revolutionized chanson and was soon omnipresent on the new mass medium, radio. **Irène de Trébert** became Mademoiselle Swing, and **Jean Sablon**, the French Bing Crosby, became the first French singer to rely on a microphone and croon intimately, unlike the operatic *bel canto* delivery still lingering in the work of Tino Rossi. And then along came **Charles Trenet**, *le fou chantant* (the singing clown), a bundle of zany energy with his trilby-topped blond curls, his taste for Gershwin and surrealism, and his flair for striking lyrics.

The Golden Age

But then, straddling the worlds of chanson and bal-musette, came **Édith Piaf**. If one artist represents the world image of twentieth-century France, it is Piaf, the Parisian sparrow. Born, according to legend, on a pavement in Belleville (actually a nearby hospital), Piaf developed into a singer of enormous charisma, taking the drama of the old realists to a new level, and retaining their fascination with the colourful poor Paris of popular myth while moving on to a more universalized treatment of human emotion. Although she was primarily an interpreter, Piaf also wrote successfully: her "La vie en rose", a simple statement of the power of love to blank out pain, is an ultra-famous example.

Piaf died in 1963, after two decades of turbulent fame. By this time, a new generation of artists was raising chanson to its peak of intellectual prestige. At its centre was the great trinity of **George Brassens**, **Léo Ferré** and **Jacques Brel**.

The first two, working from the late 1940s onward, introduced an unparalleled degree of poetic aspiration into the realm of popular song. Ferré, a musical interpreter of the verse of Verlaine and Rimbaud, became a symbol for bohemian freedom and, after the 1968 students' revolt, a counter-culture hero. Brassens, whose avuncular pipe and moustache are so hard to equate now with cutting-edge arts status, combined the bawdiness of the old chansonniers, and a solid anchor of populism, with high literary ambition.

Brel, an accomplished dissector of the human condition in the mould of Piaf, was born into a bourgeois Catholic family in Belgium. He progressed from scout troop entertainer to the cabarets of first Brussels and then Paris, where he polished his intensely emotional delivery in Right Bank establishments such as Les Trois Baudets. By 1958 he was a huge star and, until his death in 1978, a symbol of French popular music abroad, notably in the US, where the show by Mort Shuman devoted to Brel's music was a hit on Broadway. But the era was not an entirely masculine domain. The Left Bank cabaret scene, which grew up around the Boulevard St Germain, featured sultry new divas such as **Juliette Gréco**, the black-polo-necked muse of Jean-Paul Sartre and lover of Miles Davis, and **Barbara**, "l'aigle noire", with her half-murmured, half-sobbed, self-composed concoctions of nostalgic sensuality.

Édith Piaf

The Pop Age

As Anglo-American pop (converted in France into *yé-yé*) and rock swept all before them in the 1960s, chanson was forced to react, by either ignoring the new trends, mimicking them, or assimilating them creatively. Brel typified the first tendency, along with Gréco and Barbara. Elvis simulacra with anglicized stage names such as Johnny Hallyday and Dick Rivers spearheaded the mimics, to their lasting shame: though Hallyday is nowadays a grandee of show-business, a survey of young musicians by the magazine *Les inrockuptibles* in 1999 revealed Hallyday as their most reviled anti-role-model.

Other artists brought a greater individuality to the problem. In the 1950s, **Gilbert Bécaud**, "Monsieur 100,000 Volts", had adapted the dynamic proto-rock 'n' roll stage antics of Johnny Ray to his classic Piaf material, provoking the first outbreak of teenage screaming and seat-wrecking among the audience of Paris's Olympia concert hall. In 1956, **Boris Vian** began his career as a songwriter. As a teenager, he had promoted jazz concerts by visiting Americans such as Duke Ellington. A keen trumpeter, Vian had always played in big-bands, alongside his better-known surrealist novels and poetry – the most infamous being *J'irai cracher sur vos tombes* (I Spit On Your Grave). His first album as a singer, *Chansons Possibles ... et Impossibles,* was released in 1956: a collection of slightly anachronistic chanson and jazz songs with savagely satirical lyrics. Vian also worked with Henri Salvador on French rock'n'roll material, and many of Vian's oddball ditties ended up receiving surprisingly funky and swinging treatments over the course of the 1960s. The sixties also saw the arrival of the artist who most dominated French song in the later decades of the century. **Serge Gainsbourg** was born to a poor but artistic Russian-Jewish family, studied art and then entered the same 1950s cabaret circuit which nurtured Brel, Gréco and so many more. Gainsbourg shared Johnny H's fascination with all things American – and with Swinging sixties London – but his incorpora-

Tropical and World Chanson

France has always been among the first to assimilate musical styles from Latin America, the Caribbean, Africa and, of course, the Mediterranean, and part of this assimilation has been into the realm of chanson.

In terms of Latin American input, one of chanson's most eminent elder statesmen, **Henri Salvador**, had feet in the camps of *variété*, including a rich vein of slapstick and humour, and of lilting, tropical-shaded song. This is partly due to his background: he was born in Guyane, the French territory next to Brazil, and spent years working in Brazilian casinos, after having first visited with the Ray Ventura Band in the 1940s. In a similar vein, the Turkish-born **Dario Moreno** included plenty of 1950s cha cha cha influence. Artistes such as **Georges Moustaki** and **Bernard Lavilliers** brought their travellers' love of Brazil and elsewhere to their musical personalities, while **Pierre Barouh** – actor, singer and composer of the famous theme song from the 1960s hit film *Un homme et une femme* – was also responsible for the advance of the *bossa nova* shading into chanson in the 1960s. Since the worldwide vogue for Cuban music in the 1990s, French artists have been prominent collaborators with Cuban musicians, the musicality of the French language sitting well in a Latin context. The best is the singer, composer and arranger **Cyrius Martinez**, who has made outstanding albums of French language chansons infused with the spirit and music of eastern Cuba.

From the Mediterranean, the current has been equally strong, ranging from the shading of Neapolitan song contained in the work of **Tino Rossi**, one of the greats of 1930s chanson, to the North African contribution of singers from France's one-time colony Algeria. Perhaps the most interesting example of this phenomenon is **Enrico Macias**, the singer who most personifies the nostalgia of France's pieds-noirs, the French citizens who fled Algeria in 1962, after having been on the losing side in the War of Independence. Born to an Algerian-Jewish family connected with the master of eastern Maghreb *maalouf* music, Cheikh Raymond Leyris, Macias rose through the Oriental cabarets of Paris to become a national pop star, combining a musical flavour of his native territory with the catchiness of yé-yé.

It's worth noting, finally, that chanson's position as a world marque is acknowledged by a strong movement of Japanese imitators, such as the diva **Kohko Arai**, who has been known to don a black beret to thrill Tokyo audiences with her vibrato-laden versions of Brel.

---

tion of such influences, like his early espousal of tropical music (*Couleur Café*, a 1964 album featuring Nigerian drummers is a case in point), was creatively cannibalistic rather than slavishly mimicking. Gainsbourg's classically derived melodies, his clever punning lyrics, and the close-miked murmured singing style he both affected himself and imposed on many of the young female singers he wrote for, all marked him as one of the major forces of pop-era chanson. His Pygmalion role was applied to Brigitte Bardot, his long-time companion **Jane Birkin**, **Françoise Hardy**, a teen star who has matured into one of France's finest artists, and in later years Vanessa Paradis and his own daughter Charlotte.

The Rock Years and the New Wave

Although certain French artists and audiences devoted themselves to rock through the 1970s and 80s, there were some new artists producing high-quality chanson with modernized arrange-

ments. Starting in the 1960s at the influential *café-théâtre* La Vieille Grille, **Jacques Higelin** grew to combine the stage presence of a Mick Jagger with a feel of the traditional music hall and a strong hint of Trenet. **Alain Souchon** produced beautifully reflective songs on the transience of life and modern preoccupations. And **Renaud** combined a politically engaged folk-rocker image with a flair for demotic and satirical song-pictures.

By the mid-1980s, performers such as **Étienne Daho** or **Lio** were combining a chanson-imbued take on contemporary international pop with the beginnings of a cult re-appraisal of the recent past, in Daho's case the work of Françoise Hardy. Around this time, a fully fledged return to the roots of popular chanson was gathering pace, particularly among the series of artists, notably **Les Garçons Bouchers** and **Pigalle**, associated with the label Boucherie Productions run by François Hadji-Lazaro. Pigalle reprised old Damia songs, and the accordion, re-introduced into the pop charts in 1981 by the rock pasticheur Gérard Blanchard, suddenly began to crop up in groups influenced three-quarters by The Clash and a quarter by Les Compagnons de la Chanson. Some, such as the **Négresses Vertes**, included the accordion in a kaleidoscopic mix of elements from North Africa and Spain, alternative circus and Saturday night provincial dance. The group Lo'Jo, formed in 1982, surrounded the Gauloise-toasted classic chanson vocals of singer Denis Péan with Gypsy rhythms and Arabic, Berber and African influences. In 1989 the most significant group, the **Têtes Raides**, released their first album and began to refine the mixture of oblique atmospheric lyrics and sophisticated multi-faceted arrangements that would make them leaders of the movement sometimes referred to as *néo-réaliste* in reference to the realism of the Fréhel generation (although the term had been coined earlier to describe Brel and co.).

Minimalists and Chanson Buissonière

Through the 1990s, a fresh set of artists rose to the challenge of creating distinctively French music for a new generation. They included singer-songwriters such as Parisian Thomas Fersen and **Miossec** (Christophe Miossec), a Brittany-born chronicler of life's bitterer edge. The so-called *chanson minimaliste* movement was born, its leading light **Dominique A** combining sparse, home-made, noir-shaded instrumentation, all rhythm-boxes

and David Lynch guitars, with droll, half-murmured texts. Another key minimalist was Philippe Katerine, alias **Katerine**, a playful, deceptively easy-listening blender of everything from sixties Franco-Brazilian pop to faux psychedelia. As Étienne Daho had sought out past icon Françoise Hardy, so Katerine recorded with **Ana Karina**, the actress beloved of Jean-Luc Godard and *nouvelle vague* cinema.

As an antidote to the darker side of the minimalists, a school of light-hearted, flippant performers arrived, magpie-like in musical influence, who reclaimed something of the high-quality fantasy of Charles Trenet. This tendency is sometimes referred to as *chanson buissonière* (the word relates to "truant", and implies a playfully rebellious attitude); its stars are artists such as Mathieu Chedid, stage-named **M**. A new crop of female artists came forward too, usually following in the Gainsbourg/ Hardy/Birkin singing mode: breathy, murmured, occasionally fausse-gamine to the point of parody. There was even a Gainsbourg figure in the shape of the composer, singer and arranger **Benjamin Biolay**, who worked with the Dutch-Israeli-Parisian singer-songwriter **Keren-Ann** and a string of similar new chanteuses "*sans voix*" (without voice), as the phrase goes, notably his sister **Coralie Clément** and the actress **Chiara Mastroianni**, daughter of Cathérine Deneuve and Marcello Mastroianni, whom Biolay married in 2002.

DISCOGRAPHY French Chanson

⊙ **A Night in Paris**
Union Square Music, UK
A good double-CD selection of early chanson, including Trenet, Damia, Fréhel, Chevalier and post-war material from Gréco and Hallyday, unfortunately padded out with tacky cover versions.

⊙ **Les cingles du music-hall**
Fremeaux, France
A series of fifteen CDs, each devoted to one year from 1929 to 1943, from France's best archive compilation label. Top names and obscure finds, plus excellent biographical and explanatory notes.

⊙ **Cuisine non-stop**
Luaka Bop, US
A rare attempt by an Anglophone label to present modern chanson-related music, including important names such as the Têtes Raides, Arthur H, Ignatus and Louise Attaque, and world-oriented acts such as Lo'Jo.

Barbara

Monique Serf, later known as Barbara, was one of the greats of Saint Germain chanson. Having studied singing in the Paris Conservatoire, she began to make a name in the chanson clubs of the late 1950s, particularly l'Ecluse, where she earned the title "la chanteuse de minuit". Known for her intensely dramatic, virtuoso vocal performance.

★ **Master serie: Barbara**
Polygram, France
Two CDs of the greatest hits of the "black eagle", sometimes accompanied by accordion, piano and bass, sometimes by a larger group, sometimes by the full orchestra of Michel Colombier.

Benjamin Biolay (and School of)

The young singer/songwriter/producer often spoken of as the new Gainsbourg studied music in the conservatoire of his native Lyon, and worked with local groups including the successful Affaire Louis Trio before writing for himself

155

and a succession of female singers, including Gainsbourg's last companion, Bambou.

⊙ L'Origine
EMI, France

A more heavily rock-arranged exercise than his lighter, dreamier debut *Rose Kennedy*, *L'Origine* nonetheless showcases Biolay's voice and writing well, and has the advantage of a guest track from Françoise Hardy.

⊙ La biographie de Luka Philipsen
EMI, France

The hit debut album by Biolay's muse and co-writer Keren-Ann, demonstrating the chanteuse's qualifications as the new Françoise Hardy, and containing the song "Jardin d'hiver" which was partly responsible for the return to fame of the octogenarian Henri Salvador.

⊙ Bye bye beauté
EMI, France

The debut album by another Biolay muse, his sister Coralie Clément, who manages to out-Hardy Keren-Ann with her Lolita-like wisp of a voice, nicely adorned with touches of *mariachi* brass, Calexico-style.

Jacques Brel

Brel, an austere and serious young singer/guitarist from Brussels, joined the 1950s Right Bank cabaret world of Paris and transformed himself into a powerful performer and brilliant writer.

⭐ Brel: infiniment
Barclay/Universal, France

A double CD of forty remastered tracks, including all the classics – a terrific live "Amsterdam", the dark Randy Newman-esque "Ces gens-là" – plus five tracks newly released in 2003, of which at least two are as powerful as anything Brel wrote.

Dominique A

The soon-to-be leader of minimaliste chanson was an impecunious amateur rocker living in Nantes when he decided to go back to basics. "Le courage des oiseaux", recorded on a cheap Casio synthesizer, was critically acclaimed, and led to major success for his recipe: "a modern flirt with the highest traditions of Barbara and Michel Polnaroff", as one critic put it.

⊙ La mémoire neuve
Lithium/Virgin, France

This third album, from 1995, is a little richer in instrumentation but still demonstrates well the sobriety of voice and introspective, faintly sinister atmosphere of lyric that is the Dominique A brand.

Léo Ferré

Ferré started his musical career in the celebrated restaurant-cabaret Le Boeuf Sur Le Toit in 1946, on the same bill as the young Charles Aznavour. In addition to his own complex, allusive song-poems, Ferré adapted the texts of Baudelaire, Verlaine and Rimbaud, produced an opera and an oratorio, conducted richly flamboyant orchestrations of his works, and espoused the post-1968 rock revolution.

⊙ Les années toscanes
La Memoire et la Mer, Monaco

A brilliantly contemporary compilation from albums recorded during the last two decades of Ferré's life, this contains some of the most ambitiously orchestrated texts in twentieth-century chanson.

Serge Gainsbourg

Born Lucien Ginsburg, he began his career as a support act to the bohemian songwriter and novelist Boris Vian, and wrote early hits for a roster of glamorous females. His own work drew upon a huge range of sources, from classic chanson to rock and reggae.

⭐ De Serge Gainsbourg à Gainsbarre
Polygram, France

The best of dozens of compilations, combining his early cabaret work – "Le poinçonneur des lilas" – with Bardot and Birkin outings and mid-period cult album *L'homme à tête de chou*.

Françoise Hardy

Françoise Hardy was a demure and beautiful seventeen-year-old political science student when she sent an amateur recording of "Tous les garçons et les filles" to Disques Vogues. The single sold two million copies. Hardy's simple, fragile voice matured into one of the most respected in French popular music.

⊙ Dutronc, Hardy: Le meilleur des deux
BMG, France

A good collection of early songs also featuring the work of Jacques Dutronc, contemporary rock-oriented chanson star and Hardy's husband.

⭐ Clair obscur
Virgin, France

An excellent 2000 release featuring great duets with Dutronc, Étienne Daho and Iggy Pop indicates where Hardy is at today.

Katerine

Once categorized as a singer of "*chanson bébête*" – silly chanson – Katerine is a soft-voiced, irreverent faux-innocent, and a highly original foil to Dominique A. After a conservative Catholic upbringing, art college in Nantes, and writing and producing for other artists, his first CD, *Mes mauvaises frequentations*, established a reputation which has grown steadily.

⭐ Les creatures *and* L'homme à trois mains
Barclay/Universal, France

Two CDs packaged together rather than a double CD, this 1999 release shows Katerine at his most engaging, amusing and musically progressive.

Édith Piaf

Édith Giovanna Gassion, stage-named Piaf, or sparrow, rose from poverty in the workers' quarter of Belleville to consecration as France's musical ambassador and the embodiment of the passionate theatricality of a principal strand of chanson.

⊙ 30e Anniversaire
EMI, France

Numerous Piaf "Best Ofs" succeed each other on the CD racks. This is a rarity, produced for the thirtieth anniversary of the star's death, and containing a particularly good cross-section of her hits.

Alain Souchon

Born in Casablanca in 1945, Souchon's formative influence was The Beatles as much as Brel and Brassens, and, with his song-writing partner Laurent Voulzy, he has always steered a path between instrumental fascination with things Anglo-American and a serious lyrical intent.

⊙ **Collection**
Virgin, France
A good compilation from five major hit albums between 1985 and 1999, featuring his huge 1998 smash "Foule sentimentale", a classic of modern pop chanson.

Les Têtes Raides

Christian Olivier, the leader of Têtes Raides, was an art student and fan of The Clash who gradually moved closer to the world of chanson. Half-a-dozen successful albums later, the band was able to sell out a month-long season at the Theatre des Bouffes du Nord, the old music hall once home to the greats of chanson réaliste.

⊙ **Dix ans de Têtes Raides**
Tôt ou Tard, France
A selection of seventeen good tracks from seven of the Têtes Raides' most important albums, including hits such as "Un p'tit air" and the perennial show-finale "Ginette". A feast of accordions, drums, tubas, guttural vocals, more or less obscure lyrics and eccentric fun.

Charles Trenet

From his teenage fascination with jazz and musical theatre, via his huge success in the 1930s and 40s, to his rediscovery as a national treasure in the Mitterand years, the author of "La mer" dominated French song until his death in 2001.

⊙ **The Extraordinary Garden**
EMI, UK
A competent selection, with all the greats – from "Boum", "La mer" and "Douce France" to the extraordinary "Je chante" from 1937, the cheeriest and strangest post-suicide lyric ever written.

Boris Vian

Prankster, surrealist, poet and anti-establishment icon, Boris Vian wrote songs that have a kinship with acerbic romantics such as Kurt Weill and Tom Waits.

⊙ **Boris Vian chante Boris Vian**
Polygram, France
There are plenty of good Boris compilations out there, some which also include his contemporaries' takes on his songs (which are often surprisingly groovy, in a very 1960s kind of way). This one sticks to Boris's own uniquely mordant delivery of his razor-sharp *chansons*, with savage swings into tango and jazz.

FRANCE | Chanson

PLAYLIST
France | Chanson

1 ORLY Jacques Brel from *Brel infiniment*
An observed moment at an airport is worked into a majestic edifice of existential tragedy by the power of *le grand* Jacques.

2 NANTES Barbara from *Master serie*
A touching and atmospheric lament on the death of her father becomes one of Barbara's most celebrated songs.

3 L'HOMME A TETE DE CHOU Serge Gainsbourg from *De Serge Gainsbourg à Gainsbarre*
Rock-era Gainsbourg at his most verbally dextrous and inexplicably fascinating in a tongue-in-cheek tale of suburban passion and murder.

4 CLAIR OBSCUR Françoise Hardy from *Clair Obscur*
Mature Hardy, but still the same clarity and simplicity of voice, in a sensitive semi-love-song of ambivalence and muted passion.

5 POULET N.728 120 Katerine from *Les Creatures*
Can a love song to a Red Label chicken "eaten hot for lunch and cold in the evening" stand alongside Brel? Hell, yes.

6 DESERTEUR Boris Vian from *Boris Vian chante Boris Vian*
A controversial protest against the Algerian war, this song made Vian something of an anti-establishment hero, with his hangdog voice moping along to a mournful Duke Ellington-ish backing.

Germany

not what you expect

17 Hippies
Andreas Riedel

Germany's roots music scene is scarcely known abroad, yet it is actually quite a success story, ranging from the traditional to the radical, with innumerable detours en route. But what did the Germans ever do for us? For starters, suggests **Ken Hunt**, they coined the very words "folksong" and "world music", and named the "folk condition".

The gloriously hot first weekend in July 1991 was a turning point for the newly reunified Germany's roots and world music scenes. That weekend, the former German Democratic Republic (GDR) town of Rudolstadt in Thuringia hosted the first **Tanz&FolkFest Rudolstadt**. German music had never witnessed anything approaching it. This dance and folk festival inaugurated a new era in German roots and world music. The spirit of optimism and the piqued curiosity evident everywhere at that festival proved nothing less than transformative.

TFF Rudolstadt

The acts TFF Rudolstadt booked that first year were a mixture of tried-and-tested East and West German folk luminaries such as Liederjan, Folkländer and Wacholder. There was a sprinkling of old Anglo-American hands like Derroll Adams and Ramblin' Jack Elliott and Wizz and Simeon Jones. The line-up also included four world-class European folk highlights in Bulgaria's Bisserov Sisters, Sardinia's Elena Ledda e Sonos, Hedningarna from Sweden and Jablkoň from Czechoslovakia. It all succeeded well enough for TFF Rudolstadt to become an annual event and emblematic of the amalgamated folk scene, fleetingly (it now seems) called the **Deutsch-Deutsche Folkszene** in those heady early years after Reunification when neither *Ossi* (East German) nor *Wessi* (West German) knew what lay in store. That *Zeitgeist* also gave birth to *Folker!*, one of the world's most important folk and world music magazines, and the German Folk Awards, known as Ruths since 2002, a co-production of MDR Figaro (the local radio station's arts programme), PROFOLK (Germany's lobbying organization for folk, roots and world music) and TFF Rudolstadt itself. Indicative of its cultural status and economic importance, Germany's Chancellor Angela Merkel provided the salutatory introduction to the 2008 festival programme.

Since June 1955 Rudolstadt had hosted festivals reflecting the perception of comradely culture of the GDR's state party, the Socialist Unity Party of Germany (SED). (Never forget that the GDR was very narrow in its interpretation of brotherhood since, although cultural miscegenation *might* be allowed, miscegenation across races carried heavy penalties, while the slang term for gay men was the GDR penal code number.) These festivals never became an annual event, and the turnover of names was impressive: Festival of German Folk Dance, Festival of the Socialist Family and Folklore Festival of the Joy of Living are just some, summon-

ing an increasingly strong waft of SED identity and agenda. Although Rudolstadt was only one of many *Stadtfeste* (town festivals) that took place across the length and breadth of the GDR (and indeed in the Federal Republic of Germany or West Germany), it became known as the "City of Dance Festivals", as a mural on the side of a house proclaimed in 1991. The focus at Rudolstadt was on good working-class culture, *rote Lieder* (red songs) and manifestations of solidarity. Larger GDR events, notably Berlin's **Festival of Political Song**, held between 1970 and 1990, gradually got the funding to secure a range of foreign acts from Argentina, Australia, Britain, Chile, Cuba, India, North Korea and Portugal. Naturally, Rudolstadt had troupes from abroad, but these were primarily from the comrade states, from the CSSR, Hungary, Poland and the USSR. Then, as now, key to the town's flowering as a festival town was its geographic centrality.

By 1989, the year that Rudolstadt hosted its last GDR-style shebang, the old certainties were under attack. That July, Hans-Jürgen Schaefer of the state-run record label VEB Deutsche Schallplatten (the only game in town) formally declined to release **Angelika Weiz & GVO**'s astonishing and courageous deconstruction – aka desecration – of the socialist youth hymn "Unsre Heimat" (Our Home/Homeland). Weiz had expressed the unutterable and transformed it from one of the central song-pillars of SED socialism into a folk-rock ecological critique. There is nothing in the annals of European folk-rock that comes close. (Wolfgang Becker used a children's chorus version in his 2003 film *Good Bye Lenin!* to similarly double-edged effect.) Two years later, TFF Rudolstadt began its progress into a new world, in time growing to dominate Germany's roots and world music festival scene.

TFF Rudolstadt in fact became the most influential roots festival in Central Europe, partly due to its ability to put on ambitious projects such as the Global Vocal Meeting, a sumptuous collaboration between Corin Curschellas (Switzerland), Abdoulaye Diabate (Mali), Rinde Eckert (US), Mitsou (Hungary), Sudha Ragunathan (India) and Senge (Madagascar) in 2000, a souvenir CD of which was released by the German NoEthno label. Break through at TFF Rudolstadt and, the wisdom goes, an act can break through further afield. Rudolstadt has become a model of how the old certainties collapsed – and, many argue, how new, post-Reunification orthodoxies set in. It has set a new benchmark for artistic standards and resilience, especially since world music festivals tend to come and go in Germany. (For more information, see *www.tff-rudolstadt.de*.)

In the beginning was the word I: Volkslied

German **Johann Gottfried Herder** (1744–1803) did for folk music what the Swedish naturist Linnaeus did for the natural world: he put a name to what had been around since time immemorial. Herder was steeped in German Protestantism and had a lifelong interest in music (world music if you count his experience of Latvian traditional music) and philology. Like many people of his age, he was much taken by Rousseau's ideas. Harmonizing with nature and empathizing with those closest to nature became badges of Herder's world view. For him, it was a small, yet significant, step to locate a poetic essence in the ownerless songs of the people.

Herder's new word germinated in 1773. His simple compound noun joining "people" (*Volk*) and "song" (*Lied*) appeared in his Sturm und Drang manifesto *Von Deutscher Art und Kunst* (Of German Kind and Art). The word took a while to establish itself, but Herder was living in a lively era when ideas, philosophies and political theories flowed freely across regional and national borders. *Volkslied* had a plangent simplicity that resonated with Sturm und Drang (conventionally translated as "storm and stress", though "storm and drive" comes closer) and nascent nationhood.

Within forty years of Herder's death, the English language began a process of superannuating its plethora of lofty-sounding words of the "antiquary", "minstrelsy", "balladry" and "relique" kind. That seed planted in 1773 in faraway Germany took root in the UK. In 1847, the London-based *Howitt's Journal* included a piece on German dialect song. The half-page article addressed issues of common ground between "the German Volkslieder, or people's songs" and England's equivalent cultural heritage. Above it stands the first traced occurrence of "folk's song". That construction, clumsily close to the German original, had been replaced by "folk-song" by the early 1850s. Volkslied whelped descendants in most European languages. It was simply too useful a word to let go. Ultimately, that loan word changed people's perceptions of national and regional culture on many continents.

Of course, things are seldom straightforward in folk music. Nowadays it is an irony that many Germans would rather use "folk music" than *Volksmusik*. For them, "Volksmusik" is a loaded word, sullied by political and historical allegiances and associations with beerglass-thumping, sing-along camaraderie, regional costume (*Tracht*) and the televisual insincerity of popular, commercial folk fare. One has to wonder what Herder would have made of all that.

A Little History

The European and American folk movements of the 1950s and 60s were in part a distancing from the commerciality and banality of pop music. Many Germans, who could find no way back to their own folk roots, embraced Anglo-American folk and folk-blues idioms instead. A typical example of this from the 1960s might be Hamburg's **City Preachers**, fronted by **Dagmar Krause** and **Inga Rumpf**, doing material like Josh White's "Come Back Baby", Big Bill Broonzy's "Black, Brown And White" or the ubiquitous "Frankie and Johnny". But there were German initiatives too, both East and West.

In the West, a low-key wave of new folk acts emerged. **Ougenweide** reinvigorated literary traditions, taking their name from a bucolic poem by the Middle German poet Nithart (or Neidhart) von Reuenthal and drawing their musical inspiration from British folk bands Fairport Convention and Pentangle. **Lilienthal** explored a German branch of the folk-rock which Fairport Convention, Steeleye Span and the Albion Band had pioneered in Britain. **Liederjan** became early champions of singing in German with their witty, punningly comic songs – a tradition they continue. They also galvanized the GDR folk scene; the two scenes were not hermetically sealed but, of course, the Stasi dutifully logged cross-border mailings, the frightening or frighteningly banal details of which many East German folkies discovered when they gained access to their Stasi files. West German acts such as **Fiedel Michel**, **Werner Lämmerhirt**, **Hannes Wader** and **Zupfgeigenhansel** were also part of this traffic of ideas.

Interestingly, a different music culture continued around the industrial heart of West Germany, that of the **bandonion orchestra**. In the Ruhr, only one such orchestra out of the hundreds in the past has survived: the **BandonionFreunde Essen**, an array of massed bandonions and strings. Bandonion defined working-class German culture along with pigeon lofts, allotments and the Schalke 04 football team just as bandoneón defined Argentine culture, whorehouse entertainment and tango music; the original spelling is its inventor Heinrich Band's.

On the other side of the border, folklorists laboured away – **Wolfgang Steinitz** (1905–67) being the prime figurehead – and their work would illuminate Germany's folk revival. But by the 1970s, there was a really thriving independent **East German folk scene**, based around clubs, folk workshops, a circuit of *Tanzhäuser* (dance houses comparable to Hungary's *táncház* scene) and the inevitable Stadtfeste. Such was the level of interest, organization and infrastructure that **JAMS** – one of the country's finest roots bands, formed around 1980 – could comfortably play 150 to 180 gigs a year.

After the Wall came down, JAMS was the first East German band to play both Britain and the US. Their music was compellingly danceable and in no sense dependent on language – and it stood up brilliantly on disc. JAMS was a cultural Catherine wheel. The group's **Jo Meyer** is the constant in a family tree that connects **Malbrook** (Dance Devil in Low German), **Mrs Meyer's Love Affairs**, **Cathrin Pfeifer**, **Spillwark** and **Polkaholix**.

JAMS was not alone. East German acts such as **Bierfiedler**, **Folkländer** and **Wacholder**, given to jamming like everyone else, developed fearsome levels of professionalism. Iron Curtain seclusion not only made them musically hungrier, it also forced them to rely on alternative sources of repertoire. West German archives and libraries were largely denied them because of travel and currency restrictions. As a result, folkies looked to *Gesellenlieder* (journeymen's songs), the 1848 Revolution and alternative sources including Steinitz's research. Wacholder, a word-orientated band, fashioned a particularly interesting repertoire using texts from Heinrich Heine. The Nazis had denounced the Jewish poet Heine's work as unpatriotic (and when they had to publish it, published it as "author unknown"). It was not lost on Wacholder that, even though Heine was reinstated politically, his work still glinted with wicked barbs such as descriptions of Germany as a "land of oaks and stunted minds".

Performing live was the key to Ossi success. Unlike their Wessi counterparts, they had few opportunities to record and any repertoire had to be approved before going into the studio. Wacholder, for example, started auspiciously, receiving their radio debut in May 1978, a month after forming. But it took them until 1983 to release their debut album, *Herr Wirt, so lösche unsre Brände* (Landlord, that's how we put out our fires), and until 1989 to release the follow-up. By the time Wacholder disbanded in January 2001, they had clocked up a paltry five releases and a valedictory video under their own name, despite having generated enough material for dozens more. No wonder very few Wessis had vinyl experience of the Ossi scene until the first bands began to cross the border.

Regional Voices

In common with English and Spanish, German pays little deference to a "standard tongue". Go to

Profolk

JAMS

In the beginning was the word II: Weltmusik

Raise a glass to the true home of world music: Germany! Long before anyone in the English-speaking world sweated over, in record producer Joe Boyd's words, "how to persuade record shops to stock the music with strange names we were issuing on our various record labels", a German, **Georg Capellen** (1869–1934) came up trumps with a neologism that captured the Zeitgeist. His word *Weltmusik* was not chosen by vote, it had nothing to do with marketing or "file under" brainteasers and it celebrated its centennial in 2006.

The world music that Capellen described in his essay "Exotische Rhythmik, Melodik und Tonalität als Wegweiser zu einer Neuen Kunstentwicklung" (Exotic Rhythm, Melodics and Tonality as a Signpost to a New Development in Art) was premised on art and the future. "Through the marriage of Orient and Occident," he observed, "we are attaining a new style of music, 'Weltmusik.'"

Described by writers Jean Trouillet and Werner Pieper as "the doyen of the German *Weltmusik-Szene*", the broadcaster, record producer and musicologist **Joachim-Ernst Berendt** (1922–2000) was one of the first to reintroduce what Capellen had far-sightedly described in 1906. Although the concept developed wings – helped to legitimacy by, for example, Beethoven and Mozart slyly borrowing Turkish strains and sonorities – the word itself took longer to fledge. Berendt talked about the 1967 Berliner Jazztage (jazz days) festival as a meeting of musicians from different cultures under the banner "Jazz Meets The World". He was fully conversant with the complexities of nuancing what was and what wasn't when it came to world music too. Once again the German language had planted a seed of an idea and, as every good gardener knows, germination can take time. That is the fun and frustration of such matters.

Germany and Hochdeutsch (High German), the language taught in schools, will get slammed into context. Regional voices abound – whether dialects from Bavaria, Saxony or the Saarland. Furthermore, along the Baltic and North Sea coasts and further south another language is spoken. **Plattdütsch** – or, in High German, Plattdeutsch or Niederdeutsch (Low German) – is related to yet distinct from High German, much as Scots differs from English. It is a salty, earthy, predominantly working-class tongue, rich in folklore. Much of everyday Plattdütsch culture is concentrated around the coastal regions. It is a language close to the natural world and traditional crafts; its vocabulary is perfect for discussing farming and cheese-making, singing shanties, and telling tales about luggers, fishing for cod or hunting pods of whales. In East Friesland (the home of the band **Spillwark**) it intergrades with Dutch. In Schleswig-Holstein, historically a territory that switched between Denmark and Germany (and the home of **Moin**), it blurs into Danish. Acts such as **Hannes Wader** and **Piatkowski & Rieck** tapped into Plattdütsch's oral and written culture, while in Mecklenburg, in the former GDR, JAMS' *Fisch* project breathed new life into the often vilified shanty form, affirming its vigour and relevance.

In the Nazi and East German regimes, dialect artists and *Mundarten* (dialects) themselves were deemed abjectly uncultivated or questionable and often fell foul of officialdom. The songstress-poet

Lene Voigt (1891–1962) from Saxony, for example, was in effect silenced by the Nazis. Yet what was once banned is now being fêted, and in a nation where received pronunciation has long prevailed, the rediscovery of people singing in their natural voices works like mental floss. Hearing the likes of Swabian songwriter **Thomas Felder**'s captivating language or **Saure Gummern**'s blues drolleries delivered direct from the Hesse delta has generated political debate. Some voice the concern that here art might be hymning the break-up of the newly reconstituted Fatherland.

Born in 1953, Thomas Felder grew up being taught that High German was the proper way to talk, but in 1975 experienced a personal epiphany in London. Thumbing through the records at the Goethe-Institut, he happened upon an Austrian dialect singer. It connected him with dialect artforms and soon afterwards he began writing in dialect. Felder's Swabian dialect remains a pinnacle of dialect composition and eerie transcendence. One minute he is delivering a mass on a theme of flux, egged on by sublimely simple hurdy-gurdy, the next he is yelping along in "So Beni".

In a similar way to Thomas Felder, it was Austria that inspired southern Germany's **Hundsbuam Miserablige** (Dog-boys or Curs) to work in their native Bavarian, in 1996. Their model was the punkish-roots Austrian-Alpine duo Attwenger. The Hundsbuam take on Alpine music is pure Bavarian and unmistakably their own. Their

Thomas Felder

eponymous debut album begins with quacking ducks on a pond. All of a sudden searing guitar and choppy rhythms shatter the bucolic idyll and punk hell descends on the pond. The Hundsbuam, as they were generally known and to which they shortened their name, provided a direct role model for JAMS and others, even if some were just openly approving of the dialectical chutzpah. Jo Meyer and JAMS had gawped – not too strong a word – with genuine wonderment and admiration at the ability of Hundsbuam to get away with things that were not allowed in Standard German.

Alternative Postcards

Germany has a third native language, unconnected to any Germanic tongue. **Sorb** is Germany's indigenous Slav language. Talk to even university-educated Germans and the likelihood is that the name of one of Germany's longest-established minorities will still turn up a blank. The **Sorbs** or **Wends** are a Slav minority from eastern Saxony and southeastern Brandenburg out east, long pressured to relinquish their culture, but at last perhaps expe-

riencing an artistic resurgence. It's not before time for the likes of the **Serbski Ludowy Ansambl Budysin** (the Sorb National Ensemble of Bautzen), founded in 1952. But growing numbers of young Sorbs are living in both Sorb and mainstream German culture, with a corresponding need to nurture their Sorb identity. The *Liedermacher* **Pittkunings** exemplifies this dual cultural heritage, writing in both Sorb and German, while **Sprewjan**, founded in 1979, reveal and reinterpret a traditional Sorb repertoire using *wĕrowanske huslički* (wedding fiddle), *mĕchawka* (the small Sorb bagpipe) and *kozol* (big Sorb bagpipe).

In the former East Germany, opportunities for experiencing other cultures were limited. In practice this meant folkies had to look to the states on their own side of the Iron Curtain. **Aufwind**, for example, have explored and researched the post-Holocaust world of Jewish and Yiddish music, visiting Hungary, Poland and Romania. *Klezmer* naturally figures in their repertoire, but theirs is distinct from the more familiar klezmer as transplanted and played on American soil. Klezmer-based acts such as **Di Grine Kuzine** and **Massel-Tov** are also exploring this field.

One act that has taken a very different path is **Dissidenten**, which began as a spin-off from the Krautrock group **Embyro**, famed for a seminal album, *Embyro's Reise* (1980), recorded in Afghanistan, Pakistan and India. Dissidenten took the journey further, fusing traditions by immersing themselves in North African and Indian life, and taking location recording to new heights.

Kabarett and Liedermacher

Shadowing the German folk scene are two separate but related movements, the urbane roots of which are tangled up in Europe's cross-bred cabaret, literary and bohemian movements. The first is world famous. Talk of **Kabarett** and conversation instantly turns to the interwar Berlin of Christopher Isherwood and his kind, with images provided by Bob Fosse's film *Cabaret* (1972).

In the Weimar Republic, Kabarett inhabited a murky world of late-night clubs in which sexuality was opaque, petit-bourgeois conservatism was denounced and political-satirical cabaret thrived. The foremost composers and lyricists were **Mischa Spoliansky**, **Friedrich Hollaender**, **Kurt Tucholsky** and **Marcellus Schiffer**, while performers such as **Marlene Dietrich**, **Margo Lion** and **Karl Valentin** were household names. The satire was insightful, but the most popular subject was sex, often of a

Hans-Eckart Wenzel: urbane renewal

Generally speaking, when discussing German songmakers, either *Liedermacher* or *chansonnier* will suffice to describe them. The GDR songmaker Jürgen Eger upped the ante with his self-aggrandizing coinage *Dichtersänger* (poet-singer). **Hans-Eckart Wenzel**, another East German, can genuinely claim that title. In an inversion, seams of gold masquerading as fool's gold run through his songs – veins of bewilderment and *clownerie*. The befuddled and beleaguered, the drunk and the low-life people his songs. Often he plays the starring role of King Leer with a hangover piecing together last night's escapades.

Even after the fall of the Wall, Wenzel still appeared in whiteface for a while, as if loath to dump the principle that jesters can get away with murder. The US comedian Bill Hicks might have been talking about Wenzel when he said "Listen to my messages, not my words." Humour, absurdity and enigma were top tricks up his sleeve. In this he followed in the literary steps of the bourgeois-bubble burster and parodist Wilhelm Busch (1832–1908), the author of the *Galgenlieder* (Gallows Songs), Christian Morgenstern (1871–1914) and Johann Nestroy (1801–62), the Austrian playwright-actor and songwriter active during the repressive Hapsburg era.

Born in 1955 in Kropstädt in Saxony-Anhalt, Wenzel was raised in nearby Wittenberg. Like many of his contemporaries, Wenzel's take on folk music was a modern, hybridized one, a mishmash of printed and parlour arrangements of Lieder (art songs) from the pens of Goethe, Heine and Schubert, Volkslieder, GDR-approved anthems like "Unsre Heimat", songs of the Old Comrades, modern literary fare from Brecht, Eisler, Tucholsky and Weill and a residue of great songs from bygone years by the likes of Werner Richard Heymann, Friedrich Hollaender and Mischa Spoliansky. "Some people say that I'm a Liedermacher", he explains. "Others say it's Kabarett. What I do is a cross-over or a bastardized form in which many mediums are fused together. Deep down I feel as if I'm some sort of folk musician. I make music and lyrics that are to do with my fellows' everyday lives. That's folk music in the original definition."

During his GDR years, Wenzel created a body of work that juggled the present, the past and plausible deniability with a splash of Swiftian-strength satire. Artistic obfuscation is still close to Wenzel's heart. "The playwright Nestroy wrote at the time of Metternich during a period of intense censorship. He continually had to paraphrase things. In times when potatoes were in short supply, he would write about beets and everybody knew he was writing about potatoes. In that way the censor couldn't attack him. At the same time it kept things interesting for his audiences. You can still play those songs because potatoes can be substituted for beets and those "political beets" can stand for anything that one cannot get. The absolute freedom to say anything is not necessarily a good thing for art."

surprisingly liberal hue. Schiffer's "Wenn die beste Freundin" (When the Special Girlfriend), first performed by Margo Lion and Marlene Dietrich in 1928, became the unofficial anthem of the German lesbian movement. Commenting years later, **Lotte Lenya** (the Austrian singer, *Dr No* actress and wife of Kurt Weill) clarified, "People often think it was all left wing, but of course much of it was non-party and purely satirical."

More than a century on from Brecht's birth in 1898, and as Germany slouches towards what the right wing perceives as multicultural bedlam, Kabarett still retains its reputation as "the Muse with the sharp tongue". The former East German scene produced work of great political subtlety, wielding irony and ambiguity to get past censor and Stasi (the secret police). Equally importantly, Ossi acts such as **Barbara Thalheim** and **Duo Sonnenschirm** produced work after the Wall came down which packed the punch of Brecht or Tucholsky. Inequalities within the two-in-one state, envi-

ronmental and sexual issues and the perennial absurdity of politics provide enough ammunition for today's satire boom, and Berlin enjoys a thriving Kabarett club scene.

There is a somewhat blurred line between Kabarett and the **Liedermacher movement** (literally, songmakers), which, since its craft lies in the words, has received inevitably curt treatment outside the German-speaking countries. Its finest writers were able to take the French cult of the song and infuse it with a German sensibility. Although they were as far from folk as Dylan's *Highway 61 Revisited* was from folk protest, **Wolf Biermann** and **Franz-Josef Degenhardt** remain spectral godfathers to the German folk scene. Their candid, crafted material both set standards for others to aspire to and suggested alternatives to the Anglo-American mire into which the German folk scene looked like sinking. Instead of looking to America for inspiration, they looked to the French-language chanson tradition of Georges Brassens and Jacques Brel for standards.

Liedermacher singer **Joana Emetz**, for example, had her first hit in 1964 with a cover of Edith Piaf's "Non, Je Ne Regrette Rien", while Degenhardt himself produced an entire album of Brassens' material in 1986 called *Junge Paare auf den Bänken* (Young Couples On Benches). Biermann remains especially important. He really suffered for his art, being stripped of his East German citizenship in 1976 while on tour in West Germany – the GDR's equivalent of excommunication.

As their notable contemporary **Christof Stählin** admits, "Back then, in the 1960s, we thought we'd discovered a new profession. In the 1970s this movement was worldwide. There was a great expression of support from the public. We all believed, whether prominent or not, that it was all for us." The Liedermacher movement has gradually declined in popularity compared to the mid- to late-1960s when Degenhardt's *Spiel Nicht Mit den Schmuddelkindern* (Don't Play With The Grubby Children) was essential listening, but its key figures are still making music and performing their intellectually stimulating songs.

Flux and Future

The paradox of Reunification has been that many Ossi musicians have found it very difficult to break through in the old West Germany. "In the East", **Hans-Eckart Wenzel** (see box) observes, "there was a way of receiving and listening, as well as reading, that was stamped with spiritual strength. People sought out the tiniest signs in songs and that produced something highly intense." Regrettably, an appreciation of nuance seems all too often to have bypassed West German audiences with their superior Wessi attitudes. Learning to listen hard and close and learning from listening are very good tips for appreciating any music. The East German experience has demonstrated that over and over again.

Getting to understand the countless rivers, streams, brooks and rivulets of the German scene can be as instructional as it is musically revealing and entertaining. What has been apparent since Reunification is the self-renewing vitality of German music and the nation's ability to be the hothouse home of some of the world's finest musical acts.

DISCOGRAPHY Germany

⊙ **Festival des politischen Liedes: Die Siebziger (1970s)**
⊙ **Festival des politischen Liedes: Die Achtziger (1980s)**
Pläne, Germany
These two mementos of the GDR era's most international solidarity music festival present two decades of live performances. The 1970s volume includes recordings from Floh de Cologne, Dr Bhupen Hazatika, Inti Illimani, Karls Enkel and Mariam Makeba. The 1980s volume is just as historical, but has wider appeal, with sterling performances by Billy Bragg, Bruce Cockburn, Perry Friedman and Abdullah Ibrahim, plus a collaboration between the Sands Family, Dick Gaughan and Wacholder. Excellent notes, but only in German.

★ **Music! The Berlin Phonogramm-Archiv 1900–2000**
Wergo, Germany
Germany was at the forefront of ethnomusicology and world music recordings. This four-volume horn of plenty covers everything from early wax cylinder recordings to modern concert recordings, from the Americas, Asia, Australia, Europe and Oceania. German treasures include archival Sorb material (1907), a recording from a German-speaking enclave in the Czech Lands (1931) and a Bavarian *Zwiefacher* (a mixed-metre dance that switches between 2/4 and 3/4) from 1967.

⊙ **TFF Rudolstadt 2003**
Heideck, Germany
A vintage year for TFF Rudolstadt with recordings from Hubert von Goisern (Austria), Wenzel (Germany), Yggdrasil

(The Faroes), Les Charbonniers de l'Enfer (Canada) and Salsa Celtica (Scotland). Highly recommended.

★ **Travellin' Companion 3: A Musical Journey to Germany**
Weltwunder, Germany
This compilation is as accessible as it is remarkable. Its extraordinary portfolio includes BandonionFreunde Essen, Element of Crime, Elster Silberflug, Di Grine Kuzine, Polkaholix, the Schäl Sick Brass Band and 17 Hippies. Erci E's "Weil ich 'n Türke bin" and LeckerSachen's "Lass mich in Ruh" are inspired and inspirational *tours de force* (and radio mix rarities to boot). Notes in English and German.

⊙ **Von Küste zu Küste**
LAG Folk, Germany
Subtitled "Folk music from Schleswig-Holstein", this double anthology assembles 25 acts (including De Drangdüwels, Folk Rovers, Aver Liekers, Glenfiddle and Die Schrägen Vögel) from the German "land between two seas" whose history is linked to Denmark's and whose Low German borders on Danish.

BandonionFreunde Essen

At the turn of the century the bandonion was extremely popular around the Ruhr, a region famed for heavy industry and mining. As Kari-Heinz Beckedal, the band's leader, puts it: "If one was a civil servant, one had to have a piano in order to demonstrate one's position – whether one could play it or not. For the little man it wasn't obligatory and a bandonion was affordable and one could accommodate it far more easily." Essen's Friends of the Bandonion preserve a playing style from a time when the bandonion was an ensemble instrument, not a soloist's ticket to fame.

⊙ Tango dei Gruga
Satiricon, Germany

Imagine the impact of big-band bandonion in the style of the old-time mandolin or balalaika orchestras in a seventeen-piece orchestra plus conductor. The last of the Ruhr's famed bandonion orchestras is like nothing else on earth.

Notker Homburger

Based in Konstanz on the German-Swiss border, Notker Homburger mixes vocal and dance pieces, regional and original material and Swabian reworkings of standards.

⊙ Nur In Konstanz
Chaos, Germany

The CD is subtitled "indigenous music from the western Lake Constance". Homburger and an assortment of line-ups, including Notty's Jug Serenaders, produce music of great vivacity and good humour, leavened with serious scholarship. "Z'Areneberg Am Bodesee" is a ribald account of the exiled Prinz Luis Napoleon, the future Napoleon III, who chose sowing wild oats over scholastic tedium. "Lili Marleen", a Standard German renegade, gets an excellent straight treatment.

Hundsbuam (Miserablige)

The Hundsbuam polarized opinion after bursting upon the scene in 1996. Assertively Bavarian, they sing in a dialect that would bamboozle people from Oberbayern (Upper Bavaria), let alone those in the other federal states. But beyond the words, what communicates loud and clear is the band's raw energy and musical iconoclasm.

★ Hundsbuam Miserablige
BMG/Lawine, Germany

After a chorus of barnyard beasts, the Hundsbuam blast in with one of the all-time greatest album openers, "Hoizhakka Pogo" (Woodchopper's Pogo). This 1996 debut slashes a dividing line between what has gone before and what is to come. Kow-towing to nobody and tattooed with black humour, they pull off the dangerous balancing act of mad dogs savaging Bavarian conformity while remaining vehemently Bavarian.

⊙ Hui
BMG/Lawine, Germany

The humour got more savage still on *Hui*. Doffing its cap to Hitchcock and the murder ballad, "Mei Liab" (My Love) is fatal attraction terminated with extreme prejudice: its narrator knows a way to keep his obsession's love forever. "Heit" (Today), by contrast, is tranquillity in the eye of the hurricane.

JAMS

Darlings of the GDR dance scene, in 1997 JAMS – taking a lead from Hundsbuam Miserablige – unveiled Plattdütsch songs within their already strongly north German-flavoured repertoire. In Mecklenburg, band leader Jo Meyer's birthplace, Plattdütsch is many people's first language.

⊙ Fisch
John Silver, Germany

Too busy to record because of a full diary, after a personnel revamp, the discovery of their own voices and the realisation

that the Plattdütsch contingent was now a quorum, JAMS changed tack. Shanty, polka, waltz and hip-hop ferry these fisherfolk across the briny. Truly innovative, this is one of the most outstanding folk albums of 1997, worldwide.

Ko J. Kokott

Like Scarlett O', Jörg "Ko" Kokott, born in 1955, was a linch-pin in the East German group Wacholder. Even before the group's split, its members had pursued a number of extracurricular activities. Ko has worked as a soloist, as a duettist with Hans-Eckardt Wenzel and Rainer-Christof "Pascha" Dietrich (in the Bettelfolkband), and as a member of Mooncoin.

⊙ Morgen in Montreux
Cooleur, Germany

Billed as the work of the group Liedhaber, a pun on *Lied* (song) and *Liebhaber* (lover or lovers), this album is a step on from Wacholder's rock side heard on their last release, *unterwegs* (on the road). The all-original material falls between rock and Liedermacher in tone and delivery.

Wolfgang Meyering

Wolfgang Meyering, a key player in today's Plattdütsch musical revival, is also responsible for coordinating the Magic Instrument programmes at TFF Rudolstadt and is the mastermind behind the band Malbrook.

WITH MALBROOK

⊙ Malbrook
Westpark, Germany

A revelation. Malbrook mix dance and song, some traditional, some original compositions cast from a traditional mould. Meyering renews links between northern Germany and southern Scandinavia dating back to medieval trading alliances: collaborators include Kerstin Blodig, Jo Meyer, Ralf Gehler and the Swedish group Hemållt. Notes in German and English.

Ougenweide

These Hamburg-based folk-rockers have striven to escape Anglo-American influences by concentrating on German textual sources, yet their sound shows the influence of British folk-rockers Fairport, Pentangle and Jethro Tull.

⊙ Wol mich der Stunde: 1970–84
Sireena Records, Germany

This Ougenweide compilation delves deep into the archives. It includes three pieces from their breakthrough as Fairport Convention's support act in Hamburg in 1974. Ougenweide's Minnie Graw was the nearest thing Germany had to Sandy Denny. Jethro Tull-style flute, Terry Cox-style percussion, Dave Swarbrick-style fiddle, Richard Thompson/Graeme Taylor-style guitar. But utterly *ougenweide* (a feast for the eyes) nonetheless.

Polkaholix

Polka taken to extremes by one of Germany's foremost and consistently innovative dance bands.

★ Denkste!

BuschFunk, Germany

Wonderful music, with wonderfully woeful, Dada-esque booklet notes. Try, "You think German polkas are for nerds? Then check out the POLKAHOLIX, clear your minds, pull on your sweats, and … may the 2/4s be with you!"

Spillwark

Spillwark, *Spielwerk* in High German, means a "musical mechanism"; it is also a sly allusion to an idiomatic saying about getting the job done – or not. The Emden-based ensemble's focus is "Weltmusik aus Ostfriesland" (world music from East Friesland). It specializes in a Plattdütsch repertoire laced with elements from afar; witness "Czardas" (described as what happens when the Orient Express collides with a Dutch market organ) on *Hamswest* and the 11/16 instrumental "Brava Brava Bratislava" on *Sien Kurs*.

 Sien Kurs
Laika, Germany

This perfectly encapsulates contemporary, outward-looking Plattdütsch culture. It includes Wolfgang Meyering's masterful adaptation of the traditional "Lord Franklin", about his search for the North-West Passage, here in a Plattdütsch version.

Kabarett and chanson

 100 Jahre Kabarett 1901–1933, 1933–1955, 1955–1970, 1970–2001
Bear Family, Germany

These four phenomenal three-CD volumes chronicle the history of Kabarett and the nation's literate, literary song tradition as no other series has ever attempted. With its selections from Aristide Bruant to Die Nachrichter (1901–33), Willi Schaeffers to Lucie Mannheim (1933–55), Wolfgang Müller to Peter Schmitz and Werner Eichhorn (1955–70) and Lorre Lorentz to Lukas Resetarits (1970–2001), the series is unsurpassed. Notes in German only.

⊙ **Es lag in der Luft…**
edel, Germany

There are plenty of compilations of Kabarett and chanson from between the wars, but this excellent 25-track anthology is heartily recommended. A strong, representative body of work from composers Mischa Spoliansky, Rudolf Nelson, Ralph Beneatzky, Werner Richard Heymann and Friedrich Hollaender with interpretations from the Comedian Harmonists, Marlene Dietrich and the Sid Kays Fellows. Notes in German and English.

Marlene Dietrich

Marlene Dietrich (1901–92) defined the German ability to succeed with art of a transcendent nature. Just as she insisted on being lit in just the right way to make the camera adore her, she discovered ways to present her limited vocal range to immaculate effect. In 1991 the German news weekly *Der Spiegel* headlined its feature on her with the words "Hot or cold, but never lukewarm". As career summations go, it was perfect: style defined as an expression of limitations.

 Der blonde Engel/Die Retrospektive
EMI Electrola, Germany

This four-CD set with notes in German and English is the best anthology of the Blonde Angel's over-anthologized work. It gathers together her *shellac* output, her microgroove days, singles and album tracks and many, many rarities. Every aspect of her life is here, from the ambiguous to the explicit, seductress to seduced, heterosexual to lesbian, protagonist to peacenik, Blue Angel to Scarlet Devil.

Element of Crime

Element of Crime have taken literate German-language song to literary heights with their cryptic and multi-layered lyrics.

⊙ **Weisses Papier**
Polydor, Germany

Like skaters on the thinnest of ice, over and over again Element of Crime have pulled off stories in which chickens and guinea pigs collide, somebody shakes a cat until everything plops out and an old man throws worse than stale bread to/at the ducks. Their mini-manifestos should be on German-language syllabuses everywhere, beginning with Germany.

Dagmar Krause

Born on the outskirts of Hamburg in 1950, by 1964 Krause was singing on the city's world-renowned club scene, both in the dockland area and on the Reeperbahn, the red-light district. She made her name with avant-garde rock groups Henry Cow and Slapp Happy, and later recorded seminal interpretations of material by Brecht, Eisler and Weill.

⊙ **Panzerschlacht (Tank Battles)**
Island, UK

A cycle of songs by Hanns Eisler. The "Chanson Allemande" miniature is positively heartbreaking. Krause retains the edge to this material that far too many interpreters buff away.

Lotte Lenya

Born in 1898 in Imperial Vienna, Lotte Lenya still retains an almighty hold on German-language song. Her artistry was immense, her singing voice capable of transforming into a speaking voice (*Sprechstimme*) or a low growl, her subtle

Marlene Dietrich

interpretations able to invest a single world with a cosmos of meaning and possibilities.

Lenya
Bear Family, Germany

This eleven-CD career overview comes with a hefty hard-back book. The recordings include many of the most enduring works in German of the twentieth century, plus pieces with Louis Armstrong and ones in which her husband Kurt Weill has a hand. Her voice and delivery have no truck with prettification, but she detonates reverberations in the heart, mind and soul. This is unquestionably the most important release by any non-classical German-speaking singer.

WITH KURT WEILL

Berlin & American Theater Songs
CBS, US

An urban voice. An urbane voice. An urchin voice. All in one. With notes in English, German and French.

Scarlett O' (Scarlett Seeboldt)

The most sensuous voice ever to emerge from Germany, Scarlett Seeboldt was a member of Wacholder for two decades. Her repertoire includes some of the hardest-hitting feminist or lesbian song-stories of the century, as well as Protestant hymns, Leoncavallo's light operetta and the work of Element of Crime and Ton Stein Scherben. Her ability to both growl and hit the highest of notes and her emotional and intellectual grasp of her material is positively scary.

⊙ Das muss ein Stück vom Himmel sein
Duophon, Germany

Here Steffen Mensching guests as Scarlett's male foil. This testimony to the greatness and continued relevance of Werner Richard Heymann's songcraft is greatly enhanced by Jürgen Ehle, former lead guitarist of Pankow, in the producer's chair. The accompaniments include guitar, mandolin, mandola, clarinet, keyboards, basses and kit drum.

⊙ Zum Beispiel Nilpferde
John Silver, Germany

On the cover Scarlett O' is pictured before a statue by the lake in the grounds of the Brecht-Weigel-Haus in Buckow, Brecht's home. This garland of songs, interspersed with biographical and autobiographical reminiscences, is simply great art.

Gina Pietsch

The singer and actress Gina Pietsch has created a succession of musical programmes based on the work of Brecht, Erich Fried, Goethe, Heine and Theodorakis and themes of Berlin, Prague and womankind.

⊙ Pietsch singt Folkerts
G. Folkerts, Germany

With Gerhard Folkerts as composer and on piano, this labour-intensive cycle of songs corrals material from Brecht, Heine, Rilke and others.

⊙ Klampfenlieder bei Brecht
Kreutzberg Records, Germany

Klampfe is a good old-fashioned synonym for guitar. This was Pietsch's eighth programme of work from Brecht. Jointly credited to her and guitarist Dietmat Ungerank, this album contains 33 gem-like interpretations.

Barbara Thalheim

Born in Leipzig in 1948, Barbara Thalheim is one of the great voices of engaged German chanson.

⊙ Deutsch zu sein
Duophon, Germany

A re-examination of what it meant to be German in September 2002, with languid post-Piazzolla and Piaf touches. Thalheim is joined by Jean Pacelet and others.

⊙ Inselsein
Duophon, Germany

The English poet John Donne famously spoke about no man being an island. Philosophical outpourings on that subject and more.

Liedermacher

Wolf Biermann

The rebel writer who made things uncomfortable for the East German regime. Tit for tat, they made things uncomfortable for him. Far worse was to befall him before he settled in the West. An iconic figure on the German scene and one of Germany's finest ever Liedermacher. Recent work has tackled family history, Holocaust-era poetry and, on his *Das ist die feinste Liebeskunst* (2005), Shakespearian settings.

⊙ Chausseestrasse 131
Zweitausendeins, Germany

The cover of the original release on Wagenbach's Quartplatten in 1969 showed a mustachioed Biermann staring impassively at the photographer/listener. Back then Chausseestrasse was a street in East Berlin. Biermann paid for the thorny, politically embarrassing content of the songs emanating from that apartment by being stripped of his citizenship in 1976.

⊙ Grosser Gesang des Jizchak Katzenelson
Lieder Produktion, Altona/Zweitausendeins, Germany

Recorded live in Zurich in December 2003, this double-CD programme of commentary and songs in German reworks material from the Jewish poet Jizchak Katzenelson, murdered in Auschwitz in May 1944 – a little over a year after Biermann's own father died there.

Franz-Josef Degenhardt

Born in 1931 in Schweim, Westphalia, Degenhardt is one of the figureheads of the Liedermacher movement, with clarity of vision and linguistic precision – he is a doctor of law.

⊙ Café nach dem Fall
Polydor, Germany

With Degenhardt you don't necessarily know where he's going but you go along for the ride and make the most of the cultural and political scenery. The dream-like title track manages to name-check Luther and Lennon, Hendrix and Elton John, Madonna and Mozart, Karl and Groucho Marx, Günther Grass and Nina Hagen and ropes in a cast that take drugs, scoff garlic, go for piercings and get mistaken for Hannes Wader. It is one of those gathering places…

⊙ Krieg gegen den Krieg
Koch, Germany

Anti-war songs and warnings, released in 2003 with Iraq on his mind, selected from his back pages and mainly but not exclusively written by him.

Thomas Felder

Swabian dialect had a long tradition, but was the poor relation of High German. As Felder said, "I wanted to make serious poetry. There wasn't any model in Swabian." His music turns apprehension into appreciation. "It's the sound that gets across, that communicates", he explained. "If it depends on understanding the content then I don't need to sing a song: I can give a lecture."

Sinnflut
Musik & Wort, Germany

Sinnflut puns on *Sintflut* – the Biblical flood – to translate as "Sense Flood". Vocally, Felder bends notes till their eyes pop out. For fans of footnotes, this album also contains Buffy Sainte-Marie's little-known Swabian period protest song "Hald Ao Soldat" which she later translated into English for Donovan as "The Universal Soldier".

★ Vesperplatte
Musik & Wort, Germany

Co-conceived with Michael Samarajiwa, this suite was debuted in 1995 on the fiftieth anniversary of Dresden's obliteration by British bombers. Felder delivers a series of inspired performances ranging from what he calls the Klangerlebnis (sound experience) of "Pappmaschee" (papier mâché), which begins with mimicked air-raid sirens before going surreal, to the uplifting "Dag" (Day). There is no need to work hard to like Felder's Swabian vespers. His voice and hurdy-gurdy shatter the language barrier.

Christof Stählin

Christof Stählin is a poet-writer supreme, one of the most consistent and important contemporary German songwriters. His songs are distillations of refined thought. He typically accompanies himself on *vihuela*, and has created a series of themed song programmes.

⊙ Auf einem anderen Blatt
NOMEN + OMEN, Germany

Stählin's elegant prose is nowhere better illustrated than in "Deutschland nicht mehr" (a title that puns on nationalism and living in the present). In it he makes a point about cultural assimilation by describing the lass down the Turkish baker's shop talking in Swabian.

Hannes Wader

Hannes Wader is one of the greatest treasures and re-energizers of West Germany's Liedermacher movement. His peerlessly broad repertoire includes Low and High German folksongs, anthems of the politicized working class, shanties, and the work of Sweden's Burns-like poet-musician Carl Michael Bellman (1740–95) and Franz Schubert (1797–1828).

⊙ Jahr für Jahr
Pläne, Germany

An overview of Wader's career, covering the period from 1995 to 2005. Highly recommended.

Wenzel

If Wenzel were wine he would be Eiswein, the sweetest, most lusciously scented and heady wine made from frosted grapes. He fuels and dupes minds.

★ Grünes Licht
Conträr, Germany

Wenzel is a master of double-speak, in the best sense. His great talent is to talk simultaneously in phosphorescent and jettest-black terms. The DVD recording of this concert is titled *halb und halb: Wenzel & Band im Konzert*.

Sorb music

Sprewjan

Sprewjan were, so to speak, baptized in the Spree – their name derives from the river's Sorb-language name, Sprjewja. The band came together for the third Festival of Sorb Song in 1979 in their hometown of Bautzen. Prominent in their instrumentation are various Sorb bagpipes and the small three-string wedding fiddle. Currently Tomasz Nawka plays small bagpipes, Steffen Kostorz big bagpipes and Bernadette Ziesch wedding fiddle. All three sing. They represent another side of Germany, an overlooked facet of Germany's folk otherness.

⊙ Po Łužicy ze serbskim spěwom
Servi, Germany

As the characters suggest, Sorb as a language is closer to Polish than Czech. The title translates as "With Sorb song through Lusatia". Lusatia (Lausitz in German) is the historical region between the rivers Bóbr and Kwisa and the Elbe – nowadays represented by the German states of Saxony and Brandenburg and Poland's Lower Silesian voivodeship or province. This anthology draws on three decades of recordings, and a variety of line-ups and musical forms.

Volkslied interpreters

⊙ Röslein auf der Heiden
Deutsches Volksliedarchiv, Germany

Released by the Freiburg folksong archive, this collection, subtitled "Goethe und das Volkslied", views German folksong through an art-song prism. The songs are delivered by a series of "trained voices" including Markus Flaig (bass), Regina Kabis (soprano) and Frauke Schmidt (alto). A reminder of how porous Germany's musical traditions are.

Holger Saarmann

The singer and guitarist Holger Saarmann, born in 1971 in Hagen in Westphalia, follows in the quintessential German tradition of song programmers. Past programmes include an examination of Yiddish song culture (*Shalom Musik*) and an international folk double-hander with the actress Beate Weidenhammer (*Fremdwärts wider Willen*, Into the Foreign against your Will).

⊙ Hüt dich, schönes Blümelein
Top-Delta, Germany

Saarmann walks the delicate tightrope between Volkslied and Lied with very few wobbles. His choice of material encompasses songs like "Das Lied vom Brombeerenpflücken" (Bramble-picking song), music from German-speaking islands in the Ukraine and the theoretically apolitical song "Lied für die Pariser Kommune" (Song for the Paris commune) that took an overtly political guise as "Lüstig, Lüstig". A very fine anthology of German song drawing on songbook literature.

WeltBeat and Weltmusik from Germany

17 Hippies

Founded in 1996 as an outgrowth of Berlin's famed, notorious Hippie-Haus-Tanz scene, 17 Hippies have grown into one of the most accomplished big bands specializing in world music, with techno, rave, Balkan, klezmer and musette marblings. They sing in English, French and German.

★ Ifni
Hipster Records, Germany

The album opens with a wild blast in the form of "Frau von Ungefähr". Their cover of Los Lobos' "Saint Behind the Glass" is marvellous. Highly moreish music from one of the world's greatest world music ensembles.

Aufwind

The main focus for Aufwind (Up-current) is Eastern European Jewish and Yiddish music. Their repertoire reveals considerable originality and inspiring musicianship. The current line-up comprises Jan Hermerschmidt (vocals/clarinet), Claudia Koch (vocals/violin/viola), Hardy Reich (vocals/mandolin/guitar), Andreas Rohde (vocals/bandoneon/guitar) and Heiko Rötzscher (bass).

⊙ Awek Di Junge Jorn
Misrach, Germany
As Ossis, Aufwind accessed sources behind the Iron Curtain, talking to survivors of the Holocaust. "Jidisch Tango" exemplifies their highly distinctive, unorthodox vision. A world-class klezmer album, nothing less.

Nadia Birkenstock

Irish and Celtic music has had an immeasurable influence on the German folk scene in recent years, and in particular on Nadia Birkenstock. Although she sings, her primary "voice" is the harp.

⊙ Wandering Between the Worlds
SSI Records, Germany
Birkenstock avoids the "Celtschmerz" pitfalls with an assortment of English, Irish, Scottish and Welsh tunes and songs.

Dissidenten

Dissidenten grew out of the German progressive rock movement, starting life as a side-shoot of Embryo. Light years removed from the World Music tourist experience, their music dazzles with intensity and authenticity, the product of steeping themselves in various cultures – notably those of Morocco and India. The core line-up comprises Friedo Josch (flute/soprano sax/keyboards), Marlon Klein (drums/percussion/keyboards/vocals) and Uve Müllrich (bass/guitar/vocals).

★ Instinctive Traveler
Exil, Germany
This 1997 album found Dissidenten casting their cultural net further than ever. Arabic, Hawaiian, Native American, North Indian and Tamil influences ripple through the songs. The result is no stylistic Tower of Babel, rather a time capsule of musical cultures and styles blasted into space. Bajka Müllrich, daughter of Dissidenten's bassist, turns "Lobster Song" and "Instinctive Traveler" into two of WeltBeat's catchiest ever tracks.

⊙ Live in Europe
Exil, Germany
Fronted by Izaline Calister, Manickam Yogeswaran and Noujoum Ouazza, this captures one of the finest line-ups of one of the longest-lived world music bands of all time. Marlon Klein proves himself one of the greatest rhythmists of our age.

Erci E.

Erci E. (Erci Ergün) is a second-generation, Berlin-based rapper and broadcaster of Turkish extraction.

★ Weil ich 'n Türke bin
BMG, Germany
"Weil ich 'n Türke bin" (Because I'm a Turk) regurgitates a litany of racial stereotypes hurled at him, his sister and other Germans of Turkish extraction, from racial finger-pointing of the "over-here-and-stealing-our-jobs" kind to accusations of smelliness. One of the most piquant and hard-hitting political statements of recent years.

Ensemble FisFüs

This quartet of oriental and occidental musicians comprises Murat Coşkun (frame drum, percussion and voice), Annette Maye (clarinet and soprano sax), Wolfgang Maye (bass) and Karim Othman-Hassan (*oud*).

⊙ SimSim
Peregrina Music, Germany
The album title puns on sesame and opening doors (in Arabic). Oriental jazz with flavourings of Turkey, Greece and Arabia.

Steffen Basho Junghans

Born in 1953 in Vielau in Saxony, Junghans is a graduate of the East German folk scene, a steel-strung acoustic guitar virtuoso, composer and painter. His intellectually demanding music glides over borders and rivals that of Robert Basho, John Fahey, Henry Kaiser and Leo Kottke in terms of otherworldliness.

⊙ Inside
Strange Attractions Audio House, US
Although his own Berlin-based Blue Moment label has released much of his output, a steady stream of work has appeared in the US. *Inside* is devoted to a three-movement suite with the central movement divided into three parts. Twilight music that extends into the small hours.

⊙ Song of the Earth
Sublingual, US
Seven original instrumental compositions, two for twelve-string guitar, the remainder for six-string guitar. Highly impressionistic and visual soundscapes.

Die Singvøgel

Germany has its Nu-Folk scene too. Karan Braun, Duke Meyer and Sven Scholz, collectively Die Singvøgel ("songbirds", with an "ø" substituted for the standard "ö"), began as a duo in 2002 (before Scholz joined). The repertoire is a mixture of original and traditionally arranged German-language songs. The instrumentation includes guitar, electric bass, flute, keyboards and percussion.

⊙ drei
Echsenflug Sentense, Germany
Their third (2007) album catapults them forward with a stronger suite of songs, better recording values and a tighter sound.

Ulrich Kodho Wendt Band

The Hamburg-based UKW Band was founded in 1998 as a live ensemble. Its line-up since 1999 has been Karlo Buerschaper (bass), Ele Grimm (violin, vocals, trombone), Yogi Jockusch (drums) and Ulrich Kodho (accordion). There is a strong filmic quality to the band's music, even when their soundtrack work (in films such as *Let It Rain Red Roses*, *Kebab Connection* and *Krimi*) is separated from its visual counterpart.

⊙ Tango Scandale
Liekedeler, Germany
Despite its title, this acoustic quartet contains a smattering of home-grown and exotic material, not necessarily tango. Never a hodge-podge, it wafts in bandonion flavours (though bandonion is absent) from South America, a taste of the Balkans and Iran, a hit of Tom Waits' ("Tango 'Til They're Sore") and a redolent batch of OST compositions.

PLAYLIST
Germany

1 LUSTIG LUSTIG Bierfiedler from *Bierfiedler*
A journeyman's catalogue of travels, tight squeezes, laments and survival strategies, washed down periodically with a glass of something.

2 WEIL ICH 'N TÜRKE BIN Erci E. from *Travellin' Companion 3: A Musical Journey to Germany*
Erci Ergün, a second-generation, Berlin-based Turk, raps a shaming litany of racial stereotypes in German. "Because I'm Turkish…"

3 SO BENI Thomas Felder from *Vesperplatte*
Swabian-word jazz with guilt, Catholic and otherwise.

4 LASS MICH IN RUH LeckerSachen from *Travellin' Companion 3: A Musical Journey to Germany*
A heartfelt plea to be left in peace by a former lover, delivered in folk, hip-hop and pop language.

5 ICH HAB MEINEN MANN GESCHLACHTET Scarlett O' from *Zum Beispiel Nilpferde*
"I Butchered My Husband". You get the picture. Kabarett for today.

6 GRUNEWALD IS' HOLZAKTION Polkaholix from *Denkste!*
Polka at a frantic pace.

7 LĚS Pittkunings from *Z njeznatego luda*
A Sorb singer-songwriter evoking a potent symbol of Germanhood – the "deciduous wood" (Lěs) – to express Sorb cultural values.

8 DEUTSCHLAND NICHT MEHR Christof Stählin from *Auf einem anderen Blatt*
A rapier thrust of a song extrapolated from the fragrant pun "Nothing more than Germany" and "Germany no more". A true Dichtersänger (poet-singer).

9 UNSRE HEIMAT I + II Angelika Weiz & GVO from *Heimat*
In July 1989 Angelika Weiz was emphatically refused permission to release this magisterially sacrilegious interpretation of one of the most defining songs of the GDR era. Finally the Wall came down. Listen to the banned.

10 ZEIT DER IRREN UND IDIOTEN Wenzel & Band from *Grünes Licht*
A tale of what happens when it gets so hot in May that the city sweats, asphalt bubbles and even the whores get the day off.

Greece

crossroads of the balkans

Rembetes at Piraeus, 1937
Coll. Ilias Petropoulos/Kedros

The current Greek musical scene may not have the vitality and distinctiveness that it had from the 1950s through the millennium – Greece's winning entry for the 2005 Eurovision Song Contest is fairly representative of the current pop-flavoured output. But **Marc Dubin** and **George Pissalidhes** demonstrate that Greece's "backlist" – from the orientalized *rebétika* to the groundbreaking experiments of *éntekhno* – is more than enough to keep collectors busy for the foreseeable future.

The music of Greece, like other aspects of the country, is a fortuitous mix of East and West. The older songs of the folk (or *dhimotiká*) tradition are invariably in Eastern-flavoured minor modes: their antecedents lie in both Byzantine religious chant or secular song, and in Turkish music, via the centuries of Ottoman rule in Greece. The flavour of the Orient is even more immediately evident in the blues-like **rebétika** music, which had its heyday in the 1920s and 30s, and has been revived at various periods since.

Western music had surprisingly little impact until well into the twentieth century. Almost all the native Greek instruments are also found throughout the Turkish/Islamic world, though it's an open question as to whether Byzantines, Arabs or Persians first constructed them, or indeed how they spread. To this broadly Middle Eastern base, **Slavs**, **Albanians** and **Italians** have added their share of influences to various of the Greek regions or island groups. The result is an extraordinarily varied repertoire, with local and national traditions still very much alive in both music and dance.

Folk Music

The most accessible live **folk music** events are the numerous summer *paniyíria* (saints' day festivals). But there are also more tourist-oriented cultural programmes – when musicians based in Athens or city clubs during winter go touring the islands and villages. These tend to be community-based performances, often using town or village squares or monasteries.

Such music is essentially traditional; however, as throughout the world, groups have steadily adopted electric and rock instruments since the 1970s. Purists argue that much of it is heavily vulgarized and it is perhaps true that, as the oral transmission of technique from older master players has broken down, musicianship has declined. Certainly, few shows appear to match the skill and spirit shown on CD re-releases of old archival 78s material. But there are some superb revival groups attempting to recapture the musicianship of the old-timers.

Island Music

The arc of southern islands, comprising **Crete**, **Kássos**, **Hálki** and **Kárpathos** is one of the best areas of Greece for hearing live folk music at any season of the year. On Crete, in particular, there is a network of music clubs (*kendrá*) in the main towns.

The dominant instrument on these islands is the *lýra*, a three-stringed fiddle directly related to the Turkish *kemençe*. It is played not on the shoulder but balanced on the thigh; since the 1930s the instrument has been modified by having its body enlarged, drone string removed, tuning altered and bow made more violin-like, changes intended to widen its range.

Two of Crete's finest lýra players were in fact brothers: **Nikos Xylouris**, whose vocal abilities eventually surpassed his playing and earned him the nickname "The Nightingale of Crete", and **Andonis Xylouris**, who performs under the name Psarandonis.

The lýra is often backed by one or more *laoúto*, similar to the Turkish or Arab *oud* but (especially on Crete, where the Venetians ruled for several centuries) more closely resembling a mandolin. These are rarely used to lead or solo, but a virtuoso player will enter a true dialogue with the lýra, using well-chosen rhythms and melodic phrases in pleasing, chime-like tones, rather than bashing away with abrupt attack and over-frequent chord changes.

In several places in the southern Aegean, notably northern Kárpathos, you also find a simple, droneless **bagpipe** – the *askomandoúra* or *tsamboúna*. In Kazantzakis' classic Cretan novel, *Alexis Zorba*, the hero played a **sandoúri**, or hammered dulcimer – an instrument introduced to the islands by Greek refugees from Anatolia. Today, accomplished sandoúri players are few and the instrument tends to be used in a supporting role.

On most of the Aegean islands, particularly the **Cyclades**, the lýra is replaced by a more familiar-looking **violí**, essentially a Western violin. These days you're more likely to find a rhythm section of bass, guitar and drums than the traditional accompaniment of laoúto or sandoúri. Amongst violí players, **Stathis Koukoularis**, born on Náxos, and two young fiddlers **Nikos Ikonomidhes** and **Kyriakos Gouvendas** stand out.

The island of **Lésvos** occupies a special place in terms of island music. Before the turbulent decade of 1912–22, its "mainland" was Asia Minor rather than Greece, its urban poles Smyrna and Constantinople rather than Athens. Accordingly, its music is far more varied and sophisticated than the Aegean norm, having absorbed melodies and instrumentation from the various groups who lived in neighbouring Anatolia. It is the only island with a vital tradition of brass bands, and virtually every Greek dance rhythm is represented in its local music.

By way of contrast, the **Ionian islands** – alone of all modern Greek territory – never saw Turk-

Aerakis

Wedding procession with Cretan lýra and laoúto

ish occupation and have a predominantly Western musical tradition. Their indigenous song-form is Italian both in name – **kantádhes** – and instrumentation (guitar and mandolin). It's most often heard these days on Lefkádha and Zákynthos.

Island folk songs – **nisiótika** – feature melodies that, like much folk music the world over, rely heavily on the pentatonic scale. The lyrics, especially on the smaller islands, touch on the perils of the sea, exile and thwarted or forbidden love. Among the best known singers are the **Konitopoulos** clan from Náxos, while older stars such as **Anna** and **Emilia Hatzidhaki** and **Anna Karabesini** – all from the Dodecanese archipelago – offer a warmer, more innocent delivery.

Mainland Folk Music

Many of the folk songs of mainland Greece – known as **dhimotiká tragoúdhia** – hark back to the years of Ottoman occupation and to the War of Independence; others, in a lighter tone, refer to aspects of pastoral life (sheep herding, elopements, fetching water from the well and so forth). Their essential instrumentation consists of the **klaríno** (clarinet), which reached Greece during the 1830s, introduced either by Gypsies or by members of the (imported Bavarian) King Otto's entourage. Accompaniment is traditionally provided by a group or *koumpanía* comprising *kithára* (guitar),

laoúto, *laoutokithára* (a hybrid in stringing and tuning) and *violí*, with *toumberléki* (lap drum) or *défi* (tambourine) for rhythm.

Many mainland tunes are **dances**, divided by rhythm into such categories as *kalamatianó* (a line dance), *tsámiko*, *hasaposérviko* or *syrtó*, the quintessential circle dance of Greece. Melodies that aren't danced to include the slow, stately *kléftiko*, which relates, baldly or in metaphor, incidents or attitudes from the years of the Ottomans and the rebellions for freedom.

Stalwart vocalists to look for on old recordings include **Yiorgos Papasidheris** and **Yiorgia Mittaki**, both of whom were Arvanites – descendants of medieval Albanian settlers. Among the cream of the folk singers of the 1960s and 70s were **Sofia Kollitiri**, **Takis Karnavas**, **Filio Pyrgaki** and **Stathis Kavouras**. Among the musicians, clarinettist **Vassilis Saleas** is a remarkable Gypsy player. (Gypsies dominate instrumental music on mainland Greece.) Other noteworthy instrumentalists, not of Gypsy origin, include **Nikos Saragoudas** (oud) and **Yiorgos Koros** (fiddle).

The folk music of **Epirus** (*Ípiros*) exhibits strong connections with that of northern Epirus (now in Albania) and the Former Yugoslav Republic of Macedonia, particularly in the polyphonic pieces sung by both men and women. The repertoire tends to fall into three categories, which are also found further south: **mirolóyia** or laments (the instrumental counterpart is called *skáros*); drinking songs or **tis távlas**; and various danceable melodies as noted above, common to the entire mainland and many islands also. Most famous of the Epirot clarinettists are the late **Vassilis Soukas** and **Tassos Halkias**, and the younger (unrelated) **Petro-Loukas Halkias**.

In the northern Greek regions of **Thrace** and **Macedonia**, whose bewilderingly mixed population was under Ottoman rule until the beginning of the twentieth century, the music can sound more generically Balkan. Owing to the huge influx of Anatolian refugees after 1923, the region has been a rich treasure-trove for ethnomusicologists seeking to document the old music of Asia Minor. *Kálanda* (Christmas carols), Carnival dances, wedding processionals and drinking songs abound. Noteworthy singers include **Khronis Aïdhonidhis** and **Xanthippi Karathanasi** – both still active.

Among Thracian instruments, the **kaváli**, or end-blown flute, is identical to the Turkish and Bulgarian article, as is the drone bagpipe, or **gaïdha**. The **zournás**, a screechy, double-reed oboe (the same as the *zurna* used throughout the Balkans and Turkey) is much in evidence at local festivals, in combination with the deep-toned **daoúli** drum, a typical Gypsy ensemble. The klaríno is present here as well, as are two types of lýras, but perhaps the most characteristic melodic instrument of Thrace is the **oúti** (oud), whose popularity received a boost after refugee players arrived.

Unique in Greece (outside of Lésvos) are the western Macedonian **brass bands**, introduced in the nineteenth century by Ottoman military musicians. Finally there is the melancholy, harsh lýra-based music of the Pontians, refugees from the Black Sea coast. Their main dance is the *pyríhios*, a war dance described by ancient writers. The main exponents are singer and lýra player **Yiorgos Amarantidhis** and London-based young lion **Mattheos Tsahouridis**.

Rebétika

Rebétika began as the music of the Greek urban dispossessed – criminals, refugees, drug-users, defiers of social norms. It had existed in some form in Greece, Smyrna and Constantinople since at least the 1890s, but it is as difficult to define or get to the origins of as jazz or blues – genres with which (tenuous) comparisons are often made, not so much for the music as for its inspirations, themes and tone. Rebétika songs tell of illicit or frustrated love, drug addiction, police oppression

or death, and their delivery tends to combine resignation to the singer's lot with defiance of authority.

Musically, rebétika is inextricably linked with the **bouzoúki** – a long-necked, fretted lute derived, like the Turkish *saz*, from the Byzantine *tambourás*. It has become synonymous with Greek music but early in the twentieth century, prior to the popularisation of rebétika, it was used by only a few mainland musicians. As to the term "rebétika", its derivation is uncertain, the favoured candidate being the old Turkish word "harabat", a word with meanings covering "shanty town", "drunkard" and "bohemian" – all definitively aspects of rebétika culture.

Origins: Café-Amán

At the beginning of the twentieth century, in the Asia Minor cities of Smyrna and Istanbul (Constantinople), music cafés became popular. Owned and staffed by Greeks, Jews, Armenians and even a few Gypsies, they featured groups comprising a violinist, a sandoúri player and a (usually female) vocalist, who might also jingle castanets and dance. The songs were improvised and became known as **café-amán** or *amanédhes* for the frequent repetition of the exclamation "*aman aman*" (Turkish for "alas, alas"), used both for its sense and to fill time while the performers searched their imaginations for more articulate lyrics.

Despite sparse instrumentation, café-amán was an elegant, riveting art song, and one requiring considerable skill. It harked back to similar vocalisation in the *ghazals* of Persia and the East. Some of its greatest practitioners included **Andonis "Dalgas" (Wave) Dhiamantidhis**, so nicknamed for the undulations in his voice; **Rosa Eskenazi**, a Greek Jew who grew up in Istanbul; her contemporary **Rita Abatzi** from Smyrna; **Marika Papagika** from the island of Kós, who emigrated to the US where she made her career; **Agapios Tomboulis**, a *tanbur* and oud player of Armenian background, and **Dhimitris "Salonikiyeh" Semsis**, a master fiddler from Strumitsa in northern Macedonia. The spectrum of nationalities for these performers gives a good idea of the range of cosmopolitan influences in the years preceding the emergence of "real" rebétika.

The 1919–22 Greco-Turkish war and the resulting 1923 **exchange of populations** were key events in the history of rebétika, resulting in the influx to Greece of over a million Asia Minor Greeks, many of whom settled in shantytowns around Athens, Piraeus and Thessaloníki. The café-amán musicians, like most of the other refugees, were, in comparison to the Greeks of the host country, extremely sophisticated; many were highly educated, could read and compose music, and had even been unionized in the towns of Asia Minor. Such men included the Smyrniots **Vangelis Papazoglou**, a noted songwriter, and **Panayiotis Toundas**, a composer who headed the Greek divisions of first Odeon and then Columbia Records. But the less lucky lived on the periphery of the new society. Most had lost all they had in the hasty evacuation, and many from inland Anatolia could speak only Turkish. In their misery they sought relief in another Ottoman institution: the *tekés* or hashish den.

Vamvakaris and the Tekédhes

In the *tekédhes* of Athens and its port, Piraeus, or the northern city of Thessaloníki, a few men would sit on the floor around a charcoal brazier, passing around a *nargilés* (hookah) filled with hashish. One of them might begin to improvise a tune on the baglamás or the bouzoúki and begin to sing. The words, either his own or those of the other *dervíses* (many rebetic terms were a burlesque of those of mystical Islamic tradition), would be heavily laced with insiders' argot. As the *taxími* (introduction) was completed, one of the smokers might rise and begin to dance a *zeïbékiko*, a slow, intense, introverted performance following an unusual metre (9/8), not for the benefit of others but for himself.

Coll. Ilias Petropoulos/kedros

Markos Vamvakaris (right)

By the early 1930s, several key musicians had emerged from tekédhes culture. Foremost among them was a Piraeus-based quartet comprising **Markos Vamvakaris** and **Artemis** (Anestis Delias) – two great composers and bouzoúki-players – the beguilingly-voiced **Stratos Payioumtzis**, and, on baglamás, Yiorgos Tsoros, better known as **Batis**. Stratos, the lead singer, went on to perform with other great rebétika stars, like Tsitsanis and Yiannis Papaioannou. Artemis, the son of a sandoúri player from Smyrna, was a remarkable lyricist and composer, who lived a rebetic life of hard drugs, and died in the street (as his song "The Junkie's Lament" had predicted) in 1943 outside a tekés with his bouzoúki in his hand.

Vamvakaris, however, was the linchpin of the group. Born on the Aegean island of Syros in 1905, he had a tough childhood, leaving school at eight and stowing away on a boat for Piraeus at fifteen. Within six months of arrival, he had taught himself bouzoúki as a way out of a particularly grim job in a slaughterhouse, and was writing songs and playing in the tekédhes with Stratos, Artemis and Batis.

At first, Vamvakaris did not consider himself a singer, leaving the lead vocals to Stratos, but when Columbia wanted to release a record by him they persuaded him to have a go, and were pleased with his metallic, hash-rasping sound. Subsequently, he went on to sing on nearly all his records and his gravelly style became a paradigm for male rebétika singers.

Songs about getting stoned, or *mastouriaká*, were a natural outgrowth of the tekédhes. One of the most famous, composed by Batis and first recorded in the mid-1930s by Vamvakaris, commemorated the exploits of the quartet:

On the sly I went out in a boat
And arrived at the Dhrakou Cave
Where I saw three men stoned on hash
Stretched out on the sand.
It was Batis, and Artemis,
And Stratos the Lazy.
Hey you, Strato! Yeah you, Strato!
Fix us a terrific nargilé,
So old Batis can have a smoke
A "dervish" for years he's been
And Artemis too,
Who brings us "stuff" from wherever he's been.
He sends us hash from Constantinople
And all of us get high;
And pressed tobacco from Persia
The mangas smokes in peace.

As time went on such lyrics got cleaned up. For instance, the most commonly heard version of this song from the 1950s substitutes "Play us a fine bit of bouzoúki" for "Fix us a fine nargilé", and so forth.

Tough Times

This **golden age of rebétika** was short-lived. The association of the music with a drug-laced underworld would prove its undoing. After the imposition of the puritanical Metaxas dictatorship in 1936, *rebétes* with uncompromising lyrics and lifestyles were blackballed by the recording industry; anti-hashish laws were systematically enforced and police harassment of the tekédhes was stepped up. In Athens, even possession of a bouzoúki or baglamás became a criminal offence and several of the big names served time in jail. Others went to Thessaloníki, where the police chief Vassilis Mouskoundis was a big fan of the music and allowed its practitioners to smoke in private.

For a time, such persecution – and the official encouragement of tangos and frothy Italianate love songs (which had a much wider audience) – failed to dim the enthusiasm of the *mánges* (wide boys) who frequented the hash dens. Police beatings or prison terms were taken in stride; time behind bars could be used, as it always had been around the Aegean, to make *skaptó* (dug-out) instruments. A baglamás could easily be fashioned from a gourd cut in half or even a tortoise shell (the sound box), a piece of wood (the neck), catgut (frets), and wire for strings, and the result would be small enough to hide from the guards. Jail songs were composed and became popular in the underworld.

However, the rebétes suffered from all sides, incurring the disapproval of the puritanical left as well as the right. The growing Communist Party of the 1930s considered the music and its habitués hopelessly decadent and politically unevolved. When Vamvakaris was about to join the leftist resistance army ELAS in 1944, he was warned not to sing his own material. The left preferred *andártika* (Soviet-style revolutionary anthems).

Like most ideological debates, it was largely academic. World War II, with its harsh Axis occupation of Greece, and the subsequent 1946–49 civil war, put everyone's careers on hold, and the turbulent decade erased any lingering fashion for hash songs. When Greece re-emerged in the 1950s, its public preferred softer music and wanted new heroes.

Tsitsanis and Cloudy Sunday

The major figure of post-war rebétika was undoubtedly **Vassilis Tsitsanis**. Born in Thessaly,

the son of a silver craftsman, he was a very different personality to Vamvakaris, whose mantle he took on as both the most significant composer and bouzoúki master of his generation.

Tsitsanis embarked on his career in Athens, just before the war, cutting his first record for Odeon, at that time directed by rebetic composer Spyros Peristeris, in 1936. Tsitsanis spent the war years – during which time all the recording studios shut down – more comfortably than many, running his own bar in Thessaloníki and composing songs in the meantime. The most famous of these was "Synefiasmeni Kyriaki" (Cloudy Sunday):

> *Cloudy Sunday, you seem like my heart*
> *Which is always overcast, Christ and Holy Virgin!*
> *You're a day like the one I lost my joy.*
> *Cloudy Sunday, you make my heart bleed.*
> *When I see you rainy, I can't rest easy for a moment;*
> *You blacken my life and I sigh deeply.*

Although it wasn't recorded until 1948, the song became widely known after its composition during the occupation (supposedly within a week of the Germans' arrival in Athens) and became a kind of anthem for the dispossessed, occupied Greeks.

After the war, Tsitsanis obliged a traumatized public with love songs and Neapolitan melodies. This new rebétika enjoyed, for the first time, something of a mass following, through top female singers such as **Sotiria Bellou**, **Marika Ninou** and **Ioanna Yiorgakopoulou**. Tsitsanis himself remained a much-loved figure in Greek music until his death in 1984; his funeral in Athens was attended by nearly a quarter of a million people.

If Tsitsanis' "softening" of rebétika was a first key change to the music, a second, perhaps more dramatic, was the innovation in 1953 by **Manolis Hiotis** of adding a fourth pair of strings to the bouzoúki. This allowed it to be tuned tonally rather than modally. In its wake came **electrical amplification**, over-orchestration and maudlin lyrics as a crest of popularity led to the opening of *bouzoúkia* – huge, barn-like clubs where Athenians paid large sums to break specially provided plates and to dance flashy steps that were a travesty of the simple dignity and precise, synchronized footwork of the old-time zeïbékika. Virtuoso bouzoúki players Manolis Hiotis and **Yiorgos Mitsakis** – assisted by kewpie-doll-type female vocalists – amassed large fortunes while debasing the rebetic genre.

Rebétika Revivals

Ironically, the original rebétika material was rescued from oblivion by the colonels' junta of 1967–

74. Along with dozens of other features of Greek culture, rebétika verses were banned. In response, a generation of students growing up under the dictatorship took a closer look at the forbidden fruit and derived solace, and deeper meanings, from the nominally apolitical lyrics. When the junta fell in 1974 – and even shortly before – there was an outpouring of reissued recordings of the old masters.

Over the next decade live rebétika also enjoyed a revival, beginning with a clandestine 1979 club near the old Fix brewery in Athens, whose street credentials were validated when it was raided and closed by the police. These smoky attempts to recapture pre-war atmosphere – which led to dozens of rebétika clubs in the early 1980s – saw performances by revival groups such as **Ta Pedhia apo tin Patra**, **Rebetiki Kompania** and **Opisthodhromiki Kompania** (featuring Eleftheria Arvanataki), and the performers **Hondronakos** and **Mario**. In the northern capital of Thessaloníki, a leading figure was **Agathonas Iakovidhis** with his group **Rebetiko Synkrotima Thessalonikis**. Most recently, he has worked with **Glykeria** and **Babis Tsertos**.

A feature film by Kostas Ferris, *Rebetiko* (1983), attempted to trace the music from Asia Minor of the 1920s to Greece of the 1950s, and garnered wide acclaim in Greece and abroad. These days, however, the fashion has long since peaked, and only a handful of clubs and bands remain compared to the 1980s revival heyday.

New Waves

Alongside folk and rebétika, post-war Greece developed its own forms of "art" (**éntekhno**) and pop (**laïkó**) music, while since the late 1970s the scene has broadened to include roots-minded **rock and fusion** experiments, and even new explorations of **Byzantine** forms.

The Éntekhno Revolution

The Westernization of rebétika that had begun with Tsitsanis and escalated with the electric bouzoúki craze paved the way for the éntekhno music of the late 1950s. Éntekhno mixed zeïbékika, *hassápika* and ballads with Western-styled arrangements. Its first and most famous exponents were **Manos Hatzidhakis** and **Mikis Theodhorakis**, both classically trained musicians and admirers of rebétika. Éntekhno reached its peak with albums such as Theodhorakis' *Axion Esti* and **Yiannis Markopoulos's** *Eleftheri Poliorkime-*

ni where folk instruments, rhythms and melodies were interwoven into a symphonic fabric, but with a still recognizably Greek sound.

Already in 1948, Hatzidhakis defended rebétika in a lecture, suggesting that Greek composers be inspired by it, rather than bow to the prevailing left-wing, middle-class prejudices against it. In a period when most Greek tunes imitated Western light popular music, he had transcribed rebétika for piano and orchestra, keeping only the spirit and nostalgic mood of the original. Theodhorakis, a disciple of Tsitsanis, included zeïbékika tunes on his earliest albums, with **Grigoris Bithikiotsis** or **Stelios Kazantzídhis** on vocals and Manolis Hiotis as bouzoúki soloist.

The éntekhno of Theodhorakis and Hatzidhakis combined rebetic and Byzantine influences with Western ones, but – more memorably – fused Greek music with the country's rich poetic tradition. Among Theodhorakis' early albums were *Epitafios* (1963), based on poems by Yiannis Ritsos, and *To Axion Esti* (1964), a folk-flavoured oratorio incorporating poetry by Odysseas Elytis. Hatzidhakis replied in 1965 with a recording of *Matomenos Gamos*, an adaptation version of García Lorca's *Blood Wedding* translated into Greek by poet-lyricist Nikos Gatsos, and also tried his hand at rendering Elytis in song.

Together, these works changed Greek perceptions of bouzoúki-based music, popularized Greek poetry for a mass audience and elevated lyricists such as Gatsos and Manos Eleftheriou to the status of bards. The downside was that the sophistication and Western classical orchestral arrangements distanced the music from its roots, and in particular, from the modal scale which had served Greece so well since antiquity. With its catchy melodies, the genre fell prey to the demands of the local film industry – writing a soundtrack became an obligatory rite of passage for éntekhno composers – and at its worst degenerated into muzak covers that thoroughly obscured the merits of the original versions.

Theodhorakis and Hatzidhakis paved the way for successors who were generally less classicising and more pop-leaning, such as **Stavros Xarhakos**, most famous abroad for his soundtrack to the film *Rebetiko*; **Manos Loïzos**, who gave George Dalaras his start in 1968; the Cretan **Yiannis Markopoulos**, the most folk-based, and most accessible to foreign audiences; and **Stavros Kouyoumtzis** and **Dhimos Moutsis**, who collaborated with a galaxy of stellar vocalists during the early-to-mid-1970s – in retrospect, the Indian summer of éntekhno.

Laïkó: Son of Rebétika

Diametrically opposed to éntekhno was the authentic **laïkó** or "popular" music of the 1950s and 60s, its gritty, tough style a direct heir to rebétika, undiluted by Western influences. Laïkó used not only zeïbékika and hasápika time signatures but also the *tsiftetéli* – another age-old rhythm from Asia Minor mistakenly labelled as belly-dance music abroad. Once again, "debased" oriental influences dominated Greek pop, to the chagrin of the bourgeois classes and the Greek left, who also objected to it as being apolitical, decadent and escapist. This reached its high – or low – point during the brief mid-1960s craze for *indoyíftika*, Indian film music lifted straight from Bollywood and reset to Greek lyrics; chief culprit was the Gypsy singer **Manolis Angelopoulos**.

The most influential laïkó performer in the 1960s was **Stelios Kazantzídhis**, whose volcanic, mournful style was often imitated but never matched. His work, frequently in duets with Marinella (Kyriaki Papadhopoulou) and Yiota Lidhia, immortalized the joys and sorrows of the post-war Greek working class which faced a choice of life under the restrictive regimes of the time, or emigration. Among the best exponents of laïkó were also the songwriter **Theodoros Derveniotis**, the lyricist **Kostas Virvos**, the singers **Katie Gray** and **Poly Panou** and the classic duo of **Panos Gavalas** and **Ria Kourti**. A trio of other rising stars in this period were **Yiorgos Dalaras**, still the top-selling Greek pop singer, who had already attained gold sales status by 1971; and **Yiannis Parios** and **Haris Alexiou**, both of whom emerged on albums by the composer **Apostolos Kaldharas**.

Two other laïkó composers with a distinctively Greek sound were **Akis Panou** and **George Zambetas,** two bouzoúki virtuosi who never succumbed to the oriental-tsiftetéli craze. Zambetas become famous when he played bouzoúki in the soundtrack of *Never on Sunday* that led to the popularity of Greek music all around the world. He would participate in sessions of Hatzidhakis, Theodhorakis and Xarhakos, before writing sunny laïkó hits for **Vicky Moskholiou**, **Stamatis Kokkotas** and **Tolis Voskopoulos** or singing in his unique style, mixing gritty roots with influences from Athenian kantádha. Although less high profile, Akis Panou wrote excellent albums for Dalaras, **Bithikotsis**, **Stratos Dhionysiou** and Stelios Kazantzídhis. Finally there was **Khristos Nikolopoulos**, a bouzoúki virtuoso who at the age of sixteen wrote his early hits for Kazantzídhis in the mid-1960s, before their historic collaboration in the early 1970s.

Although laïkó and éntekhno represented opposite poles of the Greek music world, the extremes sometimes met. Éntekhno composers such as Yiannis Markopoulos hired laïkó singers for dates, or tried their hand at writing in laïkó style. A good example of the latter was Dhimos Moutsis' and Manos Eleftheriou's 1971 album *Ayios Fevrouarios*, which made singer **Dhimitris Mitropanos** a star overnight. But these syntheses were increasingly exceptional; after the success of *Epitafios* and *Axion Esti*, Greek record labels tried to marginalize laïkó, a trend accelerated under the military junta, when the greater portion of laïkó was banned from the radio as being too "oriental" and "defeatist". In these conditions, the genre turned into **elafrolaïkó** (light popular), in which more honeyed voices were preferred. However, the stage was set for the emergence of singer-songwriters – many of them from Thessaloníki – and groups of folk-rockers, who together arrested the descent of Greek music into anodyne pap.

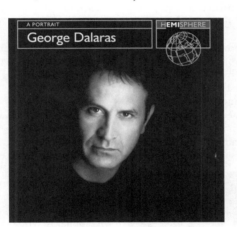

Yiorgos Dalaras

Singer-Songwriters and Folk-Rock

The first significant musician to break out of the bouzoúki mould was Thessaloníki-based **Dhionysis Savvopoulos**, who burst onto the scene in 1966 with a maniacal, rasping voice and elliptical, angst-ridden lyrics, his persona rounded out by shoulder-length hair and outsized glasses. Initially linked with the short-lived **néo kýma** (new wave) movement – a blend of watered-down éntekhno and French chanson performed in Athenian boites soon closed down by the colonels – Savvopoulos's work soon became impossible to pigeonhole: twisted Northern Greek folk with influences from Bob Dylan and Frank Zappa at his jazziest. Although he was arrested, detained and tortured, he was able to continue performing and became something of a touchstone for the generation coming of age under the junta.

Out of Savvopoulos's "Balkan rock" experiments sprung a short-lived movement whose artists alternated electric versions of traditional songs with original material. Few left much trace, apart from the folk updater **Mariza Koch**, whose *Arabas* album was the equivalent of Fairport Convention's *Liege and Lief* for Greek folk-rock, and who influenced later performers such as Kristi Stassinopoulou. Other important singer-songwriters are the Gypsy protest singer **Kostas Hatzis** and **Nikos Portokaloglou**, a disciple of Savvopoulos who started his career in the 1980s, leading the laïkó-rock group Fatme.

As an independent producer and (briefly) head of Lyra records, Savvopoulos gave a break to numerous younger artists, many of them also from northern Greece. The first of his protégés were **Nikos Xydhakis** and **Manolis Rasoulis**, whose landmark 1978 pressing, *Iy Ekdhikisis tis Yiftias* (The Revenge of Gypsydom), actually embodied the backlash of laïkó culture against the pretentiousness of 1960s and 70s éntekhno. Its spirited,

defiant lyrics – with **Nikos Papazoglou** handling many of the vocals – and tsiftetéli rhythms were both a homage to and send-up of the music beloved by Greek truck-drivers.

As with mainland folk instrumental music, Gypsies have been extremely important contributors to laïkó, both as performers and composers, though some went to considerable lengths to conceal their background. However, there are plenty of others, such as **Eleni Vitali**, **Makis Khristodhoulopoulos** and **Vassilis Païteris** who made no bones about their identity.

Beyond Laïkó

After an equally successful reprise in 1979, Nikos Xydhakis and Nikos Papazoglou went on to pursue successful independent careers. Xydhakis created a style that hardcore laïkó fans dismiss as *koultouriárika* (highbrow stuff), for its orientalised instrumentation and melody. His most successful venture in this vein was the 1987 *Konda sti Dhoxa mia Stigmi*, with **Eleftheria Arvanitaki** guesting on vocals. Arvanitaki went on to forge a successful career, and is still one of the most popular artists on the Athens club scene.

Other performers to emerge from the Thessaloníki scene included the group **Himerini Kolymvites**; folk re-inventer **Thanasis Papakonstandinou** with his Laïkadelica touring band featuring **Martha Frintzela** on vocals; the singer, author and musicologist **Thomas Korovinis** and, most recently, the Papazoglou disciples **Sokratis Malamas** and **Melina Kana**.

Back in Athens, the composer **Stamatis Kraounakis**, lyricist and producer **Lina Nikolakopoulou** and female singer **Alkistis Protopsalti** made a splash with a number of hit albums stretching into the 1990s, exploring the boundaries between rock, jazz-cabaret and éntekhno.

On the more committed laïkó side Khristos Nikolopoulos, Takis Soukas and Takis Moussafiris ignited the 1980s, writing dozens of hits for a range of singers including **Alexiou**, **Glykeria**, **Eleni Vitali**, Stratos Dhionysiou, Dhimitris Mitropanos and **Pitsa Papadopoulou**.

Contemporary artists to watch out are éntekhno songwriter **Panayiotis Kalantzipoulos**, rootsy singer-songwriter **Pandelis Thalassinos**, the éntekhno performer **Eleni Tsaligopoulou**. Ethnobeat singers such as **Anna Vissi**, **Yiorgos Alkeos** and **Despina Vandi** sing a style that mixes glitzy laïkó and oriental styles with pop and dance trends. In 2002 Despina Vandi had a huge hit on both sides of the Atlantic with "Gia".

Eleftheria Arvanitaki with Domna Samiou (left)

Byzantine and Folk Revivals

An offshoot of éntekhno during the late 1970s and early 1980s combined **folk** and **Byzantine traditions**. Influential in this was the musicologist and arranger **Khristodhoulos Halaris**, who produced a version of the Cretan epic *Erotokritos*, showcasing Nikos Xylouris and Tania Tsanaklidou and followed it with the riveting *Dhrossoulites*, which featured the late **Khrysanthos Theodhoridhis**, a high-voiced male singer of Pontian descent, on alternate tracks with Dhimitra Galani. He then lost his way with less musically successful ventures in Byzantine song.

Ottoman, rather than Byzantine, Constantinople was the inspiration for **Vosporos**, a group co-ordinated in Istanbul from 1986 to 1992 by *psáltis* (church-chanter) and *kanonáki*-player **Nikiforos Metaxas** to explore Ottoman classical, devotional and popular music. In the late 1990s the group reformed as **Fanari tis Anatolis**, with Greek and Turkish singers alternating Greek folk material with Anatolian songs or mystical Alevî ballads, before reverting to being Vosporos and collaborating with Mode Plagal in 2005.

Ross Daly, whose interests and style overlap slightly with Vosporos, is also well worth catching whether on disc, live on Crete where he runs music workshops or touring abroad. English-born but from an Irish background, Daly has updated both Greek and Turkish folk material. He plays a dozen traditional instruments and has absorbed influences not only from Crete, where he lives, but from throughout the Near East and Central Asia. Native Cretans reworking folk material include mandolinist **Loudhovikos ton Anoyion**, and the group **Haïnidhes**, who produce accessible and exciting music. A drier, more scholarly approach is undertaken by **Domna Samiou**, who has collected and performed material from every corner of the Greek world since the 1960s.

A range of other, less durable groups – for example the short-lived 1980s pioneers **Dhynameis tou Egeou** – have attempted to explore Eastern influences on Greek music with varying success. Often the eclecticism has gone too far, with many performers using bells, sitar, ney, synthesizer, et al to produce a bland, New-Agey sound that is not particularly anything. It's mirrored by a mainstream laïkó industry whose product has sounded increasingly Europop since the millennium. Individuals who have managed to avoid this trap include the innovative young clarinettist **Manos Ahalinotopoulos**, oud player **Haig Yagdjian**, the group **Notios Ikhos** (led by **Ahilleas Persidhis**) and folk interpreter **Savina Yiannatou**.

The first group which incorporated rebétika and folk with electro/hip-hop rhythms was the New York-based **Annabouboula**, whose members were of Greek-American origin; a mixture of laïkó and rock was essential to the music of the group **Pix-Lax**. This trend is best represented by the collaboration of the king of underground laïkó Yiorgos Margaritis with the rock/funk/dub outfit **667**.

These days Greek fusion covers a wide range of artists: Alexandros Karsiotis' **Greeks & Indians** (see box on p.182), the folk/Balkan experiments of jazz group **Iasis**, the neo-hippie folk-rocker **Kristi Stassinopoulou**, the percussion experiments of **Krotala**, the "new ancient" music of **Daemonia Nymphae** and the folk/world electronica of **Palyrria**. All of them have been trying to push Greek traditional music forward into the twenty-first century.

Ross Daly at his Labyrinth workshop in Houdetsi, Crete

Simon Broughton

Greeks & Indians

The home of **Saraswati Records** at Kapandríti, northeast of Athens, is a hidden, enchanted place in the hills, far from the traffic, noise and pollution of the city. There's a comfortable rambling house full of Indian artefacts, a tranquil garden with a small amphitheatre and a stream flowing through. This magical oasis of calm has produced a series of extraordinary recordings that have no equivalent anywhere else. The idea, as the title **Greeks & Indians** suggests, is simple – a creative meeting of Greek and Indian musicians - but the results are more than the sum of the parts.

The Svengali mastermind behind the project is **Alexander Karsiotis**, a Peter Gabriel and Pink Floyd fan who became fascinated with the music of India and went there for enlightenment. He came back and started to put on tours for Indian musicians, such as flautists **Hariprasad Chaurasia** and **Rakesh Chaurasia**, in Greece. A music teacher heard one of the concerts and suggested getting them together with the great clarinettist from Epirus, **Petro-Loukas Halkias**. "I'd never heard any traditional Greek music in my life", Karsiotis admits. But the seed was sown. Three years later he was asked for a concert for the Halándhri festival in Athens and suggested his Indian musicians plus Chalkias. The clarinettist arrived after playing at an all-night *paniyíri* (village festival), but he still pulled out all the stops. The concert was a great success and the first recording followed. Since then Karsiotis has produced seven Greeks & Indians CDs with traditional Greek players from different regions (Epirus, Pontic Greece, Thrace and elsewhere) plus a fairly consistent line-up of Indian musicians – **Rabindra Goswami** (sitar), Rakesh Chaurasia (bansuri) and **Shubankar Banerjee** (tabla). He convened the Master Musicians Meeting Club with Greeks, Indians and the Malian kora player **Ballake Sissoko**.

Karsiotis records the discs in his living room. There are Turkish carpets and cushions on the floor where the musicians sit. Candles and incense burn and petals are scattered. Presiding over it all is a statue of Shiva. "I've been very fortunate – the gods have smiled on these projects", explains Karsiotis. "The only skill I have is a knack for putting things together so that the musicians feel comfortable ... With Indian music and the traditional Greek music, you're latching onto the product of generations of wisdom. It's crystallised in these things of timeless value, and these don't go astray."

Simon Broughton

DISCOGRAPHY Greece

Folk/Traditional Music

⊙ **Instrumental Folk Music from Greece**
Topic, UK
A pretty good sampler of traditional dance music from the islands, Epirus and Macedonia.

⊙ **Oi Protomastores 1920–1953**
Aerakis, Greece
This is the definitive compilation of early Cretan recordings. The ten-CD set is a tad prohibitive for casual exploration, and some volumes are of specialist interest only, but fortunately discs are available individually. Go for Vol. 1 (Rodhinos and Baksevanis, lýra and small orchestra), Vol. 4 (Stelios Foustalieris, the last master of the tambur-like voœlgari, knowledge of which died with him), Vol. 5 (Yiannis Demirtzoyiannis, guitarist and epic singer) and Vol. 6 (Yiorgis Koutsourelis, on melodic laoúto).

★ **Lesvos Aiolis: Songs and Dances of Lesvos**
University Press of Crete, Greece
Two decades' worth (1974–96) of field recordings of the last traditional music extant on the island of Lesbos; a labour of love supervised by musicologist Nikos Dhionysopoulos. The quality and uniqueness of the instrumental pieces, and the lavishly illustrated booklet, justify the expense.

⊙ **Seryiani sta Nisia Mas, Vol. 1**
MBI, Greece
An excellent retrospective of vintage *nisiótika* hits and artists, mostly from the 1950s. A highlight is Emilia Hatzidhakí's rendering of "Bratsera".

⊙ **Songs of . . . (series)**
SDNM, Greece
A series of field recordings, with over thirty volumes, spanning the 1950s to the 1970s, each covering traditional music of one region or type. Quality can vary, but they're inexpensive, and all contain liner notes in English. Good choices include *Thrace 1, Epirus 1, Peloponnese, Mytilene and Chios*,

Mytilene and Asia Minor, Rhodes, Khalki and Symi, and *Kassos and Karpathos.*

⊙ Thalassa Thymisou
En Chordais, Greece

This mix of live taverna sessions and studio recordings is the superb result of a "field trip" by a Thessalonian ensemble and group of musicologists to the remote islet of Inoússes near Híos.

⭐ Tis Kritis ta Polytima
MBI, Greece

The perfect antidote to misconceptions of Cretan music as monotonous sawing on the lýra: a two-CD anthology of beautiful compositions and interpretations by post-1990 performers including the Xylouris clan, Haïnidhes, the beguiling Vassilis Skoulas and some wonderful female vocalists.

Khronis Aïdhonidhis

Born in the Évros valley of western Thrace, Aïdhonidhis moved to Athens in 1950, where he fitted recording and live broadcasting sessions around a civil service career. He is unquestionably the greatest male singer of material from Thrace and Western Asia Minor.

⭐ T'Aïdhoni tis Anatolis
Minos, Greece

That rare thing – a folk collection of sterling material flawlessly produced. This 1990 session features Yiorgos Dalaras guesting on four tracks, and Ross Daly in charge of a traditional orchestra. You can also hear Aïdhonidhis alone on *Tragoudhia keh Skopi tis Thrakis/Tunes and Songs of Thrace* (University Press of Crete, Greece), with more stripped-down instrumentation.

Banda tis Florinas

Brass bands are unique (in mainland Greece) to western Macedonia. This is probably the best of them all.

⊙ Banda tis Florinas
Ano Kato-Rei, Thessaloníki, Greece

This is wonderfully twisted brass-band music, verging on ethno-jazz territory with a nudge from guest saxophonist Floros Floridhis, one of the foremost personalities on Greece's avant-garde/improvisational scene. Their second outing, *Banda tis Florinas II* (Lyra, Greece), is more explicitly jazzy but still highly worthwhile.

Petro-Loukas Halkias

Born in 1934 in Epirus, near the Albanian border, clarinettist Halkias lived in the US for twenty years before returning to Greece in 1979 to commence his recording career. After the deaths of Vassilis Soukas and Tassos Halkias, Petro-Loukas became – until his effective retirement in 2006 – the most sought-after session player in the country, injecting new life into the tradition in the best possible taste.

⭐ Petro-Loukas Chalkias and Kompanía
Network, Germany

Halkias is at his best on this superbly recorded disc, as are his *kompanía* (group) who provide the traditional backing of laoúto, violí, kithára and percussion. There are meaty oud solos by Khristos Zotos and fiddle licks by Petro-Loukas' brother Ahileas, which realize the true sense of the kompanía: tight co-ordination, but clearly articulated instrumental voices.

Xanthippi Karathanasi

From Macedonia's Halkidhikí Peninsula, Karathanasi is one of the foremost interpretators of northern Greek folk material.

⊙ Tragoudhia keh Skopi tis Makedhonias/ Songs and Tunes of Macedonia
University Press of Crete, Greece

High quality, like all releases on this record label. The only possible quibble is that the sidemen are so good that they threaten to overshadow Xanthippi's vocals.

Konitopoulos Family

It's hard to keep track of all the siblings and generations of this musical family, originally from Náxos; basically, the late George played fiddle, while sister Angeliki and daughter Stella sing. The other sister, Irini Konitopoulou-Legaki, is a star in her own right.

⊙ Anefala Thalassina
Lyra, Greece

This is Irini on the club stage: a riveting, intimate performance, with accompaniment by octogenarian Dhimitris Fyrogenis on *tsambouna* and backing vocals.

Yiorgos Koros

Considered Greece's foremost fiddler, Koros (born 1922) has been playing music since childhood, and appeared at *paniyíria* at the age of seventeen. His discography spans three decades, but unfortunately little of it is on CD.

⊙ To Magiko Violi
BMG, Greece

This welcome re-release of an out-of-print 1982 disc features daughter Katerina and Yiannis Kondoyiannis (both of the Rebetiki Kompania) on vocals.

Stelios Petrakis

Born in Crete in 1975, Petrakis studied with Ross Daly and plays in his Labyrinth ensemble. He is also a lyra maker and his specially developed model with 22 sympathetic strings is a favourite amongst lyra players including Daly.

⭐ Orion
Aerakis, Greece/Buda, France

Sheer poetry on the Cretan lyra and convincing evidence that it's a lot more than a mere folk fiddle. With Iranian percussionist Bijan Chemirani.

Psarandonis (Andonis Xylouris)

With his low, gruff singing voice, Zeus-like presence and multi-instrumental abilities, "Psarandonis" is one of a kind. Many mainstream Cretan musicians shun him for his idiosyncratically spare and percussive lyra style, but there is no doubting his musical courage and integrity.

⊙ Palio Krassi Ih Skepsis mou
Lyra, Greece

A varied collection, with rarely heard instruments – bagpipes, oud, long-necked baglamás – well integrated into a densely textured whole. Extra atmosphere is imparted by Psarandonis' sighs and bow-scrapings.

⊙ Mountain Rebels
Raki Records/Network, Germany

A recording from 2008 with the Xylouris family band and vocals from his daughter Niki. With its barks, growls and idiosyncratic lyra playing, this is a recording to be enjoyed late at night with a raki.

Domna Samiou

Samiou ranks as the foremost living collector and interpreter of Greek folk material. Since the 1960s, she has also nurtured generations of young traditional musicians. In most other countries she would be hailed as a national treasure – and she did feature among performers at the closing ceremony of the 2004 Athens Olympics – but the following year she had to see off a mischievous criminal complaint from the Orthodox Church for singing "improper" carnival songs on television.

⊙ Seryiani
Seirios-Minos, Greece
A short but very sweet collection of songs from every corner of the Greek world, with particularly crisp instrumentation.

⊙ Apokriatika
Domna Samiou Greek Folk Music Association, Greece
This double CD of often bawdy carnival songs, was Exhibit A in the Church prosecution described above.

Nikos Xylouris

He died tragically young in 1980 but Xylouris was indisputably the finest voice of his generation, a charismatic figure who lent his considerable talent to numerous 1970s éntekhno endeavours, as well as accompanying himself on lýra for Cretan material.

★ Itane mia Fora
EMI, Greece
An almost exhaustive selection of his best 1970s work with Markopoulos and others, spread across two CDs. Includes the high points of such classic albums as Sylloyi, Anexartita, Erotokritos, Rizitika and Ithayenia. Indispensable for understanding why Xylouris is still worshipped nearly three decades after his passing.

Rebétika

⊙ The Greek Archives
FM Records, Greece
Luxuriously packaged (though with skeletal liner notes in English), this multi-disc series from the 1990s is uneven but generally worthwhile. Of the 28 discs still in print, choose from among 1: Rembetico Song in America 1920–1940; 6: Women of the Rembetico Song; Anthology of Rembetiko Songs 1933–1940; and Anthology of Smyrean Songs 1920–1938 vol. 1.

★ Greek-Oriental Rembética
Arhoolie, US
A superb rebétika collection spanning 1911–37, featuring the singers Rosa Eskenazy, Rita Abatzi, Marika Papagika and Dhimitris Semsis. Good liner notes and lyric translations.

⊙ Historic Urban Folk Songs from Greece
Rounder, US
The above-cited artists, plus many more on terrific selections (mostly from the 1930s) complement the Arhoolie disc well, with no duplication.

⊙ Lost Homelands: The Smyrnaic Song in Greece, 1928–1935
Heritage, UK
Like all the Heritage releases (sadly mostly out of print), this has excellent sound quality and editing, plus intelligent liner notes. It features lots of Dalgas, the two great peers Rosa Eskenazy and Rita Abatzi, and instrumental improvisations.

⊙ Mourmourika: Songs of the Greek Underworld 1930–55
Rounder, US
These songs of the mourmourídhes (street toughs) are considered the purest, most stripped-down forms of rebétika, with possible origins in the 1850s. An invaluable document, with good mastering and intelligent notes.

⊙ Rembetika: Baglamas, Bouzoukis and Bravado
JSP Records, UK
This four-CD set of lovingly remastered and rare material, arranged chronologically and by genre, is let down only by almost non-existent liner notes.

⊙ Rembetika: Songs of the Greek Underworld 1925–1947
Trikont, Germany
Two CDs crammed to the gills with hasiklídhika and jail songs, including many classics as well as obscure but intriguing pieces. Minimal English-language notes.

★ The Rough Guide to Rebétika
World Music Network, UK
Arguably the best single introduction to the genre, with performers from its earliest recorded days to current revivalists. The only major omission (for licensing reasons) is Sotiria Bellou. Unlike many such collections, it has thorough notes in English.

Rita Abatzi

Born in Smyrna in 1914, Rita Abatzi came to Greece as a child and began singing at sixteen. She had a huskier, more textured voice than her great rival Eskenazi, and seemed to gravitate toward meatier lyrics as well – though she often worked with the same sidemen: Semsis, Toumboulis et al.

⊙ Rita Abatzi
Minos EMI, Greece
The only surviving worthwhile disc devoted exclusively to Rita; part of the respected Arkheio series coordinated by rebétika scholar Panayiotis Koundahis. Greek-only notes, though.

Sotiria Bellou

Born in Évvia in 1921, Bellou lived in Athens from 1940 until her death in 1997. Though her forthright homosexuality, left-wing political views and addiction to gambling sometimes drew more attention than her artistry, there's no denying that on a good night she could sing the socks off most contemporaries with her searching, no-nonsense voice.

⊙ Sotiriou Bellou Ihografiseis
hellenicrecord.gr, Greece
Part of this company's series of re-released 78 classics, this five-disc set covers the peak of her career from 1947 to 1954; sound quality is unremastered but all her classic hits are here.

Rosa Eskenazi

Though born in Istanbul around the turn of the century, Eskenazi moved to Greece before the 1922 disaster and then lived in Athens until her death in 1980. Her voice inimitably combined innocence with the come-hither sensuality that was supposed to be intrinsic to all the *hanumákia* (bar girls) from Asia Minor.

 Roza Eskenazi: Rembetissa
Rounder, US

Superb renditions with her usual sidemen Semsis and Tomboulis, plus Lambros on kanonáki. An extremely varied selection of standards and rare gems make this the best of several collections available.

Dhimitris Mystakidhis

Mystakidhis, from Thessaloníki, is only in his thirties – you'd never guess from the gruff voice on the recommended disc – and a frequent collaborator with Thanasis Papakonstandinou (see p.188).

 16 Rebetika Tragoudhia Pegmena sti Kithara (16 Rebétika Songs Played on Guitar)
Music Corner, Greece

As it says – but you've rarely heard guitar (one of the less-common rebetic instruments) like this, meaty and plangent. Mostly jail, mastouriaká and love songs.

Marika Ninou

Born in 1918 in a Greek community of the Caucausus, Ninou came to Greece as a child and sung with Tsitsanis from 1948 until her premature death from cancer in 1956.

⊙ **Stou Tzimi tou Khondhrou/At Fat Jimmy's**
Venus-Tzina, Greece

Poor sound quality, since it was a clandestine wire recording, but still a classic. Performing with Tsitsanis at their habitual club in 1955, Ninou gives it her all, including two cuts in Turkish. Well worth rooting out.

⊙ **Marika Ninou & Vassilis Tsitsanis**
Philips, Greece

Not as soulful as the Venus disc, but far better sound and more than adequate renditions of their favourites, including "Synnefiazmeni Kyriaki" and the gut-wrenching "Yennithika".

Marika Papagika

Born on Kós in 1890, Papagika emigrated to the US in 1913, where she performed with her husband Gus between 1918 and 1937, for the considerable and nostalgic Greek community in New York.

⊙ **Greek Popular and Rebetic Music in New York 1918–1929**
Alma Criolla, US

Marika Papagika's best work, with Gus on sandoúri. Includes a rare, affecting kantádha duet with Marika Kastrouni.

Vassilis Tsitsanis

One of the giants of rebétika, who mellowed and popularised the style, Tsitsanis began his recording career in Athens, but spent the critical war years in Thessaloníki, where he performed live and accumulated the material that was to make him a household name. A shy, nattily dressed man, he never quite lost the air of the law student he'd once briefly been.

⊙ **Vassilis Tsitsanis 1936–1946**
Rounder, US

A fine first disc to begin exploring Tsitsanis. It features mostly male singers, but includes his reputed first recording, a *mastouriaká* with Yioryia Mittaki.

⊙ **Tsitsanis: Ta Klidhia**
EMI Regal, Greece

Tsitsanis, together with such stars of the late 1960s as Grigoris Bithikiotsis, Panos Gavalas, Poly Panou and Manolis Hiotis. This (re)popularized rebétika long before Dalaras et al did, and was the Saturday-night-party album of its day – look for the double keys (klidhiá) on the cover.

Markos Vamvakaris

The "Grandfather of rebétika", Vamvakaris was born on Sýros into a poor Catholic family in 1905. He stowed away on a freighter bound for Piraeus at age fifteen, and worked odd jobs around the port before discovering the bouzoúki and hash – more or less in that order. The rest is Greek musical history.

 Markos Vamvakaris, Bouzouki Pioneer
Rounder, US

Excellent sound quality, good notes and unusual material – not a trace of his hackneyed and over-covered "Frangosyriani" – make this a top choice.

⊙ **Afthentika Rembétika tis Amerikis No.2**
Lyra, Greece

Mostly Markos, and wonderful. The title's a wild misnomer, as Vamvakaris never went to America, though some 78s may have been simultaneously issued there and in Greece.

Stavros Xarhakos

⊙ **Rebetiko**
CBS, Greece

Soundtrack to the namesake film, available as a double LP or, in somewhat edited form, on one CD. Virtually the only "original" rebétika to be composed in the last forty years, with lyrics by Nikos Gatsos. His *éntekhno* work is best profiled on two successive discs, each entitled *Trianda Khrysses Epityhies* (Columbia EMI, Greece).

New Waves

⊙ **Ta Horeftika**
Minos–EMI, Greece

All the laïkó and tsiftetéli classics in an album that sounds like the typical working-class night out of the 1960s and which today forms the core of any programme in Athens clubs. Includes the original version of 3Mustaphas3's "Anapse to Tsigaro".

 Grecia: De Oriente Y De Occidente
Resistencia, Spain

The best one-stop tour of Greek trends in all genres up to the mid-1990s – there's hardly a duff track on this double set. Most of the big names, and quite a few surprises.

Haris Alexiou

Born in Thebes in 1950, Haris Alexiou reigned virtually unchallenged as the queen of Greek laïkó (pop) throughout the 1970s and 1980s. Her unschooled but incredibly expressive voice graced the albums of improbably varied composers.

⊙ Ta Tsilika
★ Ta Tragoudhia tis Haroulas
Minos-EMI, Greece

Of these two discs, the former includes her best rebétika interpretations. The latter is her landmark collaboration with Loizos and Rassoulis, which ignited the laïkó explosion of the late 1970s and early 1980s.

⊙ Gyrizontas ton Kosmo
Universal, Greece

A collection of live recordings from around the world, covering the more recent éntekhno/modern pop phase of her career.

Eleftheria Arvanitaki

The wondrous Arvanitaki began her career as a rebétika revivalist, moved on to frequent collaborations with Nikos Xydhakis, and is now considered the leading all-round female vocalist in the country.

★ Greatest Hits
Lyra, Greece

A fine collection from the first, best and more rootsy period of her career. It includes her collaborations with Opisthodromiki Kompania, Nikos Xydhakis, Yiorgos Zikas and Stamatis Spanoudakis

⊙ Ta Kormia ke ta Maheria
Universal, Greece

A groundbreaking Greek-Armenian collaboration with oud player and composer Ara Dinkjian and lyricist Mihalis Gonis that brought Arvanitaki international fame.

Yiorgos (George) Dalaras

Born in 1950, the son of a Piraeus rebétika player, Dalaras has appeared on over ninety recordings since his 1968 debut, spanning styles from Anatolian, dhimotiká and éntekhno. As both performer and producer, he has worked with everybody who's anybody on the Greek music scene. A national institution, Dalaras always – even under the junta – remained a staunch supporter of popular struggles, giving benefit concerts for various worthy causes. In his commitment to quality musicianship, he has scrupulously avoided the more banal corners of the pop scene.

⊙ Peninda Hronia Rebetiko Tragoudhi
Minos–EMI, Greece

The 1975 disc that helped kick-start the rebétika revival. A classic.

⊙ Latin
Minos–EMI, Greece

The only album that focuses on Dalaras as soloist brought him into collaboration with the US jazz fusion guitarist Al Di Meola.

Ross Daly

Although Irish by origin, Daly has revived the art of lyra playing in Crete, where he has lived for 25 years. Alone and with his group Labyrinth, he has recorded striking versions of traditional pieces.

★ Beyond the Horizon
Aerakis, Greece

One of the best introductions to Cretan lyra, with traditional Cretan material and explorations into nearby Middle Eastern traditions.

⊙ Mitos
Network, Germany

This is a selection of concert recordings from 1991, with Spyridhoula Toutoudhaki singing.

Glykeria

Born near Serres in 1953, Glykeria (Kotsoula) was one of the most popular and versatile laïkó singers and rebétika revivalists of the 1980s, and is equally accomplished when exploring dhimotiká and nisiótiká.

⊙ Smyrneïka
⊙ Mia Vradhia me tin Glykeria stin Omorfi Nykhta
Lyra, Greece

The two best rebétika revival albums from Glykeria. The former ignited her long career and features George Koros on fiddle and Aristidis Moskhos on santouri. The latter marked the peak of her popularity in the mid-1980s.

Greeks and Indians

The Greeks and Indians recordings are a remarkable series of collaborations between Rakesh Chaurasia (bansuri flute), Rabindra Goswami (sitar), Shubankar Banerjee (tabla), Devashish Dey (vocals) and various traditional Greek musicians like the clarinettist from Epirus, Petro-Loukas Halkias, violinist Yorgos Koros and honorary Cretan and lyra player Ross Daly. Some were recorded in concert, others in a living room studio.

⊙ Greeks and Indians 1
Saraswati, Greece

The Gypsies originally came from India, so it sounds perfectly natural when clarinettist Halkias begins improvising in an Indian raga with his warm, keening tone. Traditional Greek tunes also in the mix. High-quality music making from master musicians. All of their CDs are worth hearing and have their own character.

⊙ Master Musicians Meeting Club
Saraswati, Greece

Extending the idea even further, this album invited Ballaké Sissoko to add rippling Malian kora to the mix.

Haïnidhes

Haïnidhes is an old Turko-Cretan word meaning "bolshy layabouts". This all-acoustic group has turned the slur on its head; their rebelliousness, if anything, is against the ossification of Cretan lyrics and music.

⊙ Kosmos ki Oneiro ineh Ena
⊙ Haïnidhes
MBI, Greece

The group's first (and most would say best) albums, with the original, pre-1997 personnel. Unlike many other "revival" groups, they feature mainly all-original lyrics and compositions on traditional instruments.

Manos Hatzidhakis

Hatzidhakis was a catalyst to the acceptance of rebétika on the Greek music circuit. Like Theodhorakis, he composed many excellent soundtracks. After he turned his back on his early pop hits, he went on to release a series of mature albums with Galani, Mitsias, Lakis Pappas and Flery Dhadonaki. He also released *Reflections*, a rock album with the New York Rock & Roll Ensemble on Atlantic records.

⊙ Matomenos Gamos: Paramythi khoris Onoma
Columbia, Greece
Featuring material with Nikos Gatsos-translated lyrics, this has the added bonus of Lakis Pappas singing.

⊙ O Megalos Erotikos
Lyra, Greece
A 1972 landmark outfit, with Flery Dadonaki and Dimitris Psarianos, playing songs with lyrics based on Greek poetry from Sappho to Elytis

★ Gioconda's Smile
EMI, Greece
Produced by Quincy Jones and recorded in New York, this is an instrumental album that brought a radical sound to Greek music.

Apostolos Kaldharas

Born in the central Greek town of Trίkala in 1922, the late composer Kaldharas regularly tipped his hat to rebέtika and έntekhno.

⊙ Mikra Asia
Minos, Greece
A disc which marked Haris Alexiou's 1972 debut and, with vocals from George Dalaras, helped spark the rebέtika revival of the mid-1970s.

Stelios Kazantzίdhis

A great bear of a man, born in 1931 of Asia Minor parentage, Kazantzίdhis was an incredibly versatile performer, with a repertoire ranging from rebέtika to mainland folk, and the ability to sing in Turkish if needed.

⊙ Iy Zoi Mou Oli
Minos–EMI, Greece
A quintessential double collection of all the classics that turned Kazantzίdhis to a national institution.

Mariza Koch

One of the most underrated singers in Greek music, Koch was born during World War II on Santorini, of Greek-German origins. The early 1970s saw her making folk-rock albums featuring both rockers and folk soloists before moving to straightforward folk music and roots-inspired έntekhno.

⊙ Arambas
Minos, Greece
⊙ Aegeon 1 & 2
Sony, Greece
Arambas was Mariza's psychedelic folk masterpiece, while the two *Aegeon* albums were her two best folk efforts, consisting of island traditional songs.

Himerini Kolymvites

Led by architect Arghyris Bakirtzis, this engaging northern Greek group still performs frequently despite a limited discography.

⊙ Himerini Kolymvites
Lyra, Greece
Their 1981 debut album quickly acquired cult status, with its blend of rebέtika, laïkό and a dash of island melodies on plucked and bowed strings. The CD release has live renditions from 1986–88 concerts.

Loudhovikos ton Anoyion (Yiorgos Dhramoundanis)

Born in 1951 in Anόyia, Crete, as his pseudonym suggests, Loudhovikos was one of Manos Hatzidhakis' protégés at the Seirios label, where, arguably, his best work was to be found.

⊙ O Erotas stin Kriti ine Melangolikos
Seirios, Greece
His second album restored the mandolin – downgraded in Crete to the role of rhythm laoœto – to its rightful place.

⊙ Pyli tis Ammou
Mylos, Greece
A later evolution in a larger group than on the Seiris releases (now difficult to find) with guest appearances by Malamas, Papazoglou and Nena Venetsanou.

Yiorgos Margaritis & 667

Yiorgos Margaritis is the king of 1980s underground laïkό. He teamed up with 667, a group put together by rock musician and laïkό producer Theodoris Manikas which featured some of the best rock musicians in the Greek scene, most notably Mode Plagal's Kleon Antoniou on guitars.

⊙ Ola tha ta Diagrapso
Minos-EMI, Greece
Here, Yiorgos Margaritis reinterpets some of his best-known laïkό hits with 667 building a rock/funk/dub sound around him, making this the best laïkό-rock fusion album since Papazoglou's *Haratsi*.

Sokratis Malamas

Since the late 1980s, one of the most consistently listenable of the Thessaloníki-based disciples of Nikos Papazoglou.

★ Dhromi
Lyra, Greece
This 2007 release, with Haris Alexiou guesting on several tracks, is almost pitch-perfect in its fusion of laïkό, Balkan rock and έntekhno. A logical outgrowth of the preceding *Ena*, with just his resonant voice and guitar; 1992's *Tis Meras ke tis Nykhtas*, with Melina Kana, was the big breakthrough for both performers.

Yiannis Markopoulos

Born in 1939 in Iraklio, Crete, Markopoulos began recording in the mid-1960s and hit his peak a decade later. Certainly the rootsiest of the έntekhno composers, he has been fortunate in the range of quality artists who have sung for him: Yiorgos Dalaras, Nikos Xylouris, Lakis Halkias, Tania Tsanaklidhou and Haralambos Garganourakis among others.

⊙ Anexartita
EMI, Greece
Features an incredible range of talent, and includes the original live version of the bitter "Iy Ellada", recorded just after the junta fell.

★ Rizitika
Minos–EMI, Greece
The subtitle, *La Chante Profunde de Crète*, for the sensationally popular French edition says it all. Includes stirring anthems like "Pote Tha Kamei Xasteria", a veiled snub at the ruling junta of the time, which launched Xylouris' έntekhno career.

⊙ Thiteia
Minos–EMI, Greece
With lyrics by Manos Eleftheriou and enduring hits like "Malamatenia Loyia", this is a sentimental favourite for many.

Mode Plagal

Bursting on the scene in the mid-1990s, this Athens-based group – named for one of the modes of Byzantine chant – in fact has one of the more interesting takes on folk material.

⊙ Mode Plagal II
Musurgia Graeca, Greece
Greek folk material deconstructed as hard-driving funk, with a more-than-occasional echo of John Coltrane. It works more often than not.

Khristos Nikolopoulos

Born in northern Greece in 1947, Nikolopoulos is the most prolific and arguably most influential laïkó composer of the past three decades.

★ Yparkho
Minos, Greece
This historic collaboration with Stelios Kazantzídhis stands as the greatest laïkó album of all times.

⊙ O Salonikios
Minos, Greece
A collaboration with laïkó legend Stratos Dhionysiou, this was one of his best albums of the 1980s and gained gold status.

Akis Panou

Panou was not only a versatile composer and lyricist, but a true bouzoúki whiz. He died in 1999.

★ Ta Megala Tragoudhia
EMI, Greece
The 1993 retrospective is one of the best possible starts to a laïkó collection.

Thanasis Papakonstandinou

Papakonstandinou, arguably the most original folk-based musician working in Greece today, reinterprets material from his native Thessaly in startling ways; the name of his current touring band, Laïkadelica (i.e. laïkó + psychedelica), gives a clue.

⊙ Vrakhnos Profitis
Lyra, Greece
Check out the track "Pehlivanis", with the traditional melody emerging unelaborated from one channel and a Hendrix-like guitar version of the same from the other.

⊙ Agrypnia
Lyra, Greece
More jazz- and sampling-orientated, plus a reprise of the title track from *Ayia Nostalgia*, his 1993 debut CD which gave no hint of his future development.

Nikos Papazoglou

Born in Thessaloníki in 1948, Papazoglou was the first to successfully blend laïkó and Western-style rock, as opposed to the folk-rock endeavours of the early 1970s.

⊙ Haratsi
Lyra, Greece
An album that alternates introspective ballads with hard-driving electric jams.

⊙ Synerga
Lyra, Greece
A gentler, even mystical set, more in the mould of later Xydhakis.

★ Ma'issa Selini
Lyra, Greece
Rootsier, uptempo 2005 disc, with not one duff track, that broke a long recording silence.

Yiannis Parios

Born on Páros in 1946, Parios is the undisputed king of Elafro-laïkó, mixing Julio Iglesias-style crooning with laïkó roots.

⊙ Ta Nisiótika Vol. 1
Minos, Greece
This 1981 release, with the Konitopoulos family accompanying him, became Greece's most successful disc ever, with nearly a million copies sold to date. Though a curious chimera – authentic folk instrumentation with laïkó-style vocals – it evidently tapped a valuable vein.

Alkistis Protopsalti

Born Alkistis Sevasti Akiouzel in Alexandria, Egypt, Protopsalti started her career singing on albums of Dimitris Moutsis. However, it was her collaboration with songwriter Stamatis Kraounakis and lyricist Liana Nikolakopoulou that set new standards in Greek music.

⊙ Kykloforo Ke Oploforo
Universal, Greece
This album ignited her long and fruitful collaboration with Kraounakis and Nikolakopoulou and brought a new jazz/cabaret sound to Greek éntekhno.

Dhionysis Savvopoulos

Despite a modest discography – he took early retirement after his much publicized return to Greece's Orthodox roots – it's difficult not to overestimate Savvopoulos's effect on subsequent guitar-based songwriters (most notably Nikos Portokaloglou). The credit for much Greek folk-rock and folk-jazz can be laid at his door.

⊙ Vromiko Psomi
Lyra, Greece
Savvopoulos's masterpiece, this album mixed Greek folk and jazz-rock.

⊙ Ballos
Lyra, Greece
This is the album that ignited the short-lived folk-rock movement in Greece during the early 1970s

⊙ Trapezakia Exo
Lyra, Greece
The best of his later work, this is more digestibly folky, and features a cameo by Eleftheria Arvanitaki.

Kristi Stassinopoulou

Singer, lyricist and fiction writer Kristi Stassinopoulou and husband and songwriter Stathis Kalyviotis became both heroes of the Greek alternative scene and international stars thanks to their mix of traditional Greek rhythms, haunting Byzantine vocal lines, rebétika, psychedelica, ambient grooves and electronica.

⊙ Ifantokosmos
Thesis, Greece
Thirty years after the folk-rock experiments of Mariza Koch, Kristi and Stathis once again mix Greek folk with psychedelica, adding world music to the mix.

Mikis Theodhorakis

After his overplayed, over-covered 1965 soundtrack for *Zorba the Greek*, Theodhorakis shunned Byzantine/folk/rebetic influences in favour of overtly political symphonic works and film soundtracks dictated by his then-Communist affiliation. For the committed, there's the white-boxed, five-CD set (EMI) entitled *Mikis Theodhorakis*, comprising the highest-quality interpretations of his best-loved songs, organized roughly chronologically and by type (soundtracks, oratorios, etc).

⊙ Epitafios
⊙ Epifania
EMI Columbia, Greece
These are two of Theodhorakis' most influential, reputation-justifying works. Be sure to get the original versions only; second-rate instrumental covers abound.

★ Axion Esti
Columbia, Greece
Containing éntekhno classics that changed the face of Greek music forever, this folk oratorio ranks among the best Greek discs of all time. Get the original, white-sleeved pressing with Gregory Bithikotsis on vocals.

⊙ Canto General
Minos, Greece
Based on the poetry of Pablo Neruda, and featuring Maria Farantouri and Petros Pandis on vocals, this excellent 1975 venture into nueva canción marked the most political phase in the career of Mikis Theodhorakis.

Mattheos Tsahouridis

The lion of the Pontic lyra is based in London, where he has been making a splash of late.

⊙ Apo Ton Ponto Stin Persia
Protassis, Greece
Tsahouridis collaborates here with Hussein Zahawy on *daf* and Ardeshir Kamkar on *kamancha* to produce an excellent improvisational album of Greek and Persian music.

Nena Venetsanou

Born in Athens in 1955 and educated in France where she lived for some years, Venetsanou is an engaging yet deliberative live performer and has guested on the albums of numerous "new wave" performers.

⊙ Ikones
Anatoli, Greece
This gives a good overall idea of Venetsanou's range, from *nisiotika* to French chanson.

⊙ Zeimbekiko
MBI, Greece
An audacious but successful recasting of the rebetic genre as "profane prayer", performed on tour in various French chapels.

Eleni Vitali

Born as Eleni Lavida to a family of folk musicians, Vitali started her career at the age of thirteen, touring with folk legends Tassos Halkias, Vassilis Soukas, George Koros and Tassia Vera. In the 1980s she collaborated with songwriters Takis Soukas, Khristos Nikolopoulos and Stamatis Spanoudakis, becoming one of the greatest vocal stylists of Greek music.

⊙ Horepste Yiati Hanomaste
Minos, Greece
An essential souvenir of the laïkó explosion of the 1980s, this live album sees Vitali interpreting laïkó songs related to Gypsy women (she's dressed in Gypsy folk costumes on the cover) and features Vassilis Saleas on klarino.

Vosporos/Fanari Tis Anatolis

Vosporos was a pioneering group led by Nikiforos Metaxas, consisting largely of musicians from Istanbul, and was strictly orchestral. In 1992, Metaxas formed Fanari Tis Anatolis, showcasing Greek singer Vassiliki Papyeoryiou and (often) Turkish artist Melda Kurt in atypical renditions of Greek and Anatolian folk songs, plus instrumental interludes. Reformed as Vosporos once more, they have recently collaborated with Mode Plagal.

VOSPOROS

⊙ Vosporos
HMV, Greece
The original group underlined their 1987 debut's pertinence to Grecophiles by giving the album the sub-title *Greek Composers Of The City* (the city in question being Constantinople), highlighting the contribution of Greek and other non-Turkish musicians to the Ottoman courtly tradition.

FANARI TIS ANATOLIS

⊙ Ellenika keh Asikika
⊙ Balkania Oneira
MBI, Greece
It's hard to choose between these two albums: they constitute the best of the group's output.

WITH MODE PLAGAL

★ Beyond the Bosphorus Tou Vosporou To Pera
Hitchhyke, Greece
This tour de force from 2005 revisits Constantinopolitan and Anatolian melodies.

Nikos Xydhakis

His birth (in 1952) and early childhood in Egypt seems to have predisposed Xydhakis to Oriental influences. Critics say that since 1989 his albums have all sounded the same, but if you get hooked on the sound, you'll want them all.

⊙ Iy Ekdhikisi tis Yiftias
Lyra, Greece
⊙ Ta Dithen
Lyra, Greece
Released within eight months of each other in 1978–79, with essentially the same personnel, these inspired early works – still selling in large numbers – effectively rehabilitated laïkó.

★ Konda sti Dhoxa mia Stigmi
Lyra, Greece

With lyrics by Thodhoros Gonis, and guest appearances by Ross Daly and Eleftheria Arvanitaki, this classic 1987 album offers a particularly beguiling blend of folk, Byzantine and Asia Minor styles.

Haig Yagdjian

Syrian-born Armenian oud player Haig Yagdjian became popular through collaborations with Dalaras, Arvanitaki and Xydhakis.

⊙ Talar
Libra, Greece

One of the most popular albums of Greek fusion, this landmark album gained gold-selling status.

Savina Yiannatou

It's hard to classify Athens-born Savina, whose two decades of versatile recordings have taken her from éntekhno to folk revival by way of children's lullabies and avant-garde classical suites. Her high, penetrating voice, like those of several other female vocalists currently the rage in Greece, can take some getting used to.

⊙ Anixi sti Saloniki
Lyra, Greece

Imaginative re-workings of Sephardic songs in Ladino, with Middle Eastern instrumental backing arranged by Kostas Vomvolos.

⊙ Songs of the Mediterranean
Lyra, Greece

Encouraged by the critical and commercial success of *Anixi*, and with the same musicians and arrangers, Savina broadened her scope to include not only songs from the Aegean but Italy, Sardinia, Albania and North Africa.

George Zambetas

The greatest bouzoúki soloist of the 1960s, Zambetas became a kind of a living legend after playing the theme of *Never On Sunday* sixty times during the showing night in Cannes 1961. A favourite among the international jet set, he wrote unforgettable hits and performed in many Greek films, presenting an extrovert persona that could not hide his great musicianship.

⊙ O Pio Kalos O Mathitis
EMI, Greece

All these sunny classics were covered in schmaltzy fashion for the *Souvenirs From Greece* series, introducing millions of tourists to Greek music. Here are the originals, interpreted by Grigoris Bithikotsis, Viky Moskholiou, Stamatis Kokotas and the man himself.

PLAYLIST
Greece

1 BRATSERA Emilia Hatzidhaki from *Seryiani sta Nisia Mas*
Arguably the most beautiful of all nisiótika songs, this nautical ballad particular to Léros and Kálymnos was recorded in 1950, when Hatzidhaki was in her prime.

2 SYNEFIASMENI KYRIAKI Marika Ninou & Vassilis Tsitsanis from *Marika Ninou & Vassilis Tsitsanis*
There are several recorded versions of this 1940s anthem; this, with both Ninou and Tsitsanis singing, is perhaps the most widely appreciated.

3 STO PERIYIALI TO KRYFO Mikis Theodhorakis from *Epifania*
This poignant setting of Greek Nobel poet George Seferis' poem "Arnisi" is still a staple of gatherings around the taverna table over four decades on.

4 POTE THA KANI XASTERIA Yiannis Markopoulos & Nikos Xylouris from *Rizitika*
The apotheosis of éntekhno: this march-anthem has soaring vocals from Xylouris at the head of a choir and Markopoulos' orchestra in full tilt.

5 IY ZOI MOU OLI Stelios Kazantzídhis from *Iy Zoi mou Oli*
An existential laïkó anthem with a great metaphor of life – it's a cigar the singer does not like. He smokes it and gives it as a present to the "Great Gripper".

6 IY SMYRNI George Dalaras from *Mikra Asia*
Yiorgos hit the big time at age 23 with this elegy to the "lost homelands" of Asia Minor.

7 IY MANGES DHEN YPARHOUN PIA Nikos Xydhakis and Nikos Papazoglou from *Ta Dithen*
The two Nikos declare the rebetic era well and truly over in this much-covered song with crisp lyrics, starting with "The mánges don't exist no more...".

8 O FANTAROS Haris Alexiou from *Ta Tragoudia tis Haroulas*
One year after the success of Iy Ekdhikis tis Yiftias, Alexiou gets wild (and sensual) in a tsiftetéli- style song that has been a favourite among Greek soldiers ever since.

9 MAVRO MOU HELIDHONI Khronis Aïdhonidhis from *T'Aidhonia tis Anatolis*
One of the best laments of exile – of which there are dozens in the Greek world – making plain the links between the folk tradition and Byzantine chant.

10 FUNKY VERGINA Mode Plagal from *Mode Plagal II*
Here Mode Plagal blend Greek Macedonian folk, jazz-funk and Afro-Latin grooves in an instrumental that shows the shape of things to come.

Greenland

tradition in hibernation

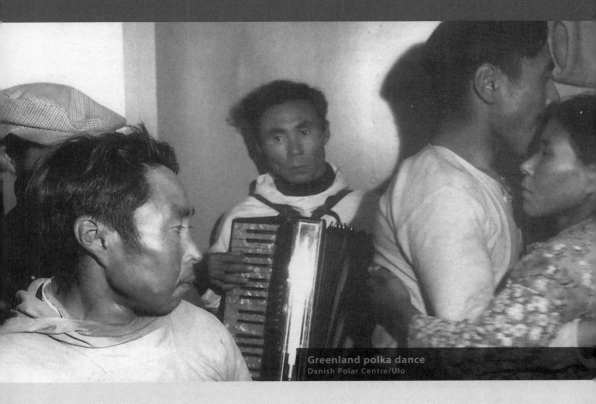

Greenland polka dance
Danish Polar Centre/Ulo

It was Erik the Red who gave Greenland its unlikely name after he "discovered" it in AD 982. The name was a deliberate attempt to make the Arctic island sound more appealing to settlers from Iceland – and it worked. According to the chronicles he "gulled twenty-five ship loads of men, women, serfs and animals and off they sailed". It must be one of the earliest PR successes on record, and Greenland can boast many such surprises – including what could once be described as the world's most successful record label. Etienne Bours fills in the details.

Since it was founded in 1973, Greenland's first record company, **ULO**, have released some 170 albums and maintained an essential presence in the market. Their CDs and cassettes of traditional music, folk songs, rock, polka, hip-hop and hymns have long provided a link between the island's scattered people. As one of the label's founders, **Karsten Sommer**, says: "The people in Greenland love to listen to their local music. Fifty thousand Inuit live in towns and villages, far from each other, and the only connection between them is by ship or plane." Through their recorded music, Greenlandic people know what is happening on the opposite coast.

ULO were once very prolific, with even their least successful recordings selling the equivalent of four times platinum in Europe. But things have changed a lot since the turn of the millennium: "Production and releases of new records have increased dramatically", observes Sommer. "Many musicians have begun to make their own recordings and many companies are producing things faster and cheaper. That means the sales are still approximately 50,000 CDs per year! But, of course, the quality in some ways has also got lower."

Many Greenlandic performers now sing in English and attempt to sound as international as possible, meaning that some of them, like **Julie Berthelsen**, have become pop stars in Denmark. Young Greenlandic Inuits seem to like the fact that their singers have an international style – but could these young artists who sing in another language, play with Danish musicians and don't even write their own songs spell the end of **Inuit rock**? Is this the end of young musicians capable of writing and singing in Inuktitut about the cultural divide and their own life experiences? There is a genuine concern that the younger generation are moving to the other side of that divide and leaving their country's cultural traditions far behind them.

Karsten Sommer says that ULO is "wintering" now, and concentrating on preserving Greenland's cultural "musical treasure". They're planning to make their music available for download on the Internet, as well as releasing quality sampler CDs. New releases might be forthcoming in the future, but for now ULO is trying to find a new role in Greenlandic music.

Drum Songs

ULO look set to become the guardians of the traditions they once recorded. They have made an effort to release **traditional Inuit music** since the 1970s, but things are now moving so fast, and it seems as though no-one will bother with **drum songs** and the like any longer, even if these traditions continue in some remote areas of the country.

The ancestral Inuit drum dances are traditionally played on a small **oval drum** with a wooden frame that is covered with a bear bladder. The player uses a stick to strike the frame of the drum, rather than the skin. The instrument is related to the Inuit drums of Canada and Siberia, but it is smaller in scale and played more intimately.

The Inuit used to sing and play the drum for occasions such as feasts and gatherings, as well as to tell stories, play games and tease or charm partners. Personal songs, **pisiq**, were bound up with daily life – similar to the *joik* songs of the Sami people. The singer is the owner of the song, and if somebody else sings it, it is often named after its original author. A passed-on song can be sung practically unchanged for decades, as you can hear on *Traditional Greenlandic Music*, which includes recordings from 1905 to 1987. Some **personal songs** don't use words, just vocables – *ay-ay-a*. That's why some people call these chants **ayaya**.

The drum was also the instrument of the **shaman**, or *angakkog*, who made magic and brought luck for hunting. It was even used to maintain the social order: when somebody's behaviour was causing problems, instead of sanctions, the community sometimes organized a **song duel** between the offender and the victim. The problem was brought in front of the village, and the spectators became the **court**, determining the winner by their shouts, exclamations and laughs. The person who made the audience laugh the most was the winner. Here's an example:

I long to answer him who stands before me
I am married, I am not like you
Maybe you would like to try them again
Try those up in the tent
I will tell who you have visited
You have visited my wife
You lay with her as I have lain with her
But you got tired of that. Toruka got tired
How strange that I should sing about that.

Recorded in 1961 on *Traditional Greenlandic Music*

Even though this system is now obsolete, some Inuit singers are keeping the tradition of drum songs alive, mainly in the northern and eastern parts of the country. They maintain a repertoire of old songs, extracts from contests and games, and personal songs. Drum songs are also performed on stage, as a way of keeping the tradition alive and attracting new interest to it.

Polka, Rock and Hip-Hop

The Inuit always liked to sing, play and dance, so they soon adapted the instruments of the **white settlers** when they arrived. The Danes colonized the island over 250 years ago and **whalers** visited from many other parts of the world, so the influences were diverse. The Inuit learnt to sing hymns from the missionaries, to play the accordian and the fiddle from the whalers, and the **polka** from the Danish settlers.

These influences had a dramatic effect, and resulted in new musical styles, such as the Inuit polka, the **kalattuut**. This new Inuit music was usually played on the fiddle or **accordion**, and danced at feasts. It was then passed from generation to generation, like the drum dance before it. The musician's relationship with their instrument is often seen as very physical, joyful and passionate. For example, people speak of the late accordion player **Louis Andreasen** talking and laughing to his instrument while he played.

A younger generation took to the **guitar** and sung about living their lives between two worlds. Their **folk songs**, **rock** and **blues** can sound like a pale imitation of Western music, but it's the words that are important. They tended to avoid ancestral instruments like the drum, but used guitars, keyboards, bass and Western drum kits to sing of their own experience. They even dared to say that their forefathers knew the way, and that the sound of the drum should be heard again:

Be aware of the power of nature
because it is the very source of life
You yourself have to revitalise
the fading sound of the drum.

The song "Inngerpalaaq" by Silamiut

Some modern musicians even sampled Inuit drums or used traditional performers in their music.

Rasmus Lyberth, one of the most powerful voices of the Arctic, sings about the experience of trying to eke out a living in Denmark as an economic migrant:

One evening alone with my thoughts,
I think of my land, so far away.
Memories of my childhood
make me want to go back,
But here I am, homeless
with no work and no money.

Some young Inuit rappers have become very successful during the last ten years, while maintaining a connection to their cultural heritage. **Nuuk Posse** even sampled drum songs from ULO's own catalogue, and their songs include their own messages about Greenlandic identity:

The city is a jungle with hunters and prey
Pale riders passing by I'm trying to find my way
Sick and tired of street signs
Written in a language that's not mine
I want to write in Greenlandic
Be proud of who you are and open your mind.

"Oqariartuut" by Nuuk Posse

Other groups, such as **Lucas** and **Prussic**, have followed in recent years, releasing albums that comment on life in Greenland. Karsten Sommer explains that these songs have "made them heroes among the young people", but left their parents "shocked". These young groups have all seen significant CD sales in the domestic market.

However, another popular domestic artist is **Angu Motzfeldt**, who sings in English and has a very international sound. He is signed to the Atlantic label, and his success demonstrates how much Greenland's music market is changing. New performers like Motzfeldt sing a kind of international **pop music**, and their music no longer has any link with Inuit traditions or culture. Until very recently, Greenland's singers and musicians made rock or pop music while still digging into their roots – but that has now changed.

Rasmus Lyberth

ULO can be contacted at P.O. Box 306, DK-3900 Nuuk, Greenland; ulomusic@greennet.gl.

⊙ Traditional Greenlandic Music
ULO, Greenland
A cross section of traditional styles recorded from 1905 to 1987 from different areas of Greenland, including Shaman songs, drum songs, epic songs and singing games. Although not an easy listen, this is fascinating and it has good notes.

⊙ Avanngarnitsat ileqqorsuutaat: Traditional North Greenlandic Accordion Music
ULO, Greenland
Fantastic accordion music played by five musicians in the 1990s, including kalattuut (Inuit polka), square dances, waltzes and the traditional Inuit dance music of Thulé.

★ Qavaat: Music from South Greenland
ULO, Greenland
Old and new music from the south: traditional drum songs, fiddle, accordion and mouth organ pieces for polkas and square dances, plus contemporary pop songs. Features fifteen tunes from accordionist Louis Andreasen.

Rasmus Lyberth

Greenland's most popular folk singer has been singing for nearly thirty years now. He is at his best accompanying himself on guitar or joined by a couple of fellow musicians.

⊙ Erningaa (To My Son)
ULO, Greenland
Lyberth's debut CD features simple, but effective, songs about life, work, love, his forefathers and snow.

⊙ Rasmus Lyberth's Bedste Sange: Når Livet Fortæller
Rasmusik, Greenland
A recent "best of" collection from this essential singer that includes some songs from his old LPs. The voice, the feeling and the engagement are all here – Lyberth is the voice of this part of the world. The only problem is the lack of translation in the CD booklet.

Nuuk Posse

Literally "the gang from Nuuk", the capital of Greenland, these six singers combine hip-hop and rap with traditional drum dance and the sound of whales, etc.

★ Nuuk Posse
ULO, Greenland
This debut CD was a big success in Greenland – and in Japan. It was the voice of a new musical generation: "We're Greenlanders, Arctic rappers, Northern funkers, Greenland rap is here to stay." Move over, Compton.

Prussic

This popular hip-hop group produced their own debut in 2004. It was distributed by Atlantic.

⊙ Misiliineq siulleq (The First Try)
Atlantic Music APS, Greenland
The songs are full of funny and amazing comments about life on the island.

Sume

Sume were Greenland's first pop group, releasing their first record, Sumut (Where To?), in 1973. It was bought by twenty percent of the population, and it kick-started the Greenlandic pop industry. They re-united in 1994 for the

ULO

Sume

hit album *Persersume* (*Snowdrift*). Their songs have always looked at the cultural confusion of Inuit life.

⊙ Sume 1973–76
ULO, Greenland

Some of the best songs from the various Sume line-ups built around composers, singers and guitarists Malik Hoegh and Per Berthelsen. As the song "Nunaqarfiit" (Restoration) says, "It's time to live again as Inuit and not as Westerners".

Zikaza

Greenland's most popular group, Zikaza comripises seven musicians playing guitars, keyboards, sax, bass and percussion and producing sophisticated rock.

★ Miki Goes To Nuussuaq
ULO, Greenland

The most successful album produced by label ULO, which won the band a "Sealskin disc". Zikaza sing about generational conflicts in the Arctic where young and old don't necessarily live in the same world.

PLAYLIST
Greenland

1 DUEL SONG Lauritz Ningâvan from *Traditional Greenlandic Music*

A great way to understand what Inuit music is – the drum struck on the frame, the ayaya vocables, the sighs and cries of the singer, the mood of a duel fought with songs as weapons.

2 SISAMAAQ (GREENLANDIC SQUARE DANCE) Louis Andreasen from *Qavaat: Music from South Greenland*

The late Louis Andreasen playing his accordion like Joseph Spence played his guitar in the Bahamas: amazing, rare and passionate.

3 KISIMEERUSAARTILLUNGA Rasmus Lyberth from *Erningaa*

The story of an old man who feels like an orphan – lonesome and rejected. The voice of Rasmus Lyberth goes right into you like a devastating wind.

4 OQARIARTUUT Nuuk Posse from *Nuuk Posse*

Living not far from the sea where the whales still sing their songs, these young rappers are proud to be Inuit and try to keep their minds open.

5 NUNAQARFIT Sume from *Sume 1973–76*

Sume were Greenland's most important Inuit rock group in the 1970s. They sing that it's time to be Inuit again, instead of trying to live in a Western world that is dying.

Gypsy Music

on the road

Taraf de Haidouks
Masataka Ishida

There's a symbiosis between Gypsies and music. From Django Reinhardt to Esma Redžepova, from the Taraf de Haidouks to the Gipsy Kings, from Andalusia to Rajasthan, Gypsies are making some of the most powerful music on the planet. Indeed, the Gypsy musician has become a symbol of musical passion embracing deep soulfulness and flashy virtuosity. But a symbol can also become a stereotype. Simon Broughton attempts to sort the myth from the reality on the thousand-year road from the Indian subcontinent to Europe.

▶▶ *While this article makes links between Gypsy music in countries from north India to the Balkans and Spain, please check the individual country entries for more details on individual artists – for example, Esma Redžepova in Macedonia, Azis in Bulgaria and flamenco in Spain.*

The journey may have started 1000 years ago, or more, but go to Frankfurt's cool Bucovina Club where DJ Shantel (see box) spins Balkan Gypsy remixes, spiced up with live musicians and free glasses of vodka, and it is clear that Gypsy music is hot in the twenty-first century. A gorgeous Gypsy girl from the crowd is dancing and Frankfurt's youth are going wild. "This music isn't just for the specialists", explains Shantel, "everybody can enjoy it. It's a marriage of anarchy and romance." That's certainly no surprise to anyone who's been to a Balkan wedding, where – as Emir Kusturica has vividly demonstrated in his films – Gypsy music is as essential as plum brandy to fire and lubricate the festivities. Whether it's a flamenco club in Jerez, Spain, a wedding in the Gypsy metropolis of Šuto Orizari, Macedonia, or an outdoor restaurant in Istanbul, Gypsies sure know how to make a musical party. But other than over-the-top *joie de vivre*, is there anything else that connects the Gypsy music in these stops along the Gypsy road?

On the opening track of Network's compilation CD *Road of the Gypsies*, the great Gypsy flamenco singer **El Camarón de la Isla** sings a Lorca poem accompanied by a sitar, rather than the expected Spanish guitar. It makes an appropriate connection between the beginning and end of the Gypsy trail, which runs from northern India to southern Spain. But this is a self-conscious statement of identity and culture. It is difficult to pin down specific links between the various types of Gypsy music in Europe, the Middle East and India. Clearly there are shared characteristics common to flamenco, Rajasthani Gypsy music and much of the music of Eastern Europe: an upfront, raw singing style, a tendency to make exaggerated slides between notes, wringing out the emotion, and a love of instrumental virtuosity. But perhaps more interesting and more important is the way Gypsies

DJ Shantel: Electric Gypsy

The traditional music may still be going strong, but these days Gypsies are just as likely to be listening to Romani rap broadcast on one of the Gypsy radio stations. **Fekete Vonat** (Black Train) was the pioneering Romani rap group, while Romano Drom have done fusions of Gypsy music and beats. If there's anything that has brought a buzz to Gypsy music in recent years, it is the way it's been remixed and renewed for the club scene. Romani rap and Gypsy Trip club nights in Budapest and Prague are one thing, but the way **DJ Shantel** and his Bucovina Club and Electric Gypsyland tours have brought Balkan music to a new audience is something else.

Shantel was born Stefan Hantel in Frankfurt, but his mother came from Bucovina, the province split between northern Romania and Ukraine. For him Gypsy music was as natural as mother's milk. "It has the same attitude, energy and power as hip-hop and house music", he says. "I'd always been disappointed when I'd heard Boban Marković in a concert hall with everybody politely sitting down. The spirit was gone." In Germany, techno, house and drum'n'bass were the dominant sounds, but for Shantel they had no soul. And then the Berlin Wall came down and the east, and its Gypsy soul, opened up. All the same, it took an act of bravado to put this music into a cosmopolitan urban environment. "It was like jumping into cold water, because nobody believed in this vision", he says. But the music, the beats, the live instrumentals and the "marriage of anarchy and romance" have become a craze. He likens the remixes and production to the dynamic attitude that Gypsy musicians themselves bring to their playing. "When I put the music together with electronics, beats and drums I don't want to copy what they do, but you have to entertain the people. If you start at 8pm and end at 4am you need a musical dramaturgy." The punk-like underground power of Balkan Gypsy music is certainly making waves. Across the Atlantic the Ukrainian-born Eugene Hutz and his group **Gogol Bordello** in New York are also exploring this Gypsy musical anarchy, winning the attention of Madonna, no less.

Harald H. Schröder/essay Recordings

DJ Shantel

in these regions have become the leading musical personalities, practising music as a trade – just as they do other caste professions such as blacksmithing, horse trading and peddling – and bringing to it a distinctive showmanship and display.

Wherever they have ended up, it seems that Gypsy musicians have an unfailing ability to absorb local styles and make them their own. Among folk musicians they tend to be much more open to new sounds and influences than the "indigenous" locals, retaining a voracious kind of musical nomadism. As professionals being hired for gigs, Gypsy musicians will play what is popular. This drives folk music purists to despair, but Gypsies like the Taraf de Haidouks are great tradition bearers and they've kept traditional music alive in the twenty-first century.

Roma Roots and Rights

The word **Gypsy**, and its equivalent in other European languages – the German *Zigeuner*, French *Tzigane* and Spanish *Gitano* – is often thought to be pejorative. It derives from the word "Egypt", which is where the Gypsies were assumed to have come from at one time, though linguistic evidence shows they in fact originated in India. *Dom* – of which **Rom** is thought to be a corruption – refers to a lower-caste group doing menial work in India today, but in the past it just meant "man", which is also the meaning of "Rom" in Romani, the Gypsy language.

It's probable there were several migrations of different groups of Rom from North India into the Middle East and Europe. There are several different dialects of Romani, which suggests different origins or different dates of departure. Broadly speaking the Roma are divided into three groups: the Domari of the Middle East and Eastern Europe (the *Dom*), the Lomarvren of Central Europe (the *Lom*) and the Romani of Western Europe (the *Rom*). The various Romani words for musician all derive from the Sanskrit "vsyate", meaning to "sing" or "make a noise". It suggests that music has been part of the Roma identity since the beginning. Today there are an estimated twelve million Gypsies outside India, with about eight million in Europe. Once they'd arrived in Europe the dispersals got ever more complex as persecution forced movement one way and then another. In virtually every European country there has been popular or state persecution of Gypsies, culminating in the extermination by the Nazis of an estimated half a million during World War II. Since the fall of Communism in Eastern Europe, there has been

a resurgent and violent racism against Gypsies across the region.

On a positive note, however, since the 1970s there has been a growing awareness of Gypsy identity and culture, and political moves to establish rights. The popular Balkan Gypsy song "Djelem, Djelem" (I've Travelled) was chosen as the **Romani anthem** (see below), and in 1979 the UN recognized the Roma as a distinct ethnic group. With the fall of the Berlin Wall and the EU accession of former Eastern Bloc countries, there have been headlines and complaints about Roma migrants in the West, but as musicians the Gypsies are highly regarded.

> ### Opré Roma (Rise Up Roma)
> *I've travelled, travelled long roads*
> *Meeting with happy Roma.*
> *Roma, where have you come from*
> *With tents on fortune's road?*
> *Roma, O fellow Roma,*
> *Once I had a great family.*
> *The Black Legion* murdered them.*
> *Come with me, all the world's Roma,*
> *For the Romani roads have opened.*
> *Now's the time, rise up Roma,*
> *We shall now rise high*
> *Roma, O fellow Roma.*
> Romani anthem, written by Jarko Jovanovic
> (* Black Legion refers to the Nazi SS)

Rajasthan?

Arab and Persian historians describe how **Shah Bahram Gur**, who ruled Persia from AD 420 to 438, invited musicians and dancers from northwest India to entertain his people. One source says four thousand, another twelve, but they were spread throughout the kingdom and left dark descendants "who are experts in playing the flute and lute". A later Persian history, written by Firdausi in 1011, tells a story about how the Shah's musicians were given corn, oxen and donkeys so they could become farmers, but ate the oxen and corn and returned after a year starving, whereupon the angry Shah told them to fit their instruments with strings of silk, put their possessions on their donkeys and wander the world.

The musicians who went to Persia in the fifth century were probably the first of several migrations. Others were perhaps prompted by the Muslim invasions of northwest India from the eighth century onwards. Linguistic evidence suggests that the ancestors of most of the Roma in Europe today left around AD 1000.

Northwest India, and **Rajasthan** in particular, still has a high concentration of nomadic tribes and Gypsies, many of whom have specific professions: the Gadia Lohar are blacksmiths (a profession associated with Gypsies everywhere), the Kamad are travelling jugglers, the Bhat are puppeteers, the Sapera are pipe-playing snake charmers and the Langa, Manganiyar and Bhopa storytellers are all musician castes in Rajasthan (see p.572).

Musafir, **Maharaja** and other groups that have brought Rajasthani Gypsy music to the West have combined musicians from several musical castes, and the same is true of many of the groups you can hear in north India today.

Of the many professional musicians of Rajasthan, the **Manganiyars**, who operate in the Thar desert around Jaisalmer, seem the closest to European Gypsy musicians; they have low social status and are always on call to provide a party. Typically they play the **kamayacha**, a bowed fiddle with four strings and a large skin-covered circular belly carved out of mango wood. Like most folk musicians from the region, they play and sing music which has the essential Gypsy qualities of declamation, emotion and ecstasy, but unusually, for percussion, they use pairs of **khartal** – hard *sal* wood clappers used just like flamenco castanets. Who knows if the Manganiyars, or their ancestors, are the proto-Gypsies? The castanets may be coincidence, but they are as strong a musical connection as you'll find on the Gypsy road.

The Baluchi Ostâ

Spread out over a vast territory comprising parts of **Pakistan**, **Iran** and **Afghanistan** are around ten million (traditionally nomadic) **Baluchi** people. Within Baluchi society, the **ostâ** caste are the music makers and share a fairly low status with other categories like blacksmiths and carpenters. They have been cited as possible descendants of the musicians cast out to wander by Bahram Gur, but they have absorbed so many different ethnic groups (who have adopted their language and customs) that it's hard to come up with hard evidence.

Like all the musician castes of the region, the ostâ are fiery performers with declamatory voices and great instrumental virtuosity. The most important instrument is the bowed **sorud** (fiddle), carved into a complicated skull-like shape

MUSAFIR | GYPSIES OF RAJASTHAN +++

Blue Flame/bmg

Musafir

with four playing strings and a number of vibrating sympathetic strings. The instrument has a soft but edgy tone with wonderful colours; it is often used to accompany songs and epic chants, but also as a solo instrument and for trance music. The **tanburag** lute often gives a rhythmic drone accompaniment.

The Road to Europe

Important linguistic ingredients in Romani come from Persian, Armenian and Greek, suggesting sustained contact with these peoples. Many Gypsies are thought to have arrived in Anatolia with the Seljuk army in the eleventh century. They would have interacted with Greeks in the Byzantine capital **Constantinople** (now Istanbul). From 1050 onwards, there are references to fortune tellers, acrobats, snake charmers and bear trainers who are thought to have been Gypsies. In their wanderings, the Gypsies encountered Christianity and they called the cross *trushul*, the same word they used for the trident carried by the Hindu god Shiva in India.

The migration of the Gypsies often seems to have been connected with Muslim invaders. The Muslims employed them as musicians (as Islamic theologians sometimes discouraged Muslims from the profession), but often persecuted them for their lack of a monotheistic faith. Gypsies in **Turkey** have long been a part of the rich ethnic mix of Istanbul and are still an important part of Turkey's musical life today.

From Constantinople the Gypsies crossed into **Europe** both in advance of and after the Ottoman conquest of the city in 1453. From the fourteenth and fifteenth centuries there are records of Gypsies in the **Balkans** – **Bulgaria**, **Greece**, **Serbia**, **Romania** and **Hungary**; Gypsies have made a huge contribution to music in all of these countries, and still do so today.

In Turkey and the Balkans the pairing of **zurna** (wooden *shawm*) and **davul** (barrel drum) is frequently heard outdoors at weddings and festivities. The insistent wailing of the zurna, usually played with continuous "circular breathing", and the driving rhythms of two furiously wielded sticks on the drum is strongly associated with Gypsy musicians, and this **shawm and drum duo** is found stretching back along the Gypsy route through Iran and into Central Asia, India and China.

The names of the instruments remain virtually unchanged across this vast territory. The word "zurna" originates from the Persian **shahnai** (from *shah*, king, and *nai*, flute), and this is the name used in India. It becomes *sornai* or *sorna* in Afghanistan, *suona* in China and *zurna* in Turkey; the Persian *dohol* becomes *davul* in Turkey and *daoúli* in Greece.

While many Gypsies went west through Turkey and into Europe, others left Persia and went south into the Arab lands and then on to **Egypt**, reaching as far south as **Sudan** in the fifteenth century. Musicians from Gypsy families have played an important role in Arabic music, in both the folk and classical fields. The late **Matar Muhammad**, for example, was one of the great **buzuq** players of the Arab world. The buzuq, a long-necked lute, is a popular instrument amongst Gypsy families of the Middle East.

There are still Gypsies – called **Nawar** – in **Upper Egypt** and they are frequently entertainers, acrobats, dancers and musicians, playing *rebab* or *rebabah* (upright fiddle), tambourines and those tell-tale castanets. Egypt's best-known group of traditional players, **The Musicians of the Nile**, includes Gypsy or Gypsy-related musicians.

It's possible that, with a migration across North Africa, it may have been Egyptian Gypsies that arrived in Moorish Spain, but most evidence suggests they came from the north.

Turkey

In **Turkey** today, the vast majority of restaurant and *gazino* (nightclub) musicians are Gypsy (called *Roman* in Turkish). They are also widely employed in the radio orchestras and for pop and arabesk recordings. However, the style of music with which Roman are inextricably linked is **fasıl** (light classical) and **belly dance** (*raks*).

With the virtuosity and panache that characterize Gypsy bands everywhere, these **fasıl musicians** are masters of the deep Turkish clarinet (*klarnet* – a metal instrument usually pitched in G), violin (*kaman* – typically played with yelping and screeching glissandos to attract attention), *kanun* (lap-top zither lending a lacy texture to the ensemble) and *darbuka* (goblet drum). The *ud* (lute) and *cümbüş* (a type of banjo) are also common. The fast fasıl tunes are driven by the darbuka while clarinet and violin weave melodies on top with furious runs and impossibly long sustained notes. The slower melodies and songs are highly ornamented, with lyrics of love, betrayal, poverty and drink.

Gypsy musicians were already in Constantinople (Istanbul) before the arrival of Mehmet the Conqueror in 1453. Throughout Anatolia, they were folk musicians and they were also involved

Selim Sesler

in the **Karagöz shadow theatre** – which is thought to have been brought from the east, and may even be about a Gypsy character as *karagöz* means "black eye". Turkish historians relate that Mehmet brought Gypsy musicians to Istanbul and into the **court orchestras**. Ottoman music was sustained by a multicultural range of musicians who were organized into guilds according to their ethnic group. There were guilds of Turkish, Armenian, Greek, Jewish and Gypsy musicians.

The **belly dance** grew out of the professional and courtly entertainments which included the **raks** dance in which female dancers, clicking finger cymbals, moved the belly, shoulders and other parts of the upper body while dancing. During the twentieth century Egyptian influences were absorbed into the dance and the style became the staple entertainment in cabarets and nightclubs, more or less erotic depending on the venue. Less showy and professional versions of the dancing can still be seen at Gypsy weddings, particularly in Thrace (the European part of Turkey towards Bulgaria), where many of the best Gypsy musicians come from.

Clarinettists **Hüsnü Şenlendirici** and **Selim Sesler** are amongst the top Turkish Gypsy performers.

Greece

Gypsies in **Greece** – known as **Yiftoi** ("Egyptians") – have long been involved in music as well as other typical Gypsy professions – horse traders, acrobats, bear trainers and Karagöz shadow puppeteers. They are found almost exclusively on the mainland and especially in Epirus, Macedonia and the Peloponnese; they are not part of the musical scene on the islands (where the communities have perhaps been too small to sustain them) and played little role in *rebétika* music, which was dominated by Greeks from Asia Minor.

Traditionally, Greek Gypsies played instrumental music and rarely sang. There were two types of ensemble, the ubiquitous **zurna and daoúli duo** and the more refined **koumpanía** music, the equivalent of Turkish fasıl, frequently heard in the coffee house or *café-amán*, and at weddings, parties and funerals. The clarinet is the lead instrument along with violin, lute or accordion. Koumpania music was frequently played by Jews until World War II, but with the devastation of the Greek Jewish communities it became the province of Gypsy musicians.

Epirus, in the northwest of Greece, has become particularly famous for its Gypsy koumpania groups. Clarinettist **Petroloukas Chalkias** is the pre-eminent player (now based in Athens), but there are other excellent local musicians like the family groups of **Grigoris Kapsalis** and **Yorgos Chalkias** (or Xalkias). More recently, with the growth of the Greek popular music industry over the past thirty years, Gypsy singers like **Yiannis Saleas** and **Kostas Pavlidis** have become popular commercial artists.

Eastern Europe

It's estimated that 47 percent of Europe's Gypsies live in the **Balkans**, which makes the region the densest concentration of Gypsies in the world. Throughout Eastern Europe, Gypsy musicians have been primary carriers of the folk tradition since the nineteenth century; indeed, most of what we think of as Eastern European folk music is almost exclusively played by Gypsies. But the form and sound of the music varies from place to place as the Gypsies have adapted to local styles; even the same band will vary its repertoire and instrumentation depending on who it is playing for.

Albania, Macedonia and Serbia

In south **Albania** it's essentially the Epirus-style koumpania music that's played on the clarinet, violin and accordion or lute. The same sort of music is called *čalgia* in **Macedonia** where it also exists in a modernized electric form largely played by Gypsies.

Emir Kusturica's film *The Time of the Gypsies* was shot in the Macedonian Gypsy suburb of **Šuto Orizari** (or Shutka), the largest Gypsy town in the world. The music from the film – and particularly the hit song "Ederlezi", a traditional tune (reputedly of Macedonian origin) catapulted to international popularity by the film – is now even more firmly a staple for Gypsy brass bands of the region and other groups in the Balkans and Turkey (where it became a hit performed by Sezen Aksu). If there's one thing that does unite the Gypsies across the Balkans, it's resentment at the film's composer Goran Bregović for ripping off their tunes. **Hindi film soundtracks** are also popular but often reworked into *čoček* forms far from the originals (*čoček* is a syncopated dance common in the south Balkans). These tunes reflect an important awareness of Gypsy ethnic origins.

Amongst the leading Macedonian Gypsy musicians are the brass **Kočani Orkestar**, the great saxophone and clarinet player **Ferus Mustafov** and the singer **Esma Redžepova** (who sings a lot of Romani repertoire). Her voice, often with the ensemble led by her late husband, clarinettist **Stevo Teodosievski**, takes you back the thousands of miles to the Gypsies' origins with its raw power and declamatory emotion.

Many of the East European Gypsy **female vocalists** like Redžepova, Slovakia's **Věra Bílá** and Hungary's **Mitsoura** have a paradoxical but winning combination of childlike innocence and long-suffering world-weariness that could be almost a defining quality of the typical Gypsy voices in Eastern Europe and beyond.

Serbian Gypsy music is, however, essentially a man's world where the brass band is king. And the Serbian brass band king is **Boban Marković** from the southern town of Vladičin Han. He's taken the Golden Trumpet prize numerous times at Guča, Serbia's three-day brass bacchanalia and the biggest and wildest musical festival in the Balkans. His band featured in Kusturica's film *Underground* (1995) and tunes from that film, "Mesečina" and "Kalashnikov", are staples of the brass band repertoire across the Balkans. With its blaring trumpets and big bass drummers, it's easy to think this Gypsy music is wild and crazy but actually Marković's band is one of the most disciplined around. Like any good Gypsy boy, his son **Marko** is following in his footsteps, and stars in the Kusturica-produced feature *Love Fair in Guča*.

Gypsy vocalists have long been popular in Serbia. During Tito's time **Šaban Bajramović** became a legend of Gypsy music and many others, including **Ljiljana Petrović** (now Buttler), were frequenting Skadarlija, the goodtime café quarter of Belgrade, making records and singing on the radio. In post-Milošević Serbia, after the years of war and heavy turbo-folk, there's something of a revival of interest in Gypsy music. Certainly Bajramović and Buttler have both enjoyed renewed success thanks to acclaimed albums recorded with Bosnia's **Mostar Sevdah Reunion** (see p.45). MSR's tour of Bosnia, Serbia and Croatia in 2003 seemed to touch deep emotions after those insane war years. The tears in the eyes of audiences spoke volumes about the power of music (particularly in the hands of Gypsies) to heal – if only people would listen.

While Bajramović and Buttler are essentially great Gypsy interpreters of Serbian (or Balkan) music, other groups are much more self-consciously Gypsy in their outlook. The **Earth-Wheel-Sky Band**'s name draws on common Roma symbols. Their music – vocals, violin, *cimbalom*, guitar and percussion – is a Gypsy stew of the many cultures that meet in the northern region of Vojvodina. **Kal** is a violin, accordion and guitar band based in Belgrade with a growing reputation.

Bulgaria

During the Communist period, Bulgaria's large Gypsy population were, like the Turkish minority, pressurized into Bulgarianizing their names. Clarinettist **Ivo Papasov**, a Turkish Gypsy, was the big name on the semi-underground wedding band circuit. More recently he has enjoyed international acclaim, winning a BBC World Music Award in 2005. These days, the popular Gypsy style in Bulgaria is *chalga*, with keyboards and programmed beats. One of the big names is **Jony Iliev**; his excellent CD *Ma Maren Ma* is a lyrical, soulful collection of Bulgarian Gypsy music for the international market. But the most colourful figure on the scene is **Azis** (see p.56). "One day I will be like Madonna!" he has said, and in Bulgaria he is. A gender-bending Gypsy and a massive star, Azis has done more to overthrow the old Communist sensibilities than anyone else in the Balkans.

Romania

Far from the stereotype of rootlessness and freedom, in Romania the Roma were subject to slavery for over four hundred years. The terms Gypsy (*ţigan*) and slave were interchangeable, Gypsies could be bought and sold and women were frequently used as sex slaves. Slavery was abolished in 1864, but there's a legacy in terms of racism to this day.

Some of the more fortunate slaves were used for their musical skills and, as everywhere in the Balkans, the Gypsies are pre-eminent as *lăutari* (professional musicians) in Romania today. Divas like **Romica Puceanu** and **Gabi Luncă** charmed Bucharest audiences from the 1950s onwards in the city's theatres and restaurants. Today, the popular style of Gypsy music is called **manele**, but it's the traditional, rural style that's become most celebrated in the West.

Apart from the brass band **Fanfare Ciocărlia**, it's string bands that dominate. The instrumental line-up includes fiddles, cimbaloms, accordions and plucked double bass. The most high-profile band internationally is the **Taraf de Haidouks**. They are (or were) a genuine village band from the village of Clejani, southwest of Bucharest, where it's supposed a music-loving *boyar* gathered a collection of musical slaves. The band includes players of several generations who have managed to transfer the vibrancy and soul of a local gig to stages across the globe. Sadly, however, the best veteran players have died in recent years. The strength of the Taraf is that they are a genuine band, with musicians used to regular wedding gigs, and not some folkloric ensemble. The old timers have kept alive some of the old traditional ballads and improvised songs. The fact that these Gypsy musicians work closely with those who are booking for weddings and parties means that they know both the old traditional repertoire and the latest fashions.

In **Transylvania**, northwest Romania, within the sweep of the Carpathians, Gypsies are still the musical providers, but the instrumental line-up is slightly different. Here it's a trio or quartet of lead fiddle over the strong rhythmic base of accompanying violin or viola playing off-beat chords and a strongly bowed double bass. Accordions and cimbaloms are less common. As the territory rises into the Carpathian mountains, Gypsy musicians thin out and "indigenous" players take over.

Poland

Generally, Gypsies are found on the lowlands and in urban areas, rarely in the highlands. They are not active in the rich folk tradition of the Tatras, for example, the heartland of folk music in **Poland**, although the country has Gypsy communities.

Slovakia

Slovakia has large Gypsy communities, although there are few musicians or singers who've become widely known. The Slovak singer **Valerie Buchačová** appears on Network's *Road of the Gypsies* compilation, but the greatest voice of the Slovak Gypsies – indeed, one of Europe's most remarkable Gypsy voices – is the formidable **Věra Bílá**, now resident in the Czech Republic (see p.81). Small in height, wide in girth, Bílá has a powerful, almost male-sounding voice that can really swing with her band **Kale**, as she expresses (in Romani) the hardship and tragedy of Gypsy life. Her song about drinking herself to death because her lover's left her, "Te Me Pijav Lačhes Rosnes", has extraordinary grief-stricken sliding between pitches.

Hungary

Hungary has been famous for its Gypsy music since the end of the eighteenth century, although Gypsy musicians were already mentioned in the sixteenth century playing "in the Turkish manner" for the Pashas occupying Hungary and "in the Hungarian manner" for the Hungarian princes in Transylvania standing out against the occupation. Again Gypsy musicians can be seen caught up in both sides of a Muslim invasion.

The first celebrated Gypsy band leader was **Czinka Panna** (1711–72) – a woman, very unusual, then as now. The most famous, however, was **János Bihari** (1764–1827), who was known as the Napoleon of the fiddle. Bihari's band usually consisted of four strings plus a cimbalom, an instrument much associated with Gypsy players. These professional musicians are known as **Romungro** Gypsies.

Many of Bihari's pieces are still in the repertoire of Hungary's restaurant ensembles today. The most celebrated fiddlers now playing in this style come from the Lakatos family – notably **Sándor Lakatos** and his nephew, the young **Roby Lakatos** – said to be direct descendants of Bihari himself. Their repertoire is essentially the light classical music of Liszt and Brahms and Vittorio Monti's Csárdás, played with lots of exaggerated rubato and up-front virtuosity. It is more slick than soul, but technically impressive.

There's a completely different style of music that the rural **Vlach (or Olah) Gypsies** in Hungary (and Romania) play amongst themselves. Oddly, considering the skill of the Gypsy musicians, it hardly uses instruments at all. It comprises slow songs called, in Romani, *loki djili* and dance songs, *khelimaski djili*. Though there are no instruments, many of these songs are accompanied by rhythmic grunts, the tapping of sticks and cans and imitations of instruments in a "doobie-doobie-doobie" sort of way called **oral-bassing**.

These "rolled songs" and dance songs which have a wild, improvised sound provided the raw material for some of Hungary's professional Gypsy groups – notably **Kályi Jag** (Romani for Black Fire), **Ando Drom** (On the Road) and **Romano Drom** (Romani Road). All have added guitars and other instruments to the vocal and percussion line-up and they have strong, dark-voiced vocalists singing in Romani. **Parno Graszt**, who've recorded some excellent albums, are a real rural Gypsy group from the village of Paszab in the run-down Gypsy heartland of northeast Hungary.

Russia

In **Russia** Gypsies became popular performers in the late eighteenth century, during the reign of Catherine the Great. It's said that Count Orlov heard Gypsy musicians in Moldavia and in St Petersburg assembled a Gypsy chorus from his Roma serfs. In 1807 he freed them to form the first professional chorus in Russia. They sang Russian folksongs, but enlivened with a romanticized Gypsy spirit. *Tsiganshchina* (Gypsyness), meaning a wild, untamed quality, became a preoccupation and stereotype in Russian literature (for instance Pushkin's *The Gypsies*), however far from the truth it may have been.

During the course of the nineteenth century Gypsy choral singing gave way to romances and urban songs which were hugely popular at themed restaurants, like Yar on the outskirts of Moscow, to which it was customary to drive in a troika in winter. While the Gypsies propagated a romanticized view of Gypsy life, they probably also created the stereotyped image of the Russian soul with sad songs, fiery dances and devil-may-care drinking.

The 1917 revolution was a blow to the Russian Gypsies and many chose to leave. Their aristocratic patrons had gone, they were persecuted as entertainers of the bourgeoisie, and the Bolsheviks introduced bans on nomadism. Even so, the love of Gypsy music didn't go away. "Dark Eyes", one of the most popular Gypsy songs, was taken up by "folk" ensembles and Red Army choirs. **Romen**, a Gypsy theatre, was established in Moscow in 1931 and still survives today.

One of the most popular Russian émigré performers, from the 1930s through to the 1950s, was **Pyotr Leschenko**, not himself a Gypsy, but a celebrated singer of Gypsy songs, romances and tangos. His recordings were smuggled into Soviet Russia and were avidly danced to and cried over round the gramophone. In Bucharest, he set up a themed restaurant with Tiffany lamps and a mural of a Russian troika harking back to the romantic days of Yar. In 1951 Leschenko was arrested on stage in his Gypsy dress, and he died three years later in a penal camp near Bucharest.

The Russian Gypsy violinist **Jean Goulesco** (who played for the Tsar for many years) left St Petersburg in 1917 with his new-born daughter **Lida Goulesco** and settled in Paris where she became another of the great Russian Gypsy voices in exile.

Many of the prominent Gypsy performers in Russia today come from the families of Erdenko and Ponomarev. These include romance singers **Nikolai Erdenko**, **Rosa Erdenko** and **Valentina Ponomareva** and the groups **Loyko**, **Jelem** and **Jung**. Their music displays the hallmarks of the Russian style: a spectacular virtuosity on fiddles and guitars, combined with a clichéd romantic approach close to kitsch. A slightly more restrained approach is taken by the Busilyov family of Siberian Gypsies, who maintained a nomadic lifestyle until the mid-twentieth century.

Spain

The most celebrated Gypsy music is, of course, **flamenco**, born of the fusion of cultures in Andalucía, southern Spain. Flamenco isn't Gypsy (*Gitano*, in Spanish) in origin, but – as with most of the music in this survey – it's a style Gypsies have made their own.

Gypsies were first recorded in Spain in 1425, and following on from the Christian re-conquest of Spain in 1492 the first anti-Gypsy (and anti-Muslim and anti-Jewish) legislation was introduced. Nonetheless, Gypsy communities grew in Spain over the following century, particularly in Andalucía, to which many migrated – from Europe, perhaps also from North Africa – to fill the gap left by the expelled Moors.

Over the years a tradition of leading flamenco families grew up in the main Andalucían cities – Granada, Córdoba, Seville – and in the nineteenth century, with the rise of flamenco cafés and *juergas* (private gatherings), Gypsies and flamenco became firmly linked in the popular imagination. There have been flowerings and declines in the music since then, but districts like the Gypsy quarter of Jerez still retain something of the traditional character.

British Gypsy Music

Gypsies reached Britain in about 1500, and since 1976 they have been legally recognized as a distinct ethnic group. Many British Gypsies (Romanies or Romanichals) still speak Anglo-Romani, whereas Travellers – also recognized as an ethnic group – are of Irish/Scottish descent and speak Cant. It is estimated that approximately 300,000 Romanies and Travellers live in Britain today, with roughly one third on legal (or – due to the lack of official spaces – illegal) Traveller sites, and the rest in conventional housing. Except when considered a social problem, the impact of these groups on British life is rarely acknowledged. Yet in 1906, Cecil Sharp (the founding father of the folk revival in England) wrote that "the finest … bit of singing I had ever heard" was that of Romanichal **Betsy Holland**, and in the 1950s the eminent folklorist Hamish Henderson remarked that collecting traditional songs from Travellers was "like holding a can under Niagara Falls in order to catch water". So why are the contributions that British Gypsies and Travellers have made as carriers and preservers of traditional song so rarely acknowledged?

Innovative and flexible, Gypsies continually select and reject songs from mainstream genres. However, their distinct historical and cultural experience leads Gypsies to approach music and song in a different way from that of the majority Gorger (non-Gypsy) population. Not bound by the same conventions as Gorgers, Gypsies often demonstrate a scant regard for rhyme and metre. Singing tends to be solo, dramatic, slow-paced and loud, while music is played on portable instruments – the fiddle, Jew's harp, melodeon, spoons, flutes fashioned out of reed or, more recently, the guitar.

Songs performed by British Gypsies tend to create a kaleidoscopic image rather than a linear narrative, and this may initially render them less accessible to outsiders. However, while they may not appear to be easy listening, the songs of Romanichals and Travellers are, according to folk singer and collector Shirley Collins, "totally fascinating". Folk artist Martin Carthy has spoken about the impact that Mike Yates' 1974 field recording of **Levi Smith** singing the seventeenth-century broadside ballad "Georgie" had on him: "It confronted everything I had thought made musical sense, and changed it." Folk singer Norma Waterson is also an admirer of the "extraordinarily varied and ultimately unique" performances of the **Brazils**, **Wiggy Smith**, **Duncan Williamson**, **Jasper**, **Minty** and **Levi Smith**, **Mary Ann Haynes**, **Phoebe Smith** and **Belle Stewart**, to name but a few of the Travellers and Romanichals recorded by Mike Yates and other collectors. It is ironic that an ethnic group that is so frequently excluded from official representations of British life became the carriers of a folk tradition that urbanization, industrialization and modernization virtually extinguished in the Gorger population.

Hazel Marsh

One of the things that characterizes flamenco is the dominance of emotion over text. Often the words are broken up and obscured by sighs and emotional outbursts; vowels are often extended into long oriental-sounding melismas which take flight as the emotion is conveyed through the performance – the singing of Pastora Pavón, known as **La Niña de los Peines** (1890–1969), is renowned for this. It is tempting to liken this declamatory style of singing with the other Gypsy styles in northwest India and Eastern Europe – and indeed flamenco and the Eastern European vocal styles share the expressive outbursts of "ai" and "yai" in the performance of the music.

The most celebrated flamenco singer was **El Camarón de la Isla** (1950–92), son of an amateur singer and blacksmith in the gitano barrios of Cádiz. Like many Gypsies he had a larger-than-life approach to performing and often glided between notes in a melismatic way. He could perform traditional Cádiz-style flamenco, but after *Le Leyenda del Tiempo* in 1979 chose to push at the boundaries and annoy the traditionalists with the celebrated guitarist **Tomatito**.

France and Catalonia

Gypsies were first mentioned in **France**, near the Rhine, in the early fifteenth century, but these days the main areas of concentration are in the south – in the **Camargue** at the mouth of the Rhône and around **Perpignan** (Roussillon).

The Perpignan Gypsies have moved back and forth between France and Spanish **Catalonia** over the years, and the music to be heard on both sides of the border – in Barcelona and Perpignan – is **Rumba Gitana** (Gypsy Rumba), made most famous by **The Gipsy Kings** (see box). It grew from the Gypsy music of Catalonia, but with a mélange of flamenco, North African music, Cuban and rock grafted on. Its essence, however, is virtuoso guitar playing, some agile clapping and those formidable declamatory Gypsy vocals – in Catalan or Spanish.

In Spanish Catalonia, the group **Ojos de Brujo** in Barcelona have updated this mix still further. Started by Gypsy guitarist Ramón Giménez and featuring the dramatic singer Marina Abad, Ojos has taken Rumba Gitana, flamenco and hip-hop and created a streetwise fusion sung in Calo, a fla-menco-Romani dialect. With its electronics and DJ scratching it's certainly a contemporary take on the tradition, but "Ventilaor R-80", one of their trademark songs, is a very danceable rumba dedicated to Camarón. Their recordings and particularly their live shows just reek of Gypsy attitude.

In France, in addition to the Gipsy Kings, there's **Chico and the Gypsies**, led by former Gipsy King **Chico Bouchikhi**, and in Perpingnan the excellent rootsy groups **Tekameli** and **Kaloomé**. In

The Gipsy Kings

The Gipsy Kings are that rare thing, a world music band who are famous all over the world. Their signature song "Bamboleo" has become over-familiar due to repeated play, so much relief greeted their 2004 album *Roots*, a sublime acoustic effort that captured the raw musical beauty of which these Provençal Gitans are capable.

The Kings' eponymous 1988 album won over international audiences with its potent blend of flamenco and Latin American rumba rhythms. They went on to sell fourteen million albums, yet the formula became sterile until a change of management got them off the treadmill of endless touring and mechanical, hi-tech recording. *Roots* found them sounding fresh, soulful and invigorated as they played the music that had shaped these sons of nomads and refugees.

The band consists of two sets of brothers, the Reyes and the Bailardos. The Reyes are the sons of flamenco singer **José Reyes**, while the Bailardos are the nephews of **Ricardo Bailardo**, a flamenco guitarist who gained international acclaim as **Manitas De Plata** (Hands Of Silver) in the 1960s when partnered with José Reyes. Their success presaged that of the Kings – they played for the likes of Picasso, Dali, Chaplin and adoring audiences internationally. After a bitter split over money, José formed Los Reyes with his four sons. He died in the late 1970s and Los Reyes incorporated their Bailardo cousins into the band. When an American admirer proclaimed, "Los Reyes? Then you're Gipsy Kings", the band had a new name. Local success spread nation-

ally, Europe was seduced, the US and Asia too. No one was more astonished than the band themselves – invited to Japan, they refused to believe the Japanese listened to them.

The Reyes and Bailardo families are descended from Spanish Gitano families who fled the Spanish Civil War for the south of France; the band's dialect is flecked with Spanish and Catalan words. The rumba rhythms they heard in Barcelona in the 1960s were blended with flamenco and Django Reinhardt guitar passages to create their distinctive sound. Living in Arles and Montpelier, the band members grew up attending the annual Gypsy pilgrimage to Santes Maries de la Mer, a seaside town, where Black Sara (the Gypsy saint) is worshipped. Today the raw, soulful expression that once went into making music there continues to inform the music of the Gipsy Kings.

Garth Cartwright

The Gipsy Kings

Swinging Gypsies

Gypsy swing or jazz manouche? Is it jazz *per se* or the music of a Gypsy community, the **Manouche** Gypsies (also called **Sinti**) who used to roam the roads of northen France, Alsace, Belgium, Holland and Germany? One thing is sure, before **Django Reinhardt** there was no Gypsy swing. In the Paris of the roaring twenties there were outstanding Manouche musicians eager to play any music for a living, including **musette**. Meanwhile, over in Montmartre, **American jazz** nurtured by a strong African American community became the rage among a few conoscenti including Django. In forming the **Quintette du Hot Club de France** with **Stéphane Grappelli**, Django created the finest string ensemble ever to come out of Europe, but he did not "mix" or "fuse" anything to do so. He had the guts and foresight to forge something totally new that has become the trademark of his own community (despite his untimely death in 1953, aged 43), and he remains highly influential to this day.

Superior musicians all playing guitar in a similar style were to be found in Django's immediate family, including his brother **Joseph Reinhardt**, his sons **Babik Reinhardt** and **Lousson Baumgartner** (all dead) and now his grandson **David Reinhardt** and great-grandson **Dallas Baumgartner**. Foremost among the myriad of Django followers are the outstanding **Rosenberg family** from Holland; **Bireli Lagrène**, **Tchavolo Schmitt** and the **Loeffler family** from Alsace; and **Patrick Saussois** and his band **Alma Sinti**. Others include **Christian Escoudé**, **Romane**, **Angelo Debarre**, **Ninine** and **Mondine Garcia**, **Raphael Fays**, **Moreno Winterstein**, the **Ferré** (or Ferret) family and **Thomas Dutronc** (gadjo son of French chanson stars **Françoise Hardy** and **Jacques Dutronc**).

The most colourful Gypsy swing festivals, attracting hordes of Manouches travelling in huge caravans and eager to jam non-stop, are the ones directly associated with Django: **Samois-sur-Seine** (60km south of Paris) where he died and is buried (end of June), **Liberchies** (near Charleroi, Belgium) where he was born (end of May) and **Salbris**, near Orleans, where he got married (beginning of June).

Jean-Pierre Bruneau

the Camargue, there's a vast annual gathering at **Saintes Maries de la Mer** where Gypsies from France and Spain congregate to celebrate the feast day of their patron saint, Sara, on 24 and 25 May. Here the music is predominantly flamenco in style with a large number making the pilgrimage from Andalucía.

An earlier French-based Gypsy star was the composer and guitarist **Django Reinhardt** (1910–53), who began a whole style of music called manouche or **Gypsy swing**. Django was actually born in Belgium, but spent most of his life in France. He was working as a guitarist, aged eighteen, when a fire broke out in the caravan where he was sleeping. His left leg and the third and fourth fingers of his left hand were badly burnt, but guitar therapy enabled him to create

his own style of playing and enjoy a hugely successful career. He formed the Quintette du Hot Club de France in 1931 with *gadjo* (non-Gypsy) violinist **Stéphane Grappelli** and, after the war, embarked on major international tours. A dynasty of French Gypsy (and non-Gypsy) musicians has continued Django's style of Gypsy swing (see box above).

Some of the most interesting Gypsy music in France has been created by non-Gypsies. Guitarist and oud player **Thierry "Titi" Robin** has frequently collaborated with gypsy flamenco artists and, harking back to Indian roots, the Rajasthani Gypsy singer **Gulabi Sapera**. The long-lived Paris-based group **Bratsch** are also honourary Gypsies who can play in any number of styles along the Gypsy road.

There is a mass of Roma information – including disc reviews – available at *www.geocities.com/~patrin*.

General

★ Gypsy Queens
Network, Germany

A daughter of Network's *Road of the Gypsies* collection (see below), this two-disc set focuses on six women singers – Esma Redžepova and Džansever (from Macedonia), Romica Puceanu and Gabi Luncă (from Romania), Mitsoura of Ando Drom (from Hungary) and La Macanita (from Spain). It's passionate and emotional stuff and, as ever with Network, nicely packaged with a full-colour booklet.

⊙ Latcho Drom
Caroline, France

The soundtrack for Tony Gatlif's rather ramshackle film about Gypsy music features fine contributions from Rajasthan, Spain, Egypt, Turkey, Romania, Hungary, Slovakia and France. Aural connections are pretty self-evident.

★ Road of the Gypsies
Network, Germany

This two-CD set of Gypsy music, stretching from Rajasthan to Spain, is a superlative compilation. It could perhaps have included more from the western end of the trail but makes up for it with Camarón's excellent homage to the Gypsies' Indian roots and a fantastic range of tracks from Eastern Europe including Goran Bregović's film music, the wonderful Esma Redžepova (singing the Roma anthem, here titled "Szelem Szelem"), the Taraf de Haidouks, Hungary's Kályi Jag and Ando Drom, and strong Greek and Turkish contributions. An essential first buy.

⊙ The Rough Guide to Gypsy Music
World Music Network, UK

If you want a single disc on Gypsy music, this compilation will do nicely. Alongside obvious choices such as the Taraf de Haidouks and Musafir, there are selections from Šaban Bajramović and Bela Lakatos.

India/Middle East

⊙ Baluchistan: Music of Ecstasy and Healing
Ocora, France

Trance-like music on a double CD which has a mesmeric power, particularly the playing on the sorud fiddle with its shimmering sympathetic strings. Whether the musicians are related to the original Gypsies or not, there seems a spiritual kinship in the music.

⊙ Gypsies of Rajasthan: Desert Charm
Sense World Music, UK

A splendid and varied collection from the Langa and Manganiyar musicians of Rajasthan, with beautiful kamayacha playing.

⊙ Inde – Rajasthan:
Musiciens Professionnels Populaires
Ocora, France

The best introduction to the various caste-musicians of Rajasthan, including Langa and Manganiyar performers.

There's more than a hint of Gypsy-style showmanship in many of these tracks. Good photos and notes.

★ The Mystic Fiddle of the Proto-Gypsies: Masters of Trance Music
Shanachie, US

A haunting collection of instrumental numbers from veteran Baluchi sarod players living in Pakistan. The music has great intensity and power, whether the musicians are proto-Gypsies or not.

⊙ Sulukule: Rom Music of Istanbul
Traditional Crossroads, US

Named after one of the Gypsy suburbs of Istanbul, this CD evokes the earthy character of urban life. The band is led by Kemani Cemal (named after his instrument, the violin – keman). There are good notes about the history of Turkish Gypsy music and translations of lyrics.

Mustafa Kandıralı

Born in Kandıralı in 1930, this Gypsy clarinet player toured the Middle East, Soviet Union and US as a fasıl band leader in the 1960s. It was in the US that he had his formative encounter with jazz. Kandıralı's performances have a quiet radicalism to them, and his melodically inventive improvisations blend seamlessly with the restless dance tunes.

⊙ Caz Roman
Network, Germany

This is the epitome of instrumental fasıl, including some of the genre's best-known musicians – Ahmet Meter (kanun), Metin Bükey (ud) and Ahmet Kulik (darbuka). The final section of dance tunes was recorded live at a 1984 concert.

Matar Muhammad

Matar Muhammad (1939–95) was born into a Gypsy family in the Bekaa Valley of Lebanon. He took up the buzuq aged seven and made his professional debut in the early 1960s on the BBC's Arabic programmes. With performances at the Baalbek Festival he became celebrated throughout the Arab world, but sadly partial paralysis stopped him playing for the last twenty years of his life.

⊙ Hommage à un Maître du Buzuq
Inédit, France

Live recordings of some of Muhammad's last performances, at the Beirut Theatre in 1972. What makes him a remarkable musician is the free-wheeling imaginative fantasy of his improvisations within the classical Arabic modes. There are four such here, and the exclamations and applause of an appreciative audience add to the extraordinary atmosphere.

Musafir

Musafir is a loose group of mainly Rajasthani Langa musicians put together by tabla player Hameed Khan. The group perform Gypsy and folk repertoire alongside spectacular circus and fakir displays.

★ Gypsies of Rajasthan
Blue Flame, Germany

Good professional performances of folk music, Sapera snake charmers' music and devotional songs to Baba Ramdev.

Instrumentation includes several flutes and pipes, sarangi and harmonium.

⊙ **Dhola Maru**
Sounds True, US
Also a fine album with good songs and instrumentals plus Sufi qawwali music.

The Musicians of the Nile

A group of fine traditional musicians from Upper Egypt with links to Gypsy families, although these things are hard to ascertain in Egypt. They are led by singer and *rababah* (upright two-string fiddle) maestro Metqal Qenawi Metqal.

⊙ **Luxor to Isna**
RealWorld, UK
The ensemble play dry, deserty music on the *zumarin* (Egyptian zurna), with drums and an unusual *arghul* (a double clarinet that can be extended to alter the pitch). There's also strong rootsy singing and playing on the rababah with lots of overtones.

Burhan Öçal

Öçal is a top Turkish percussionist, but not a Gypsy, who grew up in the Thracian town of Kırklareli. He formed the Istanbul Oriental Ensemble to play Gypsy-style fasıl music and has collaborated with many jazz musicians and other international artists.

⊙ **Burhan Öçal and the Trakya Allstars**
Doublemoon, Turkey
Öçal assembles some of his childhood friends to perform Thracian Gypsy music. It's given an interesting contemporary twist with electronics from Tunisian-born French whizz kid Smadj. Stylishly done.

WITH ISTANBUL ORIENTAL ENSEMBLE

⊙ **Gypsy Rum**
World Network, Germany
Fourteen tracks of tight instrumental playing on clarinet, violin, ud, kanun and darbuka drums. Emotional twists and lightning intensity will have your belly dancing – and listen out for the screaming shrieks from Fethi Tekaygil's violin.

Selim Sesler

Born in 1957, Sesler comes from the town of Keşan in Turkish Thrace near the Greek border, but has been working primarily in Istanbul since the 1980s. He's the best rootsy clarinet player in Turkey.

★ **The Road to Keşan: Turkish Rom and Regional Music of Thrace**
Traditional Crossroads, US; Kalan, Turkey
The best recording there is of Turkish Gypsy music from Thrace, recorded in situ. Sesler plays with a lithe band including violin, kanun, Turkish cümbüş, banjo and percussion.

Eastern Europe, the Balkans and Russia

⊙ **Golden Brass Summit**
Network, Germany
A spectacular two-CD album which captures the extraordinary history of Serbian brass through the annual festival at Guča, with recordings dating back to the inaugural year in 1961. There's plenty of Boban Marković, but many others, equally stirring, including rising star Ekrem Sajdic.

⊙ **Greece: Epirus – Takoutsia, Musicians of Zagori**
Inedit, France
Lovely recordings of an old-style koumpania Gypsy band from Epirus in northwest Greece. Various members of the Kapsalis family feature in an ensemble with clarinet, violin, lute and tambourine. There is a rare recording of elaborately ornamented funeral music, plus dance music and drinking songs.

⊙ **Gypsy Music of Macedonia and Neighbouring Countries**
Topic, UK
A good disc for those wanting to explore the characteristic Gypsy duo of zurna and drum. The title is rather misleading as there is only one track from Macedonia, but plenty more from Kosovo, Romania, Greece and Turkey. Wild stuff recorded in the 1970s and 80s.

⊙ **Kosovo Roma**
ArheFon, Slovenia
Rare field recordings made by Svanibor Pettan between 1984 and 1991. Traditional and modern music from the Gypsy communities of Kosovo before they were devastated in the Kosovo war.

⊙ **Music of Greece's Gypsies**
FM Records, Greece
A great disc recorded live at a concert featuring some of Greece's top Gypsy performers. Very strong vocals from Eleni Vitali, Kostas Pavlidis, Yiannis Saleas and others plus masterly instrumental playing, notably on zurna and clarinet. Some songs are traditional in character, others more modern. Bregovic's "Ederlezi" inevitably appears.

⊙ **Rom Sam Ame!**
Fonti Musicali, Belgium
A specialized but excellent survey of authentic Gypsy songs from six towns and villages in central and eastern Hungary. Hungarian and Romani vocals are accompanied by spoons and struck pots and tables. This is Gypsy music for Gypsies. Excellent photos and notes.

⊙ **Russian Gypsy Soul**
Network, Germany
This two-CD album is pretty much all you need to get the low-down on Russian Gypsy music. Excellent musicianship, larger-than-life colour and kitsch.

⊙ **Serbia: Romany Musical Heritage**
VDE-Gallo, Switzerland
A great selection of location recordings from across Serbia of Gypsy musicians on fiddles, *tamburicas* and accordions. The real stuff.

⊙ **Suburban Bucharest: Mahala Sounds from Romania**
Trikont, Germany
A great sampler of the music of Bucharest (recorded between 1936 and 2004), most of it Gypsy. Includes Gypsy divas Romica Puceanu and Gabi Luncă, as well as modern-day *mahala* men like Dan Armeanca and the Mahala Raï Banda.

Ando Drom

Ando Drom are one of the best of Hungary's professional Roma ensembles. Formed in the early 1980s and led by Jenö Zsigó, they have transformed the rural Gypsy traditions into a dynamic concert music.

⊙ **Phari Mamo**
Network, Germany
This is, as the subtitle says, "magnificent Gypsy music from Budapest" – and not the schmaltzy café variety. Fronted by the swarthy vocals of Mónika "Mitsou" Juhász Miczura (who

has since left the band to go solo), Ando Drom's vocal and percussion line-up has real soul and a melancholy edge. They are joined on this recording by violin and accordion players from the French group Bratsch.

Šaban Bajramović

Born in Niš in 1936, Šaban is a legend of Serbian Gypsy music. It's hard to establish what is fact and what is fiction, but certainly he spent a year on Goli Otok, Tito's prison island, for going AWOL when conscripted to the Yugoslav army. He started releasing records in the 1960s and became a sort of Balkan Gypsy Elvis or James Brown. He's made many records and written hundreds of songs, and has a voice wonderfully coarsened by Red Marlborough.

⊙ A Gypsy Legend
World Connection, Netherlands
A moody collection of Šaban's songs and Gypsy classics ("Djelem, Djelem") in Romani with Mostar Sevdah Reunion. The marvellous "Pelno Me Sam" is about Goli Otok.

Věra Bílá and Kale

Bílá is an extraordinary Slovak Gypsy singer now resident in the Czech Republic. Her band Kale provide accompanying guitars, hand claps and harmony vocals. She's the subject of an excellent documentary film, *Black and White in Colour*.

⊙ Kale Kaloré
BMG/Ariola, Czech Republic
This 1998 album, Bílá's second CD, is the most Gypsy in character, although her band have also picked up Latin and Rumba Gitana ingredients. Catchy tunes and some tragic-sounding tracks, including "Te Me Pijav Lačhes Rosnes" (I Always Drink), in which Bílá's dark voice reaches into the depths.

Ljiljana Buttler

Ljiljana was born in Belgrade in 1944. Her father (who left soon after she was born) was an accordion virtuoso, her mother a Croatian singer. Aged twelve, Ljiljana had to go out and sing for her family when her mother fell sick. As Ljiljana Petrović she was a well-known singer of the 1970s and 80s. She emigrated to Germany before the break-up of Yugoslavia. Under her married name of Ljiljana Buttler she was tracked down by Dragi Šestić of Mostar Sevdah Reunion, who has given her dark, masculine voice a new lease of life in concerts and on CD.

★ The Mother of Gypsy Soul
Snail Records, Netherlands
One of the great Gypsy discs of recent years. Ljiljana, who'd been working as a char lady in Germany for years, shows that she's still a sublime singer. Her dark, smoky vocals are backed by Bosnia's excellent Mostar Sevdah Reunion. If you want an aural definition of soul, listen no further.

Petroloukas Chalkias

Born in Epirus in 1934, Chalkias is the leading Greek clarinettist playing the Gypsy-style music of the region. He lived in the US for twenty years before returning to Greece in 1979.

★ Petro-Loukas Chalkias and Kompania
Network, Germany
Chalkias has released scores of recordings, but this is one of the best, featuring traditional repertoire with lute, fiddle and percussion. There is a distinctively Gypsy intensity to the performances.

Fanfare Ciocărlia

Romania's leading Gypsy brass band, from Moldavia in the northeast. They have recorded six excellent albums and become hugely popular on tour.

★ Queens and Kings
Asphalt Tango, Germany
This 2007 release is one of the great discs of recent years. The Romanian brass band are the backing group for a wonderful range of Gypsy performers including Šaban Bajramović, Esma Redžepova, Kaloomé and Dan Armeanca.

Gogol Bordello

Funny how the Americans seem to manage to take a lead even on the Eastern European Gypsy punk circuit. Gogol Bordello is a New York outfit led by Ukrainian Gypsy émigré Eugene Hütz. They've made wild Gypsy craziness hip.

⊙ Gypsy Punks: Underdog World Strike
Side One Dummy, US
A swaggering, over-the-top CD that really delivers. Wild playing, verbal abuse and devil-may-care attitude make this a faux-Gypsy classic.

Lida Goulesco

Born in Petrograd in 1917, Goulesco was taken to Paris by her violinist father when he fled Russia after the revolution. She grew up there in an atmosphere of decadent Russian Gypsy parties in restaurants and cabarets.

⊙ Chants Folkloriques Tziganes
Buda/Musique du Monde, France
This is probably as close as you can get to the music played at restaurants in Moscow and St Petersburg around the end of the nineteenth century. Goulesco's husky voice speaks volumes, guitars and fiddles provide the right accompaniment and lots of drunken-sounding guests make it into a party.

Kal

Kal – meaning "black" in Romani – is the leading young Gypsy band in Serbia. Founded in 2006 by Dragan Ristic, it's a six-piece with guitar, violin, accordions and percussion.

⊙ Radio Romanista
Asphalt Tango, Germany
The band's second album, from 2009, with an intense, rootsy, driving sound.

Kočani Orkestar

This Macedonian Gypsy brass band was led by trumpet player Naat Veliov and was based, as you might expect, in the town of Kočani. The line-up was two trumpets, three tubas, sax, clarinet, zurla (shawm) and drums. Veliov now leads another Kočani Orkestar.

⊙ L'Orient Est Rouge
Crammed Discs, Belgium
The title comes from the Chinese Communist anthem – totally transformed into a Balkan dance – which opens the album. Other cuts include a radical arrangement of the popular "Ederlezi" tune, with an endless slow *taksim* (improvisation) on trumpet and zurla leading into a frenetic dance, and the Roma anthem "Djelem, Djelem". Full-bodied and brash, this is the band at their peak in 1997.

Roby Lakatos

Born in 1965, Roby is one of the younger members of the famous Lakatos dynasty of professional Hungarian Gypsy musicians. He learned in the family tradition as well as at the Budapest Music Academy. Since 1985, he has lived in Belgium where he's expanded his style to include jazz and Stéphane Grappelli-style violin. The Hungarian café-style is often sneered at, but Lakatos makes it work.

⊙ **Lakatos**
Deutsche Grammophon, Germany
Classical-oriented repertoire including Brahms' Hungarian Dances, Vittorio Monti's Csárdás and Gypsy favourites like "Dark Eyes" and "The Lark".

Pyotr Leschenko

Leschenko was a hugely popular Russian exile singer from the 1930s through to the 1950s, when he was arrested and imprisoned in Romania. He was not a Gypsy, but was famed for his Gypsy songs and tangos.

⊙ **Gipsy Songs and Other Passions**
Oriente, Germany
Atmospheric performances recorded in England in 1931 and containing the best of Leschenko's Gypsy-related material, plus the odd tango and waltz. Good remastered recordings. There are several other such reissues on Oriente.

Boban Marković

The king of Serbian brass. He was born in the late 1960s in the southern town of Vladičin Han and started playing the trumpet as a child. He's played professionally since his teens but became well known with his regular Golden Trumpet awards at the Guča festival and Kusturica's film *Underground* in 1995. He's recorded several albums for X Producio in Hungary and Piranha in Germany. His son Marko is already following in his footsteps.

⊙ **Live In Belgrade**
Piranha, Germany
A brash and energetic live performance which includes two (disputed) Bregović classics: "Mesečina" and "Ederlezi".

Ferus Mustafov

Born in Štip in 1950, clarinettist and sax player Mustafov is one of the top band leaders in Macedonia and has worked for the Romani-language radio and TV in Skopje. He's in heavy demand on the wedding circuit.

⊙ **King Ferus**
GlobeStyle, UK
An excellent collection of dances and songs in catchy and seemingly unplayable rhythms. Good-time music for your Shuto Orizari-style wedding.

Palatca Band

Palatca, from the Mezőség region, are one of the best Transylvanian Gypsy bands. The line-up is two violins, two accompanying violas playing chords, and a string bass.

⊙ **Báré: Magyarpalatka**
Fono, Hungary
This is the third disc in Fono's *Final Hour* series of traditional Transylvanian music. It's the real thing, with dodgy but idiomatic intonation. There are exquisite slow dances, powerful songs and furious, fast *csárdás* dances in which the bows really lay into the battered instruments.

Shantel

It may be annoying, the way that these days the DJ becomes the artist, but Stefan Hantel (aka DJ Shantel) has done more than most to put Balkan Gypsies on the European club scene, thanks to his Frankfurt dancefloor laboratory the Bucovina Club. He was born in 1968 in Frankfurt but has drawn on his mother's Bucovina Czernowitz background for the Balkan and Gypsy sounds that characterize his music.

★ **Bucovina Club Vol. 2**
Essay Recordings, Germany
Both of Shantel's Bucovina Club collections are essential listening, featuring his own Bucovina Club Orchestra. He's at the front of a dynamic European trend bringing Balkan Gypsy music into the club scene. Shantel is also one of the producers on the equally compelling *Electric Gypsyland* (Crammed Discs), which also includes tracks produced by DJ Dolores from Brazil and Mercan Dede from Turkey.

Taraf de Haidouks

Romania's most successful Gypsy band, from Clejani near Bucharest. Clejani has been renowned as a musical centre for years and the band was first recorded by Romanian musicologist Speranţa Rădulescu before being made into international stars by the Belgians Michel Winter and Stephane Karo.

⊙ **Les Lâutari de Clejani**
Ocora, France
Great traditional repertoire recorded in 1986 which demonstrates how the Gypsy *taraf* bands are also the preservers of Romanian traditional music – in this case old ballads. Very few ethnic Romanians were performing this sort of repertoire.

★ **Dumbala Dumba**
Crammed Discs, Belgium
This 1998 recording is their most self-consciously "Gypsy" in style, with Napoléon Constantin from the bear-tamers caste adding his pots-and-pan percussion to the Taraf's incendiary fiddles and cimbalom mix.

Western Europe

⊙ **Early Cante Flamenco:**
Classic Recordings from the 1930s
Arhoolie, US
Great recordings from the seminal early flamenco artists, including Pastora Pavón, "La Nina de los Peines"; her younger brother Tomas Pavón, one of the greatest Cante Gitano performers; the flamboyant Manolo Caracol; and Manuel Vallejo, one of the first non-gypsy singers hailed as king.

⊙ **Here's Luck to a Man…: Gypsy Songs and Music from South-East England**
Musical Traditions, UK
Field recordings by Mike Yates ranging from popular Anglo-Romani songs ("All Through Mi Rakli") and Gypsy performances of traditional songs through to Derby Smith's wonderful Country and Western Gypsy protest song "Will There Be Any Travellers in Heaven?"

⊙ My Father's the King of the Gypsies: Music of English & Welsh Travellers & Gypsies
Topic, UK

Volume 11 of the extraordinary *Voice of the People* anthology of British folk music, this comprises mainly unaccompanied songs, plus melodeon and stepdance tunes. Most of the repertoire is not specifically Gypsy. And it's not easy listening.

⊙ Romany Culture in Scandinavia
Etnisk Musikklubb, Norway

Finland, Norway and Sweden aren't the first places you think of when it comes to Gypsy music. But Gypsies have been settled there for five hundred years or more. In Norway they are referred to as "Tatere" and speak a language related to Romani. Unsurprisingly, they've included some great traditional fiddlers among their number. This double CD provides a unique survey of Gypsy culture in the region.

⊙ The Rough Guide to Gypsy Swing
World Music Network, UK

This is the genre forged by Django Reinhardt, who fused his Gypsy guitar music with American swing. The CD features three tracks from Django himself, plus music from his successors including Biréli Lagrène (with the Russian classic "Black Eyes") and the New Quintette du Hot Club de France.

⊙ Rumba Flamenco
Putumayo, US

It is surprising there aren't more compilations of the very accessible Rumba Gitano repertoire. This is an engaging disc featuring veteran singer Peret, Chico and the Gypsies, Javier Ruibal, Ojos de Brujo and others, but you wonder how durable many of the others are.

⊙ Traveller's Joy: Songs of English and Scottish Travellers and Gypsies 1965–2005
English Folk Dance and Song Society, UK

This superb book/CD compilation, from the remarkable Mike Yates, is an excellent introduction to the music of British Gypsies and Travellers. The book includes words and music for fifty songs, while the CD contains twenty field recordings of Romanichals and Travellers, including the late Scottish Traveller Duncan Williamson's moving protest song "Closing Our Camping Grounds Down".

Klaus Weddig/world Network

Bratsch

Bratsch

Based in Paris, Bratsch are a five-piece new wave French roots band featuring guitar, violin, accordion, clarinet, double bass and vocals. They are not Gypsies but play postmodern Gypsy and Gypsy-style repertoire, often with Gypsy singers and musicians as guests.

⊙ Rien dans les Poches
Network, Germany

An entrancing album with guest musicians from Bulgaria and Iran, plus Hungary's Ando Drom. A couple of klezmer-style tracks underline the connections between Gypsy and Jewish repertoire, and there is also one of the best versions of the ubiquitous "Ederlezi" on record, with searing vocals from Mitsoura of Ando Drom.

El Camarón de la Isla

One of Spain's greatest flamenco singers ever, El Camarón de la Isla (born José Monje Cruz) had a voice of unrivalled passion and flair, and was unsurpassed in his interpretation and tone. He died, aged 41, in 1992 and was mourned throughout Spain, with all the national newspapers devoting their front pages to his life (troubled by drink and heroin) and career.

★ Soy Gitano
Phillips, Spain

A 1989 recording with the London Royal Philharmonic Orchestra and regular guitar accompanist Tomatito, amongst others, this begins with the dramatic and confessional "Soy Gitano" (I am a Gypsy) and ends with the song to Lorca lyrics "Nana del Caballo Grande" (Lullaby of the Big Horse). It is perhaps the most clearly "Gypsy" of Camarón's many albums.

The Gipsy Kings

Has anyone missed the Gipsy Kings? Unlikely, given their dominance at bars and cafés worldwide in the late 1980s. They are basically a Catalan rumba group, with lead singer Nicolas Reyes providing a nicely rough-edged sound accompanied by harmonies, handclaps and guitar from other members of the Reyes and Baliardo families. After many albums in which their sound was diluted with keyboards, electronics and rock drums, 2004 saw a welcome return to roots recording.

⊙ Gipsy Kings
A1, UK/Nonesuch, US

Their 1988 album featuring "Bamboleo", "Djobi Djoba" and "Bem Bem Maria" is surely a classic.

★ Roots
Sine/Sony Music, France

Roots was recorded in a farmhouse in the south of France with impassioned, grainy vocals, fizzing guitars, handclaps and stamping feet on the stone floor. Nicolas Reyes brings a distinctive growl to his vocals and there is magnificent guitar playing from Tonino Baliardo.

Kaloomé

A relatively new group featuring Gypsy musicians from the city of Perpignan, Kaloomé is led by Antoine "Tato" Garcia, formerly of Tekameli.

⊙ Sin Fronteras
Long Distance, France

Long Distance has a knack of finding new and interesting rootsy groups, but then not giving them the push they deserve. This great 2004 recording features Algerian singer

Madjid Banyagoub, violinist Caroline Bourgenot and Josép Poubill on percussion.

Ojos de Brujo

Since the early 1990s this Barcelona-based collective have been updating Rumba Gitana with urban styles including electronics and hip-hop. They won a BBC Award for World Music in 2005 and are one of the most active groups on the live circuit.

 Bari
Le Fabrica de Colores, Spain
This compelling album is a melting pot of contemporary flamenco, rumba, club culture and Gypsy attitude. Vocalist Marina "La Canillas" Abad is particularly striking.

Thierry Robin

French guitarist, oud and buzuq player Thierry Robin has consistently made interesting Gypsy-oriented recordings featuring collaborators from Rajasthan, the Middle East, North Africa and Spain. He was a founding member of Le Trio Marchand, with the Breton singer Erik Marchand, and has released ten albums, most of which feature Gypsy performers. The Rajasthani singer Gulabi Sapera has been a regular collaborator.

⊙ Gitans
Silex, France
The first of Robin's Gypsy-focused albums, this has become a classic. He brings together musicians including Gulabi Sapera, tabla player Hameed Khan and flamenco singer Paco El Lobo.

⊙ Rakhi
Naïve, France
Robin's 2002 duo album with Sapera focuses on songs from her native caste of snake charmers from Rajasthan. Deep stuff.

Phoebe Smith

Phoebe Smith (1913–2001) is one of the very few commercially recorded British Gypsies. Raised in a large Gypsy family, Phoebe spent much of her childhood travelling in southeast England before marrying Romanichal Joe Smith and settling in Woodbridge, Suffolk. She described learning songs by listening to older relatives singing around the fire, and always viewed these songs as being "made of things that really happened".

⊙ The Yellow Handkerchief
Veteran, UK
The recordings on this CD reveal an extraordinary singing style; she has a rich vocal tone, but there is always an element of abandon.

Tekameli

The name means "a message of love". Four brothers of the Espinas family from Perpignan started out singing religious repertoire before being signed up to Sony for the album *Ida y Vuelta* in 1999. Since then things have gone quiet.

⊙ Chants Religieux Gitans
Long Distance, France
This is the rootsy version of the Gipsy Kings, featuring Jérémie, Jérôme, Moise and Salomon Espinas in Gypsy Catholic repertoire. Gritty voices, guitars and handclaps.

PLAYLIST
Gypsy Music

1 PUNDELA Musafir from *Dhola Maru*
A classic Rajasthani song that's also been recorded by Ando Drom and by Gulabi Sapera and Thierry Robin.

2 SUITE OF DAMALI PIECES Mohammad Ramazan from *The Mystic Fiddle of the Proto-Gypsies*
Marvellous raw trance music on the sorud fiddle.

3 KIREMIT BACALARI Selim Sesler from *The Road to Keşan*
Great wedding dance piece from the Turkish Gypsy communities of Thrace.

4 SZELEM, SZELEM Esma Redžepova from *Road of the Gypsies*
Esma gives one of her most passionate performances of the Gypsy anthem, recorded live for WDR in 1989. The whole tragedy of a people is here.

5 MESEČINA Boban Marković from *Live in Belgrade*
"Moonlight", the hit song from *Underground* and a tune you're sure to hear at every Serbian wedding, in an exuberant version by the country's *boyar* of brass.

6 EDERLEZI Vaska Jankovska from *Road of the Gypsies*
The strange, childlike voice of Vaska Jankovska sings the song that has become synonymous with Balkan Gypsy music thanks to the film *Time of the Gypsies*.

7 CIGANKA MEDLEY Shantel from *Bucovina Club Vol. 2*
Shantel's own Bucovina Club Orchestra with female vocalist Vesna Petkovic. Ciganka means "Gypsy girl" – her eyes shine bright and she dances till dawn. With crazy brass outbursts, this lives up to the stereotypes.

8 TE ME PIJAV LAČHES ROSNES Věra Bílá from *Kale Kaloré*
This song's universal theme – I drink to forget unhappy love – is given an extraordinary deep Gypsy sensibility as Bílá slides mournfully between the notes.

9 AVEN, AVEN The Gipsy Kings from *Roots*
The grainy lead vocals of Nicolas Reyes are unmistakable and the song is one of the catchiest from their unplugged album of 2004.

10 AGNI SHA KSHI Thierry Robin and Gulabi Sapera from *Rakhi*
A sensitive guitar groove from "Titi" Robin accompanies this timeless Rajasthani song.

Hungary

magyar magic

Parno Graszt
Simon Broughton

For a country of ten million people, Hungary has a strong musical profile – two or three world-class composers, the extraordinary "dancehouse" phenomenon which finds traditional music flourishing in the capital and a dynamic Gypsy scene. It all comes down to a statement of identity about who the Hungarians are in the patchwork of Eastern Europe. Simon Broughton tells the story.

The fiddler strikes his bow on the string with enough energy to make sparks fly, a musical wizard dispensing his Magyar magic. An accompanying violin and double bass spring into action, sawing away as the dancer begins his routine of high leaps, shoe slapping and intricate footwork. The music is lithe, earthy and full of bite. The sound and the heady atmosphere of red wine and plum brandy makes it easy to ignore the air brick and brieze block walls, and you feel you're somewhere deep in rural Hungary. In fact, the location is one of several dancehouse (*táncház*) clubs dotted around Budapest, and you'd be hard pushed to find traditional music of this quality anywhere in the countryside.

Despite its globalized lifestyle, Budapest's vibrant traditional music scene reinforces a strong national identity. With origins in Siberia, the **Magyars**, as the Hungarians call themselves, are ethnically distinct from the Slavs and other nationalities that surround them, and their musical mother tongue is something sacrosanct. Though, like the people, the music is now thoroughly "Europeanized", it remains highly distinctive. In very large part, this is down to the Hungarian language, which is invariably stressed on the first syllable, lending a strongly accented dactylic rhythm to the music. Its infectious sound has been surprisingly influential on neighbouring countries (thanks perhaps to the common Austro-Hungarian history) and it's not uncommon to hear Hungarian-sounding tunes in Romania, Slovakia and southern Poland.

In Transylvania (Romania) and southern Slovakia there are also large Hungarian minorities where village music is still a living tradition – far more so than in Hungary itself (see Romania article p.324). In these areas the music as well as the mother tongue are crucially important in maintaining that all-important sense of identity. It's the music of Transylvania first and foremost that fuels the Budapest táncház scene and village musicians from the region are regularly brought over to play.

Bartók, Kodály and Roots East

Béla Vikár started collecting Hungarian folk music as early as 1895 with an Edison phonograph machine, so the composers **Béla Bartók** and **Zoltán Kodály** were not the first to systematically investigate the peasant music of Hungary. But they were the most famous and influential. On their collecting trips in the first decade of the twentieth century, they revealed the "real" Hungarian folk music – as opposed to the popular salon tunes played by Gypsy orchestras that were taken to be folk music until then. Both men were fine ethnographers as well as composers, and by using folk material in their own work they not only found their individual voices but brought the folk music to the attention of an international audience. They were also responsible for recognising the Asiatic roots of Hungarian music.

Kodály's interest was in Hungarian music and the creation of a truly national style. Bartók's concerns were more international, rooted in the peasant music of all the nationalities of Eastern Europe and beyond. By the time the First World War brought his expeditions in Eastern Europe to an end, he had collected over 3500 Romanian tunes, 3000 Slovak, 2721 Hungarian, plus Ruthenian, Serbian and Bulgarian pieces.

What Bartók and Kodály discovered on their expeditions to remote Hungarian villages was a music that was earthy, fresh and hitherto unknown. More than that, it was distinctly Hungarian and in its oldest layers stretched back to the Magyars' roots on the fringes of Europe and beyond. Exactly where the Hungarians originated is still debated; but they are not of Indo-European stock like most Europeans, but belong – with the Finns and Estonians – to the Finno-Ugrian linguistic group, whose ancestors lived over 4000 years ago in the Ural region and southwest Siberia.

Much research has been done to see if there are musical connections between the Hungarians and Finns but virtually none have been found; not surprising, perhaps, as the tribes are thought to have split around 4000 years ago. Kodály, however, found a link between the oldest Hungarian songs, with their pentatonic (five-note) tunes and descending pattern, and songs of the Mari people,

Hungarotron

Béla Bartók with his cylinder recorder in 1908

a Finno-Ugrian group who still live close to the ancestral home around the Volga and Kama rivers in Russia. Kodály came up with a substantial number of Hungarian tunes that had direct equivalents in these eastern territories: musical fossils apparently dating back to a shared past 2500 years old. "Time may have wiped away the eastern features from the face of the Magyar community", he concluded "but in the depths of its soul, where the springs of music lie, there still lives an element of the original east, which links it with peoples whose language it has long ceased to understand, and who are today so different in mind and spirit."

"New Style" and Gypsy Bands

The Hungarians' musical history evolved as they settled in the Carpathian basin (around AD 895–902), adopted Christianity (under the canonized King Stephen who ruled from 1000 to 1038) and began to come under the influence of European culture, before Suleyman the Magnificent put a stop to that in 1526 and Hungary endured one hundred and fifty years of Turkish rule. But most of the Hungarian music familiar today has its roots in the eighteenth century when the country rebuilt itself as part of the **Hapsburg Empire**. The close contact with central European culture brought "new style" music with a regular metric structure for dancing and marching instead of the free speech rhythms of the old style.

Solo bagpipers used to play these tunes for village dances but they were gradually replaced by the new **Gypsy orchestras**, and the medieval-style drone accompaniment gave way to the central European harmony of the string bands. Just as bagpipes mean Scotland, so Gypsy bands mean Hungary in the popular imagination. When nationalist composers like Liszt composed their *Hungarian Dances* and *Rhapsodies* in the latter part of the nineteenth century they took as their models the Magyar Nota music of the urban Gypsy orchestras much as you can hear it in Budapest restaurants today. Most of this repertoire, often showy and sickly sweet, was composed in the nineteenth century.

Following Bartók's lead, folklorists tend to dismiss this urban Gypsy style in favour of authentic "peasant music". Yet the music the Gypsies play is no less Hungarian, and it has more in common with peasant music than folklorists may admit. Hungarian folk song was often an influence on popular songs, and even in the remotest parts of the country urban songs have become part of the oral tradition and serve the function of folk songs. In the Transylvanian village of Szék you can still hear a *csárdás*, which pops up in Brahms' *Hungarian Dances*, often cited as prime examples of Gypsy-style fakery.

Gypsies (or more correctly Roma) were first recorded in Hungary in the fourteenth century, and the country's Gypsy musicians became famous from the eighteenth century on. "The Hungarian has a musical score which can compete with that of any nation … This score lives and travels in the form of the Hungarian Gypsy", wrote one observer in 1858. Most of the early Gypsy bands seem to have been located in western Hungary and were often invited to perform at aristocratic celebrations.

In addition to society gigs, the Gypsies also performed at recruiting ceremonies where young lads were enticed into the army with **verbunkos** music (from *werbung* – the German word meaning "recruit"). The Hapsburgs only introduced universal conscription in 1868, so before that the men were lured with dancing, music and the promise of a carefree life. Verbunkos music is strongly rhythmic, consisting of a slow dance followed by a fast one. The steps were developed from the showy men's dances of the village. Probably the most famous verbunkos tune is the "Rákóczi Song", which later evolved into the "Rákóczi March" – featured in compositions by Berlioz and Liszt.

The Hungarians, always searching for a musical identity, found it in the verbunkos music and it typified the Hungarians abroad. A German officer saw the dance in 1792: "It expresses the character of the nation in an extraordinary way. The true Hungarian dances have to begin really slowly and then continue faster. They are much more becoming to a serious moustached face than to a young lad no matter what forced capers they do. The whole art of the dancer is to be seen in the artistic movement of his legs and the rhythmic clicking of his spurs." The slow and fast dances of verbunkos music have been seen as the two contrasting aspects of the Hungarian character and in the nineteenth century, Liszt felt unequivocally that the Gypsies were Hungary's national musicians and verbunkos was the inspiration for his *Hungarian Rhapsodies*.

Amongst the most celebrated Gypsy performers of the "golden age" were the female *primás* (lead violinist) **Czinka Panna** (1711–72) and Gypsy musicians from the town of Galánta – both celebrated in pieces by Kodály. The most famous Gypsy band leader was **János Bihari**, born in

1764 and known as the Napoleon of the fiddle! "Like drops of some fiery spirit essence, the notes of this magic violin came to our ears", wrote Liszt. Bihari's band usually consisted of four strings plus a *cimbalom*, the hammered dulcimer so common in Gypsy bands.

The most celebrated fiddlers now playing in this style come from the **Lakatos family** – notably Sándor Lakatos and his nephew, the young Roby Lakatos – said to be direct descendants of Bihari himself. Their repertoire is essentially the light classical music of Liszt, Brahms and Monti's Csárdás played with a showy verve and abandon. There is lots of exaggerated rubato and up-front virtuosity. More slickness than soul, but technically very impressive.

Sadly these days in Hungary it is very hard to find real village music in the way Bartók and Kodály did. The music was already disappearing in the early years of the twentieth-century although it persisted up to the 1960s and beyond. Today, the best areas to try – at traditional weddings and similar affairs – are **Szabolcs-Szatmár** county, out on a limb in the northeast, and **southwest Transdanubia** in the south of the country bordering Croatia. Fonó Records, who have released the much-acclaimed *Final Hour* series of Transyl-vanian bands have recent recordings of various Hungarian village bands waiting for release.

A more fixed event, with a guarantee of music-making, is **Busójárás Carnival in Mohács** at the beginning of March. The music played in Mohács is basically Serbian and Croatian. The celebrated **Bogyiszló orchestra** was until recently the best in the region but is, alas, no longer active.

There's also a rich tradition of **Serbian music** from the communities in Szentendre and Pomaz north of Budapest where the excellent group **Vujicsics** is based.

Gypsy Folk

So if the music played by Hungary's ubiquitous Gypsy bands is Hungarian, what's the Gypsy music? Oddly enough, considering the number of Gypsy instrumentalists, the music of the Roma themselves hardly uses instruments at all. Most of the Romungro Gypsy musicians who play in the urban bands don't actually live amongst the (poorer) Gypsy communities and generally play for non-Gypsy audiences. Their music is professionally composed and urban in style. But there's a contrasting style of **rural Gypsy music** played by the Vlach (or Olah) Gypsies, horse-traders

Romano Drom

Romano Drom (Gypsy Road) is the hottest and coolest of the Gypsy bands in Hungary right now – and they sing only in Romani. "I'm incapable of writing a song in Hungarian, because I think in Romani" says their leader Antal "Anti" Kovács. "We decided early on just to sing in Romani because the language has to survive."

The band was started by **Antal "Gojma" Kovács** and his son **"Anti"** who both split from the group Ando Drom in the late 1990s. Half the band were Romungro Gypsies, while Gojma and Anti are Olah Gypsies and there was a divergence of opinion. "We were the ones that brought the music – traditional songs from our family – but we were kept in the background. They wanted to push the instrumentals and change the singing style. But the most beautiful thing in our culture is the singing style!" Gojma certainly had a distinctive, growly vocal style which gave a fantastic raw edge to the sound of Ando Drom and Romano Drom. Sadly, he died in 2005. The basic Romano Drom sound is the vocals, guitars and water pot, but they also have guest instrumentalists on accordion, sax and so on.

"Much of our music comes from songs sung in the family", explains Anti. "The song Phari Mamo, the title song on the *Ando Drom* CD, comes from the grandmother of my mother in Transylvania and we've sung it in the family for years. It's a song of the Tsollar Gypsies who were cloth and carpet sellers. My father Gojma recorded it first in a field recording, then we arranged it with Ando Drom and then Romano Drom too."

In the 1980s there were many Gypsy groups and folk festivals in Hungary and songs were learned and exchanged at events. Now the Gypsy music scene in Budapest tends to be in clubs rather than concert halls, with Romano Drom a pioneer of the Gypsy club scene. For live club shows they've stripped the band down to Anti (voice and guitar), percussion, the excellent female vocalist **Beáta Palya** and two guys on electronics. And in 2003, one of their tracks (on the *Romano Trip* remix album) was used for a widely-shown anti-racist advert and as a jingle by Gypsy radio stations. "A real 'live' remix. It's very Gypsy!" adds Anti.

and travelling salesmen, who came to Hungary from Romania in the nineteenth century when slavery was abolished. In recent years, their music has proved the most dynamic on the Hungarian music scene.

Traditionally, this rural Gypsy music had no swooning violins, but was accompanied by rhythmic grunts, the tapping of domestic utensils like spoons and water cans and imitations of instruments in a "doobie-doobie-doobie" sort of way called "oral-bassing". It oscillates between tragic songs about the hardships of Gypsy life and wild, upbeat numbers throwing all cares to the wind. The music was not intended for others and was only performed at Roma gatherings or celebrations until professional bands appeared in the 1970s. **Parno Graszt** (Romani for White Horse) is a real village band from Paszab in northeast Hungary that has made excellent recordings and played a few festivals. Led by guitarist and *tambura* player József Olah, they combine a rough authenticity with a musical professionalism that makes them quite unique.

Kalyi Jag (Romani for Black Fire) was the first of the Hungarian Roma groups to present their music on stage in 1978. They added guitars and other instruments to the powerful vocals of Gusztáv Varga and József Balogh and are still going strong. They've been followed by bands like **Ando Drom** (On the Road), with the extraordinary singer Mitsoura who's now gone solo, and **Rományi Rotá** (Gypsy Wheel) who have a regular tánchéz in Budapest. There are often concerts by these bands in the atmospheric Roma Parlament in the heart of Pest's Gypsy neighbourhood in the eighth district.

The most interesting group of late is **Romano Drom** (see box opposite), formed around the father and son Antal "Gojma" Kovács and Antal "Anti" Kovács Jr. Their basic vocal, percussion and guitars line-up is augmented by guest musicians on saxophone, accordion and violin and recently the female singer Matild Dobi. They're also involved in the Gypsy club scene, a new feature of Budapest nightlife. Romano Drom's music was remixed by various producers and DJs on the *Romano Trip* album. The Roma rap scene has also taken off in recent years, pioneered by **Fekete Vonat** (Black Train). Their name comes from the train (no longer running) which took migrant Gypsy workers from the deprived northeast to jobs in Budapest. (See the chapter on Gypsy Music, p.196, for the wider context of Roma music in Eastern Europe.)

The Tánchéz

The Hungarian capital Budapest is one of the best places in Europe to hear really good folk music, and the place to go is a **tánchéz** – literally a "dance house" named after traditional village dancing places (see box below). The atmosphere at a tánchéz is a cross between a barn dance and a folk club but without the self-conscious folksiness of its Western counterparts. The dress may be blue jeans and trainers with the odd Transylvanian jacket or skirt, but for the most part the clientele – teachers, doctors, lawyers – know the music and can dance to it well. Once again this is a statement of identity. Blue jeans are the same the world over, but this music and dance comes with a Hungarian designer label.

The tánchéz movement started in the 1970s as a reaction to the regimented folklore of the state ensembles. Following in the footsteps of Bartók and Kodály, musicians like **Ferenc Sebő** and **Béla Halmos** collected music from the villages, learned it and brought it back to Budapest. But whereas Bartók and Kodály had been interested mainly in songs, this new generation was interested in the instrumental music and traditional dances – **György Martin** and **Sándor Tímár** were the principal dance researchers. The idea was to bring the music back to the grassroots rather than present it on

Tánchéz in Budapest

Budapest has a great variety of dancehouse clubs, including some for Greek, Balkan and Irish music. But it's Hungarian and Transylvanian music that's at the heart of the scene. The venues are usually ugly 1970s style cultural centres, but there's always a bar and snacks are usually available. There is often dance instruction early in the evening before the tánchéz really gets underway, usually from around 8pm to midnight. Entrance fees are minimal. The **Tánchéztalálkozó** (Meeting of the Dance Houses) is the annual get together in the Budapest Körcsarnok in late March which gives an unrivalled overview of the current talent. Check *www.tanchaz.hu* for this and the regular Budapest dancehouse programmes.

Márta Sebestyén and Muzsikás

"People think that folk music is for old situations", says Márta Sebestyén. "I think that's rubbish because the basic human and emotional situations are still the same. My duty is to bring this music closer to people in an emotional way. You can't say you have to respect this music of your ancestors – people shit on that. But if it touches the heart it will be remembered forever." Márta's organic, natural voice has an uncanny power to captivate – her performance of "Szerelem, Szerelem", an old Transylvanian love song, entranced the fictional Hungarian count played by Ralph Fiennes in *The English Patient*, but also audiences across the globe. In Hungary she's received many awards, she dined with the Blairs at number 10, and counts Prince Charles amongst her admirers. But actually it's in communication with ordinary people, both in learning the songs and transmitting them, that her real skill lies. "I love to hear these old ladies sing", she explains. "Their voices are like delicate lace. They put their lives into their songs and I can remember every nuance, every ornamentation in the voice."

Márta was born into a musical environment. Her mother was an energetic musical teacher and pupil of **Zoltán Kodály**. According to her, Márta could sing before she could talk. At school she won folk singing competitions every year and in the early 1970s got involved with the "dancehouse" movement that was just taking off. Márta performed with **Ferenc Sebő** and **Béla Halmos**, two of the tánczház pioneers, and for many years sang with Muzsikás, Hungary's leading group on the international circuit. Márta's voice cutting through the swirling violins and sawing bass of traditional Transylvanian repertoire is hard to beat, although now she's exploring new directions.

Music and dance are inseparable. "If you don't know the feeling of the dance you can't make a good accompaniment for the dancers", says Muzsikás' bass player Daniel Hamar. "You have to know the music from the inside." It certainly makes their music feel natural and they keep close contact with the traditional sources, where sometimes the music isn't appreciated enough. In the Transylvanian village of Szászcsávás (Ceuas), Muzsikás decided to help.

"The Szászcsávás band has played in Europe and America and had big success", explains Hamar. "Everybody knew this, except the local people who just got resentful when their Gypsy musicians come home with more spending money. So we decided to make a concert there with technical quality as good as anywhere else in the world. We took a top-quality PA, modern lights and printed full-colour posters. We were the stars, of course, because they'd seen us on television. But after half an hour I said to the audience that we'd like to invite on stage some of the best musicians we've ever heard. And we invited the local musicians to play. It was the first time the village had seen their local musicians as stars and the reaction was fantastic."

Since their *Bartók Album* of 1999, Muzsikás have been introducing traditional music to classical music audiences and vice versa. "Some of Bartók's pieces include direct quotations of folk melodies", says Hamar. "But the spirit of folk music is there even in his most abstract pieces. For example, in the String Quartets there are no

stage and, despite the urban setting, keep it closer to its original form.

Even though it had virtually no official support, the movement grew from strength to strength. For many years it also had a political dimension. The wellspring of Hungarian tánczház music was in neighbouring Romania where the Hungarian minority of **Transylvania** has kept a living folk tradition to this day (see Romania article, p.324). Tánczház musicians often travelled there in very difficult circumstances to collect music and dances. Since the fall of Communism there's been a regular flow of great Transylvanian village performers to the tánczház of Budapest bringing a welcome rough-edged note of authenticity.

Tánczház music falls into two types. One is music from Hungary proper which, with less of a living tradition, has usually been learned from archive recordings or written collections and arranged by the groups in the manner of folk bands all over Europe. But the most popular music comes directly from the village tradition and that means Transylvania (or occasionally the Hungarian communities in Slovakia). The basic **instrumental line-up** is a lead fiddle, an accompanying violin (*kontra*) playing chords and a bowed bass – there's often a cimbalom included as well. If at first the tunes all sound similar, keep listening. The better you know this music the more rich and varied it becomes. In the right hands it has a beauty unrivalled in Europe.

Tánczház dances are played in sets, generally moving from slower tempos to fast – beginning perhaps with a verbunkos or *Lad's Dance*, giving the chance for the men to show off, and ending with a fast and furious *csárdás*. It's the *prímás*, the first violinist of the band, who keeps an eye on the

actual folk melodies, but we can feel their emotions. Bartók himself said that it was the expressiveness and feeling inherent in traditional music that inspired him to use it."

On the *Bartók Album* Muzsikás worked with the classically-trained violinist **Alexander Balanescu** and on tour in the US with the **Takács Quartet**. Approaching Bartók after thirty years of playing traditional music gives them a new approach and both Balanescu and Takács say they play differently since their collaborations with Muzsikás. "When we did our concert with the Takács Quartet in Carnegie Hall all eight of us felt that it was one music we were creating together", says Hamar. "It was like the traditional music created an energy which the string quartet took over. We interleaved our music between the movements of the 4th Quartet which had to be done very carefully to maintain the symmetry of the piece. But it was truly something special and we felt that if Béla Bartók had been able to hear it he'd have been very happy. At the end of his life he lived just a couple of blocks from Carnegie Hall."

"I respect Béla Bartók enormously", continues Hamar, "but in one thing he was not right. In 1928 he said that it was the last moment and that within a few years traditional music would die out. But in fact it has proved to be much stronger. The old musicians die and suddenly there's a young player who takes over and plays in exactly the same way. It's a fantastic thing. Whether it will still be there in 25 years I don't know, but I hope this music can find its new function in this new life. We have given it a chance because we can prove that this music is not only acceptable at a wedding in Transylvania, but in Carnegie Hall or a club in Budapest."

Béla Kása

Márta Sebestyén and Muzsikás

dancers and judges when to make the move and tempo change into the next dance. When it's done well it's thrilling.

The **csárdás** is the most famous Hungarian dance tune and you won't spend five minutes at a Budapest táncház (or a Transylvanian wedding) without hearing one. They can be fast or slow, "whirling", "quivering" or "leaping" – and there are all sorts of regional variations. All of them are couple dances which can reach great virtuosity, but at their most basic it's two steps left, two steps right followed by a turn. The music has a regular four-square rhythm with a distinctive spring.

Internationally, the best-known names in Hungarian music emerged from the táncház scene: **Márta Sebestyén** (see box), a truly remarkable singer (and not just of Hungarian music) and **Muzsikás**, one of the first of the dancehouse groups. As a band they have succeeded in keeping the fine balance between a professional approach on stage and the raw gutsy sound of the village. They have explored the links between Kodály and Bartók's music and the authentic village tradition and they remain the leading ambassadors of traditional Hungarian folk music.

Other top musicians to watch out for include fiddler **Csaba Ökrös** and his ensemble, and the **Tükrös**, **Téka** and **Kalamajka** groups who specialize in Hungarian and Transylvanian repertoire. Other notable singers are **Kati Szvorák, Beáta Palya** and **András Berecz**. Muzsikás have also introduced the Moldavian singer **Mária Petrás**.

The virtuoso Gypsy cimbalom player **Kálmán Balogh** frequently collaborates with many of these musicians and also draws on wider influ-

Kálmán Balogh and the Gypsy Cimbalom Band

ences from Balkan, Latin and American music. **Makám**, with a wide variety of eastern European and "world" instruments, are a stimulating ensemble pushing the music in a classical, chamber-style direction with the excellent singer Irén Lovász.

Clarinettist, saxophonist and cimbalom player **Mihály Dresch** pursues a much more experimental line in a jazz/folk quartet with violin, bass and percussion which probably doesn't do a lot for the dancers in the táncház, but appeals to another clientele. The young virtuoso violinist **Félix Lajkó** (a Hungarian from Subotica in Serbia) is classically trained, but with his group Zenekara plays rhythmic

and infectious concert music drawing on Hungarian, Balkan and Middle-Eastern traditions. Great playing and definitely a name to watch out for.

One of the most exciting groups in Hungary specializes in fusing Serbian and Croatian tambura music. **Vujicsics** is based just north of Budapest amongst the south Slav communities in Szentendre and Pomaz. And, as Hungary has the largest Jewish community in Eastern Europe, it's no surprise that there are fine *klezmer* groups – the **Budapest Klezmer Band** and notably **Di Naye Kapelye** who really marry the Jewish and the táncház tradition to explore little-known rural repertoire.

The Final Hour Recordings

Coined from a phrase of Bartók's, the ambitious **Utolsó Óra** (Final Hour) project aims to record the best traditional bands before they inevitably disappear. Village bands from Transylvania have been invited to Budapest for a week where academic study of the music is done and recordings are made. The project is supported by the Hungarian Academy of Sciences, the Ethnographic Museum and the Soros Foundation amongst others. The twenty CDs released so far, on the Fonó label, have all been of Transylvanian bands, but recordings have already been made of village bands in Hungary. The **Új Pátria** (New Patria) series, named after the historic Patria recordings made by Bartók, Kodály and others in the 1930s, is projected to be 45 CDs. Selected Final Hour CDs of Transylvanian bands are included in the Romania discography.

A lot of Hungarian recordings feature music from Transylvania (Romania) – played by táncház ensembles as well as real village bands. Some of the most important táncház groups playing Transylvanian repertoire are included below, while the village bands will be found in the Romanian discography (p.333).

⊙ Folk Music of the Hungarians
Fonó, Hungary
Published with Lajos Vargyas' book of the same title, this ten CD collection is the most comprehensive survey available. Recordings come from the Hungarian Academy of Sciences and the Museum of Ethnography in Budapest with the songs and music arranged scientifically into tune types.

⊙ Hungarian Instrumental Folk Music
Hungaroton, Hungary
A good two-CD set covering the typical sounds of Hungarian folk music from cow bells and horns, through bagpipes, hurdy-gurdy and zithers to various sizes of Gypsy band.

⊙ Hungary – The Last Passage
Ocora, France
An excellent survey of traditional music from Hungary itself and Transylvania played by some old-time musicians and the best táncház groups.

⊙ Listen, My Hungarians – A Survey of Hungarian Folk Music
Hungaroton, Hungary
A two-CD set of archival recordings from the five geographical areas from Transdanubia to Gyimes and Moldavia.

⊙ Musiques de Transylvania
Fonti Musicali, Belgium
One of the best introductions to Transylvanian music featuring the best musicians from Budapest's táncház scene.

★ Rough Guide to Hungarian Music
World Music Network, UK
The best single-disc introduction to the Hungarian roots music scene, compiled by the author of this chapter.

Gypsy Bands

⊙ Hungarian Folk Music from Szatmár Region
Hungaroton, Hungary
A great CD of four traditional Gypsy bands from villages in the northeast of the country playing Hungarian dance music plus some Jewish repertoire. Terrific stuff.

⊙ Rom Sam Ame!
Fonti Musicali, Belgium
A specialized, but excellent survey of authentic Gypsy songs from six towns in central and eastern Hungary – vocals, in Hungarian and Romani, with accompanying spoons and struck pots and tables.

⊙ The Rough Guide to Hungarian Gypsy Music
World Music Network, UK
A good selection that covers the bases including Romano Drom, Kalyi Jag, Parno Graszt, Kálmán Balogh and others.

Ando Drom

Ando Drom have been around since the early 1980s and are one of the leading groups performing the rural Gypsy style on stage.

★ Phari Mamo
World Network, Germany
Ando Drom in their late 1990s heyday with the swarthy vocals of Mónika "Mitsou" Juhász Miczura. There is soul and melancholy here with idiomatic instrumental contributions on violin and accordion from the French group Bratsch.

Kálmán Balogh

Balogh, from a family of Gypsy musicians, is Hungary's leading cimbalom player. As well as having his own band he is regularly pulled in to play with Budapest's best groups.

⊙ Live in Germany
Traditional Crossroads, US
With his Gypsy Cimbalom Band, this is a great showcase of the art of cimbalom playing.

Kalyi Jag

With musicians hailing from the northeast of the country, Kalyi Jag was the first of the groups to put rural Gypsy sounds on stage. Led by singer and guitarist Gusztáv Varga.

⊙ Gypsy Folk Songs from Hungary
Hungaroton, Hungary
Originally recorded in 1989, this collection is catchy and representative – traditional songs given the "Black Fire" treatment with the guitar and mandolin of József Balogh. There's another good Hungaroton CD called *I Have Still a Long Way to Go*. Translations of the lyrics included with both albums.

Roby Lakatos

Born in 1965, Roby is one of the younger members of the famous Lakatos dynasty of Gypsy musicians. He learned in the family tradition as well as at the Budapest Music Academy. He's lived in Belgium since 1985 where he's expanded his style to include jazz, popular classics and Stephane Grapelli-style violin.

⊙ Lakatos
Deutsche Grammophon, Germany
The violin swoops and sighs with the characteristic rippling of cimbalom and strings. We get "The Lark", a Brahms Hungarian Dance and Khachaturian's "Sabre Dance" which seems to have become a popular Gypsy standard.

Tcha Limberger

Limberger is actually Belgian, but this blind fiddler and singer has learned Hungarian and learned the Magyar Nota (Hungarian song) style from some of the best Hungarian players. Magyar Nota isn't very fashionable these days, but Limberger makes it sound fresh, exciting and, of course, romantic.

⊙ Bura Termett Ido
Lejazzetal, UK
Probably the best disc of Magyar Nota there is. Recorded live with a band of Hungarian players on violin, clarinet, cimbalom and bass.

Parno Graszt

A real village Vlach Gypsy band from Paszab near Nyiregyháza in northeast Hungary.

⊙ Rávágok a zongorára
Fonó, Hungary
Their debut CD from 2002, featuring fiercely catchy tunes from a group who have taken care of the local Gypsy repertoire. Voices, guitars, tanbura and the usual pots and pans plus excellent guest musicians on viola and reedy *taragot*.

Romano Drom

In the late 1990s father Antal "Gojma" Kovács and Antal "Anti" Kovács left the group Ando Drom to set up Romano drom. They specialize in the Oláh music of the Lovár and Tsollár Gypsies and are probably the leading Gypsy band on the scene today. Sadly, Gojma died of cancer in 2005 aged 51.

⊙ Ando Foro
Daqui, France
The first and gutsier of the band's international releases, although both can be recommended.

⊙ Romano Trip
Gypsyhouse Entertainment, Hungary
Romano Drom team up with various DJs and re-mixers to take their music to the club scene.

Ferenc Sánta and his Gypsy Band

Sánta trained at the Music Academy in Budapest and has led a Budapest Gypsy Orchestra since the 1970s.

⊙ Csárdás: Hungarian Gypsy Music
Naxos, Hong Kong
While Sánta isn't amongst the best-known of Gypsy bandleaders, this budget Naxos collection includes many of the favourites of the Budapest Gypsy orchestras like Monti's Csárdás and the popular encore, "The Lark". Typical of its type.

Szilvási Gipsy Folk Band

An interesting band, led by István Szilvási, that have brought together the urban and rural styles of Gypsy music.

⊙ If I Catch the Devil...
Fonó, Hungary
A compelling CD released in 2001 with the fiddle of Ernő Oláh and Jenő Setét.

Táncház and other Groups

Ghymes

An excellent five-piece band led by Tamás Szarka and based in Slovakia. Growing out of the tánchház movement, Ghymes has become more of a folk rock outfit.

⊙ Rege
Fonó, Hungary
This from 1999 and their earlier *Üzenet* (Message) are their best albums with a good mixture of traditionally based and experimental material.

Béla Halmos

Singer and violinist Béla Halmos was one of the leading figures in the early days of the tánchház movement and remains so today.

⊙ Az a szép piros hajnal
Hungaroton, Hungary
A strong collection of Transylvanian music – mainly from the central region of Mezőség. Joining Halmos are some of the best names on the Hungarian music scene, singers Márta Sebestyén and András Berecz and flautist Zoltán Juhász.

Makám

Formed in 1984, Makám specialize in a chamber-style music based on traditional Hungarian and Balkan sources.

⊙ Skanzen
Fonó, Hungary
Featuring the voice of Irén Lovász, this album composed by Zoltán Krulik takes Hungarian roots music into new areas with some excellent instrumental playing.

Mitsoura

Striking Gypsy vocalist who caught attention in the group Ando Drom (when she was known as Mitsou), but has since gone solo.

⊙ Mitsoura
Mitsoura, Hungary
Mainly traditional material, but in contemporary, electronic arrangements with Indian percussion some good instrumentalists like Kálmán Balogh on cimbalom.

Muzsikás

Now into their fourth decade, Muzsikás are Hungary's leading tánchház group featuring original members Mihály Sipos (lead violin), Péter Éri (contra, tambura, etc) and Dániel Hamar (bass). They have researched and performed Jewish tunes of Transylvania as well as music from western Hungary to the eastern outpost of Gyimes.

⊙ Morning Star
Hannibal/Ryko, UK
All of Muzsikás's albums come highly recommended, but this 1997 disc more than any other has the freshness and rough-edged feel of the village. Great songs too from Márta Sebestyén.

★ The Bartók Album
Hannibal/Ryko, UK
A beautifully produced album from 1999 in which the music that inspired Bartók is combined with his cylinder recordings and compositions for two violins, played by Mihály Sipos and Alexander Balanescu.

Ökrös Ensemble

Csaba Ökrös is a tremendous fiddler and his traditional ensemble is one of the best – working regularly with some of Transylvania's best village musicians in concert and on record. They've recorded a number of excellent CDs of Transylvanian music on small labels.

☉ Transylvanian Portraits
Koch World, US

The most widely available of the Ökrös discs with a beautiful selection of traditional Hungarian music from different regions of Transylvania. Csaba Ökrös demonstrates his extraordinary violin technique in the traditional shepherd who's lost his sheep piece and Márta Sebestyén sings.

Márta Sebestyén

Hungary's most celebrated female vocalist – bringing her distinctive qualities to the soundtrack of *The English Patient*, the popular concoctions of Deep Forest and a Hungarian rock musical amongst other things. A strong and searing voice at its best in traditional Hungarian and Transylvania repertoire.

☉ Dúdoltam Én – Márta Sebestyén Sings
Hungaroton, Hungary

A 1988 album of Hungarian and Transylvanian music with Muzsikás – featuring a beautiful "morning song" from Kalotaszeg, Transylvania, one of her specialities. Also released worldwide by Hannibal as Márta Sebestyén.

☉ The Best of Márta Sebestyén
Hannibal, UK

A compilation designed to cash in on the *English Patient* effect, but an excellent collection of Márta's work, including songs in Hindi, English and Serbo-Croat as well as Hungarian.

☉ I Can See the Gates of Heaven
Viva la Musica, Hungary

A 2008 release in a new formation with Balázs Szokolay Dongó, a multi-instrumentalist on wind instruments, and Mátyás Bolya on lutes. A transparent recording of songs sacred and secular from different regions.

Tükrös Zenekar

Formed in the late 1980s, Tükrös is one of the top táncház groups with Atilla Halmos and Gergely Koncz on violins. They also organize a regular summer music camp.

★ Szatmári Népzene
Folk Europa, Hungary

A marvellous disc of music learnt from Gypsy musicians in the Szatmár region in the northeast. Evidence, if it were needed, of the fruitful relationship between táncház groups and village musicians.

Vujicsics

One of the best groups anywhere playing Serbian and Croatian music – a six-piece ensemble with guitars, tamburas and bass from the South Slav communities north of Budapest.

☉ Southern Slav Folk Music
Hungaroton, Hungary

Their debut recording from 1981 with fast and furious *kolos* and other dance tunes. Vocals from Márta Sebestyén and others. Hannibal's *Vujicsics* from 1988 is also marvellous if you can find it.

PLAYLIST
Hungary

1 SZERELEM, SZERELEM – THE ENGLISH PATIENT SONG Márta Sebestyén from *The Best of Márta Sebestyén*
A Transylvanian love song Márta learned from cantor and fiddler Márton Maneszes in the Transylvanian village of Magyarszovát.

2 NUMA ROMANES Fekete Vonat from *The Rough Guide to Hungarian Music*
Roma rap with voices imitating instruments, turntable scratching and rattling water pot.

3 PÁVA Irén Lovász with László Hortobágyi from *The Rough Guide to Hungarian Music*
Classic Hungarian folk song in completely new clothes with *gamelan*-style instrumentation.

4 DETA DEVLA Romano Drom from *Romano Trip*
Emil Biliarski gives one of Romano Drom's traditional songs the remix treatment.

5 HAJNALI NÓTA (MORNING SONG) Márta Sebestyén and Muzsikás from *Dúdoltam Én*
Achingly beautiful slow song with keening fiddle from the Kalotaszeg region of Transylvania.

6 SHEPHERD'S SONG Csaba Ökrös from *Transylvanian Portraits*
A shepherd laments the loss and celebrates the rediscovery of his sheep. A great fiddlers' display piece.

7 RÁVÁGOK A ZONGORÁRA Parno Graszt from *Rávágok a zongorára*
A totally infectious tune from a real village Gypsy band from the northeast.

8 SAMU MIHÁLY NÓTÁI Tükrös Zenekar from *Szatmári Népzene*
Learnt from a village Gypsy musician, the sort of tunes heard down the pub late into the evening.

9 ZSA MO Ando Drom from *Phari Mamo*
Featuring the strange, childlike voice of Mitsou, one of the best groups of rural Gypsy musicians.

10 LEI TOI Mitsoura from *Mitsoura*
A 2003 recording in which the Gypsy vocalist (ex Ando Drom) brings in Indian tabla and electronic beats. Powerful stuff.

Iceland

local warming

Björk

Iceland has a strong sense of national and cultural identity, a rich musical tradition and a vibrant contemporary music scene, with a distinctive character. But until very recently, it wasn't experiencing the same roots resurgence as other Nordic countries and its traditional music had virtually disappeared. Now that situation seems to be changing and there are signs of its reappearance, sometimes in quite unexpected company. Andrew Cronshaw narrates the saga.

The tradition of singing Iceland's old folk songs, with their distinctive melodies and irregular rhythms, had virtually died out (in public, at least) by the second half of the twentieth century. The country's youth didn't prompt a renewed interest in traditional music, as they had in other parts of northern Europe from the 1960s onwards. And although songs described as Icelandic folk were still sung, they were mostly poetic works from the nineteenth and twentieth centuries set to melodies from abroad.

Religion and Decline

The influence of the **church** seems to have been the most decisive factor in altering Iceland's traditional music thread. The Reformation in the sixteenth century brought an influx of translated **Danish protestant hymns**, as well as ministers who opposed the joys of secular folk singing and dancing. But Icelandic poets increasingly wrote their own hymns, which became the most popular. Like the country's folks songs, these hymns were often in the **lydian mode**, which was unusual in European music. *Fimmundar söngur* – singing a parallel fifth above or below the melody (a way of harmonizing outlawed in western classical music) – was also used in folk singing and more formal church polyphony.

The traditional **heterophonic** ways of singing these hymns were similar to the "undisciplined" Gaelic long-psalm singing of the Scottish highlands, and their melodies retained a strong Icelandic character until the nineteenth century. However, in 1801, Magnús Stephensen, who acted as governor of Iceland on behalf of Denmark, bought the island's first **pipe organ** and published a new hymn book. He described the singing of epic ballads and song poetry as "horrendous howling", and wanted to convert Icelandic music to something he considered more intelligent and tasteful.

By the end of the 1870s, most Icelandic churches had harmoniums, and in came new Danish-syle hymns with their formal harmonizations and four-square rhythms. These were incompatible with the old singing styles, which were soon judged as cacophonous and old-fashioned. The arrival of radio in 1930 completed this "**enlightenment**", which affected not only religious music, but the whole musical taste of the population. Iceland was a modernizing nation recovering from a long famine and anticipating full independence from Denmark, and most Icelanders rejected their previous folk music as embarrassingly primitive.

Langspil and Fidla

Although usually performed acapella, Icelandic folk singing was sometimes accompanied by one of the island's two **indigenous folk instruments**, the *langspil* and *fidla*. But both of these bowed stringed instruments had fallen into disuse by the end of the nineteenth century.

The **langspil** has a fretted string and two or more drone strings stretched over a long soundbox that is either wedge-shaped or bulged on one side. It is very similar to the Norwegian *langeleik*, and closely related to the long fretted zithers found across Europe from Scandinavia to Hungary and to the Appalachian dulcimer in the US. But, unusually, the langspil is normally played with a bow.

Peculiar to Iceland, the **fidla** is also a long box zither, but it has no frets and its two strings pass over high bridges so that the player can reach in to touch them from below while bowing from above. While there are plenty of reconstructions, there are no complete original fidlas in existence. Of the two in the National Museum, one was modified early in the nineteenth century with fiddle features, and the other was made later in the century based on recollections. Therefore, some aspects of construction and playing style are conjectural.

Sagas, Rímur and Other Folk Songs

Iceland is famous for its heroic ballad poetry, the **sagas**, which date back to the Viking era and were passed down orally for centuries. They were first written down in the thirteenth century by **Snorri Sturluson**, and then began to move from the oral

A. Mayer

Langspil player, 1835

tradition into the realm of literature, where they found a permanent place in Iceland's culture and now continue as part of the consciousness of every Icelander. The country's language has also stayed remarkably unchanged for a millennium, so the sagas are much more understandable to a modern Icelander than thirteenth-century English would be to a present-day Anglophone.

The sagas have come to be seen as literature, but it's likely that the Viking bards, or **skalds**, originally sung much of their heroic poetry, a tradition that can still be found in the Icelandic folk songs known as **rímur**. These sung ballads use both internal and line-end rhyme, as well as poetic synonyms called *heiti* and intricate metaphors called *kenningar*. Although delivered orally, rímur are a poetic form passed down via the written word. The singing style, known as *að kveða*, is usually described as a form of **chanting**, since it is a recitative that falls somewhere between song and speech (depending on the musicality of the chanter).

In the nineteenth century, people began to write down the varied tunes – which often had irregular rhythms – to preserve them alongside the texts. A society called **Iðunn** was formed in Reykjavik in 1929 to protect and continue the rímur tradition, and to remember the communal spirit of life on the farms, where the rímur were sung to accompany indoor work or enliven the dark night. To this day, the society continues to meet for chanting sessions once or twice a month.

Not all Icelandic folk songs are rímur, however. As in any culture, the folk songs' form follows function, and there are song styles – lullabies, for example – related to most aspects of everyday life.

Collection, Preservation and Unveiling

While the old styles of religious song were banished from churches in the nineteenth century, they continued in people's homes. And while many ministers railed against the ballads and folk songs of the people, there were some intellectuals, even in religious authority, who could see their significance to the national culture, and committed them to paper and the new sound-recording media.

The **Reverend Bjarni Thorsteinsson** published his seminal book *Icelandic Folk Melodies* between 1906 and 1909, and church organist **Jón Pálsson** made the first audio recordings of folk singing on wax cylinder between 1903 and 1912. In 1926 and 1928 composer **Jón Leifs** made more field record-

ings, and his compositions were very much shaped by traditional folk song. With the advent of the tape recorder, recordings of stories, rímur and other folk songs became more prolific, courtesy of a handful of determined collectors who generally worked at their own expense.

All of this material is now housed at the main repository for Icelandic culture in Reykjavik, the **Árni Magnússon Institute**, and for years a visit to the Institute was the only way of hearing any of it. However, in the 1990s, *Raddir/Voices*, a CD of recordings from the archives was released, in conjunction with the Institute, by the **Bad Taste** record label. Another big step was taken in 2004 when the Institute's folklore archives, both written and audio, started to be made accessible via the Internet.

The Bad Taste label had sprung from a collective set up by a group of Icelandic musicians, including the country's most famous singer, **Björk**. *Raddir/Voices* was followed by a CD from a present-day rímur chanter, **Steindór Andersen**, on the international label Naxos. Singer **Bára Grímsdóttir** has researched and performed traditional song for some years, and in the duo **Funi** with English folk musician Chris Foster is increasingly taking the music, and the instruments fidla and langspil, to foreign audiences. After a long fallow period it seems that the country's traditional music might finally be gaining wider interest.

Björk, Bands, Rap and Rímur

For a country with such a small population – about 300,000 – it's remarkable how musically productive Iceland is. Reykjavik has a considerable image abroad for musical cool, and since Björk achieved international stardom (initially with the **Sugarcubes** and then solo), the spacious, quirky, distinctively Icelandic sounds of bands such as **Sigur Rós** and **Múm** have become internationally known, with others set to follow in their wake.

Björk is probably the world's most famous Icelander. She's hardly a traditional singer, but she's deeply Icelandic, not only in public perception, but also in her very individual art and inspiration. She clearly has a wide palette of references, but Iceland is fundamental to her music and she embraces her cultural heritage, from what she describes as the "old woman songs" played by her grandparents to the works of composer and folk-song recorder Jón Leifs (using choirs on the *Medúlla* album).

Contemporary Icelandic musicians are often well aware of traditional forms such as rímur, and sometimes make direct connections in their own music. Sigur Rós have collaborated with rímur chanter Steindór Andersen, and the latter's album, *Rímur*, was produced by Sigur Rós collaborator **Hilmar Örn Hilmarsson**, who is one of Iceland's leading producers and film composers, as well as a great enthusiast for the old traditions. Another of Hilmarsson's projects draws attention to what at first sight seems an unlikely alliance, "**rap and**

rímur". Icelandic-language rap is a popular genre, and its improvising, alliterative, rhyming and chanting word play isn't far from that of rímur, and could be seen as a direct decendant of it.

A useful source for more information on the contemporary music scene and its connection to traditional Icelandic poetry, music and culture is Paul Sullivan's recommended 2003 travelogue *Waking Up in Iceland*.

DISCOGRAPHY Iceland

While Iceland's popular, rock, progressive, avant garde and other musics are readily available on CD, there are still very few CDs relating to the island's tradition-rooted music. However, the archives of the Árni Magnússon Institute at the University of Iceland in Reykjavik contain thousands of recordings, which are gradually being made available online via the Icelandic musical and cultural heritage website: *www.ismus.musik.is*.

⊙ **Raddir/Voices: Recordings of Folk Songs from the Archives of the Árni Magnússon Institute in Iceland**
Smekkleysa, Iceland
An album of rímur extracts (in their entirety they tend to be too long) sung by housewives, farmers, carpenters and other ordinary Icelandic workers and recorded in the late 1960s and early 1970s. It features ballads in both the stanza-disciplined quatrain form and the freer, more improvised *thula* style, plus lullabies and hymns; subjects include Viking heroes, monsters, the cuckolding of a vicar, poetry, fairies, dwarves, a harp-playing mermaid and country life. There is also a fragment from Jón Pálsson's wax cylinder recordings of 1903–12.

Steindór Andersen

A fishing boat captain and president of the *Iðunn* society, Steindór Andersen is Iceland's best-known living rímur chanter. He has actively raised the tradition's profile by appearing on radio and TV, performing in Europe and the US with Sigur Rós, and teaching.

⊙ **Rímur**
Naxos World, USA
Andersen sings rímur extracts written in the eighteenth and nineteenth centuries; most were recorded in a traditional sleeping loft and small turf-roofed church, but a few were recorded in a concert hall with the addition of a second singer, didgeridoo drone or Irish harp.

Bára Grímsdóttir

From a family of traditional chanters, singer Bárá Grímsdóttir had a classical music education but remained deeply connected with traditional music, exploring the archives and performing with well-known langspil and fidla player Sigurður Rúnar Jónsson ("Diddi Fidla") and the folk group Embla.

★ **Funi**
Green Man, UK
A fine demonstration of the melodic and lyrical variety of Icelandic folk songs. Grímsdóttir sings with beauty and power, accompanied with understanding by two of the most respected musicians of the English folk revival, guitarist Chris Foster and button-accordionist and concertina player John Kirkpatrick. It is not only musically impressive, but – like the *Raddir/Voices* compilation and Andersen's *Rímur* – it also has excellent booklet material in both Icelandic and English.

Anna Thorhallsdóttir

A traditional singer, Anna Thorhallsdóttir accompanies herself on the langspil.

⊙ **Canti Popolari d'Islanda/Folk Songs of Iceland**
Albatros/King, Japan
An interesting set of folk songs in which the elderly, but still brisk and sparky, singer counterpoints the varied, word-linked rhythms of the modal tunes with dronal, percussive bowstrokes on her langspil. Recorded in the 1970s by Italian folk music collector Roberto Leydi, the LP was originally issued on the Albatros label. On the King Records CD reissue, the extensive Albatros LP notes are only in Japanese.

Ireland

the nya and the draíocht

Lúnasa in Japan
© Lúnasa 2006

Fiddler Ben Lennon says it has to have "the nya", his fellow bowman Martin Hayes reckons it must possess draoícht ("enchantment"), while accordionist Brendan Begley believes it's the "only acceptable form of madness". No matter how it is defined, as Geoff Wallis reports, Ireland's traditional music has some innate and elusive quality whose appeal has spread far beyond its shores.

Though often viewed through green-tinted glasses, especially by émigré communities, there is something intrinsically captivating about Irish music. Ireland was perhaps the first European country to be subject to musical tourism when, from the 1960s onwards, young musicians from other countries, especially France and Germany and later Japan, headed for places like Doolin in County Clare, West Cork, West Kerry and Donegal to catch a glimpse of a real living tradition in its natural habitat (and maybe learn a tune or two).

For one of the most stunning aspects of traditional Irish music is that it has survived relatively unscathed by the exigencies of poverty, famine and emigration as a fully living form. Comparatively untouched by academia and largely resisting commercial pressures, despite the global success of some of its exponents, the music essentially still belongs to the Irish people, in both urban and rural areas, at home and in communities abroad.

Dancing at the Crossroads

Just as many people believe that Guinness is brewed from the waters of the River Liffey, so there are others who suppose that Ireland's traditional music is inextricably linked to some preternatural "Celtic Twilight". In both cases, the truth is otherwise. Though some religious songs and other ballads can trace their origins to medieval times, the bulk of Ireland's **traditional music** was composed within the last three hundred years – and a substantial proportion dates from after the Great Famine of 1845–49.

Until relatively recent times, apart from the performance of solo airs and songs, the music has played second fiddle to **dancing**. In rural Irish communities the most popular form of entertainment until well into the twentieth century was the **house dance**, usually held in the kitchen of the largest house in the area, or the outdoor "crossroads" dance. The dances were either group dances, now known as "sets", based on quadrilles where two sets of two couples danced facing each other, or solo dances performed by the best dancers in the locality. Rural depopulation, Church interference, legislation, the commercial dance halls, the radio and the record player nearly killed the custom off altogether by the 1940s, though it lingered on a while in places like Clare, Connemara and Kerry.

In the early 1980s, however, there was a concerted effort to revive set dancing, though not the crossroads dances themselves. Increasing numbers of pubs and local centres made space available for dancers and a number of musicians, recognized as expert accompanists, became much sought after for the events. Although the dance tunes they use are the jigs, reels and hornpipes known to every traditional musician, playing for dancers requires special skills since during a dance it is the dancer and not the piper who calls the tune. The tunes are often played at a slower tempo than is usual at a session and the emphasis is placed firmly on the rhythm rather than on instrumental ornamentation.

It took a while longer for step-dancing to be accorded its own revival. This was famously instigated by the performance of a short piece of music, featuring the dancers Michael Flatley and Jean Butler plus a huge supporting step-dancing cast, during the interval of the 1994 Eurovision Song Contest. Composed by Bill Whelan, the music integrated Flamenco and Eastern European dance influences with Irish traditions. The dancers' electrifying performance brought immediate acclaim and, with Flatley as choreographer, Whelan set about expanding the piece into a full show called **Riverdance**. This featured singers, instrumental solos, and an eighty-strong chorus line of Irish dancers liberated from the constraining folk uniforms and rigid upper body posture of traditional dance as insisted upon by Comhaltas Ceoltóirí Éireann in its competitions. The expanded show first opened in Dublin in 1995, went on to London, and grew into three touring companies performing worldwide. Flatley went on to devise "Lord of the Dance" – a similar extravaganza with music written by the Irish composer Ronan Hardiman. While providing employment to a host of Irish musicians, the success of these two shows catalysed enormous interest in Irish music worldwide.

Ireland's economic boom during the 1990s – the rise of the "Celtic Tiger" – and its emergence as a fully fledged European state also ensured that many young musicians who might have emigrated in the past remained at home. While previous generations of city dwellers, especially those from rural areas, had rejected all trappings of a bucolic past, including traditional music, their children now had the confidence to undertake a process of rediscovery that coincided with increasing international interest in roots music. That process continues to breathe life into Ireland's music.

Pub Sessions and the Crack

For much of its life Ireland's traditional music has survived by being passed on from one person to

The Sean-Nós Tradition

Songs in the Irish language are at the heart of the Irish tradition, weighted with significance as one of the few remaining links to the culture of Gaelic Ireland. The most important of them, and many of the oldest, form the repertoire of a style of singing known as **sean-nós** (literally "old style"). An unaccompanied singing form of great beauty and complexity, it is thought to derive from the bardic tradition which died out in the seventeenth century with the demise of the old Gaelic order, though most of its songs are believed to have been written between 1600 and 1850. Since the majority of these are love songs, parallels have been drawn with other European traditions dating back to medieval times, such as the French *carole* and *rondel*. A more controversial theory points to a shared maritime culture between the coastal fringes of western Europe and North Africa and directs attention to the similarities between sean-nós and the traditional songs and music of Moorish Spain and Morocco. Whatever the case, there's no doubting that the style is deeply rooted in the rhythms and intonations of the Irish language itself.

Each *Gaeltacht* (Irish-speaking area) has a slightly different sean-nós style, although there are songs common to all regional traditions, often known as the "big" songs. The songs of Connemara, for example, have elaborate melodies that lie within a small vocal range, whereas those of Donegal are more rhythmically regular and tend to feature less ornamentation. The sean-nós repertoire is made up of **long songs** which have an allusive and delicate poetic style. There are also many less complex songs, ballads, love songs, lullabies, children's songs, comic songs, and local songs of all sorts. In addition, most sean-nós singers have English-language songs in their repertoire, including ballads of great antiquity such as "Barbara Allen", as well as more recent compositions.

Sean-Nós makes heavy demands on both singer and listener. The former must have the skill to vary the interpretation of each verse by means of subtle changes in tempo, ornamentation, timbre and stress, while the latter needs to possess the knowledge and discrimination to fully appreciate the singer's efforts. The greatest sean-nós singers all possess the ability not just to utilize these techniques within the confines of their local singing style, but also to captivate their audience through their telling of a story. Such attributes were common to Connemara's **Seosamh Ó hÉanaí** (Joe Heaney), **Seán 'ac Dhonncha**, **Máire Áine Ní Dhonnchadha**, Waterford's **Nioclás Tóibín**, **Darach Ó Catháin** (born in Connemara, but brought up in Meath) and **Róise Bean Mhic Grianna** (from Arranmore Island, Donegal).

The songs' **airs** also form a significant part of the repertoire of traditional musicians, especially uilleann pipers, as well as often being the basis for songs in the English language. Less obvious, perhaps, is the influence of sean-nós on Irish rock music. In the 1970s the band **Horslips** deliberately incorporated airs into their own compositions, while the singer **Pierce Turner** has absorbed the intricacies of sean-nós songs into his own writing – his song "All Messed Up", for instance, draws upon the well-known "Seán Ó Dúibhir a' Ghleanna". Most recently, sean-nós has had an unlikely implosion with African and dance rhythms through the **Afro-Celts**, a fusion group which features the Cork singer **Iarla Ó Lionáird**.

Sean-Nós singer Iarla Ó Lionáird

another, whether from parent to child, teacher to pupil, musician to musician or singer to singer. In that sense it is an **oral tradition** and remains largely so despite the incursions of books, recorded and broadcasting media and the Internet.

One of the best ways to learn tunes is in the company of fellow musicians and, since it plays such a focal part in Irish life, the **pub** has become the venue for such transactions via the medium of the **session**. Indeed, other than concerts or social events, it's unlikely that the visitor will hear live traditional music in any venue other than the pub and the pub itself has become synonymous with purveyance of "**crack**" (*ceol agus craic* as many pubs advertise). The whole Irish pub session phenomenon has become a global commodity, to be found in almost any city you care to mention. The "crack", of course, can't be produced to order, but when good music, good company and drink combine in the right proportions then a sort of critical mass is achieved and crack ensues. If it is really there, then not only will the music be memorable and the musicians on form but those present reckon they have participated and not been mere spectators or consumers.

Pubs actually came into the traditional music picture in Ireland as late as the 1960s. Before then, traditional music was played in a domestic setting or at loosely organized community events. The first regular pub session, as we now know it, began not in Ireland at all but in London's Camden Town in 1947. The players were Irishmen, mostly from South Sligo, all traditional musicians, and immigrants working mainly in the building industry on the post-war reconstruction of London. Packed into lodging houses and living in a city for the first time, away from their families, they did not have access to the old ways of music-making. Pubs offered the opportunity to meet and play with other musicians with the informality required by players and listeners alike. This development had long-term implications for traditional music. It removed it from the domestic or community environment and further separated it from dancing, which was not allowed in most pubs. It also brought drink, publicans and ultimately the drinks industry into an influential relationship with traditional music.

Within a decade the pub session idea had spread to Ireland and by the 1960s there were Irish pubs that were synonymous with traditional music – O'Donoghue's of Merrion Row in Dublin being one of the best known (and still in business). At the **Fleadh Cheoil**, Ireland's annual festival of traditional music which began in 1952, pub sessions became a feature of the informal or fringe events around the organized concerts and competitions. As the Fleadh moved from town to town each year the practice spread and very quickly publicans realized the opportunity presented by the session.

In the summer, during or around local *fleadhanna* (festivals) or major events such as the Fleadh Cheoil or the **Willie Clancy Summer School** held in Miltown Malbay, Co. Clare, every July, you will also find all-inclusive sessions when large numbers of musicians congregate in one place. These sessions are still "the real thing" – spontaneous, unplanned gatherings, based only on a mutual desire to make music. These can be terrific occasions when it seems the music just couldn't get any better and no one is willing to put an end to it. Space in the pub is at a premium and such sessions can feature group playing, solo playing, singing in Irish and English or any combination of these: it all depends on who's in the company and where their musical bias lies. Singers may gang up and keep the musicians from playing or vice versa.

By contrast, little of what passes for traditional music in today's Irish pubs corresponds to an authentic session. This is not to say that good traditional music cannot be heard, for many excellent young and not so young traditional musicians earn their living in pubs, and in places like **Donegal**, especially, you can still find a great session erupting. However, the pub session is essentially a business driven by tourism and the drinks industry. The music may be viewed as just another facility, like large-screen TV or pool tables, and may well have to compete with them. Pub musicians, in fact, have always had to compete with noise and clatter and the ringing of tills and have developed a kind of pub repertoire as a result – amplification, a preponderance of reels played fast and loud, almost no traditional singing, and no unaccompanied singing. Fortunately, there are pubs which are exceptions to this rule.

The real session is by definition something that cannot be scheduled, so the pub which guarantees a session is in fact offering a formal traditional music gig, where at least one of the musicians is paid, expected to turn up at a certain time and finish at a certain time. In a real session, different conventions apply, usually none of the above. Where musicians frequent a pub because the owner is into the music they are not paid, but neither are they under any obligation to play or even to turn up. It's possible to arrive at a pub known for its sessions only to find that on this particular night no one is in a playing mood. The venues of

The Tunes and the Collectors

IRELAND

Most instrumental Irish traditional music heard at sessions and concerts originated as **dance music**. It was the repertoire of the rural working people and was part of a communally expressed cultural life. Traditional music was played to accompany dancing at celebrations – usually in houses and barns or out of doors when weather permitted – including weddings, fairs, wakes and saint's day observances known as "patterns". For centuries it was the recreational and social expression of Irish people and it has not entirely died out in this form yet.

The most popular tune type in Ireland is the **reel**, closely followed by the **jig** (in a variety of forms and time signatures – the double jig, single jig, slip jig and slide) and, to a lesser extent, the **hornpipe**. Then there are barndances, flings, highlands and Germans (both variants of the Schottische) as well as tunes originating in Central and Eastern Europe such as waltzes, polkas and mazurkas. Add to these tunes formerly used to accompany long dances and set dances and a range of unclassifiable and special pieces (of which the best known is "The Foxchase", a piping tune imitating the hunt) and the overall repertoire is massive. In the 1980s the collector **Breandán Breathnach** estimated that this amounted to more than 7000 tunes, but that total has since been much augmented through the addition of newly composed melodies and the rediscovery of forgotten ones.

In addition there is also a group of instrumental pieces known as **slow airs** played without accompaniment. Most of them are laments or the melodies of songs, some of such antiquity that the words have been lost. The uilleann pipes (see instruments box) are particularly well suited to the performance of airs, as their plaintive tone and ability to perform complex ornaments cleanly allows them to approach the style of sean-nós singers. However, most good players, regardless of their instrument, will have a repertoire of airs.

The existence of such a vast body of music is almost entirely the result of periodic fears for its survival. The first actual printed anthology, John and William Neale's *Collection of the Most Celebrated Irish Tunes*, appeared in 1724, but, later that century, so great were concerns to preserve the last remnants of the Gaelic harp tradition that a festival was mounted in Belfast in 1792 and a young **Edward Bunting** charged with notating the melodies played by the **harpers** who attended. Enthused by the experience, Bunting subsequently toured various counties, meeting harpers and writing down their tunes, becoming in the process the original Irish field collector. His first collection of airs appeared in 1796 and others followed in 1809 and 1840.

Other notable nineteenth-century collections were published by **Thomas Moore** (*Moore's Irish Melodies*) and **George Petrie**, but, in terms of dance music, the daddy of them all is simply known as "the book". In 1903 **Captain Francis O'Neill**, then Chief Superintendent of the Chicago police and an émigré from County Cork, published *Music of Ireland*, consisting of 1850 tunes gleaned from Irish musicians in the US. Four years later he published "the book" itself, *The Dance Music of Ireland*, also known as "O'Neill's 1001". The work of the Chief, as he was known, remains of inestimable importance and ensured that many tunes were preserved. "The book" is still the first point of reference for many an aspiring musician.

Beginning in 1963, Breandán Breathnach published his *Ceol Rince na hÉireann*, four volumes of previously unpublished or unrecorded tunes that he had noted down from musicians. By then, however, another form of preservation – field recordings – were making their own impact. In the 1940s the uilleann piper **Séamus Ennis** was hired by the Irish Folklore Commission as a field collector, and his substantial findings were added to their archives. In 1947 he moved to Raidió Éireann and made numerous documentary programmes before teaming up with Brian George of the BBC in 1951 to undertake a vast collection scheme covering Ireland, England, Scotland and Wales. Others followed in Ennis's wake, including the Americans Alan Lomax, Diane Hamilton, Jean Ritchie and George Pickow, as well as another BBC employee, Peter Kennedy. The result was a vast collection of field recordings, many of which can be found at the focal point for Irish traditional music, Dublin's **Irish Traditional Music Archive** (ITMA). The ITMA also holds a wealth of commercial recordings and just about every single printed collection of tunes.

In recent years a number of musicians have taken advantage of the CD's relatively cheap production costs as a means of ensuring that rare and previously unpublished tunes are not lost from the collective repertoire. Notable examples include Brian McNamara's Leitrim recordings and Kevin Crehan's collection of his grandfather Junior's repertoire, as well as Garry Walsh's commercial release of *Uncovered*, whose tunes are so rare that even ITMA held no previous versions.

sessions are as changeable as their personnel and the scene is in constant flux. A new landlord, a difference of opinion or too many crowds can force the musicians out to other meeting places.

At first sight, sessions may seem to be rambling, disorganized affairs, but they have an underlying order and etiquette. Musicians generally commandeer a corner of the pub as their sacred domain. They also reserve the right to invite selected non-playing friends to join them there. The session is not open to all comers, although it might look that way, and it's not done to join in without introduction; a newcomer will wait to be asked to play, and may well refuse if they consider the other musicians to be of a different standard to themselves.

Whereas the old style of dance accompaniment featured musicians playing just one tune at a time, nowadays the session is utterly dependent on sets. While nearly all Irish tunes conform to the same basic structure of two eight-bar sections or strains, each of which is played twice to make a 32-bar whole, then repeated from the top, in a session one tune is followed by another without any appreciable break. The change or "turn" in the tune is communicated through gesture – a nod or wink or movement of some kind.

However, the pub session as we know it today may well be in danger. Steep increases in the price of a pint and the implementation of a ban on smoking throughout the Republic's pubs, not forgetting a more rigid enforcement of drink-driving laws, has led to a decline in the number of punters heading for their local. As pub takings fall, landlords may well investigate more profitable alternatives to the session, while there has already been a small but significant revival in the house session in some western counties.

Ensemble Playing

Unsurprisingly, considering musicians spend so much time at sessions, ensemble playing is largely the norm in terms of public performance, but this was certainly not the case for most of Ireland's musical history. Before the appearance of **céilí**

The 78rpm Era and the Sligo Fiddle Masters

Many of the tunes still popular today gained their currency from the enormous number of 78rpm records released in the US during the first half of the twentieth century. The presence of so many Irish immigrants in that country provided a ready market for the newly developing record companies and the fact that a significant proportion of those émigrés were musicians meant that there was no problem in supplying a demand for their product. At the same time these musicians were able to supplement their income by appearing on specialist Irish radio stations.

Amongst the early recording artists were the German-American accordionist **John J. Kimmel** who recorded from 1903 into the 1930s and influenced a host of budding musicians (though why he was attracted to Irish music still remains a mystery). In his wake came the concertina player **William J. Mullaly**, the flute player **John McKenna** and the piper **Tom Ennis**, but perhaps the most prominent were three fiddlers from **South Sligo**.

The oldest and most influential of these was **Michael Coleman** (1891–1945) from Killavil who arrived in the US in 1914 and began playing the dancehall and vaudeville circuits before making his first recordings in 1921, eventually releasing forty 78s for a variety of labels. Many of these found their way back to Ireland (brought home by returning migrants or sent as presents) and his smoothly rhythmic bowing and mellifluous ornamentation made him the most famous Irish musician of his time.

James Morrison (1893–1947) from Drumfin arrived in the US in 1918 after a spell working as a travelling teacher of Irish and dancing for the Gaelic League. He too first recorded in 1921 and released more than forty records either solo or in duet with musicians such as Ennis and McKenna or with his own band. Known as "The Professor", he taught many musicians in New York and his most famous pupil was **Paddy Killoran** (1903–65) from just outside Ballymote who went to the US in 1925. Apart from forming the hugely popular Pride of Erin Orchestra, Paddy ran a bar in the Bronx and began recording in the 1930s. Later he co-founded the Dublin Records label, one of the first to release Irish LPs.

The importance of these three fiddlers' recordings cannot be underestimated. Indeed, while some claim that the influence of the Sligo style of playing helped to undermine other regional styles and led to the dominance of one region's repertoire, there is no doubt that they played a significant role in keeping the music alive during the decades when Ireland's rural society was ravaged by emigration.

bands (groups formed specifically to accompany dancers) in Ireland from the 1920s onwards, the music was played unaccompanied. Usually a single fiddler, piper, flute-, whistle- or box-player or a pair of these played for the dancers. The single decorated melody line was the norm in playing as in singing, and the music had no rhythmic or harmonic accompaniment. However, Western ears are now attuned to playing and singing with a chordal backing, and over the past sixty years this has inevitably found its way into traditional playing and singing.

In the 1960s, two almost simultaneous currents emerged in Ireland which turned musicians increasingly towards the group format. One of the major successes of the 1950s folk revival in the US saw three brothers from Carrick-on-Suir, Co. Tipperary – **Tom, Pat and Liam Clancy** – join forces with the Armagh singer **Tommy Makem** to record several albums of boisterous ballads and rebel songs. When the band returned to Ireland that success was mirrored and resulted in a host of imitators forming their own groups in the wake of The Clancys and Makem, some even going so far

Enduring Influences: Planxty & The Bothy Band

The 1970s was an era of musical revolution in Ireland, and two bands were in the vanguard. The first was **Planxty**, which evolved from the recording of **Christy Moore**'s second solo album, *Prosperous*. The singer/guitarist/*bodhrán* player had recruited his old school friend **Dónal Lunny** on bouzouki, who brought along his then duo partner **Andy Irvine** on *mandola* and harmonica, while uilleann piper **Liam O'Flynn** had been remembered from the sessions in the Kildare village which gave Moore's album its title. Their musical rapport was instant and a band was formed, taking its name from the title of an old type of tune composed for a patron and often associated with the harper Turlough Carolan.

Their unusual combination of instruments and Moore and Irvine's powerful songs brought immediate success and radically changed their audience's perception of the folk song tradition. An eponymous debut album in 1973 enhanced Planxty's reputation, which was boosted further by its successor, *The Well Below the Valley*, after which Lunny left. Moore soon followed and the group disbanded in 1975, though the original line-up reformed in 1979 with additional members and lasted a few further years.

Ever since, the quartet has been fed "The Beatles Question", with interviewers enquiring when – never if – they would get back together. To much amazement and general joy they reunited in late 2003 and have since played a series of sell-out concerts including their first gigs in the UK for 25 years, as well as releasing a monstrously successful live album and DVD.

Dónal Lunny originally left Planxty to form **The Bothy Band**, which materialized from an ad hoc grouping called Seachtar ("seven people"). The band's members included **Matt Molloy** on flute, uilleann piper **Paddy Keenan**, singer and harpsichord/clavinet player **Tríona Ní Dhomhnaill** and her brother, singer/guitarist **Mícheál Ó Domhnaill**, plus fiddler **Paddy Glackin** (though he soon left, to be replaced by **Tommy Peoples**).

There was an innate wildness in the band's music, led by the trio of Peoples, Molloy and Keenan, whom Lunny has described as "like three horses racing across a field … the rhythm section was in tatters trying to keep up with them". This high-energy playing received a rapturous reception, as did the band's choice of songs, which

were often drawn from the singers' familial roots in Donegal. In many ways, the band's self-titled 1975 debut set a template for contemporary bands such as **Lúnasa** and **Danú**, though there are many who reckon The Bothy Band has never been bettered.

Tara Music

The band itself underwent one further change of membership (**Kevin Burke** replacing Tommy Peoples) and recorded two more studio albums and a live set before playing its last gig at the 1979 Ballysodare festival. Like Planxty, all of its members have been vital forces in Irish music over the last thirty years, though, sadly, Mícheál Ó Domhnaill passed away in 2006.

Planxty

Stephen Finnegan

Gerry O'Connor

as to sport the quartet's trademark Aran sweaters. Ireland's home-grown sensation of that time, **The Dubliners**, espoused a far more bohemian image, based on a hard-drinking, devil-may-care attitude and beards that would frighten children.

Meanwhile, the Cork-born composer **Seán Ó Riada** had hit upon his own form of ensemble playing while working as musical director of Dublin's Abbey Theatre. His concept involved one or two musicians first expressing the basic melody of a tune which would then be ornamented and explored by small groups of solo traditional instruments and the entire ensemble as a whole. He formed the group **Ceoltóirí Chualann** as a vehicle through which to explore his ideas. While Ó Riada also composed notable film scores, such as *Mise Éire*, his experiment proved immensely popular and reached even wider audiences when several members of the group first recorded as **The Chieftains** in 1963 and subsequently became the spearhead of the ensuing revival of Irish traditional music. The Chieftains continued to develop ensemble playing, but it was not until 1975 that the band decided to embark on a full-time career, becoming Ireland's best-known traditional group in the process.

By then, however, two perhaps more radical bands had emerged, **Planxty** and **The Bothy Band** (see box), who transformed the ensemble format into something far more accessible to the ears of Ireland's young musicians. Groups such as **De Dannan**, **Stockton's Wing**, **Arcady**, **Patrick Street**, **Four Men and a Dog**, **Skylark**, **Déanta**, **Nomos** and the hugely successful **Altan** (see box)

and **Dervish** continued to explore and expand the group setting, while the current cream of the crop are **Lúnasa**, **Téada**, **Beoga**, **Solas** and **Gráda**.

Nowadays, too, many prominent solo musicians opt for the group format. Among the most notable is **Sharon Shannon**, a talented accordionist from County Clare whose technical agility has enabled her to embrace all manner of musical partnerships and blend Irish traditional tunes with a range of other genres, including reggae, Cajun, Scandinavian and North American material. Equally innovative are the lightning-quick Tipperary banjo player **Gerry O'Connor**, the expressive Galway fiddler **Frankie Gavin** and the uilleann piper **Liam O'Flynn**, all of whom have worked within a variety of group frameworks.

Many other musicians, however, prefer just a simple backing, perhaps a guitar or bouzouki, when playing gigs. This allows instrumentalists to highlight all their skills in ornamentation, decoration and embellishment, the very factors which continue to breathe life into traditional music. It's a kind of controlled extemporization in which the player recreates the tune with each performance. Technical mastery is necessary, of course, but the skill with which a musician decorates a tune is the measure of creative power, and often even accomplished players will play the settings of established master players, reproducing their particular phrasing, decorations and intonations.

A quieter but perhaps equally significant course has been charted over the past couple of decades by **Mícheál Ó Súilleabháin**, who has created a fusion of Irish traditional, classical and jazz music, developing a unique piano style. Ó Súilleabháin is also a significant figure in Irish music through his work at the pioneering Limerick University music department, which offers courses in traditional Irish music and has an associated World Music Centre (see *www.ul.ie/~iwmc/*).

Shamrock 'n' Roll

Since the 1960s Ireland has had an indigenous rock scene which at times owes little or nothing to traditional music. However, even a band like **U2** – who once rejected traditional music as part of the repressiveness of Irish culture – have incorporated its strands in recent years. And London-Irish iconoclasts **The Pogues** emerged in the early 1980s playing a chaotic set of "Oirish" standards and rebel songs, bringing a punk energy to the Irish ballad. They were also blessed with one of the finest Irish songwriters of recent years, **Shane MacGowan**, who, in his subsequent

Instruments and Players

We've included mention of the best Irish musicians in this round-up of traditional instruments. If you get a chance to see any of them at the festivals, don't miss it.

Uilleann Pipes

"Seven years learning, seven years practising and seven years playing" is reputedly what it takes to master the uilleann pipes (pronounced "illun" or "ill-yun"). Perhaps the world's most technically sophisticated bagpipe, it is highly temperamental and difficult to master. The melody is played on a nine-holed chanter with a two-octave range. Air is supplied from a bag held under the left arm, itself fed by a bellows squeezed under the right elbow. As well as a set of three drones, the uilleann pipes have three regulators, which can be switched on and off to provide chords. In the hands of a master they can provide a sensitive backing for slow airs and an excitingly rhythmic springboard for dance music.

The pipes arrived in Ireland in the early eighteenth century and reached their present form in the 1870s. Taken up by members of the gentry, who became known as "gentlemen pipers", they were also beloved of the Irish **Travellers**, and two different approaches evolved, the restrained and delicate parlour style exemplified by the late Séamus Ennis, and the traveller style which, designed as it was to coax money from the pockets of visitors to country fairs, is highly ornamented and sometimes breathtakingly quick.

Some of the most acclaimed traditional musicians of the twentieth century have been pipers: **Séamus Ennis**, **Willie Clancy** and the brothers **Johnny and Felix Doran**. Today one of the country's foremost practitioners, **Liam O'Flynn**, has pushed forward the possibilities for piping, initially as a member of Planxty, and later through his association with classical composer Shaun Davey and poet Seamus Heaney. The whirlwind **Paddy Keenan** made his name with The Bothy Band, while other pipers of note include Cran's **Ronan Browne**, that superb player of slow airs **Néillidh Mulligan** and **Brian McNamara**, whose speciality is rare tunes from his native Leitrim.

Flutes and Whistles

The flute used in Irish music is of a simple wooden type, played mostly in a fairly low register with a quiet and confidential tone which means that it's not heard at its best in pub sessions. The master player of his generation is **Matt Molloy** from Roscommon, a member of The Chieftains. The most well-known of the Sligo players is **Séamus Tansey**, while Belfast has produced a slew of musicians, including the late **Frankie Kennedy**, **Desi Wilkinson**, **Hammy Hamilton**, **Gary Hastings**, **Harry Bradley** and **Marcas Ó Murchú** – The Boys of the Lough's **Cathal McConnell** was a major influence on virtually all of these players. Others to look out for include Dubliner **Paul McGrattan**, **Catherine McEvoy**, **June McCormack** and **Kevin Crawford**.

While anyone can get a note out of a tin whistle, it can take a long time to develop an embouchure capable of producing a flute tone, and so piper **Finbar Furey** introduced the low whistle, which takes the place of the flute when there is no proper flute player around. In the right hands – such as those of **Packie Manus Byrne**, **Mary Bergin**, **Gavin Whelan** or The Chieftains' **Paddy Moloney** – the whistle itself is no mean instrument, but it's also suitable for the beginner. If you're interested, make sure you get a D-whistle, as much Irish music is in this key.

Fiddles

The fiddle is popular all over Ireland and many areas still retain particular regional styles and repertoire. **Donegal** fiddle style is melodic but with lively bowing techniques, typified by the music of **John Doherty**, whereas the **Sligo** style, exemplified in the playing of the great **Michael Coleman**, is more elaborate and flamboyant. The Donegal repertoire inclines towards reels, flings, highlands and tunes with a Scots influence, while in the **Kerry** repertoire polkas, jigs and slides predominate. There are literally hundreds of fine fiddle players: **Tommy Peoples**, **Kevin Burke**, **Gerry O'Connor**, **Liz Carroll**, **Frankie Gavin**, **Seán Keane**, **Paddy Glackin**, **Martin Hayes**, **Paul O'Shaughnessy** and **Matt Cranitch** are but the tip of the iceberg, while **Ciarán Ó Maonaigh**, **Malachy Bourke**, **Andy Morrow** and **Meabh O'Hare** are just a few of the younger generation to look out for.

Accordions and Concertinas

The two-row button accordion is often found at a session, though the smaller one-row version, usually known as a melodeon in Ireland, has its devotees. The accordion gained enormous popularity in the 1950s and 60s through the playing of **Paddy O'Brien**, **Joe Cooley** and **Joe Burke**. Since then **Jackie Daly**, **Máirtín O'Connor**, **Tony Mac Mahon**, **James Keane**, **Dermot Byrne**, **Jo Marsh** and **Brendan and Séamus Begley** have taken the instrument to new heights, though **Sharon Shannon** is probably today's best-known accordionist. The undoubted king of the melodeon is **Johnny Connolly** from Connemara.

Also free reed, the concertina was a popular instrument in country houses in the last century, particularly in Clare, which produced some exemplary players such as the renowned **Mrs Crotty**. **Mary Mac Namara**, **Josephine McCarthy** and **Noel Hill** carry on the tradition of fine Clare concertina playing today. **Micheál Ó Raghallaigh** is an extraordinarily versatile concertina player, while **Niall Vallely** is one of the most innovative traditional players around on any instrument.

Banjo

Plucked with a plectrum, the four-string tenor banjo was popularized in Ireland by **Barney McKenna** of The Dubliners, who tunes his instrument to GDAE an octave below the fiddle. Rarely used as strummed accompaniment, the banjo is a melody instrument in Irish traditional music. Apart from Barney, its most influential exponent is **Gerry O'Connor**; other notable practitioners include **Kevin Griffin**, **Kieran Hanrahan**, **Angelina Carberry** and **Darren Maloney**.

Bouzouki, Mandolin and Guitar

At first sight it might seem odd to include the bouzouki on a list of traditional Irish instruments. Nevertheless, its light but piercing tone makes it eminently suitable both for melodies and for providing a restrained chordal backing within an ensemble or at a session, and since its introduction to the islands by **Johnny Moynihan** in the mid-1960s, and subsequent popularization by **Dónal Lunny** and **Andy Irvine**, it has taken firm root. In the process it has lost much of its original Greek form, and with its flat back the Irish bouzouki is really closer to a member of the mandolin family.

The mandolin itself is rarely seen at a session, though there are some notable players, including **Paul Kelly** and the US-based **Mick Moloney**, while **Garry Ó Briain** plays a larger version, the *mandocello*.

The guitar is still the most common accompaniment in traditional music and over the decades a traditional style has grown up around the instrument which is most often tuned to DADGAD. A guitarist of genius is **Stephen Cooney** whose blend of rhythm and syncopation rooted in the Kerry dance tradition has influenced many younger musicians. Other outstanding players include **Arty McGlynn**, **Alec Finn**, **Donogh Hennessy**, **Tommy O'Sullivan** and **Garry Ó Briain**.

Bodhrán

The bodhrán provokes more division in traditional music than any other instrument. One school of thought reckons that in the hands of a bad player it sounds "like a sack of spuds tipped down the stairs". Others argue that in skilful hands it adds sympathetic support to the innate rhythms of the dance tunes. The instrument itself is a frame drum usually made of goatskin and originally associated with "**wren boys**" who went out revelling ("hunting the wren") and playing music on St Stephen's Day (December 26). It looks like a large tambourine without jingles and can be played with a small wooden stick (a beater) or with the back of the hand or fingers.

Seán Ó Riada is generally credited with introducing the bodhrán to ensemble playing and today's best-known exponents include **Johnny "Ringo" McDonagh**, **Dónal Lunny**, **Tommy Hayes**, **Jim Higgins**, **John Joe Kelly** and **Donnchadh Gough**, while **Christy Moore** was one of the first to use the instrument to accompany his own singing.

Harp

There are references to harp playing in Ireland as early as the eighth century. Irish legend has it that the harp has magical powers and it has become symbolic of the country (as well as of Guinness!). The old Irish harpers were a musical elite, serving as court musicians to the Gaelic aristocracy, and had a close acquaintance with the court music of Baroque Europe. The hundred or so surviving tunes by the famed, blind eighteenth-century itinerant harper **Turlough Carolan** – which provide much of the repertoire for today's exponents, and is often heard in orchestral or chamber music settings – clearly reflect his regard for the Italian composer Corelli.

The harp these players used was brass-strung and played with the fingernails. Today's harpers play (with their fingertips) a chromatic, gut- or plastic-string version, which one of its best exponents, **Máire Ní Chathasaigh**, describes as "neo-Irish". Máire has been notably successful in adapting Irish dance music for the harp, drawing on her love for the piping tradition. Other outstanding players include **Laoise Kelly** and **Michael Rooney**.

Beware that there is also a bland, prissy harp tradition, associated with anodyne tourist versions of Ireland, and often heard at ersatz medieval banquets. About as traditional as green beer, it should be given a wide berth.

Jak Kilby

Shane MacGowan

solo career with **The Popes**, continues to capture the state of Irish exile in a series of raw pain-filled ballads.

In the early 1980s two of Irish music's greatest innovators, **Dónal Lunny** and **Christy Moore**, original members of Planxty, made a more radical attempt to fuse traditional and rock music with the launch of the band **Moving Hearts**. Their objective was to bring traditional music up to date by drawing on all the apparatus of rock, yet without compromising the folk element. It was a tall order, but they came as close as any Irish band has ever

Altan

From the late 1980s to the present day **Altan** have been at the forefront of Irish traditional music, their vivacious stage presence and outstanding recordings garnering international acclaim and a fan base that stretches to distant Japan.

The band was forged by the fiddler **Mairéad Ní Mhaonaigh** from Irish-speaking Gweedore in Donegal and the late, much-missed flute and whistle player **Frankie Kennedy** from Belfast. Together the pair recorded an outstanding duo album, _Ceol Aduaidh_, in 1983 before deciding to form Altan (named after a lough near the Donegal landmark Errigal Mountain). With the addition of **Ciarán Curran** on bouzouki, guitarist **Mark Kelly** and fiddler **Paul O'Shaughnessy**, Altan became a fully fledged touring band whose identity was strongly defined by the Irish-language songs Mairéad had learnt from childhood onwards and a classic mix of dance tunes drawn from the Donegal fiddle tradition. Another Donegal fiddler, **Ciarán Tourish**, was recruited in the early 1990s and debuted on 1992's _Harvest Storm_, the only Altan album to feature a triple-pronged fiddle attack, since O'Shaughnessy left shortly afterwards.

Sadly, Frankie, a hugely talented musician, was diagnosed with cancer in 1991, but he went on to shape the group's 1993 masterpiece, _Island Angel_, a landmark album for contemporary traditional music which combined driving fiddle and flute music with a telling variety of subtly arranged songs. This was also the first album to feature new guitarist and singer **Dáithí Sproule**, while its virtuoso guest accordionist **Dermot Byrne** became a full-time band member a while after Frankie's death in 1994.

For all its crossover success, the group's sound has remained resolutely traditional. They play within traditional structures, and though they employ the occasional Scottish tune, they have remained true to their roots, a point reinforced by the fact that Mairéad sings mainly in Irish – her first language. As a result, Altan's albums incorporate elements of contemporary arrangement and instrumentation while retaining regional and local coherence to a remarkable degree.

A **winter school** is held in Gweedore shortly after Christmas in Frankie Kennedy's memory. This has become a highlight of the traditional music year and regularly turns in memorable concerts, sessions and workshops.

done, using rock and jazz to rethink the harmonic and rhythmic foundations of Irish music. Remarkably, the line-up was led by pipes and saxophone, with backing from bass and lead guitars, electric bouzouki, drums and percussion. Their gigs were feasts of music that seemed simultaneously both familiar and new, while the lyrics, unusually in (southern) Ireland, confronted political issues head on, with a commitment to the rights of the dispossessed – in Ireland and beyond. They lost momentum when Christy Moore departed for a solo career in 1982, and the band folded in 1985, but they had created a space for future Irish groups to follow, not least Lunny's own **Coolfin**, one of the foremost bands of the 1990s.

Current bands working in the traditional/rock borderlands include the Dublin group **Kíla**, who offer an eclectic, beguiling and danceable mélange of trad, rap and funk with vocals in Irish. The Irish-American band **Solas**, centred around the nucleus of multi-instrumentalist **Seamus Egan** and fiddler **Winifred Horan**, has become increasingly exploratory, using electric instruments and backing and all manner of studio techniques. Another Irish-American band, **Black 47**, led by Wexford singer **Larry Kirwan**, harness traditional tunes to self-composed lyrics via the medium of rock with considerable success.

DISCOGRAPHY Ireland

General compilations

- ⊙ **Irish Dance Music**
- ⊙ **Past Masters of Irish Dance Music**
- ⊙ **Past Masters of Irish Fiddle Music**
- ⊙ **Round the House and Mind the Dresser – Irish Country-House Dance Music**
Topic, UK
Four sumptuous albums drawn from 78s, radio broadcasts, private collections and the Topic label itself, collated by the redoubtable Reg Hall.

- ⊙ **The Coleman Archive Volume 1 – The Living Tradition**
Coleman Heritage Centre, Ireland
Thirty-four recordings spanning the 1940s to the 1990s reveal all the glories of the Sligo tradition.

- ⊙ **Music from Matt Molloy's**
RealWorld, UK
An evocative session recording, with background chatter and glasses clinking to boot, featuring The Chieftains' flute player in his own pub as well as a pre-Lúnasa Seán Smyth, Iarla Ó Lionaird and guitarist Arty McGlynn

- ⊙ **The Rough Guide to Irish Music**
World Music Network, UK
Twenty-two tracks covering everything from North Cregg's vibrant take on the Sliabh Luachra polka tradition to Lasairfhíona Ní Chonaola's ethereal rendition of "Bean Phaidín", make this a valuable introduction to the tradition.

- ★ **Seoltaí Séidte**
Gael Linn, Ireland
All the 78s released by the label between 1957 and 1961, featuring singers such as Seán 'ac Dhonncha and Seosamh Ó hÉanaí and musicians like uilleann piper Willie Clancy, fiddlers Denis Murphy and Paddy Canny, all re-mastered on two discs and presented with a detailed one hundred page book. Essential.

Singers

- ⊙ **Buaiteoirí Chorn Uí Riada**
- ★ 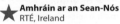**Amhráin ar an Sean-Nós**
RTÉ, Ireland
Magnificent introductions to the unaccompanied tradition, the first includes many of its most popular songs while the latter has every winner of the prestigious Ó Riada Trophy from 1972 to 1996.

Paul Brady

A member of folk group The Johnstons before joining Planxty, Brady subsequently changed tack and enjoyed a successful career in mainstream rock. However, his live repertoire still includes several numbers from the traditional canon.

- ⊙ **The Liberty Tapes**
Compass Records, USA
Taken from a 1978 concert, this includes Brady's popular renditions of both "Arthur McBride" and "The Lakes of Ponchartrain" while the supporting cast includes Liam O'Flynn, Andy Irvine, Dónal Lunny, Matt Molloy, Noel Hill and Paddy Glackin.

Karan Casey

The pure-voiced singer from Waterford first made her name with Solas, but has since released a series of acclaimed solo recordings.

- ⊙ **Chasing the Sun**
Vertical, UK
Successfully marries traditional but lyrically pointed songs, such as the epic unaccompanied "Jimmy Whelan", with contemporary material reflecting Karan's status as one of Ireland's most politically charged singers.

Cara Dillon

After spells with the Co. Derry-based Óige and the Lakeman brothers' Equation, this sublime singer has become renowned for her dulcet interpretations of traditional songs, a powerful stage presence and solo albums recorded in cahoots with her partner Sam Lakeman.

⦿ **Hill of Thieves**
Charcoal Records, UK
Her best album to date features delicate, yet ever-knowing interpretations of songs such as "Jimmy Mo Mhíle Stór" and "The Parting Glass".

Frank Harte

The recordings of the late Dubliner song-collector Harte include definitive collections of Dublin street songs as well as more recent themed collections, such as the release below.

WITH DÓNAL LUNNY

⦿ **The Hungry Voice**
Hummingbird, Ireland
A rich blend of emigration songs and those, such as "Lone Shanakyle", paying testament to the sufferings of the Great Famine of 1845–49.

Joe Heaney (Seosamh Ó hÉanaí)

From Carna in the Connemara Gaeltacht, the late Joe Heaney was one of the greatest sean-nós singers, though he also had an extensive repertoire of songs in English. His powerful voice led someone once to say, "he opened his mouth and the voice came out like an iron bar".

⭐ **The Road from Connemara**
Topic, UK
Recorded in 1964 by Ewan MacColl and Peggy Seeger, this double-CD captures Joe at his peak, revealing not just his eloquence, but an overriding sense of the tradition which imbued his singing.

Andy Irvine

London-born Andy found inspiration in Irish music and has been a driving force ever since his early days in Sweeney's Men. Membership of Planxty and Patrick Street followed, as well as his truly international band Mosaik. Releasing several solo albums, it's his collaborations which have been most influential and his bouzouki, mandola and other instrumental work has been constantly coloured by his love of Balkan music.

WITH PAUL BRADY

⭐ **Andy Irvine, Paul Brady**
Mulligan, Ireland
This 1976 album was a watershed in both musicians' careers and features Andy's stirring rendition of "Bonny Woodhall".

WITH DAVY SPILLANE

⦿ **East Wind**
Tara, Ireland
Generally reckoned to be the album that inspired "Riverdance", especially since Bill Whelan was its producer, this blends traditional Irish tunes and East European traditions to telling effect and also features Marta Sebestyen.

Dolores Keane

Once the possessor of perhaps the purest voice in Irish music, Dolores sang with De Dannan before embarking on a successful solo career. However, her choice of material often entered soft rock/MoR territory, failing to do justice to such a fine interpreter of traditional songs.

⭐ **There Was a Maid**
Claddagh, Ireland
Recorded with the band Reel Union in 1978, the songs here, especially "Seven Yellow Gypsies", exemplify all the brio and ornamentation synonymous with her singing style.

Christy Moore

Kildare-born singer Christy Moore is an Irish institution, notable both for the strength of his political commitment and a massive stage presence, though he rarely tours solo nowadays. A founding member of Planxty and Moving Hearts, he revitalised his own solo career in the 1980s. Long acclaimed for his sensitive yet highly personal interpretation of others' material, he finally recorded an album of his own songs, *Graffiti Tongue* (Columbia), in 1996.

⦿ **Christy Moore At The Point Live**
Columbia, UK
This great album captures all the vitality and contrasting moods of a Moore concert, including his tremendous distaste for hecklers and his ability to have his audience (literally) rolling in the aisles with numbers like "Joxer Goes to Stuttgart".

⭐ **The Box Set: 1964-2004**
Sony, UK
A mammoth six-album collection of, in Christy's words, the "under-belly" of his work – awesome in range and documenting many of the key moments in Ireland's recent history.

Lasairfhíona Ní Chonaola

A young sean-nós singer from Inishere, the smallest of the Aran Islands, Lasairfhíona has also worked with the innovative Hector Zazou.

⦿ **An Raicín Álainn**
Own label, Ireland
Its 2002 release announced a major new singer and one keen to explore the possibilities of the sean-nós tradition via expressive new arrangements.

Maighread and Tríona Ní Dhomhnaill

Two of Ireland's most accomplished traditional singers with a repertoire rooted in the Donegal tradition, the pair started out in the early 1970s with the highly-rated band Skara Brae. Tríona went on to be part of The Bothy Band, Touchstone, Relativity and Nightnoise while Maighread enjoyed a stint in Dónal Lunny's Coolfin.

WITH DÓNAL LUNNY

⭐ **Idir an Dá Sholas/Between the Two Lights**
Gael Linn/Hummingbird, Ireland
A feast of songs from many sources, sung in both Irish and English, with the sisters in exceptional voice and Lunny's typically understated backing.

Iarla Ó Lionáird

Iarla Ó Lionáird, a superb contemporary sean-nós singer, has consistently sought to expand the frontiers of his art, both via his solo work and the Afro-Celts (see "Groups", p.246)

⊙ **Invisible Fields**
RealWorld, UK
An astounding series of dazzling vocal soundscapes, married to the ultimate in sensuous backing.

Niamh Parsons

This rich-voiced Dubliner has produced several classy albums of traditional song.

⊙ **Blackbirds and Thrushes**
Green Linnet, US
Probably Niamh's finest to date, and impeccably arranged too.

Nioclás Tóibín

The late Tóibín hailed from the Waterford Gaeltacht of An Rinn and sang with an innate majesty.

★ **Rinn na Gael**
Cló Iar-Chonnachta, Ireland
Songs from the radio archives reveal a master of the sean-nós craft and include unbeatable versions of "Róisín Dubh" and "Na Connerys".

Instrumentalists

⊙ **The Brass Fiddle**
Claddagh, Ireland
Capturing all the strengths of the Donegal fiddle tradition, this includes the influential, but sadly departed Con Cassidy and Francie Byrne, as well as two who are still going strong, James Byrne and Vincent Campbell.

⊙ **The Drones and the Chanters, Volumes 1 & 2**
Claddagh, Ireland
The first disc dates from the early 1970s and features master uilleann pipers such as Seámus Ennis, Willie Clancy and Leo Rowsome. The second, from 1994, covered a then much younger generation, including Liam O'Flynn, Mick O'Brien and Robbie Hannan.

★ **An Gaoth Aduaidh/The North Wind**
Frankie Kennedy Winter School, Ireland
Thirteen of Ireland's finest flute players play unaccompanied in honour of the late Frankie Kennedy of Altan – stunning in places and never a dull moment!

⊙ **Kerry Fiddles**
Ossian, Ireland
Recorded live in a Kerry bar in 1952, this features the Sliabh Luachra fiddle teacher Pádraig O'Keeffe and his two foremost pupils, siblings Denis Murphy and Julia Clifford, providing a raft of effervescent tunes from the area.

Séamus Begley

Once remarking that he didn't "see much point in playing music unless there's somebody dancing to it", Séamus is a member of a notable Kerry musical family. In the late 1980s his driving accordion work and expressive voice formed a potent partnership with guitarist Stephen Cooney.

WITH JIM MURRAY
⊙ **Ragairne**
Dara, Ireland
Slides and polkas predominate as Cork-born guitarist Murray joins Begley for a sparkling album in which Séamus's rendition of the comic song "An Seanduine" plays a starring role.

Mary Bergin

Ireland's most accomplished tin whistler, the intricacies of her music belies the apparent simplicity of her chosen instrument.

★ **Feadóga Stáin and Feadóga Stáin 2**
Gael Linn, Ireland
Bergin's two solo albums are classics on which she is accompanied by long-time collaborators Johnny 'Ringo' McDonagh on bodhrán and Alec Finn on bouzouki.

Joe Burke

Instantly recognizable by his Santa-style beard, Burke's rolling B/C accordion style has been influencing musicians ever since he recorded "A Tribute to Michael Coleman" with fiddler Andy McGann in 1966.

⊙ **The Morning Mist**
New Century Music, Ireland
Backed by pianist Charlie Lennon, this is a rollicking selection of tunes, encapsulating all the drive and innate wit of Burke's playing.

Paddy Canny, P.J. Hayes, Peter O'Loughlin and Bridie Lafferty

In 1959, the Clare fiddlers Paddy and P.J. (Martin Hayes' uncle and father respectively) and flute-player O'Loughlin, together with Dublin pianist Lafferty, recorded an album which brought the "lonesome" sound of East Clare to a wider audience and went on to achieve iconic status.

⊙ **Meet Paddy Canny**
Dublin Records, US
Originally titled "All-Ireland Champions – Violin" this was a monumental release, both in terms of Ireland's recording history and its influence on musicians at the time.

Willie Clancy

The late uilleann piper, flute player and whistler from Miltown Malbay was one of traditional music's most popular and admired figures and is commemorated each year by Ireland's biggest summer school in his native town.

★ **The Minstrel from Clare**
Green Linnet, US
Issued in 1967, six years before his death, this superbly demonstrates Clancy's all-round ability and genuine warmth.

Michael Coleman

Sligo fiddler Michael Coleman was probably the most influential Irish musician of the twentieth century. Although he moved to the US in his early twenties, the many recordings he made there fed the imagination of generations of musicians back home.

IRELAND

 Michael Coleman 1891–1945
Gael Linn/Viva Voce, Ireland
Wonderful recordings of the great Sligo fiddler at his best, digitally re-mastered on a superb double CD, and complete with an exhaustive 116-page booklet.

Séamus Creagh

A wonderfully expressive fiddler from the musically barren Westmeath, Creagh (who died in 2009) lived for many years in Cork, though a spell in Newfoundland also influenced his music.

WITH JACKIE DALY

⊙ **Jackie Daly, Séamus Creagh**
Gael Linn, Ireland
This consummate 1977 album, featuring box and fiddle, unleashed a welter of polkas, slides and reels on a much appreciative world.

John Doherty

From a travelling tinsmith family, Doherty tramped the byways of rural Donegal for most of his adult life, a welcome guest in many a home thanks to his status as a fiddler nonpareil and knowledge of folklore. Though he died in 1980 the tunes he passed on form a major component of the repertoires of Donegal's musicians and those beyond its boundaries.

 The Floating Bow
Claddagh, Ireland
Taped between 1968 and 1974 in the relaxed setting of a friend's home, these recordings fully reveal the sheer majesty of Doherty's playing, based around distinctive staccato bowing and extremely rapid fingering.

Johnny Doran

One of the last of the travelling pipers, Doran was feted for his wild, unique and compelling approach to his music. He was only recorded once in his life, in 1947 by the Irish Folklore Commission.

 The Master Pipers – Volume 1
Na Píobairí Uilleann, Ireland
Originally released on cassette as "The Bunch of Keys" these re-mastered recordings are justifiably regarded as a magnificent memento of the piper.

Séamus Ennis

A master piper and a major figure in performing, collecting and preserving traditional music, Ennis still influences traditional musicians today with his quirkily joyous approach to dance, tempered by emotionally mature airs and laments.

 The Return from Fingal
RTÉ, Ireland
This magnificent survey of Ennis's life covers recordings spanning forty years, including some songs. Indispensable in describing how a giant of Irish music developed his highly personal style.

Cathal Hayden

The fiddler with Four Men and a Dog plays music in the classically driving style of his native Tyrone and is no mean banjoist either.

⊙ **Cathal Hayden**
Hook, Ireland
Hayden's rich and resonant tone is instantly recognizable and this impressive collection sees him in cahoots with Arty McGlynn on guitar and Brian McGrath on keyboards.

Martin Hayes and Dennis Cahill

With roots in the Clare style of fiddle learnt from his father and uncle (see p.243), Hayes also draws on blues and jazz to create a personal style of playing, notable for its blend of energy and lyricism. His musical relationship with Chicagoan guitarist Dennis Cahill is truly symbiotic.

 Live in Seattle
Green Linnet, US
A rousing concert performance in which Hayes and Cahill's imagination seems boundless and reaches its heights on a staggering eleven-tune 27-minute track.

Noel Hill and Tony Mac Mahon

Concertina wizard Noel Hill owes much to the piping tradition while his collaborator, accordionist Tony Mac Mahon, is one of the finer exponents of his instrument.

 I gCnoc na Graí
Gael Linn, Ireland
Recorded one memorable night at a session in Knocknagree, Co. Kerry. Hill and MacMahon play for a group of set-dancers, capturing the party atmosphere to perfection.

Paddy Keenan

A fiery uilleann piper from a musically prolific Traveller family, Keenan was schooled in the Johnny Doran fast-fingered "tight" style of playing to which he often adds his own judicious harmonies on the instrument's regulators.

 Paddy Keenan
Gael Linn, Ireland
Accompanied by his brothers John (banjo) and Thomas (whistle), along with Paddy Glackin on fiddle, this debut's resulting brew was an Irish classic where the piper's and fiddler's shared mastery of harmonics blended to memorable effect.

Dónal Lunny

Not just a leading exponent of the Irish bouzouki, but a motivational, innovative force in Ireland's music over the last forty years, Lunny has also produced more than 150 albums.

⊙ **Journey**
Hummingbird, Ireland
A double-CD retrospective spanning not just spells with Planxty, The Bothy Band, Moving Hearts and Coolfin, but including several of his own compositions and TV scores.

Mary Mac Namara

Mary Mac Namara comes from a family of East Clare musicians and her concertina playing often embodies the "lonesome" style of music associated with the area, played with a graceful pace and often in unusual keys.

⊙ **The Blackberry Blossom**
Claddagh, Ireland
Innately elegant playing, whether solo, accompanied by pianist Geraldine Cotter, or joined by her brother Andrew on accordion.

Seán McGuire

McGuire, who died in 2005, was one of Ireland's most colourful musicians. His flamboyant fiddle style was rooted in his native Cavan, but embellished by classical training, growing up in Belfast where he was exposed to Scottish music, Gypsy music and jazz. His recording career spanned some fifty years, though virtually everything is currently out-of-print.

⊙ Fiddle on the Fiddle
Emerald, Ireland
The last album released during his lifetime reveals a septuagenarian still packing a powerful punch, especially on his rumbustious version of "The Mason's Apron".

Matt Molloy

Matt Molloy, a flute player from Co. Roscommon, is a musician of consummate sensitivity. He plays and tours with The Chieftains, is the landlord of a well-known music pub in Westport, Co. Mayo, and commands great respect as a player from the critically demanding traditional hard core.

WITH DÓNAL LUNNY

 Matt Molloy
Mulligan, Ireland
This 1976 debut, when Matt was still in fiery youthful bloom, remains a benchmark for all aspiring flute players. The musicianship is sublime with consummate use of ornamentation, thoroughly enhanced by Lunny's apposite accompaniment on bouzouki and guitar.

WITH PAUL BRADY & TOMMY PEOPLES

⊙ Molloy, Brady, Peoples
Mulligan, Ireland
A largely successful "supergroup" outing featuring Brady's voice and guitar, Matt Molloy's flute and the Donegal-style fiddle of Tommy Peoples on a grand selection of jigs and reels, plus the emigration song "Shamrock Shore".

James Morrison and Paddy Killoran

Two contemporaries of Michael Coleman, these Sligo fiddlers were almost as influential. Apart from his many solo 78s, Morrison also recorded duets with the flute player John McKenna and the uilleann piper Tom Ennis. Killoran recorded solo and with the fiddler Paddy Sweeney, as well as running The Pride of Erin Orchestra.

⊙ From Ballymote to Brooklyn
Coleman Heritage Centre, Ireland
A collection of re-mastered 78s revealing two musicians at the peak of their powers.

Máire Ní Chathasaigh

Harper Máire Ní Chathasaigh (sister of Nollaig Casey) works regularly with her partner, guitarist Chris Newman, and has a particular interest in the music of Turlough Carolan.

⊙ The New Strung Harp
Temple Records, UK
Influenced by both the sean-nós tradition and uilleann pipers, Máire pioneered the playing of traditional music on the harp with great verve and resulting acclaim.

Gerry (banjo) O'Connor

One of Ireland's best-known banjo-players, thanks to his part in the success of Four Men and a Dog and three fine solo albums, Tipperary-born O'Connor's playing is notable for its velocity yet enduring ability never to lose the plot of a tune.

⊙ Myriad
Compass Records, US
Inspired playing, including a marvellous duet with whistler Vinnie Kilduff on "Cam a' Lochaigh".

Gerry (fiddle) O'Connor

The Dundalk fiddler with a mercurial touch and an ever resonant sound achieved renown via membership of both Skylark and Lá Lugh.

★ Journeyman
Lughnasa Music, Ireland
Probably the best album of Irish fiddling for many a year, O'Connor is on tremendous form throughout, exemplified by a remarkable set of a highland and reels kicked off by "The Chicken's Gone to Scotland".

Liam O'Flynn

One of the most versatile musicians of his generation and a master piper of impeccable credentials, O'Flynn excels both as a solo and ensemble player – the latter exemplified by Planxty and his pivotal role in Shaun Davey's symphonic "The Brendan Voyage" (Tara).

WITH SEAMUS HEANEY

★ The Poet and the Piper
Claddagh, Ireland
Nobel prize-winning poet Heaney reads his verse in evocative fashion while O'Flynn's magisterial piping has probably never been better.

Tommy Peoples

A fiddle player of unrivalled modern influence, Tommy first captured major attention in the mid-1970s via his fiery playing with The Bothy Band and a heady brew of tunes drawn from both his native Donegal and time spent in Dublin and Clare. Most of his recordings date from a prolific period spanning the 1970s and 80s, though also check 1998's *The Quiet Glen*.

WITH PAUL BRADY

★ The High Part of the Road
Shanachie, US
Many regard this 1976 album as Tommy's finest hour and tracks include his staggering version of the reel "The Nine Points of Roguery".

Sharon Shannon

Clare-born accordion virtuoso Sharon Shannon (a dab-hand on the fiddle too) has become one of Ireland's best-known musicians over the last two decades thanks to her exuberant music and a willingness to explore the potential of other genres.

⊙ Spellbound
The Daisy Label, Ireland
An engrossing "best of" retrospective, this includes not only some of Sharon's work with the Brixton-based dub producer Denis Bovell but also her inspired rendition of the French-Canadian "The Mouth of the Tobique".

WITH FRANKIE GAVIN, MICHAEL McGOLDRICK AND JIM MURRAY

⊙ Tunes
The Daisy Label, Ireland
A dazzling return to form after a couple of dodgy releases, *Tunes* harnesses box, fiddle and flute, with understated guitar backing, to telling effect.

Davy Spillane

A focal member of Moving Hearts, Spillane has since recorded a number of adept and sensitive solo albums exposing the often breathtaking scope of his uilleann piping and low whistling.

⊙ Atlantic Bridge
Tara, Ireland/Cooking Vinyl, UK
On this debut album producer P.J. Curtis's recruitment of guitarist Albert Lee plus US banjo and *dobro* maestros Béla Fleck and Jerry Douglas, backed by a solid Irish rhythm section, proved a masterstroke. All the conjunctions are best heard on the title track.

Séamus Tansey

From Gurteen, Co. Sligo, the larger-than-life Séamus Tansey is renowned not only for his outstanding flute playing and his championing of "pure drop" traditional music, but also his outspokenness.

⊙ King of the Concert Flute
Sound Records, Ireland
Originally released in 1976, this is Tansey's masterwork, highlighting all the dramatic flamboyance of his playing, accompanied by the mighty Charlie Lennon on piano.

Groups

Altan

A key band since the mid-1980s, Altan recorded the landmark "Island Angel" just before flute player and musical lynchpin Frankie Kennedy died tragically early (in his thirties). The band rallied from the blow, adding virtuoso Donegal box player Dermot Byrne, and remain a major force on disc and stage.

⭐ Island Angel
Green Linnet, US
The classic Altan album saw the band tap the deep roots of the Northern tradition, particularly Donegal, for a fresh and cohesive set. Their re-interpretation of regional style in contemporary idiom informs a set of great tunes and five beautiful songs from Mairéad Ní Mhaonaigh, who also plays majestic fiddle.

⊙ The Blue Idol
Virgin, UK
A monumental return to form after a couple of relatively bland releases (and only in comparison to their own high

standards), this marries vibrant musicianship, particularly on "The Low Highland Set", with some of the best songs the band has ever recorded, including a sparkling, verse-swapping "Daily Growing" featuring Mairéad and Paul Brady.

The Bothy Band

Short-lived, but still incredibly influential, this band set the template for so many others to follow and featured both astonishing instrumental interplay and a telling repertoire of songs.

⭐ The Bothy Band 1975
Mulligan, Ireland
The opening "The Kesh Jig" kicked off a feast of music while fiddler Tommy Peoples shone on "Hector the Hero" on this his only album with the band.

The Chieftains

More than forty years on, though now sadly lacking the late harper and pianist Derek Bell, The Chieftains remain the best-known of all Ireland's traditional groups, yet, strangely, they nowadays rarely make a traditional album. Instead, under the dynamic leadership of piper/whistler Paddy Moloney, over the last 25 years the band has been involved in a colossal number of collaborative projects, ranging from the Breton "Celtic Wedding" and Galician "Santiago" to the Country inspired "Down the Old Plank Road" and the rock-oriented "Fire in the Kitchen", leading some cynics to remark that they have become guest musicians on their own albums.

⭐ The Chieftains 4
Claddagh, Ireland
This all-time favourite is a classic slice of The Chieftains, dating from 1973. It was the band's international breakthrough album and the first to feature harper Derek Bell.

⊙ Water from the Well
BMG, UK
The last Chieftains traditional album to date, recorded at various locations around Ireland and featuring musicians as various as The Dubliners' Barney McKenna and the harper Laoise Kelly.

Clannad

From Donegal, Clannad take their name from a conflation of the words "Clann as Dobhair" meaning "family from Doire", a townland in Donegal. Originally comprising Máire Ní Bhraonáin and her two brothers, Pól and Ciarán plus their slightly older twin uncles Noel and Pádraig Ó Dúgáin, the band has always been strongly song-based, reworking regional repertoire in a fresh, inventive manner.

⊙ Clannad 2
Gael Linn, Ireland
This 1974 album fully captures their early spirit, blending traditional songs in Irish, Carolan tunes and jazzily syncopated arrangements.

⊙ Macalla
BMG, UK
Clannad's sound became increasingly multi-textured during the 1980s, featuring lush and determinedly ethereal arrangements of traditional and newly-written material, exemplified here by the commercially successful duet between Máire Ní Bhraonáin and U2's Bono on "In a Lifetime".

Cran

Combining eloquent vocals, uniquely resonant harmonies, and stunning instrumental arrangements Cran's line-up of Ronan Browne (uilleann pipes and whistles), Seán Corcoran (bouzouki and vocals) and Desi Wilkinson (flute and whistles) produces exuberant music with an astonishing degree of technical accomplishment.

Lover's Ghost
Black Rose Records, Ireland
Often breathtaking in its audacity, this, their third album, is Cran's magnum opus, featuring gorgeous renditions of the eerie "Stolen Bride" and the jaunty jig-song "Na Ceannabháin Bhána".

Danú

Bursting onto the scene with youthful abandon in the late 1990s, this traditional septet blended influences from counties as far afield as Donegal, Waterford and Kerry and has also unleashed two formidable singers, Ciarán Ó Gealbháin and Muireann Nic Amhlaoidh.

⊙ The Road Less Travelled
Shanachie, US
The fourth of Danú's six albums features not only splendid singing from Muireann on "Co. Down" and "Ráitachas na Tairngreacht", but also potent musicianship from accordionist Benny McCarthy and fiddler Oisín McAuley.

De Dannan

Over its almost thirty-year span, De Dannan released a host of albums, revealing seemingly constant line-up changes, but always based on the pivotal duo of fiddler and flute player Frankie Gavin and bouzouki man Alec Finn. Gavin remains one of the finest musicians of his generation while Finn's playing is characterized by elegant counter melodies and an exquisitely developed sense of timing.

⊙ How the West Was Won
Hummingbird, Ireland
This double-CD retrospective not only features nearly all of the band's many singers (including Mary Black, Dolores Keane and Tommy Fleming), but also includes their quirky arrangement of The Beatles' "Hey Jude", naturally segueing into the high-paced "St Jude's Reel".

Dervish

Formed originally to record an album of session tunes for a local Sligo label in the late 1980s, Dervish became a fully-fledged band when Roscommon-born singer Cathy Jordan was recruited. Over a series of strong releases they've remained resolutely rooted in the musical traditions of North Connaught while always providing inspired arrangements of both songs and tunes.

⊙ Midsummer's Night
Whirling Discs, Ireland
Probably the band's best album to date, this not only features magnificent vocals from both Cathy Jordan and Shamie O'Dowd, but also showcases the combined instrumental talents of fiddler Tom Morrow, accordionist Shane Mitchell and flute player Liam Kelly.

The Dubliners

Ireland's best-known ballad group have been warming the cockles and raising not only the roof, but the hackles as well (their single "Seven Drunken Nights" was banned in Ireland in the 1960s) for some forty years.

⊙ The Dubliners with Luke Kelly
Castle Music, UK
There are more Dubliners albums than hairs on a gorilla's chin, but this is still probably the best, featuring the vocal triumvirate of the late Ciarán Bourke and Luke Kelly and the still extant, gravel-voiced Ronnie Drew on classics such as "The Wild Rover" and "The Holy Ground", backed by Barney McKenna's frenetic banjo.

Horslips

Horslips singlehandedly invented "Celtic Rock" in the 1970s and the band is still remembered fondly for its treatments of Irish myths in a rock setting. After more than two decades' absence they reformed in 2004 to record a new album, Roll Back, reworking their old material.

⊙ The Best of ...
Edsel Records, UK
A double-disc retrospective, drawing material chronologically from the band's eight studio albums, this includes tracks from their two concept albums, The Táin and The Book of Invasions, both based on Irish legends.

Lúnasa

A band with a unique sound forged from the conjunction of fiddler Seán Smyth, flute player Kevin Crawford and piper Cillian Vallely, plus the resolute rhythms of double-bassist Trevor Hutchinson and guitarist Donogh Hennessy, Lúnasa are one of Ireland's most exciting and imaginative groupings (with Paul Meehan now filling the guitar spot).

Otherworld
Green Linnet, US
Of their six albums to date, this is definitely the one to track down. All the band's vivacity is captured on "The Floating Crowbar" set and their version of "The Butlers of Glen Avenue" is utterly self-defining.

Moving Hearts

A project initiated by Dónal Lunny and Christy Moore, marrying traditional music and a politically-charged song repertoire with the rhythmic energy of rock, which notably featured uilleann piper Davy Spillane and saxophonist Keith Donald. The Hearts returned to the road as a wholly instrumental outfit in 2007.

⊙ Dónal Lunny's Definitive Moving Hearts
Warner Music, Ireland
Essentially a "best of" compilation and re-mastered to boot, this includes several classic Moore songs as well as the extensive thirteen-minute traditional workout on "The Lark".

Patrick Street

Patrick Street harness the talents of fiddler Kevin Burke, accordionist Jackie Daly, singer/multi-instrumentalist Andy Irvine and guitarist/Northumbrian smallpiper Ged Foley (who replaced guitarist Arty McGlynn a decade into the band's career).

⊙ Compendium – The Best of Patrick Street
Green Linnet, US
An excellent introduction, featuring some typically effervescent polkas from Daly, classics from Irvine's song repertoire and the tune they unleashed upon a thousand sessions, Penguin Café Orchestra's "Music for a Found Harmonium".

Planxty

Unquestionably Ireland's best-loved band, a point utterly reinforced by the rapture which greeted its 2003 re-formation, Planxty's original line-up of Andy Irvine, Dónal Lunny, Christy Moore and Liam O'Flynn have each played more than significant parts in the country's musical history.

Planxty
Shanachie, US

Known as "the black album", thanks to its stark cover of that colour, this magical release redefined Ireland's musical landscape.

Live 2004
Columbia, UK

Thoroughly captures Planxty's joyful music in all its glory and the audience's ecstatic response (and there's a DVD version too) – many argue that the band was better then than ever.

The Pogues

With their unpredictable, but explosive lead singer/lyricist Shane MacGowan, The Pogues became immensely popular in the mid–1980s with a punk-influenced approach to Irish music. The band occasionally reforms for St Patrick's Day and Xmas gigs and Shane sometimes resurfaces with his band The Popes.

⊙ If I Should Fall from Grace with God
WEA, UK

The Pogues' most inspired and imaginative recording not only captures the bar-room blitz of their musical assault, but also includes MacGowan's duet with the late Kirsty MacColl on "Fairytale of New York" and guitarist Phil Chevron's evocative emigration song "Thousands Are Sailing".

Solas

Nine albums on and this Irish-American quintet, in which multi-instrumentalist Seamus Egan and fiddler Winifred Horan are the only constants, remains at the cutting edge.

⊙ Reunion
Compass, US

A fabulous live gig, convening all the band's past and present members and featuring a DVD of the entire affair too.

Sweeney's Men

Some reckon this trio of Andy Irvine, Johnny Moynihan and Terry Woods actually invented folk-rock and they might well be right!

⊙ The Legend of Sweeney's Men
Castle Music, UK

Contains both of the band's albums, plus tracks from a number of side and later projects.

PLAYLIST
Ireland

1 **THE LARK Moving Hearts**
from *Dónal Lunny's Definitive Moving Hearts*
A staggering thirteen-minute musical exploration encapsulating all the Hearts' passion.

2 **RAGGLE TAGGLE GYPSY/TABHAIR DOM DO LÁMH Planxty** from *Planxty*
The classic song and rousing pipes-led tune combination which still creates a storm thirty years on.

3 **CO. DOWN Danú**
from *The Road Less Travelled*
Tommy Sands' modern-day emigration song, vibrantly delivered by Muireann Nic Amhlaoidh.

4 **JIMMY WHELAN Karan Casey** from *Chasing the Sun*
Stunningly arranged and evocatively sung.

5 **TOMMY PEOPLES/THE WINDMILL/ FINTAN MCMANUS'S Altan** from *Island Angel*
Three sparkling reels from the awesome *Island Angel*.

6 **THE LAMENT FOR STAKER WALLACE/ THE GREEN GOWNED LASS Matt Molloy**
from *An Gaoth Aduaidh/The North Wind*
An evocative air followed by a typically sprightly reel.

7 **NA CEANNABHÁIN BHÁNA/THE BLACK ROGUE/WILLIE CLANCY'S SECRET JIG Cran** from *Lover's Ghost*
A rollicking jig-song segues naturally into two rousing jigs.

8 **NA CONNERYS Nioclás Tóibín** from *Rinn na Gael*
One of the "big" songs in the sean-nós tradition, sung impeccably.

9 **THE CHICKEN'S GONE TO SCOTLAND/ KITTY THE HARE/JIM ERWIN'S/THE DRUNKEN MAIDS OF ARDNAREE Gerry O'Connor** from *Journeyman*
This is how fiddle music should sound – a gem of a highland and three fine reels.

10 **THE BUTLERS OF GLEN AVENUE/ SLIABH RUSSELL/CATHAL MCCONNELL'S Lúnasa** from *Otherworld*
Fiddle, flutes, pipes and whistles combine to gorgeous effect.

Italy

canti della memoria

The Bottari barrel beaters, who worked
with Enzo Avitabile, at the annual festival
in Portico, near Naples
Simon Broughton

Italy only became a unified country in 1860 and its constituent parts are still struggling
to retain their local identities. Italy's regional and roots music is still awaiting wider
recognition but, as Alessio Surian outlines, it's a thriving scene.

Traditional music is one of Italy's best-kept secrets. You hear it in the hip-hop of **Almamegretta** and in the soundtracks of **Ennio Moricone**, but it gets little recognition from the Italian press or even its music industry.

The mainstream record industry has concentrated its attention on televised song contests like the Sanremo song contest, and on a few names such as **Eros Ramazzotti**, **Andrea Bocelli**, **Zucchero** and **Laura Pausini** to promote on the international scene. A list of Italian popular singers would go beyond the scope of this chapter, though it is probably worth mentioning that the likes of **Vasco Rossi**, **Ligabue**, **Lucio Dalla**, **Claudio Baglioni** and **Pino Daniele** can attract a hundred thousand people to a concert and sell hundreds of thousands of copies of a new CD. But by now, their use of a regional language or the reference to a local music tradition is rather an exception. This is why *Creuza de ma*, recorded by the late **Fabrizio De Andrè** and **Mauro Pagani** in 1984 stands as a turning point for the Italian roots scene. Showing an extraordinary ability to combine old and new sounds from Italy and its neighbours, the CD acquired such a relevance that Mauro Pagani skilfully re-recorded it to mark its twentieth anniversary.

Italy has some strong regional traditions and a lively but very local and independent roots music scene. However, only a few of the musicians mentioned here are known to the wider Italian public.

Rescuing the Past

Franco Coggiola, **Alan Lomax**, **Diego Carpitella** and **Roberto Leydi** did extensive research into traditional music from the beginning of the 1950s, recording then extant regional styles. Diego Carpitella also captured Italian musical traditions on film, including events where music can be experienced at its best: the Montemarano Carnival, Holy Week in different parts of Sardinia and the possession rituals of Puglia. In the 1950s he teamed-up with anthropologist **Ernesto De Martino** for ground breaking work on the magical aspects of traditional culture – particularly Puglia's *tarantolati*.

The Istituto De Martino, named after Ernesto and now based in Sesto Fiorentino, near Florence, was established in the early 1960s to research and document Italian oral culture and traditional music. It helped bring together the **Nuovo Canzoniere Italiano**, a versatile group including traditional musicians such as **Giovanna Daffini** (Reggio Emilia) and young composers and singers

from different regions such as **Paolo Pietrangeli** (Rome) and **Gualtiero Bertelli** (Venice). Among its leading figures were **Ivan della Mea** and **Giovanna Marini**, who, by combining traditional music and protest songs, literally documented Italian history in the 1960s and 70s.

Between 1962 and 1980 the Nuovo Canzoniere Italiano produced 276 records, mostly for the Dischi del Sole label, and about 3500 concerts. In 1964 their arrangement of the song "Bella Ciao", a symbol of the liberation struggle against Nazism and fascism during World War II, became the title track of a controversial live work and sold over one hundred thousand copies. Nuovo Canzoniere Italiano live works also include "Ci ragiono e canto" (1966 and 1969) which brought together young musicians and traditional groups, including the striking voices of **Aggius** (Gallura, Sardinia), under the direction of Dario Fo. He added a theatrical dimension to the interpretation of a traditional repertoire ranging from Piedmont to Sicily, organizing some forty songs around key themes of birth, work, war, love and marriage.

Fo's show was one of the few attempts to bring together traditions from the various Italian regions which otherwise can be loosely divided into four areas – the north, centre, south, and the island of Sardinia, not to mention specific and rich cultural traditions such as those of the Albanian and Greek communities in the south of Italy or of the people of the Val Resia, Friuli, in northern Italy. Broadly speaking, **northern Italian music** offers a rich repertoire of both instrumental dance music and monodic and polyphonic singing, often in the major mode, with many songs in a narrative, ballad-like style. The **south of Italy** might favour melody over words in its chants with ballads that don't necessarily take into account the epic-lyrical rhythm adopted in northern and central regional chants. The **central regions** combine both northern and southern musical elements, though they retain some original features, for example singing in *endecasillabo*, a song-form based on phrases of eleven syllables. Finally, **Naples** and **Sardinia** (see p.356) still offer a wide range of examples of a strong and autonomous cultural identity.

Naples

As elsewhere in southern Italy, Naples is at its best around events like saints' days, or Holy Week when the devotional music and dances bring together its pagan and Christian roots.

Canzone napoletana

There is a song from 1839, "Te voglio bene assaie" (I love you so much), which is still very popular and numbers countless interpretations. It is often considered the starting point of **canzone napoletana** (Neapolitan Song), the unique mix of popular and classical elements that cuts across Naples' social classes and musical styles.

Canzone napoletana has roots in the *villanella* of the sixteenth century, a rural style which influenced the cultivated Neapolitan composers with its polyphonic vocal harmonies and often satirical lyrics. The writers and composers of the urban canzone napoletana were poets and intellectuals as well as unschooled popular authors. Some of their songs achieved international fame thanks to performances from tenor **Enrico Caruso** (1873–1921) onwards.

In recent years this vast repertoire has found sober yet passionate new voices in **Sergio Bruni** (1921–2003) and **Roberto Murolo** (1912–2003). The wider public listen to it through popular TV faces such as **Massimo Ranieri** (who is reinterpreting the tradition with arrangements by Mauro Pagani) and **Nino D'Angelo**, while the roots scene prefers the theatrical dimension added by violin maestro **Lino Cannavacciuolo** and **Beppe Barra**. Barra, in particular, has an ability to stage traditional repertoire such as "La Cantata dei pastori" (The Shepherds' Chant) and to collaborate with outstanding voices, among them **Pietra Montecorvino**.

Campania Roots Groups

Beppe Barra and his mother Concetta collaborated with the only roots group to achieve national fame, **Nuova Compagnia di Canto Popolare** (NCCP), founded in 1967 by **Roberto De Simone**, from the Pignasecca neighbourhood. NCCP are still active today with the powerful voices of Fausta Vetere and Corrado Sfogli. De Simone has continued his own research and produced outstanding works often conceived as stage productions. Other members of NCCP such as **Eugenio Bennato** and **Teresa De Sio** pursued their own paths and have found a safe harbour within the *taranta* movement. Today De Simone's work seems to be best interpreted by guitar player and composer **Antonello Paliotti** who offers traditional material new compositions and arrangements. With strings echoing the rural and urban Neapolitan melodies, his original compositions bring out the different souls and metric ideas of dancing rhythms in the *moresca* and *tarantella*.

While canzone napoletana works best with the simple guitar and "thin" voice of Roberto Murolo, the current loud and cosmopolitan face of the city is reflected in the "thick" sound of **Daniele Sepe**'s groups, who seem to embody the city's musical versatility. As a musician Sepe is at ease as a classical flautist, jazz saxophonist or player of traditional percussion and wind instruments. What is most remarkable though, is his ability to find and play energetic traditional and protest songs from different Italian and world traditions.

Sepe began playing in the early 1970s with **Gruppo Operaio di Pomigliano d'Arco**, better known as **E'Zezi**. At that time, he recalls, "there were two different views on popular music. People like the NCCP and Roberto De Simone opted for more or less philological research. For others, such as E'Zezi, traditional music was less serious so they were convinced it was legitimate to create new texts and new sounds. In other words there was a more scientific and a more political way of interpreting things." Over the years, Sepe's ensem-

Folk Roots Archive

Daniele Sepe

Wrasse

Enzo Avitabile and Bottari

ble has gathered some of the best Neapolitan musicians, who can also be heard on solo projects by singer **Brunella Selo** and guitar player and singer **Massimo Ferrante** – a man who shares with Sepe an interest in the traditions of the Italian southern regions.

The 1990s proved to be seminal for a number of roots groups exploring the musical heritage of Campania, the region around Naples. Outstanding examples include Guido Sodo's _Cantodiscanto_; the double bass and _tammorra_ frame drum duo of Francesco and Vincenzo Faraldo who teamed up with Emilio Di Donato's mandolin and guitar as **Corepolis**; singer **Vittorio Accone**, who had already produced two very energetic acoustic CDs with **La Moresca**; **Napoli Extracomunitaria**, (nine musicians deeply rooted in the rural traditions around Mount Vesuvius); **Rua Port'Alba**, who produced three CDs featuring lyrics focusing on issues of social justice at the local and at the global level; **Sancto Ianne** who come from San Giovanni di Ceppaloni (near Benevento) and show an original approach in arranging traditional material. Older groups include **Nuova Compagnia della Tammorra** from the little Marra village and **I Musicalia**, led by brothers Amerigo and Marcello Ciervo from the Caudina valley, near Benevento.

Contemporary sounds come from jazz pianist and composer **Rita Marcotulli** and singer **Maria Pia De Vito** who toured and recorded the project "Nauplia", a convincing marriage between improvised music and Neapolitan traditions. Another distinctive trend is the _neomelodici_, the pop oriented love and satirical songs which make singers such as **Ciro Ricci** and **Ida Rendano** the stars of weddings and street parties.

Another jazz veteran, **Enzo Avitabile** has found his path to traditional sounds by playing with the **Bottari** group from Portico. Avitabile leads by singing and playing tenor sax, and is backed by a colourful seven-piece band including trumpet and baritone sax, _chitarra battente_, mandola and a rhythm section with keyboards, electric bass and his brother and long time musical partner Carlo on drums. On stage behind them, all dressed in black are the Bottari: nine percussion players solemnly hitting three enormous barrels, four vats and two scythes under the smooth and athletic direction of _capopattuglia_ **Carmine Romano**. Traditionally, peasants in Portico would hit barrels, vats and scythes in a frantic way in order to drive evil spirits out of the house.

In the Neapolitan area there is still a living tradition of dancing and singing to the accompaniment of frame drums, especially the large tammorra and the smaller _tamburello_. This has been adopted and updated in the music by groups such as Tamburi del Vesuvio and Tammurriata di Scafati, led by **Nando Citarella**, and **Paranza di Somma Vesuviana**, with the melismatic voice of **Marcello Colasurdo**, previously with E'Zezi, and **Spaccanapoli**.

Sicily

Thanks to its lively jazz scene, Sicily boasts some of the country's best instrumentalists. Based in Palermo, **Enzo Rao** (violin, electric bass and _oud_) is a skilled composer and musician. His collaboration with Glen Velez (percussion) and **Gianni Gebbia** (saxophones) has drawn on Sicilian traditions and the Arab influence that is so much a

Organetti

How much of the evocative mood of Fellini's *Amarcord* is due to Nino Rota's melodies coming from the blind *organetto* player? Probably invented by Demian in Vienna in 1829, this little diatonic accordion or melodeon has become one of the most popular instruments in Italian traditional music, sometimes teaming up with instruments like *zampogna*, *launeddas*, violin or even substituting them due to its more stable tuning, powerful volume and ability to handle both the leading and accompanying melodies at once.

The son of traditional musicians from Maranola (Latina), **Ambrogio Sparagna** made field recordings with the late Diego Carpitella, Italy's leading ethnomusicologist. A virtuoso organetto player, in 1984 he founded the **Bosio Big Band**, an orchestra made solely of (thirty) organetti and percussion. Following the example of Roberto De Simone with *La Gatta Cenerentola* he has composed several theatrical works for the orchestra including *Trillillì*, *Giofà*, *La via dei Romei*, featuring the voice of the famous Rome-based songwriter Francesco De Gregori.

One of the most gifted pupils of Ambrogio Sparagna is **Clara Graziano**. A member of the Bosio Big Band, she has taken the place of Sparagna as teacher of organetto at Scuola Popolare di Musica Donna Olimpia (Roma) and has teamed up with such oustanding jazz players as Toni Germani (reeds) and Giovanni Lo Cascio (percussions). The compositions she writes for her group, **Circo Diatonico**, are all instrumentals centred around the life of the circus, and they interact on stage with the theatrical clown Augusto.

Based in Puglia, **Mario Salvi** has been playing organetto for over twenty years and has specialized in the various forms of tarantella. He can play dozens of different traditional tarantellas and has composed several himself. Although his own recordings are fairly recent, he can be heard on the first record by Riccardo Tesi in 1983 where he plays tamburello, the frame drum which he also teaches, drawing from the techniques of different parts of Italy. With **Roberto Tombesi** of Calicanto and **Ciuma** (Bevano Est), Salvi has formed a unique organetto trio that skilfully blends friendship, musical traditions and original compositions from northern, central and southern Italian regions bordering the Adriatic Sea.

Roberto Tombesi's musical journey also mixes field research, a degree in ethnomusicology at the University of Bologna, intensive concert and recording dates and teaching activities including the writing of a seminal organetto handbook together with Riccardo Tesi. He took up the instrument in 1979 although he had been fascinated by it since childhood, when family holidays were spent in Montecarotto, a village near Ancona, a region at the core of the organetto diffusion in Italy.

Paolo Benvenuti

Virtuoso and master of diverse regional traditions, **Riccardo Tesi** has collaborated with French mandolin virtuoso Patrick Vaillant and the jazz reeds of **Gianluigi Trovesi** to name a few. Based in Pistoia (Tuscany), he is, of course, a great interpreter of the repertoire of the Apennine mountains between Tuscany and Emilia, usually involving violin and organetto ensembles. In 1998 he formed his own group, **Banditaliana**, including Ettore Bonafè on percussion, Claudio Carboni on sax and the voice and guitar of Maurizio Geri. Together they have produced four solid CDs. Tesi's masterpiece dates back to 1995 when he gathered together some outstanding folk, classical and jazz musicians for a project centred on the **liscio** dance, probably the only style which can be found in all Italian regions.

The most brilliant pupil of Riccardo Tesi, **Filippo Gambetta** has built a solid and deserved reputation as organetto virtuoso performer. With two CDs under his belt, this Genoa-based young musician has shown astonishing maturity both as a player and composer. **Raffaelle Pinelli** is following a similar path in Rome.

Amongst organetto players working in regional traditions, two of the most accomplished are **Pierino Crucitti** and **Totore Chessa** from Irgoli (Nuoro), in Sardinia, where the instrument was first introduced around 1870 and has partially replaced wind instruments such as the launeddas. He has mastered organetto styles from different parts of the island, and continues to develop the heritage of the virtuosi of the recent past such as Francesco Bande, Pietro Porcu and Tonino Masala, supporting the melodies with his extraordinary ability on the bass.

Riccardo Tesi

part of the island's history. Their group **Shamal** made its name playing distinctively Mediterranean instrumental music, as **Nakaira** is doing today. Meanwhile, since 2002 the Catania-based group **Ipercussonici** has combined outstanding vocal and percussion talents to produce a variety of world sounds. Another outstanding Sicilian percussionist, **Alfio Antico,** learned to play framedrums – another common feature of Arabic and Sicilian music – from his shepherd grandparents, and has developed a technique which bridges many styles, including the widespread tarantella.

Holy Week is one of the best times to visit Sicilian villages to hear music traditions. In places like **Montedoro,** the devotional songs connected with the passion of Christ are sung acapella exclusively by male singers, with moving four-part harmonies. **Brass bands** are also a frequent feature of religious festivities and they have developed a rich repertoire often based on operatic and classical compositions from the late nineteenth century and early twentieth century. The local *banda* was very often the product of the working people, and the only musical training for players who would later make their names known in the folk, pop and jazz music circuits.

In many places the banda is directly linked to the local Catholic church, but in the first half of the twentieth century one might have found two bandas in the same village, one of the Catholic church and the other associated with a more progressive religion. In both cases the local bandas would have a repertoire ranging from well-known traditional songs to operatic arias by Bellini and other well-known classical composers.

A collection of Easter and funeral marches from southern Italy was recorded by the twenty piece brass band **Banda Ionica**, including some of the best Sicilian musicians headed by **Rosario Patane** and Aretuska leader, trumpet wiz **Roy Paci**. "The Banda Ionica project", recalls producer **Fabio Barovero**, previously with Mau Mau, "comes from the love Roy and I share for the sounds of the brass bands from southern Italy and particularly those of the coastal regions around the Tyrrhenian Sea. They play music that can make you laugh and cry. Their way of playing awakens a collective memory that concerns not only the musical compositions and arrangements but also a certain type of interpretation: a sound that took over 150 years to mature as we hear it today."

Along with Puglia, Sicily is known as "Italy's granary" and traditionally the **harvest times** have brought together a complex mix of religious and work songs, and a cross-cultural exchange due to the coming together of reapers from different parts

of the island. It is the time when the polyphonic singing in the devotional style of "Sarvi Rigina" and "Razioni di lu Metiri" blend with party songs such as "A Nicusiana", often accompanied by guitar or organetto. A selection of religious traditional songs can be heard on *Pesah*, a CD produced in 1999 by **Carlo Muratori** from Siracusa.

Storytellers and Songwriters

Muratori's first group, **Cilliri** arrived as a breath of fresh air in 1977, suggesting new ways of interpreting traditional material and the wealth of songs collected by field researchers such as Antonino Uccello – a source of inspiration for guitar player Raimondo Minardi's **Sciroccu** as well. With the CD *Canti e Incanti* (1994), Muratori took a different path, exploring his abilities as guitar player and songwriter both with his own group and as partner of organetto maestro **Riccardo Tesi**.

The guitar is the working tool of traditional storytellers like **Ciccio Busacca**. "In Italy the blues is more popular than Italian traditional music. But we also have our Woody Guthries in the likes of Rocco Spatellaro and Ciccio Busacca. Busacca fought with his songs against the Mafia, but nobody turned up at his funeral. There is a general ignorance about the little which is being done in this field," says **Ambrogio Sparagna**, one of the leading Italian organetto players and composers. Busacca was probably at its best in his rendition of the poems of the late **Ignazio Buttitta**, a poet with a genuine passion for the Sicilian language, who has remained a source of inspiration not only for traditional groups but also for new bands such as **Agricantus** from Palermo (check their electric version of Buttita's "Li vuci de l'omini"), **Tanino Lazzaro** (now with **Asteriskos**), and the seminal **Kunsertu** from Messina, a group open to many world beats and languages featuring the superb voice of **Fahisal Taher**. Today he is laying bridges across the Mediterranean with groups such as **Al Kantara**, including **Fabio Tricomi**'s *marranzanu* (Jew's harp) and Catania-based **Dounia**, a quartet featuring Vincenzo Gangi (guitar), Giovanni Arena (double bass), and Riccardo Gerbino – also the basic line-up for the group of **Cecilia Pitino**, a gifted singer who is at home both with new compositions and traditional pieces in the footsteps of **Rosa Balistreri**.

Listen out too for the voices of the storyteller **Mario Incudine** and the **Fratelli Mancuso**, the two brothers Enzo and Lorenzo from Sutera who continue to develop a Sicilian tradition with exclusively acoustic instruments often borrowed from other

Zampogna

In Italy the bagpipe is called **zampogna** or, in the northern regions, **piva**. A multifaceted rural instrument of particular interest to ethnomusicologists, the zampogna is at the centre of an exciting musical revival, with cultural organisations such as Pucambù (Reggio Calabria), Circolo Culturale La Zampogna (Scapoli) and Archivio Aurunco (Formia) organizing events with a focus on the instrument.

The fact that the two main zampogna festivals take place in central Italy – in Scapoli in July and in Maranola in January – suggests that the instrument is mainly played in the rural areas of central and southern Italy, while it is almost an exception to find it in the northern regions. Even so, one of the best players and researchers, **Gabriele Coltri**, lives in Milan, and other young players are to be found in cities rather than villages.

Festival director **Erasmo Treglia** divides his time between touring and recording with Aquaragia Drom, managing the FinisTerre label and the various initiatives of Archivio Aurunco, including "La Zampogna". He recalls, "when we started we feared we were organizing an event that would more or less provide a picture of the end of an era, of the disappearance of the zampogna. The opposite was true. People who have come to festival year after year have witnessed how the older generation of players and makers have been able to integrate with new players and even new bagpipe makers. The best players know now that they will meet makers such as **Piero Ricci** who has introduced new holes/notes on the drone pipes, **Giancarlo Parisi** or **Gianni Perilli** whose father had introduced significant modifications in the pipes of the old instruments. The general feeling is that of living a turning point."

regions. "We discovered all of a sudden that we had very peculiar voices", says Enzo. "In reality we never paid much attention to our voices nor can we say to have had a master. It was all very much based on instinct. Back home we used to listen to the peasants singing their *lamentazioni* and monodic chants, called *alla carrettiera*, the chant sung when coming back from the fields riding a mule in the evening. Without being aware of it, as children, these chants must have entered us and burst out at a later stage. When we began to sing our music we found ourselves using this vocal style spontaneously."

Today every Sicilian city hosts oustanding roots groups such as **Tammorra** from Palermo, **Taberna Mylaensis** from Milazzo, **Strummula**, who turn Catania's sounds into folk-rock songs and **Dioscuri**, from Agrigento. Yet on a very different wavelength is the research started by **Franco Battiato** in the early seventies. His work bridges classical, traditional and rock music and resulted in a pop-oriented trilogy which began in 1979 with *L'era del cinghiale bianco* and, via *Patriots*, culminated in *La voce del Padrone*, which sold over one million copies. The composer from Catania proved his ability both with his long-term cooperation with virtuoso musicians such as violinist and composer **Giusto Pio** and by mastering such different fields as sacred music, opera, with the remarkable "Gilgamesh" (1991), and *lieder*, with "Café de la Paix". His spiritual strength and humanity became evident in the aftermath of the Gulf War – in December 1992 Battiato brought the I Virtuosi Italiani Orchestra to Baghdad where he played together with the Iraqi National Symphonic Orchestra.

Calabria

An instrument which occurs throughout Italy is the *zampogna*, a bagpipe of which there are around ten different types grouped into two broad families: double oboes and double clarinets. In Calabria alone there are five different types of zampogna, where it is usually called *ciaramedda*.

Roberto Leydi supposes that, "the double oboe type evolved from the Phrygian *aulos* or the Roman *tibia* (with pipes of unequal length), which, already in Nero's time, had been provided with an airtight skin reservoir (bag)", while "the drones were added in the Middle Ages. We may also suppose that the double clarinet type originates in the eastern Mediterranean. In this case, too, the drones were no doubt added later, perhaps in imitation of the 'Latin' instruments."

Ettore Castagna and Sergio di Giorgio of the **Re Niliu** (Wax King) group have been actively documenting and reviving this tradition. Together with musicians and researchers **Danilo Gatto** and **Salvatore Megna** they fed new arrangements and compositions celebrating the traditional repertoire of Calabria. Re Niliu's acoustic recordings in the 1980s went pretty much unnoticed, but did garner the attention and respect of anybody interested in roots music, and are today a collectors' item. The electric and eclectic 1994 CD *Pucambù* made it into the world music charts and provided Re Niliu with international exposure.

Greek offspring

While **Sergio Di Giorgio** was working hard to become a skilled instrument maker and interpreter of the traditional repertoire, Danilo Gatto and Salvatore Megna went their own way and further developed the *Pucambù* electro-acoustic elements as **Phaleg**. **Ettore Castagna** stayed acoustic and devoted his research to the Albanian and Greek-Byzantine worlds within the traditions of Calabria. He has also researched the regional *lira* (ancient Calabrian violin) tradition, resulting in a recorded anthology, and collaborated with outstanding singers such as **Peppe Voltarelli**. Castagna founded the group **Nistanimera,** which means "night and day" in Calabrian Greek – a language now disappearing from southern Italy. Passionate research and documentation of Calabrian traditions also lies at the heart of the music of **Valentino Santagati**, who has brought to attention the chitarra battente, of **Xicrò**, led by **Antonello Ricci**, and of **Antonio Critelli**'s **Agorà**.

The region is also home to energetic tarantellas or *soni a ballu*, a widespread tradition in villages such as Cardeto, kept alive by groups such as **Cumelca**, with lyrics drawing from their Greek heritage. Explained by leading organetto and tamburello player, Mario Salvi, "The **tarantella reggitana** comes from the mountain region of Aspromonte (Calabria). It is the most "acrobatic" since it is full of melodic and rhythmic variations which reflect the dynamic steps of the dance. The **tarantella di Montemarano** comes from a small village close to Avellino (Campania). It is a very complex type of tarantella due to the richness of the musical phrases, its syncopated rhythm and its frequent and smooth modulations into different keys. The **pizzica pizzica** comes from Salento (Puglia) and owes its name to the bite of the tarantula. It is characterized by the obsessive rhythms of the tamburello and singing which are contrasted with the melodic variations on the organetto."

Puglia

Traditional music from Puglia is best known for the healing ritual of the tarantolati, a complex tradition that can still be witnessed today, though it is gradually disappearing. The tarantolati, usually women who believe they have been bitten and poisoned by a spider known as *tarantola*, are healed through long hours or even days of dancing to the 12/8 ostinato rhythms of tarantella/*tarantata*, usually performed with the use of tamburelli plus guitar, organetto and violin, depending on the local musician ensemble.

Puglia's links with the Greek world are being explored by **X-Dar**, featuring Stratos Diamantis' accordion, while the multicultural **Radio Dervish** centre their energetic, electric live act on the voice of Palestinian **Nabil Ben Salaméh**. Also mixing traditional roots with modern sounds and instruments is **Tavernanova**, though other groups, such as **Canzoniere di Terra d'Otranto** (Salento) and **Uaragniaun**, with the moving voice of Maria Moramarco, have devoted their research and acoustic repertoire to specific local traditions.

Brass bands and beyond

Puglia is a region with a lively history of brass bands, probably best represented by **Banda Ruvo di Puglia**, an ensemble which sometimes collaborates with the iconoclastic jazz trumpet player and composer **Pino Minafra**. During Holy Week, they play compositions of great beauty and slow passion, with rhythm, as Minafra puts it, "practically suspended" and "a sweet, spiritual sound …with sweeping melodies, where there is no crisis of doubt or scepticism, because this music is addressed to believers." In recent years, the passion for brass bands has involved many other outstanding jazz players – **Enrico Rava, Battista Lena, Eugenio Colombo** and even Daniele Sepe who felt the need of a brass band for his arrangement of Matteo Salvatore's "Padrone mio". **Salvatore**, a source of inspiration for many contemporary musicians, was born in Foggia in 1925 and spent his youth learning, reviving, and then popularizing a canon of traditional songs, some dating as far back as the thirteenth century.

In 1959 ethnomusicologist Diego Carpitella went to Puglia to study *tarantismo* with an interdisciplinary team led by Ernesto De Martino. Their writings are still a great source of inspiration for a new wave of musicians such as **Uccio Aloisi**, and have turned Puglia into the most lively place for traditional music, the top event being the mid-August La Notte della Taranta (The Taranta Night). This large venue introduced the superb voice of **Anna Cinzia Villani** to a wider audience, while in Puglia she is well known both for her own work and for singing and playing with ensembles such as **Canzo-**

Faraualla, the striking female acapella group

niere **Grecanico Salentino**, **Striare** and **Ensemble Terra d'Otranto**. "Tradition should be kept alive", she says, "by allowing room for improvisation." She uses the same approach when singing with **Questa è la strada delle donne belle**, a female vocal trio with Raffaella Aprile (from the group Zoe) and Maria Mazzotta (who is active within Canzoniere Grecanico Salentino). Similar innovative strengths are being displayed by groups such as **Avleddha** and **Les Troublamours** and by songwriters such as **Tonino Zurlo** and **Dario Muci**.

Unlike most traditional musicians, **Mimmo Epifani** completed his mandolin studies at a Conservatory, as did some members of **Terranima** from Foggia. His mandolin and voice were features of the Taranta Power project by Eugenio Bennato's Musicanova before he founded his own quartet in 2004 with Massimo Cusato on percussion, Joe de Marco on bass and the accordion and arrangements by Giuseppe Laudanna.

There is a high concentration of groups drawing inspiration from the pizzica and the tarantismo healing in the Lecce region, including **Alla Bua** (Other Healing), Giorgio Di Lecce's **Arakne Mediterranea**, **Aramiré**, **Ariacorte**, **Avleddha**, **Canzoniere Grecanico Salentino**, **Gruppo Ghetonia**, **Mascarimirì**, **Menamenamò**, **Officina Zoè** and **Xanti Yaca**. **Nidi D'Arac** bring electronic and dub sounds to merge with tarantellas in the footsteps of bands such as **Tavernanova** and **Sud Sound System**. And the Bari province

is lively as well, including groups as diverse as **Ziringaglia**, **Radicanto**, the female acapella **Faraualla** and the Balkan influenced **Antonella Di Domenico** with **Rosapaeda**.

Basilicata and Molise

Potenza, in the Basilicata region, is home to **Suoni**, who sometimes play the Tarantismo in partnership with E'Zezi. Further explorations of this possession music have been made by **Antonio Infantino,** founder of the group **Tarantolati di Tricarico**, known for alternating the obsessive percussive patterns of tarantella with soothing melodies.

The folk music of Molise, Italy's smallest region, can be heard on the CD *Musiche tradizionali del Molise 1* (FinisTerre MTM 01). A rare opportunity to hear the unique *Fossalto* bagpipe, the recording was made by **Diego Carpitella** and **Alberto Mario Cirese** in May 1954, during the Pagliara ritual – the only opportunity to capture the *Ecchite Maje* (Spring chant).

Central Italy

The medieval tradition of *ottava rima* is a way of singing widespread in central and northern Lazio,

257

as well as in Tuscany and Abruzzo. Sometimes called the chant of the *poeti contadini* (peasant poets), it can be based on the poetic texts of Homer, Hesiod, Virgil, Ovid, Dante and Ariosto. It might address social and political issues, and it can be totally improvised, often as a competition between two singers who take turns with the eight-line stanzas. The difficulty lies in having to begin each new stanza with the last rhyme of the previous singer.

The *saltarello*, the most widespread dance in the whole of central Italy is mainly accompanied by bagpipes and tamburello. Among its different forms, the saltarella from Alta Sabina (Lazio) is considered the liveliest and most complex. It is usually structured in four different parts and danced by couples. This and other local traditions are well captured by gifted organetto players such as Riccardo Tesi and Ambrogio Sparagna, as well as by folk groups like the Rome-based **La Piazza** featuring the powerful voice of **Sara Modigliani**. La Piazza have also performed original music by **Giovanna Marini**, who brings together contemporary music and popular traditions plus a passion for polyphonic singing.

The research by Giovanna Marini and Sandro Portelli represented a turning point for the Italian "folk revival", a seminal movement which stimulated young musicians to investigate and interpret their regional traditions, as in the case of **Canzoniere del Lazio**, founded in 1972. The meeting of the Canzoniere del Lazio's **Piero Brega** with the daring vocal experiments of **Demetrio Stratos** led to the innovative music of **Carnascialia**, a group whose explosive mix of jazz and traditional musicians produced a seminal record in 1978. It took over 25 years to produce something comparable, and it was thanks to Canzoniere del Lazio's **Carlo Siliotto** and his unique composition, *'O Patrone d'o Cane* (The Dog's Owner).

Another veteran of the roots scene, **Luigi Cinque** now leads the **Tarantula Hypertext O'rchestra**, a group that displays a passion for hypnotic trance music and the use of iterative rhythms and sober tonal variations. You'll find them at their best behind the voice of **Raiz**, a passionate singer in the Neapolitan language. A key area of research and study for the Tarantula Hypertext O'rchestra is the religious and spiritual dimension of music across Mediterranean cultures. Cinque describes it as, "a matter of practising the art of reciprocal listening without losing the respective diversity. Within this perspective Italian islands offer a very stimulating past, both when the cross-cultural influences are evident as in the case of Jewish, Christian and Muslim traditions in Sicily, and

when one has to search at a deeper level, as in the case of the Phoenician influences in Sardinia. A search that provides fascinating musical results as we are discovering in our collaboration with the Coro Santu Lussurgiu."

Giovanna Marini has continued to inspire new groups through her teaching activities at Scuola Popolare di Musica del Testaccio (Rome) and at the University of Paris IV. A long-time member of Marini's Quartet, **Lucilla Galeazzi** has gone on to work in two outstanding trios: one with Carlo Mariani and Massimo Nardi, integrating different Italian and Sardinian roots elements, and a second named **Il Trillo** with the virtuoso percussion player Carlo Rizzo and Ambrogio Sparagna, exploring different types of song-formats in Italian traditional music.

Based in Rome, but performing a repertoire featuring various traditional influences and instruments, is **Acquaragia Drom**, a group focusing on Gypsy music who combine voice, organetto, guitar, violin and other traditional instruments such as the tammorra. Another stand-out of the region, **Viola Buzzi** of Viterbo has been active as a singer since 1994 and collaborated with Mario Salvi to produce one of the best live works centred around organetto, "Comunicanti". Also worth noting are **Novalia** and **Tyrrenia,** two bands that blend traditional music and instruments with electric guitars and sampling machines (the latter with their roots in Aquila, from the Abruzzo region). Novalia's singer **Raffaello Simeoni** has shown an ability to renew local traditions in a passionate acoustic way as well.

Abruzzo

Abruzzo is one of the smallest Italian regions, right in the middle of the Italian peninsula between the Adriatic Sea and the Apennine Mountains. It is a region where musical elements typical of the south blend with northern influences such as the traditional epic singing. Abruzzo has been the object of systematic ethnomusicological research since the second half of the nineteenth century, when **Gennaro Finamore** began to collect both lyrics and musical scores of Abruzzo traditional songs. Today Finamore's writings are available at the County Library in Chieti. They especially concentrate on female songs and have sparked a series of books and recordings, culminating in *La Musica di tradizione orale in Abruzzo* by **Domenico di Virgilio**, a comprehensive presentation of the variety of musical traditions concentrated in this small region.

The members of **Nuova Agricola Associazione** are based in and around Francavilla al Mare, on the Abruzzo Adriatic Sea. The group formed during the summer of 2000, and features the voices of **Graziano Zuccarino** and **Maria Alessandra Piroddi**. Although Abruzzo is rich with traditional instruments such as the *ddu botte* melodeon, bagpipes and various percussion instruments, the group makes no use of any of them. Rather, it presents a conventional rock band line-up. The name of the group means New Peasant Association, three words that represent a short artistic and cultural manifesto. Their songs employ a wide range of rhythms, from reggae to Balkan flavours, from traditional saltarello to beguine – the common element in all being a creative use of the local peasant dialect.

Another significant group is the trio **Scura Maje,** centred on the piano of Maurizio Patricelli. It has brought traditional melodies from Abruzzo to meet jazz in minimalistic arrangements.

Marche

Marche is home to two of Italy's oldest roots groups: **Canzoniere Piceno Popularia** whose first concerts date back to 1975, and Gastone Pietrucci's **La Macina,** founded in 1968. Pietrucci has conducted extensive field work and research in and around Ancona, focusing on the disappearing peasant traditions. The CD *Aedo Malinconico* recorded by Pietrucci in 2002 showcases the songwriter side of La Macina's leader, with accompaniment by diverse musicians ranging from the Severini brothers (from The Gang rock group) to pop singer Rossana Casale.

Tuscany

Tuscany's traditional repertoire seems best captured by Riccardo Tesi's and Maurizio Geri's **Banditaliana** album *Acqua Foco e Vento*. In the 1970s both musicians worked with traditional singer Caterina Bueno. Twenty-five years later they selected some of the best work songs, ottava rimas, beggar's songs, ballads and lullabies from the Apennine Mountains around Pistoia and neighbouring provinces, and also from across the sea in Corsica, where carbon miners would emigrate for seasonal work from the end of the eighteenth century.

Field recordings and traditional songs are also at the core of the repertoire by **I Viulan**, one of the oldest roots groups, and **Paulem**, one of its offshoots. **Musicanti del Piccolo Borgo** also have over 25 years experience interpreting the traditional repertoire from the central and southern Appennines Mountains.

Since the 1990s new groups and performers have elaborated on the traditional material, making use of both traditional and modern instruments, as in the case of **Bizantina**, featuring the voice of Michaela D'Astuto, and **Claudia Bombardella**'s eclectic projects.

The North

At the beginning of the twentieth century in Polesine, northeast of Italy, peasants used to dance to the sound of organetto, violins and other string or brass instruments playing *polcas* and *mazurcas*, often in odd tempos. After World War II the arrival of other types of music, combined with deep social changes, almost caused the disappearance of the traditional repertoire. Groups who have gone hunting for northern Italian repertoires in the last twenty years have uncovered many songs and dances through the stories of a few musicians already in their eighties. The results are oustanding recordings of both traditional and new material, though not many record shops stock the CDs of even key groups like **Calicanto** (Veneto), **Baraban** (Lombardy) or **La Ciapa Rusa** (Piedmont). Live concerts have remained the most effective way to keep in touch with these traditions.

Friuli and Trentino

The combination of the Alps Mountains and of the Po Valley provides a distinct character to the Italian northern music. Good examples come from the Friuli region, such as **La Sedon Salvadie**, founded in 1977 and based on the meeting between organetto player Andrea del Favero and violin and bagpipe player from Istria Dario Marusic. Like **Braul** and **Carantan**, their concerts and recordings are based on a wide variety of traditional material. Since 1994 the passionate voice of **Gabriella Gabrielli** and the group **Zuf de Zur** actively practice a mixed repertoire including Friuli, Istrian, Slovenian and Yiddish material.

Violin often plays a central role in re-interpreting traditional dances and the oral repertoire. Oustanding players and researchers include **Giulio Venier** (often in duo with guitar player **Michele Pucci**) and Mauro Odorizzi and Sandro Franchini with **Abies Alba**, from Trento – also home to the eclectic **Destrani Taraf**.

Veneto

Back in 1967, **Canzoniere Popolare Veneto** was one of the first groups to investigate and perform traditional material, notably for their album *Addio*

Venezia Addio, still available through I Dischi del Sole/AlaBianca distribution. From this group, the late Luisa Ronchini remains a reference for all researchers in this field, while **Gualtiero Bertelli** acquired national fame with the song "Nina" and is still touring and recording as a songwriter and in thematic theatre productions based on Veneto's history, often accompanied by **Compagnia delle Acque**. **Mercanti di Liquore** is another group that found its public through theatre productions, teaming up with the solo actor Marco Paolini.

Based in Padua, the group **Calicanto** grew out of the research and field recordings of multi-instrumentalist Roberto Tombesi. After five records presenting for the most part the traditional repertoire of the region, their recent concerts and recordings feature new compositions open to other Mediterranean influences. Former Calicanto members **Rachele Colombo** (voice, guitar, percussion) and **Corrado Corradi** (*bandonina*, a mix of organetto and *bandoneon*) pursued their own musical project, halfway between traditional material and original songs, as **Archedora.**

Calicanto was also instrumental in arranging **Grazia De Marchi**'s *Sporco Mondo* (Dirty World) album, actively experimenting with songwriting and traditional sounds. Unlike these groups, **Canzoniere Vicentino** always stayed within the tradition, producing thematic roots albums.

Emilia Romagna

Another group with deep roots in the tradition of the Veneto region and in the Emilian Apennines is **Piva dal Carner**, an acoustic ensemble which rapidly established a reputation in the Italian folk circuit in the 1990s before splitting to give birth to Bonifica Emiliano Veneta (BEV). The region now has a wealth of roots groups, including **Bevano Est**, founded in 1990 by organetto player Stefano "Ciuma" Delvecchio; **Enerbia**, from the Emilia region; **Fiamma Fumana** who mix traditional songs and live electronics; **Gruppo Emiliano** who have combined ethnomusicological work with over 25 years of concerts and recordings; **I Musetta**, from the Piacenza Appennines Mountains; and **L'Uva Grisa** from Bellaria Igea Marina (nearby Ravenna). The more recently established ensembles **Mundaris, Paulem, Pneumatica Emiliano-Romagnola** and **Pivari Trio** make music based on material from field research and use a variety of instruments.

From the same region, **Vinicio Capossela** is a singer who has done countless collaborations with pop, jazz, Balkan and Italian roots groups.

Lombardy

The oldest group still active today is surely **Gruppo Padano di Piadena**, founded in 1962 in Piadena, near Cremona. They feature the moving voice of Bruno Fontanella, a member of another group from the same city, **I Giorni Cantati di Calvatone e Piadena**, a male acapella quartet.

The folk and political song traditions of Lombardy (and neighbouring regions) are well represented by **Barabàn**, a group which has been active for over twenty years, at first with an exclusively acoustic approach that slowly made space for electric instruments. As the Associazione Culturale Barabàn (ACB), they have promoted extensive research ranging from the chants of rice-field workers to the dances collected by **Compagnia Strumentale Tre Violini** which reminds us of the importance of the violin in the dances and styles of the Po Valley region. Barabàn features the Ronzio brothers on percussion and plucked string instruments, multi-instrumentalist Aurelio Citelli on voice, and two masters of their respective instruments: **Vincenzo Caglioti** on organetto and **Giuliano Grasso** on violin. After exploring traditional Lombardy repertoire through five CDs, their sixth and best recording focused on the idea of borders, and especially on the lyrics of Franco Loi, whose poems serve as the basis for the tunes.

The best local tradition is probably the Carnival and the best places to experience it are Bagolino and Ponte Caffaro, home to **Compagnia Sonadur**, a string and guitar ensemble led by Barnardo Falconi, previously with Compagnia Strumentale Tre Violini.

Local instruments include the *baghèt*, the bagpipe from around Bergamo. It is the main instrument of ethnomusicologist Valter Biella, who since 1989 has led **Bandalpina**, an ensemble of over twenty musicians from Canton Ticino and Val Trompia. In Bergamo, another major project is **Cororchestra Cantarchevai**, led since 1994 by Oliviero Biella who has brought together a choir and an orchestra of traditional instruments.

More recent groups include **Din Delòn** with a repertoire of traditional dances such as *manfrine* and *matuzine*, **Epinfrai,** a quartet featuring Marco Domenichetti on *piffero*, the jazz-oriented **Simone Guiducci Gramelot Ensemble**, and Fabrizio Poggi's **Turututela**, which draws its repertoire from storytellers, and traditional singers such as **Giovanna Daffini**.

Piedmont and Val d'Aosta

The roots music of the Piedmont region achieved a national profile thanks to a dynamic and mul-

Mau Mau: they may look like bumpkins, but their global beats are wholly cosmopolitan

ticultural young group, **Mau Mau**, who mix the Piedmont language and organetto patterns with world beats, particularly with African percussion. The region offers a diverse wealth of musical traditions and interpreters.

Founded by **Maurizio Martinotti** (hurdy gurdy) and **Beppe Greppi** (organetto), **La Ciapa Rusa** has been active since 1977 mixing northern Italian traditional music and original material. While many Italian folk groups have focused first on an exclusively acoustic and traditional repertoire to later include electric instruments, La Ciapa Rusa completed the cycle by returning to an all-acoustic group in its last concerts and recordings. At the end of 1997 they chose to celebrate their twentieth anniversary in quite an original way: they split up.

Today their members are scattered amongst some of Italy's best roots groups. **Sergio Berardo** went back to his Occitanian music, reforming his old folk-rock band **Lou Dalfin,** a daring project to renew the Occitan tradition. **Lorenzo Boioli** plays with the bands **Tre Martelli**, **Ariondassa** and **Compagnia dell'Oltregiogo**. **Alberto Cesa** is the leader of the historical Piedmontese group **Cantovivo**. **Giorgio Delmastro** plays in the bands **Lun-a Növa** and **Aluachi**. **Beppe Greppi** abandoned live

performance and devoted himself to full-time work in the music business as a producer and distributor. After having played in various other ensembles, **Devis Longo** is now a member of the Celtic band **Birkin Tree** led by **Fabio Rinaudo** and cooperates with Riccardo Tesi, besides managing a recording studio. **Maurizio Martinotti** performs live with different bands such as **Ensemble del Doppio Bordone Le Vijà**, "Il viaggio di Sigerico" (a European project together with Paul James, Jean Blanchard, Carlos Beceiro and many others), the French-Piedmontese band **Dòna Bèla**, **Tendachënt** and a collaboration with the Catalan ensemble Urbalia Rurana. He also directs EthnoSuoni, an association for the organization of festivals, events, and tours of Italian and foreign bands. Together with Franco Lucà and Valerio Cipolli, he founded the label Folkclub EthnoSuoni. For many years **Patrick Novara** played an important role beside Moni Ovadia in a number of musical/theatrical shows around Italy. He also created **Tri Muzike**, one of the most capable Italian bands playing music from the Balkans. **Donata Pinti** founded a new acapella Piedmontese band, together with Betti Zambruno and Paola Lombardo. **Bruno Raiteri** is with Martinotti in Tendachënt, in the Ensemble del Doppio Bordone and in Le Vijà, and he has his new band, **Quartetto**

Robi Droli

La Ciapa Rusa

Tamborini, playing a repertoire of the so-called "minor" authors of nineteenth-century Piedmont. **Betti Zambruno**, after dabbling in Irish jazz music (with the band Kile-na-no), went back to popular music with the group **Bärtavela**. Accompanied by Tendachënt, she recently set up a live show based on the Piedmontese repertoire collected by Leone Sinigaglia.

Among female voices **Laura Conti** carries her passionate work on traditional songs with the group **Ombra Gaja**, while the **Ariondela Trio** stand out for their inspiring look at northern Italian polyphonic vocal traditions and at the cultural influences across the Piedmont region, from the Franco-Provencal of the Waldensian valleys, to the songs of the "mondine", the rice pickers who worked in the paddy fields around Vercelli and Novara. The trio recorded _Dòna Bianca_ in 1996 and participated as guests on the second CD by La Piva Dal Carner, _M'han presa_ the following year. They've also worked along with Maria Adelaide Negrin, Samuela Gallinari and Alba Spera on their _Beica_ CD. Most of the repertoire is traditional and borrows from a previous recording by **Buntemp** (Robi Droli) and from the wide collection of the Piedmont cultural association **La Cantarana**, whose repertoire draws from the Occitane and Alps influenced Pinerolo valleys.

The gifted duo of **Gabriele Ferrero** on violin and bagpipe and **Silvio Peron** on organetto are at the core of the **Compagnons Roulants** quintet and the

dancing repertoire by **Senhal**. A focus on traditional dance repertoire is kept by **Curenta Alternata** and **La Lionetta** (Torino), **L'Estorio Drolo** (Cuneo), **Meikenut** (Biella) and **Ombra Gaja**, whose repertoire is based on field recordings by Amerigo Viglierno and the Centro Etnologico Canavesano.

The region offers a wealth of diversified musical tradition, from the singer **Vincenzo "Ciacio" Marchelli**, (the heart of **Tre Martelli**, a group with deep roots in the Lower Piedmont and particularly in the Monferrato, Langhe and Alessandrino areas) to **Trouveur Valdotèn**, a group with its roots in the 1970s including French and patois lyrics. Probably the best known songwriter is **Gianmaria Testa,** who has an ability to team up with jazz musicians and improvisers, from Enrico Rava to Riccardo Tesi.

Many northern Italian groups' repertoires cut across different regions. The group **Sentiero del Sale** have a repertoire of Genoese and Lombard songs, especially from the area of Pavia, while **I suonatori delle quattro province** and **Voci del Lèsima** draw their traditional repertoire from four provinces of four different northern Italian regions: Alessandria (Piedmont), Genoa (Liguria), Pavia (Lombardy) and Piacenza (Emilia Romagna). **Voci del Lèsima** take particular inspiration from Bogli, a village that gives its name to the _buiasche_, a way of singing which is called _fermo_ (still) as it lacks a clear beat. This style of polyphonic singing usually includes five different voices – two soloists and the bass voices, often enriched by a baritone part and a *vusìn*, a bass hitting higher notes towards the end of the song.

Genoese Songs

The great seaport on the Ligurian coast, Genoa has a tavern song tradition called **trallalero,** an onomato-poeic name representing these tra-la-la laden songs. It is a polyphonic vocal style, possibly related to the nearby Sardinian and Corsican varieties, involving a complicated counterpoint by five male voices: tenor, baritone, alto, *chitarra* (guitar) and bass. The "guitar" imitates the sound of the instrument by singing in a nasal voice and putting the back of his hand over his lips. The sound of trallalero is one of the most ornate and haunting in the Mediterranean, and it is unusual, amongst polyphonic singing styles, for being urban rather than rural.

Trallalero's origins are in the urbanization process that drew rural populations to work in the city at the end of the nineteenth century. It thrived in the taverns where the men met after work and, in its heyday in the 1920s, over a hundred groups existed in Genoa. At that time the café-bar Tugini's was a famous trallalero venue, while today the Porto Franco bar, on Via Sottoripa under the arcades of the port, hosts the current leading group, **La Squadra – Compagnia del Trallalero**, led by Francesco Tanda. Another important ensemble is the **Squadra di Canto Popolare di Valpolcevera.**

It took the passion and powerful voice of **Laura Parodi** to break the male monopoly over the trallalero, and while she is now accepted by fellow male trallalero singers, she also keeps singing with **La Rionda**, a group that borrows its name from the *ballo tondo* played in Genoa during the Carnival. La Rionda's members are also active within **La Furlancia**, a group that specializes in traditional songs collected by ethnomusicologists Mauro Balma and Edward Neill.

Genoa remains the home of some of the best "modern" ballads written by the likes of **Gino Paoli** and the late **Fabrizio De André,** who knew national fame back in 1968 through the **Mina's** interpretation of his song "La canzone di Marinella". Many more of his songs became classics and often served as a poetic means of raising awareness on social and political issues. His collaboration with multi-instrumentalist, composer and arranger **Mauro Pagani** brought together the Genoese language with various Mediterranean traditions, and in 1984 they opened the eyes of an Italian public usually reluctant to acknowledge the musical wealth of its regional traditions with the recording of "Creuza de Mà".

Genoa is a fertile ground for a number of young groups seeking new directions, from the dub of **Sensasciou** to the vocal gymnastics of **Le Voci Atroci**.

DISCOGRAPHY Italy

General Compilations

★ **Atlante di Musica Tradizionale**
Robi Droli, Italy
★ **Italia 2 – Atlante di Musica Tradizionale**
Felmay, Italy
★ **Italia 3 – Atlante di Musica Tradizionale**
Felmay, Italy

The best introductions to Italy's varied traditional and acoustic groups. Featuring a good mix of different regional styles performed by Baraban, Calicanto, La Ciapa Rusa, La Piazza, Re Niliu, Ritmia, Tenores di Bitti, Tre Violini (Volume 1), Aquaragia Drom, Totore Chessa, Efisio Melis-Antonio Lara, La Piva del Carner (Volume 2).

☉ **Zampogne en Italie**
Auvidis/Silex, France
An impressive anthology of zampogne music from central and southern Italy, Sicily and of the *piva* from Istria (Croatia) edited by the ethnomusicologist Roberto Leydi. With 24 field recordings from between 1969 and 1990 and examples of both the "double oboe" and the "double clarinet" families of zampogne.

The South

☉ **Calabre: Musiques de fêtes**
Inédit, France
Atmospheric field recordings of traditional festivals in Calabria between 1983 and 1993. Processions, tarantellas and religious music with plenty of zampogna, organetto and drums.

☉ **Puglia: The Salento**
Rounder, USA
Instrumental and vocal polyphony from the Salento, sung both in the local dialects and in Griko, the ancient Greek language as recorded by Alan Lomax and Diego Carpitella in 1954. From pizzica to love, funeral and work songs.

☉ **Sicily. Music for the Holy Week**
Auvidis/Unesco, France
Songs, chants and laments in Sicilian, Latin and Italian, played and sung by different traditional ensembles reflecting the living tradition of Sicilian ceremonial music. Polyphonic chant (which some may find hard-going), brass bands and vocals with harmonium with a real sense of occasion.

⊙ Sutera. La tradizione musicale di un paese della Sicilia
SudNord, Italy

A thrilling and varied sample of the Sicilian rural repertoire, drawing from the traditions which are still alive in the village of Sutera. Featuring Enzo and Lorenzo Mancuso, Nonó Salamone and traditional singers and choir singing religious, labour and love songs.

⊙ The Alan Lomax Collection: Italian Treasury – Sicily
Rounder, USA

July 2–23 1954: in three weeks, Alan Lomax and Diego Carpitella collected over 160 songs from twelve different Sicilian locations and marked the beginning of modern ethnomusicological research in Italy. The CD presents a wide range of genres: dance music lullabies, love songs, serenades, wedding songs, funeral lamentations, religious songs, Christmas novenae, polyphonic and monodic Holy Week singing and work songs. Unforgettable highlights include the male voice and Jew's harp in "Surfarara" (in the sulphur miners' style), expressing all the desolation and painful hope of some of the most exploited Sicilian workers. Strongly recommended to anybody with a passion for southern Italian traditions.

Enzo Avitabile and Bottari

Fusion veteran Avitabile and Bottari bring together melodies and rhythmic patterns from various Mediterranean influences.

⊙ Salvamm'o o munno
Manifesto/Wrasse, UK

A very energetic CD with singing in the Neapolitan language as well as in Arabic and African languages and guests from various countries. "Paisà", based on funky rhythms sends a peaceful message to all travellers and immigrants: my home is your home. Avitabile's music conveys the feeling that there still exists a compass to navigate the Mediterranean labyrinth.

Roberto de Simone and Media Aetas

De Simone is simply the most knowledgeable and skilled Italian composer and a veteran of ethnological field recording from around Naples.

⊙ Li Turchi viaggiano
Oriente, Germany

An oustanding selection of Media Aetas' recent work, with a superb booklet that translates lyrics into four languages, providing an opportunity to fully understand both the musical and the lyrical message.

Epifani Barbers

Mimmo Epifani's mandolin is the most sought after by roots groups.

⊙ Marannui
Forrest Hill, UK

Finally an opportunity for Mimmo Epifani to arrange a varied repertoire blending his mandolin with some of the most skilled southern musicians.

E'Zezi

Neapolitan folk music and a working-class revolutionary message are the vital elements which have made E' Zezi a cult group both in Italy and France with a variable ensemble usually featuring some fifteen musicians and a large number of percussion instruments. Reluctant to participate in the market economy, E' Zezi have only produced three CDs in over twenty years.

⊙ Zezi Vivi
Il Manifesto, Italy

If you like a smashed glasses and marketplace atmosphere don't miss this recording that captures Zezi live in Napoli at the end of 1996, with a breathtaking sequence of trance-like *tammuriatas*.

Roberto Murolo

Born in 1912, the son of the poet Ernesto, Roberto Murolo was a veteran interpreter of the canzone napoletana repertoire in a style both restrained and moving. He passed away in 2003.

⊙ Napoletana – Volume 3
BMG, Ricordi, Italy

The chronological anthology of the canzone napoletana was originally recorded for the Durium label by Roberto Murolo and guitarist Eduardo Caliendo. The third volume covers the key years 1940–62 and includes over fifty songs spread over three CDs. Those looking for a more concise introduction to the art of Murolo can check the 2005 CD on Lucky Planets label entitled *Accarezzame*, including highlights such as "'O mese de 'rose", "Desiderio 'e sole" and "O vascio".

Nistanimera

Ettore Castagna, Anna Cinzia Villani, Valentino Santagati, Piero Crucitti, and Diego Pizzimenti are five researchers who are well known across Calabria and Puglia as skilled musicians with a passion for the ancient instruments *lyra*, ciarameddi (bag pipes), tambureddu (frame drum) and chitarra battente (guitar).

⊙ Chorè
Felmay, Italy

This is the first album by Nistanimera (night and day) and it is about dreams entering reality, about experiencing time as both joy and pain. The joy of a language as rich as Greek, the pain of seeing it disappearing from southern Italy after 2800 years.

Nuova Compagnia di Canto Popolare

Since 1967 the group has changed many of its members but still retains a powerful frontline with the voices of Fausta Vetere and the guitar and arrangements of Corrado Sfogli.

⊙ Incanto Acustico
CGD, Italy

Live recording, entirely acoustic, celebrating almost thirty years of Neapolitan music with an outstanding balance between traditional songs and original compositions.

Re Niliu

Based in Catanzaro, Ettore Castagna (strings and toothbrush), Sergio Di Giorgio (vocals and reeds) and fellow musicians have been researching, documenting, teaching and performing Calabrian traditions for twenty years.

⊙ Pucambu
Pontesonoro, Italy

After two records dedicated to Calabrian traditions, Re Niliu perform their own compositions with a delicate balance between roots and innovation, minority languages and visionary texts, subtle irony and plenty of energy.

Matteo Salvatore

Born in Apricena (Foggia), a street musician since the age of seven, Matteo Salvatore has not confined himself to the traditional songs from his native Puglia, developing his own narrative and original compositions over the years.

Italie: Chants de Mendiants
Harmonia Mundi, France

Matteo Salvatore was almost fifty when he recorded these fourteen "beggars' songs" in 1973. Some of them he'd been practising for more than forty years and his high voice beautifully and sometimes painfully leads the listener into the ancient art of storytelling. The selection includes "Padrone mio", which was later also recorded by Daniele Sepe with the Brass Band G. Capuozzo.

Enzo Rao – Shamal

Violinist and bass player Enzo Rao from Palermo brings together Gianni Gebbia (saxes) and Glen Velez (frame drums and percussion). Rao draws on native Sicilian music plus the jazz and Arabic influences so strong in Sicilian culture.

Acqua di Mare
Pontesonoro, Italy
Ettna
Music of the World, US

The same disc from 1993 under different names. Partly Sicilian jazz, partly Mediterranean fusion, this album has some strong dance rhythms alongside somewhat New Age doodlings.

Daniele Sepe

Sepe's relentless musical and poetic search brings together Gato Barbieri and Matteo Salvatore, Tacit and Mayakovsky. With a sound training as classical and jazz flute and saxophone player, and a passion for traditional songs and instruments, his albums are never less than compelling.

Vite Perdite
Piranha, Germany

This is where you want to start your Italian trip. Meet the iconoclastic Naples music scene in Sepe's visionary and fascinating patchwork featuring the hip-hop of Bisca and 99 Posse, the tradition and political commitment of E' Zezi, the vocal abilities of Quattro Quatti and Mariapia De Vito, the sixteen-piece roots orchestra of Tuba Furiosa and many more.

Central Italy

La Saltarella dell'Alta Sabina
Ethnica/Robi Droli, Italy

This disc brings you to the mountains of the Central Apennines, for centuries a region of cultural exchanges, beginning with the salt road between Rome and the heart of the Apennines. The saltarella is the region's most characteristic folk dance and it is performed here by zampogna, organetto and tamburello. Almost eighty minutes of field recordings, collected between1989 and 1992.

Giovanna Marini

Based in Rome, Giovanna Marini is by far the most important singer of the last three decades of Italian roots music, always combining her research, teaching and performing activities with concern and personal involvement at the social level. She has specialized in polyphonic singing, with new compositions especially suited for female quartet.

La vie au-dessus et en-dessous des mille mètres
Auvidis/Silex, France

Traditional roots and contemporary compositions rendered with passion and ability by this exceptional female vocal quartet including Lucilla Galeazzi, Patrizia Bovi and Patrizia Nasini.

La Piazza

The group produced its first CD in 1993 as a quartet centred around the voice of Sara Modigliani, former member of Canzoniere del Lazio. Over the years it has turned into a septet.

Milandè
Robi Droli, Italy

This 1997 album achieves a good balance between traditional songs and original compositions, including the opening track written by Giovanna Marini "Pi' lontano di così", with a reference to a traditional song from Calabria. The repertoire is rooted in the traditions of the Lazio region though it features some classics which cut across different Italian traditions such as "Mampresa", "Donna Lombarda" and "La Pastora e il Lupo".

Ritmia

The lasting partnership between Enrico Frongia (voice and guitar) and Alberto Balia (guitars, clarinet, *benas*, voice) is supported here by the outstanding Riccardo Tesi (organetti and tamburelli), and Daniele Craighead (reeds).

Forse il Mare
Robi Droli, Italy

Recorded in 1986, the four long tracks reveal a fresh approach to traditional roots, making extensive use of the improvisational skills of this virtuoso quartet bringing together musicians from Sardinia and Tuscany.

Riccardo Tesi

Organetto (melodeon) player and composer Riccardo Tesi comes from Tuscany and is an experienced world traveller with an impressive score of solo projects and collaborations, within and outside Italy in the past twenty years, from "Trans Europe Diatonique" to Justin Vali's recent recordings.

Thapsos
Felmay, Italy

Dedicated to the Malagasy *valiha* master, "Justin" opens the CD with the offspring of sound friendship, energy and inspired lyrics. Rooted in central Italian traditions, Tesi's compositions and melodic phrasing seem particularly at ease in the encounters with musical influences from the islands, be it dancing rhythms from Madagascar and Sardinia, or vocal harmonies and quarter tones from Sicily. In this new recording, Tesi's organetto can be heard in dynamic duos ("Fulmine", "Aria") as well as in different enlarged groups featuring twelve outstanding traditional Italian musicians in combination with his regular "Banditaliana" quartet. Three lyrics in Italian are contributed by the Sicilian composer Carlo Muratori.

The North

Baraban

A sextet which has been active since 1983 researching and performing the roots music of Lombardy: Guido Montaldo, Paolo and Diego Ronzio (wind instruments), Vincenzo Caglioti (organetto), Aurelio Citelli (guitars and mandolino), and Giuliano Grasso (violin).

⊙ Live
Robi Droli, Italy

A selection of sixteen live recordings from 1989–93, including Apennine dances, carnival tunes, narrative and religious songs, mixing the original acoustic traditional sound with a discrete use of electronics.

Calicanto

A Padua-based band led by multi-instrumentalist Roberto Tombesi. Very active since 1981 in field research, they have made several albums of largely traditional Veneto music and since 1986 have started generating their own repertoire.

⊙ Venexia
CNI, Italy

This is the eighth recording by Calicanto and a mature work indeed. Venice meets the Middle East and other Mediterranean traditions through Calicanto's energetic acoustic songs.

La Ciapa Rusa

Led by Maurizio Martinotti (hurdy-gurdy, percussion, violin, vocals) and Beppe Greppi (organetto, vocals), this group has been researching and performing traditional Piedmont and original music for over twenty years, establishing itself as one of Italy's leading roots bands.

⊙ Antologia
Robi Droli, Italy

A selection of twenty tracks from the first four records of La Ciapa Rusa, entirely acoustic and dedicated to the rich traditional music repertoire of the Piedmont region, from rice-fields chants to epic songs.

Compagnia Strumentale Tre Violini

The violinists Bernardo Falconi, Giuliano Grasso (also with Baraban) and Giulio Venier are three outstanding performers from Lombardy and Friuli, supported by the guitar of Oliviero Biella and the bass of Paolo Manfrin.

⊙ Il Ballo dei Pazzi
ACB/Robi Droli, Italy

After the convincing anthology of northern Italian violin repertoire, *Matuzine* (on the same label), Tre Violini remain in the north of Italy to give new life to a dance repertoire from printed scores of the seventeenth to nineteenth centuries.

Fabrizio De André

Born in Genoa in 1940, De André recorded his first songs in 1958 and was active through to his death in 1999. His voice and compositions are still a point of reference within the Italian music scene.

⊙ Creuza de ma
Ricordi, Italy

An exciting musical trip, sailing from Genoa to other shores of the Mediterranean. Seven original tracks with the arrangements of Mauro Pagani and offering a poetic rendition of the Genoese language, a turning point for the Italian roots scene.

La Squadra
(Compagnia del Trallelero)

In the best tradition of trallaleri, most members of La Squadra are or were Genoan dock workers; they have no formal music training and an average age of sixty. Led by

Francesco Tanda they have revived this Genoan tradition with a repertoire of sixty songs.

★ Italy: Genoese Polyphony
Buda/Musique du Monde, France

The manual workers of the Genoa docks know their tavern tra-la-las. Haunting vocal harmonies in traditional trallalero.

⊙ Chansons Génois
Buda/Musique du Monde, France

Composed songs in trallalero style from the 1920s, recorded in a wine cellar a few kilometres away from Genoa. The "sixth voice" in this polyphony is supplied by a popping cork.

Squadra di Canto Popolare di Valpolcevera

Based in Campomorone, a small town northwest of Genoa, the seven members of the Valpolcevera specialize in the oldest songs of the trallalero repertoire. They formed in 1983 as heirs to the legendary Nuova Pontedecimo and Vecchia Pontedecimo groups.

⊙ Trallalero
NewTone/Robi Droli, Italy

Eighteen classic trallaleri from one of the most representative groups.

Voci Del Lèsima

Six male voices from the northern Apennines in the Bogli vocal style with two soloists, Attilio "Cavalli" Spinetta and Stefano Valla, also a member of the Valpolcevera.

⊙ Splende la luna in cielo
Robi Droli, Italy

A lively trip to Bogli, on the borders of Piedmont and Liguria, where history is written in the *buiasche* (popular polyphonic chants), reminiscent of the Genovese vocal style, with deep drones sung in parallel fifths and the higher voices imitating string and wind instruments.

Organetti

⊙ Organetto e Tarantelle
Ethnica/Robi Droli, Italy

Edited by Giuseppe Michele Gala, this includes field recordings made between 1979 and 1991 in the southern Italian regions of Basilicata and Campania, where the organetto traditionally performs various tarantellas and other dance rhythms. Also featured are traditional songs of the shepherds, carnival, and courting repertoires.

Totore Chessa

Born in 1959, Totore Chessa is considered the best player of Sardinian organetto, a style characterized by acrobatic finger work and powerful bass lines, with the instrument usually featuring eight to twelve bass notes.

⊙ Organittos
NewTone/Robi Droli, Italy

A selection of virtuoso solo dances, though the disc also features three guests: Annamaria Puggioni (voice), Luigi Lai (launeddas), and Nicola Loi (Jew's harp).

Circo Diatonico – Clara Graziano

A former student of Ambrogio Sparagna, Clara Graziano has established herself in Rome by participating in key musical projects led by jazz piano virtuosi Andrea Alberti (who leads Orchestra Mediterranea), and Rita Marcotulli. Circo Diatonico develops her roots music in cooperation with jazz musicians Giovanni lo Cascio (percussions), Gerardo Bertoccini (double bass), Rosario Liberti (tuba, trombone).

⊙ Acrobazie
Finisterre, Italy
Entirely instrumental, the thirteen tracks are based on the collaboration between the compositions and organetto of Clara Graziano and the sax, clarinets and arrangements of Toni Germani. Based on the experience of the leader as a street musician and on her fascination for the circus and its music, this is a convincing debut.

Filippo Gambetta

The title of Gambetta's debut CD is also the name of his acoustic quartet, "Stria" (meaning "witch" in the local dialect), which includes classically trained musicians Mariana Carli (cello) and Francesco Denini (violin), plus the outstanding open strings technique of Claudio de Angeli on guitar.

⊙ Stria
Felmay, Italy
A great selection of instrumental tracks, for the most part composed by Filippo Gambetta. There is also room for original arrangements with a good sense of contrast between traditional material from Liguria and other Balkan and Mediterranean influences. The last track features the Ligurian Regional Pizzicato String Orchestra conducted by Carlo Aonzo in a new rendition of "The Long View" by Pete Sutherland.

Mario Salvi

Born in Rome in 1956, Mario Salvi has been active for over twenty years researching, interpreting and teaching southern Italian musical traditions.

⊙ Caldèra
Finisterre, Italy
A mature work presenting both traditional songs and original compositions. Featuring classical tarantellas such as "Pizzica Pizzica" and "Tarantella di Montemarano", and a wide range of traditional and electric instruments such as the flutes of Cristina Scrima, the powerful tammorra of Raffaele Inserra and the bass of Erasmo Petringa,

Ambrogio Sparagna

Born in Maranola (Lazio) in 1957, the son of traditional musicians, Sparagna has always combined his activities as musician and composer with field research and took his MA in ethnomusicology with Diego Carpitella in 1982.

⊙ Invito
BMG, Italy
Produced in 1995 after numerous live performances, this disc offers some of the best composition by Sparagna and his organetto with various instrumental collaborations ranging from the Villa Carpegna Polyphonic Choir, directed by Anna Rita Colaianni, to the thirty organetti of the Bosio Big Band. Also featuring the powerful voices of Lucilla Galeazzi and Nando Citarella.

Riccardo Tesi

Italy's leading organetto player has mastered styles as different as central Italy's saltarello, southern Italy's tarantella and Sardinian *ballu tundu*, and produced the first of a series of brilliant recordings in 1983.

⊙ Un ballo liscio
Auvidis/Silex, France
Tesi brings unexpected new life to the neglected liscio dance style. An inspired interaction between the organetto and the rest of the twelve-piece ensemble featuring diverse instrumentalists such as jazz and classical pianist Mauro Grossi and mandolin player Patrick Vaillant.

Roberto Tombesi

Based in Padova, Roberto Tombesi explored musical traditions from both sides of the Adriatic Sea with the 2001 Calicanto project *Labirinto Mare* (Sea Labyrinth, CNI). Now he is back with a trio of organettos including Mario Salvi (from Puglia) and Stefano "Ciuma" Delvecchio (Emilia Romagna).

⊙ Il Mare di Lato
By the Sea, Felmay, Italy
This live recording from August 2001 in Roncegno (Valsugana) is a remarkable opportunity to compare Italian repertoires from different regions, exemplified by the ten-minute "Suite 14 Agosto" with four sections reproducing styles from the northern to the southern Italian coast of the Adriatic Sea. "Vilote veneziane" (Venice) was arranged by Roberto Tombesi and features the voice of Claudia Ferronato (Calicanto) while "Saltarello Romagnolo" blends two traditional dances from Ciuma's repertoire. "Saltarello Marchigiano" pays tribute to Salvi's and Tombesi's central Italian roots and has as guest voice Gastone Pietrucci, the leader of La Macina. The Puglia influenced "Pizzica Pizzica" features Cinzia Villani (voice) and Carlo De Pascali (tamburello, frame drum) and skilfully mixes the minor modes from the region around Bari with the major tonality from Salento (Lecce), a delicate harmonic balance energized by the organetto.

Taranta Music

⊙ Lezioni di tarantella
DFV-EMI Music Italy
An anthology edited by Eugenio Bennato, including some of the best traditional musicians playing the *Tarantella del Gargano* (from Carpino, Foggia), *Pizzica Salentina* (Lecce), *Tarantella alla Montemaranese* (Avellino) and *Tarantella Calabrese*.

⊙ Taranteria
Finisterre, Italy
Mario Salvi's personal look at the tarantella traditions from Sicily, Calabria, Puglia and Campania accompanied by outstanding instrumentalists.

Aramirè (Compagnia di musica salentina)

Founded in Lecce by Roberto Raheli in 1996, Aramirè is a group with a passion for pizzicas and polyvocal traditions, be it work songs, love songs, or songs in the *griku* tradition.

⊙ SudEst
Arroyo, Italy
Fifteen traditional songs and dances from the Salento region, arranged for various ensembles, from a trio to a nine-piece band.

L'Arpeggiata

Under the direction of Christina Pluhar (who also plays various string instruments), this multicultural ten-piece from France approaches the taranta repertoire through a remarkable selection of key tunes and use of traditional and baroque instruments.

⊙ **La Tarantella. Antidotum Tarantulae**
Alpha, France
A classic rendition of taranta music including vocal parts by Lucilla Galeazzi and Marco Beasley, and powerful percussion by Alfio Antico.

Canzoniere Grecanico Salentino

This is Salento's historical group: they have been active since 1975 researching and interpreting the Salento traditional repertoire and taranta healing music. Since 1977 they have produced some fifteen CDs.

⊙ **Ballati tutti quanti ballati forte ca la taranta è viva e nun è morta**
Dunya – Felmay, Italy
A selection of well-known traditional pizzicas and tarantellas from a solid seven-piece band with vocals by Rossella Pinto.

Nidi D'Arac

Founded in the Salento area in 1998 by Alessandro Coppola, Nidi D'Arac are now based in Rome where they experiment with pizzicas and digital sounds

⊙ **Jentu**
V2 Records, Italy
A fresh approach to the taranta and Puglia traditions including electric and electronic arrangements with a look at the dancefloor.

Antonello Paliotti Trio

With two albums that present traditional sources in completely new and convincing clothes and countless collaborations, guitar player and composer Antonello Paliotti is the new man in town in Naples. He made his debut in Roberto De Simone's group in 1986 and is still active within the best ensembles including the Napoli Mandolino Orchestra.

⊙ **Tarantella Storta**
Dunya – Felmay, Italy
An outstanding instrumental trio featuring cello, mandolin and guitar with a remarkable ability to bring new life to tarantella through original new compositions.

PLAYLIST
Italy

1 CREUZA DE MA Fabrizio De Andrè from *Creuza de ma*
A seminal Genoese song about a mule track by the sea, shadows of seamen's faces; a place from where you can see the moon naked.

2 TARANTELLA DI SAN MICHELE Roberto De Simone and Media Aetas from *Li Turchi Viaggiano*
Traditional lyrics get an inspired and rich vocal arrangement from the Neapolitan maestro De Simone and fellow top interpreters.

3 CI CRITI O NON CI CRITI Epifani Barbers from *Marannui*
New arrangements for the mandolin "barber" technique inherited by Mimmo Epifani from pizzica maestros Costantino Vita and Peppu D'Augusta, from the barber shop in San Vito dei Normanni (Brindisi).

4 TARANTELLA STORTA Antonello Paliotti Trio from *Tarantella Storta*
Paliotti's instrumental breaks with the nineteenth-century 6/8 and 12/8 standard tarantella tempo and explores the wealth of variations offered by the oral tradition.

5 LARGO WALZER Riccardo Tesi and Banditaliana from *Thapsos*
Banditaliana displays its wide range of colours and provides a moving rendition of this medium tempo original penned by Tesi and Carlo Muratori.

6 SULLA VIA DE BATIPALI Calicanto from *Venexia*
Gabriele Coltri's bagpipe and Rachele Colombo's voice guide the listener through traditional work songs with backing vocals by Gualtiero Bertelli and Alberto D'Amico.

7 CHORÈ Nistanimera from *Choré*
A sung dialogue between Valentino Santagati and Anna Cinzia Villani, bringing a new momentum to traditional lyrics bridging the southern Aspromonte and Salento Greek regions.

8 GNICCHE GNICCHE Filippo Gambetta from *Stria*
Cello (Mariana Carli), guitar (Claudio De Angeli) and violin (Francesco Denini) provide a unique interplay with Gambetta's organetto with room for lyrical improvisation.

9 DISSIPA TU SE LO VUOI Giovanna Marini, Lucilla Galeazzi, Patrizia Bovi, Patrizia Nasini from *La vie au-dessus et en-dessous des mille mètres*
A masterly vocal acapella arrangement for Eugenio Montale's aching poem "Wipe Away If You Want".

10 MI VOTU E MI RIVOTU Banda Ionica featuring Cristina Zavalloni from *Atlante di musica tradizionale/Roots Music Atlas 3*
Roy Paci's banda gives a Sicilian traditional piece a passionate treatment and Cristina Zavalloni an opportunity to employ the German language.

Macedonia

beats over borders

Esma Redžepova
Jak Kilby

Formerly a part of the Socialist Federal Republic of Yugoslavia, Macedonia is a small but musically rich country with unstoppable sounds and rhythms flowing from a prodigious mix of nationalities. Covering the area known as Vardar Macedonia, the Republic of Macedonia is, in fact, part of a much larger cultural area that has borne the name Macedonia since ancient times, and was divided between Serbia, Bulgaria and Greece by the 1913 Treaty of Bucharest following the first two Balkan Wars. **Kim Burton** unpacks the box with seven locks.

It's still possible to sit in a café in Skopje, Macedonia's capital, and hear a conversation switching between Macedonian, Albanian and Turkish as people join or leave the company. For a state of two million, Macedonia has an amazing cultural and ethnic diversity. It contains a large Albanian minority (considerably increased during the 1999 war in Kosovo), as well as Turks, Arumanians (Vlachs), Roma (Gypsies), Serbs, Bosnians and even a small group who claim Egyptian origin. Around 65 percent of the population, however, are ethnic Macedonians who speak Macedonian, a Slavic language, as their mother tongue. When the Socialist Federal Republic of Yugoslavia disintegrated, Macedonia managed to secede peacefully, becoming an independent nation in 1991. In 2001 possible ethnic civil war between Macedonians and Albanians was averted, thanks to international pressure and the eventual flexibility of the political leaderships involved.

Naturally, the ethnic mix is reflected in the musical make-up of the area. Macedonia's Albanian population share the music of their cousins in Kosovo and Albania (see p.3); the Turkish minority maintains its own repertoire, often with a strong local accent; and there are significant contributions from the Roma, or Gypsy, communities. The music of the Macedonians themselves has a startling richness and range of mood. A large proportion of folk songs deal with historical subjects, and aspects of the struggle against foreign domination – but many are love songs, while others have a lightness of touch and a humour that on occasion tips over into the bawdy.

Old-style **dancing** remains an important social activity, even among the young urbanites frequenting the techno clubs of downtown Skopje, and at weddings, picnics and other celebrations everybody from toddlers to grannies joins in a great wheeling circle, jigging happily to complex, and initially baffling, rhythms.

Signatures for Swing

As is usually the case in southeastern Europe, the music of the towns differs considerably from that of the villages, but there is one thing they have in common: an extraordinary **complexity of rhythm**. Much music around the world can be understood as combinations of equal beats or of long and short beats in the ratio of two to one. But in Macedonia (and to a lesser extent in neighbouring countries) there are many more ways of dividing a bar, and the ratio of long and short beats is two to three.

In Western music, a **bar of triple time** – such as a waltz – has three equal beats, but in Macedonia it may be a bar of 7/8 divided up as 3–2–2 or 2–2–3 or 2–3–2 and so on. Meters of four, five, and even more beats are not uncommon. In slower tunes, the beats may be of equal length, yet still arranged in unequal patterns. Sometimes these patterns are referred to by the generic term *aksak*, limping. It's an odd choice of word, since the rhythmic energy generated by the irregularities catapults the melody forward with great verve and drive. In slower tempos, some of the older musicians subtly **stretch the time**, so that one beat lasts fractionally longer than it would if counted strictly. This technique lends the music a dramatic dignity with a massive sense of tension and release, where the movement of the dancers is momentarily suspended, and then paid forward in an unbroken chain. Current musical taste tends more to the fast and athletic, but there are still plenty of older recordings where it can be encountered.

Instruments and Ensembles

Macedonian village music, or rather versions of that music, has seen a notable **revival** in the years since independence. Some of this can be put down to a reassertion of national or ethnic identity, but there is also the paradoxical effect that as modernization has gathered pace the previous attitude that village mores were a cause for shame has receded a little. Increasing interest in Macedonian "roots" music by Western listeners has also played a part. Consequently, the younger generation feel confident in expressing an interest in what was until recently considered embarrassingly unsophisticated, and a considerable number of young women, in particular, are exploring the country's extremely rich and varied vocal heritage.

The quintessential village instrument is the **gajda** bagpipe, as proverbs such as "Without a gajda it's no wedding" testify. Deeper in pitch and softer-toned than the Bulgarian model, less suited to flights of virtuosity, but superbly suited to the rather dark aesthetic at the heart of Macedonian music, it is also capable of providing a surprisingly sensitive and delicate accompaniment to singers.

Other traditional village instruments include the double-course **tambura**, a Balkan variant on the strummed string instrument; the rim-blown **kaval** flute, slenderer and longer than the Bulgarian model and made of a single piece of wood; the **šupelka**, the kaval's baby cousin; and the fiddle-like three-stringed **ćemane**, bowed and held upright on the knee.

Festivals and weddings, particularly in the eastern and southern parts of the country, are often marked by the appearance of wild-sounding ensembles of two *zurli* and a *tâpan*. The **zurla** is a large but simple oboe with a piercing nasal sound at its best in the open air. It is always played in pairs, the first taking the lead while the second accompanies, normally holding a drone, but sometimes joining the first in a rough unison. The **tâpan**, a large cylindrical drum played with a heavy stick in one hand and a light switch in the other, drives the dance along with a flurry of syncopations.

As the above implies, much Macedonian music, vocal and instrumental alike, is drone-based. The bagpipe of course supplies its own drone, kavals are frequently played in pairs, in dance tunes or in the rhapsodic semi-improvisations known as *ezgiji*, and the tambura too tends to use one string as a drone and the other to execute the melody. After World War II, the **Ansambl na Narodni Instrumenti** (Folk Instrument Ensemble), linked to the state broadcasting service, combined all these instruments in a single group and introduced a sort of harmonic basis. Nonetheless, the arrangements still relied heavily on the drone for their effect. This group has provided the template for the younger revivalist groups, such as the **Orkestar Pece Atanasovski**, named after **Pece Atanasovski**, a fine bagpiper, dancer, arranger and teacher, who ran the Ansambl na Narodni Intrumenti. Other notable ensembles are those led by **Siniša Grujoski** and multi-instrumentalist **Stefče Stojkovski**.

Milan Zavkov

All the musicians working in this area encounter financial problems. State funding is at a woefully low level compared to what it was during the Communist period, and musicians have to fend for themselves or find sponsors. There is some work at weddings, but most of the bookings go to the amplified, electrified, hard-dancing and hard-singing pop-folk groups. Piracy is also a huge problem; bootleg CDs can be bought on the street for a euro or less, and this has also hit musicians' income. However, in Bulgaria, pressure from the EU has led to piracy being almost completely stamped out, and Macedonia's status as a candidate for EU membership has meant more serious attempts on the part of the authorities to combat piracy.

One group which does receive state support is the **Ansambl Tanec**, at one time a rather moribund example of the giant song/dance/instrumental state-run groups, but now with a new lease of life under musical director **Milan Zavkov** (himself a superb accordionist). The musical accompaniment to the ensemble's dances and songs is provided by the **Pro Etnos** group. Pro Etnos is a fine example of a *naroden orkestar*, an urban-styled group using chordal harmony, led by clarinet and accordion. As in neighbouring countries, such bands formed the backbone of the Macedonian folk-pop tradition in the 1960s and 70s.

A key influence on the sound of these bands is the traditional urban music performed by the groups known as **čalgii**. The classic line-up of a čalgija is violin, clarinet, *kanun* (Turkish plucked zither) and *ut* (lute), with a percussion section of *def* (a large tambourine with jingles) and *tarabuka* (small hourglass drum). Čalgii are the Macedonian version of a type of ensemble found from Albania to Istanbul. They used to provide entertainment for the urban merchant class, who sometimes built low stages on their verandahs to accommodate čalgii performances. Later, they performed in cabarets similar to the Greek *café-amán*, where they would accompany *čoček* dancers or play the slow tunes known as *na trapeza* (at the table).

The čalgija sound is romantic and passionate, sometimes tinged with a typical Macedonian melancholy, sometimes fiery and mysterious. The melodies are either adaptations of local dance tunes and songs or point back toward a Turkish classical or light-classical origin, with plenty of room for improvisation. One of the most important figures in the post-World War II čalgija tradition is clarinettist **Tale Ognenovski**. Although at one time such groups looked to be fading fast, they are still to be found, for example the **Stara Veleška Čalgija** in Veles, and the old Skopje radio band, now known as **Ansambl Üsref**. More recently, the young musicians of the **Kaldrma** have begun to make a name for themselves.

New Folk Music

The **narodni orkestri** have a line-up of clarinet (more recently saxophone), accordion, guitar, bass and drum kit, with synthesizer and drum machine becoming ever more common. They have a more direct and less dark-hued sound than the čalgija, which sounds to many ears less "Oriental", although like most modern Balkan music it gathers material and influences from all sorts of places. Their music is hugely popular and a vast number of more or less ephemeral releases serve the needs of café habitués, bus and taxi drivers and hard-pressed radio programmers.

As well as the enormous body of folk song collected from the villages and sung in something like its pristine form, either solo or by a group of singers in a simple drone-based polyphonic texture, Macedonia has a thriving industry based on arrangements of such songs, using either folk instruments or factory-made ones. The late **Vaska Ilieva** made a very successful career performing such arrangements, although she is probably at her best as a singer of slow, highly decorated ballads to the accompaniment of a pair of kavals.

Ilieva is also one of the best-loved singers of newly composed songs based on a folk idiom. Known as **novokomponirana**, these songs parallel the *novokomponovana* music of Serbia and have followed the same pattern of development. Many have become standards, and are regularly performed at celebrations. Great stars from the past include **Aleksandar Sarievski**, **Petranka Kostadinova**, **Nikola Badev**, **Violeta Tomovska** and **Jonče Hristovski**, while the current scene is dominated by **Naum Petreski** and the talented and versatile **Suzana Spasovska**. As in Serbia, the younger generation prefer the local **turbofolk**, which is harder-edged and draws on the rhythms of house and techno, often arriving close to a standard Europop idiom, with only the lyrics and singing style retaining much of a Macedonian identity. Names to look out for here are **Blagica Pavlovska**, **Sonja Tarčulovska** (formerly Veličkovska), **Elena Velevska** and **Goce Arnaudov**.

In recent years there has been a semi-official push to promote Western-style Macedonian pop, in an effort to make the population more Western in outlook and to counteract the "Oriental" influences of turbofolk. Despite the blandness of most of the resulting output, one singer was outstanding: the deeply mourned **Toše Proeski**, who recorded a CD of traditional, or at least old, Macedonian material shortly before his death in a motor accident in 2007.

A Synthesis of Sorts

In another trend, village instruments and traditional material have been combined with lush synthesizer or orchestral backings, and a strong dose of prog rock. Essentially this grew out of the score written for the 1994 film *Before the Rain* by the rock band **Anastasia**, whose doomy, Macedonian Gothic sound combined effectively with folk instruments played by **Dragan Dautovski**, a former rocker himself, and now a teacher of folk instruments at Skopje's Music Faculty. Veteran traditional singer **Vanja Lazarova** also took part, and found a new generation of fans in the process. The success of the soundtrack led Dautovski to form the band **Synthesis**. While this group retains the intense quasi-orchestral soundscapes of the 1990s, Dautovski is now working with his own quartet, which has a simpler, acoustic folk-rock sound.

The well-established tradition of local **rock bands** has left its mark as well. By far the most important of these is **Leb i Sol**, who have leavened their basic rock instincts with a yeasty brew of local rhythms and scales. Founded in the late 1970s, they are still worth hearing today. The virtuoso guitarist **Vlatko Stefanovski**, one of their founding members, is a fixture on the Balkan world music and jazz scene, currently working with Serbian guitarist Miroslav Tadić and Bulgarian kaval player Teodosii Spasov. Another guitarist, **Toni Kitanovski**, whose background is in straight-ahead jazz, has recently been making waves with the **Cherkezi** brass band, a folk-influenced project.

The audience for such groups is the urban professional classes. Entertainment for the average Macedonian, however, is overwhelmingly in the hands of Roma, the Gypsies.

Electric Gypsies

The **Gypsies** are thought to have arrived in the Balkans about six hundred years ago, originating from Rajasthan in the Indian subcontinent. They seem to have swiftly established themselves as skilled and adaptable musicians, and hold a musical reputation out of all proportion to their numbers. In some places they are practically the only musicians available for weddings and feasts. This is particularly true in Macedonia, where they form a substantial minority; the settlement of Šuto Orizari outside Skopje is the largest Roma town in the world.

Gypsy musicians were first to adopt the clarinet and violin – instruments that require more time and skill to master than was available to the peasants – and their relative lack of ties to land or territory allowed them to travel from place to place to meet demand. One authority estimates that in the heyday of the čalgija 65 percent of the musicians were Roma, 35 percent Macedonian and 5 percent Turkish.

The real Queen of the Gypsies

The term "diva" is a much misused one but when applied to **Esma Redžepova** it fits like the proverbial glove. Born in Skopje in 1943, Esma has risen to become the most famous Roma woman on earth.

Esma has been a professional singer since the age of thirteen, when Macedonian accordionist **Stevo Teodosievski** heard her sing. **Ansambl Teodosievski** quickly won a reputation for their dynamic sound, while the petite beauty who fronted them and sang with daring and grace quickly became an icon to all Yugoslavia. Esma scored her first Yugoslav hit with the self-penned "Čaje Šukarije" in 1959. In 1961 their "Romano Horo" – a Balkan response to "The Twist" – was a huge hit and she and the Ensemble shifted to Belgrade. Esma's biggest fan, Marshall Tito, started sending Esma and Ansambl Teodosievski abroad as representatives of Yugoslavia. She's since toured much of the world, been embraced by Nehru, played over eight thousand concerts and recorded hundreds of songs.

Esma's social activism has been unstinting. From the age of thirteen she began adopting Roma boys who were orphans or from poor families. She and Stevo provided the boys with a musical training. They married when she was 23 and remained devoted to one another until his death in the 1990s. Several of the children they adopted play in Esma's current Ansambl Teodosievski.

Esma is an eloquent critic of the nationalists who helped destroy Yugoslavia. She has used her fame to promote multi-ethnic politics, Roma education and women's rights and insisted the Macedonian government give sanctuary to Roma and Serb refugees fleeing the Albanian ethnic cleansing of Kosovo. "I've been a rebel since I was very young", she declares. "When I saw Yugoslavia disintegrating, the borders being set, dividing into smaller countries, I was the greatest rebel against it. The Balkans should be open. We should help one another. This is why I'm fighting for the peace, not to have borders, so people can love one another and the cultures can mix amongst one another." Though yet to win the Nobel Peace Prize, she's been nominated twice and has won many other awards, including a Mother Theresa Award. She prides herself on being crowned Queen of the Gypsies by Indira Gandhi in 1976 at a Roma festival in Chandigarh, India.

Esma returned to Skopje in 1989 as Yugoslavia crumbled. Today she is considered Macedonia's leading cultural ambassador. She remains popular around the world but as few of her Yugoslav recordings have been released in the West, her vocal majesty is sadly underrepresented, with perhaps her best widely available recordings being the six tracks she and the Ensemble cut in 1999 for the compilation *Gypsy Queens*. Recent releases in Macedonia have kept her in the local charts – "Magija" (Magic), a duet with **Toše Proeski**, the nation's favourite pop toyboy, was great fun.

"My message would be that the Roma people never fought anyone", says Esma, "never engaged in wars or occupied any other nation. The Roma have no country of their own and everyone should look up to them because they are cosmopolitan people."

Garth Cartwright

These days, in the bars of Šuto Orizari you can hear different styles of Gypsy music, especially on **Gjurgjovden**, the feast of St George on 6 May, which the Roma have adopted as the most important of their festivals. The typical orchestra consists of a singer, backed by electric guitar, synth or electric organ, drum kit, and maybe a saxophone or clarinet. Highly coloured, passionate, even erotic, the music may sound very Indian, particularly in vocal quality and phrasing. The Romani language is related to Hindi, and Indian film musicals are popular with the Gypsy population; some Bollywood songs have firmly entered the repertoire.

One of the most popular musics within Gypsy communities, and increasingly popular generally, is **tallava**. Originating among the Albanian-speaking Ashkali of Kosovo, in the late 1980s and early 1990s these women's wedding songs accompanied only by def and with semi-improvised lyrics passed from the walled gardens into the street, and the hands of male musicians. With the expulsion or flight of the Roma and Ashkali population from Kosovo after the NATO intervention of 1999, the base of the recording industry moved to Macedonia, and although the Ashkali at least have begun to return, there it remains. The music is now heavily electronic, with powerful vocals straining over a synthesizer drone, and the whole thing drenched in reverb and delay. Synthesizer, indeed, has become one of the favoured instruments, taking the place of the accordion, and specialist performers such as **Amza**, whose thrillingly ornate style owes much to the *zurna* tradition, are in high demand.

Battle of the (brass) bands

Kočani Orkestar

What's a name worth? Macedonia's **Kočani Orkestar** currently exists as two units, both operating out of Kočani, both playing the same Gypsy brass standards and competing for the same Western audiences. How did this happen?

In 1997 **Naat Veliov**, leader of the formidable brass band Kočani Orkestar, was signed by the Belgian management behind Taraf de Haïdouks' success. The Orkestar released a fine album, *L'Orient Est Rouge*, and looked to be winning a sizeable following. But Naat, bandleader since his teens, didn't like being produced by foreigners and felt they should issue his home recordings. The Belgians disagreed. Naat also believed he was owed considerable monies after a West European tour. The Belgians again disagreed. A split was inevitable, but what Naat did not then realize was that the Belgians had copyrighted the name Kočani Orkestar for Benelux territories and were continuing the orkestar with three members disillusioned with Naat's leadership.

The new Kočani Orkestar are a good live band but lack a dominant musician, as is evident on their slight CD *Alone At My Wedding*. Naat, now with German management, goes out as **The Original Kočani Orkestar** (featuring seven members of the original band, including his father and son). Naat's a hugely powerful trumpet player but his self-produced albums issued on Germany's tiny Plane label are no match for *L'Orient Est Rouge*. So everyone's a loser. These days Naat's Kočani Orkestar control Germany, Austria and Scandinavia while the new Kočani Orkestar dominate France, Belgium and Spain. Macedonia's a poor nation and the hard currency earned in the West means musicians in both orkestars are unlikely to relinquish a name that has proven drawing power.

Garth Cartwright

A more traditional Macedonian Gypsy style is associated with **Stevo Teodosievski** and his wife **Esma Redžepova**. Clarinettist Stevo died in 1997, but Redžepova, with her powerful voice and vast repertoire, remains Macedonia's most celebrated Gypsy performer (see box).

A much more modern approach is employed by the classically trained clarinettist, saxophonist and composer **Ferus Mustafov** – arguably the greatest Macedonian virtuoso. His music is a fascinating fusion of Macedonian, Turkish and Gypsy influences and many of his tunes have become standards. He can frequently be found playing in and around Skopje, and has managed to parlay his success into a thriving record company and recording studio. Mustafov is usually accompanied by his son Ilmi's band **Ogneni Momčinja**. Other clarinettists/saxophonists of note include **Ilija Ampevski**, **Medo Čun** and the wonderful **Tunan Kurtišev**.

Brass bands are as much a part of the Macedonian music scene as they are in Serbia. Once again, many are Gypsy, although not exclusively so. One that's made it onto the world music scene is the **Kočani Orkestar** (see box above). Drawing on popular song, traditional melodies and Bollywood film tunes, this band from Kočani, a town about 130 kilometres east of Skopje, is typical in its determined swing and readiness to adapt melodies from all over to its purposes, although it is hard to see why it has been favoured over such groups as **Asanovi** or **Mališevski Melos**.

Finally, the singer **Džansever**, who first came to prominence in the 1980s, and who unusually writes her own words to most of her songs, remains a somewhat mysterious figure. She has a magnificent voice, and a deeply serious and eclectic approach to her art. For a time she was living in Turkey, where she recorded several CDs of Turkish material (using the Turkish spelling of her name, Cansever), but has recently performed in Belgrade and in Germany.

Thanks to Nick Nasev

⊙ Gypsy Queens
World Network, Germany
This double-CD set includes fine Gypsy music from Hungary, Romania and Spain, as well as some of the best recent recordings from Esma Redžepova. It also marks the first appearance in the Western marketplace of the brilliant younger singer Džansever, recorded on top form with a hot band and some splendid Romani songs.

⊙ Makedonski Folk Hitovi
Senator Records, Macedonia
A quick trawl through Macedonian turbofolk, with an enjoyable selection from the likes of Bioritam and Sonja Tarčulovska.

★ Music from Macedonia 1 & 2
Caprice, Sweden
The first disc covers the more traditional side, with appearances by Stefče Stojkovski, two important čalgii and zurla master Mahmut Muzafer. The second features the more modern sound of Synthesis, plus tracks by the Kitka folklore society from Istibanja. A varied and well-chosen collection.

⊙ Tallava Vol. 6: Këngë dasmash
EuroLiza, Switzerland
Reissues of material by stars of the Golden Age, including Tafa, Lumi, Misini and Maxhuni. The roughness of the recording (these were originally cassette releases) somehow suits the rawness and immediacy of the performances. If you can't find Vol. 6 then any of the other volumes will provide a good introduction to tallava.

⊙ The Very Best of Macedonia
ARC Records, UK
A good range of favourite musicians, including Aleksandar Sarievski, Esma Redžepova, Vaska Ilieva, brass bands and more: not the most adventurous of selections, but solid good value.

Dragan Dautovski

With his roots in rock, Dautovski is a member of the generation that grew interested in traditional music only later on. He is nevertheless an important musician, entrepreneur and educator.

⊙ The Path of the Sun
Petar Pan, Macedonia
Scaled down, and contrasting with Dautovski's previously rather monumental approach, this group, including some of his former students, marks something of a return to his roots, with folky guitar strums and breathy vocals.

Vaska Ilieva

The grande dame of Macedonian folk music, with a career spanning fifty years, Ilieva is blessed with a plangent voice that is as effective in the most serious of traditional songs as it is in light, flirtatious popular hits.

⊙ Vaska Ilieva: Macedonian Folklore Classics
MRTV, Macedonia
Dug out from radio archives all over the former Yugoslavia, these eighteen remastered tracks display all aspects of Ilieva's great talent. The songs range from the traditional to her own compositions, including her signature hit "Zemjo Makedonska".

Kočani Orkestar

This is one of Macedonia's best brass bands – largely Gypsy, typically rumbustious, and featuring zurla as well as brass.

⊙ L'Orient Est Rouge
Cramworld, Belgium
The group have put out a number of discs, but this one, from the days before the band split in twain, is the best: straightforward, with strong playing and unfussy arrangements. An interesting choice of material, too.

Ferus Mustafov

A breathtaking performer with a seemingly inexhaustible flow of inspiration, clarinettist and saxophonist Mustafov is the leading figure in modern Macedonian Gypsy music.

★ King Ferus
GlobeStyle, UK
Recorded in Berlin with a top-class band, this is a splendid collection of old and new favourites.

Mahmut Muzafer

Romany wizard Muzafer is one of the most important and experienced zurla players on the scene. He has worked with many others, including Vlatko Stefanovski.

⊙ Makedonski Folklor so Zurli i Tapani, Svadbeni Običai
Mister Company, Macedonia
If you feel like developing a taste for the wild sounds of zurla and tâpan (it may take time, but it's well worthwhile), this is the place to start. Featuring the great Mahmut Muzafer and companions, this is a collection of melodies traditionally played during the wedding festivities, including an overwhelming version of the long and intricate showpiece (for dancers and musicians alike) "Teškoto".

Toše Proeski

A pop singer, but with a fine voice and immaculate technique, and noted for his humanitarian activities, Proeski was something of a phenomenon, and his early death in 2007 united the country in an outpouring of grief.

⊙ Ako me pogeldaš vo oči
MRTV, Macedonia
Light music, but immaculately produced, well sung and carefully crafted. No surprise, then, that this was a major hit. It includes "Magija", his duet with Esma Redžepova.

Esma Redžepova

Esma Redžepova remains the queen of Romani song, a stirring performer whose voice is still capable of the subtlest inflections and wildest passions.

★ Queen of the Gypsies
World Connection, Netherlands
A solid two-CD collection of most of Esma's hits, sung in Romani and Macedonian, and attractively presented.

Vlatko Stefanovski

With a rock background, a jazz sensibility and a deep interest in transformations of traditional material, Stefanovski is a virtuoso guitarist and one of the few Macedonian musicians so far to have made a serious name for himself outside the country.

⊙ Treta Majka
Avalon Production, Macedonia

Stefanovski and Miroslav Tadic are joined by Teodosii Spasov on kaval. Together, they give a new twist to well-known songs and dance melodies, with intricately woven arrangements played with almost telepathic sensitivity.

Stefče Stojkovski

Multi-instrumentalist Stojkovski is a performer and researcher with a deep knowledge of the various styles of Macedonian music and a creative, but not irreverent, approach to arrangement and reconsideration of the originals.

⊙ Echo from the Macedonian Mountains
Own label, Macedonia

On this recording, Stojkovski plays with a small group, in which kaval features prominently. There are several moving examples of the rhapsodic improvisations called ezgiji, brightened by dances with gajda and tambura.

Synthesis (DD Synthesis)

A young piano-driven band who combine folk instruments with lush orchestral backing. Started by Dragan Dautovski, they have now struck out very successfully on their own.

⊙ Swinging Macedonia
SJF Records, Macedonia

The arrangements are stately and grandiose rather than swinging, but they are tremendously effective all the same, with a powerful drive at times. Passionate singing from a female trio adds to the effect.

Tanec

Tanec has been through a lot of changes since its formation in 1949, but it remains the most down-to-earth of the large song-and-dance ensembles, with a good proportion of its members drawn from the countryside.

⊙ Tanec i Prijatelite: Od Ljubov ne se Bega
Tanec, Macedonia

The best place to see the group is, of course, in concert, with dancers, singers and musicians all working together to provide an impressive spectacle, but they sound good on CD too. Here, the band back up a number of prominent musicians in moving performances of urban songs.

Milan Zavkov

One of the very finest accordionists in the Balkans, a colleague of Ferus Mustafov and musical director and arranger for Tanec, Zavkov is also a successful soloist, with stunningly precise articulation and controlled fire in his playing.

⊙ Umetnički i Igraorni Ora i Čočeci
Mister Company, Macedonia

Virtuoso playing backed up by a small but all-star group, mixing concert-style showpieces with compelling dance melodies.

PLAYLIST
Macedonia

1 CHAJE SHUKARIJE Esma Redžepova from *Esma Queen of the Gypsies*
"Beautiful Girl" – one of the best-loved and best-known tunes in Esma's repertoire.

2 CHIFTE, CHIFTE, PAJTONLARI Ensemble Üsref from *Music from Macedonia 1*
A hypnotic, sinuous melody with its Turkish roots clearly showing: the classic sound of čalgija.

3 KITKA ORO Stefče Stojkovski from *Echo from the Macedonian Mountains*
A short ezgija on kaval gives way to a stately dance, in alternating bars of eleven and seven.

4 MORI MOME DD Synthesis from *Swinging Macedonia*
A gorgeous mix of sinewy singing, grandiloquent piano, bagpipe and orchestral backing.

5 ŠTIPSKI SA SA/TIKINO SA SA Ferus Mustafov from *King Ferus*
Two favourite dances, with inspired improvisations from Ferus on both saxophone and clarinet.

6 MAGIJA Toše Proeski from *Ako me pogledneš vo oči*
Sterling work from the young superstar, duetting with Esma Redžepova.

7 ZAJDI, ZAJDI, JASNO SONCE Aleksandar Sarievski from *The Very Best of Macedonia*
Possibly the greatest Macedonian song ever, in a definitive performance by its composer.

8 MESEČINA Dragan Dautovski Quartet from *The Path of the Sun*
Sweet, small-scale and acoustic Macedonian folk with gentle scat-singing and hippy percussion.

9 EDERLEZI AVELA Kočani Orkestar from *L'Orient Est Rouge*
Rhapsodic solos on trumpet and zurla, and a dance to celebrate St George's Day.

10 LINO MOME, SEVDALIJO Tanec from *Tanec i Prijatelite*
Naum Petreski and Suzana Spasovska duet in a heart-breakingly lovely folk melody, with the Tanec group providing a sensitive backdrop.

Malta

between the cross and the crescent moon

Valletta harbour
Sarah-Jane Muskett

Cast adrift between the North African coast and Sicily, Malta occupies a strategic position which has attracted a string of invading forces over the centuries. Only in the late twentieth century did this heavily fortified archipelago finally become an independent republic. With a Siculo-Arabic culture and a Semitic yet Europeanized language, the islanders have inherited the art of oral folk poetry as well as a tradition of brass bands and street busking. Andrew Alamango reports from the rock on a nation's reaffirmation of its social and cultural identity through the revival of its roots music.

Historically, the rural folk who populated this sparse archipelago had little say in the fate that befell their homeland time and time again. The constant political and cultural flux made Malta a cultural dumping ground, leading to the formation of a hybrid culture made up of the various influences of those who came and went. On a more positive note, this produced a unique blend of artistic expression reflecting the island's geographical location and uniting the European and Semitic styles.

The Maltese lack documentation of an oral music tradition, except for a few fleeting passages by visitors such as **George Percy Badger**, whose 1838 book *A Description of Malta and Gozo* mentions some musical instruments. The early twentieth century saw the importation of European instruments like guitars and accordions and the introduction of the gramophone. The production of bakelite records by the **HMV** label in the 1930s was instrumental in the diffusion of folk and popular music and in changing the perception of music by the islanders. Folk singers and guitarists, popular orchestral ensembles and singers were first recorded in 1931 in Tunis and then in HMV's Milan recording studio, by local agents. You may still stumble across some of the original 78rpms in a Sunday car-boot sale or a curio shop in the capital, **Valletta**.

Folk Poetry and Singing

With the increasing urbanization that followed independence from the British Crown in 1964, Malta lost much of its musical repertoire and many of its folk music traditions were discontinued. Even so, a strong tradition of oral folk poetry prevails to this day, and is referred to as **għana** (pronounced aa-na). Sung in octo-syllabic quatrains, it is performed regularly in bars and village watering-holes, to predominantly male audiences. Għana can also be heard at the National Folk Singing Festival in May and the agrarian feast of St Peter and St Paul in June. The songs' themes reflect the aspirations of working-class society, and performances often turn into a duel between singers who take it in turns to mock each other's shortcomings.

Folk singing is generally divided into three categories: **għana tal-fatt**, a ballad narrating tragic events with a moral; **spirtu pront**, improvised quatrains sung alternately between two or more singers; and **għana fil għoli**, high-pitched singing in which the singer displays his musical ability by embellishing the text with melismas. Għana is accompanied by two or three **guitars** which provide a harmonic background in 2/4 or waltz rhythm. Sung verses alternate with improvised music played by the *prim* (lead) guitarist. Using a variety of open tunings, the ringing sound of Maltese guitars is a twentieth-century innovation; upbeat satirical poetry is accompanied by simple major triads, while the unending tragic laments are supported by minor-key chords. **Indri Brincat "Il-pupa"** and **Carmelo Aquilina "Nofs il-lejl"** are two of the most influential guitarists, whose playing still inspires għana and guitar enthusiasts. "One must sing with heart", the late **Frans Baldacchino "Il-budaj"**, one of the finest exponents of ballad singing, would say. "Without heart you are lost and all is worthless." His somewhat husky voice and charm, coupled with his poetic lyrics, made him one of the most renowned and loved għana singers, both locally and in Australia where the għana tradition has flourished with Maltese migrants.

Traditional Feasts

The first Maltese band associations were formed in the 1860s. Reminiscent of Sicilian brass bands, they were initially non-religious but by the 1900s their primary function was accompanying the various activities at religious village feasts. The bands' repertoire includes upbeat marches, polkas and waltzes, *marċi funebri* for Holy Week celebrations and funerals, and operatic themes made popular through the dissemination of Italian culture since the nineteenth century. Band and parish rivalry has resulted in a lineage of local composers and a strong tradition of band club members who passionately defend their patron saint.

Frans Baldacchino 'Il-Budaj'
Tifkira
Mużika u Produzzjoni - Manuel Casha

Melbourne-based musician Manuel Casha's tribute to Frans Baldacchino "Il-budaj", one year after his death in 2006

Each year, carnival gathers inebriated musicians in the wine bars of Nadur on the island of Gozo. Accordions and harmonicas playing popular songs and echoes of Neapolitan tunes are accompanied by the clatter of tambourines, wooden clappers and *kastanjoli* (like castanets), and the "carnal grunting" of beer-lubricated **żafżafas** (friction drums). The remnants of this "demonic" carnival are probably the only surviving context for improvised instrumental folk music, which displays a whirling frenzy reminiscent of the trances of Puglian *tarantellas*.

Folk Instruments

Knowledge of the construction of the **żafżafa**, the **żmamar** (reed-flute) and the **flejguta** (cane-flute) is the fruit of recent research and living memory, as is the revived tradition of **żaqq u tanbur** (bagpipe and tambourine) playing. **Toni Cachia "Il-Ħammarun"**, from Naxxar, was one of the last surviving authorities on the making and playing of the five-holed, one-droned, calf-skin żaqq, which had almost faded from folk memory. His tambourine-playing friend, 74-year-old **Toni Camilleri "It-Tommi"**, pulls a toothless grin as he remembers how they used to play "Ħammarun's one and only tune" for a few coins and a bottle of wine. With a strong hand, he plays a 6/8 compound rhythm on his tambourine, hitting the instrument with his head, chin, elbow and wrist as in times of old when he would pull a crowd through his theatrical bravado, whilst the żaqq player gently swayed to the cyclical tune.

Roots Revival

Conceived in the year 2000, the **Etnika Project** was created to boost local and international consciousness of Maltese folk and popular music by gathering and reinterpreting traditional songs and melodies. Etnika embarked on a research project to define the characteristic sounds of the culture, documenting its musical instruments and existing repertoire and creating new repertoire based on recognizable tradition. Their summer showcase Etnikafe has captured the Maltese audience with a sense of nostalgia for a culture which was on the verge of extinction. Now a growing international name, Etnika blend local song and traditional instruments with jazz and Mediterranean styles, making Maltese folk music universally appealing whilst retaining its roots.

Etnika bassist Oliver DeGabriele

DISCOGRAPHY Malta

Frans Baldacchino "Il-Budaj"

The late Budaj was one of Malta's most renowned balladeers. Most of his music can be found on CD or cassette in local music shops.

⊙ **Malte: Ballades et Joutes Chantées**
Inedit, France
One of the only għana CDs released internationally, this captures a live performance by Frans Baldacchino and Karmenu Bonniċi in 1992. It contains four pieces, including two well-known Maltese ballads and two improvised spirtu pront "singing contests".

Etnika

An ethnic and roots band with a local following, formed with the intention of popularizing Maltese folk music traditions.

⊙ **Zifna**
own label, Malta
Released in 2003, this is a collection of eclectic grooves and moods by some of Malta's finest jazz, folk and classical musicians, depicting the sentiment of the Mediterranean island.

Sojceta Filarmonica Nazionale La Valette

One of the more prominent of the many band clubs to be found on Malta, Sojceta Filarmonica Nazionale La Valette produce and sell their own CDs of funeral and upbeat marches.

⊙ **Marċi Funebri**
own label, Malta
A collection of funeral marches by local composers and arrangers, usually played to accompany Easter celebrations, revealing the dramatic and sombre mood of the event.

279

The Netherlands

windmills on your mind

Amsterdam Klezmer Band

The Dutch have a tendency to embrace every other kind of music but their own. As if on the blades of a windmill, music has come in from four different directions and taken root. However, there is now a lively world music scene in all of the Netherlands' main cities, ranging from afro and flamenco to tango and rai – not to mention some exciting music coming out of former Dutch colonies such as Indonesia, the Dutch Antilles and Suriname. Stan Rijven tiptoes through the past and present, with thanks to Wim Bloemendaal.

When the Netherlands experienced a folk revival in the 1960s and 70s, groups like **Wargaren**, **Wolverlei** and **Fungus** explored the songs of pre-war generations. These had been collected by radio producer **Ate Doornbosch**, who broadcast them on his programme *Onder de Groene Linde* (*Under the Green Linden*) for almost forty years. The name was a reference to the fact that, prior to radio and records, people used to gather under linden trees in village squares to tell stories and sing songs. **Cobi Schreijer** also played a pioneering role, hosting Dutch and foreign folk artists at the De Waag club in Haarlem in the 1960s.

Frisian Folk

As the folk movement lost momentum and rock took over, many Dutch folk performers began performing in English. However, the trend was bucked somewhat in the northern province of **Fryslân**, where a handful of folk groups continued to express themselves in Frisian – a separate, older language related to Anglo-Saxon. Inspired by British examples, bands like **Irolt** created music based on Frisian folklore. For a live sample, it's worth visiting the village of Nylân on Easter Monday, when the **Aaipop Festival** takes place. There you might hear the likes of **Ernst Langhout**, **Doede Bleeker** and **Yggdrasil**; the latter are a sharp-voiced female duo, who have performed a mix of Frisian, Irish and British folk tunes since the early 1990s.

Limburg Carnival

As well as the Protestant north, the southern Catholic province of **Limburg** is known for its musical traditions. Although dialect-singers such as **Harry Bordon**, **Jo Erens** and **Frits Rademacher** have achieved wider recognition, Limburg is best known for its carnival, especially in the city of Maastricht. Since 1840, brass bands and topical crooners have caused an outburst of musical madness at Maastricht's annual street carnival, with its historic inner city creating a perfect setting for this lively folk tradition.

Dutch Revivalists

Elsewhere in the Netherlands, hardly any other original Dutch roots music is left. However, there are two active revivalist scenes: one digging into the past, the other focusing on the present. The group **Törf** re-create tunes from the early nineteenth century on the bagpipes and accordion, and **Madlot** and **Twee Violen en een Bas** play dance music from Dutch publife of the 1700s. Other revivalist groups include **Folkcorn** and **Pekel**. On the other side, there are pop bands who sing in local dialects, include references to their provinces in their songs and play folk instruments like the accordion. This wave started in the early 1990s with **Rowwen Hèze** of Limburg, followed by **Skik**, **De Kast** and **Blof**, from various other regions.

Trad Troubadours

A new kind of troubadour modelled on Anglo-American singer-songwriters developed in the Netherlands in the 1960s, blending French *chanson* and German *lieder* with regional traditions and dialects. These troubadours included **Ede Staal**, **Gerard van Maasakkers** and **Gé Reinders**. Although born in IJmuiden in the Netherlands, **Cornelis Vreeswijk** became Sweden's national hero with his rebellious songs. He died prematurely in 1987, but there is now a museum in Stockholm celebrating his life and work. **Boudewijn de Groot**, known as the "Dutch Dylan", became the national troubadour due to his poetic use of the Dutch language and his folk-pop approach.

From Tango to Django

Defining world music as "global going local", Holland offers a lively musical panorama, and foreign sounds have found fertile ground here since the 1900s. The **tango** hit The Hague as early as 1912, and in the 1930s **Malando** (aka Arie Maasland) started his own tango orchestra in Rotterdam. Malando compositions like "Olé Guapa" became worldwide hits, and his band's name a recognized brand. In the 1980s, influenced by Argentinian composer Astor Piazzolla, new tango took over and flourished, led by ensembles such as **Tango Cuatro** and **Sexteto Canyengue** which were both directed by bandonéonist Carel Kraayenhof.

Between the 1930s and 60s East European **Gypsy music** dominated city nightlife, with the superb bandleaders and violinists **Lajos Veres**, **Gregor Serban** and **Tata Mirando** being the most prominent figures. During the 1990s, a younger generation took over. Romanian *cimbalom* virtuoso Vasile Nedea rose from street to stage, and singer Marynka Nicolai introduced Russian folk in an electronic setting. With their 1989 debut *Seresta*, **The Rosenberg Trio** caused a sensation, and their guitarist Stochello Rosenberg was received as the new Django Reinhardt.

Amsterdam Global Village

Until World War II, Jewish cultural life flourished in Amsterdam, which was nicknamed "Jerusalem of the North". In the early 1990s, this musical tradition was revived, stimulated by the annual **Jewish Music Festival**. It presented the once famous **Leo Fuld**, plus newer performers such as **Rolinha Kross**, **StriCat** and the **Amsterdam Klezmer Band**. Partly influenced by Jewish tradition, but mainly by *cante napoletano*, the **Jordaan lied** genre developed in the working-class Jordaan quarter in the 1950s. **Willy Alberti**, **Johnny Jordaan**, **Tante Leen** and, in the 1990s, **André Hazes**, became national voices singing their popular tunes in the local vernacular.

The harbour city had long been a global village, but new influences were prolific in the second half of the twentieth century: migrants arrived from Southern Europe, Morocco and Turkey in the 1960s; South Africa and Latin America in the 1970s; and West Africa and Eastern Europe in the 1980s. Migrant musicians included: **Fernando Lameirinhas** of Portugal, who built a Lusophone repertoire; **Patricio Wang** of Chile, who created impressive film scores; and **Zuco 103** of Brazil and Germany, who mixed Latin beats with a jazz flavour. In addition, ex-Osibisa percussionist **Kofi Ayivor**, Ghanaian highlife guitarist **Sloopy Mike Gyamfi** and **Ifang Bondi** from Gambia all started second careers in Amsterdam, while **Noujoum Rai** and **Railand** became the first Dutch-Moroccan *rai* bands.

Meanwhile, Rotterdam developed into the musical capital of the **Cape Verde** islands, with lots of producers and studios, and bands like **Americo Brito**, **Splash** and **Rabasa**. In 2003, **Suzanna Lubrano** (a Cape Verdean who was raised in Rotterdam) won Best African Female Artist at the Kora Music Awards. And that same year, **Tasha's World**, alias Natascha Slagtand, put Rotterdam on the map by winning a British EMMA Award for Best World Music Act/Production.

Indonesia

Dutch roots music has also been strongly enhanced by the influx of people from the **former colonies** of Indonesia and Suriname, and from the Dutch Antilles. After **Indonesia** gained independence, tens of thousands of people moved to Holland in the 1950s, and The Hague became a centre of East Indian music. Lush Asian melodies merged with harsh American rock rhythms to form the electric guitar style of **Indorock**, and bands such as the **Tielman Brothers** gained a big following, especially in Germany, playing for the US army. Indorock disappeared when the British beat boom took over, but some bands still perform at the annual **Tong Tong Festival** in The Hague. The world's biggest

Herman T.

Rabasa, Rotterdam harbour

festival for Indonesian culture outside Indonesia, the Tong Tong Festival also stages a lot of **kroncong**, Hawaiian and *gamelan* ensembles.

The Netherlands also has a sizeable community of Moluccan exiles, whose music has Polynesian as well as Indonesian influences. There is a strong choral tradition, continued by bands like **Tala Mena Siwa**, as well as a more pop-based musical style, represented by **Massada** and the **Moluccan Moods Orchestra**. The adventurous duo **Boi Akih** expands the Moluccan vocal tradition by fusing it with different styles from all over the world.

Suriname and the Dutch Antilles

Migrants from Suriname exercised a strong influence on the Dutch music scene. Even before World War II, trumpeter **Teddy Cotton** and saxophonist **Kid Dynamite** were innovators in jazz circles and in the 1950s singer **Max Woiski** scored several hits. Surinamese music flourished after the country's independence in 1975. Flautist **Ronald Snijders** developed his own Suri-funk. The **Surinam Music Ensemble** and **Fra Fra Sound** invented **Paramaribop**, a blend of Afro-Surinamese, Caribbean and Afro-American traditions. Trumpeter **Stan Lokhin** emerged as the driving force behind **kaseko**, a fusion of jazz and calypso with Afro-Surinamese influences. As arranger and producer, Lokhin recorded countless kaseko albums with

acts like **The Happy Boys**, **The Twinkle Stars** and **Lieve Hugo**, who died in 1975, just before his big breakthrough. Since then **Trafassi**, **Carlo Jones** and **De Nazaten** kept the kaseko tradition alive. Singers like **Dhroe Nankoe** and **Raj Mohan** recalled Suriname's connection with their motherland India (in the late nineteenth century the Netherlands and England had exchanged contract labourers between the two then-colonies).

Antillean musicians were also engaged in the Dutch Latin and jazz scene. Bassist/composer **Eric Calmes** first branched out into other musical fields by starting his own group **Zaminokitaki**, which became a springboard for other explorers of Antillean styles such as the *tumba*. **Izaline Calister**, **Randel Corsen** and Calmes fused their tradition with elements of jazz, pop and world.

Fusion

This continuing process of crossover has yielded a lively world music scene. The Latin-jazz ensemble **Nueva Manteca** became a stepping stone for top percussionists such as **Nils Fischer** and **Lucas van Merwijk**; the latter went on to form his own **Cubop City Big Band**. **New Cool Collective** and **Sinas** blend jazz with Afrobeat and Latin; **Tarhana** mixes Gypsy grooves with Afro-Anatolian soundscapes; Arabic folk and American blues resulted in the "arabicana" of **No Blues**; while anarcho-punk band **The Ex** teamed up with Ethiopian saxophone legend **Gétatchèw Mèkurya**.

DISCOGRAPHY The Netherlands

 De Boonte Störm: Straatcarnaval in Maastricht
Frea records/M&W, Netherlands
Rooted in a Roman past and revived in the nineteenth century, carnival is still alive in places such as Limburg. This CD – with its fascinating street recordings – offers a lively inside report of the carnival in Maastricht. Military brass once defined the sound of this former garrison town, which later fell under the influence of the accordeon and, more recently, rock and world music. The album includes a 96-page booklet (in Dutch and English) and lyrics of all the topical songs.

⊙ **Jouster Boerebrulloft**
Pan, Netherlands
A recording of the Frisian farmer's wedding festival in Joure, that is inevitably artificial – people in costume playing a folk revival – but it also introduces music from Ljouwerter Skotsploech, Snitser Skotsploech and Aald Hielpen, a folklore group dating back to 1912.

 Onder de Groene Linde
Music & Words, Netherlands
Between 1957 and 1994, Ate Doornbosch recorded over five thousand folk songs, performed by farmers, spinsters and sailors, and played them on his weekly radio programme, *Onder de Groene Linde* (*Under the Green Linden*). Musicologist Louis Grijp selected 125 of these songs and compiled them on nine CDs, each reflecting a specific theme. The tenth disc in this box set is a television documentary from 1964 about Doornbosch's field work; also included is an illustrated book (in Dutch and English) containing all lyrics and biographies.

Amsterdam Klezmer Band

The Amsterdam Klezmer Band is the best example of the new wave of Jewish revival bands. Their performances are as hot as a Balkan brass band because of their daring mix of punky *klezmer* and jazzed-up arrangements.

⊙ **Zaraza**
Essay Recordings, Germany
This 2008 album offers a fresh view on the latest klezmer developments, blended with Balkan and Gypsy traditions.

Leo Fuld

At the age of eighteen, Jewish singer Leo Fuld (1912–97) earned a two-year contract with bandleader Jack Hylton. By 1936, he had become a Broadway star, and he later appeared on Frank Sinatra's TV shows, introduced Umm Kulthum in Europe, shared a stage with Edith Piaf in Paris, discovered Charles Aznavour, and toured North and South America and the Arabic world. He also wrote the English lyrics for "Wo Ahin Soll Ich Geh'n" (Tell Me Where Can I Go) and made it a million-seller.

⊙ **Leo Fuld: Shalom Israel**
Sony, Netherlands
Fuld was one of the great voices of Jewish song, and on these 1967 recordings, his voice is as strong as ever.

Johnny Jordaan

In the 1990s, *levenslied* – urban folk music sung in the vernacular – turned from low to high art, and working-class singer Jan van Musscher (1924–89), aka Johnny Jordaan, suddenly became a national hero, posthumously honoured with biographies, TV documentaries and even a statue.

⊙ **Het Beste van Johnny Jordaan**
EMI, Netherlands
This album contains his original hits; the first two, "Bij Ons in de Jordaan" and "Geef Mij Maar Amsterdam", defined the Jordaan *lied* genre with their upfront musette accordion. Johnny Jordaan's vocals were unique: Amsterdam slang with a *fado* touch, flavoured with cante napoletano sentiments.

Fernando Lameirinhas

Fernando Lameirinhas started with his brother in the 1960s in a pop duo called Jess and James, changing to a Brazilian party band (Sail Joya) in the 1970s, before finally returning to his Portuguese and Brazilian roots in the 1990s.

⊙ **Live**
Munich, Netherlands
A double-CD, recorded live at a concert in 2001, giving a taste of his considerable voice and performance qualities.

Madlot

The look of eighteenth-century Holland has been immortalized in hundreds of paintings, but revivalist group Madlot commemorate the era's sound. The music of the bars and brothels where the common folk met was first revived by Twee Violen en een Bas, but Madlot extended the idea by playing the real sounds in free form.

⊙ **Ik Hoorde dees Dagen (I Heard One of these Days)**
Pan, Netherlands
This 2005 album offers a daring interpretation of a 1716 hit parade, drawing from a print collection (*Oude en Nieuwe Boerenliedjes en Contredansen*) of popular dance tunes and tavern songs of the time. Madlot re-create the melodies in their own way, and although the harmonies and voices don't quite fit historically, their instruments (such as the bagpipe and rumble-pot) do.

Malando

When the first tango craze hit Europe in the early twentieth century, Rotterdam-born Arie Maasland (1908–80), aka Malando, became the king of ballroom tango. He composed such classics as "Olé Guapa" and "Noche de Estrellas" and was a respected bandleader. During his career he toured Scandinavia, South America and Japan, and teamed up with Osvaldo Pugliese and Mercedes Sosa in Argentina.

⊙ **Favorieten van Toen**
Mercury, Netherlands
This compilation contains most of Malando's original recordings, including "Campanillas", "La Mentirosa" and "Con Sentimiento". The original 1937 version of "Olé Guapa" was lost, but the 1948 version comes close. Malando developed a distinctive sound partly because he played accordion instead of *bandoneón* and added extra strings and brass, and partly because his tangos were slower.

Tata Mirando

The Mirando dynasty spans three generations of Gypsy music in the Netherlands. In the 1930s, grandfather Tata (1895–1966) arrived in Holland from Hungary with colleagues like Lajos Veres. They found an ideal climate for their nostalgic sound in The Hague, with its aristocratic nightlife of salons and restaurants. This type of music faded away in the late 1960s, but was revived in the 1990s.

★ **A Gipsy Played**
Philips, Netherlands
This reissue of Mirando's 1959 recordings offers a stirring example of East European Gypsy traditions at their best. The strings go wild, reminding you of Taraf de Haïdouks, but they are also played smoothly, in tempting passages full of desire. Mirando's approach is special because he replaced the cimbalom with piano and guitars.

No Blues

No Blues started as an experiment in 2004. The meeting between Dutch guitarist Ad van Meurs, bassist Anne-Maarten van Heuvelen and the Palestinian lute-player Haytham Safia became a huge success. They invented a new genre and labelled it arabicana.

⊙ **Ya Dunya**
Rounder, UK
A refreshing album that begins at the junction where Arabic music and American folk-blues meet. It sounds like Munir Bashir challenging Bert Jansch, or is it the reverse? Guest vocals by Tracy Bonham.

Rabasa

The musical capital of Cape Verde – sometimes even called the tenth island of the archipelago – is Rotterdam. From the 1960s, producers and studios catered for the home market, and the band Rabasa came to reflect the multicultural kaleidoscope of the city in the 1990s. Rabasa is made up of the Cape Verdean Ortet Brothers and musicians from Guinea, Holland and Suriname.

⊙ **Pertu di Bo**
Coast to Coast, Netherlands
Rabasa seduce with uptempo *coladeiras* and melancholic *mornas*, which they renew with catchy percussion, trumpet and accordion. Strong vocals and inventive grooves tease the mind and the feet on this 2004 album.

The Rosenberg Trio

At the age of 21, guitar virtuoso Stochelo Rosenberg was crowned as the successor to Django at the Reinhardt Festival in France in 1989. He then formed the Rosenberg Trio with his cousins Nonnie (bass) and Nous'che (rhythm guitar), and the trio quickly became an international success. In 1993, they accompanied Stéphane Grappelli – who called them "my children" – at New York's Carnegie Hall.

⊙ **Seresta**
Hot Club Records, Netherlands
The Rosenberg Trio's debut equals the fabulous guitar techniques and grooves of Django Reinhardt, who founded jazz manouche, or gypsy swing.

Sexteto Canyengue

Bandleader Carel Kraayenhof studied bandoneón with Juan Mosalini and performed with Astor Piazzolla before founding Sexteto Canyengue, for which he both writes and arranges. His performance at the wedding of Prince Willem-Alexander in 2002 gave the new tango a national boost.

⊙ **Tiburonero**
Lucho, Netherlands
This 1993 album pays a distinguished tribute to Kraayenhof's mentors Astor Piazzolla and Osvaldo Puglíese.

Gerard van Maasakkers

Gerard van Maakakkers is an enduring (and funny) singer-songwriter, who released his first album in 1977.

⊙ **20 Jaar Liedjes Live!**
I.C.U.B4.T, Netherlands
This two-disc live concert album features fresh arrangements of van Maasakkers' classic songs performed with a fine band.

Yggdrasil

Close-harmony singers Annemarieke Coenders and Linde Nijland grew up in Friesland, which is perhaps why they feel at home in the Anglo-Saxon and Scandinavian folk traditions and named themselves after a mythological tree. On their eponymous 1995 debut, their voices intertwined like branches reaching out for the wide open skies, while 2003's *Linde Sings Sandy Denny* is a highly acclaimed tribute to the late Fairport Convention vocalist.

⭐ **Nice Days Under Darkest Skies**
Pink Records, Netherlands
On their fourth album, Yggdrasil balance past and present in sober songs, crying out their laments purely and poetically. All the tracks are original, except for the traditional, acapella "Once I Had a Sweetheart" and a captivating cover of Bob Dylan's "It Takes a Lot to Laugh".

Zuco 103

Although singer Lilian Vieira is from Brazil, Zuco 103 is a Dutch band. The trio were moulded by the fertile musical climate of 1990s Amsterdam, where afro-beat, dance, jazz and Latin music happily co-existed. Out of this amalgam, they created *brazilectro*, and became an overnight success after the release of their debut album in 1999.

⭐ **Tales of High Fever**
Ziriguiboom/Crammed, Belgium
Zuco 103 really found their distinctive sound with this third album. Sensual and provocative, it aims for the ultimate bricolage. Listening to it, you could be clubbing in Amsterdam or Rio, New York or Lagos.

Dutch-Antillian

⭐ **Riba Dempel: Popular Dance Music of Curaçao 1950–54**
Otrabanda Records, Netherlands
A compilation of 78rpm discs from the golden age of the indigenous Papiamento recording industry with teasing local versions of *guaracha*, *son montuno* and *bolero* as well as waltz and danza from colonial times.

Izaline Calister

In the 1980s singer Izaline Calister came to the Netherlands from Curaçao. After replacing Angelique Kidjo in Pili Pili and touring with Dissidenten she started a solo career. Her 2000 debut album *Soño di un muhé* was an overnight success. Since then Calister has been a favourite act on both world music and jazz stages.

⊙ **Krioyo**
Network, Germany
In Papiamento, Calister's native language, Krioyo means Creole. Her third album fulfils the title by mixing a jazz idiom with the traditional styles of her island such as *danza*, *tumba* and *tambú*. Calister is surrounded by the cream of Dutch-Curaçao musicians, including pianist Randall Corsen and bassist Eric Calmes.

Dutch-Indonesian

⊙ **Indorock: The Original Recordings**
EMI, Netherlands
Among the Indonesians who moved to Holland after decolonization were teenagers who brought along the rock'n'roll

Stijntje De Olde

Zuco 103

they'd heard on American radio stations. Soon Indorock was born from a mixture of rock'n'roll, country, *kroncong* and Hawaiian sounds. Melodic electric guitars become the sound's main characteristics, and The Hague its epicentre. This compilation includes trendsetters like the Hot Jumpers, Javalins and Tielman Brothers in their heyday.

Boi Akih

Guitarist Niels Brouwer and singer Monica Akihary are the nucleus of Boi Akih. In varying coalitions they transform the heritage of the Moluccan culture into a new musical idiom. Through breathtaking and compelling concerts, they have built bridges between East and West.

⊙ Yalelol
Enja Records, Germany
Boi Akih have an unique sound that is intensely moving and spiced with virtuoso improvisations. On this 2007 album they cross borders between Moluccan, jazz and classical music.

Moluccan Moods Orchestra

This band of South Moluccan expatriates were led by guitarist Eddie Lakransy until his death in 1988.

⊙ Wakoi
Piranha, Germany
An addictive disc of Moluccan songs given a contemporary jazz-funk treatment, featuring guitars, keyboards, flutes, sax and percussion, plus some wonderful harmony singing from the three female vocalists.

Dutch-Surinamese

De Nazaten

This band of Dutch, Antillean and Surinamese musicians is named after the bastard offspring of the infamously promiscuous Prince Hendrik, husband of Queen Wilhelmina. With a line-up of saxes, trombone, guitar and percussion, they explore music from all over the Dutch-speaking colonized world.

⊙ Kownu Boy E Dansi (The Prince is Dancing)
Pan, Netherlands
A fine dance record that mixes influences from the Dutch Antilles, dixieland and even a combination of Balinese gamelan and Surinamese kaseko.

Fra Fra Sound

One of the many Surinamese musicians who came to Amsterdam in the 1970s, bandleader Vincent Henar developed the unique mix that became known as Paramaribop. A superb example of world music in the making, Fra Fra Sound have evolved into exciting ambassadors that join African, Caribbean, Latin American and funk vibes together.

⊙ On Tour: 25 Years
Pramsi Records, Netherlands
This 2004 compilation brings the best of the albums *Kultiplex*, *Mali Jazz* and *Kid Dynamite Tribute* together.

Lieve Hugo

Lieve Hugo was Suriname's first kaseko singer to become a popstar. He sang in both sranang-tongo and Dutch. He died in 1975 on the brink of his big breakthrough.

PLAYLIST
The Netherlands

1 **MORENA Rabasa** from *Pertu di Bo*
A nostalgic Cape Verdean song full of teasing trumpets and irresistible rhythms.

2 **BOSSA DORADO Rosenberg Trio** from *Seresta*
Dazzling guitar meeting between jazz *manouche* and *bossa nova*.

3 **ARMENIAN FOLK SONGS Tata Mirando** from *A Gypsy Played*
A breathtaking expression of longing for one's homeland; intense and evocative.

4 **ONE MORNING IN THE SPRINGTIME Yggdrasil** from *Nice Days Under Darkest Skies*
This stirring love ballad is sung in perfect harmony, and fuelled with feelings of loss and anger.

5 **OLÉ GUAPA Malando** from *Malando: Favorieten van Toen*
Malando's 1948 recording of his worldwide tango classic still sounds fresh and captivating.

6 **RAGEEN RAMBLING No Blues** from *Ya Dunya*
A fascinating fusion between the American folk-blues guitar and the Arabian lute.

7 **PEREGRINO Zuco 103** from *Tales of High Fever*
A happy and sultry song about migration, framed in a pulsing Afro-beat.

8 **DE PAREL VAN DE JORDAAN Johnny Jordaan** from *Het Beste van Johnny Jordaan*
A bluesy tribute to Amsterdam's Latin quarter sung in typical Jordaan dialect.

9 **BLACK EYES Tielman Brothers** from *Indorock: The Original Recordings*
Kroncong meets rock'n'roll in this instrumental Gypsy standard by the masters of Indorock.

10 **DOINA Leo Fuld** from *Shalom Israel*
The king of Jewish song at his ultimate best.

★ **The King of Surinam Kaseko**
EMI, Netherlands
This ultimate summary of Hugo's career offers both smooth ballads and irresistible dance tracks, including the fifteen-minute live version of "Langa Bere".

Norway

fjords and fiddles

Hardanger fiddle player Hallvard T. Bjørgum
Signe Dons

In the old days musical styles and tunes would travel up Norway's valleys, but less easily over the mountains between them. Because of this, each valley had – and to some extent still has – its own distinctive music. Nowadays musicians mingle in the major cities, producing music that is infused with diverse ideas but has a very strong and ever-evolving Norwegian identity, as **Andrew Cronshaw** reveals.

After a period in which traditional music was seen by many as a folksy postcard for old people and tourists, Norway seems to be coming to recognize that its cultural strength doesn't lie in copying mainstream international pop, rock or classical music, but in making its own distinctively Norwegian sounds. Norwegian pop and avant-garde music has become bolder, wittier and stranger, and the new Norwegian jazz, its airy shapes invested with a sense of the light and land, has moved far from its US antecedents. While many of these musicians choose to sing in English, hoping to broaden their market abroad, many others of today's young musicians are exploring music in which the Norwegian language plays an essential part – their country's living and growing traditional music. Given Norway's relatively small population (4.5 million), musicians working in all these genres tend to meet, so mutual influence and collaboration is increasingly common.

Land and Light

Nearly half of Norway lies north of the Arctic Circle, but the majority of its population lives in the southern part. The country borders Finland and Russia in the far north, but the thousand-mile southeast border is with Sweden, with which Norway was politically united until 1905. A much longer union with Denmark – Scandinavia's domi-nant power in the Middle Ages – lasted from 1380 until Napoleon's defeat in 1814.

Since 1917 there have been two official Norwegian languages. The twenty percent minority *Nynorsk*, based on Norwegian dialects, is found in fjordland and mountain communities, while the more Danish-rooted *Bokmål* prevails in all the cities and many other areas.

There is, of course, a completely different group of languages indigenous to Norway, those of the Sámi peoples. Sámiland, spreading across the northern reaches of Norway, Sweden and Finland and on into northwest Russia, gets its own chapter in this book (see p.348), dealing with the **joik** and other Sámi music. Norway has the largest Sámi population of the four countries, with such well-known Sámi musicians as **Mari Boine**, **Berit Nordland**, **Ailu Gaup** and the band **Transjoik**.

Despite its former Danish and Swedish links, Norway has always had a distinct culture – or rather a patchwork of cultures, the result of the country's stretched shape and mountainous topography. The high tops of the Scandinavian spinal mountain range discourage east–west communication across the border with Sweden, and north–south travel is impeded by a corrugated pattern of steep valleys. Water has been a more convenient route, and styles and fashions from outside have tended to spread up the fjords from the west and south, not always penetrating the remoter areas.

Hardingfele

A *hardingfele* is a beautiful object, usually with black pen-drawn acanthus patterns on the body, mother-of-pearl inlay on the fingerboard and a carved head, often in the shape of a lion or dragon. Compared to an ordinary fiddle, the neck is shorter, and the bridge flatter. In addition to its four playing strings, it has four or five resonating strings passing under the fingerboard and bridge.

Such sympathetic strings were found on the English *viola d'amore* in the seventeenth century – it's thought the idea came from Asia where several instruments feature them. They ring unchecked even when the bowed strings have been damped, so the hardingfele generates a ringing, silvery high overtone drone, while the fingered strings can produce a lower unstopped drone or a double-stopped effect; the flat bridge facilitates the bowing of two or more strings at once.

The tuning itself is drone-oriented. There are said to be 24 different tunings; the standard is A D A E (starting with the lowest string), with the resonating strings D E F# A. The "non-standard" tunings change the apparent tonal centre of a tune and therefore its whole feeling. The playing styles of different regions favour particular modalities, and so use particular tunings. Some have mood associations, and are named to match – for example, *grålysing* (dawn; A E A C# – one of the "troll" tunings). Another, *gorrlaus* (very slack) – in which the A is tuned right down to F and so wows in pitch as it's bowed hard – is associated with the three Setesdal *rammeslåttar* (strong tunes) only resorted to by a fiddler in times of extreme emotion.

Nineteenth-century Setesdal folklore collector Johannes Skar describes a fiddler called Peter Strømsing playing the *rammeslått* "Norafjells": "Suddenly he was caught by the ecstatic tune. He played like a madman and could not stop. They cut off the strings, and then he cried."

As a result, forms of music very different from the European mainstream have persisted among the rural population of Norway, and their isolation even from one another has resulted in greater divergence. Much traditional music shows the influence of the **natural scale** and may use microtonal intervals; it can sound either out of tune or exquisitely "on the edge" to those accustomed to twelve mathematically equal semitones. There's also an appreciation in Norwegian music – particularly apparent in the sound of hardingfele (resonant-stringed fiddle) and *seljefløyte* (no-holed pastoral whistle) – of the high, silvery frequency ranges. Indeed, there's an open, airy sound to much Norwegian roots music.

Fiddling

The best-known Norwegian instrument is the **hardingfele** or Hardanger fiddle (see box), whose resonant strings give it a distinctive high-ringing sound. It gets its name from the Hardanger region where it first caught on, but its exact genesis is uncertain. It seems to have been in use by the middle of the seventeenth century, at about the same time as the ordinary violin (*vanlig fele*) was itself being taken up in Norway. Surviving examples of early hardingfeler are more varied in design and smaller than the present-day form, which evolved in the mid-nineteenth century. Some ordinary fiddles have had their necks shortened and bridge flattened, making it possible to play in a hardingfele style. Others have been fitted with resonant strings, making what's known as a **Setesdals-fele**.

Hardingfele territory is roughly to the west of Oslo as far as the sea and as far north as Ålesund, with the triangle made by inner Hordaland, Valdres and Telemark usually regarded as the instrument's heartland. In other areas the ordinary violin prevails, also called the **flatfele** because of its longer neck and so lower tuning. Not only the playing styles but also the repertoires of hardingfele and ordinary fiddle are fairly distinct from one another, and both show great regional variation. Like Hardanger fiddlers, flatfele players use a variety of tunings.

Fiddles of all types suffered a setback during the nineteenth century as a result of religious revivalism. They were seen as instruments of the devil, and in western Norway many were destroyed. Fortunately, fiddle-burning was by no means universal.

The national movement that culminated in the dissolution of Norway's union with Sweden in 1905 increased enthusiasm for traditional music, and competitions, **kappleikar**, began at the end of the nineteenth century. These gave a new impetus

to fiddling, and the various local kappleikar, as well as the national contest, the **Landskappleik**, remain a major feature of the present-day fiddle scene, though not all of today's young musicians take the competitive route.

Though the music of solo fiddlers may sometimes seem rhythmically elusive, it's virtually all based on dance forms, and the best way to understand it is to watch, or better still participate in, dancing. The rhythms can be stretched and complex, but the player's footstamp is a guide. Sometimes, when being recorded, players have been discouraged from stamping in case it swamped the recording levels, but it's a key, heartbeat-like component.

Norwegian folk-dance music can be divided into two ages. The old dances, known as **bygdedans**, are done to an older stratum of tunes known as *slåttar*, and these make up most of the solo repertoire of hardingfele and fiddle. Slåttar subdivide into two-beat dances, including *halling*, *gangar*, *rull* and *brurmarsj*, and three-beat dances, including *springar*, *springleik* and *pols*. The halling is a male solo dance involving displays of prowess, including kicking a hat from the top of a stick held by a woman standing on a chair – the sort of thing beloved of dance-display teams. The rest, apart from the stately brurmarsj (bridal march), are normally couple dances.

The old, straightforward way of playing the tunes is as a short series of themes, each repeated, with small variations but nothing very elaborate. But during the nineteenth century some players began to play in a more personally expressive way, exploring and developing the themes, turning them from dance tunes into more evocative works. The leading name in this progression was **Myllarguten** (Torgeir Augundsson, 1799–1872), from Telemark, who was a great innovator and also travelled a good deal spreading his ideas. Though he did play for dances, he was one of the first masters of hardingfele to perform in a concert situation, to a non-dancing audience. The Norwegian classical violinist **Ole Bull** recognized his skill, and they sometimes shared a concert platform. Bull was also influential in the musical education of composer **Edvard Grieg** (1843–1907), who incorporated hardingfele music in works such as the piano piece "Slåtter", based on transcriptions of the playing of **Knut Dahle** (1834–1921). Another frequent visitor to Hardanger was **Ola Mosafinn** (1828–1912) from Voss, and his creative developments of Hardanger ideas, particularly his springar style, had considerable influence on fiddling back in his home area in the west.

There is an unbroken – if many-stranded – tradition stretching from the famous fiddlers of the nineteenth century to the present day. Quite a few of the best-known twentieth-century musicians were recorded, so their music can still be heard. Hardingfele tradition-bearers in more recent times include brothers **Hauk** and **Knut Buen** of Telemark, **Leif Rygg** from Voss near the Hardanger fjord, and **Vidar Lande** and **Hallvard T. Bjørgum** of Setesdal, near Norway's southwest tip.

Fiddlers commonly acknowledge the input of the musician who wrote the tune they're playing or (authorship usually being uncertain) the player from whose repertoire they or their predecessors learned it. Indeed, many a tune doesn't have a title other than the name of the fiddler associated with it. Though a player may be avowedly playing a tune in their predecessor's style, subtle touches of his or her own are incorporated, intentionally or not, and so the tradition creeps forward.

The repertoire and style of a particular fiddler are still strongly linked to the tradition of their home region, down to the particular valley. Musical dialects are very much valued and encouraged, not just in competitions but in forming the whole persona of a player. However, in recent years there has been a wave of enthusiasm for fiddling among young players, many of whom are learning repertoire and technique not just in their home area but also on folk music courses at regional music colleges, at the Ole Bull Academy in Voss, which was founded in 1977 by Hardanger fiddler **Sigbjørn Bernhoft Osa** and is dedicated to folk music, and at the Department of Improvised Music, Jazz and Folk Music at the Norwegian Academy of Music in Oslo. These highly skilled young fiddlers gathered in the cities are learning from one another, mingling with jazz, rock and classical musicians, and playing the tunes that excite them whatever their regional origin. In doing so, they're creating a new Norwegian roots wave, or at least accelerating one that began in the 1990s.

Dynamic, harmonizing ordinary-fiddle sextet **Majorstuen** formed at the Norwegian Academy of Music, in the Majorstuen district of Oslo. Its members, including **Ragnhild Furebotten**, **Andreas Ljones** and fiddler/cellist **Gjermund Larsen**, continue to play together, largely their own new-

Andrew Cronshaw

Annbjørg Lien

composed music, but have also developed busy solo careers. While hardingfele has traditionally been largely a solo instrument, back in the 1930s Sigbjørn Bernhoft Osa, Eivind Groven and Alfred Maurstad formed a hardingfele trio, and today's trios **Gamalnymalt** and **Trio Hardanger** expand the line-up's possibilities. **Valkyrien Allstars**, a band whose popularity reaches far beyond traditional music circles, is a hardingfele trio too, but with a very different approach, the fiddles providing an exciting, impelling shuffle supporting Tuva Syvertsen's wild and definitely un-traditional vocals in front of a meaty rhythm-section.

A particularly intense hardingfele duo is **Warg Buen** (**Per Anders Buen Garnås** and **Daniel Sandén-Warg**, the latter a well-known Swedish fiddler who moved to Setesdal and has become one of its finest players). **Benedicte Maurseth** and Trio Hardanger's **Knut Hamre** are exploring the special sounds of the oldest hardingfele instruments and repertoire. In **Utla** and other projects with saxist and bukkehorn player Karl Seglem, Gamalnymalt's **Håkon Høgemo** brings out the instrument's hypnotic pulse, sometimes intensifying it with savage valve-driven distortion to get at what he feels is the raw spirit of the music and the old players. **Nils Økland**'s work emphasizes the whispery minimalist and improvisatory possibilities of the hardingfele, as well as connecting into Western classical music with orchestral collaborations. There was some culture-crossing in the 1990s too; for example Knut Buen investigated raga connections with a sitarist, and Hallvard T. Bjørgum has collaborated with, among others, US singer-songwriter Eric Andersen, The Band's Hammond organist Garth Hudson, and Azerbaijani *kemanche* player Elshan Mansurov.

Annbjørg Lien was born in Ålesund, just outside hardingfele territory, so in competition terms she had no local hardingfele tradition; she has always played the tunes that appealed to her wherever they came from. Her recording career began at the age of thirteen, and her debut solo album appeared five years later in 1989. On it the traditional tunes she played on hardingfele and Swedish *nyckelharpa*

NORWAY

were given hefty arrangements employing reeds, electric guitar, percussion and synths. It created a lot of interest, and some controversy. Since then she has made a string of richly melodic albums, with her own band and in the "folk super-group" **Bukkene Bruse**. Like many present-day Norwegian folk musicians, she has increasingly moved to writing her own material, rooted in tradition but reflecting her present-day musical environment.

These days it's not uncommon for fiddlers to play both hardingfele and ordinary fiddle. **Sturla Eide** is one who plays both, in the powerful fiddle, accordion and drums trio **Flukt** and his solo projects and duo work with guitarist Andreas Aase. **Sven Nyhus** has a long career as player of both in both traditional solo or group contexts and as a composer and player of *gammeldans* music, as well as co-editing *Fanitullen*, a guide book (in Norwegian) to Norwegian traditional music. **Ånon Egeland**, playing both fiddles as well as traditional whistles and Jew's harp, has long been a prime mover in Norwegian traditional music and also in collaborating with Swedish musicians.

Masters of ordinary fiddle in both the past and the present are, as with hardingfele, numerous. A major figure throughout the second half of the twentieth century, winning the Landskappleik thirteen times, was **Hans W. Brimi**. Leading present-day players include **Tron Steffen Westberg**, **Knut Kjøk**, **Mari Eggen**, **Helene Høye**, and the members of Majorstuen. **Per Sæmund Bjørkum**, not only a leading folk fiddler but also a violinist with the Oslo Philharmonic, makes rich music with church-organist Kåre Nordstoga. **Susanne Lundeng**, from the Lofoten Islands in the far north, plays both traditional tunes and her own, moving between stately bridal march and roaring pols with a sophisticated band in front of which she stamps and whirls with magnetic, quirky energy.

In addition to solo artists and small groups, there are societies of traditional folk musicians, often with noted solo players among their members. These play in large groups, comprising fiddles plus sometimes accordion, guitar and bass. Some, such as **Vågå Spelmannslag** of Gudbrandsdalen, use ordinary fiddles, but a few, notably **Indre Sunnfjord Spelemannslag**, present the stirring silvery sound of massed hardingfeler, as does the Setesdal hardingfele sextet **Spelemannslaget Knut Heddis Minne**.

Gammeldans and Accordions

During the nineteenth century increasing numbers of people moved from the country to the cities where they had fixed working hours and regular leisure time. Before long, new dances, such as *vals, reinlender, masurka, polka, polkett, skotsk, englis, hamburger, galopp, sekstur, hopsa, fandango* and *feier* became fashionable. These were collectively called *runddans* (round or turning dance), but when the next new wave arrived in the 1920s runddans became known as "old dance" – **gammeldans**.

Gammeldans is still popular, and its music is dominated by the **trekkspel** (accordion), an instrument that first appeared in the nineteenth century and to an extent ousted the fiddle. First came the diatonic **enrader** or **torader** (one- or two-row melodeon) and later the bigger chromatic forms.

A typical modern gammeldans band may or may not have a fiddler, but it will certainly have accordion (usually chromatic), probably double or electric bass and perhaps guitar. Accordions – particularly the large ones when insensitively played – tend to make fiddlers pack up and walk away. Not only are the fiddle's tone and most of its stylistic turns obscured by volume, but the fixed-pitch and equal-temperament tuning, and the frequently used musette detuning of reeds to create a thicker, beating effect, are in direct conflict with the subtleties of the "floating-tone" scales of the old fiddling, in which the exact pitch of some notes varies according to the feel of the piece and whether the phrase is ascending or descending.

Recently, however, there are signs of increased lightness of touch in the gammeldans-band sound, influenced by the growing number of skilled accordionists outside the dance-band scene who have been collaborating with fiddlers with great sensitivity. Diatonic and chromatic accordionist **Jon Faukstad**'s work with Hans W. Brimi and others led the way in a more or less traditional style. The band **Over Stok Og Steen** proves that gammeldans music can sound beautifully elegant – like a summer tea-dance orchestra but with better tunes and more skill and verve – while still being eminently danceable.

One of Norway's most skilful and progressive accordionists is **Stian Carstensen**, who plays in the extraordinary band Farmers Market as well as with double bassist Arild Anderson and others. He's also a fine player of Bulgarian *kaval* and an innovator on the banjo. Accordionist **Frode Haltli** moves between composing and playing classical chamber music and working with traditional performers including the group Rusk and fiddler Ragnhild Furebotten. Another subtle accordionist is **Kristin Skaare**, who has collaborated with fiddler Susanne Lundeng and singer Kari Bremnes. The trio Flukt – hardingfele player Sturla Eide, accordionist **Øyvind Farmen** and drummer Håvard Sterten – is a delight of intelligence and drive. Accordion and drums duo **Gabriel Fliflet** (whose Columbi Egg acoustic club-night in Bergen is a great meeting-point for musicians) and Ole Hamre deliver a wild, ever-quirky take on repertoire ranging from Norway to the Balkans. Accordionist and euphonium player **Tom Karlsrud** is at the heart of the quartet **Streif**, whose unexpected interpretations of Norwegian tradition draw on *klezmer* and Balkan music. He is also a member of **Gjertruds Sigøynerorkester**, led by fiddler Gjertrud Økland, which plays Roma music including that of the Taters, Norwegian Romanies. Serbian accordionist **Jovan Pavlovic** leads Balkan band **Bengalo** and plays with the similarly skilful **Urban Tunélls Klezmerband**.

Song

The overall word for traditional Norwegian singing is **kveding** (from the old word *kvede*, "to sing"). Traditional songs – **folkeviser** – fall into a range of categories. The oldest are the **balladar**, epic and magical story-songs going back at least to the Middle Ages and sharing many themes with the ballads of other European countries as well as containing more specifically Nordic elements. At one time ballads were danced, as they still are in the Faroes. From the seventeenth to the early twentieth century printed song-sheets (**skillingstryk**) were sold bearing lyrics of some of the old ballads as well as more recent compositions, including many relating to the emigration to North America of about 75,000 Norwegians at the turn of the twentieth century.

Also dating back to the Middle Ages is the **stev**, a short rhyming-couplet song either handed down from tradition or improvised on the spot. The form known as **slåttestev** uses a dance-tune melody. Dance tunes can also be sung using non-word "tra-la" vocables, either in the absence of an instrument or by a fiddler while playing. This parallel to Scottish or Irish "diddling" is called, onomatopoeically, **tralling**.

Other forms of folksong include lullabies (**bånsuller**), game songs (**voggeviser**) and rhythmic work songs (**arbeidssongar**). Until recently animals were taken to the high pastures (**seter**) in summer, and this gave rise to striking melodic vocalizing that carried across the landscape: wordless animal-calling, **lokking**, and human-directed song-signalling, **laling**.

A very significant aspect of Norwegian music is the result of an unusually strong connection between folksong and religious music. What are known as **religiøse folketonar**, religious folksongs, draw their lyrics largely from hymn books, from **Thomas Kingo**'s and **Petter Dass**'s seventeenth-century publications onwards, but the melodies have been so folk-processed that they have been almost totally transformed. Their four-squareness is modified by the prevailing local traditions into a wide variety of rhythmically and modally complex, beautiful and deeply Norwegian tunes that are inseparable from the rest of the folk tradition.

There's a clear, floating, high-register soprano or tenor sound to most Norwegian traditional singing. Like that of many north European countries, and like hardingfele, its essence is solo and unaccompanied, though it has long been the subject of instrumental arrangements and in the current wave of interest fresh encounters and directions multiply. Like fiddlers, most of today's traditional singers centre their repertoires on the traditions of their home area.

Agnes Buen Garnås, sister of Telemark fiddlers Knut and Hauk Buen, was one of the first of this generation of singers to make links with the new Norwegian jazz, in her work with saxist Jan Garbarek, as well as her album-length ballad suite *Draumkvedet* featuring reeds, harp, brother Knut's hardingfele and Kåre Nordstoga on church organ.

Kirsten Bråten Berg is a well-known singer and silversmith from Setesdal, a region noted for its traditional music, silversmithing and making and playing of Jew's harps. She began recording in the late 1970s with wind player Tellef Kvifte and hardingfele players Hallvard T. Bjørgum and Gunnar Stubseid in the group **Slinkombas**. Among other projects are work with jazz bassist Arild Andersen, a cross-border collaboration with Swedish singer **Lena Willemark**, and combining Norwegian and West African traditions in the group **From Senegal To Setesdal** with *kora*-player and singer **Solo Cissokho**, Cote d'Ivoire singer, mouth-bow player and percussionist **Kouame Sereba** (both of them Norway-resident) and Setesdal Jew's harp player and maker **Bjørgulv Straume**. Since that project, Senegalese Mandinka griot Cissokho has become well known internationally for his duo work with Swedish fiddler Ellika Frisell, which won a BBC Radio 3 Award for World Music, while at home in Norway he leads the band Cissokho System and his family band.

Berit Opheim from Voss was a member of **Orleysa**, one of the first bands to combine traditional music with new jazz. She has worked frequently with Karl Seglem, has guested with Sondre Bratland and is a member of the trio **BNB**, as well as the groups **Kvarts** and **Fryd**.

Unni Løvlid from Sogn og Fjordane is active in a range of projects including the trio Rusk with accordionist Frode Haltli and hardingfele player Vegar Vårdal, a solo recording in the extraordinary long-reverb acoustic of Oslo's Vigeland Mausoleum, and collaboration in rural China with musicians of the Dong people.

Tone Hulbækmo of Tolga in Østerdalen has long been making elegant contemporary statements of Norwegian folksong, accompanied by her Norwegian harp. Sinikka Langeland lives in Finnskog, on the Swedish border northeast of Oslo. It's an area of historical Finnish settlement, and Langeland plays Finnish *kantele* and mixes Finnish runo-songs with Norwegian tradition, collaborating with jazz musicians such as Bjørn Kjellemyr and Arve Henriksen.

Jon Anders Halvorsen from Telemark is a rising figure in Norwegian traditional music. His work with guitarist Tore Bruvoll shows just how sensitively the guitar can be used in this music, and his role as Tamino in Norwegian Opera's folk-music version of *The Magic Flute* illustrates Norway's musical boundary-crossing. He is also a member of the vocal group Dvergmål, which specializes in religious folksongs. Another member, Øyonn Groven Myhren, grew up in Oslo but her material reflects her Telemark roots. Her solo singing is sparsely accompanied by her lyre or *seljefløyte*.

The best-known voice in religious folksong for two decades has been the calm, sonorous tenor

Karl Seglem

of Telemark's Sondre Bratland. Accompanied by many of Norway's leading traditional, rock, jazz and classical musicians, he makes connections with contemporary song, poetry and other cultural perspectives, including work with Bhutan singer Jigme Drukpa. Younger singers well known for religious folksongs include Åsne Valland Nordli, from Hardanger, and Arve Moen Bergset, who grew up in Bratland's home town of Vinje and took lessons with the elder singer. Bergset's second album, made at the age of just fifteen with Annbjørg Lien, Iver Kleive, Hans Fredrik Jacobsen and others, won a 1987 Spellemannspris (the Norwegian equivalent of a Grammy). As well as being a leading singer, he is a noted classical violin and hardingfele player, and is a member of the band Bukkene Bruse.

A former member of the Vinje folk band Blåmann Blåmann, Odd Nordstoga made a rapid but uncompromised transition from deep tradition to the high reaches of the pop charts with his 2004 debut solo album. Kim André Rysstad is a very fine light-voiced young male singer with a quiet narrative authority and musicality reminiscent of, and at least the equal of, the most magnetic singers of the contiguous Scottish ballad tradition, and sometimes using kindred tune-forms.

Other fine traditional singers include the warm-voiced Frode Nyvold (whose songs from Agder include Norwegian versions of shanties also known in the English tradition), Gunhild Tømmerås, Gunnlaug Lien Myhr from Buskerud, Eli Storbekken from Østerdalen, Kristin Gulbrandsen from Valdres, Anne Gravir Klykken of the group Vintermåne, and Camilla Granlien and Tone Juve of the trio Skrekk.

Apart from its wide range of pop, rock, country, blues and classical singers, some singing in Norwegian, some in English or other languages, Norway also has a distinctive breed of vocalists and songwriters who are very characteristically Norwegian in style, making spacious and elegant recordings. A prime example, throughout her long career, is singer and songwriter Kari Bremnes. With few overt connections to traditional music, and singing in English, but with a musical and lyrical approach reflective of today's Norwegian non-pop sound, is the avant garde-ish, quiet new-jazz and poetic work of the likes of Sidsel Endresen or Susanna And The Magical Orchestra.

Other Instruments

Although the hardingfele gets most of the attention, Norway has other distinctive instruments, and ways of playing more international instruments. The **langeleik** is a form of long box zither, with melody strings which run over frets and unfretted drone accompaniment strings. Dating back to the sixteenth century or earlier, it was once widespread, with regional forms including the dramatic Telemark design which has a high head scroll reminiscent of the prow of a Viking longship. Its use is beginning to spread again, but the only unbroken tradition of langeleik dance music is in Valdres, where today's players include **Gunvor Hegge**, **Elisabeth Kværne**, **Ole Aastad Bråten**, **Helge Myrheim** and **Marit Mattisgard**.

The **munnharpe** (Jew's harp) is widely used in Norwegian traditional music, playing the same genres of dance tunes as fiddles. Its heartland is Setesdal and noted players include **Bjørgulv Straume**, **Svein Westad**, **Frode Nyvold** and **Hallgrim Berg** (the last a European Union politician who, as a result of playing to fill up time in a radio interview, found himself making a hefty nordicgroove munnharpe album at the instigation of techno producers **Ari Thunda**).

There was a harp tradition in Norway, but it died out in the nineteenth century. In the 1970s **Tone Hulbækmo** had a copy made of a seventeenth-century example in Østerdal museum, and the resulting slim, wooden-pegged, metal-strung instrument is central to her music. Her partner in many musical projects is multi-instrumentalist **Hans Fredrik Jacobsen**, who is a particularly

fine player of **seljefløyte**. The word "selje" means "sallow", and that's what the flute – earlier called *borkfløyte* (bark-flute) – was originally made from, by animal-herders here and in other north and central European countries. In Norway it was particularly used in the high summer pastures. There are no fingerholes; the flute, or really whistle, plays two harmonic series of overtones, one made with the end open, the other, a tone or less lower, made by covering or part-covering the end with a finger. Thus a natural scale is playable; it's only complete above the first octave, so the tone is high and whispery, with a playing style of tonguing and fast shivering grace-notes.

Like many of the new ideas reaching Norway, the first European recorders arrived by sea, and that's probably how the **sjøfløyte** (sea-flute) – a huskiertoned whistle resembling a recorder – got its name. It was considered more on the side of the angels than fiddles, and so survived when they were suppressed. Notable present-day players of Norwegian folk-flutes include **Steinar Ofsdal**, **Tellef Kvifte**, **Hans Fredrik Jacobsen** and **Per Midtstigen**.

Various **clarinets** have been used in Norwegian folk music: an unkeyed shepherd's instrument known as the **Meråker** clarinet, the **tungehorn** made from an animal horn, and versions of the orchestral instrument. The **bukkehorn** ("goathorn" – but usually a ram's horn) has finger-holes and is blown like a trumpet.

Knut Bry

Terje Isungset

Events and Contacts

Norway has a large number of festivals of all genres of music, mostly in the summer. Those with major Norwegian roots or traditional music content include the folk and world music festivals at **Førde** in early July and at **Bø** in Telemark later in the month, the smaller Nordsjøfestivalen folk festival in Farsund in late August, the **Árinn** traditional music festival in Christiansholm fortress in Kristiansand harbour in September, and **Landskappleiken**, the national contest for traditional music, which moves location and date each year. **Folkelarm**, a showcase of Norwegian and some other Nordic roots music performers that to some extent parallels the rock and pop showcase/conference **by:Larm**, takes place in Oslo in September. ("Larm" means "sound".)

The websites of the **Norwegian Music Information Centre**, www.mic.no and www.musicfromnorway.com, provide a large amount of information in all musical genres on artists, events and recordings, including sample audio clips and paid-for downloads.

NRK (Norwegian Broadcasting) has a DAB and Internet channel **Alltid Folkemusikk**, www.nrk.no/alltid_folkemusikk, streaming traditional music tracks 24/7.

In the hands of **Jan Garbarek**, **Tore Brunborg**, **Bendik Hofseth** and others of the new **Nordic jazz**, the saxophone echoes these pastoral instruments. Tenor saxist **Karl Seglem** plays both tungehorn and bukkehorn in his powerful meetings between traditional music and new Norwegian jazz with the trio Utla and others.

The sound of trumpets – the small bukkehorn and long wooden **lur** – that once echoed across the summer pastures is now reflected in the veiled, floating melodic lines and spacious reverberations of Norwegian jazz trumpeters **Arve Henriksen** and **Nils Petter Molvær**, both of them with strong connections to the countryside and to traditional music. Also using traditional music in its mix is brass combo the **Brazz Brothers**.

The **church organ** isn't the most portable of instruments, but church acoustics go well with Norwegian music, so although fiddling in church was frowned upon in some places, nowadays the organs find themselves drawn into traditional music, rock and jazz. Key players in this unusual alliance are organists **Iver Kleive** and **Kåre Nordstoga**; among the high points of their work are Kleive's duets with guitarist Knut Reiersrud and Nordstoga's with fiddler Per Sæmund Bjørkum. To composer and ethnomusicologist **Eivind Groven** (1901–77), born and raised in Telemark with the natural scales of seljefløyte and hardingfele, the twelve equal semitones of the standard piano and organ scale sounded out of tune, so he built a 36-tone modified organ manual able to cope with traditional music. It hasn't caught on, but two of his instruments are still playable at the **Eivind Groven Organ House** in Oslo.

In the past the guitar hasn't played much part in Norwegian traditional music, which is a thing of melody, and sometimes rhythm, not chord progressions. Guitars are sometimes used in the relative four-squareness of gammeldans, which usually involves accordion with its bank of chords, but the microtones and natural scales of vocal, fiddle, seljefløyte, langeleik and Jew's harp music call for an approach much more subtle than chords if a guitar-player is to join in. Recently some very fine players have been doing just that, generally going for the melodic lines rather than driving chords. In the early 1990s guitarist **Øyvind Lyslo** did sensitive pioneering work in guitar accompaniment with Nordfjord fiddler **Arne M. Sølvberg**, and guitarist **Roger Tallroth** of Sweden's well-known trio Väsen has had considerable influence on Norwegian guitarists' approach to fiddle accompaniment, working with Annbjørg Lien's band. **Tore Bruvoll** has recently become the guitarist of choice in a number of leading bands, including with singer Jon Anders Halvorsen in Bruvoll/Halvorsen and with fiddler Ragnhild Furebotten. Moving between hefty acoustic and electric blues and a spacious Norwegian sound, with perfectly judged bottleneck slide playing, **Knut Reiersrud** is probably Norway's most powerful and eclectic guitarist, with a fine feel for the microtonality of Norwegian traditional music.

In the past in some regions of Norway drums were used instead of melody instruments to beat out dance rhythms at social events. In recent decades a new and distinctively Norwegian approach to drumming and percussion has developed, in the area where jazz and traditional music meet. **Terje Isungset**, whose organic kit throbs like an animated pile of jetsam, is the prime example. His bass drum is not rock music's tight, damped thud but a huge, heartbeat-booming item, evocative of a fiddler's footstamp. The hi-hat is replaced by a tangle of bells and jingles, attached by string to lines bearing slates, wooden boards and bark-stripped branches. While he has all this moving he's liable to stand up and add wild buzzing shivers of Jew's harp, or pause for a limpid bukkehorn call. He plays with Karl Seglem in the duo **Isglem** and trio Utla, with Swedish band Groupa, and in a string of other projects in music, performance

art and theatre. Recently he has become known as "the ice man", performing and recording with only instruments made of ice – percussion and trumpets – and creating a festival of ice instruments in his home town of Geilo. Other developers and leading exponents of these new Norwegian styles of drumming and percussion include **Helge Norbakken**, **Paolo Vinaccia**, **Kenneth Ekornes**, **Audun Kleive** and **Finn Sletten**.

DISCOGRAPHY Norway

⊙ **Buskerudtonar Med Tradisjonar Vols 1 & 2**
Buskerud Folkemusikklag, Norway
This musical selection is limited to the county of Buskerud, but male and female kveding, hardingfele, vanlig fele, seljefløyte, sjøfløyte, langeleik, torader, trekkspel and gammeldans are all well represented in these two CDs recorded in 1990–91.

⊙ **Meisterspel**
Heilo, Norway
Twenty-three players of hardingfele accorded the title of Master, recorded between 1937 and 1997. Includes the Buens, the Bjørgums, Leif Rygg, Knut Hamre, Håkon Høgemo, Eivind Mo, Alf Tveit, Sigbjørn Bernhoft Osa and many more.

⊙ **Norsk Folkemusikk**
Grappa, Norway
A ten-CD series of recordings, dating from the 1930s to the 1990s, from Norwegian Radio's archives of instrumental and vocal traditional music. Vol. 1 is an overview from before World War II, while each of the others deals with a different county. The expert notes are in Norwegian and English.

Hallvard T. and Torleiv H. Bjørgum

Hallvard and his late father Torleiv have long been pillars of the Setesdal music scene and prime exponents of the essence of hardingfele.

⊙ **Dolkaren**
Sylvartun, Norway
Father and son with a good display of the strong Setesdal tradition, and a pathway into the depth and differentness of unaccompanied Norwegian traditional music. Solos from each on hardingfele, plus from Torleiv some ordinary fiddle, Jew's harp and singing.

Per Sæmund Bjørkum

Bjørkum's playing of ordinary fiddle is rooted in the tradition of his home, Vågå in Gudbrandsdal, but he's also an orchestral violinist, and his four-time Landskappleik-winning traditional playing has an exquisite, soaring tone in the slow tunes.

⊙ **Den Våre Fele (The Delicate Fiddle)**
Heilo, Norway
Very shapely set of traditional tunes, based on the playing and repertoire of Bjørkum's mentor Pål Skogum (1921–90), both solo and accompanied by prominent Norwegian modern roots musicians: guitarist Knut Reiersrud, church organist Kåre Nordstoga, accordionist Jon Faukstad, wind player Hans Fredrik Jacobsen and double bassist Bjørn Kjellemyr.

Kirsten Bråten Berg

One of the pillars of today's traditional singing, Bråten Berg has long been a leader in finding interesting and sensitive ways to emphasize the strength of tradition by contrasting and combining it with other musical ideas. Whether she's alone or working with Arild Andersen, Hallvard Bjørgum, From Senegal To Setesdal or Swedish musicians, her singing has a fine richness and dignity.

WITH MARILYN MAZUR AND LENA WILLEMARK
⊙ **Stemmenes Skygge**
Heilo, Norway
Stark, noble and spacious, here are two of Scandinavia's greatest voices, Bråten Berg and Sweden's Willemark, with the latter's fiddles and the backing of US-born Danish percussionist Marilyn Mazur.

WITH ARILD ANDERSEN
⊙ **Arv**
Kirkelig Kulturverksted, Norway
This 1993 album features traditional songs from Bråten Berg among the slowly unfolding shapes of Arild Andersen's double bass, sax and keyboards, with percussion from Paolo Vinaccia and Nana Vasconcelos.

Kari Bremnes

While Bremnes' work is richly Norwegian, she isn't a kveding-style singer, more of a song-poet, with a beautiful, serene voice and a catalogue of albums of intelligent music, including her own songs and settings of poetry by painter Edvard Munch and others, always with impeccable production and classy accompanists.

⊙ **Spor**
Kirkelig Kulturverksted, Norway
She's been recording since the late 1970s, and her finest moments are spread across her albums, but this 1991 winner of the Spellemannspris has several of them. The material is the work of all three Bremnes siblings: Kari, Ola and Lars. The line-up includes Kristin Skaare, Knut Reiersrud, Stan Poplin, Finn Sletten and her brothers.

Tore Bruvoll and Jon Anders Halvorsen

Jon Anders Halvorsen is a young singer with a vocal perfection comparable to the likes of Arve Moen Bergset. A member of the traditional vocal group Dvergmål, in 2002 he won the vocal prize at the Landskappleik, and teamed up with guitarist Tore Bruvoll.

⊙ Nattsang
Heilo, Norway

A set of traditional ballads sung in Telemark within the past 150 years, some from collections and some learnt from living singers. The duo are joined by the subtle, sophisticated and well-matched tones of Per Oddvar Johansen's percussion, Gjermund Larsen's viola and Arve Henriksen's smoky trumpet.

Knut Buen

The Buen family of Telemark has been musical for generations. Brothers Hauk and Knut are leading and influential players of hardingfele. Hauk also makes the instruments, Knut's company releases traditional CDs and books, their sister Agnes Buen Garnås is a well-known traditional singer, and among the next generation there are Landskappleik winners for hardingfele and kveding, and a fiddle maker.

⊙ Seljordsmarsjen
Nyrenning, Norway

Knut Buen on solo hardingfele. The Napoleonic-like "Bridal March from Seljord" and eighteen other springars, gangars and listening tunes from the repertoires of two nineteenth-century fiddlers and craftsmen from Seljord in Telemark, Øystein Langedrag and son Leiv Sandsdalen. An excellent way to learn this music.

Agnes Buen Garnås

One of the first traditional singers to blend her art with that of jazz musicians, Agnes Buen Garnås led the way in the creation of the new Nordic-rooted music.

⊙ Rosensfole
Kirkelig Kulturverksted, Norway

A 1989 collaboration with Norwegian saxophonist Jan Garbarek on a set of traditional songs, largely ballads, with occasional herding-calls, all with a spacious, drifting, lyrical sound.

Bukkene Bruse

What started out in 1993 as a collaborative project between three star soloists for the Lillehammer Winter Olympics has become a permanent band. Hardingfele and nyckelharpa player Annbjørg Lien, singer and fiddler Arve Moen Bergset and Steinar Ofsdal, doyen of Norway's breathy and reedy traditional whistles, are now joined by keyboardist, arranger and producer Bjørn Ole Rasch.

⊙ Spel
Heilo, Norway

A live album of mostly traditional melodies, including a scattering of old favourites, this moves between powerful ensemble playing and commanding soloing.

Sigurd Eldegard

Eldegard spent his whole life, from 1893 to 1962, working and playing in the family tradition on his farm in Årdal, Sogn. He wasn't a competitive or famous player of hardingfele, but he was a great one, with a very strong, direct style, close to the way hardingfele was played before the influence of international virtuosi led to the extension of tunes into concert pieces.

⊙ Hardingfelespel Frå Årdal
Talik, Norway

Twenty tracks, including fine examples of springar, halling, *vals* and *lydarslått* (listening tune). These raw, exciting, foot-stamping recordings were made for Norwegian radio in the 1940s and 50s but still sound very fresh today, replete with the old spirit of hardingfele.

Ragnhild Furebotten

Norway is hardly short of excellent fiddlers, but Ragnhild Furebotten has a special bright-eyed, infectious energy in performance, often of her own shapely tunes.

★ Endelig Vals
Ta:lik, Norway

Furebotten is joined by the extreme articulacy and subtlety of Majorstuen colleague Gjermund Larsen's cello, viola and fiddle and Frode Haltli's never-brash accordion in a set full of strong melodies. It ranges in pace from the deep darkness of a Saltdal folksong tune, through *reinlender*, pols, light-touched Danish minuet, steaming polka, a reel and a classic arrangement of the stately "Brurmarsj from Sørfold", to a restless, twitching Furebotten polka that is by turns mischievously suppressed and exuberant.

Farmers Market

Stian Carstensen was a child prodigy on the accordion, later taking up electric guitar. At Trondheim Conservatory in the early 1990s he met guitarist-vocalist Nils Olav Johansen, bassist Finn Guttormsen, saxist Håvard Lund and drummer Jarle Vespestad. They chanced on the delights of Bulgarian music, explored Bulgaria, and made a live album, *Speed/Balkan/Boogie*, with members of Le Mystère du Voix Bulgare. Lund left, Bulgarian saxist Trifon Trifonov joined, and the Market continued to metamorphose, with Carstensen by now not only ace accordionist but also banjoist, guitarist, violinist, mandolinist and player of Bulgarian kaval and bagpipe.

⊙ Musikk Fra Hybridene
Kirkelig Kulturverksted, Norway

Rapid-fire flickering, within the same number, across a finely detailed patchwork-pastiche of tunes and songs, the music of the invented islands of the Hybrides, including snatches of spot-on Bulgarian trad, film themes and corny pop classics, all delivered with unerring accuracy, switching so quickly and often that the mind approaches multicultural meltdown.

Flukt

Sturla Eide on fiddle and hardingfele, Øivind Farmen on accordion and Håvard Sterten on drums. At the time of its first album, *Spill*, the trio included bassist Sondre Meisfjord, but by 2004's *Drufiacc* his place had been taken by Sterten, and it's a very complete, powerful-sounding formation.

⊙ Drufiacc
2L, Norway

This captures Flukt's drive and excitement but with plenty of contrasts in pace, style and texture in its repertoire of pols, *schottis*, wedding music and originals.

Iver Kleive

Kleive is probably the world's rockiest church organist, combining the big pipes with Hammond B3, piano, Paolo Vinaccia's resounding percussion, Knut Reiersrud's guitar and hot gospel choirs, as well as accompanying hardingfele and many other musical forms. He and Reiersrud magnificently typify the genre-crossing of Norway's music mafia.

⊙ Kyrie
Kirkelig Kulturverksted, Norway

An extraordinary, massive-sounding album, largely recorded in Denmark's Odense Cathedral, using Norwegian traditional and other church music and some enormous grooves, stinging slide guitar, soaring vocals and power percussion.

WITH KNUT REIERSRUD

★ Himmelskip
Kirkelig Kulturverksted, Norway

Also recorded in Odense Cathedral, Kleive and Reiersrud's "Blå Koral" was an atmospheric and very successful duet between church organ and guitar on traditional song tunes and hymns which led to an ongoing series of church concerts. This is its long-awaited and powerful follow-up.

Annbjørg Lien

Lien, from Ålesund, first recorded at the age of thirteen; five years later, playing hardingfele, ordinary fiddle and nyckel-harpa, she made her first full album, which in its modernist arrangements was so strikingly different from preceding fiddle albums that it raised a lot of interest in Norway and abroad. Since then, with her own band and as a member of Bukkene Bruse, she has made a string of elegant and energetic albums and remains a high-profile figure, an important influence on today's swelling generation of players.

⊙ Annbjørg
Kirkelig Kulturverksted, Norway

The controversial first album, full of strong, memorable traditional tunes, accompanied by Brazz Brothers trombonist Helge Førde's muscular arrangements for woodwind, saxes, cello, electric guitar, percussion and Frode Fjellheim's synths.

★ Prisme
Grappa, Norway

By 1996 Lien was writing most of her own material, drawing deep on Norwegian tradition but also influenced by other cultures, and still making nothing like a standard fiddle album. Here she is joined by keyboardist Bjørn Ole Rasch, traditional wind and oud player Hans Fredrik Jacobsen, guitarist Roger Tallroth and viola player Mikael Marin from Sweden's Väsen, and percussionist Rune Arnesen.

Susanne Lundeng

Lundeng, from the Lofoten Islands north of the Arctic Circle, is an outstanding player of the ordinary fiddle, with silky smooth tone or huge drive as the tune demands and an engagingly eccentric and energetic stage manner.

★ Drag
Kirkelig Kulturverksted, Norway

Lundeng's first album was solo fiddle; for its successors, beginning with this one, she has brought in top cross-cultural musicians – here Kristin Skaare on wonderfully subtle accordion, piano and harmonium, percussionist Finn Sletten and bassist Stan Poplin. *Drag* is a constantly interesting and varied journey of dance-impelling polsdanses, gorgeous stately bridal marches, compulsive hallings and hypnotic, ecstatic rammeslått-type pieces, as well as some unexpected, serene singing, and an underlying subtle wit.

Majorstuen

High-energy band of six hot and fine-toned young players of standard fiddle, who met at the Norwegian Academy of Music in Oslo. Harmonizing and interweaving, occasionally they expand the tonal range with viola or cello, but it's all bowed strings; the exuberant rhythmic drive comes not from any kind of rhythm section but from incisive bowing.

⊙ Joran Jogga
Majorstuen Fiddlers Company, Norway

At the time of their eponymous debut album they played mostly traditional tunes, but this second album from 2004

is virtually all their own compositions, as they continue and extend the living tradition.

Sigrid Moldestad and Liv Merete Kroken

Kroken (hardingfele) and Moldestad (ordinary fiddle and hardingfele) met in 1996 while students at the Ole Bull Academy in Voss. Since then, in duo, band and solo work, they have emerged as leading lights of the new generation.

⊙ Spindel
Heilo, Norway

Impressive debut album, produced by Tellef Kvifte, that gave its name to the band. Hardingfele and fiddle duets with strength, stamping energy and beauty, some with satisfyingly meaty band adding piano, harmonium, guitar, cittern, double bass and percussion.

Nils Økland

A traditional-skilled hardingfele player and violinist, for six years musical director of the Ole Bull Academy in Voss, and a member of BNB and other groups, Økland is creating a lot of interest in the hardingfele outside its normal circle with his impressionist, minimalist albums.

⊙ Straum
Rune Grammofon, Norway

A drifting set of his own compositions and arrangements of traditional tunes, from whispering natural-scale hardingfele harmonics through regal airs on normal violin to extreme contrasts with the sudden thunder of church organ. Contributors include singer Berit Opheim, hardingfele player Ole Henrik Moe, cimbalom player Laszlo Racz, Sigbjørn Åpeland on piano, harmonium and organ, and Økland's brother Torbjørn on trumpet and guitar.

Over Stok Og Steen

Adding clarinet, cello, harmonium, piano, dobro and the occasional song to the usual gammeldans line-up of fiddles, accordion, guitar and bass, this band turn Norwegian dance music into something exquisite. They specialize in the music of Hedemarken, the flatland villages east of Lake Mjøsa near Oslo.

⊙ Till Almuen
2L, Norway

A beautifully arranged set of Hedemarken tunes and songs, the latter appealingly delivered by guest Hege Nylund. It includes, in the band's words, "minuets from the eighteenth century, the peasant's polka, the farmer's fandango and the ballad singer's wistful love songs".

Knut Reiersrud

With his perfectly judged slide and eclecticism, guitarist Knut Reiersrud might be compared to Ry Cooder, but he has very much his own voice, based in a distinctive take on blues but embracing Norwegian traditional and other roots musics. Apart from his own projects and duets with organist Iver Kleive, collaborations include *Lullabies From the Axis of Evil* and, with Nepali classical band Vajra, *Himalaya Blues*.

★ Tramp
Kirkelig Kulturverksted, Norway, remixed as *Footwork* for Shanachie, US

This is a beautiful, airy, powerful recording, naturally crossing textures, grooves and cultures, with Alagi M'Bye's kora and vocal, Juldeh Camara's vocal and riti, Iver Kleive's church organ and Hammond, percussionist Paolo Vinaccia, bassist Audun Erlien plus the Five Blind Boys of Alabama. Full of wit and surprise.

Karl Seglem

Born and raised in Årdal in Sogn og Fjordane, tenor saxist Karl Seglem first took the jazz path, but never felt comfortable with that tradition, so turned to his own, bringing Årdal hardingfele player Håkon Høgemo into his Sogn-a-Song project, taking up tungehorn and bukkehorn and writing tunes that draw deep on tradition. The trio Utla – the two of them with percussionist Terje Isungset – followed. It's hard to capture in just audio, but immensely powerful live, with the raw, wild spirit of rammeslått. Seglem also works with his band and other musicians, releasing albums on his own NORCD label.

 Femstein
Long Distance, France/NORCD, Norway
Seglem and band – comprising Høgemo and the ex-Mari Boine rhythm section of bass guitarist Gjermund Silset and percussionist Helge Norbakken – unite in his powerful, primal melodies of air, metal, stone, wood and bone.

WITH UTLA
⊙ **Song**
NORCD, Norway
The trio are joined by traditional vocalist Berit Opheim. Isungset's rumbling bass drum is a magnified version of the fiddler's footstamp, pulsing with the natural-scale hypnosis of Høgemo's hardingfele, under which Seglem's tenor sax interjects tangential notes. Some tracks are driven by the quivering infuriated-wasp buzz of Isungset's Jew's harp.

Tango For 3

Tango is one of the dance forms that came to Norway and put down roots, though it hasn't gone native in the way it has in Finland. Tango For 3 comprises Sverre Indris Joner (piano), Per Arne Glorvigen (bandoneon), Odd Hannisdal (violin) and Steinar Haugerud (bass). It's a quartet of dazzling virtuosity, ingenuity, wit and lightness of touch.

⊙ **Soledad**
Majorselskapet, Norway
Argentinian and newly composed tangos, and three "Gringos" – an acute tango take on Grieg's tunes that the composer can't have envisaged – in the second of the group's albums.

Vintermåne

The trio of Telemark traditional singer Anne Gravir Klykken, saxist Frødis Grorud and keyboardist Torjus Vierli came together in 1997 at Agder Conservatory in Kristiansand.

⊙ **Vintermåne**
2L, Norway
In a set of traditional songs, mostly from Telemark, Klykken's clear vocals flow naturally into the calm uncluttered airiness of Norway's new roots jazz, with Grorud's limpid soprano sax matching and expanding on her lines, Vierli's piano and keyboards tastefully syncopating, and touches of guest seljefløyte and percussion.

PLAYLIST
Norway

1 SPRINGAR (FØRKJESLÅTTEN) Sigurd Eldegard from *Sigurd Eldegard: Hardingfelespel Frå Årdal*
Highlighting the difference between hardingfele music and Western violin playing, here are high-ringing strings, two or three bowed together, and a leaping, driving tune of overlapping rhythms.

2 BRURMARSJ, FRA SØRFOLD Susanne Lundeng from *Drag*
A beautiful, stately bridal march, led with perfect poise by Lundeng on violin, nobly accompanied by Kristin Skaare's accordion and Stan Poplin's bass.

3 BLÅ BOTN Karl Seglem from *Femstein*
Husky tenor sax and tungehorn, overdriven amped hardingfele, throbbing bass, and shuffling, gutsy percussion in a compelling traditional-form tune.

4 SOLFAGER OG ORMEKONGJEN Arild Andersen and Kirsten Bråten Berg from *Arv*
Clouds of drifting texture and sustained electric guitar over calm double bass, with Berg's regal voice singing traditional lyrics to Andersen's folk-hymn-like melody.

5 HIMMELSKIP Iver Kleive and Knut Reiersrud from*Himmelskip*
Electric guitar and church organ, distant and veiled at first, suddenly bursting out and up into the church acoustic with ecstatic guitar lines and mighty chords, then subsiding.

6 VILLVINTER Annbjørg Lien from *Prisme*
A characteristic Lien up-tempo track, with ringing hardingfele and nyckelharpa strings and a meaty accompaniment.

7 BERG OG BÅRE Kari Bremnes from *Spor*
A gorgeous melody of interflowing lines and hesitations, in which Knut Reiersrud's acoustic guitar slides and Bremnes' voice soars and hovers over Skaare's piano and accordion, Poplin's bass and Sletten's ticking percussion.

8 ENDELIG VALS Ragnhild Furebotten from *Endelig Vals*
A perfect waltz of her own composition, finely arranged; as memorable as anything in the tradition.

9 UNGJENTDRAUM Tore Bruvoll and Jon Anders Halvorsen from *Nattsang*
A traditional song from Telemark featuring Halvorsen's serene tenor vocal, Bruvoll's guitar and Arve Henriksen's breathy trumpet.

10 GRINGO NR. 1 Tango For 3 from *Soledad*
Grieg would tango in his grave: an exquisitely done re-rhythming of "In The Hall Of The Mountain King".

Poland

polish punks seize warsaw

Motion Trio
Izabella Pajonk-degardo

With Poland's accession into the EU in 2004, the biggest country of the former Eastern Europe became integrated with the West. Strangely enough, its music began to make an impact too, as the punkish Warsaw Village Band won a BBC World Music Award and gained a European following. Traditional music lost its credibility in Poland under Communism after World War II, with Communist fakelore tainting people's interest in the genuine article. But there are pockets of the country – notably the Tatra Mountains – that boast some of the most distinctive sounds in Europe. **Simon Broughton** and **Agnieszka Matecka-Skrzypek** outline the background and highlight some of the new developments.

An interest in folklore emerged in the nineteenth century in Poland, allied to aspirations for national independence; folk music and politics in the region often have symbiotic links. The most important collector of songs and dances from all over the country was **Oskar Kolberg** (1814–90). His principal interest was in Polish song; it's thought that instrumental music was fairly primitive until near the end of the nineteenth century. From the 1900s, progress was rapid, fuelled by gramophone recordings. However, the wartime annihilation and movement of ethnic minorities in Poland severely disrupted folk traditions, and after the war, the Communist regime – as throughout Eastern Europe – co-opted folk culture as a part of its own ideology, as a cheerful expression of healthy peasant labour.

Communist Folk

The Communist espousal of folk music was a near killer blow for the traditon. Both folk music and folk traditions were sanitized almost to irrelevance, emerging mainly through presentations by professional folk troupes – most famously the **Mazowsze** and **Śląsk** ensembles – who gave (and still give) polished virtuoso performances with massed strings and choreographed twirls, whoops and foot-stamping. Their repertoire was basically core Polish with a slight regional emphasis (the Mazowsze territory is around Warsaw, the Śląsk around Wrocław), but the overall effect was one of homogenization rather than local identity. For the most part, real folk music withered away as its image became tarnished by the bland official ensembles. Nevertheless, there was just about enough slack in the system to allow local bands to keep some genuine traditions alive.

The development of the media was another, equally important, reason for the gradual disappearance of tradition. Popular music was becoming widespread in the country as never before, and it was viewed as "better" or "more interesting".

Polish Dances

Thanks mainly to Chopin, the **mazurka** (*mazurek*) and **polonaise** (*polonez*) are Poland's best-known dances, and they stand at the core of the folk repertoire. They are both in triple time, with the polonaise generally slower and more stately than the mazurka. The polonaise is particularly associated with the more ceremonial and solemn moments of a wedding party. It was taken up by the aristocracy from a slow walking dance (*chodzony*), given a French name identifying it as a dance of Polish origin and then filtered down to the lower classes.

Another triple-time dance popular in central Poland is the **oberek**, which is interspersed with one-stanza improvised songs. Like most other dance tunes, the oberek has many possible variants – the fiddler does not reproduce the melody but improvises on a basic tune adding his or her own embellishments. Another oberek characteristic is its rubato rhythm, a performance manner based on the free shifting of accents and rhythmic durations within a bar. Consequently, the pulse of the dance seems to change from triple to duple time.

In addition to these triple-time dances, there are several five-beat dances, which are characteristic of the northeastern areas of Mazury, Kurpie and Podlasie. As you move south, somewhere between Warsaw and Kraków, you find duple-time dances like the **krakowiak** and **polka**. The krakowiak is named after the city of Kraków and the polka is claimed by both the Poles and the Bohemians as their own, although it became most widely known in Bohemia. Of course, none of these Polish dances are confined to their native areas; many have become staples across the country and abroad.

Folk Music Today

Today, with the notable exception of the Tatra region and a few other rural pockets, traditional music has virtually ceased to exist as a living tradition and has been banished to **regional folk festivals**. Several of these are very good indeed, with the **Kazimierz Festival** at the end of June foremost amongst them (see box on p.305).

Typically, the areas where the music has best survived tend to be the remoter regions on the fringes – Kurpie and Podlasie in the northeast (with their ritual songs based on four- and five-tone modal scales), the Rzeszów region in the southeast (where the *cymbały* – hammer dulcimer – is popular in the local bands), and the Podhale and highland regions in the Tatras along the southern border.

Good, active regional bands include: the **Franciszek Gola Band** in Kadzidło (Kurpie); the **Jan Gaca Band** in Przystałowice, the **Franciszek Racis Band** in Jasionowo, the **Jan Kania Band** in Lipniki (Kurpie); the **Edward Markocki Band** in Zmysłówka-Podlesie and the **Stachy Band** in Haczów nad Wisłokiem (Rzeszów); the **Świarni Band** in Nowy Targ; the **Ludwik Młynarczyk Band** in Lipnica; the **Trebunia Family Band** in Poronin and the **Gienek Wilczek Band** in Bukowina (Podhale).

Warsaw Village Band

The word "barbarian" crops up pretty quickly in conversation with **Wojtek Krzak** of the **Warsaw Village Band**. It's a description the band have adopted not only in reference to their musical style, but also in their attitude to Polish traditional music. There's no mistaking the WVB sound. It's strident, rough and in-your-face – they are the "Polish Pogues". Most groups playing traditional music tend to soften it to make it more palatable, but the WVB have done quite the opposite – they strike their strings more stridently, beat their drums more fiercely and play the tunes a good deal faster than any traditional Polish band. "We are barbarians on the violin and other instruments", says Krzak. "We use the violin like an electric guitar or the voice just shouting. There's the influence of traditional music of course, but also the sounds of contemporary life."

All six members of WVB live in Poland's urban capital, and four of them were born there. But they have a passion for Polish traditional music, and for making it vital for their own generation. In Polish they're known as *Kapela ze Wsi Warszawa*, the "Band from the Village of Warsaw", which clearly implies the collision of the urban and the rural. Take "In the Forest" from *Uprooting* (2004), their best CD to date: the tune comes from nineteenth-century collector **Oskar Kolberg**, but the vocals are shouted with a punk-like savagery, and the string-playing is aggressive, scratchy and supercharged, accompanied by powerful percussion on the frame drums and a swish of cymbal, but no drum kit. Then there's the edgy turntable scratching that gives the song a contemporary feel. The basic violin and drum sound comes directly from traditional music, but it's been designer-distressed in a distinctive way.

Three scary women front the band, yelling vocals and providing the instrumental core: **Ewa Wałecka** on violin, **Maja Kleszcz** sawing out the bass on cello, and **Magdalena Sobczak** hammering her dulcimer like she's performing a pummelling back massage. Behind them are the three guys, **Wojtek Krzak** (with his dreadlocks and sunglasses) on accompanying violin, and percussionists **Maciej Szajkowski** and **Piotr Gliński** reinforcing the sound from behind.

The band started in 1997 (with quite a different line-up) and won first prize at the "Nowa Tradycja" (New Tradition) festival, which led to them cutting their debut CD. Since then, they've had widespread success, including winning a **BBC Award for World Music** in 2004, and have toured extensively. They have sought out veteran traditional musicians, like fiddler **Kazimierz Zdrzalik** and the group **Kapela Mariana Pełki**, who can be heard on the *Uprooting* CD.

Folk music in Poland was largely devalued thanks to kitsch sanitized ensembles like **Mazowsze**, and WVB are currently the most vital force in revitalizing its credibility. "If you ask our fathers about traditional music", explains Krzak, "they won't know anything because of Communism. But if you ask our grandfathers they know it. So there is this missing generation. We're trying to make traditional music understandable and digestible for young people. Mazowsze sucks for them."

Michal Hetmanek

Warsaw Village Band with the Marian Pelka Band

Simon Broughton

Podhale

Podhale, the district around Zakopane, has the most vibrant musical tradition in the country. It has also been one of Poland's most popular resorts for years – so it defies the usual rules, being in no way remote or isolated.

Podhale musicians are familiar with music from all over the country and beyond, but choose to play their own way. This sophisticated approach is part of a sense of pride in Podhale identity which probably dates from the late nineteenth century when several notable artists and intellectuals (including composer **Karol Szymanowski**; 1882–1937) settled in Zakopane and enthused about the folk music and culture. Music, fiddlers and dancing brigands are as essential to the image of Podhale life as the **traditional costumes**, which consist of tight felt trousers, broad leather belts with ornate metal clasps and studs, embroidered jackets and black hats decorated with cowrie shells.

Musically, Podhale is very different from the other regions, and it is highly diversified in terms of both its musical style and its folk customs, such as dance, architecture, costume and dialect. What is common to all of Podhale's sub-regions, however, is the **shepherds' tradition**, which can be traced back to the sixteenth century to the cultural heritage of the Wallachian settlement, which comprises polyphonic singing and characteristic shepherds' instruments. These features of Podhale music are common to the entire Carpathian area. The influence of the Kraków region, further north, can also be heard in Podhale's wedding tunes, in which the rhythms of the dance krakowiak predominate.

The typical **Podhale ensemble** is a string band, with a lead violin (*prym*), a couple of second violins (*sekund*) playing accompanying chords, and a three-stringed cello (*basy*). The music is immediately identifiable by its melodies and playing style. The tunes tend to be short-winded, angular melodies based on the so-called **Podhale scale** with Lydian fourths.The fiddlers typically play these melodies with a "straight" bowing technique – giving the music a stiff, angular character as opposed to the swing and flexibility of the usual "double" bowing technique common in Eastern Europe. The straining high male vocals which kick off a dance tune are also typical of these ensembles.

At the heart of the repertoire are the *ozwodna* and *krzesany* **couple dances**, which are both in duple time. The first has an unusual five-bar melodic structure and the second is faster and more energetic. Then there are the showy **Brigands' dances** (*zbójnicki*), which are the popular face of Podhale culture, central to festivals and demonstrations. Danced in a circle by men wielding small metal axes (which are sometimes hit together fiercely enough to strike sparks), the Brigands' dances are a celebration of the *górale* traditions of brigandage – full of tales of colourful robberies, daring escapes, festivities and death on the gallows for anti-feudal heroes. "To hang on the gibbet is an honourable thing!" asserted the nineteenth-century górale musician Sabała, "They don't hang just anybody, but real men!"

The songs you're most likely to hear in more tourist-oriented performances are those about

Simon Broughton

Podhale wedding band outside the church

Janosik (1688–1713), the most famous brigand of them all. Musically these are not actually Podhale in style, but are in fact lyrical ballads with a Slovakian feel; countless tales of the region's most famous character are sung on both sides of the border. The most played songs are "Idzie Janko", whose tune seems to be used for many other Janosik songs, and "Krywań", which is a celebration of one of the Tatra's most famous mountains.

The mountain regions around Podhale also have their own, less celebrated, musical cultures. To the west, the region of **Orawa**, which straddles the Polish/Slovak border and the Beskid Żywiecki to the north, holds an annual festival in the town of Żywiec. **Józef Broda**, a brilliant singer and musician who mainly plays woodwind folk instruments, lives in Beskid Śląski – the part of the Beskidy Mountains reaching furthest west.

To the east of Zakopane, the music of the **Spisz** region has more Slovak bounce than the Podhale style and boasts an excellent fiddle-maker and musician in **Wojtek Łukasz**. If you can't make it to a highland wedding, music is relatively accessible in Zakopane. Many of the restaurants have good bands that play certain nights of the week, there are occasional stage shows and an annual Festival of Highland Folklore in August.

Ethnic Minorities

Post-Communism, there's been something of a revival in the music of the national minorities living in Poland. There is now a more liberal climate in which to express national differences, and travel is easier across the borders between related groups in Lithuania, Belarus and Ukraine.

Poland's **Boykos** and **Łemkos** are ethnically and culturally linked to the Ukranians and the Rusyns of Slovakia, and their music divulges its eastern Slavonic leanings in its choral and polyphonic songs. The music of the Belorussians and Lithuanians can also be heard in Poland. A number of ethnic minority groups are also now a regular feature of the **Kazimierz Festival**, at which you can hear the common heritage in types of Romanian, Ukrainian and Jewish music. The singer **Maria Krupowies**, who was born in Vilnius, Lithuania, but raised in Poland, has sung Lithuanian, Belorussian and Polish songs exploring the connections and differences between them.

World War II saw the effective extermination of **Jewish** life and culture in Poland, along with the exuberant and melancholy **klezmer** music that was an important part of weddings and festivals. Klezmer music had distinctive Jewish elements, but it also drew heavily on local Polish and Ukrainian styles. Thanks to emigration and revival, it now flourishes principally in the US. However, it has also become increasingly popular in Poland in recent years, where the greatest celebration of klezmer music is the annual **Festival of Jewish Culture** in Kraków.

The city, which attracts lots of visitors to its former Jewish district, is home to a number of klezmer bands, the best of which is **Kroke**. They started off playing schmaltzy klezmer standards to visitors on the *Schindler's List* tour, but are now one of the most inventive and exciting bands in Eastern Europe. They have proven their abilities on many concert tours, and have collaborated with top British violinist Nigel Kennedy. One of the band's members is of Jewish origin, although he didn't discover that fact until he'd been playing klezmer for several years – which says something about the pressure to assimilate in post-war Poland. Another Kraków group, the **Bester Quartet**, has made an important link to the radical New York scene through John Zorn's Tzadik label.

Revival and New Music

It is perhaps not over-optimistic to sense a reviving interest in Polish traditional music as the exhortations of the Communist troupes slip further into the distance. The band that has broken Polish folk internationally is the **Warsaw Village Band** (see box on p.302). They are a rare thing, a young, hip band who have a genuine interest in the old traditions. But, ironically, they're probably better-known abroad than they are at home; one of their

Jak Kilby

Kroke

Festivals and Events

Kazimierz Dolny: This festival of folk bands and singers, held on the last weekend in June, is Poland's biggest traditional music festival. Contact: Andrzej Sar, Wojewódzki Dom Kultury, ul. Dolna Panny Marii 3, 20-010 Lublin, Poland. tel +48 81 532 4207; fax +48 81 532 3775.

Folk Music Festival of the Polish Radio "Nowa Tradycja": This has been organized every year (usually in April) since 1998 by the Folk Culture Radio Centre of the Polish Radio. "Nowa Tradycja" (New Tradition) consists of two competitions – one for Polish Folk CD of the Year, the other for artists inspired by the folk music of Poland and its ethnic minorities. The most important folk groups from abroad perform as guests of the festival, too. Contact: Piotr Kędziorek, RCKL, Polskie Radio SA, al. Niepodległości 77/85, 00-977 Warszawa, Poland. *www.polskieradio.pl/rckl*

International Folk Music Festival "Mikołajki Folkowe": The oldest folk festival in Poland, this has taken place every December since 1991, with the aim of popularizing the folk movement. It consists of an "Open Stage" competition for debuting groups from central and Eastern Europe, concerts of folk music stars from Poland and abroad, presentations of films inspired by traditional culture, artistic workshops on singing, dance, instrumentation and handicraft, and various other exhibitions and happenings. Contact: Orkiestra św Mikołaja, ACK UMCS "Chatka Żaka" ul. Radziszewskiego 16, 20-031 Lublin. tel +48 60 173 2249; *www.mikolaje.lublin.pl*; *www.mikolajki.folk.pl*.

first tours in Poland was as support for Senegalese rappers Daara J! Another Polish group gaining international attention is **Motion Trio**. These three accordionists based in Kraków don't particularly use traditional music, but they're putting an often maligned instrument at the cutting edge of contemporary music.

The revival of traditional music in Poland is a fairly recent phenomenon – it only became a recognizable current in the late 1980s. It was, and still is, a grassroots movement created by people fascinated by folk music and culture, often self-taught, just like the old folk musicians. But they're filtering the traditional sounds through a modern artistic sensitivity, which can mean incorporating risky and unconventional ideas – like the self-described "barbarian" approach of the Warsaw Village Band. Revival groups have also been strongly influenced by Celtic and Andean music.

Not surprisingly, some of the most interesting musical developments have come out of Podhale – such as the Trebunia Family Band of Poronin. Stern fiddler **Władysław Trebunia**, and his son Krzysztof, both preserve and experiment with the tradition, as well as leading one of the best wedding bands around. In the early 1990s, they joined up with reggae musician **Norman "Twinkle" Grant**, and his brothers, to produce two albums of **Podhale reggae** or, perhaps more accurately, reggae with a Polish backing. Surprising as it might seem, once you get used to the rigid beat imposed on the Polish material, the marriage works rather well. The Trebunias

describe their style as "new music of górale". In recent years, they've sung the texts of contemporary poets from Podhale, and **Krzysztof Trebunia** has proved to be talented at writing lyrics to accompany traditional music and music composed in the traditional style by his family. They have also joined folk music with rock and even experimented with techno.

Elsewhere, contemporary folk bands to look out for include the **Orkiestra św Mikołaja** (St Nicholas Orchestra). The group is part of the Maria Curie-Sklodowska University and was started in Lublin in 1988, when the folk movement was just emerging in Poland. The St Nicholas Orchestra was the first folk group in Poland to use the music of the Hucul and Łemkos minorities. Since 1996, the Orchestra has also published the country's only folk magazine, *Gadki z Chatki*, which runs a website (in Polish and English) about Polish folk: *www.gadki.lublin.pl*.

Another interesting band is the **Kwartet Jorgi**. Based in Poznań, they take their music from all round Poland and beyond, with many of the tunes coming from the nineteenth-century collections of Oskar Kolberg. The group's leader, **Maciej Rychły**, plays an amazing range of ancient Polish bagpipes, whistles and flutes which are sensitively combined with guitars, cello and drums. The music is inventive and fun and shows how contemporary Polish folk music can escape the legacy of fakelore.

The group that has really gone back to the rural roots of Polish, Jewish and other ethnic groups in Poland is **Transkapela**. A quartet, led by cimbalom player Robert Wasilewski, they focus on the traditional music of the Carpathians in its original acoustic format and show how truly beautiful it is.

With thanks to Krzysztof Ćwiżewicz and Ewa Zabrotowicz

DISCOGRAPHY Poland

POLAND

Polish Radio has issued an excellent survey called *Sources of Polish Folk Music*. With recordings from the 1960s to the mid-90s, many of them recorded at the Kazimierz Festival, the series currently runs to 26 volumes. Each disc focuses on a different region and comes with good notes in Polish and English on the main characteristics of the region, its vocal and instrumental music and biographies of the musicians. Contact: Polskie Radio SA, Biuro Reklamy i Fonografii, al. Niepodległości 77/85, 00-977 Warszawa. tel +48 22 645 9988; fax +48 22 645 5901; email: chopin@radio.com.pl.

⊙ **Poland: Folk Songs and Dances**
VDE-Gallo/AIMP, Switzerland
A cross-section of field recordings compiled by Anna Czekanowska. Includes some recent recordings of music by ethnic minorities, as well as informative notes.

⊙ **Polish Village Music: Historic Polish-American Recordings 1927–33**
Arhoolie, US
Recordings from old 78s of Polish bands recently arrived in the US – most still have a great down-home style. Górale fiddler Karol Stoch ("Last Evening in Podhale") was the most highly regarded of his day and the first to record commercially. His music sounds astonishingly similar to that which can still be heard in the region today – which isn't true for bands from elsewhere in Poland. Very good notes and translations.

★ **Pologne: Danses**
Arion, France
The cover suggests this is one of those fakelore ensembles, but it's actually a very good collection of instrumental polkas, oberek and other dances from southeastern Poland. It's performed by two family bands from the Rzeszów district and one, the celebrated Pudełko family, from Przeworsk, and includes several solo tracks on the *cymbały* (hammered dulcimer).

⊙ **Pologne: Instruments populaires**
Ocora, France
A compilation, by Maria Baliszewska, of authentic field recordings in the best Ocora tradition. Predominantly instrumental, the music ranges from shepherds' horns and flutes, fiddles and bagpipes, to small and medium-sized ensembles.

⊙ **Polska Rootz: Beats, Dubs, Mixes & Future Folk from Poland**
Eastblok, Germany
A good introduction to the Polish roots electronic scene, with a good dose of reggae. Includes Warsaw Village Band, St Nicholas Orchestra and Trebunie Tutki.

⊙ **Sources of Polish Folk Music 8: Krakowskie – Tarnowskie**
Polish Radio Folk Collection, Poland
The discs with a good dose of instrumental music tend to be the more accessible in this series. This volume features music from the areas of southern Poland around Kraków and Tarnów, including lots of krakowiaks and other dances from string bands, often with added clarinets or trumpets.

⊙ **Sources of Polish Folk Music 10: Rzeszowskie – Pogórze**
Polish Radio Folk Collection, Poland
Not surprisingly this disc, featuring music from the southeastern region of Rzeszów, kicks off with the famous Sowa Family Band (recorded in 1976). It also includes the Pudełko family and many other local bands and cymbały players, with most of the peformances recorded at the Kazimierz Festival.

Bester Quartet

A quartet of graduates from the Music Academy in Kraków, who use klezmer music as the basis for their experiments in jazz, chamber and ethnic music.

⊙ **Bereshit**
Tzadik, US
As well as influences from many parts of the world, this CD features special guest, jazz vocalist Grażyna Auguścik. Each tune has a clear theme, long extended in rich arrangements, and dynamic songs alternate with calmer ones, but a spiritual atmosphere predominates.

Józef Broda

A genius multi-instrumentalist, Józef Broda builds his own folk instruments, teaches with charisma and participates in various musical projects. His family has lived in the Beskid Śląski mountains since the twelfth century, and the family traditions are continued by his son Joszko, whose work includes the CD *Posłóchejcie Kamaradzi*, showing the links between the traditional music of Beskid Śląski and the folklore of Hungary, using musicians from both places.

⊙ **Symfonia o Przemijaniu, Życiu, Śmierci (Symphony of Passing away, Life and Death)**
AV Studio, Poland
An album that sums up the great artistic achievements of Józef Broda. It was recorded without using any special effects, mostly in Broda's house in Wyrszczek – a part of his village Koniaków – and in the open air.

Kapela Brodów (Brodas' Group)

Led by husband and wife Witold and Anna Broda, this band could probably be classified as "re-constructors" of tradition. Their repertoire comprises unique specimens of traditional music collected from central Poland, and they see the refined beauty of Polish music as being worthy of reconstruction, with great reverence for the original sound.

⊙ Pieśni i Melodie na Rozmaite Święta (Songs and Melodies for Various Holidays)
Raz Dwa, Poland

Winner of the title of "Folk CD of the Year" in 2001. The musicians pay special attention to the ancient vocal art; the manner in which they play is traditional, yet they enrich it with their own embellishments using original instruments such as the hurdy-gurdy, dulcimer, double bass and violin.

Kroke

Kroke are Tomasz Kukurba (violin/viola), Jerzy Bawoł (accordion), Tomasz Lato (double bass) and, more recently, Tomasz Grochot (percussion). They have released six CDs on the Oriente label, plus a best-selling collaboration with Nigel Kennedy. Their early discs featured imaginative and extended workings of klezmer material inspired by their home town of Kraków, but they've since moved on to perform a much wider range of new material.

★ The Sounds of the Vanishing World
Oriente, Germany

It's still rooted in Jewish sounds, but this 1999 album marked a change in direction for Kroke. The tune "Time" has almost become a folk classic, having been covered by Serbia's Boban Marković orchestra.

⊙ East Meets East
EMI, UK

British violinist Nigel Kennedy is a big fan of Kroke, and it shows in this intriguing album which reworks some of their previous tracks (including "Time") and features Belgian singer Natacha Atlas on a gorgeous Serbian song, plus some Kennedy craziness at the end.

Kwartet Jorgi

The two permanent members of the Jorgi Quartet, Maciej and Waldemar Rychły, perform in different configurations with a guest violinist, trumpeter, saxophonist or drummer. Maciej (the leader) plays an astonishing range of old Polish pastoral instruments, pipes and flutes, and his classical background is evident in the arrangements of tunes from all over Poland.

⊙ JAM
Jam, Poland

The quartet's first release from 1990 remains their best CD, featuring lots of old tunes collected by Oskar Kolberg.

Motion Trio

Although this trio (Janusz Wojtarowicz, Marcin Gałążyn and Pawel Baranek) studied at the Music Academy in Kraków, they say that they learned much of what they know by busking on the streets. "Other instruments like the violin, guitar and piano have already been exhausted in their own ways", says Wojtarowicz, "and not much new can be done with them. It's entirely different with the accordion." This innovative trio, just in their thirties, prove it.

⊙ Pictures from the Street
Asphalt Tango, Germany

A stimulating collection of acoustic accordion wizardry, including a version of "Ajde Jano", the Serbian tune that opens Kroke and Nigel Kennedy's *East Meets East* CD.

Transkapela

Based in Lublin, this is Poland's best band playing exquisite peasant music from the diverse cultures of the Carpathians.

⊙ Over the Village
Ferment, Poland

Tunes from Polish, Ukrainian, Romanian and Jewish sources, unified by spare but richly textured arrangements for fiddles, cimbalom, guitar, cello and double bass. They also create experimental pieces from the same instrumental textures.

Trebunia Family Band

The Trebunia Family Band are, without doubt, one of the leading bands of Podhale. Based in Poronin, near Zakopane, the band comprises four or five fiddles, plus bass, with players including fiddler Władysław Trebunia, his son Krzysztof, daughter Hania and several other family members. They play for local weddings and make recordings, including some rather adventurous collaborations.

⊙ Music of the Tatra Mountains: The Trebunia Family Band
Nimbus, UK

An informal family gathering recorded in Poronin, featuring dances with feet-stamping, whistling and seemingly spontaneous outbursts of song – there's real interplay between the dancers and the musicians. This includes examples of the core górale repertoire, plus some lighter waltzes, polkas and tunes from neighbouring Spisz. It also has good liner notes.

WITH THE TWINKLE BROTHERS

⊙ Twinkle Inna Polish Stylee: Higher Heights
Kamahuk, Poland

Reggae musician Norman Grant is the Twinkle Brother bringing the reggae ingredient into this suprisingly infectious collaboration. The strong backbeat sometimes threatens to destroy the intrinsic flexibility of the Trebunia's music, but on the whole, this "góralstafarianism" works. Fans can also try the equally successful CD, *Comeback Twinkle 2*. In 2008 the bands met once again and recorded the CD *Songs of Glory*.

Gienek Wilczek

Fiddler Gienek Wilczek was born in 1943, but seems older. He was taught at a young age by woman-brigand Dziadonka, the only recognized female musician in the area. He has worked mostly as a shepherd, but spent much of his free time playing the violin.

★ Music of the Tatra Mountains: Gienek Wilczek's Bukowina Band
Nimbus, UK

An eccentric peasant genius, Wilczek's style is idiosyncratic, ornamented and sometimes wayward, but it has all the depth and excitement of a real, intuitive peasant musician. This is a disc to savour once you've absorbed the basic characteristics of highland music. Recorded at an informal party, it includes "Oh, Susanna" like you've never heard it before. A real treat.

Orkiestra św Mikołaja (St Nicholas Orchestra)

The group play only acoustic folk instruments from various cultures, including the Hungarian *koboz* and the Turkish *kemenche*, and their vocal techniques include the so-called "white voice". Their unconstrained arrangements of folk tunes are filtered through the imaginations of contemporary musicians. Not averse to experiments, they search for common denominators (such as poetry from Podhale and music from Romania) and have worked on a joint project with the Ukraine's Hucul band.

⭐ Z Dawna Dawnego (From the Far-off Times)
A.A. Nicolaus, Poland

This 2000 release is mostly songs from eastern Poland, especially the Lublin region (where members of the band live), famous for its archaic folk tunes and texts. However, this music shouldn't be regarded as authentic or "reconstructed", its the musicians' own tale about a world that has passed away, but that is extremely important to them.

The Warsaw Village Band

Thanks to a BBC Award in 2004, the Warsaw Village Band have brought Polish folk music to international attention. Their roughed-up, "barbarian" arrangements and strong female vocals are backed by fiddles, cello, cymbały and forceful percussion. Their early albums have some dodgy production, but *Uprooting* (2004) and *Infinity* (2008) are strong.

⭐ Uprooting
World Village/Jaro, Germany

Hardcore contemporary folk with attitude. The WVB also demonstrate their affection for Poland's traditional culture with an opening number from Oskar Kolberg's collection and by featuring veteran traditional musicians as guests. A remix album was later released – *Upmixing* – for those who prefer their Polish traditional music with a club-friendly dance beat or two.

Zespół Polski (Ensemble Polonais)

Aiming at the continuation and propagation of traditions from the most distant past, the group base their repertoire on historic sources and scientific documentation, playing only authentic folk instruments. Their music is both illuminating and aesthetically superb, combining artistry with the kind of improvisation typical of traditional musicians.

⊙ Muzyka Nizin (Music of the Lowlands)
MTJ, Poland

On this album, cellist Maria Pomianowska (the leader and arranger) plays reconstructed Polish folk string instruments called the *suka* and *fidel płocka* in knee-position, by shortening the strings with one side of a nail. Her singing reflects her studies of techniques from southeastern Europe, and she presents the folk motifs of Frederic Chopin's compositions as they would have sounded in his time.

PLAYLIST
Poland

1 IN THE FOREST Warsaw Village Band from *Uprooting*
The vocals are shouted with punk-like savagery, the string-playing is aggressive and scratchy, and there's powerful percussion and turntable scratching.

2 GIL GUL (THE MIGRATIONS OF SOULS) Cracow Klezmer Band from *Bereshit*
Somewhere between klezmer, classical, jazz and improv, featuring the voice of Grażyna Auguścik.

3 PIEŚNI ŚRATALNE (BLESSING SONGS) Orkiestra św. Mikołaja from *Z Dawna Dawnego*
Archaic, wedding ritual songs from the Lublin region, featuring a Lithuanian *sutartina* (polyphonic song) in the arrangement.

4 OBEREK DANCE Kwartet Jorgi from *JAM*
This improvisation on a dance from Kolberg's collection is mystical and thrilling in its lightness.

5 EARTH Kroke from *The Sounds of the Vanishing World*
A dramatic version of the traditional Jewish tune, "Behusher Chosid".

6 KRYWANIU Gienek Wilczek's Family Band from *Gienek Wilczek's Bukowina Band*
Famous górale song about a local mountain, performed by female singers with the band.

7 THE KAJOCKI OBEREK Zespół Polski from *Music of the Lowlands*
A typical example of a "trance" piece, with the recordings of outstanding folk violinist Józef Kędzierski used as inspiration.

8 KRZESANY PO DWA (GOING TO THE VILLAGE) Trebunia Family Band with the Twinkle Brothers from *Twinkle Inna Polish Stylee: Higher Heights*
Lyrics in górale and English accompanied by a fusion of górale music and the Twinkles' reggae.

9 GDY PAN JEZUS WE DRZWI PUKA (WHEN LORD JESUS KNOCKS AT THE DOOR) Kapela Brodów from *Pieśni i Melodie na Rozmaite Święta (Songs and Melodies for Various Holidays)*
A carol of good wishes, performed by singers walking from door to door, containing loose Christmas references as well as many pre-Christian motifs.

10 TORKA: ŚPIEWY PASTERSKIE (SHEPHERDS' SONGS) Józef Broda from *Symfonia o Przemijaniu, Życiu, Śmierci (Symphony of Passing Away, Life and Death)*
Józef Broda skilfully accompanies himself with the pipes and Jew's harp on these loosely linked compositions based on shepherds' songs.

Portugal

tradition, fate and revolution

Amália Rodrigues
Augusto Cabrita

Portugal is best known as the home of fado, the passionate and elegant music of Lisbon and Coimbra. However, in its regions, a rich variety of traditional styles and instruments are still to be encountered, at family or civic celebrations or in concert performance. The "intervention song" movement articulated the mood for political change before, during and after the demise of the fascist dictatorship in 1974. As the country moves away from that turning point, alongside the development of Portuguese variants of global pop, rock, rap, electronic dance music and jazz, there has been a recent upsurge in the popularity of Lisbon fado. **Isabel de Lucena** and **Andrew Cronshaw** share out the custard tartlets between themselves...

Regional Traditions

Many of the strongest survivals of traditional music in Portugal are to be found in the rural areas away from the sea, such as Trás-os-Montes, Beira Alta, Beira Baixa and Alentejo, but each region has its distinctive living traditional forms with their characteristic ensembles and instruments.

In the northeast, **Trás-os-Montes** (behind the mountains) is a ravine-carved high plateau of burning summers and icy winters. It still retains not only the language of Mirandês, a relative of the old language of Spain's León and Asturias, but also ways of making and hearing music which survive in few other regions of Europe. Neither the bagpipes found there (*gaita-de-foles*) nor the older of the traditional unaccompanied singers are enslaved by the mathematical equal-temperament scale of equal semitones which, largely because of the needs of Western classical harmony, has come to dominate the musics of the world.

The gaita-de-foles is closely related to the *gaita* of Spain's Galicia to the north, with some similar tunes, and several dances, such as the *murinheira* (milkmaid), found in varying forms on both sides of the border. There are also links with Zamora to the east – for example, the *dança dos paulitos*, a men's stick dance, which, like several dances in other parts of Iberia, is strongly reminiscent of an English morris-dance. Such dances are typically played by a gaita accompanied by a *bombo* (bass drum) and *caixa* (snare drum), or alternatively by a solo musician (*tamborileiro*) playing a three-hole whistle (*flauta pastoril*) with one hand and a small snare drum (*tamboril*) with the other.

In **Minho** and other parts of the north and west, the most common instrumental groupings, playing for dancing and celebrations, are the *Zé-Pereiras*, combining the caixa and bombo with wind instruments, and the *rusga*, which features assorted stringed instruments and percussion, often plus accordion, wind and reed instruments.

In **Beira Alta** and **Beira Baixa**, the central inland areas to the south of Trás-os-Montes, a key tradition is women singing in groups, in Beira Alta unaccompanied but in Beira Baixa self-accompanied on the *adufe* (a square frame-drum). Portuguese tradition is rich with songs for all aspects of day-to-day, festive and ritual life, and some draw on the oral ballad repertoire that was once widespread across Europe with stories dating back to the Middle Ages. Iberia has its own specific group of ballads, the *Romanceiro*, which were sung in the royal courts from the fifteenth until the seventeenth century, but continued in use in the fields and villages long after that, and in some cases up to the present day. Certain ballads were associated with specific canonical hours, giving fixed points dividing up the reapers' long back-breaking days.

A great many songs reflect the cycles of nature – lullabies, and tilling, sowing and harvesting songs. Until the 1970s they remained very much within living tradition, but while some survive, sadly, many now exist only in recordings or in the repertoire of revival and progressive folk bands which, however excellent, inevitably present the songs in a different context.

In the south, particularly **Alentejo**, there is a tradition of acapella polyphonic vocal groups, a vibrant Mediterranean sound comparable to that of the vocal ensembles of Corsica and Sardinia. In the Alentejo vocal groups, which are generally single-sex, a solo singer (the *ponto*) delivers the first couple of verses, setting the song and pitch, then a second singer (the *alto*) takes over the theme, usually singing it a third above the ponto's preamble. After one or two notes he is joined, in the ponto's pitch, by the full chorus, over which the alto sings an ornamented harmony line. As the song (*moda*) proceeds, the powerful group vocal alternates with expressive solo verses from the alto and sometimes the ponto. Essentially, this is spontaneous rather than chorally directed music-making, but there exist named performing ensembles, and it is these that are featured on most of the available recordings. They may be organized to a degree, but they're not professional show-biz entertainers, they're the real thing.

Quite a number of villages and towns have folklore ensembles known as *ranchos folclóricos*, who perform at festive occasions and sometimes on concert stages. These were encouraged by the dictatorship as exemplars of the happy colourful peasantry, and were therefore somewhat disapproved of by musicians who were opponents of the regime, but shedding those negative associations such ensembles continue to exist.

Fado

Fado is one of the most important European urban musical traditions and has, since the 1990s, become increasingly well established in the international music arena. This reflects the very healthy condition that this old genre currently enjoys at home in Portugal, where over the past few years it has re-entered the national music scene with a vengeance. Decades of stagnation caused by the influence of the fascist regime that dominated Portugal from 1926 to 1974 are now history, and a fresh generation of singers are now embracing the genre with renewed energy and passion.

Origins

The Portuguese word fado, which comes from the Latin *fatum*, translates as fate or destiny. But the meaning invested in this small word by the Portuguese is rich, deep and complex. It is their most representative traditional song, a symbol of national identity. Outside Portugal, it is the most melancholic side of fado that dominates the collective understanding of the style. Yet fado is a very diverse genre that can be either mournful or cheerful and is sung by men and women alike. This diversity is a clear legacy of its complex roots, which draw on a variety of cultures and styles.

It is impossible to be precise about the origins of fado, although many have tried. Contrary to theories that the style is an ancient art form, fado has been around for no longer than two hundred years, having emerged in the old city of **Lisbon** in the early nineteenth century. Probable influences on fado include African sensual dances such as the *lundum* and *fofa* and the Portuguese ballad form *modinha*, as well as **Portuguese folk traditions** and **art music**. It is, no doubt, an outcome of the constant interchange of cultural products between **Africa**, **Brazil** and **Portugal**, and the oldest documents that mention fado refer to the combination of music, lyrics and dance performed in the streets of colonial Brazil.

It was in the cosmopolitan working-class quarters of Lisbon, notably **Alfama** and **Mouraria** (both frequently referred to in fado lyrics), that fado first emerged in Portugal and, for a while, it was confined to the districts' bars and brothels. Fado became the favourite entertainment of the lower classes that populated this district, a crowd composed of sailors, smugglers, recently freed slaves, rural migrants, thieves, black marketeers, prostitutes and other colourful characters, including bohemian elements of the aristocracy and students. Over the following decades, the genre developed stylistically as it expanded geographically and socially across Lisbon. Having absorbed traits belonging to several Portuguese popular traditions, courtesy of the rural folk who had by then settled in the capital, fado entered the salons of Portuguese high society via aficionados among the bohemian aristocracy. It was around that point that fado adopted the **guitarra** (Portuguese guitar) as its instrument of choice. Unlike the classical guitar,

which was previously fado's main accompanying instrument, the guitarra could produce a vibrato, which greatly emphasized and complemented the moaning of the voice, a prime characteristic of the style. The typical fado combo became a trio composed of guitarra, Spanish guitar and bass.

During its first century, fado underwent a continuous metamorphosis, dropping some of its initial traits while acquiring others, but by the time of the first recordings, at the very beginning of the twentieth century, it had already adopted the identifiable set of characteristics of the fado we know today.

Repression and Relocation

At the beginning of the twentieth century, fado's popularity was such that it could be heard in venues right across Lisbon. The elite enjoyed fado in the privacy of their salons, while the lower classes could hear fado in the new working men's clubs and local associations, as well as at religious celebrations. Bullfighting was by then a hugely popular entertainment in which all sections of the population mixed without the usual class barriers, and fado was often performed at fights. Finally, fado could be heard in the *retiros* – inns along the routes into Lisbon which served the rural folk who constantly came in and out of the city in order to supply it with fresh food.

The middle class and bourgeoisie were the last to embrace fado, but in the early 1900s they caught up with the trend and were soon enjoying its performances, first in the theatre and later in cafés and brasseries. But the new political regime that took over Portugal in 1926 soon changed the whole scenario and, as early as 1927, new laws emerged restricting the performance of fado. Both artists and venues now had to hold performing licenses, and lyrics had to be officially approved before they could be sung. Most venues understood the implications of such laws and simply gave up on holding fado performances. But the great demand for the genre led to the emergence of **fado houses** – venues designed specifically for the purpose, which combined fado singing with food and drink, offering a great night out to the bohemians who could afford it, mainly the bourgeoisie. The fado houses tried to reproduce the decor of the old bars, but did so in an exaggerated manner, with all sorts of fado – and often bullfighting – paraphernalia hanging from the walls. Nevertheless, they became the genre's sanctuaries, implementing a code of conduct based on great respect for song and singer, manifested by absolute silence, no service and low lights during the performance.

The emergence of the fado house had a great impact on the development of fado. On the one hand, singers became professionals with regular venues and an established network of contacts; on the other, doors were closed to those who were not part of that set. A two-tier fado scene emerged in Lisbon – that of the established names who had regular slots at the fado houses and were given record deals, and a grass-roots scene in which the non-professionals, including most newcomers, catered for an audience that could not afford luxuries. The alternative circuit, based mainly in the local clubs and associations, was continually breaking the law as neither venues nor singers held the licenses required and lyrics were not likely to be submitted for approval. It was here that the practice of *desgarrada* (an improvised clash between singers) was kept alive, as the law would not allow lyrics spontaneously made up on the spot. The clubs were also a breeding ground for new talent, and many stars began here before breaking into the professional scene.

Fadistas

In fado, the singer's performance is of capital importance. The number of fado tunes is quite limited so all the originality lies in the singer's interpretation of those tunes, and in their choice of lyrics. This explains why from fado's very early days its greatest singers have become legends.

Alfredo Marceneiro

Maria Severa (1820–46) is generally considered to be the first great fado singer, or *fadista*. According to legend she was a prostitute from the Mouraria district of Lisbon and one of those responsible for introducing fado to the upper classes, through her love affair with the Conde do Vimioso, a bohemian count with a passion for bulls and fado, who was himself an accomplished guitarist.

Performing fado involves being able to pour out pure raw emotion in a very particular manner. This requires a certain maturity and, even though a number of fadistas start singing at a very young age and some do it brilliantly, many maintain that suffering is a compulsory rite of passage to becoming a good fado singer. Fado singing is very much about personality, and being a good fadista is more about having a certain attitude and posture than about the quality of the singing voice. The great **Alfredo Marceneiro** (1891–1982) had a very rough and somewhat weak voice, yet he was the king of fado and a defining figure for the genre. His performances focused on the words rather than the music and he was a master of the use of pauses and intensity to make the music his own.

Purists still tend to react with outrage to any deviance from what they consider to be the norm, but most of the experimentation that is going on at the beginning of the twenty-first century is hardly any more radical than that undertaken decades ago by fadistas who are now revered figures. The 1960s and 70s were a period particularly rich in experimentation. Paradoxically, those were precisely the days when fado lost its appeal for the younger generations. In the 1960s, the Portuguese youth were far more interested in keeping up with foreign models of modernity, from the Swinging Sixties to May 1968, and in the 1970s their imaginations were captured by the revolution and associated artistic movements.

The queen of fado, **Amália Rodrigues**, who had observed the rules of fado for three decades, set out in a completely different direction the moment she teamed up with composer **Alain Oulman** in 1962. Her choice of poetry, melodies and accompaniment caused great outrage at the time. Then **Carlos do Carmo** arrived. The son of fado singer **Lucília do Carmo**, he was expected to follow her traditional style, but dived into modernity almost immediately. Having grown up on a diet of *bossa nova*, Brel, Sinatra and the Beatles, Carmo blended all those influences with fado to create a unique style that became extremely popular and greatly influenced the new generation of male singers. His performances were similarly modern: proper

Amália Rodrigues

Amália Rodrigues' death in October 1999 was marked in Portugal with three days of national mourning and her remains rest at the Panteão Nacional, a place reserved for national heroes. Internationally, she is still the best-known fado singer of all time, despite the great successes that have emerged from Portugal over the past few years.

Amália's humble beginnings didn't offer great potential. Born in 1920 into a large family, she was brought up in Lisbon, left school early and became first a seamstress and later a fruit seller. The idea of singing professionally was initially met with great resistance by her family but, championed by the great guitarist **Armandinho** (a friend of her brother's), she eventually started performing at the prestigious Retiro da Severa.

Her taste for erudite poetry and her original singing style, reminiscent of Arabic chants, resulted in a sophisticated product, and she soon became the elite's favourite entertainer, gaining access to a world not available to other singers. By the early 1940s, she had already achieved a very privileged position.

Over the following four decades, Amália spread the fado gospel and a taste of Portugal across the globe, first in countries culturally close to Portugal such as Spain and Brazil, and later throughout the rest of Western Europe, Africa, the US, the Middle East, Australia, Japan and the Soviet Union.

Amália had the voice, looks, charisma and connections that allowed her to become a great international success, but her importance goes far beyond acting as an ambassador for both fado and Portugal. Her great legacy is the input she had on fado as a style – re-shaping it by bringing modernity into it, turning it into a contemporary art form. This happened after she teamed up with **Alain Oulman**, the Portuguese-born composer of French/Jewish descent with whom she established a working relationship from 1962 onwards. Together they challenged norms and pushed boundaries by (controversially at first) creating fados from poems by the great sixteenth-century poet Luis de Camões as well as contemporary writers, leaving fado a different genre to the one they first encountered. Their legacy lives on and couldn't be healthier than in the hands of the prolific new fado generation.

Isabel de Lucena

showbiz concerts, not necessarily in traditional fado venues, with all the requisite lighting, sound, wardrobe and so on. He also jettisoned the traditional guitar trio in favour of an orchestral accompaniment. Carmo championed *fado canção* like no other male singer before him. This sub-genre is closer to standard song in terms of melody and instrumentation, and takes a chorus-verse-chorus structure. It works well on radio and had been popularized through a particular type of Portuguese satirical theatre called *revista*. Carmo's voice suited it perfectly and he made it very popular.

The New Fado Scene

When Amália died in October 1999 no significant new fado stars had emerged on the scene for some time, and, with the loss of its queen, the future of fado seemed seriously threatened. An obsessive search for her successor ensued. Miraculously, this quest for a voice to fill the void seemed somehow to trigger a fado revival. Certainly, it coincided with the emergence of a new generation of fado performers who have reinvigorated the genre and brought it triumphantly into the twenty-first century.

It was at a 1999 "Tribute to Amália" concert that the present figurehead emerged. **Mariza** had started singing fado during childhood, in her parents' restaurant in the Lisbon neighbourhood of Mouraria. After a break during which she concentrated on more modern genres, she returned to fado towards the end of the 1990s, and the timing couldn't have been more right. She had a great impact, and the obvious comparisons to Amália were soon made. Such comparisons were quite common at the time, but the Mariza fad never went away and her subsequent international success suggests she truly is the heir to the fado throne.

Particularly at home, Amália shared the limelight with contemporaries including **Hermínia Silva** (1913–93) and **Maria Teresa de Noronha** (1918–93). Similarly, Mariza is just one among many talented new voices that have emerged almost simultaneously over the past few years. This new fado boom seems unreal, particularly considering the lack of interest by consecutive generations in the past. But there are several factors at stake – mainly the coming of age of a generation born around or after the revolution, whose feelings towards fado are not tainted by any memories

Isabel Pinto

Mariza

associating the genre with the dictatorial regime. There has also been a notable change of attitude towards cultural identity, which can be seen as a reaction against globalization. Finally, despite appearances, the new fado has not come out of the blue, but is the result of a gradual build-up. Since the early 1980s a number of young and sophisticated artists had been flirting with fado, incorporating its traits into their looks, posture and sound. By fragmenting the genre and using its elements on a pick-and-mix basis, these artists presented a much lighter and constraint-free view of fado, which must have looked quite appealing to the young who in previous decades tended to think of it as too dated, too serious and too distant from their reality.

The first of these artists was **António Variações** (1944–84). His first single, out in 1982, was a version of Amália's "Povo Que Lavas no Rio". With his fado-infused pop, Variações managed to appeal to a wide audience, from mainstream fado lovers to members of the most alternative tribes. The new romantic trend, so popular in the early 1980s, made Variações and his music look bang up-to-date and his celebration of national identity was in tune with the work of other successful Portuguese acts of that time, in particular **Heróis do Mar**. This Portuguese band reached unprecedented levels of international credibility in the 1980s and, having toured with Roxy Music and been voted Best European Band by youth culture bible *The Face*, their judgements and alliances were relied upon at home. They produced Variações' second album, *Dar e Receber*, which was released shortly before his premature death in 1984.

Madredeus were very successful in the late 1980s, both in Portugal and around the globe, and are still a substantial draw today. With singer **Teresa Salgueiro**, they introduced a fado-inflected style of popular Portuguese music to the world. Emerging in the early 1990s, **Mísia** was arguably the first singer of what became known as the "new fado", despite the fact that her sophisticated approach has always been better appreciated abroad than at home. Singer **Dulce Pontes** started by representing Portugal at the 1991 Eurovision Song Contest, and is now internationally renowned for her collaborations with Ennio Morricone. She has maintained an on-off relationship with fado, and Amália's beautiful "Canção do Mar" reached a world audience when Pontes' version of it was included in the soundtrack of the Hollywood film *Primal Fear*. **Paulo Bragança** enjoyed some international attention in the mid-1990s when he recorded for David Byrne's label Luaka Bop.

The international recognition of these artists prepared foreign audiences for fado and simultaneously made the Portuguese more confident about and appreciative of their national genre. But even though fado currently enjoys great popularity in Portugal, its revival has been met with immense caution by the Portuguese record industry, and many artists, including Mariza, were first signed by foreign rather than Portuguese labels.

Aside from Mariza, many other female fado singers have been leaving their mark both at home and abroad. **Cristina Branco** keeps swinging between styles, but the fado chemistry that results from the combination of her vocals with **Custódio Castelo**'s guitar playing is undeniable. **Katia Guerreiro**'s Amália-style singing is the favourite among the most nostalgic aficionados. **Ana Sofia Varela** infuses her fado with influences from her native Alentejo and from Spanish music. And there are a number of other voices, such as **Mafalda Arnauth**, **Ana Moura** and **Joana Amendoeira**, who have been around for a while and consistently offer very high-quality fado.

Because of memories of Amália, it is much easier for female singers to be accepted in the international arena, but new fado also includes a number of extraordinary male voices. **Camané** won the most prestigious Portuguese fado contest, the Grande Noite do Fado, in 1979 at the age of twelve and, after a break of a few years, matured into a great success both live and on record. Camané comes from a family of fado aficionados and his two brothers **Pedro** and **Helder Moutinho** have also been making waves in the new fado scene. Other male voices of this young generation include **António Zambujo**, whose fado is tinted with sonorities of Alentejo's typical singing style *cante*, and **Gonçalo Salgueiro**.

While a great number of artists have embraced pure fado, there are others who still prefer to flirt with the genre from a distance, for example **Ovelha Negra**, **A Naifa**, **Chillfado** and the singer **Lula Pena**. The blind triangle player and former street singer **Dona Rosa**, who has received surprisingly wide exposure outside Portugal in recent years, is often misidentified abroad as a fado singer, partly because of the sad poise of her singing, but in terms of material she's really a singer of folk songs.

Coimbra Fado

There is another side to the fado story – the fado of **Coimbra**. It was the migrant student population that introduced fado to Coimbra in the mid-nineteenth century. In those days, the university city attracted the vast majority of Portuguese-speaking students. Every year newcomers arrived from as far away as Brazil. This almost exclusively male student population came from a privileged background and often brought with them new trends that would become popular amongst fellow-students.

Soon after making its debut in Coimbra, fado began to change. Lisbon fado was a product of a very particular set of influences; it was the voice of the lower classes and the defeated. Even though that had a certain appeal to the bohemian student population of Coimbra, who embraced it without hesitation, it didn't speak for them, and when they produced their own fado, the result was naturally different. The majority of Coimbra singers and players were young, male, highly educated and, far from having lost hope in life, were starting it from a privileged position. And so, little by little, with new compositions, fado moved away from its origins.

A comparison between the first legend of Lisbon fado and her Coimbra counterpart is sufficient to illustrate the difference between the two branches of the style. Whereas Maria Severa was a prostitute from one of the poorest districts of Lisbon, **Hilário** (1864–96) was a medical student and a celebrated poet. Hilário excelled at the romantic, four-stanza songs typical of the Coimbra style, which, inspired by the international romantic trends popular amongst the students, became a serenade with melodic and harmonic characteristics very different from Lisbon fado. Many assert that "Coimbra serenade" or "Coimbra song" would better describe

the style than "Coimbra fado", which implies it is just a sub-genre or branch of Lisbon fado.

Coimbra fado had its heyday in the 1920s, with the emergence of a number of singers and musicians that became known as Coimbra's Golden Generation. Singers such as **António Menano**, **Edmundo Bettencourt**, **Lucas Junot** and **José Paradela de Oliveira** and the guitarist **Artur Paredes** refined and solidified the template laid down by Hilário and her contemporaries.

Artur Paredes adapted the Portuguese guitar, creating a new version of the instrument specifically designed for playing the Coimbra style. He also developed a number of new techniques, and attracted numerous followers and imitators. The Paredes dynasty of guitarists that had begun with his father and uncle **Gonçalo** and **Manuel Paredes** reached its highest point with Artur's son **Carlos Paredes** (1925–2004), the greatest exponent of the Portuguese guitar so far, but an artist who early on departed from fado, surpassing it and creating a unique style. Today **António Chainho** is the leading soloist on Portuguese guitar, while the brilliant **Pedro Caldeira Cabral** draws on the Coimbra fado repertoire and has explored guitarra repertoire going back to the sixteenth century.

During the 1950s and 60s there was another wave of excellent Coimbra fado singers. Yet some of these felt the need to detach themselves from the genre, as the gap between their left-wing student ideology and what Coimbra fado had to offer as an art form proved too wide to bridge. **António Bernardino** is the most representative figure of this generation. He toured extensively and saw

Casa Do Fado E Da Guitarra Portuguesa

Carlos Paredes

his records released around the globe, enjoying an international popularity previously unrivalled in Coimbra fado.

Coimbra fado has recovered from the bad press it received in the 1960s and 70s and currently enjoys fairly good health and popularity among the students. The presence of some singers and guitar players among the teaching population of the university is enough to keep the tradition alive and every year a number of new students join the group. Even so, Coimbra fado is not enjoying anything like the renaissance of Lisbon fado. It can be heard regularly at the end of the academic year celebrations and at Bar Deligência in Travessa da Rua Nova, but not at an ever-growing multitude of places like its Lisbon counterpart. Unlike Lisbon fado, Coimbra fado does not seem alive and evolving, but rather crystallized in time.

Intervention Song and Roots Groups

In the second half of the twentieth century, and particularly in the years following the revolution of 1974, a new style emerged in Portugal, *cancão de intervenção* (**intervention song**). Shaped by a wide variety of influences ranging from Portuguese traditional styles (including fado) to Brazilian music, French song, rock and jazz, this new style bore similarities to the Latin American *nueva canción* (new song). In addition, from the 1970s onwards, groups have emerged in Portugal re-exploring regional traditions and often fusing them with rock and jazz influences.

José Afonso and Intervention Song

The great figure of twentieth-century Portuguese popular music was **José Afonso** (1929–87). Born in Aveiro, he spent part of his youth in the Portuguese colonies of Angola and Mozambique, where his father had placements as a judge. Afonso later entered Coimbra University where he started singing fado. His first recordings were of Coimbra fado, but in the 1960s, he began to distance himself from the style, which did not have enough strength as a political tool to fight the dictatorial regime. He and his contemporary **Adriano Correia de Oliveira** became pioneers of the Portuguese protest song movement. In the years running up to the 1974 revolution, Afonso was the leading figure in the reinstitution of the ballad – in the sense of a set

of artistic, poetic, usually contemporary lyrics set to music.

In the final years of the dictatorship, censorship and the restriction of performing opportunities caused some songwriters to move abroad and record there. But Afonso remained, where necessary masking social and political messages with allegory, and having to combine professional and family life with censorship and imprisonment. His songs were both rallying points for those who longed for the emergence of a democratized state and standard-bearers for a new Portuguese music.

One of Afonso's songs, which oddly enough hadn't been banned by the censors, became synonymous with the Portuguese revolution: "Grândola Vila Morena" was selected by the Captains of April (the group of rebel army officers who masterminded the Portuguese revolution) as the cryptic go-ahead signal for the military coup that put an end to 48 years of fascism. A national radio station played the song at 25 minutes past midnight on 25 April 1974, so troops all over the country knew that the time had come for action.

Afonso and Adriano Correia de Oliveira were joined in the protest song movement by singer-songwriters **Luis Cília**, **José Mário Branco**, **Sérgio Godinho** and others. But after 1974 there was a need for songwriters to move from protesting under oppression to exploring the needs and possibilities of the new democracy; protest song evolved into intervention song and other related sub-movements. In shaping the new forms, songwriters drew on influences both within and outside Portugal.

Sérgio Godinho, who was born in Oporto in 1945, opted to go into exile when faced with joining the army and fighting in the colonial war. He left Portugal aged twenty, returning only after the revolution had taken place, having lived in Paris, Amsterdam, Vancouver and Brazil, thus becoming exposed to a great diversity of influences. He recorded his first two albums in exile. An outstanding lyricist, he is one of the most important Portuguese singer-songwriters and a very prolific one too. He is also an actor, writer and director. A number of his albums have become classics, among them *Coincidências*, which came out in 1983 and features collaborations with some of the most important names in Brazilian popular music – Chico Buarque, Ivan Lins and Milton Nascimento. Godinho is still going strong in the twenty-first century.

Vitorino's lyrics and particularly his titles often have a surreal tinge, suggesting the work of such

South American writers as Gabriel García Márquez, but his music is strongly linked with the traditions of his native Alentejo. His brother **Janita Salomé** brings in the Arab influence of the south of Portugal. Both are well known as solo artists, and for performances with José Afonso. Together they have performed intermittently with the group **Lua Extravagante**, with Alentejo vocal group **Cantadores do Redondo** and with **Vozes do Sul**.

Fausto's first album appeared in 1970, and he has gone on to become a major songwriting force, combining traditional forms and instrumentation with a rock sensibility. His albums feature many other leading musicians including **Júlio Pereira**, who began as a songwriter, played with José Afonso, and has become a fount of knowledge and skill on traditional Portuguese stringed instruments. Even though they are often not thought of as part of the movement, because they are instrumentalists rather than singers, musicians like Júlio Pereira and Carlos Paredes are figures of great relevance to the intervention song scene.

Younger singers and songwriters, such as **Amélia Muge**, continue to draw on a mixture of rural and fado traditions, and you'll frequently hear songs by Afonso, Godinho and other intervention song leaders in the repertoire of the new fado singers. Singer **Né Ladeiras**, formerly a member of the group Brigada Víctor Jara, went solo in 1983 and has made a string of notable pop and roots albums since then, including one devoted to Trás-os-Montes music and another featuring the songs of Fausto (one of her strongest influences), drawing them closer to traditional instrumentation and feel.

Roots Groups

It isn't just individual songwriters who have been drawing on Portuguese traditional music. In the 1970s groups began to form that devoted their attention either to the research and performance of traditional music from one or more regions, or to the construction of new music with folk roots. While sometimes such work is viewed as a quest for a lost ruralism, in a newly democratized state it is often an important part of self-rediscovery.

Portugal's rich rural musical traditions were, and to varying extents still are, alive and functioning, so the gathering of material involved a trip not to dusty archives but to the villages. Ranchos folclóricos might have had the residual scent of dictatorship approval, but the new groups were closer to the spirit of intervention song, and their members often appeared on the recordings and in the bands of the singer-songwriters.

This socially aware connection is seen most obviously in the name of the pivotal roots-with-evolution group **Brigada Víctor Jara**, formed in

Brigada Victor Jara/fRoots Archive

Brigada Victor Jara

Portuguese Instruments

Strings

The **guitarra**, with its delicate, silvery sound, is the principal instrument used in fado, to accompany a singer and also to play the lead in instrumental groups. Though known as the Portuguese guitar, its body isn't guitar-shaped but more like a fat tear-drop in outline. It's a variety of the European *cittern*, which arrived in Portugal in the eighteenth century in the form of the "English guitar" via the English community in Porto, where it was used in a style of art-song ballad known as modinha which was popular at that time in Portugal and Brazil.

There are two types – the Lisboa guitarra used for accompanying singers, and the Coimbra version, with a larger body and richer bass more suited to that city's instrumental fado. Both have six pairs of steel strings tuned by knurled turn-screws on a fan-shaped machine head. The bottom three pairs have one string an octave lower than the other, giving a chiming resonant bass supporting the silvery singing vibrato and fluid runs of the unison-tuned top three pairs.

In fado, the guitarra is usually accompanied by a **viola de fado**, a six-string guitar of the familiar Spanish classical form but which, like all fretted instruments of that waisted body-shape, is known in Portugal as a **viola**. A remarkable range of other specifically Portuguese violas are found in regions of the mainland and islands. Varying in shape, they're virtually always steel-strung, and some have soundboards decorated with flowing tendril-like dark wood inlays spreading from the bridge, and soundholes in a variety of shapes.

The version encountered most often, particularly in the north, is the **viola braguesa**, which has five pairs of strings and is usually played *rasgado* (a fast, intricate rolling strum with an opening hand). A slightly smaller close relative, from the region of Amarante, is the **viola amarantina**, whose soundhole is usually in the form of two hearts; a similar soundhole pattern is found on the **viola da terra** of the Azores.

Other varieties include Madeira's slim **viola d'arame**, Alentejo's bigger **viola campaniça** and Beira Baixa's **viola beiroa**. The last of these is distinctive in having an extra two pairs of strings running from the bridge to machine heads fixed on the body where it meets the neck; these are used in a similar way to the high fifth string on an American banjo.

Like a baby viola with four strings, and played with an ingenious fast strum akin to the braguesa's rasgado, the **cavaquinho** is not only widely played in its home country but has spread across the world, including to the biggest Portuguese-speaking country, Brazil. It has also reached Hawaii, where it has become, with very few changes, the ukulele.

The Portuguese form of mandolin, the **bandolim**, also has its role in tradition. A particularly fine player is Júlio Pereira, who is also an expert exponent of cavaquinho and the range of violas.

Coimbra in 1975. Today it contains no original members, but continues to be a major force, and former members have gone on to create new projects. In finding material, the band collaborated with a man who did a huge amount to document traditional music and make it available to listeners, ethnomusicologist **Michel Giacometti**. Together with **Fernando Lopes Graça**, this Corsican-born Frenchman made a large number of field recordings throughout Portugal, which were released on various labels from the 1950s onwards.

Some bands, such as Brigada Víctor Jara, have been a fairly steady presence on the Portuguese music scene, while others have waxed and waned, almost disappearing from view and then returning with a new line-up or new album. Notable names over the years include **Raízes**, **Ronda dos Quatro Caminhos**, **Trigo Limpo**, **Terra a Terra**, **Trovante**, **Grupo Cantadores do Redondo**, **Almanaque**, **Romanças** and **Toque de Caixa**.

Leading traditional groups including Brigada Víctor Jara, **Vai de Roda** and **Realejo** have all moved on to a more detailed exploration of sound and the possibilities for development than that which prevailed in the first wave. A powerful and innovative more recent arrival is **Gaiteiros de Lisboa**, which combines gaitas and other wind instruments with drums and Alentejo-style vocals. Bypassing the Western tradition of chordal music, they have created a modern context for the much older layer of music that's still to be heard in Trás-os-Montes and elsewhere, governed not by harmony but by rhythm and melody, free from the rigidity of the equal-temperament scale.

The diatonic accordion quartet **Danças Ocultas** explore new compositions for this versatile instrument. Although the instrument is widespread in

The **sanfona** (hurdy-gurdy) fell out of use in the early twentieth century but is now being built and used again by such groups as Realejo and Gaiteiros de Lisboa. The **rabeca** or **ramaldeira** of Amarante and Douro is a short-necked folk rebec, and in Madeira the one-stringed **bexigoncelo** functions as a bowed bass with a pig's bladder as its soundbox.

Wind

The **gaita-de-foles** is the Portuguese bagpipe (the word *fole* means "bag"), played in Trás-os-Montes. Many European bagpipes use a scale different from modern equal temperament, and the gaita-de-foles diverges more than most; since it's not played ensemble or with other pitched instruments but only with percussion, the scale of each gaita's chanter is individual, tuned by ear and to the sung scale.

The **flauta pastoril** (three-hole whistle) and **tamboril** (tabor drum with snares) are played particularly in Trás-os-Montes and eastern Alentejo. The three-hole whistle is sometimes called **pífaro**, a term that also applies to a fife or whistle, an instrument found in several regional traditions. Other wind instruments used include accordion, **concertina** (diatonic accordion – what in English would be known as a melodeon, not the English concertina), *ocarina* and clarinet.

Percussion

The thump of Portuguese traditional music is created by **bombo** (bass drum), **caixa** (small side drum with gut snares), **adufe** (square double-headed drum, sometimes called pandeiro) and **pandeireta** (tambourine) or **cântaro com abanho** (a clay pot struck across its mouth with a leather or straw fan). In Alentejo there's sometimes a grunt, too – that of the **sarronça**, a friction drum made from a clay pot with skin stretched over the mouth; rubbing a stick set into the skin produces the sound, as it does the sound of Brazil's higher-pitched *cuica*.

The clatter comes from the jingles of the *pandeireta* and from a range of other devices including the clank-ing **ferrinhos** (triangle), **conchas de Santiago** (scallop shells rubbed together), **castanholas** (castañuelas, or in Madeira a chain of ten flat shell-shaped boards), **cana** (a split cane slap-stick), **trancanholas** (wooden "bones"), **reco-reco** or **reque-reque** (a scraped serrated stick) and **zaclitracs** (a form of rattle). Finally, there is the **genebres**, a wooden xylophone hung from the neck, which features in the *dança dos homens* (men's dance) in Beira Baixa, and, lost from the mainland but still found in Madeira, the **brinquinho**, a cluster of wooden dolls each with a castanet on its back, mounted in circles on a pole.

Europe, there are distinct playing styles associated with it in some regions of Portugal, where it is known as a *concertina*. The group draws music not just from the reeds of the instrument, but also from less obvious sources such as the panting of the bellows.

At-Tambur's music fuses Portuguese and foreign traditions. Classical and jazz influences are visible in their arrangements of both their own creations and traditional music, which use concertina, violin, flute and accordion side by side with double bass, guitar and a drum-kit. The group's very comprehensive website (*www.attambur.com*) is an excellent source of information about Portuguese traditional music and musicians.

In Trás-os-Montes, the old tradition of gaita-de-foles (bagpipes) just survives, principally in the easternmost tip, Miranda do Douro, hard up against the Spanish border. Of the handful of tra-

ditional *gaiteiros* remaining there, two of the best are in the quartet **Galandum Galundaina**. This group of fine musicians and singers play their region's traditional instrumental combination of gaita (and occasionally flauta pastoril), bombo (bass drum) and caixa (side drum) as perform-ance and also to accompany the pauliteiros (male stick-dancers).

Over the past few years, all-female vocal ensembles have also appeared on the Portuguese new roots scene. Among them are **Moçoilas**, who concentrate on reviving the singing tradition of the Algarve, and **Segue-me à Capela**, an interesting group which researches traditional music from all over the country and interprets it in arrangements centred around the voice, sporadically using percussion instruments.

Groups performing rural folk music continue to emerge and make CDs. Among them are **Sons Do**

Vagar, Isabel Bilou and Susana Russo, who sing, in the traditional way, songs collected in their native Alentejo, largely in attractively empathic duet, either acapella or, on their CD, simply accompanied by the rural guitar viola campaniça with interludes of other Alentejo instruments including the friction drum *sarronça*, diatonic accordion, flutes and percussion. **Toques do Caramulo** is a skilful and assured band from Águeda in west central Portugal led by singer, accordionist and braguesa player Luís Fernandes with fiddle, mandolin, flute, guitar, bass and traditional percussion doing lively, creative arrangements of traditional songs from the local Caramulo mountains.

General Compilations

⊙ **Music from the Edge of Europe: Portugal**
EMI Hemisphere, UK
Compiled from EMI-Valentim de Carvalho's catalogue, this features Amália Rodrigues, Carlos Paredes, Vitorino, Sérgio Godinho, Né Ladeiras, António Pinho Vargas, Maria João, Madredeus and more. Fado, guitarra and intervention song, but no unadorned regional/rural traditional music.

★ **Musica Regional Portuguesa**
Strauss, Portugal
A series of five CDs of the seminal field recordings made by Fernando Lopes Graça and Corsican musicologist Michel Giacometti. There is one CD each for Minho, Trás-os-Montes, the Beiras, Alentejo and the Algarve.

★ **Musical Traditions of Portugal**
Smithsonian Folkways, US
A selection of regional traditions. From Bragança in the northeast come dances with gaita-de-foles or flauta and tamboril accompanied by caixa and bombo, as well as a solo ballad. Monsanto in the central east supplies ritual songs and chant accompanied by adufes. Also included are secular and religious songs from the village of Cuba in Alentejo, ranchos folclóricos from the Tejo valley and the northwest, plus compositions by Artur Paredes and António Portugal performed by the Quarteto de Guitarras de Coimbra.

⊙ **Musical Travel: Portugal and the Islands**
Auvidis, France
Atmospheric sound-slices made on a recording trip around Portugal in the early 1990s. These are not necessarily perfect performances but have the taste and smell of the places, including Alentejo vocals, gaita with bombo and caixa played for the pauliteiros in Trás-os-Montes, a former shepherdess with adufe in Beira Alta, a cavaquinho, braguesa and guitar trio in Minho, fado in a Lisbon restaurant, bells, goats…

★ **Portugal – Trás-os-Montes: Chants du Blé et Cornemuses de Berger**
Ocora, France
The ever-reliable Ocora gets to the heart of the differentness of Trás-os-Montes music with recordings of a fine spread of the regional traditions – gaita-de-foles with caixa and bombo, flauta and tamboril, plus songs, including several romances going back to the Carolingian Cycle and other medieval tales.

⊙ **Women's Voices of Portugal**
Auvidis, France
Female singers, solo and in groups, from around the country, including Beira Alta, Trás-os-Montes and Alentejo. There is also a touch of Lisbon fado, plus the Lisbon vocal group Cramol singing songs from other regions.

Fado and Guitarra

⊙ **Biografia do Fado de Coimbra**
EMI-Valentim de Carvalho, Portugal
An excellent introduction to Coimbra fado and guitarrada (guitar instrumentals), this CD is divided into different parts, stressing the distinction between the two main generations of Coimbra fado (the 1920s–30s and the 1950s–60s). It features most of the key names and includes an informative booklet.

★ **Fado: The Soul of Portugal**
Manteca, UK
A good-value introduction to the many faces of fado, based on songs by some of the best-known names, old and new. Listening to it is like embarking on a journey through fado's different times and schools.

★ **Guitarras do Fado**
EMI, Portugal
An exceptional double CD from a live concert in Lisbon in 2000. It features magnificent instrumental playing from Paulo Parreira, Mário Pacheco and Ricardo and Fontes Rocha, among others.

⊙ **The Rough Guide to Fado**
World Music Network, UK
A handy primer for both modern and traditional fado, from the key Lisbon and Coimbra schools. Also featured are several of the best players of Portuguese guitar, the instrument which is every bit as much a fado signature as the introspective, tortured, wholly distinctive style of singing.

Camané

After his early entry onto the fado scene as the winner of the Grande Noite do Fado at the age of twelve, Camané took a break for a few years. When he re-emerged, he swiftly became the most acclaimed male voice of the new fado generation.

⊙ **Camané ao Vivo: Como Sempre, Como Dantes**
EMI-Valentim de Carvalho, Portugal
Camané's first live CD, released in 2003, works like a "best of", including songs from his previous albums.

Carlos do Carmo

The son of fadista Lucília do Carmo and fado entrepreneur Alfredo Almeida, Carlos do Carmo is, like Amália, one of

Carlos do Carmo

those responsible for the modernization of fado. Highly influenced by foreign trends and acts like Sinatra, Brel and the Beatles, he developed a very particular style which was a huge influence on the new generation of fado singers.

⊙ Um Homem na Cidade
Polygram, Portugal
A personal favourite of Carmo's, this 1977 album features lyrics by Portuguese left-wing poet Ary dos Santos and is a good example of Carmo's contribution to freeing fado from the legacy left by the dictatorial regime which dominated Portugal until 1974.

António Chainho

Born in 1938, guitarist Chainho worked alongside some of the older fadistas like Hermínia Silva and Carlos do Carmo. He's been called the Paco de Lucía of the Portuguese guitar.

⊙ A Guitarra e Outras Mulheres (The Guitar and Other Women)
Movieplay, Portugal
Not a fado album, but it has the guitarra at its heart and includes vocalists like fadista Ana Sofia Varela and Madredeus singer Teresa Salgueiro.

Alfredo Marceneiro

Born in 1891 and a cabinet-maker by profession, Alfredo Marceneiro was the king of fado even though he only became a professional singer in 1950. His very personal style and the importance he placed on lyrics over tune were a major contribution to fado.

⊙ Biografia do Fado: Alfredo Marceneiro
EMI-Valentim de Carvalho, Portugal
Marceneiro didn't like the studio. He found recording an unnatural process and avoided it as much as possible.

Consequently, his record output is very small in relation to the longevity and importance of his career. This CD brings together twenty of his unforgettable fados.

Mariza

The best-known singer of the new fado generation, Mariza was born in Mozambique but soon moved to Lisbon where she was brought up in the neighbourhood of Mouraria. She was in the right place at the right time when the Portuguese national quest to find Amália's successor reached obsession point. Her great voice, charismatic presence and professional excellence, combined with the increasing global interest in world music, turned her into a major international success almost overnight. *Concerto em Lisboa*, a live recording of a concert at the Torre de Belén in Lisbon, has also been released as a special edition with a DVD of the excellent documentary *Mariza and the Story of Fado*.

★ Transparente
World Connection, Holland
Mariza's third CD earned her rave reviews. After a debut very close to standard fado and a second album in which she experimented with different sonorities, *Transparente* sees Mariza coming of age. It features fourteen fados enriched by string arrangements courtesy of producer Jaques Morelenbaum, the Brazilian composer renowned for his work with Caetano Veloso.

Mísia

In a subtle way, Mísia has the voice, looks and charisma of a diva. She is part of the generation of artists who opened the doors to the new fado scene, preceding it by at least a decade. Probably because she was so ahead of her time, she never got the recognition she deserved at home in Portugal, but her international career is a consistent success.

★ Canto
Warner Jazz, France
This is an excellent CD in which Mísia fulfils her old ambition of applying vocals to the music of Carlos Paredes. The challenge of re-interpreting these classics was successfully met by all involved: Mísia, the three poets who found ways of expressing in words the unpredictability of Paredes' tunes, the fado guitarists who had to master a musical language foreign to them, and the French quintet of the Camerata de Bourgogne, who added a new dimension to Paredes' music.

Mário Pacheco

Composer and guitarra player Mário Pacheco runs the high-quality Clube de Fado in the old Alfama district of Lisbon where he plays regularly.

⊙ Clube de Fado
World Connection, Holland
This album is a dream evening of contemporary Lisbon fado, liberally interspersed with guitarradas (guitar solos). Vocalists include Clube de Fado regulars Ana Sofia Varela and Rodrigo Costa Felix and current stars Mariza and Camané.

Carlos Paredes

Born in 1925 into a family of guitarists, Carlos Paredes started playing Portuguese guitar at the age of four. The Coimbra style is clearly a reference in his music, but he soon departed from it, creating an inimitable style. Averse to both the studio and the politics of the dictatorial regime, he died in 2004 after a prolonged illness, leaving only a few precious recordings.

⊙ O Melhor de Carlos Paredes: Guitarra
EMI-Valentim de Carvalho, Portugal
This twenty-track compilation from 1998 includes "Balada de Coimbra", "Movimento Perpétuo" and the masterpiece "Canção Verdes Anos".

Ricardo Rocha

Ricardo Rocha is the grandson of the great Portuguese guitarist Fontes Rocha, who for a long period accompanied Amália Rodrigues. Rocha junior started playing Portuguese guitar when he was eight years old and has accompanied fadistas since he was fourteen. He is also a talented pianist and has collaborated with some of the best Portuguese singer-songwriters, jazz musicians and fado artists. Finally, he is a highly acclaimed composer who, like Carlos Paredes, developed his own style surpassing fado.

⊙ Voluptuária
Vachier & Associados, Portugal
Rocha's 2003 debut. Fifteen of the twenty-three tracks are original compositions, while on the remaining eight he plays music by the other two main exponents of the Portuguese guitar, Pedro Caldeira Cabral and Carlos Paredes.

Amália Rodrigues

Born in 1920 and still the best-known fado singer of all time, Amália is credited with both helping to define fado as we know it today and putting Portugal on the world music map. Her alternative approach to fado developed to its full potential as a result of her karmic encounter with composer Alain Oulman in the early 1960s.

⊙The Art of Amalia
EMI/Hemisphere, UK
This two-volume introduction to Amália Rodrigues includes a selection of her best-known songs. Volume 1 includes classics like "Barco Negro", "Povo que Lavas no Rio", "Estranha Forma de Vida", "Maria Lisboa" and "Primavera", while Volume 2 includes "Abandono (Fado Peniche)", whose lyrics were said to be about political prisoners under Salazar.

★ Busto
EMI-Valentim de Carvalho, Portugal
Released in 2002 to mark the fortieth anniversary of the controversial first collaboration between Amália and Oulman, this box-set includes a digitally remastered version of the original album, *Asas Fechadas*, plus two other CDs, *For Your Delight*, recorded around the same time and previously unreleased, and *As Óperas*, featuring rehearsals of three songs and an interview with Amália, Oulman and one of the poets featured on the record, David Mourão Ferreira. The CDs exhibit the duo's unorthodox approach to fado, using erudite rather than traditional poetry, sometimes piano accompaniment instead of the usual guitar combo, and previously alien arrangements.

Intervention Song and Roots Groups

José Afonso

Unquestionably the most important name of the intervention song movement, José Afonso was and still is the greatest influence in Portuguese popular music. Born in 1935, he started his singing career in Coimbra fado and later became a pioneer of the Portuguese protest song movement and a kind of revolutionary father figure to the nation.

★ Cantigas do Maio
Movieplay, Portugal
This is José Afonso's most emblematic album. Released in 1971, it includes "Grândola Vila Morena", which became synonymous with the revolution after it was used as the cryptic signal that triggered its commencement.

Brigada Víctor Jara

Since its formation in Coimbra in 1975 this has been a flagship roots band, and many leading musicians have passed through it.

⊙ Danças e Folias
Farol, Portugal
By the time this album was recorded in 1995 none of the original members were among the band's eight musicians. Lead vocals are by Aurélio Malva and guests Margarita Miranda and the wonderfully gruff José Medeiros. The material comes from Bragança, Douro Litoral, Terra de Miranda, Azores, Gândara, Beira Litoral, Beira Baixa and Estremadura.

Fausto

Born on board ship on a journey from Portugal to Angola, Fausto grew up in Africa, assimilating influences from its cultures and rhythms. When he attended university in Lisbon, he became politically active and got involved with intervention song figures such as José Afonso, Adriano Correia de Oliveira and Luis Cília.

⊙ Por Este Rio Acima
Sassetti, Portugal
Based on Fernão Mendes Pinto's *Peregrinação* (a sixteenth-century work which, among other themes, addresses interaction between Eastern and Western cultures), this 1982 album became a Portuguese popular music classic. Fausto's sound is a melting pot of influences where traditional Portuguese and African sonorities blend to great effect.

Gaiteiros de Lisboa

This constantly innovative band make connections from roots to new Portuguese musics, using magnificent, vibrant Alentejo-style male singing, with constantly interesting and creative instrumentation including drums, gaitas, sanfona, brass, flutes and invented instruments.

★ Invasões Bárbaras
Farol, Portugal
Their 1995 debut. Gaitas-de-foles, shrill flutes, trumpet, sanfona, hefty percussion and rich grainy tenor and baritone vocals, in acute arrangements of material from Ribatejo, Alentejo and Trás-os-Montes, plus original compositions by band members and a Sérgio Godinho song.

⊙ Bocas do Inferno
Farol, Portugal
On their second album the band explore the new sounds of invented instruments such as the plumbing-tube serafina, applying them to both traditional and new music, and also wrapping kazoos, panpipes, trumpet and another invention, the *orgaz*, round a tune by the Portuguese/German-American J.P. Sousa.

Galandum Galundaina

A traditional gaita-de-foles, percussion and vocal group from Miranda do Douro in the heart of Trás-os-Montes, this talented quartet speak the old language Mirandês and play for the local pauliteiros, but also have university edu-

PORTUGAL

cations and have set up a cultural association to propagate Mirandese culture. They perform both across Iberia and abroad and are key players in the present resurgence of Trás-os-Montes music.

⭐ L Purmeiro
Galandum Galundaina Associação Cultural, Portugal
The group's 2002 debut, reflecting their live sound of two gaitas, shepherd's flute, traditional percussion and strong male vocals.

⊙ Modas i Anzonas
Galandum Galundaina Associação Cultural, Portugal
Here they widen the instrumentation, making extensive use of sanfona and adding touches of non-traditional percussion, and two guests from Spain and Scotland.

Sérgio Godinho

An outstanding lyricist and one of the most prolific of the intervention song artists, Godinho lived in exile during the last period of the fascist dictatorship. He returned to Portugal after the revolution and throughout a career that spans over three decades he has worked in collaboration with some of the greatest names in both Portuguese and Brazilian popular music.

⊙ Irmão do Meio
EMI-Valentim de Carvalho, Portugal
This 2003 CD is a showpiece of Godinho's collaborations with some of the greatest names in Portuguese and Brazilian music, including fadistas Carlos do Carmo and Camané, Madredeus singer Teresa Salgueiro, Vitorino, Caetano Veloso and Milton Nascimento.

Né Ladeiras

A member of the original Brigada Víctor Jara, singer Né Ladeiras has a serene voice with a hint of fado passion. In the course of a range of projects she has combined her fondness for traditional musics with elegant arrangements, while retaining the sounds and skills of traditional instrumentalists.

⭐ Traz os Montes
EMI-Valentim de Carvalho, Portugal
This 1994 album is devoted to traditional songs from Trás-os-Montes, giving them modern settings without losing their melodic essence. It features former Brigada Víctor Jara colleagues Ricardo Dias and Manuel Rocha, plus Fausto and others. Several of the songs are to be found as field recordings on the Ocora Trás-os Montes album, and the final track is that album's recording of Adélia Garcia singing "A Fonte do Salgueirinho".

PLAYLIST
Portugal

1 AO ROMPER DA BELA AURORA Os Ceifeiros de Cuba from *Musical Traditions of Portugal*
A slow *moda* (traditional song) on the theme of love, a sinuous tenor voice using a fascinating shifting scale, leading a male chorus who follow with strange, exciting harmonies.

2 ÇARANDILHEIRA Né Ladeiras from *Traz os Montes*
A traditional Mirandese song given a sympathetic non-traditional treatment.

3 TRÂNGULO-MÂNGULO Gaiteiros de Lisboa from *Bocas de Inferno*
Such is their variety that it's hard to find a typical Gaiteiros track. Deep, fast harmony vocals, percussion and gaitas (here Galician, not Trás-os-Montes) in a setting of traditional lyrics.

4 LAURINDINHA Raizes from *Musical Travel: Portugal and the Islands*
In Minho, the fast-strummed, high sound of cavaquinho is accompanied by viola braguesa and viola (guitar).

5 ESTRANHA FORMA DE VIDA Amália Rodrigues from *Busto*
A heartfelt rendition of a classic, featuring Amália's own lyrics and music by the king of fado, Alfredo Marceneiro.

6 HÁ UMA MÚSICA DO POVO Mariza from *Transparente*
Sung by fado's biggest star, this exquisite song composed by Mário Pacheco celebrates the strange emotional power of the genre.

7 UM HOMEM NA CIDADE Carlos do Carmo from *Um Homem na Cidade*
This is the title track from Carmo's own favourite album – a modern fado about the city of Lisbon.

8 BALADA DA DESPEDIDA Fernando Machado Soares from *Biografia do Fado de Coimbra*
A sentimental ballad about the nostalgic feelings caused by the inevitable farewell to the university city of Coimbra at the end of academic life.

9 CANÇÃO VERDES ANOS Carlos Paredes from *O Melhor de Carlos Paredes: Guitarra*
Composed in 1962 for the soundtrack of *Verdes Anos*, a film by Portuguese director Paulo Rocha, the tune is inspired by Paredes' own experience of Lisbon, his adopted home.

10 GRÂNDOLA VILA MORENA José Afonso from *Cantigas do Maio*
The anthem of Portuguese popular music. Inspired by the village of Grândola and its people's sense of fraternity, this march works perfectly as the soundtrack of the Portuguese revolution.

Romania

brigands on the fiddle

The late Sándor "Neti" Fodor, master
fiddler of Transylvania
Simon Broughton

In the frenzied fiddles of the Taraf de Haidouks and the blazing brass of Fanfare
Ciocărlia, Romania has two of the most dynamic bands on the circuit. But that's
only the tip of the haystack. Romania's rural communities, with their large minority
populations of Gypsies and Hungarians, have some of the strongest musical traditions
in Europe, as **Simon Broughton** reports.

Bucharest, Romania's capital, was known between World Wars I and II as the "Paris of the East", thanks to its elegant boulevards, café society and leanings towards French culture. Sadly, these are no longer the dominant impressions in a city that had its heart ripped out by Communist dictator Nicolae Ceauşescu and has endured economic hardship since the arrival of capitalism in 1990. However, the musical heart of the city still beats to this day.

One of the things that contributed to Bucharest's Parisian flavour during its *belle époque* was its revue theatres, night clubs and Gypsy *lăutari* musicians. However, the iconic figure from the city's golden age was **Maria Tănase** (1913–63), not a Gypsy, but the Romanian Edith Piaf, who remains a nostalgic figure today. She was born on the outskirts of Bucharest and is said to have learnt her extensive repertoire of folk songs from the women who came from all corners of the country to work in her father's garden. She also attended the **Folklore Institute** founded in 1928 by Romania's leading ethnomusicologist **Constantin Brăiloiu** (1893–1958). After making her debut on Bucharest Radio in 1938, she was soon performing at the city's famous Alhambra theatre.

There's a dark and tragic tone to Tănase's voice that seems to have resonated with subsequent generations – her contemporary admirers include singer **Angela Gheorghiu** and violinists **Alexander Balanescu** and **Nigel Kennedy**. Tănase was not a folk singer, but she successfully put folk music and popular urban song on stage in a way that was genuine and affecting – and that's what the best **lăutari musicians** have done in Bucharest's restaurants and clubs for years. Much to the annoyance of Romanian nationalists, Gypsy singers and fiddlers dominate the city's professional music scene, and they are now the best-known musicians spreading Romanian music abroad.

Two of the great Gypsy lăutari divas were **Romica Puceanu** (1926–96), dubbed the "Ella Fitzgerald of Romania", and **Gabi Luncă**, a dramatic vocalist who became popular in the 1960s, but who has only performed Pentecostal music since the death of her accordionist husband in 1997. Among instrumentalists, the name that stands out is **Toni Iordache** (1942–87), who was the leading player of the ţambal (the Romanian cimbalom). Famed for his virtuoso arpeggios and runs, he is reputed to have recorded 25 strokes per second in a test conducted in Paris. During the 1960s and 70s, all of these artists recorded marvellous discs for **Electrecord**, the Romanian state label. The music is sometimes over-dramatized and tugs at the heart strings, but it's heady stuff. The heirs to this fine tradition are singers like **Panseluta Feraru**, and musicians like the late fiddler **Ion Albeşteanu** and accordionist **Constantin Fulgerică**. These days, the best places in Bucharest for lâutari music are the Hanul lui Manuc, Pescarus and Saristea restaurants.

Taraf de Haidouks

While lăutari music is mainstream culture for visitors and those who like the old ways, Bucharest's Gypsy suburbs or *mahalas* are home to a more underground music. Since the fall of Ceauşescu, the popular Gypsy sound has been *manea* or **manele music** (see box), a cheesy but vibrant style that has an added cachet for being officially disliked. Romania's most famous band, **Taraf de Haidouks**, play rural rather than urban music, and despite their fame, they hadn't played in Bucharest (except for a small ethnographic concert at the Romanian Peasant Museum) until the terrific concert in 2000 that became their live *Band of Gypsies* album. The debut recording of **Mahala Rai Banda** in 2004 was an unusual fusion of two Gypsy styles from Bucharest's suburbs – rural Romanian brass and the fiddle, ţambal and accordion of the lăutari bands – aimed at an urban audience. There's also a Taraf de Haidouks spin-off called **Clejani Express** which is rather showy by Western standards but draws audiences in large numbers to its concerts in Bucharest.

Lowland Romania

The Carpathian mountains that sweep across Romania act as a geographical, historical and cul-

Men of Manele

Manea is the common name for Romanian Gypsy pop. During the 1990s, it was both the most-loved and most-hated sound of Bucharest, and manele (the plural) cassettes blared out everywhere, from market stalls, buses and taxis. Originally the manea was a slow love song or a slow women's dance of the Turkish minorities and Muslim Gypsies in southern Romania, and the stars of lăutari music, like Romica Puceanu, always included some of these sultry songs in their repertoire.

Dan Armeanca, "the Godfather of manele", is the man credited with creating the pop manea style. In the 1980s, the singer and guitarist was inspired by legendary Serbian Gypsy singer **Šaban Bajramović** and by oriental pop cassettes brought back from Arab countries by Romanian workers. Armeanca combined the virtuosity of

lăutari music with keyboards and guitars. While nationally sanctioned folklore with sanitized orchestras appeared on TV, manele songs were all the rage at weddings. As Armeanca was unable to record at that time, his songs were taped live at weddings and circulated as pirate recordings. In 1991, he recorded the first full-length record with lyrics in Romani, *Marel Moilo (My Heart is Beating)*, which was a huge success in the Gypsy community. Manele became the dominant style in Bucharest's suburbs, and also grew popular with Romanians. Armeanca now works as a producer for other manele singers.

Most of the manele CDs have strange and eccentric covers – the singers pose with helicopters or BMWs to show how prosperous or flashy they are (although the images are actually cheap computer graphics). The undisputed king of manele is **Adrian Minune** (formerly known as "Adrian The Wonder Child", a reference to his small stature). His 2004 hit "Discoteca Boom" effectively launched manele in the Balkans, earning Minune a fanbase as far afield as Azerbaijan. One of the more established stars is **Nicolae Guţa**, a talented Gypsy balladeer from the Banat region. Other notable artists include **Vali Vijelie** (Vali the Storm), **Florin Salam** and **Liviu Pustiu**.

This style of Balkan pop is ignored by the state media and only appears on some private TV channels. This is because the lyrics are sometimes obscene, or deal with dangerous subjects like sex, crime and gangsters. Manele is now waning. Western-oriented Romanians generally prefer rock, hip-hop and etno and dislike the oriental style, while the term "manelist" has become an insult. All the same, the Fanfare Ciocărlia version of Dan Armeanca's "Iag Bari", the Gypsy pop repertoire of Mahala Rai Banda and the remix of "Ailili" by **DJ Shantel** have brought the hybrid music style a new popularity with a world music audience.

Grit Friedrich

tural barrier separating central Europe from the Balkans, and sharply dividing the country's musical styles. In **Transylvania**, the more mountainous region in the northwest, the music is audibly central European, while on the other side of the divide it is distinctly Balkan. This lowland region includes Bucharest and three broad cultural regions – **Wallachia** in the south around the capital, **Moldavia** to the north and **Banat** in the west. It is the music of all of these rural regions, rather than that of Bucharest, that is best known abroad.

There are many regional festivals of music and folklore in Romania, although they vary considerably in quality. The largest is the **Hora de la Prislop**, which takes place in August at the Prislop Pass where the regions of Moldavia, Transylvania and Maramureş meet. As a rule,

though, Romanian traditional music isn't best experienced on stage.

The Wallachian Taraf

Wallachia is home to the quintessential Romanian band, the **taraf**, which still plays a vital function at weddings and other village celebrations. The staple dances are the *hora*, *sârba*, *brîu* and seven-beat *geamparale* – all of which are danced in a circle. The musicians are usually Gypsies and the groups are generally named after their lead fiddler. The word taraf comes from Arabic and betrays the slightly oriental flavour of this music. The bands are led by a *primaş* fiddler and include a pattering *ţambal*, which fills out the harmony and adds a plangent rippling to the texture. At the bottom

Fanfare Ciocărlia

is the double bass, which is ferociously plucked rather than bowed. In the old days you'd always find a *cobză* (**lute**) in the bands, but their place has now given way to the ţambal, guitar and accordion. Never slaves to tradition, young Gypsies are always keen to try new instruments and styles. However, in Moldavia, fiddler **Constantin Lupu** has made a conscious effort to research and play old-style tunes with cobză player **Constantin Negel**.

One of the instrumental tunes played by lăutari all over Romania is **"Ciocărlia"** (The Lark), which is also a concert piece for stage ensembles. Reputedly based on a folk dance (although sometimes attributed to composer Grigoraş Dinicu; 1889–1949), it is an opportunity for virtuoso displays culminating in high squeaks and harmonics on the violin to imitate birdsong, followed by the whole band swirling away in abandon on the opening theme. It was incorporated by **George Enescu** (1881–1955) into his first Romanian Rhapsody.

Internationally, the best-known group is the **Taraf de Haidouks** (see box on p.332), from the village of Clejani, southwest of Bucharest. They began as a real jobbing band playing music for local weddings and parties, but are now one of the most sensational bands on the world music circuit, winning plaudits from the Kronos Quartet, fashion designer Yamamoto and actor Johnny Depp. The group's success is all the more satisfying given their humble origins. Other good village bands, such as the **Taraf de Naipu** are also starting to go on tour. Ironically, it is international interest that often helps to keep the music at its traditional best.

One of the musicians who appeared as a guest vocalist and performer on Taraf de Haidouks' third album was **Napoleon Constantin** of the Ursari "bear-taming" Gypsies. Now that bear-taming is a thing of the past, they are more famous for their powerful percussion music on spoons, barrels and *darbuka* drums. With fellow Ursari musicians Tamango and Clasic, Napoleon formed the **Shukar Collective**, which combines rural Gypsy percussion with a hip-hop sensibility and beats.

Moldavia

The culture of Moldavia extends across the border to the former Soviet Republic of Moldova. Both places share similar Romanian traditions and are largely pastoral. No surprise, then, that you often hear a **shepherd's flute** in place of a fiddle, as lead instrument in an ensemble.

One key Moldavian tradition is **brass bands**. Derived from Austro-Hungarian and Turkish military bands, they are part of a musical tradition that stretches across the Balkans, most notably into Serbia and Macedonia. Generally known by the French term *fanfare*, the bands became popular in the 1940s, replacing the traditional fiddle groups. They typically feature clarinets, saxophones, trumpets, tenor and baritone horns and a tuba or euphonium, plus robust percussion on bass and side drums. The tradition has been best kept in the village of Zece Prăjini, where the spectacular **Fanfare Ciocărlia** put Romanian brass on the map.

While Taraf de Haidouks have been nurtured by Belgians, Fanfare Ciocărlia have been promoted by German producer **Henry Ernst**, who discovered them in 1996. They have recorded four albums, featured in the excellent documentary *Iag Bari:*

Brass on Fire and toured widely from Europe to Japan. Their repertoire includes Moldavian dances like the *bătută* (stamping dance) and *rusasca* (Russian), as well as the sârba, hora and geamparale. Moldavia was home to a large Jewish population before the war, so there's also a bit of *klezmer* in the mix. The Fanfare musicians play their instruments with an almost unbelievable virtuosity, and they have been responsible for both reviving a declining tradition and proving that it can be profitable.

The Banat Beat

Banat, in Romania's western corner, is ethnically very mixed, with Hungarians, Serbs, Germans and Gypsies living alongside the Romanians. The province's largest town, Timişoara, was also the birthplace of the revolution that brought down Ceauşescu. Banat has developed modern-sounding urban music with clarinets, saxophones and brass. It is a fast, exciting, virtuoso style – exemplified by the **Taraf de Caransebeş** – that has absorbed much from the *novokomponovana* (newly composed folk music) of neighbouring Serbia. The region is also where the Romanian style **etno** has its musical roots. Kitsch and trashy, etno is the electronic version of lăutari music – the ethnic Romanian equivalent of Gypsy manele. It has all the unappealing power of Serbian **turbofolk**, with its own 24-hour TV station featuring stars like **Puiu Cordeanu** and **Carmen Serban**.

The Doina

The **doina** is a free-form, semi-improvised slow song heard all over Romania. With poetic texts of grief, bitterness, separation and longing, it's the nearest Romania gets to the blues. *Dor*, in Romanian, is a pleasant feeling of melancholy which this is what this music tends to evoke. Its melodies usually follow a descending pattern, and different texts are often sung to the same melody, which may then take on a contrasting character.

Doina is essentially private music, sung to oneself at moments of grief or reflection. However, nowadays the songs are often performed by professional singers or as instrumentals by Gypsy bands. Maria Tănase was particularly celebrated for her doinas. Traditional doinas can still be found in Oltenia, between the Olt and Danube rivers in the south of the country. This one is typical:

I don't sing because I know how to sing
But because a certain thought is haunting me
I don't sing to boast of it
But my heart is bitter

I don't sing because I know how to sing
I'm singing to soothe my heart
Mine and that of the one who is listening to me!

Lost Sheep

The pastoral way of life is slowly disappearing in Romania and with it the traditional instrumental repertoire of the **fluier** (shepherd's flute). But there is one form – a sort of folk tone poem – that is still regularly played all over the country: "The shepherd who lost his sheep". This song was referred to as early as the sixteenth century by the Hungarian poet Bálint Balassi. You might hear it on the flute in Moldavia, the violin in Transylvania and on the violin and *gardon* in Gyimes. It begins with a sad, doina-like tune as the shepherd laments his lost flock. Then he sees his sheep in the distance and a merry dance tune takes over, only to return to the sad lament when he realizes it's just a clump of stones. Finally the sheep are found and the whole thing ends with a lively dance in celebration.

Some of the professional bands have adopted the story and embroidered it so that during his search the shepherd meets a Turk, a Jew, a Bulgarian and so on. He asks each of them to sing him a song to alleviate his suffering. No one succeeds until he meets another shepherd who plays a **ciobaneasca** (shepherd's dance) and cheers him up. In the end he finds his sheep devoured by wolves. Hungary's Fonó records have released lots of "Lost Sheep" recordings as part of their "Final Hour" series.

Rituals

Many of the rituals that survive all over Romania have their origins in pre-Christian rites. **Carol-singing** takes place just before Christmas, with bands of singers going from house to house performing good luck songs (*colinde*). The custom is similar to wassailing in Britain, but the songs are nothing like the religious carols of the West. These are **pagan songs** celebrating the mid-winter solstice: Christ does not feature, and the tales are often about legendary battles between folk heroes and lions or stags. What is remarkable is that so many of the pagan texts have survived undisturbed. In performance they have a fiery character rather than a pious or religious one, and they are sung with a strong, irregular rhythm. The tradition predominates in the western half of the country.

The New Year is traditionally celebrated with **masked dances** and the **capra** or goat ritual. The goat is both a costume with hair and horns and a musical instrument – the animal's wooden muzzle is articulated so its jaws can clack together in time with the music. The ritual goes back to ancient fertility rites as the old year suffers its death agony. The noise of bells and clappers was supposed to frighten away evil spirits. The goat is also mirrored in the devil figures painted in local churches. **Goat dances** thrive most in Moldavia, where the custom has expanded into full-scale carnivals with music, costumes and political satires that bring its message up to date. In the towns, groups of costumed youths have taken to leaping on board trains and intimidating passengers with their performances.

The Pipes of Pan

One of Romania's most successful musical exports is panpipe player **Gheorghe Zamfir** (b.1941). He has released over a hundred albums and his ethereal music has been used for films ranging from *Picnic at Hanging Rock* to *Once Upon a Time in America*. The **nai**, or **panpipes**, are thought to have existed in Romania since ancient times – there's a famous Roman bas-relief in Oltenia. However, the word nai comes from Turkish or Persian. The musician who made the nai famous as a solo instrument was **Fănică Luca** (1894–1968), and it was he who taught Zamfir his traditional repertoire. Zamfir started his professional career as a musician and conductor in the 1960s and soon started touring and recording internationally. Probably inspired by Soviet-style conservatoire folklore, he developed various sizes of panpipe – soprano, alto, tenor and bass – and his repertoire includes everything from Romanian doinas to J.S. Bach and Andrew Lloyd Webber. Some of his most successful recordings have been with Swiss organist and *Le Mystère des Voix Bulgares* creator **Marcel Cellier**.

Transylvania

Some people think that Transylvania, the land of Dracula, is an imaginary location. Lying within the sweep of the Carpathian Mountains, it was an independent principality in the sixteenth and seventeenth centuries, while Hungary and Romania were under Turkish rule, and then became part of the Hapsburg Empire. Thus its character is more central European than other parts of Romania, and Transylvanians consider themselves more "civilized" than their compatriots in Moldavia and Wallachia. The region's music feels as exotic as its medieval Gothic architecture, although it is recognizably part of a central European tradition.

If you want to experience a living European **folk tradition**, there is no beating Transylvania. Home to an age-old ethnic mix of Romanians, Hungarians and Gypsies, the region's music is extraordinary: wild melodies and dances that are played all night (and beyond) at weddings and other parties. Music is still a part of everyday life the way it was hundreds of years ago all over Europe, and older men and women still know the old songs and use them to express their personal feelings. But it won't be like this for much longer.

Hungarian composers **Bartók** and **Kodály** found Transylvania the most fertile area for their folk-song collecting trips in the early twentieth century, and they recognized that the rich mix of nationalities had a lot to do with it. Music forms part of the individual cultural identities of Romanians, Hungarians, Saxons, Gypsies and others, as well as part of Transylvania's distinct cultural identity. The Romanian music of Transylvania is closer to Hungarian music than it is to Romanian music outside of Transylvania. And the Hungarian music of Transylvania sounds much more Romanian than the music of Hungary proper. The **Ardealul Ensemble**, led by **Emil Mihaiu**, comprises Romanian and Hungarian-speaking Gypsy musicians who amply demonstrate the shared repertoire

The traditional ensemble is a **string trio** – a violin, viola (called a *contra* in Romanian, *kontra* in Hungarian) and a double bass, plus a **cimbalom** in certain parts of Transylvania. The *primás*, the first violinist, plays the melody and leads the musicians from one dance into another, while the **contra** and the bass are the accompaniment and rhythm section of the band. The contra has only three strings and a flat bridge so it only plays chords on the offbeat, and it's the rhythmic spring of the contra and the deep sawing of the bass that gives Transylvanian music its distinct sound. Often the bands are expanded with a second violin or an extra contra to give more volume at a noisy wedding with hundreds of guests. The dances are generally strung together into suites, lasting anything from five to twenty minutes, and generally starting slow and increasing in speed towards the end.

Wedding Parties

Music in Transylvania fulfils a social purpose – nobody would dream of sitting and listening to it at a concert. In some areas there are still regular weekly dances, but the music is played everywhere at weddings, and sometimes at funerals and other occasions, as when soldiers go off to the army.

Wedding parties last a couple of days and, if you're lucky, you'll find yourself in a specially constructed tent built from wooden beams and tree fronds and strung with ribbons and fir branches. Tables are piled high with garish cakes and bottles of plum brandy, and various courses are regularly brought round. Space is cleared for dancing and a platform is erected for the band sawing and scraping away at battered old fiddles and bass, and making the most mesmerizing sound. The bride and groom, stuck on their high table, look a little fed up while everyone else has the time of their lives.

The wedding customs vary slightly from region to region, but generally the band starts things off at the bride or groom's house, accompanies the processions to the church and perhaps plays for one of the emotional highlights, the **bride's farewell song** (*cîntecul miresei*) to her family and friends. Whilst the marriage takes place inside the church, the band plays for the young people dancing outside in the street. Once the couple come out of the church, there's another procession to wherever the wedding feast is being held. The musicians have a short break to eat, before playing all night long.

The musicians alternate between songs to accompany the banquet and dances to work off the effects of the food and plum brandy. They even play particular pieces for certain courses, such as when the soup, stuffed cabbage or roast meat are served. Late in the evening comes the **bride's dance** (*jocul miresei*), when the guests dance with the bride in turn and offer her money. Things usually wind down by dawn, when people wander off home or collapse in a field somewhere, but around lunchtime the music starts up again for another session of dancing until late in the evening.

With trends towards larger weddings and an influx of new music, all sorts of instruments have started to find their way into the wedding bands. Most common is the **piano accordion**, which plays chords like the contra, though it lacks its rhythmic spring. Very often you'll hear a clarinet or the slightly deeper and more reedy **taragot**, which sounds wonderful in the open air. Sadly, as young people have moved away to work in towns, they also often demand the guitars, drums and electric keyboards of the urban groups – along with appalling amplification, which is also increasingly brought in by traditional acoustic bands. Some band leaders might regret these trends, but they are obliged to provide what the people demand.

With the newer instruments the quality of the music is often lost and, paradoxically, the combination of guitar and drum kit is far less rhythmic than the contra and bass in the hands of good musicians. It's still possible to hear first-rate traditional bands, but they now seem to be disappearing. The "Final Hour" project organized by Fonó

Records in Hungary has been documenting the last surviving traditional bands in Transylvania, with the recordings of **Adalbert "Pilu" Lucaciu** and **Aladár Csiszár** from the upper Mureş region being particularly notable. The death in 2004 of **Sándor "Neti" Fodor**, one of the master fiddlers of Transylvania, underlines the fact that this music won't be with us for much longer. However, there are still marvellous bands to be heard – especially in the villages of Mera, Palatca, Suartu and Ceuaş.

The Hungarians

There are about two million Hungarians in Transylvania and seven million Romanians, but it is the music of the Hungarian minority that has made most impact outside the region. Hungarian group **Muzsikás** have recorded and toured extensively, and are the leading ambassadors of Transylvanian music. During the Ceauşescu years, Hungarians consciously promoted the culture of their brethren in Transylvania to highlight their suffering.

Transylvania has always held a special place in Hungarian culture because it preserves archaic traditions that have disappeared in Hungary itself. While Hungary was occupied by the Turks for 150 years, and its villages destroyed, Transylvania remained an independent principality with its own cultural identity. The old medieval settlement patterns changed very little under Ceauşescu's isolationist policies, and much of the area seems like a lost world. As a minority, the Hungarians in Transylvania felt threatened, and there was a deliberate move to wear their traditional costumes, sing their songs and play their music as a statement of identity, even protest. These days, **national costume** and dances are much more visible amongst the Hungarian minority than the Romanian majority.

The regular visits of folklorists and Hungarian dance-house musicians have also helped reinforce the musical culture. Transylvanian music is the staple diet of the Budapest *táncház* clubs (see p.219), and once the peasants saw these educated city folk taking an interest they took more of an interest themselves. Now there are two opposing trends at work in Transylvania: the continuing interest in this unique tradition and the inevitable modernization as the country catches up with the times.

Regional Styles

Within the Transylvanian musical language there are hundreds of local dialects: the style of playing a particular dance literally varies from village to village. But there are some broad musical regions whose styles can be easily distinguished. Probably the richest area for music (where many of the best bands are from) is known to the Romanians as **Câmpia Transilvaniei** and to the Hungarians as **Mezőség**. This is the Transylvanian heathland, north and east of Cluj; a poor, isolated region whose music preserves a primitive feel with strong major chords moving in idiosyncratic harmony.

In the west, the area the Hungarians call **Kalotaszeg** is home to some of the most beautiful music in the region. This area lies along the main route to Hungary and central Europe, and the influence of Western-style harmony shows itself in the sophisticated minor-key accompaniment – a development of only the last thirty or forty years. Kalotaszeg is famous for its men's dance, the *legényes*, and for the slow *hajnali* songs performed in the early morning as a wedding feast dies down. These have a sad and melancholy character all their own. There is also some fine Romanian music in this area, particularly in the Sălaj district.

Also in western Transylvania, in the **Bihor region** around the city of Oradea, a strange hybrid instrument can be found – the **vioară cu goarnă** (violin with a horn). This isn't a cow or ram's horn, but a horn from an old gramophone. Often there's no body to the violin at all, just an old-fashioned acoustic pick-up which transmits the vibrations into the horn. It's thought that the instrument was developed in the 1930s, so that violins could compete with louder wind instruments like clarinets. The sound is rather harsh and wiry, but it certainly cuts through the dancing feet, particularly when you get three or four playing together.

Further east is the most densely populated Hungarian region, **Székelyföld**. The Székelys, who speak a distinctive Hungarian dialect, were the defenders of the eastern flanks of the Hungarian kingdom in the Middle Ages. Rising up towards the Carpathian Mountains, their land becomes increasingly wild and mountainous, and their dance music is different once again, with eccentric ornamentation and very often a cimbalom in the band.

On the eastern side of the Carpathians, outside Transylvania in western Moldavia, live the Hungarian-speaking **Csángós** whose songs leave Hungarians misty-eyed for their distinctive, yet archaic, language and expression. The Csángós living in the high valley of Ghimeş (Gyimes) also play ancient instrumental music on the remarkable duo of violin or flute and **gardon**. The latter is shaped like a cello, but it is actually percussive and is played by hitting its strings with a stick. The "pipe and drum" nature of the music suggests Moldavian, pastoral origins. The fiddle-playing is highly ornamented and the rhythms complex and irregular, showing Romanian influence. Since the death of veteran Gyimes fiddler **Mihály Halmágyi**, the outstanding player is **János Zerkula**, accompanied, as per tradition, by his wife Regina on gardon.

Maramureş

In the far north of Transylvania, sandwiched between Hungary, the Carpathians and the Ukrainian border, is Maramureş one of the most extraordinary regions of Europe. It has beautiful wooden churches, carved gateways, watermills

Simon Broughton

Village dance in Maramureş

Honoured Brigands

Romanian musicologists have known about the rich concentration of Gypsy musicians in Clejani for years. The musicians are believed to be descendants of Gypsy slaves who worked at the courts of landowning *boyars* until the mid-nineteenth century. **Speranţa Rădulescu**, Romania's leading musicologist and the person responsible for the best recordings of traditional music, went to Clejani in 1986 with Swiss musicologist Laurent Albert. They recorded a CD of the old-timers' music for French label Ocora and then took them on tour to Geneva and Paris at a time when such things were virtually impossible.

It was that CD, *Les Lăutari de Clejani*, that inspired Belgian promoters Michel Winter and Stéphane Karo to go to Romania the moment they heard about the fall of Ceauşescu in 1989. They hand-picked their orchestra, which included veterans **Nicolae Neacşu**, **Ion Manole** and **Cacuric** plus an invigorating clutch of younger players, and christened the dozen-strong band the **Taraf de Haidouks** after the Robin Hood-like brigands that feature so often in the old ballads.

This music can easily seem stultified or picturesque on stage, but the Taraf pull it off. They divide into smaller ensembles for different parts of their stage show, and the traditional style of the old men contrasts with the flashier playing of the younger musicians, like fiddler **Caliu**, who also bring in jazz-style walking basslines and tricksy Bulgarian or Turkish rhythms. There's a breathtaking *joie de vivre* in the bows racing and cimbalom hammers beating and an unmistakable heart and soul in the slow music – particularly from the older players – that crosses barriers.

From the beginning, the bright-eyed fiddler and singer Neacşu became the emblematic face of the band. "I'm the one the audience come to see after the show", he chuckled. Neacşu, who bought his first violin aged twelve, was given a new lease of life by the birth of the Taraf. He improvised the song about the fall of Ceauşescu, "Balada Conducătorolui", that was recorded on the band's first album in 1991. It features his extraordinary party trick of tying a length of bow hair to the lower string of the violin and pulling it rhythmically through the fingers of his right hand, creating a deep gutteral sound like the earth breaking or a political regime cracking.

The Taraf have toured the world from Europe to America to Japan, and the musicians have been able to build new houses in Clejani or even move out of the Gypsy quarter. Their CDs have all been extremely good, with *Band of Gypsies* (2001) featuring an interesting collaboration with the Macedonian **Kočani Orkestar**. Sadly Nicolae Neacşu died in 2002, followed by Ion Manole and ţambal player Cacaurica, and the band will never be quite the same again. However, the Taraf's strength has always been its ability to sub-divide, reform and change with the times – after all, that's what traditional music has done for centuries. The DVD *The Continuing Adventures of Taraf de Haidouks* (2005) is a fine record of the greatest Gypsy band of them all.

and villages perched in the rolling foothills of the Carpathians – and a living traditional culture. Village costumes are worn for everyday life and music forms an accompaniment to every stage of life, from birth, through courtship and marriage to death. There are magic songs and spells of incantation against sickness and the evil eye, and you still find Sunday afternoon village dances, either on the streets or on wooden dance platforms.

The music, while recognizably Transylvanian, is reminiscent of that in Carpathian Ukraine. As often happens in the highland regions, it is played predominantly by Romanians, not Gypsies. The typical instrumental group is a trio of violin (locally called *ceteră*), guitar (*zongoră* – with only four or five strings tuned to a major triad) and drum (*dobă* – usually an old military-style drum with a little cymbal on top struck with a screwdriver). The music has a fairly primitive sound,

lacking the beguiling harmonies of elsewhere in Transylvania, and with a repeated chord on the zongoră played as a drone. Hundreds of years ago all the music of Europe probably sounded something like this.

The small district of **Oaş**, to the northwest, is separated from Maramureş by a range of hills, and its musical style is even more outlandish. The ensemble is reduced to a duo of fiddle and zongoră. The violin strings are tuned up several tones to make the sound project better and the melodies are all played "double-stopped" on two strings at the same time. The sound is high-pitched and harsh, as is the local singing style. It takes some getting used to, but it has a captivating power and unsettling, tragic quality. Sunday dances are still held in wooden pavilions in some of the villages – you feel as if you've stumbled into another age.

The only label releasing recordings of traditional music in Romania is Ethnophonie, produced by Speranţa Rădulescu at Bucharest's Romanian Peasant Museum. Fonó Records in Hungary (*www.fonorecords.hu*) has released scores of CDs in its "Final Hour New Patria" series documenting Transylvania's traditional ensembles. The standout discs from both labels are below (for more information go to *www.international-records.com*). With a few exceptions, only field recordings of Transylvanian bands are included here; Budapest-based dance-house groups are in the Hungary discography.

General Compilations

⊙ **The End of the Millenium in the Romanian Village**
Ethnophonie, Romania
Produced by Speranţa Rădulescu, this is the best Romanian-produced CD giving a representative selection of traditional bands from all areas of the country.

★ **Romania: Wild Sounds from Transylvania, Wallachia & Moldavia**
Network, Germany
This is the best overall anthology of Romanian music. It includes a few rather arranged Communist-style performances, but also features great ensembles from Transylvania and Wallachia (like Taraf de Haidouks), plus the Moldavian Fanfare Ciocărlia and samples of taragot and "violin with a horn".

★ **Suburban Bucharest: Mahala Sounds from Romania**
Trikont, Germany
A great sampler of the music of Bucharest (1936–2004), from Maria Tănase, through Gypsy divas Romica Puceanu and Gabi Luncă to modern-day musicians like Dan Armeanca and the Mahala Rai Banda.

⊙ **Village Music from Romania**
AIMP/VDE-Gallo, Switzerland
A three-CD box set, produced by the Geneva Ethnographic Museum, of archive recordings made by the musicologist Constantin Brăiloiu from 1933 to 1943 on his travels around Moldavia, Oltenia and Transylvania.

Lowland Romania

Ion Albeşteanu

Albeşteanu (c.1930–98) was born into a large family of lăutari musicians and learned to play all the instruments, although he became known as a violinist and singer. He worked in Bucharest in the officially promoted folklore style of the Ceauşescu period, but was also able to maintain the genuine lăutari style.

⊙ **The Districts of Yesteryears**
Buda/Musique du Monde, France
The pieces on this disc aim to recreate the music of the outlying districts of Bucharest in the years 1920–70. Albeşteanu is a good singer, with a pleasant and idiomatic voice, and an expressive fiddler. He is accompanied by a good band featuring beautifully textured ţambal, accordion, and the fine cobză playing of Marin Cotoaanţă. "At the Reed House", sung in an intimate, head voice, is quite beautiful.

Fanfare Ciocărlia

Since 1996, this band from the village of Zece Prăjini has revived the Romanian brass band tradition at home in Moldavia and on tour, recording six albums for Piranha and Asphalt Tango. However, as with the Taraf de Haidouks, Romanian musicologist Speranţa Rădulescu got there first. Her recordings feature Costică Panţiru as leader, while German producer Henry Ernst has focused on the Ivancea family, although they both draw on the Trifan family. Their DVD *Iag Bari – Brass on Fire* (Asphalt Tango) is excellent.

★ **Baro Biao: World Wide Wedding**
Piranha, Germany
Moldavian brass sharpened up for export in 1999 – the most wild and exuberant of the Fanfare recordings.

⊙ **Zece Prăjini's Peasant Brass Band**
Buda/Musique du Monde, France
Great music recorded in 1989 by one of Moldavia's finest traditional brass bands, showing the rural roots of Fanfare Ciocărlia's style. There's also an excellent recording with a comprehensive history of Moldavian brass on Ethnophonie.

Panseluta Feraru

Feraru, aged around fifty, is a Bucharest-based lăutari singer in the tradition of Romica Puceanu and Gabi Luncă.

⊙ **Lăutar Songs from Bucharest**
Long Distance, France
Recorded at a concert in Paris in 1999, Feraru performs with an excellent band, including her husband Marian Gheorghe Stefan on clarinet and a brilliant uncredited cimbalom player. "Sînt atît de Supărat" (I'm Very Sad), with its melismatic arabesques, underlines the oriental background to much of this music.

Constantin Fulgerică

Fulgerică means "lightning", which says something about the speed of this man's accordion playing. He leads a band of Bucharest lăutari musicians playing violin, clarinet, cimbalom and double bass, who provided some of the music in Tony Gatlif's film *Gadjo Dilo*.

⊙ **Fulgerica & the Mahala Gypsies**
World Connection, Netherlands
A good example of what a top Bucharest band can do, featuring stunning ţambal playing from George Miu, plus guest vocalist Cristina Turcu and manele star Dan Armeanca.

Toni Iordache

Iordache (1942–88) was Romania's most celebrated ţambal player and leading lăutari musician for years. He was also one of the few musicians touring from the People's Republic.

⊙ **Sounds from a Bygone Age Vol. 4**
Asphalt Tango, Germany
Great recordings from the 1960s and 70s with quicksilver cimbalom playing and four songs from Gabi Lunca and Romica Puceanu.

Constantin Lupu

Lupu (b.1951) is a fiddler from the Botoşani region of Moldavia who collects and performs a large repertoire of regional tunes in the old style.

⊙ Old Music from North Moldavia
Ethnophonie, Romania

A selection of mainly dance tunes performed with the late cobză player Constantin Negel and a small band. A charming, intimate collection of a kind of music that is becoming increasingly difficult to get hold of.

Mahala Rai Banda

Combining the lăutari talents of the Bucharest-based descendants of musicians from Clejani with retired military brass musicians from Moldavia, this band is a new creation from Crammed Discs, experts in Balkan Gypsy music.

⊙ Mahala Rai Banda
Crammed Discs, Belgium

A promising big and brassy debut from a band that combines traditional roots music with a dousing of contemporary Gypsy culture. With its omnipresent kit-drum, this album is clearly aimed at an urban market and its infectious stand-out track, "lest Sexy'" (You're Sexy), really kicks.

Romica Puceanu

The queen of Romanian urban song was born into a poor Gypsy family in Bucharest in 1926. She began singing in local restaurants and was "discovered" by her cousins, accordionist Victor and violinist Aurel Gore. She had a vast repertoire of *cantece de pahar* (drinking songs) and was a favourite not only of the Gypsy community of Bucharest, but also of Nicu Ceauşescu, the dictator's son. She died in 1996, but her recordings remain bestsellers today.

★ Romica Puceanu & the Gore Brothers
Asphalt Tango, Germany

Woman or werewolf? So extraordinary is Puceanu's voice, it's never quite clear what she is, but she recorded her best work between 1964 and 1973, with the Gore Brothers. Their band includes the marvellous cobză player Măslină Vetoi, spooky, atmospheric cimbalom from Marin Marangros and lots of virtuoso fiddle and accordion by the brothers themselves. All these "Sounds from a Bygone Age" discs are worth collecting.

Shukar Collective

Ursari Gypsies Napoleon Constantin, Tamango (Radu Vasile) and Clasic (Petre Panciu) join with a group of experimental musicians as the Shukar Collective to give a contemporary take on traditional rural percussion.

⊙ Urban Gypsy
Riverboat, UK

This interesting group brings a club and hip-hop flavour to Gypsy music. Napoleon's dark, craggy vocals and tracks like "Taraf", with its samples and evocations of bagpipes, ţambal and funky vocal percussion, are particularly distinctive.

Dona Dumitru Siminica

Looking like a chubby bank manager, Siminica (1926–early 1980s) was an extraordinary singer on the Bucharest lăutari circuit with a haunting falsetto voice. He was one of the few singers able to record in Romani during the Ceauşescu period.

⊙ Sounds from a Bygone Age Vol. 3
Asphalt Tango, Germany

A magnificent collection of songs (one in Romani) and instrumentals from the Electrecord archive featuring this remarkable singer.

Maria Tănase

Vocalist Tănase (1913–63), the Romanian Edith Piaf, came to fame during Bucharest's *belle époque*, and she is still revered and loved years after her early death from cancer. There's a dark and serious quality to her music.

⊙ Malediction d'Amour
Oriente, Germany

One of three Oriente archive releases, this album recorded for Romanian radio in the mid-1950s includes famous songs like the title track and "Lume, Lume", plus lăutari ballads and songs from Maramureş and Transylvania. The 1930s recordings on *Magic Bird: The Early Years* are also worth investigating.

Taraf de Haidouks

Since 1986, Romania's most recorded Gypsy band has spanned three generations of musicians from the village of Clejani near Bucharest. The Taraf de Haidouks have recorded several excellent albums for Crammed Discs, plus the 2005 DVD *The Continuing Adventures of Taraf de Haidouks*, which includes a live concert in London from 2001.

⊙ Roumanie: Les Lâutari de Clejani
Ocora, France

This was the Speranţa Rădulescu and Laurent Aubert disc that started it all off in 1986. Great songs, doinas and dance music from veterans Nicolae Neacşu and Ion Manole before they were sharpened up by international touring. Excellent archive recordings of the band are also available on the Romanian Ethnophonie label.

⊙ Musique des Tsiganes de Roumanie
Crammed Discs, Belgium

This 1991 Taraf de Haidouks recording includes Neacşu's seminal "Balada Conducătorului" (Ballad of the Dictator).

★ Band of Gypsies
Crammed Discs, Belgium

If you're new to the Taraf, this 2001 CD is the place to start, featuring excellent performances from all generations of the band plus a daring collaboration with the Kočani Orkestar. *Honourable Brigands, Magic Horses and Evil Eye* (1994) is exciting for its dynamic new Geamparale and Turcească pieces.

Gheorghe Zamfir

Born in Bucharest in 1941, this nai panpipe player must be Romania's most recorded musician. His repertoire ranges from traditional doinas to cheesy recordings with James Last.

⊙ Folksongs from Romania
Delta, US

Souped-up folk songs and doinas from around the country, with panpipe and organ improvisations with Marcel Cellier that are soft-centred but okay. Just try to avoid the popular movie and Christmas collections.

Transylvania

⊙ **The Blues at Dawn**
Fonó/ABT, Hungary
A beautifully produced CD of slow, melancholy hajnali (morning songs) from Kalotaszeg sung by two native Kalotaszegi singers, with guests Márta Sebestyén and András Berecz from Budapest. The fine fiddler Sándor "Neti" Fodor leads the band.

⊙ **Hungarian Music from Transylvania: Traditions of Gyimes and the Great Plain**
Inedit, France
A selection of recordings licensed from Fonó's "Final Hour" series featuring János Zerkula from Gyimes on fiddle, his wife Regina on gardon and an excellent string band from Suatu in Mezoseg.

★ **Musicians from Transylvania and Moldavia**
Etnofon, Hungary
The Hungarian title of this disc – *Prímások* – translates as "lead fiddlers" and sounds rather more enticing. It is a magnificent collection of tracks from some of the greatest fiddlers and bands in Transylvania, plus a few Csángó musicians from Moldavia. The real thing.

⊙ **Musiques de Mariage de Maramureş**
Ocora, France
A good selection of Maramureş dance music, captured at three village weddings.

⊙ **Musiques de Transylvanie**
Fonti Musicali, Belgium
One of the best introductions to Transylvanian music, this disc features a mostly Hungarian repertoire played by the best musicians on Budapest's tánchaz scene. It includes great music from Kalotaszeg, Mezőség and Gyimes, plus Romanian dances from Bihor and Moldavia.

★ **Romania: Music for Strings from Transylvania**
Chant du Monde, France
A great collection of dance music played by village bands from the Câmpia Transilvaniei, Maramureş and Oaş regions. Excellent notes and photos, too.

⊙ **Wedding at Méra**
Folk Europa, Hungary
Although it might seem odd to listen to a stranger's wedding, this recording of the music at the 1984 wedding of András Tötszegi and Tekla Kelemen features the best Kalotaszeg musicians, including "Neti" Sándor and "Árus" Berki. A similar recording of the Palatca band was hugely influential on Budapest dance-house musicians of the same vintage.

Aladár Csiszár

Violin primaş (b.1937) from the village of Petrilaca (aka Magyarpéterlaka) in the upper-Mureş region of Transylvania.

⊙ **Csiszár Aladár: Magyarpéterlaka**
Fonó, Hungary
This is one of the best CDs from the "Final Hour" series of Transylvanian recordings featuring a five-piece band. There's a great variety of music, including a seventeen-minute dance sequence that really creates the mood of a village dance.

Sándor "Neti" Fodor

One of the great fiddlers of Kalotaszeg, Neti (1922–2004) spent a lot of time collaborating with, and passing on his talents to, the dance-house musicians of Budapest.

★ **Hungarian Music from Transylvania: Sándor Fodor**
Hungaroton, Hungary
On this compelling disc of both Hungarian and Romanian music from Kalotaszeg, Neti plays with some of the best tánchaz musicians from Budapest – who became his disciples. The energy and bite are fantastic – this is one of the essential Transylvanian records.

Mihály Halmágyi

One of the great performers of Csángó violin music from Gyimes, the late Mihály Halmágyi played a fiddle which had a fifth string running beneath the playing strings to give resonance and overtones.

⊙ **Hungarian Music from Gyimes: Mihály Halmágyi**
Hungaroton, Hungary
Dance, wedding and funeral tunes played on fiddle, accompanied by his wife Gizella Ádam on gardon. Strange and wild music and one of the Transylvanian classics, this includes a great performance of the shepherd and his lost sheep.

Éva Kanalas & Géza Fábri

These Hungarian-based tánchaz musicians specialize in the music of the Moldavian Csángos. Singer Kanalas lived for a while with village performers in Transylvania and Moldavia, and musician Fabri learnt the *tambura* of South Hungary, before taking up the *koboz* (lute) used in Csángó music.

⊙ **Across the Water**
Pan, Netherlands
A disc of duo performances. The language is clearly a Hungarian dialect, but the music – from the region around Bacău – has strong Romanian influences, not least in the cobză-like *koboz* lute.

Mácsingó Family

One of the important musical Gypsy families from central Transylvania, the Mácsingó band are based in the villages of Báré (aka Bărăi) and Déva and led by György Mácsingó.

⊙ **Báré: Magyarpalatka**
Fono, Hungary
It may be too raw for some tastes – the bass saws, grates and slides onto its notes and the lead fiddle is heavily ornamented, drawing energy and emotion out of every note – but this is the real thing. The band comprises two fiddles, two contras and bass, and offers up Hungarian, Romanian and Gypsy dance sets plus a few songs. From the "Final Hour" series.

Palatca Band

Probably the most celebrated band of central Transylvania, the Palatca Band is led by members of the Codoba family from the vilage of Magyarpalatka.

⊙ **Magyarpalatka: Hungarian Folk Music from the Transylvanian Heath**
Hungaroton, Hungary
A beautiful two-disc selection of traditional dance sets recorded over the years by this seminal band. Their typical line-up comprises two fiddles, two contra and bass.

"Pilu" Band

Led by primaș Adalbert "Pilu" Lucaciu (b.1924), this band, from the village of Solovăstru (aka Görgényoroszfalu), is one of the most celebrated in the Upper-Mureș region.

⊙ Görgényoroszfalusi Pilu Bandája
Fonó, Hungary

Pilu was joined by second violinist Béla Moldován for this great two-disc collection of their village repertoire. It includes Romanian, Hungarian, Gypsy and even Jewish music, and is part of the "Final Hour" series.

Ioan Pop and Iza

From his home in Hoteni, singer and guitarist Ioan "Popica" Pop leads the excellent Maramureș-based group Iza made up of local fiddlers and drummer Ioan Petreu.

⊙ Christmas in Maramureș
Buda/Musique du Monde, France

Although recorded in Bucharest, this disc has all the flavour of a real Maramureș occasion. It also comes with excellent notes and translations.

⊙ Romanian, Ukrainian and Jewish Music from Maramureș
Ethnophonie, Romania

Iza explore the links between the musical traditions of Carpathian Ukraine and the Jewish heritage of Maramureș.

Szászcsávás Band

Szászcsávás (aka Ceuaș) is a predominantly Hungarian village in the Kis-Küküllő region of Transylvania. Their Gypsy band, led by István "Dumnezu" Jámbor, is one of the best in the region.

⊙ Transylvanian Folk Music
Own label, Hungary

Although not as good as their excellent Quintana recording which seems to have disappeared from the catalogue, this is a decent taster of one of the best bands in Transylvania.

János Zerkula

Zerkula is a veteran violinist and singer who comes from a long line of Gyimes musicians.

⊙ Zerkula & the Szigony Ensemble
Folk Europa, Hungary

Zerkula performs laments (a Gyimes speciality), songs and dances accompanied by Regina Zerkula on gardon and Róbert Kerényi Szigony on *furulya* (wooden flute).

PLAYLIST
Romania

1 BALADA CONDUCATOROLUI Taraf de Haidouks from *Musique des Tsiganes de Roumanie*
Nicolae Neacșu sings about the downfall of Ceaușescu.

2 IAG BARI Fanfare Ciocarlia from *Iag Bari*
The Fanfare cover one of Dan Armeanca's biggest hits with the man himself.

3 LEGENYES Sándor "Neti" Fodor from *Sándor Fodor*
Just listen to the springy tension in the playing of Kalotaszeg's greatest fiddler.

4 CAN MARRAULAN Dan Armeanca from *Suburban Bucharest*
Top manea-style Gypsy synths.

5 LUME, LUME Maria Tănase from *Malédiction d'Amour*
A bittersweet evergreen classic.

6 TARAF Shukar Collective from *Urban Gypsy*
A hip-hop flavoured electronic workover of Gypsy percussion.

7 INVĂRTITA DANCE MELODIES Ioan Pop from *Romanian, Ukrainian and Jewish Music from Maramureș*
Dance melodies from Maramureș, with Dumitru Hîrb on fiddle.

8 EȘTI SEXY Mahala Rai Banda from *Mahala Rai Band*
A truly sexy song given the Bucovina Club remix treatment by DJ Shantel.

9 VÂNTULE, BĂTAIA TA Romica Puceanu from *Gypsy Queens*
The dark-voiced Gypsy diva, accompanied by magnificent accordion and cimbalom.

10 DANCE TUNES FROM MAGYARPALATKA Téka Ensemble from *Transylvanian Folk Music*
The perfect set of Transylvanian dances, meaty and full-blooded.

Russia

from skomorokhs to ethno-techno

Sergey Starostin
Sergei Kantere

Despite decades of Communism and state interference, the deeply rooted music of the Russian people – the songs that grew naturally out of their lives – managed to survive. The developments that began behind the Iron Curtain in the mid-1980s were in tune with similar trends across Europe, and the growing openness inside the country and in its relationship with the outside world coincided with the global development of world music. In the early years of the free market, the semi-legal manufacturing of pre-recorded cassettes was a key factor in creating an audio industry for ethnic minorities, and in helping to preserve some of the forms and genres of the country's traditional culture. However, a new era also brought new styles and genres; some (ethno-punk and ethno-techno) in line with global developments, others uniquely specific. **Tatiana Didenko, Dmitry Ukhov** and **Alexander Kan** examine such contemporary trends while charting the uneasy relationship between the people's music and the state.

n Andrei Tarkovsky's great film *Andrei Rublev* (1966), there's a scene with a **skomorokh**, a Russian vagabond minstrel, who sings and dances not to make money but to entertain the people. And that's precisely why he is mercilessly beaten by the Tsar's militia and why his **gusli** (folk zither) is broken into pieces. The actor had to improvise because no original skomorokh verses survived (apart from a couple too obscene to be performed publicly). Both skomorokhs and their art were ruthlessly eradicated in the seventeenth century. Almost no one could have predicted in the mid-1980s that this largely forgotten marginal folk sub-genre (that only survived in emigration) would not only make a comeback under the new name of **Russian chanson**, but would also become hugely popular and create its own infrastructure complete with radio stations and national awards.

The Real Russia

The traditions of the Soviet Republics, music included, have long had a political dimension, and they were pressed into service by the state from the revolution on. However, the rural customs of Russia itself were less pressured. You can go into the Russian countryside today – all Russians will tell you that the countryside is the *real* Russia – and find **babushkas** singing seasonal songs at village parties or local folk groups, much as they did a century ago. There are even a few folk instrumentalists to be found, playing traditional melodies on flutes, horns, violins and accordions, though the dominant strand of Russian folk music is still **choral singing** – usually performed by women.

This singing takes on different styles depending on the region; the voices tend to move together in the north and divide into solo and chorus in the south. The repertoire ranges from plaintive laments (*plachi*), wedding songs and lyrical songs to the humorous and satirical **chastushki** (poems similar to limericks), often with backing from accordion or *balalaika* (three-stringed triangular guitar). The chief dances are the funky, foot-stomping *khorovodi* round-dances.

The areas where the strongest regional traditions survive are southern Russia (the districts of Belgorod, Voronezh and Kursk), the north around Archangelsk, the central Volga region and **Siberia** (see box), where extraordinary shamanist rites and musical styles persist. There is also a strong and distinct musical tradition in the autonomous republic of **Tuva** (see p.629), though its music and overtone singing – hugely successful on the world music circuit – is Central Asian in character.

Roots and Composers

You're very unlikely to encounter real Russian traditional music unless you know when and where to find it. What you can hear easily enough, on CD or on a visit to the country, are versions of Russian folk played by professional groups. These groups are, by no means, all just "**Communist fakelore**". Indeed, they have a surprisingly long pedigree of their own, rooted in the whole development of Russian music – folk, religious and classical.

In medieval times, the first church singers who became "composers" and used a primitive hook-like notation system for their chants were the same rural people who created folklore. These original composers inherited their modes and intonations from ritual and **calendar songs**, which is why the modal structure of **monophonic church singing** is so similar to that of folk tunes. Such "professional" musicians travelled as their lords' serfs to distant lands and brought foreign influences into their tunes, performed on traditional instruments like wooden pipes and gusli. Out of this came the first "professionally trained" Russian composers, like **Maxim Berezovsky** (1745–77).

Most of the famous Russian composers of the nineteenth century maintained close ties with the rural tradition – this is true of Glinka, Balakirev, Tchaikovsky, Rimsky-Korsakov, Musorgsky and Stravinsky. Their experiences were strongly enriched by a substantial stream of folklore. At that time, wealthy city children tended to spend their summers in the country, immersed in the natural environment of folk tunes, while country people were regular visitors to city markets and fairs.

In the years of the post-Stalin "thaw", folk scholars rediscovered ethnic musical authenticity. They were soon followed by professional academic composers such as **Igor Stravinsky**, who made a historic return visit to his homeland in 1962 (his music had been banned). His enormous influence created a so-called "**new folk wave**", led by composers **Georgy Sviridov**, **Sergei Slonimsky** and **Rodion Shchedrin**. Even though this new wave was limited to philharmonics, it paved the way for the tradition revival of the 1960s.

State Ensembles

As early as the mid-nineteenth century, Russian folklore came under the guardianship of the state, as part of Count Uvarov's campaign of "national revival". In the wake of this, musician **Vasily Andreyev** founded the first professional orchestra of traditional Russian instruments. He had heard a

Siberia's Indigenous World

There are more than twenty different ethnic groups living in *tundra* (steppes) and *taiga* (forests) in the north of **Siberia** and on the **Sakhalin islands**. They number less than half a million in an area of nearly seventeen million square kilometres, among a Russian population of over 140 million. Some of the ethnic groups comprise no more than two or three hundred people.

The Soviet system relocated Siberian villages, brought universal education and collectivized reindeer farming, breaking the traditional way of life. The music, as elsewhere, was folklorized and desacralized, as much of it was connected to **shamanism**. But shamanism is still very much a part of life; an enactment of the traditional relationship between nature and its inhabitants. People worship their environment through singing and drumming. They defy the permafrost, wind and thunder through their songs and instruments. With their voices and simple accompaniment they are the best imitators in the world, re-creating the sounds of the forest, the steppe and the animals they hunt. They drink too much and have a high suicide rate, but they keep on singing.

The biggest indigenous group in Sibera is the **Yakuts** (or Sakhas); 400,000 live in a republic the size of India. They are famed for playing the *khomus* (Jew's harp) and for their *olonkho* (epic songs). The **Buriats** in south Siberia sing

Huun-Huur-Tu with Tuvan singer Sainkho Namtchylak

unaccompanied songs and play a stately spike fiddle related to central Asian instruments. The **Tungus** people in the far east produce extraordinary imitations of animals and nature with voice, horns and drums. And the **Nganasan** in the far north are best known for their shamanistic practices.

French musicologist Henri Lecomte has produced a series of CDs for the Buda label presenting a detailed musical survey of Siberia's ethnic groups. However, the relationship between Siberia and the West's world music scene has never been simple. Siberian traditional music remains an area of interest for a few specialists, ethnomusicologists and those interested in shamanism. But apart from internationally known **Tuvan** bands like **Yat-Kha** and **Huun-Huur-Tu**, with their commercially appealing throat-singing, little is known about the music in the rest of Siberia.

These days the most interesting aspect of the Siberian musical scene is its **music festivals**, which provide unique opportunities to experience the music in the places it was created, while enjoying nature in its extremes. One of the oldest festivals is **TABYK**, which is organized every autumn in the Republic of Sakha-Yakutia. Begun at the end of 1980s as a platform for the shamanic rock movement, it was spearheaded by psychedelic rock band **Cholbon**, with their mesmerizing singer **Stepanida Borisova**. It has became one of the biggest festivals in Russia and invariably presents a multitude of local Sakha-based music, from traditional to rock and pop.

Summer festivals are also going strong in southern Siberia, mostly in the Sayan-Altai region. **The Sayan Ring Festival**, held in the picturesque village of Shushenskoye, started in 2003. It is supported by the local tourist agency and it represents a wide cultural area, from Azerbaijan to the Yamalo-Nenetski autonomous region. The **Zhivaya Voda** (Living Water) festival in the mountains of Altai was set up by **Nick Dmitriev**, a tireless enthusiast, producer and promoter who also established the Dom cultural centre in Moscow. Up to 2004, it served as the first good resource for Siberian music artists and local tourism, but it has since switched to a more pop-oriented format. Finally, there is **Ustuu Hure** festival in Tuva, which attracts interest from music lovers and new age travellers worldwide.

Etienne Bours & Misha Maltsev

balalaika played in a village and decided to reconstruct it. He made models of this three-stringed triangular guitar in different sizes, taught a company of grenadiers to play them and took them to Paris as a display of Russian exotica. The orchestra's repertoire was based on his arrangements of folk songs and dances. This was not authentic folk music performed by peasants, but arrangements performed by musicians far from the genuine tradition. As such it was a direct antecedent to Communist fakelore. Indeed, the famous **Red Army Choir** that vocally conquered the world in the 1960s and 70s was the next logical progression.

In the early 1900s, **Mitrofan Pyatnitsky** – a great admirer of Russian folk song – formed the **Pyatnitsky Choir**. It originally only recruited genuine **peasant singers** and its repertoire was a reflection of a vibrant, living musical culture, but in time it became just another state ensemble performing compositions *à la russe*. By the 1940s, such pseudo folk music was institionalized and the country was flooded with folk music and dance ensembles singing "Kalinka", "Katyusha" and the "Volga Boatman" – popular Russian songs that took their place alongside the ubiquitous matryoshka dolls.

It's sad that this attitude to tradition prevailed despite a profound perception of folk music by composers and ethnomusicologists. By the end of the century, the oral music tradition was attracting the attention of practising musicians and scholars, and the advent of the phonograph made it possible to document the peasants' music in its full authenticity. The first phonographic recordings of peasant folk songs were made by opera singer **Evgenia Lineva**. They made it easier for her to transcribe traditional **polyphonic singing**, which she then tried to re-create with her choir. From 1899, various expeditions resulted in field recordings, which were regularly published with academic commentaries. But despite this, the gap between genuine folklore and its official presentation grew. And the genuine forms, having been plundered for their melodies, were increasingly left out in the cold.

Reviving the Tradition: Shchurov and Pokrovsky

Luckily, an interest in the revival of the real tradition did not have to wait for the fall of Communism, although the death of Stalin in 1953 may have helped things along. In 1958, a young singer called **Vyacheslav Shchurov** came back from a field trip with his teacher, folk researcher **Anna Rudneva**. A gifted singer with a strong voice, Shchurov was so charmed by the singing of Arkhangelsk peasants that he took it up himself. He joined forces with two friends to put on performances as a trio and, without quite realizing what they were doing, they instigated a small revolution of authenticity.

In 1966, Shchurov, by then a professional ethnomusicologist, organized a series of concerts at the Composers' House in Moscow, to which he invited authentic singers from all over Russia. In 1968, he created his own ensemble, **Solovka** (Nightingale), with graduates of the Gnesin Musical Institute. They re-created authentic singing and performed songs from the various regions. Shchurov also paved the way for the **Dmitri Pokrovsky Ensemble** (DPE), formed a few years later. Pokrovsky's "epic" folk, unlike Shchurov's conservative revivalism, was part of a larger European wave of post-rock folk renaissance.

The DPE's repertoire consisted of Russian peasant songs brought back by its members from field expeditions. The musicians talked to the peasants, recorded their singing and transcribed their songs. By immersing themselves in the authentic scene in this way, they drew upon its wealth and were able to transfer the genuine folk tradition onto the professional stage. Pokrovsky's method was further developed by the influential folk scholar and artist **Andrey Kabanov**, with his **Kabanov Family**. Pokrovsky's ensemble also influenced musical spheres outside Russia. For instance, his impact can be seen on an all-female folk choir in Poland who look for common roots and repertoires in Polish, Russian and Ukrainian songs.

At the same time another generation of professional folk artists was gaining prominence with state backing. These ranged from out-and-out kitsch – Lyudmila Zykina, Russkaya Pesnya Ensemble and Zolotoye Koltso – to ensembles who kept a more or less respectful attitude to their material. The latter included Evgenia Zosimova's **Karagod**, Gennady Rudnev's **Slavichi**, Maria Chekareva's **Slavyanskaya Kumirnia**, Marina Kapuro's **Yabloko** and **Evgenia Smolyaninova**, all of whom managed to retain the charm of genuine and authentic musicmaking.

Since Pokrovsky's death in 1996, his ideas have been maintained by his ensemble, which is co-led by its two female lead singers, **Masha Nefedova** and **Olga Yukecheva**. The ensemble's alumni **Andrei Kotov** and **Boris Bazurov** had already started their own groups: Bazurov's **Narodnaya Opera** is more rooted in the song genre and is often accompanied by electronica, while Kotov's group, **Sirin**, tries to follow strictly religious spiritual verses. The small-

Pokrovsky Roots and Shoots

"It all began when he once joined his mother, applied art historian Nina Budanova, in an ethnographic expedition to the Russian North. In a village there he heard four old women sing. It was a revelation. He realized that out there was a different music, music neither he nor any of his friends and colleagues knew anything about. That music was not being taught anywhere and the impression was that it was a sacred, deep hidden mystery. He desperately wanted to unravel this mystery."

That's how **Masha Nefedova**, long-term member and co-leader (with **Olga Yukecheva**) of the **Dmitri Pokrovsky Ensemble** (DPE), recalls how her mentor and guru got his "conversion". A half-Jewish Moscow-born musician, **Dmitri Pokrovsky** seemed the least likely candidate for the role of catalyst for the Russian authentic music revival. At the time of his conversion, he was a balalaika player with an ambition to become a symphony orchestra conductor.

By a remarkable coincidence, the initiating expedition went to the Arkhangelsk region, the same area where **Vyacheslav Shchurov**, another pioneer of the Russian folk revival, was charmed by authentic singing. However, it was not in Arkhangelsk, but in the Belgorod region, that Pokrovsky met his teacher and guru, legendary folk singer **Efim Sapelkin**. Conducting research further south among the Cossacks of the Don river, Pokrovsky made his first scientific and artistic discoveries: he was the first to disprove the theory that Russian **polyphonic singing** was exclusively female.

For all his reverence for authenticity, Pokrovsky's ambitions couldn't be further from blind imitation. "We're young urban professional musicians, we're artists," he insisted, "and what we're singing should for us be a living music, not a museum piece." But why, as a musicologist fascinated with a new discovery, did he go the hard way? Why not just bring the old men and women up on stage as a slap in the face for tedious officialdom?

"The whole point was that they did not sound convincing," argues Masha Nefedova. "Taken out of their element and placed before a strange albeit friendly audience, they get confused and lose all of their charm. It becomes a museum piece, not a living art form. Folk music, like jazz is about improvisation, about communication."

No wonder he was looking for collaborations with jazz and improv musicians almost from the outset. Unfortunately, none of the DPE's many joint performances with the **Ganelin Trio**, **Arsenal** or singer-songwriter **Alexander Gradsky** in the 1970s and 80s were ever recorded. A rather experimental recording with the **Arkhangelsk Jazz Group** and free jazz singer **Valentina Ponomareva** has yet to be released. The only existing record of their collaborations, *Earthbeat*, documents their joint effort with the "ecological jazz" of American **Paul Winter**.

Much more striking and convincing were Pokrovsky's forays into classical music. The group's version of **Igor Stravinsky**'s *Les Noces* (The Wedding), traditionally performed by standard operatic sopranos and baritones, became a revelation, described by the *New York Times* as "a swirl of bright, raucous voices, costumes, and energetic peasant rituals".

Paradoxically, Dmitri Pokrovsky's untimely death in 1996 served as a catalyst for the further spread of his ideas. Without its founder and undisputed leader, the ensemble broke into several parts and each, like a miraculous Russian matryoshka doll, started to live a life of its own. Arguably none of them is as good and strong as the original, but instead of a tree there's now a forest – OK, a grove.

Alex Kan and Dmitry Ukhov

Dmitri Pokrovsky

est, and probably oddest, offshoot of the DPE is **NE TE** (Not the Who).

These offshoots have continued the trend that started with the seminal performance of Stravinsky's *Les Noces* (The Wedding) They also collaborate with contemporary avant-garde, minimalist or electronic composers, such as Vladimir Martynov, **Anton Batagov**, Alexander Raskatov, **Iraida Yusupova** and **Vladimir Nikolaev**. Composer **Vladimir Martynov** is known for two major opuses: *Laments of Jeremiah*, written for the Sirin choir and based on Russian Orthodox texts, and *The Night in Galicia*, the last work Dmitri Pokrovsky performed. In similar efforts, the music tended to be modernized and the lyrics traditional, but Martynov resorted to the avant-garde poetry of Russian futurist Velemir Khlebnikov for *The Night in Galicia*. **Alexander Raskatov**'s magnificent *Voices of Frozen Land* (2001), based on genuine peasant rituals, stands out among the works recorded and released by the DPE after its founder's death.

New Russia and Cultural Diversity

The social and political changes of the last few decades, including the break-up of the multinational and multiethnic Soviet Union in 1991, brought radical changes and the consolidation of sometimes strikingly antagonistic cultural tendencies. Contrary to expectations, state-sponsored fakelore did not quite disappear. "Professional folk" readily embraced a new agenda of statehood and patriotism, and groups like **Russkaya Pesnya** and **Zolotoye Koltso** became almost indistinguishable from the pop mainstream.

The **Terem Quartet**, based in St Petersburg, is a better-known example of this tendency. Quite well-known in the West – they have performed at several **WOMAD festivals** and released albums on Peter Gabriel's **Real World label** – their music doesn't aspire to be authentic or traditional. It's just wild, eclectic and great fun. The four members were trained at the Leningrad Conservatoire and play their instruments – accordion, two **domras** (a three-stringed mandolin) and a huge bass balalaika – with astonishing panache and virtuosity. Their repertoire includes Russian popular songs, Broadway evergreens, pastiches, classical arrangements and their own compositions. In November 2003, Terem launched an annual world music festival in St Petersburg called "Terem and Friends".

At the same time, the folk trends that began with Shchurov and Pokrovsky have continued to develop. In the late 1980s, the groups **Narodnyi**

Prazdnik and **Kazachy Krug** (specializing in Cossack songs) appeared on the scene. Their style is closer to that of Shchurov as they both base their work on studies of authentic folk music. **Ekaterina Dorokhova** and **Evgenia Kostina**, the leaders of Narodnyi Prazdnik, are professional ethnomusicologists who go on expeditions each year to research and record folk songs in the Kursk, Bryansk and Belgorod regions, and too add them to their repertoire. Most importantly, they also sing with authentic folk singers. It's amazing that this authentic tradition still survives – these revivalists are essentially saving the traditional songs. Even in the countryside, there are fewer and fewer people who remember and sing genuine folk music.

Since the break-up of the Soviet Union, renewed awareness of ethnic identity has also stimulated a cultural quest within various ethnic minorities. Two bands from the Finno-Ugrian ethnic groups in the Volga region and the Ural mountains, **ToRama** and **Ptitsa Tyloburdo**, strive for authenticity while remaining open to new musical trends. Better known are the performances and recordings of the Sakha-Yakut singer **Stepanida Borisova**.

Ethno Fusions: Rock, Jazz, Punk and Techno

The Pokrovsky ensemble's experiments were also a wake-up call for a number of rock and jazz musicians who tried to merge the newly found ethnicity with the more familiar patterns of their music. One of the better examples of this fusion was the *Russian Songs* album by singer-songwriter **Alexander Gradsky**. His affinity to the tradition was obvious from the name of his band, **Skomorokhi** (Vagabond Minstrels), active in Moscow's **underground rock scene** throughout the 1960s and 70s.

The St Petersburg, or rather Leningrad, scene – an undisputed hot spot for rock and new jazz in the 1980s – paved the way in ambitious, non-commercial and highly creative efforts blending genuine ethnic spirit with the best in **jazz** and improv. Probably the most striking and convincing of these efforts was the *Dearly Departed* suite conceived by rock percussionist **Roman Dubinnikov**. A great connoisseur of Russian authenticity, he put together a pick-up combo with guitars, bass, saxophone, tuba and voices, and recorded a striking non-stop forty-minute sequence with meticulously structured **polyphonic singing**. One song seamlessly flows into another linked by powerful free jazz solos. Although for a long time largely unknown, *Dearly Departed* remains unsurpassed.

Around the same time, jazz musician, trumpeter and composer **Vyacheslav Gayvoronsky** wrote his own three-movement suite called *Russian Songs*, based on imaginary folk songs. It was a challenging and strikingly rich piece, especially considering it was performed by just the composer and a bass player, **Vladimir Volkov**. Gayvoronsky later played the suite with accordion player **Evelyn Petrova**, and it became a springboard for her spectacular solo career. Her performances magically blend primeval rootsy energy, refined conservatory-trained virtuosity and the freedom of a jazz improviser. "Frank Zappa meets Valkyrie Handmaiden-on-testosterone" according to Jethro Tull's Ian Anderson, who asked her to join his band onstage.

The underground rock movement lost momentum in the 1990s, its drive and energy shifting towards ethnic projects such as traditional folk-rock (groups such as **Va-Ta-Ga**) and more radical ethno-punk. In the early 1990s, there was an idiosyncratic collaboration between folk-intellectuals from the group **Krai** and underground punks led by provocative nationalist radical **Sergey Zharikov**. Formed in St Petersburg in 2002, the all-female band **Iva Nova** play **ethno-punk**, and their aggressive vocals, quirky arrangements and dishevelled looks owe as much to Siouxsie and the Banshees as they do to a rollicking Russian village party.

There have also been attempts to capitalize on the popularity of world music by adding ethnic components to a more habitual pop, rock and techno mix. **Ethno-pop** has gained wider recognition, with artists such as child prodigy **Pelageya** and Tatar singer **Zulya Kamalova**, who regularly visits Russia from Australia, where she now lives. **Alexander Tsarovtsev**, who spent several years in the US, regularly performs synagogal chanting in Hebrew tinged with a folk-rock drive.

One of the more interesting voices in the post-folk scene has been **Inna Zhelannaya** with her band, the **Farlanders**, who managed to organically blend swinging rock rhythms with folk tunes. **Sergey Starostin** started his career with the band, playing ethnic wind and reed instruments. He later became the second vocalist, and his moody epic drones contrasted and augmented Zhelannaya's bouncing and rocky momentum. The Farlanders' greatest achievements were a result of the balance between the two leading vocalists. In 2005, Zhelannaya left the band and Starostin became lead vocalist. He and the Farlanders are two of the stellar new-ethno acts on the **Green Wave** label owned by **Alexander Cheparukhin**, one of the most active promoters and producers in world music.

The availability of music software in the late twentieth century brought to life a sub-genre that could be called **ethno-techno**. Among the pioneers were Estonian jazz musicians who used jazz arrangements as beds for archive ethnic recordings as early as the 1970s. Ethno-techno has since become a widespread phenomenon, aided in part by the rise in ethnic music festivals since 2004, in particular the **Ethno Life Festival**, a large ethno-techno festival held just outside Moscow.

After leaving industrial band Nochnoy Prospect, keyboard player **Ivan Sokolovsky** experimented with augmenting folk choir recordings with his beatbox, creating the 1992 album *Pressure: Music for Rich People*. The band's former guitarist **Alexei Borisov** founded **Volga**, one of the most interesting groups on the ethno-techno scene, with folk researcher and lead singer **Angela Manukian**. Volga explore the realm of electronics and ambience. Manukian renders traditional songs over a pulsating mix of live electronics and *zvukosuk*, an amplified monochord designed by musician **Yuri Balashov**. Their performances are usually accompanied by striking psychedelic visuals.

Although mainstream showbiz has remained largely oblivious to these new trends, the St Petersburg-based band **Ivan Kupala** are an exception. The musicians are well-educated in authentic music and their first album, the stylish *Kostroma*

Va-Ta-Ga's Alexander Leonov

(1996), featured uncharacteristically joyful singing underscored by bouncing disco rhythms. Young jazz trumpeter and sound designer **Anton Silaev** works in the same **world-techno fusion** area. His ethno remix album *Mixing Point, Moscow: World Voices Remixed* was highly regarded by critics for its remixes of Sergey Starostin's "By the Blue Sea".

Despite the relative wealth and variety of world music in contemporary Russia, it remains under-represented in both the media and the recording industry. Television has completely ignored the genre since **Tatiana Didenko**'s sad death in 1998 caused the demise of the *Global Village* programme that she produced and presented on Russian TV along with Sergey Starostin. However, since 1996, Radio Russia has continued to broadcast the weekly world music programme *Music of the Entire World / Voyage Across Three Seas*.

DISCOGRAPHY Russia

⊙ Document: New Music from Russia, the 80s.
Leo Records, UK
This eight-CD compilation is currently out of print, but Leo have made it available for download in MP3 format (along with almost all their back catalogue) on their website. It is included here mostly for one piece, the *Dearly Departed* suite which opens the whole anthology.

⊙ Korjak Kamchatka: Dance Drums from the Siberian Far East
Buda/Musique du Monde, France
This is perhaps the most accessible of Henri Lecomte's Siberian series (which currently runs to nine volumes), with its physical dance music from the Kamchatka peninsula in the far east. None of these discs are exactly easy listening, but they are well recorded and document music otherwise unavailable to the wider world.

⊙ Russian Soul
JARO Records, Germany
A 2005 "best of" compilation taken from previous JARO releases, with a few welcome tracks licensed from other labels. A good beginner's introduction to the work of Inna Zhelannaya, Sergey Starostin, Misha Alperin and Stepanida Borisova.

⊙ Songs of the Volga
Auvidis/Ethnic, France
Songs and accordion music from the Turkic Chuvash people and polyphonic songs from the Finno-Ugric Mordvin people. The recordings were made *in situ* with local groups, and it includes good notes and lyric translations.

⊙ The Horse is Galloping, the Bell is Ringing: Songs from the Arkhangelsk, Pskov and Vitebsk Regions
Boheme Music, Russia
This is just one of Boheme's fine collections of actual and "virtual" field recordings (some were recorded live during a season of ethnographic concerts at the Moscow Union of Composers in the 1980s) compiled by experienced ethnomusicologists. Each collection covers different styles of traditional songs and instrumental music from north and west Russia.

★ Zhivaya Voda (Living Water)
Salon AudioVideo
Originally issued as a supplement in Moscow car audio magazine *AvtoZvuk*, this is a comprehensive collection of contemporary folk rock. It includes tracks by Inna Zhelannaya, Va-Ta-Ga, Volga and Two Siberians (Beliy Ostrog), plus ethno-techno from Maleria, folk jazz from guitar virtuoso Ivan Smirnov and ethno-rock from Raznotravie and Dobranotch.

Mikhail Alperin

Having grown up playing the piano amid a rich mix of ethnic cultures in Moldova – Slavic, Roman, Gypsy and Jewish – musician and composer Mikhail Alperin moved to Moscow in the mid-1980s and began delving deeper into his ethnic and cultural roots. Meeting Sergey Starostin led to his forming the ethno-jazz group, Moscow Art Trio, and eventually to multi ethnic projects with Huun-Huur-Tu and the Bulgarian female choir Angelite.

⊙ Folk Dreams
JARO, Germany
Alperin's ethno-jazz album of Russian and Moldavian folk themes features the professional folk choir Russkaya Pesnya, jazz horn-player Arkady Shilkloper, who adds Swiss Alpenhorn to his regular French horn, and Sergey Starostin, whose career was propelled by the Moscow Art Trio.

Boris Bazurov and Folk Opera

Former DPE soloist Boris Bazurov is not only a talented folk singer and musician, but also a talented jazz-rock keyboard player. In the late 1980s, he formed his own band, Folk Opera, creating film music and producing major musical works that could be called ethno-folk-rock operas.

⊙ Psalmophony-2000
ARC-System, Russia
This release by the prolific Boris Bazurov is not so much an opera, as a vocal and instrumental suite that brings together elements that seemed incompatible even in the stormy 1980s: Orthodox religious singing and quality jazz-rock fusion.

Dmitri Pokrovsky Ensemble

Founded in 1973, the revivalist ensemble led by Dimiti Pokrovsky (1944–96) was the best-known group that tried to absorb the peasant singers' traditions and create an authentic village style. A key figure in Russia's authentic music revival, Pokrovsky was enormously influential, even after his death, when his ensemble divided into a number of different groups, each with its own unique sound.

⊙ Faces of Russia
Trikont, Germany
One of the Dmitri Pokrovsky Ensemble's best-known ethnic music recordings, this has a wide repertoire that includes Cossack songs, harvest and wedding songs, religious music and a bizarre instrumental featuring Jew's harp, whistle and clanging rhythms hammered out on a sickle.

☉ Les Noces (The Wedding)
Nonesuch, USA

Although truly cosmopolitan, Igor Stravinsky claimed not to use ethnic material in his "choregraphic scenes". But with *Les Noces*, Pokrovsky disproved his claim, having found folk songs lyrically and musically related to the score in villages near the great composer's home. The four tableaux of *Les Noces* are placed between these folk songs. The vocal performances are simply stunning, but it's a shame they didn't use real pianos. The piano parts recreated on Apple Macs aren't the same.

WITH PAUL WINTER

☉ Earthbeat
Living Music, USA

The first joint project between Soviet and American musicians, this was created in 1987 by the DPE and saxophonist and jazz musician Paul Winter. Although somewhat clumsy overall, *Earthbeat* is of historical interest as a rare example of Pokrovsky's collaborations with jazz and rock musicians.

Alexander Gradsky and Skomorokhi

A seminal figure in rock and pop, Gradsky displayed an interest in tradition as early as the mid-1960s, naming his underground rock band Skomorokhi (Vagabond Minstrels).

☉ Russian Songs
MTKMO, Russia

The first rock suite based on carefully selected folk material, from ritual to urban. Gradsky recorded all the vocal parts and his conservatory-trained tenor remains unique. Several tracks kept free from the heavy dominance of pompous keyboards are as stunning today as they were in 1980.

La Minor

St Petersburg-based group, founded in 2000 and inspired by the underword sounds of Jewish Odessa as depicted in Isaac Babel's stories. Lead singer Slava Shalygin with bayan (button-accordion), guitar and sax.

☉ Oboroty
Eastblok, Germany

An excellent 2009 release inspired by the subculture of the 1970s and a bitter-sweet nostalgia for things Soviet. Songs of alcohol, crime and low-life delivered in gruff vocals and fine musicianship which sounds pissed but never misses a note.

Iva Nova

The all-female Iva Nova, founded by enthusiastic and tireless drummer Katya Fedorova, is a five-piece band, complete with bayan and violin, that uncompromisingly pursues an ethno-punk path.

☉ Iva Nova
Soyuz Records

This debut from the "Russian girls' answer to the Pogues" is a mix of wild, but jolly, drunken village party and harsh angst. Rough, vigorous, driving ethno-punk.

Namgar

Namgar Lhasaranova has one of the best soprano voices the other side of the Ural mountains. She is of Buryat (Mongolian) origin, and her people are Lamaist Buddhists who preserve shamanistic Siberian folk music and round dances. In 2001, she moved to Moscow with two friends and joined two professionally trained ethno-techno musicians as the Namgar ensemble.

☉ Hatar
Sketis Music, Russia

"Hatar" is Buryat-Mongolian for dance, but Namgar's debut offers much more, including all the diverse local music styles slightly updated by Yuri Balashov who adds contemporary flavour by playing an amplified monochord he made himself.

Narodnyi Prazdnik (Pesen Zemli)

This ensemble (whose name means Folk Festivity) was founded in Moscow in 1982 by Ekaterina Dorokhova and Evgenia Kostina. Where possible, the ten female members of the choir learn the songs directly from village singers.

☉ Russia: Polyphonic Wedding Songs
VDE-Gallo/AIMP, Switzerland

It's indicative of just how difficult it is to get good quality field recordings that this label (which usually features the real thing) has gone for a trained ensemble. But these wedding songs are very hard to hear in Russia now, and there's a good spread from the west, north and south of the country.

NE TE

Although unorthodox, the duo NE TE (Not the Who) are among the most successful offshoots of the DPE. Husband-and-wife team Sergey Zhirkov and Lena Sergeeva left Pokrovsky's group in the 1990s to seek contacts in the improv community, and recorded with the minimalist pop group Ensemble 4:33.

☉ Suffering
Long Arms Records, Russia

NE TE's 2002 solo debut is heavy, moody and occasionally hysterical – a challenging, yet extraordinary album. The duo are joined by two improv musicians – free jazz saxophonist Eduard Sivkov and percussionist Mikhail Yudenich.

Evelyn Petrova

Conservatory-trained accordionist Evelyn Petrova first came to prominence in a duo with jazz trumpeter Vyacheslav Gayvoronsky, but has played solo since 2003.

★ Year's Cycle
Leo Records, UK

An ambitious twelve-piece cycle based on Russian songs traditionally performed according to season. The genre is described by ethnomusicologists as a "Calendar Cycle", as each piece represents a month in the year. Challenging, complex and breathtakingly visceral.

Vyacheslav Shchurov

Vyacheslav Shchurov pioneered the creation of a choral group that performed Russian music with some fidelity to the original folk style. He took recordings or transcriptions of village songs as his score and refused to arrange them or beautify them as other ensembles did. He started his group Solovka (Nightingale) in 1968.

☉ Solovka
Pan, Netherlands

A collection of recordings from the Melodiya label from 1978 to 1985, plus new tracks recorded in 1995, principally of south Russian and Siberian choral songs and some good chastushki. Shchurov sings lead and solo on several tracks. Real village singing can be quite demanding to listen to, so this makes a good introduction.

Sirin

This fifteen-piece mixed choir was formed in 1989 by former DPE musician Andrei Kotov. While Pokrovsky mostly explored secular music, Sirin celebrates Russian Orthodox chants and early Russian polyphony. However, Sirin aren't alien to secular music and they also often perform scores by professional composers, while Kotov undertakes even more adventurous outings into jazz, rock and improv.

⭐ **Putnik: Russian Pilgrims**
Opus 111, France

Impeccably conceived, performed and packaged, this disc includes traditional devotional songs or "spiritual poems" by Russian pilgrims in their original forms and in contemporary arrangements, plus a new work by Vladimir Martynov.

Tamara Smyslova and the Dmitri Pokrovsky Folk Music Theatre

Influenced by her husband Dmitri Pokrovsky, classically trained vocalist Tamara Smyslova mastered the ethnic "white sound" and was the primary voice of the DPE until her husband's death. In 1997, she founded the Folk Music Theatre, which, unlike the DPE, avoided collaborations with contemporary music.

⊙ **Krapiva (The Nettle)**
Ulitka Records, Russia

Although released by an indie label, this is purely a folk record. Like the DPE's recordings, *Krapiva* serves as a perfect introduction to Russian musical ethnicity, from pre-Christian *khorovods* to the polyphonic singing of Siberian sects.

Sergey Starostin

The focal point of the Russian world music scene, Starostin is ubiquitous and indispensable. Hardly any serious project involving traditional music – be it a festival, television programme or feature film – can manage without his participation in one form or another. The huge respect and authority he enjoys in the artistic community is best reflected in his nickname "Ded" (Grandad).

⭐ **At Home: Live in Dom**
CD DOMA Records, Russia

Starostin's "biography in songs" combines immaculate renditions of traditional songs with an unorthodox approach. He starts with a legendary phonograph recording of the great Russian bass Feodor Shaliapin and closes with a sort of auto-epitaph, overdubbing a Buena Vista Social Club karaoke with his own emulation of a late nineteenth-century Russian *lied*. Featuring an Armenian *duduk* player and a free jazz trumpeter.

Ulger

Ulger are the folk song and dance company of the Khakas Philharmony. The Khakas people never had a state of their own, so their national traditions (including shamanistic throat-singing) were always open to new influences.

Ulger's leader Evgeny Ulugbashev achieves a smart balance between their indigenous repertoire and Soviet-style songs arranged in a surprisingly traditional manner.

⊙ **Aidym**
CD Doma Records, Russia

The songs on this album fall into three distinctive categories: epic ballads, *yr*, in which recitation alternates with *khai* throat-singing; *thakhpakh* songs, which are both ritualistic and lyrical; and the notorious pseudo-folk songs of the Soviet Era.

Va-Ta-Ga

Along with the Farlanders and Sergey Starostin, Va-Ta-Ga are a prime example of clear-cut Russian-style world music. Leader Alexander Leonov is a singer and an avid instrument collector and maker, and the band play a huge variety of ethnic and self-made instruments from all over the world. Although based on Russian songs, their arrangements and rhythms are global, and their performances sometimes turn into outdoor avant-garde happenings.

⊙ **Strannie Liudi**
Sketis Music, Russia

Issued under the band's previous name (Reel), this disc is tinged with a neo-Celtic sound, mainly due to former member Olga Gaydamak on vocals and fiddle. Leonov's singing and the repertoire are obviously northern Russian, and there's an acoustic Arctic sound-scape and jazzy "walking bass".

Volga

The first Russian band playing ethno-techno, Volga was formed in 1997 by singer Angela Manukian and Alexei Borisov, a pivotal figure in Russian electronic noise.

⭐ **Three Fields**
Sketis Music, Russia

Manukian's angelic voice floats over carefully constructed and tasteful electronic arrangements in renditions that remain true to the traditional spirit of the original seventeenth- and eighteenth-century songs. In the words of DJ Charlie Gillet in *The Observer*, "I have a feeling that Volga's *Three Fields* is going to be the [album] that defines 2004 as the year in which we landed with both feet in the twenty-first century".

Inna Zhelannaya and Farlanders

The seminal Russian world music band, the Farlanders are on offshoot of the conventional rock band Alliance. Inna Zhelannaya quit in 2005, leaving Sergey Starostin to take over as lead vocalist and de facto leader.

⊙ **Moments**
Green Wave/JARO

This live recording from Bremen in 1999 is the group's best album, with Sergey Starostin featuring heavily as a lead vocalist alongside Inna Zhelannaya. A funky rhythmic background accompanies the ecstatic singing of both vocalists.

PLAYLIST
Russia

1 KURSKY FUNK Dmitri Pokrovsky Ensemble and Paul Winter from *Earthbeat*
A new experience in world fusion between Russian and American musicians, this song still holds the enthusiasm of discovery.

2 SNOW BALLS Volga from *Three Fields*
An almost incredible combination of a trip-hop instrumental arrangement and folk vocal lyricism.

3 FOG DMITRI POKROVSKY ENSEMBLE from *Faces of Russia*
Don Cossacks' song from World War II is proof that ethnic polyphony is not just a thing of the past.

4 PRINCESS NE TE from *Suffering*
Free jazz drums and epic medieval lyrics, saxophone and ethnic reeds, plus the severe voice of Lena Sergeeva – rough, unpolished but genuine.

5 AKHKHAN LEGEND Ulger from *Aidym*
A remarkable combination of several overtone singing styles, not at all inferior to Tuvan.

6 BEATITUDES Sirin from *Putnik*
Sudden modulations from the acapella choir

transform the stylization of this piece composed by Vladimir Martynov into a kind of magic realism.

7 HO-HO YOU, VANYA Sergey Starostin from *Live in Dom*
Cross-cultural interpretation of a song from Ryazan, with Western clarinet and Armenian duduk playing a drone inherent to an Oriental tradition.

8 THROUGH THE ORCHARD Farlanders from *Moments*
Rare recording of Starostin and Zhelannaya singing together – the groovy bouncing rhythm is a perfect example of Western-style Russian world music.

9 MARCH: THE SKOMOROKHS Evelyn Petrova from *Year's Cycle*
Untrained singer Evelyn Petrova displays an extraordinary range of vocal techniques celebrating the rough, vulgar singing of the skomorokhs.

10 OH, NE BUDITE Mikhail Alperin and Russkaya Pesnya from *Folk Dreams*
A rare example of upbeat optimism in the normally melancholic Russian song, this sounds very ethnic – mostly thanks to the folk choir Russkaya Pesnya.

Sámiland

joiks of the tundra

Mari Boine

Like that of other circumpolar peoples, the traditional music of the Sámi – formerly known by foreigners as Lapps – is almost entirely vocal, and solo, rather than instrumental. The increased profile of the Sámi and their culture in the past three decades has boosted musical confidence and activity and moved personal, unaccompanied vocalizing into the arena of performance, leading to striking encounters with rock and techno. Andrew Cronshaw shares a joik or two...

The last quarter century has seen a flowering of Sámi music, both traditional and boldly progressive. This and the equally unique visual art are strong foci of modern Sámi identity, both for the people themselves and for foreigners. Despite the relatively small number of Sámi, their art, indeed their very existence, has a far-reaching influence.

The Land and the People

"Sámi" is the name for their people used by Sámi themselves. The word "Lapp" is thought to derive from an archaic Finnish word with connotations of "outcast"; it was used by foreigners but not the people themselves, and its use is diminishing.

The Sámi arrived in the far north, it's thought, from the eastern fringes of Europe at least two thousand years ago, probably long before. A thousand years ago they still populated most of Finland, but Finnish tribes, who moved in like the Sámi from the southeast, displaced them from the southern territories. Their present-day homeland, known as **Sámiland** or **Sápmi**, includes most of the areas of Norway, Sweden, Finland and the Kola Peninsula of northwest Russia that lie north of the Arctic Circle, and also territory well south of that in Norway and Sweden. By no means everyone who lives there is Sámi, though. Estimates vary, but there are 50,000–75,000 people who might claim that distinction in terms of heredity, lifestyle or language.

These days the traditional occupation of **reindeer-herding** is followed by far fewer people, and the movement with the herds from winter to summer pastures and the annual roundups are accomplished to the roar of snowmobiles. Nevertheless, the relationship with reindeer is still an iconic defining feature of the Sámi; indeed in Sweden the Sámi are the only ones legally allowed to own the animals.

The Sámi Drum

The word "shaman" originates with the Tungus people of Siberia but what is generally accepted as shamanism is found in many parts of the world, and drums are widely used to induce the trance under which the shaman makes a spirit journey.

In Sámi custom, there is a second use of the drum, found in few other shamanic traditions – that of divination. The skin of the oval single-headed drum (**kobdas**, or in South Sámi **gievri**) bore pictographic symbols drawn in red juice from chewed alder-bark. The layout of these varied regionally. A small bone or metal pointer, sometimes with attached chains and charm-shapes, was laid on the skin, which was vibrated with a small T- or Y-shaped hammer so that the pointer moved across it, and the shaman (**nåjde** or **noaite**) drew conclusions from its movement relative to the drawn symbols.

The propagators of Christianity firmly discouraged the practices of the religion it displaced, so by the eighteenth century most of the drums had been destroyed, and the remainder were spread across the world in ethnographic collections; only about seventy of these still exist. Nowadays many new ones are being made, but their use is musical or symbolic rather than religious.

Sámi graphic art has a very strong identity, and artists frequently use symbols from the drums. One, the sun and moon circle usually drawn in the centre, is the basis of the Sámi flag, which uses the bright colours of the striking traditional costume. The flag was adopted in 1986 – as was the national anthem, a setting by Arne Sørlie of Isak Saba's 1906 poem *Same soga lavla* (The Song of the Sámi Family).

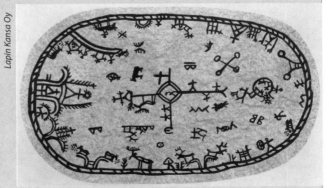

Lapin Kansa Oy

Sámi drum skin

The several **Sámi languages**, spoken today by about 20,000–30,000 people, are Finno-Ugrian, related to Finnish but not understandable to a Finn nor even necessarily to one another – they fall into three mutually non-comprehensible regional groups. The majority speak North Sámi, a language of the Central group.

There has never been a Sámi nation with its own political identity, but there is a considerable sense of solidarity and communication, with a Sámi parliament in each Nordic country, and the cross-border umbrella organization of the Nordic Sámi Council. Norway has the largest Sámi population, at about 40,000, the majority living in its northern-most county, Finnmark. (Yes, to add further confusion, the Norwegian word for Sámi is "Finn"!)

The Joik

While individual Sámi might play instruments such as fiddle, accordion or bone flute, and nowadays have access to the whole range of contem-porary instruments, there is no Sámi tradition of instrumental music, apart from the shamanistic use of the **drum** (see box on p.349).

The musical focus is on song – *lavlu* or *laavloe* in Sámi. The most characteristic type of singing is the improvised **joik**, also called in North Sámi *luohti* or in South Sámi *vuolle*. It's hard to give a watertight definition of a joik – there are wide regional differences and it is perhaps more defin-able by what it isn't than by what it is. It's not a rhyming, formal, structured song. The tune can wander, usually with some phrases recurring. A singer improvises a joik to go with whatever he or she is doing or thinking, or to remember a person, an animal or a place. Sometimes it'll be a one-off, sometimes parts of it will be repeated on another occasion and it will become more fixed in form. The singer explores vocal textures – thin, thick, high, low – normally using just a few different notes, sliding between them, chopping them with glottal stops. Sometimes there will be words, per-haps just one, a name for example, repeated from

Juho Huttunen

Wimme Saari

time to time, its sound explored and reinterpreted. There aren't usually a lot of words, or a story, but then again there can be. There are no absolute fixed rules – self-expression is the key.

Though a joik may be sung to or for another person, it's not a performance in the modern sense. A singer will make one which somehow typifies a person, living or dead, and helps remember them. Joiks are usually said not to be *about* their subject, but rather in some way to *be* the subject. "We joik, therefore we remember, therefore we are", is the way joiker and researcher **Krister Stoor** puts it. **Inga Juuso**, well-known not only for her unaccompanied joiking but also for combining it with a range of other musics, describes it as "like painting a picture, but with tunes". A joik may be a gift, for example to a new-born baby. As another leading modern joiker, **Wimme Saari**, explains: "The mother or father can do it. Then, as the child grows up, more is added to the joik – it grows up as the child grows up. A joik is like life." Though largely expressive, joiks could also have a function, for example making a sound to discourage wolves from attacking the herd, or attracting a girl across the marketplace.

The joik isn't a creature of the concert hall; its natural environment is outdoors, sung by a person alone while working or travelling, or perhaps over the usual Sámi drink – coffee – at the fireside. When Matts Arnberg, Håkon Unsgaard and Israel Ruong were recording joiks for Swedish radio in the 1950s and 60s (see discography), it was clear, as it had been to others before them (sound recordings were made as far back as 1906), that as far as possible they had to take their bulky equipment to wherever the singers felt most comfortable if the stream of consciousness was to be prompted.

As with many folk forms, researchers have regularly been told that joiking is dying out or is already dead in a particular district. It's true that religious fundamentalism – in northern Sámiland largely Laestadianism, which still has its adherents – often took a dim view of a custom which once had associations with magical, shamanistic practices. Lars Levi Laestadius of Karesuando, who preached in the nineteenth century – though mostly targeting fiddling and other modern pleasures – sometimes condemned joiking, partly because of the type of joik that tended to emerge under the influence of drink, and many followers regarded it as sinful.

Overall, Sámi art and music these days is a strong force, and a central feature has been widespread interest in *joiku*. The main focus has been on North Sámi luohti, while Swedish South Sámi vuolle has diminished, and the music and culture of the East Sámi of the Russian Kola Peninsula are close to extinction. **Wimme Saari**, who comes from Kelottijärvi in northwestern Finnish Sámiland, describes the situation: "In the border areas like ours where there are more Finns and Swedes, joiking has a tendency to vanish, but in the middle, in Sámi areas like Kautokeino, naturally it has been able to survive better, and it's very strong with young people too. Since we've been doing the new modern styles more young people have paid attention, and it's opened their eyes to the old joiking too."

Wimme himself had to piece together his own family tradition: "I started working at the Finnish Broadcasting Company in 1986. There I found some tapes including my uncles joiking. With the help of those tapes I learned some of the old tradition. Although my mother comes from an old joiking family, the direct connection from one generation to another had already been broken. Due to religious fundamentalism there was no joiking at home."

New Developments

What Wimme Saari learned was the North Sámi tradition of luohti, in which the joik normally describes a specific person or animal and the melody sticks fairly rigidly to a pentatonic scale. Since then, however, he has also moved into a freer form, and also joiks over instrumental and electronic textures and rhythms. He has collaborated in this with Finnish traditional band **Tallari**, Swedish/Finnish roots-rock band **Hedningarna**, and predominantly with Finnish saxophonist **Tapani Rinne** and members of his ambient techno band **RinneRadio**, in which the sound of the instruments becomes an environment within which to joik:

"When working with musicians, often I close my eyes and listen to what comes from the instruments and samples. Then it's like a building, a dream building in my mind. I can perhaps see a lake, or a tree, or I'm underwater like a fish, swimming against the stream. Sometimes I'm in space, with the stars. Sometimes it's colours and shapes, and I'm following them with my voice. What I do is the same as the older joikers did, but I'm in the sound world of the instruments, and I must listen".

From the 1970s until his death in 2001, the name of poet, designer, artist and singer **Nils-Aslak Valkeapää**, otherwise known as **Áillohaš**, was at the forefront of Sámi joik and other aspects of Sámi contemporary culture. Áillohaš emphasizes joik's minimalism, simultaneously archaic and contemporary, in his poems and recordings. He was a major influence in shaping present-day Sámi self-awareness and identity. His musical collaborators were saxophonist **Seppo "Báron" Paakkunainen**, **Esa Kotilainen** and other members of the Finnish exploratory-roots band **Karelia**. Since joiking is traditionally a largely outdoor activity, several recordings of joiking feature the natural or contrived sounds of nature. Áillohaš

incorporated them as accompaniments, and on his 1994 album *Goase Dušše* (The Bird Symphony) they constitute the whole piece. In 1992 he produced **Johan Anders Bær**'s album of person-joiks,

Mari Boine

The only way to fully experience **Mari Boine** is live. Her figure in the centre of the band's spacious sound becomes magnetic – the intense bright focus, her wheeling dance with outstretched arms evocative of a gliding bird. Her on-stage persona, the culture she reflects, the sound of her North Sámi language, her joik-rooted exploration of vocal sounds and the powerful, vibrant minimalism, rock-stripped-bare, of the band all contribute to her distinctive position in European music.

Boine belongs very much to the radical Nordic remodelling of jazz and rock and its open relationship with traditional music. This remodelling involves a shift from the harmonic, chordal structure which has prevailed in Europe for so long, back towards forms drawing their richness from the texture and shape of the note, and their energy from rhythmic stresses and balances. It pulls in ideas from other traditions, many of them fundamentally linear, predominantly monophonic or duophonic, and there are glimpses in the Boine band's instrumental work – only fleetingly discernible and never creating a detour – of Indian, Arabic and Native North and South American musics.

Mari Boine came to the notice of a non-Nordic audience when the album *Gula Gula* was licensed by the Sámi label Iðut to Peter Gabriel's RealWorld. At about the same time, she took part in a live worldwide TV musical special. But, as she told me, that wasn't the beginning:

"I started in the late 70s, and I think I started to sing and make music as a therapy for myself. I never planned to be an artist; sometimes, when I think about it, it's crazy that I'm here, and I'm touring, and I'm doing what I'm doing.

"I think I realized, at teachers' training school, that I felt that the culture that I came from, the Sámi culture, was not good enough, so I wanted to be Norwegian or European, I wanted to forget the culture. And then I had to ask myself 'why is this, and what does all this come from?' And after that came a lot of songs. Actually I made my first lyrics to John Lennon's 'Working Class Hero'! At that time I don't think I quite understood what he was singing about, but there was something in the music, and I think also my unconscious understood, and I wrote a song about how it was for Sámi children to be placed in the Norwegian school and learn to hate their own background."

But that's changed now, hasn't it – there are Sámi schools?

"Yes, there are some Sámi schools, and there is more room for the Sámi culture in the schools. I can see many changes in a good direction. I was working in a school in the Sea Sámi area before I started to sing, and then there were only a few children who learned the language. These days, there are many more."

Your songs are not traditional joiks – but is it a major influence on your music

"It's always there. Influences from joik and influences from the Christian hymns (I was brought up in a very Christian family), and I like this mixture. Actually we made a new piece out of six Christian hymns, and then I mixed it with a shamanistic beat, because I like this meeting, of things that you'd expect to be very different, to find the meeting points."

"Shaman" seems to be a word that blurb-writers utter whenever a Sámi bangs a drum.

"Yes, I feel that. I also was afraid of the word shamanism, and I see this stereotype. But I want to fill this word with meaning, because I think through my music I learn to understand, a bit of it, and to get in touch with the spirituality that was in our culture before. I think you can find elements of the shamanistic tradition, of shamanistic music, in my music – the beat, the spirituality. This trance, or this good feeling that I'd call it, it's a way … if you go there you can get new energy, but it's not something you just play with.

"For me, I want to have this down-to-earth relationship with the shamanism, because this is what my people had, and also other people who had this religion. I don't want to let it be something mysterious, not able to be caught, not able to be understood. There are some very healing parts in this religion, and I learned something about this in my music but I can't express it in words, I am expressing it in my music."

Festivals

There are a number of annual cultural and music festivals in Sámiland. The biggest (though not enormous) is **Riddu Riđđu**, a festival of the culture of international indigenous peoples that features music, performing arts, courses, seminars, movies, a children's festival and youth camp. It's in July in Manndalen, Kåfjord, north Norway.

Also in north Norway, **Márkomeannu** is a culture and music festival in the Sámi villages of Ofoten and southern Troms in July, and Kautokeino has a **Sámi Easter Festival**. In Sweden there's a music stage at Jokkmokk's **Winter Market**, and Finland's main Sámi music festival is **Ijahis Idja** (The Nightless Night) in Inari at the end of May. There are also Sámi events around the Nordic countries celebrating Sámi National Day, 6 February.

Ulla Pirittijärvi

Máhkarávju, which had the continuous accompaniment of a noisy gannet colony.

The best-known Sámi singer by far, indeed worldwide probably the best-known Sámi, now lauded in not just Sámi but also Norwegian national culture, is **Mari Boine** (see box). While not a joiker as such, her songs and style are uniquely Sámi, and since the 1970s she has been making albums and fronting bands that exploit the possibilities of rock instruments to open up a whole new territory.

Other Sámi musicians have been finding their own ways to expand that territory, creating music that surrounds traditional joik or uses its shapes

and sounds as a basis for new music and new encounters. Wimme Saari, Inga Juuso and Johan Anders Bær have all been involved in a variety of techno-electronic and acoustic approaches, as have **Johan Sara Jr**, **Ulla Pirttijärvi**, bands **Orbina**, **Transjoik**, **Sančuari** and **Jienat** and the sister duo **Angelit**. Transjoik keyboardist and joiker **Frode Fjellheim** is involved in a number of significant projects as producer and arranger, including Ulla Pirttijärvi's albums and an arctic mass. Nils-Aslak Valkeapää's godson **Niko Valkeapää** has had considerable mainstream success, not as a joiker but as a singer-songwriter influenced by joik and the Sámi soundscape.

DISCOGRAPHY Sámiland

Traditional joik is a creature of the outdoors, and usually a very personal and solitary thing. So recording a joik places the joiker in an unnatural position. The value of putting a string of them on record, even if recorded outdoors, is predominantly archival. Accompanied joik isn't the heart of the tradition, but it can make a much easier access point.

⊙ Dejoda
DAT, Norway
The leading Sámi label and book publisher DAT has a catalogue containing a good number of CDs of unaccompanied joiking from throughout Sámiland. *Dejoda* probably has as much feel of the joik and the outdoors as it's possible to capture in a recording session. Nils-Aslak Valkeapää and Johan Anders Bær, themselves well-known joikers, produced this

recording of Johan J. Kemi, Marit Berit Bær and Berit Inga Bær at the seaside of North Cape.

⊙ Son Vuäinn – She Sees: Skolt Sámi Leu'dd from the Kola Peninsula
Global Music Centre, Finland
Two CDs in a 100-page hardback book of lyrics and notes, the largest collection ever made of songs of the Sámi of Russia's Kola peninsula. Five women singers, all now dead, recorded by Ilpo Saastamoinen in 1994–97. Not joiks, *leu'dd* are chant-like or more melodic contemporary stories of a virtually disappeared life disrupted by war and clearance.

⊙ Yoik: A Presentation of Saami Folk Music
Caprice, Sweden

This boxed set comprises a 310-page hardback book in Swedish and English plus three CDs of field recordings – in all, 175 joiks from 34 different Forest and Mountain Sámi. The recordings were made for the Swedish Broadcasting Company by Matts Arnberg, Håkan Unsgaard and Israel Ruong, during the course of two field trips across Sámiland in 1953. While many Sámi recordings have very little accompanying written information, here the stories and texts in the book set the context. Many of these joiks have words, and often their imagery is beautiful and revealing of the old ways of life.

Angelit

Earlier called Angelin Tytöt/Annel Nieiddat (girls from Angeli), sisters Ursula and Tuuni Länsman come from the Finnish Sámiland village of Angeli near Inari. Their joik-pop was originally acoustic but more recently comes with the addition of hefty technology.

⊙ Mánnu
Warner, Finland

The keyboards and programming of Kimmo Kajasto, of techno band RinneRadio, beefed up the sound in this and their preceding album. The duo's energy was a good humanizing balance with the more impersonal techno.

Johan Anders Bær

A frequent collaborator with Nils-Aslak Valkeapää, Bær has gone on to make his own contributions to the new joik-based music as performer and producer.

⊙ Guovssu
DAT, Norway

Bær blends joik with acoustic and electric instruments and occasional rocky grooves. He is joined by Valkeapää's colleagues Esa Kotilainen (synth and accordion) and Seppo "Baron" Paakkunainen (sax and flute), plus others on electric guitar and gutsy percussion.

Mari Boine

A riveting live performer and a modern Sámi figurehead, at home and internationally.

★ Eallin
Antilles, UK; Sonet, Europe

This 1996 live album gives some idea of her magnetism and of the splendid, intense, spacious-sounding Boine band of that time: Roger Ludvigsen (guitars), Hege Rimestad (violin), Carlos Quispe (South American notch flutes and *charango*), Gjermund Silset (bass, *hackbrett*) and Helge Norbakken (percussion). It includes the popular title track (covered by Jan Garbarek and others) from the first of her albums to be released worldwide, 1990's *Gula Gula* (Iðut, Norway; remixed for RealWorld, UK).

Frode Fjellheim

Frode Fjellheim, a keyboardist/vocalist of Sámi extraction, is a key figure in new Sámi music as a producer and arranger. He led the Trondheim-based Frode Fjellheim Jazz Joik Ensemble, which after one classic album reduced to the quartet Transjoik comprising Fjellheim, guitarist/vocalist Nils Olav Johansen and percussionists Snorre Bjerck and Tor Haugerud.

★ Aejlies Gaaltije – The Sacred Source: An Arctic Mass
Vuelie, Norway

Traditional hymns, joiks, folk tunes and Fjellheim's own compositions, with lyrics in South Sámi, Finnish, Norwegian,

North Sámi and Latin. The Transjoik quartet is joined by vocalist Kristin Høyseth Rustad, ex-Hedningarna Finnish singer Sanna Kurki-Suonio, Sámi singer and joiker Ulla Pirttijärvi, and Susanne Lundeng's soaring violin.

AS FRODE FJELLHEIM JAZZ JOIK ENSEMBLE

★ Saajve Dans
Iðut, Norway

An extraordinarily effective meeting of gutsy joik with jazz-rock, heartbeat grooves and pinched harmonics. From almost inaudible to threatening, from limpidly melodic to tortured, it touches many bases including Miles Davis territory. Largely based on joiks transcribed between 1910 and 1913, it's a Sámi fusion classic.

Orbina

Orbina originally came together at Beaivváš, the Sámi national theatre, with a core trio of joiker Leif Isak Eide Nilut, keyboardist Bjørn Ole Rasch and former Mari Boine band guitarist Roger Ludvigsen, with Inga Juuso first guesting, then joining. Over the years they've gigged only irregularly but have released two notable albums.

⊙ Orbina
Iðut, Norway

Released in 1993, this is big, spacious joik rock on original and traditional themes. The core group are joined by saxist Bendik Hofseth, guest joiker Inga Juuso and the Mari Boine band rhythm section.

⊙ Orbina II
DAT, Norway

Nine years after their debut, Orbina's second album is more digital, less rocky. Fellow Sámi electric guitarist Klemet Anders Buljo replaces Ludvigsen, who still guests here, and Inga Juuso takes a more central vocal role in tandem with Nilut.

Ulla Pirttijärvi

Born in Angeli and an original member of Angelin Tytöt, Pirttijärvi has emerged as a fine solo joiker and singer, usually in collaboration with Frode Fjellheim and the Transjoik team.

⊙ Ruossa Eanan
Warner/Atrium, Sweden

On Pirttijärvi's debut album her joik-shaped songs are finely integrated with rich-toned, brooding arrangements by Fjellheim using warm, deep synth sounds, percussion and occasionally cello and soprano sax.

★ Máttaráhku Askái – In Our Foremothers' Arms
Warner, Finland

This picks up where the previous album left off, and is even more powerful. Pirttijärvi's shell-like vocals and Fjellheim's beautiful blend of samples and real instruments create constantly interesting pictorial textures with compelling pulse and memorable melodic lines. This stirred up airplay interest Europe-wide on its 2002 release; her live shows are rare but matchingly excellent.

Wimme Saari

A very fine joiker who re-learned the art upon hearing recordings of his uncles, Wimme's recorded and live work with the ambient and techno approaches of RinneRadio and his own band have made considerable international waves.

⊙ Gierran
RockAdillo, Finland

Wimme's second album, from 1997, is a robust and meaningful interaction between voice and strong sounds, with more varied joiking, more connection and point and less drifting ambience or detached grooves and bleeps than most of his other recordings. Perhaps Wimme's most beautiful recorded collaboration is the track "Iešdovddu Oiannus" on Finnish band Tallari's pan-Finno-Ugrian project CD *Lunastettava Neito* (Folk Music Institute, Finland).

⊙ Gapmu/Instinct
RockAdillo, Finland
Thirty-four unaccompanied joiks, very personal and pictorial, in which Wimme joiks people, places, a fire, sawing an ice-hole for fishing, the way he feels. The video clips included have him joiking marsh gas bubbles and a boat journey powered by outboard motor.

Johan Sara Jr and Group

Though Sara is Sámi he came to joiking relatively late, after a musical education centred on guitar. His joiking developed with an awareness of the possibilities of instrumental settings; nevertheless it is fully formed, real joik, of which he has great command, using a range of vocal sounds that make him sound like several different people.

⊙ Ovcci Vuomi Ovtta Veaiggis
DAT, Norway
This impressive 1995 debut contains a set of joiks co-produced by Nils-Aslak Valkeapää, centred on voices with the band playing pitched and unpitched percussion, bass and touches of synth, sax and Sara's guitar and flutes.

★ Boska
DAT, Norway
Nine years later, and with a completely different line-up, this is a magnificent album. Sara forsakes guitar, working with just Erik Halvorsen's synths, Geir Lysne's sax and flutes and Knut Aalefjær's percussion, joined on a couple of tracks by Buryat throatsinger Sayan Zhambalov and the soaring hard-edged female voice of Erzhena Zhambalova. Not ambient, not dance, this nevertheless employs a fine command of that technology to make explosively full-blooded music that's right inside the twists and turns of the joiking rather than overlaid on it.

Krister Stoor

Stoor teaches and researches at the Sámi Studies department of the University of Umeå in northern Sweden.

★ To Yoik Is To Live
Umeå University, Sweden
The best CD there is to explain the nature and meaning of Sámi joik. Between his joiks, plus one from Ánte Mikkel Gaup and two archive recordings of Martin Nilsson, he speaks about them, in English. His voice has a warm musicality, what he says is beautifully and concisely expressed, and there's such a fine balance and flow of speech and music that the whole thing becomes as musical a listen as any all-music album. Among the short unaccompanied joiks are some accompanied in ways that really get inside the form, featuring electric guitar and some bass, fiddle, diatonic accordion or harmonium. The CD isn't commercially distributed; contact *krister.stoor@samiska.umu.se*.

Nils-Aslak Valkeapää

Valkeapää, otherwise known as Áillohaš, was a pioneer and major figure in Sámi music, poetry and visual art. Finns Seppo "Baron" Paakkunainen and Esa Kotilainen were regular collaborators, surrounding his joiks with sound textures of sax, flutes, subtle synth and trickling, rattling percussion.

★ Dálveleaikkat: Wintergames
DAT, Norway
With Paakkunainen, Kotilainen and fellow joiker Johan Anders Bær, and centred on the joik that began the opening spectacular of 1994's Lillehammer Winter Olympics, this is a good representation of the approaches Áillohaš and his associates evolved over the years.

PLAYLIST
Sámiland

1 KYJRIE Frode Fjellheim from *Sacred Source*
Quiet space and power as singing and joiking voices overlap under a slow soaring fiddle motif.

2 DÁLVELEAIKKAT Nils-Aslak Valkeapää from *Wintergames*
The Olympic opening joik, Áillohaš against a wide soundscape.

3 IEŠDOVDDU OIANNUS Wimme Saari from *Lunastettava Neito*
Slow, almost Vaughan Williams-like shifting dronal string and harmonium chords underpin Wimme's joiking, which slides ecstatically into falsetto.

4 DE JUOIGGAS Ulla Pirttijärvi from *In Our Foremothers' Arms*
A melodic line on a Chinese *erhu* sample swoops across Pirttijärvi's joik.

5 SUMMERLAND Martin Nilsson from *To Yoik Is to Live*
A vuolle reflectively joiked by Nilsson (1904–91), from the western Sámi village of Allejaur.

6 ANÁR GILLI Angelin Tytöt from *Mánnu*
A characteristically poppy joik from the sisters, cheerfully joiking the village of Inari over hefty synth rhythms.

7 MIELAHISVUOHTA Mari Boine from *Leahkastin*
Boine and her band at their most exciting. Imagine her dancing holding her red Sámi shawl wide, wheeling like a bird of the tundra.

8 BEKKA BIERA Orbina from *Orbina*
Leif Isak Nilut joiks to spacious guitar and keyboard rock, propelled by Helge Norbakken's drumming.

9 HIMBA Johan Sara Jr and Group from *Boska*
High and low Buryat throatsinging and Sámi joik meet techno beats and harmonizing saxes.

10 ÅARJEL SAEMIEH Frode Fjellheim Jazz Joik Ensemble from *Saajve Dans*
A gradual, muttering build-up develops into joiking voice over ringing pinched guitar harmonics, then bursts into wildness. Based on a South Sámi joik.

Sardinia

an island of enchantment

Tenores di Bitti
Real World

By virtue of its location at the heart of the Mediterranean, the Italian island of Sardinia has seen countless invasions and occupations over the centuries. The Romans, Greeks, Arabs and, above all, the Spanish – with their three hundred-year domination – have all left their mark. Such influences have moulded the island's musical heritage, producing a distinctive traditional repertoire that remains remarkably intact and alive to this day. Giacomo Serreli circumnavigates a rich and varied musical landscape.

With an area of no more than 24,000 square kilometres and a population of around 1.6 million inhabitants, Sardinia is small and sparsely populated. Yet it has one of the richest and most ancient musical cultures in the Mediterranean, with unique styles of **polyphonic and monodic singing**, and several instruments found nowhere else.

The Tenores Style

The most outstanding and original vocal tradition is the **canto a tenores**, which always employs four male voices, and originates from the central mountainous areas of Sardinia. Similar forms are found in Corsican *paghjella*, and elements of the style even bear a resemblance to Tuvan and Mongolian throat singing.

The lead voice, known as *boghe*, defines the musical motif on the basis of poetic verses that contstitute the main body of the repertoire. The *bassu* keeps to the same tonality as the solo lead, but with a very accentuated low nasal tone, which distinguishes it from *sa contra* and the high-pitched *mesa oghe*. The timbre of the bassu and the contra are said to evoke the sounds of the herds of animals which the shepherds co-existed with, far from home, in days gone by, while the *mezza voce* emulates the whistling of the wind.

The leading exponents of this style are the **Tenores Remunnu 'e Locu,** better known as the **Tenores di Bitti**, who formed in the early 1970s in the small mountain village of Bitti. They have since travelled the world extensively, enjoying international acclaim – especially in the last ten years – following their appearances at **WOMAD** festivals and since recording with Peter Gabriel's **Real World label**. There are more than ninety tenores groups all over the island, and they have created a large body of recorded work. Canto a tenores has also been declared as a "**patrimony of humanity**" by UNESCO, who granted the request of the central Nuoro province to recognize and safeguard their cultural heritage.

Other major groups include **Tenores San Gavino**, from Oniferi, and **Tenores di Neoneli**, named after their hometown which is actually far from the central Barbagia region. Tenores di Neoneli are renowned for their experiments with jazz bands and Italian pop musicians, while the **Tenores di Orosei** have experimentally fused their work with that of Dutch cellist Ernst Reijseger.

Canto a cuncordu is another Sardinian vocal style – also performed with four voices – that is typically heard during holy week in the form of **liturgical chants**. The religious brotherhoods of Orosei, Castelsardo, Santulussurgiu and Cuglieri continue to keep this form alive. Yet another type of canto a tenore, known as **tasgia**, developed in the northeastern area of Gallura, and has a fifth vocal timbre called *falsittu*.

An Orchestra Inside an Instrument

If we consider the tenores and cuncordu styles as representing the rich vocal heritage of the island, the sound of the **launeddas** would represent instrumental Sardinian music. A small bronze statue found on the island that depicts a launeddas player is believed to be more than three thousand years old. The unique instrument consists of three reed canes played using circular breathing. Just as the canto a tenores tradition is concentrated in Sardinia's central regions, this "**triple clarinet**" is not native to the whole island. It belongs to the sub-regions of **Sarrabus-Gerrei** in southeastern Sardinia, the Trexenta area in the province of Cagliari and the town of Cabras on the west coast.

The most detailed studies of the launeddas were carried out from the late 1950s to the early 1960s by Danish researcher **Andreas Bentzon** (1936–71), who knew several of the great players personally. Talents such as **Antonio Lara** (1886–1979) and **Efisio Melis** (1890–1970), who represented the Sarrabus-Gerrei school, were capable of extraordinary displays of talent during long sessions of festivities. Another name worthy of note is **Dionigi Burranca** (1913–79), from the Trexenta area. He was the first to undertake fusion projects mixing jazz and the launeddas tradition, teaming up with American musician **Ornette Coleman**.

Today, the grandmaster of the launeddas is universally acknowledged to be **Luigi Lai**, who was born in the town of San Vito and originally schooled by Lara and Melis. He is a rigorous guardian of the tradition, but he also has an open mind and a perfect technique. This has allowed him to introduce the instrument into other musical contexts, for instance, recording with Italian pop star **Angelo Branduardi** or experimenting by mixing launeddas with three canto a tenores voices.

New on the scene is a young player from the southeastern town of Villaputzu, **Andrea Pisu**. He has managed to assimilate the sound of his idol Melis in an extraordinary fashion and has recently collaborated with **Basque musicians**. On his debut CD, he revived the almost lost tradition of improvised poetry in the Campidanese dialect, accompanied by the launeddas.

Curiously, the multifaceted history of the launedas – from its most traditional form in music for dancing and religious ceremonies to its more recent appearances in jazz, rock and experimental music – can be summed up in the work of a non-Sardinian performer, the Roman **Carlo Mariani**, who was educated at Dionigi Burranca's school.

The launeddas is a truly indigenous instrument, although it is similar to the Egyptian *arghul* which has just two reed canes. However, there is a theory that it may have travelled as far as **Scotland**, as rocks in the Scottish countryside bear images of a player of a triple clarinet that looks remarkably similar to the launeddas. A young Glaswegian musican called **Barnaby Brown** reconstructed the depicted instrument. He even moved to Sardinia to learn the construction techniques of the launeddas and to try to figure out how the instrument could have travelled so far from its place of inception.

In the past, the launeddas were mostly used to accompany the dancing in Sardinia's *piazze*, or town squares, but given the extreme difficulty of learning the instrument, a **diatonic melodeon** called the *organetto* gradually took its place. The current organetto grandmaster is **Totore Chessa**, from the town of Irgoli.

The New Tradition

Music and popular song has always had deep roots in Sardinia. The fairs (*sagre*) and festivals that take place across the island's three hundred or so communes have always been accompanied by **dance and music exhibitions** – which has kept the island's folk traditions alive. Therefore, Sardinia did not undergo the same folk revival as the rest of Italy during the 1970s.

During this period, the island's most important singer was at the peak of her career. **Maria Carta** (1934–94) was the first Sardinian performer to gain international recognition with a secular as well as religious repertoire, which was linked inextricably to the **Gregorian tradition**. One of her most popular performances is that of the hymn "Ave Maria". A new and fascinating rendition of the same song by Cagliari singer **Clara Murtas** was elaborately arranged by **Ennio Morricone** for a small symphonic orchestra, and it had echoes of Gregorian and minimalist traditions.

Since the 1970s, many young musicians have developed new takes on the Sardinian tradition, revisiting popular songs from fresh perspectives and creating original material inspired by it. Fore-

most in this tradition – and its most representative contemporary exponent – is **Elena Ledda**. She founded the groups Suonofficina and Sonos with her mandola player **Mauro Palmas**, and experiments with modern non-Sardinian instruments in a crossover style that incorporates jazz and other Mediterranean flavours. Albums such as *Incanti*, *Mare Mannu* and *Amargura* showcase Ledda's vocal firepower, inspired use of poetry and careful balance between tradition and innovation.

Other groups, such as **Calic** and **Cordas Et Cannas** from Olbia, have worked in a similar vein over the last 25 years. In their music, Calic have explored the **Catalan tradition**, which is still very much alive in the small northern city of Alghero. That tradition has also found a new voice in the work of former jazz singer **Franca Masu**.

Jazz instrumentalists have frequently experimented with Sardinian roots music. Double-bass player **Marcello Melis** (1939–94) was a pioneer in the free-jazz era. Following in his wake, Ornette Coleman, David Liebman, Ralph Towner and others have tried their hand at ethno-jazz fusions. Some of the better fusions are by saxophone player **Enzo Favata** on *Voyage en Sardaigne* and *Boghes and Voices*, which includes Tenores di Bitti and the **Cuncordu di Castelsardo**. His work also features launeddas, and even the Argentine *bandoneón*. Despite the jazz contexts, you can still hear the pulsating *gosos* (invocations to the Madonna and saints) and traditional dances in Favata's broad-minded creations. Even Sardinia's current international jazz superstar, **Paolo Fresu**, has ventured into tradition, with the project *Sonos 'e Memoria* (Sound and Remembrance, see box opposite).

With thanks to Pablo Farba

Maria Carta

SARDINIA

Sonos 'e Memoria

In 1993, film director **Gianfranco Cabiddu** began viewing vintage footage from Sardinia in Rome's Luce Insti-tute. Two years later, *Sonos 'e Memoria* was born. The 25-minute film documented the work of Sardinian shep-herds, farmers and miners, plus popular festivals such as the procession of **Sant'Efisio** in Cagliari and the wild horse-back chase, known as the **Ardia**, in the town of Sedilo. The director decided to synchronize the black-and-white footage, dating from the 1930s to the 1950s, with a tailor-made soundtrack that would be performed live during the projection, and he entrusted this responsibility to the renowned trumpeter **Paolo Fresu**.

One of Italy's leading jazz artists, Fresu roped in Sardinia's most respected traditional artists, including **Elena Ledda**, **Mauro Palmas**, the voices of **Su Cuncordu e su Rosariu**, and **Luigi Lai** on launeddas. He teamed them with a variety of jazz artists, including eccentric pianist and accordionist **Antonello Salis**, doublebass player **Furio Di Castri**, tabla player **Federico Sanesi** and cellist **Carlo Cabiddu**. "Each one played their own music with-out trying to blend … thus keeping a pure and emotive tie with the common traditional root," stresses Fresu.

The film premiered at the Venice Film Festival in 1995 and has since been performed to great acclaim in France, Brazil, Switzerland, Germany and Argentina. Its intense soundtrack marries jazz and roots sensibilities without any friction, and a 2001 CD of the same name records the adventure. The award-winning documen-tary *Passaggi di Tempo* (Passages Of Time) – similar in style to Wim Wenders' *Buena Vista Social Club* – gives an overview of the entire process by which this concert-film project was brought to life. Cabiddu declares that "respecting tradition is respecting yourself, so that we may face the road ahead of us instead of the one behind us".

⊙ **Sardaigne: Les Maitres de la Musique Instrumentale**
Al Sur, France

A series of in-situ recordings featuring typical Sardinian instru-ments: organetto, *pipiolu* (a small wooden flute), *triangolo*, *tamburino* and launeddas played by luminaries such as Luigi Lai, Aurelio Porcu and Mondo Vercellino. The CD booklet also contains abundant information.

★ **Sardegna: Antologia della Musica Sarda Antica e Moderna**
Dejavu Retro, EEC

Comprising two double-CD volumes (79 tracks in total), this offers an interesting panorama of a variety of Sardinian music. In each volume, one CD features a more traditional repertoire – canti a tenores, polyphonic and monodic vocals and instrumental tracks featuring the launeddas and organetto – while the other focuses on more modern forms and artists that have elaborated on the traditions in innovative ways.

Marino De Rosas

Born in Olbia, Marino De Rosas is a leading Sardinian gui-tarist who began to play during the 1960s beat period, but disappeared from the scene in 1975 to study acoustic gui-tar. He experiments with open chord systems (generally in C) and composes new tunes in classical or flamenco style, inspired by Sardinian traditional music.

⊙ **Meridies**
Amiata, Italy

This 1998 masterpiece showcases De Rosas' extraordinary finger-picking style. It alternates between soft ballads

("Transumanza", "Reina Eleonora"), lullabies ("Ninna Nanna") and Sardinian dances ("Cannonau", "Kandelera"), which really capture the ambience of the island. Guests include Totore Chessa (organetto), Rossella Faa, Andrea Parodi (vocals) and the ubiquitous Gavino Murgia on traditional instruments.

Enzo Favata

Enzo Favata began on the jazz circuit, but gradually became interested in traditional forms. He reworks these in a very personal way, often tingeing them with Indian, Mediterranean and Latin influences. His eclectic produc-tions include film soundtracks and an excellent collabora-tion with *bandoneónista* Dino Saluzzi.

⊙ **Made in Sardinia**
CCn'C, Germany

This is the natural sequel to his "Voyage en Sardaigne" project, with elements of Sardinian tradition blending with jazz struc-tures. It features the voices of Tenores di Bitti and Cuncordu di Castelsardo, and the launeddas of Giuseppe Orru.

Elena Ledda

Elena Ledda is the most expressive voice of the new Sardinian tradition. Born in Selargius, near Cagliari, in 1959, she toured Europe extensively following a period with her first band Suonofficina. She has also performed with artists such as Noa, Andreas Vollenweider, Antonio Placer, Riccardo Tesi and Paolo Fresu.

★ Amargura
Marocco Music, Italy

Ledda's 2005 album – produced by Neapolitan violinist Lino Cannavaciuolo – marks a departure from her previous work, and confirms her extraordinary versatility and vocal mastery. Of her usual collaborators, only Mauro Palmas can be heard here. With their lyrics in Sardinian, the songs include a version of "Nights in White Satin" and "Tre Madri", a classic song by Italy's legendary singer-songwriter, Fabrizio de André.

Andrea Parodi

Born in Liguria, but a true Sardinian thoroughbred, Andrea Parodi was the most popular voice of ethno-rock band Tazenda during the 1990s. After leaving the band, he followed his own singular path, touching upon the popular music of the Mediterranean basin and the Arab and African worlds, and collaborating with artists with different musical tendencies, including Al di Meola, Noa and Mauro Pagani. He died in 2006.

⊙ Abacada
Vandle 99, Italy

Parodi's solo album clearly shows his interest in the popular music of various countries, and includes adaptations of Greek and African songs into Sardinian. A versatile singer, he delivers everything from religious anthems ("Stabat Mater") to delicate ballads ("Astrolicamus"). This also features the Pugliese vocal quartet Faraualla and Gavino Murgia on launneddas.

Tenores di Bitti

This historic quartet – with more than thirty years of experience – have taken their unique tenores style from their home town of Bitti all over the world. The present line-up still includes two original members. The group have recorded on the Real World, Swiss Amori and Felmay labels.

★ Caminos de Pache
Felmay, Italia

The quartet chose the title, which means "Paths of Peace", for their 2005 CD feeling it was very representative of the times. The album shows their extreme mastery of their genre and their repertoire and, for the first time, features not just their voices, but also the organetto, played by Totore Chessa, and the launeddas, played by Luigi Lai.

Tenores e Cuncordu di Orosei

Direct heirs of the Confraternita di Santa Croce chorus, which was formed in 1978, this group comes from a town on Sardinia's east coast. They perform a rich and original panoply of religious and secular songs.

⊙ Colla Voche
Winter & Winter, Germany

Ten tracks recorded in the church of San Pietro di Galtellì, ranging from strictly religious themes to traditional dance tracks, where the sound of the additional instruments is carefully balanced and never invasive. The voices of the quartet are accompanied by the cello of Ernst Reijseger and the percussion of Alan "Gunga" Purves.

PLAYLIST
Sardinia

1 AVE MARIA Maria Carta from *Paradiso in Re*
The most important song in Sardinia's religious repertoire performed by the island's most representative voice accompanied only by an organ.

2 INGHIRIOS Andrea Parodi from *Abacada*
Based on the rhythm of traditional Sardinian dance, this features the typical instruments, plus the accordion, percussion and Elena Ledda's vocals.

3 DILLU Tenores de Orosei from *Amore Profundhu*
Led by the crystalline vocal timbre of Patrizio Mura, this song accompanies one of the oldest dance traditions of the northeastern area of Baronia.

4 KANDELERA Marino De Rosas from *Meridies*
The most refined and original guitarist on the Sardinian scene in a unique and personal recreation of traditional island motifs.

5 FILUGNANA Elena Ledda from *Sardegna: Antologia della Musica Sarda Antica e Moderna*
The most sensitive and ductile voice of the new tradition performs a novel interpretation of the music of Gallura, in the north of Sardinia.

6 ITE M'IMPORTA SA VIDA Tenores di Bitti from *Caminos de Pache*
A classic example of the *ballu lestru*; the perfect mix of voices to accompany the popular dance known as the *ballo tondo*.

7 BANDERAS Cordas et Cannas from *Sardegna: Antologia della Musica Sarda Antica e Moderna*
A good vocal mix with a strong tenores tendency and a rhythmic pulse provide the base for this hymn to the Sardinian regional flag.

8 FIORASSIU IN LA Luigi Lai from *Sardegna: Antologia della Musica Sarda Antica e Moderna*
Hear the extraordinary symphonic effect of the launeddas as performed by an unsurpassable master in an awesome *ballo sardo*.

Scotland

braver and braver

Karine Polwart

Time was when Scottish music seemed inextricably strangled by its own clichés. Hoary old tartan images of pipe bands, kilted country dancers and sedate parlour room singers died hard, so the inventive, vital and thoroughly modern edge to the nation's music comes as something of a revelation. Colin Irwin and Pete Heywood chart its development.

The end of the twentieth century was a watershed for Scotland with the introduction of its first parliament for nearly 300 years focusing minds on national identity and indigenous culture. There was an explosion of roots and dance music bands in the 1980s and 1990s: a younger crop of musicians ready, willing and able to use the passion and drive of the Scottish tradition to make a very different kind of dance culture.

Far from destroying the old traditions, it has helped rejuvenate Scottish music into a proud, vibrant force at last free of the old hang-ups and baggage of the past. The telling songs of **Brian McNeil**, the still potent voice of **Dick Gaughan**, the new contemporary sound of **Karine Polwart** and the flotilla of bands such as **Capercaillie**, **Shooglenifty** and enduring veterans the **Battlefield Band** have all given Scotland a strong sense of itself again. Indeed, with a rich grass roots scene and thriving sessions to be found in Glasgow, Edinburgh and many points beyond, it might be said to be the envy of the rest of Britain.

The Celtic Folk Band Arrives

As in much of northern Europe, the story of Scotland's roots scene begins amid the **"folk revival"** of the 1960s – a time when folk song and traditional music engaged people who did not have strong family links with an ongoing tradition. For many in Scotland, traditional music had skipped a generation and they had to make a conscious effort to learn about it. At first, the main influences were largely American – skiffle music and singers such as Pete Seeger – but soon musicians started to look to their own traditions, taking inspiration from the Gaelic songs of **Cathy-Ann McPhee**, then still current in rural outposts, or the old **travelling singers**: the **Stewarts of Blairgowrie**, **Isla Cameron**, **Lizzie Higgins**, and the greatest of them all, Lizzie's mother, **Jeannie Robertson**.

On the instrumental front, there were fewer clear role models, despite the continued presence of a great many people playing in **Scottish dance bands**, **pipe bands** and **Strathspey and Reel Societies** (fiddle orchestras). In the 1960s the most inspiring instrumental folk music was coming out of Ireland and the recorded repertoire of bands like The Chieftains became the core of many a pub session in Scotland. Even in the early 1970s, folk fiddle players were rare in Scotland, although **Aly Bain** made a huge impression when he came down from Shetland and soon after Shetland reels started to creep into the general folk repertoire.

The Scots have always had a proud dance tradition, reflected by the popularity of old school bands

Capercaillie

like **Bob Smith's Ideal Band** (a 1930s outfit who became a bit of a cult after a 1977 Topic collection of reissues), **Jim Cameron**'s band of the 1940s and, towering above them all, the patron saint of Scottish dance music, the lion of the accordion, **Jimmy Shand**. He was often lumbered with the damaging tartan'n'heather image of Scots music but in truth Shand was a brilliant traditional musician who brought many fine tunes to the table.

It still took a lot of work by vibrant young musicians with long hair to overturn the twee Scots music stereotype repeatedly exacerbated by patronising national television coverage. Even those who emerged from the early folk revival with a good understanding of folk song – the likes of **Robin Hall & Jimmie MacGregor** and **The Corries** – were moulded by radio and TV into caricatures of themselves. History doesn't look too kindly on them, though in the 1960s Roy Williamson, one half of The Corries, did write "Flower Of Scotland", a song commemorating Robert the Bruce's triumph at the Battle of Bannockburn in 1314 which is now Scotland's unofficial national anthem.

And then, in the 1970s, inspired by the example of Irish bands like Planxty and the Bothy Band, a flood of young Scots emerged to wrench away the cobwebs and take the music kicking and screaming into a new era. **The Clutha** were one of the first and most influential, particularly when **Jimmy Anderson** introduced a set of chamber pipes into the line-up. A pipemaker as well as an expert player, he invented a set of pipes to be played in the key of D, which made them much quieter than the highland pipes – a vital requisite for the pipes to be seriously incorporated as a band instrument. It opened the way for the country's national instrument – not that bagpipes are in any way exclusive to Scotland – to be incorporated into contemporary music, completely changing the outlook of both Scottish music and of bagpipes themselves.

Pibroch: Scots Pipes

Even though **bagpipes** are synonymous with Scotland, they were once to be found right across Europe. Bagpipes seem to have made their appearance in their Scotland around the fifteenth century, and over the next hundred years or so they took on several forms, including quieter varieties (small pipes) – both bellows and mouth blown – which allowed a diversity of playing styles.

The highland bagpipe form known as **pibroch** (*piobaireachd* in Gaelic) evolved around this time, created by clan pipers for military, gathering, lamenting and marching purposes. Legend among the clan pipers of this era were the **MacCrimmons** (they of the famous "MacCrimmon's Lament", composed during the Jacobite rebellion), although they were but one of several important piping clans, among which were the MacArthurs, MacKays and MacDonalds, and others. In the seventeenth and eighteenth centuries, through the influence of the British army, reels and strathspeys joined the repertoire and a tradition of military pipe bands emerged. After World War II they were joined by civilian bands, alongside whom developed a network of piping competitions.

The bagpipe tradition has continued uninterrupted, although for much of this century under the domination of the military and the folklorists Piobaireachd Society. Recently, however, a number of Scottish musicians revived the pipes in new and innovative forms. Following the lead of Clutha, The Boys of the Lough and The Whistlebinkies, a new wave of young bands began to feature pipers, notably **Alba** with the then-teenage **Alan McLeod**, the **Battlefield Band**, whose arrangements involved the beautifully measured piping of **Duncan McGillivray**, and **Ossian** with **Iain MacDonald**. These players redefined the boundaries of pipe music using notes and finger movements outside of the traditional range. They also showed the influence of Irish Uillean pipe players (particu-

Simon Hollington

Battlefield Band

SCOTLAND

363

larly Paddy Keenan of the Bothy Band) and Cape Breton styles which many claim is the original, pre-military Scottish style.

Alongside all this came a revived interest in traditional piping, and in particular the strathspeys, slow airs and reels, which had tended to get submerged beneath the familiar military territory of marches and laments. The century's great bagpipe players, notably **John Burgess**, received a belated wider exposure. His legacy includes a masterful album and a renowned teaching career to ensure that the old piping tradition marches proudly into the next century.

Folk Song and the Club Scene

Whilst the folk bands were starting to catch up on the Irish and integrating bagpipes, folk song was also flourishing. The song tradition in Scotland is one of the strongest in Europe and in all areas of the country there were pockets of great singers and characters. In the 1960s the common ground was the folk club network and the various festivals dotted around the country.

The great modern pioneer of Scots folk song, and a man who it is perhaps no exaggeration to say rescued the whole British tradition, was the great singer and songwriter **Ewan MacColl**. He recorded the seminal *Scottish Popular Ballads* in 1956, and founded the first folk club in Britain. Another of the building blocks of the 1960s folk revival were the Aberdeen group **The Gaugers**. Song was at the heart of this group – Tam Speirs, Arthur Watson and Peter Hall were all good singers – though they were also innovative in using instrumentation (fiddle, concertina and whistle) without a guitar or other rhythm instrument to tie the sound together.

Other significant Scots groups on the 1960s scene included the **Ian Campbell Folk Group**, Birmingham-based but largely Scots in character (which included future Fairports Dave Swarbrick and Dave Pegg, as well as Ian's sons, Aly and Robin, who went on to form UB40).

Other more adventurous experiments grew out of the folk and acoustic club scene in mid-1960s Glasgow and Edinburgh. It was at Clive's Incredible Folk Club, in Glasgow that **The Incredible String Band** made their debut, led by **Mike Heron** and **Robin Williamson**. They took an unfashionable glance back into their own past on the one hand, while plunging headlong into psychedelia and other uncharted areas on the other. Their success broke down significant barriers, both in and out of

Scotland, and in their wake came a succession of Scottish folk-rock crossover musicians. Glasgow's **Bert Jansch** not only set a new template for young guitarists, but launched folk supergroup **Pentangle** with Jacqui McShee, John Renbourn and Danny Thompson. Meanwhile, a more traditional Scottish sound was promoted by the likes of **Archie, Ray and Cilla Fisher**, who sang new and traditional ballads, individually and together.

The great figure to emerge from this time, however, was the singer and guitarist **Dick Gaughan**. He started out in the Edinburgh folk club scene with an impenetrable accent, a deep belief in the socialist commitments of traditional song, and a guitar technique that had old masters of the art hanging on to the edge of their seats. For a couple of years in the early 1970s, he played with Aly Bain in The Boys of the Lough, knocking out fiery versions of traditional Celtic material. Gaughan became frustrated, however, by the limitations of a primarily instrumental (and fiddle-dominated) group and subsequently formed **Five Hand Reel**. Playing Scots-Irish traditional material, they might have become the greatest folk-rock band of them all if they hadn't just missed the Fairport/Steeleye Span boat.

Leaving to pursue an independent career, Gaughan became a fixture on the folk circuit and made a series of albums exploring Scots and Irish traditional music and re-interpreting the material for guitar. His *Handful Of Earth* (1981) was perhaps the single best solo folk album of the decade, a record of stunning intensity with enough contemporary relevance and historical belief to grip all generations of music fans. And though sparing in his output, and modest about his value in the genre, he's also written some fine songs too.

Crucial contributions to folk song came, too, from two giants of the Scottish folk scene who were probably more appreciated throughout Europe than at home – the late **Hamish Imlach** and **Alex Campbell** – and from **song collectors** and academics such as **Norman Buchan**, with his hugely influential songbook, *101 Scottish Songs*, and **Peter Hall**, with *The Scottish Folksinger*.

Gaelic Rocking and Fusions

Scottish music took an unexpected twist in 1978 with the low-key release of an album called *Play Gaelic*. It was made by a little-known ceilidh group called **Runrig**, who took their name from the old Scottish oil field system of agriculture, and worked primarily in the backwaters of the highlands and islands. The thing, though, that stopped people in their tracks was the fact that they were writing original material in Gaelic. This was the first time any serious Scottish working band had achieved any sort of attention with Gaelic material, although Ossian were touching on it around a similar time, as were Nah-Oganaich.

Runrig went on to unprecedented heights, appearing in front of rock audiences at concert halls all over the world, including a memorable show (and bestselling video) at Loch Lomond. Their Gaelic input became marginal in time, but they started a whole new ball rolling, adopting accordions and bagpipes, ever sharper arrangements, electric instruments, full-blown rock styles, surviving the inevitable personnel changes and the continuous carping of critics accusing them of selling out with every new market conquered. They even made a concept album, *Recovery*, which

related the history of the Gael in one collection, provoking unprecedented interest in the Gaelic language after years of it being regarded in Scotland as moribund and defunct.

They weren't alone. **Karen Matheson** of Oban has consistently sung Gaelic material with **Capercaillie**, mostly songs learned in childhood from her grandmother, a MacNeil from the isle of Barra in the Outer Hebrides. Apparently her grandma was reluctant to sing her the songs and bewildered that Karen wanted to learn them, after years of being conditioned to assume that the modern world had no interest in such old traditions.

Mixing traditional material with the contemporary songs of **Donald Shaw**, Capercaillie achieved startling success, providing the music to the Liam Neeson movie *Rob Roy* and a series of TV programmes about Scottish heritage and inspiring one of the narrators, Sean Connery, to describe

The Battle Goes On...

Plenty of fine bands have served Scots music well over the last thirty or so years – Silly Wizard, Tannahill Weavers, Ossian, Boys of the Lough, Easy Club, Capercaillie, Jock Tamson's Bairns. But surely none has been as enduring, consistent and resilient, or produced so many quality musicians, as the **Battlefield Band**.

Formed by four students who named themselves after a Glasgow suburb, they set out to do for Scots music what the Bothy Band had done for Irish music: to drag it into a modern context and appeal to their own generation. Over thirty years later it's fair to say they've achieved that and a whole lot more. Never afraid to try new things, they've always blended instrumental accomplishment with bold interpretations of traditional material and contemporary songs too.

The one constant has been **Alan Reid**, but in the early years his main co-conspirator was **Brian McNeil**, who's subsequently written some of the most potent songs ever penned about Scotland (several of them recorded by **Dick Gaughan**) and also written several books. But apart from their own vast catalogue of outstanding recordings, the Batties – as they're rather cutely nicknamed – have almost been an academy for leading Scottish musicians and singers. Perhaps the most celebrated graduate has been **John McCusker**, who joined the band as an unknown seventeen-year-old schoolboy and left a decade later as one of Scotland's most gifted fiddle players. He subsequently went on to make a couple of fine solo instrumental albums and become the arranger and producer of one of England's best-loved singers, **Kate Rusby**.

McCusker seemed impossible to replace, but the Batties discovered another teenage fiddle prodigy, **Alasdair White,** from the Isle of Lewis, who's steadily building a reputation that may yet rival McCusker himself. Others who have been through the Battlefield's ranks include award-winning bagpiper **Duncan McGillivray**, Kentigern duo **Jim and Sylvia Barnes** and even a Scotsman raised in the northeast of England, **Alistair Russell**.

Tragedy struck in 2001 with the death from cancer of their hugely popular singer/guitarist/songwriter **Davy Steele** – subject of Kate Rusby's best contemporary composition "Who Will Sing Me Lullabies?" If there was ever a point when the very existence of this Scottish institution was under threat, then this was it. But urged on by Davy himself before he died, the band decided to continue, and into the breach stepped one of Scotland's finest young singers, **Karine Polwart**. She had already shown her superb vocal credentials with the groups **Malinky** and **McAlias** and she helped Battlefield through their crisis before she too flew the nest to embark on a solo career. For Battlefield it was business as usual, re-recruiting one of their old boys, **Pat Kilbride**, alongside Alan Reid, **Alasdair White** and the man with the longest beard in the Western world, the American **Mike Katz**, playing highland bagpipes. They march remorselessly on under the banner "Moving forward with Scotland's past". It just wouldn't seem right without them.

Matheson's voice as "surely touched by the hand of God". Their commercial success reached a peak with their *Delirium* album in 1991 which topped 100,000 sales and produced the first Gaelic language hit single, "Coisich A Ruin". The band Runrig were enjoying mass success around the same time: their *Wonderful* album reached number two in the album charts and they followed Capercaillie into the singles chart with a Gaelic hit single "An Ubhal As Airde".

Capercaillie went on to push the boat out at the other end of the scale, boldly attempting to push Scots music into new territories, embracing the brave new world of beats, samples and modern technology in the late 1990s. It wasn't entirely successful but it reflected a sea change in Scots folk music, accentuated by the band's further embracing of world music, wonderfully demonstrated on "Inexile", which integrated the sumptuous vocals of Equatorial Guinean duo Hijas del Sol into their Scots sound on the landmark album *Beautiful Wasteland*.

Martin Swan's **Mouth Music** have also been constantly innovative over a series of different line-ups and ever challenging approaches to Scottish music. Initially the band featured the ethereal vocals of **Talitha MacKenzie** and performed in a style that was tagged "Gaelic-Afro-pop". It later featured other notable singers such as Jackie Joyce and Ishbel McCaskill.

The revival of interest in the Gaelic language is not without its critics – some suggest it's mere affectation, learned phonetically without regard for the people who used it as a first language. Awareness of Scottish heritage, however, has spread into other areas of the musical psyche. The classic Scots bands like Silly Wizard, Tannahill Weavers and, especially, Battlefield Band (see box) fostered a broader awareness of the richness of the Scottish tradition, which seeped into the mainstream. If bands like Del Amitri, Big Country and Simple Minds were identifiable with a Caledonian mindset, **The Proclaimers** wore it like a badge. It was in the 1980s that Craig and Charlie Reid first emerged with their close harmonies and a geeky image, but the most significant thing about their debut hits was the pronounced Scots accents with which they sang. Such a conscious display of identity – underlined by the second album *Sunshine On Leith* – had scarcely been seen before and is surely an important factor in their longevity and their long-term heroic status. **Jackie Leven**, too, emerged from the ruins of post-punk band Doll By Doll to exorcise his own demons and embark on a solo career drawing heavily on his Celtic roots.

Those roots have never been far, either, from the work of **Mike Scott**, who took his band The Waterboys into an unexpected rootsy direction at a point when they seemed on the verge of becoming the next U2-type stadium band and, after becoming infatuated with Irish music, returned to his own Scottish heritage for a couple of well-received solo albums in the late 1990s. Meanwhile, the maverick singer songwriter **Rory McLeod** investigated his Scots background more deeply following his marital, and occasional gigging, partnership with the exquisite Orkney singer **Aimee Leonard** (former singer with Anam).

The relationship between national identity and music has never been as prominent in Scotland as in Ireland but it's more obvious than it used to be. **Dougie MacLean**, once a Tannahill Weaver, has regularly written songs about the emotional pull of his homeland, most enduringly on "Caledonia", another alternative national anthem. Yet, like Ireland, emigration has been a constant feature of Scottish history, and the music has been sustained passionately in unlikely corners of the world. **Nova Scotia** has sent a thrilling interpretation of the music back home to Scotland through the art of various brilliant young Cape Bretons, notably extrovert dancing fiddle players such as **Ashley McIsaac** and **Natalie McMaster**, teenage band **The Cottars** and Gaelic singer **Mary Jane Lamond**, whose family travelled from Skye to Cape Breton in the 1820s and kept the music close to them.

The lively session scenes in Edinburgh and Glasgow and the proliferation of fine, progressive young bands has been a further testament to the richness of Scots music. **Shooglenifty** have inventively blended a strong traditional base with a dance music-influenced rhythmic approach, while bands like **Peatbog Faeries** from the Isle of Skye, **Deaf Shepherd** and **Back of the Moon** have continued to take the music forward. The Orkney sisters **Jennifer and Hazel Wrigley**, on fiddle and guitar respectively, have produced some stirring, atmosperic compositions inspired by the landscapes and lifestyle around them.

Eddi Reader, once the voice of Fairground Attraction, went deep into the Scottish psyche to magnificent effect with her 2004 album of Robbie Burns songs, while **Karine Polwart** established herself as a singer-songwriter *par excellence* with her *Faultlines* album, after leaving the band Malinky. Scotland's *Living Tradition* magazine thrives and labels like **Greentrax** and **Iona** offer a willing outlet for the music. A plethora of vibrant young musicians seem to have been emerging from all corners of Scotland to light the flame anew for a fresh generation. Former Young Scottish Traditional Musician of the Year **Emily Smith**, for one; breathtaking Shetland fiddler **Chris Stout** for another. **Julie Fowlis** from North Uist has even given a glamorous image to ancient traditions of dancing, piping and Gaelic singing.

The spillover from rock has continued into a new generation with the emergence of the Glaswegian singer and guitarist **Alasdair Roberts**. He has proved himself a mesmerizing interpreter of murder ballads under the American patronage of cult figure Will Oldham, while also demonstrating a lighter touch on his own recent compositions. **James Yorkston** sings gentle, faintly spiritual songs and Fife's **Kenny Anderson** seems to have invented his own organic Scottish folk-rock hybrid under his alter-ego of **King Creosote**. Kenneth McKellar used to sing "Scotland The Brave", but it seems Scotland is growing braver and braver…

Julie Fowlis

The Unsung Hero

You don't go far into Scottish music without doffing your cap to **Hamish Henderson**. Whatever strand of Scots traditional music may be played today, most of it in some way will lead you back to the door of this extraordinary, much-loved and widely respected figure. A man who passed the selection process and all the formal niceties to be deemed worthy of winning an MBE for his contribution to Scottish culture … only to turn it down at the eleventh hour.

Born in Blairgowrie, Perthshire, Henderson contributed to the national culture on so many different levels – he was a poet, folklorist, songwriter, singer, collector and essentially the father of the Scottish folk music revival. In World War II he served with the 51st Highland Division in North Africa and worked with the Partisans in Italy. He returned to Scotland a war hero – and with plenty of material to inspire his writing. Songs such as "The 51st Highland Division's Farewell To Sicily" and "D-Day Dodgers" – set to the tune of "Lili Marleen" – became classics, while his book of war poetry *Elegies For The Dead In Cyrenaica* described his experiences in the Battle of El Alamein.

He attributed his interest in song collecting to his mother, a nurse who sang around the house in Gaelic, French and English, and instilled in him the unshakeable belief that songs should always be learned orally rather than through books or records. In later years he insisted that if someone wanted to learn one of his songs they must do it through the oral tradition, refusing permission for them to record it but patiently singing it however many times it took for them to remember it. He was a passionate advocate of the living tradition of Scots music and effectively "discovered" many great traditional singers like the Border Shepherd **Willie Scott** and a whole host of seminal travelling singers, most famously **Jeannie Robertson**, **Flora McNeil** and the **Stewarts of Blairgowrie**. He'd accompanied the American collector **Alan Lomax** on a field research trip in Scotland during the early 1950s, heard the great songs and singers in danger of being lost and taken on the role of bringing them to a wider public. In 1951 he established the **School of Scottish Studies** at Edinburgh University and spent the rest of his life working for the good of Scottish music.

Perhaps the finest song he ever wrote was "Freedom Come All Ye". Memorably covered by **Dick Gaughan**, it was once seriously touted as the Scottish national anthem, and Henderson was a passionate champion of the underdog and a campaigner for home rule. Yet for someone who garnered such respect and wielded such influence, his fame seems oddly muted. "He was our most important collector of folk songs yet the bulk of his work was for a university department and lies in an archive, unseen and unheard by most of the public," said Gaughan.

He died in March, 2002 at the age of 82 and left a vital legacy. But it's a shame the great Scots public remain almost wholly unaware of what he did.

Hardlands and Highlands

The death of **Martyn Bennett** at the age of 33 in 2005 robbed Scotland of perhaps its most innovative and exciting young talent. Born to Scottish parents in the Gaelic-speaking Cordroy Valley in Newfoundland, Martyn was imbued with a sense of tradition from day one. His mother Margaret brought him to live on the Isle of Mull and introduced him to the music and lifestyle of the travelling community.

A child prodigy, he mastered the bagpipes at 12, raising eyebrows at folk festivals in his early teens and winning a scholarship to the classically orientated Edinburgh Music School, where he studied violin and piano. From there he moved on to the Royal Scottish Academy of Music and Drama in Glasgow, by which time he was already balancing two apparently alien cultures, playing classical violin in a symphony orchestra by day and driving fiddle in informal traditional music pub sessions by night. In the summer of 1990 he also became captivated by the rave scene and the pounding dance beats embraced by clubbers. When out busking one day, finding himself drowned out by someone's beatbox belting out techno music, he instinctively played along with it. It triggered the idea that, far from incompatible, traditional dance tunes would work very well in company with the dance music of the rave culture.

Martyn Bennett

It set him off on an amazing musical journey, marrying the very purist Scottish instrumental tradition to a fiercely modern techno context. His debut, low-profile eponymous album was released in 1996 and by the time he released his second – the breathtaking *Bothy Culture* – a couple of years later, Bennett was already an iconic figure. With his baby face, flailing dreadlocks and dynamic piping and fiddle playing over the keyboards, sampler and mixing desk, he quickly attracted attention way beyond the confines of the folk music fraternity. He sent the crowds outside Edinburgh Castle delirious when he brought in the New Year at the Hogmanay celebrations and Sean Connery and Ewan McGregor were among those who danced on stage with him when he played at the opening of the 1998 World Cup in Paris the night before Scotland played Brazil.

His avowed intention was to introduce young Scots audiences to the beauty and wonder of their own tradition, and to some degree it galled him that he failed to achieve this. But he did move the music forward by several leaps – whether recording the great Gaelic poet **Sorley Maclean** reciting his classic "Hallaig" shortly before he died or, with his wife Kirsten, taking a live band Cuillin on the road to rock the masses. Moving to Mull, he teamed up with kindred spirit **Martin Low** and hurtled even further into the future with the furiously intense *Hardland* album, unforgettably launched with a headlining show still talked of as one of the loudest – and best – sets at the Cambridge Folk Festival.

He seemed set finally to break through into the mainstream, but weeks after that Cambridge show he was diagnosed with Hodgkin's lymphoma. Having already overcome a brush with testicular cancer in his early 20s, he fought it stoically and between operations, radiotherapy and chemo programmes he still managed two more remarkable albums. *Glen Lyon* set the singing of his mother Margaret Bennett against the natural sounds and rhythms of the Isle Of Skye, but his last one *Grit* was probably the most remarkable of all. Too ill to play any more himself in 2003, he destroyed all his instruments in a rage of frustration, but still summoned the energy and desire to sample the music of great travelling singers like **Jeannie Robertson** and **Lizzie Higgins** who'd entranced him in his childhood and surround them with his characteristic box of beats and techno tricks.

Martyn Bennett gave plenty but had plenty more to give – that's the bitterest pill of all.

⊙ **A'The Bairns O'Adam: The Hamish Henderson Tribute Album**
Greentrax, UK
An emotive tribute album to the legendary Hamish Henderson. Many leading Scots artists, including Dick Gaughan, The Corries, Gordeanna McCulloch, The Laggan and Jim Reid perform Henderson's songs and poetry and Hamish himself is included singing his classic "51st Highland Division's Farewell To Sicily".

⊙ **Future Sound of Gaeldom**
Survival, UK
Intelligent compilation showcasing bands and artists who've braved the wrath of the purists by experimenting with electro sounds. Big Sky's excellent "Las Temporadas" shares groove space with Peatbog Faeries, Salsa Celtica, Nusa, Keltik Elektrik, Shooglenifty and Mouth Music.

★ **The Rough Guide to Scottish Music**
World Music Network
A decent snapshot of contemporary Scots music with Battlefield Band, Deaf Shepherd, Salsa Celtica, Malinky, Alasdair Fraser, Croft No 5, Blazin' Fiddles, Boys of the Lough, Heather Heywood, Alison McMorland and Christine Primrose.

★ **The Scottish Tradition Series**
Greentrax, UK
A great achievement from Edinburgh's School of Scottish Studies, this vast and impressive series collects various important aspects of the tradition. Perhaps the best of them is the first CD, *Bothy Ballads*, reflecting the itinerant music and songs played by farmworkers in bothies in late Victorian and Edwardian times. Others in the series include *Music From The Western Isles*, *Waulking Songs*, *Gaelic Psalms From Barra*, *Shetland Fiddle Music* and *The Muckle Sangs*, which features many of the great travelling singers, such as Jeannie Robertson, Lizzie Higgins and the Stewarts of Blairgowrie. Many of Scotland's finest pibroch pipers also pop up on the later volumes.

Bands

Battlefield Band

A band of colossal influence and now a Scottish institution, with important figures like Brian McNeil, John McCusker, Karine Polwart and the late Davy Steele having passed through their ranks. With Alan Reid the one constant, they've survived the various changes and mostly come back stronger each time.

⊙ **Leaving Friday Harbour**
Temple, UK
This represents a peak of sorts for the band with John McCusker's compositions being a particular highlight, along with the immaculate bagpipe playing of Mike Katz and some fine songs to boot.

Ian Campbell Folk Group

The Campbell group emerged in Birmingham, England in the late 1950s out of the ashes of the short-lived skiffle boom, but it was their upbringing in the fishing community of Aberdeen that most shaped their musical and political heart. They were the first UK group to cover Dylan, and Ian Campbell developed into a potent songwriter.

⊙ **The Times They are a'Changing**
Castle, UK
Definitive 62-track double album charting the group's halcyon years between 1964–72, when Fairport Convention's Dave Swarbrick and Dave Pegg were in the line-up. An irrepressibly hearty approach with sturdy trad songs mixed with strong contemporary material of the day.

Capercaillie

Always willing to challenge themselves, Capercaillie – built around the sumptuous vocals of Karen Matheson – have been one of the most consistently successful Scots bands of the last two decades.

★ **Grace and Pride: The Anthology 2004–1984**
Survival, UK
Gaelic songs, techno, Donald Shaw's poppy material, world music, driving instrumentals – the full range of Capercaillie's broad talents.

Jock Tamson's Bairns

A band originally formed in the late 1970s, they won a lot of admirers for their feverish commitment to Scots music at a time when Irish tunes ruled the roost. They split up a few years later, only to come storming back in the late 1990s sounding better than ever.

⊙ **May You Never Lack a Scone**
Greentrax, UK
Rod Paterson's superlative version of "Bogie's Bonnie Belle" is the highlight of an immensely powerful album that includes pipe marches, Gaelic songs, mournful airs and striking strathspeys.

Malinky

A quietly compelling young band, whose role in Scots music may ultimately be overshadowed by the subsequent solo career of their main focal point, Karine Polwart. That would be a shame – far from being merely a vehicle for Polwart, they were a solid, thoughtful unit with enough confidence to move on creatively following her departure in 2005.

⊙ **3 Ravens**
Greentrax, UK
Their second album – and a big leap on from their first, *Last Leaves* – offering subtly inventive arrangements of strong traditional material. Polwart's expressive vocals won the plaudits, but the musicality around her is terrific.

Peatbog Faeries

From the Isle of Skye, the Faeries have been at the forefront of the brave new world of Scots music, using bagpipes, fiddles, whistles and the other instruments of the tradition, but blending it with hip-hop, African music and other global dance styles.

SCOTLAND

⊙ Faerie Stories
Greentrax, UK

Among the varied assortment of infectious grooves and potent rhythms, they also offer a keen wit and sense of humour on tracks like "The Folk Police".

The Tannahill Weavers

One of the bands that kicked off the thunderous "Celticisation" of Scots music in the 1970s, they are still to be found doing it with equal passion and rousing spirit 30 years later, with charismatic frontman Roy Gullane still at the helm.

⊙ Alchemy
Green Linnet, US

Blazing bagpipes from Duncan J. Nicholson, some beautiful Breton tunes and Roy Gullane at the front in epic form – this is the stirring sound of the Tannahills defying the march of time.

Instrumentalists

Aly Bain & Tom Anderson

Anderson is the great legend of Shetland fiddle playing and Aly Bain is his most celebrated student. When Bain moved to the mainland and went on the road with Boys of the Lough to become rightly celebrated as one of Scotland's all-time great fiddle players, he was always quick to pay tribute to the old master going about his business on Shetland. By the time Anderson died in 1991 – and Bain had added the titles of TV presenter and author to his CV – his own iconic status was assured.

★ The Silver Bow
Topic, UK

A historic record pitching Shetland's two most famous folk music sons together. Two other fine fiddle players, Trevor Hunter and Davy Tulloch, are also featured on the CD reissue – a definitive recording of Shetland tunes and playing styles.

John Burgess

Whenever they talk of great highland bagpipers, the name of John Burgess will always loom large. He demonstrates the wild, majestic sound of Scotland at full tilt.

⊙ King of the Highland Pipers
Topic, UK

Strathspeys, hornpipes, reels, marches, piobaireachd … music to stir the blood and fire the soul. Bagpipes at their very best.

Catriona MacDonald

From yet another new generation of brilliant Shetland fiddlers, Catriona MacDonald was, like Aly Bain before her, tutored by the great Tom Anderson in the last years of his life. She won the BBC's Young Tradition Award in 1991, but studied opera singing in London before reverting to her first love playing traditional music, and forming a successful duo with accordionist Ian Lowthian. She's since gone on to become a member of the massed fiddle orchestra, Blazin' Fiddles.

⊙ Bold
Peerie Angel

As the title suggests, Catriona's debut solo album is a proud and occasionally daring take on the tradition, full of intent and ambition. It includes several fine tunes by Ian Lowthian as well as plenty of evidence of her Shetland heritage, while

the brilliant guitarist Tony McManus is among the outstanding supporting cast.

John McCusker

The fiddle prodigy was snapped up as a teenager to travel the world with the Battlefield Band, stayed for ten years, but left to marry Kate Rusby and become an acclaimed solo artist, producer, arranger and composer.

⊙ Goodnight Ginger
Pure, UK

Surrounded by some of the finest musicians of his generation (Michael McGoldrick on flute and pipes, Phil Cunningham on accordion, Ian Carr on guitar), McCusker shows his versatility and real relish for informal ensemble playing.

Ashley McIsaac

Extrovert young fiddle player from Cape Breton who consciously takes liberties with the music applying an approach to the music that sometimes seems to owe as much to punk rock as it does to the Scottish forefathers. A colourful character whose high profile and hi-energy stage performance has introduced the music to a new young audience.

⊙ Hi How Are You
A&M, UK

He's made other albums since this 1995 debut, but this is still the best, genuinely blending his natural flair and exciting playing with an empathy for the music. He can be erratic but he gets it right here.

Tony McManus

A product of the session scenes in Edinburgh and Glasgow, McManus has effectively shifted the humble acoustic guitar towards new horizons with the combination of exquisite technique and vibrantly innovative arrangements, taking tunes of a Celtic/traditional base into the realms of classical, jazz, world music and beyond.

★ Ceol More
Greentrax, UK; Compass, US

This sublime 2002 collection encompasses everything from Robbie Burns to Charles Mingus, Breton, French-Canadian and Scottish tunes to a seventeenth-century Jewish hymn. The results are quietly stunning.

Natalie McMaster

The niece of the great Cape Breton fiddler Buddy McMaster, Natalie has inherited the locality's great inherent tradition of Scots music and – equally influenced by the outside world – taken it somewhere else. In the mid-1990s she toured the world with the Chieftains and, signed to a major label, won much acclaim in Canada and the US and, perhaps most tellingly, in the music's motherland of Scotland as an inspirational fiddler who's not a bad dancer either.

⊙ My Roots are Showing
Warners, US, UK

Jigs, reels, airs and Scott Skinner strathspeys vie for space in McMaster's impressive back-to-basics 2000 collection exploring the purest form of Scots music the émigrés took to Cape Breton. Her uncle Buddy McMaster joins the party.

James Scott Skinner

He was born in 1843 and died in 1927, but Scott Skinner's reputation as one of the key figures in the Scottish tradition remains undiminished and his individual fiddle style still earns him instant recognition as "the strathspey king". He's an iconic figure, said to have written over 600 tunes.

⊙ The Strathspey King
Temple, UK

Originally issued by Topic in the 1970s, this collection of archive recordings, made between 1905 and 1922, has re-emerged on CD to illustrate exactly why Skinner is so revered for his vigorous, highly distinctive bowing technique on this unusual style of dance music. You forgive the imperfect recording quality.

Chris Stout

From Fair Isle, Stout has taken the proud Shetland fiddle tradition into bold new territories.

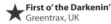 First o' the Darkenin'
Greentrax, UK

An amazingly bold and innovative demonstration of fiddle playing, it prominently features sax and double bass accompaniment on material that includes strong jazz, classical and Scandinavian influences.

Richard Wood

One of the very best of the thrilling new young generation of Celtic fiddle players from Canada, Wood was step-dancing at the age of eight, and learned fiddle soon afterwards, playing a dynamic style that made him a popular performer at festivals. He was just fifteen when he made his first album in 1991.

⊙ The Celtic Touch
Iona, UK

The album that essentially introduced Wood to the land at the source of his music and his impassioned, heartfelt approach to strathspeys, reels, jigs and hornpipes impressed greatly.

Jennifer & Hazel Wrigley

These twins from Orkney were barely in their teens when they first started playing together – Jennifer on fiddle, Hazel on piano and guitar. Their versatility and willingness to incorporate other styles and genres always makes their music fascinating, although they are probably at their best on their own tunes which evocatively mirror their own Orcadian environment.

⊙ Skyran
Geosound, UK

Their fifth album together is atmospheric, yet challenging, Hazel supplying sharp rhythmic foil to Jennifer's unusually rich fiddle technique.

Crossover

Martyn Bennett

Bennett was a tragic figure who, since his death in 2005, has been liberally referred to as a genius for his trailblazing blend of traditional Scots music and modern techno. His albums *Bothy Culture* and *Hardland* are both landmarks for the genre.

Grit
Real World

Bennett's astonishing last album was made while battling with cancer. He didn't play a note. Instead, he sampled some

of the great old singers, such as Jeannie Robertson, Lizzie Higgins and Flora McNeil, and set them in a ferociously modern setting of beats, tape loops and samples. It made perfect sense.

Alasdair Fraser & Natalie Haas

An unusual partnership featuring fiddle player Fraser – most noted for his performances with the trailblazing Skyedance – teamed with American cellist Natalie Haas playing Scottish dance music.

⊙ Fire and Grace
Culburnie Records, UK

The seemingly odd instrumental relationship works surprisingly well, even as they move into ever ambitious territory, including Scandinavian polska. It switches almost imperceptibly between darkness, serenity and joy.

Mouth Music

Formed in the early 1990s, the group named after a specific Gaelic vocal style have blazed a trail for a new and challenging take on Scottish music. With a regularly changing personnel (notable members have included Talitha MacKenzie and Jackie Joyce) they've essentially become a vehicle for the intriguing musical explorations of Martin Swan. The only thing you can be sure of is that each new album will be totally different from the last.

⊙ The Order of Things
Skitteesh, UK

Martin Swan works closely with Martin Furey and Kaela Rowan on this 2005 album which is perhaps the most accessible of Mouth Music's career. Rowan's vocals are sublime, Furey's pipes lift the whole thing and the maze of jazz , pop and traditional themes that Swan weaves around them is surprisingly inviting after the darkness of some of their previous work.

Paul Mounsey

Born in Ayrshire, based in Brazil, Mounsey saw similarities in the two cultures and the rhythms of their music and set about trying to blend them. His mastery of technology helped turn these experiments – started in the early 1990s – into a landmark for Scottish music, often overlooked but significant nevertheless.

⊙ Nahoo 3: Notes From the Republic
Iona, UK

Mounsey's third attempt at an ethnic dance style is his earthiest, and probably his best, as he adopts a more organic approach that adds warmth to the beats.

Karine Polwart

The former Malinky, MacAlias and Battlefield Band singer eventually leaped into contemporary singer-songwriter territory.

⊙ Faultlines
Neon, UK

The beauty of her voice and the unexpected emotional power of her songs have taken her a long way in a short time and this, her first solo album, won numerous awards in 2004 and 2005. She does heartbreak particularly well.

The Proclaimers

Twins Charlie and Craig Reid were dismissed by some as a novelty act when they first emerged wearing geeky specs, singing Everly Brothers harmonies in strong Scots accents. But hits such as "5,000 Miles" and "Letter From America" proved more durable than anybody ever imagined, especially when later used in movies, and they hit a particular chord with Scots. They've survived to enjoy an unexpected career as festival heroes.

⊙ The Best of The Proclaimers
Capitol, UK, US
A solid 20-track collection of the Reids most famous songs, underlining how much their Scots surroundings inspire them, typified by the splendid "Joyful Kilmarnock Blues."

Salsa Celtica

A most peculiar Scots band who do exactly what their name suggests, cleverly pulling off the unlikely marriage of mixing Cuban *charanga* with the sound of the Highlands. Brass, fiddle and percussion explode gloriously in the mix and they've won acclaim all over the world.

⊙ El Agua de la Vida
Greentrax, UK
An irresistible cross-cultural mix that features guest appearances from Cuban singer Ricardo Fernandez and Venezuelan Lino Rocha singing and rapping. A dynamic mix of styles that really shouldn't work, but does. Gloriously.

Shooglenifty

The name is a Scottish word meaning to "shake, agitate and move around" apparently and this is an explorative band that does all of those things, nudging Scots music into ever newer territories. You can't take your eyes off charismatic fiddle player Angus R. Grant while the band have played everywhere from village ceilidhs to the Olympic Games in Sydney.

⊙ The Arms Dealer's Daughter
Compass, US; Shoogle, UK
A subtly daring 2003 album that mixes Scots tunes with the rhythms of the world from Africa to South America in a dazzling hot pot of styles. Celtic music at its most eccentric.

Singers

Julie Fowlis

If Flora MacNeil is the traditional face of Gaelic song, Julie Fowlis from North Uist in the Western Isles is very much the new face. Winner of the Pan-Celtic *sean nos* singing competition in Ireland in 2004, she subsequently became a regular on TV presenting a glamorous new image for the old tradition with her cool voice and prowess on a variety of instruments.

⊙ Mar A Tha Mo Chride – As My Heart Is
Macmeanmna, UK
The first solo album by Fowlis (she's also a member of the band Dochas) is a lovingly presented collection of Gaelic songs and tunes, largely rescued from her own upbringing in the Outer Hebrides, revealing that not only is she a singer of great expression, but a pretty nifty piper too.

Dick Gaughan

Gaughan's passionate singing, inventive guitar work and uncompromising commitment to the power of song has been a beacon of excellence for longer than most people can remember. He had a stint in the folk-rock band Five Hand Reel, but Gaughan has largely pursued his own solo path with almost unblemished conviction.

Handful of Earth
Topic, UK; Philo, US
Originally released in 1981, it still stands not only as Gaughan's masterpiece, it's also one of the best folk albums ever made. Passionate, political, invigorating and provocative, Gaughan sings out of his skin on brilliant material such as "Song For Ireland", "The World Turned Upside Down" and "Worker's Song".

Ewan MacColl

He may have been raised in Salford, but MacColl was as fiercely Scottish as he was fiercely left wing, playing a defining role in the British folk revival. He effectively recognised in folk song the voice of the people and saw it as a political tool, writing a plethora of classic songs that sustains the folk club movement to this day.

★ Black and White
Cooking Vinyl, UK; Green Linnet, US
The title song refers to the Sharpeville Massacre. This collection concentrates on his own songs rather than his interpretations of the tradition, and includes most of his most celebrated songs – "Dirty Old Town", "First Time Ever I Saw Your Face", "The Joy Of Living" and "Manchester Rambler" among them. It lives up to the "definitive" tag on the subtitle.

Dougie MacLean

He first came to attention in the 1970s as a member of Tannahill Weavers, forged a popular partnership with Alan Roberts and then launched a long and rewarding solo career on the back of his rare talent for writing genuinely heartfelt songs about the environment around him, notably one of the finest songs ever written about Scotland, "Caledonia".

⊙ The Dougie MacLean Collection
Putamayo, US
"Caledonia" is here along with most of his other finest works, including "Solid Ground", "Rite Of Passage" and "Ready For The Storm".

Flora MacNeil

From the Hebridean island of Barra, MacNeil's name will always be prominent when the great tradition bearers of Gaelic song are mentioned. As interest in Gaelic culture revived towards the end of the twentieth century, so Flora MacNeil's star rose anew as one of the last living singers to have learnt from the oral tradition.

⊙ Orain Floraidh
Temple, UK
The title means "Songs of Flora" and this is a fine representation of MacNeil's timeless vocal talents. Here Flora mostly singing Gaelic songs learnt in childhood, while her daughter Maggie MacInnes – herself a fine singer and harpist – accompanies her.

Eddi Reader

From the "wrong side" of Glasgow, Reader was a session singer (who sang with Eurythmics, among others) before hitting it big as the singer with Fairground Attraction. Their single, "Perfect", hit No 1 all over the world. When they fell apart she had a few polished, poppy solo hits before being drawn into more traditional roots music.

⊙ The Songs of Robert Burns
Rough Trade, UK

Reader's exploration of Scottish roots music reached a summit with this much-acclaimed 2003 album of songs by Scotland's bard. Surrounded by top-notch musicians like Ian Carr, John McCusker, Phil Cunningham and Boo Hewerdine, she brings Burns to life with oceans of passion. And yes, "Auld Lang Syne" is one of the songs included.

Alasdair Roberts

The son of the late Alan Roberts, who at one time forged a successful duo with Dougie MacLean, Alasdair gained a cult following with the band Appendix Out. He came to the attention of maverick American songwriter Will Oldham, who produced the solo albums that took Roberts on a journey into traditional song.

⊙ No Earthly Man
Drag City, US

Stripped down to the bare bones, this 2005 album took Roberts' craft to a new level of intensity as he delivered a series of murder ballads that are all the more gripping for the sparseness of the arrangements. Roberts is a minimalist performer who demands concentration from the listener, but offers provocative rewards in return.

⊙ The Amber Gatherers
Drag City, US

Roberts has a smile on his face and a spring in his step on this full-band album that steps into folk-rock territory. His original songs sound like traditional ballads; "Where Twines the Path" is the most joyous, panoramic and witty celebration of landscape and countryside you may ever hear.

Emily Smith

This stylish and talented young singer, pianist, accordion player and songwriter from Dumfriesshire first came to attention when she won the 2002 Scottish Young Traditional Musician of the Year. She quickly established a devout following with her warm stage show and proved her instrumental mettle working with the likes of John McCusker, Karine Polwart and North Cregg, while she's also a member of the "folk orchestra" Unusual Suspects.

⊙ A Different Life
White Fall, UK

Produced by Joe Rusby, her seductive second album features Brian Finnegan on flute and Jamie McClennan on fiddle and proved this was a star of the new wave that was here to stay. A mix of tunes, traditional song and her own material, songs such as "A Day Like Today", written for her Polish grandmother, marked her out as an exceptional songwriter too.

Sheila Stewart

From a famous family of travelling singers, Sheila is perhaps the last in a line of traditional singers to have learnt the songs orally. A great storyteller and a proud, passionate singer.

⊙ From the Heart of the Tradition
Topic, UK

A definitive 20-track collection of not only a classic travelling singer, but many of the most heart-stopping ballads in the tradition. "Bogie's Bonny Belle", "Twa Brothers", "Glencoe", "The Parting Glass" … all human life is here.

PLAYLIST
Scotland

1 THE WORKER'S SONG Dick Gaughan from *Handful of Earth*
As stirring, passionate and committed a performance as you'll ever hear. It could be about Glaswegian shipyards or chimney sweeps – why would anyone want to listen to fey pop music when there's music as rousing as this around?

2 INEXILE Capercaillie from *Beautiful Wasteland*
This saw the band take a giant leap into techno and multicultural influences in a gorgeous collaboration with the African duo Sibeba.

3 MOVE Martyn Bennett from *Grit*
The soaring voice of Sheila Stewart performing Ewan MacColl's heartbreaking tribute to itinerant Gypsy life, "Moving On Song", meets Bennett's thundering backbeats and bizarre samples, making a frighteningly modern whole.

4 THE JOY OF LIVING Ewan MacColl from *Black and White*
One of MacColl's last songs, effectively seen as his epitaph – a highly moving farewell.

5 WILLIE STEWART Eddi Reader from *The Songs of Robert Burns*
The infectious stand-out track from her impassioned interpretations of Burns material.

6 CALEDONIA Dougie MacLean from *The Dougie MacLean Collection*
A very tender and beautiful love song for Scotland – an alternative national anthem.

7 THE GYPSY LADDIES Jeannie Robertson from *The Muckle Sangs*
One of the greatest travelling singers of them all at the top of her game.

8 51ST HIGHLANDERS FAREWELL TO SICILY Hamish Henderson from *A' The Bairns O'Adam*
A classic song by one of the greatest figures in Scottish music.

9 FAULTINES Karine Polwart from *Faultlines*
An emotive song, immaculately performed by a major talent.

10 HAMNATAING Chris Stout from *First o' the Darkenin'*
A wonderfully warm and pensive instrumental. Stout's fiddle and Fraser Fifield's sax echo each other and intertwine in an unlikely but inspired pairing.

Serbia and Montenegro

heavenly sounds

A brass player at the Guca festival
Jenny Matthews

Over the last decade and a half, musical life in the now independent republics of Serbia and Montenegro (united as the Federal Republic of Yugoslavia, 1992–2003, and the State Union of Serbia and Montenegro, 2003–06) has been played out against a history of oppression, resistance, political assassination, a volatile relationship between state corruption and organized crime, and a series of vicious wars. As a result, most forms of music had a politically charged identity forced upon them. **Kim Burton** reports on the region's distinctive musical styles, including its most famous product, turbofolk.

gainst the turbulent backdrop of the Yugoslav Wars in the 1990s, Serbia and Montenegro's most distinctive, influential and politically charged musical creation was born. This brash variation on commercial dance music is usually known as **turbofolk**. No approach to the region's music can avoid touching on this musical – and political – minefield, but it must also address the area's other unique styles, including etno, brass bands and the sounds of the musically influential Roma community.

The Sound of the Streets

Both turbofolk and its predecessor, *novokomponovana narodna muzika* (**newly composed folk music**), can trace their origins to the folk and popular styles of the former Yugoslavia, as well as further afield to Greece and Turkey. Both have also had such a powerful influence on neighbouring countries (particularly Romania, Bulgaria and Albania) that it makes sense to talk of a single pan-Balkan popular style sharing musical idioms, subject matter and iconography. The name turbofolk is credited to musical satirist **Rambo Amadeus**. He coined the term sardonically, but it was picked up enthusiastically by its followers.

Serbian turbofolk found itself the target of criticisms from both the right-thinking public and musicians working in more serious fields like rock and jazz, and the loaded words flung at it – "corrupted, impure, kitschy and trashy" – betray a moral, not a musical, evaluation. Yet turbofolk is so strongly identified with the hysterically nationalist atmosphere of the 1990s and the Serbian government's role in the Yugoslav Wars that it carries a unique opprobrium. It inspired such rage on the part of some, that singer **Zorica Brunclik**, who had previously been mentioned as a possible Minister of Culture, has said she was confined to her home in 2000 after receiving death threats in the wake of the ousting of Slobodan Milošević.

It's clear that the authorities made use of the music for their own purposes, but many of the performers were happy to go along with that. And, in some respects, the music lent itself to being used in such a way. According to Amadeus: "You can't make the people in the trenches listen to Disciplina Kičme, Wagner or Schnittke … the primitive impulses which drive people into tribal wars can only be woken by primitive music. And that's why, when they needed to, they brought the chavs straight from the tents to the Sava Centar [Belgrade's biggest concert hall]." Amadeus's less than nuanced use of the word "primitive" in itself shows where he positions himself in the Serbian culture wars. It should also be noted that at the time of NATO's aerial bombardment of the country in 1999, the authorities were perfectly capable of mobilizing rock music for their own purposes.

Pop singer **Ceca** is still the queen of turbofolk, and what is true for her can be taken as generally true for the rest of the field. Although turbofolk is a loose genre, its rhythms are influenced by house and techno and its often bombastic backings jumble sampled guitar riffs, trippy synth sounds and heavy basslines behind fairly standard stripped-down Europop melodies. Local influences are restricted to traces of intricate ornamentation, the symbolic presence of a splash of sampled **folk clarinet** or a guest appearance by a Gypsy brass band. Typical irregular rhythms occasionally crop up, as do chromatic turns in the melodies which reflect a more traditional urban sound from the south of Serbia or *sevdalinka* from Bosnia, but the trend is towards Western popular idioms.

Ceca also stands as an examplar for the non-musical aspects of turbofolk: the singers are mainly female, attractive, skimpily clad and unlikely to make much headway without an aspirational video displaying the trappings of ostentatious wealth. Rather too many of these singers (excluding Ceca and her arch-rival **Jelena Karleuša**) suffer from producer's girlfriend syndrome, with the most creative thing about them being the scandals that regularly surface in the entertainment magazines. Indeed, it is usually the producers who have the guiding hand in this music. Singers who are less identikit than the rest include **Dragana Mirković**, **Seka Aleksić** and **Indira Radić**, and of the few male interlopers, **Aca Lukas** and **Saša Matić**.

Blurring the Boundaries

The term turbofolk is used loosely to cover both the harder-edged, synthesizer-based music of the 1990s and 2000s and the less in-your-face **newly composed folk** of the 1970s and 80s. The term **folk-pop** has since come into use as a less pejorative description. The bridge between turbofolk and folk-pop is probably best represented by **Lepa Brena**, who has spent 25 years in the business. The singer from Bosnia and Herzegovina retains elements of newly composed folk in her melodies and vocal style, but sets them over a bouncy pop-rock beat. She was the first to pump up her star quality (and, some say, to distract attention from her vocal shortcomings) with her wardrobe, but she doesn't take herself too seriously – injecting humour into songs like "No-one Kisses like a Bos-

A Gypsy King: Šaban Bajramović

The Yugoslav Roma pantheon of heroes apparently places President Tito at number one and **Šaban Bajramović** at number two, followed by several empty spaces, then Bajramović again at ten. Apocryphal though this story may be, it illustrates just how potent Šaban Bajramović's majestic Balkan Gypsy soul music was.

Born in the southern Serbian city of Niš in 1936, he grew up in extreme poverty, working menial jobs, playing football and singing. Called up for military service in the early 1950s, he went AWOL in search of the girl he loved and was sentenced to five years in prison (spending some of this time in Goli Otok, considered "Tito's gulag"). While others perished in prison, Bajramović thrived, learning to read and write, singing in the orchestra and playing football. Once freed, he sang at *kafanas* (Serbian honky-tonks) and Roma festivities, his talent unmistakable.

In 1964, he released his first record, *Pelno me Sam* (*I Am Imprisoned*). In this original composition, the protagonist begs his mother to get him out of jail so he can see his daughter get married. No one before had expressed the Gypsy experience – or sung lyrics in Romani like, "hey another beating from the police" – and he carried great cultural weight. In the 1960s and 70s, Bajramović was to Balkan Roma what James Brown was to African Americans. Hailed as the King of *Nove Romske Pesme* (New Romani Song), he fronted the **Black Mambas**, had his teeth capped with gold, drank and fought and gambled heavily, missed gigs and embraced chaos, his liquid voice and elegiac songs carrying him forward. Legend has it that, flush with early success, he entered Niš's *mahala* (Roma ghetto) driving a white Mercedes, wearing a white suit and accompanied by two bodyguards – but left after a night of poker without money, Mercedes or bodyguards.

Šaban Bajramović

"Life inspires me to write songs", explained Bajramović. "My inspiration is life because I am a great consumer of life! I've never desired for some fortune in my life, I don't have dreams to become rich, just to live normal." He sat out the disintegration of Yugoslavia in his humble Niš bungalow, breeding pigeons, looking after his grandchildren and occasionally releasing a poorly recorded cassette for the local market. Yet his legend kept growing, and **Goran Bregović** appropriated Bajramović's melodies for his soundtracks to **Emir Kusturica**'s baroque cinematic projections of Balkan life. According to Bajramović, "Kusturica and Bregović turn everything upside down. They show the black side of Gypsy culture. The begging, the stealing. They don't show the Gypsies who go to work in the factory every day, the good ones." Yet he sang the theme for Kusturica's 1997 Gypsy comedy *Black Cat, White Cat* and performed on Bregović's *Songs from Weddings and Funerals* in 2003. Hypocrisy? No, Šaban simply recognized a good payday when it was offered.

In 1999, **Mostar Sevdah Reunion** producer **Dragi Šestić** tracked Bajramović down and produced his exceptional album *A Gypsy Legend*. Western world music stardom beckoned, but – as ever – Bajramović failed to turn up for concerts, preferring to gamble and sing in restaurants for tips. In the early years of the twenty-first century he enjoyed a big Balkan hit when he sang with Croatian salsa band **Cubismo**, and he toured the US in 2004. When the occasion arose, Bajramović remained a singer of wild, soulful abandon. The rest of the time? His pigeons demanded a lot of attention. He died in 2008.

Garth Cartwright

nian" and "Mile Loves Disco". Once a huge star and an almost inescapable presence in the bedrooms of Balkan youth, she is no longer at the peak of her popularity. However, she is still on the road, delighting fans and providing fodder for gossip magazines.

Newly composed folk music dates from before the death of the second Yugoslavia, so its singers and styles stem from all over the region – particularly Bosnia and Herzegovina, where **Sarajevo** was the centre of the music industry. It can be useful to think of it as the Balkan equivalent of Country and Western, with which it shares certain characteristics. These include the use of iconic instruments, such as the **frula** (similar to the penny whistle), accordion and clarinet, a formalized performance practice derived from true folk roots, lyrics obsessed with love and betrayal, huge doses of sentimentality and a largely urban audience with rural origins. Its origins can be traced to **Lepa Lukić**'s massive 1960s hit "Od Izvora dva Putića", with its tricky irregular phrasing and deceptively simple accordion. Lukić recently returned after a long break, with her talents undimmed.

This style ruled the roost in the late 1970s and 80s. There were several variations, with the Bosnian Krajina region being represented by **Bora Drljača** and the Morava-Šumadija area by **Miroslav Ilić**.The king of them all, **Šaban Šaulić**, conquered hearts and minds with brilliant mini-dramas like "Bio sam Piijanac" (I Used to Be a Drunkard). Most of the songs were naïve, sentimental and musically unassuming, but they usually had at least one attractive twist in the melody, harmony or arrangement. Perhaps strangely, it was this idiom rather than turbofolk that was appropriated in the 1990s to fan the flames of war. This frequently amounted to little more than hate speech by performers whose wild-eyed hyper-nationalist songs now sound more like evidence than music.

A number of singers of newly composed folk came from a Rom background, but the style also contained a separate strand of *Ciganska muzika* (**Gypsy music**), which was often sung in Romanes. It boasted such stars as the deep-voiced Ljiljana Petrović (who gained a new lease of life as **Ljiljana Buttler**, after years in exile) and **Vida Pavlović**, whose tragic death in 2005 came all too soon after she began to receive recognition. The greatest of them all was the masterful **Šaban Bajramović**, also no longer with us, who was blessed with astonishing natural talents but little discrimination – in some of his earlier work he and his band seem to be on different planets. His 2001 return to prominence with **Mostar Sevdah Reunion** (MSR) seemed to promise a new, international audience, but he may have missed his chance. Ex-rocker and composer **Goran Bregović** is not Rom, but has used Gypsy music so extensively for his atmospheric film scores and popular **Weddings and Funerals Orchestra** that he can be considered a distant offshoot of

this strain, although his music draws on wider traditions.

Between the 1930s and 60s, several fine singers of traditional songs were employed with the various *narodni orkestri* (**folk groups**) of **Radio Belgrade**. The first and most famous of these groups, led by violinist **Vlastimir Pavlović Carevac**, was formed before World War II and comprised plucked and bowed stringed instruments, plus the accordion. Later bands added the clarinet. MSR's **Ilijaz Delić** divided his time between the radio and singing in restaurants, as did many others who are only remembered by those that heard them at the time. Fortunately, in the late 1990s, the record company attached to Serbian Radio Television started to reissue some of the station's best archive recordings. These include Carevac, plus accomplished singers **Predrag Gojković Cune**, Montenegrin **Ksenija Cicvarić** and **Mara Djordjević**, who all demonstrate the kind of emotional restraint that has gotten lost in recent years. Accordionist and composer **Miodrag Todorović Krnjevac**, who also worked for the radio, deserves a mention as one of the founders of the present-day virtuoso style.

Beyond the Heartland

Vojvodina (with its capital Novi Sad) is an ethnically mixed autonomous province in northeastern Serbia that has a different musical character. *Tamburaški orkestri* (**tamburica orchestras**) of the Croatian model flourish, playing a repertoire of traditional and new songs with arrangements involving complex running counter-melodies, and driving backbeats or sentimental tremolos. **Zvonko Bogdan** is the doyen of all the singers. Vojvodina has also produced some of those working on the fringes of the contemporary etno movement.

Another regional style is found in the northeastern corner of Serbia, in the remote and haunted Vlaška Krajina area. The **Vlachs** speak a language closely related to Romanian, and retain an interesting mixture of customs, some of which are clearly pre-Christian and linked to ancient cults of the forests and the sun and moon. The French label **Ocora** has released an excellent recording of local village music for funerals, weddings and dances, ranging from solo songs, violin duets and bagpipe solos to large groups of low-pitched *frule* and brass bands. Modern **Vlach popular music** bears a strong resemblance to that of Wallachia in southern Romania in its rhythm, harmony and modality. The dance music is energetic and rapid, often in 6/8 time, but it has a melancholic aspect that is more evident in the songs. It's very much a regional music, but it's still worth exploring.

Sounding Brass

Duvački or *trubački orkestri* (**brass bands**) owe their origins to Turkish and Austro-Hungarian military bands, and are now the most popular folk instrumental groups. These bands made up of trumpet/flugelhorn, euphonium, sousaphone, bass and snare drum are sometimes imported into turbofolk as a sort of badge of authenticity. They

Boban Marković

tend to fall into two main groups: the first, from western and central Serbia, are usually ethnic Serbs, amateurs who play a mixture of bouncy two-beat **kolo dance**, folk and traditional songs and patriotic melodies; the second group, from further south around the town of Vranje, are ethnic Roma, professionals whose more complex, syncopated and chromatically inflected repertoire reflects the lingering influence of Turkey in urban music.

Trumpeter **Boban Marković** from the south is the outstanding bandleader of the moment, with his innovative approach, immaculate technique and internationally renowned band. **Fejat Sejdić**'s ensemble, the 2004 winners of the **Dragačevo Festival** at **Guča** run a close second. The late **Bakija Bakić** was one of the masters of the southern Serbian style and his recordings are well worth a listen. None of the bands who play the central Serbian style have attained this level of fame, but **Mića Petrović**, **Milovan Babić** and **Dragan Lazović** are names to remember.

Montenegrin Epics

Although the tradition of the **sung epic** flourished in Albania, Croatia, Bosnia and Herzegovina and Serbia, it has become particularly identified with the barren mountain fastness of Montenegro, where isolation, a patriarchal society and an independent spirit helped it survive. Sung, or rather intoned, in a strained and pinched voice to the accompaniment of a **one-stringed fiddle**, or *gusle*, the poems could run to thousands of lines. They speak of legendary heroes and historical figures and events, the most important being those that make up the cycle about the battle of **Kosovo Polje**, when the Serbian army suffered a catastrophic defeat at the hands of the Ottoman Turks.

Once improvised by the performer imaginatively combining set phrases, the poems are now learnt by heart from nineteenth- and twentieth-century collections, or newly written. The new songs cover diverse, but usually tragic, subjects; a number of the more recent ones deal with the flight of Serb refugees from Kosovo and the March 2004 attacks by Kosovar Albanians on Serb villages and monuments. Readers interested in sung epics should start with Albert B. Lord's *The Singer of Tales* (2000), which includes transcriptions, translations and a CD-ROM with audio and video, but they aren't all from Montenegro.

The Etno Sound

Over the last fifteen years or so, Serbia has seen a separate musical current running alongside the music already discussed. Loosely termed **etno**, it covers a number of different styles, ranging from acapella singing via acoustic instrumentals to songs using synthesizers and electric guitars. The main thing all its exponents have in common is their determination to reclaim and rework traditional music, rescuing it from both the dusty files of the academy and the poisonous nationalism of the 1990s. **Svetlana Stević** was one of the first to revive the singing traditions of the countryside and present them to an urban audience and, together with unique multi-instrumentalist **Darko Macura**, she inspired and encouraged younger musicians and singers in the early days. Stević and Macura's work is well worth seeking out in its own right.

Traditional village music still survives in some families or within the framework of amateur *Kuturno-umetnička društva* (cultural and artistic societies set up during the Communist era to help folk culture survive). Yet, despite these and the festivals at which older people and little children are

Sounds d'Serbique

Most of the etno performers mentioned have appeared on the *Srbija: Sounds Global* series put out by the label attached to **Radio B-92**, one of the pillars of resistance during the Milošević years. The brainchild of impresario, promoter and World Music DJ **Bojan Djordjević**, the series grew out of his alternative **Ring-Ring Festival**. When the audience responded enthusiastically to groups like **Ognjen i Prijatelji**, **Drina**, **Boban Marković**'s band and the stunning (if sometimes long-winded) Vojvodinan violinist **Lajkó Felix**, Djordjević released the first CD in the series.

Several important bands from the etno fringes have also appeared in the series. Of these, two are Rom: the hard-driving **Kal**, led by guitarist **Dragan Ristić** and violinist **Dušan Ristić**, who give a contemporary twist to familiar sounds; and **Olah Vince**'s long-established acoustic **Earth-Wheel-Sky Band**, who have their roots in rock and produce explosive grooves and thrilling solos. Unlike any of these, the remarkable **LaDaABa Orchest**, led by clarinettist **Boris Kovač**, rarely draws on folk forms. With echoes of the ballroom, the circus, European jazz and deformed tango, the mood is one of grim and exhausted nostalgia. Their sound is popular art music in the tradition of experimentalists like Willem Breuker.

Kal

More recently, Djordjević has brought veterans out of retirement, notably violinist **Aleksandar Šišić** whose CD *Magična Violina* marks a spectacular return after more than a decade. The old master remains – at the age of seventy – a master. New discoveries and rediscoveries are surely still to be made, so let's hope *Srbija: Sounds Global* will continue to lead them into the wider world.

dragged on stage to perform their party pieces, demographic shifts and changes in social conditions were inexorably leading to its disappearance. Fortunately, when young musicians began to seek out village music in the 1990s, there were enough older people around who could remember the songs and dances, and share their knowledge.

The women's vocal group **Moba** is probably the least compromising in their dedication to re-creating the original music. They concentrate on mastering and performing vanishing village styles in as unmediated a way as possible. However, since some of this music sounds strange to the Western ear – with its harsh vocal tone and delight in closely stacked dissonances – their sound may take some getting used to. The mostly unaccompanied **Teofilović brothers** do not claim to be returning to untouched roots, but work out their own arrangements from written music. This has earned them criticism in certain quarters,

but the hushed stillness of their performances is utterly magical. The female duo **Drina** (now disbanded) had a somewhat similar approach, although with a tougher sound. One of them, **Svetlana Spajić Latinović**, has since started to move away from a purely regional repertoire, and has worked with a variety of musicians from all over the world.

Belo Platno (which shares members with other etno groups) are all-acoustic, and use folk instruments like the Macedonian *kaval* (end-blown flute) and strummed *tambura* to produce a sense of serene enchantment. They also draw on the Kosovo Serb tradition for much of their material. **Pavle Aksentijević**, who has a magnificent baritone voice, uses a similar line-up for his band, although their rhythmic drive contrasts with Belo Platno's calm. He is a distinguished cantor of medieval Serbian Orthodox chants, music with a sense of timeless rapture. A number of etno performers

Balkan Babylon

It's riotous, trashy, nationalist and chaotic – yet there's nothing like the **Dragačevski Sabor Trubača**, the three-day brass band competition better known as the **Guča Festival**. Held every August in the small town of Guča, south of Belgrade, the festival sees top brass bands from all over the country battling it out for the coveted title of "Golden Trumpet", which may not mean a lot in terms of prize money, but is worth much more in private bookings and reputation. **Boban Marković**, the trumpet master behind Goran Bregović's *Underground* soundtrack, dominated the competition in the 1990s and is now a big name on the world music scene.

Simon Broughton

Balkan brass player

Since its inception in 1963, it's grown from a local celebration of folk music and culture into one of Europe's biggest music festivals. What makes Guča special is that most of the action takes place not on the stages, but on the streets and in the bars and restaurants during the long, drunken evenings. In any café you can find four eight-piece brass bands slugging it out side by side for the customers' attention. The plastic tables buckle under the weight of the girls' frenzied dancing, macho businessmen compete to slap ever bigger notes on the sweaty foreheads of the Roma musicians, the volume increases and the *rakije* keeps on flowing. The combined effect is like a three-day-long adrenaline shot to the head – you stagger home high and hungover with the sound of trumpets ringing in your ears. From a small village happening to Balkan Babylon in forty years – everything that is beautiful and ugly about Serbia is packed into one mind-blowing weekend at the Guča Festival.

Jonathan Walton

have heartfelt links with the Church, which has always served as a repository for ethnic identity.

Bilja Krstić and her group **Bistrik** have gone one step further, using synthesizers to produce haunting and imaginative arrangements of traditional songs. Somewhere in the middle lie **Serboplov**, a promising five-member string band plus clarinet. They have revived kolo dance and the sentimental urban *starogradski* tradition that culminated with Carevac, but reinterpret it to include sometimes surprising twists of harmony. Finally, clarinettist **Ognjen Popović**, the leader of **Ognjen i Prijatelji**, spices up already spicy southern Serbian-Macedonian sounds with touches of jazz and Latin music, and pianist **Sanja Ilić** combines rock moves and folk instruments in his **Balkanika** project.

DISCOGRAPHY Serbia and Montenegro

⊙ **Les Bougies de Paradis**
Ocora, France
This is the only recording of traditional music from the Vlach area of northeastern Serbia that's also relatively easy to get hold of – fortunately it's also still the best.

⊙ **Folk Mega Hitovi 1, 2**
PGP-RTS, Serbia and Montenegro
These two CDs give a good overview of newly composed folk and turbofolk from the 1960s to the 90s, volume one covers the women singers, volume two the men.

⭐ **Golden Brass Summit: Fanfares en Delire**
Network, Germany
A fine compilation from the Dragačevo Festival archive featuring some of the very best brass bands, including Boban Marković and Bakija Bakić, plus guest appearances by singers and instrumental groups.

⊙ **Narodna Kola**
PGP-RTS, Serbia and Montenegro
Bouncy acoustic dances from some of the best players of accordion, violin and frula, including lots of old favourites.

⭐ **Srbija: Sounds Global Vols 1, 2, 3**
B92, Serbia and Montenegro
Compiled by Bojan Djordević, these three volumes tell you everything you need to know about the etno movement, and also point you in the direction of the artists' own CDs.

Dragoslav Pavle Aksentijević

Painter, opposition politician, singer and raconteur, Aksentijević was one of those who, thirty years ago, foreshadowed the current revival. A singer with a magnificent voice and a keen musical intelligence.

⊙ **Antologija Srpske Duhovne Muzike**
Tioli, Serbia and Montenegro
This gripping collection of medieval Orthodox Christian chants has tremendous power and eloquence.

Šaban Bajramović

Bajramović was a legend. Despite a chequered past and an insouciant approach to life, he had one of the finest voices to have ever graced a stage. His phrasing and sly ornamentation of the line transformed even the most suspect songs.

⭐ **A Gypsy Legend**
World Connection, The Netherlands
This was Bajramović's return after years in obscurity. It marks an advance on earlier recordings in its integration of singer and band, and sustains a unified atmosphere throughout.

Belo Platno

A welcome antidote to the relentless party approach of some Serbian music, Belo Platno represent a younger generation and use folk instruments and beautifully focused vocals to create a sense of stillness and contemplation.

⊙ **Muzike Kosova i Metohije, južne Srbije i Makedonije**
ATOS, Serbia and Montenegro
An album of stripped-down arrangements of music from Kosovo, southern Serbia and Macedonia.

Goran Bregović

Once the frontman for the rock band Bijelo Dugme, Goran Bregović was born in Sarajevo, but is now based in Belgrade. He has managed to parlay his film scores into a recording career and vast live shows.

⊙ **Tales and Songs from Weddings and Funerals**
Universal, France
An album of lush and dramatic arrangements, as you would expect from a film composer.

Lepa Brena

An undoubted star, Brena came from the provinces to make her name in the 1980s, and is still packing them in.

⊙ **The Best of Lepa Brena**
Grand, Serbia and Montenegro
This double-CD from 2004 is a fairly exhaustive mining of her career since it began in the early 1980s.

Ksenija Cicvarić

A Montenegrin singer of an earlier generation who worked with the Belgrade radio orchestra, Cicvarić is a straightforward and beautiful performer of urban songs.

⊙ **Pesme Ksenije Cicvarić (The Song Cycle of Ksenija Cicvarić)**
PGP-RTS, Serbia and Montenegro
This is the most easily available and comprehensive collection of her music – but it's all from the radio archives.

Predrag Gojković Cune

One of the giants, he is a classy sweet-toned singer, mostly of arrangements of folkloric material.

⊙ **50 Godina sa Vama (50 Years with You)**
PGP-RTS, Serbia and Montenegro
As this anniversary compilation shows, he's been in the business a long time. There are some great classics here, including very nice selections backed up by tamburaški orkestri.

Mara Djordjević

Born in Romania of Macedonian parents, and raised in Macedonia, Djordjević is one of the stable of radio singers.

⊙ **Pesme sa Kosovo i Metohije (The Song from Kosovo and Metohija)**
PGP-RTS, Serbia and Montenegro
As she made few records, this selection from the Radio Belgrade archives comes as a welcome surprise. Very spare, very controlled singing and arrangements.

Kal

Bandleader Dragan Ristić is not merely an accomplished musician but also a political activist for the Gypsy cause, and in many ways his work with Kal combines both roles. The band display dazzling virtuosity and style in their live shows, and they tour widely.

⊙ **Radio Romanista**
Asphalt Tango, Germany
Brilliant playing and a clean production, with Romany-inflected views of many different styles, a rock attitude, and none of the sentimentality that afflicts much Gypsy music.

Boris Kovač & LaDaABa Orchest

Saxophonist Kovač is as much a philosopher and a poet as he is a musician with a gift for slightly eerie cabaret. He has recorded three albums in which the dismemberment of the former Yugoslavia is evoked in a seductive dance of death, performed by La Danza Apocalypsa Balcanica.

⊙ **The Last Balkan Tango**
Piranha, Germany
Released in 2001, this album (with its decadent George Grosz-style cover) is the first and darkest of Kovač's series of apocalyptic dance albums. It's a masterpiece of catchy and seductive tangos ironically highlighting a human tragedy. The sequels are *Ballads at the End of Time* and *World After History*.

Bilja Krstić & Bistrik Orchestra

Although Krstić had been around for some time, Bistrik didn't get going until 1998, and came to the public's attention with their score for the 2003 film *Zona Zamfirova*.

 Karpoš
Intuition, Germany
The work of Krstić and her group Dragomir Stanojević reached a real maturity in this highly imaginative CD, marked by splendid singing and a richly inventive marriage of the old and the new.

Boban Marković Orkestar

Trumpeter Marković runs a tight band, and has pretty much sewn up the international market with his inventive powerhouse arrangements. (His son Marko looks set to carry on the family tradition.)

⊙ **Srce Cigansko**
X-Produkcijó, Hungary
There are a lot of good Marković recordings available, but this album from his earlier days has a relaxed and easy charm missing from some of the later, more hard-driven, material.

Ceca Ražnatović

A phenomenon and the queen of turbofolk, Ceca is now moving into out-and-out pop and techno remixes with, presumably, an eye on the coming generation.

⊙ **Ceca: The Best Vols 1, 2, 3**
Hi-Fi Centar, Serbia and Montenegro
This widely available compilation contains all of Ceca's hits, from her start in the late 80s with the novokomponovana style through to the big hits from her 2001 album.

Aleksandar Aca Šišić

Another important figure rescued from retirement, virtuoso violinist Aca Šišić is one of the greats.

⊙ **Magična Violina**
B92, Serbia and Montenegro
These beautifully produced dances and song melodies are an echo from an almost vanished world: the sound of self-management.

Braća Teofilovići

The twin Teofilović brothers from southern Serbia take a do-it-yourself approach to their music, with very gentle and simple – yet unexpected – arrangements.

 Čuvari sna
Own label, Serbia and Montenegro
A labour of love, their first CD was entirely unaccompanied. A marvellous recording that became a word-of-mouth success.

PLAYLIST
Serbia and Montenegro

1 CRVENO Ceca from *Ceca: The Best Vols 1, 2, 3*
Cheap sampling, quick and dirty production, but a great turbofolk song.

2 PITAO SAM MALOG PUZA Šaban Bajramović from *A Gypsy Legend*
Gambling man begs a snail for shelter – passionate singing, plus inspired backing from MSR.

3 OD IZVORA DVA PUTIĆA Lepa Lukić from *Folk Mega Hitovi 1*
Striking a perfect balance between old and new – the song that started it all.

4 MARIJO, BELA KUMRIJO Braća Teofilovići from *Čuvari sna*
An emigrants' song powerfully performed with an almost hieratic air. Short and spare, but haunting.

5 OVA BRDA I PUSTE DOLINE Moba from *Srbija: Sounds Global 2*
If you want to hear old-style singing by new-style people, Moba is your best bet.

6 CRNI VOZ Boban Marković from *Scre Cigansko*

All aboard the Black Train! Boban's band are on track, with virtuoso violinist Lajko Felix as a guest.

7 TUZNO VETRI GOROM VIJU Predrag Gojković from *50 Godina sa Vama*
This man could sing the telephone directory and I'd be queuing for tickets – a heartfelt rendition of an almost perfect song.

8 THE STAR FLICKERED Bilja Krstić and Bistrik Orchestra from *Karpoš*
A song from southern Serbia is given the full Bistrik treatment, with a simple tambura opening giving way to a huge orchestral panorama, and Krstić's voice equally at home in either setting.

9 LAJ LAJ Kal from *Radio Romanista*
Perfectly pitched mid-tempo groove, with a lovely melody and gorgeous drifting harmonies.

10 PADURÂ, SORA PADURÂ Dragutin Djurdjević from *Les Bougies du Paradis*
Astonishingly powerful playing and singing on this hypnotic duet from experts from the Vlach country.

Slovenia

beyond polka

Terrafolk in *Terrafolk Production*
Bojan Stepančič

Slovenia has always existed on the fringes of larger political units, whether it was the Austro-Hungarian Empire (until 1918), Yugoslavia (until 1991) or – since 2005 – the European Union. Thus, according to transient political or cultural trends, perception of its geographical position has been shifted from the southeast end of Middle Europe to the Balkans and back. Relatively remote from the centres of state authority, Slovenes have tried to retain their cultural integrity and political raison d'être through language and traditional practices such as music. Katarina Juvančič and Kim Burton explore the old roots, nationalized pop, folk revival and current trends of what is broadly known as Slovenian folk music.

ntil the Second World War Slovenia was predominantly a rural agrarian country with diverse regional types of vernacular music reflecting its unique blend of Alpine, Pannonian and Mediterranean character. Unlike other newly established European socialist states which remained largely isolated on the eastern side of the iron curtain, the Yugoslav federation adopted a relatively liberal outlook, with an open borders policy and a well-developed industrial base.

Slovenian music, too, has been largely influenced by Western styles and genres, going back to pre-war jazz, via 1960s rock through to punk subculture. Subsequently, the avant-rock group **Laibach** initiated a provocative and experimental art collective called Neue Slowenische Kunst (NSK), which played an important role in the Slovenian civil rights movement of the 1980s.

The most distinctly mainstream strand, however, is "national pop music" (**narodnozabavna glasba**); comprising cheerful waltzes and polkas played by accordionists, guitarists, trumpeters and clarinettists in knee-breeches, and romances sung by women in *dirndls*, the popularity of national pop has been unchallenged for over fifty years. Based as it is on more traditional sounds from Slovenia's links with the Alpine region and German-speaking world, it is often mistaken for a purely rural genre, though it was in fact initiated by the urbanized post-war working classes. With its politically

correct lyrics praising simple country life and its rather kitschy sentiments, it was approved by the Communist regime and hence extensively broadcast nationwide. This party music's dominant arrangement and performance style was more or less invented by the **Avsenik brothers** (Slavko and Vilko) and the accordionist **Lojze Slak** in the 1950s. Their bands attained immense popularity at home and in Austria and southern Germany, as well as in Slovenian diasporas across Europe, the US, Argentina and Australia.

In the last few years, a new sub-genre of rejuvenated national pop with synthetic Balkan pop-folk rhythms called **Slovenian turbo folk** has hit the charts and its popularity is still on the rise. **Atomik harmonik** are its leading exponents.

Old Styles and Revivals

The popularity and commercial strength of *narodnozabavna glasba* has swept aside older styles of music, although there are some remnants in more remote areas or at the borders with Austria, Italy, Hungary or Croatia, where various cultural elements have been constantly inter-mingling. Pannonian musical influence can be traced, for instance, in the so-called *bande* (bands) of *cimbalom*, stringed instruments and woodwind. In this small field, the best exponents are **Marko Banda** and their predecessors, **Beltinška Banda** from the northeast. In the late 1990s the highly regarded singer-songwriter **Vlado Kreslin** recorded and performed with (now deceased) members of Beltinška banda which helped them gain national appeal.

Other distinctive regional styles and line-ups can still be traced elsewhere on the peripheries, from **tamburica bands** in the southeast to the coastal (Istrian) dance tunes and instruments with connections to Mediterranean and Balkan music traditions. Perhaps the most extraordinary of all is an ancient type of fiddling that has been preserved by the Slovenian speaking population in the valley of **Resia** (northeast Italy). The origin of this dance music is still fairly unknown but it is distinct from all the other neighbouring traditions. Its main characteristic is the use of quite basic and repetitive melody lines in a divided three plus two four time (also found in parts of France and Ireland), performed by a string duo of *citira* (a higher-tuned fiddle) and *bunkula* (three-stringed bass) providing a resonant drone.

Traditional unaccompanied harmony singing, once very widespread, can still be found in the villages, and there are a few players of older

Slavko Avsenik and his happy troupe

traditional instruments such as the bowed zither and the panpipes – although numbers dwindle with each year that passes. However, there are a few institutions and some individuals seeking to preserve and revive these more ancient forms. The work of musicologist **Mira Omerzel-Mirit** and her former husband **Matija Terlep**, as well as **Dario Marušič** from Istria – who collected and rebuilt old instruments, researched old songs and performed them – was perhaps the earliest example of this kind of initiative, going back to the 1970s. Over the years they have made a series of field-recordings, some of which have been broadcast or released on vinyl or CDs. However, the **Institute for Ethnomusicology** takes the leading role in recording and publishing Slovenia's music, singing and dance practices. Over the last fifty years, its staff have gathered more than sixty thousand items of folklore, making it one of Europe's largest sound archives.

Revival Bands and Individuals

Ever since Slovenia gained independence, there has been a rapid growth in the number of revivalist groups, though this process began much earlier. In the late 1970s and early 1980s acoustic bands and performers such as **Salamander, Stribor, Slovenska gruda,** and **Tomaž Pengov** took their lead from American and West European folk revivals in experimenting with traditional music.

The first intentional move towards a more genuine, if not authentic, sound (still with evident individual input and Western folk influences in their tune and song arrangements) was by the group **Istranova**, whose members (**Dario Marušič**, **Marino Kranjac** and the late **Luciano Kleva**) stimulated a renewed interest in Istrian folk music among locals. Alongside revivalists such as **Pišćaci**, **Musicante Istriani**, **La Zonta**, **Vruja** and family band **Volk Folk**, groups of source musicians and singers (**Trio Pišćaci**, **Batista family**, **Šavrinske pupe en ragaconi**) research and perform the songs and dances of the Istrian peninsula (the northernmost part of Istria lies in Slovenia, around the town of Koper); this music has a strong Italian tinge in the melody, and texts in the local dialect of Italian (though it also uses a lot of Slovene and Croatian words). Many performers also play (and some are still making) some of the area's older instruments, which can also be found in the Croatian part of Istria. These include the *meh* (a droneless double bagpipe) the *sopele* folk oboe and the two-stringed *bajs* (a bass played with a bow), as well as the more familiar button accordion, mandolin and violin. While these groups have a strong regional bias, others have a repertoire that draws on music from the whole of Slovenia.

One of the longest ongoing groups is **Katice** – twelve female singers with a sweet-toned vocal timbre who perform acapella songs from all over the country recovered from folk-song collections and field recordings. They have made three pleasant albums and add a little local colour to some records by the inclusion of the pop-oriented **Roberto Magnifico** and other familiar faces from the folk-pop scene.

Two other significant revivalist singers are **Ljoba Jenče**, who also produced a few records of source singers in her local area of Notranjska (southwest), and **Bogdana Herman**, a very influential and innovative balladeer who has worked with many local musicians over the past thirty years. There are also (or have been) some well-established revivalist groups with a stronger instrumental bias, such as **Kurja koža** – a trio best known for their vigorous versions of tunes played on panpipes – an extinct form from the northeastern region of Haloze. **Trinajsto Prase** was another trio who recreated traditional dance music for a more modern audience. Their quest is now continued by the trio **Tolovaj Mataj**, who recently released the well received *Črna kuhna* CD, recorded in collaboration with Slovenian rapper **Pižama**.

New Routes

While the folk revival protagonists are busy grasping more purist forms of Slovene traditional music, a new generation of folk music admirers, who have been socialized in popular and world music, has sprung up since the start of the new millennium. The acoustic quartet **Terrafolk** (accordion, double bass, guitar and fiddle) are the most high-profile exponents of this new approach to traditional music. Their dynamic and virtuoso delivery of cleverly arranged original and traditional material from the Balkans and beyond and energetic live shows won them the audience award at the BBC Radio 3 Awards for World Music in 2003. Terrafolk's former accordionist and double-bass player **Janez Dovč** recently released a playful record with his own post-folkloric band **Jararaja**. Two other less well known but promising young folk-orientated groups are **Brina** and **Katalena**.

Žiga Koritnik

Brina

DISCOGRAPHY Slovenia

Compilations

☉ Modern Folk Music in Slovenia vols I and II
Folk Slovenia Cultural Society, Slovenia
Recorded in 1999 and 2002, these two discs document the exciting early years of the cultural association. Rather than just reanimating old forms, the music showcased here is genuinely innovative. A must for all those interested in more pure Slovenian revival forms.

☉ Slovenian Folk Songs vols I–IV
Institute of Ethnomusicology, Slovene Academy of Science and Arts, Slovenia
This series of archival material, published between 1996 and 1998, is a gold mine of information on the rich tradition of Slovene singing styles and other genres, illustrating where many revival and young post-traditional bands sourced their ideas. Each disc's introductory booklet provides expert textual and ethnomusicological notes, with an English translation for each song.

☉ The Echo of the First Recordings
Institute of Ethnomusicology, Slovene Academy of Science and Arts, Slovenia
This sumptuously packaged overview of the history of folk music recordings in Slovenia ranges from 1898 to 2000. The selection reflects not only the variety of folk song (along with spoken rhythmic texts, nursery rhymes, supplications and apocryphal prayers) but also instrumental music from dance tunes (mazurkas, waltzes, polkas, *scottishes*, *csardases*), to bell chiming and leaf blowing. The booklet provides detailed and concise ethnomusicological information, all in English.

Artists

Brina

This group is a fairly new kid on the block, although its leading figure, the siren-voiced Brina Vogelnik was previously known for her work in the bands Šišenska bajka and String.si. Her folk family pedigree goes back to the end of the nineteenth century, when her grandfather, Dr Ivan Grafenauer, passed on to his female descendants his monumental collection, *Traditional Slovene Songs*, by the folklorist Dr Karel Štrekelj.

☉ Mlado leto
Drugodb, Slovenia
This debut reveals lightly textured and jazzy arrangements of Slovenian folk ballads and love songs. The traditional lyrics have been translated from local dialects to fit into a contemporary urban vibe.

Katalena

When Katalena appeared in 2001 they brought amplification to the world of Slovenian folk music for the first time. Combining the finest traditional tunes and songs from the archives and old vinyl records with solid rock riffs, funky grooves and strong female vocals, this six-piece created a unique postmodern folk rock style that presents the musical legacy of Slovenia's regions in an utterly new light, much appreciated even by youngsters.

Katalena

⊙ Cvik Cvak
Dallas Records, Slovenia
Their fascination with the unique music legacy of the Resia Valley drew Katalena's crew to explore new possibilities of sound, enabling this archaic language and culture to find its place in the 21st century. Their fourth album, *Cvik Cvak*, is a prime example of how to transgress musical, physical and symbolical boundaries with a true elegance, insight and subtlety.

Terrafolk

The first Terrafolk line-up formed in 2001 and soon after, this four-piece (two of whom are conservatoire-trained)

joined the European world music caravan in style, charming audiences with their unique globetrotting repertoire and bold virtuosity. In the past five years they have released four albums, undergone line-up changes, toured the world and won numerous music awards.

⊙ Pulover ljubezni/Jumper of Love
Music Net, Slovenia
Perhaps their tastiest Pythonesque cocktail of Slavic, Jewish, Celtic and classical ingredients, mixed with Terrafolk's own mad figments. The set was recorded live at various locations across the country and clearly illustrating the ecstatic connection between the band and their audience.

PLAYLIST
Slovenia

1 OD ENGA VRTA BOM ZAPEU Ančka Lazar
from *The Echo of the First Recordings*
A narrative traditionally sung at wakes, hauntingly delivered by one of the best source singers, Ančka Lazar, who is unfortunately almost completely unknown.

2 ČEGLEŠČEK Kurja koža from *Modern Folk Music in Slovenia II*
A stunning polyrhythmic instrumental piece from northeast Slovenia, performed by revivalist Drago Kunej on a primitive Jew's harp.

3 TA ALDOWSKA Katalena from *Cvik Cvak*
Katalena's own composition. Imbued with pulsating electronic beats and combining powerful

rock-flavoured female vocal sampling with a very old vocal piece of confession recital, it takes Resian dance tradition to a new level.

4 CARO PAPA Terrafolk from *Jumper of Love/ Pulover ljubezni*
An Istrian tune, which comes out sounding more like a Jewish wedding number than anything else.

5 DETECE/DIYORÈ Brina from *Mlado leto*
Based on a Guinean lullaby, Diyorè is a unique example of a musical bridge between Africa and Slovenia. The *kora* is played by a Slovenian, though.

Spain | Flamenco

a wild, savage feeling

Festival de Jerez
Finale Jerez festival, 2008

Flamenco is one of the great musical forms of Europe, with a history and repertoire that few traditional or folk cultures can match. Forty years or so ago, however, it looked like a music on the decline, preserved only in the clubs or *peñas* of its aficionados, or in travestied castanet-clicking forms for tourists. In the 1980s and 90s, flamenco returned to the Spanish mainstream, with styles infused by jazz, salsa, blues and rock making their way in the charts and clubs, and a new respect for the old "pure flamenco" artists. While flamencologists initially saw this as a sign of decline, it has, in fact, rejuvenated the scene by establishing a new generation of key musicians, and 2013 has been named as the official International Year of Flamenco. Jan Fairley catches up with the state of play.

Scratch a hot night in **Andalusia**, even on the much-maligned Costa del Sol, and you'll find flamenco. "You carry it inside you," said a man in his sixties sitting next to me at a concert in the local municipal stadium in downtown Marbella. There was not a tourist in sight, it was 2am, the sky was deep blue-black, patterned with stars, the stadium cluttered with families enjoying the most pleasant hours of the Andaluz summer, flapping their fans until dawn, children asleep on their laps.

Flamenco is the most important musical and cultural phenomenon in Spain, and its huge resurgence in popularity has seen its profile reaching far beyond its Andalusian homeland. It owes this in part to emigration from that province, which has long meant that the flamenco map encompasses Madrid, Barcelona, Extremadura and the Levante – indeed, wherever Andalusian migrants have settled.

Flamenco's resurgence in the 1980s and 90s was down, more than anything else, to the musicians – to the vitality and attitude of a younger generation of traditional flamenco clans. In the 1980s, the Spanish press hailed the group **Ketama** as the creators of the music of the "New Spain", after the release of their first album fusing flamenco with rock and Latin salsa. Ketama pushed the frontiers of flamenco still further by recording the two wonderful *Songhai* albums – an early high point of world music fusion – in collaboration with Malian *kora*-player Toumani Diabaté and British bassist Danny Thompson. Another young group, **Pata Negra** ("black leg" – the tasty bit of a leg of Andalusian ham, and a term for anything good), caused an equal sensation with their *Blues de la Frontera* album. This time flamenco was given a treatment encompassing both rock and blues.

These developments were not always welcomed by flamenco purists, who continue to keep old-time flamenco alive in their peñas or clubs. But the new Spain has become a much bigger audience. Today artists like **José Mercé** and **El Cigala** (**Diego Ramón Jiménez Salazar**) create flamenco that enters the mainstream charts, while the Barcelona-based collective **Ojos de Brujo** give new fusions hip credibility and a contemporary ethos, making flamenco much more integral to Spanish musical life. And **flamenco-rumba** – the style that first found fresh markets abroad, spurred initially by the global success of the **Gipsy Kings** from southern France – is now thriving.

The *nuevo flamenco* revolution, however, had begun towards the end of the 1960s, with the innovations of guitarist **Paco de Lucía** and, especially, the late, great singer **El Camarón de la Isla** (José

Nuevos Medios/Universal Music Spain

Paco de Lucía

Monge Cruz, see box on p.395). They both knew flamenco, but their tastes embraced international rock, jazz and blues. Paco de Lucía blended jazz, salsa and other Latin sounds, including those of Afro-Peruvian music, onto the flamenco sound. El Camarón, simply, was an inspiration – and one whose idols (and fans) included Chick Corea and Miles Davis, as well as flamenco artists.

Origins and Laws

The **roots of flamenco** evolved in southern Spain from many sources: Morocco, Egypt, India, Pakistan, Greece and other parts of the Near and Far East. How exactly they came together as flamenco is a subject of debate, though most experts believe its roots were brought to Spain by Gypsies in the fifteenth century. In the following century, it was fused with elements of Arab and Jewish music in the Andalusian mountains, where Jews, Muslims and "pagan" Gypsies had taken refuge from the forced conversions and clearances effected by the Catholic kings and the Church. The main flamenco centres and families are still to be found in areas of Gypsy and refugee origin, such as Alcalá, Jerez, Cadiz, Utrera and the Triana quarter of Seville.

There are various theories about the origins of the name flamenco. One contends that Spanish Jews migrated through trade to Flanders, where they were allowed to sing their religious chants unmolested, and that these chants became known as flamenco by the Jews who stayed in Spain. Another agrees on the derivation from the Spanish word for Flemish, but suggests the word was coined to describe the Gypsies who had served with distinction in the Spanish war in Flanders and were allowed to settle in lower Andalusia. A third argument is that the word is a mis-pronunciation of the Arabic words *felah* (fugitive) and *mengu* (peasant), a plausible idea, as Arabic was a common language in Spain at that time.

Ojos de Brujo

The impact of Barcelona collective **Ojos de Brujo** (Eyes of a Wizard) has been huge. Emerging from the larger artistic grouping La Fabrica de Colores (The Colour Factory), their genius lies in their reworking of flamenco styles to incorporate modern musical tendencies, and their passionate expression of political issues related to everyday life. Their concerns include the struggle for basic human rights like food and shelter, and they challenge corporatism and the negative effects of global capitalism on their small community. "Before, they used to complain about the landowner. Now we complain about the world bank which is the same thing in the end with every economy in its grip," declares guitarist **Ramón Giménez**.

Passing flamenco through the prism of the sounds and preoccupations of the modern city, the group's vision sees them drawing on the music of the flamenco diaspora, Latin America, the Middle East, India, the Mediterranean and North Africa. They also add an eclectic mix of Latin, ragga, reggae, hip-hop, scratch and looped sounds. "There's no leader and we try not to impose anything. We're all important and have space to express ourselves, and we try and express ourselves as a collective. That's the sound you get," Giménez continues.

Ojos de Brujo

Their song "Tiempo de Soleá" (Lamenting Time) is dedicated to all the street kids the group meet where they live. For their flamboyant singer **Marina Abad**, the song is "urban flamenco with contemporary hip-hop, a lament, for the moment in which we are living now. We took a "soleá" because that's the strong flamenco form traditionally used to express those emotions."

In the words of **DJ Panko**, another member of the collective: "Pieces evolve when we are all working together. We have an idea and we all add to it. Later we record ourselves and listen, like when we are driving in the van, and discuss what might be possible and everyone brings their own ideas and colour and it grows." Agreeing that cooperation and conversation are key to both the group's success and their sound, Giménez adds, "There are many different conversations within the mix, between guitar and percussion, percussion and scratch, with the bass, and everyone together and with the voice. They are all voices at one level."

From the outset, flamenco has been associated with the Gypsy (*gitano*) clans of Andalusia, although the singers and players are not exclusively Gypsy in origin. Its whole development and preservation was probably made possible by the oral tradition of the Gypsy clans. Its power, and the despair that its creation overcomes, seems to have emerged from the gitano experience – from a people surviving at the margins of a society which offers them little or no social status. Flamenco reflects a need to aggressively protect self-esteem.

These days there are as many acclaimed *payo* (non-Gypsy) artists as there are Gypsy artists. Following the models of legendary singers and passing on traditions is fundamental for both sets of artists, but different attitudes prevail within the scene.

As José Mercé says, "Flamenco is flamenco from Gypsy or non-Gypsy. But what happens is that Gypsies have a way of feeling that is special, different. Fernando el Teremoto summed it up when he said, 'We throw the salt on the other side.'"

The concept of dynasty is fundamental. The veteran singer **Fernanda de Utrera**, one of the great voices of the tradition, was born in 1923 into a Gypsy family in Utrera, one of the flamenco singing centres. Fernanda and her sister **Bernarda**, also a notable singer, inherited their flamenco genes from their grandmother, the legendary singer **Pinini**, who created her own individual flamenco forms. The sisters' significance as women singers in a predominantly male world was recognized in 1994 when they were awarded the Gold Medal of Andalusia. This concept of an active inheritance has not been lost in contemporary developments: even the members of Ketama, the Madrid-based flamenco-rock group, come from two Gypsy musician clans – the Sotos and the Carmonas.

It is generally agreed that flamenco's laws – its forms of expression and repertoire – were established in the nineteenth century. From the mid-nineteenth to the early twentieth centuries, the music enjoyed a Golden Age, the tail end of which is preserved on some of the earliest 1930s recordings. These original musicians found a home in the **cafés cantantes** – bars which had their own groups of performers (*cuadros*). One of the most famous was the Café de Chinitas in Malaga, immortalized by the Granada-born poet García Lorca.

Flamenco, Lorca asserted, was a way of breaking out of social and economic marginality, and this was clearly shown in 1922 when he was present – with composer Manuel de Falla and guitarist Andrés Segovia – at a legendary *Concurso de Cante Jondo* (Competition of Deep Song). A Gypsy boy singer, **Manolo Caracol**, reportedly walked all the way from Jerez and won a special prize with the voice and flamboyant personality that were to make his name throughout Spain and South America. The other key figure of this period, who can be heard on a few recently remastered recordings, was **Pastora Pavón**, known as **La Niña de los Peines**. She is popularly acclaimed as the greatest woman flamenco voice of the twentieth century.

In the 1950s, several events crucial to flamenco history took place, which opened up the music to an audience beyond the aficionados in the café cantantes. In 1954, the Spanish label Hispavox recorded all the flamenco greats on the CD collection, *Antología del Cante Flamenco*; two years later, the first national **Concurso de Cante Jondo** was launched in Cordoba; then, in 1958, a Chair of Flamencology was established at Jerez. Each of these events brought media attention and deserved respectability to the art form. They were also accompanied by the appearance of numerous *tablaos* (clubs that were the heirs of the café cantantes), which became the training ground for a new generation of singers and musicians.

The Art of Flamenco

In addition to tablaos, flamenco is played at fiestas, in bars and at *juergas* – informal, more or less private, parties. The fact that the Andalusian public are so knowledgeable and demanding about flamenco means that musicians, singers and dancers performing even at the smallest local club or festival are usually very good indeed.

At the concert in Marbella mentioned at the beginning of this article, **Tina Pavón** from Cadiz sang *fandangos* and *alegrias* (literally happinesses) and *malagueñas* from Malaga, part of the light **cante chico** and **intermedio** repertoire which paves the way for **cante jondo** (deep song). The latter is the profound flamenco of the great artists, whose *siguiriyas* and *soleares* are outpourings of the soul, delivered with an intense passion and expressed through elaborate vocal ornamentation. Tina Pavón's improvised sculpting of phrases, which draws attention to certain words and the emotions they evoke, had people on their feet shouting encouragement. To invoke such a response is essential for an artist, as it lets them know they are reaching deep into the emotional psyche of their listeners. They may also achieve the rare quality of **duende** – total communication with their audience, a moment of immortality that transcends time, and the mark of great flamenco of any style or generation.

Duende is a quality that stops listeners in their tracks, and it can have a profound emotional effect, reducing people to tears. Many of those listeners are intensely involved, for flamenco is not just music; for many it is a philosophy that influences their daily activities. A flamenco is not just a performer, but anyone who is actively and emotionally involved. As **Estrella Morente** (daughter of singer **Enrique Morente** and dancer **Aurora Carbonell**) says: "To be 'flamenco' is to understand life in a different way. It's taking art by the horns of the bull and saying, 'I will live life from the basis of art, and I am going to eat and drink that art.' So when you eat you are flamenco, even when you are ironing you are flamenco. Flamenco is a way of living, of moving your body, your hands, everything."

Luis Baylon

Estrella Morente

Flamenco Dance

Most popular images of **flamenco dance** – twirling bodies in frilled dresses, rounded arms complete with castanets – are *sevillanas*, the folk dances performed at fiestas and, in recent years, in nightclubs. While these are danced in pairs at the spring fair in Seville, classic flamenco is danced solo. Even when great dance companies take to the road, group performance exists primarily to foreground individual talent. Like the music, flamenco dance can reduce onlookers to tears in an unexpected flash, a cathartic point after which the dance dissolves. What is so visually devastating about it is the physical and emotional control the dancer has over his or her body: the way the head is held, the tension of the torso and the way it allows the shoulders to move, the shapes and angles of seemingly elongated arms, and the feet, which move from toe to heel, heel to toe, creating intricate rhythms. These rhythms have a basic set of moves and timings, but they are improvised as the piece develops, through interaction with the guitarist and singers.

Flamenco dance dates back to around 1750, moving, in the nineteenth century, from the streets and private parties into the cafés cantantes, attracting people of all social classes. This was a great boost for the dancers' art, providing a home for professional performers, where they could inspire each other. It was here that legendary male dancers like **El Raspao** and **El Estampío** began to develop the spellbinding footwork and extraordinary moves that characterize modern flamenco, while the women adopted the flamboyant *bata de cola* dresses for the first time. Only very skilled dancers can handle these glorious long-trained dresses, designed to show off the sensuous movements of the dance.

By around 1910, flamenco dance had moved into Spanish theatres, and dancers like **Pastora Imperio** and **La Argentina** were major stars. They mixed flamenco into programmes with other dances, and made dramatic appearances at the end of comic plays and silent movies. For a period, theatre flamenco – featuring single-act light comedy dramas – offered brief moments of flamenco song and dance. In 1915, composer **Manuel de Falla** created the first **flamenco ballet**, *El Amor Brujo* (Love Bewitched), for Pastora Imperio. In the 1920s, **La Argentina**, who had established the first Spanish dance company, took her version of the ballet abroad. With her choreographic innovations, flamenco dance came of age, working as a narrative in its own right. Another key figure was **Carmen Amaya** who, from the 1930s to the 60s, took flamenco on tour around the world, and into the movies.

In the 1950s, the dance found a new home in the tablaos, the aficionado's bars, which became enormously important as places to serve a public apprenticeship. Artistic developments were forged in the 1960s by **Matilde Coral**, who updated the classic dance style, and in the 1970s by **Manuela Carrasco**, who made such an impact with her fiery feet movement – continuing a rhythm for an intense and seemingly impossible duration – that a new style was named after her (*manuelas*).

Carrasco set the tone for the highly individual dancers of the 1980s and 90s, including **Mario Maya** and **Antonio Gades**. These two dancer-choreographers gave flamenco a theatrically inspired staging, most significantly by extending the role of dance dialogue and story – often reflecting on the potency, and the dangers, of love and passion. Gades was also influential in flamenco films. He appeared with Carmen Amaya in *Los Tarantos* (1963), and made his own trilogy with director Carlos Saura in the 1980s: *Boda de Sangre* (Blood Wedding), *Carmen* and *El Amor Brujo*. The films featured guitarist **Paco de Lucía** and dancers **Laura del Sol** and **Cristina Hoyos**. One of the great contemporary dancers, Hoyos also created her own superb ballet, *Sueños Flamencos* (Flamenco Dreams).

In the 1990s, everyone was talking about **Joaquin Cortés,** the top flamenco dancer of the moment. He emerged as a real phenomenon by introducing balletic and jazz-influenced choreography to beautifully designed shows, reaching new audiences across Europe and the US. The baton was then passed to innovative female dance choreographers, notably **Maria Pagés**, **Eva Yerbabuena**, **Sara Baras** (who leads a striking company of dancers for her shows *Juana La Loca* and *Suenos*) and **Rocio Molina**, one of the most extraordinary dancers of recent years. Indeed, more women now lead flamenco dance companies than men. Catalyst for new work has come from the dynamic annual Jerez Festival and the Seville Biennial Flamenco Festival.

Flamenco is still regarded by many as sacred music. It is said that **Tomas Pavón**, brother of La Niña de los Peines, would not sing cante jondo as entertainment. Before singing he reportedly meditated in church and listened to monks intoning psalms in Gregorian Chant. For the musicians, this fullness of expression is integral to their art, which is why, however many famous names one can list, there are as many lesser-known musicians whose work is perhaps just as startling. Not every great flamenco musician gets to be famous, or to record, for flamenco thrives best in live performance. Exhilarating, challenging and physically stimulating, it is an art form which allows its exponents huge scope to improvise while obeying certain rules.

The Repertoire

There is a **classical repertoire** of more than sixty flamenco songs (*cantes*) and dances (*danzas*) – some solos, some group numbers, some with instrumental accompaniment, others acapella.

These different styles, or *palos*, of flamenco singing are grouped in families according to more or less common melodic themes. The basic palos are **soleares**, **siguiriyas**, **bulerías**, **tangos** and **fandangos**, but the variations are endless and often referred to by their place of origin, for example, **malagueñas** (from Malaga), **granaínos** (from Granada) or **fandangos de Huelva**. The Andaluz provinces of Cadiz, Seville, Malaga and Granada are responsible for most of the palos, although they also come from other parts of Andalusia and the neighbouring regions of Extremadura and Murcia. Each style has a musical structure with a different melody and beat, and styles are added to the various groups according to the fashions of the period. The songs of the "*ida y vuelta*" ("coming and going" from the Americas) group are the best example, as they include the *milonga*, tango, rumba and *guajira* styles. Certain styles have achieved prominence by their link with individual singers, for example, soleares with Tomas Pavón and siguiriyas with **El Manolito**.

In all of these palos, the most common **beat cycle** is twelve – like the blues. The piece may be executed by juxtaposing a number of complete musical units called *coplas*. Their number varies depending on the atmosphere and emotional tone the *cantaor* (singer) wishes to convey. These coplas may be familiar couplets from popular poetry, or verse poetry drawn from a body of material the singers know by heart. The singers may also improvise to express their mood, experiences and the immediate context. A song such as a *cante por solea* may take a familiar 3/4 rhythm, divide phrases into 4/8 measures, and then fragmently sub-divide again, with voice ornamentation on top of that. The resulting complexity and the variations between similar phrases undermines repetition, contributing greatly to the climactic and cathartic structure of each song.

Songs

Flamenco songs often express pain, and they do so with a fierceness that turns the emotion inside out and beats it against violent frontiers. Some songs are performed *a palo seco* (acapella), but generally, the voice interacts closely with improvising guitar, the two inspiring each other, aided by the **jaleo** – the hand-clapping *palmas*, finger-snapping *palillos* and shouts at certain points in the song. The jaleo sets the tone by creating the right atmosphere for the singer or dancer to begin, and bolsters the artists as they develop the piece. Aficionados will shout encouragement when an artist is getting deep into a song – most commonly "¡olé!", but also various less obvious phrases suited to the piece.

It is an essential characteristic of flamenco that a singer or dancer takes certain risks, putting feelings and emotions arising from their own lives into their performances, and exposing their vulnerabilities. Aficionados tend to acclaim voices that gain effect from surprising and startling moves, rather than those governed by recognized musical logic. Vocal prowess or virtuosity deepened by sobs, gesticulation and an intensity of expression can have a shattering effect on an audience. Thus, pauses, breaths, body language and facial gestures of anger, pain and transcendence transform performances into cathartic events. However, for both singers and players, technique is everything. As guitarist Paco de Lucía says, "No matter how much emotion you have bottled up inside, you can't possibly transmit any of it if you haven't got the vehicle."

The **siguiriya** flamenco style, whose theme is usually death, has been described as a cry of despair in the form of a funeral psalm. In contrast, songs and dances such as tangos, sevillanas and fandangos capture great joy for fiestas. The **sevillana** originated in medieval Seville as a spring country dance, with verses improvised and sung to the accompaniment of guitar and castanets (these are rarely used in other flamenco forms). **El Pali** (Francisco Palacios), who died in 1988, was the best-known and most prolific sevillana musician. He combined an unusually gentle voice and strummed guitar style with an enviable musical pace and an ease for composing the popular poetry of the genre. In recent years, dancing sevillanas has become popular in bars and clubs throughout Spain, but their natural habitats are Seville's **La Feria de Abril** (April Fair) and the spring **Romería del Rocío** – a pilgrimage to a shrine in Rocio, near Huelva. Each year, specially composed new sevillanas are performed live at the Seville fair.

Another very important, but specifically seasonal, flamenco form is the **saeta**. These are songs in honour of the Virgins, who are carried on great floats in the processions of **Semana Santa** (Easter Week), and they are, traditionally, quite spontaneous. As the float is passing, a singer will launch into a saeta, a sung prayer, the procession will stop and everyone will remain silent while it is sung.

Singers

El Camarón de la Isla (see box) was by far the most popular and commercially successful modern flamenco singer of the twentieth century. Collaborating with guitarists **Paco de Lucía**, the late

Camarón, Paco de Lucía and El Lebrijano

Ramón de Algeciras and, latterly, **Tomatito**, El Camarón raised cante jondo, virtuoso deep song, to a new art. He almost singlehandedly revitalized flamenco song, inspiring and opening the way for the current generation of artists.

Among those regarded as the best **contemporary singers** are Enrique Morente, El Cabrero, El Lebrijano, the Sorderos, Fosforito, José Menese, Duquende, El Potito, José Mercé, El Cigala and Miguel Poveda. The most revered women include Fernanda and Bernarda de Utrera, Carmen Linares, Remedios Amaya, Estrella Morente, Montse Cortés, La Macanita and Carmen Amaya. In particular, **Enrique Morente** is considered one of the great artists of his generation, thanks to his renovation and adaptation of modern and classic poets. Similarly, **Carmen Linares** has been a major figure since the 1990s, her deep, rich voice expressing melodies with complex attack and searingly intense emotion. Rigorous and uncompromising, she innovates from within the tradition. **Miguel Poveda**, who grew up in Barcelona in a non-fla-

menco family and is today based in Seville, won many awards at an early age and has become the most significant flamenco singer of the twenty-first century, noted for his impassioned and delicate singing.

Flamenco Guitar

The flamenco performance is filled with pauses and the singer is free to insert phrases on the spur of the moment. The **guitar accompaniment**, while also spontaneous, is precise and serves one major purpose – to mark the *compás* (measures) of a song and organize the rhythmical lines. **Instrumental interludes**, which are arranged to meet the needs of the cantaor (creative singer), not only catch the mood and intention of the song, but also allow the guitarist to extemporize *falsetas* (short variations including quotations from master musicians) at will. When the singer and guitarist have a rapport, the intensity of a song develops rapidly, the one charging the other, until the effect becomes overwhelming.

The **flamenco guitar**, with its body usually made of cypress wood, is lighter than most acoustic guitars, and often has a pine table and wooden pegs, rather than machine heads. This is so that the guitar produces a bright responsive sound that does not sustain too long, as opposed to the mellow, longer sustaining sound of a classical guitar. If the sound did sustain, chords would carry over into each other, particularly in the fast pieces. The other important feature of the guitar is a **diapason** placed across the strings to enable returning. This was an important development in the relationship between guitarist and singer, as, before its introduction, a singer often had to strain to adapt to the guitarist's tone.

Guitarists

During the nineteenth century, guitars were used primarily to accompany the voice and as rhythmic support for the dancers, and some singers even accompanied themselves. Gradually, the players developed their own short instrumental melodic interludes. One of the most influential early musicians was **Ramón Montoya**, who revolutionized flamenco guitar by shifting the role of the guitarist from mere accompanist to solo instrumentalist. Montoya's main innovation was to enrich the guitars language using new scales, harmonies, arpeggio and playing techniques. Along with **Niño Ricardo** and **Sabicas**, he established flamenco guitar as a solo medium, an art extended in the

El Camarón de la Isla

José Monge Cruz – known throughout his career as **El Camarón de la Isla** – died on July 2, 1992. Flags were immediately dropped to half mast in his home city of San Fernando, near Cadiz, and every single Spanish newspaper carried his photo and obituary on their front pages. The leading Madrid daily, *El País*, devoted no less than four pages of homage to his memory. "Camarón revolutionized flamenco from the point of absolute purity," it concluded.

Only 41 years old when he died, El Camarón (the nickname referred to his bony frame, likened to the shrimps – *camarones* – of the San Fernando peninsula) was acknowledged as a genius almost from the moment he first sang publicly in the late 1960s. His high-toned voice had a corrosive, rough-timbred edge, cracking at certain points to release an almost ravaged core sound. His vocal opaqueness and incisive sense of rhythm, coupled with a near-violent emotional intensity, made him the quintessential singer of the times, with a voice that seemed to defy destiny.

Even at its gentlest, El Camarón's voice would summon attention – "a fracture of the soul", critics called it – and he would phrase and match cadences in astonishing ways, yet always making the songs appear as if they were composed for exactly that manner. His voice evoked "the desolation of the people", according to his guitarist-collaborator, **Paco**

El Camarón de la Isla

de Lucía: "My soul left me each time I heard him – he gave to flamenco a wild, savage feeling." This verdict was echoed in almost Christ-like terms. As one of the obituaries put it: "Camarón's despair was our consolation. His desperation soothed us. The infinite sadness of his voice gave us tranquility. He suffered for us. His generosity liberated us from misfortune."

Of mythical standing in his lifetime, El Camarón has become a kind of flamenco saint since his death, for he seemed to live out the myths of his music. His death left an unfillable void in the flamenco world, which even now continues unassuaged, as is vividly expressed by Paco de Lucía in the song "Camarón", from *Luzía* (Polygram, Spain):

con lo mucho que yo quería
se fue para siempre,
Camarón, Camarón

(with all my love for him,
he went forever,
Camarón, Camarón)

1960s by **Manolo Sanlucar**, whom most aficionados consider the most technically accomplished player of his generation. Sanlucar has remained within a classical orbit, uninfluenced by jazz or rock, experimenting instead with orchestral backing and composing for ballet.

The best-known of all contemporary flamenco guitarists is, undoubtedly, **Paco de Lucía**, who made the first moves towards new, or fusion, flamenco. A payo, or non-Gypsy, he won his first flamenco prize at the age of fourteen, and went on to accompany many of the great traditional singers,

including El Camarón de la Isla. He started forging new timbres and rhythms for flamenco following a trip to Brazil, where he fell in love with bossa nova, and he established a sextet with electric bass, Latin percussion, flute and saxophone in the 1970s. A trip to Peru introduced him to the Afro-Peruvian **cajon** – a kind of box drum, sat on as it is played – which he also incorporated into flamenco.

Over the past twenty years, Paco de Lucía has worked with jazz-rock guitarists like John McLauglin and Chick Corea, while his own regular band (featuring his brother, the singer **Pepe de Lucía**)

Flamenco Trails

It is still possible for visitors to find real flamenco in Spain, as opposed to clichéd tourist fare. If you want to see live flamenco in small bars and picturesque villages, and have the chance to hear experts talking about this extraordinarily powerful music, you could go on one of the **flamenco trails** from the *Guide to Andalusian Flamenco*. Its rather wacky English translation outlines seven different flamenco trails to follow by car, train, bus or on foot, taking you to key places in flamenco history and intimate venues where you can still find local flamenco today.

Commissioned and promoted by the **Andalusian Tourist Board**, due to the passion of **Manuel Macías**, these five-day trails include free introductory workshops on flamenco and its styles in Seville, talks and demonstrations on song, guitar and dance in the different villages on the routes and performances in local flamenco peña clubs. Each route has a different focus, such as flamenco song, guitarists, the miners' routes or Huelva's fandangos, and one can include a visit to the Jerez Festival. The accompanying book has beautiful photographs evoking the sights, sounds and smells of the scene over the years.

For more information on the trails (including routes, itineraries, accommodation, etc), or to get hold of the guide, see the tourist board's website (*andaluciaflamenco.org*), which is in English, Spanish and several other languages. If you want to follow one of the trails, you must book in advance via the website or by contacting the tourist board (flamenco@andalucia.org; +34 951 29 93 00).

remains one of the most original and distinctive sounds on the flamenco scene. Of his fusion, he says: "You grab tradition with one hand, and with the other you scratch, you search. You can go anywhere and run away but must never lose the root, for it's there that you find flamenco's identity, fragrance and flavour."

Other modern-day guitarists have equally identifiable sounds and rhythms, and fall broadly into two camps, being known either as accompanists or soloists. The accompanists include Tomatito (El Camarón's last accompanist), Manolo Franco and Paco Cortés. Among the leading soloists are **Enrique de Melchor**, **Gerardo Nuñez**, **Vicente Amigo**, **Jerónimo Maya**, the **Habichuela brothers** (Pepe and Juan) from Granada, and **Rafael Riqueni**, an astonishing player who is breaking new ground with his classical influences.

Nuevo Flamenco

One of flamenco's great achievements has been to sustain itself while providing foundations and inspirations for much of the new music emerging in Spain today. In the 1960s, rock largely displaced traditional Spanish music, but the work of El Camarón de la Isla initiated a flamenco revival. In the 1980s, flamenco almost reinvented itself, gaining new meaning and renewed public interest through its absorption of influences from Brazilian and Latin music. For **José Soto** ("El Sordo", Deaf One), Ketama's lead singer, there were implicit connections: "our music is based on classic flamenco that we'd been singing and listening to since birth. We just found new forms in jazz and salsa: there are basic similarities in the rhythms, the constantly changing harmonies and improvisations. Blacks and Gypsies have suffered similar segregation so our music has a lot in common."

Paco de Lucía set new parameters of innovation in guitar-playing in the 1960s and 70s, and went on to have considerable commercial success. He was followed by other innovative musicians, such as **Lolé y Manuel**, who updated the flamenco sound with original songs; **Jorge Pardo**, Paco's sax and flute player who was originally a jazz musician; and **Salvador Tavora** and **Mario Maya**, known for their flamenco-based spectacles.

Meanwhile, **Enrique Morente** and **El Lebrijano** (**Juan Peña**) worked with North African musicians and with **Andalusian orchestras** from Morocco, while **Amalgama** recorded with southern Indian percussionists, revealing stylistic unities. Most recently, Pepe Habichuela has worked with the Bollywood Strings. Another interesting fusion of forms came with **Paco Peña**'s 1991 album, *Misa Flamenca*, which set the Catholic Mass to flamenco forms. Participants included established singers like Rafael Montilla "El Chaparro" from Cordoba, and a classical academy chorus from London.

Flamenco's encounter with rock and blues was pioneered at the end of the 1980s by Ketama and Pata Negra. Ketama used rock and Latin sounds to add a kind of rock-jazz sensibility, or "flamenco cool", as they put it. **Pata Negra**, a band led by

Radio Tarifa

Creating magical music has been the life of the three men known as **Radio Tarifa** since the early 1990s, when **Faín Sánchez Dueñas**, **Benjamín Escoriza** and **Vincent Molino** decided to record an album in Dueñas' bedroom. The result was the mesmerizing *Rumba Argelina*, which rocketed them to cult fame throughout Europe and placed them firmly on the map of world music innovators. The album is an irresistible fusion of stunning erotic melodies, with a pattering of percussion, drums, undulating pipes and funky guitars, and the smoky flamenco-esque rumba voice of Escoriza grabs you and never lets you go. It's music with emotions and vitality that you can simply never tire of.

The group's music is summed up by their name, which evokes an imaginary radio station, As Dueñas explains: "Tarifa is the southernmost point of Spain. If you turn the dial of a radio there you can pick up sounds from North Africa, the Arabic early morning call-to-prayer, and from there you reach out into the whole of Mediterranean Europe, to the Middle East and beyond to the Americas. Our music is a meeting point between all the cultures that have come through and continue to come through that part of Spain. We don't make fusion music. We explore the inter-relationships between the mix of cultures that lie by side – Arabic, Jewish, Christian, Muslim – and we have this strong medieval background of making music without chords."

Their music is very fluid: "Think of it like watching a shoal of fish swimming. From a distance it looks like a unit until you look closer, then you see they are all moving slightly differently. Almost all our music is modal, which means it is totally melody based. Modal means it's not chromatic, so it doesn't use all the black and white notes of the piano like classical European scales, and the scales

Radio Tarifa

do not necessarily have seven note patterns either. We all play single melody lines with different rhythmic phrasing, and the flow and the delicacy and density of what we do comes from that. The harmony is always there, but we reach it another way: instruments like the winds and strings are playing single lines but there are maybe three notes in the same moment sounding together, which makes a kind of chord if you want to think of it that way. We play like an ensemble, listening hard to each other, with lots of eye contact all the time on stage, so we dovetail in and out of each other."

Bassist **David Purdye** regularly tours with the group, and he has a clear feeling as to why Tarifa are different: "They let things happen, evolve and grow organically. Even when the pressure is on, they're always relaxed and very human. But then Spanish culture is like that. We sit round tables and eat and talk about what we are doing and feeling and everyone gets to know everyone else better all the time, and understands where they are coming from in their life and their music. It is very warm this Tarifa culture, and you take that closeness and rapport with you onto the stage. That's why it's great."

Sadly, the Radio Tarifa project officially ended in 2006; however, their music can still be heard on some excellent recordings.

brothers Raimundo and Rafael Amador, introduced a more direct rock sound with a bluesy electric guitar lead, giving a radical edge to traditional styles like bulerías. The creativity of this generation has focused on the lighter, more festive flamenco forms, such as rumbas, tangos and bulerías, introducing upbeat, often poppy, choruses without losing their root intensity.

In the 1990s, these young, iconoclastic musicians became known as nuevo flamenco; the movement particularly associated with the Madrid label **Nuevos Medios**. They form a challenging, versatile and musically incestuous scene in Madrid and Andalusia, with the various musicians guesting at each others' gigs and on each others' records. For instance, members of Ketama crop up, along with guitarist Tomatito, on an album by **Duquende**, another powerful singer of flamenco's new wave.

Flamenco became a regular sound in night-clubs, thanks to the appeal of young singers like **Aurora**, whose salsa-rumba song "Besos de Cara-melo", written by **Antonio Carmona** of Ketama, was the first flamenco number to crack the pop charts in the 1980s. Pop singer **Martírio** (**Isabel Quiñones Gutiérrez**) is one of the most flamboy-ant personalities on the scene, performing in a lace *mantilla* scarf and shades like a character from a Pedro Almodóvar film. Martírio's songs are often Almodóvar-like too, with their ironic, contempo-rary lyrics, full of local slang, about women's lives in the cities. Martirio's producer, **Kiko Veneno**, who also wrote one of El Camarón's most popu-lar songs, is another key artist on the scene. His own material is basically rock, but it has a strongly defined sense of flamenco. Similarly, **Rosario**, one of Spain's top female singers, brought a flamenco sensibility to Spanish rock music.

Other more identifiably nuevo flamenco bands and singers include **La Barbería del Sur** (who add a dash of salsa), **Raímundo Amador** (of Pata Negra fame) and **José El Francés** (from Montpe-lier in France). In the mid-1990s, **Radio Tarifa** emerged as an exciting group. Starting out as a trio, they expanded to include African musicians, and mixed Arabic and medieval sounds onto a fla-menco base. They also had a fine feeling for the popular song side of the genre, bringing flamenco to an even wider world music audience.

The twenty-first century has seen further devel-opments in flamenco, with musicians of all ages (such as **Miguel Poveda**, **José Mercé** and **Estrel-la Morente**) showing that they can easily move between the traditional and the new, small peña clubs and large concerts, serious world festivals and more commercial work. The female singer **Concha Buika**, has cut a striking figure, bring-ing in a husky bluesiness and also rehabilitating the piano as a flamenco instrument. Taking into account the witty songs of **Diego Carrasco**, as well as this versatility, flamenco is certainly thriving.

DISCOGRAPHY Spain | Flamenco

In addition to the recommendations below, enthusi-asts should be aware of four major series: EMI España's *Antologia de Cantaores* (twenty five volumes), the Hispavox *Magna Antología del Cante Flamenco* (ten volumes), RCA España's *Gran Antología Flamenco* (ten volumes) and the French label Chant du Monde's *Grandes Cantadores du Flamenco* (twelve volumes). Discs are available individually for each of these series which cover most historic figures, styles and epochs.

⊙ **Al aire de Jerez: La herencia cantaora de tres familias gitanas**
Nuevos Medios, Spain
Unbeatable tradition, bristling with the vitality of Los Moneo, Los Zambo and Los de la Morena, three Gypsy families from Jerez, the most vibrant Gypsy stronghold left.

⊙ **Beginner's Guide to Flamenco**
Nascente, UK
These three CDs cover the essentials, from the classic palos (styles), through innovative contemporary fusions to re-mixes introducing key musicians past and present. Sourcing much material from Spain's pioneering Nuevos Medios label, they're brimful of groundbreaking songs.

★ **Duende: The Passion and Dazzling Virtuosity of Flamenco**
Ellipsis Arts, US
This is a terrific introduction to flamenco: an excellent and well-illustrated booklet offering a succinct introduction to the tradition, genre, singers and musicians, and three CDs cover-

ing pretty much the full range of artists from La Niña de los Peines to Radio Tarifa.

★ **Flamenco Woman**
Boa, Spain
Seventeen stunning songs by some of the best women flamenco singers, from the finest voices of the present day to the greatest classic names of the recent past. Indispensable.

⊙ **Grandes Maestros del Flamenco**
Sonifolk, Spain
A timely remastering of the greatest names in flamenco born in the nineteenth century, including many who attended the pivotal first *Concurso de Cante Jondo* in 1922. Excellent biographies.

⊙ **Los Jóvenes Flamencos: Vols I–5**
Nuevos Medios, Spain
The pioneering label presents the very best of the innovative young artists on the 1990s scene who brought jazz, blues and a rock sensibility to the flamenco tradition. Each artist can be followed up through their various solo albums.

Agujetas (aka Manuel de los Santos Pastor)

Born in Jerez in 1939, this master of the old school per-sonifies flamenco Gypsy "outsider" mythology. Singing since the age of eight, he won the national prize in 1977, and was one of stars of the film *Flamenco* (1995). In 1999,

French director Dominique Abel made the award-winning documentary about him, *Agujetas, Cantaor*.

⊙ El Rey del Cante Gitano
Boa, Spain
Flamenco that ploughs the emotional depths, showing Agujetas' rough, rusty-edged voice at its best.

Vicente Amigo

Vicente Amigo (b.1967) is the outstanding concert guitarist of the moment. With various key guitar prizes under his belt, he set Rafael Alberti's poetry to music, working with Cuban guitarist Leo Brouwer. He has also produced discs for Remedios Amaya and Jose Mercé.

⊙ Ciudad de ideas (City of Ideas)
BMG, Spain
This 2001 album won Vicente Amigo the Latin Grammy for Best Flamenco Album, and it is quite superb.

Buika

Buika Concha is a black flamenco singer from Majorca, who in her short recording career so far has already caused quite a stir.

⊙ Nina de fuego
Warners, Spain
Javier Limón on guitar and Iván 'Melón' Lewis on piano are the perfect foil to Buika's husky tones.

El Camarón de la Isla (José Monge Cruz)

Spain's greatest flamenco singer of the second half of the twentieth century, El Camarón de la Isla was unsurpassed for interpretation and tone, and for pushing flamenco into new areas. With a voice of unrivalled passion and flair, he died tragically in 1992 at the age of 41. All his discs are worth hearing, from those with just pared-down voice and guitar to those with full orchestral accompaniment.

★ La Leyenda
Universal, Spain
A magnificent 4-CD anthology (75 songs), ranging from El Camarón's 1969 debut to his final 1992 recordings, remastered to emphasize the music's raw power and passion. An accompanying 48-page book contains many photos and fascinating text (in Spanish). Essential.

⊙ Camarón Potro de Rabia y Miel
Polygram, Spain
The disc includes a heroic poetic tribute to El Camarón from Joaquin Albaicin which really shows just how significant the singer was for flamenco. One of his last recordings, this is, for many, the most cherished.

Diego Carrasco

A key singer and composer from Jerez, Diego Carrasco is equally respected by flamenco purists and innovators; his wit and vitality are evident in his songs and performances.

⊙ Diego Carrasco
Nuevos Medios, Spain
"Yo Marinero" and the breathtaking "Nana de Colores" from this album explain just why Carrasco is so popular.

⊙ Mi ADN Flamenco
Nuevos Medios, Spain
Jerez-born Carrasco is a key figure in the flamenco world. This CD demonstrates his mastery of the compás, with inventive references to flamenco history and plenty of wit.

El Cigala (Diego Ramón Jiménez Salazar)

One of the premier young flamenco stars of his generation, thanks to his legendary collaboration with Cuban pianist Bebo Valdés, El Cigala has been dubbed "the Sinatra of flamenco". His stage name means "the little crayfish", perhaps inviting comparisons with El Camarón de la Isla.

AS BEBO & CIGALA

★ Lágrimas Negras
BMG
A sublime collaboration between émigré Cuban pianist Bebo Valdés and El Cigala giving a flamenco interpretation to Latin and Spanish classics. Placing them firmly on the international map, this won a 2005 BBC World Music Award and sold massively worldwide. Also recommended is *Black and White*, the DVD of their 2003 concert in Valdemossa, Mallorca.

Duquende

Duquende is one of the singers most often described as a successor to El Camarón de la Isla.

⊙ Duquende y la Guitarra de Tomatito
Nuevos Medios, Spain
Duquende is accompanied here by Tomatito, El Camarón's last accompanist and one of Spain's most respected young flamenco guitarists.

WITH FAÍZ ALI FAÍZ, MIGUEL POVEDA AND CHICUELO

⊙ Qawwali Flamenco
Accords Croisés, France
Double CD plus DVD. The twenty-first century's most exhilarating collaboration comes in this sublime dialogue between the mighty Arabic *Qawwali* and flamenco: ecstatically spine-tingling live and on disc.

El Indio Gitano

El Indio Gitano has a voice like bitter chocolate that can deal with anything from tangos to *granadínas*.

⊙ Nací Gitano por la Gracia del Díos
Nuevos Medios, Spain
El Indio Gitano is accompanied here by the jazz-sensitive guitar of Gerardo Nuñez.

Ketama

By introducing rock and Latin sensibilities to flamenco, Ketama exerted a seminal influence in the 1980s. Formed by young Gypsies José Soto, Ray Heredia and brothers Juan and Antonio Carmona, Ketama brought flamenco bang into the twentieth century. Their reputation spiralled when they recorded the groundbreaking *Songhai* with Malian kora player Toumani Diabaté and bassist Danny Thompson.

⊙ Ketama
Nuevos Medios, Spain
An essential CD that made Ketama the crossover group that helped establish the foundations of contemporary world music, featuring collaborations with guitarists Pepe Habichuela, Moraíto Chico and bassist Carlos Benavent.

El Lebrijano (Juan Peña)

Born in Lebrija in 1941, singer El Lebrijano is an essential figure in flamenco history. Following the school of Antonio Mairena, he toured with Antonio Gades' troupe, and was one of the first people to bring together flamenco and North African music, most notably on *Encuentro* (1985). He is a genial man with an earthy voice, and his innovations have made him one of the most admired singers.

⊙ Yo me llamo Juan
Flamenco Duende, Spain
An album with a wonderfully contemporary feel to it, this affirms El Lebrijano's flamenco identity.

⊙ Casablanca
EMI, Spain
This stunning collection of Arab-flamenco songs matches El Lebrijano's voice with a host of distinguished Arab singers.

Carmen Linares

Carmen Linares is one of the top contemporary female singers. A counterpoint to El Camarón, she has a fierce edge to her voice, a passion that borders on anger and fury before catharsis. Her concerts are a stunning live experience, not to be missed.

⊙ Antología: La Mejor en el Canto
Universal/Mercury, UK
Linares focuses on the cante jondo deep forms in her albums of rich, emotional and dynamic flamenco singing. There is no better way to hear this enormously expressive singer – one of the best in the world – than in this anthology.

Federico García Lorca

Lorca, a poet and playwright killed by Franco's men, was a keen flamenco enthusiast and excellent pianist. He worked hard to win intellectual respect for this unique genre and his interest brought it to new audiences in the 1930s.

⊙ Colección de Canciones Populares Españolas
Sonifolk, Spain
Here García Lorca accompanies female singer La Argentina on piano, with a repertoire of ten classic Spanish songs, including flamenco numbers, recorded in 1931.

⊙ Federico García Lorca: de Granada a la Luna
Sombra, Spain
An eclectic group of musicians pay homage to the murdered poet who championed flamenco, including Enrique Morente, Martirio and Imperio Argentina.

Martírio (Isabel Quiñones Gutiérrez)

Martirio is a pop singer who has flirted with flamenco and sevillanas, performing in mantilla scarves and dark glasses in the 1980s, like a symbol of the new Spain.

⊙ Estoy Mala
Nuevos Medios, Spain
The lyrics expose the hardship and frustrations of life (particularly for women) at the margins of Spanish society, and the hypocrisy of both bourgeois society and Catholicism in relation to the female experience. Martirio also uses untranslatable local slang with great verve and humour.

José Menese

Born in Seville in 1942, José Menese was a crucial figure in flamenco, retaining its integrity during the Franco dictatorship (1950s–70s) and regenerating orthodox styles.

⊙ A mis Soledades Voy, de mis Soledades Vengo
Boa, Spain
In this live recording from Seville in 2004, Menese sings a cycle of Golden Age classic poetry set to different flamenco palos, partnered by singer Laura Vital.

José Mercé (José Soto Soto)

With the handsome looks of a rock star and a voice with that treasured, torn, parched-leather quality, Mercé has followed in the footsteps of El Camarón, who encouraged him in his early teens. Born in Jeréz in 1955, he appeared in the Antonio Gades company's *Bodas de Sangre* (*Blood Wedding*) and in Carlos Saura's *Flamenco*. Moving fluently from classic deep cante jondo to upbeat poppy styles, his albums have beaten all previous flamenco sales records, and he is, undoubedly, one of the best present cantaores.

★ Aire (Air)
Virgin, Spain/UK
The ten mesmerizing songs on this album literally blew everyone away, from the infectious rumba "La Vida Sale" (recorded with Cuba's Cuarteto Patria) to the flamenco cover of Luis Eduardo Aute's "Al Alba". Featuring brilliant Jeréz-style guitar from El Moraíto Chico, this CD is essential listening.

Enrique Morente

Enrique Morente is considered one of the great artists of his generation because of his revivals and adaptations of modern and classic poets.

⊙ Negra, si tú Supieras
Nuevos Medios, Spain
Innovative arrangements of lyrics by various important poets.

★ New York and Granada
BMG, Spain
This collaboration with the late guitarist Sabica – one of his last recordings – became an instant classic.

Estrella Morente

Guided by her father, the great innovator Enrique Morente, Estrella has fulfilled the destiny of her name by becoming the new star of Spanish flamenco. While her nightingale voice places her in the footsteps of Pastora Pavón, she has the ability to sing the most complex flamenco styles with the maturity of someone beyond her years.

★ My Songs and a Poem
Real World, UK
Aided by a posse of seminal guitarists, this glorious disc moves from the upbeat to the soulful, and includes "Moguer", the exquisite exile poem written by Spain's Nobel Prize-winning poet Juan Ramón Jiménez.

⊙ Mujeres
EMO, Spain
Estrella pays dazzling tribute to innovative women singers from flamenco and related musics, including the tango mimed to by Penelope Cruz in Pedro Almodóvar's film *Volver*.

Gerardo Nuñez

Gerardo Núñez (b.1961) is one of the great guitarists of his generation. After studying flamencology at Jerez and touring with Paco Cepero, he formed an artistic partnership with his wife, the dancer Carmen Cortés. His collaborations with jazz musicians and with a large number of famous non-flamenco artists (including Plácido Domingo and Joaquín Sabina) has taken his work to a wide audience.

⊙ Andando el Tiempo
ACT, Germany
Including the talents of Paolo Fresu, Perico Sambeat and Mariano Diaz, this is a great flamenco-jazz disc.

Flamencos en Nueva York
Accidentales Flamencos, Spain
Gerardo Nuñez shows off his stunning technique – there are few faster guitar runs to be heard on any disc.

Ojos de Brujo

Barcelona's cutting-edge collective have brought a new audience to flamenco, and rapidly become a world-class act. Their dynamic, award-winning fusion, involving DJs, percussionists, guitarists and singer Marina Abad, draws on the music of the flamenco diaspora and beyond, their lyrics address contemporary political issues – and they party too!

Barí
La Fábrica de Colores, Spain
"Tiempo de Soleá" is just one of the stop-you-in-your-tracks songs this gifted group have sent travelling around the world. This is a fast-paced, yet soulful, album full of spontaneous, beautifully structured, songs. These superb musicians deliver spot-on accounts of everyday life with infectious energy.

⊙ Aocaná
Warner Music, Spain
A beautifully boxed mature set of new songs composed by singer Marina from the leading lights of European world music with a host of subtle collaborations with musicians from Spain, Cuba and India.

Paco de Lucía

Spain's leading and best-known flamenco guitarist, Paco de Lucía has a unique intuitive style, whether playing solo, accompanying others or working on jazz- or Latin-inflected material with his sextet. He has worked closely with El Camarón and has often collaborated with jazz guitarists such as Al di Meola, John McLaughlin and Pat Metheny.

Sirocco
Philips, Spain
A landmark album which set new standards for solo flamenco guitar – even now, it has few rivals.

⊙ Luzia
Polygram, Spain
This 1998 solo outing is a reflective and potent set, including pieces inspired by the memories of the late El Camarón de la Isla and by his own mother, Luzia.

SEXTETO PACO DE LUCÍA

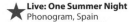
Live: One Summer Night
Phonogram, Spain
An irresistible, innovative recording courtesy of Paco de Lucía's band that, for all its fusion with jazz and Latin music and its big concert audience, still captures the essence of all that flamenco can be. If you'd prefer to hear their studio material, plump for *Solo Quiero Caminar* (Philips, Spain).

Pata Negra

Brothers Raimundo and Rafael Amador broke barriers by mixing flamenco with blues and rock'n'roll. Unanimously considered the best Spanish pop of its time, their 1980s music still sounds good today.

⊙ Pata Negra
Nuevos Medios, Spain
A key disc – a must-have – that kicks off with the ground-breaking "Blues de la Frontera".

Pastora Pavón

Born in Seville and known as La Niña de los Peines (the Girl of the Combs), Pastora Pavón was one of flamenco's most important early twentieth-century singers for introducing new styles. She was posthumously honoured by the Andaluz government as a national asset.

⊙ Voz de Estaño Fundido
Sonifolk, Spain
A remastering of key pieces from the "Queen of Flamenco aong", including the *bamberas*, *peteneras*, bulerias, soleares, seguiriyas and tangos she made her own.

Paco Peña

Twenty years ago, Córdoba-born Paco Peña won the Ramon Montoya prize for best concert guitarist. Organizer of the annual Córdoba guitar festival, his spirit of musical adventure has led him to forge new flamenco fusions, most notably with Argentine Eduardo Falú, Chile's Inti Illimani and the UK's John Williams.

Paco Peña, Flamenco Master: Essential Flamenco Recordings
Manteca, UK
This CD maps the gamut of Peña's art, including guitar solos, duos with Argentine Eduardo Falú, accompanying singers on his theatre pieces, and his flamenco Mass with The Academy of St Martin's in the Fields.

Miguel Poveda

Born in Barcelona in 1973, Poveda broke into the scene in 1993 when he won three prizes at the prestigious Festival de las Cantes de las Minas de La Unión. A formidable young talent, he has worked in film with Bigas Luna and in theatre with Calixto Bieito, and also created his own shows.

Suena Flamenco
Harmonia Mundi, Spain
From the show of the same name, this brilliantly captures the singer in various dynamic musical contexts, from guitarist, handclaps and simple piano to more upbeat arrangements.

⊙ Poemas del Exilio: Rafael Alberti
Harmonia Mundi, Spain
Live recording of Poveda's flamenco song cycle based on the poems of Rafael Alberti. Music by Enric Palomar; with accompaniment from a small chamber ensemble.

⊙ Tierra de calma
Discmedi Blau, Spain
Poveda is a young genius and has become the voice of the twenty-first century. The artist of choice for many other flamencos, he is capable of the most extraordinary emotional intensity. With amazing guitar from Romero, every song here is a pearl, including a vital duo with Diego Carrasco.

Radio Tarifa

In the early 1990s, Faín Sánchez Dueñas, Benjamín Escoriza and Vincent Molino created *Rumba Argelina* – one of the world music hits of the decade. An irresistible blend of erotic melodies and Mediterranean sounds, infused with Arabic, Sephardic and medieval influences, the album was just the first of Radio Tarifa's musical innovations.

⊙ Rumba Argelina
World Circuit, UK
Imaginatively interweaving snatches of music from an imaginary radio station playing sounds that evoke the straits

linking southern Spain to north Africa, this desert-island disc rocketed Radio Tarifa to cult fame.

Cruzando el Río
World Circuit, UK

Radio Tarifa ventured further afield for inspiration for their third album, looking to France and Japan, as well as drawing on Castillian, Andaluz and Galician folkloric traditions. Short but sublime, *Cruzando el Río* also features the inspired introduction of electric guitar.

Son de la Frontera

In their brief lifespan this acclaimed group made only two discs, *Cal* and *Son de la Frontera*.

⊙ Son de la Frontera
Nuevos Medios, Spain

In 2008 Son de la Frontera won a BBC Award for World Music for their pioneering introduction of the sound of the Cuban *tres* guitar into flamenco.

Manuel Soto, "El Sordero"

Manuel Soto is another great flamenco voice.

⊙ Grandes Cantaores de Flamenco: Manuel Soto, "El Sordero"
Chant du Monde, France

This is music to bring tears to your eyes, and it features a breathtaking recording of a Holy Week saeta.

Tomatito

Virtuoso guitarist Tomatito remains best-known for having been El Camarón's last accompanist, which is reason enough to cast him as one of the most fluent, imaginative and fiery contemporary guitarists.

⊙ Barrio Negro
Nuevos Medios, Spain
A superb solo album.

⊙ Tomatito
Nuevos Medios, Spain

As well as lovely solo work, this includes El Camarón singing "La Voz del Tiempo" (Voice of the Times), plus pieces with contemporaries Remedios Amaya, Potito and Duquende.

Fernanda and Bernarda de Utrera

Granddaughters of the legendary Pinini, sisters Fernanda and Bernarda de Utrera are fabulous both live and on disc, with a natural, earthy passion and lyricism.

Cante Flamenco
Ocora, France

These briliant recordings made for French radio include the Cantinas de Pinini, plus siguiriyas, bulerías, por solea and fandangos, with Paco del Gastor accompanying on guitar.

PLAYLIST
Spain | Flamenco

1 ENTRE SABANAS DE HOLANDA La Niña de los Peines from *La Niña de los Peines Voz de Estaño Fundido*
The key voice of twentieth-century flamenco sings a glorious folk piece.

2 LA VOZ DEL TIEMPO Tomatito & El Camarón de la Isla from *Tomatito*
With the upbeat chorus echoing El Camarón's voice and Tomatito's guitar underpinning it all, this proves Camarón to be "the voice of the time".

3 MOGUER Estrella Morente from *My Songs and a Poem*
A poem by Juan Ramón Jiménez set to music by Estrella Morente's father Enrique.

4 LA VIDA SALE Jose Mercé from *Aire*
The rough-edged chorus, trumpet blasts, vamping piano, percussion and, above all, Mercé's corroded, rusty voice – full of yearning – make this unbelievably sexy.

5 JARABI Ketama with Toumani Diabaté from *Ketama*
The passion and energy of the 1980s are captured in this beautiful encounter between Ketama and Malian kora player Toumani Diabaté.

6 DAME TU BOCA Javier Ruíbal from *Sahara*
Erotic seduction from flamenco-influenced singer-songwriter Javier Ruíbal.

7 EL YEDDI HAG ENNAS Radio Tarifa from *Fiebre*
Radio Tarifa's unbeatable live version of this compelling song, featuring wild sax solo.

8 CORAZÓN LOCO Bebo y Cigala from *Lágrimas Negras*
Classic Latin dilemma of a man torn between his wife and his lover; his pain and madness are made real in this sublime flamenco rendition.

9 TIEMPO DE SOLEA Ojos de Brujo from *Bari*
A flamenco solea written for the Barcelona street kids by this cutting-edge collective.

10 COGE LA ONDA El Lebrijano con la Orquesta Arábigo Andaluza from *Casablana*
The whole Arabic-Spanish fusion is consummated here in the earthy voice of Juan Peña, partnered by Hassan Jebelhbibi and an Arabic chorus.

Spain | Regional Musics

hot scenes

Amparanoia's Amparo Sánchez

Spanish music is known almost universally for flamenco but – popular though it is – for many of the country's musicians (and listeners) it's an exotic, almost alien strain. The "new Spain" of the 1990s and beyond was very much about its regions, and music is still an integral part of the country's multiple identities. There are bagpipes and Celtic sounds to be heard in the northwest, accordionists in the Basque Country, and, dotted around, fine singer-songwriters like the Catalan Lluís Llach or Mallorca's María del Mar Bonet and even a raft of medieval revivalists. However, Spain's thriving scene also bubbles with collaborations both between regions and with artists from abroad. Jan Fairley takes a tour.

"The party I carry within me, I bring to you, I bring to you", sings **Amparo Sánchez**, the sassy leader of the award-winning Spanish group **Amparanoia**. Her irresistible music is the sound of modern Spain: eclectic, socially conscious, raucous, defiant and fabulously entertaining. And this line from her song "La Fiesta" sums up the present exciting and confident state of Spanish music. The scene has transformed dramatically in the past ten years and is incomparable with the situation twenty years ago. Back then, Spanish groups mostly sang to local audiences in the regions; now the scene is red hot, with everyone not only making their own music but also engaging in a world of collaborations and exchange with artists in and outside the country.

Ana Belén and **Víctor Manuel** sing with **El Grupo SAF** in the celebratory "Contamíname", which merges West African Wolof language with Spanish, "Tell me your stories… Contaminate me, mix yourself with me." And what a lot of mixing is going on: **Enrique Morente** singing with **Les Voix Bulgares**, **Xosé Manuel Budiño** with **Capercaillie**, **Berrogüetto** with **Djivan Gasparan**, **Diplomáticos** with **Julian Hernández, Uxía** and **Batuko Tabanka** and **Bebo Valdés** with **Diego "El Cigala"** to name just a few.

This is in sharp contrast with the Spain of the Franco years when regional musics were a force for resistance against the censorship and grey commercialism of the dictatorship. During the post-Franco years this music acted as a springboard for the regeneration of Spain's culture, both locally and nationally, and of the individual identities of the autonomous regions such as the Basque Country and Catalonia. Now while regional musics thrive, with artists of all ages creating new material and enjoying popularity, the scene has become more complex.

The region's folk song and dance traditions which once buttressed regional identity in the face of oppression are now accepted as the norm by younger generations who enjoy the practices but use them as the basis for newer things. Dances such as *jota*, *fandango* and *seguidilla* continue to cut across several regions with variations. Others remain unique to (and often emblematic of) particular communities, for example the *muiñeira* in Galicia, the *zortziko* in the Basque Country and the *sardana* in Catalonia. While these are not as "ancient" as people think, they remain an integral part of the cultural scenery, still a key expectation during the annual pilgrimage to home villages of those who have left to work in the metropolitan centres. The celebration of **patron saint fiestas** continues as an essential reaffirmation of extended familial and historic bonds – and a guaranteed way of having a good time!

Today, festivals all over Spain not only celebrate local musics but also mix together the musics of different regions, and Cartagena's annual Mar de Musicas festival celebrates international sounds.

Galicia and Asturias

Folk or regional music is well developed in the country's northwest – **Celtic Spain** – with many vibrant voices and bands in the region. The **Festival del Mundo Celta** at Ortiguera, which played a leading role in the folk music revival, goes from strength to strength, and there is a thriving summer scene of local festivals in the **Basque Country**, **Asturias** and **Galicia**. The country's Celtic musicians take an active role in pan-Celtic festivals across Europe and further afield, with many attending Glasgow's mid-winter Celtic Connections Festival. Asturian piper **Hevia** was among those first off the starting block when his 1998 album *Tierra de Nadie* (featuring a digital electronic version of the local bagpipe, dubbed a MIDI *gaita*) clocked up reputed sales of two million.

These days Galician music is in particularly fine fettle, rooted in traditional ensembles of pipes, bagpipes and drums. The early pioneers like **Milladoiro** continue to find keen audiences, while a whole new generation of musicians like **Mercedes Péon** have followed in their spiritual footsteps,

Mercedes Péon

heading out into the villages to learn from old music practitioners who have kept the music alive there. Bagpiper **Carlos Nuñez** was one of the first to gain an international reputation, following his work with Ireland's Chieftains in the 1990s. His enthusiasm and charisma paved the way for others such as Péon, **Xosé Manuel Budiño**, **Susana Seivane** and the group **Berrogüetto**. This generation of musicians are highly inventive in approach, having grown up steeped in tradition while absorbing wider influences from contemporary pop, rock and world music.

Other Galician musicians who have helped revitalize the scene include **Na Lua** (who combine saxophones with bagpipes); **Doa**, **Citânia**, **Trisquell**, **Fía Na Roca** and **Xorima** (all traditional and acoustic); **Palla Mallada** (hyper-traditional); and **Alecrín**, **Brath** and **Matto Congrio** (electric folk). **Emilio Cao** switches back and forth between traditional folk and more modern singer-songwriting. Watch out also for the *pandeireta* (tambourine) groups like **Leilía** and **Faltriqueíra**.

A Celtic movement also exists in Asturias. Most groups there are fairly traditional, but **Llan de Cubel** can be challenging. There are also some talented Asturian harpists, among them **Herminia Olivarez** and **Fernando Largo**.

Basque Country (Euskadi)

The Basque Country (or Euskadi, as Basques call their land) is home to **trikitixa** (literally "devil's bellows") – a traditional pipe music transposed for the accordion. Trikitixa maestro **Josepa Tapia**, who was taught the instrument by his uncle and now plays with pandeireta player Leturia in the **Tapia Et Leturia Band**, is one of the most popular stars in this genre. **Kepa Junkera** has taken trikitixa further afield, working with Carlos Nuñez, and creating an exciting disc, *Bilbao 00:00h*, in collaboration with musicians from Madagascar, Sweden and beyond.

Junkera now enjoys a fine reputation in Spain, where his music has been used by Nacho Duarte for the Spanish National Ballet. He is also very popular internationally, particularly with Celtic music audiences. He has helped champion the playing of the ancient *txalaparta* xylophone, particularly the group **Oreka TX** who beat out rhythms on this unique instrument made out of loose planks of tuned wood. He is also involved in a summer school for budding musicians back home in Donostia-San Sebastián.

The best-known Basque roots band, **Oskorri**, are a politicized electro-acoustic group. They were

Marc Masschelein/M&M

Carlos Nuñez

instrumental in keeping Basque music publicly alive in the latter years of the Franco regime and have since gone from strength to strength. Also impressive are **Ganbara**, **Azala** and the singer-songwriter **Benito Lertxundi**, whose energies are generally devoted to traditional Basque music but who has also recently experimented with the Celtic sounds of the northern coast. Another singer-songwriter, the rock-influenced **Ruper Ordorika**, has recently worked on a collaborative venture using the poetry of **Bernardo Atxaga** (the first Basque to win Spain's National Prize for Literature). Atxaga has previously written lyrics for rock and folk bands.

There is also a thriving Basque tradition of **bersolari** – improvising rural poets – and now a younger generation move freely between village and city, encouraged by Basque radio and TV competitions and festivals.

Catalonia

Catalonia shares with French Rousillon the roots of a language and a number of music and dance styles, including Rumba Gitana (Gypsy Rumba), made famous by the Perpignan-based Gipsy Kings (see Gypsy music chapter). Catalonia's top star in the genre is **Peret**, who opened the Barcelona Olympics. The late Gato Perez was also hugely popular, producing a kind of rock-rumba. And rumba has gained new prominence through the work of flamenco-hip-hop collective **Ojos de Brujo**.

The province also has a couple of national (and indeed international) stars – **Lluís Llach** and **Joan Manuel Serrat**. Serrat sings in both Catalan and Castilian, and enjoys a huge reputation in both Spain and Latin America. Llach started out in a group called **Els Setze Jutges** before going solo as a singer-songwriter. He was a political writer in the late Franco years, composing songs in the repressed Catalan language – songs such as the clandestinely distributed "País Petit" (My Small Country). He spent four years in exile in France. More recently he has led a village life and his lyrics have had an acute political awareness of the problems of life in rural areas, notably in his 1997 suite of songs, *Porrera*. Now retired, he toured Europe until recent years with a superb group, mixing elements of jazz and rock in his arrangements, while at home he's become part of the national establishment, invited to give recitals of his settings of poetry at key literary awards. A recent project involved setting the work of key Catalan poets to music.

Catalonia also has a number of orchestras who play traditional dance music: some closer to salsa, such as the **Orquesta Platería** and the **Salseta del Poble Sec**, others more traditional, such as **Tercet Treset** and the **Orquesta Galana**.

The emblematic **sardana dance** remains important at every local festival, as does the popular singing tradition known as **habanera**, which thrives today on the coast at summer festivals, linking Catalonia with Cuba. The maritime connections between the countries through merchant seamen and the navy were strong throughout the nineteenth and twentieth centuries, and are reflected in the music of *ida y vuelta* – coming and going, greeting and farewell.

Barcelona is now one of the cultural hotspots of Europe and has a thriving, cutting-edge musical scene involving many Brazilian and Cuban immigrants, among others. The scene is fuelled by a fresh generation of musicians whose anti-corporate, ethical politics, eclectic tastes and strong friendships take them back and forth between Barcelona, Madrid, Granada and Seville as they move in and out of each other's bands. Key groups include Ojos de Brujo, who came out of the **Fabrica de Colores** artistic collective, and **Macaco**, led by music activist Dani "El Mono Loco" Macaco. Macaco's description of his group's music as mixing earth and space perfectly sums up the ingredients: Latin, flamenco and Catalan rumba plus hip-hop and electro.

The now defunct **Dusminguet**, from the nearby town of La Garriga, were another typically eclectic outward-looking Catalan group, unafraid to mix sardana with Tex-Mex, reggae, East European and North African grooves. Barcelona was also where ex-pat French singer **Manu Chao** fermented many of the ideas and influences which would lead him to global fame. But the Catalan knack for thinking outside the box isn't just a recent phenomenon, as exemplified by the **Companyía Elèctrica Dharma**, whose pioneering work electrifying *cançó catalana* traditions has its roots in the late 1970s.

The annual Barcelona Grec festival is a good window on the contemporary scene in the region and further afield. Nearby **Manresa** on the Ignatian pilgrimage route now hosts the November **Fira d'Espectacles d'Arrel Tradiciones** (Traditional Roots Fair) where local artists such as Valencian singer **Miquel Gil** and **La Banda d'En Vinaixa** play alongside musicians from neighbouring cultures.

Mallorca

In Catalan-speaking **Mallorca** singer-songwriter **María del Mar Bonet** was, with Lluís Llach, a part of the 1960s singer-composer group Els Setze Jutges, and a prominent figure in the *nova cançó* (new song) movement which incurred the displeasure of Franco's censors.

Bonet's most popular songs include Mallorca's unofficial hymn, "La Balanguera", as well as lively dances like "La Jota Marinera" and the apocalyptic medieval "La Sybilla", sung only on Christmas Eve in certain churches in Mallorca. Some of her arrangements of Mallorcan work songs have been choreographed as ballets. She has delved into Mallorca's connections with what Turkish poet Omar Zülfü Livaneli has described as the "sixth continent": all the countries embraced by the Mediterranean, from Mallorca, Sardinia and North Africa to Sicily, Italy and Greece. As well as recording Livaneli's songs, she has worked closely with Greek composer Mikis Theodorakis. In recent years, Bonet has seen her career take off again internationally, particularly stimulated by her "green" album *Raixa*, a tribute to Mallorca which confronted the politics of land ownership on the island.

Other Mallorcan musicians of interest include the superb guitarist **Joan Bibiloni**, who embraces folk, jazz and picking styles, and the singer-songwriter **Tomell Penya**, always disguised under a cowboy hat.

Manuel Dominguez/Nubenegra

Luís Delgado

Andalusia

Andalusia is not only the home of flamenco. Musicians like **Kiko Veneno** and **Joaquín Sabina**, for example, play a witty, catchy rock with youthful lyrics. Andalusia also has two further significant singer-songwriters, the popular **Carlos Cano**, who has revived the traditional Andalusian *copla* (a form of popular song), and **Javier Ruibal**.

Sephardic (medieval Iberian Jewish) music is also to be found in the region – a cross between folk and traditional styles. Singers **Rosa Zaragoza** and **Aurora Moreno** have produced interesting work in this field, as has the outstanding musician **Luís Delgado**. Moreno has also recorded Mozarabic *jarchas* (Arabic-Christian verse set to music), while the groups **Els Trobadors** and **Cálamus** have, like Radio Tarifa (see Flamenco chapter), experimented with medieval traditions.

Elsewhere

Musicians move freely in and out of Madrid, Barcelona, Granada, Santiago de Compostela, Vigo and other cities, mixing with others from the Americas and the Caribbean such as Cuba's **Pancho Amat** and **Pablo Milanés**. **Eliseo Parra** is just one versatile Madrid-based multi-instrumentalist who works with groups all over Spain. Rock singer **Santiago Auserón** is also an active collaborator, notably with Cuban musicians, while **Luís Eduardo Aute**, based in Madrid, enjoys a wonderfully creative relationship with Cuban troubadour **Silvio Rodríguez**. The long-standing singing partnership of **Ana Belén** and her husband **Víctor Manuel** has been consistently creative. Belén's songs – including popular settings of poems by the Cuban Nicolas Guillen – are unsurpassed, her mobile, lively voice forging a new Spanish-Cuban style.

From Valencia, **Al Tall** is an interesting band who have collaborated with the Moroccan Berber group Muluk El Hwa. From Aragon, roots groups include **Hato de Foces**, **Cornamusa** and the **Orquestina del Fabriol**, while the Zamora-based **Habas Verdes** perform spirited, vivid versions of traditional tunes on instruments such as the hurdy gurdy, the *dulzaina*, cello, organ and guitar. Finally, singer **María Salgado** has made fine recordings of the habanera tradition found outside Catalonia, and has recorded the album *La Sal de la Vida* (The Salt of Life) with two other women musicians, Uxía from Galicia and Rasha from the Sudan, exploring the similarities and differences between their cultures.

Piping Hot

Pipers lead the way in Galicia. In the words of one of the key musicians involved, **Susana Seivane**, "In Galicia the bagpipe means everybody dancing and singing, getting together in a neighbour's house, rather than anything military. We have a lot of rich rhythms in our culture. The muiñeira is the most characteristic one; you could compare it to a Scottish reel. Then we have *pasadobles* and *xotas*. It has a lot to do with emigration, as we Gallegos have gone everywhere in the world and other parts of Spain, bringing new music back home, and over the years we have made it distinctly our own."

One of the trailblazers was **Carlos Nuñez**, whose 1987 album *Irmandade das Estrellas* (Brotherhood of Stars) went platinum in a matter of months in Spain. It set the vogue for collaborations, as it involved North American guitarist **Ry Cooder**, Cuba's **Vieja Trova Santiaguera** and Ireland's **The Chieftains**. Voted one of Galicia's leading figures in a recent poll, Nuñez was the first of a generation of musicians to gain world fame not just as a result of talent and technique (they championed the rediscovery of ornamentation and grace notes), but through their passion and attachment to their Galician and Spanish roots.

Increasingly, through the work of pipers like Susana Seivane, **Xosé Manuel Budiño** and **Mercedes Péon**, reinterpretation has given way to original composition. Seivane was born to play: "When I was tiny I played my father's bagpipes and used to fall over they were so heavy. When I was four my family made a special set just for me so I could play properly. My body has grown with the pipes. It's not misshapen but you can see how they have evolved together." For Seivane her music is "Music that walks. And it's true we have been looking for our musical pathway, what we enjoy doing and what we don't, creating our own style."

Xosé Manuel Budiño's *Zume de Terra* takes the renaissance still further. Totally conversant with technology, Budiño did all the composing, arrangements and samples in his home studio, sending mock-ups of complete pieces for the album to the various musicians who he'd asked to collaborate with him – people like Cape Verde's **Sara Tavares**. The first track, "Nós", which samples the voice of exiled Galician intellectual Alfonso Castelao, establishes the concept for the album and acts as a larger metaphor for much of what is happening in Galician music. "Castelao says that work needs to be universal and understood by the rest of the world, that his work is made with 'zume de terra' – the juice of the earth – and 'mel de tradicion galega', the honey of Galician tradition." For Budiño, that means exploring Galician roots with all the influences of his travels, working with musicians from India to Scotland.

Like Peón, Budiño has done source collecting from people who only sang for families and friends and not commercially. While he knows that Galicia did not originally have harmonic instruments, just pipes, percussion and voices, today like the others he uses harmony, while offering catchy, danceable melodies, marrying his rich Galician heritage with something experimental and techno. Budiño's desire is to offer people "an image of Galicia so that even someone who has no idea about the place feels identified with its rhythms and melodies. Last summer during our gigs we had a video-jockey projecting old black and white photo images of Galicia with modern video images. It was beautiful."

DISCOGRAPHY Spain | Regional Musics

⊙ **Barcelona Zona Bastarda**
Organic Records, UK
A vital two-CD cross-section of one of the most vibrant musical scenes in Europe, with a huge Latin undertow abounding in exciting and experimental collaborations and fusions.

★ **Discopolis 5000**
Boa, Spain
Spanish radio DJ José Miguel López's programme *Discopolis* has played a key part in opening Spanish ears to the richness of Spanish music. This CD celebrates one thousand editions of his award-winning show with seventeen glorious pieces of the million or so played since 1987. A must have.

⊙ **Federico García Lorca: De Granada a la Luna**
Sombra, Spain
An eclectic group of musicians, from Enrique Morente to Compay Segundo, Neneh Cherry to Santiago Auserón, mark the centenary of the birth of the great poet Lorca, who was killed during the Spanish Civil War.

⊙ Valencia, Cant d'Estil
Ocora, France

A charming recording of non-professional street singers from Valencia. The *cantadoras* and *cantadors* perform *valencianes* in the old high-pitched *cant d'estil* manner, accompanied by small *rondallas* – orchestras using trumpet, clarinet and trombone, as well as guitars strummed in a fandango rhythm. There are also *albaes*, backed only by a *dolçaina* (shawm) and snare drum.

Amparanoia

Granada singer Amparo Sánchez has a truly international musical spirit, fusing influences from Europe, Cuba, Mexico and the Latin Caribbean with plenty of techno touches in her own inimitable way. A fiery songwriter, she often takes a women's perspective on life's struggles, including those of Mexico's Zapatistas. Her band, Amparanoia, was formed in 1996.

★ Rebeldía con Alegría (Rebellion with Fun)
Virgin/EMI, UK

This is an exhilarating compilation of some of Amparanoia's greatest moments to date, wittily drawing on hip-hop, ska, punk, thrash dub, reggae and rock'n'roll. Watch out for collaborations with Manu Chao and Calexico.

Berrogüetto

This seven-piece group craft beautiful roots pieces with a real cosmopolitan feel to them. With a mix of old and new sounds from pipes, guitars, piano, bass, bouzouki and accordion, they benefit from the glowing voice of Guadi Galego.

★ Hepta (Seven)
Boa, Spain

This beautifully packaged album, full of fabulous pieces, is a tribute to this cool yet fiercely talented band.

Xosé Manuel Budiño

Proving to be the most exciting of his generation of pipers, Budiño uses the tradition he is steeped in as a springboard to new sounds. His passion for technology and collaborations gives him fresh ideas and has led him even deeper into his roots.

★ Zumo de Terra
Boa, Spain

A feast of gorgeous pieces with great guests like Sara Tavares. Watch out for the hidden "Galicia Vente Xa", his haunting song for Spanish TV's *Fiesta en Finisterre*, which involved Capercaillie's Karen Matheson and Mercedes Péon.

Manu Chao

Born in France to Spanish parents, Manu Chao is based in Barcelona, where he has lived for over ten years.

⊙ La Radiolina
Because, France

Asking "What now?", Chao shows that his commitment to anti-globalism, the plight of migrants, and the people of Africa and the Americas is stronger than ever.

Luís Delgado

Luís Delgado is an exceptional musician – a multi-instrumentalist, producer and composer who has explored medieval, traditional and regional music and worked with all kinds of groups in creative and daring fusions.

⊙ El Hechizo de Babilonia
Intuition, Germany

Delgado and female guest singers including María del Mar Bonet and Marien Hassan sing his spellbinding settings of songs based on the poetry of six women poets from the eleventh to the thirteenth century.

Faltriqueíra

These five exuberant women singers and pandereta players from Pontedeume sing in harmony and mix Galician and Basque cultures, crossing the border to work with Basques Kepa Junkera and Oskorri to make music that defies any notion of regionalism or national borders.

⊙ Faltriqueira
Resistencia, Spain

Recorded in the Basque Country's Donostia-San Sebastián, this features songs learned from Galician families and friends plus a few songs for neighbouring Portugal.

Miquel Gil

A gruff-voiced veteran of several well-known bands, including Al Tall and Terminal Sur, Gil is the leading figure of Valencian song.

★ Orgànic
Sonifolk, Spain

This impressive 2001 solo debut is full of beautifully nagging melodies set to the words of contemporary and traditional poetry. Gil's music reflects his love of *rondallas* (Mediterranean string bands) as well as the distinctively Valencian *dolçaines* and *grallas* (shawms), which lend a shrill sound reminiscent of Radio Tarifa in places.

Kepa Junkera

A virtuoso player of Basque trikitixa, Junkera is unusual for achieving success while not being a native Basque speaker.

⊙ Bilbao 00:00h
Resistencia, Spain

The trikitixa ace successfully collaborates with veteran Basque group Oskorri, Portuguese singer Dulce Pontes, The Chieftains' Paddy Maloney, the Swedish band Hedningarna and Madagascar's Justin Vali.

⊙ Maren
EMI Odeon, Spain

Dedicated to sea journeys and to Junkera's own navigation of different musics, *Maren* offers a multi-ethnic context for trikitixa. Collaborators include Oreka TX, Bulgarka Junior, Albania's Tirana, the brass of Canada's La Bottine Souriante, Madagascar's Justin Vali and Mallorca's María del Mar Bonet.

Ibon Koteron

Koteron plays the ancient *alboka*, the double-reeded, twin-piped cow horn originally played by shepherds in the hills of the Basque Country, partnering it with accordions, *duduk* and the txalaparta cider plank xylophone.

⊙ Airea
Elkar, Spain

Produced by Kepa Junkera, this intriguing disc shows the versatility of the alboka. Basque music meets influences that accentuate its Mediterranean connections.

Leilía

All-women group Leilía are reviving the Galician rural tradition of pandeireta (women tambourine players) and their repertoire of dance songs, many with double-entendre. A band with great energy and a sense of innovation.

⊙ Leilía Exuberant
Discmedi, Spain

A disc of jotas, muineiras and *mazurcas*, with the original six women joined by various guests including the six-man Pandeiromus group.

Lluís Llach

A key singer of Catalan nova cançó, Llach has succesfully moved from embodying the spirit of opposition to Franco to success with new themes and audiences in the 1990s. Now retired, he is nevertheless a major Catalan cultural figure.

Poetes
BMG, Spain

A live recording of Llach and his ace band performing a tribute to his literary heritage and poetic passions. His settings of the work of eight Catalan poets are full of gorgeous lingering melodies flowing with emotional nostalgia.

Llan de Cubel

Headlining the Celtic movement in Asturias, Llan de Cubel produce challenging versions of traditional music.

⊙ Un Tiempu Meyor
Fono Astur, Spain

Contemporary texts and Asturian melodies played on fiddles, flutes, accordions and bagpipes.

Macaco

Led by visionary eclectic producer-composer-musician Dani "El Mono Loco" (the Mad Ape) Macaco, this band are a force in the region and way beyond. Drawing members from Cuba, Argentina, Brazil, Colombia, Venezuela and Spain, they merge hip-hop, techno and a huge rock sensibility with Catalan rumba, flamenco and Latin sounds.

⊙ Rumba Submarino
Edel, Spain

A blend of witty lyrics, catchy melodies, found sounds, samples, Spanish and Caribbean-Latin rhythms and snatches of reggae, hip-hop, scratching and roots styles. Irresistible.

María del Mar Bonet

Known as the "Mermaid of the Mediterranean", Mallorca's María del Mar Bonet (Mary of the Sea) is one of Spain's major singers.

Raixa
WorldMuxxic, Spain

Recorded live in the open-air Plaça del Rei at Barcelona's Grec Festival, this is a feast of story-songs that celebrate the garden within and without, its underpinning politics the sale of wild mountain scenery dating back to Muslim-Arab times.

⊙ Amic Amat
Galileo, Switzerland

With a Catalan choir adding subtle touches, this is a sublime recording of Ramon Llull's mystical poetry "The Book of the Lover and the Beloved", based on King Solomon's "Song of Songs" with Koranic, Talmudic and Eastern influences.

Milladoiro

Galicia's foremost band have many years' experience pioneering the Galician sound on a multiplicity of pipes and other instruments.

As Fadas de Estraño Nome
Green Linnet, US

Recorded live in April 1995 in Buenos Aires, this features a brilliant set of invigorating tunes and rhythms.

Fermín Muguruza

A veteran of the Basque cultural-political scene and punk bands, Muguruza fuses challenging lyrics with hip street sounds and roots in his own special way.

⊙ FM 99.00 Dub Manifest
Piranha, Germany

Multi-faceted, multi-ethnic music that fuses Basque heritage via singers Mikel Laboa and Ruper Ordorika with a host of contemporary hip sounds. Club to "Men Without Guns" and "Reunite the World".

Carlos Nuñez

Galicia's – and Spain's – foremost bagpiper and flautist, Nuñez has a feel for the diaspora of Spanish and Galician music reaching as far as Cuba.

⭐ A Irmandade das Estrelas
Ariola, Spain

A superb disc of lively and moving melodies with a great band and terrific arrangements, this established Nuñez's potential for worldwide fame.

⊙ Os Amores Libres
RCA Victor, US

Recorded in ten countries with over a hundred musicians, this ambitious disc pursues connections between apparently distinct musical traditions with great tenacity and some success.

Domingo Rodrígues Oramas "El Colorao"

Domingo Rodrígues Oramas is the Canary Islands' leading player of the *timple* (a small five-stringed instrument). The islands' folkloric music hints at many Latin American styles – especially those of Cuba and Venezuela, to which many Canary Islanders once emigrated.

⊙ Aulaga
Colorado Producciones, Spain

This two-CD set from 2003 is a treasure trove of acoustic waltzes, *aires*, *folías malagueñas*, etc, on which Oramas is accompanied by numerous other local singers and musicians on guitar and percussion (including limpet shells!). It was recorded in atmospheric outdoor settings, with chirping sparrows for accompaniment.

Oskorri

Oskorri are the Basque Country's essential folk group, forging a clear musical identity for themselves at home and abroad over the past couple of decades.

⊙ Desetore
KD, Spain

This veteran multi-instrumental group refuse to sit back on their laurels but instead remain crisp and innovative, proving they are one of the best of their generation. Watch out for the guests!

Eliseo Parra

Parra's eclectic innovations reinvent tradition. Based in Madrid, he draws from every region of Spain, but having been a part of the Barcelona scene for many years he also performs everything from Latin to jazz.

⊙ Viva Quien Saber Querer (Long Live Those Who Know How to Love)
Boa, Spain
Each song is a world in itself, revealing Parra's optimistic take on life.

Mercedes Péon

Composing, singing, playing pipes and dancing, Péon is at the cutting edge of folk music in Spain as well the renaissance of the Galician scene. A great source collector of tunes from old village musicians, she's a magnetic performer with a voice that radiates every conceivable emotion.

⊙ Isué (This Is It)
Resistencia, Spain
This debut disc, full of raw energy, knocked everyone sideways as much for the power of its vision as for Péon's voice. Once heard, it's never forgotten.

⊙ Ajrú
Trompo, Spain
With a hint of shamanism in the brew, there is a kind of primeval power to some of these songs, while others hint at gentle French romance and reggae touches.

Port-Bo

Port-Bo are one of several Costa Brava groups singing the surviving habanera tradition which links these Catalonian fishing villages with Cuba.

⊙ Canela y Ron
Picap, Spain
Celebrated in annual festivals held on the beaches of Catalonia, these are old and new, mostly romantic habaneras.

Joaquín Sabina

The inimitable Madrid-based songwriter does not dabble in world music but, as the Peter Pan of Spanish music, he articulates the left-field soul of activists from the 1960s onwards in Spain and Cuba. Today he enjoys very young audiences who know his songs by heart.

 Cantautores
Epic/CBS, US
Contains "Pongamos que Hablo de Madrid" (Let's Talk About Madrid) and the achingly beautiful "Calle Melancolia" (Melancholy Street).

María Salgado

Castilian María Salgado is one of mainland Spain's most interesting contemporary singer-songwriters.

WITH UXÍA AND RASHA
⊙ La Sal de la Vida
NubeNegra, Spain
Salgado, Galician vocalist Uxía and Sudanese singer Rasha come together to sing their own traditions and exchange songs, including recordings of largely unheard songs from Galicia and Asturias, from lullabies to songs of leaving for Havana.

Susana Seivane

The youngest in a hitherto male dynasty of pipe makers and players, the attractive and amiable Seivane has been playing since she was a small child and is a rising star of Galician music.

⊙ Mares de Tempo
Boa, Spain
Aided by a rock-influenced band, Seivane sings and plays her pipes, transforming traditional xotas, muiñeiras and polkas with the odd rustic sound like the saw!

Joan Manuel Serrat

Serrat is one of Spain's key singer-songwriters, with a huge international following in Spain and Latin America.

⊙ Nadie es Perfecto
Ariola, Spain
A 1994 live album that found Serrat in exuberant, serenading form.

⊙ Sombras de la China
Picap, Spain
This one is a must, especially the witty truth of "I Love All of You, But Not You".

WITH ANA BELÉN, MIGUEL RIOS AND VICTOR MANUEL
⊙ El Gusto es Nuestro
Ariola, Spain
In 1996 four of Spain's top singers united for an exciting world tour, which this CD commemorates. The songs include stunning covers of American 1960s rockers, revealing their true eclecticism.

Tapia Et Leturia

Basque trikitixa duo Tapia Et Leturia are the masters of the genre, maintaining and revitalizing the tradition.

⊙ Nueva Etiopia
Colección Lcd el Europeo, Spain
Subtitled "Songs, Conversations and Poems", this is an exciting collaboration, with texts by the Basque and Spanish national prize-winning author, poet and lyric writer Bernardo Atxaga. Featuring Tapia, Leturia, folk-rocker Ruper Ordorika, giant Basque singer Mikel Laboa, Itoiz and Gari, this is inspiring medieval troubadour music.

PLAYLIST
Spain | Regional Musics

1 CONTAMÍNAME Ana Belén, Víctor Manuel, El Grupo SAF from *Discopolis 5000*
Invigorating collaboration fusing rough and raucous Wolof with Spanish.

2 LA FIESTA Amparanoia from *Rebeldía con Alegría*
A trip to Mexico to hook up with the Zapatistas inspired this cabaret-style song, which reminds us that in the darkest times we're our own best resource.

3 ALQUIMISTA DE SONOS Berrogüetto from *Hepta*
Guadi Galego's lyrics for "Alchemist of Dreams", written with guitarist Guillermo Fernández, are about her father's death.

4 EL EMIGRANTE MIX Celtas Cortas from *Discopolis 5000*
Fabulous quasi-heavy-rock Andean fusion with pithy political lyrics about the treatment of immigrants.

5 VAMOS DANÇAR Faltriqueira from *Faltriqueira*
You'd be hard pressed to know exactly where these five girls came from – the sound is a heady fusion of Spain and Galicia with something African, north European and Mediterranean too!

6 VIATGE A ITACA Lluís Llach from *Poetes*
Strings give way to jazz funk sax on this epic version of Llach's prophetic "Journey to Ithaca".

7 BURBUJO ROJA Macaco from *Rumba Submarino*
The seductive, laconically sexy and beautiful "Pink Bubbles", from the guys at the cusp of the Barcelona scene.

8 MADONA DE SA CABANA María del Mar Bonet from *Raixa*
An acapella version of the Mallorcan traditional song to the Madonna and the morning sun rising "red as a pomegranate".

9 MARABILLA Mercedes Péon from *Isué*
An unforgettably beautiful song that shows Péon's voice at its very best.

10 NA LINA DA MARE Xosé Manuel Budiño from *Zumo de Terra*
Cape Verde's Sara Tavares sings this exquisite song of the sea.

Sweden

a devil of a polska

Swåp
Thomas Fahlander

Swedish bands play the international pop and rock game with considerable success, but Sweden is also rich in traditional music, with a strong heritage of fiddle and nyckelharpa playing, and some distinctive uses of the voice. It is a world of fascinating dance rhythms, microtonal scales and high skill. Andrew Cronshaw takes a journey of discovery.

As elsewhere in Europe, it was the youth radicalism of the late 1960s and early 1970s that sparked a revival of interest in Sweden's roots music. A new wave of young musicians took up folk instruments, predominantly the **fiddle**, learning where possible from older tradition bearers. Sweden's traditional music is a patchwork of regional styles and repertoires of music and dance, and there was a strong desire to learn the dances, tunes and techniques of one's own locality. Many joined or formed a **spelmanslag** (traditional musicians' club), and also rediscovered the social delights of couple dancing; many of the dance tunes, particularly those for the very popular **polska**, are hard to understand rhythmically unless one dances. **Spelmansstämmor** – traditional musicians' gatherings – multiplied across the country, courses sprang up for making and playing traditional instruments, and roots music began to feature in live events and on radio and TV. There was an upsurge in entries for the auditions for a Zorn badge – the award to traditional musicians which, if gold or silver, bestows the title *riksspelman*.

As the scene grew during the 1980s the music was largely instrumental, with the fiddle to the fore, but the 1990s saw a flowering of new approaches, bringing in more vocals and other instrumentation. Some bands combined traditional instruments and modern electronics with great success, both musically and in reaching a new audience.

Since 2000 some of the electric bands – never numerous but extremely powerful and looking set to take on the world – have gone quiet, partly it appears because of the difficult economics and logistics of touring. The new ones arising are largely acoustic, as the skills gained and developed in the earlier days of the revival evolve further in the hands of both a new generation and the prime movers of the previous thirty years. Bands may come and go but this is music of the individual; indeed much of the tradition is of solo playing or singing.

Fiddling

The violin arrived in Sweden in the seventeenth century and was widespread as a folk and concert instrument within a hundred years, though it suffered a setback in some rural areas in the nineteenth century as a result of religious fundamentalism; some preachers saw music and dancing as ungodly and the fiddle as an instrument of the devil.

Today the most famous fiddling region, with a very much living tradition and a great variety of music, is the county of Dalarna, particularly the townships near Lake Siljan such as Rättvik, Boda, Bingsjö and Orsa, each of which has its own tunes and style.

The Addictive Polska

There are a wide range of dances in Swedish tradition, but by far the most popular is the **polska**. The style of playing and dancing varies regionally and even from township to township, but essentially it's a couple dance in which side-by-side, hesitating walking steps alternate with exciting bouts of tight-embraced wide-stepping turning. Exactly when the change comes, and the details and elaborateness of the steps, is chosen by each couple rather than being in synchrony with others. It's nominally in 3/4 time, but the three beats aren't necessarily equal in length; in some local traditions they get stretched or shortened. This lurch in the rhythm is most in evidence in polskas from the region of Dalarna.

Musicians, as well as dancers, become fascinated by the rhythmic and melodic possibilities of polska, and at first listen a Dalarna polska, in particular, can be rhythmically confusing and unsettling, particularly when played, as it often is, by a solo fiddler, either for his or her own amusement or for dancing. As with the dance tunes of Norway, the player's footstamp, usually on the first and third beat, can give some clue, but the only way to really grasp it is to dance.

Polska evolved from the "Polish-style" dances **polonaise** and **mazurka** that swept across Europe in the seventeenth century. (Sweden had particular exposure to Polish fashions at the end of the sixteenth century, when both countries were ruled by Swedish king Sigismund Vasa.) It's not to be confused with the **polka**, which is a more recent 2/4 dance that spread across Europe and beyond in the nineteenth century, including to the Nordic countries; its origins are Czech and – unlike the polska – the polka is danced in Poland too.

Other forms of tune that crop up frequently in Swedish traditional music include the **gånglåt** (a walking tune traditionally played for the wedding procession on the way to church), the stately **brudmarsch** (wedding march), and the **halling**, a tune for a high-kicking male showing-off dance that's still danced that way in Norway but rarely in Sweden. Like the polska, it's well suited to the drive of modern roots bands.

Falun Folk Festival

Hjort Anders Olsson

The styles of individual musicians were major factors in shaping the way Swedish fiddling evolved. Notable fiddlers of the nineteenth century, whose names are still associated with particular tunes or versions, include **Lapp-Nils** (Nils Jonsson, 1804–70) from the county of Jämtland and two Dalarna fiddlers: **Lejsme-Per Larsson** (1822–1907) from Malung and **Pekkos Per** (d.1877) of Bingsjö.

Their music is known only from reputation and as passed down by those who knew them, but the next generation lived into the era of sound recording. Most famous by far was **Hjort Anders Olsson** (1865–1952), who was born in Bingsjö and played many of Pekkos Per's tunes. His success in a fiddle competition launched his concert career, and he became well known in Stockholm as resident player at the Skansen outdoor museum. He made many radio broadcasts and a number of recordings. His grandson **Nils Agenmark** (1915–94) learned from him and tried to reach back in his playing to the style of Pekkos Per; he in turn directly influenced many of the present generation. So did **Päkkos Gustaf** (1916–2000), who lived all his life in Bingsjö, a village which since 1969 has annually thronged with fiddlers and others during one of the country's most popular spelmansstämmor. Gustaf was the model for a brilliant modern wood-sculpture, on display in the Dalarnas Museum in Falun, which perfectly captures the essence of an old fiddler, his work-hardened hands pouring out music of great delicacy and complexity.

The styles and skills of these and other fiddle tradition-bearers have been taken up by today's myriad fiddlers; there are probably more excellent fiddlers now than at any time in history, each with a distinctive style that's the result of location, preference in role model, repertoire and personal inspiration. Leading names include **Kalle Almlöf, Pers Hans Olsson, Björn Ståbi, Per Gudmundson, Mats Edén, Ellika Frisell, Jonny Soling, Kjell-Erik Eriksson, Hans Kennemark, Ola Bäckström, Mats Berglund, Ole Hjorth** and **Sven Ahlbäck**, but there are many more of equal skill and characterfulness. Some have taken up other forms of the fiddle – for example **Mikael Marin** on viola. **Magnus Stinnerbom, Daniel Sandén-Warg, Mats Edén** and quite a few of the current generation play deep-sounding fiddles with extra sympathetic strings, like the Norwegian Hardanger fiddle, to enhance the drone effect. Derived from the seventeenth-century European *viola d'amore*, these go under a variety of names including *bordunfiol* (drone fiddle), *stakefiol* and *låtfiol*.

Nyckelharpa

The folk revival was the perfectly timed salvation of Sweden's most distinctive indigenous instrument, the **nyckelharpa** (keyed fiddle). In size and construction, it's some way from a standard fiddle – more like a thinner hurdy-gurdy without a wheel; it has a long, boat-shaped soundbox tapering to a thick neck bristling with keys operating tangents which press against one or more of the four bowed strings. Its sound is enriched by a set of sympathetic strings which ring like a silvery reverb behind the played notes.

The earliest known depiction of the instrument is a carving of circa 1350 on a gate at Kälunge church in Götland. It is also depicted in murals in late-fifteenth-century churches in Denmark and Uppland. The oldest preserved nyckelharpa is dated 1526: its body shape is waisted like a guitar's, but during the seventeenth century the boat shape came to prevail. The sympathetic strings were added in the eighteenth century.

The county of **Uppland** was a nyckelharpa stronghold right through to the twentieth century, and is also the centre of the instrument's modern renaissance. The best-known nyckelharpa spelman of the nineteenth century was **Byss-Calle** (Karl Ersson Bössa, 1783–1847) from Älvkarleby. In 1925 fiddler **August Bohlin** built a chromatic nyckelharpa; player and maker **Eric Sahlström** (1912–86) of Tobo made further developments and so emerged the form of the instrument now most commonly played.

Despite the flexibility and possibilities of the new design, as Sweden's social emphasis moved from rural to urban the occasions at which the nyckelharpa would normally be played declined so much that by the 1960s the number of players had dwindled to perhaps twenty. Sahlström, however, was an exceptionally fine player, a writer of memorable tunes and a proponent of the instrument. He carried it through the thin times until, as the folk boom gathered steam in the 1970s, there was a major national upsurge of interest in folk instruments. The nyckelharpa presented a fascinating new challenge for players and woodworkers alike, and the courses organized and led by Sahlström, who received a state artist's salary from 1977, became very popular.

At the end of the 1970s the television appearances and high record sales of **Åsa Jinder** – at the time a remarkably skilled teenager – had a significant effect in broadening awareness of and enthusiasm for the instrument. Though the rather "commercial" arrangements of some of her work caused her to be viewed with disdain by some on the nyckelharpa scene, her contribution and her role as a pioneering female player have come to be recognized.

The nyckelharpa's spread continues today, with many makers and thousands of players worldwide. The **Eric Sahlström Institute**, providing teaching and a national gathering point for folk music and dance, was opened in Tobo in 1998. The main annual gathering is the *nyckelharpstämma* at **Österbybruk**, the weekend before midsummer.

The range of designs of nyckelharpa played has also expanded. Some players have turned to older, simpler variants of the instrument such as the *silverbasharpa*, so named because of its silver-wound bass string, and the *kontrabasharpa*, which has a smaller range and brighter tone than the chromatic instrument and a drone string that's bowed along with the melody strings. Innovative musician and instrument-maker **Anders Norudde** has made a series of instruments based on the 1526 nyckelharpa in the museum at Mora, extending the principle as far as a bass model, very suited to the drone-emphasizing music made since the 1990s by the band **Hedningarna**, of which Norudde is a member. One of today's most skilful and exploratory players, **Johan Hedin**, has collaborated with makers to create other new-old forms including a tenor nyckelharpa that produces an even richer low end than the standard modern instrument.

As with fiddlers, today fine, questing players of the nyckelharpa are legion. Leading names include **Olov Johansson** of the well-known nyckelharpa-viola-guitar power-trio **Väsen**, **Niklas Roswall** (of another prime folk band, **Ranarim**), **Marcus Svensson**, **Esbjörn Hogmark**, **Peter Hedlund** and **Daniel Pettersson**. Hedin, Johansson, Roswall and Svensson are all members of the mighty nyckelharpa sextet **NHO** (**Nyckelharporkestern**), which originally formed for the *Till Eric* recording project to celebrate the compositions of Eric Sahlström.

Other Instruments

Various wind instruments were played by animal herders in the days when flocks and shepherds moved up to high pastures for the summer. Farming practice had changed in most places by the middle of the twentieth century and so such instruments fell from use, but they have been taken up by some players in the revival. The **spelpipa** or **spilåpipa** is a small wooden whistle, usually with eight equal-sized, equally spaced fingerholes. A variant is the **härjedalspipa**, which is slightly larger, with just six fingerholes. It's more recorder-like in appearance but not in sound, usually having a pleasingly husky tone – certainly in the hands of multi-instrumentalist **Ale Möller**, one of Swedish roots music's greatest activists.

Also part of the armoury of Möller and others is the **sälgpipa** ("willow-pipe"), Sweden's version of the no-holed overtone whistle widespread throughout Europe and beyond as a pastoral instrument. Traditionally it was an ephemeral instrument made from a tube of willow-bark, but these days another easily available and more robust material is used – plastic plumbing tube. The player opens or closes the end to produce a scale built on the natural harmonic series. Cow's or goat's horns, usually pierced with a few fingerholes, and longer horns (**näverlur**) made of wood and birch-bark, produce a similarly non-equal-temperament scale.

Sweden has a **bagpipe** (*säckpipa*) too. In Dalarna it persisted, just about, in living tradition into the twentieth century; the last player there died in 1949. The säckpipa is small, mouth-blown, with an unkeyed cylindrical-bored chanter to play the melody and a single drone pipe (though some makers have recently been exploring the addition of more drones and other elaborations). The tone, reedy but relatively non-strident, is largely the result of the fact that, as with most eastern European pipes but unusually in western Europe, the chanter, like the drone, has a single-blade reed. The main step in its revival came with the pipes made, from 1981 onwards and now running into hundreds of sets, by **Leif Eriksson**, and their playing by his co-investigator, well-known Dalarna fiddler **Per Gudmundson**. Gudmundson's 1983 bagpipe album *Säckpipa* won a Swedish Grammy. Since then there hasn't exactly been a boom, but now there are several makers in Sweden and abroad supplying quite a few players, the pipes have become a feature of bands including Hedningarna, in which **Anders Norudde** has been prone to wave the chubby little säckpipa around like a squealing piglet, and there has been a considerable amount of research and development on construction and reed-making. The booklet notes by **Olle Gällmo** to his 2008 säckpipa CD are particularly enlightening, and there's abundant well-presented information and links at his website, *www.olle.gallmo.se*.

Revival players' liking for drones and grainy textures has led them to take an interest in Sweden's version of the bowed lyre, the **stråkharpa** (akin to Finland's *jouhikko* and Estonia's *hiiu-kannel*), and also to take up the **hurdy-gurdy** (*vevlira*). Leading explorers of the possibilities of the latter in modern roots music are Hedningarna's **Totte Mattsson** and Garmarna's **Stefan Brisland-Ferner**. Another string-drone instrument is the **hummel**; a strummed fretted long-box zither with close kin across Europe including the Norwegian *langeleik*, it is occasionally played but hasn't yet gained new life. In contrast, the **Jew's harp** (*mungiga*), while not having the strong regional smithing and playing connections it has in Norway, is a significant member of the Swedish drone-instrument toolkit. Other instruments, either still in use or reinstated from Swedish history, include the rectangular **chord-zither** (*ackordcittra*), **hammered dulcimer** (*hackbräde*) and **shawm** (*skalmeja*).

Since its introduction into this realm of music by Totte Mattsson when he was a member of Groupa (and later Hedningarna), variants of the baroque **lute**, often amplified, are finding increasing use. New instruments have been developed too, most notably a variety of **microtonally fretted mandolas**. Ale Möller came to Swedish folk music as a bouzouki player (having been deeply involved in Greek music), then transferred to the flat-backed octave mandola that – also as a result of the initial introduction of bouzouki – was becoming a staple instrument on the Irish and Scottish folk scenes. He found semitone frets inadequate to accompany the quarter-tones and blue notes of Swedish folksong and fiddling, so had mandolas made with partial or full-width intermediate frets. An extra feature of some of these is stud-capos that peg into the fingerboard between frets to allow individual pairs of strings to be shortened. The use of mandolas and citterns, with the new features plus others such as extended bass strings, is now spreading to other musicians such as Daniel Fredriksson, playing with Daniel Pettersson's nyckelharpa, and Jens Engelbrecht of the band Ranarim.

Accordions arrived in Sweden in the nineteenth century, and as soon as mass-production brought the price down they caught on. Sweden's most famous accordionist was **Carl Jularbo** (1893–1966), a skilled piano-accordionist, author of 1500 compositions and a vast number of recordings. The big chromatic accordions, with either piano keys or buttons, are a key instrument in **gammeldans** bands. The term means "old dance", but actually in tradition terms it's relatively new: the popular dances that spread across Europe in the nineteenth century. The repertoire consists largely of waltzes, *hambos*, polkas and *schottises*, with the occasional mazurka, tango or other dance. The typical line-up of a gammeldans band is one or more chromatic button-key or piano-key accordions, and perhaps a fiddle, backed by guitar and bass.

The role of these big accordions in gammeldans, coupled with their potential for loudness and unsubtlety, meant that they were viewed with suspicion in folk music revival circles, though they are sometimes to be heard behaving themselves behind the massed fiddles in spelmanslag ensembles. But the smaller diatonic button accordions with just one or two melody rows – known as melodeons in Britain – crept into acceptance in the hands of sensitive players well aware of the melodic and harmonic delicacies of polskas and other pre-gammeldans tunes. Fine players such as **Erik Pekkari** and **Mats Edén** are well respected; Edén, well known as a fiddler and a member of key revival band Groupa, was in 1979 the first to receive a Zorn badge for playing diatonic accordion. British piano-accordionist **Karen Tweed**, playing with fiddlers Ola Bäckström and Carina Normansson in the quartet **Swåp**, has shown that in skilled hands the big chromatic can integrate in fine detail with Swedish music.

Not a traditional instrument, but increasingly making itself one, is the **saxophone**. Lower-pitched saxes made strong first appearances in the 1980s in the orbit of the pioneering band **Filarfolket**, and the fluid, vocal tone of the **soprano sax** is increasingly a feature of today's roots music, as to a lesser extent are **clarinets**, both standard and bass. The **guitar** – winding through the tunes or impelling them with deep understanding of the underlying rhythms, not a simplistic strum – is also finding a significant role in the hands of such skilful, innovative players as **Roger Tallroth**, **Mattias Pérez** and **Ian Carr**.

Song

The first decades of the folk revival were very much concerned with instrumental music, and there were relatively few singers. Sweden has a rich store of folksong, however, including its share of the body of great ballad stories that are found across northern Europe, many of them traceable back to the middle ages. They tell epic stories of heroic exploits, love and magic. There are also songs of love, emigration, the sea, work and all the other aspects of life, as well as songs telling folktales, dance songs, *kulning* (herding calls) and *tralling* (wordless vocalizing of dance tunes). In the last decade or so the number of singers has increased, and they have been finding material in written collections, from among the printed ballad-sheets, *skillingtryck*, sold by itinerants until as late as 1910, or from recordings of traditional singers made during the twentieth century by folksong collectors such as **Matts Arnberg**. Of the singers he recorded, three in particular – **Svea Jansson** (1904–80), **Lena Larsson** (1882–1967) and **Ulrika Lindholm** (1886–1967) – sang from memory remarkable funds of songs and ballads that they'd learned through the oral tradition, the most impressive being Jansson, who sang over 600.

Lena Willemark, prime among today's singers of traditional songs, first learned from the old people in the northwest Dalarna village of Evertsberg where she grew up. As well as being a wonderfully passionate singer of ballads and folksongs, with an absolutely distinctive voice and exquisite command of the microtonal "blue notes" of Swedish traditional song, Willemark is a highly regarded singer in the jazz world and an excellent, fiery fiddler. She is also an outstanding exponent of **kulning**, a form of traditional vocalizing that is one of the most show-stopping elements of the contemporary folk music scene. It's the hollering that was used by women to call the cattle on the summer pastures, a penetrating, high-pitched, controlled scream that in the revival has become popular as both performance and voice-liberating personal catharsis among women singers.

The majority of the most active singers emerging during the folk revival have come to traditional music as a choice rather than in the old way of being brought up in a traditional community. Several have taken the new opportunities to study folk music, particularly at Stockholm's Royal College of Music, where the courses are taught by leading performers. Today's notables include **Ulrika Bodén**, **Sofia Karlsson**, **Emma Härdelin**, **Sofia Sandén**, **Susanne Rosenberg**, **Carina Normansson**, **Gunnel Mauritzson**, **Marie Axelsson**, **Anna Elwing**, the harmonizing vocal quartet **Kraja** and, from western Finland's Swedish-speaking minority, **Jenny Wilhelms**. It's noticeable that these singers (several of whom are also strong fiddlers) are all women; there are male musicians who sing well but few make the voice their main instrument.

Pulling the Threads Together: the 1960s and 70s

In the 1960s, before the folk revival gathered steam, some Swedish jazz musicians began to explore the possibilities of using folk song and dance tunes as themes. The most influential of them was pianist **Jan Johansson** (1931–68). His work, capturing and exploring the nuances of traditional music, was a formative influence in the development of today's Nordic jazz, and a signal that folk music was no embarrassing museum piece but a fount of melodic and rhythmic ideas.

In the early 1970s a series of free all-music festivals in Stockholm triggered what came to be known as the **Swedish Music Movement**, an upsurge of live and recorded music activity which included the founding of a slew of new largely musician-run Swedish rock and roots record labels.

Those young Swedes whose interest in folk music was fired at this time sought out older musicians to learn from, and got together at home, in spelmanslag and at spelmansstämmor to develop and perform their music. A fiddler learning a tune from another fiddler is inevitably playing a duet, and a pair of fiddles offers the possibility of drones, harmonizing and intertwining melodic lines. In this way were formed fiddle duos such as **Pers Hans Olsson and Björn Ståbi** and **Mats Edén and Leif Stinnerbom**.

Some played with jazz or rock musicians. Fiddle trio **Skäggmanslaget**'s collaboration with rock band **Contact** in 1971 resulted in a number-one hit with a polska from Hjort Anders, "Gråtlåten", Contact backing the trio's playing with a splashy, somewhat behind-the-beat folk-rock bash. Hammond organist **Merit Hemmingson**'s "Svensk folkmusik på beat" recordings featured a series of fiddlers including Kalle Almlöf, Ole Hjorth, Pers Hans and Björn Ståbi. Improvising band **Arbete och Fritid**'s flexible line-up included fiddlers Kalle Almlöf and Anders Rosén. **Kebnekajse** began as a hard rock band, but lead guitarist Kenny Håkansson's exposure to the traditional music played by Björn Ståbi and Pers Hans while they were all in the touring band of singer Cornelis Vreeswijk resulted in a change of direction for Kebnekajse to electric-guitar-led instrumental folk tunes.

During the 1970s folk bands began to appear, a few playing songs as well as fiddle tunes. **Folk och Rackare** was the first major revival band to focus on Swedish traditional ballads, drawing partly on the approach of contemporaries in Britain such as Steeleye Span. It began as a duo of singer **Carin Kjellman** and guitarist (later Hedningarna producer and national radio big-wig) **Ulf Gruvberg**. Fiddlers Kalle Almlöf and Jonny Soling joined them for one album, then multi-instrumentalist Jørn Jensen and fiddler Trond Villa (both from Norwegian folk band Folque), arrived to make up what became the band's stable line-up for nearly a decade.

From Norrbotten in the Arctic north came **Norrlåtar**, with material founded on the Finnish-language songs and dance music of their region. Also from Norrbotten, but an instrumental band, **J.P. Nyströms** formed in 1977 when its members were teenagers and is still performing with a rich, swingy fiddles-and-harmonium sound that bears similarities to the music of the *pelimanni* bands of Finland's Österbotten. The most famous of those, JPP, was influenced by Västergötland fiddle band **Forsmark Tre**.

The 1980s

In the 1980s **Filarfolket** ("the fiddling people") and **Groupa** made another big click of the evolutionary ratchet. They both put together fiddles and flutes with bouzouki or lute, trumpet and the deep honk of bass clarinets or baritone or bass sax. With their immensely muscular, danceable and intricate polskas and hallings, they were joint powerhouses of the new-roots scene throughout the decade. Their members have gone on to spawn a slew of other bands, and many of these musicians are now among the best-known and most respected on the scene.

In Filarfolket's slightly flexible line-up were bouzouki player and later multi-instrumentalist Ale Möller, percussionist Tina Quartey, saxist/flautist Sten Källman, flautist Thomas Ringdahl, clarinettist Dan "Gisen" Malmquist, guitarist/bassist Lars Bomgren and fiddlers Ellika Frisell and Katarina Olsson.

Filarfolket disbanded at the end of the 1980s, but Groupa has carried on, changing and developing throughout three decades. Founded on the fiddle duo of Mats Edén and Leif Stinnerbom, the cast has included bass clarinettist Bill McChesney,

lute and guitar player Totte Mattsson, trumpeter Gustav Hylén, saxist/flautist Jonas Simonson, keyboardist Rickard Åström and percussionists Tina Quartey and Helge Norbakken. Like Filarfolket, it has largely been an instrumental band, but singer Lena Willemark guested for one album and, more recently, Sofia Karlsson was a member. The current line-up is Edén, Simonson and Norwegian percussionist Terje Isungset.

Benny Andersson of **ABBA** is, among other things, a player of chromatic button accordion, and in 1987 he began a collaboration with fiddlers from the long-established Orsa Spelmanslag. The first album, *Klinga Mina Klockor*, a collection of Andersson and Björn Ulvaeus compositions in a variety of non-ABBA styles, sold 100,000 copies. He and the fiddlers, who became the group **Orsa Spelmän**, still play together.

The 1990s and Onward

Filarfolket and Groupa led the way in a broadening of approaches to the music, and the involvement of a wider range of instruments and musicians from other fields of music. During the 1990s and on into the new millennium that process continued and evolved.

Having worked together variously during the 1980s, in 1991 Filarfolket multi-instrumentalist **Ale Möller**, singer **Lena Willemark** and fiddler and bagpipe pioneer **Per Gudmundson** made an album together called *Frifot*, which became the name of their trio. It's a magical, intuitive combination, full of extraordinary, communicative vibrancy and wit, and continues to be a must-see

Frifot

419

for Swedish roots music in its many live performances in Sweden and around the world. Despite its members' many other projects and areas of musical activity, they're all still very grounded and involved in the life and people of traditional music and spelmansstämmor. In the mid-1990s, at the request of German jazz record label ECM, Möller and Willemark put together the **Nordan** project, recruiting Mats Edén, percussionist Tina Quartey, soprano saxist Jonas Knutsson and bassist Palle Danielsson for two albums of traditional ballads.

Möller has always been full of ideas and can be relied upon for the energy to carry them through. When asked to come up with a project for Stockholm's year as European City of Culture in 1998, he and Jonas Knutsson delivered the **Stockholm Folk Big Band**, whose members he drew from the various communities of the country's now very multicultural capital. It was a tough thing to organize, but it worked. Its members were keen to carry on, and it has now condensed and intensified as the six-piece **Ale Möller Band**, whose members have origins in Senegal, Mexico, Greece, Québec and Sweden.

Also back in the 1980s another trio had formed that was going to be a big influence. Lutenist **Totte Mattsson** from Groupa teamed up with **Anders Norudde**, instrument maker, inventor and player of gutsy bowed and wind instruments (hurdy-gurdies, fiddle, early forms of nyckelharpa, bagpipe, bass *sälgflöjt* and more) and percussionist **Björn Tollin**, whose main instrument was tambourine, from which he extracted remarkably meaty rhythms using Turkish and south Indian techniques of pressing on the skin to vary the pitch. They named themselves **Hedningarna** ("the heathens"), and their first album was based on music they'd made for a stage play. For the second they stepped up the power with extensive use of amplification and midi-triggered samples, and recruited two Finnish singers, **Sanna Kurki-Suonio** and **Tellu Paulasto**, who brought with them songs from Finland's runo-song tradition. These made up the bulk of the song material on *Kaksi* ("two" in Finnish), while the instrumentals came from the Swedish tradition or new composition. Produced by Folk Och Rackare's Ulf Gruvberg, with attendant videos and promotion, it made waves in Sweden and gained Hedningarna an international audience. The third album, *Trä*, was at least its equal. It was followed by an instrumental album that returned to the core trio. Tellu left the band, and was replaced by fellow Finn Anita Lehtola. After the 1999 fifth album, *Karelia Visa*, Sanna left and was replaced by Finn Liisa Matveinen. Since then the band's appearances have been intermittent, and its line-up, now

instrumental again, has varied – fiddler Magnus Stinnerbom, who also plays in the Ale Möller Band, was a member for several years – but Mattsson and Norudde are at its heart.

A third key trio, **Väsen**, released its first album in 1990. The line-up is simple – **Olov Johansson** on nyckelharpa, **Mikael Marin** on viola and **Roger Tallroth** on twelve-string guitar (joined for a time by percussionist André Ferrari) – and acoustic, but they make an extraordinarily powerful polska-fuelled sound, and from the beginning have been very popular at home and abroad. For a time in the mid-1990s they were involved in the **Nordman** phenomenon: nyckelharpa player and producer **Mats Wester** recruited metal singer **Håkan Hemlin** to make a sort of folk-metal with nyckelharpas taking the place of lead guitar. The debut album sold over half a million copies, and the members of Väsen joined for spectacular live shows. Nordman's name and imagery and Hemlin's skinhead look were, to the band's chagrin, sometimes interpreted as linked to viking-metal and even white-power, but though perhaps he should have seen it coming they were just Wester's utilization of graphically and commercially effective symbols.

The period from 1990 to the present has seen a proliferation of excellent younger musicians, the continuing strength and influence of the older ones, and, inevitably, the deaths of some of the oldest. Players and singers have moved in and out of a panoply of bands, some continuing for years, others just short-term projects. Quite a few appear in this chapter's discography and there are more details there, but here's a brief overview of some of the most important.

Avadå Band, formed in the late 1980s in Malmö in south Sweden and led by ex-Filarfolket Dan "Gisen" Malmquist's clarinet, mix Swedish dance tunes with the styles of Klezmer, European tango and folk-rock. Early in the 1990s, storming in to show how powerful can be an application of all-out rock to the lurching beat of polska, came the fiddle-fronted **Hoven Droven** and ex-Filarfolket saxist Sten Källman and Groupa bass clarinettist/flautist Jonas Simonsson with **Den Fule**. **Garmarna** from Sundsvall brought the wild abrasive sound of hurdy-gurdy, rock and sequencing technology to the strong, often dark stories of traditional ballads and gained an enthusiastic young following at home and abroad.

As the 1990s turned into the 2000s, developments in the close-miking and amplification of acoustic instruments made it possible to make a full sound in concert without necessarily taking the rock route. **Gjallarhorn** from west Fin-

Carl Hjelte

Bazar Blå

land's Swedish-speaking enclaves constructed a sort of acoustic drone-rock sound from fiddle, viola, percussion and bass-growling didgeridoo, fronted by singer Jenny Wilhelms, later replacing the didg with the even more unusual bass of a multiple-miked sub-contrabass recorder. **Triakel** is the acoustic trio of Garmarna singer and fiddler Emma Härdelin, Hoven Droven fiddler Kjell-Erik Eriksson, and former Hoven Droven organist Janne Strömstedt on harmonium. **Harv**'s core is the duo of Magnus Stinnerbom and Daniel Sandén-Warg playing hypnotic new-composed duets on deep-toned resonant-stringed fiddles. **Swåp** united, with sparklingly creative result, two leading Dalarna musicians, fiddler Ola Bäckström and fiddler/singer Carina Normansson, with two leading Brits, accordionist Karen Tweed and guitarist Ian Carr.

Events and Contacts

At the heart of Sweden's roots music scene are **spelmansstämmor**, festive meetings of amateur and professional folk musicians to play together, gathering near their tents in fiddling, nyckelharping, sometimes even accordion-playing clusters at every opportunity, or dancing (most Swedish traditional musicians dance as well as play) to solo fiddlers or groups on dancefloors set up on the site, which is usually a suitable green area near a village. In recent years the larger spelmansstämmor such as Bingsjö and Ransäter have also begun to stage ticketed concerts, but the essence is still playing and summer socializing.

There are other festivals either devoted to or including folk and roots music around the country, most in the summer such as the world music festival **Urkult** at Näsåker in Ångermanland, **Korrö** folk music festival in Småland and the classical, folk, jazz and popular music festival **Musik vid Siljan** in Dalarna, but the folk music festival further north in **Umeå** is in the snows of February (indoors, naturally).

The website of **RFoD** (Riksförbundet för Folkmusik og Dans), *www.rfod.se*, has links to most aspects of traditional music including festivals and spelmansstämmor. It also runs the venue **Stallet** in Stockholm (*www.stallet.st*), which presents Swedish and foreign roots performers most nights of the week. Sweden's main glossy magazine covering roots, jazz, and world music is *Lira* (*www.lira.se*).

Incidentally, Swedish Radio broadcasts a 24-hour DAB and Internet channel of well-programmed world music, **SR Världen**.

Bazar Blå is the trio of nyckelharpa player Johan Hedin, acoustic bass guitarist Björn Meyer and percussionist Fredrik Gille. The duo of two Daniels, **Pettersson and Fredriksson**, makes intense polska-based dialogues on nyckelharpa and mandola. **Ellika Frisell** and **Solo Cissokho** interweave, with remarkably natural and indeed danceable result, two disparate traditions – the complexities of deep fiddle polska and Senegalese griot Solo's kora and vocals – and are the only Nordic-based performers to have won a BBC Radio 3 Award for World Music.

In addition to solo projects with the music of her native Ångermanland, singer and flute player **Ulrika Bodén** has been in a string of notable bands and groups including Sälta, Kalabra and Rosenbergs Sjua. In the current line-up of **Ranarim** she's joined by fellow singer Johanna Bölja Hertzberg, Niklas Roswall's nyckelharpa, guitarist Daniel Ek and percussionist Christian Svensson. **Alwa**, with the vocals of Anna Elwing, twin fiddles, big tunes, deep sax-honking lines and lyrical, free-tempo spaciousness, released an excellent album in 2002 but dissolved after a disappointingly brief career. **Sofia Karlsson**, singer with Groupa between 1998 and 2002, now has a solo career and has made a series of richly elegant albums, largely setting the works of major Swedish poets and songwriters.

The trio **Ni:d** make wonderfully intelligent, satisfying music with just two melody instruments – Hanna Wiskari's soprano sax and Mia Marin's fiddle – and Petter Berndalen's percussion. Showing the rise and rise of the soprano saxist, **Horn Please!**, put together by Jonas Knutsson, has six of them including Hanna Wiskari, playing as tight and structured as any fiddlers, but with multiple lines and rhythmic offsets that can open out into more improvisational blowing sections that snap-twist back to polska or spread into lyrical melodies.

Fiddler and multi-instrumentalist Magnus Stinnerbom of Harv, the Ale Möller Band, ex-Hedningarna and more, is the son of Groupa founder-member Leif Stinnerbom. For his father's fiftieth birthday Magnus put together the **Outhouse Allstars**, including guitarist Mattias Pérez and more of his pals, to play the tunes from Leif's Groupa period in the 1980s. Their subsequent gig at Ransäter Spelmansstämma became a TV and radio event, a live album and an ongoing, next-generation band.

The Sámi

Sweden's arctic north, like the north of Norway and Finland and the Kola Peninsula of Russia's extreme northwest, is the homeland of the Sámi peoples. Their music is covered in a separate chapter.

DISCOGRAPHY Sweden

The Giga label was founded in 1976 by fiddlers Per Gudmundson and Magnus Bäckström and run from soon after that by one dedicated man, the late Mats Hellberg (d. 2006). Devoted to traditional music, particularly fiddling, its catalogue of over eighty releases includes albums by just about every great fiddler in those thirty years, and some from earlier, including a triple CD set of Hjort Anders' recordings. To record for Giga was an accolade. There's no compilation CD; such a thing, anyway, wouldn't allow the listener to get to grips with a particular player, and the substantial booklet notes open up the music, not just with the stories of the tunes but by revealing the enthusiasm, humanity and self-effacing dry humour of those who play them.

⊙ **Årsringar: Svensk Folkmusik 1970–1990**
MNW, Sweden
A double-CD compilation which gives a pretty comprehensive overview of Swedish traditional and new-roots music of the 1970s and 80s, compiled from many labels by the knowledgeable Ale Möller and Per Gudmundson. A first listen can give the impression of wall-to-wall fiddles; it isn't quite, but bowing is at the heart of the tradition and revival, and this sampler, released in 1990, doesn't cover the subsequent widening of textures.

⊙ **Musica Sveciae: Folk Music in Sweden, Vols 1–25**
Caprice, Sweden
Twenty-five CDs, with extensive notes, of archive recordings covering traditional musical genres, regional instrumental styles and songs from across Sweden (including Sámiland). The CD releases were spread through the 1990s, based largely on LPs issued by Swedish Radio and Caprice from the 1960s to the 1980s, so they don't cover the more recent traditional master-players, and only touch on evolutions during the revival on a couple of discs. These include orchestral and jazz arrangements, Jan Johansson, Folk och Rackare, an early Hedningarna track and an atmospheric 1995 kulning and horns recording. One disc, *Traditional Folk Music*, is a series sampler.

★ **Nordic Roots, Vols 1–3**
NorthSide, US
Three remarkable-value compilations from NorthSide, which specializes in licensing and promoting the music of the most prominent Nordic new-roots bands. Swedes predominate, and tracks from the vast majority of the key bands from the 1990s and 2000s, plus some otherwise unreleased live material, make these samplers an excellent continuation of the story begun in the MNW *Årsringar*

compilation. (Since NorthSide concentrates on bands and evolutions they don't, however, continue Årsringar's coverage of the more traditional fiddlers; for that one has to go to Giga releases.)

Ale Möller Band

Möller's magnificent multi-ethnic band comprises, as well as its leader on mandola, various flutes and whistles, shawm, accordion, harmonica and vocals, Magnus Stinnerbom on fiddles, mandolin and guitar, Greek-born singer Stellas, Senegal-born Mamadou Sene on vocals and *riti*, Québec-born double bassist Sébastien Dubé and Mexican-born drummer Rafael Sida Huizar.

★ Djef Djel
Amigo, Sweden

A mighty, dizzying roller-coaster ride through a rainbow of cultural references. Combining disparate traditions, new composition and inventive instrumentation with extraordinary life and energy, it unites them into a completely meaningful, and definitely Swedish, whole.

Alwa

Alwa's line-up is singer/fiddler Anna Elwing, Karin Ohlsson (fiddle/viola), acoustic and electric guitarist Jonas Göransson, saxist/flautist Torbjörn Righard and, on percussion including her characteristic *berimbau*, Tina Quartey.

⊙ Alwa
Amigo, Sweden

In the big tunes and deep sax-honking lines that underpin them, there are echoes of Filarfolket. But while Filarfolket was an instrumental band playing mainly dance music, Alwa features a singer, calmly melancholic but well capable of power-surges. The band drives when it needs to, but there's plenty of lyrical, free-tempo spaciousness in its music which, while strongly rooted in traditional forms and often using traditional texts, is largely written by band members.

Ellika & Solo

Ellika Frisell is a fine fiddler rooted in the Bingsjö tradition but with wide experience of taking it into other musics. Kora player Solo Cissokho is from Casamance in Senegal. Double-billed for a small Stockholm concert in 1998, they duetted with no rehearsal and found a remarkable affinity, Ellika's Swedish fiddle tunes and rhythms interweaving with Solo's kora and singing in the Casamance tradition.

⊙ Tretakt Takissaba
Xource, Sweden/Proper, UK

The first album, a natural coming-together which caught the ears of the world music scene and gained the duo a BBC Radio 3 Award for World Music.

Filarfolket

Along with Groupa, Filarfolket pioneered and galvanized the new wave in Swedish roots music during the 1980s. It combined bowed strings, saxes, bass clarinets, trumpet, flutes, harmonica, bouzouki, guitar, bass, percussion and more in a powerful new instrumental polska and halling sound, built of traditional tunes and new compositions, including some of Ale Möller's best known. The team featured Ellika Frisell, Katarina Olsson, Ale Möller, Sten Källman, Dan Gisen Malmquist, Ulf Johansson, Thomas Ringdahl, Lasse Bomgren, Tina Quartey and others.

⊙ Vintervals
Xource, Sweden

A compilation from the band's albums from 1980 until the diaspora of its members into other interesting projects at the end of the decade. It still sounds richly melodic, energetic, fresh and relevant.

Folk och Rackare

Sweden's first major band of the new roots wave. Like British folk bands of the time, it was much more dedicated to song than later groups such as Filarfolket and Groupa. It consisted of singer Carin Kjellman, guitarist Ulf Gruvberg and two Norwegians: fiddler Trond Villa and multi-instrumentalist Jørn Jensen. Kjellman's airy vocals and the acoustic instrumentation gave it an appealing lightness of touch.

⊙ 1976–1985
Xource, Sweden

A compilation of tracks from the band's four albums.

Didier François

Nyckelharpa player Didier François may be Belgian, but he's an excellent player and arranger, and in 2001 delivered a glorious new perspective on largely Swedish music.

★ Falling Tree
Long Distance, France

The vocals are by Sweden's Ulrika Bodén, the instrumentation is François' nyckelharpa and violin with hurdy-gurdy (Gilles Chabenat), double bass (Renaud Garcia-Fons), *theorbo* lute (Jan van Outryve), *duduk* (Levon Minassian) and *ney* (Haroun Teboul). The result is rich-textured and magnificent.

Frifot

Multi-instrumentalist and innovator Ale Möller, singer and fiddler Lena Willemark and fiddler/bagpiper Per Gudmundson have been central figures in Swedish roots music for the past thirty years. You have to see Frifot live to fully appreciate the band's appeal: the tight physical and musical energy with which they grip every moment, their total involvement with the power and humanity of the traditions they draw on, their mighty instrumental and vocal skill, their good humour. The albums only give part of the picture.

★ Järven
Caprice, Sweden

Tradition, development and new composition. Central sounds are voice (mainly Willemark's, but all three sing), octave mandola (Möller) and fiddles (Gudmundson and Willemark), with Gudmundson also on Swedish bagpipes and Möller on harmonica, hammered dulcimer, harp, sälgpipa, härjedalspipa and other flutes. All effortlessly negotiate the music's shifting stress-patterns and microtones.

Garmarna

In a sense, Garmarna brought Folk och Rackare's "big" epic ballads into the 1990s, the era of Hedningarna's drone-rock, surrounding them with dark acoustic and electronic textures, samples and muscular (but sympathetic) beats. Singer/fiddler Emma Härdelin is joined by Stefan Brisland-Ferner, Gotte Ringqvist, Rickard Westman and Jens Höglin on hurdy-gurdy, alto låtfiol, lute-guitar, guitar, Jew's harp, samples and drums.

⊙ **Guds Spelemän**
Massproduktion, Sweden
Occasionally bigness of sound has seemed to dominate proceedings, but on this second album the arrangements, hefty as they get, really support the stories of the songs.

Groupa

Since its formation in 1980 by Mats Edén and Leif Stinnerbom, Groupa has been a beacon on the Swedish folk music scene, using and making tunes and bringing together instruments in ways that have influenced the whole course of the music. The current members are Mats Edén, Jonas Simonson and innovative Norwegian percussionist Terje Isungset.

⭐ **Månskratt**
Amigo, Sweden
The 1990 album, featuring Lena Willemark. The extraordinary wild intensity of Willemark's singing is matched by Mats Edén's driven bow, Totte Mattsson's furious lute, Gustav Hylén's cornet, the grunting block bass of Bill McChesney's bass clarinet and Jonas Simonson's bass sax, and the energetic percussion of Tina Johansson (later Quartey).

⊙ **Fjalar**
Amigo, Sweden
Their seventh album (from 2002) is another high point, featuring the exuberantly hefty halling/polska swing that Groupa pioneered, wild extemporizations lurching into heartland traditional playing, and limpid pools of stillness too. Isungset's wood, skin, metal and stone percussion kit is rolling thunder, breath and clatter under and around the rich drones and surges of Mats Edén's fiddles, the airiness of Jonas Simonson's harmonic and other flutes, and Rickard Åström's natural-toned keyboards. On top of that are the just-right vocals of Sofia Karlsson.

Hedningarna

Hedningarna created a whole new genre of Swedish music – drone-rock. They began as an acoustic instrumental trio – Anders Norudde (then Stake), Totte Mattsson and Björn Tollin – then added two Finnish singers – Sanna Kurki-Suonio and Tellu Turkka (then Paulasto) – and became a massive-sounding band combining the raw, wild sound of amplified old and invented instruments with sample-expanded percussion and dynamic stagecraft. Most of the songs have been Finnish, the instrumentals Swedish, either traditional or original.

⊙ **Kaksi**
Xource, Sweden/NorthSide, US
Their second album (1992) was the first onslaught of the new sound, full of memorable songs. It won a place in the Swedish charts and a Swedish Grammy, and brought a new wave of energy into the already lively Swedish-rooted music scene.

⭐ **Trä**
Xource, Sweden/NorthSide, US
The 1994 follow-up, a work of even more overwhelming, all-firing intensity, went straight into the Swedish top ten. It did what British folk-rock had once seemed to promise, and did it without kit drums or bass guitar but with a whole new armoury of noise weapons: voices silky and grinding, joik, chainsaw and falling tree, percussion thunder, breath-rhythms, and at last icy running water.

Ole Hjorth and Sven Ahlbäck

These two fiddlers are both from Uppland, but from different generations. Hjorth was a pupil of Hjort Anders Olsson. Ahlbäck was one of the first to study folk music on the course which Hjorth initiated at the Royal College in Stockholm, and now heads the folk music department there.

⊙ **Arabiskan**
Giga, Sweden
The masterly Ole Hjorth and Sven Ahlbäck take turns playing lead and second fiddle, their rich woody tones surging, pausing, twisting, turning and tumbling. This is music that not only provides functional accompaniment for Sweden's rhythmically fascinating, subtle and expressive couple dancing, but also bears comparison with Bartók's tradition-inspired Hungarian violin duets. It deserves to be held in high regard.

Hoven Droven

A screamingly high-energy instrumental folk-rock band with deep traditional skill, Hoven Droven consists of Offerdal traditional fiddler Kjell-Erik Eriksson, Jens Comén (saxes), Bo Lindberg (guitars), Pedro Blom (bass) and Björn Höglund (drums).

⊙ **Groove**
NorthSide, US
A compilation of the first two albums, 1994's *Hia Hia* and 1996's *Grov*, recorded when trumpeter Gustav Hylén was still a member. Strong tunes played as full-on as they get, cathartically loud and wild, but also with some finely lyrical moments.

Ni:d

The silky roundness of Hanna Wiskari's soprano sax and the friction of Mia Marin's fiddle complement one another, tracking in unison, harmony or diverging melodic lines with quick response and tremendous empathy. Using a very individual and beautifully integrated percussion kit, Petter Berndalen picks out and intensifies the twists and turns of the melody, and is as able to contribute as meaningfully to a tune with stretched rhythms as to one with a steady pulse.

⊙ **[ni:d]**
Academus, Sweden
The 2006 debut album, of traditional Swedish and Norwegian and new-made tunes, with a lot of those stretched, lurching, hesitating rhythms.

Norrlåtar

Norrlåtar, from the northern county of Norrbotten, formed in 1972 and made several albums with very varied approaches to the Swedish- and Finnish-language music of the region.

⭐ **En Malsvelodi**
MNW, Sweden
Their 1990 album is an inspired gem little known outside Sweden but well worth seeking out for its quirkiness, wit and bold variety. Wide instrumentation including brass, accordion, fiddle, harmonium, nyckelharpa, piano, synths and drums accompanies unusual male vocals ranging from guttural to abandoned.

Nyckelharporkestern

Six of Sweden's foremost nyckelharpa players – Olov Johansson, Niklas Roswall, Marcus Svensson, Johan Hedin, Ola Hertzberg and Henrik Eriksson – playing a range of versions of the instrument: "old" chromatic, octave, alto, tenor and *moraharpa*. The nyckelharpa equivalent of a chamber group, they play powerful, elegant and complex arrangements that would astonish any classical audience. But unlike with most chamber orchestras, the members are also the composers and arrangers, and fine ones.

⊙ N.H.O.
Drone, Sweden
Their first album was dedicated to arrangements of Eric Sahlström's tunes, the second to those of Byss-Calle. This, their third, comprises new compositions for the ensemble by its members.

Ranarim

There's great charm and freshness to Ranarim's music, particularly its live shows: light, attractive female duet vocals set against the nyckelharpa, guitar and percussion in well-found, infectiously melodic traditional songs and ballads.

⊙ För Världen Älskar Vad Som Är Brokot
Drone, Sweden
Traditional and new-made ballads, songs, kulning and instrumentals from the 2003 album when the line-up was singers Ulrika Bodén and Sofia Sandén, Niklas Roswall on nyckelharpa, Jens Engelbrecht on frets, with bassist Anders Johnson and percussionist Sebastian Notini.

Swåp

Two Swedes, Dalarna fiddlers Ola Bäckström and Carina Normansson, and two Brits, accordionist Karen Tweed

and guitarist Ian Carr, playing a perfectly blended mix of Swedish traditional and ingenious original compositions that lead the tradition onward.

★ Du Da
NorthSide, US
This 2005 album, studio-recorded but full of the energy, wit and strong tunes of their live performances, expands on an aspect only hinted at in the past – the excellence of Carina Normansson as a vocalist.

Väsen

Acoustic, but with extraordinary power and energy in their combination of nyckelharpa (Olov Johansson), viola (Mikael Marin) and driving guitar (Roger Tallroth), this trio has had a tremendous influence on the image of the nyckelharpa and its possibilities, creating music of simultaneous intricacy and swing.

★ Live in Japan
NorthSide, US
Including many of their strongest numbers, this captures something of their live energy. A bonus DVD contains interviews in English with Johansson and Tallroth about the band's compositional process, the nyckelharpa and collaborations with foreign musicians, plus some footage of concerts.

PLAYLIST
Sweden

1 VALLMUSIK KRING STÅNGTJÄRN Various artists from *Musica Sveciae Vol. 8: Lockrop & Vallåtar – Ancient Swedish Pastoral Music*
Cow horns and the kulning voices of Eva Rune, Susanne Rosenberg and Agneta Stolpe echo across the calm evening waters of the lake near Falun.

2 TIMAS HANS Hoven Droven from *Groove*
A huge, irresistibly danceable swinging traditional waltz.

3 KRAFTHALLING Groupa with Lena Willemark from *Månskratt*
Mats Edén's wild fiddle and Totte Mattsson's driving Arabic-sounding lute are joined by deep-chugging bass sax, bass clarinet and Lena Willemark's full-on vocals.

4 GORRLAUS Hedningarna from *Trä*
Sinuous vocals, gutsy percussion, overdriven hurdy-gurdy and moraharpa evoke Finnish runo-song and the spirits of hypnotized Norwegian fiddlers.

5 KÖPMANSPOLKAN Ole Hjorth and Sven Ahlbäck from *Arabiskan*
The two fiddles intertwine and lurch in a fine polska from the repertoire of Hjort Anders, who got it from Pekkos Per, passed down from a Boda fiddler called Köpman.

6 GYRISSVITEN Frifot from *Järven*
From Lena's home district of Älvdalen, two polskas with Frifot's trademark tense, stretched rhythms and sudden note-flurries, plus a short song, in Älvdalen dialect, to a heifer.

7 BAIL Ale Möller Band from *Djef Djel*
The Greek traditional "Vasilikos", with rich bass, high harmonica, grainy fiddles and ecstatic vocals, morphs into the West African lope of "Djef Djel" then, with screaming shawm, into Möller's "Dancing Tune".

8 BRUDPOLSKA FRÅN ORSA EFTER MINU PER Swåp from *Du Da*
A bridal polska from Orsa, in which Carina Normansson sings about a civil engineer with a ring in his ear.

9 ISABELS JUL-JIGG Nyckelharporkestern from *N.H.O.*
The jig isn't normally found in Swedish music; this composition by Marcus Svensson shows how interesting the form can become in six pairs of nyckelharpa-playing Swedish hands.

10 COWBOYHALLING Filarfolket from *Vintervals*
An Ale Möller composition, one of Filarfolket's best-remembered numbers.

Ukraine

the bandura played on

Carpathian ska reggae punk kings
Haydamaky

Ukraine, the second-largest state to emerge from the wreckage of the Soviet Union, is undergoing something of a cultural renaissance. Despite the country's history of war, collectivization, rapid industrialization and cultural oppression from Moscow, all across the country unique vocal and instrumental village traditions still survive. After a decade of post-independence government neglect, a new generation has started to revive and reinterpret this cultural heritage. **Alexis Kochan** and **Julian Kytasty**, continuing a tradition in exile, explore the roots of their music and **Jonathan Walton** checks out what's happening today.

Given Ukraine's position, it's not surprising that it shares Carpathian musical traditions with Romania and Poland to the west, and rich polyphonic song styles with southern Russia to the east. But it also has music that is uniquely its own, notably that of the impressive **bandura** – a cross between a zither and a lute – and its associated bardic repertoire. A strong village **instrumental tradition** also persists in the western part of the country, although the customary ensemble of fiddle, *tsymbaly* (hammered dulcimer) and drum – a combination known as **troista muzyka** – is rapidly losing ground to drum machines and synthesizers.

At the beginning of the twentieth century a wave of emigrants from western Ukraine brought the troista muzyka tradition to **North America**, where its most famous exponent was **Pavlo Humeniuk**, "King of the Ukrainian Fiddlers", who recorded in New York in the 1920s. Even today on the Canadian prairies no Ukrainian wedding band is complete without a tsymbaly, and a small local recording industry there continues to produce recordings of hybrid **troista-country** bands.

Hutsul Melodies

The prairies aside, the best place to hear real Ukrainian roots music is in the Carpathians, where the **Hutsuls**, a mountain people speaking an archaic Ukrainian dialect, have clung tenaciously to their distinctive music. This is the home of the *kolomeyka* (named after the town of Kolomyya), a widespread circle dance in duple time, and in the highland villages around the towns of Rakhiv and Kosiv, the full assortment of Hutsul instruments can still be heard.

These include not only fiddle and tsymbaly, but a bewildering array of flutes (*sopilka*, *frilka*, *floyara*, *tylynka*) reflecting the Hutsuls' traditional pastoral occupation. The *trembita*, a long mountain horn, has a repertoire of calls used for signalling between mountaintops. The melody instruments play in a wildly ornamented unison over the rhythmic underpinning of the tsymbaly, creating an instantly recognizable sound.

Many of the ensembles in this region – as elsewhere in Ukraine – are organized around families of master musicians spanning many generations. Among them, the **Tafiychuk Family** ensemble from Bukovets is especially highly regarded.

Choirs and Rituals

Elsewhere in Ukraine, **vocal music** predominates. "Bring together two Ukrainians and you have another choir" goes an old Ukrainian saying. And, despite everything that the twentieth century threw at the country, those choirs have survived, or are sprouting anew.

In **Polissya**, a region of forests and swamps northwest of the capital Kiev, an archaic repertoire of seasonal **ritual songs** dates back to pre-Christian times. The nuclear accident at Chernobyl left a deep wound, and wasn't just a disaster for public health and the environment. The rich local culture of Polissya was irreparably affected as a large area was evacuated overnight and its communities scattered across the country. It's a bitter irony that, before the tragedy, music scholars had considered the area's musical traditions to be so well established that documenting them was not a priority.

In **western Ukraine** choral singing is delivered in unison, while in **eastern and central Ukraine** there's a rich tradition of mainly two-part **folk polyphony**, sung mostly by women. In the latter tradition, the beginning of a verse is often sung by one or two singers (the *zaspiv*) and then the verse, or chorus, is taken up by the rest of the choir (*pryspiv*). The solo lines are more ornamented and sometimes improvised, while the lower choral lines take the melody. The traditional singing style is strong and open-throated and the harmony quite bare.

Sadly, the elderly grannies heard on today's field recordings are in most cases the last carriers of the tradition in their village and will have no successors. However, several excellent ensembles of university folklore students have recently begun performing and recording recreations of regional vocal styles based on fieldwork and archival recordings. Kiev-based **Drevo** is the first and probably the best of these; other ensembles with an excellent reputation for attention to detail are **Hilka** from Kirovohrad and **Bozhychy**, also from the capital. All three can be heard on various recent compilation CDs.

Eastern Ukrainian polyphonic singing was also exported to the Kuban region in southern Russia, settled by descendants of Ukrainian Cossacks from the eighteenth century. Striking examples can be heard on the recordings of the professional **Kuban Cossack Chorus**, which had professional status in the Soviet era.

Another big Soviet group, based in Ukraine, was gathered by folklorist and composer Hryhory Veriovka, who in 1944 followed the advancing

Red Army westward across Ukraine, picking the best singers from the ruined villages for a State Folk Chorus. For forty years, this group – known after the founder's death as the **Veriovka State Folk Chorus** – was practically the only recorded source of Ukrainian traditional music, showcasing stunning examples of women's polyphonic singing and brilliant instrumental soloists.

Singer **Nina Matvienko** began her career as a soloist with the choir in its heyday in the 1970s. She has gone on to record on her own and with her vocal trio Zoloti Kliuchi on the new Ukrainian label Symphocarre.

The Bandura

The **bandura**, a kind of zither, is unique to Ukraine and is considered the national instrument. Unlike the Scandinavian and Baltic zithers, it is plucked held upright and has a lute-like neck for the longest bass strings.

The bandura owes its special position in Ukrainian culture to its association with a tradition of epic songs – *dumy* – that survived into the twentieth century. Most of them were historical tales of Turkish captivity, daring escapes and the deeds of Cossack heroes. Their performance was the special province of the *kobzari*, blind singers formed into secretive guilds. The bandura was the accompanying instrument of choice, though at least one prominent nineteenth-century kobzar still used the older lute-like *kobza*, while **hurdy-gurdy players** – *lirnyky* – performed a similar repertoire of dumy and religious and moralistic songs.

In the early years of the twentieth century urban musicians took up the instrument and by the time of the Russian revolution there were professional ensembles in Kiev and Poltava performing choral music with bandura accompaniment. The subsequent history of the bandura is a case study in the way the cultural politics of the Soviet regime could shape and deform the development of a musical tradition. The one or two blind singers who survived the Stalinist terror of the 1930s (there is considerable evidence of a Congress of Traditional Singers from which the participants did not return) paid for their survival with pseudo-dumas about Stalin and Lenin. Meanwhile, the Kiev and Poltava ensembles were lumped together into a **State Bandurist Chorus** performing party anthems and merry folk ditties.

After World War II the bandura, like other folk instruments in the Soviet Union, was "developed and improved" to a standard 60-plus-string chromatic instrument with complex and bulky key change mechanisms. Conservatoire courses in Kiev and Lviv trained many technically proficient players, but neither the instrument nor the playing technique – still less the repertoire, heavily oriented towards classical transcriptions – has much connection with the earlier tradition.

In fact, a more traditional take on the instrument can be heard today in Detroit or Cleveland. There, an instrumental style evolved out of the style of exiled players from the Kiev ensemble. The **Ukrainian Bandurist Chorus**, a group containing most of Ukraine's best surviving players, made its way west in an incredible wartime odyssey that included forest concerts for Ukrainian insurgents, close calls from Allied bombing, and hungry months in a Nazi labour camp. Coming to the US in 1949 and settling in Detroit, the group maintains an unbroken performance tradition going back to the original Kiev and Poltava ensembles and has issued a steady stream of recordings (over twenty at the last count) beginning with albums of 78s in the 1940s and now including several CDs.

Together with other original members of the group, its long-time director **Hryhory Kytasty** (1907–84) trained a generation of North American-born players. Today's North American bandurists cultivate a repertoire and a style of playing based on the professional school of the 1920s and 30s and markedly different from that taught in Ukraine. New York-based **Julian Kytasty**, a third-generation bandurist, has built on his great-uncle's work to create new music for the instrument. He has made several recordings, including an independently produced CD of Hryhory Kytasty's solo music.

In terms of re-discovering an older style, the Smithsonian Folkways Institute is carrying out restoration work on a priceless archive of wax cylinder recordings of kobzari from the beginning of the twentieth century and there is work being done on recordings of **Zynovij Shtokalko** (who died in New York in 1968), arguably the one bandurist of the twentieth century who achieved a professional standard of performance without in any way classicizing the instrument or the music.

New Ukrainian Music

The contemporary Ukrainian **pop scene** was conjured into existence in the space of one September week in 1989 in Chernivtsi. The occasion was **Chervona Ruta** (named after a red flower in the Carpathians that is said to bloom just once a year), the first festival of modern Ukrainian music. Surmounting considerable obstruction from the authorities – performers had to thread their way to venues through rings of military checkpoints – the festival assembled hundreds of musicians from every corner of the country, performing in genres ranging from singer-songwriter to heavy metal.

Since independence, Chervona Ruta has been repeated, each time in a new city, at two-yearly intervals. Although in recent years the protest songs of 1989 have given way to a predominance of techno-oriented dance genres, the festival organizers continue to seek out and showcase new music that connects to traditional roots.

Today the most interesting traditional music is happening where efforts are being made to bridge the gaps and disruptions of the Soviet period: for example, the revival of the **epic singing tradition**. This is centred on the single performer who carried its unbroken thread into the 1990s: **Heorhiy Tkachenko** (1898–1993), who learned the art of duma singing in his youth from blind kobzari. In his old age, he passed on his songs and an authentic style of accompaniment on a traditional 21-string bandura to several students. The movement has since spread to include several informal kobzar schools and workshops building traditional banduras and other ancient instruments. The best performers are lira player **Mykhailo Khai**, kobza player **Volodymyr Kushpet** and Tkachenko's student **Mykola Budnyk**, a fine singer, kobza player and musicologist who sadly passed away in 2001

just before some of his excellent work, compiled on the definitive *Bervy* CD, could finally be made available to a wider audience.

Some of **Ukraine's minorities** have been engaged in bridging formidable cultural disruptions of their own. A significant **Jewish revival** has been taking place in recent years. Impossible during Soviet times, the appearance of the annual Klezfest series of concerts and masterclasses (run by Yana and Boris Yanover of the Centre for Jewish Education in Kiev) has provided an invaluable platform for old Yiddish singers and instrumentalists who experienced pre-war Jewish cultural life to pass their knowledge on to the younger generation. Particularly worth mentioning are **Khaverim**, a trio of septuagenarian Yiddish tango aficionados from Simferopol in Crimea; **Natalya Kasyanchik**, who plays virtuoso klezmer on the *domra*, a four-stringed round-bodied mandolin, and the **Kharkov Klezmer Band**, who are fast earning a reputation as the best traditional klezmer band in Europe. Alik Kopyt, leader of **Poza** (and the Amsterdam Klezmer Band), is a kind of Ukrainian Jewish Tom Waits, growling his way through the wonderful body of larger-than-life *blatnye pesni* (underworld songs) that celebrate ducking and diving in pre-war Odessa, the USSR's great multi-ethnic melting pot. Thanks to Poza's seminal 1997 recording *Odessa*, these songs are now a staple part of the traditional repertoire in the Jewish music scene across the ex-USSR.

Julian Kytasty

Heorhiy Tkachenko (third from left) with students at his ninetieth birthday concert

429

Crimean Tatar guitarist **Enver Izmailov** is perhaps the Ukraine's best-kept musical secret – his mastery of various folk and jazz styles, combined with his astonishing double-handed finger tapping style, has given him such a reputation inside former Soviet cultural circles that he is now something of an international ambassador for the Krymsky Tatary. From his home in Simferopol he builds his own double-headed guitars with and without frets, which allow him to imitate all manner of instruments: Indian sitar, Afghan rubab, even the Japanese koto. The entire Crimean Tatar population of some 200,000 was deported by Stalin to Central Asia in 1944 on a pretext of wartime collaboration, and not allowed to return until the late 1980s. With the exception of Enver and stodgy Soviet-era folk song and dance ensembles, it is not easy to find identifiably Crimean Tatar music within Ukraine, although there are several good music Internet pages amongst diaspora communities in Romania, Bulgaria and Turkey.

Largely thanks to Stalin's brutal austerity policies and the onset of World War II, the Ukrainian diaspora spread across the globe, and currently numbers approximately 10 million, including such unlikely sons as Argentine accordionist **Chango Spasiuk**. Other diaspora musicians, such as the New York-based bandurist **Julian Kytasty** and the British band **The Ukrainians**, continue to have a notable impact on the music scene back home. Indeed, it is said in some circles that if it hadn't been for that group of lyrical Yorkshireman led by ex-pat Ukrainian Pete Solowka, the current explosion of folk-based Ukrainian rock might never have happened. Other musicians from the large North American diaspora currently experimenting successfully with their heritage include mandolinist **Peter Ostroushko,** jazz pianist **John Stetch** and singer **Alexis Kochan**.

One of the most interesting things about the domestic Ukrainian music scene in recent years is the way in which rock and hip-hop have started to draw on folk influences. One of the main figures in this movement is renaissance man Oleg Skripka and his band **Vopli Vidopliassova**. The group played many gigs for Viktor Yushchenko's opposition party Nasha Ukraina, often acting as a "warm-up act" at his speeches and rallies at a time when doing so meant facing open hostility from the police and authorities. At a gig in Kontraktova Square, Kiev, for an audience of around 100,000 people, the police cut the band's lighting cables. "Let's not beat around the bush here," Skrika said. "You see what they are doing to us. Today they cut the lights, tomorrow our throats…" VV are not just a band famous enough to be known merely by their initials: they have become a national treasure.

Also well worth a listen among contemporary Ukrainian sounds are the Carpathian ska of **Haydamaky**, folk-rock band **Mandry**, rising reggae stars **5Nizza** from Kharkiv, Carpathian underground folk-pop group **Ocheretyany Kit** (or Komyshovy Kot in Russian) from Vynnytsa, hip-hop crew **Tanok Na Maidani Kongo** (TNMK) and **Greenjolly** from Ivano-Frankivsk, whose people power anthem "Razom Nas Bohato" (Together We Are Many) was downloaded more than 100,000 times during the first days of the mass protests during the controversial 2004 presidential elections that launched them into the stratosphere.

If you are travelling to Ukraine and want to visit a **festival**, there are two recent additions to the scene that come highly recommended. **Kraina Mriy**, organized by Vopli Vidopliassova frontman Oleg Skripka, takes place on the banks of the Dnipro river in Kiev on the first weekend in July. **Sheshory Festival** in the Ivano-Frankivsk region, near the Carpathian mountains, is an eco-festival that takes place every July and has garnered much praise for the beautiful surroundings and atmosphere. At both festivals the focus is on top-quality world music, traditional folk from Ukraine with special guests from neighbouring countries.

Eduardo Torres

Ukrainian-Argentine accordionist Chango Spasiuk

⊙ Bervy
ArtVeles, Ukraine

An encyclopedia of Ukrainian folklore on one CD, this gives a representative sampling of the best traditional performers and regional styles from around the country. It also contains a wealth of computer-viewable documentation, photos and articles about not only the music but other related topics such as traditional decorative arts and folk architecture.

★ Musiques Traditionelles d'Ukraine: Vol. 1 & 2
Auvidis/Silex, France

These two CDs of recent field recordings (mainly the work of Hubert Boone) provide a valuable picture of traditional music in Ukraine today. Vol. 1 includes polyphonic singing from central Ukraine featuring the Hilka choir, excellent Hutsul music from the Tafichuk family, and string bands from western Ukraine. Vol. 2 boasts excellent tracks by the Drevo choir, various old singers, the rare sound of the *lira* and intimate old-style bandura playing by Mykola Budnyk.

⊙ Oleh Skrypka Presents Songs from the Barricades: The Songs of Orange Revolt
Moon Records, Ukraine

Skripka has gathered together most of the leading musicians who performed on the frontlines to produce this, by far the most interesting compilation to emerge from the 2004 "Orange Revolution". The best of the bunch is Greenjolly performing their anthem "Razom Nas Bohato I Nas ne Podolati" (Together We Are Many and We Will Not Be Defeated) as an unplugged café session on voice and guitars.

⊙ Treasures of Jewish Culture in Ukraine Vol.1 (Sokrovishcha Evreiskoi Kul'tury v Ukraine)
Institute for Information Recording, Vernadsky National Library of Ukraine, Ukraine

This unique snapshot of pre-war Ukrainian Jewish music was collected from the priceless Edison cylinder archive in the Vernadsky Library in Kiev recorded by the pioneering ethnographers Moishe Beregovsky, Zinovy Kiselhof and Semyon Ansky between 1912 and 1947. The scratchy but delicately restored recordings are the first in a planned series of twelve CD reissues.

⊙ Ukrainian Village Music: Historic Recordings 1928–1933
Arhoolie, US

Down-home recordings by fiddlers and bands fresh off the boat from western Ukraine: polkas, kolomeykas and the odd Jewish number.

⊙ Zeleniy Shum Polissya (The Green Murmur of Polissya)
ArtVeles, Ukraine

The people of Polissya (Forest Land) in the northwest are considered to have the best-preserved and most archaic vocal repertoire in Ukraine. Focusing on ritual songs, this disc contains 35 audio tracks recorded from village performers, alongside 13 articles and over 400 photographs.

Haydamaky

Named after a historical eighteenth-century rebellion, Haydamaky are the Carpathian ska reggae punk kings of the Ukraine scene – the Pogues meet Burning Spear over a bottle of homebrew *horilka*. With members drawn from all parts of Ukraine, including a former member of Moldova's top band Zdob Si Zdub, their socially informed outlook was born out of their experiences in the anti-globalization underground music scenes in Germany and Poland.

★ Haydamaky
Comp Music/EMI Ukraine

Folk sounds and instruments from the Carpathian Hutsul, Bukovyna and Zaporozhye traditions are laced with a heavy dose of funky horns and dubby basslines. Vocalist and band-leader Oleksander Yarmola has a strong voice and conscious lyrics, which combine with accordionist Ivan Leno's deft arrangements to elevate them far above most of the other nu-folk rock bands out there.

⊙ Ukraine Calling
Eastblok, 2006

This, their excellent first release on a Western European label, features new tracks plus some greatest hits, and should win some richly deserved international recognition. The cocktail of Carpathian folk, punk rock and ska is unchanged, but the production is that bit crisper and the tunes more focused. High-energy trumpet-led ska tracks like "Sing Even If You Got No Bread!" show this is a band who know how to party. Hard.

Pavlo Humeniuk

Born in western Ukraine around 1884, Pavlo Humeniuk, "King of the Ukrainian Fiddlers", went to America around 1902 and started recording "village-style" music in 1925. He died in 1965, leaving over 250 recordings behind him.

⊙ King of the Ukrainian Fiddlers
Arhoolie, US

Recordings made in New York in the 1920s. Quite a few include orchestral instruments like piano or trombone, but the best, with tsymbaly and double bass or violins and accordion, are classic examples of the old village style.

Enver Izmailov

The great ambassador of Crimean Tatar culture has been well known within the former Soviet jazz scene for twenty years but is only just gaining recognition in the West. He has featured on dozens of collaborative jazz projects and released four albums in his own right.

WITH BURHAN ÖÇAL

★ Kara Deniz (Black Sea)
Unit Records, Switzerland

One of Turkey's most prolific percussionists head to head with one of the world's great guitarists. The duo format provides ample space for Izmailov to showcase his inimitable multi-textured folk jazz sound. At times it is difficult to believe there is only one melody instrument playing: harmonies and bass counterparts dance around the Oriental lead lines complemented by Öçal's intricate rhythmic patterns. But to be honest, Enver doesn't need him. A gem.

⊙ Minaret
Boheme Music, Russia

Tunes and traditions of the Crimea are here deconstructed and rebuilt in Izmailov's unique style. Of all Izmailov's jazz collaborations this one stands out: percussionist Rustem Bari and Narket Ramazanov (sax and clarinet) are old friends, and the latter's Oriental soprano sax sounds like no other jazzman.

Kharkov Klezmer Band

Klezmer music has been slowly creeping back to its ancestral homeland since the break-up of the USSR, and this fabulous quintet from Kharkiv in Eastern Ukraine are testament to the strength of the current revival.

Ticking Again
Fréa/Music and Words, Netherlands
With gutsy virtuoso fiddling from leader Stas Raiko and superb Turkish-inflected clarinet from Gennadiy Fomin, this is raw, passionate, emotion-laden klezmer that hits the spot so many more polished Western ensembles seem to miss.

Alexis Kochan

Winnipeg-born singer Alexis Kochan has a particular interest in giving songs from the oldest layers of Ukrainian culture a contemporary twist. Each of her *Paris to Kiev* CDs took years to prepare, allowing musicians from different traditions time to learn each other's musical language so as to create a seamless, unforced fusion of disparate elements.

⊙ **Paris to Kiev: Prairie Nights and Peacock Feathers**
Olesia, Canada
The vocal and improvisational styles are distinctly jazz-based, over a textured base of string instruments that is richly detailed.

Kuban Cossack Chorus

The Kuban state choir, under the Ukrainian director Victor Zakharchenko, used the freedoms of the 1990s perestroika era to stretch the boundaries of the choral form. They spent a lot of time in the villages collecting material and stimulating a revival of village singing in the region. In their own work, the chorus had an intensity and commitment that occasionally allowed one to forget that it was a show song and dance chorus like all the rest.

⊙ **In the Kuban: Folk Songs of the Black Sea and Linear Cossacks**
Melodiya, Russia
Nina Matvienko is the featured soloist on two of the cuts on this exemplary album of the Ukrainian folk song repertoire of the Black Sea Cossacks.

Julian Kytasty

Julian Kytasty is an American-Ukrainian bandura player, actively exploring the old tradition. Based in New York, he is the grand-nephew of Hryhory Kytasty, the great bandurist who emigrated to the US after World War II.

Black Sea Winds: The Kobzari of Ukraine
November Music, UK
Kytasty's delicate and understated style never fails to make his instrument sing. It's a real solo album, with Kytasty playing several sorts of bandura and wooden flute, and singing exceptionally. A beautiful exploration of historical material from one of the diaspora's most talented performers.

⊙ **Hryhory Kytasty: Music for Solo Bandura/Songs**
Kytasty, US
A tribute to Hryhory Kytasty, this develops the bandura style of the first generation of professional Ukrainian players of the 1920s and 30s. Although composed for a classicized chromatically tuned instrument, they are informed by the modes, ornamentation and textures of the kobzar tradition.

Nina Matvienko

Originally a soloist in the Veriovka State Folk Chorus, Matvienko's subsequent career has made her *the* diva of Ukrainian folk song.

⊙ **Zolotoslov**
Symphocarre, Ukraine
Features a contemporary choral composition from Kiev composer Lesia Dychko, and 21 unaccompanied folk songs. The interpretations are unrivalled.

Peter Ostroushko

Mandolin, guitar and fiddle player Ostroushko blends American and Ukrainian sensibilities. He was born in northeast Minneapolis to parents from Ukraine and for many years he was a regular performer and then musical director of Garrison Keillor's radio show *A Prairie Home Companion*.

◉ **Down the Streets of My Old Neighbourhood**
Rounder, US
A loving, humorous, sentimental 1986 recording in tribute to the people, food and music of his immigrant neighbourhood. Some Ukrainian love songs, a drunken polka, and the memorable "B-O-R-S-C-H-T" dedicated to the women of the local Orthodox church.

Poza

A short-lived but influential group, whose Odessa-born lead singer Alik Kopyt went on to form the excellent Amsterdam Klezmer Band.

Odessa: Jewish Music from Russia
Playasound, France
A simple line-up of voice, accordion, guitar, clarinet and tuba in a fabulous faux-drunken recording of underworld songs from pre-war Odessa. Kopyt's glorious sandpaper voice brings humour and tragedy to the gallery of loveable Yiddisher pimps, prostitutes and dealers, with the raucous clarinet as his sidekick. Also released under the title *Crazy Balkans* by AirMail Music.

5Nizza

A superstar band in the making, 5nizza (pronounced Pyatnitsa) are a Kharkiv-based duo whose languid, acoustic, Russian-language reggae anthems caused a sensation in Russia and Ukraine when their eponymous debut album was released in 2003. Their second, *05*, expanded their sound to include beatboxing and hip-hop, confirming them as one of Ukraine's most exciting and distinctive new bands.

Pyatnitsa
Vdoh, Russia
With just one guitar and two soulful male voices, this is a statement of intent: pure sun-drenched good-time vibes that could not be further away from their environment in arty but industrial Kharkiv. Lead singer San's voice is sweet as coconut bread and the songs have a laid-back spring in their step that recalls Manu Chao at his best.

Mariana Sadovska

A contemporary singer who manipulates traditional ritual songs and singing techniques to wonderful effect, Sadovska has a powerfully delicate style reminiscent of the first lady of Czech experimentalism, Iva Bittova. She spends most of her summers living in the isolated villages where Ukraine's vocal traditions are maintained.

⊙ Songs I Learned in Ukraine
Global Village Music, US

Accordion, strings and Sadovska's striking voice create a powerfully raw, intimate atmosphere during this sparsely arranged cycle of wedding songs, mainly from the Polissya region on the southeastern slopes of the Carpathian mountains.

John Stetch

Born in Edmonton (one of Canada's strongly Ukrainian cities) in 1966, jazz pianist Stetch grew up in a Ukrainian musical environment. He currently lives in New York.

⊙ Kolomeyka Fantasy
Global Village Music, US

Carpathian polkas and other tunes in solo piano arrangements (with some bass and drums), and with excursions into Bartók, boogie-woogie, blues and impressionism.

Tafiychuk Family

With a family line from the Hutsul village of Bukovets in the Carpathian mountains, the Tafiychuks have been cultivating local music traditions for decades. Their repertoire is recognized as a canon of Hutsul folklore.

⊙ Hutsulshchyna No. 2
Koka, Poland

Although slightly more "produced" than the first volume of family recordings – with occasional atmospheric reverbs – what gives this the edge is the fantastic village trumpet sound of the trembita, the village herding horn. Elsewhere the ensemble of tsymbaly, sopilka flute, violin and drum creates an otherwordly village fair atmosphere.

The Ukrainians

A legendary BBC Radio 1 session for iconic DJ John Peel back in 1988 inspired Pete Solowka from the Leeds rock band The Wedding Present to rework some traditional Ukrainian folk tunes, and a new brand of modern Ukrainian music was born. The Ukrainians are a classic example of the power of the diaspora to inspire cultural developments back home.

⭐ Istoriya
Zirka, UK

A greatest hits album bringing together twenty of their finest Ukrainian-language head-banging hymns to the motherland. Big rock guitars meet Western Ukrainian vocal harmonies and instruments, and once you've heard their uproarious indigenous cover versions, the Smiths, Sex Pistols and Velvet Underground will never sound the same. Mad but inspired.

Vopli Vidopliassova

Now in their tenth year, VV are undoubtedly Ukraine's top rock outfit. Led by the intellectual Kurt Cobain-alike Oleg Skripka, they have released seven albums, maturing into a sophisticated outfit who subtly rework a variety of folk material into satisfying rock anthems.

⭐ Fayno
Misteriya Zvuka, Russia

Recorded in Moscow and Kiev and mixed in Paris, VV's superbly produced seventh album brings together Skripka's bohemian range of influences in unerring style. Hard-dancing funky rock, introspective ballads, punk, electro-pop and a ska-laced, dirty reworking of a classic western Ukrainian folk melody are all in the mix. Skripka's voice and accordion soar over the cranked-up guitars and violins; Carpathian flutes remind us of the music's roots; and even the Ukrainian Armed Forces Song and Dance Ensemble are brought in, to rousing effect.

Tony Woolgar

The Ukrainians

PLAYLIST
Ukraine

1 RAI Vopli Vidopliassova from *Fayno*
Almost oriental-sounding violin and guitar riffs weave in and out of the slick rhythm section in an all-round belter of a song.

2 200 YEARS Haydamaky from *Haydamaky*
A "sensitive yet street" take on traditional Carpathian sounds: the plaintive folk harmonies beguile and soar, but you know the dub bass, ska trombone and delay guitar are ready to rock in at any moment.

3 ANARKHIYA The Ukrainians from *Istoriya*
Head-banging Ukrainian-language cover of the Pistols'"Anarchy in the UK". All together now: "Ya je anarkhist/Ya ne antikrist".

4 RAZOM NAS BOHATO Greenjolly from *Oleh Skrypka Presents Songs from the Barricades*
A now legendary hip-hop street protest anthem is here reborn as an unplugged bardic song.

5 SOLDAT 5Nizza from *Pyatnitsa*
Funky, soulful acoustic reggae anti-military anthem that established their burgeoning reputation.

6 THE SAME ROOT Enver Izmailov from *Kara Deniz*
Imagine John McLaughlin brought up in the steppes of Central Asia – this is mindbendingly brilliant Eastern guitar playing.

7 LONDONER NIGN Kharkov Klezmer Band from *Ticking Again*
An achingly beautiful slow Hassidic tune from Europe's best traditional klezmer ensemble.

8 SHOPA NEBRITAYA Poza from *Odessa: Jewish Music from Russia*
A brilliantly filthy Odessan version of "Miserlou" – the clarinet soars as Ailk Kopyt growls about the last time he had a good wash.

9 COSSACK LAMENT Julian Kytasty from *Black Sea Winds: The Kobzari of Ukraine*
A wonderfully evocative musical trip back in time: the harp-like, cascading sound of the bandura is complemented perfectly by Kytasty's delicate and quite beautiful voice.

10 EARLY ON SUNDAY Village singers of Kriachkivka from *Bervy*
A striking example of vocal folk polyphony from the Poltava region.

UKRAINE

434

Wales

gwerin: the red-hot, soaring dragon

Young Welsh-Irish band Uiscedwr
Jak Kilby

Welsh traditional music is rich and varied, but many are unaware that it even exists, largely because the rest of non-Celtic Europe subscribes to a well-worn myth that the fire-and-brimstone preachers stamped out Welsh folk culture long ago. While it's very true that English suppression and a religious revival nearly did just that, there are hundreds of traditional dance tunes surviving, alongside a plethora of marches, jigs, hornpipes and beautiful airs, preserved by inspired and visionary collectors, while balladeers still sing their achingly beautiful old songs. There's a renewed interest in the often frenzied folk fiddling tradition, while musicians are striving to revive the use of ancient instruments and preserve the tradition of Wales' national instrument, the triple harp. There's also an exciting buzz about Welsh rock bands, in a nation whose music has too often been commercially overshadowed by the Celtic giants of Ireland, Brittany and Scotland. Mick Tems reports from the valleys.

There's a word in the Welsh language, *Cymraeg*, which all aspiring Welsh speakers will have to learn if they wish to properly get to grips with Welsh culture – *sesiwn* (session). Traditional Welsh music sessions, in which fiddle, harp, melodeon, bagpipe and *crwth* players join in the *hwyl* (what the Irish might call the *craic*), are blossoming. The sleeping dragon is waking up, scratching itself and roaring again.

Despite New Labour's draconian licensing laws, these past few years have seen a Welsh music renaissance. In the 1960s and 70s a few artists and collectors were quietly tending the seedling that became the Welsh music revival – **Ar Log**, **Dafydd Iwan**, **Merêd Evans**, **Tomi "Trumpet" Jenkins** and his group **Cromlech**, the legendary band **Swansea Jack**, **Robert Evans** and **Calennig**, to name but a few.

Today, the US is still the main outlet for Welsh artists. The small but enterprising label **Fflach Tradd** broke out of Wales to distribute Welsh CDs across Europe and in the States. But while the US and the rest of Europe might be welcoming it, Wales remains a mystery to many English monoglots, even though Calennig, who had toured in US, New Zealand and Europe many times, and the stunning Brynmawr-based **Huw** and **Tony Williams** (who have since gone their separate ways), made some inroads in the 1980s and 90s and played on both sides of Offa's Dyke.

It's often said that the Welsh love singing but ignore their native instrumental music. Certainly, Welsh **folk song** has always been close to the heart of the culture, acting as a carrier of emotions, political messages and social protest, while traditional Welsh music and dance have had the difficult task of fighting back to life from near-extinction following centuries of political and religious suppression. Unlike their cousins in Ireland, Scotland and Brittany, folk musicians in Wales largely learnt their tunes from books and manuscripts rather than from older generations of players, although in recent years a surprising and encouraging series of links with "source" performers has been revealed.

The triple harper **Robin Huw Bowen** broke new ground in 1987 with his company Gwasg Teires (Triple Harp Press) by publishing **Tro Llaw**, a collection of 200 traditional Welsh hornpipes. He also published 200 Welsh folk dance tunes, which had been recorded by the Welsh Folk Dance Society. After its rediscovery by musician Simon Owen, a very rare nineteenth-century dance book (*The Cambrian Trifles* by **W. Burton Hart**) became available again. The fiddle and crwth player **Cass Meurig**, from North Wales, published 200 tunes of the celebrated eighteenth-century musician **John Thomas**, and several interesting Welsh tune collections dating back 120 years or more.

Language has traditionally been more of an issue in Wales than in other Celtic countries; today, the Welsh language is spoken by half a million of the country's 2.5 million population, and the national attitude to the language has undergone a remarkable renaissance. In some parts of the anglicized south, up to 33 percent of children now attend Welsh-language schools and their monoglot parents are rushing to evening classes in a bid to keep up.

This headlong rush to learn Welsh threatens to swamp the English songs of South Wales, however. In response, **Celfyddydau Mari Arts** has created a 400-song Internet archive – some of it in Welsh but the majority of it in the English language. The aim, a maxim of the song collectors **Calennig**, is to preserve local folklore in Gower, Pembrokeshire, Monmouthshire and the mining valleys which would otherwise disappear and be lost.

Ar Log

The Triple Harp

Wales can claim to have the only unbroken harp tradition in Celtic countries. Simple harps have been played in Wales since at least the eleventh century. These were ousted by the triple harp, imported from Italy in the eighteenth century, which has three rows of strings, the outer two in unison to each other, the middle for accidentals, making it a fully chromatic instrument. It was popular for a time throughout Europe, in art music as much as traditional circles, but was later superseded by the pedal harp (which uses the pedal for accidentals). The triple harp survived only in Wales, where it was extremely popular, and the Welsh Gypsies and Roma found it much cheaper and more portable than the heavy pedal harps. It became thought of as the Welsh national instrument in the nineteenth century.

The great triple harper Nansi Richards (1888–1979) of Penybontfawr, Oswestry, always maintained that the greatest influences on her life were her father, the Gypsies who stayed on their farm and Tom Lloyd (Telynor Ceiriog) who taught her to play the harp. She was a keen eisteddfod contestant who won the harp competition three times in succession, and recorded several times for the BBC – Sain records have released a CD called *Brenhines y Delyn*. Nansi's pupil **Llio Rhydderch** can claim an unbroken line of student-teacher tradition going back for many years. Llio, from Anglesey, has her own students now and her playing is documented on several CDs.

The most exciting move of recent years has been the emergence of **Fflach Tradd**, a label devoted to capturing the key roots sounds of Welsh music and giving it the same international profile as that enjoyed by the Celtic giants. A string of excellent albums has been released and actually made it on to the shelves of shops in Brittany, the US and elsewhere in the Celtic world, to the delight of musicians who have been frustrated at the lack of sales outlets for their work outside Wales.

Spurred on by this rocketing interest in Welsh "roots", **Sain** (of Llandwrog, Llyn) has released CDs of triple harper **Nansi Richards** (1888–1979) and the family of **Stabl Lloft** (Stable Loft), while the great traditional singer **Merêd Evans** has been honoured with a 50-track double CD, called *Merêd*. The **Plygain Carols** (traditional three and four-part midnight and early morning carols, sung to the composer's manuscript) have also made it to CD, years after they were recorded.

Bards and Eisteddfods

The **bardic** and **eisteddfod** traditions have long played a key role in Welsh culture. Medieval bards held an elevated position in Welsh society and were often composers rather than performers, employing a harpist and a *datgeiniad*, whose role was to declaim the bard's words. The first eisteddfod appears to have been held in Cardigan in 1176, with contests between bards and poets and between harpists, players and pipers.

It was a glorious but precarious tradition. Henry VIII's Act Of Union in 1536 – designed to anglicize the country – saw the eisteddfodau degener-ate, while the rise of Nonconformist religion in the eighteenth and nineteenth centuries, with its abhorrence of music and merry-making, almost sounded the death knell for Welsh traditions. Edward Jones, Bardd y Brenin (Bard to the King), observed sorrowfully in the 1780s that Wales, which had once been one of the happiest of countries "...has become one of the dullest".

Folk music, however, gained some sort of respectability when London-based **Welsh Societies**, swept along in a romantic enthusiasm for all things Celtic, revived it at the end of the eighteenth century. Back in Wales, in the 1860s, the **National Eisteddfod Society** was formed. These days three major week-long events dominate the calendar: the **International Eisteddfod** at Llangollen in July, the **Royal National Eisteddfod** in the first week of August and the **Urdd Eisteddfod**, Europe's largest youth festival, in May.

Today a host of non-competition festivals champion Welsh music alongside the best from around the world, including **Sesiwn Fawr** at Dolgellau (July), Ceri Rees Matthews' September **bagpipe festival** held at Pencader, Ceredigion, the **Cwlwm Celtaidd** pan-celtic festival at Trecco Bay caravan park, held approximately on St David's Day, the annual dance-oriented **Tredegar House Folk Festival** in Newport, kicking off in May, and the August **Pontardawe International Festival**.

Gwerin Sounds

In terms of world popularity, four names stand out – **Crasdant** (a breathtaking quartet of red-hot musicians that features the triple harper), **Robin Huw Bowen**, **Julie Murphy** and the group **fernhill**. A gloriously eclectic band, fernhill produced several beautiful and amazing CDs, *Ca' Nos*, *Llatai*, *Whilia* and *Hynt*, featuring singer Murphy, piper and guitarist **Ceri Rhys Matthews**, piper and woodwind player **Jonathan Shorland** and ubiquitous young English diatonic accordeon maestro **Andy Cutting**. Murphy is a breathtaking vocalist and sings equally well in Welsh, Breton, Gallo (a form of Romano-French) and in English. She sang solo on the CD *Black Mountains Revisited*, with jazz guitarist **Dylan Fowler** on the CD *Ffawd* and with band members on the CD *Lilac Tree*, her most adventurous yet.

Within the Welsh-language scene, bands can be hugely popular without ever breaking through to the wider world. **Ar Log**, however, with the wonderful harp-playing brothers **Dafydd** and **Gwyndaf Roberts**, were the first to cross the divide more than 25 years ago, and their occasional concerts today can still whip up a fury, even if the original bleak wildness of their sound has been replaced by a smoother big-band approach. In North Wales, the visionary **Bob Delyn A'r Ebillion**, led by the enigmatic Twm Morys, plough a path fusing Welsh, Breton and rock influences. Other northern bands include **Moniars**, who have a raucous electric bass-and-drums approach to Welsh-language song, and **Gwerinos**, descendants of the late lamented Cilmeri. One southern band breaking through to an international audience from the

Welsh-language scene is Cardiff-based **Carreg Lafar**, though the most heartening sounds must be those of the Brittany-based Welsh-Breton six-strong band **Twm Twp**, led by melodeon player **Mike James**.

On the more traditional gwerin scene, the acknowledged father of Welsh folk is politician, songwriter and Sain Records founder **Dafydd Iwan**. He began as a singer-songwriter in the Dylan/Seeger mould in the mid-1960s and has been popular and prolific ever since, providing a musical voice for Plaid Cymru (the nationalist Party of Wales.) He has since stepped down from singing, and from Sain, following his election to the post of Plaid Cymru President (2003–06) and is now head of the voluntary wing of the party. From the same school, singer-songwriter **Meic Stevens** has consistently produced good work on the borderlines of folk, blues and acoustic rock.

Singer/harpist **Siân James**, from Llanerfyl in mid-Wales, has produced four albums which have won the acclaim of Welsh and English speakers alike and have now been released in Japan. Her influences are wide-ranging and her pure-voiced harp pieces were always offset by sporadic appearances with the rock-oriented **Bwchadanas**. She even cropped up playing harp with the London roots-reggae band, One Style.

Another quality Welsh-language singer is Cardiff-based **Heather Jones**, who has worked both solo and in with the now sadly defunct group **Hafren**.

A recent casualty has been the rich-voiced Rhondda singer **Siwsann George** – of pioneering band **Mabsant** – who died of cancer in 2005 at the age of 49. Siwsann recorded several albums (including Saydisc's *Traditional Songs Of Wales*), published songs she had come across, and was the mainstay of **The Siwsann George Road Show**.

Harmony songs in three or four parts were a traditional feature in mid-Wales, where the *plygain* carol-singing tradition still survives at Christmas. Small parties of carol singers, each with its own repertoire, would sing in church from midnight to dawn on Christmas morning. The group **Plethyn**, formed in the 1970s to adapt this style to traditional and modern Welsh songs,

Robin Huw Bowen with Mabsant

still perform occasionally. Singer **Linda Healey** (who has also developed a solo career) led the harmony trio, who were influenced by the mid-Wales Plygain tradition; lately they have been back in the Sain studios, re-recording many of their favourite songs.

A visionary duo/trio/quartet from Llantrisant in Glamorgan, **Calennig** was formed out of the **Swansea Jack** band in 1978 and made eight albums and CDs (including *A Gower Garland, Trade Winds* and *Dwr Glân*) before serious illness brought their career to an unexpected end in 2001. They blended fiery Welsh dance sets with English-language songs and ballads from the Valleys and Gower, much of it stemming from their own research – they championed the diatonic accordeon (the melodeon), the anglo-concertina and the spoons, proving by their own research that these ubiquitous instruments were commonplace in Wales. Elsewhere, **The Calennig Big Band** still continues, playing for *twmpaths*; Calennig member **Pat Smith** also teamed up with guitarist **Ned Clamp**, the duo are regular festival guests and specialize in hard-hitting songs.

There's a plethora of Welsh sounds just vying for your attention. **Toreth** consist of Guto Dafis (melodeon) and Gareth Westacott (fiddle); their eponymously titled first CD is highly recommended. Swansea's **Boys From The Hill** are also a band well worth a listen. One of their members, **Martin Leamon**, has joined the Estonian violinist and *huii-kannel* (bowed lyre) player **Sille Ilves** in a duo called **Sild** ("Bridge"). Fflach Tradd have released their debut CD, *Priodi*. **Rag Foundation** exploded onto the Swansea folk scene, but seemed to have lost their path shortly before they went their separate ways, leaving behind the *Uplands* album. Fiddle diva **Siân Phillips** recorded *Gramundus* and quickly polished up her art (*Jac Tô Bach* with **Danny Kilbride**). Siân is now a member of Irish-Welsh group, **Celtish**. As far as piping goes, **Ceri Rhys Matthews** and **Jonathan Shorland** are quite stunning on the album *Pibau*.

Tragically, the fantastic group **Ffynnon** had to curtail their activities when **Dave Reid**, whose ambitious bass playing formed the crux of the band, died of a heart attack in New York. Their only published recording, *Celtic Music From Wales*, serves as a precious epitaph. Equally tragic was the death in a house fire of the South Wales rock musician **Robert "Tich" Gwilym**, who had spent much of his time accompanying Siân James and Heather Jones. An estimated 500 people attended the funeral.

HTV Wales

Calennig

Another musician worthy of note is **Cass Meurig**, from England, who went to Bangor University and stayed in North Wales, where she organizes a fiddle festival. A class fiddler, Cass – who learned Welsh – studied the medieval and rectangular **crwth**, defunct for 400 years, but which is now enjoying a spectacular revival. The label Flach Tradd have released her CD *Crwth*, in which she demonstrates all the nuances of the six-stringed instrument. She's a member of **Pigyn Clust**, working together with fiddler **Idris Morris Jones** and stunning singer **Ffion Hâf**.

On the straight folk circuit, **The Hennessys**, led by broadcaster and songwriter Frank Hennessy, still have a huge and well-deserved MOR following in the south. Frank, too, has done great work by bringing Welsh and other Celtic music to mainstream attention with his various radio and TV shows.

Other notable performers have never been recorded, such as the Welsh-Irish couple **John** and **Briege Morgan**, Bargoed songwriter **Jeff Hankins** and Cardiff harpist **Elonwy Wright**.

The Mari Lwyd

The **Mari Lwyd** (in Welsh, *Y Fari Lwyd*, or the horse's head) is one of the strangest and most ancient of a number of customs with which people in Glamorgan and Gwent used to mark the passing of the darkest days of mid-winter. Pre-dating Christmas, New Year, and even earlier Roman winter festivals, the long cold nights had been the time of fire festivals in Wales and across the Celtic World for generations.

The Mari Lwyd is unique to Wales. In its purest form (still to be seen at Llangynwyd, near Maesteg, every New Year's Day) the tradition involves the arrival of the horse and its party at the door of the house or pub, where they sing several introductory verses. Then comes a battle of wits (known as *pwnco*) in which the people inside the door and the Mari party outside exchange challenges and insults in rhyme. At the end of the battle the Mari party enters with another song.

In some places, like Llantrisant, the pwnco disappeared and the Mari party sang only their arrival verses, adding Christmas carols to the repertoire. In other areas, such as Llanharry, Cowbridge and the Vale of Glamorgan, the parties interspersed English-language verses with Welsh-language rhymes.

The Nonconformist religious revivals and the coal boom, which led to many different nationalities settling in predominantly Welsh-speaking areas, spelt doom for the Mari – but for a stroke of luck. The preacher **William Roberts** (Nefydd, 1813–72) was from Denbigh and he hated the Mari, but he recorded a full version as a warning for his congregation not to stray from the narrow path. Today the Mari is flourishing again across South Wales.

DISCOGRAPHY Wales

★ **Ffidil**
Fflach Tradd, Wales

An in-depth look at the work of thirteen of Wales' leading fiddlers, almost all of excellent quality. The range of styles, from north to south and from old to innovative, is impressive.

⊙ **Megin**
Fflach, Wales

The title translates as "Bellows", and this is a sample of the best squeezebox players in Wales. Though some accomplished musicians are noticeable by their absence, there's a delightful duet from concertina player and fiddler John Morgan, a measured, thoughtful piece by Guto Dafis and a joyous set from Neil and Meg Browning. Sheer squeezebox heaven.

★ **The Rough Guide to the Music of Wales**
World Music Network, England

Compiled by Ceri Rhys Matthews, this is an absorbing 71 minutes. Though triple harper Llio Rhydderch kicks things off with her mesmerizing "Melangell", and Capel Rhydwilym catapult us back with their primitive, electrifying chanting, any notions about Wales being all harps and choirs are pleasantly dispelled; there are bagpipes and Bray harps, rock bards such as Meic Stevens and Siôn Williams, electrifying fiddlers, scintillating melodeon and concertina players, traditional Welsh-language singers and ambitious, innovative alternative-folk bands like fernhill.

Bragod

Robert Evans, a master on the fiddle and an inspiration to many other musicians, has concentrated his attentions on the crwth, a medieval rectangular six-stringed welsh instrument, played with a bow. Juxtaposed with the rasp-ing voice of Mary-Anne Roberts, Evans' work shows medieval music and the crwth in all its possibilities.

⊙ **Kainck**
own label, Wales

Not easy listening, but thoroughly educational – the crwth sings hypnotically in the hands of Evans, making a perfect foil for Roberts.

Bob Delyn A'r Ebillion

Led by enigmatic poet Twm Morys on vocals and harp, and Gorwel Roberts on guitar and mandolin, Bob Delyn fuses Welsh, Breton and rock influences. The other players are Nolwen Korbell (voice), Edwin Humphries (sax, clarinet, bombarde), Jamie Dore (bass) and Hefin Huws (drums, vocals).

⊙ **Dore**
Crai, Wales

Celtic harp meets the bardic beatbox: a delightful collision between Wales and Brittany with just a smattering of American influences too.

Carreg Lafar

Four-piece band (Linda Owen Jones, Rhian Evan Jones, Antwn Owen Hicks and James Rourke) based in Cardiff, and with a sizeable following among the city's hip generation. Their three CDs on the Sain label so far are *Ysbryd y Werin*, the award-winning *Hyn* and *Profiad*.

Hyn
Sain, Wales

Swelling voices and instruments form a stunning Celtic back-drop on which this collection gets motoring.

Calennig

The 25-year collecting and performing career of this vision-ary duo/trio/quartet from Llantrisant, Glamorgan has been cut short by serious illness – but the songs and dance tunes they have researched live on.

⊙ A Gower Garland
Wild Goose, UK

A tribute to Gower traditional singer Phil Tanner, recorded on the 50th anniversary of his death. Calennig draw you into bygone Gower's culture and traditions on a riveting tour.

Crasdant

A truly amazing quartet, with Robin Huw Bowen (triple harp), Andy McLauchlin (flute, whistles, pibgorn), Steven Rees (fiddles, accordion, pibgorn) and Huw Williams (gui-tar, clog stepping). They have three enjoyable CDs on Sain.

★ Dwndwr/The Great Noise
Sain, Wales

Welsh airs, hornpipes and jigs come sparklingly alive when they are treated with this much tender loving care.

Merêdydd Evans

Born in 1919, Evans has been a lifelong activist for Welsh song. As a child, he listened to his mother singing old Welsh folk songs she had learnt from a farmhouse nearby. Merêd went to America, where he got a job as a university lecturer, and made a made a record for Folkways, which *The New York Times* carried in its Top 10 listings.

★ Merêd
Sain, Wales

A stunning brace of CDs, with 50 tracks of Merêd singing in that wonderfully controlled voice. The first CD is from Merêd's 1977 recordings and the second covers four tracks from *Canu'r Werin*, 16 tracks from *A Concert of Welsh Folk Songs* (1962) and two from *Folk Songs*. It sounds as fresh today as it did then.

fernhill

Formed in 1996, they have become ambassadors for a movement of talented bands injecting new life into Welsh traditional music. The spectacular singer Julie Murphy paints soundscapes with her voice; her husband and lead-er, Ceri Rhys Matthews, concentrates on ambitious acoustic guitar and the current line-up is Tomos Williams (trumpet), Christine Cooper (fiddle, crwth) and Tim Harries (of the June Tabor band) on double bass.

★ Hynt
Beautiful Jo, UK

Experts in pared-down, sparse albums, fernhill have taken their sound to the limit here, on their fourth album. Six tracks, each with a stark one-word Welsh title except "Grey Cock", on which Murphy's solo interpretation of the lyrics is a work of art.

Siwsann George

A singer and collector with a voice of Welsh gold. Born in Treherbert, Rhondda, Siwsann loved Welsh music and the Welsh language, and formed the group Mabsant and

the Siwsann George Road Show (SGWRS) before she suc-cumbed to cancer in May 2005 at the age of 49.

⊙ Traditional Songs of Wales
Saydisc, UK

Part of a series of albums of British music, "Songs of Three Nations", this features Siwsann working alongside Ray Fisher and Jo Freya. Siwsann initially sold 20,000 copies, and the public are still buying it.

Gwerinos

Seven-strong North Wales twmpath/concert band, with Ywain Myfyr (guitar, bodhran), Tudur Huws Jones (banjo) and Idris Morris Jones (fiddle) all gelling together.

⊙ Lleuad Llawn
Sain, Wales

Gwerinos are having a ball, no doubt about it. Celtic tradition-al influences merge into inspiring and original songs, with a trio of writers. Tongue-in-cheek it may be, but the humour is strengthened by the fact that these are cracking musicians.

Siân James

James is a classical, traditional and contemporary harp player, with a wonderful and at times spine-tingling voice. Her atmospheric music has won her deserved praise beyond Welsh-language circles.

⊙ Pur
BOS, Wales

"Pure" is the translation, and of all the immaculate Siân James' productions, this is arguably the best. She confidently returns to her Welsh roots, competently and confidently moulding each note. This is one of Siân's own BOS label recordings.

Tudur Huws Jones

Serial band member (Odyn Galch, Cilmeri, Y Cynghorwyr, 4 Yn y Bar and Gwerinos), writer and one of the most accomplished session musicians for Sain, Tudur's first loves are the banjo and the mandolin. With so much time spent in the studio, it was inevitable that Sain would ask him to record a solo CD of his favourite compositions.

⊙ Dal I Drio
Sain, Wales

Tudur's lifelong influences from Welsh tunes to modern country, or, as he puts it: "Nansi Richards to Nancy Griffiths." A heartwarming and scintillating collection.

Kilbride

The Kilbride brothers were the sons of Jenny and Gil Kilbride, of Castleton, Gwent, who played accordion and fiddle in their family band, Juice of Barley. Danny took up guitar and bass while the other two brothers were deft and expert fiddle musicians. Jenny tragically died of cancer, and Juice of Barley gradually evolved into that monster band Juice.

⊙ Sidan
Fflach Tradd, Wales

Two fiddles and guitar blend, overlap and enfold in a cohe-sive and triumphant climax. Joyously danceable.

Cass Meurig

A class fiddler by trade, Cass has learned Welsh and studied the crwth. She's a member of Pigyn Clust, who recorded promising CDs for Sain and Fflach Tradd.

⊙ Crwth
Fflach Tradd, Wales

Cass demonstrates all the nuances of the six-stringed instrument from strange old airs to dance tunes.

Julie Murphy

The English-born lead singer of fernhill became fluent in Welsh after moving to the Teifi valley in the mid-80s. However, she sings entirely in her native language on her solo debut.

⊙ Lilac Tree
Beautiful Jo, England

Murphy collaborates with Richard Llewellyn (acoustic and electric guitars, vocals) on ten stunning original songs, ranging from the fiercely passionate "Kiss Like That" to the quiet joy of "Cilgerran" (Glory Of Love). A truly moving and intelligent album.

Never Mind The Bocs

A family group from Caernarfon: Neil Browning (former guitarist with Welsh folk-rockers Bluehorses, master melodeon player and instigator of Sain's CD, *Scwîsbocs*) and his wife Meg Browning, plus youngsters David and Kate and Pete Walton (who plays fiddle with Cajuns Denbo, the exhilarating Bangor-based Welsh-language Cajun band).

⊙ Never Mind The Bocs
Joscyn, Wales

Sheer Welsh-music joy, with Neil's box coaxing, caressing and cajoling the tunes along.

Pigyn Clust

Singer Ffion Hâf's delicious soprano soars like a bird, augmented with fiddle players Cass Meurig (ex-fernhill and Pondman) and Idris Morris Jones (Gwerinos). If you want an easy night out listening to well-worn Celtic chestnuts, this five-strong group are not for you – they're continually probing for the outer reaches of your mind.

★ Perllan
Fflach Tradd, Wales

A strikingly mysterious and beguiling CD, with Ffion coming into her own and Cass and Idris trading licks and proving that the whole can be greater than the sum of its parts.

Rhes Ganol

For the first time since 1913, a triple harp "choir" played at the Newport National Eisteddfod in 2004. Formed in 2000 by five Welsh musicians who wanted to recreate the Llanover Triple Harp Choir of 100 years ago – Rhiain Bebb, Huw Roberts, Robin Huw Bowen and father and son Wynn and Steffan Thomas. Lady Llanover, of Llanover House in Gwent, became the sole patron of the Llanover "choir". She died in 1896 and her daughter assumed responsibility, until her death in 1913. The harp "choir" played at the Eisteddfod in the year of her death, but it too disappeared.

⊙ Yn Y Gwaed
Tant, Wales

Translated as "In The Blood", Rhes Ganol have produced an important, educational and inspirational CD – not just mirroring the music, but leading it to new places.

Llio Rhydderch

Anglesey-born triple harper Llio is at last being recognized for her remarkable talent and musicianship. She represents a 600-year tradition, and was taught by Nansi Richards (Telynores Maldwyn), whose vibrant, rhythmic style she copied and in turn teaches to her own pupils in Wales' only unbroken triple-harp tradition.

★ Enlli
Fflach Tradd, Wales

Influenced by Bardsey Island (Ynys Enlli), Llio interprets her heritage with panache and style. The mysterious, magical and holy island was reputed to be the burial place of 10,000 saints. Llio uses the unique quality of the triple harp to compose a stunning celtic soundscape. This is Fflach Tradd's most ambitious work and on the accompanying DVD *Meic Shoring* captures some amazing pictures and film.

Nansi Richards

Nansi Richards, or to give her her bardic name, Telynores Maldwyn (the harper of Montgomeryshire) was undoubtedly the outstanding influence in the field of twentieth-century traditional harp-playing in Wales. She not only brought the triple harp back into prominence, but inspired a whole generation to master the national instrument of Wales.

⊙ Brenhines y Delyn
Sain, Wales

Forty-four tracks recorded between 1947 and 1972, which show Sain's appreciation and gratitude for the tunes and airs she left. Nansi was influenced by the Welsh Roma who called at her house, and the triple harp must have made an impression on her. The bulk of these tracks are short, and the recording quality is badly faulted, but Nansi shines through.

Phil Tanner

Phil (1862–1950) lived in Llangennith on Gower's west coast, and was a striking traditional tenor. One of a seven-strong weaving family, he soaked up songs like a sponge and his chief influences were his Llangennith surroundings and its traders. The darling of the BBC (especially broadcaster Wynford Vaughan Thomas), Phil had an amazing memory – at the King's Head in Reynoldston, Gower, he started singing and was only prevented by closing time, 88 songs later. On his death, however, the BBC deleted almost all Phil's recordings, leaving just a handful.

★ The Gower Nightingale
Veteran, England

Calennig campaigned to have Phil Tanner more widely recognized, and this is the result – a breathtaking, comprehensive tribute by Veteran's John Howson, belatedly released on the 50th anniversary of his death. Digitally enhanced, with copious notes and never-before-seen photographs, Phil's old recordings take on a new life again.

Uiscedwr

This young Welsh-Irish band were lauded as one to watch when they first hit the scene as a trio. Recipients of a BBC Radio 2 Folk Award, they became a quartet with the recruitment of fiddler Ben Broughton, Uiscedwr turned heads everywhere with their debut CD. Fiddler Anna Esselmont and guitarist Ben Hellings, who both come from North Powys, and bodhran-ace Cormac Byrne play a satisfying hotchpotch of Celtic-cum-world music.

⊙ Everywhere
Yukka records, UK

Anna's beautiful fiddle swoops and soars around Cormac's bodhran soundscapes, while Ben's non-folk background breaks down traditional ideas and reworks them into a completely relevant vision.

Rachel Williams

Singer and harpist Rachel Williams comes from Letterston, Pembrokeshire, though she has made her home in Cornwall. Her harp was fashioned for her in the same village by harpmaker Alun Thomas. She coaxes her instrument with a unique, soothing voice.

⊙ **Both Sides**
Sain, Wales
Supported by top musicians Stephen Rees (fiddle) and Ywain Myfyr (bodran), Rachel's voice soars and takes flight in a most beguiling and relaxing manner.

PLAYLIST
Wales

1 **WASSAIL SONG** Phil Tanner from *The Gower Nightingale*
Tanner died in 1950; here Veteran Records have lovingly restoring his Columbia and BBC recordings to glorious pristine audio fidelity.

2 **GWALCH** fernhill from *Hynt*
Julie Murphy's golden voice swoops between butterfly-like delicacy and steely strength on a track featuring Swansea rapper Nobsta Nuts.

3 **PIBDDAWNS TREFYNWY** Crasdant from *Dwndwr/The Great Noise*
Virtuoso triple harper Robin Huw Bowen starts off this delicate hornpipe before the rest of the band join in for the swelling chorus.

4 **SOULING SONG** Calennig from *A Gower Garland*
Hypnotic concertina, melodeon and voices make for a startling combination of long-lost and ancient Gower incantations.

5 **MALLTRAETH** Llio Rhydderch from *Enlli*
Irish guru Donal Lunny asked the triple harper – somewhat bewilderingly – for a "Celtic intermix", to which she responded with this beautiful and stately traditional tune.

6 **DYDD CALAN** Cass Meurig from *Crwth*
The ancient six-stringed crwth, forerunner to the fiddle, gets a new joyous lease of life.

7 **O WRECSAM I FACHYNLLETH** Tudur Huws Jones from *Dal I Drio*
A sheer celebration from two stunning musicians, Tudur (mandolin) and Paul Airey (guitar).

8 **EI DI'R DERYN DI** Sian James from *Pur*
A magnificent harper with a controlled, strong voice and a vibrant personality.

9 **BOB BENGOCH** Kilbride from *Sidan*
A lovely, mysterious tune, the addition of oboe giving it a Breton flavour. With Dean Ryan and Jonathan Shorland as members, Kilbride are almost transformed into that wonderful band, Juice.

10 **PERLLAN** Pigyn Clust from *Perllan*
A delight from astounding singer Ffion Hâf, with verses by the eighteenth-century poet Lewis Morris, celebrating sensuous love. Idris Morris Jones and Cass Meurig create exquisite fiddle harmonies.

Part 2

Asia

This map is drawn on the Peter's projection which shows the correct relative size of countries

Asia

Afghanistan

asian crossroads

Mahwash and Ensemble Kaboul
Pascal Lafay

The fall of the Taliban regime in 2001 brought a rebirth of music in Afghanistan. Among the two or three million exiles who have since returned to the country are many musicians, and, despite continued fighting in the south of the country, there is new musical life in the country and new interest abroad. **Simon Broughton** and **Veronica Doubleday** report.

The ruins of the musicians' district of **Kharabat** in Kabul are like a symbol of Afghanistan's musical life. Those who knew it in its heyday speak of a vibrant place with musicians vying for trade. But it was reduced to rubble during fighting between rival mujahideen factions after the departure of the occupying Soviet forces in 1992. Islamist elements then imposed a ban on female singers and increasing restrictions on music, leading many musicians to leave the country. As the **Taliban** took control of Afghanistan, reaching Kabul in 1996, music was completely outlawed and instruments were destroyed. Musicians faced a stark choice: shut up or get out. Television (which broadcast a lot of music) was totally banned for its idolatrous images, and the only music permitted on radio was religious chants (*nat*) or unaccompanied songs in praise of the Taliban (*tarana*). These forms did not use instruments, so were not officially regarded as "music".

After 9/11, coalition troops brought a swift end to the Taliban regime. Within 48 hours, television was back on air and Radio Afghanistan assembled a team of musicians and began broadcasting to a population hungry for music. Cassettes and CDs flooded in from the exile community in Peshawar in neighbouring Pakistan. Musicians, too, started returning and before long a **rubab** player and a maker of rubabs (the Afghan national instrument) had settled back in the ruins of Kharabat. The arrival of commercial radio and TV stations, notably Arman FM and Tolo TV, completely transformed the scene by broadcasting Western music and promoting contests, such as *Afghan Star*, which generated a new interest in Afghan popular music. Although hampered by political constraints on music broadcasting, Radio Afghanistan saw its role as uniting the country, where the cultures of Persia, Central Asia and the Indian subcontinent meet.

The **Pashtuns**, to the south and east, are the dominant and largest group. Broadly speaking, their music is highly dramatic, with exciting climaxes and pauses, and a strong rhythmic emphasis. Speakers of **Afghan Persian (Dari)** inhabit the west, centre and northeast. Much of their music is nostalgic and romantic. In the north, **Turkic** speakers – mainly **Uzbeks** – form a third cultural group. Rather flamboyant, their music includes epics and coquettish dance pieces. These various regional styles have fed into a melting pot, contributing to two more widely disseminated types of music: classical art music and popular genres which are sometimes now quite Westernized in their instrumentation. But Afghanistan is also a heartland of Sufism, where music and Islam meet in praise of God.

Sufi Music

Rather ironically, given the conflicts in the country over music and religion, Afghanistan is crucial in the story of **Sufi music** – the mystical music of Islam that helps devotees get closer to God. Many of the great Sufi saints originated in the region. Moinuddin Chishti (1142–1236), the most revered Sufi saint in the Indian subcontinent, was born in western Afghanistan, while the celebrated mystic Jalaluddin Rumi (1207–73), who established the Mevlevi brotherhood of "whirling dervishes", was born near Balkh in the north.

Sufism remains a strong presence in modern Afghanistan. The **Naqshbandi** Sufis, followers of Baha'uddin Naqshband (d. 1390) from Bukhara in present-day Uzbekistan, are active in Kabul and elsewhere. Rather than using musical instruments, they create impressive trance-like states as they bend and sway, rhythmically chanting invocations to God in incredibly powerful and heartfelt vocal performances. Regular ceremonies are held on Fridays, notably at the shrine of Tamim-e-Ansar near the Shohada-e Saleheen cemetery and the grave of Ahmad Zahir in Kabul. One meeting-place for **Chishti** Sufis is Shur Bazaar, close to Kharabat, where musicians sing devotional music, including Pakistani-style *qawwali* and *ghazals* with harmoniums and tablas.

Both brotherhoods have suffered persecution. The Naqshbandis were persecuted by the Soviets in their campaign against

Simon Broughton

Naqshbandi Sufis in Kabul

Islam, while Chishti practices were outlawed by the Taliban, because they use musical instruments. Now a visit to a Sufi ceremony is one of the most powerful musical experiences on offer in Afghanistan.

Klasik

Afghan **classical music** is known as **klasik**, from the English word. There are several genres: sung poetry (especially **ghazals**) and instrumental pieces: **naghmehs** and **ragas**. The music is predominantly urban and has close historical links with India and Pakistan. Many of the Kabuli professional "master-musicians" (known as **ustad**) are directly descended from musicians who came from India to play at the Afghan court in Kabul in the 1860s. They maintain cultural and personal ties with India and use Hindustani musical theories and terminology, for example raga (melodic form) and **tala** (rhythmic cycle).

Many of the main Afghan ragas are similar to those in India. In performance, however, Afghan ragas are slightly different from their Indian equivalents, placing more emphasis on rhythmic variation. For rhythmic accompaniment, **Indian tablas** have eclipsed other local drums like the *zirbaghali* (goblet drum), *dohol* (hand-played barrel drum), and *daireh* (frame drum). The **Afghan ghazal** is a close cousin of the ghazal as sung in Pakistan and North India. With its romantic and mystical texts, it is an important vehicle for Sufi sentiments. Afghanistan's much-loved classical singer Ustad **Sarahang** (1923–82) was a remarkable exponent of all classical vocal styles, including ghazals, which he sang with great spiritual understanding.

The defining Afghan instrument is the **rubab**, a short-necked, fretted, plucked lute that was originally a folk instrument, probably from the mountainous Afghan-Pakistani borderlands. Here the Afghans have contributed to Indian music, since the rubab is the forerunner of the Indian *sarod* (see p.542). The latter has a steel belly and no frets – a design that favours the sliding microtonal effects common in Indian music. Afghans have a special feeling for the rubab, describing it as the "lion" of instruments. Its double-chambered body is carved from a single piece of mulberry wood and the lower part covered with skin. Its three main strings are played with a plectrum of wood, bone or ivory, but its rich, echoing sound comes from sympathetic strings, which vibrate and give a full, resonant quality – dreamy sometimes, or ecstatic. The most famous rubab-player was **Ustad Mohammad Omar** (1905–80) of the Kabuli school. Among the most celebrated contempo-

Simon Broughton

Ghulam Hussain

rary players are **Mohammed Rahim Khushnawaz** from Herat and **Ghulam Hussain**, who has returned to Kharabat and now teaches rubab in the school set up by the Music Initiative of the Aga Khan Trust for Culture. Other notable players are **Essa Kassemi** and **Daud Khan Sadozai**, both resident in Germany, and **Homayun Sakhi** in the US.

Popular Music

Afghan **popular music** is based on singing. The modern style was created at the Kabul radio station in the 1950s when the country first began broadcasting in earnest. In imitation of Indian and European styles, an official radio orchestra was established. This included some Afghan folk instruments, such as the **dutar** and **tanbur** (fretted, plucked lutes) and the bowed **ghichak** and **sarinda**. Indian instruments, like harmonium, tabla drums, sitar and **dilruba** (bowed lute), and European instruments including the violin, clarinet and guitar, were also part of this slick, massed sound.

At **Radio Afghanistan**, singers and musicians composed new material and created a specific genre structured around a verse, chorus and melodically stereotyped instrumental section, which, in typical Pashtun style, usually built up to a climax and then paused precipitously before launching into the next verse. The textured orchestral backing was hitherto unknown in Afghan music, but makes it very accessible to Western ears.

Radio Afghanistan played an important role in bringing Afghans together through music and was an influence for social change. One of the first women to broadcast on air (in 1951) was **Par-**

win, who came from an aristocratic background. Another aristocratic ground-breaker was **Ahmad Zahir**, showing that music could be a vaguely respectable career. Long after his death in 1979, he remains the most popular singer in Afghanistan today (see box). Perhaps the most notable singer is **Mahwash**, whose reedy voice and studies in classical music earned her the official title of "ustad", despite being a woman. In 1977 she had great success with a popular song called "O Bacheh" (Oh Boy), devoting each verse to a different area of Afghanistan and singing in the corresponding regional style. Although she now lives in the US, Mahwash has maintained her place as the most respected of Afghanistan's female singers, and returned to perform in Kabul in 2007. She has performed and recorded with many musicians living in exile, including the Geneva-based **Ensemble Kaboul**, formed by rubab-player Khaled Arman during the Taliban years to try and keep Afghan music alive during its time of crisis. They won a BBC Award for World Music in 2003 and are the leading group playing popular Afghan instrumental music and songs outside Afghanistan.

Weddings and Folk Music

In Afghan culture, music plays an important function in advertising and celebrating marriage, with ritual wedding songs bestowing blessings on the bride and groom. Traditionally, weddings were also a prime source of income for professional musicians.

Marital celebrations are usually gender-segregated, but both feature dancing. Entertaining the men at a city wedding, a male singer typically used to accompany himself on the Indian portable harmonium, sitting on a decorated bandstand surrounded by three or four other musicians, but nowadays, the most popular line-up features a singer with electronic keyboards. Whatever the band, the sound of drums is integral: tabla drums or the barrel-shaped **dohol** are both traditional, while the modern-style bands make heavy use of synthesized beats. In a traditional band, the melodic accompanists play local types of lutes like the rubab or **tanbur**, but a modern line-up will achieve various melodic effects on its keyboards. Popular songs and dances are the regular fare.

The traditional rituals involve processions and displays of gifts in the bridegroom's house (where the marriage is consummated). The bridegroom's sisters and their friends usually lead the music and dancing, all the surrounding women clapping in time to the rhythm. In some parts of Afghanistan,

professional bands entertain at women's parties and play for the rituals. Herat still has its female bands, whereas in Kabul and some eastern areas young boys are allowed to do the work.

All over Afghanistan, in the privacy of their homes women have been used to playing, singing and dancing to the sound of the **daireh** or frame drum. This particular drum is sanctioned by the scriptures – authentic accounts attest that the Prophet Mohammed listened to the Arab frame-drum (called *duff*) with tolerance and pleasure. As the only instrument considered suitable for women, it is indispensable for their music at weddings.

Traditionally, frame drums are made by Gypsy-like specialists known by the derogatory name of "Jat". Some of them are musicians in their own right. The men traditionally work in pairs, always outdoors, playing loud, driving music on the **shawm** and a dohol played with two sticks. This duo is often called *sazdohol* (*saz* simply means "instrument") and the musicians are ritual specialists with a semi-outcast status – no outsider will touch these instruments. (Gypsies and Gypsy-related groups play this instrumental duo in a wide area stretching from China, Central Asia and North India through Iran, Iraq and Turkey to the Balkans.)

The Afghan Jat duos often work as barbers and shave the bridegroom and circumcise boys, as well as playing music for circumcision celebrations and wedding processions. In villages they sometimes accompany men's stick dances (**chub-bazi**) and circle dances (**atan**). In the north they play at the winter game known as *bozkashi* – "goat-dragging" – in which a goat carcass is contested by teams of skilled horsemen. Sazdohol players also appear in the streets at religious festivals and at New Year, brashly demanding tips.

The **Afghan New Year** at the spring equinox is traditionally a very important time for music and festivity. Afghans love to celebrate the advent of greenery and warm weather after the bitterly cold winter by going outdoors for mass fairs called **melehs**. Most famous for this is the shrine of Ali in **Mazar-i Sharif** in the north. Its forty-day "tulip festival" with music and healing has its roots in pre-Islamic history, and in the past few years an officially staged televised music festival has been organized with local and international performers. Whether at Mazar or at other shrines or gardens, people love to sit outside playing or listening to music as they drink tea.

Tea-houses were also important male venues for music-making, especially in the north. Some areas of the northeast were never conquered by the Taliban and remained in control of the muja-

Ahmad Zahir

Ahmad Zahir

In June 1979, on his thirty-third birthday and out on a country spree with friends, the handsome Afghan pop idol Ahmad Zahir lost his life in circumstances that remain mysterious to this day. The official cause of death was a car accident, but he was known to have enemies and had already received death threats for criticizing the communist government. Rumours about his turbulent love-life flew around Kabul, claiming he had been murdered by a vengeful rival, but nothing was ever proved. The unresolved tragedy of his death is part of his legend, enhancing his image as a charismatic, talented person who lived life to the full, only to be cut down in the flower of his youth. His grave in the Shohada-e Saleheen ("Pure Martyrs") cemetery was the site of an annual pilgrimage until it was vandalized, allegedly by mujahideen, in 1992.

As a singer, songwriter and composer, Ahmad Zahir is still enormously popular and famous today, loved by Afghans all over the world, young and old. He broke with tradition: when he grew up it was unheard of for an upper-class Pashtun like him to become a professional musician. His father was a prominent politician with a family reputation to protect, but Zahir was headstrong and fiercely independent. In 1960, as a student at Kabul's Lycée Habibiya, he formed a radical new Western-style pop group and soon became famous as Bolbol-e Habibiya – "the nightingale of Habibiya". The following year they made their first recordings at Radio Afghanistan and were known as the *Amaturi* ("Amateurs"): educated young men challenging the monopolies and style of the established hereditary professionals. With his sensuous face, rousing mellifluous voice and dapper Western clothing, Zahir attracted a frenzied following among Kabul's fashionable youth, spearheading a new craze for Westernized modernity. He was the first to accompany himself on the electric organ, pioneering this instrument on the Kabul scene, and his sound was appealing and fresh.

Ahmad Zahir's upper-class background and social connections enabled him to commission work from the best songwriters and instrumentalists. These included the esteemed composers Salim Sarmast, Naynawaz and Taranasaz, the saxophonist Ustad Ismail Azimi, and the trumpeter Ustad Nangiyaly. Immensely active and prolific in his short career, Zahir left an important legacy of songs that remain bestsellers today. Mostly romantic and sometimes philosophical, they present varied and original approaches to instrumentation. His voice is filled with emotional intensity, and many of his songs are autobiographical – one such being his famous elegy to his mother on her death: "Madaram" (My Mother). Over the decades other singers have continued to sing Ahmad Zahir's songs, such as the popular "Leili Jan" (Leili, My Beloved), but they remain his own, and the public invariably seems to go back to the original recordings. His legendary fame endures in his music and in fan clubs and on websites that continue to discuss the radiance of his voice and spirit.

Simon Broughton

Ahmad Zahir's destroyed grave

hideen, who enjoyed rousing ballads about their heroes and their religious struggle. On market days before the civil war, musicians would perform epics or popular songs. The singer might strum a long-necked lute like the tanbur, or weave a wayward melodic accompaniment on the ghichak spiked fiddle, the whole sound punctuated with the zirbaghali drum or the regular chinking of tiny cymbals. The ghichak is a specifically northern instrument, with a quaint recycled tin-can soundbox. **Taj Mohammad** is one of the popular traditional musicians of the region.

Since the return of public music-making in Afghanistan, the one issue that has remained contentious is the participation of women. With the fall of the Taliban in 2001, CDs of exiled female singers like Naghma were hugely popular in the markets of Kabul. But women singers were not heard on radio or seen on TV until 2004, when the Pashtun singer Rita Wazhma recorded for TV and also performed in concert.

May 2004 saw the biggest concert in Kabul for years with the return of the most celebrated exiled singer, **Farhad Darya**. His CD *Salaam Afghanistan* had been the biggest seller for weeks and his concert in the Kabul football stadium before 40,000 people had a symbolic value, as this was where the Taliban had conducted their public executions. Farhad Darya, like many of the Afghan musicians in exile, wasn't returning to Afghanistan to live, but the concert marked an important step in making music part of normal life again. Tolo TV's *Afghan Star* competition started in 2006 and, although it has attracted criticism from Islamic leaders, it is hugely popular and has featured many female singers.

DISCOGRAPHY Afghanistan

Very few recordings of popular Afghan artists have been released internationally. Tracks and albums by Ahmad Zahir can easily be found online; otherwise it's a matter of picking things up locally in Afghanistan or cities like Peshawar in Pakistan.

⊙ **Afghanistan: A Journey to an Unknown Musical World**
Network, Germany
Excellent collection of recordings made in 1974 with the aid of Abdul Wahab Madadi, a music director at Radio Afghanistan for many years and a fine singer in his own right. Covers the various regional styles of Afghanistan: Northern Afghanistan is particularly well represented, plus the remote semi-pagan region of Nuristan. The emphasis is on vocal music, but there's also a track by rubab master Ustad Mohammad Omar. Good notes.

⊙ **Afghanistan Untouched**
Traditional Crossroads, US
A fine two-CD collection of field recordings originally made in 1968 by Mark Slobin. It's mainly folk music from the north of Afghanistan from tea-houses as well as Afghan radio. Very nicely packaged with good notes and photos.

⊙ **Anthology of World Music: Afghanistan**
Rounder, US
Recordings by the finest musicians from Radio Afghanistan in the late 1960s, including the legendary singer Biltun, who accompanies himself on tanbur. A great sample of folk music from different regions.

★ **Rough Guide to the Music of Afghanistan**
World Music Network, UK
The only compilation of Afghan music that cherry-picks the highlights of folk, popular and classical music from artists inside and outside the country. Includes tracks by Ahmad Zahir, Mohammad Omar, Farad Darya, Mahwash, Ensemble Kaboul and others.

⊙ **The Traditional Music of Herat**
Audivis/Unesco, France
A valuable collection of traditional pieces collected over five years of fieldwork in the 1970s. It includes an unaccompanied devotional song recorded in the echoing precincts of the Friday mosque; a passionate Sufi song about a local saint, with dutar accompaniment; sazdohol music (rarely represented in commercial recordings); a woman's lullaby and women's singing with frame-drum accompaniment; and fine examples of urban-style music. Extensive notes.

Farhad Darya

Darya became one of the most popular Afghan singers during the Soviet occupation of the 1980s, performing several duets with the respected female singer Mahwash. He left the country in 1990, living first in Europe and then in the US. His song "Kabul Jan" (Beloved Kabul) was played heavily by Radio Afghanistan after the fall of the Taliban and he returned to Kabul for a massive concert in 2004.

⊙ **Salaam Afghanistan**
TriVision, US
Darya's bestselling and most successful album to date. "I am the voice of a martyred nation", he sings on the title track. It was top of the charts in Afghanistan for weeks in the spring of 2004.

Ensemble Kaboul

Formed by Hossein Arman and his son Khaled in Geneva in 1995, the group's aim during the Taliban years was to keep Afghan music alive while it was suppressed at home. They remain the leading ensemble playing traditional Afghan music outside the country, and have recorded with Mahwash (see below); Khaled Arman has also released a CD of solo rubab music, *Rubab Raga* (Arion).

⊙ Nastaran
Ethnomad, France
Their debut CD, with instrumental tracks and good vocals by Hossein Arman.

Daud Khan

Born in 1955, Khan studied rubab with Mohammad Omar and also plays sarod, the Indian descendant of the rubab. He now lives and teaches in Germany.

⊙ Tribute to Afghanistan
Felmay, Italy
An excellent solo recording of classical and folk rubab pieces.

Mohammed Rahim Khushnawaz

Rahim comes from a family of hereditary musicians in Herat and is regarded as one of the city's finest rubab players. Now one of Afghanistan's veteran musicians, he has a soulful depth of interpretation.

⊙ Afghanistan: The Rubab of Herat
VDE Gallo/AIMP, Switzerland
On these 1974 recordings, Rahim turns local folk tunes into exquisite Persian miniatures, and plays two classical pieces ("Rag Bihag" and "Rag Ahir Beiru") with tabla accompaniment from his brother Naim. Good notes.

⊙ Afghanistan: Rubab and Dutar
Ocora, France
Here Rahim is joined by Gada Mohammad, the finest exponent of the Herati dutar, and a cousin on (under-recorded) tabla. The duets and solos include a masterly twenty-minute "Rag Beiru" by Rahim, as fine an example of Afghan classical instrumental music as you will find, recorded when these two outstanding musicians came to Europe in 1995.

Ustad Mahwash

Born in 1947, Mahwash is Afghanistan's leading female singer. She studied under old masters like Sarahang and became popular thanks to radio broadcasts in the 1970s, gaining the title "ustad" (master) in 1977. She left Kabul in 1991 and now lives in the US.

WITH ENSEMBLE KABOUL

★ Radio Kaboul
Accords Croisés, France
Subtitled "A Homage to Afghan Composers", this album revisits the repertoire popularized by Radio Afghanistan in its heyday. It includes lyrics by Rumi and well-known songs like "Mola Mamad Jan" and "Leili Jan". A nice booklet with pictures from the old radio station in Kabul.

Ustad Mohammad Omar

Born into a musical family in the Kharabat district of Kabul, Omar (1905–80) was largely responsible for raising the status of rubab from much-loved folk instrument to a classical solo instrument. Joining the staff of Radio Afghanistan at 32, he eventually became director of the National Orchestra and taught at the University of Washington in Seattle in 1974.

⊙ Virtuoso from Afghanistan
Smithsonian Folkways, US
A concert given in Seattle while Omar was in residence there with Zakir Hussain, no less, on tabla. Not the best sound quality, but a rare recording of historic value.

Homayun Sakhi

Born into a musical family in Kabul in 1976, Sakhi left for Peshawar in 1992, where he developed his virtuoso instrumental skills. Since 2001 he has lived in California, where he plays and teaches the rubab.

★ The Art of the Afghan Rubab
Smithsonian Folkways, US
The best available recording of contemporary Afghan rubab playing. Two lengthy ragas plus a folk-style piece to finish. Comes with a DVD and excellent notes.

Zarsanga

Born in rural Pakistan in the early 1950s, Zarsanga is one of the great traditional Pashtun singers. For many years she has lived in Peshawar, where she became known as the "Voice of the Pashtun" due to her radio performances.

⊙ Songs of the Pashtun
Long Distance, France
Raw and lively love songs, accompanied by Sultan Mohammad on rubab, plus tabla and dholak drums.

PLAYLIST
Afghanistan

1 MOLA MAMAD JAN Mahwash and Ensemble Kaboul from *Radio Kaboul*
One of the most popular songs in Afghanistan, describing the New Year celebrations at the shrine of Ali in Mazar-i Sharif.

2 SALAAM AFGHANISTAN Farhad Darya from *Salaam Afghanistan*
A lyrical song from 2003 celebrating, perhaps prematurely, the return of peace to Afghanistan.

3 JAM-E NARENJI Rahim Khushnawaz and Gada Mohammad from *Afghanistan: Rubab and Dutar*
Lovely instrumental track featuring rubab and dutar in the Herati style.

4 KATAGHANI Homayun Sakhi from *The Art of the Afghan Rubab*
A short folk-inspired track from the contemporary master of rubab.

5 LEILI-JAN Ahmad Zahir from *Rough Guide to the Music of Afghanistan*
Another of Afghanistan's most popular melodies, by the country's most popular singer.

Australia | Aboriginal Music

following the songlines

Yothu Yindi at the Garma Festival

With a remarkable history that stretches back at least 50,000 years, the indigenous people of Australia are part of one of the world's oldest cultures. Preserving their ancient heritage through a complex oral tradition of mythological "Dreamtime" stories, music has always played a central role in maintaining cultural identity, ancestral lineage and an enduring connection to the land. From the traditional sounds of voice, *bilma* (clapsticks) and *yidaki* (didgeridoo) through to contemporary singer-songwriters, rock bands and the latest Aboriginal hip-hop, Australia's indigenous music continues to evolve in fascinating ways. **Seth Jordan** tells the story.

In the Dreamtime

Aboriginal **creation myths** tell of legendary totemic beings who wandered over the continent in the **Dreamtime**, singing out the name of everything that crossed their path – birds, animals, plants, rocks, waterholes – and so singing the world into existence. The **songlines** are paths which can be traced across the continent, linking sacred spirits that have returned to the land – a kangaroo that has turned into an outcrop of rocks, perhaps, or a giant lizard into a mountain range. Tribal groups regard these totemic beings as ancestors and thus may have, for example, a local Rainbow-Serpent Dreaming or a Honey-Ant Dreaming which incorporate the story of their creation and can be depicted in art or retold in song.

The songlines define the intangible relationship between Aboriginal music, beliefs and the land. As **Mandawuy Yunupingu** from the popular band **Yothu Yindi** explains: "The role of song in Aboriginal or Yolgnu Creation is what creation is all about. The song is creation. The art is creation. The specialness in that is that we have a heart-and-mind connection to Mother Earth. Songlines are entrenched within the land itself, the journey of the songlines is from the east to the west, the journey is about following the sun."

According to Bruce Chatwin's book *Songlines*, the ancestors are thought to have scattered a trail of words and musical notes along the lines of their Dreaming-tracks. An ancestral song is thus both map and direction-finder, an essential requirement in the unforgiving environment of Australia's outback: "Regardless of the words, it seems the melodic contour of the song describes the nature of the land over which the song passes. One phrase might say, "Salt-pan", another "Creek-bed", "Spinifex", "Sandhill", "Mulga-scrub", "Rock-face" and so forth. An expert song-man, by listening to their order of succession, would count how many times his hero crossed a river, or scaled a ridge – and be able to calculate where and how far along a songline he was."

Chatwin also maintained that while a songline might pass through the country of various language-groups, the melody may intrinsically remain the same. In this way, if two neighbouring groups are allied and agree to trade the geographic "lyrics" of their songs, members of each group can safely travel through the country of the other. Having learned a new "verse", the extended song simply covers more territory. Some songlines reportedly stretch across the entire continent.

As the name songlines suggests, music and song are central to Aboriginal identity. Through singing, dancing, painting and ceremony, people become co-participants in the ongoing creation and re-animation of life. Songs can contain the history and mythology of a clan, the practical instructions for the care of land or advice about dangerous foods and animals.

Traditional Aboriginal music is strongly rhythmical, with a dependence on natural sounds – handclaps, body slaps, the stamping of bare feet on the ground, or the clapping together of **bilma** and boomerangs. The best-known instrument is, of course, the **didgeridoo** (see box overleaf), which gives either a pulse or sustained accompaniment to a dance, sacred ceremony or *corroboree* – a meeting of neighbouring tribes. The instrument's deep, resonant sound is instantly recognizable and has become the most popular and distinctive feature of contemporary Aboriginal bands.

Emmo Reiss

Mandawuy Yunupingu of Yothu Yindi

The Didgeridoo

The **didgeridoo** (didjeridu is the scholarly spelling, while *yidaki, yiraki, magu, kanbi* and *ihambilbilg* are among its alternative Aboriginal names) is the traditional instrument unique to Australia's Aborigines. It is made from the limb of a eucalyptus tree, naturally hollowed out by termites, and is often finely decorated with carvings and painted symbols. To perfect the required circular breathing method, players are encouraged to spend time listening to the sounds and spirit of the bush, so as to imitate and respect insects, animals and nature.

Originally found among the Aboriginal clans of northern Australia, the didgeridoo is now used all over the country, and often by non-Aboriginal performers. Traditionally, the didgeridoo was played only by initiated men, selected by tribal elders, and on ceremonial occasions. In keeping with this role, the didgeridoo was handled with the utmost respect, and recently there has been debate in the Aboriginal community about its use by women musicians, and to a greater degree white Australians.

Among the best-known Aboriginal players today are **Mark Atkins**, **David Hudson**, **Richard Walley**, **Tjupurru** and **Joe Geia**. Their repertoire ranges from traditional to electronica to collaborations with symphony orchestras. A noted white player is **Charlie McMahon**, who has brought the music to white audiences with his electrified band **Gondwanaland**.

A Bit of History

The indigenous people of Australia are thought to have arrived between 40,000 and 100,000 years ago. Clans may have migrated through Southeast Asia, though this has not been proven. There is genetic evidence which indicates a common link with East Coast Africans and southern Indian Dravidian peoples, which may suggest an original arc of migration from Africa. There are also strong genetic and linguistic similarities between some Aborigines and the peoples of modern-day New Guinea, although this may be as a result of more recent trade and intermarriage.

While some of Australia's northern indigenous peoples traded successfully for centuries with visiting Macassan seafarers from Sulawesi (formerly Celebes), European exploration of the continent only began in the early 1600s, with Dutch, Portuguese, Spanish and French sea captains. It wasn't until 1770 that English explorer James Cook claimed the continent for Britain, which he justified by the legal concept of *terra nullius* ("no man's land" or "empty land") – a distinctly European idea defined as "an absence of civilization", since no other colonial power had previously laid claim to it. This was despite the fact that the continent already had somewhere between 300,000 and a million inhabitants, speaking at least six hundred distinct languages.

From 1788, the indigenous people were driven off their ancestral lands and resettled, or simply hunted and killed like animals. Such brutal practices persisted until well into the twentieth century, and discrimination has continued, with the recognition of Aboriginal rights a relatively recent development. European settlement also meant the suppression of traditional languages, ceremonies and culture, the denial of identity, the importation of European diseases and the forced removal of Aboriginal children from their families.

In the late nineteenth century, Christian missionaries established mission stations in remote areas, rejecting the "heathen" music and culture of the Aboriginals and teaching them European hymns. The strong influence of gospel singing can still be heard in Aboriginal choirs and the work of some indigenous singer-songwriters.

There are currently over 450,000 people in Australia who identify themselves as indigenous (2.4 percent of the population) and some two hundred surviving languages. As well as the mainland Aborigines, the Torres Strait Islanders – of Melanesian descent – inhabit the islands between the coast of Queensland and Papua New Guinea. The vast majority of Aboriginals are scattered across the continent in country towns and settlements, with concentrations in the urban centres. While in some areas Aborigines are well integrated into Australian society, elsewhere there is continued deprivation, unemployment, high rates of incarceration and domestic violence, and ongoing problems with education, health and alcoholism.

Since the late 1970s, Aboriginal music has become an important vehicle for expressing the struggles and concerns of Aboriginal people, and in educating listeners from the outside world. Modern Aboriginal music is often closely aligned with the political struggle over **land rights**. Music has consolidated its place as a cultural glue, holding the people together and educating the public.

On the 1995 compilation album *Our Home Our Land*, Yothu Yindi's song "Mabo" celebrated the historic 1992 legal case in which the Australian High Court overturned the *terra nullius* doctrine:

Terra nullius, terra nullius,
Terra nullius is dead and gone
We were right, that we were here
They were wrong, that we weren't there . . .

Preserving the Past

The first known wax-cylinder recordings of indigenous Australians were made in 1898, on islands in the Torres Strait. Recordings were also made in Tasmania in 1899 and 1903, and in South Australia and the Northern Territory in 1901 and 1912. An important modern cultural development for Aboriginals was the establishment in 1964 of the Institute of Aboriginal Studies in Canberra, now known as the **Australian Institute of Aboriginal and Torres Strait Islander Studies** (AIATSIS). This has sponsored research into all aspects of traditional Aboriginal life, including a priceless archive of over 7000 hours of indigenous music, collected from 1898 to the present. An exhaustive directory titled "Recordings of Australian Indigenous Artists 1899–1998" is available at *nfsa.afc.gov.au/pdf/collectionguide_indigenousartists1899-1988.pdf*.

For most white Australians, traditional Aboriginal music has been a primary, if marginal experience of Black Australia. Its otherworldliness has maintained the image of Aboriginal issues being on the periphery of "Australian" life, and it has received very little mainstream attention outside anthropological or ethnomusicological circles.

One in-depth study of traditional Aboriginal music is the book *Songs, Dreamings and Ghosts* by Professor Allan Marett. Much more than a dry academic exercise, it gives a detailed analysis of the *wangga* (song and dance) of the Daly River region of Northwestern Australia. Marett's work with senior songmen and women sets a benchmark for future research into Aboriginal music.

Country Roads

Since the 1950s one of the strongest influences on contemporary Aboriginal music has been **country music**. Considered unlikely musical bedfellows by some, the two genres actually have a lot in common. As most Aboriginal people continue to live outside the major urban centres, the appeal of rural subject-matter is obvious, and for many years country artists were the only musicians who

regularly toured and performed in those regions. As documented in Clinton Walker's definitive book (and accompanying CD/DVD) *Buried Country: The Story of Aboriginal Country Music*, "Not only did Aborigines share a large part of country's roots (gospel music, minstrelsy, bush ballads), they were also attracted because country songs are story songs, and in traditional Aboriginal society this is what songs did too – told stories."

Adapting the tradition of campfire singing, Aboriginal singers began to make small inroads into the music industry. **Jimmy Little** began releasing albums in 1956, and his 1963 hit "Royal Telephone" made him the first Aboriginal pop star; he has remained popular ever since. Other prominent country-influenced performers/songwriters from the 1960s and 70s include **Bob Randall**, **Herb Laughton**, **Lionel Rose**, **Gus Williams**, **Auriel Andrew**, the **Soft Sands** band and early rocker **Vic Simms**. In the 1980s, **Roger Knox** became the unofficial King of Koori Country, and more recently artists such as **Bobby McLeod**, **Warren H. Williams** and **June Mills** have attracted well-deserved attention. Western Australia's Broome-based **Pigram Brothers** (who in a former incarnation were rock band **Scrap Metal**) continue to release relaxed country-folk albums, and singer **Troy Cassar-Daley** has achieved enormous commercial success, winning national praise at the annual Country Music Awards in Tamworth NSW – Australia's version of Nashville.

Reggae Roots

The real revolution in Aboriginal music began in the late 1970s, with the documentary film *Wrong Side of the Road*. For the first time, the idea of Aboriginal music was seen to encompass a contemporary scene, as well as its purely traditional and country forms. The film showed the Aboriginal rock bands **No Fixed Address** and **Us Mob** struggling to get exposure for their reggae-influenced songs. It marked the beginning of a public recognition of music as a tool in the fight to communicate the Aboriginal story. In particular the No Fixed Address song "We Have Survived", written by the band's frontman **Bart Willoughby**, made the point that the Aboriginal people would not simply disappear into the background:

We have survived the white man's world
And the torment and the horror of it all
We have survived the white man's world
And you know, you can't change that!

Skinnyfish Music

Nabarlek

Bob Marley, who toured Australia in 1979, had a marked influence in the early days of this Aboriginal contemporary music scene. As throughout Africa, Marley's socially conscious music, with its "Get Up, Stand Up" assertions, had a strong resonance and a number of Aboriginal-based bands began using reggae and rock formats to express their connections with the other black peoples of the world.

The Rock Circuit

The number of **Aboriginal rock bands** formed over the past three decades is phenomenal, on a scale similar to that of the punk explosion in Britain or the US, and more lasting. Even in the sparsely populated Northern Territory, virtually every remote community has its own band.

The two most notable bands of the 1980s were **Warumpi Band** and **Coloured Stone**. The desert-bred Warumpis attracted attention as the first mixed Aboriginal and white band, singing in both tribal languages and English. Fronted by the late George Rrurrambu, their flamboyant lead singer, and white songwriter/guitarist **Neil Murray**, Warumpi's 1983 single "Jailanguru Pakarnu" (Out from Jail) was the first rock song ever recorded in an Aboriginal language. Their 1984 debut album *Big Name, No Blankets* contained the singles "Blackfella/Whitefella", "Breadline" and "Fitzroy Crossing", which all received national radio airplay. They followed up with *Go Bush* in 1987, which included the iconic song "My Island Home". Their next album, *Too Much Humbug*, didn't appear until 1996, and the band officially retired in 2000, though Murray continues to pursue a creative solo career.

Coloured Stone, led by **Buna Lawrie**, originated in South Australia in 1978 and was one of Australia's longest-lasting indigenous bands. Their mid-1980s albums *Kooniba Rock, Island of Greed* and *Human Love* caught the ear of mainstream radio with the catchy singles "Black Boy" and "Dancing in the Moonlight". Lawrie continues to perform with his latest group The Peace Tribe.

Since 1990 there has been continuous development within the indigenous rock/reggae scene, with most new bands coming from the regions around Darwin, Alice Springs and Aboriginal-controlled Arnhem Land. While many have only been locally popular, others have gone on to record and undertake major tours. The most prominent groups have been **Mixed Relations**, **Blek Bala Mujik**, **Letterstick Band**, **Sunrize Band** and **Lajamanu Teenage Band**. Current Arnhem Land favourites include **Nabarlek**, **Saltwater Band** and **Yilila**.

Yothu Yindi

Yothu Yindi ("Mother Child") have been far and away the most successful exponents of distinctively Aboriginal rock, both at home and abroad, and are inseparably associated with the struggle for Aboriginal rights. Former schoolteacher **Mandawuy Yunupingu** and his fellow band-member **Witiyana Marika** are sons of leaders of the Gumatj and Rirratjingu clans in Northeast Arnhem Land.

Yothu Yindi's first album, *Homeland Movement*, was released in 1988, Australia's bicentennial year – an event which provided a focus for their protest. Their second release, *Tribal Voice* (1991), spawned the massive hit single "Treaty", which has become an Aboriginal anthem.

In concert, the band has continued to address social injustice as well as the wish for harmony and reconciliation between black and white. The band itself symbolizes this, with its mix of Aboriginal and white (*balanda*) musicians, and Western and indigenous instruments (clapsticks and didgeridoo). Yunupingu was declared "Australian of the Year" in 1992 for his work in promoting Aboriginal culture and inter-racial harmony.

While no longer the musical force that they once were, Yothu Yindi still offer a unique live experience, with their body-painted dancers and a repertoire that includes arrangements of traditional and sacred songs, giving a strong spiritual dimension to their music.

Kev Carmody

Singer-songwriters

Perhaps the most important development in Aboriginal music over the last thirty years has been the emergence of a number of individual singer-songwriters. Able to eloquently express themselves by sharing their often traumatic life-experiences, their personal perspectives have acted as a bridge between cultures, and educated many listeners about Australia's history.

Assimilation was the euphemistic term for a policy, practised up until the 1960s, of taking children from their parents and raising them in white foster homes or institutions. Many of these children, some of mixed race, were literally kidnapped and told that their parents were dead. The institution responsible was called the "Aborigines Protection Board" – an astonishing piece of doublethink. The theory was that children reared away from traditional influences would choose to become like whites. In fact, a good many children felt compelled to try and track down their families and rediscover their roots.

Three of them – **Kev Carmody**, **Archie Roach** and his wife **Ruby Hunter** – have become major singer-songwriters, and are today among the most powerful indigenous voices of Australia.

Kev Carmody, who was taken from his family when he was ten, has become the leading balladeer

of Aboriginal concerns and has been dubbed Australia's Dylan. The angry, insightful lyrics of his 1990 album *Pillars of Society* were informed by his doctoral research into the white treatment of Aborigines. He is especially contemptuous of the hypocrisy of British colonizers, a theme brilliantly developed in the song "Thou Shalt Not Steal":

*1789 down Sydney Cove the first boat people
 land
And they said sorry boys our gain's your loss
 we're gonna steal your land
And if you break our new British laws you're sure
 gonna hang
Or work your life like our convicts with a chain
 on your neck and hands
They taught us Oh black woman thou shalt not
 steal
Hey black man thou shalt not steal
We're gonna change your black barbaric lives
 and teach you how to kneel
But your history couldn't hide the genocide, the
 hypocrisy was real
'Cause your Jesus said you're supposed to give
 the oppressed a better deal
We say to you yes our land thou shalt not steal,
 Oh our land you better heal*

Carmody's subsequent albums have sustained his strong vocal style with hard-strummed guitar and occasional didgeridoo, and his 1993 duet with Australian troubadour Paul Kelly, "From Little Things, Big Things Grow", remains a much-loved national classic. His influential voice has found a wide audience, notably in schools.

Archie Roach was taken from his parents at the age of three and told that his family had perished in a fire. As a teenager he discovered that his mother had died only recently, and the shock was devastating. Dispossessed and rootless, like thousands of Aborigines he resorted to drink and spent the next ten years in an alcoholic haze. "I went from city to city, living on hand-outs. Playing music was my way of getting money to drink. Finally I stopped drinking and music seemed the natural thing to fill up the void. It was therapeutic. Still is."

Roach's expressive songs, often simply written for voice and guitar, sound confessional and many come directly from his own experience. "Took the Children Away" made his name and appeared on his 1990 debut album, *Charcoal Lane*:

Told us what to do and say
Told us all the white man's ways
Then they split us up again

And gave us gifts to ease the pain
Sent us off to foster homes
As we grew up we felt alone
Cause we were acting white
Yet feeling black

The recognition that some of the evils committed against Aboriginal people are at last being overturned was an important theme in Roach's second album, *Jamu Dreaming*. The title track celebrated the rediscovery of lost ancestral values by urban-dwelling Aborigines. His more recent albums, *Looking for Butter Boy* and *Sensual Being*, share the recurring twin themes of hurt and hope.

Roach's wife **Ruby Hunter** pursues a solo career, as well as performing alongside her husband. With her deep husky voice and folk style, Hunter offers unique insights from the perspective of an older Aboriginal woman – especially noteworthy given the silence that Aboriginal women can be bound to in traditional contexts. Her 1994 debut album *Thoughts Within*, its follow-up *Feeling Good* (2000) and the stage presentation *Ruby* (2005) have all served to solidify her reputation as Australia's most articulate indigenous female voice.

Skinnyfish, CAAMA and Indigenous Media

Although generic didgeridoo and clapstick soundtracks are frequently used in both advertising and tourist promotion, the mainstream recording industry has always been reluctant to take Aboriginal music seriously, claiming there is insufficient public interest, and most commercial media outlets have ignored all but a handful of indigenous pop hits. This has meant that the Aboriginal music industry has had to develop outside the mainstream. While the independent Australian record labels **Mushroom** and **Larrikin** released a number of landmark indigenous albums in the 1980s and 90s, in recent years, most Aboriginal recordings have come from **Skinnyfish Music** and the **Central Australian Aboriginal Media Association** (CAAMA).

Founded in 1999, **Skinnyfish Music** is a labour of love for two Darwin-based "whitefellas" – Michael Hohnen and Mark Grose. Often recording in isolated Arnhem Land locations, the Skinnyfish team continually deals with unusual music industry difficulties – like culturally based family and ceremonial commitments, a reluctant attitude towards lengthy touring and the lack of adequate instruments in the bush. They promote everything from individual singer-songwriters to Arnhem hip-hop crews.

CAAMA was created in Alice Springs in 1980. Today CAAMA is a multimedia organization operating its own radio station and TV network, Imparja, as well as managing a recording and music publishing label. Not as active as they once were, the formidable CAAMA back catalogue includes seminal releases from Warumpi Band, Coloured Stone, Frank Yamma, Lajamanu Teenage Band and Bart Willoughby.

Aboriginal media often runs on a shoestring budget, but is still quite effective. The **National Indigenous Radio Service** (NIRS) is a satellite system that provides programming to over 160 Aboriginal radio stations, often in remote locations. In addition there are over two hundred urban and regional community radio stations, many of which regularly feature Aboriginal music, including the long-running networked programme *Deadly Sounds*. Australia's national government-funded public broadcaster, the ABC, broadcasts Aboriginal news and music on their weekly radio programme *Awaye*, and the television show *Message Stick*. Likewise, the national multicultural broadcaster SBS airs their own indigenous television programme *Living Black*. Music is also given regular coverage in the Aboriginal print media, which includes *Vibe Australia*, *The Koori Mail* and the *National Indigenous Times*.

The rise of female Aboriginal performers has greatly broadened the perspective of Australian indigenous music. The vocal trio **Tiddas** ("Sisters") enjoyed a popular decade-long career of close harmonies before disbanding in 2000, and the **Stiff Gins** currently occupy similar musical territory. Singer-songwriters **Kerrianne Cox**, **Lou Bennett**, **Shellie Morris** and **Emma Donovan** have all found enthusiastic audiences for their work, and Emma's cousin **Casey Donovan** won the 2004 *Australian Idol* TV programme.

Other notable male singer-songwriters who have emerged in recent years include **Frank Yamma**, **Dan Sultan**, **L.J. Hill** and actor/musician **Tom E. Lewis**. However, the most recent indigenous success story has been the phenomenal rise of Elcho Island singer and guitarist **Geoffrey Gurrumul Yunupingu**. Blind from birth, Yunupingu first came to prominence in his cousin Mandawuy's band Yothu Yindi, and then went on to form his own Top End group, the Saltwater Band. But it was his 2008 solo album *Gurrumul*, featuring Yunupingu's remarkably pure and gentle voice in an acoustic setting, that has propelled him to the forefront of the Australian indigenous music scene, and made him a household name across the country. Praised by one music journalist as "the greatest voice this continent has ever recorded", Gurrumul won two ARIA Awards (the Australian Grammys) for Best World Music Album and Best Independent Release.

The Torres Strait Connection

The Torres Strait archipelago is made up of over a hundred islands. Its first inhabitants are believed to have migrated from Indonesia thousands of years ago, when there was still a land bridge between New Guinea and Australia.

The discovery of pearl shell in the 1860s led to an influx of people from all over the Asia/Pacific region, concentrating on Thursday Island. The colony of Queensland officially annexed the islands in 1879, but they have maintained their own distinct culture and identity, with strong links to both the mainland Aboriginal people and the tribal groups of New Guinea.

The Mills Sisters – Rita, Cessa and Ina – formed in 1970, and performed their traditional island songs around the world. Perfectly summing up the relaxed Torres Strait Islander lifestyle, these swinging island grannies' 1993 album *Frangipani Land* still makes for essential listening. Rita began performing solo in 1995, and died in 2004.

Without a doubt, the best-known Torres Strait Islander performer is singer/dancer/actor **Christine Anu**, who brought a youthful pop sensibility to her first single, "Monkey & the Turtle" (1994). Her 1995 remake of Neil Murray's Warumpi ode "Island Home" has remained her signature tune ever since:

I come from the saltwater people
We always lived by the sea
Now I'm down here living in the city
With my man and my family
My Island home/my island home
My island home is waiting for me

Anu has remained in the public eye with her follow-up albums *Come My Way* (2000), *45 Degrees* (2003) and the live set *Acoustically* (2005). She's also pursued an acting career.

A favourite Torres Strait Islander performer at present – both at home and on the mainland – is septuagenarian crooner **Seaman Dan**. Other notable musicians include **King Kadu** (Richard Idagi), storyteller **Getano Bann** and local Thursday Island band **Totemic**.

Here Come the Hip-Hoppers

Like young people all over the world, in recent years many young Aborigines have been attracted to hip-hop. Adapted to their own culture and environment, hip-hop has encouraged a whole new generation of indigenous Australian musicians to come forward. While some of the beats, hand-gestures and baseball caps may be borrowed from abroad, there's no denying that Aboriginal hip-hop is establishing its own distinct style.

Whether it's the urban wordplay of inner-city rappers like **Wire MC**, **Local Knowledge** and **Radical Son**, the hardcore sound of Central Desert rockers **NoKTuRNL** or the sassy raps of female Arnhem Land crew **Wildflower**, indigenous hip-hop seems here to stay. While many young Aboriginal hip-hop artists are yet to properly record their work, every year sees a few more releases, and the live scene is booming.

Blackfella/Whitefella

Over the years there have been numerous musical partnerships between black and white Australian musicians. While Yothu Yindi and Warumpi Band are the best-known examples, a couple of others deserve special mention. Inspired by renowned Aboriginal actor David Gulpilil, the band **Waak**

Jak Kilby

Drum Drum

Waak Jungi is an occasional collaboration between Arnhem Land songmen and rurally based white musicians from Victoria. Their 1997 album *Crow Fire Music* was a successful blend of traditional vocals and ambient soundscapes. Warren H. Williams has regularly collaborated with fellow Aussie country star John Williamson, and their musical partnership yielded the classic 1998 hit single "Raining on the Rock". The 2001 album *Corroboration: a Journey through the Musical Landscape of 21st Century Australia* featured collaborations between an all-star cast of indigenous and non-indigenous pop performers.

The careers of several other white Australian musicians have been closely associated with indigenous issues. Among them are ex-Warumpi singer-songwriter **Neil Murray**, Goanna band founder **Shane Howard**, Gondwanaland's didge virtuoso **Charlie McMahon**, and veteran rock band **Midnight Oil**. Singer/keyboardist **David Bridie** has produced a number of albums for Aboriginal artists, and with his own band Not Drowning, Waving he has forged ties with indigenous musicians from Papua New Guinea and West Papua. In 2008, a mixed-race, all-star indigenous group – the **Black Arm Band** – emerged, featuring some of Australia's finest musicians. Fronted by Archie Roach and Shane Howard, this large group has appeared at major festivals in both Australia and the UK, and a stripped-down version of the ensemble, Liyarn Ngarn ("the coming together of the spirit") has also toured extensively.

Australia's World Music Scene

Multicultural Australia has also become the adopted home for a substantial number of first- and second-generation migrant musicians from around the world. The result has been a vibrant local world-music scene in most of the major cities, with urban venues regularly presenting African, Asian, European, South American and other acts. Adelaide has hosted **Australia's annual WOMAD Festival** since 1992, and many of the country's other regional festivals often contain a strong world music component.

Currently prominent non-indigenous acts include Australian/Kazakh guitarist **Slava Grigoryan**, Tatar/Russian singer **Zulya**, cheesy gypsy band **Monsieur Camembert**, the Eastern European-influenced group **Mara!**, soulful Tongan sisters **Vika & Linda**, Papuan troupe **Drum Drum**, female acapella quartet **Blindman's Holiday**, Australian/Egyptian oud player **Joseph Tawadros** and multi-ethnic party band **The Cat Empire**.

Aboriginal Festivals and Awards

Festivals celebrating all aspects of Aboriginal community life continue to be a focus for music around Australia. While some take place in the capital cities – often as part of larger Arts Festivals – many of the more rural-based gatherings are not easily accessible to outsiders, although it is possible to visit Aboriginal lands in Central and Northern Australia when events are held.

One of the most important is the annual **Garma Festival of Traditional Culture**, organized through the Yothu Yindi Foundation, which takes place each August near the community of Nhulunbuy on Arnhem Land's Gove Peninsula. The **Laura Dance Festival** occurs biannually in June in far North Queensland's Cape York region, while the newest and most easily accessible indigenous event is the annual **Festival of the Dreaming**, which began in 2005. This professionally run event takes place in June at Woodford, northwest of Brisbane. A number of concerts featuring Aboriginal performers occur each year on Australia Day, 26 January (which some indigenous people refer to as "Invasion Day"), the largest being Sydney's **Yabun Concert**.

Australia's main national awards for Aboriginal and Torres Strait Islander music are the annual **Deadly Awards**, which began in 1995 and take place in Sydney. In recent years the Darwin-based **Music NT Awards** have also gained increased attention, particularly for musicians based in Alice Springs, Darwin and the remote Arnhem Land communities.

DISCOGRAPHY Australia | Aboriginal Music

Useful websites for information on traditional indigenous music include The Australian Institute of Aboriginal and Torres Strait Islander Studies (*aiatsis.gov.au*), and for contemporary sounds, Vibe Australia (*vibe.com.au*) and Message Stick (*abc.net.au/message/links.htm*).

⊙ **Budal Lardil**
Larrikin, Australia
The title means "songs of the Lardil people", who live on Mornington Island off Queensland, and this is one of the more approachable collections of traditional Aboriginal music. Includes Dreaming songs from a traditional and contemporary perspective and great didgeridoo.

⊙ **Culture: Music from Black Australia**
ABC/EMI, Australia
Released by Australia's youth radio network Triple J, this is a hipper-than-usual collection of contemporary indigenous music. Artists represented include the hard-rocking NoKTuRNL, urban female trio The Stiff Gins, Arnhem Land bands Saltwater and Nabarlek, and The Pigram Brothers.

⊙ **From the Bush: CAAMA Sampler**
CAAMA, Australia
This was the disc that inspired a generation of Aboriginal musicians, with its songs celebrating all the styles of Central Australia. It now feels like a historical collection, but remains a fine introduction to the contemporary music of Central Australia's desert regions.

⊙ **Meinmuk Mujik: Music From the Top End**
ABC/EMI Music, Australia
One of the best introductions to popular Aboriginal music, specifically from the Northern Territory. Recorded in remote Arnhem Land communities, its mix of Aboriginal and English-language recordings conveys the depth of styles currently flourishing.

⊙ **Our Home Our Land**
CAAMA, Australia
A miscellany of performers and styles gathered to celebrate the Mabo High Court Case victory in favour of land rights. This 2-disc set includes songs from Christine Anu, Yothu Yindi, Blek Bala Mujik, Warumpi Band and Coloured Stone.

⊙ **The Rough Guide to Australian Aboriginal Music**
World Music Network, UK
A good sampler of Aboriginal sounds both traditional and contemporary. Featured artists include Archie Roach, Ruby Hunter and Christine Anu.

⊙ **Songlines: Acoustic Sounds from Black Australia**
ABC/EMI Music, Australia
A solid collection of mainly individual singer-songwriters, including tracks from Frank Yamma, Toni Janke, Archie Roach, Troy Cassar-Daley, Kev Carmody, George Djilaynga and Kerrianne Cox.

⊙ **Spirit of the Outback**
Manteca, UK
A diverse compilation ranging from the solo didgeridoo of Richard Walley through ambient, dance fusion, country, rock and hip-hop from the likes of Coloured Stone, Warumpi Band, Frank Yamma, Blekbala Mujik, David Hudson and Charlie McMahon.

Christine Anu

A dancer and actor as well as a singer, Torres Strait Islander Christine Anu seems to have it all – looks, talent and grace. Her 1995 debut album *Stylin' Up* cracked the pop charts with her gorgeous remake of the Warumpi Band classic "Island Home", with her version almost becoming an alternative national anthem. An indigenous pop star for the MTV generation.

Stylin' Up
Mushroom, Australia

Includes "Island Home", "Wanem Time", "Monkey & The Turtle". Probably the most commercially successful indigenous album so far.

⊙ **Acoustically**
Liberation, Australia

A live acoustic 2005 set, which includes most of her past hits, some new material, and worthy versions of Marley's "Redemption Song" and "No Woman, No Cry".

Mark Atkins

A descendant of the Yamatji people of the western desert, Atkins is one of the key contemporary didgeridoo players, noted for his muscular tone and traditionally based style.

⊙ **Didgeridoo Dreamtime**
Arc, UK

A repackaged version of a Larrikin album which highlights Atkins' solid playing as well as innovations such as the use of guitars and the unusual sound of the "bullroarer".

Kev Carmody

A powerfully articulate singer-songwriter and a relentless critic of white Australian society. Carmody's albums are essential to any Aboriginal music collection.

 Pillars of Society
Larrikin/Festival, Australia

Carmody's unexpected and stunning 1990 debut, featuring the blistering title track and "Thou Shalt Not Steal".

⊙ **Mirrors**
Independent, Australia

This 2005 release proves that Carmody's songwriting skills and poignant delivery remain undiminished. In addition to the expected political material, there are several reflective tunes about the land.

Coloured Stone

One of Australia's longest-surviving bands, Coloured Stone are from the Mirning people of South Australia. Fronted by singer-songwriter Buna Lawrie, their much-loved 1980s hits like "Black Boy" and "Dancing in the Moonlight" are considered staples of contemporary Aboriginal music.

⊙ **The Best of Coloured Stone**
CAAMA, Australia

A good compilation featuring all of their classic hits from the now hard-to-find original albums *Kooniba Rock*, *Island of Greed* and *Human Love*.

Ruby Hunter

Evocative personal perspectives from the first Aboriginal woman to engage with these issues as a solo recording artist. Hunter's folk-blues style and remarkable smoky voice is full of passion and emotion. A consistently brilliant artist.

 Thoughts Within
White Records, Australia

A slow-burning fuse, Hunter's impressive 1994 debut is still massively relevant.

Tom E. Lewis

Best known for his teenage lead role in the classic 1978 Australian film *The Chant of Jimmy Blacksmith*, this impres-sive actor/musician's debut solo album displayed a new side to his multi-faceted career. After years of living in urban Melbourne he returned to his mother's country in the Northern Territory, finding inspiration and a renewed sense of place.

 Sunshine After Rain
Skinnyfish, Australia

With his half-spoken, half-sung lyrics focusing on country, family and a personal struggle for optimism, Lewis's melancholic gift for storytelling heralds him as a major new indigenous voice. This 2006 release won the Music NT Award for "Album of the Year".

Jimmy Little

With a career spanning six decades, Jimmy Little is the gentle giant of Aboriginal music, whose repertoire ranges from his early 1950s country and gospel hits to more recent crooning cover versions. A quiet legend who deserves massive respect.

⊙ **Passage 1959–2002**
Festival, Australia

A definitive double-CD overview of Little's extraordinary career.

 Messenger
Festival, Australia

This 1999 "comeback" album saw Little ambitiously covering songs from a number of well-known Australasian artists, including Nick Cave, Neil Finn, Paul Kelly and Warumpi Band.

Charlie McMahon

The most visible white practitioner of the didgeridoo, McMahon has a lifelong commitment to Aboriginal causes. He understands the mix of the Australian bush and the place of the didgeridoo in its culture.

⊙ **Gondwanaland – Wide Skies**
Warner, Australia

McMahon rocks along with synthesizer and percussion backing on this 1991 recording. Active since the early 1980s, the Gondwanaland band was the precursor to many of today's didge-based soundscape projects.

⊙ **Bone Man**
Log, Australia

A 2002 release showcasing McMahon's more recent work, which has been heading in a beat-oriented dance/trance direction.

Mills Sisters

The swaying tropical songs of The Mills Sisters reflect the relaxed Torres Strait Islander mood, and the good Sisters' deep love for their Thursday Island homeland.

Frangipani Land
Newmarket, Australia

Their classic 1993 collection of island songs. Perfect.

⊙ **Mata Nice**
Independent, Australia

One of Rita's two solo albums, this 2001 release kept the island vibe alive, even though her sisters had already retired.

Nabarlek

Billed as "the garage band that never had a garage", Nabarlek hail from the Central Arnhem Land community of Manmoyi. Founded in 1985, Nabarlek have gone on to become one of the Northern Territory's premier indigenous rock bands. With a sound and instrumentation not dissimilar from Yothu Yindi, Nabarlek's outback rock maintains a professional edge that sets them apart from many Arnhem Land bands.

⊙ **Bininj Manborlh (Blackfella Road)**
Skinnyfish, Australia
Their 2001 album finally brought their music out of the Northern Territory to a wider audience.

⊙ **Manmoyi Radio**
Skinnyfish, Australia
This 2007 release raised the bar once again, with solid new songs and slick production.

Pigram Brothers

Originally known as rock band Scrap Metal, The Pigram Brothers have carved out a laid-back country/folk musical niche, with a swag of finely crafted acoustic songs. Based in their Western Australian coastal hometown of Broome, the seven-piece band records at their own home studio, led by brothers Alan and Stephen.

⊙ **Saltwater Country**
Independent, Australia
Classic 1998 album featuring "Nowhere Else But Here" and "Saltwater Cowboy".

⊙ **Under The Mango Tree**
Independent, Australia
More Broome magic. Winner of the national 2006 Deadly Award for "Album of the Year".

Archie Roach

Roach's warm emotive voice and strong personal recollections give all of his songs a poignancy and power unmatched in Aboriginal music. Roach remains Australia's most heartfelt indigenous voice.

★ **Charcoal Lane**
Mushroom Records, Australia
An album that stunned listeners when first released in 1992, with its tales of street life and stolen children, set to simple acoustic melodies. The folk style works to convey the deep emotions behind contemporary urban Aboriginal experience.

⊙ **Sensual Being**
Mushroom, Australia
His 2002 offering had Roach in great voice and in a more upbeat mood, with bigger production and lyrics strong as ever.

George Rrurrambu

The former lead singer for the Warumpi Band was dubbed "the Johnny Rotten of Aboriginal music" for his wild onstage persona. Following the break-up of Warumpi, his solo career saw him stage an impressive one-man theatre show based on his life. Rrurrambu died in 2007.

⊙ **Nerbu Message**
Transmitter, Australia
A solid reggae-influenced outback album.

Saltwater Band

Hailing from Elcho Island, off Arnhem Land, the Saltwater Band has rapidly become one the Northern Territory's most popular groups. Fronted by blind singer/guitarist Geoffrey Gurrumul Yunupingu and showman Manuel Dhurrkay, their music is an intoxicating mix of traditional vocals, island reggae and desert blues. Terrific live and very creative on disc.

★ **Djarridjari/Blue Flag**
Skinnyfish, Australia
The better of their two albums so far, it ranges from atmospheric traditionalism to full-on rock/reggae. Excellent production.

Seaman Dan

Henry Gibson Dan, a.k.a. Seaman Dan, is the undisputed King of the Torres Strait Hula Blues. Born in 1929 on Thursday Island (T.I.), Gibson's grandfather was a Jamaican boat captain and his great grandmother a chief's daughter from New Caledonia. After a career spent as a deep-water pearl diver and boat skipper, he entered a recording studio for the first time at the age of 71. Four albums into his second career, he continues to champion Australia's rich multicultural musical heritage, charming with his Soother Band at schools and major festivals around the country.

⊙ **Follow the Sun**
Hot/Didgeridoo UK/Australia
His 2001 debut album is a delightfully smooth blend of blues, jazz, hula and traditional Torres Strait songs, and includes classics like "T.I. Blues" and "Island Lady", Lazy Pacific hula blues at its best.

★ **Perfect Pearl**
Hot/Didgeridoo, UK/Australia
This 2003 release deservedly won Australia's Grammy, the ARIA, for "Best World Music Album".

Tiddas

The three women – Lou Bennett, Sally Dastey and Amy Saunders – who made up Tiddas enjoyed enviable success until they broke up in 2000. Their close vocal harmonies and beautifully penned lyrics took their acapella/acoustic folk style into the pop charts. Sweet Honey in the Ayers Rock!

⊙ **Sing About Life**
Id/Phonogram, Australia
This 1993 ARIA award-winning album was their best studio effort.

Bart Willoughby

One of the true originals of the contemporary Aboriginal rock sound, and a survivor, both musically and culturally. Active since the late 1970s (he appeared in the documentary *Wrong Side of the Road*, as part of No Fixed Address), Willoughby then formed the influential 1990s band Mixed Relations. He continues to make his presence felt through his solo work.

⊙ **Pathways**
CAAMA, Australia
This 1997 solo album contains an excellent acapella recording of the old No Fixed Address song "Sunrise", which features Tiddas.

Frank Yamma & Piranpa

A talented Pitjantjatjara singer/guitarist from Alice Springs, Yamma is a songwriter and performer with exceptional vocal strength and a penchant for a variety of modern styles.

⊙ Playing With Fire – Warungku Inkanyi
CAAMA, Australia
When coupled with the funky playing chops of his tight multicultural band on this 1999 debut release, Yamma's music sounded both irresistible and very contemporary.

Yilila

Led by Grant Nundhirribala, Yilila are the latest stars of the vibrant Arnhem Land music scene. Based in the remote community of Numbulwar on the Gulf of Carpentaria, the band's music is based on the story of Dhumbala or Red Flag – which chronicles their ancestors' centuries-old relationship with Macassan traders from Indonesia.

⊙ Manilamanila
Independent, Australia
With their energetic mix of pulsing didge, screaming guitar solos, funky bass and painted traditional dancers, Yilila's future looks exceptionally bright.

Yothu Yindi

Galvanized into being by the Australian bicentennial celebrations in 1988, Yothu Yindi are Australia's veteran multi-ethnic band. They had their first big hit with their timely song "Treaty" in 1991 and subsequently exploited the dance-music craze for agitprop purposes, using every trick in the studio book. Quiet on the recording front in recent years, the band continues to perform occasionally and still plays an important symbolic role in Australia.

★ Tribal Voice
Mushroom, Australia
Includes their mega-hits "Treaty" and "Tribal Voice".

⊙ Garma
Mushroom, Australia
With their trademark strong rhythms and ever-present didgeridoo, this 2000 offering showcased singer Jodie Cockatoo-Creed.

Geoffrey Gurrumul Yunupingu

A former member of Yothu Yindi, this amazing singer-songwriter now alternates playing with his popular Elcho Island group Saltwater Band with his own solo acoustic work. Blind since birth, he possesses an incredibly beautiful voice.

★ Gurrumul

Skinnyfish, Australia
His breakthrough, multiple-award-winning album has broken all records for Australian indigenous music. A hauntingly gorgeous and melodic masterpiece.

PLAYLIST
Australia |
Aboriginal Music

1 **TREATY Yothu Yindi** from *Tribal Voice*
Classic indigenous anthem from 1991, asserting prior Aboriginal occupancy of the country and advocating the restoration of land rights.

2 **TOOK THE CHILDREN AWAY Archie Roach** from *Charcoal Lane*
Moving story of the forced removal of indigenous children from their parents, which awakened many to this long-standing government policy.

3 **BLACKFELLA WHITEFELLA Warumpi Band** from *Big Name, No Blankets*
A grassroots call for racial reconciliation and social empowerment, typical of the 1980s rock style of this crucial Central Australian band.

4 **THOU SHALT NOT STEAL Kev Carmody** from *Pillars Of Society*
A quick history lesson and a scathing indictment of Aboriginal dispossession and Christian hypocrisy from Australia's best indigenous singer-poet.

5 **ISLAND HOME Christine Anu** from *Stylin' Up*
Massively popular 1995 remake of Neil Murray's ode of transition from island life to city living – a metaphor for the entire Australian island continent.

6 **PITJALA WANGKANYI Frank Yamma** from *Playing With Fire – Warungku Inkanyi*
Soaring and thoroughly modern slab of Aboriginal funk, sung in Yamma's native Pitjantjatjara language.

7 **BAPA Geoffrey Gurrumul Yunupingu** from *Gurrumul*
A dreamy Elcho Island mourning melody, enhanced with strings and sung in Yolngu language.

8 **A CHANGE IS GONNA COME Ruby Hunter** from *Thoughts Within*
Rollicking country-rock tune highlighting an indigenous woman's perspective on domestic violence.

9 **PERFECT PEARL Seaman Dan** from *Perfect Pearl*
Easy-going Torres Strait island ode to beauty and the ongoing quest to find what you're looking for.

10 **BOOMERANG Tom E. Lewis** from *Sunshine After Rain*
Thoughtfully spoken, eight-minute story/song of generational change, cultural knowledge and the land, with reflective guitar-picked backing.

Bangladesh

melodies of the soul and soil

An exuberant Purna Das Baul
Jak Kilby

In the popular imagination, the region known as Bangladesh and West Bengal is known for many things – a lot of them negative, due to disasters such as cyclones, flood and famine. But in cultural terms, it is one of the subcontinent's richest and most fertile grounds for folk, film, devotional and classical music. Ken Hunt gives an finds out more.

Appropriately, the act that opened George Harrison's famous Concert for Bangladesh in August 1971 featured the two most famous Bengali – or Bangla – musicians in the world, though few people in the West would have identified them as anything other than "Indian". The piece that the sitarist Ravi Shankar and his brother-in-law, the sarod player Ali Akbar Khan, performed was a Bengali *dhun*, or folk air. In the subsequent triple-album set and film, the piece was not given any specific name, simply given the generic title "Bangla Dhan". That decision symbolized the region's cultural commonalities rather than political divisions. A shared musical bedrock linked the Indian state of West Bengal and the emergent state of Bangladesh.

The region's music can sound downright obscure to some listeners. Musicians across the continent are often labelled as "Indian" in a blanket sort of way, and outsiders rarely bother to differentitate between the particular regional roots. Relatively few people assciate the likes of Ali Akbar Khan or Ravi Shankar – and tranches of their music – with Bangla roots. Yet the region's interwoven musical continuities – the folk, religious and classical traditions – have deeply influenced Bengali maestros of the calibre of Allauddin Khan, Nikhil Banerjee and Annapurna Devi.

Bangla music also permeates some of the most creative periods in twentieth-century film. The Bombay work of S.D. Burman, his son R.D. Burman and Hemant Kumar, and the art films of the celebrated filmmaker and composer Satyajit Ray (1921–92) often drew melodically or lyrically on traditional musical themes. And just as Tagore and Allauddin Khan were influenced by the songs of the Bauls of Bengal, so Bangla music informs the work of acts such as India's Kailash Kher and Bangladesh's Habib Wahid, and diaspora acts such as Joi, Zoe and Idris Rahman, State of Bengal, Arun Ghosh and Honey Hasan. Unlikely as it may sound, Bangla music has also shaped the creativity of, amongst others, Bob Dylan, Allen Ginsberg, The Band and the Kronos Quartet.

Bangladesh and West Bengal

When the Concert for Bangladesh benefit took place to generate relief funds for Bangladeshi refugees, the breakaway state of East Pakistan was still striving to throw off Pakistani shackles, fighting a war of liberation and singing Azam Khan's songs of struggle. After Partition and self-rule in 1947, Bengal was divided into provinces along imprecise, though topographically useful, faith lines. The western part went to India and the eastern part joined Pakistan as a province called East Bengal –later renamed East Pakistan. The shared faith of Islam proved to be not enough of a glue for Bangladeshis. In late 1971 a much bloodied independent Bangladesh formally came into being after Indian armed forces intervened to tilt the balance and defeat Pakistani troops.

The word Bangladesh simply means "Bengal country" –much like the Indian state of Madhya Pradesh means "middle country". West Bengal and Bangladesh have a mainstream culture in common which transcends the faith barrier of their dominant Hindu and Muslim faiths, and which revolves around the dominant language in cultural terms – namely Bengali or Bangla.

This eastern region of South Asia has an enduring and desrved reputation for its folk, literature and cultivated performing arts. Topographically, the region is varied. It has mountain and hill territorie, marshland and forest, and many mighty rivers flowing into the Bay of Bengal. Much of its musical character is riverine, with a strong tradition of work songs associated with particular livelihoods, such as those of the fishermen and boatmen – notably the *shaari* and *bhatiyali* (boatmen songs). Watery themes appear in Bengali film songs and in the music of the Bauls. Reflecting countless waves of settlement from prehistoric times, this heavily populated region is one of the most linguistically, religiously and ethnically diverse places on the planet.

Praise songs and Patriotic songs

During the twelfth century and thereafter the Hindu Vaishnava movement flourished. Vaishnavism focuses on the worship of Vishnu or his associated avatars, notably Rama and Krishna, and the tradition imbued a particular strain of poetry to Sanskrit and Bangla devotional texts. Out of this movement came **Jayadeva**, a court poet and composer whose texts focused on Radha-Krishna themes, the so-called *Gita Govinda* (Songs About Govinda) in which Govinda (like Kanu later) is an alternative name for Lord Krishna.

At the same time, the mystical Islamic practice of Sufism arrived and spread. It found favour to the extent that, right up to the present, the faithful may follow and accommodate twin Hindu and Muslim practices, much like how, in the northwest of the country, Sikhs may also have Hindu shrines in their households.

The next development was the evolution of another genre of *kīrtan* (Hindu devotional songs) on similar themes of love, surrender and devotion. **Baru Chandidas** created a devotional song-drama called *Shri Krishna*, a spiritual song "portfolio" dating back to the second half of the fifteenth century. Its importance is heightened by the fact that it constituted a major work in Bangla literature, as opposed to the Sanskrit canon. It brought about a flowering of devotional lyricism, a poetry that used music to take flight.

Cartwheeling down the years came a succession of Bangla musical forms based on praising Hindu deities and Sufi *pirs* (holy men). Notable among these musical forms were *padāvali* kīrtan, which concentrated on themes such as Radha-like everlasting love (Radha being the principal consort of Krishna) and *shāktapaga sangeet*, songs devoted to divinity symbols of the female creative force, especially the Goddesses extraordinaires Kali and Durga. Kali, whose name is at the root of Cal-

cutta and Kolkata because of her famous temple in Kalighat, is, as Balraj Khanna points out in his book *Kalighat: Indian Popular Painting 1800-1930*, "a living presence" in the city.

Vaishnava themes also coloured the region's folk entertainments such as *putul-nāch* (puppet dance), now in decline but a popular rural entertainment well into the second half of the twentieth century. In tandem with this, there was a number of popular manifestations of religious themes in folk-drama – *jatra* or *yatra* – themed on particular deities such as Candi (or Chandi), the serpent goddess Manasā and Kamala Kamini. Candi is a divinity that is an amalgamation of several mainstream Hindu and local deities, and that blurring pattern is repeated throughout this region with Hindu and pre-Hindu gods, summed up in the Bangla saying that in Bengal there are thirteen religious festivals for every twelve months of the year.

In contrast to the prevailing religiosity of previous musical forms, a wind of secularism blew

Lalon

Properly speaking, fakir is a word originally specifically applied to Muslim ascetics, meaning "one poor in the sight of God" from the Arabic fakīr or "poor". Lalon Fakir or Lalon Shah – also spelled Lalan – was a Bengali pilgrim poet-philosopher about whom little is known biographically beyond the year of his death – 1890 – and that he settled in the Kushtia district of modern-day Bangladesh, then a part of the Bengal Presidency. Various decades ranging from the 1770s to 1790s are given for his birth.

He was silent or evasive about his origins. In one lyric he sang, "People ask if Lalon Fakir is a Hindu or a Mussulman [Muslim]/Lalon says he himself doesn't know who he is…" This obfuscation was central to his belief in overturning prejudice and conducting life with a clean slate. Though "Fakir" and "Shah" seemingly point to an Islamic connection, they may be misleading or later additions or accretions. Similarly, Awul Chand, another influence on the Bauls and the founding guru of eighteenth-century Kartabhaja sect combining Vaisnavism and Sufism, shed his lineage for posterity. Caste, familial lineage, faith were "baggage" – to use the modern idiom – when taking mystical paths.

What is indisputable is that his poeticism remains a cornerstone of Bangla music's mysticism. Just as it moved Tagore, it motivates Baul maestros such as Purna Das Baul ("the Emperor of the Bauls") and the blind Baul singer Shāhjahān Miah from his village northwest of the Bangladeshi capital Dhaka (formerly Dacca) who specializes in the repertoire of Lalan Shah. According to Lalon Fakir – and Awul Chand – it is the present and the future, not the past, which matter.

Baul painting

in with the classical vocal form *tappa*, which revisioned divine love through a romantic mortal prism. The tappa composer-musicians **Nidhu Babu** (a.k.a. Ramnidhi Gupta [1751–1839]) and **Kalidas Chattopadhyay** (1750–1820) showed the way forward and many others followed. New musical genres which emerged in the wake included *Brahma sangeet* (Brahma songs). During the period 1905 to 1911 an independence movement for self-rule blossomed and a genre of patriotic songs called *swadesi gaan* became massively popular. New urban musics arose in which fixed composition rather than extemporised spontaneous creativity, of the interpretative *raga* kind, was favoured. By 1868, India was being portrayed as a weeping woman under foreign rule in a **Dwijendranath Tagore** song

Songs of the "Madmen" – the Bauls

One of the most remarkable of all the subcontinent's folk traditions traces its roots to the time of the de facto Hindu Reformation. Like the Christian Reformation, the **Bhakti** (Devotion) movement unfurled over centuries. Fundamental questions about faith and religiosity, Brahminical doctrine and malpractice were asked. Tantric Buddhist and Sufi thought provided fresh angles from which to view Hinduism and its practices – whether to do with *varna* (Hinduism's four castes and the bulk of humanity beneath them) or the control-freak aspects of Brahmanism. This melting-pot of ideas created the Baul philosophy of how to behave, how to view life and how to ponder greater truths and dominions beyond the sword. And in its utter, unapologetic "Bengaliness", it profoundly coloured the greatest Bengali writer and thinker of historic times, **Rabindranath Tagore**.

The Bauls are a mystical brotherhood of wayfaring minstrels, at pains to sidestep society's conventions and religious orthodoxies. Theirs is a syncretic philosophy: they borrow from mystical Hinduism, Islam and Tantric Buddhism. They search for *maner manush* – the "man of the heart", or the ideal within us – and strive for ecstatic communication with the divine while dispensing with any need of God or gods. With a typically contrary logic, the Bauls describe their path as *ulta*, meaning "reverse" or "the wrong way round". They have no scripture or doctrine in any conventional sense. Baul philosophising is in many ways as patchwork as their garb.

Parallel and interchangeable bodies of song reflect their mystical Hindu or Sufi origins and often the historical faith allegiances of the individual Baul. In this last respect, the quip goes, in a riot a Baul knows which direction to run.

The Bauls' name is said to derive from *batul*, the ancient Sanskrit for "wind" or "mad" from which, incidentally, English ultimately obtains the word "aubergine". The unorthodoxy of the Baul faith is not dissimilar to Sufism; the Bauls describe themselves as "mad about the soul of God within [themselves]" and seek mystical union with the divine through ecstatic singing and dance. Female Bauls sing and dance in public alongside the men, indicative of their equal status.

Typically they accompany their songs with the *dotara* lute, the *khamak* (a hollow tension drum with one or two strings attached that allows the pitch to be changed whilst playing and slithery percussive effects), the *ektara* (a one-string drone instrument often played by mendicant holy men) and assorted percussion such as the trademark *napur* (ankle rattles). They promenade with sashaying steps, pirouetting or dancing in tight, concentric circles as they sing.

Actually, many Bauls have long adopted settled lifestyles with generations living in villages or following the more meditative tradition of the *akhra* (religious centre) which by its very nature implies a sedentary rather than an itinerant life. This reflective Baul approach is reflected well on **Shāhjahān Miah**'s highly recommended *Chants Mystiques Bâuls du Bangladesh* (1992).

With free abandon Baul repertoire takes from historical, reforming poet-philosophers such as **Kabir** and **Lalon Fakir** (see box on p.469) as well as adding and updating as they go. Songs with many levels of meaning are handed down from guru to *shishya* (student); they come cloaked with the deceptive simplicity of nursery rhymes or children's songs. Prosaic images conceal aphorism and present paradox. "I am blind, I cannot see the darkness", goes one song. In another, a light bulb refers to deeper illumination. An airport's runway is used as a metaphor for a spiritual path; the jackfruit's sticky juice stands for higher love. For those who don't understand the words, it's the music that connects. To appreciate the Bauls' non-conformity – at least on a surface level – you need only see a live performance.

Rabindranath Tagore

One of the people whose life was transformed by Baul thought was Rabindranath Tagore (1861–1941). The Bard of Bengal, he became Asia's first Nobel Laureate for Literature in 1913 and composed songs that were adopted as national anthems of both India (1911's "Jana Gana Mana") and Bangladesh (1906's "Amar Shonar Bangla"). For Tagore, the Bauls were a culturally rich signpost to the true path. Although Tagore grew up in a privileged family, he also grew up in questioning era in which the arts played a huge role.

In many ways, Tagore *was* the modern age. When the singer **Pankaj Mullick** (1905–78) tentatively contacted him about including his work in a film – it included a setting by Mullick of one of Tagore's poems – Tagore responded enthusiastically. He proffered further material for inclusion and even suggested the name for the film. It became *Mukti* (1937), in which Mullick also sang, acted in and was director of music. Mullick's work in *Mukti* presented Tagore's lyricism to a new cinema-literate generation and, with the magic wand of technology, Tagore's influence expanded exponentially in pre-Partition India. Then and now, Tagore represents something more. He is the living breath of Bangla nationhood and even has a song form named after him – *Rabindra sangeet*. Tagore is an icon about as core to the Bengali experience as it is possible to imagine.

Bangla Music for Modern Times

Tellingly, Tagore was open-minded enough to really listen to **Narbani Das Baul** sing and talk at Santiniketan near Bolpur, about 180 kilometres north of modern-day Kolkata. He used Narbani Das Baul's Baul melodies too, setting new words to old tunes. In so doing he transformed perceptions and Bangla arts. His acknowledgment of the cultural importance of the Bauls was transforma-tive, a vindication of Bengal's folk traditions and a signal that it was perfectly in order to treat Baul songs and dhuns as worthy.

Narbani's son, **Purna Das Baul** (Purnachandra, or "Full Moon", in full) was born in Ekchakka village, near Rampurhat in West Bengal during the springtime Holi mela – the Festival of Colours – in 1933. Nobody ever did more to further the acceptance of Baul culture in the wider world. The Indian government officially anointed Purna Das Baul the **Baul Samrat** (Emperor of the Bauls). Around 1967, thanks to nudging by **Allen Ginsberg**, awareness of the Bauls blossomed. Purna Das was one of the two Bauls – the other was his brother, Luxman Das – flanking **Bob Dylan** on the cover of *John Wesley Harding*, while an ecstatic image of Nabani Das appeared on the cover of *Bengali Bauls at Big Pink*, a recording by Garth Hudson of The Band. The family's musical lineage is unbroken today – Purna Das' son **Bapi Das Baul** is creating new music in a traditional Baul vein with his group Baul Bishwa, as well as DJing.

Diaspora acts have revisited Tagore's material, such as the paean to the Bengali motherland "O Amar Desher Mati", that clarinettist **Arun Ghosh** (of Bengali and Sindhi ancestry) performed on his 2008 album *Northern Namaste*. Brother-and-sister piano-and-clarinet team **Zoe** and **Idris Rahman** (of a Bengali and English family) have reinterpreted Tagore's "Auld Lang Syne"-like "Purano sei" and Gauri Majumder and Hemanta Mukherjee's "O Nodi Re" on their *Where Rivers Meet* (2008). It's no wonder Messrs Khan and Shankar were perfectly at ease beginning that concert at New York's Madison Square Gardens all those years ago with a simple Bangla folk air.

DISCOGRAPHY Bangladesh

⊙ **Bauls de Bengale**
Dacqui, France
A good selection of rustic-style Baul music from singer Viswanath Das Baul and his two sons Anando Gopal and Nitya Gopal. The traditional Baul instrumentation includes dotara, khamak and small cymbals.

⊙ **Bengal: Traditional Folk Music**
Auvidis/Unesco, France
A good introduction to the traditional sounds of Bengal, this features Baul material from Purna Chandra Das Baul and a *bhatiyali* (boatman song) from Haripado Deva Nath, plus flute tunes, and folk and religious songs.

⊙ **Inde: Kobiyals, Fakirs & Bauls**
Buda, France
Recorded at the Boral festival in 1999, these recordings present the region's folk music in a microcosm. Rebel poets make mystic, cross-faith detonations and declarations, while the *kobiyals* protest social injustice and cultural iniquities in song.

⊙ **Music of India, Volume 1**
Frémeaux & Associés, France
The second CD of Deben Bhattacharya's two-CD set concentrates on Bengali art music. Recorded in a *jalsaghar* or *salon de musique* setting, and sung by Himaghna Roy Chowdhury, the material includes songs by Tagore and Najrul Islam and

Hindu devotional material addressing themes of Lord Krishna and the Goddess Kali.

⊙ River Songs of Bangladesh
ARC Music, UK

Watery imagery percolates through Bengali and Bangladeshi culture, poetry and music. The lovers that swore they'd never separate but are separated by the funeral pyre and the river between them is but one of many favoured poetic images. These recordings made in 2001 by the musicologist Deben Bhattacharya tap into that sort of symbolism with a variety of river songs that extend well beyond the tradesmen's *bhatiyali* genre.

Paban Das Baul

Paban Das Baul (no relation to Purna Das Baul, below) was born in the village of Mohammedpur, West Bengal in 1961. He has performed at WOMAD and mixed traditional music making with crossover collaborations with Sam Mills and The State of Bengal. His wife, Mimlu Sen, is author of *BaulSphere* (Random House), a personal view of the minstrels and their culture.

★ Real Sugar

Real World, UK

British guitarist and producer Sam Mills (of indie band 23 Skidoo) has spent a lot of time in West Bengal and first got to know Paban in 1988. In this 1997 collaboration, their friendship and respect for the other's work preserves the integrity of the Baul songs in music directed towards a global audience.

Parvathy Baul

Born into a family of Hindu astrologers and farmers from Bangladesh's Chittagong District in 1976, Parvathy went to Tagore's Santiniketan at the age of 15 and discovered the world of the Bauls. Female Bauls figure in many recordings but Parvathy Baul is particularly good. Her musical career is a great example of the guru-shishya (master-pupil) principle of Baul knowledge and transmission.

⊙ Radne Bhava
Arion, France

A beauteous recording in an informative package. The notes reveal her sources and inspirations – Phulmala Desi, her guru Sanathan Das Baul and others.

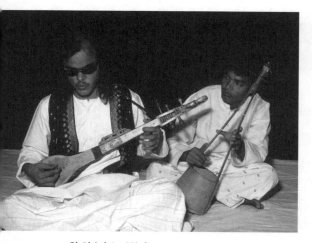

Shāhjahān Miah

Crammed Discs

Purna Das Baul (middle) with son Bapi Das Baul (left)

Purna Das Baul

⊙ The Bauls of Bengal
Legacy International, USA

Not wholly the reissue this masterpiece deserves, but it takes nothing away from the sheer artistry of its musicians. The most represented soloist here is Purna Das, although Hare Krishna Das, Luxman Das and Sudhananda Das get one solo apiece. On its original release in 1968, with Baul releases thin on the ground, the Elektra album proved revelatory - both as a musicological document and for introducing the world to the majesty of Purna Das's high-soaring voice and consummate artistry. It still has that power.

⊙ Bauls of Bengal
Crammed Discs, Belgium

One of the best recordings of Baul music around – a dozen representative tracks of Purna Das Baul and family in 1994. There's vibrant percussion on the distinctive khamak drum and evocative flutes played by Gour Pal.

Shāhjahān Miah

Muhammed Shāhjahān Miah is a Baul musician in the more meditative tradition of the akhra (religious centre), rather than that of the wandering minstrels. He lives in the village of Taota northwest of Dhaka. Blind since the age of 14, he specializes in the repertoire of Lalon Shah.

⊙ Chants mystiques bauls du Bangladesh
Inedit, France

Gentle, intimate music in the Baul Muslim tradition, which underlines the Sufi connections, although there are Hindu subjects like Krishna and Radha here too. Accompanying himself on the dotara lute, plus a small ensemble of bells and percussion, Miah is less colourful and more serious than many of the Baul performers.

British Bangladeshi pianist Zoe Rahman

Zoe Rahman

Nominated for a Mercury Award in 2006, pianist Zoe Rahman, daughter of a Bengali father and English mother, is a prominent figure on the UK jazz scene.

⊙ **Where Rivers Meet**
Manushi Records, UK
Zoe and her brother Idris Rahman take up repertoire from their father's record collection reworking Bengali folk and film songs in this 2008 release.

PLAYLIST
Bangladesh

1 **AGUN PANI Purna Das Baul** from *Bauls of Bengal*
Fire and water, two of the elements that make up the human body.

2 **KI DIE PUJIBO HARI CHARANA TOMAR The Bauls of Bengal** from *The Bauls of Bengal*
The opening track from the Elektra album that propelled them into people's imagination.

3 **ASHARH MAISHYA Muhammad Jasimuddin Hiru** from *River Songs of Bangladesh*
"Through a floating screen of sand and the wind, as I gaze at the sails of the river-boats, full of hope, I await someone," he sings to string, wind and percussion accompaniment – no doubt with the purl of the river in his ears.

4 **SHAON ASHILO PHIRE Himaghna Roy Chowdhury** from *Music of India Volume 1*
A Calcutta recital with melodic and rhythmic accompaniment of a monsoon song by Najrul Islam. The recording is one made by the musicologist Deben Bhattacharya in late 1972.

5 **BAUL MELODY Nikhil Banerjee** from *Lyrical Sitar*
This performance from one of the greatest of sitarists shows the porous nature of art and folk music in Bangladesh and West Bengal. Banerjee (1931–1986), accompanied by Anindo Chatterjee on tabla, reworks the Baul melody to spontaneously create something sublimely classical during which time slips away and has no meaning.

6 **PILGRIM'S SONG Zoe & Idris Rahman** from *Where Rivers Meet*
An instrumental dialogue between Zoe (piano) and her brother Idris (clarinet) with their father on vocals and Kuljit Bhamra on tabla.

Burma

secret scenes

Village folk performers in Ngabutaw
Ernest Hariyanto

Pro-democracy protests in Burma (or Myanmar as the ruling regime has renamed it) have highlighted the political situation in the country, which has been isolated under rigid military rule since 1962. The music of Burma, however, remains largely undiscovered by the outside world. Yet Burmese classical music offers a distinctly original and exotic sound, as mysterious and intriguing as the country itself, and Burma's numerous ethnic groups perform on rare instruments in timeless rural tradition. Meanwhile, modern urban musicians defy strict government censors to get their music out of Myanmar. Jack Chance takes us inside.

Classical Music

Burmese classical music can be difficult to grasp for the first-time listener, appearing to shift abruptly from frenzied, complicated rhythms to delicate and spacious melodies, modulating and shifting tempo in unexpected places. It can sound like free jazz, but actually relies on complex rhythmic and melodic forms, as well as a unique system of tuning. Burmese classical music is of two types – loud "outdoor" music with circular drum and gong ensembles, with frenzied melodies and complicated rhythms which can be difficult to grasp for the first-time listener, and softer "indoor" courtly music (harp, xylophone and vocals) with delicate and enchanting melodies.

Mahagita (literally "great song") is a collection of songs (about 500) that comprised the classical repertoire until the last king was exiled by the British in 1885. Mahagita songs are typically performed on the *saung gauk* (harp) or *hsaing waing* (circular drum and gong ensembles). The saung gauk has been around for perhaps a thousand years, since the early Burmese kingdom of Bagan, and there are stone carvings in the ancient capital depicting its precursors – arched harps with between five and seven strings. The saung gauk today has sixteen strings between its arched neck and resonator body. A deerskin covers the soundbox and the harp is ornately decorated with nature motifs and intricately inlaid glasswork. **Hsaing** ensembles are led by the *pat waing*, 21 tuned drums arranged in a circle around the performer. The pat waing creates an incredible and unique sound: legend has it that it's supposed to mimic the sound of mangosteen fruit falling into a river. The 21 drums of a pat waing are tuned by smearing *patsar* ("drum food" – a mixture of rice flour and ash) on the heads. Other instruments in classical ensembles include *maung waing* (a circular set of tuned gongs), *patala* (bamboo xylophone) and *hne* (oboe).

Virtuosic singing typically accompanies the orchestra, featuring poetic lyrics about natural beauty, love and loss, and the occasional subtle political message. Sadly, due to government restrictions, new Mahagita works are rarely composed these days.

Burma was administered as a province of British India between 1886 and 1948. When Western instruments began arriving with British colonizers, Burmese musicians adapted these instruments to perform in these local musical forms. Musicians such as **Ko Ko** and **U Yee Nwe** have taken the European piano in a new direction, improvising Mahagita-style melodies while using non-tempered tunings on the *sandaya*, as the piano is called in

Mandalay Thein Zaw

Burmese. Another odd import into Burmese classical music is the **Hawaiian slide guitar**, or *guitar gyi*, which has taken a strange and different path in the hands of Burmese classically trained musicians.

Folk and Religious Traditions

The traditional Burmese instruments often accompany **pwe**, an outdoor evening performance not to be missed. On auspicious days at the local Buddhist pagoda, Burmese families bring picnic provisions for an all-night carnival of music, dancing, comedy and opera. A typical pwe stage-show features a **zat min thar**, a central male character who is actor, singer and dancer throughout the performance. The singing is boisterous and unrestrained, while the dancing features highly acrobatic movements, complete with tremendous leaps, somersaults and even the occasional hoop of fire.

Po Sein, **Shwe Man Tin Maung** and **Mandalay Thein Zaw** are some of the best-known pwe dancers, while **Po Chit** is among a younger generation of zat min thar. Comedians are traditionally part of this vibrant cabaret, and comics like **Mos** and **Modi** have risen from the pwe stage to become nationally known film actors. But comedy can be no laughing matter in Burma: members of **The Moustache Brothers** of Mandalay served several years in prison for performing outside incarcerated president-elect **Aung San Suu Kyi**'s house.

Do bad waing is another type of folk/religious ensemble featuring *do bad* (small drums), *wah lah ko* (bamboo handclapper), and *linkwin* (cymbals). A singer, or sometimes a male-female duet, leads the chorus, improvising lyrics to comment

Jack Chance

Young Karen girl plays the thana harp in a Thai refugee camp

on recent events. During **Thingyan** and **Tazaung Daing festivals** and for family events such as a son entering a monastery, do bad waing performers parade through the streets in celebration. Unfortunately, the government cracks down hard on social commentary, and do bad waing is now usually banned in major cities.

Ethnic Music

Burma's geographic perimeter is home to over a dozen indigenous and migratory ethnic groups, each with a decidedly different culture from that of the Burmese majority. While tourists are rarely allowed into these areas (which are sometimes active war zones), places like Shan and Karen States contain rich traditions that have changed little in the past century.

A good place to find traditional **Karen** music is the Thai-Burmese border, where Karen refugees play the *thana* (folk harp), *kana* (fretless mandolin), *gwe* (buffalo horn), *bi* (mouth harp) and various drums and gongs. Karen folk singing, *taday ta'oo*, has a mellow bluesy sound, and the lyrics often reflect the dire situation that the Karen face after six decades of war with the Burmese military. At festivals, such as Laku Kisu (a wrist-tying ceremony), *dohn* dances are held in Karen villages. Vibrantly choreographed to a simple drumbeat, dohn dancers sing the stories of neighbours (or sometimes neighbouring armies) who have done wrong.

The **Mon** ethnic group of southern Burma is known for the *kyam*, a three-string zither carved in the shape of a crocodile. *Batt kine* is a set of tuned gongs, arranged in a vertical crescent shape. Drum ensembles (*hta bone pone pon*) and *kha dae-kha bart* (cymbals), provide the rhythm for traditional Mon performances.

Shan and Thai cultures are closely related; you can probably find more Shan recordings in Thailand than inside Burma. For those intrepid enough to enter Shan State, watch for the social dance *ram wong*, accompanied by a parade of bamboo flutes, drums, cymbals, and gongs.

Rocking the Junta

The Myanmar government bans all political songs, so artists have learned to cleverly disguise subversive messages through their lyrics. For example, Shan rock legend **Sai Htee Saing**'s "Wheel No. OK0122L" is ostensibly about a bicycle wheel. But the numbers refer to 12 February, the date that the **Panglong Agreement** was signed, promising autonomy to several ethnic groups; a promise which the Burmese government never kept.

On 8 August 1988, thousands of university students, democracy activists, Buddhist monks and workers staged massive protests in Rangoon, demanding democratic reforms after then ruler General Ne Win, in a move against the country's thriving black market, suddenly declared all the country's high-denomination banknotes invalid. Overnight, three quarters of the currency in circu-

"Copy" Songs

Burma is overrun with songs that sound conspicuously similar to the latest hits from other countries, but with Burmese lyrics. Whether it's the government restricting foreign influences or people just wanting to hear songs in their own language, the "copy" song phenomenon is said to have been started in the late 1960s by recording studio owner **Peter Ba Dain**. Today the practice is so widespread that when they hear the original English-language version of a song, many locals think that it's a copy of a Burmese song because they heard the version in their language first.

During the 1988 democracy movement, a Burmese version of Kansas's "Dust in the Wind" was given new lyrics by an unknown democracy activist, becoming an unlikely anthem for the movement as "Gabar Ma Jae Boo".

lation became worthless. When government forces responded to the protests by firing on the crowds, killing thousands of civilians, musicians like **Dennis Mun Aung** and the late **Htoo Ain Thin** fled to the Thai-Burmese border to join student groups organizing against the government. Htoo Ain Thin eventually returned to Rangoon, where he is remembered as having bravely remained true to his roots, writing and singing songs that were clearly against government policy. **Khaing Htoo**'s song "Last Dream" has a profound resonance for many democracy activists and student protesters who witnessed their peers gunned down during the protests.

For fifteen years after the 1988 uprising, if you wanted to release an album in Burma, you needed to include one song praising the regime. **Policy thachin** (policy music) became a standard requirement for any album to get past the censors. These songs flattered the government but were unpopular. At the time of writing, Policy thachin were no longer required, most likely because of an agreement between record producers and junta officials. But if you pick up a Burmese-produced album, count on the first few tracks to be public service messages praising the regime. **Phardae gita** (propaganda songs) are also commonly ignored by the average Burmese citizen. As Orwellian as music can be, these are happy songs about the happy state of affairs for all the happy people of Burma.

Popular Music

When it comes to rock'n'roll, the people's choice is **Iron Cross**. The long-running heavy metal stars from Rangoon have a massive following throughout the country. Singer **Lay Phyu** was frequently banned from the stage and has since retired from public performances, but Iron Cross continue to record albums with scorching guitar tracks by **Chit San Maung**.

BPM and their late singer **Doh Lone** were pioneers of the alternative rock scene in Burma, a much-needed departure from the 1980s rock so

The late great songwriter El Pew

often copied by other Burmese artists. **The Ants** are less popular but produce original rock'n'roll, with outstanding lyrics by late songwriter **El Pew**. **Big Bag**, **Antibiotic** and **Black Hole** are heavily promoted, but tend to imitate American pop-punk and new metal.

Hip-hop has taken off in Burma and the Burmese language flows well when rapped. Sound engineer **Myo Kyaut Myain** brought hip-hop to Burma in the early 1990s and has gone on to produce many of Burma's electronic tracks. Like much Asian hip-hop, there's a lot of copying Western styles (see box), but rappers/producers like **J-Me** have a huge following. There's some political rap, but with government censorship, it's fairly underground.

DISCOGRAPHY Burma

⊙ **Green Tea Leaf Salad: Flavours of Burmese Music**
Pan Records, Netherlands
A well-rounded sampler of Burmese traditional music, including the guitar-playing of U Thein Soe, as well as crocodile zither and the gamut of Burmese percussion.

⊙ **Guitars of the Golden Triangle: Folk and Pop Music of Myanmar**
Sublime Frequencies, US
Psychedelic 1970s rock from the poppy-fields of Shan State, lifted from old cassette tapes to capture this "lost scene" from northeast Burma.

⊙ **Kyu Aye Nyeit Nyeit [Saung Hlaing Win Maung]**
Unknown label (available via *shwemyanmar.net*), Burma
Burmese-produced (and thus difficult to find), this recording features saung gauk harp played by the virtuoso Hlaing Win Maung.

★ **Mahagita: Harp and Vocal Music of Burma**
Smithsonian Folkways, US
An excellent introduction to Burmese traditional music, well produced and featuring the elegant vocals of Daw Yi Yi Thant and the subtle saung gauk harp playing of the late Inle U Myint Maung.

⊙ **Pat Waing: The Magic Drum Circle of Burma**
Shanachie, US
Featuring master drummer Kyaw Kyaw Naing, this album showcases Burma's most unique instrument, the pat waing.

⊙ **Sandaya: Spellbinding Piano of Burma**
Shanachie, US
Featuring the delicate piano artistry of U Yee New with accompanying percussion and vocals.

⊙ **White Elephants and Golden Ducks: Enchanting Musical Treasures from Burma**
Shanachie, US
A broad mix of traditional Burmese instruments, including saung gauk, pat waing, sandaya (piano), mandolin and guitar gyi (Hawaiian-style slide guitar), professionally performed and produced.

The Ants

Alternative-style rock'n'roll with thoughtful lyrics and original arrangements from a relatively unknown band.

⊙ **First, Second, Third**
unknown label
Western-style rock featuring tracks written and sung by the late great El Pew.

Doh Lone

The late pioneer of Burmese alternative rock and leader of the popular band BPM.

⊙ **A Kaung Sone Tay Myar**
unknown label
Solo album from rocker Doh Lone.

Iron Cross

By far Burma's most popular rock band, fronted by Lay Phyu, and with Chit San Maung on guitar, Ka Yang (drums), Khin Maung Thant (bass), Ba Nyar Naing (keyboards).

⊙ **Butterfly**
PTL Studio, Burma
Officially Lay Phyu's solo album (but featuring Iron Cross as backing band), a modern rock offering from Burma's best.

Sai Htee Saing

Longtime rebel rocker from Shan State, Sai Htee Saing's music remains popular throughout Burma.

⊙ **Unplugged Live**
unknown label
This energetic retrospective performance captures the spirit of Shan State's musical hero.

Win

A relatively undiscovered singer-songwriter with an amazing vocal range, Win would be a heartthrob in any other country.

⊙ **Song for Peace**
unknown label
A mix of Western and Burmese covers with a few original tracks and simple acoustic guitar accompaniment. This is hard to find, but ask around in the bars on the Thai border.

PLAYLIST
Burma

1 TAUN TO/ THA JA Hlaing Win Maung from *Hlaing Win Maung*
Happy melodies on the saung gauk harp.

2 LAKE THAY MAH SHOKE Saing Saing Maw from *Guitars of the Golden Triangle: Folk and Pop Music of Myanmar*
You can almost taste the opium in this laid-back 1960s-style groove from this psychedelic guitarist from Shan State.

3 PAT WAING LET SWAN PYA Kyaw Kyaw Naing from *Pat Waing: The Magic Drum Circle of Burma*
The uniquely odd sound of the pat waing circle drum at its best.

4 GOLDEN BROWN HAWK Kyaw Kyaw Naing/Ko Ba Htay/U Kyi/U Tin Maung from *White Elephants and Golden Ducks: Enchanting Musical Treasures from Burma*
Flute weaving over pat waing circle-drum accompaniment.

5 NAO SOWN The Ants from *First, Second, Third*
Smooth ballad from late great songwriter E. Pew.

6 NGA NAY JAL Lay Phyu from *Butterfly*
Slow rocker with Iron Cross backing their legendary frontman.

7 CHIT OO MAY Doh Lone from *A Kaung Sone Tay Myar*
A swinging ballad from one of the main singers in Burma's alternative rock scene.

8 THAN LWIN CHONG CHAR Sai Htee Saing from *Unplugged Live*
A love song about the much-contested Salween River.

9 SONG FOR PEACE Win from *Song for Peace*
Reggae-themed roots music from a young singer with an amazing voice and a small but extremely loyal following.

Cambodia

from dancing angels to dengue fever

US-Cambodian rockers Dengue Fever

If you visit Angkor Wat, Cambodia's vast temple complex and one of Southeast Asia's biggest tourist attractions, you'll experience two sides of the country's music – the celestial and the human. While the walls of Angkor are covered in reliefs showing angels playing heavenly instruments, along the processional paths that lead to the temples you can hear traditional music played by orchestras of musicians who were disabled under the murderous Khmer Rouge regime (1975–79) or by left-over landmines. Although many musicians were among the million-plus victims of the Khmer Rouge, Cambodia is steadily rebuilding its musical culture. John Clewley reports.

Although Cambodia is a small country sandwiched between larger neighbours – Thailand (formerly Siam) and Vietnam – its Khmer kings ruled over much of mainland Southeast Asia between 802 and 1431. Under their rule, spectacular temples were built around the Angkor site (one of the world's largest temple grounds): Angkor Wat, Bayon, Baphuon, Ta Prohm, Banteay Srei and many others. During this period, a delicate classical dance style and accompanying court music were developed from the dances of maidens (**apsaras**) who performed at the temples to honour the gods, and the dance style the Khmer created went on to influence classical dance across the region.

Khmer music remains an essential part of Cambodian life. Each region has distinctive folk dances and many villages still have their own classical and folk ensembles which play at funerals, weddings and Buddhist ceremonies, using many of the same instruments depicted on the bas-relief murals on the walls of Angkor Wat – harps, gong circles and drums. You can hear this music as you leave the temples of Ta Prohm and Banteay Srei, where classical and folk bands play for the visitors and sell CDs for the charities supporting disabled musicians.

Pre-Khmer music still exists in the countryside, for example in the form of dances for spirits in Koh Kong and the *nang meo* rain dance in Siam Reap. Ancient epic storytelling (*chareng chapey*) and trance dances can be found in the north of the country. Cambodia also has a call-and-response folk style, *lakhon ayai*, which involves verbal jousting between a male and female singer, not unlike the *lam* found in Laos and the *mor lam* of northeast Thailand.

The collective term for Cambodian folk music is *Phleng Khmer* (Khmer music) and the musician at the centre of the music-making is usually the **chapay** (long-necked lute) player. Chapay players are also itinerant bards, wandering the countryside to sing bittersweet, comic or satirical songs, not unlike the travelling bluesmen of the Deep South in the US. Only a handful of ageing master chapay musicians, like **Kong Nay**, have survived the Khmer Rouge era, but Nay, who recently toured the UK, continues to travel around the country and teach a new generation.

Classical Dance – Heavenly Forms

There are two major forms of **Cambodian dance** – **classical** and the much-older traditional **folk styles** (the latter with roots in animism and magic, together with Hindu forms from the first century). You can see the roots of traditional dancing whenever Cambodians have a social get-together and form a circle (*ramvong*), around which they move slowly, with graceful hand-movements. The classical form (*lakhon kbach boran*) borrowed much from the Indian tradition and earlier folk styles,

Jak Kilby

Chapay musician Kong Nay

John Clewley

Carved apsara dancers at Angkor Wat

but by the thirteenth century the style was more Khmer than Indian. Carved bas-reliefs at Angkor show musicians and dancers, some of whom are apsaras. Estimates suggest that there were 3000 apsaras at the court of the twelfth-century king, Jayavarman VII.

Apsaras and tontay dancing, the latter depicting early myths, are the two main elements of classical dance. The **Dance of the Apsaras** and **Tep Monoram** are non-dramatic ballets where the dancers are "sewn" into silken bodices and skirts, and adorned with tall spiked golden headdresses. The dancers move to the rippling and haunting cascades of sound provided by a **pinpeat orchestra**, which consists of a bamboo xylophone (**roneat**), chapay, flute (**pia au**), oboe (**srlay**), two-stringed violin (**tro**), temple hand-cymbals (**ching**), tuned bronze gongs (**ghong**) and various drums. Today, there are some sixty pure dances and forty dance-dramas.

Tontay is a form of dance drama. Here the graceful dancing of the ballet gives way to pantomimic moves, humour, clowning around, ad-libbing and action dancing styles. For tontay, extracts from the Indian epic *Ramayana* are performed. Female dancers play the parts of queens, princesses and demons, while male dancers play those of religious figures and clowns, with boys playing monkey roles.

Classical dancing has been revived several times this century, most noticeably in the 1960s by the great "white apasara" dancer **Princess Norodom**

Buppha Devi, the daughter of King Norodom Sihanouk. The genocidal rule of the Khmer Rouge, however, left the tradition in tatters, as some ninety percent of all classical performers were killed, along with anyone who had a "bourgeois" musical background. When the few artists who were left returned to Phnom Penh, they found that all the centuries-old written records of Hindu epics had been destroyed.

Older Cambodians regard the classical and folk traditions as the "soul of Cambodia" and a dedicated band of teachers have devoted themselves to reviving them. It takes great dedication, discipline and up to ten years' training to master the classical and folk arts. Interestingly, the Cambodians combine teaching both the classical and folk traditions under the same roof, whereas in Thailand, classical dance is separated from folk styles, being seen as "high art".

Cambodian classical music has greatly influenced the similar traditions found in Thailand and Laos, and to a lesser extent Burma (Myanmar). The Cambodian, Thai and Laotian classical musical scales are almost identical, for instance. When Thais from Ayuthaya sacked Angkor in 1400, apasara dancers and musicians were taken to the Thai court, and when the Burmese sacked Ayuthaya in turn in 1767, they took Thai musicians and dancers with them, with the result that Burmese classical music was indirectly influenced by what were originally

Cambodian styles. All of these traditions can be traced back to the "heavenly dancing" at Angkor hundreds of years earlier.

In addition to apsara and tontay, Cambodia has ancient traditions of **mask dancing** (*lakon khol*) and **shadow plays** (*nang sbek*), both of which can be seen throughout the country. Performances of classical ballet and other styles can be seen at major hotels and at the Chatomuk Theatre near the Royal Palace in Phnom Penh.

Apart from the Khmer majority, Cambodia has minority ethnic groups such as Chinese, Cham and Vietnamese, as well as numerous hill-tribe groups (*Khmer Loeu* or "highland Khmer"). Each hill-tribe group has its own musical traditions, based around propitiating spirits, courtship and important social ceremonies; many groups use gongs and home-made instruments, from bamboo reed-pipes and zithers to the unique *k'longput*, a rack of bamboo pipes which are played by a musician clapping his hands to force air into the tubes. The best place to hear this music is in the villages during New Year festivities, although the National Theatre Company of Cambodia in Phnom Penh maintains a wide range of ethnic-minority dances in its repertoire.

Popular Traditions

Given Cambodia's recent history, it is amazing that any traditional music exists at all, but **folk songs** (*ayai*) and **wedding songs** (*phleng kar*) are still commonly played. Drums and the ubiquitous two-stringed fiddle are the chief instruments, and are often home-made. Despite the difficult circumstances – poverty, a shattered economy, the legacy of civil war – and a younger generation increasingly seduced by pop music, some ancient tunes and melodies are being passed on. With the assistance of UNESCO, the Cambodian government is currently trying to gather and collect material from old Cambodian folk singers.

Lakon Bassak, the popular theatre of Cambodia, was created by Cambodians living near the Bassak River in Vietnam at the beginning of the twentieth century. It sounds at times like the Vietnamese popular operetta *cai luong*, with its strange mix of pinpeat and Vietnamese music. Dances are often popularized versions of classical styles and the plays feature *jataka* stories based on the life of the Buddha. Lakon bassak can be found in Phnom Penh and major cities, particularly at festival times. You might also see *lakon tammada* or *yeekay*, a bawdy folk-drama, similar to Thailand's *likay*.

Cambodia Rocks: the Rise of Popular Music

As with many Asian countries, Western music entered Cambodia in the middle of the nineteenth century. Filipino musicians were among the first to bring Western instruments into Cambodia to play military marches, anthems and fanfares; locally, this was known as "Manila music". By World War I, the Frenchman François Perruchot had been hired to teach Western music at the Palace, which led to written forms of Khmer music and the setting of Khmer tunes to Western orchestration. In the 1920s and 30s, Western music also entered the country through travelling theatre troupes; by the 1930s and 40s, many kinds of music were being played at entertainment venues and distinctive modern Khmer songs (*jamrieng samai*) were developed by composers like Mer Bun, Peo Sipho and Puong Bopha.

Independence from France in 1953 gave the entertainment industry a shot in the arm, and the period between 1955 and 1970, known as *Sangkum Reastr Niyum* (Popular Socialist Community), was a golden era for songwriters and singers like **Sinn Sisamouth**, the legendary "King of Khmer Music". Sisamouth was both prolific and versatile, able to write folk songs, mambo, rock'n'roll or movie soundtracks (such as the epic *Au Euil Srey An* or "Khmer after Angkor"), and using both classical poetry and popular idioms in his lyrics. He was most popular for his duets with leading female singers like **Ros Sereysothea** and **Pan Ron**. None of these artists survived the murderous Khmer Rouge, but their influence lives on, and Sisamouth remains an important figure for Cambodians, comparable to Malaysia's superstar of the same era, P.J. Ramlee.

The "King of Khmer Music" Sinn Sisamouth

Cambodian Festivals

Cambodia shares many Buddhist festivals with its neighbours Thailand and Laos. Festivals like mid-April New Year (*Bonn Chaul Chhnam*) and the November Water festival (*Bonn Om Tuk*) are good times to catch live performances of popular and traditional music. A Ramayana festival is also held every two years in the month of December at Angkor Wat, but this was replaced in 2007 with a light and sound spectacular.

Locally brewed modern styles like **ramvong** and **ramkbach** also use electrified Western and sometimes traditional instruments. Ramvong songs are slow dance numbers for the circle dance described earlier (the modern form originated in Thailand), while ramkbach is similar to *luk thung* or Thai country music, with its slow, moody rhythms and bittersweet vocals. The musical backing is full of sweet melodies, while the wavering top notes of the singer hold the attention. The top performer in this Cambodian country style is **Song Senghorn**, ably supported by newcomers like **Noy Vanneth**, **Touch Sreynich** and **Oeun Sreymom**.

In the 1960s, local pop and rock music took off. Garage rock, surf rock, the Cambodian take on calypso and ska, and fuzzy organ sounds were cranked out by stars and no-name bands alike. In the mid-1990s, some enlightened Western backpackers brought back fading cassettes of 1960s Cambodian psychedelic pop/rock, and the compilation *Cambodian Rocks* was released on Parallel World, quickly becoming a cult classic. It also inspired a US-Cambodian band, **Dengue Fever**, to play covers of Cambodian pop (see below).

After the Khmer Rouge were deposed by the invading Vietnamese, a new generation of singers led by **Preab Sovath**, **Ieng Sithol** and **Keo Pich Chanda** emerged, joined more recently by **Him Sivorn**, **Preab Sovath** and **Meng Pichinda**.

One exciting new development outside the capital comes from the province of Siam Reap. This is the emergence of a Cambodian version of the funky Thai-Cambodian roots music **kantrum** (see Thailand p.760), sometimes called *Khmer Ler* or *Khmer Surin*. Siam Reap is close to the border with Thailand, where Thai-Cambodians mix with their Cambodian counterparts, sharing a common language and culture. Look out for cheap local compilations of Khmer Surin music and "non-stop" dance compilations which feature the style.

Perhaps the most intriguing development in Khmer popular music, however, is the growth of "transnational music" from the Cambodian diaspora (more than 200,000 Cambodians left the country in the 1970s and 80s to settle in the US, Canada, France and Australia). Cambodian heartthrobs like **Heng Bunleap** tour the US and Europe, but it is the younger generation from the diaspora who are influencing Khmer musicians in Cambodia. **Prach Ly** (stage name: **praCH**) set about dealing with the tragic recent past of Cambodia from his parents' garage in the US, concocting a heady brew of Khmer classical, Western rock, rap, Khmer-language speeches and found sounds. His 2000 debut album, *Dalama: The End'n Is Just the Beginnin'*, which was bootlegged and renamed *Khmer Rough Rap* in Phnom Penh, catapulted him to instant nationwide fame.

By contrast, US-Cambodian rockers **Dengue Fever** took on covers of 1960s Khmer pop and have developed their own unique sound from this root, adding the wonderful vocals of Chhom Nimol, Middle-Eastern jazz and even spaghetti Western guitars. They seem to be developing a cult following in the US and Europe. As with Laos, the transnational scene seems likely to produce the most interesting Khmer music over the next few years.

DISCOGRAPHY Cambodia

⊙ **Cambodge: Musique classique khmère, théâtre d'ombres et chants de mariage**
Inédit, France
Pinpeat music for classical dance and shadow theatre and a smaller ensemble of oboe, lutes, spike fiddle and percussion accompanying wedding songs.

⊙ **Cambodian Cassette Archives: Khmer Folk & Pop Music Vol. 1**
Sublime Frequencies, US
An eclectic selection of Khmer pop and rock classics, featuring scratchy guitars, fuzzy organ sounds, garage rock and upside-down ska. Glorious and totally essential, but worth

buying just for Sinn Sisamouth's "A Diamond Ring" or Pan Ron's "Hippie Men".

⊙ City of Ghosts OST
Lakeshore, US
Matt Dillon's 2003 directorial debut was surprisingly good, as was the excellent soundtrack, which features Dengue Fever's Khmer-language version of Joni Mitchell's "Both Sides Now", *chanson* and Ros Serey Sothea's sublime "I'm Sixteen". Deleted, but available for download.

⊙ Ethnic Minority Music of Northeast Cambodia
Sublime Frequencies, US
Animist rituals and ceremonies, gong ensembles, home-made bamboo instruments and haunting singing from the hills of Cambodia's northeastern region.

⊙ Music of Cambodia Vols 1–3
Celestial Harmonies, US
Volume 1, *9 Gong Gamelan* features a rural pinpeat orchestra and other sounds of Siam Reap, beautifully recorded in Angkor Wat itself. Volume 2 presents the courtly version of pinpeat, a *mahori* folk orchestra (fiddles, flutes, xylophone and percussion) and tribal music. The third volume features solo instrumental music. Essential.

Dengue Fever

A six-piece band formed by two Californian brothers, Ethan and Zac Holtzman, who became fascinated by Cambodian pop from the 1960s and early 70s. Looking for a Cambodian lead singer, they chanced upon Chhom Nimol, who had performed for King Sihanouk before settling in the US. In 2006 they went on a highly successful tour of Cambodia, and in 2008 released the eclectic *Venus on Earth*, which was picked up by Real World.

★ Escape from Dragon House
M80 Records, US
The band's second album, released in 2005, included self-composed new material alongside covers of Cambodian 1960s pop hits like Sinn Sisamouth's "Sweet Sixteen". Chhom Nimol's vocal style is perfect.

Musicians of the National Dance Company of Cambodia

A group of master musicians, dancers and singers sponsored by the Arts Department of the Cambodian Ministry of Culture. The company has made many overseas tours, including one in the UK in 1990, the first for thirty years, from which this recording came. They feature a stripped-down pinpeat orchestra.

⊙ Homrong
RealWorld, UK
A fabulous collection representing many styles of Cambodian classical and traditional music, from pinpeat to wedding songs to folk songs (mahori ensembles). While the classical music transports the listener back a thousand years to Angkor and the "sound of clouds", the folk and wedding tunes are down to earth, with catchy rhythms and plaintive singing. Highly recommended.

Kong Nay

Born in 1946, Nay went blind aged four due to smallpox. One of the few chapay (lute) playing troubadours to survive the Khmer Rouge. The chapay is a fantastic-looking lute made out of jackfruit wood with a long teak neck and two or three strings. Nay has devoted himself to passing on his skills to a new generation of players, although he admits his kids are more interested in karaoke and Cambodian pop. The closest thing to the Delta blues in Southeast Asia. He toured the UK in 2007.

⊙ Kong Nay: A Cambodian Bard
Inédit, France
Eight intimate tracks recorded in 1997 with Nay on chapay and vocals. There are useful English and French translations of the lyrics, but the music may be an acquired taste.

PLAYLIST
Cambodia

1 HOMRONG Musicians of the National Dance Company of Cambodia from *Homrong*
An act of worship played before weddings and parties, featuring haunting vocals and a wailing fiddle.

2 SOMPOUGN KLAY Taam Ming from *The Music of Cambodia Vol. 1*
Sparse and ritualistic-sounding small ensemble with nine-gong instrument, recorded in the Angkor complex.

3 ROAP SOMPHIREAK (INVENTORY OF EVERYDAY THINGS) Kong Nay from *Kong Nay: A Cambodian Bard*
Nay gets down with a list of all the things his extended family needs for a decent life.

4 SWEET SIXTEEN Dengue Fever from *Escape from Dragon House*
The sultry vocals of Chhom Nimol on Sinn Sisamouth's catchy 1960s number.

5 QUANDO, MY LOVE Sinn Sisamouth from *Cambodian Rocks Vol. 1*
Latin-tinged 1960s love song featuring Sisamouth's smooth voice and twangy guitars.

Central Asian Republics

sounds of the stans

Kyrgyz ensemble Tengir Too
Via Kaboul

Since becoming independent amidst the collapse of the Soviet Union in 1991, the Central Asian Republics of Kazakhstan, Kyrgyzstan, Tajikistan, Turkmenistan and Uzbekistan have been forging their own autonomous identities. Although the region has mainly attracted attention in the West because of its valuable natural resources and some megalomaniacal leaders, **Razia Sultanova** and **Simon Broughton** suggest that its rich musical heritage is well worth exploring.

n his novel *The Day Lasts Longer than a Hundred Years*, written during the time of perestroika, the Kyrgyz writer Chingiz Aitmatov refers to a legend about a tribe who left their prisoners lying in the sun with raw camel hide stretched over their heads. As it dried, the camel hide would compress the prisoners' skulls and so destroy their memory and mind. The prisoners were then known as *mankurts*. In Aitmatov's words: "A mankurt did not know where he was from. He did not know his name, did not remember his childhood, his father and his mother – to put it more simply, a mankurt did not realize that he was a human being." For centuries, "mankurt" has been a frightening concept of misfortune for Central Asian people. And after years of cultures and ethnicities mixing, after the heavy hand of the Soviet Union and now rampant capitalism, it's easy to forget who you are.

The **Central Asian Republics** share a common historical and cultural background in the Islamic faith and – except for Tajikistan which is **Persian** – their **Turkic** roots. In the fourteenth century all these states were part of the powerful empire of **Timur** (Tamberlaine the Great), who built his capital in Samarkand. The capital moved to Bukhara in the sixteenth century, but the Golden Age was disrupted by regional conflicts, which continued until Russian domination began in the nineteenth century. The Soviets created rather artificial states out of the various ethnicities in the region – and there are strong links with the Turkic-speaking **Uyghurs** in Chinese Turkestan (see p.509). Broadly speaking, the Uzbeks and Tajiks were settled, urban people, while the Turkmen, Kazakhs and

Central Asian Instruments

The instruments found in Central Asia are common throughout the Turkic countries and the Middle East. The most popular are the long-necked **lute** – called the **saz** by the Turks, the **dutar** by the Uzbeks and **dombra** by the Kazakhs – and the **rubab**, which in Central Asia, Iran, Afghanistan and Pakistan is a plucked lute (not a bowed fiddle, as in many other parts of the Arabic and Asian world). Variants – and other significant instruments across the region – include:

Dombra A much shorter Kazakh version of the dutar without frets, typical of nomadic culture.

Doira Circular frame-drum held in the hand and played with the fingers.

Dutar Long-necked plucked lute with two strings and frets (*dotar* is Persian for "two strings"), found in the area extending from Kurdistan to Xinjiang. The most widespread instrument in Central Asia for both professional musicians and amateurs, it is used for classical maqam, ghazals and both popular and mystical melodies, and is played in a wide variety of styles with great sophistication and virtuosity.

Gidjak Spike-fiddle with a round, parchment-covered body and cylindrical neck. It usually has four strings and is identical to the Persian and Azeri *kamancheh*.

Karnay A ceremonial brass trumpet two metres long, frequently used for weddings, parties and important events in Uzbekistan.

Kobyz Two-stringed Kazakh fiddle, also known as kyl-kobyz. Known as *kiyak* in Kyrgyzstan.

Komuz Kyrgyz long-necked fretless lute, with a pear-shaped sound box carved from apricot wood.

Rubab Long-necked five-string lute with a skin-covered sound box. The Central Asian instrument probably came from the Uyghurs and is often called the Kashgar rubab to distinguish it from other forms like the Pamir and Afghan rubab.

Sato Bowed version of the tanbur, played upright on the lap.

Setar A long-necked Tajik tanbur carved from mulberry wood. It originally had three strings (setar means "three strings" in Persian), but now usually has four. It has moveable frets (like the Indian sitar), made from gut or nylon knotted onto the neck.

Surnay Conical oboe (*zurna*) generally used for outdoor festivities.

Tanbur Long-necked three-stringed lute found all across Central Asia. The melody is plucked on the upper string with a plectrum worn on the tip of the index finger, while the other strings act as drones.

Târ Fretted lute with a figure-of-eight shaped body of mulberry wood and three double strings. Common in Azeri and Persian music.

Kyrgyz were traditionally nomadic, although in the contemporary context these distinctions are breaking down.

Today, traditionally settled Uzbeks are migrating to Russia and to Kazakhstan to earn a living for themselves and their families. As a result, new songs of a humiliated diaspora have arisen. A pop group with the paradoxical name **Obmorok I Mama** (Faint and Mother) sings:

I cannot remember when I moved to this land / I might have been drunk / When a cop stops me / "You don't have a work permit!" / I answer him / "Hang on! My address today is...".

This mocks the pan-Soviet hit "Moy Adres Sovetskiy Soyuz" (My Address is the Soviet Union), a rock anthem symbolizing the Soviet people's friendship. As Obmorok I Mama's hits have become the face of immigrant Uzbek music in Russia, paradoxically it's the once nomadic Kazakhs, with their booming oil revenues, who are happier to stay at home. The same is true in gas-rich Turkmenistan, where there have been signs of liberalization since the death of the megalomaniacal President Niyazov (known as Turkmenbashi) in 2006. In Uzbekistan, as international human rights organizations have reported, the regime of Islam Karimov has cracked down on both secular and religious dissenters. Although Tajikistan and Kyrgyzstan are poorer than their neighbours, they are freer. The new ethno-pop music, which is evolving throughout Central Asia, has acquired its richest forms in these two small but proud nations.

One Soviet legacy in all these states is that of **conservatoire training**, which ironed out many of the distinctive tunings of regional music, introduced a Western "tempered" scale and a formal concert style of performance. In many of the Central Asian ensembles the legacy of folklore troupes lives on, and although their governments never miss an opportunity to celebrate state holidays with music, there is less state support for musical culture and education. Significantly in Central Asia, the Music Initiative of the **Aga Khan Trust for Culture** has helped found schools, institutions and make recordings.

Uzbekistan

Uzbekistan is home to the three most spectacular historic cities of the Silk Road: Samarkand, Bukhara and Khiva. In the late sixteenth century, **Bukhara** became the Emirate capital, and a cultured, cosmopolitan city with flourishing trade routes fuelling its bazaars. From this court came **shashmaqam**, the most elevated musical form

of Uzbek and Tajik culture, of whom many celebrated performers were Bukharan Jews. It began as a royal music of princesses and pavilions, with musicians, sitting on the floors, playing on lutes (like the tanbur, gidjak and dutar) and doira (see instrument box).

Shashmaqam literally means "six maqams" referring, as with the related Uyghur *muqams*, to suites of pieces in different musical modes. The six maqams are called "Buzruk", "Rast", "Nava", "Dugah", "Segah" and "Iraq" and take their names from classical Persian modes. The maqam begins with an instrumental prelude (*mushklilot*) followed by vocal settings of classical Sufi poems (*nasr*) sung by a soloist or small group of singers. The texts express a rich variety of emotions – love and despair, sadness and regret, passion and hope. The singer generally begins in a low register, passes through a middle range and then ascends through increasingly higher sections to the musical culmination known as the *awdj*, after which the music relaxes and descends to the low register where it began. This rising towards a spiritual and musical climax comes directly from the Sufi nature of the music.

A Shashmaqam ensemble of the classical period might contain two tanburs, a dutar, a gidjak and doira plus two or three singers. Although the Soviets promoted large ensembles and choruses, today's groups have largely returned to this intimate chamber style. The pre-eminent Uzbek performer of Shashmaqam and Uzbek classical traditions is **Munadjat Yulchieva**. Her name translates as "ascent to God" – the true meaning of Sufism. One of the important Sufi beliefs is in the continuity of a spiritual chain (*silsila*) and Yulchieva has inherited her musical knowledge from generations of spiritual and musical *mur-*

Munadjat Yulchieva

shid or masters. Despite Soviet influences on the poetical texts, the music preserved its traditional form and, now that the classical texts can be used once again, Yulchieva widely performs Sufi ghazals of classical Uzbek poets, with her teacher Shavkat Mirzaev as accompanist.

Yulchieva's voice has a wide range and is beautifully understated, although you can still sense a conviction beneath the measured delivery. She started singing in early childhood and was once advised to give up Uzbek music and become an "opera star". But Yulchieva refused: "I am a singer of my culture", she said, "and I do my songs for my people."

Turgun Alimatov (d. 2008) had a long career as a performer of **instrumental maqam** music – he was a master-performer on the dutar, tanbur and **sato** (bowed tanbur lute), an instrument he himself revived. His playing was refined and skilful, eschewing virtuosity, but redolent of his status as a philosopher of music with an ascetic way of life. He played with his son Alisher Alimatov and included maqam repertoire from different areas of Uzbekistan – Bukhara, Khorezm and Ferghana – as well as mystical and lyrical songs like the famous "Giria" (Weeping).

The main focus for Uzbek (and all Central Asian) music is the **toi** – a rite of passage celebration. Uzbeks have a **beshik-toi** (celebrated forty days after the birth of a baby), a **sunnat-toi** (for circumcision or initiation into Islam), a marriage toi and so on. All of these occasions reflect important elements in Central Asian life, such as deference to the older generation, respect for Muslim sensibilities and the gender divide (women don't sit next to men).

A **toi** is also an important musical academy where musicians gain their experience of practical music-making. In Central Asia, two thirds of the population is rural, so traditional toi and weddings are common. Every city has its celebrated **wedding musicians and singers** and people attend weddings to see their favourite performers. The singer and târ (Persian lute) player **Sherali Juraev** (see box) is a celebrity – one of the most popular singer and composers in Uzbekistan.

There's also an important Uzbek tradition of female wedding entertainers – singing and playing doira and giving protective blessings to the bride and groom. In the Bukhara-Samarkand region they are known as *sozanda*, in Khorezm *khalpa* and in Tashkent-Ferghana *otin-oy*.

After Sherali, one of the most famous wedding poets and singers is **Dadahon Hasanov** from the Ferghana Valley. Born in 1941, he showed song-writing skills from childhood and became famous for songs that commented on everyday events. Under the Soviets, Hasanov was regularly harassed by the authorities because his songs didn't conform to ideological requirements and in 1976 he was arrested for singing nationalistic Uzbek songs. His situation hasn't improved since independence: his licence has been suspended since 1992 and he is not supposed to perform in Uzbekistan. Hasanov became famous as the only songwriter to comment on the 2005 massacre in Andijan, when hundreds of protesters were killed by government forces. In 2006 he faced impris-

Sherali Juraev

Much to the annoyance of Uzbekistan's political leaders, Sherali Juraev – the nation's favourite wedding-singer – was also voted the country's hero in a popular poll. Juraev brings together the beauty of traditional narrative ballads and the infectious power of contemporary compositions, combining patriotic praise of the motherland (Uzbegim), with deeply sincere love songs (Caravan) and classical-style songs based on poems by Hafiz and Navoi. His performances at wedding celebrations (toi), where he plays the role of master of ceremonies, are astonishing: he opens a wedding, leads it, introduces the parents of the bride and groom to each other, blesses elderly relatives, instructs the newly-weds on how to behave in married life and seeks to protect them from future mistakes by using songs, proverbs and sayings, accompanied by his group members. Although Juraev performs widely in Uzbekistan and abroad, the state's attitude to him is inconsistent, ranging all the way from hostility to high appreciation. Officially, the singer is not allowed to perform in concert halls or participate in festivals. On the other hand, no foreign embassy private party in Uzbekistan today takes place without Juraev. Despite the obstacles, he has found a way of carrying on with his mission: recreating ancient court tradition, running old-style evenings to commemorate famous poets of Central Asia, when all the local stars of literature and the arts are brought together to commemorate the spirit of Rumi (Rumiyhonlik) or Hafiz (Hafizhonlik) in all-night performances. Video recordings of these events then pop up on YouTube.

onment, but due to his age (66 at the time), he was sentenced instead to three years of house arrest.

The most popular female singer is **Yulduz Usmanova**, who sings in Uzbek and many other languages. Her songs are catchy and contemporary, but often keep a traditional flavour or use traditional instruments in the arrangements alongside a strong influence from Turkish pop. The classically trained **Sevara Nazarkhan** is the new name on the block and came to prominence in 2003 with a recording for Real World which combined traditional influences and electronica. Her follow-up in 2007 was more poppy.

Sevara Nazarkhan

Uzbekistan has an international showcase for music in the form of **Sharq Taronalari** (Eastern Tunes), which has been held in Samarkand every two years since 1997. However, as Westerners who have attended have attested, it is heavily state controlled and is unlikely to gain much international credibility. More interesting is the regular folk festival **Boysun Bakhori** (Boysun's Spring), held in the mountainous Boysun district in Surkhandarya province. It demonstrates an archaic style of music and life that survives in this area. There are ritual songs and dances, performances by *akyn* (bards) along with the heroic epic *Alpamysh*. In 2001, the Boysun district and its music were included in the UNESCO List of Masterpieces of the Oral and Intangible Heritage of Humanity.

Tajikistan

Although the **Tajiks** are of Persian rather than Turkic stock, the musical links with neighbouring Uzbekistan are strong. Tajiks and Uzbeks used to share the same classical shashmaqam repertoire, although with the creation of separate republics, the Soviets began a separation, with Uzbek material and Tajikistan concentrating on Uzbek material and Tajikistan taking on the Tajik, Persian-derived texts.

In Tajikistan today, the leading musical scholar is sato player **Abduvali Abdurashidov**, who leads the **Academy of Maqam** in the capital Dushanbe, despite the fact that there was no historical tradition in this new city. Established with support from the Aga Khan Music Initiative in Central Asia, the Academy provides an intensive four-year course of study in shashmaqam. Like much art and courtly music, it's not easy listening for those unfamiliar with its sound world. "A fundamental aspect of the Academy's curriculum is the study of maqam as a musical cycle or suite", Abdurashidov explains. "I learned from my own experience that performing and listening to the maqam as an integral cycle can lead to an entirely different understanding and experience of the music – to a kind of self-purification. You cannot get that simply by listening to individual pieces extracted from the cycle, which is how maqam is mostly performed these days."

While the rural music of the plains and river valleys is closely related to that of the Uzbeks, in the mountainous south of Tajikistan there's another, more popular style known as **falak** (literally "celestial dome") performed at weddings, circumcisions and the *nowruz* spring festival. A falak is a suite made up of a collection of sung poems and instrumental pieces played on the lute or spike-fiddle – a sort of popular maqam. The leading performer is conservatoire-trained **Davlatmand Kholov**. He's a fine singer and a particularly good instrumentalist on the gidjak, dutar and setar (three-string lute).

In the Pamir mountain region of **Badakhshan** bordering Afghanistan, there's also a rich variety of music, including folk poetry and Persian influenced ghazals and praise songs.

There's also a very active popular music scene, with groups and singers like **Nobovar and Shams group, Farzin, Nigora Holova, Shabnami**

The Aga Khan Music Initiative in Central Asia

Supported by the Aga Khan Trust for Culture, the Aga Khan Music Initiative in Central Asia (AKMICA) was formally inaugurated in 2003. One of its aims is to overcome the heavy-handed legacy of the Soviet Union and to encourage a more sustainable musical culture in the region. It aims to bring outstanding musicians from Central Asia to the attention of audiences round the world, and – through the release of high-quality recordings – to help bring prestige for these musicians at home. There are also local schools, education centres and more ambitious institutions like the Academy of Maqam in Dushanbe.

Tanbur player Kamaliddin Hamdamov of the Academy of Shashmaqam at an Aga Khan Trust for Culture performance at the English National Opera

Philip Ryalls

Surayyo and others, who draw on local traditions as well as Russian-style *estrada* (folk-pop).

Kazakhstan, Kyrgyzstan and Turkmenistan

Although the Kazakhs, Kyrgyz and Turkmen are traditionally nomadic, Kazakhstan – the ninth largest country in the world, with rich supplies of oil – has now become the dominant state in Central Asia. It attracts workers from across the region, as well as high-profile international architects to design buildings in Astana, the new capital created by **President Nursultan Nazarbayev** in 1997. Others might argue that it is Borat that really put the country on the map. The *Borat* movie used music from the Balkans, but there are some notable contemporary groups, including **Roksonaki** and **Ulytau**.

The rural and nomadic music of the Kazakhs, Kyrgyz and Turkmen, however, has a closer connection with pre-Islamic and **shamanic** culture. Related to this is the art of the bard or **bakshy** – a branch of the widespread Turkic *ashik* tradition. Often the bakshy is a shaman, acting as healer, magician and moralizer. All three countries have

traditions of **sung epics** performed by akyn (Kazakh), *manaschi* (Kyrgyz) or bakshy (Turkmen).

Of these, the Kyrgyz **Manas** epic is said to be the longest in the world – twenty times longer than the *Iliad* and *Odyssey* combined, and two and a half times the length of India's *Mahabharata*. The Manas epic is the pillar of Kyrgyz culture, telling of the warrior Manas and his descendants and battles with the Chinese. It's not easy to listen to if you don't understand the words: its monotonous repetitive phrases require some knowledge of the cultural background of Kyrgyzstan, of the land of endless steppes and high mountains, where people and animals are equal heroes of the same epics. Sayaqbay Karalaev (1887–1971), the most famous manaschi, was reputed to know all 500,000 stanzas, and most Kyrgyz can recite at least some of them. The Manas epic is traditionally recited rather than sung, but **Rysbek Jumabaev** performs graphic musical versions with the **Tengir-Too** ensemble.

Kazakh, Kyrgyz and Turkmen epics and songs are either sung solo or accompanied by dombra (Kazakhstan), komuz (Kyrgyzstan) or dutar (Turkmenistan), all two- or three-stringed lutes found throughout Central Asia. The dombra and komuz are strongly linked to nomadic culture and there are certain pieces (*kui*) which can represent an animal, a person, a state of mind, a landscape or even a journey. These are also played on the amazing **spike fiddles** like the Kazakh kobyz and Kyrgyz *kiak*, carved out of a single piece of wood and played on the lap. Because these are not popular folk instruments (like the dombra and komuz) and because of their shamanic association, they declined in Soviet times, but have returned in the post-Soviet period. Photographs of traditional players often show a mirror in the soundbox through which they were said to see into the spirit world. The kobyz is linked to the figure of Korkyt Ata, the ancestor of the bakshy shamans. His playing on the kobyz was said to be so powerful that even Death was entranced, and it was only when he stopped playing to have a drink that Death could take him into the spirit world. Per-

formed by top players like **Raushan Orazbaeva**, both composed and traditional kui, like "Akku" (White Swan), can have the power and intensity of Bach's cello suites.

The only widely known group from Turkmenistan outside the country is **Ashkabad** (named after the Turkmen capital), basically conservatoire-trained musicians who created an infectious wedding-band style with violin, clarinet, târ (Persian lute), accordion and frame-drum percussion. The group have recorded for Real World and appeared at WOMAD festivals.

Since the death in December 2006 of President Turkmenbashi, who promoted the most extreme of personality cults and even attempted to ban recorded music on radio, TV and at weddings, the environment for new musical developments seems to have become more favourable.

DISCOGRAPHY Central Asian Republics

⭐ **Bardic Divas: Women's Voices in Central Asia**
Smithsonian Folkways, US
The fourth in the Aga Khan's AKMICA series, featuring great female vocalists and instrumentalists from across the region. Beautifully produced, like all the discs in the series, with good photos and an accompanying DVD.

⊙ **Central Asia: Classical Traditions**
Ocora, France
A fine collection, bringing together classical pieces from Uzbekistan and Tajikistan played by performers such as Munadjat Yulchieva, Turgun Alimatov and Tajik singer Barno Itzhakova.

⊙ **Central Asia: The Masters of the Dutar**
VDE-Gallo/AIMP, Switzerland
A fascinating survey of different instruments and styles of dutar playing, with comprehensive notes. It includes Uzbek, Tajik (and Pamir), Persian Khorasan and Turkmen styles and is an inspiring document of the artistry of the players of this instrument, which is central to the tradition.

⊙ **Inner Asian Pop**
Colours, Italy
A collection of contemporary pop tracks from all five Central Asian states, produced by Benetton's *Colours* magazine.

⭐ **Rough Guide to the Music of Central Asia**
World Music Network, UK
The best introduction to the region's music, featuring popular, folk and classical performers. Includes Munadjat Yulchieva, Yulduz Usmanova, Sevara Nazarkhan and Sherali Juraev from Uzbekistan; Davlatmand, Farzin and Shams group from Tajikistan; Ulytau, Edil Husainov and Raushan Orazbaeva from Kazakhstan, and some great traditional performers.

⊙ **Saz**
Kalan, Turkey
An interesting compilation tracing the various types of saz or lute from Central Asia to Turkey and beyond – the Uzbek dutar, Tajik tambur, Kyrgyz komuz, Kazakh dombra, Iranian tanbur, Azeri saz and various Turkish varieties. A useful and listenable survey with photos and a few notes in English.

⊙ **The Silk Road: a Musical Caravan**
Smithsonian Folkways, US
A splendid double CD of folk and traditional performances from the whole region. Recommended.

Uzbekistan and Tajikistan

⊙ **Badakhshan: Mystical Poetry and Songs from the Ismailis of the Pamir Mountains**
Pan, Netherlands
A delightful collection of music from a small but fascinating area of Tajikistan. The Ismailis belong to the Shiite branch of Islam and this contains religious music, ghazals, folk songs and some great instrumental playing on rubab, tanbur and sitar. Extensive notes and photos.

⊙ **Bukhara: Musical Crossroads of Asia**
Smithsonian Folkways, US
Not easy listening this one, but a serious survey of musical life in this cosmopolitan city in 1990. It features the female sozanda musicians for a toi, classical music and Jewish and Muslim liturgical music.

⊙ **Falak: The Voice of Destiny**
Topic, UK
A good double-CD compilation of traditional music from Tajikistan, played by different musicians from various regions, plus contemporary groups and orchestral compositions.

⊙ From Samarkand to Bukhara
Long Distance, France

A good survey of musical styles recently recorded across the country, including dutar maestro Turgun Alimatov and gidjak player Ahmed Djan Dadaev in Tashkent, folk singer Mardan Moulanov in Samarkand, the Maqam Ensemble of Khorezm and the Women's Ensemble of Ferghana singing Sufi songs.

⊙ Tadjikistan: Songs of the Bards
VDE-Gallo/AIMP, Switzerland

A disc celebrating the art of the *hafiz*, the Tajik bards recorded in various towns and villages in the early 1990s. Falak, ghazals and other forms sung by male vocalists with accompaniment on dombra, dutar, setar, gidjak and so on. A specialized disc, but interesting.

⊙ Tadjikistan-Uzbekistan: Erudite Shashmaqam Tradition
Buda, France

Tajik performers Mastâne Ergasheva and Jurabeg Nabiev perform the classic shashmaqam repertoire, including the Persian Sufi poetry of Hafez and Bedil.

⊙ Uzbekistan: The Art of Dutar
Ocora, France

A near-definitive collection for dutar devotees, featuring three current star players: Abdorahim Hamidov, Soltan-Ali Khodaverdiev and Shohrat Razzaqov.

⊙ Uzbekistan: Les Grandes Voix du Passé, 1940–1965
Ocora, France

Archive recordings from Tashkent Radio focusing on the Ferghana region. Five male and two female singers perform, most memorably in the duets by brothers Akmal-Khan and Baba-Khan Subhanov, both devout Sufis, who perform in a wonderful devotional style, despite the Soviet persecution of the time. Obviously of specialist appeal, but a valuable collection and with excellent notes.

⊙ Uzbekistan: Instrumental Art Music
VDE-Gallo/AIMP, Switzerland

A thorough survey of classical Uzbek music, with the usual examples of wind ensembles as well as string playing on sato, tanbur, dutar and so on. The Shavkat Mirzaev Ensemble are the main performers, with several other groups and musicians.

★ Uzbekistan: Maqam Dugah
Inédit, France

One of the best recordings of shashmaqam, with the fine singers Nadira Pirmatova and Mariam Sattarova, Abdurahim Hamidov on dutar and a small ensemble.

⊙ Uzbekistan: Music of Horezm
Auvidis/Unesco, France

A fine collection of various genres – oral epics, women's music, religious songs, classical and popular music – from the Khorezem oasis in the heart of Central Asia.

The Academy of Maqam

Led by sato player Abduvali Abdurashidov, the Academy of Maqam in Dushanbe probably plays the most historically authentic style of shashmaqam.

⊙ Invisible Face of the Beloved
Smithsonian Folkways, US

With an intimate eight-piece group of vocalists and instrumentalists, this is the only recording of a complete shashmaqam suite in Rast. The poetry is mostly by Hafiz. A beautifully produced AKMICA disc with good pictures and accompanying DVD.

Turgun Alimatov

Alimatov (1921–2008) was a master performer on the dutar, tanbur and sato. He was instrumental in reviving the sato (bowed tanbur), worked for many years in the ensembles of Tashkent Radio, and was the leading player of his generation in the professional style.

⊙ Ouzbekistan: Turgun Alimatov
Ocora, France

Folk and classical music expertly played on the main string instruments of Uzbek music. Features several duets with his son Alisher on dutar.

Ari Babakhanov and Ensemble

Ari Babakhanov, born in 1934, comes from a dynasty of Jewish Bukharan musicians specializing in shashmaqam. He leads one of the most respected ensembles of singers and instrumentalists.

⊙ Shashmaqam: The Tradition of Bukhara
New Samarkand Records, Netherlands

A selection of vocal and instrumental pieces in Buzruk, Rast, Nava and Dugah maqams. The instrumental music is particularly beautiful. Good historical notes.

Badakhshan Ensemble

Founded by Soheba Davlatshoeva in the early 1990s, the ensemble has a slightly folkloric character, but performs both traditional acoustic and modern music of the Badakhshan region, centred on Khoroq. "We don't perform folklore at weddings", admits Soheba. "If we did no one would hire us. What people want to listen and dance to is pop music."

⊙ Song and Dance from the Pamir Mountains
Smithsonian Folkways, US

Volume five in AKMICA's series, a beautifully recorded set of traditional songs accompanied by gidjak fiddle, Badakhshani rubab (similar to the Afghan variety), Pamiri rubab, tanbur, setar and *daf*.

Davlatmand

Davlatmand Kholov was born in 1950. He studied classical music at the Dushanbe conservatoire, but was drawn back to the folk styles of southern Tajikistan and the Pamir mountains. He's now a well-known instrumentalist (gidjak, dutar and setar) and singer.

⊙ Davlatmand: Musiques Savantes et Populaires du Tadjikistan
Inédit, France

An appealing selection of little-known music from southern Tajikistan, including the falak repertoire and classical music.

Sevara Nazarkhan

Born in the Ferghana valley, but resident in Tashkent, Sevara Nazarkhan is a young dynamic singer (and dutar player) who started in Sideris, once described as the Uzbek Spice Girls, but soon went solo. She released her international debut *Yol Bolsin* on Real World and a follow-up *Sen* in 2007.

★ Yol Bolsin

Real World, UK

A stylish disc from 2003, mixing traditional and modern ingredients, although the production by Hector Zazou makes Nazarkhan sound much cooler than her lively stage shows.

Yulduz Usmanova

Born in 1963 in Margilan, Ferghana Valley, Usmanova studied music at the local pedagogical institute and later at the Uzbekistan State Conservatory. Winning first prize in the Voice of Asia competition in 1991, she is probably Uzbekistan's most popular female singer and has released a large number of recordings. She has also been a member of parliament.

⊙ The Selection Album
Blue Flame, Germany
An excellent greatest hits album from 1997, opening with the sultry "Schoch Va Gado" (The Rich and the Poor) with stylish tanbur and gidjak playing.

Munadjat Yulchieva

Munadjat Yulchieva was born in 1960 into a peasant family in the Ferghana Valley. The senior Uzbek musician Muhammadjan Mirzaev said: "Her voice is like a flying dove, turning over in the currents of warm spring air." Yulchieva is currently Uzbekistan's most respected vocal artist.

⊙ Munadjat Yulchieva and Ensemble Shavkat Mirzaev
Network, Germany
This collection is a great introduction to Uzbek classical music. It begins subdued and introverted, a melancholy melody turning in on itself sung by Yulchieva's dark alto voice and widens out into a passionate declaration of love. Great instrumental playing including Shavkat Mirzaev on the rubab and there are also instrumental tracks and some vernacular songs to lighten the tone.

Kazakhstan, Turkmenistan and Kyrgyzstan

⊙ Le Chant des Steppes
Éditions du Layeur, France
A handsome book and CD written (in French) by Xavier Hallez, with great archive pictures and an excellent accompanying CD, including Raushan Orazbaeva on kobyz and Hamid Raimbergenov on dombra.

⊙ Kazakhstan: Music from Almatï
VDE-Gallo/AIMP, Switzerland
Recordings made in 1994 of conservatoire-trained musicians, so this doesn't reflect the real folk style, but an interesting collection of Kazakh music nonetheless.

⊙ Music of Kyrgysztan
Buda, France
A rather specialized collection of the nomadic-style music played and sung by amateur musicians: extracts from the Manas epic, lyrical songs with komuz accompaniment, kiyak fiddles and lullabies. One highlight is a song about the inspiring power of the komuz in war, including a whistling shell striking the sound-box of the instrument!

⊙ Music of Kyrgyzstan
Inédit, France
A rather serious, but representative selection of Kyrgyz folk performers and instruments.

Yulduz Usmanova

⊙ Songs from Steppes: Kazakh Music Today
Topic, UK
A good collection of traditional-style pieces, including the extraordinary Folk Ensemble of the Presidential Orchestra.

⊙ Turkestan: Kyrgyz Komuz and Kazakh Dombra
Ocora, France
Another reflection of the nomadic character of Kyrgyz and Kazakh music featuring kui (instrumental pieces said to narrate a musical journey). Performed by Abdurahman Nurak (komuz) and Hamid Raimbergenov (dombra).

⊙ Turkmenistan: The Music of the Bakshy
VDE-Gallo/AIMP, Switzerland
A scholarly survey of Turkmen bard music for singer and accompanying dutar, gidjak and *tuiduk* flute. The recordings (made in 1988–90) are not as good as they might be, but the music is genuine and intimate. Includes excellent notes and photos.

Ashkabad

Five-piece supergroup made for export from the city of Ashgabat, Turkmenistan.

★ City of Roses
RealWorld, UK
A great debut release from 1993, with audience-friendly tunes in stylish arrangements that remain true to the character of the music. Excellent târ, violin, accordion and percussion, showing how Central Asian music can swing.

Raushan Orazbaeva

Born in 1973, Orazbaeva is the leading kobyz player in Kazakhstan, classically trained in Almaty but originating from a family with a shamanic tradition. Kobyz isn't a common instrument for a woman.

⊙ Akku
Felmay, Italy
Not an easy disc to listen to, but the intense performances on the bowed instrument with its shamanic associations are incredible. "Akku" and "Kaskyr" are vivid depictions of a swan and a wolf respectively, while "Aral Muny" laments the ecological destruction of Lake Aral. Extraordinary.

Roksonaki

Formed in the early 1990s, this trio is one of the best groups combining traditional and contemporary music in Kazakhstan.

⊙ Evolution
Mosaiqa, US
A good "best-of" album including dombra and kobyz with contemporary influences and sensibility.

Tengir-Too

Named after the Kyrgyz word for the Tien Shan mountains, Tengir-Too is led by Nurlanbek Nyshanov, a graduate from the Kyrgyz National Conservatoire in Bishkek. One of the best traditional ensembles.

⊙ Mountain Music of Kyrgyzstan
Smithsonian Folkways, US
The first of the AKMICA discs, with some great vocal and instrumental performances on komuz, kiyak and a fragment of the Manas epic from Rysbek Jumbaev.

PLAYLIST
Central Asian Republics

1 TARONA 1 Academy of Maqam from *Invisible Face of the Beloved*
A *tarona* is a short folk-like song which links the longer shashmaqam compositions.

2 EI NOZANIN Sevara Nazarkhan from *Yol Bolsin*
A nice mixture of ancient and modern in this beautiful love song.

3 LALY YAMAN Munadjat Yulchieva from *A Haunting Voice*
A song about separation from the Uzbek singer's Sufi repertoire.

4 KARIYA Roksonaki from *Inner Asian Pop*
Lots of reverb, growly throat singing and rock drums from leading Kazakh group.

5 AQQU Hamid Raimbergenov from *Kyrgyz Komuz and Kazakh Dombra*
A famous kui about a swan performed on Kazakh dombra.

6 AKKU Raushan Orazvaeva from *Akku*
The same swan kui in a hair-raising bird-like performance on Kazakh kobyz.

7 BAYATY Ashkabad from *City of Love*
Luscious, lyrical music from Turkmenistan's supergroup.

8 KÖKÖTÖIDÜN ASHY Rysbek Jumabaev from *Mountain Music of Kyrgyzstan*
A fragment of the Manas epic with music from Tengir-Too.

9 OZ'BEGIM Sherali Juraev from *Rough Guide to the Music of Central Asia*
A sing-along patriotic song from this Uzbek star.

10 FALAK Badakhshan Ensemble from *Song and Dance from the Pamir Mountains*
A lament-like song with words by Hafiz and Rumi: "Ignite the fire of love and burn all wisdom."

China | Han Traditional

a well-kept secret

Ritual musicians perform before god
paintings, Gaoluo village near Beijing
Stephen Jones

Despite massive urban migration since the 1980s, the rural population of China still
outnumbers city dwellers by two to one. Chinese pop may dominate urban areas,
but the countryside still echoes with the sound of traditional music accompanying
ceremonial rituals – a legacy from imperial times that has largely been ignored by
record companies. **Stephen Jones** examines the continuing energy of Han Chinese
traditional music.

The scene is a scorching summer's day in a poor and dusty village in northwest China, where the local temple is holding its annual fair. Outside the gate, strung with pennants, a shawm band plays raucous versions of local opera. Peasants are kowtowing with incense before the main altar and having their fortunes told with divining sticks, while a Buddhist sect intones ancient liturgy with percussion accompaniment. Joking and smoking, teenagers eye each other up; firecrackers are let off, soup kitchens feed the pilgrims, people cluster round stalls selling local goods. Beggars and bards entertain the crowds with songs. On a stage opposite the temple, an opera troupe performs for the gods, while in the courtyard, a group of lay Daoist priests act out a cosmic drama, alternately solemn and bawdy. Later, the shawm band, augmented by a female singer, plays cheesy pop music, including revolutionary songs from Maoist times, adding trumpet and sax. Then, with the Daoists, they process to a nearby well in a symbolic water-fetching ritual that brings blessing to the community.

Such is the common experience of live music for the country-dwellers who still make up two thirds of China's population. Whether it's temple fairs, funerals, New Year celebrations or house-building, music-making is linked to local ceremonies. It's here that you find the full range and depth of China's musical heritage, and it's a world away from the well-mannered concerts of folk arrangements given by urban professionals in hotels, concert halls and conservatoires.

A stereotypical Western image of China might incorporate vague elements of Confucianism and Daoism, the enforced conformity of the Cultural Revolution and the current surge of economic development. But traditional music-making (at least in rural China) survived the ideological pressures of Maoism and is now facing an uncertain future under market liberalization, with new competition from pop music.

Far from the standardization of the urban professional troupes, rural China offers as much variety of regional styles as Africa or Europe, as you'd expect from an area containing almost a quarter of the world's population, extending from the steppes of Inner Mongolia south to the borders of Myanmar and Vietnam, and from the border with Siberia to the Himalayas and the deserts of Central Asia. Here we survey some of the traditions of the Han Chinese, who comprise about 92 percent of the population within the borders of the People's Republic of China. (For the ethnic minorities, see the following article and that on Tibetan music; see also the article

on Taiwan, the island off the southeast coast where a separate regime has ruled since 1949.)

For the Chinese, vocal music takes pride of place, with – in increasing order of stylistic complexity – **folk song**, **narrative-singing** and **opera** being the major forms. Instrumental music generally accompanies ceremonies and vocal performances. Chinese melodies are basically pentatonic, but this doesn't convey the rhythmic subtlety or the tone of voices and instruments – and you might find more than one pentatonic scale in a single melody. Ensemble music is mostly heterophonic, with the musicians playing different versions of the same melodic line. **Percussion** (notably drums, gongs, and cymbals) plays a major role, both in independent ensembles and as an accompaniment to opera, narrative-singing, ritual music, dance and political campaigns.

The recent monumental collection of local traditions *Zhongguo Minzu Minjian Yinyue Jicheng* (Anthology of Chinese Folk Music) consists of around 300,000 pages, mainly of transcriptions – alas, the recordings on which it is based are still unpublished – which is less than a tenth of the material collected, which in turn is only a tiny fraction of the music out there. With so much Chinese music still undocumented, this can only be a frantic dash around some of the better-known styles.

History and Living Styles

Chinese music dates back millennia – among extraordinary archeological finds are a magnificent fifth-century BC set of 64 bronze bells from a princely tomb in Hubei province – replicas of which have been used for recent concert renditions of pieces from later epochs, as well as by avant-garde composer Tan Dun. The **Tang dynasty** (AD 618–907) was a frequently cited golden age, indeed hosting the first world music boom, with several ensembles from the Central Asian kingdoms all the rage at court. The great Tang poets such as Li Bai and Bai Juyi were also avid musicians and several *qin* zithers from this period are still played today. Living genres are often claimed to have links with the Tang, and the industry in fake antiques extends also to music, where tourists may be regaled with glossy routines marketed as the music and dance of the Tang court. In recent years, the rather soulless Confucian rituals of the bygone imperial courts have been revived in Qufu and some other towns like Nanjing, again largely for tourists.

The reality, of course, is that there are no "living fossils", and most traditional forms in the countryside are the product of gradual accretion over the centuries. After the Opium Wars of the mid-nineteenth century, China was continually humiliated at the hands of foreign imperial powers, and in the turbulent years after 1911, when the last dynasty, the Qing, was overthrown, Western ideas became prestigious, at least in the cities.

Musically, some intriguing urban forms sprang up, such as the wonderfully sleazy **Cantonese music of the 1920s and 30s.** As the movie industry developed, people in Shanghai, colonial Canton (Guangzhou) and nearby Hong Kong threw themselves into the craze for dance halls, fusing the local traditional music with Western elements, notably jazz, adding saxophone, violin and xylophone to Chinese instruments such as the high-pitched *gaohu* fiddle and the *yangqin* dulcimer. Composers **Lü Wencheng** and **Qiu Hechou (Yau Hokchau)**, the violinist **Yin Zizhong (Yi Tzuchung)** – who played in London in 1924 – and **He Dasha** (Thicko He), guitarist and singer of clown roles in Cantonese opera, made many wonderful commercial 78s during this period. The official Maoist line castigated the music of composers like **Li Jinhui** and his star singer **Zhou Xuan** as decadent, unhealthy and pornographic – making it rather fashionable in China now. More often heard nowadays in modern arrangements, some of the 1930s classics are still great, but around heavily industrialized Guangzhou, if you can find anything older than Cantopop at all, it's more likely

Zhou Xuan film poster

to be a slick institutionalized troupe than an amateur band.

After the Communist victory of 1949, the whole ethos of traditional musical performance was challenged. Anything "feudal" – including a lot of traditional folk customs and music – or "superstitious" was severely restricted, while Chinese melodies were "cleaned up" with the addition of rudimentary harmonies and bass lines. New **"revolutionary" music**, composed from the 1930s on, was generally march-like and optimistic. The anthem "The East is Red" is a typical example: having begun life as a folksong from north Shaanxi province, birthplace of Mao's revolution, its local colour was ironed out as it was regimented into a march-like communist hymn.

The "conservatoire style" of **"national music"**, which for many urban listeners still represents Chinese music, is a modern pan-Chinese fabrication designed for the concert hall. It derives from the official ethos of twentieth-century urban reformers, with composed arrangements in a style akin to light music, often showcases for soloist and orchestra. The plaintive pieces for solo *erhu* fiddle by musicians from before the Communist era such as **Liu Tianhua** and the blind beggar **Abing** (also a Daoist priest) have been much recorded by (female) virtuosos like **Min Huifen** and younger players like **Ma Xiaohui** and **Song Fei**. For atmospheric meanderings on the *dizi* flute, older-generation (male) players like **Lu Chunling** or **Zhao Songting** are giving way to younger ones like **Zhang Weiliang** and **Zhan Yongming**.

Although conservatoire musicians have a lot of young pupils, performances of traditional music can hardly be said to be popular in the cities. In recent years, polished professional versions of traditional pieces have occasionally found their way into the concert hall, though all too often they suffer from the deadening hand of official control. Enterprising musicologist Tian Qing has invited an itinerant troupe of blind beggars from Shaanxi to perform on stage in Beijing, but their heart-rending ballads largely fall on deaf ears in the cities.

Folk music has a life of its own, and rural traditions have always been deep-rooted, somehow surviving collectivization and famine until the outbreak of the Cultural Revolution in 1966. Even then, although only eight model operas and ballets were permitted on stage, local musical traditions persisted underground. Since the liberalizations around 1980, local traditions have revived but are now threatened by the new pan-Chinese pop culture that offers an alternative that is more tempting than Maoism was ever able to provide.

Vocal Traditions

Vocal and dramatic styles have dominated Chinese music for many centuries. Traditional **folk songs** (as opposed to ball-gowned divas warbling sentimental bel canto arrangements in a concert hall or on VCD) are performed for local festivals, drinking parties and the completion of new houses; groups of beggars sing for weddings and funerals. Though more difficult for the casual visitor to find in Han Chinese areas than among the ethnic minorities (see next article), the beautiful songs of areas like northern Shaanxi and Sichuan are thankfully represented on disc. Call-and-response work-hollers called *haozi* have long been rare, but **shan'ge** (mountain songs) are haunting free-tempo songs sung at full belt; **xiaodiao** ("little tunes")

are more rhythmic songs often accompanied by a small ensemble.

Narrative-singing, again sadly neglected in recordings, is often performed by one solo bard accompanying himself on a plucked lute and/or percussion, although many styles have accompanying instruments. Like Chinese opera, the repertory is based on long classical stories about scholars and beauties, emperors and outlaws. Again, rural styles, based on ritual healing, are little known. In the towns, you may still find a teahouse full of old people following the story avidly, particularly in Sichuan, where one popular style is accompanied by the yangqin dulcimer. In Beijing, or more often in Tianjin, amateurs sing traditional **jingyun dagu ballads**, accompanied by drum and *sanxian* banjo. In Suzhou, **pingtan** is a beautiful genre. In Beijing

Chinese Opera

Traditional **Chinese opera** combines music, singing, dialogue, pantomime, acrobatics and the martial arts. Rooted in village rituals to appease gods or celebrate men, this form has subdivided into intricate regional genres from north to south, from coastal regions to mountainous interior. While there are fans who couldn't live without it, even some who become avid amateur performers (*piao you*, literally "ticket friends"), Westerners may initially experience Chinese opera as a jarring, high-pitched aural onslaught, with little to grasp in terms of plot, characters and musical content.

Indigenous opera has long been responsible for connecting people to their history and folklore. Stories of fairies and ghosts, historical legends of valiant warriors and kings are enacted on stage, often teaching moral lessons of fidelity and filial piety. In the countryside, they remain an important part of calendrical fairs where the operas are performed on a stage opposite the temple. All performances, however, assume familiarity with the storyline, so those going to Chinese opera for the first time – in the city or the countryside – need to be prepared. Read up on the plot and be prepared for an onslaught of often strident-sounding voices with accompanying high-pitched gongs, cymbals and bowed *huqin* fiddles in Peking and Cantonese operas.

Currently, the most famous among the regional forms are **Peking opera** (still known as Peking rather than Bei-

Frank Kouwenhoven

A local opera performance at a temple fair in Yulin, N.Shaanxi

and elsewhere there is also **xiangsheng**, a comic dialogue with a know-all and a straight man which subtly parodies traditional opera.

Whether performed by state or folk troupes, the several hundred types of regional opera are mainly staged at the innumerable temple fairs which punctuate the rural calendar.

The Qin and Other Solo Traditions

Despite the popularity of vocal music in China itself, Chinese instrumental music somehow has a higher profile in the West. Most is for ensemble: the many short virtuosic pieces that you may hear on the erhu fiddle or dizi flute are mostly the product of modern composers writing for the concert hall in a pseudo-romantic Western-influenced style. But more authentic solo traditions of plucked instruments, derived from the literati of imperial times, also live on in the conservatoires, with musicians trained as virtuoso soloists on the pear-shaped *pipa* lute and the *zheng* and *qin* zithers.

The oldest and most exalted of these instruments is the **qin** (also known as *guqin* – ancient qin). This seven-string plucked zither has been a favourite subject of poets and painters for over a thousand years, and it is the most delicate and contemplative instrument in the Chinese musical palette. It is the most accessible, too, producing expressive slides and ethereal harmonics. Though primarily associated with the moderation of the Confucian scholar, the qin is also steeped in

jing Opera) and **Kunju** (Kun opera, from the Kun mountains near Suzhou). The latter can be traced back more than four hundred years to the Ming dynasty and writer Tang Xianzu (author of such Kun classics as *Peony Pavilion* and *Peach Blossom Fan*). Peking opera evolved about two hundred years ago, not only in the Chinese capital but also around the country and beyond, and is now acknowledged as the "national" opera. Among other forms, **Yueju** hails from Shanghai and its environs, while **Chuanju** (Sichuan opera) is most famous for lightning speed face-changing techniques. **Cantonese opera** is still popular in Guangzhou, Hong Kong and even in southern Chinese diaspora communities as far-flung as America and Australia.

Character roles are currently divided into four main types according to the sex, age, social status and profession of the character. *Sheng* refers to male roles, subdivided into *lao sheng* (middle-aged or old men), *xiao sheng* (young men) and *wu sheng* (men with martial skills). *Dan* refers to female roles and is subdivided into *qing yi*, women with a strict moral code; *hua dan*, vivacious young women; *wu dan*, women with martial skills; and *lao dan*, elderly women. *Jing* refers to the roles with painted faces. They are usually warriors, heroes, statesmen or even demons. *Chou* is a comic character and can be easily identified by his special make-up (a patch of white paint on his nose).

For the uninitiated, probably the most accessible types of opera in any regional genre are action-based pieces like *Monkey King* or romantic comedies about mistaken identities. If nothing else, you can sit back and watch the acrobatics, or enjoy the fast-paced routines of the comic stars.

The instrumental ensemble that accompanies traditional opera performs without a conductor, with the head percussionist cueing the rest of the musicians and actors with his drums, cymbals and a wood-clapper. Apart from percussion, major families of instruments are divided into **bowed fiddles** (*jinghu, gaohu, zhonghu* with different pitch ranges), **plucked lutes** (*yueqin, sanxian, ruan*), and **wind instruments** including mouth organs (*sheng*), shawms (*suona*) and bamboo flutes (*dizi*).

In the old days, audiences sat and enjoyed good food and chatted with friends while being stirred by the huge variety of emotions emanating from an elevated square-shaped stage, listening to the sad strains of *Farewell My Concubine* one night and watching fairy tales and fierce battles the next. Nowadays, large theatres in China have created a need for "grand" operas. New works (often politically required) appear on stages that emulate Broadway. Not long ago, the national company of Peking opera – the China Peking Opera Company – put on their version of *Turandot*, with seventy people on stage. A few avant-garde directors who have absorbed the essence of traditional opera have also created a **"new drama"** trend, in which Stanislawski meets Chinese tradition. Among the leading directors is Li Liuyi, who between 2003 and 2008 created a trilogy of war heroines – *Mu Guiying, Hua Mulan, Liang Hongyu* – questioning the role of women in a postmodern style. Instead of the "one table, two chairs" of stage convention, for example, Li replaces "one table" with "one modern bathtub".

Joanna Lee

Daoism – not the earthy Daoism of later folk ritual but the mystical Daoism of ancient philosophy, the contemplative union with nature, where silence is as important as sound. The only instruments which may occasionally blend with the qin are the **xiao end-blown flute**, or the voice of the player, singing ancient poems in an introverted style.

With its literate background, qin music has been written in a unique and complex notation since the Tang dynasty. Today the earliest score commonly used is the *Shenqi Mipu* (Wondrous and Secret Notation) written by the Ming prince Zhu Quan in 1425, and including many pieces from earlier dynasties. Most qin pieces today have been transmitted from master to pupil since at least the eighteenth century, though since the 1950s the recreation of early pieces such as those in the 1425 score, whose performance tradition has been lost, has become a popular pastime somewhat akin to the early music movement in the West.

Despite its exalted status, the qin is little-known outside the conservatoires. Few Chinese have heard its sound, or even heard of the instrument, and there can only ever have been a few hundred qin players in the whole of China. Great musicians active before and after the Cultural Revolution like **Zha Fuxi**, **Guan Pinghu**, **Zhang Zijian**, **Wu Jinglue** and **Wu Zhaoji** embodied the refinement of the older generation, but today's senior players are accomplished too, such as **Li Xiangting**, **Wu Wen'guang**, **Lin Youren**, **Gong Yi** and **Dai Xiaolian**. There are also many ancient instruments around: a few Tang qins are over a thousand years old, while fifteenth- to seventeenth-century Ming instruments are commonplace.

The qin is best heard in informal meetings of aficionados rather than on the concert stage: Qin associations meet regularly in Beijing, Shanghai, Hong Kong, London and New York. There is a vast discography compared with the neglected folk traditions, and a number of fine websites.

Modern traditions of the **pipa lute** and **zheng zither** also derive from regional styles, transmitted from master to pupil, although "national" repertoires have also been developing during the twentieth century. For the zheng, the northern styles of Henan and Shandong and the southern Chaozhou and Hakka schools are best known, while the pipa has thrived in the Shanghai region. The current design of the pipa lute goes back to the seventh century. It makes riveting listening, with its contrast between intimate "civil" pieces and the startlingly modern-sounding martial style of traditional pieces such as *Shimian maifu* (Ambush from All Sides) with its frenetic percussive evocation of the sounds of battle.

The Temples

The revival of religious practices has been very much in evidence since the end of the Cultural Revolution. Buddhist and Daoist temples have been restored and musical traditions revived.

All over China, temples are not just historical monuments for tourists, but living sites of worship. In temples with resident priests, such as the great mountain temple complexes at **Wutaishan**, **Taishan**, **Qingchengshan**, **Wudangshan**, **Emeishan** and **Putuoshan**, morning and evening services are held daily, with larger calendrical or requiem rituals for special occasions. The priests mainly perform vocal liturgy accompanied by ritual percussion – few now use melodic instruments. They intone sung hymns with long melismas, alternating with chanted sections accompanied by the relentless and hypnotic beat of the **"wooden fish" woodblock**. Drums, bells, gongs and cymbals also punctuate the service.

In Beijing, temples with fine ritual traditions include the Baiyunguan (though beware its spurious recent instrumental ensemble), Guangjisi and Guanghuasi. Southern temples are more lively. In Shanghai, active Buddhist temples include the Longhuasi and Yufosi; Daoist ritual is thriving not just in the central Baiyunguan temple, but, amazingly, in the glitzy new industrial area of Pudong east of the river. Nearby in Changzhou, the **Tianningsi Buddhist temple** is an influential centre of vocal liturgy.

Smaller rural temples hold fairs where all kinds of music are performed as well as the rituals of lay specialists. Melodic instrumental music tends to be added when priests perform rituals outside the temples, the style becoming more earthy and accessible. The Daoist priests from the **Temple of Sublime Mysteries** (Xuanmiaoguan) in Suzhou, for example, punctuate their rituals with some wonderful and varied instrumental music, including mellifluous pieces for silk-and-bamboo instruments, gutsy blasts on the shawm, some spectacularly long trumpets and a battery of percussion.

Traditional instruments

Percussion

In general, percussion is the engine-room of Chinese music, with a dazzling array of large and small drums, clappers, woodblocks, gongs and cymbals.

yunluo: a frame of ten pitched gongs whose melodies give a beautiful halo to ritual ensembles.

Strings

erhu (huqin, jinghu, erxian, huhu, zhuiqin, yehu, gaohu): two-string spike fiddle with many regional variations. The soundbox is usually covered with skin and the hair of the bow runs between the two strings.

pipa: pear-shaped plucked lute with four strings.

qin (guqin): delicate plucked zither with seven strings. Players in Hong Kong and Taiwan still often use silk strings, which have mostly been replaced by metal ones in mainland China.

sanxian: three-string banjo with a long neck.

yangqin: hammered dulcimer, similar to Indian *santoor* and Iranian *santur*.

zheng: plucked zither with sixteen or more strings, each with a tuning bridge, related to Japanese *koto* and Korean *kayagum*.

Wind

dizi: transverse flute with membrane, giving it a buzzing, nasal tone.

guanzi: short wooden pipe with a large double-reed played by ritual specialists in north China, similar to the Japanese *hichiriki* and Armenian *duduk*.

sheng: free-reed mouth-organ with seventeen pipes in a wind-chamber.

suona: double-reed shawm with pirouette and flared metal bell. The Chinese form of the Turkish *zurna*, which extends across Asia into the Balkans and beyond. The most common melodic instrument in China, played by low-caste musicians.

xiao: an intimate-sounding end-blown flute.

Jaime Gramston

Pipa player Wu Man

The poetic titles of many solo pieces – like "Autumn Moon in the Han Palace" or "Flowing Streams" – are often programmatic, relating to nature or a famous historical scene. Such aesthetic imagery is indeed significant in music for these solo instruments, products of the literati of imperial times. The titles of pieces played by folk ensembles, however, are largely irrelevant to their content, serving only as identification for the musicians, rather like jazz standards.

The North: Blowers and Drummers

Today what we might call classical traditions, derived from the elite of imperial times, live on not just in these solo instruments but even more strongly in the folk ensembles. Traditional music can be found even in ugly modern county towns, but if you can, visit the villages, where it can be heard as an accompaniment to life-cycle ceremonies and calendrical rituals for the gods.

The most exciting forms of music are played at **funerals and temple fairs** – at weddings, traditional styles have given way to karaoke. Most common are shawm and percussion bands called **chuigushou** ("blowers and drummers") – the amazing **Hua Family Shawm Band** has appeared in the US, Europe and on CD, but there must be well over ten thousand active bands. The professional musicians are peasants, but virtual outcastes and uneducated, formerly opium smokers and often blind. They are like Chinese Gypsies who pass on magnificent traditions once patronized by the imperial elite. The piercing double-reed **shawm** (the name suona reveals its Central Asian

Stephen Jones

Hua Family Shawm Band leading a funeral procession

origin from the Turkic zurna, but it's commonly known by local names such as *laba* or *weirwa*) is played in pairs, accompanied by a rhythm section of drum, cymbals and gong.

Even funerals include lively pieces to entertain the guests, adding extra instruments like **sheng mouth-organ** and **plucked and bowed lutes**. The "blowers and drummers" play not only lengthy and solemn ancient suites and instrumental versions of local opera, but also the latest pop hits and theme tunes from TV and films, now often adding trumpet, sax and drum kit. They milk the audience by sustaining notes for ever, using circular breathing; by keeping on playing while dismantling and reassembling their shawms; or by balancing plates on sticks on the end of their instruments while playing. Nobly laying down their lives for their art, shawm players also love to play while successively inserting cigarettes into both nostrils, both ears, and both corners of the mouth.

Rituals performed by lay Daoist priests for the well-being of a family or a community are hardly less operatic, entertaining both gods and mortals. A popular act at funerals in Shaanxi villages, performed by both Daoists and shawm bands, is a routine in which the leading wind-player pretends to smear the snot from a kid's nose over the face of one of the other musicians as he keeps playing.

In northern villages, apart from the blowers and drummers, ritual **sheng-guan ensembles**, often lay Daoists, are common, with an exquisite combination of **oboes** and **mouth-organs**, as well as darting flutes and the shimmering halo of the **yunluo gong-frame**, accompanied by percussion. Apart from this haunting melodic music, they play some spectacular ritual percussion, with balletic

cymbal-playing. Derived from the temple music of imperial Beijing (the Zhihua temple was one influential site), Tianjin, Wutaishan, and Xi'an, folk ensembles still perform at funerals and calendrical rituals. Though most of the several hundred amateur ritual "music associations" on the otherwise drab plain just south of Beijing still cater for funerals in their home village, villages like Qujiaying and South Gaoluo have tried to make a name for themselves further afield.

Around Xi'an, ritual groups performing music misleadingly dubbed **Xi'an drum music** (*Xi'an guyue*) are active for temple festivals not only in the villages but even in the town, especially in the sixth moon, around July. And if you remember the tough shawm bands and haunting folksong of the film *Yellow Earth* (directed by Chen Kaige), or the harsh falsetto of *The Story of Qiuju* (directed by Zhang Yimou), go for the real thing among the barren hills of northern Shaanxi (Shaanbei). These were not only the base for Mao's revolution at Yan'an, but the home of fantastic folk-singers, local opera (such as Qinqiang and Mihu), shawm bands and folk ritual specialists. Aim for counties such as Suide, Mizhi, and Yulin, and try and get to the spectacular **Baiyunguan temple** high above the Yellow River, ideally for the fourth moon festival, generally around late May, where vocal liturgy is punctuated by cymbals and sheng-guan music, with shawm bands, story-tellers and opera performing all around the temple complex.

The South: "Silk-and-Bamboo"

More renowned and mellifluous than the outdoor wind bands of the north are the *sizhu* **"silk-and-bamboo" ensembles** of southeastern China, who play in several distinct styles using bamboo flutes and plucked and bowed strings (until recently, these were made of silk, hence the name). The easiest way to hear this music live is to pay a visit to a Shanghai **teahouse**, where old-timers – and some youngsters too – get together in the afternoons, sitting round a table and taking it in turns to play a set with Chinese fiddles, flutes and banjos. You can't help thinking of an Irish pub session, only with Chinese tea instead of Guinness. The many amateur clubs dotted around the city meet up on a fixed afternoon each week. The dovetailing of the phrases is always subtle, far from the black-and-white four-square rhythms of the conservatoire style. Many pieces consist of successive elaborations on a basic theme, beginning with the most ornate and accelerating as the embellishments are gradually stripped down to a fast and bare final statement. Above the chinking of teacups and the subdued chatter of the teahouse, you can listen to the gradual unravelling of the piece *Sanliu*, or feel the exhilaration of the dash to the finish of *Xingjie* (Street Parade), with its breathless syncopations. With a bit of persistence you should be able to find **amateur silk-and-bamboo clubs** through the whole lower Yangtze area, including Nanjing and Hangzhou. Although in its urban form the music is secular and recreational, sizhu instrumentation originated in ritual ensembles and is still so used in the villages and temples of southern Jiangsu. Indeed, amateur ritual associations are found all over southern China, as far afield as Yunnan, punctuating ceremonies with sedate music reminiscent of the Shanghai teahouses, while often adding the yunluo gong-frame of north China.

Another fantastic area for folk music is along the coast of southern Fujian, notably the bustling cities of Quanzhou and Xiamen. Here you can find not only opera, ritual music and puppetry, but also the haunting **Nanguan ballads**. Popular all along the coast of southern Fujian, as in Taiwan across the strait, Nanguan features a female singer accompanied by end-blown flute and plucked and bowed lutes. The ancient texts depict the sorrows of love and particularly of women, the music is mostly stately, while the delivery is restrained yet anguished. Further south along the coast, Chaozhou and the Hakka area, inland around Meixian and Dabu, have well-known string ensembles featuring a high-pitched **erxian bowed fiddle** and zheng plucked zither, as well as large and imposing **ceremonial percussion bands**, sometimes accompanied by shrill flutes, accompanying processions of god statues around their parish.

Overall, the resistance of rural traditions to official ideology during more than three decades of Maoism is remarkable. Pop music may be encroaching more on traditional repertoires than revolutionary music ever did, but despite remaining a well-kept secret, a robust traditional musical life persists in the ceremonies of rural communities.

DISCOGRAPHY China | Han Traditional

Good traditional recordings of opera are available in China itself, but conservatoire-style recordings of instrumental music with souped-up arrangements still predominate over more authentic recordings of local Chinese instrumental and religious music.

★ Songs of the Land in China: Labor Songs and Love Songs
Wind Records, Taiwan
A double CD of beautiful archive recordings of folk singing, mostly unaccompanied, from different regions of China, including rhythmic songs of boatmen, passionate *huar* songs from the northwest, and the plaintive songs from northern Shaanxi. A varied and captivating selection.

★ Voice of the Dragon: A Journey through Musical China
CHIME/Stemra, The Netherlands
The only really worthwhile overview of Chinese music as a whole. This features styles from Chinese pop and rock to opera, from puppet theatre music to the "silk-and-bamboo" repertoire, from minority vocal polyphony to village shawm bands, and from temple rituals and narrative-singing to contemporary conservatory traditions, all eloquently introduced in the notes by Frank Kouwenhoven.

Ballads, Narrative Singing and Opera

⊙ The Beauty of Chinese Folk Opera
Wind Records, Taiwan
Two CDs of excerpts from diverse regional operas, mostly recorded before the Cultural Revolution, including not only Beijing opera (such as a chilling extract from "Farewell My Concubine" sung by Mei Lanfang) and Yu Zhenfei's extraordinary *Kunqu*, but also rare examples of the genre from Hunan and Sichuan provinces. Northern "clapper" operas are specially featured, with *yangge* dance-dramas composed to rouse the peasants at the Communist base against the Japanese in Shaanxi in the 1940s, and a stirring puppet drama from the same area.

⊙ The Best Collection of Nanyin
Hugo, Hong Kong
Rare recording of the little-known Nanyin Cantonese style of narrative-singing in Hong Kong, related to Cantonese opera, with restrained singing (described as "miserable and expressive") supported by a delicate filigree of *yehu* fiddle, qinqin lute and zheng zither.

⊙ An Introduction to Chinese Opera
Hong Kong Records, Hong Kong
A series of four CDs illustrating different styles, including Beijing, Cantonese, Shanghai, Huangmei, Henan, Pingju and Qinqiang operas.

Nan-Kouan: Chant Courtois de la Chine du Sud
Ocora, France
Haunting chamber ballads with a female singer accompanied by end-blown flute and plucked and bowed lutes. This beautiful first volume was recorded in Paris in 1982; there are five further discs.

⊙ Opéra du Sichuan: La Légende de Serpent Blanc
Buda, France
A double CD of traditional opera from the spicy southwestern province of Sichuan, featuring a distinctive female chorus, and ending with the attractive bonus of a "bamboo ballad" on the same theme sung by a narrative-singer.

⊙ The Peony Pavilion: Chinese Classical Opera: Kunqu
Inédit, France
A double CD of excerpts from the great opera by the early seventeenth-century writer Tang Xianzu. The vocal sections give a better idea of the tradition than the kitsch harmonized orchestral arrangements.

⊙ Shuochang: The Ultimate Art of Storytelling
Wind Records, Taiwan
A valuable 2-CD overview of an otherwise neglected genre, with archive recordings of some major regional traditions, from the urban drum-singing styles of Beijing and Tianjin, and mellifluous singing from Suzhou and Yangzhou, to rarely heard narratives from the more remote Hubei, Guangxi, Gansu and Qinghai provinces.

Instrumental Ensemble and Temple Music

⊙ China: Chuida Wind & Percussive Instrumental Ensembles
UNESCO, France
Three traditional ensembles from southern China recorded by the indefatigable Francois Picard in 1987, including some unusual silk-and-bamboo from Shanghai and ceremonial music for weddings and funerals from Fujian and Zhejiang.

⭐China: Folk Instrumental Traditions
AIMP/VDE-Gallo, Switzerland
A double CD of archive and recent recordings of village ensembles from north and south, including earthy shawm bands, mystical sheng-guan ritual ensembles, mellifluous silk-and-bamboo, and some awesome percussion. Features some master musicians from before the Cultural Revolution, such as Daoist priests An Laixu on yunluo gong-frame and Zhu Qinfu on drums.

⊙ China: Ka-le, Festival of Happiness
AIMP/VDE-Gallo, Switzerland
Instrumental music from the exquisite puppet operas of southern Fujian, featuring the Quanzhou Puppet Troupe.

⊙ Chine: Chant Liturgique Bouddhique
Ocora, France
A selection of music from Buddhist temples, including vocal liturgy from Quanzhou and Shanghai.

⊙ Jiangnan Sizhu: Beautiful Traditional Music from Southeastern China
Hugo, Hong Kong
A somewhat polished yet intimate selection of some of the lesser-known repertory of silk-and-bamboo, played by senior masters from Shanghai, mostly in chamber versions.

⊙ Rain Dropping on the Banana Tree
Rounder, US
Reissue of 78s from 1902 to 1930 featuring early masters of Cantonese music such as Yau Hok Chau, as well as excerpts from Beijing and Cantonese opera.

⊙ Shawms from Northeast China. Vol.1: Music of the First Moon; Vol. 2: The Li Family Band
Buda, France
Ear-cleansing shawm-and-percussion bands have long thrived in the northeastern provinces, with these discs featuring groups from the port of Dalian. Vol. 1 features several earthy bands accompanying New Year's yangge dance and stilt-walking processions, while Vol. 2 has a spectrum of music from the Li family band, from the doleful funeral style for large shawms to more popular pieces using an array of instruments, including some wild glissandos on the zhuiqin fiddle.

⭐Sizhu/Silk Bamboo: Chamber Music of South China
Pan Records, Netherlands
Several styles of chamber ensemble along the southeastern coast, with silk-and-bamboo from Shanghai, refined Nanguan from Xiamen, Chaozhou and Hakka pieces featuring zheng zither, and examples of the more modern Cantonese style.

⊙ Tianjin Buddhist Music Ensemble
Nimbus, UK
The temple music style as played around Tianjin, on the coast near Beijing, with some wonderful guanzi oboe playing.

⊙ Xi'an Drums Music
Hugo, Hong Kong
Majestic wind-and-percussion music performed for funerals and calendrical pilgrimages around Xi'an, including some rarely heard vocal hymns (strangely translated as "rap music").

The Hua Family Shawm Band

A family of peasant musicians from a poor village in the northern province of Shanxi, the Hua band perform wild music for funerals and temple fairs within a small radius of their home. Tours of the US and Europe since 2001 haven't changed their style, but the demand for Chinese pop at their local ceremonies has!

Walking Shrill: The Hua Family Shawm Band
Pan Records, Netherlands
This disc concentrates on the classical repertory of the band, evoking the real spit and sawdust of north Chinese life with searing laments and wild syncopations. Think Chinese Coltrane.

Instrumental Solo

⊙ Chine: Musique Classique
Ocora, France
A selection of solo pieces featuring the qin, pipa, sheng, guanzi, dizi, xiao, erhu and yangqin, played by outstanding instrumentalists of the 1950s, including Guan Pinghu, Cao Zheng and Sun Yude.

Special Collection of Contemporary Chinese Musicians
Wind Records, Taiwan
A more comprehensive double CD of archive recordings of some of the great 1950s instrumentalists, including masters of the qin, zheng, pipa, suona and guanzi.

Dizi, Erhu and Zheng

Lin Maogen

Born in 1929, Lin Maogen represents the Chaozhou style of zheng playing, having studied with the master Zhang Hanzhai. After the Communist "Liberation" he maintained the traditional style while taking part in official troupes.

⊙ Jackdaws Gambol Water
Hugo, Hong Kong
A disc that shows the plaintive style of zheng played in the Chaozhou area, with some pieces accompanied by the earthy yehu fiddle of Lin Jiheng. The minor-mode melodies like the title piece are particularly evocative, and modal and metrical variation technques are illustrated by three exquisite (and very different) versions of the standard "Liuqingniang", each in gradually acccelerating tempos. This is part of a major series of zheng masters from Hugo.

Lu Chunling

Former trishaw driver Lu Chunling (b. 1921) later became dizi professor at the Shanghai Conservatoire, and has led the way in establishing the dizi as a solo instrument, playing a polished version of his local style of Shanghai silk-and-bamboo, trilling away jovially – his quartet versions of the local silk-and-bamboo repertory are both more slick and more romantic than the local amateur tradition.

⊙ Lu Chunling: The Art of Dizi
Marco Polo/Naxos, Hong Kong
Featuring Lu Chunling as soloist with orchestral accompaniment in easy-listening arrangements of traditional tunes.

Min Huifen

Min Huifen (b. 1945) is the grande dame of erhu solo music, whose expressive and technically fluent playing inspired the younger generation of conservatoire erhu virtuosos.

⊙ The River of Sorrow
Marco Polo/Naxos, Hong Kong
This disc features peerless recordings of the plaintive modern erhu classics, including the immortal "Reflections of the Moon on Erquan Spring", first recorded by the blind beggar Abing in 1950.

Pipa

Lin Shicheng

Lin Shicheng (b. 1922), a former doctor and amateur pipa player from near Shanghai, has become the main pipa educator in China, based at the Central Conservatoire in Beijing.

⊙ Chine: l'Art du Pipa
Ocora, France
Classical pieces for the pipa played by the senior pipa master.

Wu Man

Wu Man (b. 1963) has become the international ambassador for the pipa. From the southern town of Hangzhou, Wu Man studied with masters such as Lin Shicheng in Beijing. Since making her home in the US, she has championed new – including new Chinese – music, working with the Kronos Quartet and composers such as Philip Glass and Tan Dun.

⊙ Chinese Traditional and Contemporary Music for Pipa
Nimbus, UK
A double album including some of the best traditional pieces – including the martial and descriptive "The Tyrant Removes his Armour" and "Ambush on All Sides", and "civil" pieces which Wu Man performs with a sensual elegance. There are also contemporary compositions for pipa and Wu's ensemble of Chinese instruments.

Qin

⊙ An Anthology of Chinese and Traditional Folk music: Music Played on the Guqin
China Record Co., China
These eight CDs reissuing the great masters of the 1950s are a must for serious qin fanatics.

Dai Xiaolian

Dai Xiaolian is a female qin player and scholar based at the Shanghai Conservatory.

⊙ Chine: L'Art de la Cithare Qin / The Art of the Qin Zither
Ethnic/Auvidis, France
Dai Xiaolian has maintained the contemplative ethos of the qin while appearing on the international concert stage. In this album she displays her mastery of the instrument.

Guan Pinghu

Born in Suzhou, Guan Pinghu (1897–1967) was long resident in the harsher northern capital Beijing. Also a respected painter, he was the grand master of qin players in the 1950s, an outstanding teacher and scholar, leading the qin through difficult times. He also led the way in recreating ancient pieces from early scores such as the 1425 *Shenqi Mipu*.

Roi Productions

Guan Pinghu playing qin

Favourite Qin Pieces of Guan Ping-hu
ROI Productions, Hong Kong

This lavishly annotated and illustrated double CD includes recordings that have become the benchmark for many qin players since, including Guan's own realizations of pieces not heard for many centuries, notably "Guangling San". His classic version of "Liushui" (Flowing Waters) was chosen to go into orbit on the spaceship *Voyager* in 1977. Part of a great series of qin masters from ROI that also includes players like Wu Jinglue.

Lin Youren

Lin Youren, an eccentric Shanghai-based qin master, prefers to play for his friends over a bottle or three of wine, another ancient qin tradition.

⊙ **Music for the Qin Zither: Lin Youren**
Nimbus, UK

An intimate recording made on Lin's 1998 UK visit, featuring classics like "Evening Song of the Drunken Fisherman", and rare gems like a "qin song" with Lin crooning and an improvisation inspired by Michael Owen's World Cup goal against Argentina!

Wu Zhaoji

Wu Zhaoji (1908–97), from the canal city of Suzhou, embodied the all-round culture of the Chinese scholar: with his long white beard, practising *qigong* breathing exercises and calligraphy daily, he was also a professor of mathematics.

⊙ **Wumen Qin Music**
Hugo, Hong Kong

Wu's qin playing typified the contemplative ethos of the instrument, eschewing mere technical display. This fine CD set of some of the great qin masters in regional styles also includes masters like Zhang Ziqian and representatives of the middle and younger generations.

PLAYLIST
China | Han Traditional

1 DAHEINIU JINGDI LI HUANGTU Zhang Eryinhu from *Songs of the Land in China*
Gorgeous unaccompanied free-tempo folk-song from the barren mountainsides of the "yellow earth" of Shaanbei in poor northwest China, sung at high pitch and volume by a male peasant.

2 KANG-KUN TOAN-JOK Tsai Hsiao-yueh from *Nan-kouan: Chant Courtois de la Chine du Sud, Vol. 1.*
Passionate yet restrained ballad singing from Taiwan in the Nanguan style popular in southeast China.

3 FAREWELL MY CONCUBINE (EXTRACT) Mei Lanfang from *The Beauty of Chinese Folk Opera*
Beijing opera music sung by the great Mei Lanfang in 1954. The tragic denouement where the concubine bids farewell before committing suicide.

4 SHUILONGYIN IN MEIHUADIAO The Hua Family Shawm Band from *Walking Shrill*
From the wailing slow opening in this bluesy scale, the long gradual accelerando to a wild climax is irresistible, embodying the sheer macho grit of north Chinese peasants.

5 XIAO HUAYAN Former Monks of the Zhihua Si Temple from *China: Folk Instrumental Traditions*
Haunting sounds from 1953 in a perfect combination of oboes, mouth-organs, flutes and gong-frames.

6 ZHONGHUA LIUBAN Huxinting Teahouse Ensemble from *Sizhu/Silk Bamboo: Chamber Music of South China*
Evocative live recording of this gentle ensemble piece, capturing the bustle of the Shanghai teahouses.

7 FORGETTING THE VULGAR IDEAS Guan Pinghu from *Favourite Qin Pieces of Guan Ping-hu*
A simple piece to evoke Daoist mysticism, played on a silk-strung qin by a master from the generation before the Cultural Revolution.

8 THE TYRANT REMOVES HIS ARMOUR Wu Man from *Chinese Traditional and Contemporary Music*
The martial side of the traditional pipa, with brilliant and avant-garde-sounding effects evoking the sounds of battle.

9 MOON REFLECTION IN ERQUAN SPRING Min Huifen from *The River of Sorrow*
A modern classic of the conservatoire style of erhu fiddle.

10 JACKDAWS GAMBOL WATER Lin Maogen from *Chaozhou Zheng Music*
Soulful solo zheng zither playing from southeast China.

China | Minorities

sounds of the frontiers

Uyghur Muqam Ensemble
Jak Kilby

Although they make up less than ten percent of the population of China, there are nearly one hundred million people divided among the country's fifty-five officially recognized "minority nationalities". The heaviest concentrations of these are found in the areas where most Western backpackers tend to head: the northwest and southwest. Minorities in the north include the Central Asian Kazakhs and Uyghurs, the Manchus and the Mongolians; in the southwest, the Dai, Miao, Naxi, Yi and Zhuang, to name but a few. All of China's minorities speak different languages, and their musical traditions are very different from those of the Han Chinese majority, though some share languages and culture with groups in Burma, Laos, Thailand and Vietnam. Rachel Harris gives an overview of China's rich diversity of minority musical traditions. (Note that Tibetan music is covered in a separate article on p.766.)

China's minority nationalities and their different musics have virtually nothing in common except their official minority status. Many visitors to China head directly to the remote and beautiful northwest and southwestern regions which these ethnic minorities inhabit, and can easily seek out live performances on their travels. In recent years, these regions and their exotic minority cultures have also become a magnet for mass Chinese tourism, and music is a key part of the way in which they are marketed. It's a cliché in China that minority peoples are good at singing and dancing – in fact, talking to people in China, you sometimes get the impression that the Han majority have no musical traditions of their own at all.

Although China may have a somewhat patchy record with its minority policies, it has invested incredible energy in researching, documenting and promoting its minority musics. Many of the classic 1950s Communist songs like "Salaam Chairman Mao" are based on minority folk-songs and are still warmly welcomed by Chinese audiences. A disproportionate amount of contemporary Chinese composition is based on minority traditions, and numerous professional troupes offer staged performances of minority folklore, which are popular on TV and regularly served up to tourists. These can look cheesy to the average Westerner, but things are beginning to change as Chinese tastes adapt to the global market, and there is currently a drive to promote more authentic traditions. There are also a disproportionate number of minority rock stars, singing in both Chinese and their own languages, from the heartfelt 1990s Mongolian rock of **Tengger** (see box below) to the more recent Uyghur flamenco guitar of **Arken Abdulla** (see box opposite). Even **Cui Jian**, China's most famous rocker, belonged to China's Korean minority, although he never really emphasized his ethnicity. Maybe minorities do rock in a way that the Han Chinese just can't manage.

It's impossible to do justice to so many peoples and musics in a short article, so what follows is a sample of some of the better-known traditions and recent trends.

The Northeast and Inner Mongolia

The largest minorities in the far northeastern provinces of Heilongjiang, Jilin and Liaoning are the ten million or so **Manchu** – who ruled China during the Qing dynasty (1644–1911) – and the almost two million **Koreans**, whose ancestors migrated from Korea in the nineteenth century, and who still preserve many Korean customs and

Tengger: Mongolian Rough

Tengger, a singer-songwriter from Inner Mongolia, first made his name in 1986 with the song "The Mongolian". His music combines hard guitar-rock and traditional Mongolian sounds, especially the **morin huur fiddle** and thrilling women's **long-songs**, all underpinning his famously growling vocals in Chinese and Mongolian. It's a voice so raw that it leaves Tom Waits in the shade, nurtured by a diet of Chinese cigarettes and evil-smelling *baijiu*

liquor. Tengger's brand of minority macho made him very popular in China in the 1990s: he recorded songs for several famous Chinese films, including the early Zhang Yimou classics *Yellow Earth* and *Red Sorghum*, and he starred in and wrote an award-winning soundtrack for *A Mongolian Tale*. Tengger trades heavily on his Mongolian identity, with lyrics full of themes of freedom, nature and the emptiness of the grasslands. His band **Blue Wolf**, formed in 1993, is named after the totemic ancestor of the Mongols. An icon for Mongolians in China, Tengger has used his position to make nationalist statements through songs like "The Land of the Blue Wolf" and interviews on the near-disappearance of the nomadic lifestyle in Inner Mongolia. His many releases are available on the Hong Kong-based Wind label: probably the most attractive for Western ears are those which find him delving deeper into traditional Mongolian sounds.

Tengger

Arken Abdulla: Uyghur Flamenco

Arken Abdulla grew up in Kashgar, where he taught himself the guitar, scouring the bazaars for cassettes of Beijing rock, Cantopop and Bollywood. One of the few Uyghurs to gain a university place in Beijing, he formed a band playing Chinese and American rock in the capital's bars. Arken's first two albums feature songs in Chinese and in Uyghur, and they made him popular in Xinjiang, as well as with the larger Chinese market where he is now the biggest selling minority star. His selling point is "a blend of Latin and traditional Uyghur music, with a distinct, modern and international sound". Flamenco underpins his songs far more than Uyghur traditions; indeed it's hard to discern much of these traditions in the music at all, although his videos draw heavily on grainy images of Uyghur peasant musicians. That aside, Arken has produced some great songs with slick production values. His second album *Arken: Guitar King* (2005) is a riot of musical influences, with acoustic reworkings of everything from salsa to bluegrass to Balkan Gypsy fiddle, plus a touch of bouzouki and (of course) belly dancing. Arken has been laden with awards and often appears on national TV, not only because his music is pretty good but because he manages to be popular with Chinese and Uyghur youth and (most importantly) to keep clear of politics. Although his CDs are as yet unreleased in the West, his videos are easily found on YouTube.

Arken Abdulla

musical styles. While many Manchu have been assimilated into mainstream Chinese life, some still practise traditional **shamanistic rituals**, in which a magic drum and waist-bells are used to communicate with the gods.

Nearly five million **Mongols** live in China, most of them in the Inner Mongolian Autonomous Region. The rich variety of Mongolian music includes overtone singing (*xöömii*), epic songs and "long-songs" (*urtyn duu*), with their slow, extended melodic line, often accompanied by the Mongolian horse-head fiddle (*morin huur*). Singers from Inner Mongolia have become popular in China and in the West by bringing their traditions into contemporary frameworks: the best-known in China is the rocker **Tengger** (see box opposite). In Europe, **Urna Chahartugchi** is beginning to attract critical attention. Born on the grasslands, Urna made her way to Shanghai, then to Bavaria, where she has combined her Mongolian long-songs and more avant-garde explorations with traditions ranging from Eastern Europe to India and Iran.

A new Beijing-based Mongolian group called **Hanggai** are currently making waves in the UK. Lead singer Ilchi disbanded his punk group in 2003 and started exploring the authentic sounds of the grasslands. With horsehead fiddles, throat singing and the funky Mongolian *tobshuur* lute underpinned by a rock aesthetic, Hanggai is a fresh and fun take on tradition, and part of a wider movement coming out of Beijing which is now being dubbed "Chinagrass".

(For more on Mongolian music, see the Inner Asia chapter on p.628.)

The Northwest

The **Xinjiang Uyghur Autonomous Region** in China's far northwest, once a staging post on the Silk Road, has long been a meeting point for Chinese and Central Asian culture. The **Uyghurs**, a Turkic Muslim people numbering around ten million, are renowned for their music and dancing, which accompany weddings, traditional *mashrap* parties and festivals. The major Uyghur instruments are various long-necked lutes (*dutar, tambur, satar*), the spike fiddle (*ghijak*), dulcimers (*chang* and *qalun*), and the frame drum (*dap*) – all variants of instruments found throughout Central Asia (see Central Asian Republics article, p.485). The best music comes from the various **Muqam**

Jean During/Ocora

Dap and dutar players, Xinjiang

traditions, which are closely related to Uzbek and Tajik music, and indirectly to *maqam* traditions found across the Islamic world. The most prestigious of these are the **On Ikki Muqam** (Twelve Muqam) which contain some truly ravishing music. The large-scale professional performances usually seen on Chinese TV may lack charm, but there are several great recordings available in the West. One truly roots-style Muqam tradition that has received a lot of attention recently is the **Dolan Muqam**. With its raw male voices, driving rhythms and jazz-like riffs on fiddle and dulcimer, this is the most accessible of the Uyghur traditions, and it has recently been parachuted out of the villages and onto the international stage. There is a thriving Uyghur recording industry which deals mainly in VCDs, covering the spectrum from rural traditions to hip-hop (the bazaar in Urumchi is the easiest place to find them).

In Urumchi, there are nightly performances of traditional music in the top-end Uyghur restaurants, and the many dance restaurants featuring live Uyghur pop are great places for watching (and joining) urban Uyghurs at play. Song-and-dance shows are staged daily in the bazaar for tour groups, but not recommended. You're much better off catching informal music sessions in Kashgar, the old Silk Road town with a famous Sunday market in southwest Xinjiang. Musicians often gather in the musical instrument shops around the main square in front of Idgah mosque. If you arrive in Kashgar during one of the major religious festivals you may be lucky enough to catch the **Sama**: a mass whirling dance with obvious Sufi links that is performed in the main square to the sounds of shawms and kettle drums (*naghra-sunay*). Even if you only make it as far as Beijing, you can find Uyghur music of a sort in the fashionable and up-market Uyghur restaurants, which put on lavish stage shows featuring Uyghur pop singers and other not very authentic items such as Uyghur belly dancing.

Another famous northwestern tradition is the **Hua'er** song festivals. These are attended by Han Chinese as well as **Hui** Muslim Chinese, **Salar**, **Tibetans** and other groups in Gansu, Qinghai and Ningxia. Hua'er festivals usually take place between June and July, and they feature unaccompanied, competitive songs sung either between two singers or between groups. Singers improvise flirtatious or boastful lyrics or insult their competitors, often for comic effect and using some truly rude language. The songs begin in a comparatively low register then hurtle upwards, taking male singers into a falsetto yell, and the women higher still. In Gansu, festivals take place at Erlang Mountain (fourteenth to nineteenth days of the fifth lunar month), and Lianhua Mountain (second to sixth days of the sixth lunar month); when I last went it was necessary to hire a jeep to get there. At night, fires dot the mountainside and you can hear snatches of song and laughter floating down to the main festival site. Cars leaving the festival are held hostage by groups of children holding ropes across the road and demanding songs from the passengers.

Southern China

There are some large groups in the central south, of whom the most numerous are the **Zhuang** of Guangxi Zhuang Autonomous Region, numbering around thirteen million. The Zhuang are known for their "song fairs", held during festivals such as Chinese New Year, at which young people get acquainted by singing love songs and question songs.

The million or so **Li** of **Hainan Island**, off China's south coast, east of Vietnam, have distinctive, though now declining musical traditions, including a two- or three-bar xylophone strung from a bamboo trestle or between trees, and the "pole dance" – nothing to do with pole dancing – in which girls rhythmically clap together bamboo poles parallel to the ground, while boys leap between them.

The Southwest

Many minority groups in the remote, mountainous areas of **Sichuan**, **Guizhou** and **Yunnan** provinces still preserve traditional musical cultures. **Yunnan**, which borders on Burma, Laos and Vietnam, is home to 25 minority nationalities. A recent discovery is the two- to eight-voice singing of rice-transplanting songs by the **Hani** people of Honghe prefecture, famous for cultivating terraced rice-fields which rise hundreds of feet up steep mountain slopes. Men and women of all ages sing together, with voices entering successively to create an extraordinary dense, microtonally coloured chordal effect. Better known are the courtship songs and enormous **lusheng** (mouth organs) of the **Miao** of **Guizhou**, which may have several pipes extending up to five or seven metres in length.

The **Naxi** of Lijiang County in Yunnan are proud of their **Baisha Xiyue** genre, a suite including song, dance and instrumental music, said to have been brought by Mongol conqueror Kublai Khan in 1253. They also borrowed Confucian-style ritual music associations from the Han, and play **Dongjing music** derived from Chinese silk-and-bamboo music. With its rich variety of string, wind and percussion instruments performed by ancient-looking bearded sages, you can hear this beautiful music at nightly tourist concerts in Dayan Town.

Using instruments to "talk" is widespread among Yunnan minorities. Courting couples of the Naxi, Yi, or other groups often express their love through the Jew's harp; the **Wa** consider their **wooden drum** capable of communicating with Heaven, and some groups use it to declare war, send news, congratulate hunters and so on, with each drum pattern representing a signal with a particular meaning.

Regional festivals are often the best time to catch music-making in Yunnan. The Third Month Fair held in April in Dali brings out a variety of local Han, Bai and Yi performers, and in Lijiang County festive occasions such as New Year's day see folk singers, instrumentalists and ritual groups all performing informally across Dayan Town.

With thanks to Helen Rees

DISCOGRAPHY China | Minorities

⊙ **Music of Chinese Minorities**
King, Japan
Somewhat arbitrary selection of top-class solo instrumentalists performing on the Kyrgyz *komuz*, Uyghur *rawap*, Mongolian morin huur, Korean *haegum* and Miao bamboo pipes.

North

⊙ **Mongolian Epic Song: Zhangar**
King, Japan
Beautiful long-songs contrast with typically jolly song-and-dance troupe offerings. Of most interest is a 25-minute recording of the Oirat epic "Zhangar".

⊙ **Mongolian Tale**
Wind, Hong Kong
This award-winning 1995 soundtrack finds Mongolian rocker Tengger exploring traditional Mongolian sounds.

⊙ **Urna: Amilal**
Trees Music and Art, Taiwan
The Chemirani Trio join Urna on this 2005 release, with a spare approach to traditionally inspired songs, ranging from ballads to the avant-garde.

Hanggai

Hanggai are a group of Inner Mongolians, based in Beijing, where they currently play monthly gigs. Leader of the band is ex-punk singer Ilchi, although the Ghengis Khan lookalike Hurcha is the star, alongside morin huur player Hugejiltu.

⊙ **Introducing Hanggai**
World Music Network, UK
An excellent debut album from 2008 featuring horsehead fiddle and the guttural Mongol singing style, underpinned by cool beats and Tarantino-esque guitars.

Northwest

⊙ **Bu Dunya / This World: Song and Melodies of the Uighurs**
Pan, Netherlands
A good sample of folk songs and extracts from the classical Twelve Muqam repertoire performed by the virtuoso Shadiyana Ensemble from Urumchi.

China. Xinjiang: The Silk Road
Playasound, France

Attractive Anderson Bakewell field recordings from the mid-1980s, featuring *muqam* traditions, instrumental pieces and folk songs.

The Muqam of the Dolan: Music of the Uighurs from the Taklamakan Desert
Inédit, France

Live recordings made in Paris in 2006; this most recent Uyghur release in the West captures the raw, funky energy of the village-based Dolan tradition.

Turkestan Chinois / Xinjiang: Musiques Ouïgoures
Ocora, France

This two-CD set of field recordings from the late 1980s made by Sabine Trebinjac and Jean During includes excerpts from the Twelve Muqam, plus more popular repertoire; includes some rare traditional performances, useful notes and great photos.

The Uyghur Musicians from Xinjiang: Music from the Oasis Towns of Central Asia
Globestyle, UK

Studio recordings made by some of the greatest living masters of Uyghur music during their 2000 UK tour; includes excerpts from the local muqam traditions of Ili and Turpan.

Mamer

An ethnic Kazakh living in Xinjiang, Mamer made his name as an alt-country singer and guitarist before his return-to-Kazakh-roots career.

Eagle
RealWorld, UK

A well-produced 2009 album with evocative grassland songs in Mamer's growly voice accompanied by plucked *dombra*. They're given a contemporary feel with guitar, beats and other sampled ethnic traditions plus a duet with banjo maestro Bela Fleck. More magic from the Chinagrass movement.

Southwest

Alili: Multi-Part Folksongs of Yunnan's Ethnic Minorities
Nanwoka: Multi-Part Folksongs of Yunnan's Ethnic Minorities
Pan, Netherlands

Two epic double CDs of extraordinary field and studio recordings by Zhang Xingrong and Li Wei, featuring unaccompanied polyphonic folk songs of the diverse peoples of Yunnan Province. Notes and lyrics translated and edited with loving care by Helen Rees. A joy for the specialist.

Buddhist Music Of Tianjin / Naxi Music from Lijiang
Nimbus, UK

A double CD featuring one Han Chinese and one ethnic minority group playing essentially the same style of ritual ensemble music. The elegant Han-derived Dongjing ensemble music on the second disc was performed by the Naxi Dayan Ancient Music Association from Yunnan during their 1995 British tour.

Naxi Music from Lijiang
Nimbus, UK

This earlier release contains two contrasting forms of Naxi music: the same recordings of the Dayan Ancient Music Association as above, plus dance-tunes played on the Naxi pipe by Lijiang folk musician Wang Chaoxin.

South of the Clouds: Instrumental Music of Yunnan Vol. 1
Manu, New Zealand

Another double CD of field recordings from the bottomless archives of Zhang and Li, featuring instrumental music from Jew's harps and leaves to shawm ensembles; produced in collaboration with the Australian researcher and composer Jack Body. Useful notes and photos, and some truly extraordinary sounds.

PLAYLIST
China | Minorities

1 GANGANG HARA Tengger from *Mongolian Tale*
From the film soundtrack, featuring fantastic female vocals and morin huur fiddle.

2 PENJIGAH MUQAM OF ILI Riyazidin Barat, Musajan Rosi, Husanjan Jami, Yasin Muhpul from *The Uyghur Musicians of Xinjiang*
Stunning folky rendition of this popular Ili Muqam, sung by the old masters of the tradition.

3 WU CHU A CI (RICE-TRANSPLANTING SONG) Farmers of Azhahe Township from *Alili: Multi-Part Folksongs of Yunnan's Ethnic Minorities*
The Hani of Yunnan have recently become famous within China for these haunting polyphonic songs. Here a large ensemble of voices, lutes and flutes – all performed by peasant farmers – weaves a magical texture.

4 CHARIGAHNING TAZISINING MARGHULI Dolqun Sapar from *Bu Dunya*
Exceptional virtuosic instrumental solo excerpt from the Uyghur Twelve Muqam played on the ghijak spike fiddle by Dolqun Sapar.

5 A MU GU (I LOVE MY MOTHER) Ma Guoguo from *South of the Clouds Vol. 1*
Fantastic example of multi-bladed Jew's harp playing from an eighteen-year old Yi-nationality chamber maid.

6 TEN OFFERINGS Dayan Ancient Music Association from *Buddhist Music Of Tianjin/ Naxi Music from Lijiang*
The Dayan Ancient Music Association performs ritual chant accompanied by fiddles, flutes and lutes.

7 YISUN DALAIIN HOVOOND Urna from *Amilal*
An interesting collaboration between the Inner Mongolian vocalist Urna and the Chemirani Trio.

8 JULA Hesen Yahya, Huseyn Yahya, Supi Turdi, Muhammad Mutallip from *The Muqam of the Dolan*
The raw energy of this group of Uyghur village musicians playing live in Paris in 2006 electrifies the crowd.

China/Hong Kong I
Pop and Rock

from bubblegum to protest

予適堡

Aaron Kwok, live in concert: 2008 poster

Unsurprisingly, Cantonese pop or Cantopop is particularly popular among the Cantonese-speaking population of the south and in Hong Kong, from where it originated. Since the reversion of Hong Kong to China in 1997, however, government-sanctioned Chinapop – derived from Cantopop, but sung in the official Putonghua (northern dialect, also known as Mandarin) – has morphed into a multi-million enterprise and is beamed to every television set, even in remote villages. Chinese rock, on the other hand, is still very much an underground, urban phenomenon, having its roots in the protest music of Cui Jian, whose songs were taken up by the students in Tiananmen Square in 1989. **Joanna Lee** sketches the history and introduces the stars.

Cantopop

Western-influenced music first came to China in the 1920s, and local singing stars emerged with the rise of the middle class in urban areas, especially in Shanghai. One of the most famous was **Zhou Xuan** (1918–57), who acted in films and recorded popular songs with salon orchestra accompaniment. One can only imagine the musical revolution in 1949 when the Communists took control of the city. Shanghai was purged, and all such entertainment forms of the corrupt capitalist world were denounced as "pornographic".

In many ways, **Hong Kong's Cantopop** owes its existence to Shanghai's popular music – thanks to the influx of Shanghai composers and singers in the 1950s, not to mention the transplanting of nightclubs, dance halls and a major film industry. The catalyst for the Cantopop boom, however, was the meeting of East and West in the 1970s.

Cantopop Beginnings

Back in the 1960s, there were two popular music scenes in Hong Kong: Western music – Elvis, Johnny Mathis and The Beatles (who visited in 1964) – imported for the Western-educated youth; and **Shidaiqu** (contemporary song), which followed the tradition of 1930s Shanghai and was sung in Mandarin (a second language for Hong Kong's 95-percent-Cantonese population). In the China of the Cultural Revolution, meanwhile, there were just the eight revolutionary operas approved by Madame Mao.

Hong Kong was different. As the British colony transformed itself into an industrial-cum-financial powerhouse, it built its own music industry. **Cantopop** (Cantonese pop) began to appear in the 1970s – an amalgam of Western soft rock and mellow Cantonese lyrical singing – "Southern China-meets-the West", a musical equivalent of Hong Kong itself. It developed around the time when TV became a household fixture in the mid-1970s, and stations commissioned theme songs for prime-time soap operas. Radio stations were also important in advancing careers, holding songwriting competitions and talent contests.

Joseph Koo and **James Wong** were the groundbreakers, composing Cantopop for TV themes in the 1970s. If you want to get the feel of the era, try and get compilation discs including singers **Adam Cheng** (Cheng Siu Chau) and **Lisa Wang** (Wang Ming Chuen), famous prime-time soap opera stars who sang much of this material. The scene then took off further with bands such as **Lotus** and the **Wynners** (initially named the Losers – the change of name paid off), who sang Abba covers and original songs in English.

Glory Days

It was in the 1980s, when artists began singing in Cantonese, that things really got going. The glory days of the early part of the decade saw the creation of a host of stars, all in their twenties. They included **Anita Mui**, **Sam Hui**, the late **Leslie Cheung**, **Jacky Cheung** (no relation), **Danny Chan**, **Kenny Bee** and **Alan Tam** (these last two formerly of the Wynners). Almost all of them combined a singing career with roles in prime-time soaps, and went on to make movies. New songs were often featured in films to further boost the performer's career.

By the end of the 1980s, four male stars – **Jacky Cheung**, **Andy Lau**, **Aaron Kwok** and **Leon Lai** – dominated the Cantopop scene so completely that they were known as *Sei Dai Tin Wong* (the Four Heavenly Kings). These rival singing deities created a boom in sales of their respective solo albums, as well as an incessant flurry of media exposure via film roles. Jacky Cheung, the most accomplished, even premiered the first-ever Cantonese Broadway show in 1997. But after the millennium, a few well-connected record labels crossed the borders into China, the most prominent being the Emperor Group, with such teeny-boppers as **Cookies** (a

Andy Lau *Warlords* film poster

seven-girl group), **Twins** (two young girls) and **Sun Boyz** (two young men). The big labels have raised Cantopop to a new level of sophistication in marketing, packaging and production. Yet the music itself is often haphazard: the hit process tends to involve rushed commissioning of composers and lyricists, with producers occasionally selecting Japanese and American covers, and singers recording in long sessions to beat production deadlines.

Cantopop has become the dominant pop style throughout the whole of Greater China: sometimes a Cantonese song will have a Putonghua version with similar packaging. Musically, Cantopop remains a close cousin to Anglo-American soft rock and a younger sister of Japanese pop – a bit heavy on synthesizers and drum machines. The songs are always in a moderate tempo and the lyrics are formulaic (happy/sad love). A few stock English phrases remain amid the "oohs and aahs" of the backing vocals: "I love you", "You love me" and "Oh yeah".

Hearing Cantopop in Hong Kong

It's hard to escape the synthesized accompaniment of Cantopop and Chinapop songs on the streets of Hong Kong or Beijing, blasting from shops and car radios. You can surf the channels on TV (Asian MTV and VH1 on cable) for music videos and pop music programmes, while online there are plenty of streaming websites. If you want to **buy Cantopop**, you can take your chance on what's displayed at the neighbourhood CD shop or Hong Kong branches of HMV: sample a few tracks and pick what you like. For a bargain, try the night markets in Temple Street and Tung Choi Street in Kowloon. Go into little shops and street stalls where they sell cheap DVDs, VCDs, CDs, tapes and laser discs, and pick through their selections.

If you want to experience Cantopop as **live entertainment**, visit Television City (an offshoot of Universal Studios) in Clearwater Bay, or try and track down concerts at the Hong Kong Coliseum. Tickets for Coliseum concerts range from HK$150 to $480, which will get you comfortably close to the singers. You can also sample radio programmes or listen online (*www.rthk.org.hk* – Radio 2 is the pop music channel). Call up the local radio stations (Commercial Radio 2, Radio Hong Kong 2, and Metro Radio's Hit Radio) and ask if they have any special public events in parks or shopping malls with star appearances. At any of these live events, you'll be surrounded by screaming

teenyboppers trying to present bouquets to their idols. Soak up the sugared quality of the music, wallow in the soothing voices of those stars, and swing and wave and clap and hold candles (or little electric torches), like everyone else around you.

Cantopop is marketed worldwide and sells wherever there are Chinese communities – indeed, the large HK émigré populations in North America provide major concert tour stops for Cantopop singers. As you might imagine, Cantopop also has a big presence on the Internet, with fan pages devoted to all the major stars: to explore, try *www.hkvpradio.com*.

Chinese Rock and Chinapop

Hong Kong's enterprising spirit has broken down the barriers of the Chinese government-approved entertainment industry. A recent trend in Cantopop, which began during the countdown to Hong Kong's return to China, is the proliferation of **Chinapop** – Cantopop-style music with Mandarin lyrics for the market in mainland China, as well as the smaller market of Taiwan. Pop may once have been banned as "pornographic", but it no longer raises an eyebrow in post-reform consumerist China. And Hong Kong-based entertainment corporations have been quick to sign on Chinese artists, to package them and sell them to the global Chinese market.

Although the Chinese market is tapped by the Cantopop industry, only a small percentage of "creative capital" has been injected into the local Chinese rock scene. After all, Hong Kong moguls are keen to keep their toehold and keep mainland Chinese competitors out. China's indigenous rock, although often connected to the Hong Kong/Taiwanese entertainment industry, is a different beast. One which has its traditions in passionate and fiery protest, and which still struggles to preserve a cultural and political self-awareness.

Protest Rock: Cui Jian

Chinese protest-rock really began with singer-trumpeter-guitarist, **Cui Jian**. He is now regarded as the grandfather of **yaogun yinyue** (rock'n'roll), thanks to his hit "Yiwu suoyou" (Nothing to my Name), picked up by worldwide media during the democracy movement of May–June 1989.

The rock scene was non-existent in China until the mid-1980s, when foreign students on cultural exchange brought tapes of their favourite rock and pop music (and their own electric guitars) to the Chinese mainland, and shared them with their fellow students. Their music quickly caught the imagination of Chinese university youths and the urban vanguard. Cui Jian cited the Beatles, the Rolling Stones, the Sex Pistols and Sting as his major influences.

Cui also credits the influence of the Taiwanese singer **Teresa Teng** (1953–95), known to the Chinese by her original name, Deng Lijun. Teng's singing style can be directly traced to Zhou Xuan and 1930s Shanghai. She was probably the most popular Chinese singer of her time: her recordings were circulated in China on the black market from the late 1970s, when such music was officially banned. The reasons for the ban were, in part, that it represented bourgeois ideas such as paid entertainment and social dancing, and that the lyrics were thought to lower sexual morals. The ban was lifted in the late 1980s, when the state loosened its grip on the popular music market, seeing it as a sign of "openness to capitalism".

The openness of China's authorities to Hong Kong and Taiwanese pop, however, goes hand in hand with a suspicion of indigenous Chinese rock. The scene therefore remains low-key, with bands playing in private bars (recently the government did approve one Cui Jian concert at the Beijing Workers Stadium). Top bands at the end of the 1990s included **Cobra** (an all-female band), **Tang**

Teresa Teng's album *I Want Coffee*

Chao (Tang Dynasty), **Heibao** (Black Panther), **Lingdian** (Zero Point), **Zhinanzhen** (Compass), and solo singers **Dou Wei** (formerly of Heibao) and **He Yong**. Although these artists did not take dangerously political oppositional stances, they were outside the Chinese mainstream. To pursue rock music as a career is seen as rebellion, and the music is nothing like Cantopop, with lyrics voicing a youthful angst. Musically, Tang Chao and Heibao leaned towards hard rock (with the former doing a heavy-metal version of the "Internationale"). Lingdian modelled itself on the early Police, especially their lead singer, Zhou Xiaoou, who was a veritable Chinese Sting. The Chinese rock scene has seen the birth and death of thousands of bands in the past decade. Post-Olympic Beijing hotspots include D-22 and Yu Gong Yi Shan, presenting bands as diverse as **Carsick Cars**, **PK14**, **Buyi** and **Hanggai**, the last combining Mongolian singing technique in their rock renditions.

Chinese rock has a strong national flavour: apart from the standard drums, synthesizers, electric and bass guitars, you will hear Chinese instruments such as the **suona** (shawm) and **zheng** (zither), and colourful gongs and cymbals borrowed from traditional opera. Tang Chao was noted for the latter and He Yong's father, a **sanxian** banjo player, played alongside him on stage. In addition, the vocal melody of much Chinese rock has pentatonic and modal qualities that are clearly rooted in tradition. Although excluded from the official media, Chinese rock reaches its audience via mostly legitimate cassettes and CDs that can be bought anywhere in urban and occasionally even rural China.

Modern **Chinapop**, meanwhile, has begun to absorb rock influences to distinguish itself from the staid and restrictive Cantopop formula. **Second Hand Rose**, featuring a male lead who always sings in drag, went from being underground to signing with Hong Kong's Music Nation (yet another entertainment empire). The music of established Chinapop stars Liu Huan, Na Ying and Sun Nan can be heard everywhere there is a CD player or television, paving the way for stadium-filled concerts in large and medium-size cities. The Internet has created yet another channel for dissemination: in 2004, "Laoshu ai Dami" (Mouse Loves Rice) by the unknown Wang Qimin became a chart-topper, receiving six million hits in one day.

Chinese rock and Chinapop have yet to really break through to international markets. Up until the millennium, the only artist to gain a Western contract was **Dadawa** (the Tibetan stage name of Zhu Zheqin), a southern Chinese new-wave

Leslie Cheung: The Dreamboat

Praised by Hong Kong's *Film Comment* as "the dreamboat of Hong Kong singers and a stalwart of the island's vital movie industry", the late **Leslie Cheung** followed a career that closely parallels Hong Kong's pop trends from the late 1970s to the millennium. In 1977 Cheung won a TV talent contest with an English-language rendition of the Johnny Mathis hit "When a Child is Born". He was immediately drafted into television dramas, and later, films.

Cheung was one of the first singers to launch Cantopop as a genre, finding immediate success in 1981 with the title track of his first Cantopop album, *The Wind Blows On* (the music was taken from a Japanese hit). Unusually for Cantopop, Cheung composed some of his own songs and lyrics, which sometimes mixed Chinese and English, though he also performed cover-versions: a Cheung favourite of the 1980s was Rod Stewart's "Sailing".

In 1990 Cheung retired from the Cantopop scene after a series of sold-out farewell concerts at the Hong Kong Coliseum. Devoting himself to his film career, he became the darling of Cannes for his subsequent roles as a homosexual Beijing opera singer in *Farewell My Concubine* (1993) and as a drifter in *Happy Together* (1997).

In the late 1990s, Cheung returned to music, though singing largely in Mandarin. His last public concert series (again at the Hong Kong Coliseum) took place in 2001. Cheung's suicide on April Fools' Day in 2003 – he jumped from the top of Hong

Leslie Cheung

Kong's Mandarin Oriental Hotel – only served to cement his popularity. His death was universally mourned by fans worldwide: every year on April Fools' Day, thousands still gather near the Mandarin Oriental in Hong Kong, where the street is filled with floral bouquets and handwritten notes.

singer who was marketed by Warner in the mid-1990s. Dadawa sings in a high register, in a style akin to traditional opera. Her melodies are full of melisma (some are pure vocalizations) and there is an otherworldliness about her voice that is very appealing. Recording songs tailor-made for her by Chinese pop composer He Xuntian – who also heads the composition faculty at the Shang-

hai Conservatory of Music – she explores (and exploits) Tibetan themes with song titles such as "Ballad of Lhasa" and "The Sixth Dalai Lama's Love Song". These have angered many Tibetans in exile, who see them as a further Chinese appropriation of their country. Dadawa has since explored many other minority traditions, turning herself into a contemporary new-age phenomenon with

Chinese Karaoke

The **karaoke** culture hit China big time in the 1990s and has become an established part of the music scene. Typically, karaoke DVDs will feature Cantopop, Taiwanese pop, US hits, a couple of Chinese rock songs, **tongsu** (state-approved Chinese pop) bestsellers, and, bizarrely, a plethora of disco/pop instrumental tracks of songs from the Cultural Revolution. How about praising Maoist Communist ideals by performing "The East is Red", the revolutionary anthem of 1966–76, with synthesizer accompaniment in front of an inebriated audience? This fun-packed way of sampling Chinese music and a collage of odd, often unrelated images on video screens can cost as little as a single drink (ranging from US$1 to $15, depending on the city and venue), or a little more if you want to take the limelight and sing a few songs yourself. You can find karaoke bars in county towns in remote provinces, with images of Hong Kong on screen, and famous stars frequent VIP karaoke rooms, singing their own songs with their closest friends (one famous venue is Beijing's Party World on Chaoyangmenwai Dajie).

Cui Jian: Breaking Eggs

Cui Jian was born in Beijing of parents of Korean descent. He studied the trumpet at an early age, trained as a classical musician and joined the Beijing Symphony Orchestra in 1981. After being introduced to Anglo-American rock in the mid-1980s, however, he took an independent path and his gritty voice became the benchmark for Chinese rock.

Ostensibly a love song, Cui's "Nothing to My Name" became a democracy-movement anthem, with lyrics that could be interpreted as indirect political commentary:

> I used to endlessly ask
> When will you go away with me?
> You laugh at me always.
> I have nothing to my name.
>
> I want to give you my dreams
> And also my freedom.
> You laugh at me always.
> I have nothing to my name.
>
> I must tell you, I have waited too long.
> I'll tell you my last request:
> I'll hold your two hands
> To take you away with me.

The song evoked a memorable complaint from General Wang Zhen, a veteran of the Long March: "What do you mean, you have nothing to your name? You've got the Communist Party haven't you?"

Even though Cui's lyrics have always been ambiguous, his voice has occasionally been muffled in the 1990s. A nationwide tour was cancelled halfway through because of his stage appearances in a red blindfold – the colour of Communism. He upset the authorities again with his recording of "Nanni Wan", a revolutionary song closely associated with the Communist Party and its ideals, glorifying Chinese peasants and their contribution to society. Cui's rock version was interpreted by many as a challenge to – or mockery of – the Communist establishment.

Like most of China's rockers, Cui became more introspective as the 1990s progressed. His 1994 album *Hongqi xiade Dan* (Eggs under the Red Flag) reflected the shifting concern of China's youth from politics to the realities of earning a living. But the powerful title-track neatly encapsulated both:

> Money floats in the air,
> We have no ideals.
> Although the air is fresh,
> We cannot see into the distance.
> Although the chance is here,
> We are too timid.
> We are wholly submissive,
> Like eggs under the red flag.

On his 1998 album, *Wuneng de Liliang* (The Power of the Powerless), Cui continued to explore similar themes with songs such as "Bird in the Cage". His 2006 CD *Geini Yidian Yanse* (Give You Some Colours, meaning "teach you a lesson") reveals a mellower artist. Over the years, Cui has had successful tours in Europe and the US. When the Rolling Stones eventually toured China in 2006, Cui Jian accompanied their performance of "Wild Horses", while in 2007 he made his first-ever visit to Taiwan, appearing at the Ho-Hai-Yan Rock Festival.

her 2006 release "Seven Days". Dadawa's success has prompted clones such as **Sa Ding Ding**, who also exploited Tibetan themes in her 2008 debut album *Alive*. The "indie" label is a new phenomenon in China, the largest being **Modern Sky** (*www.modernsky.com*), which has helped nurture a new generation of bands, singers, and even electronica-savvy DJs. The company has already made headway in the international market, and within China, Modern Sky artists are active on university campuses.

DISCOGRAPHY China/Hong Kong | Pop and Rock

A *Spinal Tap*-inspired "mockumentary", *Sei Dai Tin Wong* (The Heavenly Kings) is a spoof on the Chinese music industry. About a fictional boy-band called Alive, the film is directed by movie-star Daniel Wu in his debut as a director. Depicting piracy, greedy agents and fanatical fans, as well as the paparazzi, its interactive site (*www.alivenotdead. com*) plugs you right into the excitement of Asian entertainment media. The film has been touring the international film-festival circuit since 2006, but a DVD is available. Catch it if you can!

⊙ **Hottest Cantopop Selection**
Polydor, Hong Kong
This 1998 compilation features hits by an impressive array of singers, among them Jacky Cheung, Leon Lai (both of "Four Heavenly Kings" fame), Alan Tam and Faye Wong. There's a song from *Snow Wolf Lake* (see next entry) and the last track features a television soap-opera theme song, the genre that started Cantopop way back in the 1970s.

⊙ **Snow Wolf Lake**
Polygram, Hong Kong
The original 1997 cast album of the first Cantopop musical, which despite the megastar power of Jacky Cheung (who played the "wolf"), was only a moderate success on stage. A fairy tale about nature, love and death and partly set in Vienna, the inspiration may have come from Broadway but the numbers are almost all written in Cantopop mode, pulled together by sophisticated pop orchestral arrangements.

Eason Chan

A singer-songwriter, Chan is one of the most accomplished of current Cantopop singers. Having studied in Britain, his English is great – and you can hear that in the various songs with English phrases.

⊙ **Shall We Dance? Shall We Talk?**
Music Plus, Hong Kong
The music on this 2001 album shows tremendous depth and sophistication. "Shall We Dance?", a tribute to Fred Astaire and Ginger Rogers, features lush orchestration recorded by the Hungarian Symphony Orchestra. Another track draws its themes from *2001: A Space Odyssey*, with Richard Strauss's *Also Sprach Zarathustra* opening the song.

Jacky Cheung

With his buttery voice and impeccable Cantonese diction, Jacky Cheung is the best singer of the "Four Gods" of Cantopop and is famous for his love songs. A superb crooner and award-winning actor, he has appeared in many notable films, such as Tsui Hark's *A Chinese Ghost Story*.

⊙ **Jacky in Concert 93**
Polygram, Hong Kong
Recorded at the Hong Kong Coliseum in 1993, this live double CD has all the atmosphere of a real Cantopop event, complete with screams, laughter and whistles. Unlike studio-recorded Cantopop, which is heavy on synthesized sound, this extravaganza employed not only a full band but a string quartet (and sixty dancers). Plenty of spine-tingling ballads and photos of Jacky's elaborate costumes.

Leslie Cheung

One of the founding fathers of Cantopop, the late Leslie Cheung remains revered by many thousands of fans.

⊙ **Guangrong Suiyue (Glorious Years)**
Capital Artists, Hong Kong
This 1998 greatest hits compilation is a testament to early 1980s Cantopop, containing Cheung's legendary Japanese remakes "The Wind Blows On" and "Monica", plus "Love of Years Past", a Joseph Koo–James Wong collaboration. Complete with accompanying VCD.

Anita Mui

Mui came to prominence in 1982 after winning a TV-sponsored talent contest and went on to act in films (notably *Rouge*, opposite Leslie Cheung, and *Rumble in the Bronx*, with Jackie Chan). Having completed a record-breaking series of concerts just a month before, Mui died of ovarian cancer in December 2003.

⊙ **Qingge (Love Songs)**
Capital Artists, Hong Kong
Prime romantic Cantopop, this 1998 double CD contains all of Mui's biggest hits – including film and TV theme songs – from 1983 to 1997. Based on a pentatonic melody, the theme song from *Rouge* is one of the most beautifully eerie examples of the genre (Mui played a ghost in the film).

Softhard

A pair of leading Hong Kong DJs who pioneered the short-lived genre of Cantorap. Bubble-rapping without a hint of violence, they transformed an American genre into something so entertaining that they were mobbed by young female fans everywhere they appeared in 1993–94. The duo reunited in 2006 with greater commercial than artistic success.

⊙ **Guangbodao Sharen Shijian (Broadcast Drive Killer)**
Cinepoly, Hong Kong
Thanks to strong beats and even reggae rhythms, this 1995 album is still refreshing. Lyrics range from safe sex ("Bring

519

Your Own Bag"), political satire ("Absolute China" samples the "Internationale"), to a retirement-home anthem ("Gala Gala Happy"). And since Cantonese is a tonal dialect, the inflections of the words give the lyrics a built-in melody.

China

⊙ **Shanghai Lounge Divas Vols 1 and 2**
EMI, Hong Kong
A selection of the best Shanghai – and later Hong Kong – hits of yesteryear, these double-CD compilations include remastered historical recordings by Zhou Xuan, Bai Guang, Ge Lan, Li Xianglan, Zhang Lu, Bai Hong and Wu Yingyin (the extra CDs are updated remixes). Transport yourself back to the dance halls and nightclubs of half a century ago, and follow the lyrical melodies.

⊙ **A Tribute to Teresa Teng**
Hubei/Jinlin/Golden Melody Music, Hong Kong/Beijing
Taiwanese singer Teresa Teng (1953–95) was among the most popular singers in China from the late 1970s on. Her hits were so well-known that the rock generation grew up knowing her songs, despite government bans in force until the late 1980s. This album features Chinese rock bands – including Tang Chao, Heibao and Lunhui – doing covers of her most popular songs and jamming together on the final track.

Cui Jian

Born in 1961, Cui is the remarkably young "grandfather" of Chinese rock. He began his musical career as a trumpeter in the Beijing Symphony Orchestra and his trumpet-playing is always impressive, remaining a distinctive feature of his performances. Cui renamed his band "Balls under the Red Flag" ("Eggs under the Red Flag" in the original Chinese) in 1993–94, a self-mocking allusion to the powerlessness of rock musicians.

⊙ **Hongqixia de Dan (Eggs under the Red Flag)**
EMI, Hong Kong
This innovative 1994 album marked Cui's arrival on the global rock scene, adding timbres such as Chinese flute, suona, trumpet, saxophone, gigantic ritual drums, gongs and cymbals. Wind-player Liu Yuan crosses seamlessly from one instrument to the next, creating memorable riffs. Although less varied musically than Cui's earlier albums, the lyrics echo China and its youth in their search for an identity in the 1990s.

⊙ **Yiwu Suoyou (Nothing to My Name)**
EMI, Hong Kong
The most important album in the short history of Chinese rock music, and one that is also musically appealing to non-Chinese listeners. Cui has a real melodic gift and an urgency in his voice, bringing a Chinese flavour to some of the music with a zheng (zither) and other Chinese instruments.

Ding Wei

After graduating from the Shanghai Conservatory of Music as a composer, Ding Wei was signed by BMG in the late 1990s, but now records and produces her own albums in her Beijing studio.

⊙ **Dear Ding Wei**
BMG, Taiwan
A ballad singer who really captures China's contemporary ethos, Ding Wei enjoys a sizeable following in her own country. She has also branched out into television and film music. Her voice is well-calibrated and the songs are refreshing (think Tori Amos).

Heibao

This five-strong band is one of the best of the post-Cui Jian generation and toured the US in 1999. They write great lyrics on love lost and found, frustrations at changing social values and urban loneliness, and feature expressive ballads and playing (especially from drummer Zhao Mingxi and lead guitarist Li Tong).

⊙ **Heibao III: Wushi Wufei (No Right No Wrong)**
JVC/ISRC, China
Heibao's third album was a bestseller in 1995 and remains a classic. The band's post-Dou Wei lead singer, Qin Yong has a much more resonant voice than Cui Jian, but puts a deliberate Cui-style strain into his vocal delivery – a trademark of Chinese rock angst. There's a distinctly Dylanesque feel to the opening verses of "For All People Who Love Us".

Second Hand Rose

After releasing their debut album on an independent label, Second Hand Rose were signed by Music Nation, and lost some of their rougher rock edges. Nevertheless, this is still a fun band, especially live, as the lead singer Liang Long always appears in drag and heavy makeup.

⊙ **Yule Jianghu (Entertainment World)**
Music Nation, China
Despite being more commercial, this 2006 album still contains plenty of innovation: Chinese gongs and cymbals, *erhu* and traditional wind-instruments (*guanzi* and suona) feature prominently. The lyrics comment ironically on urban life, especially the title track, which is about the darker sides of the entertainment world.

Wang Lee Hom

Signed by a Taiwanese record company as a teen idol, this classically trained Chinese-American then conquered Hong Kong (with his good looks) and China (with his tremendous musicality). Singing fluently in English, Cantonese and Putonghua – often flipping between them in mid-sentence – he has since made outstanding Chinapop albums that constantly cross boundaries, combining traditional and modern elements. In 2008 Lee Hom made his film debut as an actor in Ang Lee's *Lust, Caution*.

⊙ **Gai Shi Ying Xiong (Heroes of Earth)**
Sony/BMG, Hong Kong/China/Taiwan
Although most of this 2005 album follows the Chinapop formula, the title-track and the rap song "Zai Mei Bian" (By the Peony Tree) use elements of traditional *kun* opera. The instrumentation includes Chinese two-stringed fiddle (erhu) and electronica alongside the standard guitars and keyboards.

PLAYLIST
China/Hong Kong | Pop and Rock

1 ABSOLUTE CHINA Softhard from *Broadcast Drive Killer*
You don't have to know Cantonese or Putonghua, the sounds are just wild and fun. Softhard even sampled a famous phrase – "I don't know anything, I don't know" – from the Gang of Four trial in 1980.

2 SAN NIAN Li Xianglan from *Shanghai Lounge Divas Vol. 2*
The mellifluous voice of this legendary singer born in Manchuria of Japanese descent, who later became the darling of 1940s Shanghai, was captured in this song.

3 LANG XIN GOU FEI Second Hand Rose from *Yule Jianghu*
A great mix of folk, rock and pop, featuring the captivating, androgynous voice of lead singer Liang Long.

4 SHALL WE DANCE? Eason Chan from *Shall We Dance? Shall We Talk?*
Hong Kong Cantopop at its most innovative, this song broke the mould by introducing Hollywood glamour and style.

5 YIWU SUOYOU Cui Jian from *Yiwu Suoyou*
Stemming from the folk-singing tradition of the northwest region, this revolutionary cry still moves and shakes. Students protesting in Tiananmen Square were listening to it every day.

6 ROUGE Anita Mui from *Love Songs*
Mui had a deep, soulful voice, and this Cantopop hit shows her at her best. Taken from a legendary film which won international acclaim for Mui as an actress.

7 GAI SHI YING XIONG Wang Lee Hom from *Gai Shi Ying Xiong*
Combines rap, hip-hop and Peking opera, while Lee Hom sings and speaks in Putonghua, Cantonese and English. A veritable smorgasbord of instrumentation and rhythmic patter.

8 QIN AI DE Ding Wei from *Dear Ding Wei*
A contemporary-style ballad, produced and composed by Ding Wei herself. An ideal way to appreciate Putonghua, with vowels and consonants all melting into each other.

9 JIUZUI DE TANGE Lunhui from *A Tribute to Teresa Teng*
The Teresa Teng original was much more lyrical, but Wu Tong's distinct vocal and narrative style and his mastery on Chinese wind instruments match his band Lunhui very well on this 1996 rock remix.

10 DANG NIAN QING Leslie Cheung from *Glorious Years*
Written by Joseph Koo with lyrics by James Wong, this theme song from John Woo's 1986 film *A Better Tomorrow* is a Cantopop classic. The harmonica (a Wong favourite) adds large doses of bittersweet nostalgia.

Hawaii

sweet sounds of the islands

The late Hawaiian megastar Israel Kamakawiwo'ole

From the moment Europeans first reached the Hawaiian islands in 1778, Hawaiian music has been world music, constantly adapting and changing as new waves of immigrants and visitors have introduced their own traditions and instruments. A century ago, indeed, Hawaii provided perhaps the earliest world music craze of all, when its distinctive slide-guitar sound and hula dances were taken up first across the US and subsequently all over the world. But despite the islands' lengthy entanglement with tourism, their music has continued to follow its own highly individual path. **Greg Ward**, author of *The Rough Guide to Hawaii*, surveys the scene.

Although Hawaii was formally annexed by the United States in 1898, and has been the fiftieth state since 1959, it remains in many ways distinctly un-American. The archipelago lies deep in the Pacific, nearly 4000km west of San Francisco; its original inhabitants were of Polynesian origin, and its musical roots stretch back to traditional Polynesian chants and drum dances. Its famous **hula dance** and **mele** (poetic chant) were forms found throughout Oceania – a music that was essentially voice and drums.

Roots

Ancient Hawaiians were devotees of meles, but they had no specific word for "song". Meles were composed for various purposes, ranging from lengthy genealogies, put together over days of debate, through temple prayers, to lullabies and love songs. Unaccompanied chanting was known as **mele oli**; when the chant was accompanied by music and dance, the combined performance was known as **mele hula**.

Musical instruments included gourds, rattles and small hand- or knee-drums made from coconuts. A larger kind of drum, the **pahu**, made by stretching shark skin over hollow logs, was said to have been introduced by Hawaii's final wave of settlers from Tahiti, around 1400; legend tells of the voyagers booming out this menacing new sound as they pulled towards shore.

As a rule, the tonal range was minimal and the music monotonous, though occasionally bamboo pipes may also have been played. Complexity was introduced by the fact that the dance, the chant and the music were all likely to follow distinct rhythmic patterns.

The telling of the story or legend was of primary importance: the music was subordinate to the chant, while the feet and lower body of the dancers served mainly to keep the rhythm and their hand movements supplemented the meaning of the words. Dancers underwent training in a *halau hula* – part-school, part-temple – and performances were hedged around by sacred ritual and *kapus* (taboos).

Missionaries and Immigrants, Kings and Queens

When the first Christian missionaries reached Hawaii in the 1820s, they saw hula as a lascivious manifestation of the islands' general lack of morality, and set about destroying what they saw as a "heathen" culture. Their own church music, however, served to introduce Western instruments, concepts of harmony and vocal styles. Inspired by the *himeni* they learned from the first Hawaiian hymn book, local musicians were soon creating their own songs in the Western tradition.

The population of Hawaii changed rapidly, as a massive influx of settlers and sailors, whalers and labourers was matched by a precipitous decline in its indigenous peoples, exacerbated by new diseases. Specific immigrant groups exposed the islands to a wide range of musical influences: thus

---

The Ukulele: a Portuguese Gift to the Pacific

Now so prominent in Hawaiian (and Polynesian) popular music, the **ukulele** is essentially the *braguinha*, a small four-stringed instrument that originated in the Portuguese island of Madeira (and a variant of the more common *cavaquinho* of the Portuguese mainland).

In September 1878, 120 Madeira islanders arrived in Honolulu as Hawaii's first Portuguese immigrants, ready to work on the sugar plantations. They were joined a year later by another four hundred settlers, including one **João Fernandes**, who had borrowed a braguinha from a fellow passenger and learned to play it during the five-month voyage. When the boat finally arrived in Honolulu, the passengers celebrated their safe arrival with a dance, and Fernandes played the instrument, to the delight of both settlers and Hawaiians. He soon became a fixture at balls and parties and eventually formed a group, which played on occasion for the Hawaiian royalty.

A fellow passenger on that same boat, **Manuel Nunes**, opened a shop where he made and sold braguinhas – by now renamed ukuleles. He and other craftsmen began to use local kou and koa wood and before long the braguinha became a national instrument. The Hawaiian word ukulele literally means "jumping flea", and is said to originate from the nickname of a small Englishman, Edward Purvis, who played the instrument with quick, jerky movements.

Ad Linkels

the Mexican cowboys (known as *paniolos*) who came to work the cattle ranches of the Big Island introduced guitars, while Portuguese sugar farmers arrived from the Azores with the braguinha, an early form of **ukulele** (see box on p.523).

Towards the close of the nineteenth century, and championed especially by the Hawaiian royal family, a new and distinctive kind of Hawaiian music emerged. The coronation in 1883 of King David Kalakaua – the so-called "Merrie Monarch", who had his own ukulele group, and co-wrote Hawaii's national anthem, "Hawaii Pono'i" – was marked by the first public hula performance in two generations. Kalakaua also recruited bandleader Henry Berger from the Prussian army to establish the Royal Hawaiian Band, a brass band that performed arrangements of Hawaiian songs as well as marches and ragtime compositions. For good measure, Berger also taught yodelling, which helped to add an idiosyncratic twist to Hawaii's already developing tradition of falsetto singing, in which the **hai**, or break in the voice between falsetto and normal singing is emphasized rather than hidden.

King David was succeeded in 1891 by his sister, Queen Liliuokalani, who remains the most celebrated of all Hawaiian composers. She was deposed by a US-inspired coup in 1894 and subsequently imprisoned in her own palace on charges of trea-son; small wonder that she is remembered for such haunting songs as the much-covered "Aloha Oe".

Thanks in part to their strong association with the much-mourned royal family, and despite the fact that they already mixed Polynesian forms with musical influences from all over the world, the songs from this era are now thought of as typifying traditional Hawaiian music.

Slack Key and Steel Guitar and Hapa Haole

In conventional guitar tuning, strumming the open strings produces a discord. In the late nineteenth century, however, Hawaiians started to retune the strings to create a harmonious chord. A whole range of open tunings developed, in a new style they called **ki ho'alu or slack key**. A further innovation soon followed, with the development of the **Hawaiian steel guitar** (*kika kila*), leading to a new guitar sound and a new guitar posture, with the instrument played on the lap or on a stand. The steel guitar took over from the violin or flute as the lead instrument in Hawaiian music, while slack key strumming maintained the rhythm.

After the islands were annexed by the US in 1898, the **hapa haole** (half-white) style of song began to emerge, as Hawaiian musicians strove

Slack Key and Steel Guitar

Slack key guitar, as its name suggests, involves slackening or loosening the strings in order to re-tune the guitar to achieve an open chord. Thus, if you take the standard guitar tuning (from high to low – EBGDAE) and slacken the first string from E to D, the fifth from A to G and the sixth from E to D, you get a tuning of DBGDGD. This produces an open chord of G when strummed, while placing a finger (or steel bar) across the strings at the fifth and seventh frets will give you the other two chords you'll need for any three-chord song, like a blues.

This is one of the simplest tunings. During the pre-war craze for the music, Hawaiian guitarists made an art out of different tunings, some of which were closely guarded secrets. They also developed two ways of playing with open tunings – slack key and steel guitar. Slack key involves picking the strings, with the thumb providing a constant bass while the other fingers play a melody on the upper strings.

The fact that Portuguese guitars often used steel rather than gut strings, and the creation of the National Steel guitar in the 1920s, to aid Hawaiian musicians in the days immediately before electric amplification, have obscured the reality that the "steel" in **steel guitar** is simply another word for "slide". And although many people think that slide guitar originated with blues musicians, it's a Hawaiian invention. **Joseph Kekuku**, an eleven-year-old Oahu schoolboy, realized in 1885 that if he slid a solid object up or down the strings after plucking or strumming them, the chord would slide up and down in a glissando. He tried all kinds of objects before settling on the hand-tooled steel rod that gave the style its name; further experiments led him to play seated, with the guitar placed horizontally across his lap, and also to raise his strings so the steel would not touch the frets.

The first electric guitar – a Rickenbacker nicknamed the "frying pan" – was actually a Hawaiian lap-steel guitar made in 1931. In the US, this developed into the pedal-steel guitar, with its mechanical devices to change tunings and volume. This became the characteristic sound of US country music, though it is less favoured by Hawaiian musicians.

both to please visiting Americans and to win audiences on the mainland. Though hapa haole is often characterized as a form in which English or nonsense lyrics were set to traditional Hawaiian melodies, in truth the music too was heavily influenced by whatever was currently popular in the US. Indeed, at the peak of its popularity, much of it was actually written on Tin Pan Alley by songsmiths who had never visited the islands. Thus, while the earliest hapa haole songs owed much to ragtime, they shifted towards jazz and blues by the 1920s, big-band sounds in the 1930s, and even rock'n'roll by the late 1950s. Often there was a comedy or novelty element, in which the real or supposed sounds of the Hawaiian language were exaggerated for comic effect, as with the "Hawaiian War Chant".

At San Francisco's Panama-Pacific Exposition in 1915, the new Territory of Hawaii invested heavily in its pavilion. America fell in love with the sounds of Hawaii, and by 1916 more Hawaiian records were being sold in the US than any other genre. This was one of the earliest world music crazes, outdoing even the tango in popularity. Groups such as the **Kalama Quartet** introduced four-part falsetto harmony singing with two steel guitars playing counterpoint, while other recordings featured virtuoso Hawaiian steel guitarists.

Another cultural collision occurred as these musicians discovered jazz. **Bennie Nawahi** was a key figure in this early fusion – a steel-guitar wizard who performed with equal dexterity on mandolin and ukulele. He started out as a busker, then worked a cruise ship, and developed an extraordinary showmanship, playing the steel guitar with his feet and the ukulele behind his head with one hand. Nawahi played the vaudeville circuit with huge success in the 1920s, was dubbed "King of the Ukulele", and launched a recording career that was to stretch nearly fifty years.

During his early days, Nawahi also worked with steel guitarist **Sol Ho'opii**, who played a technically brilliant synthesis of American jazz and traditional Hawaiian music. Early in his career, Ho'opii developed the tuning that led to the development of the pedal steel guitar and the Nashville country-

music sound. He too recorded extensively, from 1925 up until the 1950s, and his advanced use of chords, harmony and phrasing had a lasting effect on a whole generation of island musicians

Inspired by such figures, musicians the world over explored the Hawaiian sound. From the 1930s, Hawaiian-style bands and steel-guitar players appeared as far afield as Britain and Germany, Japan, India and Indonesia. In London, for example, the **Felix Mendelssohn Hawaiian Serenaders** were a hugely popular radio and dancehall act, performing a mix of traditional Hawaiian, hapa haole, jazz and popular songs.

Rock'n'roll, Tourism and the Sons of Hawaii

As tourism to Hawaii increased, Hawaiian music became an essential part of the experience. Visitors were lured to the islands by such means as the "Hawaii Calls" radio programme, broadcast around the world from 1935 onwards from the Moana Hotel on Waikiki Beach, and entertained once they arrived by grass-skirt revues that emphasized entertainment over education.

An even greater tourist boom followed after Hawaii became the fiftieth US state in 1959, and the simultaneous arrival of jet travel from the US. By the time Elvis Presley filmed *Blue Hawaii* in

Sol Ho'opii

1961, young Hawaiians were turning away from steel guitar towards rock'n'roll. And yet the seeds of a revival of the old-style music were already being sown.

The major figure in the resurgence was slack key guitarist **Gabby Pahinui**. By the late 1950s, his virtuosity, honed through twenty years' of playing in Waikiki's clubs and revues, meant he was ready to step to the forefront and play slack key as a lead rather than simply a rhythm instrument. He joined with ukulele virtuoso **Eddie Kamae** to form the **Sons of Hawaii**, and together they championed the traditional music of Hawaii, performed with respect as well as joy.

Kamae travelled the remote backwaters of the islands in search of old songs and performers, seeking out Hawaii's heritage before it was lost forever. So few people speak fluent Hawaiian that only elders and experts could tell him the true meaning and pronunciation of many lyrics. Hawaiian is an intensely poetic language, and traditional songs often work on several levels, perhaps celebrating some beautiful place while also hymning the beauty of a loved one, all overlaid with sexual innuendo.

During the 1970s, many of the bands that sprang up in the wake of the Sons of Hawaii began to write new songs about contemporary island issues, as well as performing older Hawaiian-language material. This new generation was also hugely inspired by growing feelings of pan-Polynesian unity (which have had the side-effect of meaning that even the hula now considered most authentic has come to incorporate elements from elsewhere in Polynesia, especially Tahiti and Samoa). Among groups who came to prominence during this Hawaiian Renaissance were the **Sun-**

Eddie Kamae

day Manoa, consisting of Peter Moon alongside brothers Robert and Roland Cazimero, and **Hui Ohana**, another trio comprising Ledward and Nedward Kaapana and Dennis Pavao. By now, the hapa haole label had become an embarrassment to younger musicians, and ceased to be applied to newly made music, although arguably Hawaiian music remained as susceptible as ever to outside influences, including the soft rock then sweeping California.

Meanwhile, Gabby Pahinui had left the Sons of Hawaii for a solo career that saw him team

Iz: 20 May 1959–26 June 1997

In 1997, the Hawaiian music scene lost its biggest star. **Israel Kamakawiwo'ole**, who sang in the Makaha Sons of Ni'ihau before going solo in 1990, died of respiratory difficulties in a Honolulu hospital. During his twenty-year career, "Iz" epitomized the pride and the power of Hawaiian music. His extraordinary voice adapted equally well to political anthems, love songs, pop standards and Hawaiian reggae rhythms, while his personality shone through both in concert and on record. Like his brother Skippy – also a founder member of the Makaha Sons – Iz eventually succumbed to the health problems caused by his immense size. At one point, his weight reached a colossal 757 pounds; he needed a fork-lift truck to get on stage, and could only breathe through tubes. His strength in adversity did much to ensure that he was repeatedly voted Hawaii's most popular entertainer, and after his death he was granted a state funeral. His enduring legacy will be his four solo albums – *Ka Anoi* (1990), *Facing Future* (1993), *E Ala E* (1995), and *'n Dis Life* (1996). His medley of "Somewhere Over the Rainbow" / "What A Wonderful World" has become a staple of movie and TV soundtracks, while his haunting rendition of "Hawai'i 78" became the anthem of campaigners seeking to restore native Hawaiian sovereignty.

up with other slack key legends like **Atta Isaacs** and **Sonny Chillingworth**; with his four sons, Martin, Bla, Cyril and Philip; and, famously, with **Ry Cooder**. Gabby's recordings with Cooder crossed slack key over into the US mainstream for the first time. Worn out by a life of hard labour and hard liquor, however, Gabby died aged 59 in 1980.

Hawaii Live

The best way to experience Hawaiian music is to hear it on its home ground, though it can be hard to track down the finest practitioners amid the tourist revues. A handful of hotels and restaurants, especially in Honolulu and Waikiki, feature authentic performers, and there's a rich year-round programme of festivals. There's also always the radio: **KINE** (105 FM; *www.hawaiian105.com*) and **KCCN** (110.3 FM; *www.kccnfm100.com*) are both full-time Hawaiian music stations with online streaming, while **Hawaiian Rainbow** (*www.hawaiianrainbow.com*) and **Mountain Apple** (*www.mountainapplecompany.com*) are online only.

Venues

Oahu

Banyan Veranda Sheraton Moana Surfrider, 2365 Kalakaua Ave, Waikiki Once home to the Hawaii Calls radio show, this open-air beach bar offers steel guitar and hula dancers nightly from 5.30–7.30pm, followed by small Hawaiian ensembles from 7.30–10.30pm.

Chai's Island Bistro, Aloha Tower Marketplace, Honolulu Smart Thai restaurant that books the very finest Hawaiian musicians, including regular appearances by the Cazimero Brothers and Hapa. Nightly from 7–8.30pm.

Duke's Canoe Club, Outrigger Waikiki This rumbustious beach bar with surf-hero decor features music (including slack key), nightly from 4–6pm and 10pm–midnight.

Honey's at Ko'olau, Ko'olau Golf Club, Kaneohe Ukulele wizard Eddie Kamae is joined by other big names for Sunday-afternoon jam sessions at this unlikely hangout on the Windward (east) coast. Sundays 3.30–6pm.

House Without a Key, Halekulani Hotel, Waikiki Music and hula dancing from a classic ensemble, on the beach as the sun goes down, 5–8.30pm nightly.

Moana Terrace Waikiki Beach Marriott, Waikiki. A consistently good roster of Hawaiian musicians perform at this open-air, third-floor cocktail bar, but the biggest treat is on Thursdays, when family and friends of the late legend Auntie Genoa Keawe hold an informal jam session. Nightly at sunset.

Big Island

Beach Tree Bar and Grill, Four Seasons Resort, Kona Local musicians perform Tuesdays–Thursdays & Sundays.

Palace Theater, Hilo The venue of choice for big-name Big Island artists to perform one-off concerts.

Maui

Napili Kai Beach Resort The place to see Hawaii's finest slack key guitarists. Regular performers at the Wednesday-evening "Masters of Hawaiian Slack key Guitar" concert series include Dennis Kamakahi, George Kahumoku Jr, Cyril Pahinui and Ledward Kaapana.

Festivals

April/Big Island: Hilo's wonderful Merrie Monarch Hula Festival draws major *halau* (hula troupes) from all the islands, the US and Japan. Book well in advance.

May/Oahu: The Brothers Cazimero host a May Day event at the Waikiki Shell with a mix of traditional and contemporary acts.

May/Molokai: The Molokai Ka Hula Piko Hula festival, celebrating the birth of hula on the island, is held on the third Saturday in May at Papohaku Beach Park.

June/ Maui: Kihoalu slack key guitar festival, Maui Arts and Cultural Center, Kahului.

July/Big Island: Big Island Hawaiian Music and Slack Key Festival is held at Hilo on the third Sunday in July.

September–October/all islands: Held successively on each island in turn, Aloha Week features grassroots performances with free concerts, parades and parties.

Hawaiian Music Today

Typically, today's Pahinui-inspired Hawaiian groups consist of guitars, ukulele, steel guitar, bass and vocals, but no drums. Most mix traditional music, with country, rock covers, pop, pan-Pacific styles and reggae. The musicians don't tour outside of the islands too often, and most discs are local releases, so you really have to go there to hear Hawaiian music at its best. Hula remains an integral part of performance; Gabby himself was an expert dancer, for example, and musicians will often appeal to the audience "does anyone know the hula to this one?"

Among the finest currently active performers are falsetto harmony group **Na Palapalai**; **Hapa**, consisting of sweet-voiced singer-guitarists Barry Flanagan and Nathan Aweau, plus chanter Charles Ka'upu; the Maui-based *kumu hula* (hula teacher) **Kealii Reichel**, equally acclaimed for a succession of fine albums and his charismatic performing style; and **Amy Gilliom**, whose crystal-clear voice brings out all the beauty of her classic Hawaiian-language material, backed by quick-fire guitarist Willie K. Eddie Kamae still performs regularly as well, though most of his energies in recent years have gone into making compelling documentary movies about Hawaiian music and musicians.

Newer names to look out for include **Raiatea Helm**, a young female falsetto singer from Molokai; **Kaumakaiwa Kanakaole**, a chanter, dancer and singer from the Big Island who is keeping up a great family tradition; and **Jake Shimabukuro**, now a mature version of the teenage ukulele whiz-kid who fronted the group Pure Heart.

DISCOGRAPHY Hawaii

Rounder, the Boston-based American roots-music label, is one of the few US record companies to feature Hawaiian music. Another is Dancing Cat Records, based in Santa Cruz, California, whose series of "Slack Key Master" CDs has grown to include pretty much every slack key guitarist of note. Also in California, Cord International are steadily re-releasing classic Hawaiian recordings from yesteryear. For Hawaiian music online, see *www.mele.com*.

⊙ **Hawaiian Drum Dance Chants: Sounds of Power in Time**
Smithsonian/Folkways, US
A record of the earliest known forms of Hawaiian music, some of it from old cylinder recordings. As close as you can get to the stuff Captain Cook would have heard.

⊙ **Steeling Round The World**
Harlequin, UK
This utterly delightful, if bizarre, chronicle of how the world went mad for Hawaii features Hawaiian-esque performances recorded in the 1930s and 40s by soloists and groups from as far afield as Sweden, Indonesia, Greece, Hungary, India, South Africa and New Zealand, plus home-grown Hawaiian acts like the great Kanui and Lula, recorded in Paris in 1934.

⊙ **Vintage Hawaiian Music: The Great Singers 1928–1934**
Rounder, US
A hugely seductive collection of slack key classics compiled by Bob Brozman, featuring Mme Riviere's Hawaiians, the all-male Kalama's Quartet and Sol Ho'opii Trio, and lots more besides. Plenty of falsetto vocals and steel guitar.

⊙ **Vintage Hawaiian Music: Steel Guitar Masters 1928–1934**
Rounder, US
A companion volume highlighting the golden age of acoustic steel guitar. Tracks from Tau Moe, Sol Ho'opii, King Benny Nawahi and Jim & Bob the Genial Hawaiians.

⊙ **Vintage Hawaiian Treasures Vol. 7**
Cord International, US
A reissue of the first commercial releases of slack key from the 1940s, including seminal Gabby Pahinui cuts. Other standout tracks include Tommy Blaisdell pieces that stomp along like barrelhouse blues.

Mahi Beamer

All-round musician Mahi Beamer comes from one of Hawaii's great musical dynasties, and has spent much of his fifty-year career playing piano and guitar, as well as dancing hula, but he's most renowned for his stunning falsetto voice.

⊙ **The Remarkable Voice of Hawaii's Mahi Beamer In Authentic Island Songs**
Hula Records/EMI Music, Hawaii
Seldom can an album have been more accurately named. Originally released in 1959, it showcases the extraordinary male falsetto of Mahi Beamer, performing songs exclusively in Hawaiian and mostly written by his grandmother. The hauntingly minimal backing includes traditional hula implements.

Sol Ho'opii

Sol Ho'opii (1902–53) made his fame in the US after stowing away on a liner to San Francisco. Most famous for his classic acoustic recordings, he switched to electric guitar in 1934, then in 1938 became an evangelist and gave up secular music.

⊙ **Sol Ho'opii – Vol. 1: 1926–1929; Vol. 2: 1927–1934**
Rounder, US
Classic tracks from probably the most influential of all Hawaiian steel guitarists. Both albums are recommended.

HAWAII

Israel Kamakawiwo'ole

As described on p.526, the solo career of Hawaii's much-loved megastar Iz was cut short by his tragically early death, but his mid-1990s success raised the profile of Hawaiian music around the world.

⊙ **Facing Future**
Mountain Apple Company, Hawaii
Iz's 1993 masterpiece is an unqualified delight, showcasing the extraordinary power and resonance of his voice on "Hawaii 78", his sprightly ukulele work on island favourites like "Amaama" and "Henehene Kou Aka", his take on Hawaiian reggae-pop on the hit "Maui Hawaiian Suppa Man", and his delicacy on "Somewhere Over The Rainbow". *E Ala E* (1995) was a worthy follow-up.

Edith Kanaka'ole

Born in 1913, Edith Kanaka'ole trained as a child in the art of oli (poetic chant) and hula, and went on to epitomize the synthesis of ancient and modern traditions and values in Hawaiian culture.

⊙ **Ha'aku'i Pele I Hawaii**
Hula Records, Hawaii
The strongest available commercial recording of traditional chant. A major factor in Edith Kanaka'ole's art is her fluency in the Hawaiian language – and her understanding of the oli's hidden meanings.

Lena Machado

As she grew up in Honolulu a century ago, Lena Machado's adoptive parents disapproved of her singing. Nonetheless, she cut her first record in 1927, and enjoyed a fifty-year career. Her ukulele playing, jazzy songwriting and unique falsetto style still hold an elevated place in Hawaiian hearts.

⊙ **Hawaiian Song Bird**
Cord International, Hawaii
Most of this lovely CD dates from 1962, but it also includes a few earlier numbers, including Lena's 1927 debut and a version of her trademark "Keyhole Hula" backed by Sol Ho'opii in 1935. Her falsetto is a constant joy, especially on her own sassy, jazz-tinged material like "E Ku'u Baby Hot Cha Cha".

Bennie Nawahi

Bennie Nawahi (1899–1985) was a key figure in the acoustic era of Hawaiian guitar. He played the cruise ship and vaudeville circuits with his brother before pursuing his own career as singer and "King of the Ukulele".

⊙ **Hot Hawaiian Guitar 1928–1949**
Shanachie/Yazoo, US
A lovely disc of Nawahi performing jazz-inflected Hawaiian numbers with fellow master Sol Ho'opii.

Gabby Pahinui

Slack key guitarist Gabby Pahinui (1921–80) has been the biggest influence on modern Hawaiian music from the moment he released the first commercial recording ever of slack key, "Hi'ilawe", in 1946. He is remembered for his solo guitar skills and arranging for multiple guitar combinations, as well as his unique vocal qualities and on-stage personality.

★ **Gabby Pahinui Hawaiian Band Vols 1 and 2**
Edsel, UK
Breathtaking discs of slack key guitar, steel guitar and bass from a band of legends – Sonny Chillingworth, Atta Isaacs and the Pahinui Brothers, Cyril, Bla, Phillip and Martin – as well as Gabby himself and a little fairy dust from Ry Cooder.

BMG

The Pahinui Brothers

The Sons of Hawaii

Conceived in the late 1950s by Gabby Pahinui and Eddie Kamae, who were subsequently joined by bassist Joe Marshall and steel guitarist extraordinaire David "Feet" Rogers, the Sons Of Hawaii spearheaded a revolution in Hawaiian music. Although Pahinui left in the early 1970s, and the other original members have now all passed away, Kamae has continued to use the name on and off, and a roster of greats have passed through the ranks, including slack key maestro Dennis Kamakahi.

⊙ **The Folk Music of Hawaii**
Panini Records, Hawaii
This totally irresistible classic of Hawaiian music was the fruit of a reunion of the Sons' original quartet in 1971, joined by Moe Keale on ukulele and vocals. Everything is just perfect, from Gabby's singing and playing to the long-lost songs rediscovered and burnished by Eddie Kamae, but if one

element makes it truly transcendent, it's the staggeringly understated yet precise fills provided by "Feet" Rogers on steel guitar.

Tau Moe Family

Born in Samoa in 1908, steel guitarist and singer Tau Moe embarked on an astonishing fifty-year world tour in the 1920s. His wife Rose joined Mme Riviere's Hawaiians (Tau and his three uncles) in 1927, for a tour of Asia that lasted from 1928 until 1934; they then toured India and the Middle East until the late 1940s when they moved to Europe, performing there through the 1950s and 60s, and finally retired back to Laie on Oahu in the late 1970s. Then,

in the mid-1980s, Moe ordered his own 1929 recordings from American steel guitarist Bob Brozman. Brozman called up and discovered to his amazement that it was the self-same man.

WITH BOB BROZMAN

★ **Remembering the Songs of Our Youth**
Rounder, US

Although this amazing disc dates from 1989, it reprises the songs, style and instrumentation of the 1920s and 30s. Octogenarian Rose Moe handles the lead vocals, backed up by Tau and their two kids Lani and Dorien, and the hugely talented Bob Brozman on steel-guitar parts learnt from Tau.

PLAYLIST
Hawaii

1 OUA OUA Kanui & Lula from *Hawaii's Popular Songs*
Strange but true: this irresistible 1929 slice of ukulele-backed doggerel was a number one hit in Austria in 2001.

2 LEPE ULAULA Sam Alama & His Hawaiians from *Hawaii's Popular Songs*
A lovely early Hawaiian classic, this time from 1936.

3 HI'ILAWE Gabby Pahinui from *Legends of Falsetto*
The first major recording by the father of contemporary Hawaiian music, from 1947.

4 ALIKA Genoa Keawe from *The Waimea Music Festival*
Deliciously enjoyable 1974 live performance by one of Hawaii's greatest falsetto singers.

5 HAWAII '78 Israel Kamakawiwo'ole from *Facing Future*
The signature tune of the sadly-missed Iz, a rousing call for Hawaiian sovereignty from his seminal 1993 album, *Facing Future*.

6 KAWAIPUNAHELE Keali'i Reichel from *Kawaipunahele*
Maui-based hula teacher Reichel has released a

succession of beautiful albums since this first 1994 hit.

7 HANAIALI'I NUI LA EA Amy Hanai'ali'i Gilliom from *Hawaiian Tradition*
The leading modern exponent of the falsetto tradition, on fine form in 1997.

8 PUPU HINUHINU Mahi Beamer from *The Remarkable Voice of Hawaii's Mahi Beamer in Authentic Island Songs*
This beautiful lullaby, written by his grandmother Helen Desha Beamer, is the highlight of sublime falsetto singer Mahi Beamer's landmark 1959 album.

9 E KU'U BABY HOT CHA CHA Lena Machado from *Hawaiian Song Bird*
This perfect 1962 blend of Hawaiian charm with jazz pizzazz finds "Hawaii's Songbird" in fine falsetto form.

10 KU'U PETE The Sons Of Hawaii from *The Folk Music of Hawai'i*
Only Hawaiian speakers would know this is actually a song about a donkey but, like everything from the Sons' classic early 1970s recordings, it's infectiously joyful.

India | Indian Classical Music

how to listen – a routemap of india

Ravi Shankar teaching George Harrison in India, 1966
Angel Records

In August 1971, George Harrison, Eric Clapton and Bob Dylan were among the gala attractions of the the Concert For Bangladesh, held in New York to raise money for the stricken nation. Ravi Shankar and Ali Akbar Khan were to perform a *jugalbandi* (duet), and according to Indian classical practice, they began tuning up on stage. As the musicians finished, they were greeted with a ripple of clapping which swelled into full-scale applause. Good-naturedly, but with an edge, Shankar observed "if you appreciate the tuning so much, I hope you'll enjoy the playing more". The story has been repeated enough times to have become a mantra, but the moral remains: don't travel in Indian music reading a Western map. Robert Maycock and Ken Hunt get out the compass.

To enjoy a concert of Indian classical music, it helps a lot to have knowledge of the basic traffic rules. Most concerts are solo vehicles for an instrumentalist or vocalist, and unlike most Western music, which is harmonically based, Indian music is monodic, with a single melody line. At first, the soloist explores the road – or *raga* – alone, with just a drone accompanying; later they are joined by rhythm players – most commonly *tabla* drums. Throughout a performance, which may last for several hours, there is an altogether un-Western attitude to time. You may begin by staring at a rug on an empty platform – all part of the preparation.

Settling In

When they are ready, the performers come on in reverse pecking order: drone instruments first, accompanists (including percussion) next, the big name last. **Tuning** will take just as long as it needs and will sometimes merge imperceptibly into the first forays of the performance itself: a few notes played in earnest, some more tuning, then a leap forward.

If the accompanying drum is a **tabla**, the player's first act is usually to bring out a hammer and tap obsessively at the tuning wedges at the edges – not a repair job, just making sure the high-pitched drum is exactly in tune with the soloist. Later on, tabla players frequently retune on the hoof, hammering away without losing the rhythm.

Underlying the main instruments will be a stringed instrument called a **tanpura**, which provides a steady drone through the performance. It is often played by a student of the soloist who is given the honour of learning at close quarters – compensation for having to strum thanklessly through a concert of several hours.

Setting Off

It's one note at a time to start with – and a 'note' is a many-splendoured thing, approached from above or below and fantastically ornamented. Rhythm is a hidden asset. Watch the percussionist sit listening as the melody unfolds, often for half an hour or more. Gradually the pitch will rise; then fall, then move up again. The chosen **raga**, or theme (see below), is taking shape. You are listening to the initial exploration of a musical scale and a state of feeling, inseparably fused to make a raga. Each has its own way of ascending and descending, its special decorative features and its local variants, which depend on the performance tradition the musician belongs to.

In north Indian (Hindustani) music, a raga usually opens with the **alap** section; in south Indian classical music this is called *alapana*. Played by the soloist in free rhythm with tanpura or drone accompaniment, it is the alap which reveals most about a musician's mastery and prowess. It's the most bewildering part for an uninitiated Western listener, but the part that educated Indian audiences love best – its length is often contracted or extended accordingly. Since the alap is the distilled essence of the raga, it can also function as the sole movement in a recital.

In a fine alap the singer or player will conjure up phrase after phrase of intense beauty, vocally acclaimed by ardent followers. Singers reinforce the emotion by vigorously tracing shapes with their hands and gesturing towards the listeners – a visual translation of the music and the very act of communicating it. Feedback from the audience is important, and a gesture or eye contact returned from a listener who obviously appreciates the music is highly valued. Many musicians lament Westernized shows of approval (now encountered even in the subcontinent), when audiences will burst into applause during a solo as if they were in a jazz concert. Traditional etiquette calls for murmurs of approval like *wa-wa* (excellent) and the raising of hands.

As the alap progresses, ornamentation grows more complex or flamboyant, the intensity builds, and a climactic high note is achieved – a moment whose emotional and musical power is greater for the long, long delay. The music winds down briefly, and then introduces a slow, almost lazy pulse for the so-called **jor** section. The speed of articulation gradually increases, melody evolves, and the pace stirs. Rhythmic animation follows, and the speed steps up in discreet stages. There is a brilliant climax, the music stops and everybody applauds. Still, though, the percussionist sits silent. It's just traffic lights – a temporary halt.

Gear Changes

Once the pace drops, solo and percussion start to interact. If the percussionist is a respected virtuoso, the soloist will briefly turn accompanist and let drumming skills take centre stage. Then the soloist steps on the gas. This part of the performance will usually be based on a **gat** (a fixed musical figure), and you will hear the same melodic phrases come back again and again. It is also based on a rhythmic cycle with hugely long "bars" of four, seven, eight, thirteen – anything up to sixteen beats.

Drum-maker, Vrindavan, Uttar Pradesh

First beats of a cycle are key moments, and you will see performers glance or nod at one another to keep in touch, or using a system of downturned and upturned palms of the hand to count. Listeners to recordings learn to pick up the shape of the cycle by ear alone, usually from the emphases of the deeper-toned drum strokes. When the music is playing with intricate patterns and cross-rhythms, the first beat is always the point of culmination, especially thrilling when reached after a process that has lasted for some time.

As the speed and excitement grow, the musicians become spontaneous and competitive as they move into the climactic **jhala** section. Quick-fire "question and answer" exchanges between instrumentalists can occur towards the end – a great opportunity for witty performers, especially when a drum imitates a melody instrument. Somebody may launch another composition or change rhythmic cycle if there's a chance of heightening the action still further. Tabla players often rattle off compositions as a speech-song – a virtuoso performance in itself – and then imitate themselves on the drums. To round off, the performers will usually deliver a set-piece cadence which plays elaborately with threefold repetitions – emphatically conclusive when played with panache.

Southern Routes

It's a subtly different experience if the musicians belong to the traditions of **south India**. Performances are shorter and they rarely linger in a slow tempo for any length of time. Rhythmic patterns, melodic decoration and the instruments themselves are different, and the moments of high excitement are more evenly spread through the music. More is fixed and calculated; improvisation is more subtle. Body language varies too: whereas a north Indian performer will acknowledge a colleague's passing inspiration with a gentle shake of the head, nothing less than a full-scale wobble from shoulders upward will do in the south. But the underlying principles and motivations have plenty in common, and the fundamental idea of profoundly exploring a mood and a set of notes still drives the music.

The opening piece, called a **varnum**, is comparable to an *étude* in Western classical music and allows the musicians to warm up. An invocatory piece ordinarily follows, both devotional and a request for a blessing. The pace of a recital builds with contrasting **ragams** and **thaalams** (see below), often of increasing complexity and always of increasing intensity, using short **kritis** (Hindu hymns), of between three and ten minutes.

The exception is the fuller **ragam-thanam-pallavi** form. This sequence opens with pure, unmetred melody (confusingly, ragam is alapana by another name) before moving into *thanam* (the jor equivalent). The sequence concludes with rhythmically measured improvisations on the *pallavi* theme, the heart of a composition whose voiced or unvoiced lyrics inform the performance.

The pallavi may be unfamiliar to the percussionist and the principal soloist therefore states the theme, following that with lines based around it which are bounced back by the percussionist or the violin player, who usually accompanies the main melodicist in *Karnatic* music. The ensemble elaborates on the theme before the principal soloist restates the main theme to bring the pallavi to a close. After the ragam-thanam-pallavi, musicians will frequently perform *tillana* (a text of meaningless syllables, often voiced as rhythm mnemonics, similar to scat singing in jazz) or *javali* (an erotic song form), both of which are far lighter than the kriti form.

The Highway Code: Raga and Tala

Raga is a word woozy from the anaesthetic of familiarity – borrowed and adapted by many languages. The word is of Sanskrit origin, meaning "that which colours the mind", and it is the fundamental organizing principle and melodic paradigm of both the Hindustani (north Indian) and Karnatic (south Indian) musical systems. In the south, it goes under the name of **ragam**.

Raga is an immensely intricate system of scale-like melodic patterns and their various permutations. There are some two hundred main ragas, each defined by its unique combination of scale-pattern and dominant notes, by the specific rules to be obeyed in ascending or descending, and by certain melodic phrases associated with it. Both the Hindustani and Karnatic systems share a love of melodic invention within the routes and boundaries that each raga proscribes. This is coupled with a joy in the complexities of **rhythm**. Karnatic music, for example, boasts the most sophisticated rhythmic organization on the planet in **thaalam**. The northern equivalent for such a rhythmic cycle is known as **tala**. Each combines mathematical intellectuality with rugged muscularity.

The hallmark of the subcontinent's two classical music systems is the judicious management of melody and rhythm in the form of raga and tala, ragam and thaalam. In a concert, a convention (attributed to Ravi Shankar) is for the principal soloist to announce the raga's name, and to give information about it and the tala or talas about to be played.

Absolutely central to a great performance is the way in which the musicians imbue the raga or ragam with a sense of their own identity or personality while observing strictly defined rules. Improvisation occurs as a matter of course. Great musicians capture the spirit of their age as certain ragas capture the mood of their optimum time. Their art is not so much to describe a mood as to create and explore it with renewed sentiments and inspiration.

Raga Road

All ragas stem from 72 parent ragas known as the *janaka* or *melakartha* ragas. Each of these boasts a character so developed and distinctive that the attuned ear can discern the raga's mood or moods. Identifying or naming the raga may take longer – paralleling the experience in European music when it comes to naming a particular polka or concerto. Ragas have counterparts called *raginis* whose alliance to a primary raga corresponds to a Hindu deity's female consort. Mathematicians have calculated that some 34,776 raga permutations can be developed from this melakartha raw material. Even if mere hundreds are in common circulation, the nightmare is compounded by the variants that can be factored in.

A raga must have a minimum of five notes in a fixed sequence in ascending and descending order. This order is immovable. Within each raga certain notes are stressed and, in a music without harmony, it's the relation of the notes of the raga to each other, and to the "tonic" *sa*, that defines its mood.

Traditionally, many ragas have a set **time of day** for playing, the product of age-old analysis and scrutiny, especially from studies in the south. The evening raga Marwa, for example, has a range of moods: it touches upon devotion, peace and heroism. The psychological characteristics of particular notes combine to develop a personality – perhaps a feminine blush, a sky blue or an uplifting sensation. In raga the seasons too carry cultural resonances. *Megh* means cloud and hence Raga Megh belongs to the monsoon season, while another popular raga, *Hemant*, simply means winter. Down the centuries the sense of a raga belonging to a particular hour or season became codified.

An example of the creative use of these moods is *The Call of the Valley*, the best-selling album by Shivkumar Sharma (*santoor*), Brijbushan Kabra (guitar) and Hariprasad Chaurasia (flute). In this

CALL OF THE VALLEY
Shivkumar Sharma, Brijbushan Kabra and Hariprasad Chaurasia

HEMISPHERE

recording's scheme the day's course is matched by a cycle of ragas. *Todi's* mood reflects the early morning. *Bhairavi's* time is late morning, *Shri* is of the afternoon, *Pilu* is day turning to evening and *Kannada* suits the night. It is peculiar how rarely raga names are explained and listeners tend not to observe such niceties as the time or season appropriate to a raga. Diehards lament this erosion of tradition.

Mishra, another commonly encountered word, indicates a mixed raga conventionaly requiring a less formal exposition. Other names give clues to authorship: for example, several variants of popular ragas are popularly attributed to **Miyan Tansen**, a pre-eminent musician in the court of the Mughal Emperor Akbar. In tribute their names include Miyan or Miya to indicate the variant's author. The *surbahar* maestro **Imrat Khan's** *Rag Miya ki Todi and Rag Bilaskhani Todi* album (on Nimbus) illustrates this principle with two variants of Todi, the first credited to Tansen, the second to Tansen's son, **Bilas Khan**. For a thorough guide to Hindustani ragas, invest in Nimbus's invaluable *Raga Guide*.

Tala: Make Way for Rhythmic Cycles

Tala – also *tal* or *taal* – is the northern name for a rhythmic cycle corresponding to the southern thaalam. They are terms heard at nearly every concert or read in most CD booklets. Tala combines with raga to make music somewhat as cadence joins with words to create speech; it does not mean rhythm. Each of the 100-plus talas builds over a specific number of *matras* (beats) before generally coming to a point of release called – in northern India – the *khali*. Tension and release is a science in Indian percussion.

The south's mathematicians pondered thaalam permutations for centuries, but in general only a dozen or so favourites will pop up in a performance. although in percussion summits the number of variants used can be bewildering. Initially listeners may find the time periods over which talas unfurl baffling so the best approach is to treat them as opportunities for stretching the imagination – even a newcomer can experience multiple rhythmic frissons during a tabla solo.

Improvisation

A raga's notes are inviolate, with a prescribed order of ascending and descending. If an errant note slips in, the mood may shift, be dissipated or shatter. The performer's **melodic invention** must stay strictly within the codes – a Western parallel might be the way jazz players have to make their melodic invention fit the harmonic pattern of the song they are improvising on. On some occasions great virtuosi will raise the game by deftly quoting from, or alluding to, another raga, so long as doing so adds or heightens insight into the mood or exposition. More often they will introduce set melodic compositions that have been passed down through their tradition, or which they have composed themselves.

Both the melodicist and rhythmist will tap into rhythmic cycles of astonishing finesse based on centuries of musicological and mathematical study. Talas may be alternated to create variety. As with melody, improvisation is not the only kind of spontaneous performance. Short, fixed rhythmic compositions are often presented by percussionists in the course of a recital, particularly when the tabla is itself the solo instrument. South Asian extemporisation, by being so highly structured can make Western improvisation appear airy-fairy.

Indian music also has a lighter performance form called *ragamala* (*ragamalika* in Karnatic terms), meaning "garland of ragas", in which a performer moves through a series of different ragas in one piece (see box overleaf on ragamala paintings). In order not to detract from the seriousness of a recital, a ragamala performance will tend to end a concert. A soloist may similarly close a concert with a *dhun*, or a *deshi* (folk) air, characterized by a lightness of mood or emotion and fewer intellectual strictures. Typically dhuns will be set in core repertoire Hindustani ragas such as Bhairavi, *Kafi, Khammaj* or Pilu. Hariprasad Chaurasia's *Four Dhuns* (Nimbus) is unusual in being an album focusing on these.

Driving School: Gharanas

Indian musicians are expected to employ their musical wit to reveal new insights, even within core repertoire items, but an individual's interpretative style will generally adhere to rules handed down the generations. Before notation or recording this was exclusively oral, often transmitted down bloodlines. If a child showed promise, more accomplished teachers would be sought out to round and develop the child's education.

The southern system is renowned for producing child prodigies, often with whispered agendas of reincarnation. In the north the oral transmission of knowledge went from *guru* to *shishya*, teacher to disciple. The teaching could be severe, as indicated by shishya's root in the Sanskrit for "punish". This system gave rise to the Hindustani **gharana** tradition.

Traditionally gharanas (schools) took their names from their location – examples being **Bhendi Bazar** (a district of Mumbai), **Kirana** (near Saharanpur in Uttar Pradesh) and **Maihar** (Madhya Pradesh). Gharana means a "school of playing" in much the same way as people talk about schools of painting. Each gharana's particular playing style was jealously guarded and its musicians were highly proprietorial about their tradition. For all that, Hindustani music is changing, with some musicians' names now being cited rather than the name of their gharana.

Ragamala Paintings

Ragamala paintings, frequently used on CD covers of Indian music, were produced in India from the fourteenth to the nineteenth century. Ragamala (literally "garland of ragas") is the name given to collections of these paintings, typically thirty-six in number, each depicting a different raga (or ragini – the so-called "consorts" of the ragas). In musical terms, the word is used to describe a player moving through a range of ragas within a single piece.

Each miniature illustration, painted on paper or palm leaves, acts as an interpretation of raga music in images, aided by a traditional set of poems. Although ragas are abstract musical entities, poets and painters sought to personify them. They described situations where the emotions evoked by a particular raga could be expressed. Deities, birds, animals, flowers and lovers are shown in a spectrum of emotions ranging from disappointment and jealousy to longing and blissful union.

This painting (in Mughal style, from the early seventeenth century) depicts **Ragini Asavari**, a slightly plaintive mode said to originate in a snake-charmer's melody. The raga is characterized by a five-note (pentatonic) ascent and seven-note (heptatonic) descent. Asavari is designated as a consort or wife of **Raga Shri** in this raga-ragini system (there were several) used by many ragamala painters. But the scale and melodic outline of Shri and Asavari are quite different. Asavari is a morning raga and should create a gently erotic atmosphere, at the same time tender and melancholy. In the painting, a dark-skinned girl from a tribe of snake-charmers is sitting on a rock in the mountain forest. Dressed in a leaf skirt, she communes with a cobra while thinking about her absent lover. Although painters from different regions may have varying interpretations of ragas and raginis, this depiction of Asavari is fairly standard.

Jane Harvey

Ashmolean Museum

Ragamala painting

The Harballabh Sangeet Sammelan

"Music conferences" (look out for the words *sammelan* and *samaroah* too) are fixtures in the Indian music calendar. Many such gatherings are long established, but the claim to host the subcontinent's longest continuous celebration of this kind goes to Jalandhar in India's Punjab. First held in 1875 and now called the **Harballabh Sangeet Sammelan**, the event has long since outgrown its village origins. It takes place every December, attracting the cream of Hindustani musicianship – and increasingly the south's finest musicians too. And it is free.

Baba (Father) Harivallabh founded the celebration in the village of Bajwara, northeast of Jalandhar. The Punjab was, and is, a crossroads for devotional music, packed with *sant* (Hindu and Sikh saint) and *pir* (Muslim holy man) shrines and associations. Harivallabh was a follower of Swami Tuljagiri, who inculcated scripture, Sanskrit and *sur* (melody) into his disciple. To mark the first anniversary of his guru's death in 1875, Harivallabh inaugurated a celebration in his honour – a common practice across the subcontinent's religions, perhaps most familiar through annual *'urs* (death anniversary) celebrations for Sufi mystics or *qawwali* maestros. Harivallabh died in 1885, but his disciple Tolo Ram took the helm, and single-handedly maintained this celebration of vocal music into the early 1920s. (In keeping with the times, the festival only welcomed instrumental music in 1929.)

In 1908 Vishnu Digambar Palusker (1872–1931) happened by and was so moved that he asked to sing. Steeped in the Gwalior tradition, he was completely unknown there in the days before mass communications. He blew everyone away. Through appearances like his, the gathering's reputation spread. When Gandhi attended in 1919, welcoming crowds delayed his journey from Amritsar to Jalandhar. With time running out, three of the age's major soloists – Bhaskar Rao, Ram Krishna Bua and Krishna Rao – gave an egoless trio performance in his honour.

The Harballabh Sangeet Sammelan grew and grew. Under a succession of custodians, it has given musical platforms to generations of musicians of the highest renown, including Vishnu Digambar Palusker, Ram Krishan Bajaj, Bade Ghulam Ali Khan, Imdad Khan, Omkar Nath Thakur, Ravi Shankar, Pannalal Ghosh, Vilayat Khan, Hariprasad Chaurasia, Amjad Ali Khan, Vishwa Mohan Bhatt and Kala Ramnath.

Like most of the subcontinent's *mela* (festival or fair) celebrations, musical gatherings generally happen on specific dates in calendrical or lunar cycles. Think about timing trips to coincide with them. Many have their own websites. And check regional tourist information sites for leads.

Ken Hunt

So Where Are We?

Clearly in the democratic, technological India of today, the gharana system has certain disadvantages. Budding musicians of great brilliance may not have the means or inclination to spend years of their life cloistered away in a fusion of a medieval guild and a Victorian apprenticeship. The system can be seen as nepotistic, although defensible when considering the gifts of a child who has lived, breathed and slept the life of a musical family. The northern system is undeniably sexist, and women have a hard time getting anywhere except as singers; even daughters of famous players have been rare on the scene until Aruna Narayan and Anoushka Shankar. Some have not even tried to get in, but instead have gone to the West to study Western music.

Schools of music and a more open, conservatoire-like system look like the way ahead, as they have been in the West where it is now possible to study at least the elementary stages at one or two colleges in the UK and, particularly, the Netherlands. Traditionalists will deplore their development as undermining the intense master-and-pupil relationships that the virtuosi of the past knew. Perhaps they should take heart from the experience of Western classical music, where a more open system has led to far more musicians with a far wider spread of abilities, but no apparent drop-off in skill and imagination at the top of the tree.

The gharanas are likely to keep going alongside newer methods, but these have already affected the way classical Indian music is performed. There are more **instruments**, for one thing. The Kashmiri folk zither, the santoor, has been made a classical concert instrument almost single-handed by **Shivkumar Sharma**, one of the great players by any measure. The *sarangi* was liberated by **Ram Narayan** from its subservient role in supporting singers. Saxophones, mandolins and guitars have followed.

In the twentieth century the existence of limited-length records and fixed half-hour broadcasts by All India Radio brought a new awareness of

537

clock time into performers' minds. Short, event-packed alaps are one outcome; so, less happily, is the growing number of performers who seem able to fill an hour with continuous music but not to deliver a coherent, impactful realization of musical imagination. There is also concern about a perceived attitudinal undercurrent among musicians, whereby a minority of performers believe that when they perform abroad before non-Indian audiences anything goes and they will be applauded no matter how they play. However, what is also quite clear is that serious international interest is at an unprecedented high, and the top players are now taking their art to the world's capitals to be applauded and appreciated without so much as an ounce of artistic compromise.

India | Hindustani Instrumental Music

ragas and riches

Sitar Master Ravi Shankar
Carolyn Jones

The Hindustani classical music of northern India is one of the world's great art forms. It is immensely complex in structure and performance, yet if you surrender to its artistry, its effect can be emotional and astonishingly direct. Once the privileged preserve of a society's elite, the music has now touched the hearts and minds of people around the world. Ken Hunt investigates.

What many people casually refer to as Indian music is actually the classical music of the north of the Indian subcontinent, embracing the expansive cultural and religious diversity of India, Pakistan, Bangladesh, Nepal and even Bhutan. *Karnatic* (south) Indian music is older and represents the Hindu tradition before the Afghan and Mughal invasions of the north created one of the great hybrid musical styles of the world.

Players and Instruments

Hindustani music has been characterized as the "house with four rooms" of the Indian proverb, catering to the physical, mental, emotional and spiritual. It is in many respects much more than a concert music, more indeed than the sum of its players. However, the players provide a way in to understanding both instruments and styles – and, it must be said, Hindustani music is replete with the names of its illustrious musicians.

Among this pantheon, sitar maestro **Ravi Shankar**, born in 1920, remains a good starting point for listeners in the West. Ravi Shankar's career has often encouraged a merging of his identity and achievements with the larger canvas of history, and his finest work is the stuff of immortality. Indeed, if he had lived before recorded music, or

even before musical notation, the oral tradition of earlier generations would likely have preserved his music. As it is, his career has been comprehensively chronicled and he has recorded prolifically, acquiring a worldwide reputation as a great interpreter, innovator and popularizer of Indian music in general and the **sitar** in particular.

In India, vocal music tends to receive most attention – notably the classical styles of *dhrupad* (see p.560) and *khyal* (see p.561). In the West, **instrumental music** is the top draw and the sitar stands above all other instruments (in India it shares the top ranking with *sarod*). It is probably the sitar's sonorities that work the charm. The sympathetic strings that resonate the notes of the *raga* behind the melody notes are common in Indian music, but particularly strong on the sitar.

Alongside Shankar himself, **Nikhil Banerjee** and **Vilayat Khan** are the best-known sitarists of the post-Independence years, responsible for innovations in sitar design and exponents of a singing style of playing called *gayaki ang* which each seems to have developed independently. Performers such as these have made Hindustani music a primary colour on the world music palette.

For those that find the sitar's incessant buzzing hard to take, the **bansuri** (bamboo flute) is a first-rate alternative introductory instrument, especially in the hands of **Hariprasad Chaurasia**, **Ronu**

Navras

Bansuri player Hariprasad Chaurasia

Majumdar or **G.S. Sachdev**. And so, too, is the **sarod**, an instrument which has a star equivalent to Ravi Shankar in the veteran **Ali Akbar Khan**, a towering figure who provided the West with Hindustani music's first major concert recitals and first long-playing record. Among *rasikas* – connoisseur-listeners – it is no exaggeration to say that when it comes to instrumentalists, Ali Akbar Khan remains the absolute benchmark. No less a figure than Yehudi Menuhin hailed him as the greatest musician on the planet. The magnificent Amjad Ali Khan is another sarodist of rare distinction.

Historical Sources

If **Karnatic** music, now found in southern India, is the Hindu and Sanskrit rootstock, then Hindustani music is the product of grafting Muslim and Persian influences onto that root. Historically, the ebb and flow of cultural tides which washed over the subcontinent caused immense changes.

Music, poetry and dance forms such as *kathak* had played important roles in the Hindu Vaishnavite cult (based on the worship of Vishnu). With the arrival of **Muslim** conquerors in the thirteenth century and the creation of the Mughal Empire in the sixteenth century, life over a broad stretch of northern territory was changed forever. Traditionally, Islam frowned on the integration of worship with such frivolities as sculpture, the pictorial arts, music and dance. In such manifestations they detected pleasure-seeking which distracted and detracted from true religion. The arrival of the Mughals (alternatively Moguls or Moghuls) brought profound changes to religion, the arts and gastronomy alike. Yet the Delhi Sultanate, which preceded it as the major political force in the north, had already seen a stylistic synthesis of Islam and Hinduism, of north and south. Its most notable musical practitioner was the legendary **Amir Khusrau** (1253–1325). The far-seeing Khusrau melded Persian and Sanskrit, Islamic and Hindu, *maqam* and raga, classical and light classical elements and incorporated them into new music forms. *Qawwali* and khayal are popularly attributed to him.

The spirit of Khusrau's more conciliatory age had long departed when the Mughals began consolidating their empire. Countless Hindus fled southward to avoid Muslim persecution and conversion at the point of a sword. Since the Mughals never penetrated the southern heartland, to this day south Indian culture, music and dance remains suffused with the life force of Hinduism. Karnatic music never evolved into the propertied

man's plaything that Hindustani music became. It stayed at once devotional, classical and everyday.

The Mughal empire was at its peak between 1526 and 1707, during which time intermarriage caused something of an Indianization of Mughal culture. During the reign of the reforming emperor **Jal ad-Din Akbar** (1556–1605), who married a Rajput princess (amongst other wives), the arts flowered, and the name of one of his court musicians in particular is still spoken with awe: **Tansen**.

It is said that Tansen was ordered to sing Deepak, a raga capable of causing lamps to ignite. Against his will he agreed, but ensured his daughter Saraswati sang the rainy season raga Megh in an adjacent palace wing at the same time. When he sang, the lamps lit of their own accord, as predicted, but with such a ferocity that it was only the downpour caused by Megh which saved him from burning alive. Stories such as this permeate Hindustani music's fabric. Few musicians treat them as the literal truth. Most view them as accretions of mythology or as musicological metaphors. Tansen's variations on raga themes remain popular today: they might be likened to Bach's *Goldberg Variations*. The *surbahar* and sitar player Imrat Khan's *Rāg Mīyā kī Todī/Rāg Bilāskhānī Todī* (Nimbus, 1989), consisting of variations on Todi by Tansen and Tansen's son Bilas, illustrates this perfectly.

The Mughal empire lingered on nominally until 1857, though it was a spent force after 1707. Nevertheless, its linguistic, literary and musical legacy persists, handed down the generations from *guru* (teacher) to *shishya* (disciple). Nowadays, whether a musician follows an Islamic, Hindu or other path, it is this cross-cultural tradition which sweetens the breath of Hindustani music. As the sitarist **Rais Khan** puts it, "Music has got a different religion which doesn't go with any religion that is made by human being. It is not Hindu. It is not Muslim. The music doesn't have anything to do with Parsee or Sikh, with Christianity or Judaism. It has got its own religion which has come directly from God."

The Twentieth Century

In the first half of the twentieth century, royal courts existed in abundance, even if they no longer thrived, and many great musicians first saw service as court musicians. Appreciating Hindustani music came to be a badge of intellectual refinement, and such connoisseurship was displayed prominently, for it embodied wealth, power, discernment and exclusivity. But as the power of the maharajahs and nawabs declined, so did their patronage. Fortunately Aakashvani or **All India**

Hindustani Instruments

Stringed instruments

The best-known Hindustani instrument is the **sitar**, said to have been invented, or rather developed from the **veena**, by **Amir Khusrau**, in the thirteenth century. They are generally made from teak, with the main resonator made from a seasoned gourd. Many sitars also have an extra gourd at the top of the neck which further amplifies the sound. Played with a wire plectrum, the instrument has six or seven main strings, of which four are used for the melody and the other two or three to supply a drone or rhythmic ostinato. In addition there are nine to thirteen sympathetic or *taraf* strings which give the sitar its distinctive "jangling" sound. Around twenty moveable (usually brass) frets are arranged on the long neck and these can be slid to adjust to the raga's required tuning. The player can alter the pitch by pulling the string sideways, causing the gliding portamento so characteristic of Indian music and the **gayaki** (singing) style popularized by **Vilayat Khan** and **Ravi Shankar**, two of the best-known sitarists of recent years. Other leading names include Shahid Parvez, Rais Khan, Debu Chaudhuri and Purbayan Chatterjee.

The **surbahar**, whose name derives from the Urdu for "springtime of notes", is effectively a bass sitar and is played in the same way. Said to have been developed by **Sahibdad Khan**, the great-grandfather of Vilayat and Imrat Khan, it produces a deep, dignified sound. The neck is wider and longer than that of the sitar and its frets are fixed. Because the instrument is larger and has longer strings, the sound can be sustained for a longer time, and the range of the portamento is wider. **Imrat Khan** is the best-known player, although he played both surbahar and sitar. The most mysterious living player is **Annapurna Devi** (b. 1927), who has shunned publicity for decades. During the late 1940s and early 1950s she performed highly acclaimed surbahar-sitar duets with her then-husband Ravi Shankar.

The **sarod** is a descendant of the Afghani *rubab* (no relation of the Arab fiddle of that name). Smaller than a sitar, it is made from one hollowed-out piece of teak with a goatskin-covered soundbox. It has a metal-clad fingerboard and no frets. There are eight or ten playing strings, plucked with a wooden or coconut-shell plectrum. Four carry the melody; the others are used to accentuate the rhythm. The strings are stopped with the left hand, using either the fingertips or the fingernails. There are also a dozen or so sympathetic strings lying underneath the main strings. The sarod has a strong, crisp and characterful sound. Its leading modern exponents have been **Ali Akbar Khan** (the *khalifa*, or head, of the Maihar gharana, to which Ravi Shankar also belongs) and **Amjad Ali Khan** (from a famous dynasty of sarod players in Gwalior). Other names to look out for are **Buddhadev Das Gupta**, **Aashish Khan** (son of Ali Akbar Khan), **Brij Narayan** (son of *sarangi* maestro Ram Narayan) and Ken Zuckerman (an expert Medieval lutenist and a sarod pupil of Ali Akbar Khan).

The **rudra vina** (also called the *bin* or *been*) is an ancient string instrument associated with Saraswati, the goddess of learning. It's a fretted stick zither with two large gourd resonators towards each end of the bamboo sound board which forms the body of the instrument. The lower resonator is rested on the ground, the other on the left shoulder, and the fretboard is angled across the chest. It is plucked with metal fingerpicks. The rudra vina once held an exalted place in the pantheon of Hindustani stringed instruments (Rudra is another name for Shiva, its supposed inventor), but its influence has declined since its heyday, which stretched from medieval times to the nineteenth century. It has some twenty-four frets and seven strings; four carry the melody, two are *chikari* strings for rhythm and the last is a *laraj* or drone string. The rudra vina's voice is rich in overtones. Leading players include **Asad Ali Khan** and **Bahauddin Dagar**. The **vichitra vina** is an unfretted cousin (the counterpart of the Karnatic *chitra vina* or *gottuvadyum*) played with a slide.

The **sarangi** is a fretless bowed instrument with a broad fingerboard and rather awkward-looking belly carved out of a single block of wood and covered with parch-

Sarod maestro Amjad Ali Khan and his sons Amaan and Ayaan

ment. There are three or four main strings of gut and anything up to forty metal sympathetic strings. Some claim it to be the most difficult instrument to play in the world. Certainly the technique is highly unusual. While the right hand wields the bow as on a violin or cello, the strings are stopped not by the fingertips of the left hand, but by the nails and flesh immediately above them. The sarangi is capable of a wide range of timbres and its sound is likened to that of the human voice, so it is usually used to accompany vocal recitals. Originally this was its only function, but it transcended its courtesan or folk associations to attain the status of a solo instrument in its own right, due to the accomplishments of **Sabri Khan**, **Sultan Khan**, **Ramesh Misra**, **Ram Narayan** and his daughter **Aruna Narayan**.

The **santoor** is a hammered zither of trapezoid shape, thought to be Persian in origin. It has over a hundred strings, pegged and stretched in pairs, parallel to each other. Each pair of strings passes over two bridges, one on each side of the instrument. The strings are struck by two wooden sticks which curve upwards at the end. The santoor has only been accepted in the last forty years as an instrument for classical music, thanks to the virtuosity and persistence of its leading player **Shivkumar Sharma** and his son **Rahul Sharma**.

The **surmandal**, sometimes spelt *swarmandal*, resembles a zither and is used by vocalists to accompany themselves in performance. Even though its primary function is to provide the drone, singers sometimes also play melodic splashes on this instrument.

The **tanpura** (or *tampura*) is the stringed instrument that provides a steady drone on the tonic and other important notes of the raga. Strumming (or more accurately stroking) continuously throughout the recital, the tanpura player has a humdrum yet essential role. It's considered a privilege to be so close to a great soloist and the place is usually occupied by the soloist's shishyas (disciples). These days it's sometimes replaced by an electrical drone called a *shruti* box.

Wind instruments

The **shehnai** (or *shahnai* – emperor's flute) is a double-reed *shawm* with up to nine finger holes, some of which are stopped with wax for fine tuning to the scale of a particular raga. It was associated with grand or ceremonial occasions and in India it remains the traditional instrument for wedding music. A drone accompaniment is always provided by an **ottu**, or drone shehnai. The instrument demands a mastery of circular breathing and an enormous amount of breath control, particularly for long sustained passages. The veteran master of the shehnai, **Bismillah Khan**, died in 2006, but **Ali Ahmad Hussain Khan** follows his tradition.

The word **bansuri** (or *venu*) is used to refer to a wide variety of flutes, all made from bamboo (*banse*). The great popularity of this flute is enhanced by its association with the Hindu god Krishna, who is regularly depicted playing the flute (or *murli*) while enticing his devotees. Although the bamboo flute offers a limited range of just under two octaves, in the right hands it offers great expressive power. In the reflected glory of Krishna, it has become an important solo instrument on the concert platform. Among the leading players have been **Hariprasad Chaurasia**, **Pannalal Ghosh**, **Vijay Raghav Rao** and **G.S. Sachdev**.

Percussion

The **tabla** is a set of two small drums played with the fingertips and palms, capable of producing an incredible variety of sounds and timbres over a range of about one octave. Strictly speaking, the name tabla is a synonym for the *dayan* or *dahina* (literally, right hand) drum, played with the right hand, while the larger *bayan* (literally, left hand) or *duggi* is the bass-toned drum on the left. The most popular of the many drums of north India, its invention is – seemingly like everything else – attributed to Amir Khusrau. Both drum heads are made of skin, with a paste of iron filings and flour in the centre, but while the body of the tabla is all wood, the bayan is made of metal. The tabla is usually tuned to the tonic of the raga by tapping tuning-blocks, held by braces on the sides of the instrument. Top players include **Zakir Hussain** (son of Alla Rakha, one of the all-time great tabla players), **Anindo Chatterjee** and **Sharda Sahai**.

Predating the tabla, the **pakhawaj** is a wooden barrel drum nearly a metre long. It has two parchment heads, each tuned to a different pitch. Like the tabla, it is tuned by adjusting the drumhead tension using side wedges. A paste of boiled rice, iron filings and tamarind juice is applied to the smaller head, while a wheat flour paste on the larger head helps produce the lower notes. These paste roundels, unlike those of the tabla, have to be removed after each performance. The pakhawaj has a deep mellow sound and is used to accompany dhrupad singing and kathak dancing. The **mridangam**, the most widely used barrel drum in Karnatic music, is similarly capable of great subtlety.

Kala Ramnath: scion of a unique violin dynasty

Born in 1967, **Kala Ramnath** is one of the leading Hindustani instrumentalists of her generation. Her touch and tone on the violin are haunting, her phrases sinuous and as sheer as silk, her phraseology as consistently logical as it is surprising. Her playing can break your heart or make you believe you can fly. In 2006 she became the first violinist from either of the subcontinent's musical systems to be the subject of a feature in *The Strad* – a periodical viewed as the "Violin Bible". It was appropriate because she belongs to a violin dynasty which uniquely has created major soloists in both art music traditions. Kala Ramnath and her violinist cousin **Sangeeta Shankar** are the seventh generation of musicians in a dynasty beyond compare.

Sense World Music

Kala Ramnath

The violin is probably India's greatest metaphor for musical inclusion. It was first brought to the subcontinent by European colonists, mariners and traders. In the Hindu heartland down south, vina player **Baluswami Dikshitar** (1786–1859) had a musical epiphany: he found the latent Voice of India in the violin. For centuries it doggedly remained a south Indian instrument; in the north it remained the poor cousin of the sarangi. But that began to change in the twentieth century, especially with **V.G. Jog** and Kala Ramnath's paternal aunt, **Dr N. Rajam**.

Kala's grandfather bridged the north–south divide like nobody before or since. All five of his children – four sons and one daughter – learned violin with him. Two became full-time musicians and their names are luminescent: N. Rajam and **T.N. Krishnan**. Each was fully versed in both systems but eventually Krishnan took the Karnatic path and Rajam the Hindustani, meaning they would never be forced to compete. Kala Ramnath learned both systems from childhood (in fact beginning her studies at the age of two), but opted for Hindustani music. Her first violin teacher was the visionary **A. Narayana Iyer** (1897–1995), himself a product of south India's court musician system, and she later studied with her aunt.

Kala's epiphany occurred when the tabla maestro **Zakir Hussain** visited to pay his respects after her father's death. He simply suggested that, instead of playing like her aunt and forever being compared to her cousin, she should produce something new. Since 1989 she has studied with the vocalist **Pandit Jasraj** and in 1994 they went through the formal *ganda-bandan* (thread-tying) ceremony that symbolically binds guru to disciple. (The fact that she is an instrumentalist and he a vocalist is by no means unusual.) To gain a measure of their oneness of voice and violin, listen to *In Concert, Volume 1* (Eternal Music, Canada), recorded in Vancouver in 1996.

Naturally Pandit Jasraj teaches compositions with lyrics. "That was very important for me", Kala says, "for one, because I could bring out the mood or feeling (*rās* or *rasa*) of the *rāg* with the words there. One thing about learning with Pandit Jasraj was I learned Braj Bhasa. Not only did I learn the language, I was also able to understand how these compositions were created; which words would be apt for a particular raga; and how to compose. I do my own compositions now."

Kala Ramnath took Hussain's advice about finding her own voice to heart. Outside of the strict classical field, she has repeatedly put herself on the line, stretched herself. The new-agey *Fusion* (2002) may have been less successful, but she vindicated herself with the Yashila group's *Drive East* (2006) and her work with Fareed Haque's Flat Earth Ensemble. She has also contributed to Edward Zwick's film *Blood Diamond* (2006) and together with Zakir Hussain performed the music for his and Alonzo King's modern-day fusion ballet *Rasa* (2007).

Fittingly, *kala* means "art" in Sanskrit, Tamil and other Indian languages. As an artist, Kala Ramnath is in a class of her own.

Radio (AIR) stepped in as a substitute. Radio exposure, together with income from recordings (ordinarily a one-off payment with no sight of royalties, mechanicals or library lending rights), replaced royal patronage.

The second half of the twentieth century witnessed profound changes to the Hindustani music scene. Oral transmission of knowledge still continues in face-to-face tuition, but the rise of literacy and the wider availability of recording equipment have provided new methods of teaching. Once a *gharana* (school) was sited in a physical location. Now top-ranking musicians are globe-trotters, and ever more international students have become mail-order disciples, with recorded lessons supplemented by occasional personal tuition. Inevitably traditionalists believe that standards have plummeted. While it is true that exposure to Western traditions has increased dramatically, it can be fairly said that Indian classical music has a larger audience than ever before.

Recording

For decades Hindustani music has suffered from a surfeit of nostalgia, perhaps encouraged by the tradition of oral transmission. Forebears such as Khusrau and Tansen have become mythic figureheads, yet nobody knows how they would compare to today's musicians.

The first recordings of Indian music in India were made in 1902 by **Fred Gaisberg** for the Gramophone Company, and with them India's first recording star, **Gauhar Jan** (c. 1875–1930), was born. Jan was an accomplished singer of khayal and *thumri* and her recordings are an important stylistic link back to the old world of courtly musical patronage. But with recording, a new

commercial "patron" appeared and, for the first time, the very personal art of making Indian music could be documented. We can now review from a historical distance celebrated virtuosi such as **Kesarbai Kerkar** (vocals), **Allauddin Khan** (sarod), **Hafiz Ali Khan** (sarod) and **Imdad Khan** (sitar) – for example in the Gramophone Company of India's **Great Gharanas** series.

As elsewhere, these performers had to adapt to the constraints of contemporary recording equipment. India suffered particularly in this respect, as the late singer/producer **G.N. Joshi** recalled in his biography *Down Memory Lane* (1984). He describes his dismay at discovering that nobody at the Gramophone Company of India had realized its "state-of-the-art" machinery was fobbed-off obsolescence from Britain. The limitations that **78s** imposed had a dramatic effect on Indian music, as musicians were forced to distil their artistry into soundbite length. However deftly this was done, the result was even less representative of live performance than in other genres like *rebétika* or blues. Yet their craft shines through and the recordings are hardly quaint oddities.

While LPs were appearing in Europe and America in the early 1950s, in India 78s were still being released well into the 1960s. While the older form only gave a maximum of four minutes' uninterrupted music, LPs gave around twenty, meaning Hindustani performances could breathe again. The CD has improved things further, with longer recording time available and no distracting crackles to spoil the listening pleasure.

Today, Indian classical music is more popular and more available than ever. Top artists appear regularly in concert the world over and labels like Nimbus, Navras, Chhanda Dhara and Moment are releasing substantial live and studio performances on disc.

DISCOGRAPHY India | Hindustani Instrumental

As with any record industry, things can be volatile in this area of music. Catalogue items regularly go into discographical hibernation. The best example is *The Original Uday Shankar Company of Hindu Musicians, Recorded During its Historic 1937 Visit to the United States*. Originally released in 1937, it was reissued in 1968 and 2007. Like record labels themselves, many recordings vanish completely. This applies especially to new recordings on small labels. Many labels are repackaging old catalogue items or unearthing archival recordings. All India Radio sessions and private archives are typical sources. Perhaps the one constant in this wheeling Hindustani firmament is the

exemplary *Call of the Valley* (see below), which has always stayed in print.

⊙ **Anthology of Indian Classical Music**
Auvidis/Unesco, France
This presciently starrily-cast double-CD of north and south Indian classical music first appeared in the 1950s. Recorded by the French musicologist and Hinduist Alain Daniélou, it boasts contributions from a Hindustani and Karnatic elite including Ali Akbar Khan, Ravi Shankar and M.S. Subbulakshmi. Following his death, it now also acts as a memorial to Daniélou.

⊙ Anthology of World Music: North Indian Classical Music
Rounder, US

An important four-CD set re-issuing Alain Daniélou's survey of Hindustani music originally released by Bärenreiter/Musicaphon. Features top-quality performances of the main forms of vocal music and the main instruments – sitar, surbahar, vichitra vina, sarod, sarangi, flute and shehnai. Extensive notes with some inaccuracies.

★ Call of the Valley
Saregama, India

A late-1960s collaboration between Shivkumar Sharma (santoor), Hariprasad Chaurasia (flute) and Brijbushan Kabra (guitar), this is probably the most influential Hindustani album ever made. The idea is simple but effective: using various time-related ragas to depict the passage of a Kashmiri day. Fans of this will also want to seek out *The Valley Recalls* and *Rasdhara*, the two sequel *jugalbandi* (duet) recordings Sharma and Chaurasia made for Navras.

⊙ The Raga Guide
Nimbus, UK

An ambitious introduction to the raga system with bite-sized portions of 74 of the most performed ragas in recordings specially commissioned to show off their essence. Divided over four CDs, with the ragas arranged alphabetically, the performances are by flautist Hariprasad Chaurasia, sarod player Buddhadev Das Gupta and vocalists Shruti Sadolikar and Vidyadhar Vyas. A two hundred-page book gives comprehensive analytical descriptions, transcriptions and forty ragamala paintings.

Nikhil Banerjee

Banerjee (1931–86) was one of the finest sitarists of his generation, famed for the purity and elegance of his style. He studied with Allauddin Khan and later with Khan's son, the sarod maestro Ali Akbar Khan. His remains a singular voice in the annals of sitar, as eminent as Vilayat Khan and Ravi Shankar.

⊙ The Hundred-minute Raga: Purabi Kalyan
Raga Records, US

Banerjee, accompanied by tabla player Swapan Chaudhuri, is excellent on this two-CD recording made in California in 1982. After Banerjee's death many recordings appeared of questionable provenance but this one finds him in top form.

WITH ALI AKBAR KHAN

⊙ Rag Manj Khammaj & Rag Misra Mand
AMMP, US

Released in 1994, long after Nikhil Banerjee's death, this moving jugalbandi (duet) pairs Banerjee with sarod player Ali Akbar Khan, his guru's son.

V.M. Bhatt

Vishwa Mohan Bhatt (b. 1950) came to international fame when Kavi Alexander of Water Lily Acoustics paired him with Ry Cooder for 1993's *Meeting by the River* (see p.594). A disciple of the great sitarist Ravi Shankar, he has been a recording artist in his own right since 1970, creating some of the most enduring testimonies to the vibrancy of raga – in his case often tinged with Rajasthani themes, most notably on *Desert Slide* (see p.577). He plays a rebuilt guitar he calls Mohan vina. Anything of his on Water Lily Acoustics or Sense World Music is recommended.

⊙ Samadhi
Sense World Music, UK

This live recording made at the 2004 Saptak Festival in Ahmedabad, Gujarat, reveals many new twists to an old tune – raga "Maru Bihag". There is nothing not to love about the performance. Listen out for Bhatt's figures and phrases that dance away like dust devils.

⊙ Gathering Rain Clouds
Water Lily Acoustics, US

A last gasp of plangent creativity: Bhatt plays ragas "Miya ki Malhar" and "Gavati". This album really made ears prick up. Like all truly inspirational greatest performances, it banishes time.

Debashish Bhattacharya

Born in 1963, Bhattacharya plays one of India's adopted instruments, slide guitar. It was introduced by the Hawaiian guitarist Tau Moe, who toured India in the 1930s and was based in Kolkata in the 1940s. Bhattacharya plays three different instruments which he has designed and built himself.

⊙ Calcutta Chronicles: Indian Slide Guitar Odyssey
Riverboat, UK

A marvellous solo album, inspired by Bhattacharya's home city.

Kumar Bose

From the 1970s onwards, Kumar Bose came to worldwide fame as one of Ravi Shankar's most enduring choices for percussion accompanist. He was grounded in tabla through studies with, amongst others, his father Biswanath Bose and Kishan Maharaj, the greatest Benares-style tabla player of his day. Bose ranks as one of the most articulate and rhythmically seductive percussion maestros.

⊙ Live from Darbar Festival 2006
Sense World Music, UK

The UK Darbar Festival has maintained a tradition of showcasing percussion. Accompanied by Ramesh Mishra on sarangi in a style called *lehara* or *lehra* – a performance convention that inverts the more usual rhythm instrument accompanying melody instrument – Kumar Bose really delivers the goods.

Hariprasad Chaurasia

Hariprasad Chaurasia (b. 1937) overcame establishment prejudices to become the best-known north Indian flautist. Chaurasia has achieved more, in terms of both popularity and artistry, than any flautist in the Hindustani pantheon since Pannalal Ghosh (who studied with Allauddin Khan). In recent years he has become one of Indian music's most successful ambassadors.

★ Venu
Rykodisc, US

A live recording by Mickey Hart (of the Grateful Dead) from December 1974, with the excellent Zakir Hussain on sitar. A compelling exploration of the early-morning raga "Ahir Bhairav", with its mixture of romantic and devotional moods.

⊙ Four Dhuns
Nimbus, UK

Chaurasia is one of the most versatile of instrumentalists, playing in various fusion groups. A *dhun* is usually a folk tune or a light piece that doesn't strictly adhere to the rules of a raga, and often concludes a concert.

Bahauddin Dagar

The rudra vina player Bahauddin Dagar (b. 1970) is the twentieth generation of one of the most illustrious musical families. They specialize in dhrupad, renowned for its slow-fuse Hindu style of delivery.

Live from Darbar Festival
Sense World Music, UK

An exemplary concert recording from the 2006 Darbar Festival with pakhawaj accompaniment by Ravishankar Upadhyay. The instrument Bahauddin plays on this interpretation of the multi-purpose raga Bhairavi is the modified "Dagar been" developed by his father. While his name reveals him to be Muslim, the Dagarbani school remains firmly rooted in deepest Hinduism, musically speaking.

WITH WASIFUDDIN DAGAR

⊙ Vedanta
Sense World Music, UK

A rudra vina and vocal dhrupad jugalbandi, from the 2006 Saptak Festival in Gujarat. Over two CDs they reveal the living, beating heart of Malkauns, in a performance that rivals that of *Raag Malkauns: Bombay 1968* below and illustrates the unflagging stamina of the Dagarbani tradition and the high standard of Dagarbani musicianship.

Zia Mohiuddin Dagar

One of the great stringed instrument virtuosi, Z.M. Dagar (1929–90) is best known for playing rudra vina. Drawing on the style of dhrupad vocal music, his playing had an austere and refined integrity.

⊙ Raga Yaman and Raga Shuddha Todi
Nimbus, UK

Dagar made these recordings of two of his favourite ragas in the spring of 1990, the year he died. The music unfolds slowly, and has an incredible depth. Dagar goes in for extended *alap* sections, exploring the ragas in depth, and doesn't indulge in fireworks. Two beautifully recorded CDs for the price of one.

WITH Z.F. DAGAR

⭐ Raag Malkauns: Bombay 1968
Country & Eastern, Sweden

A dhrupad colloquy with Z.F. Dagar singing and Z.M. Dagar playing the text on rudra vina at its very finest. This is grandeur on a scale rarely achieved. Imagine eavesdropping on a slowly unfurling conversation on a par with Blind Willie McTell talking to the angels.

Zakir Hussain

Zakir Hussain (b. 1951), son of the late master tabla player Alla Rakha, is the foremost tabla player of his generation. He has contributed enormously to the worldwide popularity of Indian music with his percussion-led albums and fusion work (see p.596).

WITH ALLA RAKHA

⊙ Parampara
Saregama, India

Seven pieces recorded between 1955 and 1986 that show off father and son. They play together in 1972, and accompany Vilayat Khan in 1955 and 1980 respectively.

WITH SHAMIM AHMED

⊙ India's Great Shamin Ahmed: Three Ragas
Smithsonian Folkways Archival, US

Originally released on Monitor, here a superb master of the sitar is captured performing with Zakir Hussain. It is clear from their "Bageshwari", "Nat Bhairav" and "Khamaj" that each is destined for great things.

Ali Akbar Khan

Sarodist Ali Akbar Khan (1922–2009) is hailed as one of the greatest musicians on the planet, irrespective of genre. A master melodist, he is steeped in the Maihar (or Senia) *gharana*, his father Allaudin Khan's style of playing. From the 1950s to the 1980s, his duets with brother-in-law Ravi Shankar were the sensation of the day.

⊙ Signature Series Vols 1 and 2
AMMP, US

Accompanied by one of the finest tabla players of his generation, Mahapurush Misra, Khan delivers "Gauri Manjari", "Jogiya Kalingra" and the night raga "Chandranandan" (on Vol. 1), and Medhavi, Khammaj and Bhairavi Bhatiyar (on Vol. 2). The remastered Signature Series restores these exemplary Connoisseur albums to the catalogue, some of the most sublime Hindustani recordings ever released.

Allauddin Khan

The multi-instrumentalist Allauddin Khan lived in an age of giants. No wonder then that facts about him became distorted. He died in 1972, having celebrated his centenary in October 1962, but nobody knew his exact age, least of all Khan himself. Fortunately, the quality and importance of his music are incontestable.

⊙ Late Ustad Allauddin Khan Saheb Vols 1–5
T-Series, India

These recordings derive from All India Radio broadcasts between 1959 and 1960, and are the best introduction to the master's work. They are broadcast-length, most well over twenty minutes.

Amjad Ali Khan

The sarodist Amjad Ali Khan (b. 1945) is the son of the sarod maestro Hafiz Ali Khan. His playing has a remarkable depth to it and any concert performance offers guaranteed satisfaction. His recorded oeuvre is frustratingly extensive and scattered over many domestic and foreign labels.

⊙ The Legendary Lineage
Navras, UK

Three generations of one of the most illustrious families in Hindustani music gathered on one volume. It begins with Hafiz Ali Khan, continues with his son, Amjad Ali Khan, and closes with Amjad Ali Khan's sons, Amaan and Ayaam Ali Bangash. A memorable treasury of the past, present and future of Gwalior-style sarod playing.

Bismillah Khan

One of Hindustani music's foremost virtuosi, Bismillah Khan (1916–2006) was the acknowledged master of the shehnai. His breathtaking jugalbandi with Vilayat Khan inaugurated EMI's impressive Music of India series.

⊙ Live in London Vols 1 and 2
Navras, UK

Two marvellous albums recorded in London in 1985. The first includes Kedar and Rageshwari while the second encompasses the raga Malkauns and a dhun.

Imrat Khan

Khan (b. 1936) is a distinguished sitar player but is equally known for his mastery of the surbahar (the bass-voiced equivalent of the more familiar sitar). He is a virtuoso performer, as was his elder brother, Vilayat Khan.

⊙ Ajmer
Water Lily Acoustics, US
A 1990 recording featuring surbahar and sitar. Khan plays raga "Alhaiya Bilaval" and his own composition, "Imratkauns".

Rais Khan

Rais Khan (b. 1939) is arguably the most impressive sitarist of the post-Nikhil Banerjee years. His playing has a gloriously romantic resonance to it.

⊙ Together
Audiorec, UK
Rais Khan's solo work is exemplary but thin on the ground. This release is noteworthy for its rare pairing of sarangi and sitar. Rais Khan is joined by Sultan Khan on sarangi, with raga "Bilaskhani" as their chosen centrepiece. Sabir Khan accompanies on tabla.

Sabri Khan

Sabri Khan (b. 1927) was one of the first sarangi players to become a principal soloist. The instrument (of folk origin) had traditionally been viewed as less worthy, through its use accompanying *tawaifs* (courtesan entertainers) and its "low-caste" construction. Khan brought himself and the instrument a new profile in accompanying top vocalists.

⊙ Raga Darbari/Raga Multani
Auvidis Ethnic, France
A 1991 release showing off the maestro's exquisite playing, including a *khyal* interpretation of raga "Darbari" which builds over forty minutes to achieve a rare intensity. Also twenty minutes of glorious improvisation in raga "Multani".

Shujaat Hussain Khan

The son of Vilayat Khan, Shujaat Hussain Khan (b. 1960) sets the standard for his generation of sitarists. He has Himalayan sensitivity as a musician. Every single recording – solo or duet – he has made for India Archive Music glows.

⊙ Amoré
Navras, UK
Everything that contemporary sitar interpretation should be. This recording serves as a fitting souvenir of a magnificent concert at St John's in London's Smith Square in August 1995. A valentine cloaked in raga "Jhinjoti". Anand Gopal Bandopadhyay is on tabla.

WITH TEJENDRA NARAYAN MAJUMDAR

⊙ Shujaat Khan/Tejendra Narayan Majumdar: Raga Charukeshi
⊙ Shujaat Khan/Tejendra Narayan Majumdar: Raga Lalit
India Archive Music, US
Shujaat Khan and Tejendra Narayan Majumdar enthral with their sitar and sarod interpretations of raga "Charukeshi", made spontaneously on their first meeting in 1995, and raga "Lalit", recorded in 1997.

Sultan Khan

Sarangi player Sultan Khan (b. 1940) first came under the international spotlight at the time of the 1974 Dark Horse tour with Ravi Shankar and George Harrison. He consolidated his international career with work on the soundtrack to the film *Gandhi*. His touch is as distinct from those of Ram Narayan and Sabri Khan as Ravi Shankar's is from those of Rais Khan or Shujaat Hussain Khan.

⊙ Sarangi
Navras, UK
Sultan Khan's sarangi reveals eloquent insights into ragas "Jaijaiwanti" and "Mishra Shivranjani" that few could match in this release from a dizzy-making London concert in 1990 with Shaukat Hussain Khan on tabla.

WITH IKRAM KHAN

⊙ Sarangi
Sense World Music, UK
Khan is joined by his Rajasthani pupil Ikram Khan. Sarangi takes the foreground with tabla (Nandan Mehta and Hanif Khan) supporting tabla in seven-beat (*rupak tal*) and eight-beat (*kaharva*) cycles.

Vilayat Khan

Vilayat Khan (1928–2004) and his younger brother Imrat may have derived their musicality from their genes and the Imdadkhani gharana (named after their grandfather), but Vilayat was his own man and a legend in his own right. His most outstanding contribution to his gharana's tradition was the gayaki, or vocal, style of sitar playing.

⊙ Sitar
India Archive Music, US
Everything one could wish for. Good old raga "Bhairavi" performed with such flair and compassion that the senses tingle. A studio recording from 1989.

WITH IMRAT KHAN

⊙ A Night at the Taj
Gramophone Company of India, India
A classic jugalbandi combination – sitar and surbahar – with his younger brother Imrat. Also recommended are two double CDs: *Ragas Shahana & Bageshree* (Navras, UK), a sitar duet with his gifted son Shujaat Khan, and *Eb'adat* (Navras, UK), the historic reunion duet with shehnai player Bismillah Khan.

Gopal Krishnan

Vichitra vina is an unfretted stick zither. Its southern cousin, known through the playing of Chitravina Ganesh, Chitravina Ravikiran and Budalur Krishnamurti Shastri, is the chitra vina. Gopal Krishnan, a rare exponent of this northern Indian instrument, recorded relatively little, but his legacy is singular.

⊙ Inde du Nord: L'art de la vichitra vîna
Ocora, France
The passage of time has rendered this performance all the more poignant. This two-CD release, recorded in April 1985 in Paris, finds the maestro in the good company of Latif Ahmed Khan on tabla.

Kamalesh Maitra

Maitra (1924–2005) grew up in Calcutta and started playing tabla in 1940. He joined the Uday Shankar Ballet troupe in 1950 and was asked to learn the *tabla tarang* – a semi-circular set of tablas tuned to play ragas. He worked with the company for twenty years and in 1977 settled in Berlin. He was the acknowledged master of this rare but beautiful-sounding instrument.

★ Tabla Tarang: Melody on Drums
Smithsonian Folkways, US
This music performed on tuned tabla is absolutely compelling. In this 1996 recording, Maitra plays four forms of the early morning raga "Todi", accompanied by Trilok Gurtu on

the conventional tabla. Two ragas are associated with Tansen and his son Bilas Khan. Excellent accompanying notes.

Ronu Majumdar

Ronu Majumdar, born Ranendra Nath Majumdar in 1965, has risen to become one of the finest flautists of present times. His father Dr Bhanu Majumdar studied flute with the man responsible for giving the instrument a new identity, Pannalal Ghosh (1911–60), and like Ghosh the family is Bengali.

⊙ A Sacred Space
Sense World Music, UK
The perfect introduction to a great maestro. It includes a composition by his guru, the noted flautist Vijay Raghav Rao, in the south Indian ragam "Charukeshi".

Gaurav Mazumdar

Born in Allahabad in Uttar Pradesh in 1965, Gaurav Mazumdar is one of the most outstanding contemporary sitarists. His vision of the instrument has been honed by years of study with Ravi Shankar.

⊙ Gaurav Mazumdar
Global Records, UK
At the heart of this recording are explorations in the late-morning raga "Todi". The second track, a *gat* (a musical figure used as the foundation for sitar, sarod and percussion improvisation employing mnemonic phrases as signposts), is especially fine. The third performance is of a folk air or dhun derived from the Sindh region bedded in Bhairavi.

Sadanand Naimpali

Born in 1946, Sadanand Naimpali is an engineer by training, a musician by leaning, having studied with the tabla maestro Pandit Taranath Rao (1915–91). Naimpali later applied his mind to developing a series of *taals* (rhythm cycles) with a half-beat kilter – something endemic in the south Indian system – for example, *shani taal* (7½), *nand taal* (8½) and *adashuttaal* (10½).

WITH MOHAN BALVALLY
★ Live at Trinity Club: Bombay 1967
Country & Eastern, Sweden
A tabla duet recording that distils a bygone era. With harmonium accompaniment by their guru Pandit Taranath. Tear over with nostalgia for something you never experienced in person. The much over-used word "magic" applies.

Ram Narayan

Yehudi Menuhin once said, "I cannot separate the sarangi from Ram Narayan, so thoroughly fused are they, not only in my memory but in the fact of this sublime dedication of the great musician to an instrument which is no longer archaic because of the matchless way he had made it speak." The sarangi is one of the most eloquent melody instruments on the planet, capable of extraordinary vocal mimicry. Narayan's daughter, Aruna Narayan Kalle, has since come through the ranks as an excellent sarangi player, making history in her own right as a female exponent of the instrument.

⊙ The Art of the Sarangi
Ocora, France
Although Narayan has recorded for many labels, the first, vinyl edition of this album was a turning point. This edition has added a 1979 recording of raga "Shankara" to the original 1971 album's versions of "Bairagi-Bhairav", "Madhuvanti" and "Kirvani".

Dr N. Rajam

Recognized by audiences, fellow musicians and the Indian government alike as one of the finest musicians of her generation, Padmashree Dr N. Rajam is the most senior living violinist of the Hindustani system, although, like her brother T.N. Krishnan, she was raised playing south Indian-style violin too. Her style is greatly informed by the vocalist Omkarnath Thakur, himself a student of Vishnu Digambar (see p.537).

⊙ Radiant
Sense World Music, UK
Radiance indeed, with excellent readings of "Malkauns" (the main piece) and a *thumri* set in Khamaj, the rare "Nilambari" and "Bhairavi" as the farewell piece.

Alla Rakha

"All life is rhythm", said tabla maestro and classical legend Alla Rakha Qureshi (1919–2000). The first tabla player to give solo concerts, he rose to fame as Ravi Shankar's right-hand man during the 1960s. He was highly versatile, working prolifically as a composer in the Indian film industry as well as collaborating on the pioneering percussion fusion album *Rich à la Rakha* with jazz drummer Buddy Rich. With his sons Zakir Hussain, Fazal Qureshi and Taufiq Qureshi he has created a lasting pedigree.

★ Maestro's Choice: Tabla
Music Today, India
This recital with Zakir Hussain illustrates the potency of Hindustani rhythm, exploring *matta taal* (a nine-beat cycle) and *jai taal* (thirteen beats), with a concluding number in *pashto* (seven beats). Sultan Khan supports melodically on sarangi.

Kala Ramnath

Born in Chennai in 1967, Kala Ramnath is a musician's musician, with a fluency and maturity beyond her years. She studied violin with her aunt, Dr N. Rajam, before beginning tutelage with the celebrated vocalist Pandit Jasraj in 1989.

★ Nectar
Sense World Music, UK
Kala Ramnath's phenomenal artistry and imagination shine through here, while Vijay Ghate accompanies her on tabla. Her interpretations repay repeated listening; essential listening.

WITH PURBAYAN CHATTERJEE
⊙ Samwad
Sense World Music, UK
A groundbreakingly violin and sitar duet, released in 2005, and one of the best recordings of Indian classical music in years.

Anoushka Shankar

Being Ravi Shankar's daughter placed Anoushka Shankar (b. 1981) in a privileged position. She enjoyed a considerable head start as a musician but also had to endure a good deal of grumbling. More recently, her extra-curricular activities in film and on fusion albums have received greater publicity than her classical work.

⊙ Anourag
Angel, US
Anoushka Shankar's contract with Angel was unprecedented on several counts for a young Hindustani musician. This second album may be largely pre-conceived (she admits she had yet to develop improvisatory skills of any note) but is nevertheless a demonstration of great playing promise.

Ravi Shankar

Ravi Shankar (b. 1920) is the foremost figure in Indian and Hindustani music, as well as being among the four best-known Indians of the twentieth century (along with Gandhi, Nehru and Tagore). Beyond the sheer exquisiteness of his sitar playing, he has proved one of the genre's great innovators, working in film, dance and theatre as well as cross-cultural work of many kinds. His English-language autobiographies, *My Music, My Life* (1969) and *Raga Mala* (1998), are highly recommended.

★ Ravi Shankar and Ali Akbar Khan in Concert 1972
Apple, UK

Pyrotechnics and profundity recorded in New York, matching sitar and sarod in Hindustani music's greatest jugalbandi. The concert was dedicated to their mutual guru Allauddin Khan, who had died just a few weeks before.

☉ In Celebration
Angel, US

This four-CD set is an excellent retrospective of Ravi Shankar's unmatched recording career, although it omits his important early shellac recordings for HMV and any jugalbandi with Ali Akbar Khan (a partnership that made them the hottest ticket in Hindustani music). Released in 1996, it also contains his daughter Anoushka's debut ("Adarini"), with the marvellous Zakir Hussain on tabla.

★ In Portrait
BBC/Opus Arte, UK

This two-disc DVD offers an expanded edition of Mark Kidel's TV documentary *Between Two Worlds*. Also included is *Benares Ghat*, a fly-on-the-wall view of Shankar teaching five pupils the new composition of the title, a concert from July 2002 with his daughter Anoushka Shankar, and the outstanding twenty-minute film *The Sitar and Indian Music*.

Shivkumar Sharma

Shivkumar Sharma (b. 1938) is responsible for the birth of a new classical instrument, previously deemed worthy only of folk or regional music. Having taken up the Kashmiri santoor at his father's behest, he developed it into a soloist's vehicle in classical concerts. His name is now synonymous with that of the santoor and, beyond that, with a powerful musical vision.

☉ Sampradaya
RealWorld, UK

An excellent santoor duet performance of raga "Janasammohini" with Sharma's son Raul – the ringing notes interlace and hover in the air. The range of articulation is glorious, from delicate, feathery whispering to arresting staccato punctuations, although it is all quite restrained until the end.

Baluji Shrivastav

Born in Usmanpur in Uttar Pradesh, the sitar, surbahar, *dilruba* and surmandel player Baluji Shrivastav's instrumental playing style does not derive from any particular gharana and he has no guru to name as his lineage or pedigree.

☉ Shadow of the Lotus
Arc Music, UK

Well-chosen material, skilfully executed. Particularly notable is the round-about-midnight "Shahana" played on surbahar in an eighteen-beat taal that he and tabla player Vishnu Sahai mutate into a nineteen-beat rhythm cycle.

PLAYLIST
India | Hindustani Instrumental

1 AHIR BHAIRAV AND NAT BHAIRAV Shivkumar Sharma, Brijbushan Kabra and Hariprasad Chaurasia from *Call of the Valley*
The sunrise overture from the trio's innovative suite painting a Kashmiri day. It has never gone out of print.

2 HEM BIHAG Ravi Shankar and Ali Akbar Khan from *In Concert 1972*
An early-evening raga as a sitar and sarod duet that illuminates the idea that sitar and sarod project, respectively, female and male attributes.

3 BHUPAL TODI Kamalesh Maitra from *Tabla Tarang: Melody on Drums*
Multiple tuned tablas playing raga that rolls over the listener like waves of sound.

4 RAAG MALKAUNS Z.M. Dagar and Z.F. Dagar from *Raag Malkauns: Bombay 1968*
Rudra vina and voice prove the fundamental truth that two minds can work harmoniously without relying on harmony.

5 BIHAGADA Kala Ramnath from *Nectar*
Smell the waft of jasmine that her bow strokes release on the air. A heady violin performance to overwhelm the senses.

6 TABLA ENSEMBLE Jnan Prakash Ghosh from *Drums of India, Volume 2*
A magisterial percussion track, to be lapped up as much for its melodicism as its rhythmicality and tonal range.

7 AMRIT G.S. Sachdev from *Jasmine Nights*
Swapan Chaudhury accompanies the great flute maestro on this night-time-is-the-right-time raga. "Amrit" means "nectar".

8 RAGA PAHARI (DHUN) Shujaat Khan from *Sitar*
Seventeen minutes of rhapsodic playing – and singing – from the most consistently inspirational sitarist of his generation. A folk-derived raga hitched to a Holi story.

9 JAIJAIWANTI Sultan Khan from *Sarangi*
Live in London, 1986. Shaukat Hussain Khan on tabla. An exquisite evocation of a romantic midnight raga.

10 RAAG MADHUWANTI Bismillah Khan and Bageshwari Qamar from *Shehnai-Jugalbandi*
The maestro and one of his senior pupils greet the evening. Shehnai, it must be said, is an instrument unlikely to charm nightjar or owl from the night skies.

India | Karnatic Instrumental Music

sounds of the saints

Violin Maestro L. Subramaniam

The Karnatic music of south India might be labelled "classical", but it's nothing like classical music anywhere else in the world. Rather than being the province of an urbane elite, it's an explosion of colour, sound and Hindu worship. Ken Hunt explores the lifeblood of south Indian culture.

Karnatic (Carnatic, Karnatak) music was once the musical language of the entire subcontinent, grounded in Hinduism and boasting a history and mythology thousands of years old as the articulation of Dravidian culture.

In the fifteenth century, the Mughal conquest of north India divided the subcontinent. The Hindu culture of the north was uprooted and Muslim practices replaced the old ways – or at least were grafted onto the old stock. The two musical systems retained their allegiance to the dynamics of *raga* and rhythm, but in other respects they were to diverge – one important difference being in their audience. While Hindustani music developed close associations with court and palace, Karnatic music remained part of the warp and weft of the south Indian culture, both religious and secular.

The other major difference is that Karnatic music, lacking written notation, is taught by demonstration and learned by ear or, in the case of its highly sophisticated rhythmic system, taught by a marvellous, mathematical structure of "finger computing" which enables a percussionist to break down a complex *thaalam* (rhythmic cycle) into manageable units. Indian percussion maestros readily admit the supremacy of Karnatic concepts of rhythm, and increasing numbers of Hindustani percussionists have studied in the south.

Hindu Roots

Much to the annoyance of Karnatic musicians, Hindustani music from north India is better known internationally, although the music of the south is by far the more ancient. Its tenets, once passed on only orally, were codified in Vedic literature between 4000 and 1000 BC, long before Western classical music was even in its infancy. One of the four main Vedic texts, the **Sama Veda**, is the basis for all that followed.

The music and the faith which inspired it have remained inseparable. Visitors to the vast temples of south India are much more likely to encounter music than they would be in the north. It's usually the piercing sound of the *nagaswaram* (*shawm*) and the *tavil* (barrel drum). More than likely it accompanies flaming torches and a ceremonial procession of the temple deity.

While devotional and religious in origin, Karnatic music is as much a vehicle for education and entertainment as for spiritual elevation. **Kritis**, a genre of Hindu hymn, are hummed and sung as people go about their daily business. In their tunefulness and recognizability, they hold a similar position in popular culture to Christian hymns.

The association of music and **dance** with Hindu thought has a long heritage, beginning with Shiva himself as Nataraja, the Cosmic Dancer, whose potent image is ever-present in Hindu iconography. His temple at Chidambaram, for example, is rich with sculptures of *natya* dance poses, music-making and musical instruments, and the *devadasis*, the servants of God, were traditionally temple dancers.

Simon Broughton

Nagaswaram players at a temple, Kanchipuram, Tamil Nadu

Karnatic composers, too, are looked upon with some reverence. Indeed, the music's three great composers – **Tyagaraja** (1767–1847), **Muttuswamy Dikshitar** (1776–1835) and **Syama Sastri** (1762–1827) – are known as the *Trimurti* or "Holy Trinity" and are regarded as saint-composers. Between them, the trinity were responsible for hundreds of compositions – Tyagaraja alone is credited with some six hundred kritis.

Indians compare the music of the Trimurti to the grape, the coconut and the banana. Tyagaraja can be consumed and enjoyed immediately; appreciating Muttuswamy Dikshitar is like cracking open a shell to get to the kernel; and with Syama

Traditional Karnatic Instruments

Stringed instruments

The **vina** (or *veena*) is the foremost Karnatic stringed instrument, the southern equivalent (and ancestor) of the *sitar*. A hollow wooden fingerboard with twenty-four frets is supported by two resonating gourds, one at each end. The vina has seven strings, four used for the melody and the other three for rhythm and drone. Notable players of recent times include **Chittu Babu**, **E. Gaayathri**, **Geetha Ramanathan Bennett**, **Dr Karaikudi Sambasivayer Subramaniam**, **Rajeshwari Padmanabhan**, **S. Balachander** and **Sivasakti Sivanesan**.

Vina player Geetha Ramanathan Bennett

The **chitra vina** (or *gottuvadyum*) is an unfretted 21-string instrument with sets for rhythm and drone as well as sympathetic strings. It has a characteristic soft voice which, before amplification, meant it was best suited to intimate surroundings. The best-known player is the young **N. Ravikiran**, who has switched to a hollow cylinder of teflon for his slide.

Wind instruments

As in the north, the transverse bamboo flute goes under the name of **bansuri** or **venu**, although it is typically shorter and higher in pitch than the Hindustani instrument. Watch out for recordings by **N. Ramani** and the younger **S. Shashank**.

The **nagaswaram** (or *nadaswaram*) is a piercing double-reed oboe-like instrument. It's longer (up to two and a half feet) and more deep-toned than the Hindustani *shehnai* and is associated with weddings, processions and temple ceremonies. It's often paired with a drone nagaswaram or *ottu*. Besides its ceremonial functions – and it is perhaps best heard in the open air – it is sometimes employed in formal classical concert settings. Leading players include **Karukurichi P. Arunachalam**, the brothers **M.P.N. Sethuraman** and **M.P.N. Ponnuswamy**, and **Sheik Chinnamoulana**.

Percussion

The Karnatic counterpart to the tabla is the **mridangam**, a double-headed, barrel-shaped drum made from a single block of jackwood. Both heads are made from layers of hide and can be tuned according to the ragam being performed. **Patri Satish Kumar**, **Vellore Ramabhadran** and **Mysore Rajappa Sainatha** are among the top players.

Other percussion instruments include the **tavil**, a folk-style barrel drum commonly found in ceremonial nagaswaram ensembles, and the **ghatam**, a clay pot tuned by firing. The latter is frequently found in south Indian ensembles, and unlikely as it may seem, in the hands of a top player like **T.H. "Vikku" Vinayakram** it can contribute some spectacular solos. The **morsing** (or *morching*) is a Jew's harp, often part of the accompanying ensemble, but frequently dropped when groups tour to save on the air fare!

The **jalatarangam** (or *jalatarang*) is something of a curiosity, a melodic percussion instrument comprising a semicircle of water-filled porcelain bowls. It can create a sound of extraordinary beauty as the lead melody instrument in a typical Karnatic ensemble with violin, mridangam and ghatam. Players include **Mysore M.S. Chandrasekharian** and the brothers **Anayampatti S. Dhandapani** and **Anayampatti S. Ganesan**.

South Indian Names

Once you've cracked the code, south Indian musicians' names can provide a wealth of information. A typical name begins with an initial, but this does not necessarily stand for the musician's own name. **Initials** in the names of N. Ravikiran and L. Subramaniam, for instance, denote their fathers' names – Narasimhan and Lakshminarayan respectively. One recent trend is for married female musicians to replace their father's initial with their husband's.

Sometimes the musician's name is prefixed by the name of their instrument – **Clarinet Abbayi**, **Chitravina Ravikiran**, **Mandolin Srinivas** and **Vina Gayatri** – an inexpensive way to advertise. Another variant is for a place name – such as Srirangam, Chennai or Tanjore – to be added. In the past this would often have implied a courtly connection, when places like Mysore, Tanjore and Trivandrum were major centres of employment for musicians. The court of Serfojee of Tanjore (1798–1833) was reputed, for example, to boast a musician for every day of the year. This place name may also be abbreviated to a single letter.

A **caste name** such as Iyer (or Ayyer) may appear as a suffix, and often acts as a geographical or cultural pointer. Sarma, for instance, is a caste name associated with Tamil Nadu, Panikkar with Kerala, and Naidu with Telugu-speakers. The abandonment of caste designations is, however, a growing trend.

Brahmins and high-class non-Brahmin castes have long followed a calling as musicians, as have the barber-musician Pillai caste. To this day, Pillais are inextricably linked with nagaswaram and tavil and, more recently, with the clarinet. Certain instruments – flute, mridangam, *kanjira* (a small frame drum) and *morsing* – have traditionally been associated with the non-Brahmin dance-music tradition.

Sastri you have to remove the soft outer layer to get to the fruit. Their era has become known as the **Golden Period**, and their music is revered and celebrated year in, year out, at various music conferences (festivals) and on a never-ending stream of recordings.

In Performance

In concert, Karnatic music often seems to lack Hindustani music's showmanship and flamboyance. But neither does it require the same sustained level of concentration. A Karnatic *ragam* (raga) might be said to resemble a miniature beside a large-scale Hindustani canvas.

Karnatic musicians will distil the essence of a **ragam** into six to eight minutes. In part this is because a kriti, the base of many performances, is a fixed composition without improvisation. Karnatic musicians' creativity lies in their ability to interpret that piece faithfully while shading and colouring the composition appropriately. The words of a kriti affect even non-vocal compositions: instrumentalists will colour their interpretations as if a vocalist were singing along; the unvoiced lyric determines where they place an accent, a pause or melodic splash.

Improvisation has its place too, most noticeably in a sequence known as **ragam-thanam-pallavi** (see p.534). This is a full-scale flowering of a Karnatic ragam and is every bit the equal of a Hindustani performance, although it is employed more sparingly, tending to be the centrepiece or climax of a Karnatic concert.

Whereas Karnatic music tends to break down into three strands – temple music, temple dance-accompaniment, and music for personal and private devotional observance – **sabha**, or paying concert performances, have somewhat blurred these distinctions. During the 1890s, the sabha associations in **Madras** (now Chennai) took an innovative path, moving from music performances into dance recitals. Madras remains a centre of excellence and its music conferences, especially around December and January, attract devout audiences each year.

Concert-giving led to other changes: microphones came into use during the 1930s. They lent soft-voiced instruments such as members of the vina family a new lease of life, and replaced full-tilt vocal power with greater subtlety, granting new opportunities which led to new standards of stagecraft, and subtleties over stridencies.

Nowadays, concerts will typically feature a named principal soloist (either vocal or instrumental) with melodic and rhythmic accompaniment and a *tanpura* or drone player. Percussionists of standing are often included in concert announcements and advertising as they are attractions in their own right. Female musicians involved in a principal role tend to be vocalists, vina (or veena) players or violinists. Male musicians have access to a wider range of musical possibilities as well as outnumbering female principal soloists or accompanists by roughly three to one.

New Instruments

Both of the subcontinent's two classical systems give pride of place to the voice while melodic instruments, to some degree, are played to mimic it. Nevertheless, Karnatic music makes use of a fascinating array of stringed, wind and percussion instruments, many unique to the subcontinent (see box on previous page).

From the nineteenth century, Karnatic music began to appropriate **Western instruments**, notably the violin and clarinet. More recent additions include the mandolin and saxophone. In the south – where the northern *sarangi* is a stranger – the violin's fluidity, grace, speed and penetrative volume guaranteed it a complement of converts during the nineteenth century, most notably **Tanjore Vadivelu** of the Tanjore Quartette.

Nowadays Karnatic music without the **violin** is inconceivable. Credit for introducing it and adapting its Western tuning is given to **Baluswami Dikshitar** (1786–1859), younger brother of the saintly composer – though some traditionalist scholars claim it as really a descendant of the earlier *dhanur vina*. Maestros such as **Lalgudi G. Jayaraman**, **V.V. Subrahmanyam** and **L. Subramaniam** are major artists, while **A. Kanyakumari** typifies the female violinists who have come to the fore. The brother duo of **Ganesh & Kumaresh** are excellent representatives of male players coming through the ranks, though in accordance with southern tradition they had made their hundredth stage appearance before the younger brother had reached ten years of age. In south India, the violin is played sitting on the floor with the body of the violin against the upper chest and the scroll wedged against the ankle, leaving the left hand free to slide more freely up and down the strings. **Shankar**, brother of L. Subramaniam, has devised his own electric double violin with an extended bottom range and dark tone.

 The introduction of the **clarinet**, or to give it its local name *clarionet*, is credited to Mahadeva Nattuvanar, in around 1860. Until around 1920, the clarinet was mostly used as an ensemble instrument in *cinna melam*, a dance accompaniment form. Thereafter, it was gradually established as a soloist's instrument. **Balaraman** of the Nada-

Mandolin prodigy U. Srinivas

muni Band was one of the twentieth century's first clarinet maestros and his work has been continued by musicians like **A.K.C. Natarajan** – nicknamed the "Clarinet Everest".

The **mandolin** has gained acceptance thanks to another of south India's child prodigies, **U. Srinivas**, often known as Mandolin Srinivas. He started playing the instrument aged six and has since toured worldwide and proved that the solid-body mandolin is highly effective at spinning gossamer webs of Tyagaraja improvisations. He is a very devout musician and his performances usually retain a devotional element.

The **saxophone** is another recent import and its champion, **Kadri Gopalnath**, is one of south India's most popular musicians, with dozens of recordings to his credit. Gopalnath demonstrates Karnatic music's particular ability to be ancient and modern at the same time. His *Evolution* (Sense World Music) with flautist Ronu Majumdar is nothing short of spectacular in north-south jugalbandi terms. When he plays the Karnatic ragams the powerful sound of the saxophone echoes the ancient nagaswaram, but its tone and attitude are also distinctively contemporary.

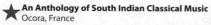

★ An Anthology of South Indian Classical Music
Ocora, France

A substantial work compiled by the eminent violinist Dr L. Subramaniam. Reissued in 2007, this four-CD primer gathers many of Karnatic music's vocal and instrumental giants, with detailed descriptions of the music they make and the instruments they play. M.S. Subbulakshmi (vocals), T.R. Mahalingam (flute), A.K.C. Natarajan (clarinet), Raajeshwari Padmanabhan (vina), N. Ravikiran (*chitra vina*), Subashchandran (morsing), V.V. Subrahmanyam (violin) and T.H. Vinayakram (ghatam) are among the concentration of virtuosi.

S. Balachander

The vina maestro S. Balachander (1927–90) was one of the best-known Karnatic instrumentalists, having been one of the influential World Pacific label's major artists, with groundbreaking issues such as *Sounds of the Veena*, featuring the flute of Ramani, and *The Magic Music of India*. Unlike most Karnatic performers, his recorded work is peppered with interpretations of ragams that are longer than normal.

⊙ The Virtuoso of Veena
Denon, Japan

Ragam Chakravaakam is at the centre of this disc. Track one comprises *alapana* and *thanam* while track two explores Tyagaraja's devotional use of the same ragam. Taeko Kusano's touching notes marvellously capture the spirit of this maverick musician.

Geetha Ramanathan Bennett

Her father was the pioneering musician-musicologist Dr S. Ramanathan (1917–85) but she blazed trails of her very own, being one of the first female vina players to make a mark beyond the subcontinent.

⊙ Veena Virtuosa
Oriental Records, US

Dikshitkar's "Vallabanayakasya" and Papanasam Sivam's "Paraathpara" are gems of concision and perfection. No wasted phrases, whatever the piece's length. Poovalalur Srinivasan and S. Kartik accompany on, respectively, mridangam and ghatam. However miserly this CD's packaging, its music remains something else.

Chidambaram Temple Musicians

This famous Hindu temple in the town of Chidambaram, Tamil Nadu, is dedicated to Lord Shiva. Its *periya melam* ritual music ensemble plays an important role in temple life.

⊙ Inde du Sud: Periya Melam – Temple de Chidambaram
Ocora, France

A recording made in 2000 and 2001, this welds together Tamil culture on many levels. The album's longest track, "Sanmukhapriya Rakti Mejam", is one of the greatest nagaswaram-tavil recordings you could hope to hear. Achalpuram S. Chinnatambi Pillai and T. Ramanathan play the nagaswaram, M. Janagiraman its ottu drone counterpart, G. Murukesan and C. Gurunathan or S. Ramamurthy and J. Kumar the first and second tavil and M. Krishamurthy *talam* (a castanet).

A.S. Dhandapani

Anayampatti S. Dhandapani and his younger brother S. Ganeshan are the leading players of the jalatharangam. The instrument may be something of a musical curiosity, and live performances are hard to come by, but the music is extremely beautiful on disc.

★ Jalatharangam
Magnasound, India

Here Anayampatti Ganeshan accompanies his brother on violin with Thinniyam Y. Krishnan on mridangam in compositions by Tyagaraja and Dikshitar, among others.

Kadri Gopalnath

Gopalnath started on his father's instrument, the nagaswaram, but got turned on to the saxophone after hearing the palace band at Mysore. He studied initially under N. Gopalkrishna Iyer of Mangalore and the vocalist and mridangam player T.V. Gopalkrishnan and pioneered saxophone in a Karnatic classical setting. He typifies the duality of Karnatic music in playing a modern instrument in a tradition that goes back centuries.

★ Gem Tones: Saxophone Supreme, South Indian Style
Globestyle, UK

A fervent and thrilling collection with accompaniment by A. Kanyakumari on her low-tuned violin, sounding for all the world like a tenor sax, plus mridangam (M.R. Sainatha) and morsing (B. Rajasekhar).

Lalgudi Jayaraman

Violin may only be a relatively recent south Indian import – merely a few centuries old – but it is difficult to imagine Karnatic music without it and Jayaraman is one of the finest contemporary violinists.

⊙ Violin Waves
Felmay, Italy

Pure stream of consciousness. Aside from the opening composition by Jayaraman himself, the compositions are Tyagaraja's. The longest piece, "Vaddane", is a masterpiece of swirling melody. Better, maybe, is the concluding "Brova Baarama". The line-up is Lalgudi G.J.R. Krishnan (violin), Karaaikudi R. Mani (mridangam) and Vikku Vinayakram (ghatam). Originally released on the Pallavi Cassette label.

N. Ramani

The flautist Dr N. Ramani (b. 1934), like Balachander and M.S. Subbulakshmi, came to attention through Richard Bock's World Pacific label. Born in Tiruvarur in Tamil Nadu, the birthplace of Tyagaraja, by the age of twelve he was accomplished enough to be appearing on All India Radio.

⊙ Classical Karnatic Flute
Nimbus, UK

A recording with a great deal of presence dating from 1990. Ramani is accompanied by violin from T.S. Veeraraghhavan, mridangam from Srimushnam Rajarao and ghatam from E.M. Subramaniam in pieces by Tyagaraja and Ramani himself.

N. Ravikiran

The magisterial Ravikiran (b. 1967), who gave his first vocal recital at the age of five, is the foremost exponent of the chitra vina. In his hands, it is a joy, capable of arcane and ethereal sounds that in the West are associated with electronic instruments such as the *theremin*, but are typically Indian melodic properties.

⊙ Young Star of Gottuvadyam
Chhanda Dhara, Germany
Accompanied on mridangam by Trichur R. Mohan and on ghatam by T.H. Subashchandran, Ravikiran's repertoire and performances here are mesmerizing. The nearly nineteen-minute long performance of "Shankara Bharanam" is especially good and after the kriti the piece goes into a percussion duet. A northern *bhajan* in "Sindhu Bhairavi" closes.

L. Shankar

Early in his career, L. Shankar (b. 1953) played in a violin trio with his brothers L. Vaidyanathan and L. Subramaniam and accompanied Karnatic vocalists. He later embarked on a solo career and founded the Indo-Jazz fusion group Shakti with guitarist John McLaughlin. He is renowned for creating his own ten-string double violin with a startling extended range.

★ Raga Aberi
Music of the World, US
A spectacular ragam-thanam-pallavi performance growing out of the growling low notes of Shankar's extraordinary violin. The performance also features spectacular vocal percussion and solos from Zakir Hussain (tabla) and Vikku Vinayakram (ghatam).

Umayalpuram K. Sivaraman

One of the foremost present-day exponents of the mridangam, Umayalpuram K. Sivaraman was born in 1935 in the city of Tanjore.

★ Rhythm Fantasies
Sense World Music, UK
Here mridangam, as played by Umayalpuram K. Sivaraman, is placed at the forefront of a mixed percussion ensemble with violin and morsing accompaniment. The recording was made "up north" at the 2004 Saptak Festival in Gujarat. An exemplary place to begin an appreciation of south Indian ensemble drumming.

U. Srinivas

Rather than the eight-string Western mandolin, U. Srinivas (b. 1969) uses a five-string, solid body instrument, akin to a cut-down electric guitar, which he claims is ideally suited to the ragas of south Indian music. Like many Karnatic musicians he was a child prodigy and he has excited listeners the world over, notably in the West, with a successful fusion album, *Dream* (1995), with Michael Brook. He sometimes performs mandolin duets with his brother U. Rajesh.

⊙ Rama Sreerama
RealWorld, UK
A well-recorded and inspiring introduction to Srinivas' music, including pieces by Srinivas himself and Tyagaraja. Strongly devotional in character, with violin, mridangam and ghatam accompaniment.

L. Subramaniam

L. Subramaniam (b. 1947) is from a dynasty of violinists (his brothers are L. Vaidyanathan and Shakti founder L. Shankar). He is one of the most recorded Karnatic artists in the West and has regularly played in non-Karnatic contexts – with Hindustani musicians, jazz-fusion groups and Western orchestras and in films (including Mira Nair's *Salaam Bombay* and *Mississippi Masala*).

★ Inde du Sud: Le Violin de l'Inde du Sud
Ocora, France
The violinist's relationship with Ocora has been a long and fruitful one. This recording presents longer pieces than is usual. It opens with a glorious performance in ragam "Mohanam" (Hindustani music's Bhopali) that runs to nearly nineteen minutes. Subramaniam then trumps himself with a magnificent rendition of "Kirvani" (or Kirwani) performed as a coruscating ragam-thanam-pallavi, followed by a garland of ragams or *ragamalika*. Beautifully conceived as one thematic whole, the entire performances, recorded in December 1980, clocks in at just under an hour.

Kunnakudi Vaidyanathan

Violin plays such a central role in the songs of the south that hearing it in a non-classical context brings new insights. Kunnakudi R. Vaidyanathan was born in 1935 in Kunnakudi, Tamil Nadu. His large *kumkum pottu* (saffron spot) and *vibhooti* (sacred ash that he wears in the broad band on his forehead) are distinctive trademarks, but his violin playing is more distinctive still. Since 1968 he has worked in film music. He has also recorded extensively for AVM, Koel, Sangetha, Saregama and Silver Disc.

⊙ Puthiya Vaanam Puthiya Bhoomi: Film Tunes on Violin
Saregama, India
Very few albums begin like this one. It totally thwarts expectations. Hybridized south Indian – Tamil – film tunes on violin with more sample-worthy moments than probably any other south Indian album.

T.H. "Vikku" Vinayakram

The most famous ghatam magician the world has ever known – whether through his long and illustrious work with classical musicians from both of the subcontinent's art music systems or through his fusion work with Shakti and Remember Shakti (see p.596) and Planet Drum (see p.590). He has largely renounced international touring; in his stead his percussionist son V. Selvaganesh has soared, not as a ghatam player but as a major rhythmist on kanjira.

⊙ Vikku: 60 Years Celebration
Navras, India
Recorded live in London in November 2001, Vikku, one of the most self-effacing virtuosi and rhythmic geniuses on the planet, takes the stress of mental computation out of drumming. What could be bewildering becomes fun. He is joined by Selvaganesh on kanjira (frame drum), A. Sivamani on drums and Shridhar Parthasarthy on mridangam.

1 PANCHASAT PITHARUPINI Karukurichi P. Arunachalam from *Nadhaswaram*
Only a fanfare could start a Karnatic playlist and the instrument most fit for purpose is nagaswaram.

2 RĀGAM-TĀNAM-PALLAVI IN RASIKAPRIYA Chittu Babu from *The Art of Veena*
A lengthy exposition captured in a Tokyo studio in 1993.

3 KRITI "SARASAMUKHI" Ravikiran from *Madras*
Ethereal sounds from the chitra vina's foremost exponent and a notable addition to Hinduism's canonical literature as updated by Harikesanallur Muttaiya Bhagavatar (1877–1945).

4 RAGAM TANAM PALLAVI Dr T.N. Krishnan and Dr N. Rajam from *The Vibrant Violin of "Sangeetha Kalanidhi"*
From the foremost musical dynasty to straddle the south–north divide. T.N. Krishnan plays in the south Indian violin style and his sister N. Rajam in the Hindustani style.

5 VINAYAKUNI NINNU Kadri Gopalnath from *Gem Tones*
Devotional saxophone – and utterly convincing with it.

6 RAGAM CHAKRAVAAKAM Balachander from *Balachander: The Virtuoso of Veena*
Enduring inspiration handed down through the generations. A 1984 release from one of Karnatic music's greatest, most unorthodox minds.

7 TALKING FINGERS T.H. "Vikku" Vinayakram from *Vikku*
Count off a nine-and-a-half-beat cycle and flow. South Indian rhythmicality; hypnotic and sensuous.

8 BROVA BHAARAMAA Lalgudi G. Jayaraman, Lalgudi G.J.R. Krishnan and Lalgudi J. Vijayalakshmi from *Singing Violins*
A triple violin extravaganza rooted in a Thyagaraja composition.

9 ĀLĀPANAM – TĀNAM Rajeswari Padmanabhan, Dr Karaikudi Sambasivayer Aubramaniam and Tanjore Upendran from *Śambhō Mahādēva: Music for Vina, South India*
The everyday devotional and the everyday demotic tapping into the wellspring of south Indian musicality.

10 MAMAVASA DAVARATHE Karukurichi P. Arunachalam from *Carnatic Nadhaswaram*
No apologies for finishing where this playlist began. Any devotee of wind instruments will intuitively grasp the grandeur, any musician the breathing finesse and lung power required.

India | Vocal Music

the sacred and the profane

Rising performer Kaushiki Chakrabarty with tabla player Yogesh Samsi
Sense

Indian musicians have an old saying: "music without ornamentation is like a river bed without water". If so, devotional inspiration is like the source of the river. Performing the austere classical form of *dhrupad* is virtually considered meditation in itself, but in vocal forms the sacred and the profane are often intimately linked, as **Ken Hunt** explains.

The songs of the north can be divided into two strands: classical and light classical (also known as semi-classical). Classical requires a serious raga exposition such as dhrupad or *dhamar* provide, while the lighter forms relish freer expression in various degrees. A recital may keep to one repertoire or be mixed, the lighter forms frequently closing a classical concert on a more relaxed note.

As a general rule of thumb, musicians stick to forms appropriate to their faith. Thus a Hindu performer might close with a *bhajan* and a Muslim *qawwali* performer (see Pakistan) with a *ghazal*. Bhajans and *kritis* are essentially devotional songs, but in the hugely popular *thumri* and ghazal repertoire love for the divine and profane is frequently blurred. In the south the differences between the exposition of a Karnatic *ragam* and a kriti (the south's most typical Hindu hymn genre) are less distinct. A ragam and kriti performance amounts to one and the same thing.

Dhrupad

More than any other classical genre, **dhrupad** is regarded as a sacred art – an act of devotion and meditation rather than entertainment. It is an ancient and austere form which ranks as the Hindustani system's oldest vocal music genre still performed. The form enjoyed a golden age in Gwalior during the fifteenth and sixteenth centuries and is strongly connected with the famed singer **Miyan Tansen**, one of the seven jewels of Mughal emperor Akbar's court. (Many compositions credited to him are prefixed by "Mian ki…".)

Traditionally, dhrupad is performed only by men, accompanied by *tanpura* and the *pakhawaj* barrel drum. Nowadays it is most often set in a *tala* of twelve beats called *chautal*. A dhrupad lyric (usually in a medieval literary form of Hindi called Braj Bhasha) may be pure panegyric, praising a Hindu deity or local royalty, or it may dwell on noble or heroic themes. Less discussed are the non-devotional and non-heroic songs, dealing with metaphysical, philosophical and erotic themes. Since dhrupad's character is intrinsically intellectual, with each note applied as painstakingly as paint on a pointillist canvas, it is not a first port of call for newcomers or listeners with short attention spans; indeed its stately precision has been uncharitably likened to watching paint dry. While historically dhrupad was embedded deep within the Hindu psyche, as evidenced by **Candanji Caube** (1869–1944), Muslim musician lineages such as the **Dagar** dynasty have played profound roles as custodians of the dhrupad tradition. The twist is that this most Hindu of vocal genres is dominated by Muslims. The sublime maestro F. Wasifuddin Dagar, for example, is as much at ease praising Lord Krishna, Lord Shiva or the goddess Durga as he is discussing yoga or Islam.

The related **dhamar** form employs more *gamakas* (grace notes or ornaments) than dhrupad. Generally, gamakas in the Karnatic tradition are deemed essential elements in the melodic structure and are only rarely omitted, whereas in Hindustani music they are used far more sparingly, being reserved as a vehicle for personal expression. Usually set in a tala of fourteen beats, dhamar has largely been displaced by *khyal*, and to a lesser extent by thumri and *tappa*.

Bhajan

The **bhajan** is the most popular form of Hindu devotional composition in north India. Lyrically, bhajans eulogize a particular deity and frequently retell episodes from the Hindu scriptures. Devotion alone as the source of release is a tenet underlining many bhajan texts. You will hear them intoned by groups of pilgrims along the Ganges, at temples and on countless cassette players at festivals. **Mirabai** (a mystic saint-composer whose compositions in praise of Lord Krishna are of enduring popularity and who had "Raga Mirabai ki Malhar" named after her), **Kabir** (the faith-bridging, caste-shattering *bhakta* or devotee) and **Tulsidas** (often viewed as the northern Tyagaraja) are all notables who've contributed to the canon over the centuries and whose work is still performed every day.

Many bhajans date from the time of the Hindu Reformation and arose out of the **Bhakti** (devotionalism) movement that had begun with the **Tamil Alvars**, or poet-philosophers, in the ninth and tenth centuries AD and gradually radiated northwards. In Bengal, the movement reached its apogee during the fifteenth and sixteenth centuries. In that fertile and ever-changing region, mystic Hindu and Sufi sects found common ground in cross-connecting spirituality and worship centred on devotional love. Such exchanges led to the founding of the **Baul** philosophy in present-day Bengal and Bangladesh (see p.470) and on the other side of the subcontinent helped shape reforming Sikhism in the Punjab.

Given this background, it is unsurprising that divine love and spiritual emancipation figure prominently as the subject matter of bhajan lyrics. The musical elements of bhajans are usually

N.Rajam and her daughter Sangeeta Shankar

simple – uncomplicated rhythms and melodies which can be learned and sung by a congregation. Percussion and harmonium are the typical accompanying instruments.

The bhajan has gained wide popularity, particularly in the Hindustani repertoire. Solo instrumentalists incorporate bhajans in their repertoires – an excellent example can be heard in **N. Rajam**'s version of "Thumaki Chalat Ram Chandra" on *Gaayaki On Violin* (Gramophone Company of India). The instrumentalist's art lies in capturing the sonorities, syllables and devotional mood of the unsung words. In the South, bhajans tend to retain their original Hindustani raga but are set in Karnatic talas, as the Karnatic violinist **V.V. Subrahmanyam**'s exquisite recordings for the Gramophone Company of India show. Bhajans figure in the repertoires of most male and female Hindu vocalists, notably Jitendra Abhisheki, Bhimsen Joshi, Girija Devi, Pandit Jasraj, Lakshmi Shankar and Shobhu Gurtu.

Hindustani music also employs other devotional forms such as the *chaiti* (or *chait*), a seasonal hymn form associated with the month of Chaitra (March–April) and devoted to Krishna and Radha themes. An evocative instrumental performance of the chait "Maasi Saiiaan Nahin Aaye" appears on *50 Glorious Classical Years* (Gramophone Company of India), played by violinist N. Rajam.

Khyal

Less formal than dhrupad, **khyal** (also *khyel* or *khayaal*) is generally translated as "imagination" or "fancy". It is semi-classical in nature and allows the expression of emotion when improvising on its lyrical and musical themes. Its origins are uncertain, although many date it from the late fifteenth century and the rule of Hussain Shah Sharqi. By the eighteenth century it was popular at the Mughal court of Mohammed Shah in Delhi. Many khyals still in the repertoire today are attributed to **Sadarang**, the pen-name of **Niamat Khan**, one of the emperor's court musicians and the leading *rudra vina* player of his day. Sung by both men and women, khyal is more elaborate, showy and romantic in character than dhrupad. It has a lengthy *bada khyal* form, which is slow (*vilambit*), meditative and soul-searching, followed by the *drut* (fast) *chhota* (little) *khyal*.

Since the nineteenth century khyal has been the most popular classical vocal style in Hindustani music. **Abdul Karim Khan** (1872–1937), **Faiyaz Khan** (1886–1950) and **Amir Khan** (1912–74) are all leading names of the twentieth century who helped to establish its position. **Bade Ghulam Ali Khan** (1902–68) was loved for his exhibitionist waywardness: he might extend an ornamentation over three octaves and on one occasion incorporated a passing train whistle outside the venue into his performance in such a way that members of the audience were unsure whether they had heard or fantasized the passage. One of khyal's greatest current interpreters is the male vocalist **Bhimsen Joshi**, whose vocal ornamentations are a special delight. A true improviser, he is a master at confounding expectations by delivering an inspired phrase where a lesser vocalist would sing a standard one. Notable female khyal singers include **Arati Ankalikar**, **Shweta Jhaveri** (a teacher at the Ali Akbar College in San Anselmo, California, whose modernizing treatment of the form is most intriguing) and **Shruti Sadolikar** (a singer deeply rooted in khyal's traditional form).

Thumri

Thumri is the other light-classical song form which shares the pre-eminent place in Hindustani music. It is more immediately accessible than dhrupad and even khyal, both of which involve the abstract exploration of a raga. Thumri concentrates on the emotion of a song, exploring the sentiment through improvisation and ornamentation. Expression is more important than technique.

The origin of thumri is sometimes ascribed to the court of **Nawab Wajid Ali Shah**, who ruled Lucknow (Oudh) from 1847 to 1856, although its roots go back centuries earlier. Wajid Ali Shah was little interested in matters of state, but he was a great patron of the arts and during his reign music, dance, poetry, drama and architecture flourished. He composed thumri under the pen name **Akhtar Piya** and his famous "Babul more naihar chuto ri jaye" (Father, I can't bear to leave your home) is said to reflect his grief at being forced to leave Lucknow for Calcutta, where thumri subsequently also flourished.

The two predominant thumri styles are known as **Lucknavi** (i.e. from Lucknow) and **Punjabi**. Lucknow emerged as the major Indo-Muslim cultural centre in the eighteenth century, taking over from Delhi, then war-torn and ravaged by political and imperial intrigue. Thumri was a favoured form of *tawaif* (female courtesan) performers who became the first recording stars of the subcontinent. **Gauhar Jan** in Calcutta and **Jankibai** in Allahabad were able to command high fees. With the decline of tawaif culture, thumri, which had been closely identified with the sleazier aspects of the profession, underwent an image makeover, thanks in part to the gramophone. In its new incarnation as music played in well-to-do drawing rooms,

thumri emerged as a much cherished art form, predominantly wistful and nostalgic.

Although classical instrumentalists frequently perform a thumri in concert as a relaxation from the intensity of the pure classical style, most thumri is vocal. It is generally sung in Braj Bhasha, a literary dialect of Hindi spoken in the Mathura area, the heartland of the Bhakti movement and Krishna worship. The singer is usually accompanied by *tabla*, and the *sarangi* and harmonium are also common. The lyrics of thumri are usually romantic love songs, usually written from a female perspective, which dwell on the sadness of separation, quarrels, reconciliation, meetings with a husband or lover and often the love and exploits of Krishna.

Top singers include **Girija Devi** (b. 1929) and **Shobha Gurtu** (1925–2004). Despite the lyrics' concentration on the woman's perspective, some of the greatest singers of thumri have been men, notably Bade Ghulam Ali Khan. As male singers are frequently middle-aged and overweight, there is a certain initial incongruity in the evocation of the gentle and delicate emotions of a beautiful young woman. Yet a fine artist, fat and balding though he may be, can make a song like this one sublimely affecting: "My bracelets keep slipping off/My lover has cast a spell on me/He has struck me with his magic/What can a mere doctor do?"

Tarana and Tillana

In the **tarana** song genre, meaningless rhythmic syllables are substituted for a lyric, much as in jazz scat singing, but with greater rhythmic precision. While the concept is simple, maintaining artistic integrity and keeping ideas fresh so as to hold the listener's attention is not. Typically a tarana passage will close a khyal performance, maybe in place of a fast chhota khyal. Tarana's southern counterpart, the **tillana** (thillana), will do the same, on a more playful note, enabling the vocalist to express delight in pure sound articulated through rhythm. These forms are wonderful opportunities for a vocalist to show off. The Hindustani vocalist **Amir Khan** (1912–74) was renowned for his skills in the form, while maestro **M. Balamuralikrishna** (b. 1930) best demonstrates the southern equivalent.

Kriti

The Karnatic **kriti** (or *krithi*) is a song of praise or adoration for a particular Hindu deity in the south Indian tradition. The languages used are most commonly Telugu, Tamil or Sanskrit. Kritis are especially associated with three Hindu saint-composers: Tyagaraja, Muttuswamy Dikshitar and Syama Sastri (see p.553). Usually seated in a specific ragam, kritis usually last from five to eight minutes, but can be developed into a full-length classical performance lasting up to an hour, as with **M. Balamuralikrishna**'s recording for the Moment label. Balamuralikrishna is one of the recent notable male vocalists, along with **D.K. Jayaraman**, **P.S. Narayanswamy** and **T.V. Sankaranarayanan**. An exquisite female vocalist is **M.L. Vasanthakumari**. Most Karnatic instrumentalists will also dip into the kriti genre during a recital or on disc, with the standard accompaniment of *mridangam* and tanpura, and maybe a violin. For boundless creativity within south Indian forms including kriti as well as more esoteric fare, the late **M.S. Subbulakshmi**, **Aruna Sairam** (the vocalist popularly regarded as her successor) and **Sudha Ragunathan** epitomize the exquisite nature of Karnatic female creativity.

Ghazal

Found in related forms in Central Asia, Iran and Turkey, the **ghazal** was introduced to India by Persian Muslims. It is more song-like than its Urdu counterpart, thumri, being intrinsically a poetic rather than a musical form, and it is hugely popular among northern Hindus too. There has always been allegorical blurring of the distinction between erotic and divine love. The archaic form of the ghazal can be very refined, but although some ghazal tunes are raga-based, many do not follow any specific mode with consistency. The rhythms are clearly derived from folk music and at times the ghazal shades into the area of sophisticated pop song. Indian film music, in its insatiable appetite for new sensations, has assisted ghazal's popularity by co-opting (some would say vulgarizing) its poetry and form.

The ghazal has played an important part in many musical (and literary) cultures from the Middle East to Malaysia since the early eighteenth century, when singing was one of the accomplishments required of a courtesan. Ghazal singers of modern times usually come from more "respectable" backgrounds.

Each era of the ghazal tradition has contributed so-called *sha'irs* or master poets, stretching from Delhi's **Amir Khusrau** in the thirteenth century to Bombay's **Shakeel** today. Since the mid-1930s, poets have addressed secular and political themes, notably Faiz Ahmad Faiz (1911–84). While thumri singers take on a female persona, emotions in the ghazal are almost always expressed from the male point of view. Yet many of the finest ghazal performers are female. Their approaches vary enormously from the old-style majesty of **Begum Akhtar** (1914–74) and **Shobha Gurtu** via the transitional traditionalism-into-modernity accomplishments of Indo-Pakistani ghazal specialists

George Whiteside

Rising Canadian-Indian ghazal singer Kiran Ahluwalia

such as **Iqbal Bano** (1935–2009) and **Farida Khanum** (b. 1935) to the new-style ghazal of **Najma Akhtar** and **Kiran Ahluwalia**.

The blossoming of **Kaushiki Chakrabarty** (daughter of the acclaimed vocalist **Ajoy Chakrabarty**) and **Sangeeta Bandyopadhyay** has been a wonder to behold. Perhaps the most

wondrous aspect of all when it comes to Indian vocal music is the continual arrival of new "discoveries" building on traditions thousands of years old. As Kaushiki Chakrabarty confides, "Indian music can never be old. The performers can be old: the music is evergreen. It's so modern. It has an all-time appeal."

Hindustani vocal music

⊙ Ragamala
Gramophone Company of India, India
The cliché of one track warranting the price of an entire album applies here – a delicious version of "Raga Marwa" sung by Amir Khan in 1960. Niaz Ahmed Khan and Fayyaz Ahmed Khan, K.G. Ginde, Bade Ghulam Ali Khan and Surshri Kesar Bai Kerkar complete the all-star classical line-up.

⊙ Vintage Music from India
Rounder, US
An anthology by Peter Manuel concentrating on northern traditions, and vocal music in particular, recorded between 1906 and the 1920s, featuring India's first celebrity recording artist Gauhar Jan. It includes forms as different as qawwali (Sufi devotional music) and tawaif or *nautch* (female courtesan) music.

Kiran Ahluwalia

Born in 1965 in Patna, Bihar, Ahluwalia has long been based in North America, but nothing prepared listeners for the paradigm shift in Indo-Pakistani diaspora music that she launched with her *Beyond Boundaries* (2003). Of utmost significance for her and ghazal is her engagement with the poeticism of contemporary writers such as Rasheed Nadeem and Rafi Raza.

★ Beyond Boundaries
Kiran Music, Canada
Impossible-to-resist performances – Ahluwalia has the magical touch. Importantly, she is not delivering traditional music. This is contemporary music poured into old bottles, both in literary and musical terms. Like the sonnet, the ghazal is an enduring form. After all, ghazal can be rendered in English as "to talk to women" and "to talk of women".

Najma Akhtar

Singer Najma Akhtar (b. 1964) made an enormous impression on fans of world music with her second album *Qareeb* in 1987. In 1989 *Atish* (fire in Urdu) confirmed her place in modern Hindustani fusion music.

⊙ Qareeb
Triple Earth, UK; Shanachie, US
Having one track included in the soundtrack to Stephen Frears' acclaimed 1987 film *Sammy and Rosie Get Laid* helped get Akhtar's debut noticed, but it is the lyrical gift, innovative arrangements and fine instrumental playing (including violin, sax and *santoor*) that sets *Qareeb* (Nearness) apart. The

hit track "Dil Laga Ya Tha" has some catchy melodic and harmonic twists. This is a modern ghazal classic.

Kishori Amonkar

Born in 1931 in Bombay, Kishori Amonkar is one of Hindustani music's greatest stylists. Totally rooted in tradition, she is a national icon, just as Edith Piaf is for France, Marlene Dietrich is for Germany and Katalin Karády is for Hungary. Especially admired for her khyal interpretations, which have a heartfelt, sensual phrasing, she represents the consummate artistry of the Jaipur gharana and the Hindustani spirit of innovation within tradition.

⊙ Maestro's Choice
Music Today, India
Two superb khyal performances in "Ahir Bhairav" and "Sampurna Malkauns". The final composition in Sampurna Malkauns is by Amonkar's guru-mother, the acclaimed vocal-

George Ward

Asha Bhosle with sarod maestro Ali Akbar Khan

ist Moghubai Kurdikar (1904–2001). Sultan Khan plays sarangi and Balkrishna Iyer tabla.

Sampradya
Navras, UK; Navras/Sony, India

Recorded live at Kensington Town Hall in 2000, this double CD not only supplies the goods musically with khyal performances in "Alhaiya Bilawal" (or Alihya Bilawal), "Bhairavi" and "Jeevanpuri" (also known as Jaunpuri) but also comes with extensive notes and an interview about Amonkar's thoughts on making music.

WITH HARIPRASAD CHAURASIA

⊙ Kishori Amonkar and Hariprasad Chaurasia
Navras, UK

In an inspired jugalbandi duet, voice and flute interweave on two khyals set in raga "Lalit" and an especially fetching thumri in "Sindhi Bhairavi". This double CD was recorded live in Bombay in 1995.

Asha Bhosle

Younger sister of Lata Mangeshkar, and almost equally acclaimed as India's favourite female playback singer.

Legacy
AMMP, US

The Grammy-nominated collaboration between Bhosle and the great *sarod* player Ali Akbar Khan, who traces his classical music ancestry back to Tansen himself. This collection of classical and light-classical vocal gems was learned from Khan's father and previous generations of his dynasty. An extraordinary beautiful opening Guru Bandana (prayer) initiates a very special collection of khyal, tarana, *holi* and *sadra* performances, with superb accompaniment from Khan and Swapan Chaudhuri (tabla and pakhawaj).

Ajoy Chakrabarty

Chakrabarty (b. 1953) is a leading exponent of the Patiala *gharana* (the same style as Bade Ghulam Ali Khan). He has recorded in a variety of styles including bhajan, *dadra*, khyal and thumri.

⊙ Vocal
India Archive Music, US

Recorded in 1992 and released in 1995, this collection of four compositions (bandishes) in Khamaj is too beautiful for words. Sultan Khan plays sarangi to die for and Samar Saha plays perfect tabla.

Kaushiki Chakrabarty

Born in 1980, Kaushiki Chakrabarty is the daughter of Ajoy and Chandana Chakrabarty. She was clearly marked out to be a formidable talent. Although she had made recordings before her association with Sense World Music, it was their getting behind *Pure* (2004) that propelled her into the wider consciousness. Her triple CD *Kaushiki* (2007) consolidated her standing.

Pure
Sense World Music, UK

Quite simply, an essential addition to a well-balanced musical diet.

⊙ Kaushiki
Sense World Music, UK

One-third studio, two-thirds live at the 2007 Saptak Festival in Ahmedabad, Gujarat. The climax is the third CD and its thumri in the light mixed raga "Mishra Pilu". Thumri is associated with allegory and musical play-acting and here Chakrabarty truly shines.

The Dagar Brothers

Born into a family of court musicians in Indore, the Dagar Brothers are the most important communicators of the intellectually demanding and dignified dhrupad vocal form. The family's dhrupad *vani* (or *bani*; the word literally means "sayings of saints", but it is akin to gharana) is one of the four main schools.

⊙ Shiva Mahadeva
Pan, Netherlands

In 1978 the Royal Netherlands World Service recorded the brothers Zahiruddin Dagar (1932–94) and Faiyazuddin Dagar (1934–89) performing "Malkauns", "Darbari Kanada", "Adana" and "Bhatiyar", interspersed with explanations about dhrupad and how time or season conditions the appropriate raga. This resulting double album concludes with a dhamar composition in "Behag". Stateliness personified.

Wasifuddin Dagar

Faiyaz Wasifuddin Dagar (b. 1969, New Delhi) has breathed new life into the dhrupad form and, contrary to the long-standing familial arrangements, he sings solo. His appearances at the 2008 Harballabh Sangeet Sammelan in Punjab's Jalandhar City and the 2009 Darbar Festival in London were exemplary.

⊙ Dagar: The Pathway
Navras, UK

The title of this album reminds us that the family's adopted name dagar means "path" or "pathway", and this performance from 2007 exemplifies everything that is magical and connecting about his singing and artistry. Dhrupad that honours the past yet ushers the form into its future.

Kumar Gandharva and Vasundhara Komkali

Nowadays, Kumar Gandharva (1924–92) is an overlooked vocalist. Yet he studied with B.R. Deodhar, one of the great shapers of Hindustani music in the twentieth century. He was a great, natural talent. Vasundhara Komkali was his second wife.

⊙ Bhajan – Triveni
Gramophone Company of India, India

Bhajans (hymns) from a triumvirate ("triveni") of saint-composers from the Bhakti (Hindu Reformation) movement that pitted its wits against, to quote the notes, "the tyranny of ritualism, casteism, untouchability and other aberrations which had crept into formal religious practices". The three are Surdas, a sightless poet with a different vision of Krishna consciousness, Tulsidas, the author of the *Ramcharitmanas*, and Kabir, a saint-poet who preached about a caste-free society and whose vision profoundly informed the true Sikh faith, sadly a religion increasingly reverting to caste discrimination. Simply gorgeous interpretations of three historic composers of songs for emancipation and change.

Gundecha Brothers

Umakant and Ramakant Gundecha are major vocalists, deeply versed in the dhrupad style of singing. They also follow the Jain faith, one of the subcontinent's great faiths. Jainism is generally overlooked, but it has a long tradition of religiosity told through musicality.

⊙ **Bhaktamar Stotra**
Sense World Music, UK
Subtitled the "Sacred Chants of Jainism", these interpretations revisit the *Bhaktamara Stotra* of Manatunga, the founding Jain poet-monk whose singing is claimed to have cured the Hindu poet Mayura of leprosy. Thereafter, the legend says that Mayura's fellow poet Bana ordered Manatunga's hands to be severed from his body, but after he sang praise songs to the Hindu goddess Chandhi, the goddess restored him. Regrettably, the gorgeous package does not include an English-language translation, only notes in English.

Shweta Jhaveri

Jhaveri (b. 1965) has a richly hued voice, well suited to khyal and bhajan. She sang the voice of Pallavi to Shanti Hiranand's Karuna Devi in Rajan Khosa's much-recommended film *Dance of the Wind* (soundtrack Navras, UK). While she has a high profile for her contemporized, "cosmic" khyal approach, her classical work is exquisite.

⊙ **Avishkar**
21st Century Cosmos, US
Khyals based on Lord Krishna's enamouring ways, the turning of the seasons and the seasonal *mela*, composed by Jhaveri herself in "Abhogi", "Chandrakauns", "Rageshree" and others. She is accompanied by tabla and pakhawaj, harmonium and tanpura.

Bhimsen Joshi

Bhimsen Joshi (b. 1922) is one of India's greatest vocal maestros and a supreme khyal interpreter. He learned from many sources but is primarily associated with the renowned Kirana gharana. An uncompromising yet far from hidebound classicist with a warm, lived-in voice.

 In Celebration
Navras, UK
One of Hindustani music's most lauded masters captured in his accomplished prime. On this 1993 recording, Joshi performs "Maru Bihag" and "Abhogi".

⊙ **Raga Yaman Kalyan; Raga Gara; Bhajan**
Chhanda Dhara, Germany
A 1999 release that confirms Joshi's position as a heavyweight, with a khyal, thumri and bhajan. His vocal displays in the faster sections of "Yaman Kalyan" weave a hypnotic tapestry of variations, while the bhajan features the lyrics of sixteenth-century mystic poet Mirabai and Joshi proves there is no male vocalist to surpass him in this genre.

Amir Khan

Amir Khan (1912–74) was *ananya* – "nonesuch" or "unique". He ties with Bhimsen Joshi as supreme contender for the male vocalist award when it comes to spontaneous creativity and influencing his and modern times. He is shamefully under-represented by commercial releases.

 Ananya
Navras, UK
These performances of "Yaman", "Hamsadhwani", "Puriya" and "Abhogi" from the undated 1960s demand repeated revisiting. As an example of continuity, the composition "Charana dhara aayo ri", which he sings in "Abhogi", also went into the repertoires of Bhimsen Joshi and Rashid Khan.

Rashid Khan

Rashid Khan (b. 1966) has deservedly risen to become a major new voice in Hindustani khyal music, widely hailed as the most promising male vocalist of his generation. He is a superb craftsman and manipulator of feelings in song.

⊙ **Khyal**
Moment, US
"Bageshri" and "Kedar" recorded in Buffalo, New York, in 1993. "Bageshri" is a fully fledged khyal performance totalling almost fifty minutes, moving from an opening alap into a bada khyai performance wrapped up with two *chhota khyal* compositions.

Mallik family

Less heavily promoted in the West than the Dagar family, the Mallik family are immortalized in the mythology of Indian music for averting a famine with the power of their performance of "Megh", a rainy season raga. As a reward they were given land in Darbhanga in northeastern India, where the family still resides. Until Independence they were court musicians for the Maharajas of Darbhanga and since 1947 they've become highly respected vocalists in the arts of khyal, thumri and especially dhrupad.

⊙ **Dhrupads from Darbhanga**
VDE-Gallo/AIMP, Switzerland
Much of this repertoire is unique to the Mallik family, with austere but rhythmic and charismatic performances by Bidur Mallik, the head of the family, and his two sons Premkumar and Anandkumar.

Shruti Sadolikar

Shruti Sadolikar (b. 1951) is one of the next generation of khyal singers, brought up in the style of the Jaipur gharana.

⊙ **Ragas Marwa, Hamsakankini & Thumri**
Navras, UK
This disc contains one of the finer khyal performances of "Raga Marwa", an evening raga. Sadolikar sings with a dignified restraint that still conveys the emotion and restlessness of the raga. "Hamsakankini" is a morning raga, and the thumri is sung to a lilting Punjabi rhythm. Accompaniment comes from the tabla of Partha Sarathi Mukherjee and the harmonium of Dr Arvind Thatte.

Lakshmi Shankar

Lakshmi Shankar (b. 1926) is a glorious singer. Married to the scriptwriter Rajendra Shankar, an elder brother of Ravi Shankar, she joined her brother-in-law Uday Shankar's artistic circle during the early 1940s as a classical dancer. Poor health forced her to give up dancing for singing and the world was a better place for it.

★ **Live in London Volume 1**
Navras, UK
Recorded at a 1992 concert of devotional and light-classical repertoire, with tabla and harmonium accompaniment. "Mishra Kafi" shows off both her glorious voice and thumri's artistic suppleness.

Jagjit and Chitra Singh

The names of this husband and wife team are synonymous with ghazal. Being previously something of a middle-class phenomenon, the Singhs' 1976 album *The Unforgettables* established them as the popular face of ghazal. In 1991 tragedy struck with the death of their nineteen-year-old son and Chitra withdrew from performance. Her husband Jagjit (b. 1941) continues to sing, notably on *Sadja* (Gramophone Company of India), the duo album with Lata Mangeshkar.

The Golden Collection
Gramophone Company of India, India
These 29 solo and duo tracks over two CDs are terrific, with tasteful sarangi and tabla work.

Parween Sultana

Contrary to typical Muslim practice, Parween Sultana (b. 1950) was encouraged by her father, debuting on stage at the age of nine and recording her first LP in 1967. She is acclaimed for the cultured tone she brought to Indian movie soundtracks such as *Ashary*, *Kudrat* and, especially, *Pakeezah*.

⊙ Live from Savai Gandharva Music Festival, Pune '92
Alurkar Music House, US
Recorded at an Indian music conference, Parween Sultana reveals her class with remarkably insightful interpretations of "Gujari Todi" and "Jaunpuri". Closing this classical recital on a lighter note, she finishes with a tarana, a wordless exercise in rhythm.

Karnatic vocal music

M. Balamuralikrishna

Born in 1930 into a musical family, Balamuralikrishna was a child prodigy. He is also credited as a composer of new ragam formulations and some four hundred classical compositions.

★ Vocal

Moment, US
A kriti in Lathangi lasting nearly an hour, followed by a spectacular tillana performance using four different ragams in succession to create a *tillana ragamalika* (garland of ragams). Zakir Hussain (tabla) and T.H. Vinayakram (ghatam) provide rhythmic support.

Jon Higgins

The presence of an American vocalist here may seem peculiar, but Higgins (1939–84) was a commanding Karnatic vocalist and still regarded as one of the most important ambassadors for Indian arts by the south Indian community. His recordings reveal a vocalist of great sensitivity.

⊙ Jon B. Higgins: Carnatic Vocal
Gramophone Company of India, India
Accompanied by violin, mridangam and *kanjira* (hand-drum), the nine tracks here reveal how Higgins made himself at home in a kriti repertoire. The performance of Muttuswamy Dikshitar's "Tyagaraja Yoga Vaibhavam" is exemplary. He closes with a tillana.

Sudha Ragunathan

On very rare occasions along comes a new musician whose presence and musicality simply transport the listener. Since her debut, Sudha Ragunathan has proved herself to be one of the most illuminating female singers in Karnatic music. Although she has recorded for labels such as EMI India and Inreco, her prime work is to be found on Winston Panchacharam's New York-based Amutham label.

⊙ Kaleeya Krishna
Amutham, US
Released in 1994, this album of devotional music finds Ragunathan in the company of a full Indian orchestra conducted by Vazhuvoor R. Manikkavinayakam. The record celebrates the work of the composer Ventatasubbaiyar (1700–65), whose muse was Krishna. An uplifting performance, even for non-Hindus.

Aruna Sairam

Born in Bombay in 1952, Aruna Sairam grew up in a musical family. Her first teacher was her mother Rajalakshmi Sethuraman and the household played host to guests such as the vocalists Amir Khan and M.S. Subbulakshmi and the *bansuri* player T.R. Mahalingam. She has recorded for a variety of labels. In 1996 she recorded *Aruna und die 1000 Namen der göttlichen Mutter* (Aruna and the Thousand Names of the Divine Mother, Lichthaus-Musik, Germany) with Michael Reimann and Christian Bollmann, a project bringing together raga and overtone singing.

⊙ Inde du Sud: padam, le chant de Tanjore
Ocora, France
An album in the Tanjore style of singing and the relatively uncommon *padam* song form. Padam is a sung poetry, which builds tension by toying with beats and using spurts of energy to "destabilize" expectations. The lines are composed. The music goes between set and spontaneously conceived composition. This masterpiece introduced this marvellous singer to the wider world. Recorded by Radio France in September 1999 and released the following year, it was reissued in 2007. Sairam is accompanied by violin, mridangam, ghatam and tanpura.

M.S. Subbulakshmi

M.S. Subbulakshmi (1916–2004) was one of the foremost cultural ambassadors for Indian arts in her lifetime, and certainly the greatest ambassador for Karnatic music. In the 1960s she enjoyed a great deal of attention by virtue of her albums being available on the World Pacific label. But unlike Ravi Shankar she did not support her recording career with constant touring, although she appeared at the Edinburgh Festival (1963) and at Carnegie Hall (1977). She has been heaped with honours, and is considered a national treasure.

⊙ M.S. Subbulakshmi at Carnegie Hall
Gramophone Company of India, India
This double CD captures Subbulakshmi in New York in October 1977 with her daughter Radha Viswanathan, the violinist Kandadevi Alagiriswami and the percussionist Guruvayur Dorai.

⊙ Legends: M.S. Subbulakshmi
Saregama, India
The definitive five-CD boxed set released in 1998. It includes film and devotional material that became so popular it might be considered popular music.

M. Yogeswaran

The Sri Lankan singer Manickam Yogeswaran (b. 1959) had his early tutelage with Thitu P. Muthukamaraswami and Thiru S. Balasingam. He is a disciple of T.V. Gopalkrishnan of Chennai. Long based in Britain, in addition to singing in traditional Tamil contexts, he is arguably the Tamil singer whose voice has reached greater audiences than anyone since M.S. Subbulakshmi in her heyday. He is a featured vocalist in the soundtracks to Stanley Kubrick's *Eyes Wide Shut* (1999), Spike Lee's *25th Hour* (2002) and Sarah Gavron's *Brick Lane* (2007). He has also worked with Dissidenten (see p.170), The Shout, the Shobana Jeyasingh Dance Company and the composer Jocelyn Pook.

Much of the subcontinent's culture is bound up in codes of conduct and morality. Much of it is enforced, allowing little leeway for free will. Thiruvalluvar created 133 aphoristic entreaties and injunctions about living one's life correctly that were set to music in order to make them easier to memorize. Yogeswaran delivers the sage's guidance on Aram (virtue), Porul (wealth) and Kamam (love).

PLAYLIST
India | Vocal

1 **PIYA MOHE ANANT DES** Amir Khan from *Ragamala (Classical Vocal Compilation) Vol. 1*
Amir Khan's 1960 reading in "Raga Marwa" remains haloed as one of the most beautiful Hindustani vocal performances of all time.

2 **GANESA PANCHARATNAM** M.S. Subbulakshmi from *Legends: M.S. Subbulakshmi*
The most influential south Indian female vocalist of our era delivers a wonderfully supple, utterly ageless performance.

3 **RAJASTHANI FOLK SONG IN RĀG BHŪP MĀND** Sultan Khan from *Sarangi*
More than a traditional lullaby: Sultan Khan turns it into a vocal and sarangi *tour de force*.

4 **KRITI IN RAGA LATHĀNGI** Dr M. Balamuralikrishna from *Vocal*
A great sweep of a performance lasting almost an hour, unusual for a Karnatic performance.

5 **DHUNDHAN JAAVU** Shweta Jhaveri from *Khayal-Saga*
The sheer power of Jhaveri's focused imagination in this example of the bada khyal (big khyal) form set in "Puriya Dhanashree" is revelatory.

6 **RĀGAM-TĀNAM-PALLAVI** Ramnad Krishnan from *Ramnad Krishnan: Vidwan*
Rāgam-Tānam-Pallavi is the sequence most closely corresponding to the standard Hindustani unfurling of a raga.

7 **RĀG DARBĀRI KĀNRĀ** Pandit Jasraj from *Invocation*
A recording from 1992 of crystal clarity and tangible presence. Shweta Jhaveri accompanies her guru on tanpura.

8 **SHAMBHO MAHADEVA** Bombay S. Jayashri from *Shambho Mahadeva*
Pace, rhythm and vocal acrobatics in ample measure, south Indian-style.

9 **THILLANA IN RAGA KUNTANAVARALI** Kaushiki Chakrabarty from *Kaushiki*
An exercise in northern Indian rhythmic musicality and melodic athleticism.

10 **PADAM "KONTEGADU"** Aruna Sairam from *Inde du Sud: padam, le chant de Tanjore*
Padam is a stately style of singing requiring extraordinary vocal control and powers of enunciation. It's like a present from the subcontinent's primeval past that is wholly contemporary.

India | Folk and Adivasi Music

tunes from the dunes

Ger dance being performed by folk artists at the Mehrangarh Fort in Jodhpur
Jodhpur RIFF

It's India's new-found economic prowess that tends to grab the headlines these days. But, according to the 2001 census, 72 percent of India's population remains rural and it's in the villages where a vibrant proportion of music has its heart in a living tradition that goes back centuries. Life for rural musicians is getting harder and harder. While the urban population leaps forward economically, the rural population gets marginalized and becomes poorer. Ken Hunt and Simon Broughton reveal the highlights of Indian folk music and some efforts being made to sustain it.

Poverty and under-development tend to preserve and nurture traditions, but it doesn't take long for technology to destroy them. In Indian folk music, you can date this process back to the 1930s, when traditional folk drama lost out to the movies, and traditional backcloths across the subcontinent were replaced with projection screens. Nowadays, for instance, although you still find itinerant snake charmers at regional fairs and festivities, they are more likely to be playing the popular "snake charming" tune from the 1950s film *Nagin* than any traditional repertoire.

The arrival of recorded sound has had a more mixed effect. While it has weakened the supremacy of live music, India's wholesale adoption of **cassettes** – from the 1970s – has hugely encouraged local music. While HMV India focused on high-art Indian music and recorded the big-name classical artists, local cassette companies like Venus and T-Series (the latter founded by Gulshan Arora in 1979) sold hundreds of regional pop and folk titles, mainly at kiosks and in grocery stores. Regional folk music, which had never been recorded before, also became available, thanks to dozens of small producers based in Delhi, Mumbai, Calcutta and elsewhere.

By contrast, recordings of more traditional folk and Adivasi music are comparatively rare, and most ethnographic recordings have been issued on Western labels – and even then in a very limited way.

Desi and Marga

Folk music in India is often described as **desi** (or *deshi*), meaning "of the country", to distinguish it from art music, known as **marga** (meaning "chaste" and, by extension, classical). Desi, a catchall term, also embraces folk theatre and popular music of many colours.

Many traditionalists and academics view folk music as a corrupted legacy of an earlier, higher form, thus aligning themselves with the scholar Bharata Muni, who demarcated all music as either marga or desi. In fact, desi music bolsters the classical Hindustani repertoire. It has lent its instruments, notably the bowed *sarangi* (still played by folk musicians to accompany songs in Rajasthan) and the *santoor* (a Kashmiri hammered dulcimer), both of which are now established classical instruments in their own right. It has lent its forms: *dhuns* (folk airs) and *kajaris* (folk songs from Uttar Pradesh) are often performed as light relaxation after the rigorous performance of a raga, rather like an encore at the end of a concert. And it has lent its style, as when Hindustani vocal maestro Bade Ghulam Ali Khan rejuvenated popular *thumri* music by flavouring it with folk stylings, typically Punjabi in nature.

Some of the ragas in classical music are named after particular regions, suggesting the influence of a local folk style. For example, the ragas Gujari (Gujarat), Mand (Rajasthan), Bangal (Bengal) and Pahari (the foothills of the Himalayas in the

Blue Flame

Rajasthani folk band Musafir

Desert Slide

The best-known legacies of the British in India are the extensive railway network, some imposing architecture and a lumbering bureaucracy. A more curious, but significant legacy are the ubiquitous brass bands, which have replaced the earlier ceremonial ensembles of *shehnai* and drums. Every large town in India will have dozens of competing "band shops" – usually identifiable by a brightly painted cart bristling with loudhailers standing outside – where a band can be booked and assembled for a wedding. In India, a wedding simply doesn't happen without a brass band. In large cities whole streets of the town or *chowk* (bazaar) may be dedicated to the business, just as you'll get an area for spices or cloth. The cities of Bhopal, Jhabalpur, Jaipur and Calcutta are noted for their wedding bands. In Bhopal, the state capital of Madhya Pradesh, strolling down Itwara Road you'll pass any number of band shops with trumpets, horns and tubas advertising their trade, plus liveried caps and formal photos of the band in uniform on the walls.

A *barat*, or wedding procession, through the streets is a spectacular sight. The groom is often on a magnificent white horse preceded by a band of perhaps a dozen musicians playing trumpets, large baritone horns, tubas, saxophones and a couple of side drums; they're usually led by a wild clarinet. Alongside, small boys stagger in procession with heavy electric candelabras joined together by cables stretching to a generator somewhere at the back.

The bandwallahs (musicians) are often migrant workers, hired in from the country for the wedding season, which lasts for five or six months through the winter. Rampur, a town northeast of Delhi, is particularly famous as a source of musicians. It's been estimated that across India there are between 500,000 and 800,000 people earning a living in the band party business. The music is brash and tuning is wayward, but it's the mood of celebration and public display that counts. A typical band can get by with less than twenty songs a season – half of these will be the current film favourites and the other half will be classic film songs that have more or less become the new folk tunes of contemporary India.

Interestingly, the Indian-style brass band has now been exported back to Britain in the shape of the Bollywood Brass Band, an act that is hugely popular at weddings and music festivals in the UK.

Simon Broughton

northwest) are named after regions whose tunes may have suggested the raga. The popular raga Desh (meaning "country") may refer to an area of Rajasthan, a region where some of the folk tunes are described as being in Sorath and Bhairavi, and share many features with those classical ragas.

Celebration and Devotion

In the Indian subcontinent, music is used extensively for ritual purposes. It marks rites of passage, logs the course of the seasons and sanctifies religious ceremonies. Any **festival** in India will include music, from the great temple festivals in the south – with curling trumpets, massed drums, elephants and ceremonial chariots – to the more ascetic conch shells and ringing bells of the Himalayan foothills, to say nothing of the sung mantras of the pilgrim groups that flock to the thousands of holy sites across the country. Religious festivals come complete with buskers, snake charmers and folk theatre troupes, and, despite rampant modernization, such practices are very much alive. Of all rites of passage, the most important for music

are weddings. In urban India the music will be provided by a brass band (see box), but in the countryside it will be more traditional.

While there is extraordinary folk music to be found all over India, there are three areas where it is particularly rich and easy to access as a visitor – Rajasthan, Kerala and Bengal, where the Bauls are the inspirational music providers. Rajasthani groups and Baul musicians are popular performers on the world music circuit. The music of the Bauls is covered, however, in the Bangladesh chapter.

Punjab and Gujarat

The harvest is celebrated in every culture and in the Punjab it gave rise to **bhangra**, a folk dance which, in its British commercial form (see p.113), has transmogrified into a form of Asian pop. In its Punjabi form, bhangra was originally an exclusively male preserve. Nowadays, female artists compete for record sales, though male Punjabi pride is too macho to be seen performing women's music, so women's music is tagged as **giddha**, or **dafjan**, another Punjabi women's song style.

571

Under the pressure of social change, certain styles of folk music, like bhangra, have displayed an adaptability which nobody would have predicted. Who would have thought that diaspora Punjabis based in England could have repackaged a *dhol* drum-driven harvest celebration and sold it back to India, even while agricultural communities still celebrated it the old-fashioned way? No one pretends that the old ways are eternal, but they are proving extraordinarily resilient.

Following on from the crossover success of bhangra, **dandiya**, a new folk-based genre, has emerged as a new phenomenon with a club-based following in India. Based on Gujarati folk music, the albums by **Falguni Pathak**, the leading female performer on the live dandiya circuit, have sold in their millions. Dandiya music is normally set to Gujarati lyrics, but Pathak sings in Hindi and gives the sound a pop sensibility for mass appeal.

Rajasthan

The northwestern desert state of Rajasthan, with over twenty million inhabitants, is one of the regions most visited by tourists. It also has the liveliest folk tradition, and not just because musicians are employed in restaurants. While the tourist industry has tapped the musical heritage – buskers play the two-stringed *ravanhatha* beneath the magnificent walls of the Jaisalmer citadel, and troupes of Manganiyar musicians can be requisitioned to play for camel safaris and barbecues in the desert – the fact is that music is a vital part of Rajasthani culture.

Most celebrated in Rajasthan are the **Langa**, caste musicians who also deal in camels and spices. Centred around Jodhpur, they converted to Islam in the seventeenth century and played for Muslim patrons. There are two sub-castes of Langa, the **Sarangi Langas**, who sing accompanied by a bowed sarangi, and the **Surnai Langa** who don't sing and only play wind instruments like the *surnai* (oboe), *satara* (double flute) and *murali* (a double clarinet with a reservoir of air in a gourd).

The **Manganiyar** caste are based around Jaisalmer, the great walled city of

the Thar desert, and serve both Muslim and Hindu patrons. They play the *kamayacha* (bowed fiddle), harmonium and *khatal* (hardwood castanets). Manganiyar means "one who begs", and this caste has a lower social status than the Langa. It's from itinerant musicians such as these that the Roma (Gypsies) may have originated. Every autumn, the Gypsies of Rajasthan gather in the town of Runija (on the road from Jodhpur to Jaisalmer) for a festival at the temple of Baba Ramdev, their chosen saint. The painted wagons on the road headed for the fair are a sight in themselves and the event itself gives the most vivid, if overwhelming, insight into contemporary Indian Gypsy life and culture.

But the Langa and Manganiyar are by no means the only musicians of Rajasthan. There are several other itinerant castes, including the **Sapera**, traditional snake charmers who play the *pungi* (a double flute). The **Jogi** are wandering mystics, and any opportunity of seeing one playing the extraordinary one-stringed *bhapang* with wild glissandi shouldn't be missed. The **Bhopa** are epic bards, whose instruments include the two-stringed ravanhatha, played with a bow with jangling bells, and the big *jantar*, a zither supported on two gourds. Traditionally, the epics are sung and danced at night in front of a painted canvas while an assistant illuminates the scenes illustrating the sung episodes in the story. These Bhopa ballads are one of the forms that has been hit dramatically by the cinema.

As the new India looks forward with its IT specialists and call centres, traditional arts – like music – are becoming neglected. But there are several organizations that have started to highlight the value of India's folk culture. Beat of India

Folk perfomers at the Rajasthan International Folk Festival, Jodhpur

Jodhpur RIFF

Beat of India

Chetan Karnani wrote eloquently in his *Listening to Hindustani Music* (1976) of "the great regard in which folk music is held", yet drew a distinction between India's "living folk music" and its "museum piece" face during Republic Day celebrations. Folk music of any authenticity has enjoyed a chequered history as far as its recorded legacy is concerned. All India Radio (AIR), HMV India and EMI Pakistan, in all their various incarnations, have done exceptional work in promoting indigenous folk music but most recordings have relatively short catalogue lives. That is why the emergence of **Beat of India** has proved such a revelation.

Launched in New Delhi in 2000, the label began as green as green can be. They started collecting in Uttar Pradesh and in what has since become Uttaranchal. Someone at AIR's Almora station eventually gave them some leads – though it was made plain that they were unsure whether any of the source

Maitrayee Patel's album *Navi Vahwani*

singers or musicians mentioned were alive or dead. It led to an early major and morale-boosting discovery. "Anandi Devi and Sant Ram sing for alms at the bus stop", Beat of India's **Shefali Bhushan** explains. "They have some of the most experienced, yet untrained voices. The kind of voice quality that both of them have and the kind of communication that they share with each other when they sing together – and they sing together mostly – is rare. Even among trained classical musicians." **Anandi Devi** and **Sant Ram** typify the wow factor that Indian folk music can bring.

Other label notables include **Jhusia Damal**, a singer of epics from the Dunga toli community from Pithoragarh in Uttaranchal; **Anita Bhandari** from Himachal Pradesh, whose voice is framed with shehnai in its folk form and dhol; **Mundri Lal**, a Punjabi singer who accompanies himself on *tumbi* and *chimta*; and the superlative singer **Urmila Srivastava** from Mirzapur in Uttar Pradesh, with her *kajri* (monsoon song) repertoire. Expanding into new worlds, the array of Gujarati bridal and wedding songs from the silver-voiced, US-based **Maitrayee Patel**'s *Navi Vahwani* ("New Bride", 2004) is a treat.

Nothing like this spread and splendour has ever been available before. For the first time in modern times, the subcontinent's traditional folkways have a true champion as Westerners would understand it. Beat of India combines pukka CD and DVD releases with CD-R releases, downloads and website responsiveness and updateability. Its remit is an expanding gazetteer of regions including Bengal, Gujarat, Himachal Pradesh, Madhya Pradesh, Punjab and Rajasthan, and regional towns including Allahabad, Almora, Delhi, Ghazipur, Jharkhand, Mathura, Mirzapur, Naintal and Varanasi.

Shefali Bhushan speaks eloquently: "A lot of people ask me why it's not beats of India because beats of India is more consonant with music in a sense. My answer to them always is that beat of India is more like the heartbeat or pulse. It's not necessarily that we will restrict ourselves to music. We want hopefully in the next eight lifetimes" – she pauses to laugh – "to expand into other areas – old historic traditions, theatre traditions, other traditions. That's why it's Beat of India."

Ken Hunt

(see box) is one of these, as is the Rajasthan-based Jaipur Virasat Foundation (JVF) who are trying to make music sustainable in the rural areas. "Small village audiences today can't pay the money that can sustain the music," says JVF's John Singh who, with his wife Faith, started the fashion company Anokhi, a pioneer in ethnic chic. "We need to raise the profile and respect for the music – and tourism is helpful here – otherwise, we're going to lose the fantastic resource we have." What JVF recognizes is that without local interest the folk music will inevitably die, so they are setting up a network of local festivals and a database of artists – they've documented around 3000 in Rajasthan alone.

Just getting musicians from one area to play to a new audience in another area already stimulates an interest. And in 2007 they held the first Jodhpur RIFF (Rajasthan International Folk Festival), which showcased Rajasthani folk musicians in the spectacular setting of Jodhpur's Mehrangarh fort. With Mick Jagger amongst the international audience, this quickly earned a reputation as one of India's most spectacular music festivals. It's become an annual event and hopefully the benefits will filter down to the grassroots where they're needed.

Kerala

Another state fantastically rich in music is Kerala in the southwest. It has some spectacular forms of ritual theatre – the best-known of which is *kathakali*, although *teyyam*, in a village or temple setting is more fun. Both feature elaborate masks. Kerala's most spectacular forms of folk music are *chenda melam* and *panchavadyam*, both percussion-led styles that are performed at Hindu temple festivals. Witnessing this music is a physical, not just an aural experience, as there are huge numbers of musicians involved. More than likely there will also be elephants carrying a statue of the god or goddess and flaming torches. *Chenda* is the name of the most common drum in Kerala, a barrel drum slung on a strap around the shoulders and played in a virtuoso manner with either one hand and one stick or two sticks. The other instruments involved are bronze cymbals, the oboe-like *kuzhal* and the spectacular C-shaped brass trumpets (*kombu*) which emphasize and prolong the drum beating. The concept is more like a jazz big-band than a European classical orchestra. During the performance the elephant, musicians and crowd process round the temple precinct. After more than two hours of continuous performing, the excited crowd and sweating musicians celebrate the conclusion and follow the elephant and deity into the inner temple. Panchavadyam means "five instruments" and the orchestra comprises three types of drums, cymbals and the kombu trumpets. They participate in the same temple festivals and the music is organized around a series of complex rhythmic cycles getting faster and faster. There will also be smaller improvised solo performances on drums and kuzhal oboe – making it a feast for the ears and senses.

Adivasi Music

The Adivasi ("original inhabitants") are also known as Tribals or Tribal Peoples, aboriginal peoples or, in the constitution, "Scheduled Tribes". They are one of the Indian subcontinent's best-kept secrets. Census data are notoriously approximate but the 2001 census identified the Adivasi as making up 8.3 percent of the population, a figure representing 84 million people. With the exception of **Arunachal Pradesh**, in the extreme northeast, the rapid growth in population and exploitation of resources of the past half-century has led to Adivasi being turfed off their ancestral land or pushed into remote and inaccessible areas and deprived of amenities. Numerically the largest groups are the **Santal** in the northeast, the **Bhil** in the northwest and the **Gond** in central India.

The complexity of Adivasi culture is something to marvel at. Many cultures and communities teeter precariously on the brink of survival and the abyss of cultural assimilation. Topography is their primary safeguard, since many Tribals are associated with forested or hill territory. Bureaucracy and conversion from tribal faiths to the main religions present unrelenting, ever-present erosions of cultural identity. Their languages point to patterns of ancient settlement and prehistoric migration, and are markedly different philologically from those spoken by local or regional neighbours or state majorities. In the case of the Adi, a hill tribe from Arunachal Pradesh, the linguistics goes one step further. In day-to-day speech they converse in Adi Agom. When chanting in rituals they use a separate language, Miri Agom. That surely is an alternative take on a musical language, if ever there were one.

Ask most educated city-dwellers about the Adivasi and they will either look blank or smile the smile of the titillated and pass remark on sexual practices. These peoples, as **Sunil Janah** wrote in his photo-essay *The Tribals of India* (1993), live "remarkably free of the established and puritanical norms of traditional India". Adivasi villages frequently make a form of home-brew (relatively uncommon in mainstream Hindu and Muslim India) and this fuels many celebrations and dances. Hindu missionaries considered the Adivasi as "junglies", little more than wild beasts. Verrier Elwin's book *The Muria and their Ghotul* (1947) remains a model of illumination, focusing on the **Muria**, a branch of the Gond. Nowadays the Muria's *ghotuls* (communal village dormitories) are more likely to be the butt of prurient interest owing to their "custom of teenage mating" (*India Today*, 1997).

Like many Adivasi, the Muria treat music as fundamental to their history and mythology. The neighbouring **Maria** have a spectacular marriage dance – to the thundering of big cylindrical drums, the boys dance in circles, masked like bisons, while the girls dance in a row, beating iron bell-sticks on the ground. Much of the music is drum-led, but there are also some exquisite strings, flutes and impressive horns.

Illustrative of more positive attitudes and a widening awareness of Adivasi culture are Raul de la Fuente's documentary film *Nomadak TX* ("Nomads TX", 2006), which includes footage of two Basque txalaparta musicians taking their ancestral, four-handed percussion instrument to an Adivasi settlement – alas unspecified – as part of a sequence of visits from Samiland via the Algerian Sahara to Mongolia, and Deben Bhattacharya's documentary film *Faces of the Forest: The Santals of West Bengal*, released commercially in 1980. In Shamla Hills near Bhopal in Madhya Pradesh the National Museum of Man (**Indira Gandhi Rashtriya Manav Sangrahalaya**) mixes open-air museum and indoor exhibit. While its main focus is not on music, it has a significant amount of musical material. Once again, new technology is working for, rather than against, old traditions.

See also the Pakistan, Bangladesh, Nepal and Tibet articles for related traditions.

DISCOGRAPHY India | Folk and Adivasi

★ Ganga: The Music of the Ganges
EMI/Virgin Classics, France
A wonderful introduction to Indian folk and devotional music which evokes the location and context. The three CDs trace the course of the river from the Himalayas to the Bay of Bengal and feature sounds of the river alongside performances beautifully recorded in temples, at the water's edge, on boats and so on. Much of the music is devotional, but other highlights include snake charmers' music, a festival percussion ensemble, a virtuoso toy-seller's song, Baul songs and a great shehnai (shawm) dhun performance at dawn. Well presented music rarely found on disc.

⊙ "Hori Hai": A Festival of Colours
Beat of India, India
In the song set in Phagun (February–March), "Mora Phagun Mein Jiyra", Lallan Singh Gahmari paints an episode for Holi, the Festival of Colours. Sucharita Gupta's "Mori Chunar Bhijal Jaye" adds a womanly touch. A remarkable anthology from Benares, Mirzapur, Malthura and Allahabad.

⊙ Inde: Peuples du Kutch
Buda/Musique du Monde, France
Music of various nomadic and sedentary castes in the Kutch region in the northwest of Gujarat, with double flute solos, drumming and a wide variety of songs accompanied by Jew's harp, lute or drum. It's not exactly easy listening, but includes instructive notes.

⊙ Lagna Mangal
Navras, UK
Wedding songs from the northern Indian state of Gujarat sung by top singers Hema and Ashit Desai, plus chorus. Specific songs are designed for the various stages of the wedding – welcome for the groom, entry of the bride, send off, etc. Contemporary-style folk accompanied by harmonium, cymbals, guitar and keyboard, with tabla and dholak percussion.

★ "Priye" (Dearest): Love Songs
Beat of India, India
Love songs from Benares, Mirzapur and Allahabad. A thematic anthology "from flirtation to sublime union", this also details the pitfalls along the path of love. Witness Mohan Lal Kanskar singing "Ram Kare Mor Devra". Its lyrics state bluntly, "God, let my brother-in-law be happy whether my husband returns or not."

⊙ Voices for Humans, Ancestors and Gods
Topic, UK
Another set of Rolf Killius's recordings, this time concentrating on the east and northeast from Andhra Pradesh to Arunachal Pradesh. The volume captures Adivasi community singers alongside semi-professional and professional folk singers. A most important contribution to the literature and another Topic–British Library Sound Archive collaboration.

⊙ Women's Songs From India
Rounder, US
Recordings made between 1995 and 1999 in Bhojpuri- and Maithili-speaking populations in Uttar Pradesh, Bihar and Nepal. A minor classic in the field, it presents devotional (Mother Goddess and village deity), bridal and wedding songs, songs timed for birthing and fasting ceremonies and to ward off spells.

Adivasi

⊙ Bangladesh: Les Garo de la Forêt de Madhupar
Ocora, France
The Garo are a people of Tibeto-Burman origin whose stronghold was the far west of the Meghalayan plateau known as the Garo Hills. The music here is ritual and social, song-stories backed by a trumpet that plays only one note, a horsehair fiddle and unusual percussion. Very different from people's usual expectations of Indian music.

575

PLAYLIST
India | Folk and Adivasi Music

1 **TAWAR Harijan** from *Inde: Peuples du Kutch (India: The Kutch Peoples)*
Kutch. A heartfelt *jodia pava* (double flute) solo to call the cattle home. The Harijan are Dalits ("Oppressed"), a name preferred by those tradition-ally called "Untouchables".

2 **JUGANI Gurmeet Bawa** from *Love and Life in the Punjab*
Punjab. A trans-religious song to the god that resides in the heart of anyone of faith, this also reaf-firms the fleetingness of humanity.

3 **THUMRI Pilgrim band from Jabbalpur** from *Music from the Shrines of Ajmer & Mundra*
Madhya Pradesh. A love song for a Sufi pir (saint). Wonderfully rousing, open-air music played by pil-grims on shehnai, *mashak* (bagpipes), dhol (barrel drum) and *khanjari* (small frame drum).

4 **HELO MHARO SUNO Vishwa Mohan Bhatt** from *Desert Slide*
Rajasthan. A praise song for Baba Ramdev, revered by Hindus and Muslims alike, this is a mélange of Hindustani classical and Rajasthani folk music.

5 **TOMAR HRIDAYA RANGE BHARAA Mehbooba Band** from *Fanfare de Calcutta*
West Bengal. A wind and percussion instrumental ensemble at full blast. Wailingmost clarinet.

6 **HAMKE SAWAN MEIN Urmila Srivastava** from *Priye (Dearest)*
Uttar Pradesh. A material girl's rainy-season love song pleading coquettishly for pampering, dia-mond-studded earrings and a decorated swing.

7 **THE NAMING SONG Simpun, Kumuti and Soranti** from *Voices for Humans, Ancestors and Gods*
Orissa. A Saora Adivasi ceremonial song celebrating a child reaching two years of age in a community blighted by infant mortality. A skilfully delayed off-unison technique creates an echo effect.

8 **ATHANTA MELAM Peruvamam Kuttan Marar and Orchestra** from *Drumming and Chanting in God's Own Country: The Temple Music of Kerala in South India*
Kerala. Ritual music played standing, promenading and to an assembly of elephants. It builds in inten-sity with demented Woody Woodpecker drumming, kombu brass horns and kuzhal shawms.

9 **PUNGI Unnamed musician** from *Ganga*
Uttar Pradesh. Time just slips away listening to this pungi piece. Pungi is a snake charmer's pipe fashioned from bamboo and gourd.

⊙ **Bangladesh: Ritual Mouth-Organs of the Murung**
Inédit, France
A Tibeto-Burmese people from western Bangladesh play-ing an extraordinary music that sounds like it could almost be played on an electronic organ. Each of the album's three studio-quality tracks feature the *plung*, a set of bamboo and gourd pipes that look like dangerous fireworks ready for lift-off. Shifting sounds knit together into a trance-inducing rhythm in the two instrumental tracks, while the third features male and female voices to a bamboo mouth organ accompaniment. Extraordinary sounds probably related to the Laotian *khaen*.

⊙ **Musical Traditions of the Gond**
VDE-Gallo/AIMP, Switzerland
Various groups of Gond (numbering four or five million) are widely settled in Central India, mainly in Madhya Pradesh. This recording comes from the Bastar district and includes examples of the Maria "bison-horn" dance, Muria music and a variety of ceremonial and social music, including wedding and harvest songs, love songs and a rain dance. Good notes.

⊙ **Honeywind: Sounds from a Santal Village**
Schott/Wergo, Germany
An atmospheric disc presenting the music of the Santal, who inhabit the forested areas of Bihar, Bengal and Orissa, in the context of the natural sounds of their village. Bamboo flute, drums and the beautiful bowed *dhodro benam* carved from a single piece of wood.

Brass bands

★ **The Bollywood Brass Band**
Own label: eea.org.uk/bollywood_brass_band.htm
This British-based band play idiomatically (having been tutored by Jhabalpur's Shyam Brass Band), if a little more in tune than most of their Indian counterparts. There are eleven pieces in all, with a formidable array of percussion. The band play arrangements of hits from Bollywood films like *Bombay* and *Raja Hindustani*, plus a Bally Sagoo hit and some UK dancefloor remixes. British music migrates, transforms and bounces back.

⊙ **Fanfare de Calcutta**
Harmonia Mundi, France
A full-tilt musical experience from the Mehbooba Band, cap-tured by the Bengali ethnomusicologist and filmmaker Deben Bhattacharya. Plentiful clarinet, cornet, trumpet, euphonium and percussion sonorities, tonalities and timbres. Everything a mutant *mehbooba* ("sweetheart") brass band should be. Its patriotic "Hai Mere Watan Ke Logon" is a good starting point.

Kerala

⊙ **Drumming and Chanting in God's Own Country: The Temple Music of Kerala in South India**
Topic, UK
Recordings documenting the vibrant traditions found in Trichur and Malapuram districts collected by Rolf Killius. A

collaboration between Topic and the British Library Sound Archive.

⊙ India: Ritual Percussion of Kerala. Vol. 1: Kshetram Vadyam
VDE-Gallo/AIMP, Switzerland
The best introduction to the ritual percussion styles of Kerala. Frankly, this music is best experienced *in situ* with all the atmosphere and drama of the occasion, but this album is a lot more than just an ethnographic record. It includes a huge *chempata melam* performance, a panchavadayam and a gripping, atmospheric *kuzhal pattu* performance from veteran oboe player Kombath Kuttan Paniker. Excellent notes.

⊙ India: Ritual Percussion of Kerala. Vol. 2: Tayambaka
VDE-Gallo/AIMP, Switzerland
A great recording by chenda player "Pugatri" in an ancient rock temple, but essentially for percussionophiles. A single 71-minute track.

⊙ Kerala: Pulluvan Songs
VDE-Gallo, Switzerland
Rare and atmospheric recordings the itinerant Pulluvan musicians who perform music for the serpent gods. Accompanied by one-stringed fiddles and cymbals.

⊙ South India: Ritual Music and Theatre of Kerala
Le Chant du Monde, France
Kathakali theatre, the most famous art form of Kerala, plus Vedic recitation and other ritual music including a panchavadayam performance. Hard work.

Rajasthan

⊙ Desert Slide
Sense World Music, UK
Featuring Jaipur-born classical slide guitarist Vishwa Mohan Bhatt and some great Rajasthani folk musicians, this is a great meeting of art and folk music traditions with vocals from Anwar Khan and instrumentalists on kamayacha and Sindhi sarangi.

★ Inde: Rajasthan
Ocora, France
The best and most varied survey of the various professional musician castes with excellent Langa and Manganiyar performers, solo and in groups. Also includes *bhopa* performances with jantar and ravanhatha and a showstopping bhapang solo played by Jogi musician Jahur Khan. Excellent notes and photos.

⊙ Rajasthan: Music from the Desert Nomads
Network, Germany
The renowned Kohinoor Langa Group from Jodhpur in action, with vocals, sindi-sarangi, harmonium and dholak. As with many Rajasthani ensembles, it should be mentioned that in concert in the West many named ensembles' line-ups are variable, deliberately changing personnel in order to allow others to see the world.

India | Film Music

soundtrack to a billion lives

Lata Mangeshkar, the most famous
playback singer of them all
Jeremy Marre/Harcourt Films

Stop at any roadside eaterie in India and *filmi* songs will be belting out from a boom-box or some tinny transistor radio while waiting for *chai* (tea) and *paratha* (flat breads, often stuffed). Pop round the local Gujarati or Tamil greengrocer's anywhere from Berkeley, California, to Bradford, England, and, likely as not, the woman behind the counter will be singing along to Hindi playback songstress Kavita Krishnamurthy or the Tamil singer Unni Menon's hottest new film hit. Hire a taxi for that haul in Kerala and chances are the driver will be happily beating time to Yeshudas' latest Madras film hit as he drives along. Indian films play to the largest audiences in the world and project their dreams. Filmi, as Ken Hunt explains, is the soundtrack to those dreams.

To describe filmi as soundtrack music is to miss the point. It neither captures its allure and potency nor explains its uncanny ability to tempt filmgoers to shell out to see the same film over and over again. Indian films often succeed because of their songs, so filmi is subcontinental shorthand for pop – the terms filmi and pop music are virtually interchangeable. Sure, the subcontinent has other forms of popular music – including the established female artist Alisha Chinai, the Colonial Cousins and Junoon, and the imported power pop of the British-based Bally Sagoo. But it's impossible to overstate the impact of the film industry on Indian music – or, for that matter, of filmi on the world's popular music.

South Asia's film industries have become a byword for quantity over quality. That is unfair. Production standards now often exceed Hollywood's – and are far removed from the ultra-fast turn-arounds and low production values of Nigeria's film industry, reputed to be the world's fastest-expanding film industry. But despite the numerous centres responsible for producing regional, non-Hindi or Urdu cinema, one stands out.

The Los Angeles of the Indian film industry is **Mumbai**, the decolonialized Bombay, hence the common shorthand **Bollywood** – a film industry in-joke that stuck and went international. It has even developed a Pakistani counterpart, **Lollywood** based in Lahore. In fact these days Mollywood, the film industry of Madras (Chennai), is reputedly bigger than Mumbai's, but Bollywood is still the main draw. With an eye on the main prize, even southern mainstays such as playback singer **S.P. Balasubramaniam** and **A.R. Rahman**, India's best-known composer, made a point of breaking into Bollywood.

Bollywood Business

Top-notch "music directors" such as **Anu Malik**, **Ilaiyaraaja**, **A.R. Rahman**, **Raamlaxman**, **Rajesh Roshan** and duos **Anand-Milind** and **Jatin-Lalit** are sometimes composers, sometimes arrangers, but certainly all-important, and can command fees beyond the dreams of most of the population. A "name" music director will ping-pong from one commission to the next, juggling any number of films at any given time. Their magician feats mirror the deadline-defying madness of Bollywood's biggest stars, who similarly flit from film to film, sometimes getting it in the can in a few days, sometimes taking years to piece it together scene by scene.

Nowadays, the majority of Hindi film productions propagate a fantasy world, and filmi interludes are essential for this magic to grow. **Karan Johar**'s *Kuch Kuch Hota Hai*, one of the highest grossers of 1998 in India and the UK, was a picture-postcard from fairytale India – real India made only a cameo appearance – with state-of-the-art, unpretentious choreography from Farah Khan and music by Jatin-Lalit. The formula continued with 2000's blockbuster *Dil Hai Hindustani*, also with music by Jatin-Lalit, in which the lyrics scream "Love, Laughter, Freedom".

Most plots are wafer-thin variations – or remakes – on themes of true love and romance, or of virtue rewarded and villainy avenged, but a catchy *filmi sangeet* (film song) can make filmgoers forget the make-do screenplay. It is commonplace for actors to begin shooting before the script has been finished and hence character development is ramshackle and makeshift. Few films pretend to offer any insights into the human condition. Stars get stereotyped and rarely find roles outside, say, romantic lead, swashbuckler, comic light relief, baddie and so on. What's more, these highly paid actors and actresses lip-synch to pre-recorded songs sung by vocal superstars such as Lata Mangeshkar and **S.P. Balasurahmaniam**, off-camera. After these superstars, **Kavita Krishnamurthy**, **Alka Yagnik** and **Udit Narayan** are among the crowd-pulling names.

Alka Yagnik

When the huge, hand-painted hoardings advertising the latest film are trundled through Mumbai's streets, it is done with the same fervour as the temple juggernauts in Orissa or Madurai, designed to cause maximum disruption and maximum exposure for the picture. It is hardly an exaggeration to describe Indian film as a religion, with its stars and singers as the deities. Indeed, several film stars have turned politician, further blurring the dividing lines between screen deity and real-life role, fantasy and reality.

Filmi also reflects and defines Indian culture. When the longing voice of **Lata Mangeshkar**, the most famous playback singer ever, implored "Come close to me for I may not be reborn again and again…", the essence of India was being distilled. Love blended with Hinduism in one memorable image. Similarly, today's songs, a confection of Indian and Western sounds and styles, are showing off the urbane face of Indian city life. When **Yeshudas** or S.P. Balasubramaniam sing in Malayalam and Tamil, they are the voices of the south.

The Filmi Sound

Many of the classic film scores and the filmi sound date from the 1950s and early 1960s, popular Indian film music's **Golden Age**, with the playback stars at the centre of the filmi music industry. The leading trio which dominated the Hindi cinema for over thirty years were **Mukesh** (1923–76), **Mohammed Rafi** (1924–80) and Lata Mangeshkar (b. 1929). Dreamy strings provide the lush backings, an Indianized account of Hollywood strings, but bursting with touches that could only come from the subcontinent. A *sarangi* might provide the lead-in and a *tabla* hold the rhythm together. The favoured vocal timbre of the female singers is high-pitched, nasal and childlike, very different from that in the West. Although film composers use Western-style harmony in their compositions, they often don't follow Western notions of harmonic progression and most film songs concentrate on melody and rhythm. Great banks of violins swirl through the tune in unison, interrupted by the contrasting sounds of *sitar* and tabla bringing unmistakable colour. Of course, those banked string sections also masked the deficiencies of individual instruments.

First Flicks

In December 1895, the Lumière brothers' invention, the **Cinématographe**, was demonstrated for the first time at the Salon Indien (a nice coincidence) in Paris. By July 1896, the brothers' apparatus, heralded in a *Times of India* advertisement as "The Marvel of the Century", was set up in Watson's Hotel in Bombay. For the princely sum of one rupee – enough to keep the masses from the marvel – it offered the future and the present wrapped up in one.

In the India of the Raj, "living photographic pictures" took slightly longer to take off than elsewhere. They had to compete with another form of projection already up and running which had been going under various names, including **Shambarik Kharolika** – the Marathi language's representation of "magic lantern". In their emphasis on music, these shows were an important precursor of filmi.

Within a few years, the magic lantern shows of **Mahadeo Gopal Patwardhan** (who had started his experiments in 1890) had set certain artistic and presentational conventions: a *sutradhar* (narrator) and singers set the stage for the main feature. With time came multiple (three) screens and the shows became a great success in the Bombay Presidency (today's Maharashtra and Gujarat). At least until 1918, the Patwardhans were able to co-exist with other travelling shows – traditional theatre, puppet shows, the new-fangled Cinématographe and the patented machines that followed it. The idea of having musicians playing – and drowning out the noise of the projectors – was therefore lifted straight out of the subcontinent's theatrical traditions. Tradition eased the transition, so to speak.

The makers of **silent films** had no intention of messing with a winning formula. Folk drama companies had entertained the poor with mythology and melodrama. These were upstanding, moral tales of piety and wonderment from the Hindu scriptures, and early Indian films concentrated on this genre. The stories were already familiar to the illiterate and, in the absence of speech, linguistic differences across the country did not matter. The flickering image did little more than upgrade the magic lantern's tales of Lord Krishna or scenes from the *Ramayana*, but did it so dramatically that people fainted, squealed with delight and feared sorcery. Most important of all, they handed over money. Still keeping faith with the past, "live" music often accompanied the action. In the north, tabla and harmonium was the Indian equivalent of the cinema pianist or organist.

Talkies and Singies

March 1931 ushered in a new era. It came courtesy of the "Father of the Indian Talkie", **Ardeshir M. Irani** (1886–1969). His film *Alam Ara* (Light of the

World), adapted from a Parsi theatre piece, deliberately retained the original's songs. His decision maintained a continuity with its folk theatre origins and its song segments instigated what would become the institution of film song, although whether this was a calculated or an inspired idea is not known. Irani also gave Indian cinema its first singer in **Wazir Mohammed Khan** and the first filmi sangeet, whose author is forgotten. *Alam Ara* in fact only narrowly beat *Shirin Farbad* into the marketplace. There is no point hypothesizing what might have happened if it had been the other way round because it and its songs trounced **J.J. Madan**'s talkie.

Alam Ara really did live up to its name. Its success shone out all over India as well as in Ceylon (Sri Lanka) and Burma (Myanmar). In January 1933, less than two years after its release, HMV India astutely identified "the key to prosperity" as being "Indian Talkie records and Radio-Gramophones". That was the speed with which filmi sangeet caught on.

Of course, the talkies brought with them a problem in a territory as large as the Indian subcontinent – the mutual incomprehensibility of **languages**. By the government's official 1931 estimate, there were 225 current in India, and once recorded dialogue was introduced, films became less universal and less profitable. W.M. Khan had already signposted a solution to this – the film song. Song could pull in crowds who barely got the gist of the scratchy dialogue. It could wipe out linguistic, caste and religious differences – and it was an efficacious lubricant for box-office tills.

It did not take the industry long to develop filmi's cash-generating formula and, with very few exceptions, movies were stuffed with songs. The craze peaked in 1932 with J.J. Madan's *Indrasabha*. Derived from a play written in 1853 for the Lucknow court of Nawab Wajid Ali Khan, it included seventy songs – although one commentator, who may have dozed off, claimed a total of 69. Thereafter a running total of between twenty and forty became too unremarkable to comment upon. Nowadays, the total has dropped to between six and ten. Quite regardless of plot, filmi was in, whether it was soppy-romantic comedy like **Raj Kapoor**'s *Awara* (1951), historical drama like *Moghul-e-Azam* (1960), dippy romance in an exotic location, as in *Love In Tokyo* (1966), or a nationalist classic like *Kismat* (1943).

In the early days, anonymous **playback singers** put their honeyed lyrics on the lips of actors and actresses – tone-deaf or otherwise. On set, actors mimed to these pre-recorded performances "played back" over loudspeakers. While film shoots were the stuff of illusion, they were not necessarily the stuff of high fidelity or big budgets. One film-maker had to use a single microphone to capture simultaneously the actor's voice and the percussion soundtrack, so the tabla player was strapped to a tree branch and instructed to play while the actor was reciting.

Quite when it began is unclear, but the habit of dubbing singing voices had gradually crept in and, for a time, fewer and fewer actors sang their own songs. The presence of playback artists became an open secret but still went unmentioned when the credits were rolled. Only later were any playback singers billed on screen because the industry was terrified that, once word leaked that the singing was faked, the public would shun the matinée idols. **Kamad Amrohi**'s *Mahal* still credited Lata Mangeshkar merely as Kamini (the part played by actress Madhubala) as late as 1949. Not that Bombay, Lahore or Madras enjoyed a monopoly in this field of playback artifice – next time the 1957 Hollywood film *Funny Face* comes on television, watch Audrey Hepburn lip-synching "How Long Has This Been Going On?" as Marni Nixon delivers the goods. (Nixon also hits the parts that Marilyn Monroe couldn't reach in "Diamonds Are a Girl's Best Friend".)

Despite the power of playback, there were people for whom faking was unnecessary. Among those with wonderful speaking and singing voices were the actress-singer **Shante Apte** (1916–64), the Marathi-Hindi actress **Shahu Modak** (1918–93), **Zubeida** (1911–90) – a genuine princess who played the eponymous female lead in *Alam Ara* – and, greatest of them all, **K.L. Saigal** (1904–47), a renowned actor, singer and larger-than-life hero.

Golden Voices

In 1934 the Hollywood film industry was hit by the **Hayes Code**, which prescribed what could be said and how far actors could go on the silver screen. It revolutionized Hollywood film as directors became more inventive and judicious in their use of symbolism. India created a similar filmic symbolism, largely still intact today, supported by the Golden Age of filmi sangeet. Screen kissing was taboo (although the 1933 Hindi-English film *Karma* included Himansu Rai and Devika Rani sharing lips improperly), but figurative romancing was everywhere. At the crucial moment a romantic song would waft in on the breeze, sometimes with watery images from fountains (where Hollywood might have gone for waves on the beach).

The year 1947 brought major changes. It brought Independence, partition and, in August that year, the very month in which India broke free, Lata Mangeshkar made her first playback recording. Other artists took their parting bows: K.L. Saigal died – his life became the raw material of Nitin Bose's *Amar Saigal*, alternatively titled *The Immortal Singer* (1955) – and the uncontested Queen of Melody, the *Malka-e-Tarannum*, **Noor Jehan** (1926–2001), departed to reign supreme in Pakistan. With her decision to forsake Bombay's multilingual, cosmopolitan film industry for Lahore's mainly Punjabi and Urdu one – Pakistan boasts far fewer name songwriters – there was a power struggle for the abdicated throne, which Lata Mangeshkar would unequivocally win. Her rise coincided with the decline of the first generation of top-ranking female playback vocalists such as **Zohrabai**, who had been able to capitalize on old *tawaif* (courtesan)-style performance skills.

As India marched into an uncertain future, playback songs offered something unique: they helped create a sense of belonging to one nation, something that the divisive "Hindi, Hindu, Hindustan" chanting of today's right-wing Bharatiya Janata Party never will. When they sang a duet, nobody cared that **Mohammed Rafi** was Muslim and Lata Mangeshkar Hindu. Great music, cliché though it may sound, bridged the gap better than politicians ever could.

There was another element, the rise of truly great film **composers**. Even *Alam Ara*, the first sound film, had someone in charge of music – Phirozshah M. Mistry. While there were plenty con-

tent to churn out songs at piece rate, a new breed was intent on raising standards. The most visionary of them all was **Naushad Ali** (1919–2006). A master of melody, he disdained the Westernization of so many film scores and looked to Hindustani classical music and folk music (from Uttar Pradesh and elsewhere) as an inspiration. He also pushed the genre's boundaries with *Aan* (1952), insisting on a huge orchestra for what he had in mind.

The number of top playback vocalists has been small, not, one suspects, through lack of talent, but through an unwillingness to try new names. A handful of illustrious singers dominated the Golden Age – Mohammed Rafi, **Mukesh** and **Kishore Kumar** and female counterparts such as **Geeta Dutt**, Lata Mangeshkar and Asha Bhosle. The last two are sisters, and remain the highest of the high. In 1967, **Satyajit Ray**, the Bengali filmmaker and film music composer, acidly pondered aloud how the public could unquestioningly accept "the voice of half-a-dozen popular singers who seem to have cornered the playback market", regardless of who was breaking into song.

In fact, **Asha Bhosle**'s ability to change the colour of her voice remains positively uncanny. She is convincing as the ingénue, the matronly middle-aged woman or the old lady looking back wistfully. She has also sung with the bhangra group **Alaap**, Indian rapper **Baba Sehgal**, Boy George and the Kronos Quartet. No one compares, not even her sister Lata Mangeshkar who was famously listed in the *Guinness Book of Records* as the most recorded artist in history, with no fewer than 30,000 solo,

Navras

Mohammed Rafi (standing left) and Naushad Ali (standing right)

Asha Bhosle and Lata Mangeshkar

When it comes to the pantheon of female playback singers, history will always remember Lata Mangeshkar and Asha Bhosle as the greatest of them all. Their kaleidoscopic versatility and vocal virtuosity shaped and defined much of what generations and continents of people understand by filmi, the subcontinent's visionary and visual film music. The sisters' arc of creativity was beyond extraordinary in terms of artistry, variety and longevity.

Both sisters are multi-million sellers, comparable in terms of worldwide influence to The Beatles, Elvis Presley and Umm Kulthum. Unlike their Hollywood equivalent "ghost singers" or "vocal doubles" – whose names only serious film buffs sit around to read on the end credits – they are superstars, household names, the stuff of legend. Playback singers were once like stuntmen and -women: anonymous. But from the early 1950s their names grew in prominence in the opening credits.

Asian Music Circuit

Asha Bhosle

They were cinema audience attractions in their own right and could tip the balance and turn a picture's fortunes.

Before 1949, when the existence of playback singers was still a leaky film-industry secret, Lata Mangeshkar was one of many anonymous artists whose pre-recorded singing was "played back" on the sound stage for leading actresses to mime to. Lip-synching had become an actorly art form in itself. Anonymity didn't preclude record sales, but, for instance, when *Mahal*'s "Aayega Aanewala" started shifting units, cannily the credits on the 78-rpm records were to the character that the actress Madhubala played – Kamini – not Lata Mangeshkar. But the response was so strong that Radio Goa broke the taboo and revealed the mystery voice's identity. Compared to All India Radio or Radio Ceylon, it was a low wattage station – think ethnic community pirate radio for a comparison. But in one bound of the imagination things changed forever. In 1956 Asha sang "Ina Mika Dika", a blast of rock'n'roll and swing jazz. She told me, "If a male singer had sung it, they wouldn't have minded. Asha Bhosle, a girl singer, couldn't sing it!" A pause. "I was Elvis Presley!"

Born in 1929, Lata Mangeshkar was the eldest of five children; Asha, the third, was born in 1933. Their father Dinanath Mangeshkar (1901–42) was a singer and actor-manager in the Marathi Sangeet Natak theatrical tradition, while their mother Shrimati was a Gujarati mother-tongue speaker. This inherent bilingualism, musicality and grounding in theatre presaged much of what followed. There is a saying that every language confers a different soul on the speaker. It is not a philological cliché. It equips. It equipped the sisters to sing in a dozen or so languages between them.

Lata Mangeshkar was the first member of the family to break into the film industry. After *Mahal* she landed plum singing roles. Asha took the harder path. She married against the family's wishes, hence the Bhosle surname. (Incidentally, "Bhosle" is the family's preferred spelling over, for example, "Bhonsle".) It meant musically leaner and often considerably more daring roles, as well as what she calls "luggage songs" – makeweight filler material that paid the bills to support her family.

For decades lazy journalism continually "raked up" – fabricated – stories of division and sibling rivalry. Rather than fuel the debate or perpetuate press speculation by speaking, the family stopped commenting. More important was their track record as musicians and how they fought against studio malpractice and threats of career shutdown and battled for recognition and royalties. Between them, the sisters transformed the industry.

583

duet and chorus-backed songs recorded between 1948 and 1987. Her record was contested by Mohammed Rafi, but the Guinness figures were shown to be hopelessly exaggerated anyway: journalist Raju Bharatan calculated that there were "only" 35,000 Hindi film songs recorded in total over that forty-year period. Bharatan states that in the first sixty years of Hindustani sound movies the total number of recorded songs was 50,000. Of those, around 5250 were recorded by Lata Mangeshkar, around 7500 by her sister Asha Bhosle and a massive 10,000-plus by male vocalist **Sunil Gavaskar**.

Filmi-ghazal and Masala Music

Apart from the folk theatre, another traditional musical and poetic form to be co-opted by the cinema was the *ghazal*. The ghazal has a thousand ways of expressing the agonies and ecstasies of love and, as a result, the songs of the Hindi film actually depended quite heavily on the poetic traditions of Hindi's sister language Urdu. As filmi grew, the ghazal (see p.563) was transformed into something quite different from the original. Composers of **filmi-ghazal** used Western harmonies and inserted lush orchestral interludes. Naturally, the art of improvisation, so important in true ghazal singing, was redundant. A standardized vocal style was introduced by filmi-ghazal's main exponent, **Talat Mahmood**.

In the 1970s the form evolved into the more modern **ghazal-song**. Its first popular exponents were Pakistan's **Mehdi Hassan** and **Ghulam Ali**, while **Pankaj Udhas**, **Anup Jalota** and **Jagjit** and **Chitra Singh** have been leading lights of the ghazal-song in India. The slow tempo, soothing melodies and sentimental lyrics are a welcome contrast to the racy disco style of the action-packed *masala* (spice) movies, popular from the mid-1970s. Two superlative examples of the genre are "Dil Cheez Kya Hai" and "In Aaankhon Ki Masti" in the first *Umrao Jaan* (1981).

Most film scores are designed to be throwaway, and few have claimed to be anything more. Some major films and mega-hit scores occasionally surface and leave more than a passing ripple, such as 1994's *Hum Aapke Hain Kaun* and 1995's *Bombay*. The former, with music by Raamlaxman, was a slight comedy (centred on weddings and a funeral) with songs mostly sung by stalwarts Lata Mangeshkar and S.P. Balasubramaniam, and is thought to be one of the Hindi hits of the century.

The 1990s saw the irresistible rise of **A.R. Rahman**, with soundtracks for the politically

Bombay Dreams

controversial *Bombay* (1995) and the percussion-loaded *Taal* (1999). He became the first composer from the subcontinent to enter the Western arts vernacular, through his collaborative work on the stage musicals *Bombay Dreams* (with Andrew Lloyd Webber) and *The Lord of the Rings* (co-credited to him, the Finnish group Värtinä and Christopher Nightingale) and the film *Slumdog Millionaire*.

Bollywood is bigger than ever. Certainly it's more than an unholy cash cow generating crores (tens of millions) of rupees, with all the attendant tales of Bollywood Babylon. The Indian film industries are a cultural phenomenon generating tittle-tattle and gossip-orientated populist writing on an industrial scale within and outside the subcontinent. But there's serious literature too, including sumptuously illustrated coffee-table books on the industry and its idols. Like Bollywood karaoke clubs and work-out DVDs, it's all indicative of how far this music-driven cultural phenomenon has come since 1931.

Rahman and the resurgence of Indian film music

In the context of contemporary Indian music, one music director has indisputably journeyed further than any other. **A.R. Rahman** is one of the first-call composers for Hindi- and Tamil-language film. And a strong films score with catchy or unusual songs can still tip the balance and turn a good film into a blockbuster. The major difference with Rahman is (a) what he brings to the party; and (b) the breadth and innovation of his music-making. His curriculum vitae is extraordinary by any standard. Not for nothing did *Time* magazine dub him the "Mozart of Madras". That also indicates the depth and extent of his penetration into the people's consciousness worldwide. Rather than philandering with crossover collaborations and Western sonorities, as is too frequently the case, Rahman has crossed boundaries and is amongst the most-heard and biggest-selling artists in the world.

Savage & Savidge

A.R. Rahman

Rahman was the first music director to be equally at ease in Western and Indian musical frameworks, having graduated from London's Trinity College of Music. In 2001 Andrew Lloyd Webber entrusted him with composing music for the Bollywood-inspired musical *Bombay Dreams* (2002). It proved a substantial stage hit with transferability. Next, he was recruited to compose for the stage adaptation of Tolkien's *Lord of the Rings*. He joined Christopher Nightingale, the English composer with whom he had worked on *Bombay Dreams*, and the outstanding Finnish folk group Värttinä. What indisputably put him on the map was his score for the British film set in Mumbai, *Slumdog Millionaire*, which won Oscars for Best Score and Best Song.

Born in Chennai (Madras) in Tamil Nadu in 1966, Rahman had leaped many divides. His father, K.A. Shekhar, was active in Malayalam-language cinema as a composer and conductor. He died when A.S. Duleep Kumar – as Rahman was named before converting from Hinduism to Islam – was aged nine. The family business hired out instruments and musical equipment. Rahman was drawn to keyboard instruments and keyboard technology in particular. His musical apprenticeship was spent playing keyboards in rock bands and in the film studio. By eleven he was playing keyboards for film composer Ilaiyaraaja. He also worked in advertising, creating jingles.

Incidental music composition for television led to working on film composition. Almost immediately he hit pay dirt with one of the greatest and most tuneful soundtracks of the 1990s. Director Mani Ratnam's *Roja* (1992) combined tunefulness, a heightened way with percussive and rhythmical elements and Western instrumental sonorities nestled into domestic song-making and sounds. These became the hallmarks of his compositions whether working in the Madras or the Bombay film industries.

As has happened over and over again with the Indian film industries, Rahman has occasionally overstretched himself. Like potters say, some pots can be blessed, others cursed by fire. On the whole, though, his orchestrational decisions have proved remarkable and unconventional. Frequently, filigree touches are so subtle they can be missed, such as the *shawms* on "Tauba Tauba" on his 1997 *Vande Mataram* album. Which brings us to another point. Rahman is also a "name" recording artist in his own right. His *Live In Dubai* (2000) is a prime example of his compositional and performance skills.

DISCOGRAPHY India | Film Music

There is a superabundance of domestic and foreign compilations of Indian film music. Many have contractually short lives and therefore soon slip out of catalogue.

⊙ **The Music of Bollywood**
Universal Music International
A skilful three-CD compilation that casts its net wide to capture Asha Bhosle, R.D. Burman, Kishore Kumar, Lata Mangeshkar, Mohammed Rafi and Jagjit Singh. It brings mat-

ters full-circle with Chitra, Remo Fernandes, Sonu Nigam and Sunidhi Chauhan, Shailendra Singh and Alka Yagnik.

⊙ **The Unforgettable Madhubala**
⊙ **Golden Girl Helen**
Saregama, India
One of the oddities of the playback singer set-up is the release of CDs such as these: compilations of songs collected under the name of the star who lip-synched to them rather than the

artists who recorded them. Madhubala (1933–69) was one of the most glamorous Hindi-Urdu actresses. *Unforgettable* includes Lata Mangeshkar's breakthrough song "Aaayega Aanewala" (1949) – the melody stolen for the Incredible String Band's "White Bird". The actress, dancer and cabaret artist Helen (b. 1938 or 1939) was a Hindi film industry synonym for risqué. Her mixed-race (Burmese, French and Spanish) parentage meant she got roles denied "good Indian" stereotype actresses – and got to act out songs by her soul twin, Asha Bhosle.

Soundtracks

1942: A Love Story
Saregama, India

The final flowering of R.D. Burman's creative genius. "Genius" is not used lightly. Shivaji Chattopadhyaya, Kavita Krishnamurthy, Lata Mangeshkar and Kumar Sanu sing Javed Akhtar's lyrics.

⊙ **Dil Se**
Venus, India

A soundtrack that ran counter to Bollywood's doldrums 1990s. Music by A.R. Rahman, Hindi lyrics by Gulzar, lyrics in Malayalam from Girish Pulthencheri and Punjabi lyrics by Tejpaul Kour, playback by Sapna Awasti, Lata Mangeshkar, Udit Narayan, Sonu Nigam, A.R. Rahman, Sukhwinder Singh and M.G. Sreekumar.

Hare Rama Hare Krishna
Saregama, India

The film's backdrop and narrative concern the Kathmandu hippie trail, the abuse of the Hindu belief system and the narcotic influence of Western ways. With songs from R.D. Burman and Anand Bakshi sung by Asha Bhosle, Kishore Kumar, Usha Iyer and Lata Mangeshkar, this is an ideal soundtrack for beginners.

⊙ **Mughal-e-Azam**
Saregama, India

A benchmark in Bombay soundtracks enhanced by a singer who didn't do playback – the classical vocalist Bade Ghulam Ali Khan (1902–68). Naushad (1919–2006) and Shakeel Badayuni match the grandeur of the royal court in Urdu song. Playback by Shamshad Begum, Bade Ghulam Ali Khan, Lata Mangeshkar and Mohammed Rafi.

Pakeezah
Saregama, India

Kamal Amrohi's film *Pakeezah* is one of the wonders of world cinema and the scale of its influence unimaginable. (Fun-Da-Mental, closely associated with social commentary, even sampled its skyline train's lonesome whistle.) Music by Naushad, Hindi lyrics by Ghulam Mohammed and playback by Vani Jairam, Lata Mangeshkar, Mohammed Rafi, Rajkumari and Parveen Sultana.

Roja
Magnasound, Canada

A sensation! A new era for Bollywood and A.R. Rahman. With Hindi lyrics by P.K. Mishra. Rahman's melodies are catchy, clever and reveal a command of theatrical music techniques. *Roja* makes plain he was pretty much ready for the big time from the beginning. S.P. Balasubramaniam, Chitra, Hariharan, Minmini, Baba Sehgal and Shweta sing their hearts out.

Playback singers and music directors

Asha Bhosle

Mumbai's most versatile, most chameleonic vocalist, Asha Bhosle is probably the most recorded artist in the world.

⊙ **The Rough Guide to Asha Bhosle**
World Music Circuit, UK

The only anthology in which she assisted in the track selection and commentary. Working with its compiler Ken Hunt was the catalyst for the Kronos Quartet and Asha Bhosle's Grammy-nominated "You've Stolen My Heart".

⊙ **Legends: Asha Bhosle the Enchantress**
Saregama, India

This definitive five-CD artistic overview of her career takes 85 performances of the highest significance for the Indian subcontinent and the diaspora.

R.D. Burman

While the music director, musician and singer Rahul Dev Burman (1939–94) imbued some compositions with classical touches or drew on his father, music director S.D. Burman's love of folk melodicism, in his heart he was a populist. Melodically and sonically, he brought unheard-of innovation to Bollywood with *bossa nova* rhythms, rock timbres and sound effects like blowing into a Listerine bottle and the sound of a striking match. The rumours that he received *sarod* lessons from Ali Akbar Khan are true.

⊙ **The Golden Years: Panchamda**
Universal, India

Forty-seven tracks over three CDs from *Abdullah*, *Bhola Bhala*, *Rocky*, *Saagar*, *Sholay* and others combine to reveal many alternative pictures, though *Sholay*'s "Mehbooba Mehbooba" with him as a Louis Armstrong-influenced vocalist is prominent. Saregama's double-CD *A Bollywood Legend: Best of the EMI Years* provides a shorthand version.

Ilaiyaraaja

For anyone luxuriating in La-La Land delusions about Bollywood's monopoly when it comes to generating musical nuggets, this Chennai-based composer's output is an ecstatic counterblast.

⊙ **Wings (Vol. 1)**
I Dischi di Angelica, Italy

The *bansuri* player Hariprasad Chaurasia is the main soloist on "Singing Self", the opening instrumental fantasia. Other contributors include Arunmozhi, Chitra, Mano and Yesudas and Chitra. The Hariharan-sung highlight "En Manavanil" masterfully combines accordion, pin-point hand drums, arcing flutes and aching strings.

Kishore Kumar

The hugely versatile, visible and industrious Kishore Kumar (1929–87) sang many of the greatest male leads. An allrounder, he wrote screenplays and song lyrics, acted in 101 films and also directed and produced. Manna Dey, Mukesh, Mohammed Rafi and he wrote the gospel of male playback artistry.

⊙ **The Golden Years: Kishore Kumar**
Universal, India

A magic 45 from the almost 3000 recordings he made.

Lata Mangeshkar

Over-estimating the scale and depth of the influence of India's most popular singer is impossible. Come Partition in 1947, Noor Jehan relocated to Pakistan. Two years later Radio Ceylon blew the Bombay film industry's open secret and Lata Mangeshkar officially became the "first" – in time the leading – female playback singer. A singer as iconic for the Indo-Pakistani subcontinent and diaspora as Umm Kulthum is for Egypt and the Arab world.

⊙ Lata Mangeshkar: The Legend
Manteca, UK

An excellent two-CD, 33-track set that dodges many of the standard choices. Compiler Bhagwant Sagoo begins with *Gajre* (1948) – that is, before she or playback singing were "outed" – and finishes with a choice from *Lekin* (1990), a film dear to her heart because her brother Hridaynath Mangeshkar was its "music director".

Asha Puthli

From a walk-on part as a jazz singer in Ved Mehta's book *Portrait of India* (1970), through acting roles in the Merchant-Ivory film *Savages* (1972) and Bruno Corbucci's *Squadra Antigangsters* (1979), to her albums as a disco queen or worldbeat leader, Asha Puthli knows much about reinvention.

⊙ New Beat of Nostalgia
Asha, USA

Seven reinterpretations of Indian film hits with a preponderance of S.D. Burman stalwarts with beats (and a smidgen of Dusty Springfield). She reinterprets Lata Mangeshkar's beauty "Tum Na Janey" from the S.D. Burman/Sahir team's *Sazaa* (1951) with an exemplary update balancing sensuality and discreet beats.

A.R. Rahman

India's only film composer to have truly entered the outside world's consciousness – through *Bombay Dreams*, *Lord of the Rings* and *Slumdog Millionaire*. *Thiruda Thiruda/ Pudhiya Mugam* (Magnasound, Canada) is also highly recommended as proof of where he came from as a Tamil composer.

⊙ Live in Dubai
Sony Music, India

An important outgrowth of Indian film music has been Bollywood-style arena spectaculars. This 2000 show revisits glories like "Gurus of Peace" with the recorded voices of Nusrat Fateh Ali Khan and the girls' choir who had sung the original on Rahman's similarly recommended studio album *Vande Mataram* (1997). It heralded his elevation to headlining musician-composer, outstripping even Burman's achievements in this field.

⊙ The Best of A.R. Rahman
Bollywood Records/Sony, India

Released after the success of Slumdog Millionaire (although it doesn't include anything from the film), this is a good selection of Rahman's work over the past decade, including the *Bombay Dreams* hit "Shakalala Boy".

PLAYLIST
India | Film Music

1 JAANE DO NAA Asha Bhosle and Shailendra Singh from *Saagar*
A plea to be set free – it means "Let me go" – with flute, santoor and pointillist electric guitar from the great writing partnership of R.D. Burman and Javed Akhtar. From *Saagar* (1985).

2 YUNHI GATE RAHO Kishore Kumar and S.P. Balasubramaniam from *The Music of Bollywood*
The wildest, most courageous pastiche ever created – with Indian percussion, massed strings, folk, mariachi, psychedelia, flamenco castanet, jive, rock'n'roll, can-can and circus music, plus male vocal exhortations to "Keep singing".

3 AAP JAISE KOI Nazia Hassan from *Qurbani*
Nazia Hassan's defining disco-era song became a rallying cry, while its post-Abba devices have dated in a very good way. Much like Abba.

4 PYAR HUA CHUPKE SE Kavita Krishnamurthy from *1942 – Love Story*
Sumptuous in its romanticism, the title means "Fell in Love Quietly" – a brilliant performance from the last ever R.D. Burman/Javed Akhtar collaboration.

5 SUN JA DIL KI DASTAAN Hemant Kumar from *The Rough Guide to the Music of India*
Swoon under the moon as the man with the light Latin touch croons, "Come close, my heart's desire."

6 THEE THEE Caroline from *Thiruda Thiruda*
A sprawling canvas of a song from A.R. Rahman and Mehboob over which Caroline's voice soars.

7 EK LADKI KO DEKHA Kumar Sanu from *R.D. Burman: A Bollywood Legend*
Pent-up emotion exploding. "I saw a girl", sings Kumar Sanu in a voice that captures the thrill and rush of love at first sight.

8 BREATHLESS Shankar Mahadevan from *Introducing Shankar Mahadevan*
The singer's calling-card taken at helter-skelter pace.

9 CHANDNI RAATEN PYAR KI BAATEN Lata Mangeshkar and Hemant Kumar from *The Rough Guide to Lata Mangeshkar*
"Heed the story of my heart…" A forever duet from Guru Dutt's 1952 film *Jaal*.

10 RISHTE BANTE HAIN Asha Bhosle from *Dil Padosi Hai*
Sheer melodicism. Doubly a work of extraordinary imagination since R.D. Burman and Gulzar's balmy "Rishte Bante Hain" comes from an imaginary film.

India | East–West Fusions

meetings by the river

Mohan veena (Indianized Spanish guitar)
player Vishwa Mohan Bhatt
Sense

Up until the 1950s Indian music was virtually unknown in Europe or America, beyond the occasional strand of exotica – like the novelty song "Indian Love Call", a Raj romance hit – and to hear Indian musicians meant visiting the subcontinent. All that changed in the following decade, when The Beatles met Ravi Shankar and the *sitar* entered mass Western consciousness. In its wake came Indo-fusions with British, European and American rock, jazz and folk music – a process that is still very much evolving, as Ken Hunt documents.

All stories are approximations and East–West fusions didn't entirely begin with The Beatles. India exerted influences on Western classical music over the course of the entire twentieth century. The ideas that India planted ranged from the philosophical and religious to the organizational (melody and rhythmicality) and organological (the use of Indian instruments). Among the composers of note touched in this manner were **John Cage**, **Henry Cowell**, **John Foulds**, **Philip Glass**, **Gustav Holst**, **Oliver Messiaen** and **Karlheinz Stockhausen**. It was a two-way street, however. Certain Indian composers steeped in both Indian and non-Indian classicism, such as **John Mayer** and **Naresh Sohal**, made sure the traffic flowed in two directions. During the 1960s India's music, philosophies and culture touched signal jazz musicians like **John Coltrane**, **Don Ellis**, **John Handy** and **Sonny Rollins**.

While there are many claims for originator of the East–West Fusion form, John Mayer (1930–2004) laid a solid, documented claim to the title. Schooled in an appreciation of both systems, both musically and in a business sense, he had the wit to copyright his 1952 composition *Raga Music for Solo Clarinet* (Georgina Dobrée's interpretation appears on *This Green Tide*, 1995). In addition, he and **Yehudi Menuhin** were in discussion about performing Mayer's work a decade before Menuhin's acclaimed collaborations with **Ravi Shankar**, and he went on to compose the *Shanta Quintet for Sitar and Strings* that the Lansdowne String Quartet and Diwan Motihar released in 1967.

Each of these were individual and enduring strands in the development of Indian–Western fusion, and you could just as well look at a mirror narrative: the arrival of Indian musicians on US and European stages, and their motivations for seeking to collaborate with Western players. Foremost among these players were the sarodist **Ali Akbar Khan**, who arrived in New York in 1955 at the invitation of Yehudi Menuhin to give the first true Indian classical recital in the US and who soon recorded the first Indian music LP, and his brother-in-law Ravi Shankar, who performed the following year in Europe and the US.

Norwegian Wood: Rock, Folk and India in the 1960s...

Ravi Shankar is the pivotal figure in Indian music's popularization in the West, and in its fusion with Western music. George Harrison

(1943–2001) described him as "the godfather of World Music" – and his influence can hardly be overstated. For example, in Indian classical music sitar and *sarod* have more or less equal status yet the fact that Shankar played the former has made the sitar almost synonymous with Indian music in Western minds.

Born in 1920, in Uttar Pradesh, Shankar made his first professional appearance aged thirteen, and he had been giving solo recitals and directing the All-India Radio Orchestra for more than a decade when he first played in Russia, Europe and the US. These concerts from 1954 onwards – beginning in Russia – greatly influenced musicians in the West. Shankar, too, benefited from the West, finding a wide audience through his work with Yehudi Menuhin, with whom he recorded the 1966 album *West Meets East*. This won a US Grammy award – the first for an Asian musician – and led to further collaborations with Menuhin, André Previn (*Concerto for Sitar & Orchestra*, 1971), Zubin Mehta (*Raga-Mala*, 1981) and Philip Glass (*Passages*, 1990). Shankar also looked East himself, producing the excellent Indo-Japanese fusion of *East Greets East* (1978).

But it was Shankar's most famous sitar pupil, **George Harrison**, who brought Indian music real global attention. When he played the instrument on "Norwegian Wood" (1965) it was the first time most Western listeners had heard sitar. For George it was the beginning of a lifetime's commitment and interest, early landmarks of which were his sitar-based composition "Within You Without You" on the huge-selling *Sgt. Pepper* album (1967) and his organization, with Ravi Shankar, of the charity Concert For Bangladesh (1971). This introduced Shankar as a special guest to a rock audience – and showed both its receptiveness and distance when they gave rapturous applause to the musicians' tuning (see p.531). His duet with Ali Akbar Khan (on sarod) filled a side of the ensuing million-selling triple-LP, bringing Indian classical music to a huge new audience.

The 1960s were a prime time for incorporating Indianesque elements or Indian-inspired tonal colour into pop and rock music. Sandy Bull created Indian inflections on "Memphis, Tennessee" (1965) with Western instrumentation. The Rolling Stones used sitar to drive "Paint It Black" (1966), while Traffic used sitar, *tanpura* and sarod as exotic guitars circa *Mr. Fantasy* (1967). Donovan and The Beatles used sitar and *tabla* on, respectively, "Three Kingfishers" and "Love You To" (both 1966). The phenomenon finally got saddled with a name in the spring of 1966 when Jim, later Roger, McGuinn called the Byrds' Coltrane-inspired "Eight Miles High" "raga rock". In January 1967 Sandy Pearlman of the New York-based rock magazine *Crawdaddy* wrote that it was being attached "as a catch-all description to any rock that sounded even vaguely 'Indian' or 'Eastern.'"

In the folk realm, Indian instrumental textures and modality found favour with British musicians such as **Davy Graham**, **The Incredible String Band** and **John Renbourn**. The ISB notably brought in sitarist **Nazir Jairazbhoy** to play on the quintessential hippie-era masterpiece *The 5000 Spirits or The Layers of the Onion* (1967). On the other side of the Iron Curtain acts such as **Hutka** in Czechoslovakia and **Creatív Stúdió Öt** (Creative Studio Five) and their successor **Makám és Kolinda** in Hungary took the otherness of Indian music to new places.

...and Beyond

In the US, **Mickey Hart** (drummer/percussionist with **The Grateful Dead**) and the composer **Philip Glass** studied Indian rhythmicality with **Alla Rakha Qureshi**. The longest-lived flowering, however, would be a series of collaborative projects between Hart and **Zakir Hussain**, son of Alla Rakha. The father-and-son tabla team participated on Hart's *Rolling Thunder* (1972), and Hussain joined Hart in the drum fusion ensemble **Diga Rhythm Band**, on the soundtrack to *Apocalypse Now* and in **Planet Drum**. This last project's eponymous album won a Grammy in 1991, making it the first recording with Indian participants – Hussain and *ghatam* (tuned clay pot) maestro **T.H. "Vikku" Vinayakram** – to be thus honoured since *West Meets East*. Owing to legal entanglements with the name, although they released another album – *Supralingua* (1998) – the ensemble that next emerged went under the name **Global Drum Project**, which released its eponymous debut in late 2007. An alternative East–West partnership saw Hart produce the Japanese drum ensemble Kodo's *Mondo Head* (2001).

The third Indian artist to win a Grammy – in 1994 – was a disciple of Ravi Shankar's, **V.M. (Vishwa Mohan) Bhatt**, who plays an Indianized Spanish guitar called the *Mohan veena*. He is arguably the most experimental and successful of the subcontinent's fusion maestros and won his award for the album *Meeting by the River*, a serendipitous venture with US guitarist and roots aficionado **Ry Cooder**. Bhatt subsequently worked in a variety of new contexts with musicians from other cultures including, most memorably, bluegrass *dobro* player

Jerry Douglas (*Bourbon and Rose Water*, 1995) and the Palestinian *oud* master **Simon Shaheen** (*Saltanah*, 1996).

In Europe, the most coherent fusion from the "rock" world emerged from multicultural German band **Dissidenten**, who released a spellbinding album of South Indian themes, *The Jungle Book*, in 1993. The product of many years spent living on and off in India, it was, like their debut *Germanistan* (1982), co-credited to the **Karnataka College of Percussion**. Following the album, the group have worked with the classically trained Tamil vocalist **Manickam Yogeswaran**. Yogeswaran went on to become arguably the most travelled voice in Tamil music since M.S. Subbulakshmi (1916–2004) through his contributions to such films as Stanley Kubrick's *Eyes Wide Shut* (1999), Spike Lee's *25th Hour* (2002) and Sarah Gavron's *Brick Lane* (2007). He is also associated with the composers Orlando Gough (through his work with the Shobana Jeyasingh Dance Company and The Shout) and Jocelyn Pook (through soundtrack sessions).

From the late 1990s onwards, Britain's second- and third-generation diaspora musicians melded new musical forms that drew on the old and the new. Some of these musicians became lumped together under the post-*bhangra* catch-all "**Asian Underground**" (see p.115). The best transcended the label. Among those that endured are the hip-hop/dub fusion band **Asian Dub Foundation**, **Joi** (who emerged from the Bangladeshi diaspora), **M.I.A.** (aka Mathangi Arulpragasam, who often leaves her Tamil roots behind in a welter of samples), **Bally Sagoo** (who refashioned bhangra and Bollywood forms), **Nitin Sawhney** (whose compositions mixed the subcontinent's melodic and rhythmic colours on a palette with flamenco, jazz and other shades), the tabla player **Talvin Singh** (whose drum'n'bass-meets-*taal* stylishness landed him work with Björk and Madonna) and **T.J. Rehmi** (trip-hop). Several genuinely eye-opening projects emerged from this maelstrom. The English National Opera and Asian Dub Foundation's collaboration *Gaddafi: A Living Myth* (2006) provocatively mixed orchestral and rap elements, political declamation, choreography and video in epic theatrical fashion. Nitin Sawhney emerged as a revealing composer capable of succeeding with canvasses small or vast. His music for the 2006 re-release of *Prapancha Pash* (A Throw of Dice, 1929) with the London Symphony Orchestra provided new twists to the grand tradition of silent movie

Ishq Records

Bally Sagoo

accompaniment. Taking the terrorist attacks of 7 July 2005 as its pivot, his *London Undersound* (2008) created a portrait of a changing London tangled up in blue funk and sky-blue optimism – with contributions from Anoushka Shankar and Ojos de Brujo.

Indo-jazz Fusions

Jazz, like Indian classical music, has improvisation at its heart and so it is little surprise that meetings of its musicians have created some of the most enduring of all East–West fusions.

Despite the wide-ranging influence of certain jazz musicians on film music, one of the great unsung stories of Indo-jazz fusion is India's indigenous jazz scene. Bollywood music-directors Laxmikant-Pyarelal paid tribute to the Goan composer-musician **Anthony Gonsalves** (who had previously worked with **S.D. Burman** and **Naushad Ali**) in the blockbuster *Amar Akbar Anthony* (1977), while another film *The Real Anthony Gonsalves* (2008) made the debt plainer still. **Sebastian D'Souza** similarly worked closely with the Shankar-Jaikishen team. The Goan and Bombay jazz clubs, haunts and niteries became vital forcing grounds for the nation's jazz talent. As early as the 1930s the **Rhumba Boys**, led by saxophonist **L.A.**

Abreu, were operating out of Goa. Later notables include **Chic Chocolate** ("the Louis Armstrong of India"), the violinist **Ken Cumine**, the drummer **Leslie Godinho**, the alto saxophonist **Braz Gonsalves** (who toured internationally with the **Jazz Yatra Sextet** and **Asian All Stars**) and the multi-talented **Chris Perry** (who reinvigorated Kokani-language song in Goa).

Almost inevitably, **Ravi Shankar** brokered the first exchange, combining with jazz flautist **Bud Shank** on *Improvisations and Theme From Pather Panchali* (1962). This showed how well jazz and Indian music could complement each other, using Shankar's acclaimed score for Satyajit Ray's film as a theme. Fascinatingly, at the same time, **John Coltrane** had fallen under the sway of Indian spirituality and, shunning meat, drugs and alcohol, reformed his jazz. Regrettably his mooted collaboration with Ravi Shankar never occurred, but Coltrane explored modal themes, titled one composition "India" (to be heard in various renditions on the 1961 Village Vanguard recordings), and named his son Ravi. **Miles Davis** also looked briefly towards India, cutting a track featuring **Khalil Balakrishna** and **Bihari Sharma** on sitar and tanpura (at the suggestion of the group's guitarist, John McLaughlin) during the *Bitches Brew* sessions in 1968.

Other pioneers of Indo-jazz fusion included the trumpeter and arranger **Don Ellis**, who formed with **Harihar Rao** the **Hindustani Jazz Sextet** and explored Indian rhythms in highly complex Western big-band time signatures, and the gifted Indian violinist and composer **John Mayer**, who partnered Jamaican saxophonist **Joe Harriott** in a group called **Indo-Jazz Fusions**. This employed both Indian and jazz compositions as vehicles for improvisation, notably featuring sitarist **Dewan Motihar**. The group worked on the soundtrack to Michelangelo Antonioni's film *Blow Up* and recorded two seminal albums in 1967–68. In a time of great experimentation **Ali Akbar Khan** set Baudelaire's poetry to music for Yvette Mimieux's *Flowers of Evil*, and with saxophonist **John Handy** went on to record *Karuna Supreme* (1975) and *Rainbow* (1980) with the Karnatic violinist **L. Subramaniam** (who himself bequeathed a handful of Indo-jazz albums).

One jazz player, however, stands out above all others in these fusion experiments. **John McLaughlin** had become hooked on Indian music, and after his stint in New York with Miles Davis had become a follower of the Bengali mystic Sri Chinmoy (1931–2007). His 1971 solo album *My Goal's Beyond* explored Indian musical scales and structures, and these continued to inform his jazz-rock band, the intense speed-playing **Mahavishnu Orchestra**, over the next couple of years. But it was in the acoustic group **Shakti** that his exploration of Indian music found its greatest expression.

Shakti was a meeting not only of East and West, but also of north and south India. Alongside McLaughlin, the group featured tabla player **Zakir Hussain** from the Hindustani tradition, as well as violinist **L. Shankar** (younger

Shakti

If the Hindustani and Karnatic music systems are like a single organism's two lungs, then in **Shakti** and its successor **Remember Shakti** that organism discovered new synergies, new ways to voice sound. Of all the East–West (and, remember, North–South) fusion acts, Shakti and Remember Shakti remain the apogee in terms of creative endeavour, artistic achievement and commercial success. Their approach to improvisation in its South Asian and jazz contexts is unparalleled.

Shakti is a Hindu deity and concept, embodying feminine creativity. At the group's helm are two musicians: the Mumbai-born tabla maestro Zakir Hussain and the Yorkshire, England-born guitarist John McLaughlin. Speaking

Moment Records

Shakti

of McLaughlin, Hussain says, "It's like playing with an Indian musician … It's just perfect the way it all works. Nobody's trying to squeeze things so that it'll all fit. It flows. It's a piece of cloth being spun, all these different threads being woven together in various ways."

Summing up the Shakti era, he says, "Shakti had two faces. One was with Raghavan, the *mridangam* player on the very first album; and the other was with Vinayakram, the ghatam player. It comes together and that definition fits very well in 'Joy'. We hadn't rehearsed. We just had this melody and a bridge in our head. We just walked on the stage and played. It was boom, top gear from the first time. It just gelled."

Twenty years after Shakti's enforced retirement, Hussain, McLaughlin and Vinayakram convened with the renowned Hindustani flautist Hariprasad Chaurasia for four English concerts. The resultant live album – *Remember Shakti* – ushered in a new era for the band, though the line-up was no longer stable. Ever afterwards, they would be joined by a shifting line-up of Indian maestros. This inaugurated what became known as the Remember Shakti phase.

Speaking after a Remember Shakti soundcheck, Hussain enthused, "What you've just heard us play, it's not a piece that we have worked on. It's an idea that we were singing along to in the bus. It's *raga*-based but it's also a scale. With John playing we can do any sort of approach, whether it's a raga- or taal-based idea. It's uncanny how he's able to fix himself on a path without him really having to concentrate on which notes he has to play or which beat he is on. This is something we [Indians] are trained in from our childhood … If I'm playing a sixteen-beat cycle, my head will move on nine and my knee will move on eleven but the point is the body has already become so attuned to it that it keeps the rhythm for me. It becomes something that you don't think about. It's amazing to see John, who probably does not have that kind of training in the West, can follow exactly … Maybe in a past life he was south Indian."

Shakti merits its reputation as the finest East–West improvising ensemble. No matter who is playing in the band, it provides a refreshing counterblast to the musical mix-and-match sweetie counter of most cross-cultural projects, with people having separate conversations in different languages. Remember Shakti communicates in many tongues and is eloquent and listenable in every one.

brother of L. Subramaniam) and T.H. "Vikku" Vinayakram from the more fiery Karnatic tradition. The quartet toured and recorded a trio of albums between 1974 and 1977, when their record company – used to massive-selling albums from McLaughlin – withdrew support. At a time when "fusion" was becoming an all too abused concept in jazz, the group produced wonderful music that grew organically out of their individual styles. Prior to forming the group, McLaughlin had attempted to learn the south Indian *veena* but, feeling he was unable to master two instruments, turned instead to applying its aspects to the guitar. He developed an instrument with sympathetic strings and a scalloped fingerboard so he could play the notes of Indian ragas. Shakti burst back in the early 2000s as the floating line-up **Remember Shakti** with Hussain and McLaughlin at its core.

In the wake of Shakti, McLaughlin and Zakir Hussain continued to influence jazz and Indian fusions, often in association with percussionist **Trilok Gurtu**, who trained in Bombay as a tabla player. Gurtu is perhaps more of a jazz player than any of his peers. He was inspired to play jazz by John Coltrane, and moved to New York in 1976, where he played with everyone from Don Cherry to Archie Shepp, and was a part of the group **Oregon**, led by **Collin Walcott**, a New York jazz musician who had studied with Alla Rakha and Ravi

Shankar. Gurtu went on to work with Italy's **Arkè String Quartet**, the Malian superstar **Salif Keïta**, Benin's **Angelique Kidjo**, guitarist **Pat Metheny** and saxophonist **Pharoah Sanders**.

In 1987 McLaughlin and Hussain joined with Norwegian saxophonist **Jan Garbarek** and Hindustani flautist **Hariprasad Chaurasia** to record *Making Music* for the ECM label – one of the great East–West fusion albums. The players' contrasting wind sounds worked perfectly and the sure-footed accompaniment and solos from McLaughlin showed Garbarek a crucial mediator. Garbarek returned to Indian music in the following decade with his *Song for Everyone* album, featuring a quartet with L. Shankar, Zakir Hussain and percussionist Trilok Gurtu, while the acclaimed *Ragas and Sagas* (1990) moved into rather different territory with a group of Pakistani musicians – singer **Ustad Fateh Ali Khan**, *sarangi* player **Nazim Ali Khan** and tabla player **Shaukat Hussain**.

In terms of reminding how snugly Indian and jazz elements can fit together, several post-millennium acts typify the way forward. These are composer-clarinettist **Arun Ghosh**, the pianist **Zoe Rahman** (often the glad company of her clarinettist brother **Idris Rahman**) and the groups **Nataraj**, **Samay**, **Shastriya Syndicate**, **Shiva Nova** and **The Teak Project** – the sitar-guitar-tabla trio of, respectively, Jonathan Mayer, Justin Quinn and Neil Craig.

Jak Kilby

Trilok Gurtu

Almost parenthetically, it must be said that rock music hasn't generally transplanted well to subcontinental soils. By far the majority of acts that are recording sound derivative. An exception is Pakistan's **Mekaal Hasan Band** with its blend of rock and indigenous musical forms. Their work might be likened to – high praise – Café Tacuba's treatment of Mexican forms in a rock context, in the way they source folk and devotional genres.

Where this fusion affair's future will go is anybody's guess. The game, at least on a commercial level, is changing and responding to change. Asian chill-out and Asian Massive are as big as they are faddish. The club-pleasing sound-textures, drum loops and samples of **Karsh Kale**, **Midival Punditz** and **Anoushka Shankar** are taking East–West fusion into new places. Only time will tell if these pied pipers are creating something with the stamina and longevity of the trail-blazing fusion masters back in the 1950s and 60s.

Midival Punditz

DISCOGRAPHY India | East–West Fusions

The discography below covers mainly jazz (and some rock) fusions with Indian music. For contemporary Asian-British dance fusions see the Bhangra/Asian Beat discography on p.119.

V.M. (Vishwa Mohan) Bhatt

Born in Rajasthan in 1950, V.M. Bhatt began playing sitar, studying under Ravi Shankar, then moved onto guitar, and created a kind of fusion of the two which he called the Mohan veena. He recorded his first fusion album, *A Meeting By the River*, with Ry Cooder in 1993 and has since worked with bluegrass musicians Béla Fleck and Jerry Douglas, oud player Simon Shaheen and bluesman Taj Mahal.

WITH RY COODER

⭐ **Meeting By the River**
  Water Lily Acoustics, US

One of the most successful East–West recordings ever, with Bhatt and Cooder sure-footed veena/slide guitar partners on

a disc that feels steeped in the Hindustani melody system. It rightly won a Grammy.

WITH SIMON SHAHEEN

⊙ **Saltanah**
Water Lily Acoustics, US

Arabian art music and Hindustani classical music share many commonalities. Harmonizing the differences is down to the wit of the performers. Two masters demonstrate their agility, and art, with Ronu Majumdar (flute) and Sangeeta Shankar (violin) assisting.

Bitter Funeral Beer Band

A Swedish band with international leanings, particularly Ghanaian tribal drumming traditions, the Bitter Funeral Beer Band are led by master percussionist Bengt Berger. Their output is to be found on ECM, Dragon and Country & Eastern. Musically, they incorporated jazz, world music and non-Western classical music elements but also collaborated with the acclaimed sarodist K. Sridhar.

⊙ Live in Frankfurt 82
Country & Eastern, Sweden

K. Sridhar's sarod is well integrated on this live album but particularly well on "Bitter Funeral Beer" and "Funeral Dance". The pioneering world-fusion maestro Don Cherry is also well to the fore. Afro-Indian-European fusion.

George Brooks

The US saxophonist and clarinettist George Brooks is an under-recorded yet exceptional Indo-jazz fusion practitioner. He is also a member of Bombay Jazz, originally convened in 2003, whose line-up as of 2007 comprised Brooks, Larry Coryell on guitar, Vijay Ghate on tabla and Ronu Majumdar on flutes.

⊙ Night Spinner
Moment, US

Among the guests that make this 1998 release so priceless are the rhythmist Zakir Hussain, Aashish Khan on sarod and Sultan Khan on sarangi. The title track – a sax and tabla chase with Jack Perla supporting on piano – and "In the Grotto" with sarod to the forefront are especially recommended.

Dissidenten

Dissidenten are in some respects a German variant of Britain's 3 Mustaphas 3, but with India and Morocco rather than Eastern Europe as prime influences. They share the Mustaphas' confidence and seriousness of approach (beneath the jokes). For more on them, see the chapter on Germany on p.158.

★ The Jungle Book
Exil, Germany

An East–West fusion masterpiece, created by musicians sympathetic to each other's cultures, traditions and aspirations. Dissidenten take Kipling's *Jungle Book* as a loose theme, weaving elements of Coltrane (*Love Supreme*), "sound-pictures" (Bombay street-sound and Puja celebration) and cross-cultural collaborations with the Karnataka College of Percussion. A Disneyfication of India it is not.

Don Ellis

Don Ellis (1934–78) was a Los Angeles-based trumpeter and composer who applied to jazz conceptual lessons learned from Indian music. He formed the first Indo-jazz fusion group, the Hindustani Jazz Sextet, in the early 1960s, and the complex Indian time signatures resonate throughout his work.

⊙ Electric Bath
Columbia, US/UK

Ellis's importance is beautifully demonstrated on this 1967 Indo-jazz-rock album. His is no East–West fusion in the sense of vogueishly employing sitar (although Ray Neopolitan plays sitar and bass) but an exploration of Indian rhythm in much the same way as Coltrane explored modality. "New Horizons" in seventeen-time receives a typically Indian solution – 5-5-7. Re-released in 1998, this remastered and extended volume captures the 21-piece band in action.

Jan Garbarek

Norwegian-born Jan Garbarek forged an initial reputation as part of a great quartet with Keith Jarrett in the 1970s. In subsequent decades he has explored a range of music – Nordic folk and early music as well as Indian and Pakistani music – with great success, underpinning each project with his characteristic spare phrasing.

★ Making Music
ECM, Germany

A dream team of flautist Hariprasad Chaurasia, guitarist John McLaughlin and saxophonist Jan Garbarek join tabla maestro Zakir Hussain. Actually it's Hussain who gets headline billing on this 1987 album and who is credited as composer of the majority of the eight tracks. One suspects that much of it is improvised, with each musician defining their territories from the opening title track on, with John McLaughlin impressively occupying the meeting ground.

⊙ Ragas and Sagas
ECM, Germany

Garbarek teams up with Pakistani musicians Ustad Fateh Ali Khan (vocals), Deepika Thathaal (vocals), Nazim Ali Khan (sarangi), Shaukat Hussain (tabla) for an album that sees him venturing into South Asian territory more than fusion. Garbarek outlines the raga of the opening track and then Ustad Fateh Ali Khan takes it up as Garbarek adopts an accompanying role along with the sarangi. "Saga", the one track credited to Garbarek, sounds like a sort of *ghazal* fantasy with dreamy sax and vocal melodies.

Ghazal

Ghazal was an Indo-Persian fusion group, featuring the leading Iranian *kamancheh* (spike-fiddle) player Kayhan Kalhor and sitar player Shujaat Hussain Khan, son of master sitarist Vilayat Khan. They released three albums on Shanachie and one on ECM.

★ Moon Rise Over the Silk Road
Shanachie, US

Ghazal's common ground is the Indo-Persian poetic form ghazal. This, their third release, came out in 2000, rose to poetic heights. Reinforcing its Persian ancestry, Pejman Hadadi plays the *tombak* (Iranian goblet drum) while Shujaat Hussain sings in Persian.

Arun Ghosh

On his father's side Arun Ghosh is of Bengali stock, while his mother is of Sindhi stock. Conceived in India, born and raised in England, he has composed extensively for Kathak and Orissi dance and for the theatre – examples being 2007 productions for the Royal Exchange, Manchester's *The Tempest* and the Salisbury Playhouse's *Indian Ink*.

★ Northern Namaste
camoci records, UK

The material's inspirations run from Manchester with "Longsight Lagoon" to Bengali Renaissance man Rabindranath Tagore and his paean to the Bengali motherland "O Amar Desher Mati".

Trilok Gurtu

Trilok Gurtu was born in 1951 into a musical family in Bombay. Son of celebrated ghazal and *thumri* singer Shobha Gurtu, he learnt tabla at an early age. He played in Bombay's annual jazz festival in the mid-1970s and then accompanied filmi star Asha Bhosle on tour to New York. Settling there and later in Germany, he has worked with Collin Walcott (in Oregon), Archie Shepp, Don Cherry, Joe Zawinul and Pat Metheny, amongst others. His *Usfret* (1988) kick-started the UK Asian Underground scene.

⊙ The Definitive Trilok Gurtu: Twenty Years of Talking Tabla
Manteca/Union Square Music, UK

The best overview of Gurtu's canon, this is a laurelled garland of issued and hitherto unreleased collaborations with the likes of Neneh Cherry, Shobha Gurtu, John McLaughlin, Pharoah Sanders and Joe Zawinul.

WITH THE ARKÈ STRING QUARTET

 Arkeology
Promo Music, Italy
Sheer moreishness with Carlo Cantini (violin, *dilruba*, recorder, *kalimba*), Valentino Corvino (violin), Sandro Di Paolo (viola) and Stefano Dall'Ora (double-bass, ukulele, Eminence bass/Aptflex). Ten magisterial compositions from a circle in which two traditions of extemporized music meet – the Indian tradition and the overlooked tradition of improvisation in Western classicism. Gurtu's "Folded Hands" ranks as one of the new millennium's most impressive and haunting East–West compositions.

John Handy & Ali Akbar Khan

Saxophonist and reedman John Handy (b. 1933) played with Charlie Mingus on his classic album *Mingus Ah Um*, before forming his own bands from the 1960s on. He formed the group Rainbow in the mid-1970s with Ali Akbar Khan, the legendary north Indian sarod player (see p.542) whose work in popularizing Indian music in the US was perhaps equal to that of Ravi Shankar, and whose fusion-minded pupils at his California college included Mickey Hart and Carlos Santana.

⊙ **Karuna Supreme/Rainbow**
MPS, Germany
Two ground-breaking Indo-jazz fusion albums repackaged and re-released as a single CD. *Karuna Supreme* dates from 1975, while *Rainbow*, on which Handy and Khan are joined by violinist L. Subramaniam, was recorded in 1981.

Shweta Jhaveri

Blessed with a sensual and rich vocal style, Shweta Jhaveri (b. 1965, Ahmedabad, Gujarat) has generated some of the most consistently satisfying and comeliest recordings within both the classical and the fusion fields.

⊙ **Anāhitā**
Intuition Music & Media, Germany
This recording broke new ground and remains one of the centrepieces of East–West fusion. Very much striking out for new territory, very much sensitive to old ways, it has several apogees. "To a Beloved" is one of the most mellifluous East–West fusion pieces ever.

⊙ **Huge**
21st Century Cosmos, US
Released in 2007, *Huge* again seeks out new territory. Its self-composed originals are set in raga frameworks, with English lyrics, a Western rhythm section of kit drums and electric or acoustic bass. "Street Café", a composition based on raga "Jana Sammohini", is the stand-out track on an ambitious album.

John Mayer's Indo-Jazz Fusions

Indian classical violinist John Mayer (1930–2004) and Jamaican saxophonist Joe Harriott (1928–73) set so much in motion with their double-quintet, Indo-Jazz Fusions. Mayer led the Indo side of the band on violin, with sitar, flute, tabla and *tambura*; Harriott the jazz side on alto sax, with trumpet, piano, bass and drums. The group disbanded on Harriott's death in 1973 but was reformed by Mayer 25 years later, with his son Jonathan on sitar.

⊙ **Indo-Jazz Fusions Vols 1 & 2**
Verve, UK
These two discs of pioneering Indo-jazz fusion from 1967 and 1968 are required listening.

⊙ **Asian Airs**
Nimbus, UK
The 1996 version sees a looser, less jazz-focused group improvising around the raga framework.

John McLaughlin/Shakti

Guitarist John McLaughlin has been a lynchpin of East–West fusion since introducing Miles Davis to Indian music back in the 1960s, moving through solo work, the jazz-rock Mahavishnu Orchestra and, most impressively, the all-acoustic group Shakti, formed in 1974 with tabla player Zakir Hussain. With L. Shankar (violin) and T.H. Vinayakram (ghatam), Shakti toured and recorded to great acclaim until 1977, when Columbia withdrew support. Returning as Remember Shakti in the 2000s, the group continues to flourish.

MAHAVISHNU JOHN MCLAUGHLIN

⊙ **My Goal's Beyond**
Rykodisc, US
This adventuresome, musically substantial album connects McLaughlin's jazz temperament with his Indian philosophical interests. In East–West terms it is a milestone, while for McLaughlin it was a bridge between his Miles Davis work with Indian guest musicians and Mahavishnu Orchestra on the path to Shakti.

SHAKTI

 Best of Shakti
Moment, US
Drawing on the quartet's three Columbia albums, the music really fires here. The first track, "Joy", just bursts with energy as the frenetic, spiritual intensity of a virtuoso Karnatic ragam is transformed into a sensational eighteen minutes of tight ensemble jazz. The rest of the nine superb tracks here bring contrasting moods and textures.

⊙ **Remember Shakti**
Polygram/Verve, France
A two-CD concert recording of a very different Shakti, with *bansuri* (bamboo flute) player Hariprasad Chaurasia taking the place of Shankar. The first disc is made up of just two lengthy Hindustani-style improvisations with drone and tabla accompaniment, and it's only on the second disc that the whole group comes together for an hour-long workout.

DVD **The Way of Beauty**
Universal Music, France
This DVD from 2006 charts the band's history through music and biographical documentary. The cast includes U. Srinivas, V. Selvaganesh, Shankar Mahadevan, T.H. Vinayakram, L. Shankar, Shivkumar Sharma, Debashish Bhattacharya, A.K. Pallanivel, Sivamani Bhavani Shankar, Roshan Ali Aziz and Taufiq Qureshi. The footage covers the period from 1976 (Shakti) to 2004 (Remember Shakti).

Zoe and Idris Rahman

Like her younger brother Idris (b. 1973), Zoe Rahman (b. 1971) is of mixed Bengali-English stock. She first introduced Bengali elements into her music on *Melting Pot* but on *Where Rivers Meet* she really flew the flag.

 **Where Rivers Meet**
Manushi Records, UK
Released in 2008, this represents a personal milestone in Rahman's creativity and a major one in East–West fusion. The only thing that capped it was the November 2008 premiere of the work at London's Purcell Room, which brought still more Bangla elements.

INDIA | East–West Fusions

Ravi Shankar

Ravi Shankar's hugely influential career – which began with a tour of France aged ten – has touched almost every Western musician interested in Indian music. His major Hindustani classical discs are reviewed on p.550. Below is one of his fusion outings.

⊙ Towards the Rising Sun (East Greets East)
Deutsche Grammophon, Germany
Typically Ravi Shankar's fusion projects brought together Indian and Western musicians in a Western quasi-classical situation. Better known under its original title of *East Greets East*, this brought together Shankar and his long-standing tabla player Alla Rakha with Japanese musicians Susumu Miyashita on *koto* (long-necked zither) and Hozan Yamamoto on *shakuhachi* (end-blown bamboo flute).

Baluji Shrivastav & Re-Orient

The UK-based trio of Baluji Shrivastav (sitar, dilruba, *bulbul-tarang*, Indian percussion, keyboards), Linda Shanovitch (vocals) and Chris Conway (keyboard instruments, synthesizer, low whistle, guitar) is known collectively as Re-Orient.

⊙ Baluji Shrivastav & Re-Orient
Arc Music, UK
Here the trio is bolstered by three guests on selected tracks, namely Guy Barker (trumpet) on "In Candlelight" and "Spirit of Joy", Hossam Ramzy (Egyptian percussion) on "Taal Manjari – Flowering of Rhythm" and Andy Sheppard (soprano saxophone) on "Blessings".

Southern Brothers

The Southern Brothers – Kadri Gopalnath (sax), James Newton (flute) and P. Srinivasan (mridangam) – were an inspired one-off masterminded by Kavi Alexander. They took as their springboard the work of Ahmed Abdul Malik (the bassist with Thelonious Monk) and saxophonist Jimmy Griffin's *Jazz Sahara* (1958).

⊙ Southern Brothers
Water Lily Acoustics, US
Spontaneous creativity and composition. Newton's "Rahsaan Breathes Freely Now" takes Rahsaan Roland Kirk as its inspiration, while ragam "Ganamurte" illustrates what can happen when Karnatic music's melody and rhythm cycles meet jazz.

Rajan Spolia

Rajan Spolia (b. 1960, Ludhiana, Punjab) is a UK-based guitarist. He plays an acoustic six-string modified with fifteen strings across the top of its body. However, these don't act as typical sympathetic strings. Instead, the effect might be likened to sounds finding their natural resonances within the body of the guitar.

⊙ Good Fortune
Bass Lord Records, UK
Spolia's breakthrough came in 2004 with this, his third album release. "Sadness Revisited", "Good Fortune" and "Raj's Dhun" are remarkable calling-cards. Manjit Singh Rasiya plays tabla.

The Teak Project

Comprising Jonathan Mayer (sitar), Justin Quinn (guitar) and Neil Craig (tabla), this trio is very much new old-school and none the worse for that.

⊙ The Teak Project
First Hand Records, UK
An outstanding debut. Mayer's concluding composition "Slow Down" and Craig's "Yamanish" are especially fine.

Dominique Vellard and Ken Zuckerman

Dominique Vellard is a tenor specializing in Europe's medieval and Renaissance music. He teaches voice at the Schola Cantorum Basiliensis in Basel, Switzerland. The sarodist and lute player Ken Zuckerman teaches improvisation in medieval music at the same college and is also head of the Ali Akbar College of Music in Basel.

★ Meeting: Two Worlds of Modal Music
Harmonia Mundi, France
East–West music finds common ground in modal music. Europe's medieval past and raga are brought together in the present, courtesy of Schola Cantorium Basiliensis and Schweizer Radio DRS2. Don't be daunted by words flying around like Dorian, Lydian and Phrygian or Bhimpalashri, Paharri, Manj Khammaj, Bihag or Bhairavi. The musicians do all the work. The listeners and the musicians get all the pleasure.

PLAYLIST
India | East–West Fusions

1 CALCUTTA BLUES Dave Brubeck Quartet from *Jazz Impressions of Eurasia*
Was this impressionistic masterpiece really released in 1958? Joe Morello's fake tabla drumming tells it like it was and is a harbinger of much to come.

2 FOLDED HANDS Trilok Gurtu and the Arkè String Quartet from *Arkeology*
The apogee of a modern-day East–West journey. A composition by Trilok Gurtu.

3 JOY Shakti from *The Best of Shakti*
The high-soaring Shakti at their most high-flying. Rarely do eighteen minutes pass so swiftly and with so many cliff-hanging moments.

4 TO A BELOVED Shweta Jhaveri from *Anāhitā*
A song of yearning sung by Shweta Jhaveri, set in the late-night raga "Bagashree" with Western instrumentation.

5 LOBSTER SONG Dissidenten from *Live in Europe*
Funk, Tamil and North African rolled into one with vocalists Izaline Calister, Manickam Yogeswaran and Noujoum Ouazza and the grand master of Indo-jazz saxophone Charlie Mariano.

6 RISHTE BANTE HAIN Kronos Quartet and Asha Bhosle from *You've Stolen My Heart*
Composer R.D. Burman's earworm in a string quartet setting, with the original's sarod counter-melody transposed to *pipa* played by Wu Man and the lyrics revisited by the song's original vocal interpreter.

Indonesia | Gamelan

from palace to paddy field

Gamelan orchestra in a central Javanese village
J Highet/Lebrecht Collection

The shimmering sounds of the gamelan have fascinated and delighted Western visitors to Indonesia for half a millennium. Sir Francis Drake, who visited Java in 1580, described music "of a very strange kind, pleasant and delightful" – which still sums up most people's initial reaction. The structural complexity of the music and its sonorous and ethereal sound have inspired twentieth-century composers such as Debussy, Messiaen, Britten and John Cage, and in recent years there's been an enthusiastic growth in playing in gamelan ensembles in the West. Jenny Heaton, Simon Steptoe and Sophie Clark explore tradition and practice.

A gamelan has been described as "one instrument played by many people". It's essentially an ensemble of tuned percussion, consisting mainly of gongs, metallophones (similar to xylophones, but with metal instead of wooden bars) and drums; it may also include singers, bamboo flutes and spike-fiddle. In Indonesia the ensembles and their sounds are diverse, ranging from Central Java's bronze court gamelans to the bamboo village orchestras in Bali.

Ensembles of drums, gongs and other percussion instruments are common throughout the vast Indonesian archipelago, but the gamelan tradition is unique to the islands of **Java**, **Bali** and **Lombok**, east of Bali. The island of Java is long and thin in shape, and is divided geographically, culturally and linguistically into Central, Eastern and Western regions, each of which has its own distinctive style of gamelan music and dance.

While musicians from different regions work happily together in the music academies, outside them the Javanese and Balinese are not too keen on each other's music. To the Balinese, Javanese music is too soft, too slow and lacking in vitality while the Javanese dismiss Balinese music as harsh, unrefined and too loud.

Central Java

The Mangkunegaran Palace, Surakarta: a cool, gentle breeze wafts through the spacious entrance hall. Birds flutter in and out. Inside, it is still and peaceful in contrast to all the noise and activity outside. Across the cool expanse of the marble dance floor sit musicians, sipping tea, chatting and smoking clove cigarettes. Two dancers appear wearing long, brightly coloured sashes and armed with shields and daggers. After a short introductory melody, the dozen or so musicians start playing the richly carved and deeply sonorous instruments of the gamelan "Kyai Kanyut Mesem" whose name means "Swept Away by a Smile". The music is measured and refined. Welcome to the stately, court tradition of Central Java.

The Javanese Gamelan

The largest bronze gamelans in Indonesia are found in **Central Java**. A complete Javanese gamelan is made up of two sets of instruments, one in each of two scales – the five-note *laras slendro* and the seven-note *laras pelog*. The two sets are laid out with the corresponding instruments at right angles to each other. No two gamelans are tuned exactly alike and a Javanese musician will often prefer the sound and feeling of a piece played on one gamelan to that produced on another. Gamelans are traditionally given a name, such as "The Venerable Ambassador of Harmony".

All the instruments in the gamelan have a clear role to play and this is reflected in the layout of the ensemble. Basically, the musical texture is made up of three elements: a central melody played on the metallophones in the middle of the gamelan; an elaboration of the melody, played on the instruments at the front; and slow "punctuations" by gongs at the back.

The **gong ageng** (large gong) at the back of the gamelan is the most important instrument in the ensemble and it's believed that the spirit of the gamelan resides within it. A large gong can be over one metre in diameter and is made from a single piece of bronze. The skilled gongsmiths of Central Java are highly respected and receive orders from the whole of Java and Bali.

In addition to the large gong, there is an array of **kempul** – smaller hanging gongs, one for each note of the scale in a large gamelan – and horizontally mounted kettle-gongs onomatopoeically named **ketuk** and **kenong**. No piece of music can begin or end without a stroke on one of the larger gongs, while the kenong, ketuk and kempul mark shorter melodic phrases. A Javanese gamelan has more hanging gongs than a Balinese gamelan, giving depth and resonance to the music.

The **metallophones** are arranged in the centre of the gamelan. They cover a range of four octaves: the lowest pitch is the soft-toned **slenthem**, which has resonating tubes under the keys and is played with a padded mallet. The large **demung** and smaller pair of **saron**, played with hard wooden mallets, cover the middle range, while the highest-pitched is the **peking**, or **saron panerus** (small saron), played with a mallet of buffalo horn. These instruments play together the **balungan** or "melodic skeleton" of a piece. Many Javanese compositions are considered to be derived from vocal melodies, which are not played on any gamelan instruments but are "sung by the musicians in their hearts".

The instruments at the front of the gamelan are the most complex in the ensemble. These include a pair of **bonang** (a set of small kettle-gongs mounted in a frame), **gendèr** (a metallophone with ten to fourteen keys), **gambang** (wooden xylophone), **siter** (zither), **rebab** and **suling** (bamboo flute). The bonang, gendèr and rebab are all leading melodic instruments in the gamelan.

CMP Records

Rebab player from Gamelan Sekar Tunjung

In the centre of the ensemble is a drummer with a selection of double-headed drums. The full ensemble also includes a **gerong** (male chorus) and **pesindhen** – solo female singers.

Although a large gamelan is co-ordinated to an extent by the drummer, its musicians (who can number as many as thirty) have neither a conductor nor any visual cues, as they all sit facing the same way. Musical notation, although now used extensively in teaching, is never used in performance. Gamelan musicians learn all the instruments and so develop an understanding of the music and flexibility in ensemble playing. During an all-night shadow play, for example, you may see musicians changing places and special guests invited to play. Gamelan is a communal form of music-making – there are no soloists or virtuosos – and although the female singers tend to use microphones they are not considered soloists in the Western sense.

Javan Traditions

Today, nearly ninety percent of Java's population is Muslim. The traditional arts of gamelan music, dance and theatre, however, have their roots in Java's **Hindu-Buddhist** past. Hinduism and Buddhism came from India to Java in the first century AD and were mixed with older Javanese religious beliefs. The temples of **Borobudur** (Buddhist) and **Prambanan** (Hindu) near

Yogyakarta are significant monuments from Java's Hindu-Buddhist past. In the fifteenth century, Islam arrived from the north, but before reaching Java, the Islam of the Middle East had mixed with Indian Hinduism, which made it more accessible to the Javanese. The new religion also included Sufi beliefs, which acknowledged the power of music and tolerated musical and artistic expression.

European colonialism was another major influence on Javanese thought and culture, through the Dutch East India Company, established in the early seventeenth century. The Dutch worked closely with the aristocracy in Central Java. This European influence stimulated experiments with notation in gamelan circles and a number system called **kepatihan** was developed for recording the music. Gamelan notation did not become widely used, however, until the early twentieth century. It is today used to outline the skeleton melody of a composition and act as an *aide memoire* during performance; it does not form a full score and accomplished musicians usually play from memory. Notations of individual instrumental parts are increasingly used in the academies to speed up the learning process but are not conducive to general performance practice.

In 1755 the Mataram kingdom of Central Java was divided between the two **royal courts** of **Surakarta** (Solo) and **Yogyakarta**. Two smaller courts soon followed: the **Mangkunegaran** court in Solo and the **Pakualaman** court in Yogyakarta. Under Dutch rule these courts did not have much political power, but the arts of gamelan, dance, literature and *wayang* (shadow plays) flourished. The sultans owned the finest gamelans and employed the best musicians and dancers. Pieces were composed by court composers although credited to the reigning sultan. Rivalry between the courts led to distinctive styles of dance and gamelan-playing. To this day the Solonese are known for the subtlety and refinement of their music and dance while the Yogyanese style is bold and strong in character.

Court Gamelans

Some of the finest gamelans in Java are housed in the courts, including a number of **ceremonial gamelans**. The largest and loudest, known as **gamelan Sekaten**, are still played once a year in the palace mosques of Solo and Yogya. The story goes that these large gamelans were built in the early days of Islam in Java to draw people in to the mosques. To this day a pair of gamelan Sekaten are played almost continuously for a week during the **Sekaten festival**, to commemorate the birth and death of the prophet Mohammed. Their powerful sound draws huge crowds into the mosques, where the calls to prayer mingle with the gamelan music, incense, offerings and the hubbub of the fair outside.

Within the palace walls gamelan playing is traditionally regarded as a spiritual discipline – a way of reaching enlightenment. The Javanese hero is always in control of his emotions and dispenses with his raging enemies – giants, ogres and demons – with a flick of a dagger. The refined austerity of the court compositions best conveys this sense of calm and contemplative detachment.

Some of the ceremonial gamelans are believed to be magically charged or linked to spirits of ancestors. The gongs are the most sacred instruments, and are given offerings of flowers and incense before performances. These gamelans are only played at special ceremonial occasions, such as Javanese New Year and royal birthdays. In the past, different gamelans were played on different occasions. For outdoor ceremonies loud ensembles in the pelog scale were played in specially built pavilions. For indoor entertainment an ensemble of gentle, soft-toned instruments in the slendro scale was played. Slendro and pelog sets were kept separate until the eighteenth century, when the combining of the two became increasingly common. The standard modern gamelan has developed from this practice.

The rise of Indonesian nationalism in the early twentieth century challenged both the Dutch colonialists and the Javanese aristocracy. Following independence, under President Sukarno, in 1945 academies of performing arts were set up to train new generations of musicians, dancers and puppeteers, away from the royal courts. Some academies, however, remained closely linked to the courts: in Solo the original campus of the academy was within the palace walls. Concepts of Western classical music and performance greatly influenced the early directors of the academies, who introduced exams, recitals and concert performances.

Gamelan Performances

Gamelan music is today played by a wide range of people in Central Java. Most village halls and neighbourhoods in major towns have a gamelan for use by the local community. The majority of schoolchildren learn basic gamelan pieces and can continue their studies in conservatories and academies of performing arts in the major towns of Solo and Yogyakarta. Radio Republik Indonesia (RRI) employs professional studio musicians and broadcasts a wide range of gamelan music – live late-night sessions from

Javanese court gamelan

the palaces, dance-dramas, shadow plays, and light-hearted listeners' request programmes, to name but a few.

The repertoire and instrumentation of gamelan music is astonishingly versatile. A piece which is normally played on a bronze gamelan, such as the well-known "**Gambirsawit**", may also be arranged for a small group of zithers and vocalists (a *siteran* ensemble). When played on a gamelan, it could accompany a dance or part of a shadow-play, or simply be enjoyed by a group rehearsing on the village gamelan. It can be played in either slendro or pelog, on a full gamelan with vocalists, or on a small *gadhon* ensemble of soft-toned instruments. Many other Javanese pieces can be played in a number of different ways: this is the essence of the gamelan tradition.

Dance and Shadow Plays

In Java, gamelan music is inseparable from the arts of **poetry**, **dance** and **drama**. There is a large repertoire of sung poetry – **tembang** – and a number of poetic texts used by both male chorus and female singers. Dances accompanied by gamelan music range from the elegant and refined palace *srimpi* dance, solo or duet "showpiece" dances, to lively village dances (*tayuban*), though over the years there's been a fair bit of interchange between the two. **Dance-dramas** (*wayang orang*) and **shadow plays** (*wayang kulit*) are always accompanied by gamelan music.

The all-night **wayang kulit** is one of the most popular forms of theatre in Java. A large screen is illuminated by a single lamp so the shadow puppets are silhouetted on the screen. The puppeteer (*dalang*) sits beneath the lamp with the gamelan behind him, and an array of intricately carved and painted leather puppets carefully arranged on his right and left embedded in a log from a banana tree. From an early age children learn to recognize the wayang characters by the shape of the head-dress and the size of the eyes, nose and body of the puppets. Javanese dance movements have been heavily influenced by the movements of these two-dimensional puppets. A wayang performance is very much a social occasion. Invited guests sit on the puppeteer's side of the screen where they can see him at work, and are served food and drink throughout the night. Uninvited guests sit on the shadow side of the screen or squeeze in to see the clowns and battle scenes at 2 or 3am. During the night people eat, drink, chat and fall asleep. Often the gamelan players fall asleep too!

Originally associated with ancestor worship in the pre-Hindu era, the wayang later adapted stories from the Hindu epics Ramayana and Mahabharata, which have formed the basis of Javanese (and other southeast Asian) dance and drama for nearly a thousand years. Gamelan music is an integral and varied part of the performance, providing gentle accompaniment for narrative and dialogue, loud vigorous pieces to accompany battle scenes, lively songs for the clowns and longer compositions to introduce important sections of the drama. The musicians take their cues from the puppeteer and the gamelan players have to respond quickly and accurately to the puppeteer's signals.

There's a localized gamelan tradition in the Betawi area of northwest Java around Jakarta. This is called **Ajeng** and is generally used for **wayang kulit Betawi** (shadow-puppet theatre performed in the Betawi dialect). The gamelan itself is similar in style to the Central Javanese form, but in place of the soft rebab as melodic leader, the Ajeng has what's called a **tarompet**. It is not in fact a trumpet, but a piercing shawm or oboe which gives a distinctive sound.

Gamelan music is a vital part of important **ceremonial occasions** – there is an old Javanese saying: "It's not official until the gong is hung". No wedding ceremony is complete without gamelan music – although nowadays it is often from a cassette recorder rather than a live ensemble. Significant moments in the wedding ceremony are accompanied by specific pieces, and at the reception special "opening" and "closing" pieces are played, many of which were originally composed for the arrival and departure of the sultan at palace ceremonies. The opening notes of a "leaving" piece are all that most people know as they will get up to leave as soon as they hear them! There are also a few pieces believed to release magical power when played, to ward off evil spirits.

In Central Java there are frequent **street performances** by **siteran groups**, made up of zithers, vocals, a drum and a large end-blown bamboo tube used as a gong. Unlike the large bronze gamelans, these instruments are cheap, portable and often home-made. The music is usually drawn from the gamelan repertoire and, with as few as four or five musicians, the ensemble recreates with astonishing resourcefulness the musical texture of the gamelan. In the quieter residential streets a lone siter player may perform in the evening, accompanying traditional songs on an instrument he made himself.

Java's Bamboo Gamelan

The western end of Central Java, traditionally known as **Banyumas,** and with its economic centre in the city of Purwokerto, boasts its own very special performing traditions. Central Javanese gamelan music is prominent and the area's indigenous and distinct brand of wayang kulit synthesizes elements from both Yogyanese and Solonese gamelan styles. However, it is the **calung** (bamboo ensemble) that is most closely associated with the region.

The word calung means "hitting to make a sound". Lightweight and portable, the instruments mimic those of the gamelan, and, indeed, were originally devised as a substitute in areas where bronze instruments were unavailable. Each instrument is constructed from a number of bamboo tubes split lengthways and suspended over a wooden frame. Even the largest of the gongs (gong ageng) is imitated; the player blows a raspberry down a large bamboo tube and produces the gong's characteristic vibrations through gentle oscillation of the air pressure.

The traditional drumming for this ensemble is found only in Banyumas and uses a small *kendang ciblon* (used in Central Java to accompany dance) in conjunction with a smaller drum known as a *kendang ketipung* or *kuluntar*. The resulting patterns are extremely dynamic and more clearly repetitive than elsewhere. Influences from Sunda are strong and some of the best performers now use the Sundanese set-up of three drums, the largest being placed on the floor at an angle to enable the player to change the pitch with his foot.

This difference in drumming style derives partly from the use of calung as accompaniment to the folk dance known as **lengger**. Nowadays performed by women, lengger is thought to have originated from dances associated with fertility rituals. Like others of its type, for instance tayuban in Central and East Java, the dance has also been connected with prostitution. Remnants of this past are still evident in the sensual movements of the dancers and their flirtatious facial expressions.

Despite its relation to gamelan, the sound of the calung is quite unlike anything else and a world away from the gentle textures and delicate refinement of the Central Javanese court traditions. The timbre of the bamboo is sharp and clipped and its short sustaining power is overcome through repetition and interlocking of instrumental parts. The overwhelming spirit of the music is one of boisterous humour, a joyful zest for life, and a refreshing openness and directness of expression.

Gamelan in Java Today

Life is changing rapidly in Java. For much of the youth population, the gamelan represents the values of the past and is rejected in favour of Western or Indonesian pop (for more on which, see the following article). In the towns and cities short, two-hour shadow plays are becoming popular in place of the all-night variety. Older puppeteers complain that their young pupils no longer understand the spiritual teachings and philosophy of the wayang.

But for many people the gamelan tradition is alive and well. In **Solo** and **Yogya**, music-making continues to play a role in community life. The local gamelan contest at the radio station in Solo draws a huge number of enthusiastic gamelan groups from the town and surrounding area every year. Men and women generally play in separate groups, with the exception of the pesindhen, female singers. Some of the larger batik shops have a gamelan upstairs for the employees to play after work and a number of schools and

local government buildings or offices have their own gamelan.

In the twentieth century **gamelan composers** have become less anonymous. **K.R.T. Wasitodiningrat,** director of the Yogya court gamelan, had one of his pieces sent up with the Voyager spacecraft amongst the samples of earthly music. Also in Yogya the music and dance of **Bagong Kussudiardja** is well known and his fame as a composer and choreographer has spread throughout Indonesia. And many groups enjoy playing popular pieces and lively arrangements of older pieces by the late **Ki Nartosabdho,** a greatly respected musician and puppeteer.

Much artistic experimentation, innovation and exchange is going on in the **academies.** Musicians and dancers from different regions of Java, Bali and Sumatra work together on new choreography, storytelling and puppetry, as well as new musical sounds, styles and techniques. Western composers work with Indonesian composers and musicians, some of whom travel abroad to study, teach and collaborate with

Western musicians, and a number of composers are writing for both gamelan ensembles and Western instruments.

West Java: Sunda

The island of Java is inhabited by several ethnic groups. The Javanese live mainly in Central and East Java, while the main inhabitants of West Java, or Sunda, are the **Sundanese**. The chief Sundanese gamelan style, **degung**, is well known, but there are other styles that have rarely been recorded.

The northern coastal plain of West Java is flat and hot, with the capital city, **Jakarta**, densely populated and full of urban squalor. The contrast with the highlands of the **Priangan** (Abode of the Gods) or **Tanah Sunda** (Sunda Lands) could not be more dramatic. This mountainous plateau covers the central and southern parts of West Java – an area of lush green valleys and high volcanic peaks. It is also the heartland of the Sundanese people, the second largest ethnic group in Indonesia, who are culturally and linguistically quite distinct from the Javanese of Central and East Java. **Bandung**, also known as *kota kembang* (city of flowers), is

the area's principal city, cultural centre and home to many of Sunda's finest musicians.

Sundanese performing arts and musical traditions are more obviously diverse than those of Central Java and have developed into three main branches: **gamelan Degung**, **gamelan Salendro** and **tembang Sunda**.

Gamelan Degung

The sound of **degung** is perhaps the most accessible gamelan music to Western ears. Its musical structures are clear and well-defined, and the timbres of the instruments blend delicately with one another without losing any of their integrity or individuality. The ensemble is small, consisting of only a few instruments, but includes the usual range of gongs and metallophones. However, the very special character of degung, which uses its own five-note version of the pelog scale found in Java, owes much to the additional presence of the **suling** (bamboo flute), which is regarded as a signature for Sundanese music. In fact, no other instrument more perfectly exemplifies the musical heart of Sunda or better conjures up its gentle, picturesque rice paddies and village life.

Contemporary Sundanese gamelan orchestra Sambasunda led by composer Ismet Ruchimat

Degung is unique to Sunda and was developed during the last century in the courts of the Bupadi (local rulers under Dutch control). Deriving from a court tradition, it has a more exalted place among the performing arts than gamelan Salendro (see below) – although the best musicians frequent the circles of both – and is now mainly used in concert form for wedding receptions and other social events. Nevertheless, examples of degung for **tari topeng** (masked dances) exist, and, more recently, augmented forms of the ensemble have been used to accompany performances of **wayang golek** (three-dimensional rod puppets). In addition, it has made inroads into popular culture through "**pop-Sunda**" (using Western pop instruments), which achieved immense popularity during the 1980s in the hands of composers such as **Nano S** (see the following chapter).

Gamelan Salendro

Nowadays, **gamelan Salendro** is used primarily to accompany performances of **wayang golek** – classical dance – as well as the more recent social dance **jaipongan** (see p.619). Compared to gamelan Degung and tembang Sunda, it has a lowly, unaristocratic status. Wayang golek is considered less refined than its Javanese counterpart, wayang kulit (shadow puppets), and the raucous and rowdy atmosphere that pervades performances, together with its emphasis on comedy and references to bodily functions, would seem to confirm this. Nonetheless, gamelan Salendro has much to offer; often energetic and exciting, lyrical and expressive, it can display a technical brilliance and virtuosity rarely heard in Central Java.

Of great importance to contemporary gamelan performance in Sunda is the **juru kawih**, the female vocalist. As elsewhere in Java, singing has become increasingly important during the twentieth century, and in popular genres such as jaipongan becomes the main focus of interest. In addition, there is the male **juru alok**, who sings during the interludes between verses and contributes cries, shrieks and yelps as appropriate.

The instruments of a Sundanese gamelan Salendro resemble those of a small Central Javanese gamelan. Much of the music's expressive character is conveyed, not just by the juru kawih, but also by the **rebab** (a two-stringed spiked fiddle, similar in construction to its Javanese counterpart) and particularly the **kendang** (a set of three drums of varying sizes). These instruments play with a degree of crispness and clarity not generally associated with the classical traditions from Central Java.

The drums, played by a single player, are unique to Sunda, with the largest of the three placed at 45° to the floor. This enables the player to change the pitch of the drumhead with his foot and obtain a "talking drum" effect.

Tembang Sunda

Although related, **tembang Sunda** is, strictly speaking, not a gamelan genre at all. It was developed at the Kabupaten (Regent's court) of Cianjur, a town between Bandung and Jakarta, during the colonial era, and consists of sung poetry – both female and male vocalists are used – accompanied by one or two *kecapi* (zithers) together with a suling or a rebab.

Spreading from its point of origin, where it was known as *mamaos* (singing), it is now referred to as *cianjuran* or tembang Sunda (the word tembang is used throughout Java to denote vocal genres). The original style consists of songs sung in free rhythm, but a more recent development, *panambih*, is metrical and consists of songs that may derive from either gamelan Salendro or gamelan Degung repertoire. Pieces can be in one of several tuning systems.

Although often used today to enhance the atmosphere of foyers in Bandung's more exclusive hotels, tembang Sunda is suited to a more intimate setting. Perhaps played in the home, late at night, and often for the sole benefit of the performers themselves, the music has the ability to transport performer and listener alike far away from the hustle and bustle of everyday life.

The vocal quality of **Sundanese singing**, particularly striking in tembang Sunda, is one of the more unusual features of music from this region. Beautiful and haunting, it is quite unlike Javanese vocal music and not only complements the nuances of the spoken language but also enhances its emotional and expressive power. Once heard, it is never forgotten.

A related instrumental form, **kecapi suling**, with the suling taking the place of the voice, has become extremely popular in the cassette industry in recent years. It is lighter in mood than the vocal genre and allows the suling greater freedom to improvise.

East Java

The performance traditions of West and Central Java are now well represented in the West on CD and cassette. The same cannot be said of those

605

from the province of **East Java**. This is a pity, as the region has a rich diversity of performing arts.

The variety stems, in part, from the greater number of ethnic groups living in the region, including **Javanese**, **Madurese** (from the island of Madura), **Osinger** (from the town of Banyuwangi), and **Tenggerese** (from the Tengger mountains). Each of these groups has its own performing traditions, and while all have some relationship to the classical gamelan traditions of Central Java, or in the case of the Osinger, Bali, they represent fascinating art forms in their own right. Javanese-gamelan are found throughout the region, but as one travels progressively eastwards, the prevailing musical style becomes marked by increasing dynamism and aggressiveness.

Gamyak drums

Perhaps the most dramatic element of East Javanese gamelan music, and certainly one not found outside the region, is the **gamyak drum**. Larger than its Central Javanese equivalent, its drumheads are made from buffalo rather than goat skin, and the piercingly sharp sound produced is immediately recognizable. It is especially associated with the *ngremo* dance – the drumming for which is considered some of the most technically demanding anywhere in Java – and various forms of tari topeng (masked dance) popular around Malang.

In addition, **tayuban** – dances where male spectators may request pieces from the gamelan and, for a small gratuity, have the pleasure of dancing with one of the *tandhak* (female dancers) present – have helped steer the popular gamelan repertoire away from the classical refinement associated with Central Java. Once common throughout Java, these are rowdy affairs and only continue to exist in areas where Islam has a limited influence on daily life. As a consequence it is still popular in the **Tengger region** where the prevailing religion synthesizes elements of Hinduism with pre-Hindu beliefs.

Madura

Gamelan music from the island of **Madura** is, in some respects, closer to the traditions of mainland Central Java. In previous centuries bloodlines were established between the royal palace of **Sumenep** (the main town on the island) and the courts of Surakarta, and this relationship is reflected in the performing arts. Nevertheless, the peculiar roughness of expression found elsewhere in East Java is still evident. Of particular note is the **topeng dalang**, unique to Madura, in which the great Indian epics of the Mahabharata and Ramayana, as well as the Javanese story of Panji, are recounted by a single storyteller (*dalang*) with the action being recreated by a company of masked actors and dancers.

Osinger

The **Osinger** of **Banyuwangi** represent yet another branch of East Javanese music and dance, with the two main forms, *gandrung* and *angklung*, displaying influences from neighbouring Bali (Banyuwangi is the departure point for the ferry crossing from Java to Bali).

Gandrung is performed by professional musicians at all-night social events (weddings, circumcisions, and so on) and consists of a small group of instrumentalists (two violins, drums, a triangle, gongs and gong-chimes) together with a female singer-dancer (the gandrung).

Angklung, played by young boys through amateur organizations which perform at local carnivals and competitions, are bamboo xylophones and can be combined with a selection of iron gamelan instruments (metallophones and gongs) in the gamelan **bali-balian**. This ensemble, truly reminiscent of gamelan in Bali, is commonly used for *angklung caruk*, in which two such ensembles compete to outdo each other with displays of skill and virtuosity.

Bali

A Balinese temple, late evening: in the main courtyard a hundred men sit in circles, only the sound of crickets breaking the silence. Suddenly, with several short cries the men rise up, then sink down again, making a hissing sound. A single short shout follows and the men break into a rhythmic chant, "*Uchak-a-chak-a-chak...*", swaying from side to side, hands waving in the air. A solitary voice rises above the rhythmic chattering of the chorus, singing a quivering, wailing melody. Another short cry and the men sink down again. This is the famed Balinese **kecak** or monkey-chant.

In the kecak, the chorus of men imitates the chattering and jabbering of the monkeys (there are several monkey forests in Bali), while the complex rhythms are taken from the gamelan. The Balinese

Balinese dancers with a gamelan orchestra in 1941

love to take something from elsewhere and incorporate it into their art. In the stone temple carvings of north Bali, among the ornate mythical beasts and flowers, there may be a Dutchman in colonial uniform on a bicycle, or in the middle of a traditional painting by a young artist you may find a car. In a similar way, the kecak was adopted in the twentieth century from an ancient trance dance into a drama using the **Hindu Ramayana** story. The chorus represents the monkey army helping King Rama rescue his queen, Sinta, from Rahwana, the ogre-king.

The kecak is performed as a spectacle rather than a ceremony and new versions are commissioned for festivals and TV. However, much of Bali's abundant music, dance and theatre continues to play an essential role in the elaborate temple ceremonies central to life on the island.

Hindu Bali

In the late fifteenth century the Hindu-Javanese Majapahit Empire fell to Muslim rulers and many of the Javanese princes fled eastwards across the narrow strait to Bali, taking with them their priests, dancers and musicians. To this day the Balinese practise their own **Hindu-Balinese religion**, a unique blend of Hinduism and traditional Balinese beliefs.

The village temple is at the heart of Balinese life and culture. Hardly a week passes without several **temple festivals** happening all over the island. Important island-wide festivals, such as **Galungan**, which comes once every 210 days (a Balinese year), call for ten days of prayer and festivities. At Galungan the spirits of the ancestors visit the island and they must be greeted with offerings, prayers, music and dance.

In the larger villages all the different gamelans are brought out for Galungan. The four-note **gamelan Angklung** (commonly associated with temple festivals) is played by the older boys of the village, as part of the long procession of women bringing the family offerings to the temple. Further down there are the clashing cymbals of the processional **gamelan Bebonangan**. Within the open-air temple itself several different gamelans are played all at once in separate pavilions. Only the gods and spirits are listening. Like the carefully arranged fruit and rice, like the flowers and incense, the music is an offering.

Later on, though, in the cool air of early evening, crowds will gather to watch a dance drama – perhaps the brilliant *Baris* **dance** with lightning movements representing a warrior, or the *Barong* dance, symbolic of the eternal conflict of good and evil, in which the dragon Barong battles with Rangda, the witch. There might also be **gambuh** theatre, an ancient form accompanied not by tuned bronze, but by deep flutes and percussion. This **gamelan Gambuh** is described in one of the earliest accounts of Balinese music and is thought to have preceded the ensembles of tuned percussion. The evening might end with a night-time performance of wayang kulit, accompanied by the intricate music of a quartet of **gendèr wayang**.

Most villages in Bali boast several gamelans owned by the local music club. The club members, all men, meet there in the evenings to rehearse.

They are almost all amateurs, earning their living as farmers, craftsmen or civil servants. Gamelan playing is considered a part of every man's education, as important as the art of rice growing or cooking ceremonial food.

The **village gamelan** is kept in a public place and rehearsals usually draw an interested audience of onlookers who offer comments and suggestions. Many villages have a distinctive style or speciality: Peliatan is known for the refinement of its courtly *legong* dance and music, Sukawati for the complexity and brilliance of its gendèr playing. It's said that

Gamelan Performances

There is no better way to experience gamelan than to visit Java or Bali and seek out performances. There are plenty of opportunities, including temple performances and regular *klenengan* (gamelan-only) performances that are open to tourists and foreign students of gamelan.

JAVA

Jakarta

The performance of traditional community gamelan music (*karawitan*) not connected to famous musicians, *campursari* performances (a popular genre often using customized diatonic gamelan instruments with Western brass and keyboards) or wayang troupes is often difficult to seek out in Jakarta. However, professional musicians do rehearse on Wednesday nights at Sanggar Dwidjolaras (7.30–11.00pm) in Kemang, South Jakarta. For up-to-date information, contact the sponsor at ekathryn@hotmail.com.

Surakarta (Solo)

There are regular **live RRI broadcasts** of gamelan music from the two palaces: the **Kraton Hadiningrat** and the **Mangkunegaran**. Listeners are welcome and this is a great opportunity to see the palace gamelans being played. Broadcasts take place at lunchtimes and late evenings (10pm–midnight). Dates are determined by the 35-day month of the Javanese calendar – some auspicious events do require spectators to wear respectful or formal attire. Go to the RRI and check the noticeboard for details of all live broadcasts.

Similarly dependent on the 35-day calendar are monthly **wayang kulit** performances at the **Bale Agung Kraton**. These occur from 9.00pm to midnight and alternate between two respected puppeteers Ki Tristuti and Ki Toto Atmojo.

ISI (Institut Seni Indonesia), the "Institute of Indonesian Arts", is a bus-ride from the centre of town. Wayang, dance and gamelan exam recitals and performances take place at the end of each semester.

There are all-night **wayang kulit performances** each month at **Taman Budaya Surakarta** (on the campus of ISI) and **RRI**.

Dance rehearsals take place at the **Mangkunegaran** every Wednesday morning and **dance performances** are held on the 26th of each month at **SMK8** (a local performing arts high school) from 8.00pm to 11.00pm.

Nightly **wayang orang** (dance-drama) performances take place at the **Sriwedari Amusement Park** and there are regular tourist performances at the larger hotels, such as **Hotel Kusuma Sahid**.

Klenengan "Pujangga Laras" – a free-form get-together of around fifty of the most respected musicians in Solo – happens monthly from 8.00pm-2.00am. The date and location varies but sponsors can be contacted at ekathryn@hotmail.com for up-to-date information.

Yogyakarta (Yogya)

There is lots going on in Yogya: much of it is geared to the large number of tourists who visit the town each year, so if you're not staying long you'll find performances more easily here than in Solo.

Daily gamelan and dance performances for tourists are held at the **Kraton**, and nightly two-hour wayang performances take place at the **Agastiya Institute**. Other central venues include the **Kepatihan**, **Taman Budaya** and

people can find their way around the island in the dark by recognizing the distinctive tones of the local gamelans shimmering across the rice fields in the night air.

Kebyar – the new style

When the Dutch took control of Bali in the early twentieth century the island's courts all but disappeared. Many royal families decided to sacrifice themselves in the cannon-fire rather than submit to Dutch rule. This had an enormous impact on the musical life of the island. The court gamelans had no function outside the palace walls and were sold or taken to the villages where they were melted down to make new gamelans for the latest style that was taking Bali by storm: **kebyar** – a word that means "like the bursting open of a flower".

Kebyar replaced the slow, stately court pieces with a fast, dynamic music, full of dramatic contrasts, changes of tempo and sudden loud outbursts. It was not long before Bali's most famous dancer, **I Mario**, choreographed the first

Pujukusuman, the dance school where the late Romo Sas (one of Yogya's top dance teachers) taught until recently. A live RRI broadcast takes place at the **Pura Pukualaman** each month.

There are also regular tourist performances of dance and gamelan in the hotels; the performers are often students from **ISI** Yogya.

Further out of town are the **Lembaga Studi Jawa**, a foundation set up recently for the study and performance of Javanese arts; **Bagong Kussiardja**'s dance foundation, where you may be able to watch rehearsals; and **ISI**, where exam recitals and performances of new dance and gamelan music are held. Performances of the **Ramayana** ballet are held regularly at **Prambanan Temple** (outside Yogya) – pricey but worth seeing.

Festivals

Annual festivals to look out for in Java are the **Festival Kesenian Yogyakarta** (gamelan, dance and wayang), the **International Gamelan Festival** (includes new compositions and groups from abroad), and the week-long **Sekaten** and **Kraton festivals**. Sekaten is held each year in both Solo and Yogya from the 6th to the 12th of the third month in the Javanese calendar.

BALI

There is always lots going on in Bali. The easiest performances to find are those arranged for tourists; the more interesting ones take a bit more searching for, and the most memorable occasions will be the ones you come across unexpectedly. The best way to find out what's happening where is to go to the Tourist Board in Denpasar, buy a Balinese calendar, and get a list of the major **odalans** (village temple ceremonies). The major temple festivals **Galungan** and **Kuningan** are held every 210 days. Odalans are held more frequently.

There is always lots of gamelan and dance in **Ubud**, **Peliatan** and **Teges**. Other places to visit if you have more time are **Sabah** (on the coast, there is a legong troupe), **Sukawati** (gendèr wayang), **Batur** (gong gedé) and the villages of **Sawan** and **Jagaraga** in north Bali.

In **Denpasar**, the **Bali Arts Festival** is held in July/August each year, and performances are held at **STSI** (Sekolah Tinggi Seni Indonesia), the high school – or academy – of Indonesian Arts, throughout the year.

Sophie Clark

Gunungan offerings at the Sekaten festival

CMP Records

Bali's Heavenly Orchestra

kebyar dance, in which the intricate and beautiful movements of the dancer's eyes, head and hands mirror the dazzling display of the music. This dynamic virtuoso style makes much Balinese gamelan music today sound utterly different from the Javanese.

While the new kebyar style swept across the island, the poorer villages in western Bali could not afford expensive bronze metallophones and so created "copies" of traditional gamelans, replacing metal keys with bamboo. These instruments were (and are) made from a series of bamboo tubes on a simple frame, often including a double "gong" made of two lengths of bamboo suspended over a large earthenware jar, which produces a deep gong-like sound.

Bamboo ensembles include the stunning **gamelan Jegog**, in which the longest bamboo tubes may be up to three metres in length. The instruments are tuned to a four-note scale and are struck with thick rubber beaters. Players sit astride the largest instrument, the **jegogan**, which sounds a deep sonorous melody beneath the interlocking patterns of the other instruments. The sound is enormously powerful, especially when two or more groups play against one another in one of the ever-popular regional competitions!

Another popular ensemble is the **joged Bumbung** ("bumbung" means bamboo). This style was born in the 1950s in west Bali and was based on the **joged**, an old flirtatious dance where the female dancers invite men from the audience to take turns dancing with them.

The older **court ensembles** still remaining in Bali sound closer in style to Javanese gamelan; slower, and without the sudden changes of tempo, texture and dynamics which are so characteristic of kebyar. There's the stately ceremonial **Gamelan Gong Gédé** from the mountain temple of Bator. And there's the sensuous and delicate **Gamelan Semar Pegulingan** (Gamelan of the Love God). The semar pegulingan includes bamboo flutes and a pair of gendèrs, played with hard mallets. Originally played near the sleeping chambers in the palace, this beautiful ensemble is now often played for the legong dance.

Sacred gamelans in Bali include the **gamelan Gambang**, frequently played for cremations, with wooden xylophones bringing a more brittle sound, and the ethereal **gamelan Selunding** from the village of Tenganan in east Bali. Although the keys of the latter are made from iron slabs, the sound is sweet and pure. It is thought to be the oldest type of gamelan on the island, possibly pre-Hindu, and is reserved for ritual occasions.

Balinese Rhythms

While Javanese music is contemplative and restrained, Balinese is loud and extrovert. It is, after all, outdoor music. Like the elaborate temple carvings and paintings, the music is intricately detailed. Just as the harmony of village life depends on the delicate balance of opposing forces of good and evil, night and day, so in the gamelan the instruments appear in pairs, even the drums, which are called male and female.

The rhythmic vitality of Balinese music comes from interlocking patterns played on the pairs of instruments. These patterns, or **kotekan**, are played on bronze *gangsas* (similar to the Javanese gendèr but struck with hard wooden mallets), a pair of drums and the *reong* (a row of small kettle-gongs, played by four people). Apart from the rhythm, there's another kind of beat in Balinese gamelan music. The pairs of instruments are tuned slightly "out" with each other, so that when two instruments are played together, there is a "harmonic beating". This gives the sound of the Balinese gamelan its characteristic shimmering quality.

The Canadian composer **Colin McPhee**, who lived and studied in Bali in the 1930s, writes in his delightful book *A House in Bali* of the stir his Steinway grand caused in the village where he lived for ten years. When he played a waltz his Balinese friends were dismayed. "Where's the beat?" they asked, "There's no beat! Like a bird with a broken wing!" **Benjamin Britten**, who was introduced to Balinese music by McPhee, was captivated by the music he heard on a visit in 1956, finding it "fantastically rich melodically, rhythmically, texturally (such orchestration!!) and above all formally". In his ballet score *The Prince of the Pagodas* Britten created a small, Western "gamelan" from the percussion section of the orchestra, which plays a version of "Kapi Raja", a well-known Balinese piece.

The island has changed a lot since the 1950s, of course. Bali is Indonesia's prime tourist attraction and draws around a million people each year (more than a third of Bali's population). The roads buzz with motorbikes, *bemos* (local transport) and huge tourist buses. But the arts continue to flourish and grow, the traditional temple festivals go on and more modern festivals, such as the annual **Bali Arts Festival** in Denpasar (mid-June to mid-July), have become an important feature of cultural life on the island. On any night of the week, if you're lucky you can hear a number of different gamelans in a temple or at a festival, a wedding, a tooth-filing ceremony or a cremation. Go there – and keep your ears open!

DISCOGRAPHY Indonesia | Gamelan

Indonesia has a large recording industry but until recently many of its major labels, such as Lokananta and Kusuma Recordings, had limited exports to the West. Cassettes are very cheap to buy in Indonesia and there are literally thousands to choose from, but good-quality commercial recordings of gamelan music are relatively hard to come by in music shops in the UK and Europe. CDs are gradually replacing cassettes as the favoured format in Indonesia and old recordings are at times remastered and re-released. Notably, more recordings by non-Indonesian labels are available to download over the Internet from major international music retailers and institutions concerned with the preservation of traditional world music.

Java

★ **Banyumas Bamboo Gamelan**
Nimbus, UK
The only widely available recording of Banyumas calung music, the Javanese bamboo gamelan. Traditional dance pieces with vocals and some more contemporary styles drawing on jaipongan and *dangdut*. Great frog imitations on track 3.

⊙ **Chamber Music of Central Java**
King, Japan
One of the few discs of Javanese gamelan that isn't a large court ensemble. This is a chamber gadhon gamelan of soft-toned instruments, without the big line-up of gongs, played by top musicians from Solo. More intimate instrumental music.

★ **Gamelan of Central Java IV: Spiritual Music**
Felmay, Italy
Explores themes of mysticism and spirituality encompassed in Javanese gamelan music. Its meditative repertoire includes powerful gamelan Sekaten compositions, sacred palace music from Solo and a unique version of a traditional piece incorporating the Muslim call to prayer. This album – although not a perfectly balanced studio recording – lacks a little of the atmosphere of live ceremonial gamelan performance but is a great document of this genre. Offers translations of the Javanese sung text.

★ **Gamelan of Central Java IX: Songs of Wisdom and Love**
Felmay, Italy
This is a definitive collection of ancient Javanese poetic texts sung in a variety of contexts. Examples range from sung

macapat poems accompanied by solo gendèr to ceremonial pieces with texts in differing poetic metres. The listener is also given a taste of the poetry used in shadow-puppetry with the full gamelan accompaniment.

⊙ Gamelan of the Kraton, Yogyakarta
Celestial Harmonies, US

The most atmospheric and beautifully recorded of Javanese gamelan discs. This royal gamelan is one of the cultural and historical glories of the island. Here the court musicians play grandiose ceremonial pieces, elegant dance repertoire and the extraordinary music, peculiar to the Yogya *kraton*, of the *bedhaya* dance with added snare drums and brass.

⊙ Gamelan of Surakarta
JVC, Japan

This is the best introduction available to the Surakarta style of Javanese gamelan. Three pieces played by the Surakarta Institute of Indonesian Arts from serene music with choral singing to dynamic and varied instrumental playing co-ordinated by the virtuoso drumming of Rahayu Supanggah, the composer. The final piece, composed to accompany traditional dance drama, reveals a developing tradition.

★ Indonesia, Central Java: Solonese Gamelan, A Garland of Moods
Inedit, Maison des Cultures du Monde, France

A four-disc document of field recordings made by ethnomusicologist Marc Benamou in July 2003 at the home of eminent musician Rahayu Supanggah. Showcasing the most influential musicians in Solo, this collection spans a huge variety of repertoire from serious meditative pieces to lighthearted playful songs and wayang (shadow-puppetry) accompaniment. Contains excellent notes and explanations of playing style for each piece.

⊙ Indonesia: Madura, Musique Savante
Ocora, France

This disc gives a rare opportunity to listen to the unique and dynamic gamelan traditions from the island of Madura as well as extracts from a performance of topeng dalang. It features master dalang Sabidin, descended from several generations of a storytelling family.

⊙ Java: Palais Royal de Yogyakarta Vol. 2, Instrumental Music
Ocora, France

This is the second volume of four recorded in the Yogyakarta palace. As many of the other discs selected here include vocals, this is a good choice if you want gamelan alone. The other volumes are also recommended, particularly Vol. 4, *Concert Music*.

⊙ Java the Jasmine Isle: Gamelan Music
Nonesuch Explorer, US

An interesting and eclectic collection of recordings originally released in 1969 but remastered and released on CD in 2003. Unusually, the collection features versions of well-known pieces in the Javanese and Sundanese style for comparison and also solo instruments performing out of context to show the complexity of the embellishing lines. The large gong sounds amazing in the pieces for full gamelan, and outdoor sounds of frogs give an authentic feel to the recording.

★ Javanese Court Gamelan
Nonesuch Explorer, US

Gamelan of the Paku Alaman palace in Yogyakarta. Recorded in the early 1970s, this highly atmospheric CD has a timeless quality. A varied choice of pieces played on a celestial traditional gamelan set within the audible ambience of an open-air pavilion, complete with bird song!

⊙ Shadow Music of Java
Rounder, US

An excellent presentation of the kind of music heard at wayang shadow puppet performances with different styles for different parts of the show. Edited from a two-hour wayang given by Widiyanto S. Putro (dalang) and the Hardo Budoyo gamelan from Wonogiri in Central Java while on tour in the US. One of the few CDs on the market showing Javanese gamelan music as it is most commonly heard today.

Sunda

★ Bebar Leyer: Gamelan of West Java
Lokananta – Sunda Series, Indonesia

Released in 2006, this CD is a remastered version of a 1973 recording of gamelan degung from RRI Bandung under the direction of E. Tjarmed. It features traditional repertoire but with the more unusual element of female choral singing. In track 5, classic degung repertoire incorporates melodies and playing styles from Cirebon featuring the ornate playing of the Sundanese fiddle in place of the melodious suling (bamboo flute) and rippling drum patterns to give extra flavour to this colourful collection.

⊙ Classical Tembang Sunda
Celestial Harmonies, US

Singer Ida Widwati and her group from Bandung in tembang Sunda swing (solo and choral styles) accompanied by a pair of Sundanese kecapi (zither) and suling. The pieces selected give a good indication of the range of poetic expression and nuance in this music. Translations included.

⊙ Flutes and Gamelan Music of West Java
Topic Records, UK

A rare glimpse of gamelan music from Cirebon, a city on the north coast of West Java, as well as a selection of kecapi suling. It features Sulaeman, a player of the Sundanese suling with a recording career stretching back to the days of 78s.

⊙ Gamelang Degung
Pan, Netherlands

Traditional degung music is beautiful and compulsive. This disc features the famous Jugala orchestra with Euis Komariah and Ida Widawati.

⊙ Java – Pays Sunda, 2: L'art du Gamelan Degung
Ocora, France

One of the definitive recordings of gamelan Degung currently available in the West, this contains a fine representation of pieces from the classical repertoire as well as new compositions. Features the bamboo flute playing of Ono Sukarna.

★ Sundanese Traditional Music, Kecapi Suling: Arang-Arang
Equinox DMD/ Pro Sound, Indonesia

A haunting collection of traditional kecapi suling repertoire by Gapura Group Bandung featuring the accomplished suling playing of Endang Sukandar.

⊙ Tembang Sunda
Nimbus, UK

Mellow performances from male and female vocalists, Imas Permas and Asep Kosasih accompanied by zither and flute. Refined classical repertoire and more easy-going love songs. Translations included.

Bali and Lombok

★ Anthology of the Music of Bali
Buda/Musique du Monde, France

This set of four double CDs, available separately, contains some of the best recordings of the various Balinese gamelan styles with excellent notes and photos. Vol. 1 (*Popular Traditions*) features vocal music, Jegog and other bamboo styles. Vol. 2, (*Virtuoso Gamelan*) features kebyar, suling and anglung. Vol. 3 (*Ritual Music*) features the archaic forms, selunding, gambang, gong gédé and others. Vol. 4 (*Classical Traditions*) includes *gambuh* and music for dance and puppet performances.

⊙ Bali: A Suite of Tropical Music and Sound
World Network, Germany

Volume 35 in World Network's ambitious global survey, this is an ideal introduction to the varied sounds of Balinese music, beginning with frogs and cicadas. It includes many of the lesser-known gamelan styles – gambuh, selunding, jegog, joged bumbung, plus kecak etc. The only thing missing is the straight kebyar sound, but there's plenty of that to be found elsewhere.

⊙ Bali: Musique pour le Gong Gédé
Ocora, France

The gong gédé of the Batur temple, dating back to the fifteenth century, the oldest in Bali and a more recent ensemble in Tampaksiring. Ceremonial music of the old, pre-kebyar style. Softer and more stately than most other Balinese gamelan music.

⊙ The Bali Sessions: Living Art, Sounding Spirit
Rykodisc, US

A well-packaged and documented three-CD set that highlights some of the lesser-known areas of Balinese music. Disc 1 ranges through the ancient gamelan selunding, gong Suling (featuring flutes), gamelan Genggong (with Jew's harps) and the bamboo gamelan Jegog. Disc 2 features gamelan Joged Bumbung and an epic kecak performance, and Disc 3 new compositions for traditional ensembles.

⊙ Gamelan Batel Wayang Ramayana
⊙ Mahabharata: Music for the Balinese
CMP/Silva Screen, UK

The first is a lovely recording of Balinese theatrical music for a wayang performance of the Ramayana. A quartet of gendèr plus drums and flute recorded in a temple pavilion in the village of Sading. The second is a beautiful recording of music for a wayang Mahabharata on four gendèr.

⊙ Gamelan Gong Kebyar
King, Japan

Three pieces of contemporary Balinese kebyar music, including a Baris warrior dance, performed by the Eka Cita gamelan in Denpasar district.

⊙ Gamelan Gong Kebyar, Vols 1–3
JVC, Japan

Volume 3 of this series is the best introduction to the kebyar style from the gamelan of Tejakula in northern Bali, noted for its large ensemble of instruments. Bold and glittering with strong percussion and drums, the CD notes say "This disc should be played at maximum volume to appreciate the essence of this ensemble's music to the full." Volume 2 features the smaller gamelan of the Academy of Art and Dance in Denpasar in contrasting kebyar and gambuh pieces.

★ Gamelan Music of Bali: Gamelan Angklung and Gamelan Gong Kebjar
Lyrichord, US

A great introduction to the classic repertoire of Balinese Angklung and Gong Kebyar ensembles. These incredibly synchronized groups play at ferocious speed with maximum intensity. The result is exciting as short bursts of energy build up to virtuosic flourishes; pounding drums drive interlocking bronze melodies and cue sudden and dramatic pauses. The players seem to think and breathe as one in a masterful example of musicianship of the highest calibre.

⊙ Gamelan Semar Pegulingan (II)
JVC, Japan

Semar Pegulingan group from Peliatan village. Another exquisite recording without the bamboo flutes but with atmospheric insects in the background.

⊙ Gamelan Semar Pegulingan Saih Pitu: The Heavenly Orchestra of Bali
CMP/Silva Screen, UK

The "love gamelan", a sort of gamelan "hump-tape"; the ethereal, tinkly sound of this sort of ensemble accompanied the king while he slept with the queen. Gamelan, flutes and drums in a lovely clear recording of a 29-strong ensemble from Kamasan, eastern Bali.

⊙ Jegog: Gamelan Jegog Wardi Santana
CMP/Silva Screen, UK

Top-quality bamboo gamelan recording with deep booming bass notes.

⊙ Jegog of Nagara
King, Japan

The best jegog disc around. Thunderous sound, lots of atmosphere and the competing of two groups from west Bali. Turn it up loud and enjoy the thrill.

⊙ Lombok, Kalimantan, Banyumas: Little-known Forms of Gamelan and Wayang
Smithsonian Folkways, US

Part fourteen of Smithsonian Folkways' extensive survey of Indonesian music features *wayang sasak* from Lombok, a theatrical form related to Balinese gambuh; masked and shadow theatre music from South Kalimantan (Borneo); and *Jemblung* from Banyumas which comprises amazing vocal imitations of gamelan!

⊙ Music for the Gods
Rykodisc, US

Recordings made (mostly in Bali) in 1941 by Bruce and Sheridan Fahnestock weeks before World War II and subsequent tourism changed the island forever. The story of the expedition and the survival of this material is incredible. These unique recordings include Semar Pegulingan, kebyar, a gendèr quartet for wayang and kecak plus three tracks of fascinating stuff from the island of Madura.

⊙ The Roots of Gamelan
World Arbiter, US

It was these 1928 recordings which inspired Canadian composer Colin McPhee to settle in Bali. Represented here by the piece "Kebyar Ding", the once-forgotten Gong Kebyar style is considered so historically important that in 1975 the Balinese reconstructed it from this very recording. A fascinating document featuring several gamelan styles plus recordings of McPhee's gamelan transcriptions for two pianos played by McPhee and Benjamin Britten in 1941.

New Gamelan Music

⊙ American Works for Balinese Gamelan Orchestra
New World Records, US

Music by three American composers following in the footsteps of Colin McPhee: Evan Ziporyn, Wayne Vitale and Michael Tenzer, author of a great book on Balinese music. Played by Californian Balinese gamelan Sekar Jaya plus assorted Western instruments from saxophone to violin and mandolin.

⊙ Asmat Dream
Lyrichord, US

One for gamelan or new music specialists perhaps, but ample illustration of the radical experiments underway with gamelan and other traditional instruments. Includes music by four Sundanese composers including Nano S. There are two other volumes in this series: Vol. 2 *Mana 689* features composers from central Java and Vol. 3 *Karya* on the work of Balinese composer I. Wayan Sadra.

⊙ Harrison: Chamber and Gamelan Works
New World Records, US

A CD of works by the late American composer Lou Harrison whose music was inspired by the sounds of Indonesia. This recording features Harrison's compositions for gamelan and Western instruments and features the US-based Gamelan Sekar Kembar with the Kronos Quartet and Manhattan Percussion Ensemble.

⊙ The Music of K.R.T. Wasitodiningrat
CMP/Silva Screen, UK

Rebab player and composer Wasitodiningrat was associated with the Paku Alaman court gamelan of Yogyakarta. The eight compositions on this disc are within the traditional framework of Central Javanese gamelan.

*Thanks to Penny King and Maria Mendonça
for help with the discography.*

PLAYLIST
Indonesia | Gamelan

1 LADRANG TURUN SIH Musicians of STSI Solo (now ISI) from *Gamelan of Central Java IV: Spiritual Music*
The voice of Rustopo leading the call to prayer over the haunting sounds of the gamelan interwoven with the sensitive rebab (spike fiddle) of Suraji is sublime.

2 JINEMAN ULER KAMBANG Solonese gamelan musicians from *A Garland of Moods*
The soothing and subtly flirtatious voice of pesinden Nyi Suparni invites the listener to "take it easy" with this popular song in *jineman* form. Rather than the full gamelan, she is accompanied by soft embellishing instruments, tinkling zither and an attentive male chorus.

3 LADRAK Musicians of RRI Bandung from *Beber Layar*
This upbeat song is intended to motivate the listener to be less complacent and more productive. The playful vocals coupled with the floating suling melody are infectious and the rippling degung motives inspire rhythm and movement.

4 PALARAN DURMA Solonese gamelan musicians from *Gamelan of Central Java IX: Songs of Wisdom and Love*
A sedate and calming version of this text accompanied in the style of the wayang. Be mesmerized by the seductively beautiful voice of Nyi Cendani Raras as she advises us to adhere to the wisdom of our ancestors before acting rashly.

5 DHOBER Banyumas calung ensemble from *Banyumas Bamboo Gamelan Traditional Music from Central Java*
The party is in full swing with this exuberant track of fast and furious bamboo xylophones, provocative female singing and raucous vocal interjections signalled by some incredible funky drumming!

6 LADRANG GEGOT Solonese gamelan musicians from *A Garland of Moods*
With catchy vocal melodies and sections of contrasting mood and style, this piece showcases the richness and diversity of Solonese gamelan music with coquettish female singing, humorous drumming and striking metallic bronze interjections.

7 KEBJAR HUDJAN MAS Various artists from *Gamelan Angklung and Gamelan Gong Kebjar*
Entitled Hudjan Mas or "Golden Rain", this piece is a masterful example of ensemble playing. Short virtuosic bursts of melody interspersed with silent pauses build in intensity to a flourishing crescendo of bronze, gongs and pounding drums.

Indonesia | Pop and Folk

beyond the gamelan

Bandung singer Detty Kurnia
John Clewley

With its three thousand inhabited islands and more than three hundred ethnic groups, the sprawling archipelago of Indonesia has a population of nearly 250 million, the world's fourth largest. It's hardly surprising, then, that it should have a bewildering range of folk styles, nor that its pop-music scene should be the most exciting in Southeast Asia and the Far East. Colin Bass introduces the world of *dangdut*, *jaipongan*, *kroncong* and more.

Contrasts, Contradictions and Parallel Worlds

To begin with, some revealing statistics: 87% of the Indonesian population describe themselves as Muslim, while nearly half live on the island of Java, which comprises just 7% of Indonesia's land area. According to a 2006 study, nearly 18% of the population lives below the poverty line, and a large proportion of the rest not far above it. Against this background, the removal of the late President Suharto in 1997, the ensuing currency meltdown, the increasing need for foreign oil supplies and the cost of rebuilding after the tsunami of 2004 and other natural disasters, coupled with the irresistible spread of information technology and the penetration of global businesses, have brought many challenges to Indonesia.

Cultural globalization is on the march too. That the traffic has been one-way is shown by the fact that, while the vast world of Indonesian pop music is still practically unknown in the West, equally vast amounts of Western pop music are available and being consumed in the country. No survey of Indonesian pop music can overlook the effect that this has had on the local music scene. In the mid-1990s, changes in trade regulations enabled the major global record companies (BMG, Sony and so on) to fully take over their Indonesian distributors. Since then, they have been investing in local talent, but mainly in acts which fit international templates. Name any contemporary style of music and there will be an Indonesian version of it. Alongside the seemingly inexhaustible supply of good-looking young singing stars there are boy-bands, girl-bands, indie-rock bands, hip-hoppers and rappers, and heavy metal groups of all persuasions: death, thrash, hard-core, grindcore and any other core you like.

This isn't to say that Western-style music has been imposed on the populace. Far from it: there's a vital and growing local scene, mainly in the major cities of Java: Jakarta, Bandung, Surabaya. MTV Indonesia is given a couple of hours' airtime daily on one of the national TV channels, during which all these styles are featured. Those who can afford a satellite dish can watch it all day. The groovy young vee-jays look the same as their counterparts around the world, and Indonesian artists interchange easily with established Western stars. In 2007 the biggest-selling Indonesian artists were the band **Peterpan**, whose melodic, guitar-led rock anthems with a strong element of local melancholy officially sold over two million CDs and cassettes and presumably kept the pirates busy

with a lot more. The band **Gigi** (Tooth), whose fine, Beatles/Stones influenced rock has recently taken on a U2-like proselytizing stance from an Islamic standpoint, share a similar stature. And so on.

Meanwhile in a parallel universe, the home-grown pop music born before the current information overload still entertains millions, even though you may not see any of it on MTV wherever you are. It remains to be seen what the next affordable, music-carrying medium will be, but for the time being, cassettes are still an important medium throughout the archipelago.

Many cassette shops in Jakarta also stock CDs, but these are more expensive and therefore luxury items for many. Video CDs are very popular in Indonesia, but cassette shops may not have many in stock because thousands of pirated copies are available on street-market stalls, proliferating parasitically just outside the door. If you find a good cassette shop, though, the shelves can take you on a musical tour of the islands once you decode the names of the proliferating genres. If a song is successful in any major genre it will be swiftly followed by scores of cover versions in a variety of regional and crossover styles, sporting descriptive double-barrelled names such as **tarling-jaipong**, **Batak-house**, **minang-dangdut** and many more. But, not to get ahead of ourselves, let's approach the subject from a historical perspective.

Kroncong

It is said that the roots of *kroncong* (pronounced "ker-ong-chong") go back several centuries to when the Portuguese were busy trading in and colonizing Africa and South Asia. Freed Portuguese slaves of mostly African and Asian origin, referred to as *mardika* or *mardikers*, established settlements in various parts of the archipelago, bringing with them guitar-like instruments and Portuguese songs. The introduction of European musical instruments laid the basis for what later became the first major urban folk-style. By the early 1900s, kroncong was associated with the underclass of the cities, and was arguably the rap music of its day, often featuring verbal duelling between sharply-dressed singers known as either a *buaya* (crocodile) or a *jago* (rooster). In the 1920s, respectability loomed through recordings and popular theatre. Kroncong musicians also found employment playing in hotels for the growing number of Dutch expatriates, business travellers and tourists. What could be called a "palm-court orchestra" style developed, incorporating popular Western songs and dance-styles, particularly the two big crazes of the day, the beguine and Hawaiian music. Later use by the new Indonesian film industry established kroncong as a national popular music. During the independence struggle of 1945–48, many inspirational patriotic songs were set to kroncong and it developed through the 1950s as a leading popular style, remaining the Indonesian elite's music of choice to this day.

A typical classic ensemble might consist of two *kroncong* (three- or four-string ukulele-like instruments), guitar, violin, mandolin, flute, percussion and a cello and a double bass, usually played pizzicato, accompanying a singer, usually female. The distinctive kroncong rhythm is set up by the two ukuleles – one known as the **cak**, the other as the **cuk** – playing alternate strokes of the beat. The medium-pace tempo, the diatonic melodies and the languid, crooning singing-style invite comparison with East African Taarab music and Portuguese Fado – and of course Hawaiian music. Kroncong is rich in both influences and originality.

A good example and a must-hear item is "Bengawan Solo", the most celebrated kroncong song (and probably the most covered Indonesian pop song); written by singer-composer Gesang Martohartono in 1940, during the time of the Japanese occupation, it tells of the beauty of the Solo River. Gesang was a penniless, untrained musician at the time, but the song found its way onto the radio and began its journey to become the national classic it is today. It was also much-liked by many Japanese soldiers and after the war a number of Japanese versions were made. A version recorded in the 1960s in Hong Kong by Rebecca Pan can be heard on the soundtrack of Wong Kar Wai's film *In the Mood for Love*. Gesang himself has recorded many versions, including one recorded in Tokyo while on tour with Waldjinah in 1994 and the last one on an album celebrating his 82nd birthday in 1999.

In and around the city of Solo, there's also a regional style of kroncong called **langgam jawa,** in which the seven-note *pelog* scale and textures of gamelan music are imitated by the kroncong ensemble. It has an enchanting and sentimental sound. Established artists still releasing kroncong albums include **Hetty Koes Endang**, **Sundari Sukotjo** and the diva of the related langgam jawa style, **Waldjinah**.

Today, kroncong appeals mainly to an older audience and has become refined and respectable, enjoying, as musicologist Philip Yampolsky

has noted, "a prestige that would surely amaze the 'crocodiles' of 1910". A suggestion of how it may have sounded in its wild days, however, may perhaps be found in another genre with a venerable history.

Gambang Kromong

Gambang Kromong developed out of the type of kroncong music featured in an urban folk theatre form called **komedi stambul**, popular in the early decades of the twentieth century. If you travel to the town of Tanggerang, about two hours' drive from Jakarta, you may be able to catch the modern-day equivalent called **lenong**, or get yourself invited to a wedding. In either case the music will be gambang kromong played on a bewildering array of Chinese, Indonesian and Western instruments.

A typical ensemble might bring together two-string fiddle, bamboo flute (**suling**), xylophone (**gambang**), pot-gongs, drums and percussion from the Javanese gamelan, plus one or more Western instruments such as trumpet, keyboards, electric bass guitar, clarinet or Hawaiian guitar. Melodies weave in and out and against the loping percussive backdrop, sounding at times like a Dixieland Jazz band jamming with a gamelan, with all of the instruments and voices that can be amplified cranked up to distortion level. The repertoire is mainly drawn from a collection of time-honoured tunes, known as **lagu sayur**. *Sayur* means vegetables and in this context could be translated as the "bread-and-butter" repertoire (see Philip Yampolsky's essay in Vol. 3 of the Smithsonian Folkways' Music of Indonesia series). Throughout the festivities a number of female singers, known as *wayang*, will take to the microphone to improvise versions of familiar four-line verses known as *pantun*, afterwards resuming their generally languid dancing routines, while the often increasingly inebriated male guests dance more ostentatiously around them and sometimes take their turn at the microphone for some live karaoke-style fun.

Any self-respecting local cassette shop should have a wide selection of gambang kromong to discover. The Paragon label has an extensive catalogue, with many cassettes for some reason displaying pictures of polar bears, penguins and other arctic scenes on the inserts (*Rindu Malam* by Hongkian's Ensemble is a personal favourite).

You will also find a category called **gambang moderen** or **gambang kromong pop**. The style was pioneered in the late 1960s by the late

Benyamin S., a nationally popular singer, film actor and TV comedy star. His recordings are mainly three-minute comedy sketches set to music, highly entertaining even if you can't understand the language. His *100% Gambang Kromong*, featuring female sidekick Ida Royani, is highly recommended.

No doubt there will be a few cassettes of **gambang kromong dangdut** or even **bang dhut**, incorporating rhythms of the most popular pop style of the last thirty years: **dangdut**.

Dangdut

Dang-dut-dang-dut-dang-dut-dang-dut. You can't mistake it and you'll hear it all over the place. **Dangdut**, Indonesia's equivalent of danceable Latin music, has been thriving since the mid-1970s. It grew out of kroncong and **Orkes Melayu** – the Indonesian version of the sort of music typified by Malaysia's P. Ramlee, itself influenced by Indian film music and Arabic pop – mixed with influences from the West, particularly British and American rock. The sum of the parts though, is uniquely Indonesian.

Like many Indonesian musical terms, dangdut is an onomatopoeic word, derived from the rhythm usually played on the **gendang** (which can be a pair of Indian tabla-drums or a pair of bongo-like drums tuned to sound like *tabla*). So that you know your *dang* from your *dut*, count in fours and hear the low dang note struck on the fourth beat and the high dut note struck on the first beat of the following bar.

Alongside the gendang, the classic dangdut line-up consists of electric guitar, bamboo flute, bass, mandolin, drum kit and keyboards. But the real stars are the **singers**: glamorous men and women singing of love found, lost or wanted, or of moral issues, family matters and the everyday and fantasy life of the dangdut audience.

Following on from Orkes Melayu crooners like Munif and Ellya Agus came the first superstars of dangdut. **Rhoma Irama** and **Elvy Sukaesih** are still known today as the King and Queen of dangdut. They made many successful recordings as a duo in the early 1970s and both have many million-selling albums to their credit. Rhoma Irama has always been identified as a "working-class hero" and has starred in several films, often playing the underdog who eventually wins through without compromising his Islamic principles: rags-to-riches with honour intact. *Struggle and Prayer*, his 1980 film debut, is available on DVD.

Starting out as a long-haired rebel, Rhoma Irama soon found his true artistic direction after his Haj to Mecca. In his live shows, backed by his **Soneta Group**, he puts over his inspirational messages with all the paraphernalia of a full-blown rock-show. After a period in the 1980s as a critic of the government, he switched camps to join the ruling party and is now, in the post-Suharto democracy, said to have political ambitions himself.

In 2003, Rhoma led the protests against the young singing star, **Inul Daratista**, who had burst upon the scene with her up-tempo heavy-rock dangdut style and, more controversially, her bottom-gyrating dancing which became known as "the drill". Immediately recognized by conservative Muslim organizations as a threat to the nation's moral well-being, she has been immured in controversy ever since, while becoming the highest-paid dangdut star ever. There are several CDs and cassettes of her music available, but it's the (mostly pirated) video CDs of her performances which have sold in the millions. Her success has led naturally to a boom in young sexy singers making what is known as **goyang putri dangdut**.

John Clewley

Elvy Sukaesih

Between the polar extremes of Rhoma and Inul lie any number of dangdut hybrid styles jostling for attention: **dangdut koplo**, as purveyed by **Didi Kempot**; **dangdut house** as heard in the dangdut discos of Jakarta; **dangdut manis** (dangdut sweet); **Mandarin dangdut** and so on.

Jaipongan

Just occasionally in the dangdut dancehalls and discos the drum machines and bendy guitars may be interrupted by a percussion-based style whose unpredictable tempo changes fail to deter some inventive dancing from those left on the dance floor. This will be **jaipongan**, a style that has no detectable Western influence, using only instruments from the Sundanese gamelan tradition (see Gamelan article, p.598).

The **rebab** (two-stringed bowed fiddle) plays the introduction, while the **khendang** (a large two-headed barrel drum) improvises in free time underneath. Then, with whooping cries, the rest of the orchestra enters: *Blak-ting-pong-blak-ting-pong-blak-ting-pong*. The khendang sets about building and releasing tension through a cyclical pattern marked by a single stroke on a large gong, while a smaller gong, a **kempul**, beats out one-note basslines. The mellow sounds of the **bonang rincik** and the **panerus** (sets of pot-shaped gongs) play stately cyclical melodies, as the **saron** (a row of seven bronze keys set over a resonating box) hammers out faster arpeggios. The rebab anticipates, accompanies and answers the singer (**pesindhen**) as she floats like a butterfly through tales of love, money and agriculture, while throughout, various members of the orchestra indulge in more whooping, wailing and rhythmic grunting known as **senggak**.

Jaipongan is part of the rich culture of the **Sundanese** people. Sunda covers a large area of West Java and its regional capital, Bandung, is a university city and thriving cultural centre. It was in Bandung that jaipongan first appeared in the mid-1960s, and by the end of the decade it had become a national dance-craze – all without an electric guitar in sight.

It's possible that jaipongan would not have happened had it not been for an attack from President Sukarno on the prevalence of Western music. He called on artists and musicians to shun foreign influences and revitalize indigenous art-forms. Restrictions were placed on the importation and broadcasting of foreign music, particularly the dreaded rock'n'roll, sowing the seeds for the Sundanese roots revival, led by

Gugum Gumbira. Taking up Sukarno's call, he travelled around Sunda collecting ideas and regional stylings, which he eventually, with the input of a little rock'n'roll-style energy, fused into jaipongan.

Jaipongan is still popular today and its dance moves and drumming styles have been incorporated into other genres such as **dangdut jaipong**. Internationally, there are a few excellent, if not exactly new, recordings available by **Idjah Hadidjah**, **Euis Komariah** and an unusual curiosity on the Japanese Meta label called "Break Pong", which features **Yayah Ratnasari** and the great **Karawang Group** having lots of fun with a drum machine. A rare recent release comes from the Italian label Felmay, presenting singer **Uun Budiman**. In Indonesia itself, there a number of excellent new jaipongan cassettes being released. One highly recommended album is *Bungsu Bandung* by the **Galura Group**, produced by Wahyu Roche. Billed as **jaipong dangdut** it deserves to be sampled by any adventurous DJ looking for unusual but irresistible groves.

Degung and Pop-Sunda

If the gongs and bonangs of jaipongan have worked their magic, it will be time to get really relaxed and investigate the soothing sounds of **degung** and **kacapi suling**. Wistful, melancholic, meditative, the sound of degung embodies the feeling Indonesians describe as *sakit hati*. The literal English translation is "sick liver", but this loses its romantic connotations. In Bahasa Indonesia, the poetic organ of affection is the liver rather than the heart, and sakit hati describes a feeling of longing and sadness.

Gamelan degung developed as a court music for playing while guests were arriving at social occasions, and **modern degung** music performs a similar function today in Bandung's upmarket hotels. It has also found a whole new audience among tourists in Bali where degung cassettes provide the ambience in many cafes and restaurants. Peaceful and harmonious, it's characterized by gentle percussion, delicate improvising on the suling and soft arpeggios played on the bonang and saron and underpinned by the warm tones of the hanging gongs which give the music its name. (See Gamelan article for more on degung.)

A mark of quality with degung releases is the name of **Nano S**. This amazingly prolific composer is also responsible for some of the best examples of the **pop-Sunda** style, in which degung meets modern technology. Sequenced drum and bass

Sambasunda: "Rhythmical in Sundanese People"

Bandung, the cool, hillside capital city of Sunda, is a city of contrasts. A BMW glides past the bicycle taxis waiting by the roadside food stalls; motorbikes buzz like mosquitoes from every direction; school-children in white and red uniforms pour out of the school gates. Take a taxi downtown to the main square, the *alun-alun*. The domes of the newly enlarged central mosque gleam brilliant white in the sun, which also lends its light to the large purple, pink and white sign proudly proclaiming the presence of a Dunkin' Donuts station next door.

Jak Kilby

Sambasunda

Around the corner in Dalem Kaum Street, the convergence of cultures continues: Satay, rice and tea. Burgers, fries and coke. It's all here. Also here are the cassette shops, almost hidden behind the stalls of the pirate CD vendors clustered on the street outside. Music fills the air. Dangdut, hip-hop, Indonesian pop, Western pop… the mainstream dominates. But occasionally you may hear local *Pop-Sunda* or the mellifluous tones of **degung** – the distinctively Sundanese small gamelan-ensemble style with its gentle and melancholic moods.

It's against this background that **Sambasunda** have brought traditional Sundanese music face-to-face with today's globalized pop styles. At a time when many young Indonesian musicians only want to copy the riffs, poses and hairstyles of Western rock gods or to assimilate the attitude of hip-hop coolness, Sambasunda have stayed respectful of their roots without being afraid of tapping into the urban energy of their hometown. But instead of adding loops, beats and other electrickery, they have created something new by bringing together a huge array of instruments not usually played together: **angklung** (tuned bamboo rattles) meet gongs and **metallophones** of both the Javanese and Balinese gamelan traditions; a Sumatran **terompet** exchanges melodies with a Western violin (played in a very Sundanese style) and the whole is driven along by a percussion section brandishing not only the Sundanese **khendang** (two-headed barrel drum) and Javanese frame-drums, but also African *djembe* and Latin timbales. Floating on top of that come the distinctively Sundanese sounds of **kacapi** (plucked zither) and **suling** (bamboo flute), the wild vocal chanting known as **senggak** and the breathtaking vocal skills of singer Rita Tila. A recipe that is both familiar and innovative to their home audience.

The founder and leader of Sambasunda is the multi-instrumentalist and composer Ismet Ruchimat. In 1991, as a student at Bandung's STSI School of Music, Dance and Dramatic Art, his precocious talents brought him to the attention of Gugum Gumbira, the man credited as the inventor of the Jaipongan dance-style, who invited Ismet to join his Jugala Orchestra. Over the next few years he toured with them in Japan, Malaysia, Korea and Sumatra and became the group's main composer. After graduating in 1994, he travelled to Iceland and Norway as a guest teacher of Sundanese music at the Universities of Reykjavik and Oslo, also collaborating with local jazz musicians. Returning to Bandung in 1995, he took up a post as teacher at STSI and soon set about forming a group with some of his best students. Ismet recalls:

"I had developed an obsession to take Sundanese music in new directions. It was very hard at first but with all my friends we kept experimenting. In the early days it was difficult for young people to try something new. We got many hard critics but it was Gugum who always supported us. Gugum was always open for new ideas. He encouraged me to take up the challenge."

The challenge duly taken, Sambasunda have been developing their unique sound and taking it in ever new directions. On their five domestically-released albums, they have explored different influences each time, mixing their Sundanese roots with jazz, Balinese gamelan, reggae and samba rhythms. In 2005 their first international release, *Rahwana's Cry* (Network Medien) saw them reach a new level, refining all these elements into a trademark style.

To date they have toured in Sri Lanka, China, Malaysia and Taiwan, Europe, Australia and the US. When asked what Sambasunda want to do in the future, Ismet says: "To keep introducing Sundanese music to the world".

patterns accompany the traditional-style melodies and often all the Sundanese instruments are replaced by synthesized sounds. If you can take that on board there is much to enjoy here. Two of the greatest pop-Sunda hits are "Cinta" (Love) by **Hetty Koes Endang** and "Kalangkang" by **Nining Meida** – both million-sellers and both written by Nano S.

Another popular composer whose work is performed in both classical and pop settings is **Mang Koko**. Seek out *Kawih Sunda Abadi Karya Mang Koko* (Dian), a two-volume cassette of his songs sung by **Ida Rosida** and **E. Sonjaya**. With virtuoso accompaniment on khendang, kacapi and rebab, this is both pop and classical at the same time – dynamic, melancholic and bubbling with harmonies that seem familiar even if you've never heard them before.

Hetty Koes Endang made her recording debut in 1973 and has since released scores of albums encompassing kroncong, dangdut, langgam jawa, degung and pop-Sunda. Rice Records of Japan recently reissued a compilation of her earliest recordings in the **Pop-Melayu** style. Still at the top, she gave a series of rapturously received performances in Holland in 2007. There are also two albums available internationally from Bandung singer **Detty Kurnia**, *Dari Sunda* and *Coyor Panon*, produced in the 1990s for the Japanese market by Makoto Kubota, who set the pop-Sunda and jaipongan selections in modern pop arrangements. Although not strictly representative of the music as heard in Indonesia, they are still an excellent intro-

Nining Meida

duction to the Sunda sound. Detty Kurnia remains popular at home and regularly releases cassettes both as a solo Pop-Sunda artist and together with the leading name in the **Calung** genre, **Darso**.

If the melodic melancholy of Pop-Sunda grabs your interest, seek out a couple of cassettes on the MC Records label bearing the description "Album Nostalgia Pop Sunda". These are wonderful compilations of recordings from the 1960s, made before the invention of the drum machine and synthesizers. Pop productions featuring real drum-kit, bass guitar, twangy electric guitars and occasional vintage organ and the young incarnations of singers who became widely popular, such as **Tati Saleh**, **Euis Komariah**, **Upit Sarimanah** and the unmistakable, characterful voice of the late and much revered **Titim Fatimah**. It's a shame that not a lot more material from this era is available, but perhaps original tapes no longer exist. Thankfully these two cassettes have been in print for many years and are still around.

It should also be noted that in Bandung, Jakarta and Surabaya there are many excellent musicians who look to Western jazz for their inspiration. Anyone interested in jazz history should try to find an album called *Djanger Bali* by **Tony Scott & the Indonesian Allstars**, featuring the great bebop pianist from Surabaya, **Bubi Chen**, who is still a fixture at the annual Java Jazz Festival in Jakarta. Bandung is home to two excellent jazz-fusion combos who incorporate local elements: **Krakatoa** and the *gambus*-based global mix of **Debu**.

Qasidah Modern

Qasidah is a classical Arabic word for epic religious poetry, traditionally performed by a

---

"Coyor Panon" (Sensual Eyes)

Sensual eyes are moving, not resting
A beautiful vision
Wrapping a silk scarf around her neck
And putting on yellow sandals
She is a gentle philanderer

If there is distance between us
Just call out my name
And let the words build a bridge
In the empty night
You may be far from me
But in my heart I hear your call

Sensual eyes are moving, not resting
A beautiful vision
That is far from me
But still I feel so close

Detty Kurnia, from Conyor Panon (Wave)

storyteller-singer, accompanied by percussion and chanting. Indonesian Muslims practise their own versions of this, improvising lyrics in local languages that address contemporary concerns and moral issues.

Qasidah modern places this in a pop-song form, adding electric guitars, mandolin, keyboards, violins and flutes. Rhythms and melodies from dangdut and Arabic pop are used, while the lyrics frequently offer moral advice to young lovers (don't do it!), extolling a virtuous life and warning against corruption and other temptations like smoking (sometimes the lyrics even tackle environmental issues such as pollution and nuclear power). Here's an example, "Bila Ingin Bahagia" (If You Want to Be Happy) from the group Nasida Ria:

Everywhere is the scent of jasmine,
The bees suck the flowers,
Many young girls forget themselves,
Not yet married they make love.
If you want to be happy,
Don't spoil this pure love,
The honeymoon should satisfy your hearts

From Nasida Ria (Piranha)

Nasida Ria, a nine-woman orchestra from Semarang, Central Java, are the pioneers of qasidah modern. They have released more than 25 albums and have twice toured Germany. At home they perform chiefly at Muslim weddings throughout Java or occasionally at open-air rallies sponsored by religious groups, where the proceedings are opened by a sermon or two before the orchestra take the stage. In their colourful headscarfs and close-fitting dresses that cover them from head to foot they manage to look simultaneously alluring and modest and the occasional heavy-metal posturing of the guitarists is also conducted with great decorum.

Qasidah modern or pop Qasidah is a growth industry in today's Indonesia. Lilin Herlina, Dwi Romansyah, Dita Arizona, Ike Widuri are just some of the singers putting across moral messages to the accompaniment of contemporary electro-pop sounds and dance grooves.

If the strong Arabic influence of this music is to your taste then you might want to plan a trip along the north coast of Java to **Surabaya**, home of gambus music.

Gambus

Gambus is the Indonesian word for the Arabic lute, the *oud*, but it is now used to denote both a style of music and the orchestra that plays it. The oud was brought to Indonesia along with Islam and much of the music and dances associated with it were introduced by settlers from the Yemen. Visit the Arab quarter in Surabaya and you may hear the voice of Umm Kulthum wafting out of one of the shops in the bazaar, or it could be Surabaya's own diva, **Soraya**. You may also hear what sounds like a typical modern pop production from Saudi or Kuwait, but it is more likely to be one of the local stars of the gambus modern scene, such as **Abdullah Hinduan** or **Ali Alatas**.

Many gambus songs are lifted straight from imported Arabic cassettes and given a local interpretation. Some retain the Arabic texts, but many are rewritten in the local language. All the hallmarks of great Arabic pop are there: rolling rhythms on the *derbuka* and the oud, sinuous melody lines on flute and violins and, regardless of the language, much silky ornamentation of the vocal lines from the singer. Although loved by millions, gambus is hardly known outside Indonesia and there are still no recordings available internationally.

Lagu-lagu Banyuwangi

Banyuwangi is the most eastern province of Java and the city of the same name is where you can catch a ferry for a pleasant or hair-raising trip (depending on the weather and the cargo-load of the ship) across the straits to Bali. The province is home to a number of different ethnic groups including the Osing, who see themselves as descendants of the Majapahit, the Hindu empire state that flourished in West Java between c. 1200 and 1500 AD. Sixteenth-century Islamic invaders pushed the surviving Majapahit east to Bali, founding today's Balinese Hinduism. There are also a number of Balinese immigrants living in Banyuwangi. Lagu-lagu Banyuwangi (literally "songs of Banyuwangi") augments dangdut and kroncong rhythms with the sounds of Balinese gamelan, creating a recognizable local sound. Female singers predominate here, with Kusniah, Ida Farida and Sumiati among the most prolific and popular.

Bali

Parallel worlds exist on the island of Bali. In the tourist enclaves of the south and particularly the inland traditional artistic centre of Ubud, there is a thriving club scene. There are many excellent local jazz-fusion groups and some of these bring in traditional and global influences. Worthy of note are the jazz-funk-blues-gamelan stylings of Komang Layang and Sekehe Bali Funk, and the smoothly groovy bamboo-gamelan jazz of the Duotones collective.

There is also much locally produced pop music that is less visible to most tourists. Digital recording technology has enabled a boom in locally produced cassettes, from the somewhat sweet pop with sampled or synthesized Balinese motifs of artists like Dek Arya and Ari Sinta or A.A. Raka Sidan to the funkier bamboo-gamelan with drum-machine grooves of local star Bayu Kasta Warsa. The many works of veteran songwriter A.A. Made Cakra are also worth getting to know.

Sumatra

West of Java, a variety of different musical styles are to be found on the neighbouring island of **Sumatra**. In the north the **Batak**, concentrated around the area of Lake Toba, have a long tradition of percussion-based music with additional flutes and reed-trumpets – **seruling** and **serunai** – to accompany healing and other ceremonial occasions. Sometimes lasting for days on end and designed to induce trance-states in the participants, this is exciting stuff. Much more European-sounding are the Batak folksongs, which presumably grew out of the first contact with Protestant missionaries at the end of the nineteenth century. Certainly, the small wooden churches around the lake reverberate to the enchanting sound of communal harmony singing on Sunday mornings.

The group **Marsada** from Samosir Island mix traditional and pop influences and instruments and excel in delightful harmony vocals. They are the only contemporary Batak group with a CD release on a European label (see discography).

Moving south from Lake Toba you reach the Tapanuli region where you can hear **tapanuli ogong** music – lively dance-tunes played on flute, reed-trumpet and a small two-string lute called the **hasapi**. Rhythm is provided by a set of hand-drums (**tagaling**), normally suspended in an ornately carved frame, and by a bamboo xylophone (**garattung**). Basslines are picked out on a set of gongs.

There is a particularly wonderful, locally available CD called *Tapanuli Ogung* on the GNP label on which **Turman Sinaga** and his group race joyfully through a set of traditional dance-tunes, managing to seamlessly insert quick takes on the dreaded football anthem "olé olé" and "La Paloma" along the way. Disconcerting for purists, but in Tapanuli they know a catchy tune when they hear one.

The **Minangkabau** are one of the world's few matrilineal societies and to check out their music it's necessary to visit Bukkittinggi, a hill-town north of the sea-port capital of Padang. While

Marsada

Moluccans in Exile

In 1950, after the war of independence, President Sukarno dissolved the short-lived federal structure, which had been imposed on him by Dutch pressure, in favour of a republic ruled by a central government in Jakarta. Army soldiers from the predominantly Christian South Moluccan islands, who had fought on the side of the Dutch colonial army, feared the worst and proclaimed the independent Republic of South Moluccas. The movement was swiftly put down by the Indonesian forces and the Dutch assisted in the evacuation of some twelve thousand soldiers and their families to the Netherlands, where a government-in-exile was formed. The dream of a return home was shattered in 1970 when the Dutch government finally gave up the idea of a return to Indonesia and tried to convince the Moluccans that their future lay in the Netherlands. Many felt abandoned and betrayed and a series of bloody hi-jackings in the mid-1970s briefly brought their plight to the attention of the world.

In the mid-1980s, guitarist **Eddie Lakransy** formed the **Moluccan Moods Orchestra** with other Dutch-born sons and daughters of Moluccan exiles and fused a jazz-funk style with the almost forgotten songs of a homeland most had never visited. Sadly, Eddie Lakransy died in a plane crash in 1988. One great album on the Piranha label stands as a reminder of a project that never achieved its full potential.

sharing many of the same traditional roots as the Batak, their music is influenced by the predominance of Islam. It also reveals similarities with some Madagascan styles and many of the songs carry a discernible Polynesian flavour. Both Batak and Minang music display influences assimilated from centuries of trade with Arabic, Indian and East African cultures.

The Moluccan Islands

A distinct Polynesian influence can also be heard on the **Moluccan Islands** towards the eastern end of the archipelago. There is an interesting tradition of farewell songs here that are stylistically related to kroncong, and much music that sounds remarkably similar to the Batak pop-folk style.

As in the Batak region of Sumatra, the predominant religion is Christianity, but the balance has been shifting due to an ongoing influx of migrants from Java. Ensuing political and religious contentions have caused some bloody conflagrations in recent years.

Pop-Ambon with its major-key melodies and up-tempo rhythms can sound like a meeting of Hawaiian music and *zouk* and a few years ago it enjoyed a period of popularity as a fashionable item in the clubs of Jakarta.

DISCOGRAPHY Indonesia | Pop and Folk

Kroncong / Langgam Jawa

Gambang Kromong

Sometimes sounding like a Chinese Dixieland jazz band jamming with a gamelan orchestra, the freewheeling sounds of Gambang Kromong are hard to find on CD but these two are available through www.farsidemusic.com.

⊙ **Gambang Kromong Sitia Muda**
Wishnu, Indonesia
Compilation of different orchestras and singers demonstrating the extraordinary mix of interweaving instruments. Good overview of the music of the Jakarta suburbs.

⊙ **Benyamin S. & Ida Rosida: 100% Gambang Kromong**
GNP, Indonesia
Shorter, more tightly arranged pieces showcasing the talents of the late Benyamin S., much-loved singer, actor and comedian together with his sidekick, singer Ida Rosida.

Gesang

In his long lifetime Gesang Martohartono has composed hundreds of songs, but it's for "Bengawan Solo", written in 1940 and now practically an unofficial national anthem, that he is truly famous.

WITH WALDJINAH

Bengawan Solo
JVC, Japan

Recorded in the JVC studios in Tokyo during their 1994 Japanese tour, Gesang, Waldjinah and a family ensemble run effortlessly and expertly through some of their greatest hits. Excellent sound.

⊙ **Sandang Pangan Campur Sari**
GNP, Indonesia

Album of Gesang songs recorded in 1999 to celebrate the master's 82nd birthday. He sings in duet with his niece, Asti Dewi Christiana, and gives a special solo rendition of his greatest hit.

Waldjinah

Veteran singer of Kroncong and Langgam Jawa.

⊙ **Anoman Obong**
GNP, Indonesia

Langgam jawa with caks and cuks and gamelan. The title track relates an episode of the Ramayana story. Other tracks offer a variety of styles, from stately classical to more easygoing pop songs that all contrive to be slow and fast at the same time. High-quality stuff.

Ratu Jawa
Rice Records, UK

Excellent Japanese production of kroncong songs with some tracks augmented by musicians from Brazil, Japan and Malaysia.

Dangdut

Original Road to Dangdut
Meta Company, Japan

Fascinating collection of recordings by various artists from the 1940s to the 1960s charting the progress from the Arab-influenced pop of the Orkes Melayu style to the first dangdut songs recorded by Rhoma Irama and Elvy Sukaesih.

Inul Daratista

Hailing from East Java, Inul burst upon the scene in 2003 with her bottom-gyrating dancing to her speeded-up heavy dangdut style. Reviled by the moral guardians, loved by millions of adoring fans, she's still at the top and has spawned an army of imitators.

⊙ **Goyang Inul**
Blackboard, Indonesia

Collection of songs that brought her to fame. Drum-heavy dangdut where fuzzy speed-metal guitar meets bamboo flute head-on while Inul squeaks, sighs and sings beautifully throughout.

⊙ **Mau Dong**
Blackboard, Indonesia

Inul takes Dangdut into the twenty-first century with a sparkling production mixing elements of Bollywood bhangra, hip-hop and heavy metal (!) into a global disco pop-dangdut party.

Smithsonian Folkways' Music of Indonesia

Few countries, particularly in Southeast Asia, can boast an ethnomusicological survey as ambitious as the twenty volumes the US label **Smithsonian Folkways** has released in their **Music of Indonesia** series. The discs are masterminded and recorded by **Philip Yampolsky**: "People's ideas of Indonesian music were limited to Central Javanese and Balinese gamelan", he explained. "But I knew from the research I'd already done that there was an astonishing amount of other music out there, and I wanted to bring it to people's attention – not only in Europe, America and Australia, but more importantly in Indonesia itself."

The project started with the Festival of Indonesia in the US in 1990, for which Yampolsky was asked by the Smithsonian Institution to make two CDs, with financial help from the Ford Foundation. "No, I said, two albums isn't enough to do anything meaningful about Indonesia. I wouldn't consider a project with fewer than twelve albums. Smithsonian gulped and said, write up a proposal, we'll submit it to Ford and see what they say. So I did, and somewhere along the line I decided twelve wasn't enough and it would have to be fifteen. This was in 1990. Later I revised the plan and upped the number of albums to twenty, which is the final figure. (Now I wish I had asked for twenty-five!)

"I have tried to find genres of music that I thought would be impressive and interesting to the open-minded, non-specialist listener – somebody who wanted to hear something new and wouldn't be put off if it wasn't gamelan (or Mozart). This means that certain kinds of music often get left out of the series: sung narratives that use one or two melodies over and over all night – the aesthetic interest is in the words, not the music, but non-specialists won't know the language so can't appreciate the text. Dance music also often gets left out, when the music is a simple repetitive formula and the fun is in watching the dancers' movements (which you can't do on CD). There are additional criteria: trying to represent the main islands and culture areas of Indonesia; trying to include all of the main instruments and ensemble types.

"One important thing to say is that this project is not a one-man show. It's a collaborative project of Smithsonian Folkways and the **Indonesian Society for the Performing Arts (MSPI)**, and many excellent Indonesian ethnomusicologists have worked with me in the field; some have also contributed to the published commentaries."

Of the twenty CDs in the series, the stand-outs are *Vol.1: Songs Before Dawn: Gandrung Banyuwangi*, *Vol.2: Kroncong, Dangdut and Langgam Jawa* and *Vol. 20: Guitars of Indonesia*.

Rhoma Irama

Dangdut's original pioneer and proclaimed king of the genre, Rhoma Irama has progressed from rebel to establishment figure.

WITH ELVY SUKAESIH

⊙ Raja dan Ratu
Rice Records, UK

The title translates as "king and queen" and these are early recordings of the first dangdut superstars in their days as a dynamic duo.

⊙ Begadang, the Greatest Hits 1975–1980
Meta Company, Japan

Just what it says on the packet. Rhoma in peak form defines 1970s-style dangdut.

Elvy Sukaesih

In the 1970s she was known as "the queen of dangdut". And she still is.

⊙ The Queen of Dangdut
Rice Records, UK

Excellent quality remastered selection of Elvy's greatest hits from the golden 1970s.

Jaipongan

Uun Budiman

Uun started out singing with puppet theatre troupes around Bandung before joining the famed Karawang group, where she was spotted by Jaipongan godfather Gugum Gumbira, who invited her to sing with his Jugala Orchestra.

⊙ Banondari
Felmay, Italy

This 2006 album marks the return to the producer's chair after a long absence by Gugum Gumbira. Budiman floats both serenely and soulfully over fresh sounding Jaipongan arrangements by Sambasunda leader Ismet Ruchimat.

Lagu-lagu Banyuwangi

⊙ Seru Gatine
Nirwana, Indonesia

Selection of Lagu-lagu Banyuwangi songs from East Java featuring the top three local female singing stars: Kusniah, Ida Farida and Sumiati. Haunting, mainly mid-tempo pop-songs with keyboards and bamboo flute complementing the vocals, powered along in the expressive and dynamic Balinese style by gamelan gongs, wooden xylophones and wild drumming.

Sumatra

Marsada

Folk-pop Batak style from engaging Lake Toba sextet excelling in harmony singing.

⊙ Pulo Samosir
Dug Up Records, UK

Tuneful and uplifting songs, with excellent ensemble harmony singing accompanied by guitars, bass and percussion, and interspersed with up-tempo traditional instrumental dance tunes featuring bamboo flute and wooden xylophones.

Sunda

Hetty Koes Endang

From Bandung, West Java. A star for over three decades, she has scored successes in a variety of genres.

⊙ The Best of Sundanese Pop Songs
PT Musica, Indonesia

Only available in Indonesia, but an essential buy if you're there: sweet, haunting melodies with pop arrangements. Includes the multi-million-selling hit "Cinta".

⊙ Pop Melayu
Rice Records, UK

Collection of her earliest recordings from the 1970s. Bouncy Indo-pop productions, good songs, sparse instrumentation, excellent musicianship and the young Hetty's already confident singing.

Nining Meida

Another great female singer from Sunda, adept in both pop and classical styles

⊙ Tibelat – Kacapian – The Music of the Sundanese People
BAS, Indonesia

Composer Nano S. leads an ensemble of three kacapis, suling, reba, kendang and gong through a wonderful selection of modern traditional style songs as Nining Meida shines on top.

Sambasunda

Bandung's best-known musical export boldly take traditional instruments where they've never been before.

⊙ Berekis
Kartini Music, Germany

Debut album of instrumental pieces from the innovative Bandung ensemble. Bamboo xylophones, gongs, melodic percussion, violin, bamboo flute. Dynamic, driving, haunting, ethereal. Unplugged urban sounds with deep roots.

⊙ Rahwana's Cry
Network Medien, Germany

The group's sixth album shows them on top form with a fine collection of compositions displaying their ability to mix varied traditional influences into a sparklingly fresh whole. Features recording debut of their remarkable young singer, Rita Tila.

SABAH HABAS MUSTAPHA & THE JUGALA ALLSTARS

⊙ So La Li
Kartini Music, Germany

Lively collaboration between the ex-3 Mustaphas 3 bassist (alias the author of this article), various Sambasunda members and singer Teti Ani Mogiono. Jaipongan-laced global pop mix-up in a West Javanese Style. Nominated for a BBC Radio 3 World Music Award in 2003.

1 ECEK (MOVE) Sambasunda from *Rahwana's Cry*
Bandung's most innovative ensemble bring together bamboo and metal gamelan instruments with kacapi, flute and wild chanting, powered by driving percussion and sonorous gongs. Breathtaking stuff.

2 BANONDARI ULAH CEURIK Uun Budiman from *Banondari*
Gugum Gumbira's return to the producer's chair sets Jaipong in a new direction with the addition of Ismet Ruchimat's electric bass. Uun Budiman sings, the orchestra grooves.

3 CINTA Hetty Koes Endang from *The Best of Sundanese Pop Songs*
It's been over a decade since this song sold its first million and it's still a classic slice of melancholic Pop-Sunda.

4 TIBELAT Nining Meida from *The Music of the Sundanese people*
Nining Meida beguiles while composer Nano S. leads kacapi suling ensemble through a Sundanese rockabilly groove.

5 YA MAHMUD Munif from *Original Road to Dangdut*
Male singing star of Orkes Melayu style with amusing 1950s novelty number of Egyptian origin.

6 HAK AZAZI Rhoma Irama from *Begadang*
Rhoma Irama plays around with funk influences on this danceable piece of political polemic calling for basic rights for all.

7 MANDI MADU (HONEY BATH) Elvy Sukaesih from *The Dangdut Queen*
Classic early 1980s dangdut, a huge success then and still sounding fresh. Typical mid-tempo rhythm with Elvy sighing playfully on top.

8 MAU DONG Inul Daratista from *Mau Dong*
The new pretender to the dangdut throne takes it into the digital age with a sparkling pop production.

9 MATANIARI BINSAR Marsada from *Pulo Samosir*
Joyful folk-pop from Lake Toba in Sumatra. Acoustic guitars, bass and percussion drive along the creamy Batak doo-wop harmony singing. Uplifting.

10 BENGAWAN SOLO Gesang and Waldjinah from *Bengawan Solo*
The most famous Indonesian pop song ever, sung by the composer and kroncong diva Waldjinah. Shimmering, sinuous and sparkling, like the Solo River of the title.

Inner Asia

throat-singing, timbral tapestries, sonic spirits

Tuvan supergroup Huun-Huur-Tu

Inner Asia lies between Central and East Asia at the intersection of verdant rolling steppes and snow-capped mountain ranges. The area is distinguished by its nomadic pastoralist and mountain peoples, its use of extraordinary throat- and overtone-singing techniques, the same timbral aesthetic for its stringed, wind and percussion instruments and an overlap between folk religion, shamanism and Buddhism. The region's many indigenous Turko-Mongol peoples have been subsumed within the different geo-political systems of Mongolia, the Russian Federation (Khakassia, Tuva, Altai, Buryatia) and China (Inner Mongolia and Tibet). Pockets of Inner Asian music are also found elsewhere, such as in Xinjiang and among Kalmyks (Western Mongols) by the Volga River in Russia. When the musics of the area gained wider exposure during the 1990s, they had an incredible impact. Tuvan and Mongolian throat-singing in particular have wowed international audiences, and Khakas and Altai styles are following in their wake. **Carole Pegg** introduces the sounds of the Inner Asian mountains and steppes.

The peoples of Inner Asia share a stunning environment of high plateaus, rolling steppes, virgin forests, great lakes, hidden river valleys and snow-capped mountains, backed by the vast Gobi Desert. The lives of these nomadic herding and hunting peoples are hard: the terrain is often dangerous and temperatures are liable to plunge to minus sixty degrees in winter.

During the Soviet period, the whole of Inner Asia was subjected to the straitjacket of Communism, with herding, hunting and farming being centrally planned rather than a tribal or family concern. All forms of religion were brutally suppressed: important lamas were liquidated, monks were made to join the army and monasteries destroyed. Shamans were purged and had their instruments confiscated, and folk-religious rituals were banned. In order to eradicate differences in status and ethnicity, the traditional music, songs and dances of different peoples were synthesized and subordinated to the style of the majority group (for example, **Khalkhas** in Mongolia, **Sagais** in Khakassia). They were also adapted to the European scale system. Military units formed music circles in which soldiers learned the new "national" instruments – modified and standardized to enable production of the new European scales and sounds that could fill the concert hall. The skin body of the **horse-head fiddle**, for instance, was replaced by wood, and its size, tuning and playing position changed. All music was doctored to become "national in form and socialist in content", and playing it necessitated training within an accepted, European-style conservatoire system. In the post-Soviet period, however, the different peoples of Inner Asia are reasserting their own ethnic and musical identities.

Borders, Not Boundaries

Culturally and musically speaking, Inner Asia is not bounded by the various state borders across which its people are scattered. The size of Western Europe, independent **Mongolia** is the world's least densely populated country, with only 2.8 million people to herd its 26 million horses, camels, cattle, sheep and goats. Across its northwest border lie three small republics: **Tuva**, **Khakassia** and **Altai**; across its northeast border lies the republic of **Buryatia** and across its southern border, **Inner Mongolia**. Rural Mongols, Tuvan, Khakas and

Altai peoples use music in every aspect of their daily lives: to lure animals during the hunt, to control them when herding and to encourage them to give milk or accept their young. Music permeates domestic and public celebrations such as the "Festival of the Three Manly Sports", when the **garuda** (eagle) dance accompanies wrestling, rhythmic calls form part of archery competitions and ritual songs are performed by child jockeys before horse-racing. Music expresses and creates relationships with human partners and is used in folk-religious, shamanic or Buddhist contexts to communicate with spirits of the land. Musicians who now play on the global stage carry with them a distinct sense of place, geographical and historical.

The current political boundaries of Inner Asia are comparatively recent. Mongols perceive themselves as **"Western"** or **"Eastern"**, a label that relates to historical confederations and includes a range of different peoples or ethnic groups. From 1630 to 1911, **Western Mongols** were part of the Jungar State, which encompassed the areas now known as Khakassia, Tuva and Altai. There are many similarities in the musics of these areas. Western Mongols are now located in West Mongolia, and in Xinjiang and western Inner Mongolia (autonomous regions of China), as well as along the Volga River (Russia). The **Eastern Mongols** – found in East Mongolia and eastern parts of Inner Mongolia and Buryatia (Russian Federation) – have fought periodically against the Western Mongols since (Genghis) **Chinggis Khan**'s great Empire fell in the late thirteenth century. The majority of **Tuvans** live in Tuva (formerly known as Tannu-Tuva, Urianghai or Tangno-Urianghai) although they are also found in West Mongolia and Xinjiang.

Harmonic Timbres

Unlike Western Europe, where music is primarily pitch-centred, the musical aesthetic of Inner Asia focuses on the creation of **timbres** rich in distinct **harmonics**. These harmonic tapestries are woven from the sounds of nature, every manifestation of which is believed to have its own spirit. The production of simultaneous harmonic voices is particularly striking in **throat-singing**, but also evident in the music of the horse-hair fiddle, end-blown flute, flat-board zither, plucked lute and Jew's harp. Timbres and **intervals** are used to evoke the contours of the wild steppes and mountains, and the sounds of birds, animals and rivers.

Throat-singing: styles and origins

Inner Asian throat-singing includes **overtone-singing**, the extraordinary vocal technique in which, as if by magic, a single performer creates ethereal, shimmering melodies high above fundamental drones to create a one-person choir. It also includes deep growling sounds, fat in harmonics, used for epic performance. Harmonic melodies are created with precise movements of the lips, tongue and larynx. Traditionally performed by herders and hunters in Tuva (*khöömei*), West Mongolia (*höömii*), and the republics of Altai (*kai*) and Khakassia (*khai*), it has spread to areas such as Buryatia and Kalmykia as professional musicians have travelled freely and influenced each other in the post-Soviet period.

It's been suggested that there may be a connection between throat-singing and **Tibetan Buddhism**, which became the state religion of both Mongolia and Tuva and also made inroads into Khakassia and Altai. This is because Tibetan lamas of **Gyume** and **Gyöto monasteries** produce harmonics when they use extreme bass voices during **Tantric ritual performances**. Mongols recall, however, that Buddhist lamas did not approve of höömii, which raises the possibility of an association with folk-religious practices that Buddhism was anxious to quash.

Tuvan throat-singing is the best-known form of a phenomenon investigated by Russian researchers, and then introduced to the West by Ted Levin's field recordings and the work of the group Huun-Huur-Tu (see box opposite). Classifications vary, but most agree on the following three main styles: khöömei (Mongolian for "pharynx" and the generic Tuvan and Mongol term for overtone-singing), which may generate up to three clearly distinguishable simultaneous harmonics; *sygyt* (whistle), which always amazes listeners because of the clarity of the whistle-like melody created above its drone; and the low, guttural, growling *kargyraa*. Sub-styles (or additional styles) include *ezenggileer*, likened to the clicking of a rider's boots in stirrups; *borbangnadyr*, which imitates the sounds of a brook; and *dag* (mountain) or *khovu* (steppe) kargyraa, which evoke a particular landscape. There are also individual styles. For instance, **Radik Tülüsh** performs *chylandyk*, which mimics the chirping of crickets, while **Aldan-ool Sevek** specializes in *khat* kargyraa, which imitates the dynamics of the wind.

Mongolian throat-singer **Tserendavaa**, who first toured in the UK in 1987, distinguished five types of overtone-singing according to the parts of the body from which they emanated – nasal, labial, palatal, glottal/throat, and chest cavity/stomach.

In the West, New Age practitioners hold overtone-singing workshops for the uninitiated, claiming that it promotes natural healing. Mongols warn, however, that while listening to höömii is beneficial, producing it can be harmful to the body. Traditionally, men performed at the peak of their strength (champion wrestlers make excellent overtone-singers), but even professionals may suffer ill effects such as blood vessels bursting around the eyes and loss of consciousness.

The Western Mongols recount a myth of origin for overtone-singing that suggests a connection

Shamanic Music

The post-Soviet era has seen a huge revival in the music associated with shamanism, the indigenous religion of Inner Asia. Performers use a wide range of vocal sounds (including throat-singing) as well as the **frame drum** or **Jew's harp** – both of which create a rich overtone field – in traditional contexts, such as healing. Some also perform for small tourist groups, at local festivals or on foreign tours. In the Tuvan capital Kyzyl, where there are shamanic clinics, shamans are more willing to perform in non-ritual contexts than in other areas of Inner Asia. **Ai Churek** is the most famous, having been part of Alexander Bapa's Pure Nature Music stable, produced a CD and toured in Europe and the US. Other shamans, such as **Nikolai Oorzhak** and **Lazo Mongush**, are venturing abroad to give workshops and to heal. Some musicians are adopting the "shaman" label, and some shamans are beginning to appear on secular stages both domestically and abroad. At an event held in Kyzyl in 2005, for instance, the experimental trio **K-Space** joined with **Radik Tülüsh**, two local shamans and the traditional Russian vocal group **Oktai** to combine ritual Inner Asian music with free jazz. Not for the fainthearted, it was a truly unique experience and sound. Shamans from related Siberian cultures are also making a mark internationally: **Chyskyyrai** from the Sakha Republic (formerly Yakutia), for example, recently visited London as part of the "Siberia Extreme" project.

Huun-Huur-Tu and Yat-kha

Still dazzling people throughout the world with their recordings and concerts are the Tuvan bands **Huun-Huur-Tu** and **Yat-kha**. The line-ups of both bands fluctuate. Original Huun-Huur-Tu members **Albert Kuvezin** and **Alexander Bapa** both left, Kuvezin to form Yat-kha, and Bapa to concentrate on production work. **Anatoli Huular**, who replaced Kuvezin, delighted audiences with his unique borbangnadyr throat-singing style, and his expertise on the Jew's harp and four-stringed *byzaanchi*. The current line-up comprises the superb khöömei, kargyraa and *igil* player **Kaigal-ool Khovalyg**

Jak Kilby

Yat-kha founder Albert Kuvezin

INNER ASIA

and *doshpuluur* lute and guitar player **Sayan Bapa**, together with percussionist, sygyt singer and string-instrumentalist **Alexei Saryglar** and igil-player and throat-singer **Radik Tülüsh**. Formerly with Yat-kha, Radik's sweet singing voice and wide throat-singing range also add new colour to the group's sound and he has now released a superb solo album. Since their classic album *60 Horses in My Herd*, Huun-Huur-Tu has experimented with fusion, working first with musicians such as Frank Zappa, Ry Cooder and the Chieftains. More recently, they have worked with the Bulgarian Women's Choir Angelite under the direction of Mikhail Alperin (*Fly, Fly My Sadness* and *Mountain Tale*), explored the relationship of Tuvan traditional and old Russian music with Sergei Starostin, and engaged in a Scottish-Canadian collaboration with Niall MacAulay and guest artists (*Where Young Grass Grows*).

Named after the long Tuvan zither, **Yat-kha** first emerged in 1991 at the Voice of Asia Festival in Alma-Aty, Kazakhstan, when Brian Eno invented a "Special Prize" for Albert Kuvezin's super-deep *kanzat kargyraa* throat-singing. A founder member of Huun-Huur-Tu, Kuvezin astonished Western listeners with the classic Yat-kha album *Yenesei Punk* (1995) and was signed by Paddy Moloney of The Chieftains to his Wicklow label; the more traditional *Dalai Beldiri* won the German Critics prize in 1999. Particularly impressive were the contributions of **Aldan-ool Sevek**, who comes from the remote mountainous Tuvan region of Möngön Taiga.

The next two albums lacked the distinctiveness of these two, but with the help of UK-based film event producer and director Marek Pytel, Yat-kha developed a radical new live soundtrack for the Soviet director Vsevolod Pudovkin's 1928 silent classic *Potomok Chingis Khana*, which was received with great success at London's National Film Theatre. Yat-kha also won the Asia/Pacific category of the BBC Radio 3 Awards for World Music in 2002. Their most recent album, *Re-Covers*, takes yet another new direction, with Kuvezin covering songs by the likes of Led Zeppelin, Motörhead, Kraftwerk and Joy Division in his inimitable ultra-bass vocal style.

with the spirits of nature. **Chandman** district in Hovd region is bordered to the west by a range of Altai mountains, including Mount Jargalant, and in the east by a huge lake, Har Nuur. Mount Jargalant, they say, catches the wind as it comes from the east and sets up a drone that crosses their area, which is then swallowed by the lake. It serves to warn herders in the valley below of the impending strong winds and is said to have a magical effect: the steppes become extra-fertile, the animals particularly fine and the people sing

and perform better. Since Mongols believe that spirits take form in all natural phenomena, the spirit of the mountain was probably thought to be producing this sound.

The timbres and contours of overtone-singing are frequently compared to specific aspects of nature, such as the entrancing sounds of the mythical River Eev (among Mongols) or the vertical separation of light rays seen on the grasslands just after sunrise or before sunset (among Tuvans). Other instruments and vocal techniques

Carole Pegg, 2005

Radik Tülüsh singing for the spirits of his land and playing in *tevee igil* style at a ritual cairn (*ovaa*), Khondergei Pass, Tyva

In recent years, throat-singing has become increasingly familiar in the West through CDs and tours by Inner Asian musicians. After Tuva's **Huun-Huur-Tu** and **Yat-kha** (see box on p.631) came Mongolian groups such as **Egshiglen** and **Altai-Hangai**. From Khakassia came **Sabjilar** (Sergei Charkov, Slava Kuchenov and his wife Anya), **Ailanys** (led by Alexandr Samozhikov), **Khyrkhaas** (Sergei Charkov and his daughter Julia), and soloist **Yevgeni Ulagbashev**; from Altai, the groups **AltaiKAI** and **New Asia**, and soloists **Sarymai Urchimaev, Nogon Shumarov, Bolot Bairashev** and **Raisa Modorova**; and from Kalmykia, **Okna Tsahan Zam**.

Long-songs and Instruments

Long-songs (*urtyn duu*) are performed primarily by Mongols, both Eastern and Western. They sound extremely sad and serious and are technically highly accomplished. Among **Eastern Mongols**, such as Khalkhas, a solo vocalist is accompanied by a horse-head fiddle (*morin huur*) and sometimes a side-blown flute (*limbe*), which follows – often into falsetto range – the soaring melodies and intricate decorations of the vocal line, with its extremely elongated musical phrases and syllables. **Namdziliin Norovbanzad**, a female singer with extraordinary range and power, typifies the Central Khalkha concert style.

Textual **themes** depend on the occasion: on state occasions or in monasteries they may be philosophical or religious; in folk-religious rituals, they will often praise nature; in weddings and other celebrations they may praise the charismatic heroes of the group, reinforce social relations or express love of family or sweetheart. Although song titles often relate to horses ("Horse of the Narrow Gobi", for example), only the opening two lines are usually about the horse, thereafter getting down to the real subject. "Tümen Eh" (First of Ten Thousand), the long-song that begins all Borjigin Khalkha celebra-

use overtones to imitate nature and communicate with the spirits within it: the **end-blown pipe** (see opposite) is used to ward off evil spirits at New Year celebrations; the **Jew's harp** (Mongol *aman huur*, Tuvan *khomus*, Altai *komus*) is used to call spirits by **shamans**; and the low-pitched, declamatory **häälah** vocal style is used by Altai Urianghais during performances of epics to create an imaginary space in which the epic-hero's spirit can enact the events described by the bard, and cure illness or bad luck.

In Khakassia and Altai, both overtone-singing and the special vocal tone used for **epic performances** are called khai (kai). In Khakassia, epic performance was traditionally used to accompany the soul of a dead person to the next world. In Altai, the bard also had supernatural abilities and kai is used by some shamans. In both places, the link with this musical and spiritual past is being re-established and recreated.

tions, refers to Genghis Khan in religious terms, but as he was decreed a "non-person" during the Communist era, the song was said to refer to a fast horse so that it could still be performed.

The long-song style of **Western Mongols** is quite different from that of Eastern Mongols. It is performed without instrumental accompaniment, but with everyone present providing verses and choruses in unsynchronized, overlapping layers of melodic improvisations (see CD accompanying *Mongolian Music, Dance and Oral Narrative*). Texts relate to their Western Confederation, the homeland from which they migrated, or their charismatic heroes, such as Shonnu or Janggar.

Although a kind of long-song exists in Tuva, it is not as elongated and elaborate as that of the Eastern Mongols. Absent from most current recordings, the only available example (on *Tuva, Voices from the Center of Asia*) is reminiscent of West-Mongolian long-song style, with angular melodies, little elongation of syllables or vowels and no ornamentation of the vocal line. Long-songs are not performed by Khakas or Altai peoples.

The **horse-head fiddle** is played throughout Inner Asia. Traditionally its two strings are made of bundles of black or white horse hairs and the top face of its body made from hide. The contemporary concert instrument has gut strings and a wooden body. It is held between the knees and bowed rather like a cello to produce a soft and mellow tone laden with harmonics.

The **morin huur** or Mongolian horse-head fiddle, formerly a symbol of ethnicity, then of national socialist identity, and now an icon for independent, democratic Mongolia has a trapezoidal body, with a horse's head carved at the upper end of the pegbox. The morin huur is a spike fiddle (its neck spikes the body and passes through it to protrude at the bottom). There is debate about whether the horse's head signifies that the fiddle was once a shaman instrument, since a shaman's staff often also bears one.

The **igil** (Altai *ikili*) or Tuvan horse-head fiddle also sports a horse's head but its body is usually heart-shaped and, like its neighbour the Khakas *yykh*, its body and neck are carved from a single piece of wood. This instrument, which is also played by Western Mongols (*ikil*), is strung in reverse order from the Mongolian horse-head fiddle, with the lower string on the left when viewed from the front. Tuvans say that "igil" invites a person, while in West Mongolia, the name is said to derive from *ih hel* meaning "large language", a tongue superior to that of humans used to communicate with and influence animals, natural

phenomena and spirits. It is used to accompany narrative songs and the *biy*, a West Mongolian dance that primarily uses the top half of the body.

The Mongolian **huuchir** is a two-string tube spike fiddle with bow hairs that interweave its strings. The larger version, a four-stringed instrument which Tuvans call byzaanchy ("calf") and which is associated with cattle rather than horses, is known as the "four-eared fiddle" (*dörvön chihtei huur*) among Mongols, and played by men in Southern Mongolia and Inner Mongolia (China) to accompany praise-songs and tales. The strings are sounded from below, which makes it unusual.

West Mongolia, Tuva, Khakassia and Altai share the two-string **plucked lute** (Altai Urianghai *topshuur*, Tuvan *doshpuluur*, Khakas and Altai *topshur*) and three-string plucked lute (Mongolian *shanz* or *shudraga*, Tuvan *chanzy*, Khakas and Altai *khomys*).

The ancient three-holed, **end-blown pipe** – used to amplify melodic overtones while simultaneously producing a vocal drone – is called *shöör* by Tuvans and Altaians, *khobyrakh* or *syylas* by Khakasses, *tsuur* by Altai Urianghais and *sibizgi* by Kazakhs (the latter two groups are both found in West Mongolia). In Mongolia, this instrument, being an identity symbol for specific ethnic groups, was not chosen by the regime to be a "national instrument" and thereby fell victim to cultural ethnic cleansing. **Narantsogt** of the Altai Urianghais hid his tsuur in the mountains to preserve it, and it was only in recent years that he was able to openly teach his son how to play it.

New Developments

In the post-Soviet era, Inner Asian groups are no longer employed by the State and are now able to determine their own musical sounds, repertoires and directions. Some draw inspiration from their ethnic, tribal and religious traditions, while others are reacting to the influx of new sounds by crossfertilizing their music with that of the West.

A striking new development in Tuva, Khakassia and Altai is the emergence of **female throatsingers**, a brave act given the dire consequences traditionally believed to ensue if the gender taboo was broken. In 1998, the multi-instrumentalist **Choduraa Tumat** put together some gifted musicians (Aylangmaa Damyrang, Sholana Denzin, Ayana Mongush, Aylang Ondar) to form **Tyva Kyzy** ("Daughters of Tyva"), the first all-female throat-singing group. Performing diverse throatsinging styles and playing all the instruments, they

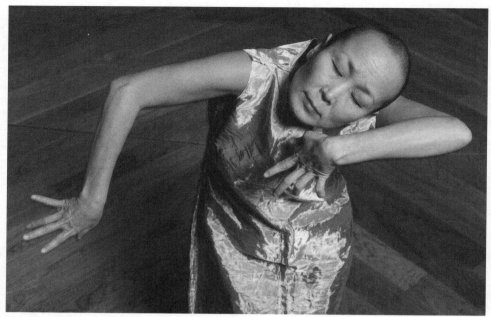

Sainkho Namchylak

are more than a match for the boys. Choduraa's superb solo CD *The Gift* (Beleg) displays her own vocal and instrumental dexterity. As she puts it in "I'm a Girl who is Never Sad":

In my chest full of music
Given by my mother,
I'll create a melody,
And offer my gift to the people.

Born out of pride
For my people's khöömei
I present you with
The treasure of my soul.

The band **Chirgilchin** ("Mirage") also boasts a female throat-singer, Aidysmaa Kandan. In Khakassia, **Julia Charkova** of **Khyrkhaas** has taken up the mantle, and in Altai, **Raisa Modorova** has also challenged the male prerogative of epic performance.

Kongar-ool Ondar, co-founder of the **Tuvan Ensemble** and a champion sygyt performer and experimenter, has been nurturing a new group, **Alash**, made up of his former students. Gutsy and

committed, they are definitely a group to watch. Meanwhile the superb Tuvan igil fiddler and throat-singer **Radik Tülüsh** has recently stepped out as a solo performer.

At the avant-garde end of the Tuvan spectrum stand **Sainkho Namchylak** and **Gendos Chamzyryn**. Sainkho has moved in modern jazz and even New Age circles, and her experimental improvised vocals, inspired by traditional Tuvan musical, spiritual and natural sounds, can evoke a screaming banshee or a velvety seductress. Chamzyryn, an expert in the deep kargyraa throat-singing style has joined up with two Brits – Ken Hyder and Tim Hodgkinson – to form the trio **K-Space**.

Mongolian throat-singing master Tserendavaa has recently re-emerged with his son **Tsogtgerel**, performing versions of the classic West Mongolian repertoire.

Urna Chahar Tugchi from the Ordos region of southwest Inner Mongolia engages in collaborations with Bavarian zither and Chinese *guqin*, and the Beijing-Inner Mongolian group **Hanggai** flirts with Chinese and electronic colorations.

Altai

⊙ Altai: The Song of the Golden Mountains. Siberia 10
Buda/Musique du Mond, France
Mostly devoted to the music of the Altai Mountain Telengits, this disc includes some gems. Listen, for instance, to the son and grandson of the famous epic bard Aleksei Kalkin: Elbek Kalkin's offering to the spirit of the fire and Alexei Kalkin's praises of his topshuur lute. It is the singing of the older women, though, that stays with you, for – whether in unison or solo – their hard, uncompromising voices express both the beauty of life and the strength needed to endure its hardships.

⊙ Central Asian Tales: Sabjilar, Chirgilchin, Sarymai
Pure Nature Music, US
This CD revisits earlier recordings by the Khakas group Sabjilar and the Tuvan group Chirgilchin. Despite its spurious shamanic packaging and lack of personnel information for the tracks, it's worth buying to hear the incomparable Sarymai Urchimaev, a Buddhist lama who really does seem to shape-shift as he sonically summons up the spirits of birds and animals.

AltaiKAI

With their snow-capped peaks, hidden valleys, ancient standing stones, burial mounds and wildlife, the Altai Mountains are sacred to their human inhabitants. This six-piece collective – unusually including two female musicians, giving their sound an unusual texture – is dedicated to countering the threat they feel to the Altai, which is integral to their indigenous identity.

★ XXI Century
AltaiKAI, Russian Federation
The group interweaves indigenous natural sounds with their own vocals and instruments on their best album to date. Their distinctive and ancient kai throat-singing summons up epic warriors, offers blessings to nature and praises the Altai, which is both a mountain range and a spirit-master or "lord" (Khan-Altai).

Nogon Sumarov

A powerful performer and musician, Nogon praises the three-peaked mountain Üch Sümer, the highest in Altai and considered the most sacred.

⊙ Altai Maktaal
Face Music, Switzerland
Mixing his own and his family's songs, Nogon summons up the culture and spiritual landscape of Altai. Detailed, accurate and informative notes.

Inner Mongolia

Urna Chahartugchi

Born in the Ordos region, Urna joined Robert Zollitsch's Gaoshan Liushui ensemble when studying *yangqin* hammered dulcimer at the Shanghai Conservatoire.

⊙ Tal Nutag: Songs and Improvisations from the Mongolian Grassland
KlangRäume, Germany
Urna has a beautiful voice with an incredible range. She is accompanied here by Zollitsch's Bavarian zither and classical guitar.

Hanggai

Bursting onto the scene in 2008, these enthusiastic young musicians from urban Beijing and rural Inner Mongolia bring energy and freshness to their recreation of Mongolian traditions.

★ Introducing Hanggai
World Music Network, UK
Hanggai use a combination of Eastern and Western Mongol instruments (morin huur horse-head fiddle; topshuur lute) to evoke and recreate the sounds and feel of the Inner Mongolian grasslands. Thankfully, electronics and sounds of the city enhance rather than dominate these, which will serve to both comfort their beleaguered minority people and make the music accessible to a wider audience.

Kalmykia

Okna Tsahan Zam

Okna Tsahan Zam's evocative horseback journey takes us along a "White Road": from Stalin's 1943 deportation of the Kalmyks to Siberia to life as herders on the Eurasian steppes, and then as participants of global culture. He intersperses the roots sounds of Mongolian stringed and wind instruments and throat-singing styles with natural steppeland sounds before moving on to urban pop remixes.

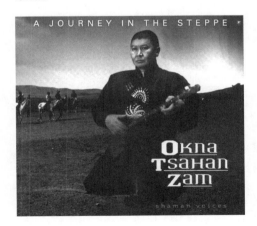

★ Shaman Voices
Buda Records, France
The orchestral arrangements of the "Djangar" epic are unnecessary, and the shamanic links less than convincing. That said, the variously textured soundscape of the first CD and

the DVD content of the second (dramatic reconstructions in stunning steppes and the musician in the studio) make this a striking contribution.

Khakassia

⊙ Khayjïlar: Chatkhan (Long Zither) and Khay (Throat singing)
Nihon Koukin Kyoukai – Japan Jew's Harp Association, Japan
Three outstanding Khakas musicians – Vyacheslav Kuchenov, Sergei Charkov and the rarely recorded Yevgeny Ulugbashev – come together on this CD. Recorded in concert in Japan, the atmosphere nevertheless captures that of ritual epic performance. There are two long epic extracts, some improvisatory *takhpakhs* and two weeping songs featuring the distinctive Khakas two-string *yykh* fiddle. An unusual offering, with excellent notes.

Khyrkhaas

Master instrument-maker Sergei Charkov and his daughter Julia honour their elders by tracking them down in the mountain steppes, rebuilding their instruments, encouraging them to play the *chatkhan* zither, yykh fiddle, *khomys* lute and khobyrak/syylas end-blown pipe, and performing khai throat-singing.

★ Songs of our Elders: Music from the Mountain-Steppes of Khakassia
Seven Star Records, UK
Using a great variety of sounds, Khyrkhaas's music expresses the undulating contours of the northern steppes, the traditional homeland of their Khaas ethnic group. Listen, for instance, to the spectral sounds and eerie glissandi of Sergei's yykh horse-hair fiddle on "Uibat Chazy" (Steppe), and the weeping song "Khuu Khustar" (Swans) addressed to the singer's late loved one.

Mongolia

⊙ Altai-Hangai
Most Mongolian music heard abroad is in the "national" style based on that of the Khalkhas (Eastern Mongols). As their name suggests, this group is refreshingly different in its specialization in West Mongolian styles (the Altai-Hangai mountain ranges are in West Mongolia).

⊙ Gone with the Wind: Songs of Mongolian Steppes
Window to Europe, Netherlands
More varied than their first album (*Naariits Biilye, Let's Dance!*) which brims with rhythmically angular Bait, Hoton and Dörbet dance tunes, this album also includes songs, rituals, praise-songs and legends. Listen particularly to the praise-song "The Nicest Auburn Horses" and the ode to the legendary female commander Mandukhai Khatan.

⊙ Mongolia: Living Music of the Steppes
Multicultural Media, US
After the first tracks of tinny Soviet-style ensemble music, there are some surprising delights. Central Khalkha long-songs are performed by the celebrated female vocalist Norovbanzad. Other Eastern Mongol music includes a huuchir (two-string tube-fiddle) ensemble and wonderful Jew's harp playing from east Gobi. Western Mongol traditions are represented, among others, by Tserendavaa's overtone-singing and a sparsely decorated long-song from Jamcha in Urumchi (Xinjiang).

⊙ Musiques de Mongolie
Buda/Musique du Monde, France
A superb and diverse collection. Herders perform traditional praise-songs and long-songs during festivals (accompanied by snorting horses) and sing to a she-camel to persuade it to feed an orphan calf. Eastern Khalkha Tserendorj performs the musical tale of "Cuckoo Namjil" and Western Khalkha Gereltsogt demonstrates six types of overtone-singing. Other delights are an ensemble that performs "court music", chanting lamas, and Kazakhs who demonstrate the improvisatory basis of their music.

Tserendavaa and Tsogtgerel

The master throat-singer and multi-instrumentalist Tserendavaa now plays with his talented son Tsogtgerel.

★ Xöömij Overtone Singing from Mongolia
Buda/Musique du Monde, France
Tserendavaa's soaring Mongolian tenor overtone-singing is complemented by his son's deeper, edgy tones as they create fluid, interweaving harmonic soundscapes. Both play morin huur (horse-head fiddle) rather than West Mongolian ikil, but Tserendavaa plays in the dance-oriented West Mongolian biy style, while Tsogtgerel uses the smoother Eastern Mongol Khalkha listening style. A bonus DVD shows part of their concert at the Les Orientales Festival, 2006.

Tuva

⊙ Tuva: Voices from the Center of Asia
Smithsonian Folkways, US
These classic field recordings by Alekseev, Kyrgyz and Levin contain a range of Tuvan throat-singing styles as well as sounds on the periphery of our understanding of music: imitations of animal sounds, and rhythmically intoned speech for domesticating animals, lulling children to sleep or communicating with spirits. Excellent notes.

Choduraa Tumat

Choduraa set a shining example by breaking the traditional Tuvan taboo on women performing throat-singing. She has also released an excellent CD with her group Tyva Kyzy, *Setkilimden sergek yg-dyr* (A Cheerful Song from my Soul).

★ Belek: The Gift
Sketis Music, Russian Federation
Choduraa slips with ease between the glottal gymnastics of different throat-singing styles to the plaintive tones of a lullaby or love song and the ritual imitative calls of animal husbandry. Her instrumental skill is equally impressive as she conjures up the mountains and steppes of Tuva with the igil fiddle ("Long and Soft") and doshpuluur lute, and sings of her love with the *demir khomus* (iron Jew's harp).

Huun-Huur-Tu

Led by co-founder Kaigal-ool Khovalyg, this well-known Tuvan ensemble performs a variety of instrumental music and throat-singing and has been involved in many collaborative projects.

WITH SAINKHO

★ Mother Earth! Father Sky!
Jaro, Germany
Two titans of Tuvan music meet. Huun-Huur-Tu's traditional nomadic soundscape and Sainkho's experimental vocals – glacier-pure, hail-hard, snowflake-soft, eagle-soaring – skirt around one another before embracing and reaching out.

Sholban Salchak's double-headed drumbeats also add new dimensions to the mix.

Radik Tülüsh

After making his mark as the wild igil fiddle experimenter with Yat-kha, Radik joined Huun-Huur-Tu in 2005. His first solo album is a real eye-opener.

Tyva: Spirits of My Land
Seven Star Records, UK

We accompany Radik as he journeys to his birthplace in the Tangdy Uula mountain range of Övür, close to the Mongolian border, to re-energize himself after touring by playing and singing for the spirits of the land. Radik transports us there with deep growls topped by spectral overtone melodies in five different styles of throat-singing, as well as heart-wrench-

Yat-kha

Best known for the unbelievably deep vocals of their leader Albert Kuvezin, the personnel and albums of this group have varied considerably.

⊙ **Tuva.Rock**
Yat-kha Recordings, France & UK

This 2003 line-up included igil player and throat-singer Radik Tülüsh and Russian "Old Believer" Zhenya Tkachoiv on percussion, with guests "Little Bird" Sailyk Ommun and Makhmus Skripal'schikov, both of whom become fully-fledged members for the later *Re-Covers* album.

ingly sweet songs and masterly improvisations on a range of traditional instruments.

PLAYLIST
Inner Asia

1 EPIC BARDS Khyrkhaas from *Songs of our Elders*
A traditional song in which Sergei Charkov and his daughter Julia both use khai throat-singing to pay homage to the epic bards of Khakassia.

2 UYARAVAS URUG BOOR MEN Choduraa Tumat from *Belek: The Gift*
Choduraa has added verses to this popular Tuvan traditional song. Her pure hard voice covers a range of impressive throat-singing styles as she accompanies herself on the doshpuluur lute.

3 JEBREN KAI LA TUNGUR. DREVNII KAI I BYBEN Altai Kai from *XXI Century*
The peculiarities of Altai throat-singing, together with their ritual shamanic traditions, and the use of two female voices make for a potent combination.

4 JARGALANT ALPIN TSUURAI Tserendavaa and Tsogtgerel from *Xöömij Overtone Singing from Mongolia*
Transport yourselves in this meditative three-voice throat-singing improvisation (including field recordist Johanni Curtet) to the mountains of your choice: the famous West Mongolian Mount Jargalant – from where Mongolian höömii mythologically originates – or the Alps.

5 CROSSING THE STORMY RIVER Tatiana Mashpevna Kurdepova from *The Song of the Golden Mountains*
Tatiana's sensitive intonation summons up the consequences for a young girl of braving the stormy river to spend a night of passion with her loved one.

6 THE ROCKY MOUNTAIN'S HEAD CAN'T BE SEEN Radik Tülüsh from *Tyva: Spirits of My Land*
Radik learnt this from his grandmother, who believes that if you sing beautifully in the Tangdy Uula mountain range, the spirit-master of that place will reward you in some way.

7 YEKUL SONG Hanggai from *Introducing Hanggai*
Combining the deep growls of the West Mongolian epic bard with rhythms of West Mongolian biy dance, the singer takes us on the hero's magnificient black steed, as it beats with its thunderous hooves a pathway through twisted steppeland roots and jagged stones.

8 SAMARINE Okna Tsahan Zam from *Shaman Voices*
A contemporary adaptation of a traditional song about a herder who rides with his fetish horse across the infinite steppes, both of them attuned to nature.

9 CHASHPY HEM Huun-Huur-Tu featuring Sainkho from *Mother Earth! Father Sky!*
Glorious textures here as the unusual tones of the four-string byzaanchy fiddle come to the fore and, with shamanic drum, horse-hair fiddle and a range of throat-singing styles, weave around Sainkho's seductive meanderings in praise of her birthplace.

10 TUVA.ROCK Yat-kha from *Tuva.rock*
Kuvezin gives a deep-bass Leonard Cohenish delivery on this English-language song about his mixed ancestry, prefiguring the latest *Re-Covers* album.

Japan

in the mix

Enka star Harumi Miyako (left)
John Clewley

In the West, the popular image of music in Japan has tended to range between two extremes: on the one hand, an austere and inaccessible classical tradition, and on the other, enthusiastic imitation of every Western genre imaginable. Times have changed, however. These days, Japanese musicians have a new confidence in their own identity, leading not just Asia but increasingly the world in using their own and other cultures to create exciting new directions in popular, jazz, avant-garde and roots-based styles. John Clewley and Paul Fisher look behind the mask.

Japanese musicians have always excelled in concocting all sorts of fascinating mixtures. Since the 1930s and even before, traditional Japanese melodies have been combined with Hawaiian music, jazz, mambo, samba and other Latin rhythms – a trend that has continued until today. During the first "world music" boom that began in the late 1980s, however, Japanese musicians increasingly looked to what their own culture had to offer. While local folk music (*min'yo*) had largely died out on the mainland, down in the southern islands of Okinawa, it was still very much alive, and – uniquely in Japan – a part of everyday life. Japanese musicians began to incorporate Okinawan elements into their music, something that a few, notably **Haruomi Hosono** and **Makoto Kubota** had done in the mid-1970s. Groups such as **Shang Shang Typhoon** emerged at this time, setting the benchmark for popular roots mixtures, while Okinawan groups **Shokichi Kina and Champloose**, **Nenes** and **Rinken Band** headed a generation of modern Okinawan artists during the 1990s. In the twenty-first century, Japanese musicians are as comfortable with their musical heritage as they have ever been: traditional instruments are incorporated into all kinds of music and *shamisen* (lute) players have become household names. Young musicians such as **Yoshida Brothers** and **Agatsuma** have been at the forefront of revitalizing Japan's northern *tsugaru shamisen* tradition, while **Michiyo Yagi** and other *koto* zither players have been pushing the boundaries of their instrument with collaborations and experimentations. Even on the dance and club scene, **DJ Krush** and others find it totally natural to record or perform with a *shakuhachi* (bamboo flute) player.

Ancient Roots

The many musical styles found in Japan have their roots in its particular historical circumstances – China, Korea, Central and southeast Asia all exerted considerable influence on the early development of music. There is evidence of music from around the third century BC, but the key events were the arrival of eighty Korean musicians in AD 453 and the introduction of Buddhism in the seventh century. **Gagaku**, court music and religious music (see box) survive from this period, and Buddhist chanting (**shomyo**) can still be heard in temples today.

Japanese scholars tend to say that all music prior to the Meiji Reformation of 1868 is traditional, but each preceding epoch had its characteristic forms. Early history (400–1200) produced religious and **court styles**. In the years to 1500, as society became more militarized, theatrical genres like **noh** drama developed (see box) and itinerant monks chanted long historical narratives to the **biwa**, a Japanese lute whose origins can be traced back to the Silk Road in Central Asia.

Between 1500 and 1868, Japanese rulers imposed a period of near-total isolation. The **repertoire of traditional instruments** like the koto and shakuhachi continued to develop, but outside influences were minimized. However, it was the three-stringed plucked lute, the **shamisen** – which came from China via the smaller Okinawan *sanshin* – that came to represent new styles, reflecting the development of a sophisticated pre-modern urban culture. The shamisen provided the perfect musical accompaniment for popular music, dance and drama, as well as the narrative folk-styles often called **min'yo** (see below). The *nagauta shamisen* style for **kabuki theatre** also developed at this time, as did the **sankyoku**, an instrumental ensemble typically consisting of koto, shamisen, shakuhachi and *kokyu* (bowed fiddle). During the Edo period (1615–1867), folk songs featuring shamisen, shakuhachi, drums and flutes were very popular.

Min'yo – Folk Music

Japan's **min'yo** (folk) tradition is long and rich. Distinctive vocals are accompanied by shamisen, shakuhachi and drums. Each region has its own style, perhaps the most famous being the instrumental shamisen style from Tsugaru. The continued popularity of min'yo is partly due to the nostalgia felt by city-dwellers for their home towns and villages, and many Japanese not only listen to min'yo, but are able to sing a song or two, particularly from their home region.

Like much traditional music, the form is tightly controlled by various guilds, a system called *iemoto*. Long apprenticeships are the norm for musicians, and family-based teaching ensures transmission to the next generation. Shamisen master and singer **Umewaka Kiyohide**, whose father started a guild in the 1950s, says the dedication required to master the form means that there are few professional players. "You must study many instruments and be certificated by the NHK min'yo school", he says. His father taught top min'yo singer **Asano Sanae** and the spellbinding young shamisen player **Shinichi Kinoshita**, who played a major role in the **shin min'yo** (new min'yo) wave led by singer Takio Ito.

Shinichi Kinoshita

A rebel with many causes, **Takio Ito** broke away from the rigid control of the guilds to make his own way. The son of a fisherman, Ito has become well known for his passionate singing style and willingness to experiment. Many older min'yo people disapprove, but **Umewaka** disagrees: "It's a good thing. The young stars are trying to make new min'yo. Min'yo has to be free. We have to think about the future."

As far as tsugaru shamisen is concerned, the future has never been brighter. The brothers **Yoshida Kyodai** were the first of the recent players to gain national fame and international recognition for their lightning-fast shamisen playing, sexed up with a punky image. A host of other hopefuls have followed in their wake, including **Agatsuma**, **Masahiro Nitta**, **Syo Asano** and **Keishi Ono**. All of these artists have flirted with rock, jazz and other styles at some point, as well as new hairdos, but all have learnt their craft in the traditional manner and are equally at home playing tsugaru shamisen standards in the orthodox style.

Traditional drumming from the island of Sado, where the percussion-based **Earth Festival** is held annually, has now become internationally famous. **Ondekoza**, the original group of drummers, and its offshoot **Kodo,** who organize the Earth Festival, are capable of playing very powerful, rootsy gigs with just various drums (**taiko**), from the massive ōdaiko to small hand-drums, but more often than not use other instruments. It's also worth checking out ex-Kodo and Ondekoza members who have struck out on their own. Foremost among these, and probably the greatest taiko player of them all is **Eitetsu Hayashi**, closely followed by "futuristic" taiko player Shuichi Hidano and US-born **Leonard Eto**, who has played on soundtracks including *The Lion King*, *The Thin Red Line* and *JFK*.

Taiko too has gained popularity both at home and abroad with mixed Japanese/foreign groups active in various countries such as the UK, US, Canada, Germany and Holland. In Japan, recently formed taiko groups who tour at home and abroad include **Bonten, Hinoki-ya** – the self-proclaimed "happiest taiko in the world" – and the punk/metal/taiko fusion band **Gevil**.

One of the very best places to catch traditional music is at a local festival or **matsuri**. At ancient Buddhist O-Bon festivals, held to celebrate ancestors, locals get down to a **bon odori** (bon dance) and you'll be dragged to your feet if you try to sit out. The dancing – to live or recorded min'yo of classic bon dances – centres on a bamboo tower with a big drum in the middle. You may catch the **mikoshi procession** where young men dressed in what look like jockstraps struggle to carry a portable shrine. Such festivals are all about music, cementing community bonds and having a good time, Japanese-style.

Kayokyoku

As Japan began the process of modernization under the Meiji Reformation of 1868, there was already a large pool of traditional music – classical, folk and urban – available for development or incorporation into newer styles. A further influence was added to the mix in the mid-nineteenth century, with the arrival of Western **military bands** – the first Western music to arrive in Japan. These laid the foundations for the Western music that followed, from classical to popular genres like jazz and chanson.

Two short song-forms, *shoka* and *gunka*, developed during the Meiji period. **Shoka** are songs composed to introduce Western music and singing to schools, while **gunka** are military songs with strong Japanese elements, acting as a prototype for later Japanese/Western syntheses. Popular from the Sino-Japanese war to World War II – when Western music was banned – you can still hear these patriotic songs blaring from the trucks of right-wing activists in Tokyo.

At the turn of the century, another immensely popular song form was **ryukoka** (literally "songs that are popular") which developed from street entertainers in the Osaka region, and was set to a shamisen backing. Japan's first recording stars, **Kumoemon Tochuken** and **Naramuru Yoshida**, were ryukoka performers and their throbbing vocal styles prefigured later developments.

With Western culture – movies and music – now flooding Japan, local musicians started to catch on. The **Hatano Jazz Band** were the first Japanese to play jazz, following a trip to the US in 1912. Tango, foxtrot, rumba, Tin Pan Alley, blues and Hawaiian all followed.

The potential for a fusion between Japanese and Western music was most fully realized by two composers, **Nakayama Shimpei** and **Koga Masao**, both of whom were major figures in the development of Japanese popular songs. Sometimes using the Japanese *yonanuki* pentatonic scale with Western arrangements, Shimpei hit the bigtime with "Kachusha no Uta" (Katherine's Song), while Koga pioneered the use of single-line guitar accompaniment in the 1931 hit, "Saké wa Namida ka Tameiki ka" (*saké* is a tear or a sigh), also using traditional *yuri* ornamentation.

The resultant style became known as **kayokyoku**, a catch-all term for Japanese popular songs that originated in the 1930s but only came into use after World War II. In the devastation and famine of the post-war period, people turned for solace to songs like the influential 1945 hit "Ringo no Uta" (The Apple Song), sung by **Michiko Namiki** and **Noburo Kirishima**. Despite the arrival of more Western styles like R&B and boogie

woogie, some artists emerged singing kayokyoku in a Japanese style. In 1949, **Hibari Misora**, the greatest popular singer of the modern era, made her debut at the tender age of 12.

Hibari, a precocious child who could memorize long poems and mimic adult singers, was remarkable for her versatility, with a voice that could handle natural **jigoe** singing as well as the wavering **yuri** folk style. The undisputed queen of **enka** (see box), her powerful, sobbing **kobushi** vocal technique created a highly charged atmosphere, but she was also talented enough to cover jazz, min'yo, Latin, chanson and torch songs in the thousand recordings she made before her death at 52 in 1989. In many ways, she was Japan's greatest popular cultural icon of the twentieth century, appearing in 160 films.

As Hibari was starting her career, others like **Michiya Mihashi** and **Hachiro Kasuga** were incorporating Japanese elements into popular song. Meanwhile, American songs were spreading across Japan, helped no doubt by the Allied occupying forces. Japanese composers like **Ryouichi Hattori** picked up on the trends with the shuffle-rhythm inspired "Tokyo Boogie Woogie", even managing a shamisen version. Other styles like bluegrass, rockabilly, Hawaiian (again), doowop, R&B and jazz all caught on.

In the 1950s, **Latin music** flourished, although it had taken root at least twenty years before. During the 1950s and early 1960s, many Cuban-style bands like the **Tokyo Cuban Boys** were formed. Singers such as Keiko Ikuta and Tomoko Takara also became huge stars, even recording in Brazil and Argentina. The tradition has been maintained, first with the success of the now defunct **Orquesta de la Luz**, followed by a host of other musicians. These include bandoneon player **Ryota Komatsu**, a fantastic interpreter of tango and especially Astor Piazzola, bossa nova player **Lisa Ono, Willie Nagasaki & Afro-Japanese All Stars,** while Orquesta de la Luz founder Carlos Kanno formed the **Nettai Tropical Jazz Big Band**.

Kayokyoku gradually became associated with styles that used traditional scales, like **enka**, while the more Western-sounding pop became known as **Japanese pops**. This latter form was defined by songs like "Sukiyaki" and by the many Western-style groups that developed in the 1960s, known as **Group Sounds**. Japanese pops mirrored all the Western moves – Beatles imitators, rock, folk, folk-rock and psychedelic groups were all the flavour of the day.

Japanese Rock and Sounds of the Underground

Many 1960s Japanese pop bands sang in English, but towards the end of the decade, some underground rock bands turned to their native language. Led by composer **Haruomi Hosono** and lyricist **Takashi Matsumoto**, the pioneering folk-rock band **Happy End** experimented with Japanese lyrics about love and politics, inspiring an entire generation of rockers. Similar artists that emerged at the end of the 1960s and into the mid-1970s included **Nobuyasu Okabayashi, Sadistic Mika Band** (who have recently reformed), **Sugar Babe** and **RC Succession**.

The **Southern All Stars**, whose way of singing Japanese as if it were English helped them to be Japan's biggest-selling band in the late 1980s, were another influential group. This period also produced a wave of "alternative" rock acts like Tama and Little Creatures.

The most successful international and domestic band of the 1980s, however, was **Yellow Magic Orchestra** (YMO), formed by **Haruomi Hosono**, Ryuchi Sakamoto and Yukihiro Takahashi. Heavily influenced by German band Kraftwerk and computer-game sounds, YMO's brand of technopop inspired many followers, notably The Plastics and Melon. Sakamoto went on to a successful international career as a soloist and Oscar-winning soundtrack composer. Hosono, regarded as a pioneer in Japan for his incorporation of exotic sounds into his music, has been working in diverse fields – songwriting, soundtracks, music documentaries for TV and international collaborations. In 2002, Hosono got back together with Takahashi to form the "electronic folk" duo Sketch Show, with Sakamoto joining them in a later reincarnation, Human Audio Sponge. At the Live Earth concert in Tokyo in July 2007, they performed once again as Yellow Magic Orchestra.

Hosono's massive influence on the new roots generation in Japan cannot be overestimated. He became one of the first Japanese musicians to look south to the islands of **Okinawa** for inspiration: in 1980 both Hosono and Ry Cooder performed on **Shokichi Kina**'s second, Okinawan-influenced album, *Bloodline*, as did Makoto Kubota of Yuyake Gakudan.

With the addition of vocalist Shoukichi Suzuki, Yuyake Gakudan transformed into **Sandii and the Sunsetz**, another band that found international

Sandii

success in the 1980s. Led by powerful singer **Sandii** and composer/producer **Makoto Kubota**, the band blended Okinawan music with reggae. But shortly after the band split up, Kubota turned his attention to producing Asian popular music, working with Indonesians like dangdut singer Elvy Sukaesih and pop sunda artist Detty Kurnia. Kubota's most recent project, **Blue Asia**, has been one of his best and most successful.

Sandii, meanwhile, has devoted herself almost exclusively to Hawaiian music, opening her own school of hula dance and releasing four successful Hawaiian albums to date.

Apart from some of the world's most banal pop music, Japan is paradoxically also the home of some of the world's most compelling underground music. Avant-garde rockers include **The Boredoms** and **Rovo**. The latter feature some members from **Dub Squad**, dub being another genre that has become something of a Japanese speciality, with artists including **Dry & Heavy**, **Audio Active** and **Little Tempo**. Dub has also featured on some albums by one of Japan's most interesting artists, female singer **UA**. Although ostensibly a pop singer, UA's albums have featured a variety of influences and performers from Balinese gamelan to Hawaiian guitar. Although the scene is constantly in transition, one of the latest groups to cross over into the mainstream while keep their artistic credentials intact is **Quruli**, who play a kind of pop, punk and lo-fi electronica fusion.

Underground jazz is another fertile scene. Many of these artists have played at some point with the new-jazz experimental big band **Shibusashirazu**, who have also toured Europe several times. Yet more members of Shibusashirazu perform with the ten-strong baritone saxophone group **Tokyo Chutei Iki**, who have appeared in London, while **Pascals**, who incorporate various toy instruments, have become particularly known in France. One of the originators of the underground scene is sax player **Kazutoki Umezu**, who now fronts his own band, the jazz-rock outfit **Kiki Band**, while other saxophonists to watch out for are the extraordinary **Yasuaki Shimizu**, known particularly for his interpretations of Bach's Cello Suites and **Akira Sakata**, who plays a lot with Jim O'Rourke of Sonic Youth. An important figure on the improvised electronic scene is **Yoshide Otomo** and **ONJO** (his New Jazz Orchestra).

More commercial, but equally dynamic in their own way, are **Soil & "Pimp" Sessions**, much championed by Gilles Peterson in the UK, while in the same vein, **Pe'z** have dubbed their music "samurai jazz".

The Roots Boom

While commercial *idoru kashus* ("idol singers") and singer-songwriters like the hugely successful **Yuming (Yumi Matsutoya)** seemed to dominate the 1980s, new sounds did begin to emerge. Many world-music acts arrived in the mid-1980s, exposing the Japanese to non-Western sounds. Each summer that followed would produce the trend of the year, be it Latin, reggae or Indonesian.

The Japanese genius for assimilating foreign sounds into a new form is well known, and the influx of world music has had a similar effect. The first "world music" group was probably the extraordinary **Geinoh Yamashirogumi**, a collective of about two hundred artists led by Shouji Yamashiro, who took over the group in 1966. They studied and mastered musical traditions from around the world, from Balinese gamelan to Bulgarian choir singing, and in the mid-1980s went on to create a hi-tech ethnic fusion on a series of groundbreaking albums and the soundtrack to the classic anime film *Akira*.

Reggae was considered "underground" for years, but is now part of the mainstream, as is ska, following the success of the **Tokyo Ska Paradise Orchestra**. **Latin** music has also had a big impact, propelling the talented **Orquesta de la Luz** to the top of the Billboard Latin chart in the early 1990s. **The Boom**, led by **Kazufumi Miyazawa**, who had helped to spawn the Okinawan music boom in 1993, started to experiment with Brazilian music in the mid-1990s, which opened up a new generation's ears to Brazilian music. In 2006 he formed a new band, **Ganga Zumba**, with Brazilians Marocs Suzano and Fernando Moura as members, again playing a mix of Brazilian and Latin-inspired pop.

At the end of the 1980s, **roots bands** like Shang Shang Typhoon, and Okinawan artists and bands, particularly Rinken Band, Nenes and Shokichi Kina broke onto the scene. Inspiration came from both within Japan (Okinawan and local popular culture) and outside.

The Okinawans' practice of taking their local traditions and updating them with other forms of music has been reflected in a wave of new bands. **Soul Flower Union** are a rock group from Kansai led by **Takashi Nakagawa** and Hideko Itami. Following the earthquake that struck the Kobe region in 1995, the group took to the streets to play for the victims. Forced to go "unplugged" they played Okinawan sanshin and added clarinet and other wind instruments, accordion and the *chindon* drum, used in chindon advertising groups that used to ply the streets in pre-war Japan. They released the now-classic single "Mangetsu no Yube" (A Full Moon Evening), co-written with Hiroshi Yamaguchi of the group Heatwave. The group called this project Soul Flower Mononoke Summit and released *Asyl Ching-Dong* on an independent label, as their record company at the time didn't take kindly to the politicized lyrics.

Several other groups inspired by chindon also emerged during the 1990s. Initially, **Compostella** became champions of a style that combined chindon and experimental jazz, although the group's leader Masami Shinoda died just as they had begun to establish themselves. Members of Compostella went on to form **Cicala Mvta**, who added Balkan, klezmer and other world brass-band music to the mix, while the explosive **Asakusa Jinta** blend chindon, punk, rockabilly, Balkan and polka into a heady brew. More orthodox chindon groups include Ching-Dong Tsushinsha and Adachi Sendensha.

Another updated local style is **kawachi ondo**, a narrative folk-genre from the central Kansai region. The leading modern exponent is **Kawachiya Kikusuimaru**, who mixed kawachi ondo with reggae and many other styles but has released little in recent years. Traditionally, kawachi ondo performers dress in colourful kimonos and play at their local bon odori summer festival: a kawachi ondo festival for Tokyo's migrant Kansai workers has become a permanent fixture in the calendar. From a nearby region comes **Tadamaru Sakuragawa**, who sings in a similar style called **goshu ondo** and who reworked the genre with striking results on his album *Ullambana*.

Nagauta, *kouta* or *hauta* singing styles, most closely associated with geisha, have also been revamped in recent years. **Umekichi** is a young singer and shamisen player who incorporates Western instruments into a joyful, upbeat sound, while the collaboration of veteran singer **Eishiba** and Toshinori Kondo on electric trumpet, programming and synthesizers brings together ancient and modern Japan.

Rokyoku (storytelling) has also been updated, especially by **Takeharu Kunimoto**. Kunimoto is a fantastic shamisen player who has been fascinated by American bluegrass since he was a child. He finally got to live out his dream by combining the two genres on *Appalachian Shamisen*, recorded with Tennessee bluegrass group The Last Frontier.

Ainu – Indigenous Music of Japan

Although they are virtually unknown in the West, Japan has an indigenous people with their own culture and music. The exact origins of the Ainu are not known, but they appear to share similarities with the inhabitants of Central Asia, although some argue for a link with the Ryukyuans of Okinawa and even with native North Americans. It was only in 1997 that the Ainu were officially recognized by a Japanese court as an indigenous people. Ainu culture, which was transmitted orally, had been dying out, preserved in a few museums and Ainu "villages" in Hokkaido, the northernmost of Japan's main islands. It is believed that there are about 150,000 Ainu in Japan today, although the exact figure is uncertain, as many either hide their origin or are unaware of it. One such person was **Oki Kano**, who set about updating Ainu music for the new generation when he discovered his own Ainu ancestry at the age of 24. After listening to archive recordings, Kano set about learning ancient Ainu songs and the **tonkori**, the long

Jak Kilby

Oki Kano

skinny stringed instrument of the Sakhalin Ainu, the island above Hokkaido belonging to Russia. He released his first album in 1996, collaborated with Japanese sax player **Kazutoki Umezu** on his follow-up *Hankapuy* and with the veteran female Ainu singer **Umeko Ando**. Oki went on to produce two albums by Ando, who died in 2004. He has subsequently combined Ainu melodies and the tonkori with dub and other world sounds. His **Dub Ainu Band** have played at festivals around the world, and Oki has also collaborated with the Irish group Kila. As well as gaining a reputation overseas, Oki has done much to raise awareness of Ainu music and culture in Japan. His albums have gained rave reviews, while young Japanese dub and reggae fans have become fascinated with his hypnotic sounds. In Hokkaido there are now hundreds of students, both Japanese and Ainu, learning the tonkori. Ainu music, it seems, has never been in such a healthy state.

Okinawa

If you want some musical magic in Japan, head for the deep, deep south and **Okinawa**'s balmy heat. It might be a min'yo performance in a small club or the massed troupes of the annual **Ei-sa festival**, but you'll find graceful dancing, haunting vocals, all kinds of drumming and stunning playing on the sanshin, the three-string Okinawan banjo. The performers, dressed in spectacular costumes, may be anything from a solo sanshin player to a hundred-strong street band complete with conch shells, sanshin and ranks of synchronized hand-drummers.

The sub-tropical Okinawan island chain, known as the Ryuku islands by *uchinanchu* (Okinawan people), is found in the East China Sea, some 500km from mainland Japan. Okinawa was under US administration after World War II and was only returned to Japan in 1972. Blending traditions of mainland Asia with those of the Pacific, the archipelago of seventy islands has a thriving traditional culture which is just as exotic to the Japanese as to anybody else.

Okinawa Roots

Okinawa was settled by people from both northern Asia (via China and Korea) and the southeast. Trading links were established first with China and then with the rest of the region, and many cultural influences were absorbed during this time. Spurred by the expectation of vast profits, the Japanese soon followed, invading and annexing the islands in 1609. Thus began a long period of foreign domination, a process some Okinawans claim is continuing to this day through the Japanese administration in far-off Tokyo and the massive US military presence.

For more than four hundred years, Okinawans have developed folk and court styles of music that are unique in Asia. Social and cultural life, centred on the village and family, has always been based on music, poetry and dance. In 1690, Englebert Kaempfer noted that peasants carried their musical instruments into the rice fields, always ready for a jam session after work. Each region has its own music and the folk tradition is very much alive. In some villages, **umui** (religious songs) are still sung at festivals to honour ancestors. Work songs that reflect communal agriculture techniques can still be heard, and various kinds of group and circle dances, some performed exclusively by women, can be found in the smaller islands.

Popular entertainment is known by the general term, **zatsu odori** (common dance), though everyone calls these songs **shima uta** (island songs). The best-known style, and one no wedding would be complete without, is called **kacharsee**. Set to lively rhythms laid down by the sanshin,

which plays both melody and rhythm, and various drums, the dance is performed with the upper body motionless and the lower body swaying sensuously, accompanied by graceful hand movements that echo similar dances in Thailand and Indonesia.

The Asian connection can be clearly seen in the history of the **sanshin**. This three-stringed lute began life in China as the *sanxien* and was introduced to Okinawa in around 1392. Local materials were quickly exhausted, so Thai snakeskin was used for the soundbox and Filipino hardwood for the neck. Once introduced to mainland Japan, the sanshin became bigger, produced a harder sound and was renamed the shamisen, one of the quintessential Japanese instruments.

While the rest of Japan rapidly modernized during the Meiji era, Okinawa was left under-developed. Even today, it has the highest unemployment rate in Japan. But go to Okinawa City (but call it by its local name when you get there, Koza City), produce a bottle of saké and someone will start playing music.

Although the relationship between the US military and Okinawans has never been as close as in the Philippines, **American culture** has certainly influenced local musicians. Local musicians started to copy US pop styles in the 1950s, sometimes mixing in folk music. Rinsuké Teruya, late father of Rinken Teruya of Rinken Band fame and a popular comedy singer, remembers constructing a four-string electric *yonshin* in the 1950s, and he owned an old recording featuring mambo and Okinawan folk music.

Rockin' Ryukus

Okinawa's early post-war music was dominated by local folk recordings, led by the legendary singer/sanshin player **Shouei Kina** and **Rinsho Kadekaru**, both of whom followed in the footsteps of pre-war star **Choki Fukuharu**. While Shouei Kina was singing, his son **Shokichi Kina** was absorbing both his father's folk music and the local rock played around the US bases by bands like Condition Green. He formed a band while still at high school, taking the name **Champloose** from the name of a traditional Okinawan stir-fry and combining Okinawan min'yo and rock on his song "Haisai Ojisan" (Hey Old Man).

Kina's music attracted attention from Western musicians like Ry Cooder and Henry Kaiser – the former played guitar on several songs on Kina's 1980 *Bloodline* album. Japanese pioneer **Haruomi**

Hosono was also on the same disc. Later, **Ryuichi Sakamoto**, **Makoto Kubota** and **Koryu** of Shang Shang Typhoon would all dip into Kina's music for inspiration. His song "Subete No Hito No Kokoro Ni Hana O", more usually just called "Hana", is an Asian favourite.

After a seven-year break, Kina made his comeback at an ecstatic 1990 concert in Shinjuku. Since then, however, his well-known "difficult" personality has led to frequent changes in band personnel and record companies. Live, Kina still maintained the charisma that has led to him being compared with Bob Marley, but in the studio his creativity seemed to dry up and his albums became rather patchy and invariably contained re-workings of "Hana" and "Haisai Ojisan". He opened his own club in Naha, called Chakra, where he and his group would perform for a few tourists every night. Kina's loss of interest in music, coincided with a growing interest in politics, culminating with his election in 2004 to the Japanese parliament's House of Councillors as a member of the Minshuto (Democratic Party).

Meanwhile ex-Champloose guitarist **Takashi Hirayasu** turned solo and released probably the top-selling Okinawan CD outside of Japan, *Jin Jin/ Firefly*. Recorded together with American guitarist Bob Brozman, the album was simple, acoustic, recorded in a traditional house on a small island and seemed to capture the atmosphere of Okinawa – classic children's songs, some charming and jaunty, others tragic and beautiful.

In January 1990, **Rinken Band** played their first dates in Tokyo. **Rinken Teruya**, a sanshin player who grew up playing with his father and maestro uncle, moved in a different direction to Kina by ignoring rock and creating instead bright pop songs that fused min'yo and *ei-sa* festival songs. These music-hall revue-style shows were packed with madcap antics, **kachashii** dance songs and plaintive haunting ballads that featured the remarkable voice of Rinken's wife, **Tomoko Uehara**. Rinken Band are still going strong and in 2006 opened a new "live house" next to their swanky studio in Chatan, called Karahai. Rinken Band are regular performers, as are Rinken's protégés, such as female duo **Tink Tink**.

Sadao China first came to public attention in 1977 with his hit "Bye Bye Okinawa". He went on to record his own solo min'yo album and produce other artists, most notably the all-female group, **Nenes**. He co-produced and played sanshin on Nenes' 1991 debut album, *Ikawu*, which

John Clewley

Sadao China

featured traditional vocals set to textured layers of keyboards from **Kazuya Sahara**. Released in 1994, *Koza Dabasa* featured **Ry Cooder**, fellow-guitarist David Lindley, drummer Jim Keltner and David Hidalgo of Los Lobos. The four original female singers have long since departed and although a new Nenes exists in name, they are but a poor shadow of their former self. The original members are now pursuing solo careers, most successfully **Misako Koja**. "Warabi Gami" in particular, a song written by her partner and Nenes co-producer Kazuya Sahara, has become a modern classic, covered by Okinawan pop stars such as **Rimi Natsukawa** and many others.

After over a decade's absence, Sadao China himself returned to the studio in 2004 to record with one of Okinawa's greatest living musicians, **Seijin Noborikawa**. After a traditional solo album, *Utamaii*, China worked with the legendary singer **Misako Oshiro**, dubbed the "female Rinsho Kadekaru" for her distinctive voice, on her 2007 comeback album "Uta Umui".

Another artist to make a splash at the beginning of the 1990s was the sanshin player and singer **Tetsuhiro Daiku** from Yaeyama island, in the deep southwest, close to Taiwan. **Yaeyama min'yo** is based on work songs, called **yunta** and **jiraba**, which follow a call-and-response pattern.

Also from Yaeyama, **Yasukatsu Oshima** can be regarded as the new keeper of the traditional music flame. Oshima didn't even consider a career in music until he arrived in Tokyo and met the members of **Begin**, who had become well known for their Okinawan folk pop. He recorded an album with Orquesta Boré, a group of underground jazz and world musicians, and then set about recording albums of traditional material mixed in with a few of his own originals. Irish trad group Altan joined him on some songs, while his latest album, recorded in New York, is a glorious collaboration with the pianist Geoffrey Keezer and other American jazz musicians.

The most in-demand young musician, though, has to be **Toru Yonaha**, whether as a session musician, producer or an artist in his own right. He has released several albums in recent years, the last two themed around Kachashii dance tunes and Eisa festival songs. The most popular artist Yonaha has played sanshin for is **Rimi Natsukawa**, who has become a superstar in Japan with her albums of soft Okinawan ballads performed in a pop style. Her biggest hits include "Nada Sou Sou" written by Begin, "Kana Yo Kana Yo", written by Kazufumi Miyazawa, and "Warabi Gami", originally performed by Misako Koja.

Okinawan music has lent itself well to various experiments. **Kenji Yano** mixed traditional Okinawan songs with surf music on his project **Surf Champlers**, which most notably produced a classic cult Okinawan/Surf version of the James Bond theme. Yano's other experiments have included The Sanshin Café Orchestra and Sarabandge, who play Okinawan trance music. Other innovators include **Wataru Kohsaka**, who puts his sanshin through various effects and plays it with Indonesian and Indian instruments. UK/US duo **Ryukyu Underground** successfully combined various dance beats and rhythms, initially with samples of traditional songs, before recording with local musicians such as Toru Yonaha. **Takuji a.k.a. Geetek** has done something similar, but the most successful in terms of sales are **Ryukyudisko** with their Okinawan techno, which has proved a hit at all the big festivals on the mainland.

Okinawa has also proved to be Japan's leading breeding-ground for indie rock groups. **Mongol 800** sold an unprecedented (for an indie band) two million copies of their first record. Other popular punk and hardcore groups include **HY** and **Duty**

Paul Fisher

Ryukyu Underground taking a break

Free Shopp, while **Orange Range** had the biggest-selling record in Japan in 2003 with their hip-hop/rap/pop mixture.

In Between – the Music of Amami

The culture and music of the Amami islands reflect their location, roughly halfway between the mainland of Japan and Okinawa. While the main instrument, as in Okinawa, is the sanshin, the Amami islanders sing **shima uta** (island songs) in a minor key, as in Japan, in contrast to the major-key songs of Okinawa. What is unique is the falsetto style of singing, which doesn't exist in either Japan or Okinawa. Less developed than Okinawa, traditional music is being kept alive here by a young generation of artists, probably more than anywhere else in Japan. Born in 1975,

Rikki was one of the first of the current crop to emerge. Her recorded output includes an eponymous Makoto Kubota-produced album from 1995 and probably her best yet, the simple *Miss You Amami*, although she is best-known for "Suteki Da Ne", which was used in the computer game *Final Fantasy X*. Younger artists recording traditional material include **Marika Yoshihara** and **Mizuki Nakamura**, who also record together as **Maricamizki**, and **Nami Makioka**, probably the pick of the bunch. Young male singer **Kohsuke Atari** started off performing traditional songs, but after signing to a major label, plays more of a pop mix, probably in the hope of emulating the enormous success of female singer **Chitose Hajime**, whose first album of Amami-inspired pop sold over a million copies. The success of the young players has brought a few veterans out of retirement, most notably another female singer, **Ikue Asazaki**.

Traditional Instruments

Shakuhachi

A bamboo flute with five finger-holes – four on the front and one on the back – the **shakuhachi** has a full range of chromatic notes, obtained by adjusting the position of the flute and partially covering the holes. The colour of its tone, while always soft and pure, depends on the bamboo used. During the Edo period (early seventeenth to mid-nineteenth centuries) it was used primarily in chamber ensembles with koto and shamisen, although more recently there's been a revival of the more ancient solo repertoire as an aid to meditation.

Biwa and Shamisen

A pear-shaped plucked lute with four or five strings, the **biwa** originated in China. It was played both in gagaku ensembles and solo, but had almost fallen out of use by the end of World War II, until Toru Takemitsu, Japan's most famous contemporary composer, started writing for it, precipitating a revival.

A three-stringed lute, the **shamisen** also came to Japan from China, via Okinawa. The earliest shamisen music is credited to biwa players in the early seventeenth century and it has become one of the most popular instruments in Japanese music.

Koto

The Japanese long zither, or **koto**, usually has thirteen strings with moveable bridges and is played with fingerpicks. It is thought to have originated from the Chinese *zheng* and to have arrived in Japan in the eighth century. Similar instruments are found in Korea (*kayagûm*) and Vietnam (*dan tranh*). It is found in gagaku ensembles, but has developed a rich solo tradition. It is also used to accompany songs and in small "chamber music" ensembles, together with a second koto, a shamisen or a shakuhachi.

Enka – Japan's Soul Music

If you ask a Japanese person what **enka** means, you're likely to get the answer that it is "*Nihonjin no kokoro*", the soul of the Japanese. They may say it's about themes of lost love, homesickness or simply drowning the sorrows of a broken heart with saké. They may talk of songs that feature fog or rain, a smouldering cigarette that means loss, a wedding ring dropped into a glass of saké or the sad, unbearable farewell at a desolate port, somewhere far from home. This is the world of enka.

Enka (from *enzetsu*, meaning public speech, and *ka*, meaning a song) is more than a hundred years old, and despite what some younger Japanese say, it is still enormously popular in Japan. Originally it was a form of political dissent, disseminated by song sheets, but it quickly changed in the early twentieth century as it became the first style to truly synthesize Western scales and Japanese modes. **Shimpei Nakayama** and **Masao Koga** were the trailblazing composers: Koga's first hit in 1931, "Kage Wo Shitaite" (Longing For Your Memory), remains a much-loved classic.

The term "enka" came into common usage in the early 1970s, to describe slow to medium kayokyoku with strong Japanese elements. Enka seems to be everywhere in Japan: special television programmes pump it out, and you'll hear it in restaurants and bars. And, of course, it received a major boost with the invention of karaoke, which helped to spread the genre's popularity both with younger Japanese and foreigners. The classic image is of enka queen **Hibari Misora** decked out in a kimono, tears streaming down her face as she sobs through Koga's "Kanashi Saké" (Sad Saké), with typically understated backing and single-line guitar. Hibari had the *nakibushi* (crying melody) technique and a stunning vibrato-like kobushi that makes the listener's hair stand on end.

When Hibari died in 1989, **Harumi Miyako** inherited her position as the top singer. She is famed for her growling attack and the song "Suki ni Natta Hito". Many enka stars have long careers, and veterans like **Suburo Kitajima** are still going strong, as are **Shin'ichi Mori**, **Aki Yashiro** and **Sachiko Kobayashi**, all of whom are in the current top bracket of singers. However, probably the most popular singer currently is the sprightly **Kiyoshi Hikawa**, who has introduced enka to a young audience who previously thought it the domain of an older generation. Hikawa's brand of enka is fun, dance-oriented and pop-influenced, but with a voice to match those of his predecessors, he is a worthy successor to the enka crown.

DISCOGRAPHY Japan

A good source for information on and CDs by Japanese (and other East Asian) artists is Far Side Music (www.*farsidemusic* .com), run by Paul Fisher, who compiled the *Rough Guide* anthologies of the music of Japan and Okinawa.

★ The Rough Guide to the Music of Japan
World Music Network, UK

The best introduction to the Japanese music scene, including all the types of music covered in this article except kayokyoku and enka. Includes Soul Flower Mononoke Summit, Takio Ito, Makoto Kubota and his band in Shoukichi Kina's classic "Hai Sai Oji-San", plus a strong Okinawan presence. Classical and traditional artists include the quartet Koto Vortex, shakuhachi player Shozan Tanabe, biwa player Yukihiro Gotoh and shamisen virtuoso Michihiro Sato.

Traditional and Classical Music

★ Have a Big Bite of Japanese Music
Victor, Japan

A great sampler of all types of Japanese traditional music. From gagaku to noh, Okinawa to Ainu, all the major instruments – shakuhachi, shamisen, biwa, koto – and much more. Excellent English notes.

⊙ Lullaby for the Moon
EMI Hemisphere, UK

Intimate chamber-music performances for solo koto, koto/shakuhachi duets and various ensembles of the two instruments. Slow-moving and restful.

⊙ Japanese Traditional Music Vols 1–3: Gagaku; Nogaku; Kabuki
King, Japan

Three separate CDs with English notes. The rarely performed gagaku is one of the strangest musics in this discography. Based around the length of a breath, the music can be ethereal or discordant, but is always engaging. Nogaku, the austere but powerful noh music, has some similarities with gagaku, but includes the *fue* pipe, whose unstable pitch gives the music a strangely compelling sound. The third disc, *Kabuki*, is a live recording of the famous *Kanjincho* (Subscription List) play, based on the immensely popular noh drama *Ataka*.

Chikuzan Takahashi

Great shamisen master, who helped to popularize the exciting tsugaru shamisen style.

⊙ Tsugaru Shamisen
Sony, Japan
Recorded live during Chikuzan's 1970s heyday.

Goro Yamaguchi

Goro Yamaguchi (1933–99) was a national treasure, and master of the shakuhachi bamboo flute.

★ A Bell Ringing in the Empty Sky
Nonesuch Explorer, US
A cult classic. Just two solo tracks from the Kinko school, which originated among Zen Buddhist monks.

Michio Miyagi

A legend of Japanese hogaku (traditional music) Miyagi (1894–1956) is credited with creating a new style of music based on Western ideas.

⊙ Ikuta-ryu Soukyoku
Victor, Japan
Includes Miiyagi's most famous composition, "Haru no Umii" (Spring Sea), a koto and shakuhachi duet and five other classic pieces.

Ondekoza

With the younger group Kodo, Ondekoza have done much to bring the dramatic drumming styles of traditional Japanese music to wider audiences.

⊙ Fujiyama
Victor, Japan
Features a good range of drumming techniques and other instruments as well.

Tadao Sawai

Tadao Sawai (1937–97) was one of the greatest contemporary players and composers of koto (sokyoku) music, known for the intensity and dramatic quality of his compositions.

⊙ Gendai Soukyoku
Victor, Japan
Features five Tadao masterpieces, including the classic "Tori no Yoni".

Tsuru to Kame

Shamisen-player Katsuaki Sawada and min'yo singer Shigeri Kitsu perform old min'yo songs in their original style, complete with bawdy lyrics.

⊙ Shakkitose
Victor, Japan
A brilliant album of min'yo and ondo songs. Also features Haruomi Hosono (of YMO fame) playing various traditional flutes and percussion instruments.

Roots Music

★ Kawachi Mondo

Nippon Columbia, Japan
Held in Kawachi in the Kansai region, Kawachi Ondo is one of the most vibrant summer festivals. Based on a standard tradi-

tional tune, the music has always been updated through the years. This amazing CD collects long-deleted recordings from 1970s disco to 1980s dub-style Kawachi Ondo, plus more traditional versions from all the top singers.

Chanchiki

Led by multi-instrumentalist Tsutom Tanaka, Chanchiki's take on min'yo is a wild mix of traditional Japanese sounds and rhythms with rock, jazz, Latin, African and other elements.

⊙ Gokuraku
Tacotsubo-Kogyo, Japan
One of the latest groups to update min'yo, Chanchiki play shamisen, taiko drums and shakuhachi, and feature female vocalist Makiko Ikeda. Their sound is augmented by electric bass, guitar, tuba, sax and trombone. Pulsating, dynamic versions of songs from Aomori in the north to Okinawa in the south.

Hozan Yamamoto, Katsuya Yokoyama, Tadao Sawaii

Hozan Yamamoto and Katsuya Yokoyama are masters of shakuhachi, while Tadao Sawaii is one of the great koto maestros.

⊙ Standard Bossa
King, Japan
The three musicians collaborate with band leader Toshiyuki Miyama and New Herd Orchestra on a selection of bossa nova classics, jazz and European tunes including "Girl from Ipanema", "Mas Que Nada" and "Un Homme et une Femme".

Shang Shang Typhoon

Originally a singer-songwriter, Koryu ("Red Dragon"), the group's leader, changed direction after a trip to Okinawa. Unable to play the Okinawan sanshin, he decided to use the banjo, with great results, adding vocalists, a keyboard player and percussionist.

⊙ Shang Shang Typhoon
Epic-Sony, Japan
SST's 1990 debut heralded the rise of roots music in Japan. The songs rush through the Okinawan-tinged "As Time Goes By" to the kawachi-ondo/reggae blend of "It's Alright Buddha Smile". Only SST could get away with the Latin madness of "Dancing Cha Cha Cha with Bitter Tea".

Shisars

From the mainland, Shisars feature the female vocals and sanshin of Yoshie Uno and Akemi Mochida and are mainly influenced by Okinawan music, which they update into something fresh, new and exciting.

⊙ Ta Hua Gu
Mangetsu, Japan
Left-field, radical reworkings of Okinawan and Japanese folk songs, performed by Yoshie and Akemi with electric guitar and Cicala Mvta's Wataru Ohkuma on clarinet, plus accordion, mandolin and percussion.

Soul Flower Mononoke Summit

Takashi Nakagawa is one of the few Japanese musicians with a social conscience. After starting out with the band Newest Model, he formed the influential Soul Flower Union with Hideko Itami of Mescaline Drive. Soul Flower Mononoke Summit is the acoustic version of the group.

Asyl Ching-Dong
Respect, Japan
First acoustic Soul Flower album, featuring old popular songs and combining Okinawan sanshin and chindon elements. Mostly live; the two studio tracks include the classic "Fukko Bushi".

Tadamaru Sakuragawa

A goshu ondo singer from Shiga Prefecture, Sakuragawa was unknown before he recorded an album with Osaka's Spiritual Unity and performed at WOMAD in Japan in 1991.

★ Ullambana DX
Disc Milk, Japan
Infectious versions of traditional tunes, accompanied by percussion, slide guitars and more. Also features the Indonesian "Bengawan Solo", with Okinawan female quartet Nenes, and more plaintive numbers. Includes a bonus CD of live and previously unissued recordings.

Takio Ito

The *enfant terrible* of the conservative min'yo tradition, Ito abandoned his early musical training to go it alone. A very powerful and colourful voice, equally at ease in a simple setting or with an electric band.

⊙ Ondo
VAP, Japan
This 1996 album is the best of his independent-label releases and includes a version of the beautiful Hokkaido classic "Soran Bashi", along with "Toraji", a Korean tune.

Umekichi

One of the new stars of Japanese roots music, the classically trained Umekichi found her vocation after attending a geisha concert. She learnt shamisen, going on to study at a traditional Japanese music school, and has since become known for giving a modern twist to traditional Japanese music and songs.

⊙ Ohedo Shusse Kouta
Omagatoki, Japan
Twelve modern Edo-era folk tunes. Umekichi is marketed as a kind of modern geisha, with her singing and shamisen-playing augmented by Western instruments to produce a generally upbeat and infectious sound.

Enka

★ Enka Best

Victor, Japan
The only compilation that not only features many of enka's biggest contemporary stars, but also includes English notes that give some insight into why it is the emotional pulse of the nation. Artists include Johji Yamamoto, Sayuri Ishikawa, Shinichi Mori, Aki Yashiro, Hiroshi Itsuki and Yoko Nagayama.

⊙ Enka-Kayo – Best of 50s
King, Japan
An overview of the revival of the dark pre-war enka songs in the 1950s, when Japanese melodies and traditional instruments such as the shamisen were combined with Western string orchestras. Artists include Isao Hayashi, Atsuro Okamoto, Hachiro Kasuga, Tsuzuko Sugawara, Michiya Mihashi and Hibari Misora.

Harumi Miyako

Harumi's unique quavering voice and trademark rough-edged attack have set her apart from other enka singers since her 1968 debut.

⊙ Greatest Hits
Nippon Columbia, Japan
Like Hibari, Miyako Harumi has the ability to make a song completely her own. This set includes her famous monster hit "Suki ni Natta Hito" (a staple karaoke favourite), which begins with her gravel-throated intro before swooping into the song. Stirring stuff.

Hibari Misora

"Hibari-chan" was the Enka Queen of post-war Japan. Making her debut at the age of twelve with "Kappa Boogie", she rose to the top and stayed there until her death. One of the twentieth century's great voices and a performer of great emotional range and power.

★ Greatest Hits
Nippon Columbia, Japan
The obvious starting-point, including her most famous songs, such as "Ringo Oiwake" and "Kanashi Saké" (Sad Saké).

Kiyoshi Hikawa

Currently the biggest young enka star.

⊙ Kiyoshi no Zundoku Bushi
Nippon Columbia, Japan
The album that turned the young enka singer into a superstar, appealing across the generations. The title track is still his most famous song.

Rock & Pop

⊙ Japanese Pops – Very Best of 50s–90s
Nippon Columbia, Toshiba, Pony Canyon, GT Music, Avex, all Japan
These 2-CD sets offer an excellent overview of the Japanese pop scene of the last fifty years. Includes 1950s recordings of Shizuko Kasagi and Hibari Misora; 1960s kayokyoku, rock 'n' roll and groups with Kyu Sakamoto, The Tigers and others; soul and disco sounds of the 1970s with Pink Lady and Finger 5; stars of the 1980s such as Hikaru Genji and Seiko Matsuda; and in the 1990s, J-pop from Ayumi Hamazaki, Namie Amuro and L'Arc-en-Ciel.

Blue Asia

The brainchild of producer Makoto Kubota, together with Yoichi Ikeda and the top Malay production team of Mac Chew and Jenny Chin, Blue Asia have recorded with local musicians around the world on a series of "Hotel" albums. Starting off in Bali, they have subsequently visited Hawaii, Vietnam, Thailand and Morocco.

⊙ Hotel Bangkok
King, Japan
A mix of Thai morlam, dub and electronic sounds, featuring some excellent local musicians, not least the blind vocalist Lady Nan.

The Boom and Miyazawa

In 1986, four Kofu City schoolmates formed a ska group. Three years later, as The Boom, they headlined the Budokan in Tokyo. Kazufumi "Miya" Miyazawa quickly established himself as the band's leader, developed a solo career and has since formed a new group, Ganga Zumba.

⊙ Shima Uta – Grandos Exitos
Sony, Japan
The pick of several greatest hits albums, this one contains the Brazilian and Indonesian-influenced material from the mid-1990s, as well as the million-selling title-track from 1993.

⊙ Tokyo Story
Far Side, UK
Compilation of Miyazawa solo tracks from the Brazil-recorded *Afrosick*, the UK-recorded *Sixteenth Moon* and the Arto Lindsay-produced *Deeper than Oceans*, recorded in various locations. Also includes three tracks from *Spiritek*, including a new version of "Shima Uta".

Geinoh Yamashirogumi

An extraordinary group of over two hundred performers who mastered various musical traditions from around the world and gradually melded them into their own unique sound.

⊙ Ecophony Rinne
Victor, Japan
Released in 1986, this blends Japanese Buddhist chants, noh, Balinese gamelan and Tibetan percussion with synthesizers into an astonishing hi-tech wall of sound. A concept album in four parts based on the eternal cycles of birth, death and rebirth.

Haruomi Hosono

Arguably modern Japan's most creative musical genius, way ahead of his time in pioneering everything from Japanese folk, rock, world and dance music in various guises and groups.

Bon Voyage
Crown, Japan
Before forming YMO, Hosono released three albums that combined Okinawan and other disparate musics into a glorious mixture. This mid-1970s set is probably the best, if only for the brilliant "Roochoo Gumbo", which combines Okinawan music with New Orleans.

Kazufumi Kodama

Trumpet-player Kodama is Japan's original dub pioneer.

⊙ Kodama (Echo) from Dub Station 1982–2002
Speedstar, Japan
Excellent compilation from throughout Kodama's career with Mute Beat, solo and with his Dub Station band, backed by and in collaboration with illustrious names such as Yashiki Gota on drums and singer UA.

Ryouichi Hattori

Perhaps the most influential composer of modern Japanese music, Ryouichi Hattori (d. 1993) laid the foundation for popular songs and enka.

 Boku no Ongaku Jinsei
Nippon Columbia, Japan
This 3-CD set includes "Wakare no Blues", Hattori's 1937 composition for Noriko Awaye, Shizuko Kasagi's "Tokyo Boogie Woogie" and Hamako Watanabe and Noboru Kirishima's "Soshu Yakyoku". Masterpieces of Japanese popular music.

Shibusashirazu

Shibusashirazu (roughly "Never Be Cool") combine elements of jazz with rock, enka, Japanese pop, Latin, dance and experimental avant-garde. The group comprise some of the most skilful and creative players in Japan, plus singers, *butoh* dancers, groovedance girls, artists and actors.

⊙ Shibuboshi
Chitei, Japan
The free-jazz orchestra at their glorious best, as the thirty-piece group on various brass and wind instruments, violin, guitar and percussion are joined by three members of the Sun Ra Arkestra. A kaleidoscopic wall of sound of screaming saxes, wailing guitars and pulsating rhythms.

Shizuko Kasagi

The singer, dancer and film actress Shizuko Kasagi (d. 1985) was one of Japan's greatest entertainers. Following the war she had numerous hits with songs influenced by American jazz and boogie-woogie, mostly composed by Ryouichi Hattori.

⊙ Queen of Boogie
Nippon Columbia, Japan
This three-CD set contains nearly all Kasagi's recorded output, including hits such as "Tokyo Boogie-Woogie", "Rappa to Musume" and "Jungle Boogie", the theme of the Akira Kurosawa film *Yoidore Tenshi* (Drunken Angel).

Soil and "Pimp" Sessions

An explosive six-piece jazz band, Soil and "Pimp" combine the highest musicianship with the coolest of cool sounds and atmosphere. Their brand of jazz is rough around the edges, unadulterated entertainment and constantly kept at boiling point.

⊙ Pimp Master
Victor, Japan; Brownswood, UK
High-octane jazz from the Gilles Peterson-championed outfit. Searing brass and tight beats.

Soul Flower Union

After starting out with the band Newest Model, Takashi Nakagawa formed the influential Soul Flower Union with Hideko Itami of Mescaline Drive. Though originally a rock band, the music has all kinds of roots influences.

⊙ Electro-Asyl-Bop
Ki/oon Sony, Japan
Their best-ever album, from 1996, combining acoustic and electric elements in a kind of swirling psychedelic roots rock played with unbridled energy and passion. Highlights include the brilliant "Eejyanika" and a new version of the classic "Mangetsu no Yube" (A Full Moon Evening).

Yellow Magic Orchestra

Formed in 1978 by Ryouichi Sakamoto, ex-Happy End bassist Haruomi Hosono and ex-Sadistic Mika Band drummer Yukihiro Takahashi, YMO pioneered techno pop. A major influence on many musicians both in Japan and internationally.

⊙ Solid State Survivor
Sony, Japan
For many, quite simply the greatest Japanese album by the greatest Japanese group, combining their synth and drum-

machine sound with memorable tunes such as the classics "Technopolis" and "Behind the Mask".

Okinawa

 The Rough Guide to the Music of Okinawa
World Music Network, UK
An ideal companion to *The Rough Guide to the Music of Japan*. Similarly wide-ranging, from traditional to contemporary, and with tracks by many of the artists discussed in this article, including Rinsho Kadekaru, Tetsuhiro Daiku, Rikki, Seijin Noborikawa, Nenes and the Surf Champlers.

 Ryukyu Rare Groove – Shima Uta Pops in 60s–70s
Pid, Japan
Brilliant retrospective anthology of singles of traditional Okinawan tunes mixed with Western and other styles. Tracks include "Bossa Nova Jintoya" and "Shirahama Blues" from the top local acts of the day, including Four Sisters, Hoptones, and Yara Family.

⊙ **The Songs of Okinawa**
Victor, Japan
Excellent compilation, with artist names, track-titles and notes in English. Traditional music from Rinsho Kadekaru, Misako Oshiro and Tetsuhiro Daiku, plus some updates, including enka-style singer Yoshimi Tendo's version of "Hana".

Nenes

In 1990, China Sadao, worried that the younger generation were forgetting traditional music, set up a four-piece female band, Nenes ("sisters" in Okinawan). China's sanshin playing, the massed vocals of Nenes (led by Misako Koja), keyboards and percussion completed the line-up.

⊙ **Koza Dabasa**
Ki/oon Sony Records, Japan
Partly recorded in Los Angeles, with Ry Cooder, David Lindley, Jim Keltner and David Hidalgo of Los Lobos. Not a dud track, and "Shima Jima Kaisha" is sublime.

Rinken Band

Founded by Rinken Teruya, the band features his wife Uehara Tomoko's fabulous singing, a fast-action three-man chorus line, keyboards, bass and Teruya's own sanshin playing. Takes a different line from Kina in modernizing Okinawan min'yo by using a more pop approach.

⊙ **Urizun – New Best**
Sony, Japan
The definitive 21-track best of, featuring all their hits from the early 1990s and onwards, including "Arigatou", an early live favourite. Bright, fresh pop ditties that blend ei-sa festival music, min'yo and Rinken's plonking sanshin.

Rinsho Kadekaru

Rinsho,Kadekaru (d. 1999), the "Godfather of Shima Uta", was one of the most revered traditional musicians in Okinawa. A truly great solo performer.

⊙ **Jiru – Rare Tracks of Rinsho Kadekaru**
Victor, Japan
Brilliant album of recordings from the 1950s on, with rare photos.

Sadao China

Son of min'yo legend Teihen China, Sadao China is one of the "Big Three" of contemporary Okinawan music (Kina and Rinken being the others).

⊙ **Utamaii**
Respect, Japan
From 2006, China's comeback studio album. Pure traditional material with help from Yasuko Yoshida (ex-Nenes) and his son, Sadahito.

Seijin Noborikawa

Seijin Noborikawa (or "Seigwa" as he is sometimes referred to) is known as the "Okinawan Jimi Hendrix" for his fast sanshin playing. Born in 1930, he formed an association with the late great Rinsho Kadekaru and taught the young Sadao China.

⊙ **It's Only Seigwa – The Best of Seijin Noborikawa 1975–2004**
Respect, Japan
The current granddaddy of Okinawan shima uta. From his traditional earlier recordings to collaborations with Japanese jazz musicians and Soul Flower Union through to his most recent duets with Sadao China.

Shokichi Kina & Champloose

Bad boy Shokichi Kina, the leader of Champloose, started a new direction in Okinawan music with "Haisai Ojisan".

⊙ **The Music Power from Okinawa**
GlobeStyle, UK
Live set recorded in Okinawa in 1977. Driving sanshin, great vocal backing (with "ay eya ay eya ay eya sa sa" shouts) and Kina on vocals. Includes a wonderful version of "Haisai" and "Tokyo Sanbika," a song co-written by Rinsuké Teruya, Rinken's father.

The Surf Champlers

The one-man project of Osaka-born Kenji Yano, now based in Okinawa. In the 1980s, Yano played with Rokunin Gumi, one of the few bands to match Champloose's passionate live performances. He always seems to be ahead of his time.

⊙ **Champloo A Go Go**
Qwotchee Records, Okinawa
Yano recorded these mostly kachashii and min'yo songs in what sounds like his bedroom. His stroke of genius was to use drum machines and a surf-style guitar. The most brilliant track of all is his cover version of the James Bond theme

Takashi Hirayasu

Hirayasu started out playing blues and R&B in the bars around the American bases in Okinawa, and took up the sanshin in his early twenties. He joined Shoukichi Kina's band Champloose and played on the *Bloodline* album, among others. He began a solo career in the 1990s.

WITH BOB BROZMAN

⊙ **Jin Jin/Firefly**
Respect, Japan; Riverboat Records, UK
This is a fine, intimate collaboration with Bob Brozman, the Californian master of Hawaiian slide guitar. Based around a dozen Okinawan nursery rhymes, Hirayasu's vocals have a gentle naivety about them, while Brozman's slide burns on the title track.

Tetsuhiro Daiku

An award-winning sanshin player, singer and teacher of traditional and Okinawan folk music, Daiku has had an enormous influence on keeping the min'yo tradition alive. He has an experimental side too, having recorded with saxophonist Kazutoki Umezu and *chindon-ya* (Japanese street musicians).

⊙ Jinta Internationale
Off Note, Japan
This 1996 album shows the new Daiku sound maturing and developing the perfect combination of Okinawan and chindon music. Includes a wonderful version of the Internationale.

Toru Yonaha

Much in-demand young sanshin-player, singer and producer.

⊙ Kachashii a Go Go
Respect, Japan
Yonaha in duets with eight vocalists on eleven classic kachashii tracks, including the climax of any self-respecting kachashii party, "Tohsin Doii". Although the songs are arranged in an orthodox style, they sound fresh in the hands of this talented musician and his supporting cast.

Yasukatsu Oshima

Oshima grew up listening to his father and grandfather playing min'yo on their sanshins. Like no other Okinawan musician from his generation, he seems to embody a living tradition, with his rich, expressive voice and the delicate, brittle sound of his instrument.

⊙ Island Time
Victor, Japan
Although still young, Oshima sounds like he's been around for years. On this, his fifth album, he is joined by musicians playing violin, guitar and percussion. Excellent English notes.

Ainu

Oki

The most prominent Ainu musician, revitalizing an almost forgotten tradition.

⊙ Dub Ainu
Farside, UK
Oki's dub remix album of his own recordings became a cult hit. Brittle tonkori sounds mixed with electronica, dub and reggae into something unique.

Oki Dub Ainu Band

Oki Dub Ainu Band
Chikar Studio, Japan
First album by the band that toured in Europe and Japan, successfully managing to recreate their dynamic live sound. Traditional tunes featuring Oki's vocals and tonkori, with percussion, guitar and funky bass lines.

Umeko Ando

Veteran Ainu singer who died in 2004.

⊙ Upopo Sanke
Chikar Studio, Japan
Ando's last and finest album. Traditional songs, with tonkori and production by Oki, but centred on Ando's hypnotic and charming vocals.

Amami

Ikue Asazaki

A veteran singer who made her first recordings late in life, on the wave of a boom in Amami island music.

⊙ Utaba Utayun
Universal, Japan
Asazaki's voice drips with character, and the sympathetic piano accompaniment makes for a quite beautiful and relaxing album.

Nami Makioka

One of the best of the younger generation of Amami island singers.

Nanka
Jabara, Japan
This album of Amami island standards is devoid of sanshin – instead, Makioka's vocals are surrounded by tasteful layers of keyboards, mandolin, violin, bouzouki, piano and a variety of percussion.

Rikki

Rikki (Ritsuki Nakano) began singing Amami shima uta when she was just four years old, and took part in a min'yo competition at the age of five. She won for the next seven years, and at the age of fifteen, was the youngest-ever winner of the National Folk Award.

⊙ Miss You Amami
Rice, UK
Simple arrangements of traditional songs featuring Hawaiian guitar, Malaysian accordion and Brazilian percussion, as well as the sanshin of her mentor, the great Shunzo Tsukiji.

PLAYLIST
Japan

1 HANA Shokichi Kina from *Bloodline*
The heartbreakingly beautiful vocals of Tomoko Kina and Ry Cooder's guitar on the original of this much-covered classic have never been bettered.

2 MANGETSU NO YUBE Soul Flower Union from *Ghost Hits 93–96*
Composed for the victims of the Kobe earthquake. Rock meets chindon with attitude and a timeless melody.

3 RINGO OIWAKE Hibari Misora from *Greatest Hits*
One of Japan's most famous songs, based on an old folk tune, performed by one of the country's greatest-ever singers.

4 TOKYO BOOGIE-WOOGIE Shizuko Kasagi from *Queen of Boogie*
Japanese music meets boogie-woogie in the post-war years. A classic Hattori composition sung by an early pop legend.

5 ROOCHOO GUMBO Haruomo Hosono from *Bon Voyage*
A mid-1970s stroke of musical genius as Okinawan music gets a New Orleans piano riff.

6 SOKAKU-REIBO Goro Yamaguchi from *A Bell Ringing in the Empty Sky*
Classic solo shakuhachi from one of the great masters, inspired by Zen Buddhism.

7 SHIMA UTA The Boom from *Shima Uta – Grandos Exitos*
The song that cemented the 1990s Okinawa music boom. Rock band turns south for inspiration and comes up with a classic.

8 SANOSE Tadamaru Sakuragawa from *Ullambana DX*
Growling ondo singer gets the feet moving with ten minutes of infectious musical madness.

9 SHIMA JIMA KAISHA Nenes from *Koza Dabasa*
The glorious sound of the four Okinawan women singers set to a slow and sumptuous backing that includes Ry Cooder.

10 TOPATUMI Oki Dub Ainu Band from *Oki Dub Ainu Band*
An ancient Ainu tune gets a radical dub reworking with a pulsating rhythm and Oki's hypnotic tonkori.

Korea

sweet seoul music and beyond

Korean gayageum (plucked zither) master
Byungki Hwang
Kuk Sooyong

Too often overshadowed by its neighbours, this small divided peninsula on Asia's northeast coast retains its own proudly distinct music styles. South Korea has a vibrant and stylistically wide-ranging musical life, and is home to the third largest music market in Asia. North Korea, by contrast, echoes to ideologically approved music that tends towards the banal, and is politically straitjacketed in a "light music" style. Although this seems imitative of Soviet pop, in reality it has its roots in 1930s Korean pentatonic songs. **Rob Provine** introduces Korea's ancient traditions, while **Keith Howard** looks, south and north, at the distinctive contemporary sounds.

distinct Korean musical identity can be traced to the fifth century, and has been well documented since the fifteenth century. State institutions charged with preserving and teaching court music have been in operation since the seventh century; their current direct descendant is the National Center for Korean Traditional Performing Arts in Seoul (*www.ncktpa.go.kr*). Japanese colonization in the first half of the twentieth century left a large recorded legacy of Korean music, early popular songs and Western imports.

The subsequent widespread adoption of Western culture has ironically fuelled nostalgia for local arts, which have enjoyed revival and updating in recent decades. This began in the 1960s with government sponsorship of performance arts as "Intangible Cultural Assets", and as student demonstrations against military rule appropriated folk music, updating it as *minjung munhwa*, a "culture of the masses". By the early 1970s, **p'ungmul** (farmers' band percussion music) had almost died out, but now you can find it everywhere, among students and striking factory workers, and in an updated urban staged form, **samulnori**. Shops in Seoul, meanwhile, are bursting with traditional musical instruments, and music teachers are enjoying prosperous times.

Traditional Music

Korean traditional music has several strands, the most formal of which are **court**, **aristocratic** and **religious music**.

Court Music

Korean **court music** is mostly orchestral, highly refined, and an acquired taste. But it has a majesty and integrity all its own and a very long heritage, dating back to the Chosŏn dynasty (1392–1910).

The main place you'll hear live court music today is the **National Center for Korean Traditional Performing Arts** in Seoul, where highly-trained musicians preserve, perform, and teach traditional music and dance. Regular performances there feature the better-known court music and dance pieces, which can be bought on dozens of CDs at the shop inside. Court rituals are still performed annually at the shrines to Confucius and Royal Ancestors. Mixed court and folk performances regularly take place for tourists at several other concert venues in Seoul, while each province and city, and some twenty universities have traditional performing orchestras.

Court music was originally divided into Chinese ritual music (*aak*), Koreanized music of Chinese origin (*tangak*) and indigenous music (*hyangak*). **Aak** was introduced to Korea from China in 1116 and has since been revived and transformed. Contemporary aak traces its ancestry back to a reconstruction of 1430, using Chinese written melodies from the twelfth century. Today, there are just two surviving melodies totalling about eight minutes of extremely slow, stark and stately music, played only at the semi-annual **Rite to Confucius** in Seoul and in concerts at the National Center. This music uses only ritual instruments of Chinese origin, including the extraordinary sets of sixteen tuned bronze bells *(p'yŏnjong)* and stone chimes *(p'yŏn'gyŏng)*. The **tangak** repertoire also consists of only two short orchestral pieces, known as *Nagyangch'un* (Springtime in Luoyang) and *Pohŏja* (Pacing the Void).

A good example of **hyangak** is the fifteen-minute banquet piece *Sujech'ŏn* (Long Life According with Heaven). Its lead instruments – none of which are used in aak – are the loud, oboe-like *p'iri*, the two-stringed *haegŭm* fiddle and the seven-stringed *ajaeng* zither, the latter bowed with a rosined stick instead of horsehair, producing a strikingly raspy and penetrating sound. Other important orchestral pieces are the slow-moving eighty-minute *Yŏmillak* (Pleasure with the People), which employs the largest traditional orchestra, complete with bells and chimes, and *Ch'wit'a* (Blowing and Beating), regularly paced music originally for military use. A special type of hyangak is the two suites of pieces performed at the annual **Rite to Royal Ancestors**: *Pot'aep'yŏng* (Preserving the Peace) and *Chŏngdaeŏp* (Founding the Dynasty). Originally composed and arranged in the fifteenth century to replace supposedly Chinese aak with something more appealing to the royal ancestors in question, the music now performed is still closely related to five-hundred-year-old notations.

Aristocratic Music

Aristocratic chamber music (*chŏngak*) was originally intended as informal entertainment for members of the ruling class; by the eighteenth century, however, it had become associated with an emerging middle class. It comprises both instrumental ensemble music and vocal music.

The purely instrumental repertoire consists almost entirely of various versions (for strings, wind or mixed ensembles) of one suite of pieces called **Yŏngsan hoesang** (Preaching on Spirit Mountain). The music starts at an amazingly slow pace, but towards the end – about fifty minutes later – builds to more cheerful dance pieces known as *T'aryŏng* and *Kunak*. The chief **aristocratic vocal music**, known as **kagok**, comprises 25 complex and lengthy pieces for singers accompanied by strings, wind and percussion. The lyrics of another genre, **shijo**, consist simply of three-line poems. Often performed only by a singer and drummer, and lasting around four minutes, the aristocracy once composed and sang shijo at parties.

Religious Music

The music played for the Rite to Confucius and the Rite to Royal Ancestors is in the Confucian tradition – ceremonial but not, strictly speaking, religious. Korean religious music belongs to the native shamanistic and imported Buddhist traditions, although in recent decades attempts have been made to create a Korean Christian music, notably through the group **Yegahoe** (Christian Praise Society).

The traditional repertoire of **Buddhist chant** consists of three main types: highly complex, extended chants (*pŏmp'ae*) performed by highly trained singers; rapid sutra chanting (*yŏmbul*) performed by monks and followers; and Korean-language folk-style music (*hwachŏng*) on Buddhist themes. Today, pŏmp'ae is rarely heard outside formal services, but yŏmbul is everywhere, usually sung on recordings by a solo monk accompanied only by a small wooden bell (*mokt'ak*) or gong (*ching*). Beginning with the meditative album *Son* by Kim Young Dong in 1989, Buddhist "light music" setting sutras as children's songs and hymns proliferated during the 1990s and today is sold in most temples.

Shamanistic music comes in two main forms: vocal chanting of texts (*muga*) and instrumental improvisation (*shinawi*) – the latter may include a vocalist singing lexically meaningless syllables. **Shinawi** can be rather like Dixieland jazz, with animated rhythms on *changgo* (a double-headed hourglass drum) coupled to several melody instruments playing simultaneously, creating a raucous, swaying and danceable polyphony. Shinawi spawned a concert form during the first decades of the twentieth century, moving it away from ritual, and this latter form features on many CD releases.

Korean Folk

In Korea, "**folk music**" spans the gamut from what ordinary people play and sing to highly professional genres. What holds it together is a consistent and easily recognizable set of rhythmic patterns and a less well-defined set of melodic modes. You can see regular performances of local folk songs, percussion bands, mask-dance plays and staged shamanic rituals at several outdoor venues in Seoul and its environs. Shinawi, *p'ansori* and *sanjo* are essentially indoor forms performed in standard concert venues and at annual festivals in Chŏnju and Namwŏn, cities to the south of Seoul.

P'ansori and Sanjo

One of the most striking folk genres, **p'ansori** is performed by a single singer and drummer (playing a *puk* barrel drum). A story, presented in song, mime and narration, may continue for five or more hours. For each song, the singer cues the drummer to a particular rhythmic cycle. The drummer (and often the audience) reacts to the singer with shouts of encouragement.

There are only five traditional stories in the active p'ansori repertoire, supplemented by a rapidly evolving contemporary repertoire. Years of difficult training are required for this demanding form: singers, by tradition, practise near a loud waterfall or in large caves to develop the powerful voice required. It really is grassroots music – intricate, rough-edged, enormously appealing and popular. Famous p'ansori singers include **Pak Tongjin** (d. 2003), **Sŏng Ch'angsun**, **Cho Sanghyŏn**, and **Ahn Sooksun**.

The instrumental form **sanjo** arranges rhythmic patterns and melodic modes in a standard order from slow to fast. Drawing melodic and expressive inspiration from p'ansori and shamanic shinawi, sanjo sets a melodic instrument against a changgo rhythmic accompaniment. A single sanjo lasts anything from ten minutes to an hour, and is popularly played on the *kayagŭm*, a twelve-stringed plucked zither; the *kŏmun'go*, a six-stringed plectrum-plucked zither; the *taegŭm*, a transverse bamboo flute; the p'iri, the haegŭm and the ajaeng. Although there are different schools of sanjo, they are all traced back to Kim Ch'angjo (d. 1918). Performers to look out for include **Chaesuk Lee**, **Yang Seung Hee**, **Mun Chaesuk** (all kayagŭm), **Yi Saenggang** (taegŭm), and **Wŏn Kwangho** (kŏmun'go).

Describing the instrumental ornamentation in these solo styles, **Byungki Hwang** (see box on p.663) observes: "What is essential when playing a melody on the kayagŭm is the vibrato and the microtonal shading on the notes. If a melody drops down you can think of it like a waterfall: the bottom note needs to vibrate in the way that water bubbles at the bottom of a waterfall. This is something that gives Korean music its special character."

Folk Song

Korean folk song comes in several varieties – chief among them being local **min'yo** (folk songs proper), categorized according to several regional melodic modes corresponding to dialect areas; the professional **shin min'yo** (new folk songs); and **chapka** (miscellaneous songs) with more fixed melodies. Min'yo from Seoul and the central area are generally in a lyrical and simple pentatonic mode and have a gently moving tempo. Those from the southwest are more expressive and often very sad, using a mainly tritonic melodic mode called *kyemyŏnjo* (also much used in p'ansori and sanjo), while the northwest uses a more nasal voice with considerable rubato. Favourite songs are the central "Arirang", the southwestern "Yukchabaegi" and the northwestern "Sushimga".

P'ungmul

One of the most appealing and increasingly international forms of Korean music is **p'ungmul** (in older texts called *nongak*). This raucous, complicated genre has dirt under its musical fingernails. In its full form, it consists of twenty or more percussionists playing small gongs (*kkwaenggwari*), large ching gongs, puk and changgo drums, and acrobatic dancing.

Since the late 1970s, small samulnori percussion groups deriving their style from p'ungmul have become very popular among Korea's urban population, with some travelling widely abroad. The best known is the quartet **SamulNori**, which created and gave its name to this new genre. These groups play complex percussion music at a professional level, and many contemporary concerts of traditional music feature it as a climax. To see these musicians dancing, wearing hats with long swirling ribbons, is truly spectacular. SamulNori have continued their pioneering role, joining forces with rock and jazz musicians such as SXL and Red Sun to create fusion music, and performing as soloists in concertos with Korean and Western orchestras.

Contemporary Traditions

Since 2001, **GugakFM** (99.1 FM in Korea or streamed from *www.gugakfm.co.kr*) has broadcast traditional Korean music with a twist. Much of the programming consists of new versions of older music: for the 2002 World Cup, one of its programmes mixed jazz piano and Korean percussion, rock, opera, samulnori and new compositions. Today, close to half of all traditional Korean concerts include one or more new compositions, which are celebrated in an annual **Gugak Festival**.

CMP Records

Percussion quartet SamulNori

Flautist and composer **Kim Young Dong** initiated many of the creative moves, starting with songs in the 1970s, moving to film and TV drama scores, then to instrumental compositions and ambient meditation music. Most of his music neatly combines East and West by juxtaposing melodies sung or played on iconic Korean instruments with guitar and keyboard harmonies. **Kim Soochul** followed suit with his million-selling soundtrack to the 1993 film *Seopyonje*.

Over a twenty-year period, the crossover group **Seulgidoong** have produced a series of vocal and instrumental albums that mix old and new. "Shin paennorae", a West Coast fishing song arranged by **Won Il**, is perhaps their greatest success to date. Their haegŭm player, **Soonyon Chung**, has single-handedly popularized her instrument among teenagers, and in 2003 their former singer **Yong Woo Kim** reached the pop charts with his album of updated folksongs, *Chilkkonaengi*. Other significant groups are **The Lim**, **Dasureum**, **Kuunmong**, and anything involving jazz pianist **Yang Bang Eun,** Won Il, or composer/pianist **Lim Dong Chang**.

Fusion is increasingly the name of the game. The traditional kayagŭm zither is now heard in quartets (notably **Sagye**), for whom arrangements of Bach and Vivaldi are as fashionable as Korean arrangements and original compositions, while a kayagŭm orchestra recently released an album of Beatles songs. Not all of these experiments work: the pentatonic tuning of Korean instruments hampers the playing of heptatonic Western scales. Composers have attempted to develop traditional instruments, increasing pitch ranges, making them heptatonic and increasing their volume. The twelve-stringed kayagŭm, for example, first became larger (for theatre use), then smaller (for children to play); then it evolved into seventeen, nineteen, twenty-one and twenty-five stringed versions.

Korean Pop

"Korea wave" (*Hallyu*, also known as "K-wave") swept Asia at the dawn of the new millennium. As *Time* reported in July 2002:

Teenagers from Tokyo to Taipei swoon over performers such as singer **Park Ji Yoon** and boy band **Shinhwa** ... "Korea is the next epicenter of pop culture in Asia", says Jessica Kam, vice-president for MTV Networks Asia.

That year, **BoA** became the first Korean solo artist to have both a debut single and album top Japan's pop charts, and the Korean domestic music market had a turnover of $300 million, primarily from pop music by the likes of boy bands **god** (**G**roove **O**ver **D**ose) and **H.O.T.**, who sold ten million albums in their seven-year existence.

Ppongtchak

Think of a constantly repeating foxtrot rhythm (*ppongtchak, ppongtchak*), and this onomatopoeic word becomes clear. It was formerly called *yuhaengga* and *taejung kayo*, a song style akin to Japanese *enka* that emerged in Korea in the 1920s. Ppongtchak are fixed in solid duple meter, contrasting with the dominance of triple meter in traditional music. The first examples set Korean words to foreign melodies, "Glorification of Death", recorded by the soprano **Yun Shimdŏk** in 1926 and using a melody by Ivanovich being particularly well-known. Ppongtchak blossomed with the growth of the recording industry, continuing after the defeat of Japan brought Korean independence in 1945.

One of the most prominent singers in recent decades has been **Lee Mi-ja**, whose career began in the 1950s. Her "Tongbaek Agassi/Camellia Maiden", released in 1964 but later banned by the South Korean ethics committee because of supposedly overt Japanese "colour", is particularly typical. Today, ppongtchak remains popular where the elderly gather to gossip and dance. It is often the background music played in cafés and on buses, and a staple of local karaoke machines. Famous singers include **Nam Jin**, **Na Huna**, **Choo Hyun-mi** (the "Queen of Trot") and **E-Pak-Sa** (the stage name of Yi Yongsŏk).

American Influences

The Korean War (1950–53) brought many American servicemen to Korea, and from 1951 the American Forces Korea Network (AFKN) broadcast American popular music across the peninsula. Many Korean stars such as **Patti Kim**, **Yun Pokhŭi** and **Hyŏn Mi** began their careers singing in military clubs. They imitated popular styles across the Pacific and added supposedly "Oriental" songs such as "Slow Boat to China" and "China Night". The **Kim Sisters** went on to travel to America; they were known for playing Korean instruments and singing folksongs such as "Arirang" and "Toraji t'aryŏng/Bellflower Song", as well as American songs. By the 1960s, American styles were Koreanized in, for example, "Toraji Mambo" and "Nilliri Mambo".

The American folk revival was mirrored in Korean **t'ong guitar**, songs accompanied by

Politically outspoken singer Kim Min'gi

acoustic guitar. From the late 1960s, this style often fused covers of American songs with elements of the earlier ppongtchak. Rather than war and nuclear destruction, the lyrics spoke of love, or the emerging urban youth culture. More political songs arose away from the mainstream, within what became known as the **Norae Undong** (Song Movement). Political oppression led college students to develop alternative styles, fuelled by pro-democracy movements and festivals that promoted the local over the foreign. **Kim Min'gi** (b.1951) was arrested for fomenting anti-government sentiment in 1972 by singing his "Kkot p'iunŭn ai/A Child Growing a Flower".

By the 1980s t'ong guitar had transformed into ballads sung by teen heart-throb stars, which have remained a permanent feature of Korean pop, often coupled with soft rock. **Cho Young Pil** was perhaps the best-known male singer in the 1980s, while **Kim Hyun Chul** and **Shin Seung Hoon** led in the 1990s. **Lee Sun-Hee** is one of the most enduring female ballad singers.

Rap, Punk and Dance

In March 1992, **Seo Taiji** devised a grammar for Korean rap and kick-started contemporary pop production, launching a solo career in 1996. An underground heavy metal scene had developed in the 1980s, and Seo started his career in one such band, **Shinawe**. As travel restrictions were lifted and satellite TV introduced, Koreans began to learn about contemporary American pop trends. Albums by **015B** and **Shin Hae Chul** and his group **N.EX.T** freely mixed jazz, metal, latin, acoustic and rap. The 1990s pop scene was characterized by appropriation, diversification and expansion

of the market. Music videos arrived with the first domestic reggae track, **Kim Gun Mo**'s "P'inggye/Excuse". In 1994 the group **Roo'ra** combined reggae with rap. Later, hip-hop, dance and techno came to dominate.

Punk took to the underground in the mid 1990s, with bands such as **Crying Nut, Yellow Kitchen** and **No Brain** laying claim to Koreanized punk. The mainstream has remained much softer, with dance groups such as **CLON**, H.O.T., **Shinhwa**, **S.E.S.** and the female **Fin.K.L**, and soloists such as **Yoo Seungjun** dominating video space before BoA's debut. Today, chasing shrinking album sales in the world's most broadband-savvy country, Korean pop is ever-changing. Current stars **M.C.Mong**, **Rain**, **Se7en** and **SG Wanabee** are likely to be history by the time you read this.

North Korea – Follow-my-Leader

North Korean music is difficult to obtain beyond the hermetically sealed borders of this totalitarian state. Occasional websites in Japan and elsewhere, and the Pyongyang-based Korea Publications Exchange Association, offer songs to download or buy on CD, but the massive output of the state-run recording company, KMC, has proved impossible to track down in its entirety. Between them, the two state-sponsored pop groups, **Wanjaesan Light Music Band** and **Pochonbo Electric Ensemble**, claim to have published 180 CDs. Both bands have existed since the 1980s and, continuing a Stalinist socialist tradition, are named after supposedly famous battle sites where the founder of North Korea, Kim Il Sung, allegedly defeated hordes of Japanese imperialists during 1930s colonial rule. Other recordings appear on the **Songs of Korea** series (which ostensibly runs to 64 albums).

After World War II, many left-leaning artists moved to the northern state; many were mercilessly purged as ideology shifted towards the notion of proletarian artists. Kim noted that musicians had "lost touch with life" and lagged behind "rapidly advancing reality". The first new song to meet his approval, "The Song of General Kim Il Sung", was written in 1947 by the farmer **Kim Wŏn'gyun** (b. 1917); the same composer then wrote the (northern) national anthem. Revolutionary songs and orchestral tone poems became the only music permitted until the late 1950s, when, following the Chinese Great Leap Forward, musicians were sent to the countryside to learn (and rewrite the words to) folk songs. In the 1970s came "revolutionary operas" and "people's operas", with the former extolling "immortal" triumphs of the leadership, and the latter, achievements of the populace. The first opera was *Sea of Blood*, followed by *The Flower Girl* and *A True Daughter of the Party* – these are still performed today by a collective known as the Sea of Blood Opera Company.

Traditional instruments have all been revised in keeping with official dogma: North Koreans refer to these as "improved" (*kaeryang*) instruments, capable of playing both Korean and Western music. Thus, the kayagŭm zither has grown from twelve to twenty-one strings, with nylon replacing the silk strings of old, while the single two-stringed haegŭm fiddle has developed into four distinct four-stringed instruments corresponding to the violin, viola, cello and bass of a Western orchestra. The kŏmun'go zither, long associated with the aristocracy rather than with popular culture, was abandoned. These adapted traditional instruments feature in operas, are sometimes used to accompany folk songs, and are taught and performed at "children's palaces" and at the Pyongyang Music and Dance College.

Strict ideological control is maintained over all music production and performance. Apart from those already mentioned, the best-known groups are the **Mansudae Art Troupe** and the various bands and choirs attached to the People's Army;

the primary Western orchestra is known either as the **State Symphony Orchestra** or the **National Philharmonic Orchestra**.

Ideology favours songs, which by definition are popular, and thousands have been written that mix the earlier ppongtchak style with conservative Western styles. Song titles give a taste of the joys: "Tankers and Girls", "My Homeland is Bright under the Star and Sun", "We Shall Hold Bayonets More Firmly", "Song Of Snipers", "The Joy Of Bumper Harvest Overflows", "The World Envies Us" and so on. Even today, there can be no mention of political oppression, economic collapse, or the desperate hunger that many millions have faced. Indeed, some songs cock a snook at the world outside, such as Wangjaesan's "Socialism is Ours", popularized after the unification of Germany:

We go straight along the path we have chosen,
Though others forsake, we remain faithful.
Socialism is ours, socialism is ours,
Socialism defended by our Party's red flag is ours.

Even love songs must be ideologically correct, so "The Girl I Love" runs:

It is good if a girl has a nice figure,
But better if she is an able worker and good-
*   natured with it;*
I like a girl who makes life pleasant
By singing the songs of creation!

Korean Music in China

Jilin Province in northeastern China is home to the Korean Autonomous Region of **Yanbian**. In the 1930s, Koreans settled here in what was then Japanese-controlled Manchukuo, joining others who had migrated earlier (other Korean diasporic communities are found in North and South America, Uzbekistan and Kazakhstan). The region sits across the Tumen River from North Korea, so North Korean influence was mixed with Chinese political ideology to create "Korean music with Chinese characteristics".

The Yanbian branch of the Chinese Music Association has for the last three decades campaigned for local production, supporting a policy whereby the Yanbian People's Radio should devote fifty percent of airtime to Yanbian music. Since 1984 Yanbian TV has produced its own programmes, including weekly concerts, and so includes local content, but as state funding has declined, so all media companies have had to become more consumer-driven. Jilin Nationalities Audiovisual Publishing produces local recordings, but in the past supplemented these with North Korean and Chinese recordings. One notable singer was **Granny Swallow** (Kim Insuk), named after her trademark "Chebiga Torowanne / The Swallow's Return", who recorded yuhaengga and folk songs on a 1995 cassette. Since 2000, CDs and VCDs have gradually replaced cassettes and videos, mostly appearing on the Arirang label.

Cui Jian, one of China's best-known rock musicians, is ethnically Korean, but made his name in Beijing. In Yanbian, the conservatism of cultural officers hampered the development of local pop into the 1990s, which meant that South Korean pop made considerable inroads. **Jin Haixin** and **Pak Sŭngnyŏng** were two early local pop musicians who moved to Beijing to try to develop their careers. More recently, **Pop Boy** emerged from a Yanbian pop training centre and, as **Arirang**, found fame across China in 2002. Upcoming groups include the hip-hop band **S.T.** and the singer **Kim Ae**.

Byungki Hwang

Perhaps Korea's most widely revered traditional musician, Byungki Hwang is certainly one of the most likeable artists I've encountered. He has a wonderfully calm manner, simultaneously learned and down-to-earth. His dour features readily crinkle into a smile and a sense of the mischievous never seems far away.

He's fond of using elaborate and often humorous imagery redolent of nature to describe Korean music – and by extension, his own. This ranges from a deeply traditional sanjo to wildly avant-garde pieces that find him worrying the strings of his kayagŭm with changgo sticks or even a cello bow. His sparse, minimalist oeuvre is something of an antidote to the high-speed world modern Koreans find themselves in:

"My hope is to create music like a fountain of water from the mountainside. Even though I know modern people like Coca-Cola, 7-Up or Fanta, I like no taste! Just pure water! But I think people have some unconscious hope to drink pure water", he chuckles.

For Maestro Hwang, less has always been more. He began to play kayagŭm at the age of fourteen in Pusan during the ruinous Korean War, eventually studying both court and folk music.

"I never dreamt to live on music. So I just naturally studied law while I continuously practised music. After the war, Korea was very poor and tragic, so we had no room in our minds to think about our own culture."

As the country recovered, interest in culture blossomed, and Hwang was appointed to a post at the newly established Department of Korean Traditional Music at Seoul National University in 1959. Prestigious international appearances followed and he recorded his first album in 1965. Though a magnetic performer, he gives only a handful of concerts each year.

"The thing I like most is to play kayagŭm in my room. I don't like letting people hear my music. It's the least performance. That's my style. I don't know why", he admits with a grin.

Jon Lusk

Songs become the basis for mass gymnastics and dancing displays for holidays, festivals and the birthdays of the Great Leader (Kim Il Sung) and the Dear Leader (his son Kim Jong Il); distributed to artistic units in every school and factory, activists teach them with appropriate dancing steps.

Kim Il Sung died in 1994, just as CD publishing got going in Pyongyang, and the resulting impasse allowed KMC to briefly publish albums of folk songs and foreign songs (on Wangjaesan's 23rd–45th albums) until Kim Jong Il gained absolute control. In 1997, production resumed its sound ideological footing with Wangjaesan 46, Pochonbo 84 and *Songs of Korea* 56. And there it solidly remains, caught in a veritable time warp of denial.

DISCOGRAPHY Korea

Traditional

There are many good CD compilations of traditional Korean music, although few are easily available abroad. The major Korean music distributor, Synnara (*www.synnara.co.kr*), has the largest catalogue of traditional music, while Seoul Records (*www.seoulrecords.co.kr*) has several hundred albums in its catalogue. The National Center for Korean Traditional Performing Arts produces annual CDs devoted to court, folk or shaman music. Along with MBC's mammoth 102-CD set of folk songs (published between 1989 and 1994), these are never sold, but distributed worldwide to libraries and institutions.

 Corée/Korea: Chants Rituels de l'Île de Chindo
VDE-Gallo/AIMP, Switzerland
Three characteristic southwestern folk song repertories: rice-cultivation songs, funeral songs, and the women's song-and-dance genre *Kanggangsullae*.

⭐ **The Selection of Korean Classical Music, Yŏmillak**
Edition RZ, Germany
A double CD with a complete eighty-minute performance of this magnificent court piece plus its variant pieces.

⊙ **Shamanistic Ceremonies of Chindo**
JVC, Japan
The most successful of JVC's shaman music releases, featuring a team of "holders" of the Intangible Cultural Asset – the preserved form of the shaman ritual.

⊙ **Yŏngsan Hoesang**
Synnara, Korea
The classic performances of this aristocratic suite, in all its versions, on four CDs recorded by veteran musicians. Austere yet calming.

Lee Chaesuk

Alone amongst Korean musicians, Lee has mastered all six of the major schools of sanjo for the kayagŭm zither, performing and documenting them during her long career.

 Korean Kayagŭm Sanjo
SOASIS, UK

A full, 56-minute digital recording, with changgo drum accompaniment by Kim Sunok, of the most famous sanjo school, that of Kim Chukp'a (the granddaughter of the originator of the genre). Links to a book including a full notation.

Seoul Ensemble of Traditional Music

A conservatoire-trained group of musicians founded in 1990, who perform both court and folk music.

⊙ Korea: Seoul Ensemble of Traditional Music
Network, Germany

Aesthetically pleasing and top-notch collection of aristocratic chamber music and sanjo, with a concluding shinawi for ensemble.

Yang Seung-Hee

Recently appointed by the government as "holder" of the Intangible Cultural Asset for sanjo, and widely acknowledged for her sensitive performing.

⊙ Gayagum Sanjo
Seoul Records, Korea

Like the SOASIS release, a recording of the Kim Chukp'a sanjo school, but with an abbreviated introduction and penultimate movements.

Contemporary

⊙ Endless Song, Arirang
Gugak Festival, Korea

This is what the folk song "Arirang" has become: jazz, blues, hip-hop, rap, ensemble and orchestral arrangements. Tracks by Cho PD (the son of SamulNori leader Kim Duk Soo) and One Sun are particular favourites. Includes an English-language booklet.

⊙ Songs of Korea Vol. 34
KMC, DPR Korea

Instrumental versions of songs designed for visitors to Kim Il Sung's mausoleum, so that the sequence matches the time

spent standing on moving walkways, waiting to enter the chamber, praying before the embalmed cadaver, and exiting to the "Internationale".

⊙ Yusŏnggira Tŭttŭn Kayosa (History of Korean Popular Song)
Synnara, Korea

A collection of 185 popular songs on ten CDs originally recorded between 1925 and 1945. "Glorification of Death" is on the first CD. Unfortunately, the highly informative booklets are in Korean.

BoA

BoA was seventeen when she topped the charts in 2002. Singing in Korean, Japanese and English, she went on to dominate Korea's "soft" cultural exports to East and Southeast Asia, receiving numerous awards.

⊙ Atlantis Princess
SM Media, Korea

This remains BoA's best album to date, neatly encapsulating the world of Asian teen pop.

Byungki Hwang

Korea's best-known contemporary composer for the kayagŭm, and a fine performer.

★ The Best of Korean Gayageum Music
ARC Music, UK

Two previously unrecorded 1970s works coupled to recent compositions, with Hwang as zither soloist. A mix of meditative music, music for the tea ceremony and flowing song-like melodies.

Kim Min-Ki

The best-known political singer of the 1970s. While most t'ong-guitar vocalists avoided controversial issues, Kim Min-Ki went straight for the jugular.

⊙ Kim Min-Ki Vols 1–4
Seoul Records, Korea

Kim Min-Ki's best songs. Vol. 1 includes "A Child Growing a Flower", his notorious protest against military dictatorship. The flower is a metaphor for democracy.

Kim Soochul

Kim came to attention as a guitarist in the early 1980s before settling into a role as a composer and performer, following the path of Kim Young Dong with crossover and fusion scores for TV dramas and films. He received important commissions for the 1988 Seoul Olympics and the 2002 World Cup.

⊙ Seopyonje
Seoul Records, Korea

This is the most successful Korean soundtrack ever. The film, released in 1993, is a dramatization of the life of p'ansori singers, and the score mixes vocals sung by the accomplished Ahn Sooksun, Kim Myŏnggon and others with synthesizer and traditional taegŭm flute.

Pochonbo Electronic Ensemble

A band, or rather a franchise to which state authorities assign musicians, which has the largest album output of any in North Korea. Some albums have titles, and some feature specific "people's artists" – singers of merit. The "electronic" in the title refers to an instrumentation strong on synths and electric guitars.

☉ Pochonbo Electronic Ensemble, Vol. 29
PEE (KMC), DPR Korea

In a sense, it doesn't matter which of the 120-plus CDs you listen to, since the song style and the instrumental arrangement remain much the same throughout. This one has long-term favourites including "We Are Glad", "My Country is the Best" and "Tankers and Girls".

SamulNori

The original and by far the best quartet playing the contemporary urban form of p'ungmul.

★ Kim Duk Soo SamulNori
Synnara, Korea

A set of two CDs giving the core SamulNori canon of six pieces which assemble rhythmic patterns from around the peninsula. These are the recordings budding Korean musicians use to learn the repertoire.

☉ Then Comes the White Tiger
ECM, Germany

For two decades, SamulNori has developed new repertoire by combining with jazz musicians – here the group Red Sun, featuring Wolfgang Puschnig on sax and singer Linda Sharrock. Many of the tracks build on the SamulNori canon.

Seo Taiji and Boys

Seo Taiji and two other youngsters. With the liberal use of English lyrics and agile dance movements, they became an instant hit among teenagers and introduced the era of Korean rap.

★ Seo Taiji & Boys II
Bando, Korea

This 1993 album features one of their greatest hits, "Hayoga", and a couple of fusion attempts that add Lee Jeong Sik on jazzy sax and Kim Duk Soo on SamulNori instruments.

Seulgidoong

Founded in 1985 to perform Korean songs with a mix of traditional and Western instruments, and now in its fourth incarnation, this group has launched a number of solo careers and spawned many imitators.

☉ Seulgidoong
Rock Records, Korea

The first five albums, digitally remastered and repackaged as a set. Two CDs feature songs mixing Westernized vocals with Korean instruments, one showcases the student songs of Kim Young Dong and two are instrumental.

Yong Woo Kim

Kim trained as a singer of aristocratic songs, but during university vacations travelled to the countryside, working with elderly folk singers. He made his name by updating songs, taking out the vibrato and raspiness of regional styles and replacing it with a blend particularly popular amongst today's urban youth.

☉ Chilkkonaengi
Universal, Korea

Kim's chart-busting fourth album, from 2003. Some of the folk songs are immediately recognizable, while others are so transformed that they appear to be contemporary pop.

PLAYLIST
Korea

1 KYŎNGNOKMUGANG CHIGOK Orchestra of the National Center from *The Selection of Korean Classical Music, Yŏmillak*
A shortened variant on the most respected of Korean court compositions, "Yŏmillak", featuring the full orchestra including clapperless bells and stone chimes.

2 CHINYANGJO Lee Chaesuk from *Lee Chaesuk: Korean Kayagŭm Sanjo*
The slow and highly emotional first movement of sanjo, sensitively played on the twelve-stringed zither in an authoritative performance.

3 DARHA NOPIGOM Byungki Hwang from *Best of Korean Gayageum Music*
A meditative work based on an old children's song excellently combining the world of today with ancient traditions.

4 YONGCH'ŎN'GŎM Yong Woo Kim from *Chilkkonaengi*
An old folk-song associated with travelling performance troupes, learnt from an elderly singer in Cheju, now given a contemporary vibe.

5 WORLD WIDE ARIRANG Mr J, Cho PD and others from *Endless Song, Arirang*
This brilliant update of what is virtually Korea's national folk song opens with very non-Korean didgeridoo, moving through rap accompanied by changgo drum, and settling on a full-bodied quasi-traditional rendition.

6 NANJANG (THE MEETING PLACE) Red Sun and SamulNori from *Then Comes the White Tiger*
An update of farmers' percussion bands of old, based on a prayer for blessings known as "Pinari", but here reborn within a frame of jazz and scat vocalizations.

7 PAN'GAP SŬMNIDA/WE ARE GLAD Pochonbo Electronic Ensemble from *Pochonbo Electronic Ensemble Vol. 29*
I once got thrown out of a restaurant on the Chinese side of the North Korean border for not being adequately appreciative of the lyrics ("Thank you, Great Leader, for this paradise on earth") after two waitresses insisted on singing this song.

8 HAYŎGA Seo Taiji and Boys from *Seo Taiji and Boys II*
Seo's most successful track from the early 1990s. Rap meets traditional music, but it works.

9 ATLANTIS PRINCESS BoA from *Atlantis Princess*
Reaching for the stars in a fantasy wonderland that encapsulates much of Korea's teen pop.

Laos

lam sessions

Khaen and ching players at rocket festival
John Clewley

Although Laos remains a communist state, tourism and trade have brought rapid change to this once sleepy land. Bridges now span the Mekong River north and south, and the final section of the country's first railway, connecting the capital Vientiane with Bangkok, will open in 2009. Vientiane is a bustling city nowadays, with new buildings going up everywhere, and the old Morning Market has been replaced by a plaza (thankfully the music stores remain). But despite the increasing pace of life, Laotians still find time for festivals and holidays, which enable visitors to sample the lively urban music scene and many different provincial styles of folk music. John Clewley dons his *pha salong* (sarong) and joins the party.

Tiny, land-locked Laos has a population of nearly six million, spread thinly over a mountainous country slightly larger than Britain. Its fertile valleys, including the mighty Mekong River, are inhabited by the lowland Lao (Lao Loum), who make up sixty percent of the population, followed by the Lao Thueng (highlanders) with over thirty percent and finally the Lao Soung (hill tribes). Across the Mekong in northeast Thailand, the Isan region is home to another eighteen million ethnic Laotian speakers who share a common culture, including music.

On the Lam

The Laotians have a saying to describe themselves: they are the people who live in stilt houses, eat *pa daek* (raw, fermented fish) and *khao niow* (sticky rice), and blow the **khaen**, the Laotian bamboo-reed pipe. Swirling around the epic tales told by the **mor lam** (singer), the **mor khaen** (master of the khaen) creates a pulsing, rhythmically hypnotic sound full of organ-like chords.

The khaen is played all over Laos and northeast Thailand, part of an Asian tradition of reed pipes that includes the ancient *sheng* pipes of china, the *sho* in Japan and Korea's *saenghwang*. Many mountain-dwelling tribes of Southeast Asia have their own version, and it is found from the Bangladesh-Burma border to Borneo, but the **Lao khaen**, which can feature sixteen pipes taller than a man, is the most sophisticated of all the bamboo-reed mouth-organs.

The instrument is used to accompany performances of call-and-response folk-songs known as **lam** (**khap** in the northern and central regions), whose lyrics draw on anything from long epic narratives to current events in the news (*lam pheun*). When pairs or groups of mor lam singers perform courtship-style verbal jousts (the most common is a male-female pair), the khaen provides the basic musical pulse, supporting the melody. Typical ensembles feature two mor lam, a mor khaen, a **phin** (plucked three-stringed lute), **so** (fiddle), drums, **khui** (bamboo flute) and **ching** (small temple bells). As the mor khaen pumps out the music, the singers often make demonstrative gestures about or at each other, and the mood is light-hearted and often bawdy – a style originally known as *lam pa nyah*, but which has since developed into the more theatrical *lam glawn*, associated in Laos and Thailand with all-night mor lam sessions.

There are regional differences in Lao folk-song styles, owing to the fact that the present-day Lao People's Democratic Republic essentially combines three ancient kingdoms – Luang Prabang in the north, Vientiane in the centre and Champassak in the south. Each province in Laos has its own style, the most influential being **lam Saravane**, from the southern town of that name, which is also popular in Thailand. Also look out for **khap tham** and the slower, moodier **khaplam wai** in Luang Prabang, the beautiful old northern capital, **lam toei** and **lam long** in Vientiane and **lam Siphadone** in the south. Lam/khap styles seem to be common to most groups in the country in one form or another.

Well-known traditional acoustic performers include **Deng Duangjduan, Malewan Duangpoomee** and **Acharn Sanaan, Lasmy Kalothong** and **Acharn Sangsawan**. Outside Laos, the best-known traditional mor lam ensemble is the Paris-based **Molam Lao**.

A modern development of this musical form is called **mor lam sing**, which began in the mid-1980s in Thailand and has since also taken root in Laos, though it is less bawdy than its Thai equivalent. The emergence of this faster, electrified version, played by a stripped-down band, reflected a resurgence in Lao identity, the challenge of small Western-style pop combos and the popularity of

John Clewley

Rare 1957 Laotian stamp depicting a khaen player

Festival Phalluses

Savannakhet, southern Laos. It's the end of the dry season and a big **boun bung-fai** festival is underway, centred around the banks of the Mekong River and a revered temple, Wat Saiyaphum. This pre-Buddhist festival is held all over Laos and northeast Thailand in May or June, when locals make huge gunpowder-powered rockets (*bung-fai*), which are launched to persuade the sky god, Payah-taen, to send rain.

Processions of drummers appear, followed by khaen players madly vamping for a shot of *lao-lao* (rice whisky) and groups of dancers in the most outrageous and lascivious costumes – men dressed as giant phalluses or pregnant women, a throwback to ancient fertility rites. Some carry wooden hand-puppets that are equally lewd and designed to shock young women; one man is in the costume of a CNN media man, complete with cardboard video camera.

Rockets explode from trees and flash upwards. Music pulsates everywhere. It's a time of summer madness. Inside the temple grounds, games of all kinds are on offer. Monks chant and tell epic tales and a mor lam troupe plays long into the night. To raise money for the temple, a *ramwong* (circle dance) is set up for anyone willing to pay a a small fee to see a young woman dance.

If you want to experience real Laotian music, check out a *boun*, or temple festival. But first get used to those flowing hand movements (*fon lam*) because there is no way the Laotians will allow you to be a wallflower.

mor lam ploen (celebratory narratives) and **mor lam mu** (folk opera) with younger audiences, though the latter style is now rare.

A new generation of traditional lam artists is taking the music on, led by the wonderful **Nouhouang Brothers**, **Noymany Sokeosy**, **Chanto Sopha**, **Thongvone Khunnara**, **Vanvisa Phothiraj** and **Kularp Maeungpiey**. They are much more versatile than their counterparts in Thailand and many of their albums mix different styles. Another interesting development is the fusion of lam with hip-hop by performers such as **Gumby**, **Laos Family**, **Supasang** and **Doeboy**.

Lao country music (the Laotian equivalent of Thailand's *luk thung*) is also developing rapidly. Old stars to look out for include Kuntung Lathparkdee (stage name: **Kor Viseth**); other artists include **Tukta Southala, Doungleudy Symeaungxay** and **Sabaidee Tukta**.

Lam luang, popular operetta with dancing, is still found in Laos. Myths and legends, narratives, epics and even development issues are presented in a gaudy revue style that developed from Thai *lam ploen* and *lam mu* in the 1960s.

Lao **classical music** is less interesting than Lao folk music, mainly because it has not been developed to the same extent as in Thailand. It was originally played at royal court dances (*lakhon prarak pharam*) and to accompany classical dance-dramas like the *Ramakien* – a version of the Hindu epic *Ramayana*. The basic format is an ensemble called the **sep nyai**, which features gongs, xylophones, bamboo flutes and sometimes the khaen (introduced after the 1975 revolution).

Each ethnic minority group has its own distinctive folk music, used for community rituals, worship and social events. Bronze drums and gongs and bamboo-based instruments feature, as does a version of the khaen reedpipe (see p.667).

Modern Music

The French introduced various kinds of Western music from the end of the nineteenth century. By the 1920s, dancehalls and clubs featured tango and French styles, but also emerging local romantic ballads (still hugely popular). A key composer during this period was Dr Thongdee Sounthonevichit, who wrote the music for the Laotian national anthem "Pheng Xat Lao".

In 1959, Western-style music studies were offered for the first time at the newly-opened National School of Music and a new generation of composers and musicians emerged as a result – composers such as Sor Sengsirivanh (Chanh Som) and Voradeth Dittavong wrote songs for singers like Khamteum Sanoubane, Malivanh Voravong and Kor Viseth.

After Laos achieved independence in 1975, revolutionary songs and anthems dominated the music scene in the country's towns and cities. Recently, however, this dominance has faced a threefold challenge: from the popularity of Thai TV and pop music in towns around Laos's river valleys; from the relaxation of restrictions on the movement of musicians and on music production by independent labels (the album that started the ball rolling was *Heavy Lao* by Sapphire, released and subsequently banned in 1994); and from the influence of the Laotian diaspora (mainly located in the US, Canada, France and Australia). Singers Ketsana Vilaylack and Phone Phoummithone tour from their stateside base, as does rocker Noy Sydanon and Canadian-based rock band The Exile (signed to Thai label GMM Grammy). US-based hip-hop artists Supasang and Gumby rap in Laotian, vying with locals like Laos Family.

The result is that Laos is buzzing with new record companies, teeny pop superstars like **Alexandra Bounxouei** and **Pan**, and heavy rock bands like **Cells** and **Virus**. The Morning Market in Vientiane may have become the air-conditioned and shiny new Morning Plaza, but the range of albums available in its many music stores show just how much the Laotian music scene has developed over the past decade.

Alexandra Bounxouei

Even in a small Lao town, never pass up the opportunity to find the local CD, VCD (mainly karaoke) and cassette sellers in the local market. Often with titles like *Lao Folk Music* and *Best of Lao Lum*, some albums are great and some are lousy, so it's worth asking for a listen. Many artists release new albums every few months and their back catalogue quickly disappears from the racks, so, if you're in Laos, look for the latest release from the musicians you're interested in. Based at the National Library in Vientiane, the Archive of Traditional Music in Laos (ATML) is a project to research, document and develop traditional Lao music. Examples can be heard at *www.seasite.niu.edu/lao/culture/tradition-al_Music/music_collection.htm* and many more at the library itself (see *www.culturalprofiles.net/laos/Units/398.html*).

⊙ Bamboo on the Mountains
Smithsonian Folkways, US
The mountainous regions of Southeast Asia are like a bamboo world – almost all everyday objects can be made from it, including musical instruments like flutes, mouth-organs, tube zithers and even fiddles. This beautiful disc features field recordings of the music of the Kmhmu tribes, whosemembers can be found in Laos, Thailand, Vietnam and even California.

⊙ Laos – Molams and Mokhenes: Singing and Mouth Organ
Inedit, France
New set of field recordings from the three main regions and covering the two main folk genres: lam from central and southern Laos and khap in northern Laos. Structured like a journey from north to south, the music goes from the cool, sonorous khaen playing up north to the spicy, raucous dance styles of the south. A brilliant collection.

⊙ Music of the Hmong People of Laos
Arhoolie, US
A disc of specialized interest, featuring traditional New Year songs, wedding songs, courtship music and funeral music. Most interesting is the soft subdued sound of the *gaeng*, the Hmong varient of the khaen, with six curved bamboo pipes and a mouthpiece.

⊙ Music of Laos
Inédit, France
Music from ten different ethnic groups in Laos, most featuring some sort of bamboo mouth-organ. Intimate recordings made in village houses, at a rocket festival and during ritual ceremonies in 1997 and 2001.

⊙ Music of Laos: The Buddhist Tradition
Celestial Harmonies, Germany
A collaboration between the Ministry of Information and Culture and the University of Applied Sciences in Germany, this album features a fascinating selection of field recordings and archival gems of Laotian music, from every region. Excellent liner notes.

★ The Music of Laos
Rounder, US
Reissued from old Bärenreiter-Musicaphon LPs, this gives a good overview of Laotian styles, including classical, ensemble music for the Ramakien and mor lam. Begins with a spellbinding solo khaen piece.

Alexandra (Thidavanh) Bounxouei

The country's first teen idol emerged as a superstar during a Vientiane concert in 2002, when she introduced songs from her first album, *Dream*. Recently a star on Thai TV soaps, she released her second album, *Luem Saa* in 2006.

⊙ Dream
Lao Art Media, Laos
A good example of contemporary Lao pop.

Molam Lao

Top-flight group featuring singer Sengphet Souryavongsay and khaen virtuoso Nouthong Phimvilayphone, plus other Laotian singers and musicians based in Paris since 1976.

Perhaps this has led to their performing style being more concert-like than many bands back home.

Lam Saravane: Music for the Khene
Ocora, France

Very fine khaen playing and top-class singing from veteran Nang Soubane Vongath and Sengphet Souryavongsay. The 45-minute-opener "Lam Saravane" (ancient music for a large, deep-toned khaen) is outstanding, and is followed by show-piece khaen playing from Nouthong Phimvilayphone.

⊙ Music from Southern Laos
Nimbus, UK

Excellent sampler of traditional styles, including another version of "Lam Saravane", long narratives and instrumental tracks with xylophone and lute. A good recording, but this music is best experienced live to appreciate the frequent duelling between singers.

Nouhouang Brothers

Try to find anything by the Nouhouang Brothers, who rose to the top of the local lam charts with songs like "Sao Dong Dok" and "Saosy Vientiane" and have stayed there ever since. Hugely popular with overseas Lao audiences.

⊙ Hit Collection #3: Borg Jan Hi Lam Lao
PK Productions, Laos

The latest release from this talented trio of singers. A new album and an Australian tour were due at the time of writing.

Noymany Sokeosy

A lam singer from the younger generation, Noymany had a huge hit with his *Yamae Mobile Phone* album.

`DVD` Yamae Mobile Phone
BK Studio, Laos

Unfortunately only available in VCD format, but it's worth it for the killer title-track and "Kid Hot Jing Toma", both of which are popular all over the country and overseas.

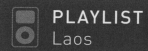

PLAYLIST
Laos

1 YAMAE MOBILE PHONE Noymany Sokeosy from *Yamae Mobile Phone.*
Topical lam hit about a female friend who just can't seem to get off her mobile phone.

2 KHAP SAMSAO KHU/KHAP THUM LUANG PRABANG KHU from *Music of Laos: The Buddhist Tradition*
A two-part "court of love" duet; if you've never been to the ancient northern capital Luang Prabang, this is the next best thing.

3 TEUM SONG WITH SNGKUUL MOUTH ORGAN Kmhmu Highlanders from *Bamboo on the Mountains*
Contrast the soft accompaniment of the Kmhmu reed-pipe mouth-organ with the Laotian khaen.

4 LAM SARAVANE from *Lam Saravane: Music for the Khen*
Mesmerising khaen, flute, small drum and Molam Lao singer Sengphet Souryavongsay take you into the rhythms of the deep south.

5 PHENG SAT NIAO Molam Lao from *Music from Southern Laos*
A spellbinding khaen solo, featuring the virtuoso skills of Nouthong Phimvilayphone.

Malaysia

music at the crossroads

Malaysian pop star Sheila Majid
Jak Kilby

Malaysia lies at the hub of global trade routes which have brought a rich mixture of cultural influences, most significantly Islam from the Middle East, and its music betrays a similarly wide range of sources. Although Malaysian traditions are threatened by rapid globalization, there's still a lot to enjoy, from local diva Siti Nurhaliza to the hidden delights of the indigenous music of East Malaysia's Sarawak and Sabah. Heidi Munan, a long-time resident of Sarawak, reports.

The Federation of Malaysia is really a political construct. Its peoples share in the wider heritage of Indonesia, Malaysia and the Philippines, whose cultures have been borrowing and transmuting elements from pre-Islamic times down to the present day. The aboriginal inhabitants of the Peninsula and Borneo contributed strong rhythms, reed flutes, and a wooden xylophone to the modern-day "national music", and over the centuries it has been enriched by instruments and tunes brought by Chinese, Indian and Arab traders.

Orang asli music is only just being recognized. It took outsiders to bring the deeply moving vocal and instrumental music of the Temuan people of interior Selangor, Pahang and Negri Sembilan out of the jungle. **Mak Minah**, Keeper of the Dragon Line, may have passed on, but her music has been preserved for posterity, and her descendants are keeping up the good work.

The Mah Meri people of Carey Island are only just taking their place on the world-music stage. The shaman is in charge of the musicians, the masked spirit mummers and the rhythmic movements of the leaf-clad dancers. Music, dance and ancestral rites merge into one: sometimes the performers seem oblivious of the audience.

The bronze gong is thought to be part of the Chinese influence, which has been adapted over the centuries, the Indonesian gamelan being one of its most refined derivatives. The skin drum in its many forms was first brought in by seafaring Arabs, who also introduced the three-string spiked fiddle (**rebab**), lute (**gambus**) and the choral tradition of *hadrah* (religious songs accompanied by tambourines). A species of oboe (**serunai**) is thought to be of Indian origin.

Portuguese music was quickly adapted after the fifteenth century: its Moorish intervals and rhythms sounded familiar to the Indian-Arab trading communities, even if the "Franks" (all Europeans) were sometimes treated as enemies or grudgingly tolerated competition. The policy of borrowing and adapting has continued, and today, traditional styles like **asli**, **ronggeng** and **joget** are still played on "foreign" violins, accordions, clarinets and hand drums. Contemporary bands perform them on electric guitars, electronic keyboards and a battery of percussion, but the old tunes remain.

Authentic traditional Malaysian music exists, but it is hard to find – it doesn't have a big popular following and is generally performed by and among connoisseurs. Asli literally means "original", but when specifically applied to music usu-ally means slow-tempo traditional music played by the small ensembles (which might include violin, gambus, accordion, gongs and percussion) that also play the faster **zapin** and joget dances.

Each of the former royal courts of Kedah, Perak, Selangor and Trengganu has its ceremonial **nobat** ensemble of oboe, drums, valveless trumpet and gongs. But these only perform their mournful strains for ceremonial occasions from which the public are usually excluded. The ethnic music of **Borneo** may be heard during harvest festivals in May and June in Sarawak and Sabah – and, since 1998, at the annual Rainforest World Music Festival held in mid-July in Kuching, Sarawak.

Sights and Sounds of the East Coast

Kelantan, Terengganu and southeastern Thailand share a distinctive **Malay culture**. Seaborne traffic linked this region to the traditions of the South China Sea more than to the west coast of Malaya, and the east coast has been less exposed to Western influence as a result.

Visitors heading for the main tourist destinations in the KL-Penang-Malacca triangle are apt to miss what traditional music there is (at weddings and festivals), but the **backpackers' route** which follows the east coast from north to south offers a liberal supply of no-frills "homestay" accommodation, local music and food in villages and small towns strung along the palm-edged shore. At Pantai Batu Burok in Kuala Terengganu, performances of traditional dance, the fighting-dance **silat** and occasionally the **wayang kulit** shadow-puppet plays are given at weekends from April to September, before the monsoon puts a seasonal stop to these open-air shows. In Kota Bharu, the capital of Kelantan, such shows are held two or three times a week.

Silat is generally called "the Malay art of self-defence", but it isn't unique to the Peninsula and the moves resemble t'ai chi. A Kelantan silat performance is accompanied by a small ensemble of long drums, Indian oboes and gongs, which generate a loose set of cross rhythms. Two Malay men in baggy dark costumes, topped by a draped headcloth, face each other in the sandpit where this dance-exercise is usually held, though for weddings and other entertainment it can be performed on a mat indoors. The initial passes are dignified, almost slow, but as the music intensifies, the flowing movements change. The combatants grip each other and the first to throw his opponent to the ground is the winner. The music rises to a crescendo as the silat intensifies, the serunai screeching atonally while the drums and gongs quicken their loose rhythm.

In a very different sort of ensemble, six to twelve men play pentatonically tuned wooden xylophones. The rhythmic melody they hammer out in unison is fast and jolly and all the players end each piece at precisely the same time, raising their beaters overhead as they do so. This kind of music, known regionally as **kertok**, originated with the native peoples of the Malay Peninsula, the orang asli (original people).

The **wayang kulit** (shadow puppet play) is an ancient artistic tradition of Southeast Asia whose roots may be traced to the Hindu epic *Ramayana*. Indonesia, in particular, is famous for its many variants of wayang, usually accompanied by gamelan ensembles. In Malaysia, however, gamelan orchestras are replaced by something similar to a silat ensemble, enhanced by the wood xylophone and sometimes small hand-drums. The puppet master sits onstage beside the musicians, hidden by a screen. As he chants the epic, he manipulates the leather puppets to act out the dramatic sequence for the audience seated in front. Wayang kulit serves as a good example of the meeting and intermingling of cultures in the Malay Peninsula. The Hindu story came from India, the craftsmanship of the puppets is Indonesian/Malay, the core of the music is Arabic – each element distilled and refracted through a Malaysian prism.

Another form of Malaysian drama, **mak yong**, is of east-coast origin but hardly ever seen there today (although it appears in a recording in Smithsonian Folkways' "Music of Indonesia" series). Mak yong is a dance-drama accompanied by the music of rebab or violin, oboes and percussion, which was traditionally performed as entertainment for the court ladies of Kelantan. Before each show the stage has to be ritually cleansed with incense and incantations. Both male and female characters in the romantic drama are portrayed by women, with the exception of one aged clown whose lines tend to be ribald.

Mak yong is certainly a pre-Islamic art form, and is disapproved of by many. In religiously conservative Kelantan, it is currently banned. Moderate Muslims, however, challenge this ban and advocate performances without the preliminary ritual (which approaches spirit-worship), without bawdy ad-libs, and with more modest costumes. These modified performances occasionally take place in Terengganu. Traditional drama enthusiasts in Kuala Lumpur get up a performance of mak yong once in a while, but even here these shows are becoming more and more rare. On the cultural scale, wayang kulit and mak yong are considered highbrow, to be enjoyed on special occasions only.

The popular traditional music of the East Coast is **Zikir Barat**. After evening prayers, when villagers stroll along the outdoor food stalls, some of the more musically inclined may strike up an impromptu zikir. Zikir Barat is an Islamic, particularly Sufi, style of singing. In its traditional form two singers perform, alternating verses in praise of Allah, to the beat of a single tambourine, sometimes accompanied by hand-clapping. As practised at evening markets or neighbourhood parties, teams of men sing the impromptu verses on topics of local politics, village gossip, or any subject of general interest. Zikir Barat has its own stars, like Drahman, Dollah, Mat Yeh, and the style of singing is also frequently recorded by Indian and Chinese vocalists.

Kuala Lumpur: Ghazal and Dondang

Kuala Lumpur rose from a ramshackle mining settlement along the banks of a couple of muddy streams (the town's name means "muddy confluence") to become the capital of modern Malaysia. Its shopping malls and markets are awash with music: Western, Eastern and anywhere in between. Shopkeepers, it seems, firmly believe that music will attract customers, but most shoppers put up with the ear-splitting noise without paying the slightest attention to it. Besides the music blaring forth from shops, there are teams of blind buskers who sing and accompany themselves on electronic keyboards; most of them will produce anything from Christmas carols to Country and Western, as well as a sentimental form of folk pop derived from Indian **ghazals** – the poetic love songs of Indian light-classical music.

More professional ghazal artists are to be heard on cassette or in concert. The great star of this genre remains the late **Kamariah Noor**, whose tapes are still available and whose voice, both intense and languid, enabled her to bend and hold notes, milking them for every last drop of emotion. Kamariah often sang with her husband **Hamzah Dolmat**, Malaysia's greatest rebab player, famous for his slow, rather mournful style, combined with a wonderful melodic creativity. As well as Kuala Lumpur, ghazal is associated particularly with Johor State.

Alongside the rebab, the other stringed instrument of Arabic origin is the **gambus**, used as an accompanying instrument for singers of ghazal and asli music as well as in ensembles for dance music. In the right hands, the six-stringed lute has a beautifully refined tone redolent of intimate, domestic music-making. Malaysia's recognized master of the gambus was the late **Fadzil Ahmad**, who started performing in the 1950s and later assisted in the formation of several cultural groups dedicated to preserving traditional Malay-Arabic music. His most famous compositions are "Joget Cik Siti" and "Dia Datang".

Islam is an integral part of Malay culture, and Arabic music has always held an important place in the Malay musical tradition. In an interesting new development of globalization, well-known Arabic musicians are invited to perform in Kuala Lumpur, where they share the stage with local musicians of the same genre, thus reinvigorating and perhaps influencing Malaysia's traditional music scene.

Malacca: Ronggeng

The old trading town which gave its name to the Malacca Strait lies southwest of Kuala Lumpur. It is a beautiful old settlement along a narrow, rather dirty river, and a strange mix of Portuguese, Dutch and Chinese architecture tells the tale of its history. The town's music, too, is a confluence of and compromise between styles. Modern Malaysia accepts the Malaccan **ronggeng** as its own "folk music" – played on the violin and the button accordion, accompanied by frame drums, hand drums and sometimes a brass gong. The melodies speak of their Portuguese origin, with faint echoes of Moorish intervals and motifs. The fiddle holds the floor until the singers join in, when it recedes to a plaintive accompaniment.

The Portuguese introduced the European custom of mixed dancing, now best known as the **joget**: couples move gracefully with and around

Gongs and Lutes: the Indigenous Music of Borneo

Two of Malaysia's States, Sabah and Sarawak, share the island of **Borneo** with Indonesian Kalimantan. The music of the various tribal groups on the island has been preserved almost pure, without the admixtures of European and other Asian styles that have entered into Malay music. The indigenous people of Borneo used to live in longhouses where music played an important part in communal life. The music now hangs on by a thread, fighting for survival against social change and against the radios, televisions and cassettes that have made their way into the remotest river tributary or mountain valley. It is unusual to find a young person proficient in his or her people's traditional music nowadays.

However, a recent interest in Borneo's culture – both on the part of tourists and the urban middle class – may yet help to reverse this decline. There has been a conscious attempt to revive the art of playing the **sapé**, the guitar or lute of the Orang Ulu people, but the only place where children can take organized traditional music lessons is in a mid-town office block in Kuching, Sarawak's capital city of 400,000 people. The number of those who learn at grandfather's feet, in the longhouse, is dwindling.

The largest of the indigenous groups in Sarawak is the **Iban** and their traditional music is played on the bossed **gongs** that are widespread all over Southeast Asia. The lead instruments are heirloom pieces in sets of six or eight, laid in a wooden frame over a bed of string and played with two beaters – these are the "melody gongs". The larger gongs are suspended singly, and beaten to keep the rhythm. Gong ensembles play for traditional dancing, and in a longhouse everybody and their grandmother can play the gongs.

The other major ethnic group is the **Orang Ulu** (Up-river People) and their principal instrument, the sapé, is one of the joys of Sarawak music when played by a real master. **Tusau Padan**, the man usually cited as the best, died in 1996. **Kesing Nyipa** from Belaga is one of the famous sapé players of the older generation.

The sapé is fashioned from one block of wood from which the body is hollowed out, and often painted with geometric designs resembling jungle ferns. It has three or four strings, of which the lowest is the melody string and the others drones. Sapés are commonly played in pairs, or even larger groups, possibly because they are rather soft in tone despite their large size. In an ensemble, they are sometimes joined by a wooden xylophone. This can be strung like a ladder with the top end fastened to an upright support (in a longhouse, one of the house pillars), and the lower end tied to the performer's waist. In the Orang Ulu longhouses you often see old "mouth-organs" made from a gourd into which are fixed bamboo pipes. These are called **keluré** or **kediri** – instruments once used to accompany dances or processions – but nowadays you really have to hunt to find anybody who can play one.

each other but never actually touch. Joget is a lively dance, ending in a final passage where the beat quickens, and the dancers skip heel-toe from one leg to the other like dancing cockerels. The traditional ensembles might contain flute, gambus, harmonium and drums, but there's also a ten-instrument joget-gamelan of gongs and metallophones in Trengganu which originally came from the Riau islands of Indonesia.

Zapin is yet another music considered typically Malay (and popular throughout the peninsula), which is actually of Arabic origin. In their traditional form, zapin dances or songs are accompanied by the gambus and a couple of two-headed frame drums beating out an interlocking rhythm. These are often supplemented by violin and harmonium or accordion, and in urban areas with flute, keyboards and guitars. The zapin tempo begins slowly, but quickens abruptly as the accor-

dion provides the cue for the dancers to improvise around their steps.

Perhaps Malacca's most prominent group is the ensemble **Kumpulan Sri Maharani**, who play **dondang sayang**, a slow, intense, majestic music led by sharp percussive drum-rolls which trigger a shift in melody or a change in the pace of rhythm. This is a typically Malaysian style, in fact an amalgam of Hindu, Arabic, Chinese and Portuguese instruments and musical styles. Tabla and harmonium, double-headed *gendang* drum and tambourine create the rhythm, while the violin, and sometimes the accordion, carries the melody. Dondang traditionally accompanies classical singing, usually duets with romantic lyrics. Maharani's band integrates electric keyboard and snippets of guitar into the traditional framework. Once incredibly long, the songs are shorter nowadays, starting with fast, expressive drumming which slows down when the soloists

Well-known younger sapé performers include Tusau's friend **Uchau Bilong, Tegit Usat, Asang Lawai, Jerry Kamit** and **Mathew Ngau Jau**. Tegit and Asang are the two loinclothed performers who electrified the 1997 WOMAD in Marseille, and incidentally provided the impetus that resulted in the Rainforest World Music Festival.

The Rainforest World Music Festival, held annually since 1998, started out as a showcase for the formerly almost unknown music of Borneo, combined with a few world musicians who could be bothered to travel to this out-of-

John Clewley

Sapé player Jerry Kamit

the-way destination. Now in its tenth year, the RWMF has become a fashionable place to be in mid-July – the 2007 line-up included Black Umfolosi, Ensemble Kaboul, Foghorn Stringband, Huun-Huur-Tu, Inka Marka, Khac Chi, Mas Y Mas, Shannon, Shooglenifty, Tammorra, the Doghouse Skiffle Group, Tarika Be and Fady, alongside East and West Malaysian world musicians.

There are many types of mouth and nose flute all over Borneo. The **Lun Bawang** people are particularly active players and have formed "bamboo bands" incorporating every flute known to man, including a bass "flute" that looks more like a bamboo tuba than anything else. Schools and villages of east Sarawak and west Sabah have resounding bamboo bands, playing anything from "Onward Christian Soldiers" to the patriotic march "Malaysia Berjaya".

More accessibly, Kuching's **Sarawak Cultural Village** has excellent examples of tribal houses and artefacts, including musical instruments. There are often sapé players in the Orang Ulu house and tapes of sapé and other indigenous music are on sale in the village shop. Interested visitors can take short or longer courses in traditional music and dancing at the Village.

enter, only to accelerate for dramatic emphasis towards the finale.

Crooners and Pop Singers

Despite the common language, Malaysia's pop music has always been regarded as the poor relation by the Indonesian music industry, and only a few Malaysians manage to break into this closed scene. Alongside the historical Insulindian rivalries, there's also the demography to consider: for every talented Malaysian there are ten talented Indonesians and for every music-buying Malaysian, there are ten music-buying Indonesians – and while the average Malaysian is more affluent, he is also likely to spend his money on Western music. In comparison with Indonesia, Malaysia has lost much of its own culture and music in the rush to develop economically.

Until the late **P. Ramlee**'s mellifluous baritone sang its way into Malaya's heart in the 1950s, modern music in Malay was almost entirely Indonesian – of the sentimental **kroncong** variety. Penang-born Ramlee used popular melodies new and old, or adapted from the Western crooners of the day, usually supplying new lyrics which catered for popular taste. Musically, he adapted the folk-instrument repertoire, often recording with a dance-hall orchestra, and reflecting the influence of the Latin ballroom music favoured in the post-war period. Ramlee is the hero of a large number of Malay films now revered as classics. He lived and worked for many years in Singapore (which is where the film and popular music industry was based) before returning to Kuala Lumpur, where he died in 1973.

P. Ramlee

Ramlee's singing style was a Europeanized version of classical dondang; his great duets with his wife Saloma are Malaysian pop's glorious dawn. Ramlee launched a new movement in modernizing traditional Malay singing, largely by abbreviating the songs and employing Western instruments. His critics felt, however, that the purity of Malay music was desecrated by its performance in popular halls devoted to such wickedness as drinking and mixed dancing.

The descendants of Ramlee's detractors still make themselves heard today, and occasionally manage to get rock and rap concerts banned, or female performers arrested, on religious grounds. But Ramlee's style lives on. Today's best known singer of "modern classical" Malay songs is **Sharifah Aini**, whose strong, sweet voice seems to improve with the years. Younger musicians tend towards more modern styles, though many intersperse a soft-rock or **balada** disc with a few P. Ramlee covers.

Young Malaysians, however, buy a lot more rock and pop than traditional music – inevitably, perhaps, given the education policy with its strong emphasis on IT and computer literacy, which includes the skill to download music from the Internet. The Malaysian pop/rock scene today is

Sharifah Aini

dominated by young musicians singing in Malay or English, following the world's styles with their own individual interpretations, often with a shot of tradition cleverly injected.

Sheila Majid, one of Malaysia's best-known pop stars, was the first Malaysian to penetrate the Asian market, particularly in Indonesia. Her foundation in classical music has stood her in good stead as she sings her way from soft rock towards jazz – mostly in the Malay balada genre, though she is equally at home in English.

A few years ago a young singer, **Siti Nurhaliza**, adopted a much rootsier style with a band featuring *rebana* (drums), tabla and bamboo flutes. Her album *Cindai* sold 200,000 copies in 1998. She is still popular, but she is drawing back from the cutting edge towards a broader, "sure-to-sell" style; much of this singer's publicity today is devoted to her personal life.

Rock singers **Awie** and **Ella** keep their standing in the local and ASEAN charts, as does the enfant terrible of Malaysian music, **M. Nasir**. This singer-poet-writer-director is given to public criticism of political figures, or anything else that arouses his ire, but an outstanding talent is hard to silence. His "Ghazal Untok Rabiah" (Love Song for Rabiah), sung in duet with **Jamal Abdillah**, has won awards, and is a moving example of what ghazal means to a creative, modern Malay mind.

If M. Nasir can't be silenced, "socially unacceptable" bands like the rapping brothers **KRU** have been banned from performing – the objection being to their "irreverent" demeanour, mode of dress and rapped comment on social issues. A 1997 tour was called KRUmania, and when the authorities consulted their dictionaries to find that "mania" meant "madness", they declined to issue performing permits in an effort to "avoid any negative effect on youths".

The two main sounds on the general Malaysian scene are **dangdut** and **nasyid** (pronounced "nah-shid"), which are about as far apart as musical genres can be. Both have been around for a long time – at the village party and mosque level respectively – and have now suddenly blossomed out and hit the charts with a bang. **Dangdut** has long been a great success in Indonesia and in its Malaysian incarnation is a sensuous, pulsing, frankly amorous music generally sung by women. Singer **Amelina** is Malaysia's recognised Dangdut Queen, while everywhere in the country dangdut lounges and similar venues advertise Indonesian artistes.

Nasyid, sung chastely by all-male or all-female groups to the accompaniment of drums and tambourines, is the Muslim equivalent of gospel pop – religious songs in Arabic or Malay rendered to appeal to the young, pop-fed generation. The group **Raihan** sold 600,000 copies of *Puji-Pujian*, a smoothly produced and engineered album which owed quite a debt to percussionist Yusuf Islam (Cat Stevens).

For more about dangdut and Indonesian qasidah, see the Indonesia article on p.615.

DISCOGRAPHY Malaysia

For up-to-date information on artists and discs, check the excellent Malaysian music website at *www.music.upm. edumy/Malaysia*.

Traditional

⊙ Dream Songs and Healing Sounds: In the Rainforests of Malaysia
Smithsonian Folkways, US
Recorded among the Temiar people, one of Peninsular Malaysia's Orang Asli (indigenous peoples). Ethnographic recordings of healing ceremonies, bamboo-zither, nose-flute and Jew's harp, and wonderful jungle sounds. Very detailed liner notes.

⊙ Melayu Music of Sumatra and the Riau Islands
Smithsonian Folkways, US
Actually volume eleven of Smithsonian Folkway's Music of Indonesia series, this is Malaysian music from Sumatra where some of the more traditional forms still exist. Includes zapin, ronggeng, mak yong and some lovely gambus playing.

⊙ Muzik Tarian Malaysia
Life, Singapore
Two-CD set of joget, zapin and other traditional dances played by a small instrumental ensemble including violin, flute, lute, harmonium and drums. Classical and refined.

⊙ Sawaku: The Music of Sarawak
Pan, Netherlands
An excellent survey of indigenous music from Sarawak, recorded and compiled by Randy Raine-Reusch. Features numerous previously unrecorded musical styles from the

Iban, Bidayuh, Orang Olu and Melanau peoples, as well as the gong and sapé music for which the region is famous.

Fadzil Ahmad

The late Fadzil Ahmad is still revered as Malaysia's most celebrated gambus player and outstanding ghazal interpreter.

 Raja Gambus Malaysia
Ahas Productions, Malaysia
"King of the Gambus" says the title of this album, a great illustration of Fadzil's art with instrumental tracks as well as songs. Malaysians usually play "Joget Memikat Janda" (Merry Widow joget) first, a catchy, rhythmic tune.

 Irama Ghazal Malaysia
Ahas Productions, Malaysia
Featuring the master and an array of well-known ghazal artistes, this is well worth hearing. Includes the classic "Dia Datang" (Here comes!), powerfully sung by S. Fauziah.

Kumpulan Sri Maharani

The best contemporary exponents of the dondang sayang style.

⊙ **Dondang Sayang Iringan**
EMI, Malaysia
The group's slow, emotional rendering of dondang sayang has kept them in the spotlight for a long time.

Mak Minah

Mak Minah (1930–99) belonged to the Temuan people, aboriginal inhabitants of the Malay Peninsula. Her music lay somewhere between ritual and art.

 Akar Umbi – Songs of the Dragon
Magick River, Malaysia
Minah's work had an almost hypnotic quality in live performance. Luckily for posterity, much of it was recorded by writer-musician Antares and his team.

Mathew Ngau Jau and Uchau Bilong

Jau and Bilong are part of the new generation of traditional musicians. Like his predecessors, Jau makes and decorates his own sapé, dances and sings.

 Lan-e Tuyang – Ngorek: Keeper of the Songs
Self-produced – available from www.jungleartsandflora.com
Lan-e Tuyang means "True Friends", and this collection of mainly Kenyah music includes a number of drinking or "friendship songs" for which this sub-group of the Orang Ulu is famous. Solos, duets with Uchau Bilong and vocals accompanied by sapé and percussion.

Tusau Padan

Tusau (1930–96) was Sarawak's most famous traditional artist, excelling as painter, sculptor and master of the sapé. Examples of his artwork are found throughout Borneo, from longhouses to museums.

⊙ **Masters of the Sarawakian Sapé, featuring Tusau Padan**
Pan, Netherlands
Although Tusau often performed overseas, these are the only recordings that have been preserved – traditional dances

played on the sapé, plus a couple of duets with younger players.

Modern

Aseana Percussion Unit

This group of four to ten performers spans the Malaysian spectrum of modern world music. The leader, Edwin Nathaniel, is a Malaysian Indian who has attracted musicians with Chinese, Indonesian, Sikh and Portuguese-Malaccan roots into this truly switched-on group.

 Colours of Rhythm
Rhythm Support, Malaysia
Living up to the title, APU perform on a variety of traditional drums and gongs, flutes, strings, electric keyboard and voice.

Sharifah Aini

Considered today's main interpreter of classic Malay singing by her many fans, although there are plenty of Arabic overtones in the orchestrations.

⊙ **Nostalgia Aidil Fitri**
EMI, Malaysia
Released just in time for the feast of Aidil Fitri (Id al-Fitr) in 1997, this album contains sentimental, nostalgic, uplifting numbers like the very popular "Dendang Perantau".

Amelina

Amelina's concerts and albums have brought dangdut into the spotlight of the Malaysian music scene.

⊙ **Asyik**
Warner Music, Malaysia
A powerful voice and sophisticated, traditional orchestration make this very appealing. It won Amelina Malaysia's Best Traditional Album award in 1995.

⊙ **Cinta O Cinta**
Warner Music, Malaysia
Dangdut for dancing, dangdut ballads, dangdut cha-cha-cha – this 1997 album consists of ten songs recorded in Bandung, Indonesia.

KRU

A crew of three musical brothers, Abdul Halim, Norman Yusri and Edy. A spirited rap in support of their favourite football team caught the public's attention, and they haven't looked back. They have performed and recorded by themselves and together with other groups.

⊙ **KRUmania**
EMI, Malaysia
The record of the tour which created a sensation; a mix of straight-out pop, rap, G-funk and a few more sedate ballads.

Sheila Majid

Since her debut in 1985, Sheila's soft silky voice has appealed to Southeast Asian audiences in her Malaysian music with a Western format. After a quiet spell (she has two children), Sheila is back in the spotlight, having recently recorded with the Sydney Symphony Orchestra (and a jazz band), and sung at the Royalty Theatre in London.

⊙ Legenda

EMI, Malaysia

The 1992 album of her successful Asia-wide tour.

⊙ Ratu

Warner Music, Malaysia

Easy-listening Malaysian style, but superbly produced. The album justifies Sheila's claim to being one of Malaysia's few jazz singers. Ratu, suitably enough, means "queen".

M. Nasir

An intense, gifted young singer, composer, lyricist and producer. His work often has a political edge.

⊙ Suratan Kasih

Warner Music, Malaysia

His best collection, including the famous "Ghazal Untok Rabiah" with Jamal Abdillah.

Raihan

Five young singers – Azahari Ahmad, Nazrey Johari, Abu Bakar Mohd.Yatim, Che Amran Idri and Amran Ibrahim – sing the praises of God (Puji-pujian) in contemporary nasyid style.

⊙ Puji-pujian

Warner Music, Malaysia

This 1996 album sold 600,000 copies, an unprecedented success in Malaysian music. Fresh young voices, sophisticated percussion.

⊙ Syukur

Warner Music, Malaysia

This more recent CD has more of an eye on the international audience, with a couple of tracks in English.

P. Ramlee

The Harry Belafonte of Malaysia. P. Ramlee was the best-loved singer and composer of modern music with a Malay soul.

⊙ Sri Kenangan Abadi Vols 1–3

EMI, Malaysia

Any of these volumes are recommended as an introduction to P. Ramlee's most popular tunes.

⊙ Di Mana Kan Ku Cari Ganti
⊙ Senandong Kaseh

EMI, Malaysia

Duets sung with his wife Saloma in the 1950s and 60s. Considered to be among the highspots of popular music in Malaysia.

PLAYLIST
Malaysia

1 SI DATANG Fadzil Ahmad from *Irama Ghazal Malaysia*

A spirited classic of Malaysian joget.

2 RAJAH PERAHU Mak Minah from *Akar Umbi*

A haunting vocal solo tells of the great king who sailed across the sea long ago to settle among the Mah Meri.

3 TITIK TITIK KENA UJAN Tusau Padan from *Master of Sarawakian Sape*

The raindrops of the title are fluidly reproduced in the mesmerizing rhythm.

4 LEILING Mathew Ngau Jau and Uchai Bilong from *Lan-e Tuyang-Ngorek*

The classic Sarawak drinking chorus, known well beyond the longhouses of the Kenyah.

5 JUNGLE WALK Aseana Percussion Unit from *Colours of Rhythm*

The elephant's heavy footsteps underscore the jungle and jingle of Malaysia's traditional musics.

MALAYSIA

Melanesia

bamboo boogie-woogie

Papua New Guinean star George Telek

The island chains known as Melanesia include Fiji, New Caledonia, New Guinea, the Solomon Islands and Vanuatu. Musical diversity is a highlight of the region, from traditional instrumental and vocal music to contemporary rock and reggae. **Steven Feld** and **Denis Crowdy** untangle this skein of sounds.

New Guinea

Musically, the best-known part of Melanesia is the island of New Guinea. This is divided in two: **Papua New Guinea** (PNG), the independent, eastern half of the island, and Papua, the western half, often called "West Papua" by indigenous inhabitants seeking independence from Indonesia. Prior to 1962, Papua was a Dutch colony, while PNG, until its independence in 1975, was divided into two Australian trust territories (British and German colonies before World War I). These colonial histories have strongly influenced the music heard today in New Guinea, as has the strong impact of missionaries.

There is considerably more documented and recorded material from the Papua New Guinea side, particularly since independence. This is partly a result of foreign interest in the country's stunning cultural and geographical diversity – more than eight hundred languages are spoken by just over five million people – but also Indonesia's hostility to the celebration or promotion of indigenous Melanesian culture in Papua.

There are clear continuities between traditional music from West Papua and PNG – from similarities in dance, song and instrumental characteristics in the highlands to bamboo flutes and wooden and bamboo end-blown trumpets closer to the coast. Contemporary popular music includes string-band music, reggae, gospel and influences from PNG music and Indonesian pop.

PNG's Popular Music

Papua New Guinea's exposure to Western sounds began in the last quarter of the nineteenth century, with the part harmony of church hymns sung in local languages. By the turn of the century, mission songs, colonial songs and gold-rush songs had also made their mark. From the 1920s, 78s of Western popular songs were played around plantations and colonial towns and broadcasting began in the late 1930s. A further foreign influence arrived during the war, when foreign servicemen played and taught songs locally.

Guitars and ukuleles became popular. **String bands** – groups of acoustic guitars and ukuleles playing a hard-strummed and lightly swinging style already in broad Pacific circulation – were first recorded in the early 1950s, and were commonplace ten years later. By the late 1960s, rock'n'roll cover bands like the **Kopikats** were performing at hotels in PNG's main cities, and string bands like the **Paramana Strangers** had become well-known.

In the mid-1970s, the boogie-woogie **bamboo band** style spread to PNG from the Solomon Islands, featuring open bamboo tubes played by hitting them with flip-flop sandals. This began among villages around Madang, and spread from a band at the Teachers College there to other colleges and high schools. The **Wagi Brothers**, complete with bamboo tubes and fuzzy rock'n'roll electric guitar (played through transistor radios), are one of the highlights of David Fanshawe's Pacific compilations.

A local **recording industry** began to develop in PNG after independence. Musical exchanges were promoted by the National Arts School and other national institutions, as well as regional and international festivals. **Sanguma** were the first PNG group to actively mix traditional songs and instruments with rock and jazz-derived styles. In the early 1980s, Sanguma toured the Pacific region, Europe and the US. Around the same time, recording studios became established in Rabaul and Port Moresby, the capital, and radio programmes featuring PNG pop styles, both in *Tok Pisin* (pidgin), the lingua franca, and in *Tok Ples*, (other local

ARC

Boogie-woogie bamboo band The Wagi Brothers

languages), spread widely. TV and radio stations, however, tend to play local rock, reggae and string-band music, also the focus of the cassette industry.

George Telek has made international waves through his work with musician and producer David Bridie, first appearing with Bridie's band Not Drowning, Waving on the album *Tabaran*. Telek hails from the village of Raluana near the town of Rabaul (destroyed by a volcanic eruption in 1994) and his songs reflect everyday village and spiritual life. He tours internationally, so keep up with his schedule at *telek.com*.

Traditional PNG Music

In 1898, some of the world's first field-recordings were made along PNG's south coast. However, music research did not begin seriously until the 1970s, with independence and the establishment of the Institute of Papua New Guinea Studies music department and recording series. Traditional PNG music also received a huge boost in 1991 when the Grateful Dead's drummer Mickey Hart produced anthropologist (and chapter co-author) Steven Feld's **Voices of the Rainforest**, the first widely available CD of traditional PNG music. It shows a rich traditional musical culture, although its diversity has doubtless been greatly diminished by colonization, missionaries and industrial development. Certain types of traditional songs, singing styles, instruments and their performance were targeted for eradication by **missionaries** who disapproved of the spiritual or erotic power of the music. Length of contact with missionaries – just over a hundred years on the coasts and under sixty in the central highlands – has played a part in how well local or regional indigenous musical traditions have survived, as did the church involved: the Catholics and Lutherans were generally quite tolerant, while the Baptists and Evangelicals were more hostile and restrictive.

Singsing is the general Tok Pisin name for village ceremonies which involve feasting, elaborately costumed song and dance, and exchanges of objects and food within and between communities. Singsings often involve entire clans or communities performing together. Songs are often sung with a leader and chorus, in unison or with an overlapping and staggered approach to the same text and melody, producing something like an echo effect. Performers exuberantly decorated in paints and plumes often accompany the singing with regular hand-drum pulses, while bouncing and swaying in dance lines, clustered groups or semicircles.

Some singsings associated with preparing for warfare or secret initiations have been abolished or were banned by colonial government officers or missionaries; others were abandoned by the communities themselves because of social and economic change. In some areas they have disappeared completely, or have been modified or replaced by newer forms, often held only in conjunction with national events like Independence Day, school holidays or Christian festivals. Singsings are the public and celebratory side of PNG culture most likely to be seen by foreign visitors. Large competitive shows with costume and dance contests attract regular audiences, and have been held regularly in Port Moresby and in the Highlands towns of Goroka and Mount Hagen since the 1950s.

Alongside these powerful displays, the more private, sometimes mystical music based on vocal poetry doesn't easily cross linguistic and cultural boundaries. Many song texts in PNG evoke the power of place, describing the local landscape, flora and fauna. These are often full of metaphors about spirits, and their meanings can be extremely difficult to grasp and translate.

Fiji

Although the Republic of the Fiji Islands is officially part of Melanesia, and the indigenous Fijians are physically similar to other Melanesians, Fijian culture shares a number of features with the culture of Polynesia: hereditary chiefs, patrilineal descent and a love of elaborate rituals, while music and dance are closely related to the western Polynesian varieties.

Meke is the generic term for dance, and the most important types are: *meke wesi* (spear dance for men) *meke i wau* (club dance for men), *meke iri* (fan dance), *vakamalolo* (sitting dance) and *seasea* (standing dance for women). The dances are accompanied by a choir singing in parts, as well as **lali ni meke** (slit drums) and **derua** (bamboo stamping tubes). Another popular style is **sere ni cumu** (literally "bumping songs"), which frequently accompanies kava-drinking sessions (the basis for a controversial herbal remedy in the West, the kava plant is used to make an intoxicating liquor of the same name).

One currently prominent traditional performing arts troupe which occasionally tours abroad is **Veivueti Ni Medrau Sucu**. In the 1980s, **Laisa Vularoko** enjoyed popularity with her *vude* pop style, which incorporated meke rhythms, and

Black Rose in concert

more recently the popular group **Black Rose** have used traditional songs in modern pop contexts. Giant lali drums were traditionally used to announce a wide variety of important events, and are still used to summon churchgoers. There is a rich vocal tradition of church music as well as styles such as *same* and *polotu*.

With albums difficult to obtain, the best way to hear Fijian music is to go there. Although there has been some political unrest in Fiji recently, this is largely confined to the capital, Suva. Since a series of coups beginning in 1987, the proportion of the population made up of **Indo-Fijians** has fallen below forty percent as a result of ongoing discrimination, although locally produced **bhajan** and **qawwali** music can still be heard.

The Solomon Islands

Independent from Britain only since 1978, the **Solomon Islands** are sparsely inhabited. About four hundred thousand people, mostly Melanesians, live on almost a thousand islands, most on the principal half dozen.

Musical life in the Solomons reveals a variety of solo and group vocal styles. Large slit-drum ensembles (like those in PNG on the islands of Manus or Bougainville) are found, but the most distinctive sounds are the solo and group **panpipe ensembles**, particularly those from Guadalcanal and Malaita Islands. The most famous ceremonial groups, from the **'Are'are** people in Malaita, feature up to ten performers with instruments of several sizes. These have unique tunings and play a powerful repertory of polyphonic songs associated with natural sounds like water, insects and birds, as well as work and other human activities.

From the 1920s a kind of **bamboo music** developed, where tubes of different lengths and diameters were struck by coconut husks to create a twangy, bouncing, island-music sounding remarkably like an ensemble of ukulele and bass. The Americans had bases around the capital Honiara, and – just as their abandoned oil drums were tempered into instruments for steel bands in Trinidad – in the Solomon Islands their footwear kick-started the modern bamboo bands: plastic or rubber thong-sandals replaced coconut husks in the 1960s, when the bamboo-band sound spread from the Solomons to PNG, and became a favourite in schools and colleges. There are some contemporary urban bamboo-band albums available on cassette.

Other bands specialize in popular **local-language music** (also well known in PNG towns), particularly the Polynesian- and Christian-influenced guitar and ukulele string-band sound usually called **island music** and local varieties of rock and reggae. Distinctive fusion developments

683

New Guinea's Indigenous Instruments

Principally found in the Sepik region in the northwest and surrounding islands like Manus, New Britain, New Ireland and Bougainville, the **garamut** is a wooden slit drum, between one and twelve feet long and often elaborately carved. Struck with wooden beaters, the drums can produce different tones, and ensembles make a powerful, thundering sound. Sometimes the garamut is used strictly as a message-signalling device for long-distance communication over both land and sea.

By contrast, the smaller **kundu**, an hourglass-shaped hand drum with a lizard, marsupial or snakeskin head, is generally associated with singsings and found throughout the country. Like garamuts, kundu can be elaborately carved and painted and produce sounds associated with spirit voices; their throbbing pulse can have a deeply moving and hypnotic effect.

Bamboo flutes, or **mambu**, are end- or side-blown and range from one to over three feet long. They are generally found in the Sepik area and parts of the highlands. The most famous variety are played in pairs at male initiation rites, and are kept in the men's cult house, the *haus tambaran*, away from women and uninitiated men. Both the carved designs and the sound patterns of these flutes are symbolically important, making present the voices of ancestral and place spirits. The **Sepik flutes**, said to be the longest in the world, have ethereal, breathy tones rich in harmonics. They are always played in groups with perhaps five or seven players, but never with less than two. Although these are the best-known and most widely recorded bamboo flutes, other types of end-blown flutes and panpipes can be found in the PNG highlands.

Of the less formal instruments, the best known is the **susap** or bamboo Jew's harp. It is particularly associated with young boys and men, and often played for fun, accompanying and mimicking rhythms of insects, birds, water and other environmental sounds.

are represented by groups like the **Narasirato 'Are'are Pan Pipers**, who join the indigenous bamboo sounds of the large Malaitian 'Are'are panpipe ensembles to the rubbery basslines of large bamboo tubes whacked by flip-flops. They perform live at cultural centres in the islands, and in recent years have also toured Australia, New Zealand, Canada and the UK. Their cassettes are locally available in Honiara.

Vanuatu

With around one hundred languages and a population of about two hundred thousand people, Van-

uatu music is characterized by cultural diversity. Instruments include bamboo and wooden voice-modifiers, panpipes, coconut-shell ukuleles and unique log drums (some huge) placed vertically in the ground. **Reggae** is very popular and there is a vibrant local recording scene. String-band groups are very common with their tight swinging groove and percussive, syncopated ukulele playing. **Fes Napuan** is a large annual music festival in the capital Port Vila, featuring rock, reggae, traditional and string-band groups. As throughout Melanesia, gospel music of various kinds is popular, with cassettes widely available locally. One of Vanuatu's finest musicians is **Vanessa Quai**, who has a growing international profile.

DISCOGRAPHY Melanesia

PNG music is released mainly on cassette, with production dominated by the National Broadcasting Commission and two companies, Chin H. Meen and Pacific Gold. Since 1990, music videos have also been locally produced and aired on *Mekim Musik* and *Fizz*, programmes broadcast on PNG's EM-TV, while Chin H. Meen has produced a series of compilations, PNG Super Sound Videoclips. For videos, cassettes, CDs and other information about PNG music, check *www.chmsupersound.com/companyProfile.aspx*. For a wide selection of Melanesian music, try *www.mangrove.ws/*.

New Guinea

⊙ **Bosavi: Rainforest Music from Papua New Guinea**
Smithsonian Folkways, US
A fascinating three-CD collection that explores the musical world of a community in the Southern Highlands province of PNG. Recorded and produced by chapter co-author Steven Feld.

⊙ Music from Mountainous West New Guinea, Irian Jaya
Volkerkunde Museum Collection, Germany
Important CD compilation with an extremely detailed booklet devoted to the everyday and ritual music of the Eipo, Mek, Yali, Dani and Moni. The best effort to date at a musical survey of the West Papuan Highlands.

⊙ Music of Biak, Irian Jaya
Smithsonian Folkways, US
Volume 10 in Smithsonian Folkways Music of Indonesia series: older indigenous celebratory songs, now in decline, plus hymns sung by female church choirs, and youthful string-band music. Excellent historical notes.

⊙ Papua New Guinea: Huli (Highlands)
Philips, France
This otherworldly disc recorded by Charles Duvelle in 1974 among the Huli ("wigmen") of the Southern Highlands includes healing, recreational, initiation and other songs, with drumming, chants, pan pipes, Jew's harp and musical bows.

⌗ Papua New Guinea Music Collection
Institute of Papua New Guinea Studies, PNG
The best introduction to the whole world of musical variety in PNG. Eleven cassettes and a comprehensive booklet illustrate the extraordinary range of styles, instruments and ensembles found throughout PNG, from turn of the century recordings to the post-independence string-band sound of the 1980s. Available from *ipgns@global.net.pg*.

★ Papua New Guinea Stringbands with Bob Brozman: Songs of the Volcano
Riverboat, UK
Five different bands from East New Britain team up with guitarist extraordinaire Bob Brozman. Includes a great DVD documentary.

⌗ Riwain: PNG Pop Songs
Institute of Papua New Guinea Studies, PNG (ipgns@global.net.pg)
A classic PNG pop roots anthology. Two cassettes and accompanying booklet of lyrics and guitar chords for some of the most popular songs of the 1970s and early 1980s, recorded by bands like Paramana Strangers, Kalibobo Bamboo Band, Sanguma, Black Brothers and Painim Wok.

⊙ Sacred Flute Music from New Guinea: Madang Vols 1 & 2
Rounder, US
These reissues of classic LPs are the best recordings available of the PNG secret flutes, whose ceremonial performance evokes the presence of spirits. Although better known in the adjoining Sepik river region, the paired flutes heard here are from the surrounding areas of Madang and nearby Manam Island. On some tracks they are accompanied by garamut slit gongs, kundu skin-drums, rattles and singers. The pulsing cries of the flutes are absolutely mesmerizing.

⊙ Voices of the Rainforest
Rykodisc, US
A day in the life of Bosavi, in the central Papuan plateau. A vivid and atmospheric soundscape where vocal and instrumental sounds of work, leisure and ritual are inspired by and blend with the noises of birds, water and insects of the surrounding rainforest.

Black Paradise

A group from West Papua intent on communicating their vital indigenous culture to an international audience.

Black Paradise in the city

⊙ Spirit of Mambesak
Blunt, Australia
Vibrant string-band music from West Papua – a valuable insight into everyday life and the plight of Melanesians at the hands of a murderous Indonesian regime.

George Telek

A tremendously popular Rabaul-based composer, singer and string player who led PNG's famous rock band Painim Wok, as well as the Moab Stringband. He was the first Papua New Guinean musician to reach a worldwide audience.

★ Tabaran
WEA, Australia
A breakthrough collaboration with musicians from Rabaul and Melbourne-based rock band Not Drowning, Waving. Combines PNG lyrics, instruments, and string bands with Australian rock songs, some exploring Australia's colonial past in PNG and expressing solidarity with the West Papua freedom movement in Irian Jaya.

⊙ Amette
Blunt, Australia
His most recent album, with a strong string-band focus and flavour.

Solomon Islands

★ Solomon Islands: 'Are'are Intimate and Ritual Music
Chant du Monde, France
Polyphonies and polyrhythms of 'Are'are slit-drum percussion ensembles, solo panpipes and amazing ensembles of bamboo tubes struck against rocks. Beautiful recordings, excellent notes.

⊙ Solomon Islands: 'Are'are Panpipe Ensembles
Chant du Monde, France
There are many recordings of Solomon Islands panpipes, but this is the best. A superb double CD featuring ensembles of four, six, eight and ten panpipes who perform for feast music. The groups are unique in their tuning and compositional style, and astonishing in their virtuosity.

⊙ Solomon Islands: Fataleka and Baegu Music from Malaita
Auvidis/Unesco, France
Excellent sampler of panpipe, flute and vocal music. Includes the original recording of the lullaby "Rorogwela" sung by Afunakwa; the sampled version of this melody became the Deep Forest hit "Sweet Lullaby" and later the Jan Garbarek adaptation entitled "Pygmy Lullaby".

Other Islands

⊙ Kanak Songs: Feasts and Lullabies
Chant du Monde, France
Short but interesting sampler of indigenous songs whose musical techniques suggest the complex ways Melanesian and Polynesian influences collided in New Caledonian chant, whistling and other vocal styles.

⊙ Kaneka. The Kanak Music
Oceania, France
Compilation of nine New Caledonian artists/groups from 2001, showcasing distinctive local harmonies and rhythms, often with a pop/reggae feel and even some politicized English lyrics.

⊙ Music of the Fiji Islands
Arc, UK
Singing accompanied by ukulele, lali, derua, clapsticks and *cobo* (clapping), and some very pleasant acapella pieces from the Rewasese and Nawaka Entertainment Groups. Includes the evergreen folk anthem "Isa Lei".

⊙ New Caledonia: Kanak Dance and Music
VDE-Gallo/AIMP, Switzerland
Important and thorough anthology of historical and contemporary Kanak styles, with excellent notes.

⊙ Vanuatu: Custom Music
VDE-Gallo/AIMP, Switzerland
Recorded in the 1970s but still the best examples available of the incredible slit-drum ("tam-tam") ensembles; other selections indicate the range of solo and group ceremonial vocal styles.

⊙ Vanuatu: The Music Tradition of West Futuna
Auvidis/Unesco, France
Enjoyable guitar and ukulele groups from Southern Vanuatu, plus contemporary hymns from the missionary repertoire.

Black Rose

One of the most popular groups in Fiji and other parts of Melanesia in recent times.

⊙ Rosiloa
Mangrove, New Caledonia
This 2005 compilation of "hits, videos and remixes" includes a DVD showcasing the group's danceable mix of traditional and original tunes with more commercial reggae/dancehall and dance grooves. Lyrics in English and Fijian.

Tropic Tempo

A great example of local musical innovation from the Banks Islands in Vanuatu.

⊙ Vois Blong Ol Bumbu
Available from *www.mangrove.ws*
Traditional women's songs using both *kastom* (traditional elements) and reggae and rock arrangements and textures. The first local "world music" release, it's an interesting indication of how Vanuatu music might develop.

PLAYLIST
Melanesia

1 RAUDE **Black Rose** from *Rosiloa*
An uplifting traditional song with an infectious dance groove.

2 PASKA **George Telek** from *Amette*
Classic East New Britain Tolai string-band style – a song in the Tolai language discussing gossiping.

3 TOU RA VUI **Gilnata Stringband** from *Papua New Guinea Stringbands with Bob Brozman: Songs of the Volcano*
A unique guitar and vocal texture from the beautiful Duke of York Islands.

4 KOHI **Various artists** from *Five Key Bands from PNG*
A fascinating blend of thick vocals, bamboo and panpipes.

5 SONG CEREMONY **Various artists** from *Bosavi: Rainforest Music from Papua New Guinea*
Ceremonial music featuring a unique textural quality, that is described locally as "lift-up-over-sounding".

6 METAMANI **Black Paradise** from *Spirit of Mambesak*
The string-band sound of Black Paradise at its best, with rich, thick, combined voices over a solid string groove.

Nepal

mountain music

Wandering minstrel Mohan Gandharba
Jacob Penchansky/Mountain Music Project

After a decade of political strife, Nepal is once again emerging as a trekker's destination, with a plethora of outdoor activities in the world's highest mountain range. But few visitors are aware of the country's rich musical traditions. These are rarely encountered outside Nepal and to experience the full range of Nepali music, of course, you really need to go there. Some non-traditional artists have, however, begun to break into the world-music charts. Jacob Penchansky explores.

A small mountainous nation of 28 million people, sandwiched between India and Tibet, Nepal has a culture that inevitably is greatly influenced by these neighbouring countries. But it also has styles all its own – notably the itinerant *gaine* musicians who also played their part in the protests demanding that King Gyanendra reinstate the government in 2006 – which he did. These minstrels have long sung of historical and everyday events of concern to ordinary people.

Classical and Religious

The history of Nepali music has not been well documented. One of the earliest influences, however, must have been **Indian classical music**, dating back to a time when there was no distinction between India and Nepal. Classical music of a north Indian style flourished at the courts of the Malla kings and reached its zenith in Nepal under the Rana prime ministers in the eighteenth and nineteenth centuries, who patronized Indian musicians to the exclusion of Nepali folk performers. Although it was always primarily an aristocratic genre, there is still a lively classical music network in Kathmandu, with tourist cultural shows supplementing public performances and private recitals.

Newar Buddhist priests still sing esoteric **tantric hymns** which, when accompanied by **mystical dances** and hand postures, are believed to have immense occult power. Although the secrets of these are closely guarded by initiated priests, a rare public performance is held on Buddha Jayanti, a festival when five *vajracharya* in Pancha Buddha costumes dance at Swayambhu.

The layman's form of sacred music is **bhajan** – devotional hymn-singing, usually performed in front of temples and in rest houses. Bhajan groups gather on auspicious evenings to chant praises to Ram, Krishna or other Hindu deities; during festivals they may carry on through the night. The haunting verses are repeated over and over to the mesmeric beat of the tabla and the drone of the harmonium.

Sherpas and other highlanders have their own ritualistic music rooted in **Tibetan Buddhist** traditions. Rhythm is more important than mel-

Music and the People's Movement

During the 2006 pro-democracy demonstrations, folk singers including Rubin Gandharba, Raju Pariyar, Badri Pageni, and Manoj Gajurel found themselves at the forefront of massive political protests, calling on corrupt members of the government to step down. These unofficial voices of the "People's Movement" have inspired Nepalis throughout the country and the singers have been repeatedly jailed for their poignant verses directed toward King Gyanendra.

Teenager **Rubin Gandharba**, a member of a lowly *Dalit* caste has been hailed as Nepal's answer to Bob Dylan. Like many Gandharbas, as a child Rubin sang for change at bus stops in his home town of Gorkha. When a local student union representative discovered him and brought him to the stage at political protests at the age of 12, Rubin's singing and sarangi playing quickly became the voice of the dispossessed and the democracy movement. His poignant lyrics have landed him in jail 16 times by the age of 15.

Jacob Penchansky/Mountain Music Project

Rubin Gandharba

In April 2006, Nepal's political unrest came to a boil with massive demonstrations in Kathmandu. Police were ordered to shoot any violators of the 24-hour curfew and thousands of Nepalis massed outside King Gyanendra's palace. While the rocks and rubber bullets flew, Rubin sang:

Listen all Nepalese sisters and brothers,
The rich people are dancing, wearing the skin of the poor.

Political protest songs from the gandharbas are nothing new. Old *dalit* songs such as "Am I not Nepali?" and "Fire in the King's Palace" date back to the 1950s and continue to be used by singers of Nepal's democracy movement.

Weddings

Until recently, no wedding could be complete without **paanchai baajaa** (five instruments): a traditional Nepali ensemble of *shanai* (shawm), *damaha* (large kettledrum), *narsinga* (C-shaped horn), *jhyaali* (cymbals) and *dholaki* (two-sided drum). Despite the name, bands ideally consist of nine members. Eleven is the legal maximum, set to keep wedding costs down. "They got married without paanchai baajaa" is still a euphemism for living together. However, town and city folk nowadays prefer the more modern sound of **band baajaa**, in which the musicians trade their traditional instruments and ceremonial dress for Western brass horns, clarinets and military-style uniforms.

Raucous and jubilant, paanchai or band baajaa is considered an auspicious accompaniment to processions, Hindu rituals and life-cycle rites. During a **wedding** the band accompanies the groom to the home of the bride, plays during the ceremony and then again during the return procession. Apart from performing popular folk songs and film favourites, the musicians have a traditional repertoire for specific occasions. Examples are the "bride-requesting tune", in which the shawm player mimics the bride's wailing as she departs from her family home, and the music of the rice-transplanting season, which imitates the body rhythm of the workers.

ody in this crashing, banging form, which is the exclusive preserve of monks. There's a hierarchy of instruments in the lamaist orchestra, from the *ghanti* (bell), *sankha* (conch shell), and *jhyaamta* (small cymbals), through the *bugcham* (large cymbals), *kangling* (small trumpet, made from a human thigh bone) and *dhyangno* (bass drum), to the *gyaling* (jewel-encrusted shawm, or oboe) and *radung* (a ten-foot-long telescopic trumpet, which looks like a Swiss alpenhorn and sounds like a subsonic fart). The human voice forms a separate instrument in the mix, as monks recite prayers in deep dirge-like chanting.

Folk Music

For Nepalis with no access to electricity, **folk songs** (*lok git*) and dancing are still just about the only forms of entertainment available. On holidays and festival days, the men of the village will typically gather in a circle for an evening session of singing and socializing. As a rule, only the men perform on these occasions while the women look on.

The **sarangi** is considered the national instrument of Nepal. A four-stringed upright fiddle, it is carved from a single piece of wood, and is much simpler than the Indian sarangi. The musical accompaniment typically consists of a **maadal** (barrel drum), and often includes other drums, harmonium, *murchunga* (mouth harp) and *murali* (bamboo piccolo) or *bansuri* (flute). After some preliminary tapping on the maadal, a member of the group strikes up a familiar verse, and all will join in on the chorus. The first singer runs through as many verses as he can remember, at which point someone else takes over, often improvising comical verses to suit the occasion. Members of the

group dance along with swirling body movements, facial expressions and hand gestures.

Both men and women sing improvised, flirtatious call-and-response duets known as **dohori**; the woman may even take the lead in these, forcing the man to come up with rejoinders to her jesting verses. Similar to the dohori is **rodi ghar**, the Gurung equivalent of a sock hop: an informal, musical means of courtship. In addition, women also sing in the fields to ease the burden of manual work, especially during **ropai** (rice transplanting) which has its own traditional songs.

Folk-music traditions vary among Nepal's many ethnic groups, but the true sound of Nepal may be said to be the soft and melodic but rhythmically complex music of the hills. Of the several hill styles, **Khyali** and **Jhyaure**, the maadal-based rhythms of western Nepal, have emerged as the most popular. **Selo**, the musical style of the eastern Tamangs, which is performed to the accompaniment of the *damphu* (a flat, round drum), has also been adopted by other ethnic communities. The music of the **Jyapu** (Newar farmers) has a lively rhythm, provided by the *dhime* (big two-sided drum) and a host of other drums, percussion instruments and woodwinds. The singing, however, has a nasal quality that's hard for outsiders to appreciate. In Tibetan and Sherpa communities, the **danyen** or **thungna** (banjo-lute) accompanies folk singers with galloping rhythms and a bluesy tone.

Although folk music is, by definition, a pursuit of amateurs, two traditional castes of professional musicians exist in Nepal. Wandering minstrels, known as **gandharbas** (or the derogatory term *gaine*, meaning "to hassle") have always served as an important unifying force in the hills, relaying

Jacob Penchansky/Mountain Music Project

Akal Bahadur Gandharba

not only news but also songs and musical styles from village to village. Accompanying their singing on sarangi or the rare *arbaj* (hollow-necked banjo), gandharbas once thrived under patronage from local chieftains whose deeds were the main topics of their songs. Although on the decline nowadays, a few gandharba still ply their trade in the villages north of Pokhara, in the far west, Lamjung, Gorkha and in Kirtipur in the Kathmandu Valley. Their repertoire includes sacred songs in praise of Hindu deities, bittersweet ballads of toil and triumph, great moments in Nepali history and even government propaganda.

More numerous are the **Damai**, members of the tailor caste, who for generations have served as wedding musicians (see box), and may also be employed at shrines to play during daily offerings and blood sacrifices. The tailor-musician combination isn't as strange as it might sound: Nepalis traditionally used to have just one set of clothes made each year, for the autumn Dasain festival, so tailors needed an occupation to tide them over during the winter and spring. Conveniently, these are the wedding seasons when musicians are much in demand.

Festivals in Nepal

Musically, the best times to visit Nepal are during the major festivals: Newar New Year in the Kathmandu Valley (March/April); Dasain all around the country, but especially in the Kathmandu Valley and Gorkha (September/October); and the Newar festival season in the Kathmandu Valley (August/September).

If you're interested in the sex lives of the gods as well as music, the **Newar New Year Festival** (*bisket jatra*) in Bhaktapur is the place to be. A glorious two-week celebration of fertility and renewal, it begins with a massive chariot tug-of-war and continues with the erection of an enormous pole and divine procreation all over town. All the local music groups accompany the sexual activities of the deities, as well as playing for them daily. New Year's morning begins early with a musical procession around the town.

Not recommended for vegetarians or animal rights campaigners, **Dasain** is a two-week festival in honour of the Mother Goddess in all her manifestations. Her lust for blood is satisfied by thousands of animal sacrifices, intended to keep her well disposed during the coming year. At larger shrines the decapitations are accompanied by special sacrificial music, and throughout the season, the dasain music (**malasri**) is played and sung everywhere, as well as being broadcast on Radio Nepal.

At the end of the rice-transplanting season in August, the Newars of the Kathmandu Valley celebrate a series of **agricultural festivals** – so many that almost every other day is a public holiday. Each festival has a different purpose – to drive away demons, to honour one's deceased family members, to mark the end of the Newar Buddhist time cycle, to ensure the success of the rice and to stop the rain. The festivals normally involve musical processions around the towns, and are generally extremely lively and colourful.

Tibetans and other highlanders have their own form of dance-drama, **cham**. Tengboche hosts the most famous of such performances, **Mani Rimdu**, on the day after the full moon of October-November (another performance is held at Thami in May), when monks wearing masks and costumes represent various good and bad guys in the story of Buddhism's victory over the ancient Bön religion in Tibet. Monasteries at Bouda and Swayambhu also present cham dances around Losar (Tibetan New Year).

Carol Tingey

Modern Music

Up until 1951, Nepal had no radio and no recording industry, and the few artists who travelled to Calcutta to record their songs on 78rpm were known only to a handful of aristocrats with record-players. The dawn of modern Nepali music came in 1952, the year after the fall of the Ranas, when **Radio Nepal** was established. Only a year later, Dharma Raj Thapa made recording history, selling 3000 copies of a novelty song about the conquest of Everest by Edmund Hillary and Tenzing Norgay.

A home-grown recording industry took root under King Mahendra (1955–72), himself something of a patron of the arts, and with it came Nepal's first wave of recording stars. Still the best loved of these, though he died in 1991, is **Narayan Gopal**, whose songs are praised for their poignant *sukha-dukha* (happiness-sadness). The late **Aruna Lama** is also remembered for her renditions of sad and sentimental numbers. **Kumar Basnet** remains popular for his folk songs, while **Meera Rana** is still in her prime, belting out classical, folk and even pop tunes. Several of Nepal's foremost composers came out of this era, including Amar Gurung, Nati Kazi, and the late Gopal Yonjan.

More recently, the growth of the Nepali **film and television industries** has opened up new horizons for composers and singers; bringing with it new recording studios and cassette- and CD-reproduction businesses. That said, cinema and TV have also done their share of harm. By copying third-rate Indian productions, Nepali films have turned audiences and musicians away from traditional styles and opened the floodgates to slick, Indian-produced **masala** music ("spicy" music: a little of this, a little of that).

Narayan Gopal

Other recent developments have also cut both ways. Tourist culture-shows have inevitably led to the commercialization of Nepali culture and music, yet they've also helped preserve folk arts by providing a source of income for musicians and dancers. Even Radio Nepal gives with one hand and takes away with the other by providing an important outlet for musicians but at the same time blurring regional differences.

A few Nepali groups have recently achieved cross-over success with East-meets-West **fusion music**, employing traditional instruments in non-traditional arrangements and recording to high production standards. **Sur Sudha** has defined this sound, with an increasingly talented scene of new players following suit.

Pop music is the sound of choice for young urban Nepalis. Locally produced material has made huge strides with music videos on Nepali TV and websites. Hip-hop and electronic music are now being produced locally and this "remix culture" is keeping at least snippets of Nepali folk melodies alive for another generation. For the electronically inclined, check out **DJ Tenzing** and **DJ Tantric** performing in Kathmandu.

DISCOGRAPHY Nepal

⊙ **Gaines de Hyangja: Songs and Dances of Nepal**
Buda, France
Nice intimate recordings of singers and sarangi players recorded in the village of Hyangja, near Pokhara. Atmospheric backgrounds of kids and dogs barking. No translations and minimal info though.

⊙ **Musique de fête chez les Newar**
AIMP/VDE Gallo, Switzerland
A good collection comparing Newar music of the Kathmandu valley across two decades with music recorded in 1952 and 1973.

⊙ Nepal: Ritual and Entertainment
Auvidis Unesco, France
The best selection of traditional folk music covering most of the genres discussed in this chapter. Recorded in the mid-1990s, it features Damai, Gaine and, from the Kathmandu Valley, Newar music, alongside various other ethnic groups.

Sur Sudha

The pioneers of Nepal's fusion-music scene, Prem Rana (flute), Bijaya Vaidya (sitar), and Surendra Shrestha (tabla) have done much to advance Nepali music by establishing a musical institute and producing albums by other artists.

⊙ Melodies of Nepal
Sur Sudha Music, Nepal
Nepal's musical ambassadors weave traditional and modern instruments into well-produced renditions of typical Nepali folk songs, with Bijaya's sitar making a very pleasant addition to the usual lok-git style

Trikaal

A soulful and infectious collaboration between producer Sachida Nand Rauniyar, Navaraj Gurung (tabla), Santosh Bhakta Shrestha (*ishraj*), Sujay Shrestha (guitar), and including cameo appearances from Nepal's other great fusion artists, including virtuoso sarangi player Shyam Nepali.

⊙ Past, Present, Future, Vols 1–3
SAC Music International, Nepal
Bluesy, soulful and rhythmic explorations featuring guitar, tabla and the rare Bengali ishraj (half-sitar, half-sarangi).

PLAYLIST
Nepal

1 ONE NIGHT IN GOREPANI Heart Sutra from *Bliss and Serenity*
Chilled-out Nepali instrumental fusion, the perfect soundtrack for your yoga session.

2 RESHAM FIRIRI Tirha Gandharba from *Saaj – Famous and Typical Nepali Folk Tunes*
Nepal's most infectious and ubiquitous folk song.

3 TAMANG SELO Kutumba from *Forever Melodies from Nepal*
Bansuri flute and damphu drum create a traditional tribal trance of eastern Tamang.

4 BHEDAKO OON JASTO Nepathya from *Bhedako Oon Jasto*
Groovy folk-rock from Nepal's most popular lok-pop band.

5 BHAIRAVI Sur Sudha from *The Third Eye*
Dark and mysterious groove from the kings of Nepali fusion.

6 RHYTHMIC JOURNEY Nava Raj Gurung from *Rhythmic Journey*
Funky fusion featuring tabla and didgeridoo.

7 TRIKAAL Trikaal from *Past, Present, Future*
Slow-cooking acoustic concoction mixing sarangi, tabla and guitar.

8 MAKURI JALAIMA Simsime from *Glorious Monsoon: Folktune of Nepal*
Cool instrumental rendition of a recent folk hit.

9 SINGHA DARBAR JALAYMAH Akal Bahadur Gandharba from *Folk Songs of Gorkha, Nepal*
An old protest song "Fire in the King's Palace"; rural folk sarangi at its finest.

NEPAL

New Zealand / Aotearoa

kia ora kiwiana

Moana Maniapoto of Moana and the Tribe

As Aotearoa/New Zealand was one of the last parts of the world to be inhabited, its folk music has a short history. The contemporary music of the indigenous *tangata whenua* / Māori people is the most distinctive and widely recognized, but many other Polynesian people have arrived more recently from all over the Pacific and made important contributions to popular and roots music. Less well known is the music of the *pākeha* (European/non-Māori) settlers, most of whom brought their cultural traditions from the British Isles over the last two centuries, and in some cases preserved them. **Jon Lusk** enjoys some long-distance listening.

Sea shanties sung by sealers and whalers in the early nineteenth century are the first examples of European folk songs in New Zealand. Popular culture never stands still, and local narratives soon arose. The rapid development of gold-mining, logging, kauri gum digging and farming after the 1870s meant an incoming tide (some would say invasion) of immigrants with their own musical traditions from Ireland, the UK, the US, Australia and elsewhere.

As a famous Canadian once sang, you don't know what you've got till it's gone, and the concept of documenting the local pākeha oral traditions was late in arriving. Although the historian James Cowan made efforts as early as 1912, New Zealand had no Alan Lomax figure to collect or record examples. Serious amateur collecting took place from the 1940s, but by the time the New Zealand Folklore Society was established in 1966, much of the oral tradition had been lost. There are recordings at Wellington's Alexander Turnbull Library, and several published collections such as Neil Colquhoun's book *New Zealand Folksongs*, but unfortunately, no authentic field recordings are commercially available.

Ballads, Brass and Pipes

The next best thing can be heard in the reconstructions of collector and musician **Phil Garland**, a Kiwi balladeer and singing historian active since the mid-1960s. He also contributed to the work of songwriter **Peter Cape**, whose affectionate and often comic portraits of rural life ("vernacular ballads") were popular in the early 1960s, paving the way for performers such as **John Clarke** (a.k.a. Fred Dagg) in the 1970s and contemporary artists like the **Warratahs** (especially notable for their collaboration with folk poet **Sam Hunt**) and the **Topp Twins** – a national treasure since their busking days in the early 1980s.

Early pākeha instrumental folk traditions fared considerably better, as shown by the ubiquity of long-established **brass bands** and, in particular, **pipe bands** (of which there are, incredibly, twice as many in New Zealand as in Scotland). Far less prominent are the few Bohemian and Dalmatian **community bands** in Northland towns, some of which were founded before 1900, and the famed **Kokatahi Band**, a "folk orchestra" founded in 1910 in the West Coast town of the same name. For homesick contemporary revivalists, there's a thriving acoustic folk club scene that includes a number of **Morris dance**, **uillean pipe** and **Welsh folk** groups and even a **bluegrass** society. On a more professional level, a small **klezmer scene** has most notably produced the well-travelled **Jews Brothers Band**.

Pacific Origins

The first Polynesian settlers probably arrived between AD 800 and 1300 from what are now called the Cook Islands, Tahiti and possibly as far away as Hawaii. The sound world of the **Māori** before the arrival of European colonists is little known, although descendants of the various forms of **waiata** (song), **haka** (chants) and microtonally inflected oration and song poetry that took place in formal situations such as *tangi* (funerals) and *powhiri* (greeting ceremonies) can still be heard on modern-day *marae* (community meeting areas). The use of body-percussion also pre-dates European contact, but the apparent absence of any significant drumming tradition has yet to be fully explained. What is certain is that the highly militarized, agriculture-based society that European settlers encountered had been through several major cultural shifts from the initial hunter-gatherer ("moa hunter") lifestyle of the first Polynesian settlers, so some musical traditions were inevitably lost or discarded. But there were also obvious links with Pacific cultures in the various *taonga pūoro* (Māori instruments) that had survived.

Kapa Haka Roots

As in the Pacific, Māori adoption of Western harmony and melody were no doubt speeded by the spread of Christianity in the nineteenth century. Tourism in the Rotorua geothermal area also fostered the **concert party** tradition of presenting Māori performing arts. **Makereti Papakura** ("Guide Maggie") was the first to take this abroad, to Sydney and London in 1910–11.

New Zealand's earliest recording star **Ana Hato** arose from the same Whakarewarewa community, first recording with her long-term artistic partner Deane Waretini for Parlophone in Sydney in 1927. In 1930, **Te Whānau Tahiwi** (the Tahiwi family), whose roots were in the Otaki Māori Brass Band, founded in 1891, followed suit. Their early fusions of Māori waiata and contemporary European styles are still available on CD, but it was the work of the politician **Sir Apirana Ngata** that ensured the documentation of older, more "purely" Māori oral traditions with the publication of his four-volume *Ngā Mōteatea* in the 1930s, reissued as recently as 2007. Ngata also played a role in stimulating the Māori cultural revival of that decade, as did the activist **Te Puea Herangi**, on extensive tours with her performing arts group **Te Pou o Mangatawhiri**. Their action songs and other waiata helped sow the seeds of today's huge **kapa haka** (performing arts) scene, in which many contemporary Māori musicians got their musical grounding.

The 1940s saw composers such as **Henare Waitoa** and **Tuini Ngawai** fuse swing by the likes of Glen Miller with often political Māori lyrics in their waiata. The following decade, the baritone **Inia Te Waiata** launched a twenty-year international career in light opera and musicals, although his recorded legacy includes more traditional material. The **Howard Morrison Quartet**, a vocal group, with concert-party roots were another success story from the late 1950s.

Wai

Urban Drift

Rural to urban drift of the Māori population in the second half of the twentieth century meant increasing contact and and cultural exchange with pākeha, one outcome of which was the **Māori showband** era, with its heyday in the 1960s. These bands drew on popular styles of the time, including R&B, show tunes and Hawaiian music, but also often had significant Māori musical content – as well as comedy. Many based themselves in Australia, working nightclubs and casinos and touring as far as Asia and the Pacific. Major names included the **Māori Hi-Fives**, **Quin Tikis** and **Māori Volcanics**.

The 1970s saw the launch of several solo careers by showband graduates such as the late **Billy T. James**, **Prince Tui Teka** and **Dalvanius Prime**. Polynesian immigrants, who had begun to arrive in significant numbers during the 1960s, were also involved in this scene or alongside it, most notably Samoan Supremes soundalikes **The Yandall Sisters**.

In the 1980s, Dalvanius joined forces with the songwriter **Ngoi Ngoi Pewhairangi** (a niece of Tuini Ngawai). Dalvanius was a catalyst in the setting up of Māori radio, while Pewhairangi was one of the key figures in the *kōhanga reo* movement, a national network of Māori-language (*te reo*) pre-school facilities that has been pivotal in the Māori cultural renaissance of the past two decades

(Māori was finally acknowledged as an official language in 1987). By 1984, Dalvanius was performing with the **Patea Māori Club**, whose disco/funk/kapa haka smash hit "Poi E" topped the charts for a month, and was a massive influence on a whole generation.

The importance of soul, reggae and hip-hop to Māori and Polynesian musicians is hard to overestimate. The mid-1980s witnessed the emergence of te reo-based reggae by bands such as **Dread Beat and Blood**, **Sticks & Shanty** and the pioneering Pacific soul/reggae group **Aotearoa**, whose founder **Ngahiwi Apanui** later made solo recordings. In 1988, Upper Hutt Posse's "E Tu" became the first hip-hop record in te reo and English, paving the way for groups like **Dam Native** in the following decade.

The 1990s saw the formation of **Moana & The Moahunters** (later Moana & The Tribe) fronted by **Moana Maniapoto**, a veteran of Aotearoa. When one of Moana's backing singers, **Mina Ripia**, teamed up with (also ex-Aotearoa) drummer/producer **Maaka McGregor**, they became **Wai**. Other notable names from this period included the commercial dance fusion of **Oceania**, whose 2000 debut made use of traditional instruments played by the late **Hirini Melbourne**. The following year, twins **Ruia & Ranea** recorded an album of Bob Marley songs in te reo, and **Ruia** did another before continuing as a skanking solo artist. **Trinity Roots** were another short-lived but seminal reggae-influenced band of the early noughties.

Reprising a late 1970s stint with the Māori Volcanics and work in early nineties with the all-female group **Tuahine Whakairo**, the singer **Whirimako Black** emerged as one of the leading post-millennial voices in Māori music. **Toni Huata** and the late **Mahinarangi Tocker** are among several other leading female performers who combine aspects of Māoritanga (culture) in their music, while male solo artists such as **Adam Whauwhau**, **Te Reotakiwa Dunn**, Tiki Taane, Ladi 6, Kora and **Tama Waipara** are other recent arrivals.

The continued and increasing popularity of **kapa haka clubs** is likely to have a steady knock-on effect on the mainstream. There are around six hundred scattered throughout New Zealand, with several in Australia, the UK and the US.

Teams of up to forty performers drawn from each region compete every two years at **Te Matatini** (first held in 1972 as the Aotearoa Traditional Performing Arts Festival), which now has UNESCO recognition and funding. A youthful, more radical offshoot is the annual National Kapa Haka Super 12 Festival, featuring twelve-minute programmes by groups (you guessed it) of twelve.

Urban Pasifika

New Zealand was once a colonial power in the Pacific, and Auckland is now the unofficial capital of Polynesia. These days there are large expat communities from Samoa, the Cook Islands, Tonga, and Niue, with smaller numbers of people from Fiji, Tokelau, Kiribati and Tuvalu. Although not as numerous or unified as the Māori kapa haka clubs, there are scores of Pacific Island performing-arts groups, most associated with churches, sports clubs and the like in larger towns, especially in South Auckland suburbs. Despite being largely amateur, most are spurred on to surprisingly high levels of professionalism by participation in various competitive events, and they feed into and interact with the commercial pop scene. Two examples of groups active on this front are **Mt Vaea Band** and the **Vai-**

Glenn Jowitt

Te Vaka

mutu String Band, whose lightning ukuleles back many artists on the Vaimutu label.

Pacific Islanders have made a disproportionately large contribution to mainstream pop since the 1980s. Pioneeering Pacific reggae band **Herbs** led the way, sagely catching the national mood in 1982 with their anti-nuclear message on "French Letter". Niuean Paul Fuemana scored an international hit as **OMC** with the laconic "How Bizarre" in 1996, and the multi-ethnic **Te Vaka** have been the most successful touring band in the Pacific for much of the noughties. On the hip-hop/R&B scene the likes of rappers **King Kapisi**, **Tha Feelstyle**, **Che Fu**, **Scribe**, **Savage**, **Ardijah** and **Adeaze** have all topped the local charts, as have boy-bands **Nesian Mystic** and most recently **Spacifix**. Despite the number of migrants from Asia (now over ten percent of the population) over the last 25 years, homegrown Asian-influenced roots music has a negligible mainstream profile. This may reflect the fact that immigration policies have favoured those from middle and upper income brackets.

It's hardly surprising that the biggest band to come out of New Zealand since **Split Enz** are the wonderful **Fat Freddy's Drop**. Their slinky "high-tech soul" combines Māori, Pacific and pākeha culture with seemingly effortless ease, sounding sweetly laid-back to a stressed-out world.

I'm an Ordinary Joker: Songs by Peter Cape
Kiwi Pacific, New Zealand

Peerless, unreconstructed depictions of mid-twentieth century rural life, most recorded in the late 1950s and early 60s, just as they began circulating among folk-singers. Songs about "sheilas", gumboots and talking sheep dogs, interpreted by Pat Rogers, Phil Garland, Arthur Toms, Cape himself and his son Christopher. The ultimate "Kiwi ballad" collection.

⊙ **Patea Māori Club and Dalvanius**
Jayrem, New Zealand

A 2003 double CD offering career retrospectives of New Zealand's most influential kapa haka group ever and the solo work of its erstwhile leader – mostly rather cheesy soul. The Patea Māori Club compilation is more interesting, with intriguing if dated fusions of kapa haka styles with disco and soul.

⊙ **Te Whaiao: Te Kū Te Whē Remixed**
Rattle, New Zealand

A reasonably sensitive multi-artist remix of the classic 1994 album – a spooky, austere showcase for the traditional instruments played by Hirini Melbourne and Richard Nunns. Thankfully, the original album is included on a separate disc, allowing a pure appreciation of *purerehua* ("bull roarer") *koauau* and *putorino* flutes and various percussion instruments.

Apanui

The founder member of the group Aotearoa has recorded two solo albums; the second is the better.

⊙ **E Tau Nei**
Jayrem, New Zealand

Inspired by his Ngāti Porou (East Cape Māori) ancestry, Apanui sings a *poi* song, a haka and the official song of Māori Language Week 2002 among others. Styles include reggae, soul and electronica. Production and beats by Maaka McGregor.

Whirimako Black

A composer of contemporary waiata, Black is also known for reviving and reinterpreting traditional material, and styles ranging from soul and jazz to electronica. She has collaborated with the UK-based One Giant Leap project.

 Tangihaku
Mai Music, New Zealand

Black's beautiful, vibrato-laden voice is showcased better here than on any of her other solo albums, with sparse, simple backing on acoustic guitar (Joel Haines) and subtle touches of traditional instrumentation (taonga pūoro) from Justin Kereama. A sublimely relaxed recording.

Rangi Te Kura Dewes

Rangi Te Kura Dewes was the leading exponent of mōteatea among the Ngāti Porou when she recorded this album in 1974.

▦ **Ngā Mōteatea**
Kiwi Pacific, New Zealand

Timeless and entrancing traditional acapella song-poetry drawn from Apirana Ngata's anthology; a lullaby (*oriori*), love songs (*waiata aroha*) and laments (*waiata tangi*), with a definite emphasis on the latter. Once heard, unforgettable.

Fat Freddy's Drop

Wellington's "seven-headed soul monster" features the silky croon of Dallas Tamaira, with MPC beats by Chris Faiumu, plus keyboards, guitar and brass.

⭐ **Based on a True Story**
Kartel, UK

An irresistible mix of dub/reggae, soul, funk, and hip-hop, marinated in jazz and served with a distinctly Pacific swing. This sublime studio debut was a multi-platinum smash at home in 2005, and a cult hit abroad.

Ana Hato

With an authentic hotu (catch or sob) in her voice, Hato was known in Rotorua as the Māori who taught Gracie Fields to sing "Now Is the Hour".

⊙ **Legendary Recordings**
Kiwi Pacific, New Zealand

These 33 recordings (some very scratchy) in Māori and English range from 1927 to 1949. Hato's extraordinarily operatic voice is often accompanied by her cousin Dean Waretini, with piano, violin, cello, ukulele and choral backing on waltzes, "love ditties", "slumber songs" and war songs.

Manawatu Scottish Society Pipe Band

New Zealand's leading pipe band was founded in 1925, and has won awards in Australia and Scotland, including a ninth placing in the World Pipe Band Championships.

⊙ **The Calling**
Greentrax, UK

Hornpipes, jigs, reels, marches, strathspeys and more on the band's sole recording, licensed by this renowned Scottish label in 2004. Not quite coals to Newcastle, but pretty close.

Te Matarae i o Rehu

This kapa haka group from Lake Rotoiti were formed in 1994, won the Aotearoa Traditional Performing Arts Festival competition in 2000, and made a big splash at WOMAD in the UK in 2007.

⊙ **2002 Live**
Maori Music, New Zealand

A typical kapa haka set, including an action song, poi dance, choral item, chants and haka.

Te Vaka

This multicultural group led by Opetaia Foa'i (of Tuvalu-Tokelau heritage) blends influences from all over the Pacific with elements of Western rock and pop, using a uniquely innovative range of log and skin drums.

⊙ **Tutuki**
Warm Earth Records, New Zealand

Their fourth and possibly best album, this 2004 offering features a typical mix of warmly swinging, heartfelt ballads and driving dancefloor-friendly workouts, punctuated by explosive percussive interludes.

Te Whānau Tahiwi

Henare, Hinepou and Weno Tahiwi never made a living from their music, but they did make an impact with their fine three-part harmonies.

⊙ The Tahiwis
Kiwa Productions, New Zealand

Exuberant waiata recorded in Sydney in 1930, with jaunty arrangements featuring piano, violin and mouth organ. A mixture of contemporary popular (English-language) material, traditional and original songs in Māori.

Topp Twins

Out-and-proud lesbians who combine politics and music with irresistible humour, Joolz and Lynda Topp are not just show-business twins. Their sibling harmonies have graced national TV series and international stages for nearly three decades. The opening of their 2009 documentary film *Untouchable Girls* broke all records.

⊙ Flowergirls and Cowgirls
EMI, New Zealand

A 2005 album that combines old favourites and newer numbers, from waltzes to hoedowns, with a yodel or two thrown in.

Wai

Singer Mina Ripia and programmer/producer/beat-maker Maaka McGregor have toured the world since their stunning debut in 2000, but have yet to release a follow-up.

★ 100%
Jayrem, New Zealand

Ripia is joined by ten guest singers, while McGregor mixes hip-hop and dance beats with a kapa haka sound palette (samples of breaths, body slaps and the whir and thud of poi percussion balls) and electronica. Still sounds groundbreaking.

PLAYLIST
New Zealand / Aotearoa

1 POKAREKARE Ana Hato from *Legendary Recordings*
Based on a "soldier ditty" and arranged by Paraire Tomoana for his concert party in 1917, this love song has become one of the most famous Māori songs.

2 RAUKAWA Te Whānau Tahiwi from *The Tahiwis*
An autobiography in rollicking waltz-time: "We are travelling musicians representing and honouring our tribe, Raukawa … going to Australia to record our songs."

3 DOWN THE HALL ON A SATURDAY NIGHT Peter Cape from *I'm An Ordinary Joker*
A revealing account of a typical night out: "Had a schottishe with the tart from the butchers/Got stuck for a waltz with the constable's wife…".

4 MĀORI CLUB Poi e Patea from *Patea Māori Club/Dalvanius*
The stomping 1984 chart-topper compares the flight of the poi to that of the fantail (flycatcher) and Māori youth searching for a path in the pākeha world.

5 E RANGATAHI MĀ Wai from *100%*
Julian Wilcox's rap-like take on the ancient oriori chanting style, accompanied by Mina Ripia, sampled breaths, beats and the slap of poi.

6 WHARIKIHIA Apanui from *E Tau Nei*
A reggae groove with poi percussion and a romantic theme in Apanui's tradition-influenced vocals.

7 TARAHATI Whirimako Black from *Tangihaku*
Based on a traditional chant Black learnt from her mother as a five-year-old, this is a wonderfully hypnotic piece.

8 LAKILUA Te Vaka from *Tutuki*
Infectiously ecstatic cries and satisfying, earthy thunks on skin and wood – hard-core Pacific polyrhythms.

9 LOCAL FARMHAND Topp Twins from *Flowergirls and Cowgirls*
A typically swinging, but socially and historically aware slice of country-flavoured sunshine – with lyrics in English and Māori.

10 THIS ROOM Fat Freddy's Drop from *Based on a True Story*
A catchy Pacific-flavoured rhythm track, stabs of brass, choppy reggae guitar, dubby effects and a coolly soulful vocal from Dallas Tamaira.

Pakistan | Folk, Pop and Film Music

dhol, disco and digital

Noor Jehan, iconic legend of film song in the Indian subcontinent
EMI Pakistan

All across South Asia, there are fantastically rich regional folk traditions. Many of them are devotional and are covered in the following chapter on Sufi music. Here, Jameela Siddiqi outlines some of the regional styles and the more recent developments in film and pop music.

As a nation, Pakistan is just over sixty years old, having been created as a result of the partition of India in 1947. The drawing and re-drawing of political boundaries, however, to say nothing of the shifting of populations, haven't essentially changed the musical cultures of the region, which are far older than these boundaries and extend beyond them. In fact, all four provinces of Pakistan – Punjab, Sindh, Baluchistan and the North West Frontier Province (NWFP) – share ethnic groups, languages and musical traditions with neighbouring states. Punjab, pre-independence India's richest province, was sliced in half by partition, but both parts share the same language and culture. Sindh shares many musical characteristics with Rajasthan; the Baluchis, with their strong musical traditions, are found in Iran as well as Baluchistan; and the Pashtun culture of NWFP extends into Afghanistan. Yet each of the four territories has its own distinctive traditional sound.

Regional Folk Traditions

The best-known music from **Punjab** is **bhangra**, from the cannabis (*bhang*) which laces the drink downed by farmers to celebrate harvest time. It is based on the rhythms of the **dhol** (a large, cylindrical drum played with sticks) and also gives its name to a dance that has spread from a rural harvest celebration to the urban dance-floor in every country where south Asians form a significant community. Apart from the uniquely Punjabi dhol, other instruments include flute and *toumba*, the latter a simple plucked instrument also known as an *ektara*. In traditional settings, bhangra is often accompanied by the *chimta*, a percussion instrument resembling tongs, made of two long flat pieces of metal, with bells loosely strung down the sides.

Although not as widely known or popular as bhangra, one of Punjab's most important and enduring musical styles is **Heer**, which takes its name from the tragic love legend of Heer-Ranjha (Heer being the daughter of a chieftain and Ranjha a cowherd), immortalized by the verse of Sufi mystic-poet and musician Waris Shah (1722–98). The verses which narrate the legend are constructed to contain a particular musical form and are sung (usually without musical accompaniment) in a variation of the north Indian classical raga Bhairavi. While Heer is known and loved all over Pakistan (and north India), one has to witness a group of Punjabis listening to it being sung to fully appreciate its impact on the Punjabi soul. In

many villages, there are regular "Heer evenings" (usually at full moon), when people gather round camp fires to listen to their favourite love-story being sung.

One of the more colourful traditions – popularized by groups which have travelled abroad like the **Multan Local Dance Party** (from Multan, the City of Saints, in south Punjab) – is that of mock animal-dances in which dancers get dressed up in horse and camel costumes. Such groups are frequently hired for weddings or festival openings when the popular *jhoomer* dance is performed.

Sindh is home to Pakistan's biggest city, Karachi, but there's a rich rural tradition as well. Apart from the abundance of Sufi music, there's a strong regional folk culture, much of it with a Gypsy-like character, as this is possibly one of the ancestral homelands of the Roma. (The Pakistani musicologist Aziz Baloch claims to have found direct links between Sindhi melodies and Spanish *cante jondo*.) Among the more common instruments characteristic of Sindh are the *yaktaro* (like a one-string ektara, but often with two or more strings) used by minstrels and storytellers, the long double-flute (*alghoza* or *beenu*) and the *murli* double-flute with a gourd (like the Rajasthani *pungi*), which is used in the Thar Desert for much more than snake-charming.

Baluchistan is the largest of Pakistan's provinces, but with a population of barely four million, making up just four percent of the total, with Quetta the only city of any size. Many of the people of this vast, dry, rugged landscape are nomadic. The Baluchis are themselves a minority in the province and their music is dominated by the professional Luri caste of musicians with devotional and trance music to the fore (see p.714).

For musical purposes, the **North West Frontier Province** (NWFP) and the area known as "Federally Administered Tribal Territories" (FATT) can be grouped together. Despite the somewhat troublesome political boundary, Afghanistan can also be included within this bloc. Pashto is the dominant language, spoken by the Pakhtun (northern) or Pashtun (southern) people, and the main instrument is the **rubab** – the ancient lute of Afghanistan and ancestor of the classical *sarod*. Regional song-forms include *loba* (also a collective term for any kind of folk song, but mainly composed as a dramatic dialogue, narrating legendary love stories); *charbeta* (long epic poems); *neemakai* (traditional women's songs); *shaan* (celebratory songs, especially for birth and wedding rituals); and **tappa**. Of these, the tappa – a song style as well as poetic meter – used to be the most widespread: it's believed to be one of the oldest forms of Pashto poetry. One of the most celebrated folk singers, who started out on Peshawar Radio, is **Zarsanga**, who has been invited to several festivals abroad. Hard-line Islamic parties in the local government, however, have campaigned against and restricted local music-making.

Oddly enough, while the people of NWFP and FATT are in danger of losing their musical heritage, elsewhere in Pakistan, particularly in the cities, pop music has turned into a massive and lucrative industry in a fairly short time.

Pakistani Pop and Film

It is generally agreed that Pakistani pop music was born in 1986 when four young lads, clad in jeans and calling themselves **Vital Signs**, appeared on Pakistani television screens with a catchy patriotic song that caused an instant sensation. This was extraordinary in a society still coming to terms with severe censorship rules imposed by a repressive military dictatorship (General Zia ul Haq) which had definite ideas of its own on what qualified as culture. Although jubilant young Pakistanis celebrated the arrival of the newcomers as a breath of fresh air, the state and self-appointed custodians of morality predictably cited the guitar-clutching boys as a prime example of all that was wrong with Pakistani youth – allegedly ignorant of their own culture and slavishly aping the West. While adulation and condemnation raged, nobody could have guessed that Vital Signs, led by vocalist Junaid Jamshed, and their massive hit song "Dil Dil Pakistan" (voted the world's third most popular song of all time in a 1989 BBC World Service Poll) would trigger a major music revolution in the country, giving rise to a fully-fledged pop music industry catering exclusively for the youth of Pakistan.

It is because of their role in triggering a lucrative recording industry that Vital Signs are generally accepted as the founding fathers of modern Pakistani pop music. In fact, there were already any number of underground "Anglo Bands" (as they were called) inspired by the Western stars of that time – Cliff Richard, The Shadows, Engelbert Humperdinck, Tom Jones and The Carpenters – mostly led by Christian Pakistanis and usually only churning out cover versions. The Karachi-based **Keytones** and **Ivan's Aces** and the Dhaka-based **The Iolites**, were all the rage in the big five-star hotels where the teenage offspring of the Pakistani elite could afford to hang out. Meanwhile, **Runa Laila** – newly arrived from what was East Pakistan and subsequently became Bangladesh – had become the first Pakistani pop superstar in 1971, only to be quickly annexed as a film playback singer.

The decline of the Pakistani film industry during the 1980s coincided with the new video age, when Pakistanis preferred bootlegged videos of old Indian films that could be viewed at home and cinema halls all over Pakistan started emptying out. It is said that this decline of Pakistani cinema – formulaic, loud and gaudy as it was – also created a vacuum in which the kind of pop music being offered by Vital Signs was able to take hold. A decade later, the Pakistani film industry and its music had almost disappeared and television in its new satellite format, free of state intervention, had arrived. The advent of MTV and other foreign music channels had a major impact on how Pakistani pop groups packaged and presented their acts. Swanky videos featured montages alternating between MTV-like dance routines and nostalgic scenes from the rural idyll of Pakistan – brightly-clad and veiled women grinding wheat and pounding chillies.

The success of Vital Signs inspired a host of other groups – far too numerous to mention individually here – many of whom became overnight sensations. Various pop stars emerged: Ali Haider, Abrar-ul-Haq (famous for "Billo de Ghar" (To Billo's House)), Faakhir, Fareeha Parvaiz, Jawed Ahmad, Rahim Shah and Sajjad Ali all became

Salman Ahmad of Junoon

Noor Jehan (1926–2000)

With her beautiful face, distinctive voice, beautifully controlled lower octaves and – if the film journalists of the time are to be believed – endless tantrums, Noor Jehan (sometimes spelt Noorjahan) was the definitive diva of the 1940s. Born Allah Wasai, literally meaning "placed here by God", she began her career as a child artiste in Lahore, in pre-partition India. Early success brought her to Bombay, at a time when singing stars – those who could sing *and* act – were the order of the day. Noor Jehan appeared in landmark films like *Zeenat* (1945), *Anmol Ghadi* (1946) and *Jugnu* (1947) – all runaway successes at the box office, with their music as popular today as it was in the 1940s. Film-music historians have often speculated how things might have turned out if there had been no partition and Noor Jehan had not gone to live in the newly created Pakistan in 1947.

Noor Jehan

The Indian playback singing phenomenon Lata Mangeshkar has admitted that it was only on listening to Noor Jehan that she herself was able to develop a style that completely departed from the light-classical singers who still followed the courtesan tradition of *thumri*, *dadra* and *ghazal*. They had already been toppled by Noor Jehan who, according to Lata and others, had a special talent in enunciating Urdu words – perhaps because she was also an actress. Noor Jehan's departure to Pakistan had a significant impact on Indian film music and brought the era of singing stars to a close, with acting and singing now considered two different departments. The emergence of Lata Mangeshkar in India is often directly linked to the departure of Noor Jehan, in that she was able to provide more than adequate vocals for a number of excellent actresses who could not have produced a musical note to save their lives.

Of all the Indian Muslim film artists who migrated to Pakistan, Noor Jehan was the only one who went on to have a brilliant career in the new country, first as a singer-actress-director (with some hugely successful Pakistani films including *Anarkali*, *Intezaar* and *Koel*) and later, when she was older, as a playback singer for younger female stars. Almost up until the end of her life, Noor Jehan's name on any concert billing was guaranteed to make the show a sell-out. She was always in huge demand for concerts in Pakistan as well as abroad, continuing to please her fans with her charismatic personality and the ease with which she moved between film, devotional and semi-classical songs. In an interview with the BBC in the early 1980s, when asked whether she missed acting, she replied: "It was great while it lasted. Acting has a definite shelf-life but singing is my soul, it is eternal."

Noor Jehan's title Mallika-e-Tarranum (Queen of Melody) was richly deserved. When Faiz Ahmad Faiz, an outstanding Urdu poet, heard her rendition of one of his ghazals, he refused to recite it in public any more, saying that he had relinquished the verses to Noor Jehan. It was the ultimate accolade, from the nation's number one poet to the nation's First Lady of Melody.

household names during the late 1980s and early 1990s as they churned out dozens of nondescript though hugely successful, easily hummable numbers. But some stood out from the rest, like the group **Junoon** (Passion), led by Pakistani-American Salman Ahmad, who were inspired by the Sufi poetry of Bulleh Shah and Baba Farid. Dubbed Pakistan's first "Sufi Rock" group, they became one of the most popular bands in South Asia, scoring their biggest hit in 1997 with "Sayonee". Junoon still re-group for events like their groundbreaking concert in Indian Kashmir in May 2008.

Not surprisingly, film producers from India – where the film industry had not only survived the VHS and satellite-TV age, but was actually going from strength to strength – began to look for new Pakistani singing talent. At a time when, for political reasons, travel between India and Pakistan itself was unthinkable, London became a vital link, with young Pakistani pop musicians often having a base there. It was in London, for instance, that Indian film producer Feroz Khan ran into the gifted and beautiful **Nazia Hassan**. She may have died tragically young (at the age of just 38), but her "Aap Jaisa Koi Meri

Zindagi Mein Aaye" (If Only Someone Like You Would Come Into My Life) is as popular today as it was in Khan's 1980 Indian film *Qurbani* (Sacrifice). The song had a tremendous impact: not only did it pave the way for a brand-new pop scene in Pakistan (of the kind that Vital Signs could cash in on later in the decade), but it also revolutionized *Indian* film music, ushering in the "disco age". Hassan's album *Disco Diwane*, also released in 1980, was an instant success, not only in India and Pakistan but also the Middle East and South America – most curiously in Brazil, where the title track climbed the charts to number one and remains enormously popular. In the 1990s, **Adnan Sami** – also British born and bred – emerged with a completely different voice on a pop scene where everybody had begun to sound the same. Coupled with razor-sharp lyrics, Sami's somewhat subdued vocals rocketed him to instant success in Pakistan as well as India. After releasing a number of catchy tunes and pop videos, he was, of course, quickly signed up to sing in Indian films.

More recently, the pop group **Strings** has experienced something of a revival, having re-formed with two of its original four members, Bilal Maqsood and Faisal Kapadia. Their albums *Duur* and *Dhaani* have proved a resounding success in Pakistan as well as abroad. Although a fairly recent addition, pop music is now an established genre in Pakistan, with a vibrant sound and video recording industry – much aided by the advent of YouTube – to match.

While young Pakistanis listened to pop, the top Pakistani musical export remained the **ghazal**. Essentially consisting of couplets in Urdu (either from the eighteenth and nineteenth century Gold-

Mehdi Hassan

en Age of Urdu poetry or from more modern and contemporary Urdu poets), the enormous popularity of ghazal has done much towards keeping the study of Urdu alive in the South Asian diaspora. Pakistan has always had some of the best ghazal singers in the world – many would say far superior to their counterparts in India – and the popularity and number of recordings of ghazals has continued to rise through the vinyl, cassette, CD and now the mp3 eras. Singers like **Mehdi Hassan** and **Ghulam Ali** – deeply rooted in the north Indian classical tradition – found large international audiences from the younger generation in this period, while ghazal diva **Farida Khanum**, although now well past her prime, still performs to packed houses in Pakistan and India as well as abroad, as did **Iqbal Bano** until her death in 2009.

DISCOGRAPHY Pakistan | Folk, Pop and Film

Folk

⊙ Halla-Gulla! Popular Traditions of Pakistan
Radiant Future, UK

A CD produced for the Pakistani Music Village held in the UK in 1995, including snake charmer Misri Jogi, the Multan Local Dance Party, Pathan singer Zarsanga, double-flute player Urs Bhatti and *qawwali* group Mehr and Sher Ali. A good disc if you can find it.

★ Pakistan: Musique du Pendjab – Chants et Danses (Pakistan: Songs and Dances from the Province of Punjab)
Arion, France

An excellent selection of Punjabi folk music, including ghazal diva Farida Khanum, Sadiq Masih & Party with real bhangra, a chimta recital and a brilliant "Raga Malkauns" from maestro Ghulam Hassan Shaggan. The high point is a superb track recorded at a shrine in Lahore, with the group leader frantically beating the *dholak* drum while others whistle, cry out in joy and (apparently) dance with carefree abandon.

Rough Guide to the Music of Pakistan
World Music Network, UK

Compiled by the author, this includes many of the artists from this chapter – Mehdi Hassan, Noor Jehan, Vital Signs and Adnan Sami.

Sounds of the Hindu Kush
Playasound, France

A rare recording of music of the Kailash people (reputedly descended from the soldiers of Alexander the Great), who inhabit three valleys close to the Afghan border. Festival music, songs and instrumental pieces, plus the music for a polo match. A good souvenir for anyone who's visited this beautiful corner of the country.

Trésors du Pakistan
Playasound, France

A region-by-region survey of Pakistan's instrumental folk music, including the Punjab style of *sarangi* (a bowed lute), and its predecessor the *sarinda*, rarely heard these days. There's lots of rubab (the most popular instrument in Pashtun districts) and the harmonium-led Gypsy-style music of Hyderabad-Sindh.

Zarsanga

From Peshawar, in Pakistan's Northwest Frontier province, Zarsanga is the district's most popular traditional singer.

Songs of the Pashtu
Long Distance, France

Songs of struggle and love, sometimes fierce, sometimes wistful, accompanied by harmonium, rubab and percussion.

Pop and Film

The Sound of Wonder
Finders Keeps, UK

One of very few compilations of Pakistani film music. Drum machines, cinematic surf and Urdu funk from the 1970s: a wonderful assault on the senses. Artists include Noor Jehan, Ahmed Rushdie, Nahid Akhtar and Runa Laila

Sajjad Ali

Probably the only Pakistani pop singer who began his career as a classical vocalist, Sajjad Ali came into the limelight after appearing on Pakistani television in 1983. Moving on to lighter classical songs, including excellent cover versions of some of Lata Mangeshkar's semi-classical film songs, he eventually made a name for himself in pop. He is still recording, and his earlier albums remain best-sellers.

Aik Aur Love Story
Oriental Star, UK

The soundtrack from a 1998 film of the same name, with a good range of some of Sajjad Ali's biggest hits including "Jhoole Lal", "Lari Ada" and "Marina Marina".

Chief Sahab
Oriental Star, UK

Another soundtrack, the title song was a massive hit in Pakistan as well as abroad. Also includes other hits like "Bolo Ali Ali" and "Tum Naraz Ho".

Abrar-ul-Haq

Former geography teacher Abrar-ul-Haq (also spelt Ibrar) shot to fame with his very first album, *Billo Day Ghar*, released at a time when Pakistan was in the grip of a newly acquired pop fever (it's reported to have sold sixteen million copies). Thereafter Abrar concentrated mainly on Punjabi and bhangra songs.

Billo Day Ghar
Oriental Star, UK

Haq's 1995 debut album is still his best and remains a firm favourite. The catchy title-track became an instant hit, quickly annexed by Bollywood, where an almost exact version appeared soon after.

Mehdi Hassan

From a long line of "Kalawants" (artistes), Hassan was trained as a classical singer from the age of eight. A 1955 radio recital led to numerous contracts including several ghazal-like playback numbers for Pakistani films. Following the decline of the Pakistani film industry, Mehdi Hassan re-emerged as a leading ghazal singer during the late 1970s and early 1980s with a successful international career and many foreign tours as well as collaborations. The ultimate accolade came from India's nightingale, Lata Mangeshkar, who compared his singing to the "Voice of God".

Live in Concert: Classical Ghazals
Navras, UK

A great three-CD collection of Mehdi Hassan's outstanding classical and semi-classical ghazal and thumri numbers, including a brilliant raga Mand song, "Kesariya Balma", from his native Rajasthan. There's also a DVD.

Nazia Hassan

When the fifteen-year-old London-born Nazia Hassan made her first recording for the 1980 Indian film *Qurbani*, it topped the charts in both India and Pakistan. Her follow-up album, *Disco Deewane*, broke all previous sales records in both countries and sold millions of copies in Brazil. Other successes followed, but after qualifying as a solicitor, getting married and giving birth to a son, she was diagnosed with cancer. Her death in 2000 was mourned by millions of fans.

Disco Deewane
Saregama, UK

Recorded with her brother Zoheb, this includes many Hassan favourites, including two versions of the title song, "Lekin Mera Dil", "Mujhe Chahe" and "Gayen Milkar".

Noor Jehan

Born Allah Wasai, Noor Jehan (1926–2000), was the leading vocalist in Pakistani films. See box on p.702.

 **Mallika-e-Tarranum**
EMI, Pakistan

One of numerous greatest hits compilations, but this has some of the very best of her older film hits like "Jis Din Se Piya Dil Le Gaye", from *Intezaar* (1957) and "Dil Ka Diya Jalaya" from the blockbusting *Koel* (1959).

Junoon

Formed in 1990, Junoon are easily Pakistan's most successful rock band to date, selling over twenty million albums worldwide. Raising awareness of tough issues like AIDS, they won an Outstanding Achievements in Music and Peace Award from UNESCO. In 1996, their single "Jazbe-e-Junoon" became the theme song of that year's Cricket World Cup, soon after which a controversial video resulted in a government ban, on the grounds that the images referred to the corrupt Pakistani political elite. Following 9/11, the band travelled to the US for a series of shows promoting peace and tolerance, after which the Pakistani government decided to embrace the band again, with President Pervez Musharraf even joining them on stage.

Inquilaab
EMI Arabia, United Arab Emirates
Probably the best Junoon album, with tracks like "Saeen" and "Husn Walo" clearly influenced by qawwali maestro Nusrat Fateh Ali Khan.

★ Dewaar: The Best of Junoon
EMI Arabia, United Arab Emirates
A good compilation released in 2003 including the hits "Pappu Yar", "Taara Jala" and "Sayonee".

Adnan Sami Khan

Born in Pakistan in 1973 and raised in the UK, Khan paid no attention to formal music lessons, but was reported to be playing the piano like a professional by the age of seven. The American magazine *Keyboard* dubbed him "The Keyboard Discovery of the 1990s". His album *Badaltey Mausam* was released in India in 1997, leading to great fame and the opportunity to work with Bollywood composers like A.R. Rahman. The album was subsequently re-released under the new name *Bheegi Bheegi Raaton Mein*, also the title of one of his hit songs.

⊙ Bheegi Bheegi Raaton Mein
Oriental Star, UK
The Indian press dubbed this album "pop with a classical twist" and many of the tracks, including the title song but most notably "Lift Karade" – which urges the Almighty to send pounds and dollars raining down – are as popular today as they were in 1997.

Farida Khanum

Known as "Maillka-e-Ghazal" (the Queen of Ghazal), Farida Khanum has a distinct semi-classical style of her own, blending ghazal-*gayaki* (singing) with *tarranum* (poetry recitation). Always popular, she enjoyed further success after her famous "Aaj Jaane Ki Zidd Na Karo" (Don't Insist on Leaving Me Today) was featured in the 2001 film *Monsoon Wedding*, resulting in several cover versions, including one by Asha Bhosle.

⊙ The Excellence of Farida Khanum
EMI, Pakistan
A definitive selection of Farida Khanum's distinctive style and repertoire, including the much-loved "Aaj Jaane Ki Zidd Na Karo" as well as outstanding songs with lyrics from Pakistan's most important poet, Faiz Ahmad Faiz and nineteenth-century Urdu poets Dagh and Momin.

Vital Signs

Pakistan's first widely-known pop band rocketed to fame in 1987 with the patriotic song "Dil Dil Pakistan" and produced four very successful albums. The original line-up consisted of Junaid Jamshed (vocal), Rohail Hyatt, Nusrat Hussain (keyboards), and Shehzad Hassan (bass), but after various arrivals and departures and their fourth album, *Hum Tum* (1995), the band gradually disintegrated.

⊙ Vital Signs I
EMI, Pakistan
1989 release featuring the hits "Dil Dil Pakistan" (in two versions, vocal and instrumental) and the immensely popular "Chehra", "Tum Mil Gaye" and "Ye Shaam".

⊙ Vital Signs 2
EMI, Pakistan
Best remembered for the massive hit "Sanwali", which was also released as a pop video.

PLAYLIST
Pakistan | Folk, Pop and Film

1 GULA STA DE KILIE Zarsanga from *Songs of the Pashtu*
A Pashto love song with lively rubab accompaniment from Peshawar's great folk singer.

2 MERA ISHQ VI TUN Patthane Khan from *Rough Guide to the Music of Pakistan*
Covered hundreds of times, but this is the best version.

3 UMARD GHUMARD GHIR AAYE RE Mehdi Hassan from *Mehdi Hassan in Concert*
Better known for his ghazals, but this thumri in raga Desh takes some beating.

4 JIS DIN SE PIYA DIL LE GAYE Noor Jehan from *Mallika-e-Tarranum*
A young Noor Jehan at her sweetest and best, with some exquisite string interludes.

5 LIFT KARA DE Adnan Sami Khan from *Bheegi Bheegi Raaton Mein*
One of the funniest Pakistani pop songs ever, urging God to rain down only strong currencies, or perhaps even write out a cheque.

6 SAYONEE Junoon from *The Best of Junoon*
The song that inspired the term "Sufi Rock" remains a firm favourite to this day.

7 DIL DIL PAKISTAN Vital Signs from *Vital Signs 1*
The song that rocketed the band to worldwide fame and made pop patriotism respectable.

⊙ Hum Tum
EMI, Pakistan
The band's fourth, last and bestselling album, which has drawn comparisons with Pink Floyd. The fervently patriotic "Jeetain Ge" and the title song were huge hits.

Pakistan/North India | Sufi Music

songs of praise

Nusrat Fateh Ali Khan at WOMAD
Yokohama, 1992
WOMAD

Unlikely as it may seem, the Islamic devotional music of Pakistan has become a major strand of the world music scene, thanks principally to the late Nusrat Fateh Ali Khan, whose *qawwali* music became a big hit at WOMAD festivals and in concerts around the world. Qawwali may be the best-known of the South Asian Sufi styles, but there are many others throughout Pakistan. As a form of Islamic music espousing peace and tolerance, Sufi music has a cultural importance in the 21st century, countering the forces of extremism. **Jameela Siddiqi** takes us into the world of qawwali and the other Sufi sounds of Pakistan.

Qawwali is music with a message – the Sufi message of love and peace – sung to catchy melodies dating back as far as the thirteenth century. Although qawwali is a recognized musical genre in its own right, the bulk of the repertoire consists of religious poetry – often disguised as love poetry because these are songs devoted to a loving, rather than a punitive God – set to music which shares a great deal with the light classical music of India and Pakistan. A vital part of worship in both Pakistan and India, qawwali has a rhythmic intensity that has made it extremely popular in Indian films, as well as in clubs and at weddings in India and abroad. Beyond the subcontinent, the music became hugely popular at world music festivals after the late **Nusrat Fateh Ali Khan** (1948–97) first performed at WOMAD in 1985. Qawwali remains popular at festivals round the world, with younger male members of Nusrat's family like **Sher Miandad Khan**, **Rahat Fateh Ali Khan** and the **Rizwan-Muazzam** duo following in his footsteps, but no other singer has matched the success of the genre's biggest star.

Qawwali Themes

The term "qawwali" refers both to the genre and its performance. Groups of **qawwals** – singers and musicians – can consist of any number of people, but always include a lead singer, one or two secondary singers (who also play the harmonium) and at least one percussionist. Every member of the group joins in the singing, and junior members also clap rhythmically. Under the guidance of a religious leader, or sheikh, these groups of trained musicians present a vast treasure of poems in song, articulating and evoking a mystical experience for the spiritual benefit of their audience.

As an occasion, qawwali is a gathering for the purpose of realizing the ideals of Islamic mysticism through the ritual of listening to music (*sama*). By enhancing the message of mystical poetry, and by providing a powerful rhythm suggesting the ceaseless repetition of God's name (*zikr*), the music is designed to arouse mystical love and even divine ecstasy – the central experience of Sufism.

Islamic musicologists wrote about the use of music to achieve a trance-like state and gain spiritual insight as early as the ninth century. Qawwali in its present form, however, is thought to have originated with **Amir Khusrau** (1253–1325), an exceptionally talented Sufi poet and composer whose poems and melodies form the core of the classical qawwali repertoire. Khusrau was the favourite disciple of the great Sufi saint Nizamuddin Auliya in Delhi, and legend has it that he invented both the *sitar* and the *tabla*. Following Khusrau, the Sufi communities of the Indian subcontinent have preserved the musical tradition of

Jak Kilby

Rizwan-Muazzam Qawwali

Mahfil-e-Sama (Assembly for Listening), which remains the central ritual of Sufism.

Through sama, the Sufi seeks to activate his link with his living spiritual guide, with departed saints and ultimately with God. The music serves to kindle the flame of his mystical love, to intensify his longing for mystical union and even to transport him to a state of ecstasy. Words like "longing" and "ecstasy" reveal the sensuality of much of the Sufi repertoire. Many texts use earthly images of drunkenness and physical love to express their divine counterparts – something that often generates criticism from more Orthodox Muslims.

> Our eyes met
> And all my finery, my decorum
> Came to nothing
> As your eyes met mine

Khusrau's image, in one of his most popular classical Hindi compositions, is that of a young woman who has painstakingly worked on her appearance for a meeting with her beloved. When she comes face to face with him, her make-up is smudged, her fine clothes crushed and her jewellery made redundant in the ecstasy of union. The imagery is powerfully erotic, but the message is that all this finery and beauty counts for nothing in the joy of union with God. With images like this in mind, perhaps Nusrat's embracing of dancefloor culture was in keeping with the broad-mindedness of Sufi tradition.

The Music

Qawwali, like other north Indian song styles, has three components: the melodic line, sung by one or more singers, the rhythm – which is articulated on the drum (traditionally the **dholak**) – and the

Nusrat's Last Interview

Jameela Siddiqi visited Nusrat Fateh Ali Khan in March 1997 and recorded the last interview he was to give to a Western journalist before his death.

Nusrat Fateh Ali Khan's house, in a well-to-do suburb of Lahore, was to all intents and purposes a modest family house, even though Nusrat was viewed in Pakistan as that country's number one cultural envoy. An armed guard at the tall, padlocked gates was the only indication that behind the high walls resided someone of national importance and international fame. His soft, gentle, unassuming manner in conversation was just as soothing as some of the full-throated, powerful, high-pitched scales which came to be associated with his specific style of qawwali. But in speech he was as economical as he was generous in song.

What does it mean to be a qawwal?
The duty of a qawwal is to reduce the distance between the Creator and the created. Those who feel cut off from their source can be reminded of their true roots through qawwali. That is what a qawwal must do. If I am singing a particular kind of verse, then whoever that verse is praising, that reality is before me. It takes me over – it becomes part of my being. The sign of a good qawwal, or any other musician, is his ability to absorb his listeners into the reality of that essential message which is being sung. A good qawwal does not himself exist when he is performing. He simply becomes a vehicle through which that message passes.

You are undoubtedly the best known qawwal in the world. Is this kind of fame and the adoration that it brings consistent with being a Sufi?
Name, fame, wealth, honour. All these things are a gift from Allah. Otherwise we qawwals are basically the kind of people who belong with the fakirs. That is where we really belong. It is only by the grace of Allah that I am given this honour of being well-known, wealthy, honoured and respected. But you don't need any of those things to be a good human being. What makes you a good human being is to be aware of other people's feelings and to never become arrogant about your own talent or fame. The most important thing is to never hurt anyone's feelings, because if you hurt someone's heart, than you hurt God, because God resides in all human hearts. That is what we say in Punjabi.

How do you feel performing qawwali on a concert stage, as opposed to its original context?
Qawwali's real setting is at the shrines of the great Sufis – in any other context it becomes merely a thing of entertainment, just like any other music. Even so, there is always hope that it will touch some of those listeners in a special way.

pitch outline of the melody, which is constantly reinforced on the harmonium. The usual style of delivery consists of singing poetic verses, which are punctuated with a choral refrain and instrumental phrases. The harmonium is now established in qawwali and seems to have permanently replaced its less practical predecessors like the *sarangi* (which requires extensive re-tuning between numbers). The tabla is increasingly used alongside the dholak and is played using a flat-hand technique (*thaap*), as opposed to the normal fingering technique (*chutki*) of north Indian music.

Qawwali is sung in many languages, but its original repertoire consists of verses in Persian (Farsi) and an old literary form of Hindi known as Braj Bhasha – the two main languages used by Khusrau. There is also an extensive repertoire in Punjabi, drawn chiefly from the verses of Punjabi mystic poets like **Baba Farid, Baba Bulleh Shah** and **Sultan Bahu**. These verses, whose natural home is in the *kafi* song-form, had always been sung by the fakirs and wandering minstrels of the Punjab and were introduced into the qawwali repertoire by Nusrat's ancestors, who composed and sang them side by side with Khusrau's classical songs, also known as "Delhi qawwali".

In recent times, there has been a growing tendency to use Urdu (a relatively modern language of northern India and Pakistan) and, nowadays, even Arabic, although the Arabs themselves have no musical affinity with the genre. An artist like **Bahauddin Qutubuddin** is fairly typical of current Pakistani fashions in his use of Urdu lyrics with melodies reminiscent of popular Middle-Eastern music.

The religious function of qawwali music gives it special features which make it distinct from all other north Indian musical forms. The qawwals see themselves as entrusted with the duty to convey the message of Allah, and it is this sense of active religious involvement that distinguishes them from other north Indian musicians.

Shrines

Qawwali is at its most splendid in its traditional setting: at the tomb of a Sufi saint on the occasion of his **urs** (the commemoration of his death and reunion with God). This is the music in its true religious context, and attending such a performance is a powerful experience (outsiders are welcome). While the sound system may not amount to much – various background noises add to the texture of the music, while mosquitoes bring their own buzz to the occasion – the whole atmosphere is charged with rhythmic energy.

Qawwalis may assemble anywhere, but do so particularly at shrines dedicated to Sufi saints, since saints symbolize that nearness to God which the Sufi seeks to achieve in a sama. Although the prime occasion for a qawwali is the anniversary of the saint's death, they are also held weekly on Thursdays (the day for remembrance of the dead) and Fridays (the day of congregational prayer). In addition to these regular events, spiritual leaders often convene special qawwali events either for themselves or for visiting pilgrims.

Many people come to these shrines, notably the shrine of Khwaja Mohin-ud-din Chishti, known as the Dargah (shrine), in **Ajmer**, Rajasthan, to pray for solutions to their problems. Childless women hope for children, mothers pray for the well-being of their offspring, others hope for success in love. As their wishes are granted, devotees return to the shrine for thanksgiving. These practices are often considered heretical by fundamentalist Muslims who reject the concept of saints as intermediaries between the supplicant and Allah.

Each shrine has a particular family group of performers attached to it, quite often direct descendants of the original saint, or at least of members of their spiritual family of followers and devotees. Distinguished visiting qawwals are permitted to perform at the shrines, particularly if they have stated an affinity with that particular saint. There is a complicated protocol governing the hierarchical system of "resident" and "visiting" qawwals and defining the seniority of different groups.

The **Nizamuddin Auliya** dargah in Delhi has a wide variety of qawwali rituals and attracts pilgrims including significant numbers of non-Muslims – Hindus, Parsees, Sikhs and Christians. The hereditary qawwali community at this shrine traces its descent to the original singers supposedly trained by Amir Khusrau himself. They are known as *qawwal bachche*, literally, the qawwal offspring.

Training and Performance

A qawwal receives his training from his family. Boys are instructed at an early age by their male elders (women have no part in qawwali singing at any stage). First they are taught the fundamentals of classical music, after which they must memorize the text and tunes of the basic repertoire. A qawwal is not considered capable of being a lead singer until he has gained a full understanding of the purpose of his music. This means a thorough knowledge of Sufi beliefs as well as practical experience of performing in different roles in the group.

With the move in the West towards concert-hall performances which cater for mass audiences from the Asian communities, qawwali adheres less and less to its traditional form. Such gatherings tend to be spectacular, glittering occasions, usually held in massive halls where the qawwals perform on a concert stage which separates the audience from the performers. This can cause some difficulties. The singers lose their interaction with their audience in a darkened auditorium. Traditionalists also argue that sitting upright in a seat physically prevents the listener from experiencing those spiritual heights which are only attainable when seated on the floor, close to and at the same level as the performers. Musicians are usually quick to single out a handful of real devotees, and quite often direct their whole performance towards this "senior" audience.

The dialogue between the audience and the musicians is central to the performance. The impact of vigorous hand-clapping tends to produce a trance-like state described by those who have experienced it as a feeling of flying. Flight is also the image used by Sufis in their endeavour to achieve union with the divine. A famous Khusrau verse proclaims: "To each his own courage. It is the power of flight – some fly up yet remain in the garden, others go beyond the stars."

A Visit to a Mahfil

Genuine aficionados usually avoid concert-hall performances. Many of them take it upon themselves to arrange a smaller, more intimate gathering (**mahfil**) in their home for an invited audience of spiritually aware listeners. Such gatherings are musically more satisfying for the performers as well as the audience, and it is argued that the giving of **nazar** (a gift), a small amount of money handed to the performers in appreciation of a particular verse, is more easily and spontaneously done in an intimate chamber atmosphere than when scrambling over rows of seats in a large hall.

The tradition of giving nazar is an integral part of the qawwali performance and dates back to the days before recording contracts and overseas tours, when it was the musicians' main source of income. A successful qawwal, with hundreds of recordings and a healthy bank balance to his credit, still displays the humble gratitude of a fakir when a five-pound note is pressed into his hand in appreciation of his art. In that moment, a wealthy and sometimes world-famous musician is reminded of his humble duty as a qawwal.

The running order of a sama is strictly laid out. The performance gets underway with an instrumental prelude, usually played on harmonium and accompanied by percussion. Once the last strains of the prelude die away, it is customary to begin the singing, quietly at first, with "**Hamd**", a hymn in praise of Allah, followed by "**Naat**", which is sung in praise of the Prophet Muhammed. Only after this is it appropriate to sing the praises of Hazrat Ali, by tradition the first Sufi and son-in-law of the Prophet. The song usually performed at this stage is Khusrau's famous "**Man Kunto Maula, Fa Ali-un-Maula**" (whoever accepts me as master, Ali too is his master), in the classical Indian raga Yaman. Although relatively short, it is one of the earliest and best-known of all qawwali songs, and it embodies a central tenet of Sufism: that there is an uninterrupted chain of master-pupil relationships stretching back to the time of the Prophet. Once these introductory songs have been performed the singer is free to choose from a huge variety of poems set in various ragas, many written by Khusrau and other great Persian poets like **Rumi** and **Hafez**.

Khusrau's Hindi compositions often draw their imagery from the Hindu folk idiom, illustrating the openness to other religions that is typical of Sufism. The story of the god Krishna and his attendant milkmaids (*gopis*) provides an appropriate setting for exploring the feeling of separation brought about by being in love with an unseen god. A popular Khusrau poem in the classical qawwali repertoire alludes to a famous episode between Radha, one of the gopis, and her beloved Krishna.

The way to the water well is a tough path to
*   traverse*
How can I walk this path to fetch the water?
He may be lying in wait for me
And cause my water pot to break.

In the original story Krishna throws a stone at the water pot Radha is carrying on her head from the well. The pot breaks and she gets drenched with water. Although the story has been interpreted as having various sexual connotations, its sacred message is undisputed. The well represents a body of knowledge and the pot the heart that has the capacity to carry this knowledge. However, the path that leads to this knowledge is strewn with unseen hazards.

A sama is concluded by singing "**Rang**" (colour), composed by Khusrau to celebrate becoming Nizamuddin's disciple. Qawwals and their audiences may enter a state of *haal* (or pure ecstasy)

Sikh Devotional Music

Shabad kirtan ("word chant") is the central communal worship ritual of **Sikhism** – a religion based on the realization of the oneness of God, through singing (and listening to) mystical poetry. The songs have evolved over the past five hundred years, absorbing a number of influences from the north Indian classical and Punjabi folk traditions.

One of the youngest world religions, Sikhism was founded by **Guru Nanak** (b. 1469), who was vehemently opposed to the Hindu caste system and what he saw as the sectarianism of Muslims. He urged both to follow the way of "oneness" and to realize that the name of God is truth (*satnam*), which he believed could be realized by singing mystical verse. Guru Nanak's new religion took hold in the Punjab and his followers became known as "Sikh" ("learner").

The verses sung as shabad kirtan are drawn from the Guru Granth Sahib (the Sikh holy book), consisting of verses from founder Guru Nanak as well as the poetry of the Sufi saint Baba Farid (1173–1266). Subsequent gurus – all of whom were poets as well as musicians – added more mystical verses, with a clear indication of the various **raags** (ragas or melodic templates), that had to be used to sing each of the poems. There are a total of 31 *shuddh* (pure) raags and another thirty or so *mishr* (mixed or composite) raags contained within the Holy Book.

Sikh devotional singers or **raagis** only perform in the presence of the Sikh holy book, whether in a **gurudwara** (Sikh temple) or a private house. They receive the same training as other classical Indian vocalists and perform along similar *gharana* (family/hereditary style) lines to those found in other north Indian classical vocal music. Although the original classical form has become diluted, there are a number of performers, notably **Bhai Sahib Bhai Avtar Singh Raagi**, who still sing in the traditional style.

At the other end of the spectrum is the hugely popular, Australian-based **Dya Singh**, who has very successfully taken shabad kirtan to the world concert-stage, with ten immensely successful albums in nine years. Using shabad kirtan as his base and concentrating solely on the Sikh holy verses, Dya Singh has integrated numerous musical influences: blues, jazz, folk (Eastern and Western), country & western, native Australian and so on. Apart from the traditional harmonium and tabla, his instruments have included Vietnamese zither (*dang thranh*), southern European gypsy violin, European flute, Persian hammered dulcimer (*santoor*), electric guitar, bouzouki, didgeridoo, Nepalese drums and the Irish fiddle – all producing quite an enchanting sound and mostly retaining the spiritual content of the music, but nevertheless causing much exasperation in purist circles.

Sung correctly, shabad kirtan can provide a transformational experience, having the power to give the listener an almost instant feeling of joyful calm. There are usually two principal voices and a supporting chorus backed by harmonium and lute (**sarangi** or older variants like *dilruba* or *sarinda*), with tabla for percussion. Devotees sway gently to the melody and rhythm, but given the religious nature of the performance, refrain from expressing any public appreciation of the singers.

The finest exponents of shabad kirtan reside at Sikhism's holiest place, the **Golden Temple of Amritsar** (completed 1601). The temple has a haunting, timeless quality as it stands shimmering majestically in a marble courtyard, surrounded by the holy waters of a small lake and accompanied by the sound of non-stop shabad.

If you can't make it to Amritsar, shabads can be heard in gurudwaras around the world. Although heads must be covered and shoes left outside, a tradition borrowed from Sufi shrines means that a free ritual vegetarian meal (*langar*, literally "anchor") is served every evening.

during the performance of "Rang" – the song evokes a mood of sheer joy and exuberance.

Songs are usually extended by inserting additional verses called **girahs**. Qawwals normally have a large stock of verses from which they can draw an appropriate girah, which may be in a language different from the main body of the song. It is this practice of adding appropriate verses when the opportunity presents itself that gives qawwali

its flexibility and spontaneity. Qawwals are often judged by their ability to add the right girah at the right moment – the more unexpected the better. It is these inserted verses that make every qawwali performance a unique creation.

One current trend in Pakistan is to end qawwali performances with a song of the Qalandar sect, **"Dama dum mast qalandar"**, instead of the traditional Delhi "Rang" of Khusrau. The

Qalandars are a group of itinerant Sufi dervishes who reject conventional standards of behaviour in order to remain "joyous in God". This song, sung in praise of Lal Shahbaz Qalandar, is entirely rhythmic, making it enormously popular outside the qawwali context and on dance floors in Pakistan as well as India – Nusrat's "Mustt Mustt" is the most famous version.

Qawwali Today

Twentieth-century qawwals, notably Nusrat Fateh Ali Khan, were quick to diversify their performances to match the current trends in East-West fusion. One of qawwali's important ingredients, **tarana**, has readily lent itself to the development of disco/jazz tarana, which can be heard on many of Nusrat's more popular recordings. Tarana is a kind of rhythmic recitation used originally to express esoteric religious ideas in a secret manner by stringing together Persian syllables which made no overt sense but were given a private meaning. Now used for musical reasons, rather than coded messages, it has often been likened to the scat style of jazz singing.

The intensity of Nusrat's voice, conveying sensitivity, emotion, power and abandonment where necessary, marked him out as one of the greatest musicians of his time. He also pushed the boundaries furthest in qawwali fusion, squandering – as the purists saw it – his art on film soundtracks and commercial dance mixes with Michael Brook and Massive Attack. But for Nusrat, spreading the word was all, and his music, even if in a diluted form, certainly reached millions.

Another qawwali group to have gained a worldwide reputation in the same period was the **Sabri Brothers**. Haji Ghulam Farid Sabri (d. 1994) and his younger brother Maqbool were particularly noted for their highly original style of rendering well-known numbers from the traditional qawwali repertoire, as well as for their distinctive style of percussion. The senior Sabri was renowned for the spirituality he brought to the songs, and his periodic chanting of "Allah" between verses became a signature. After his death, the group slowly disintegrated, while another group of the original qawwal bachche, notable for its strong affiliations with the classical Khusrau tradition and led by the legendary **Munshi Raziuddin** of Delhi (who migrated to Pakistan in 1952), began to emerge. After Raziuddin's death, his Karachi-based sons Farid Ayaz and Abu Mohammed continued to perform to packed concert halls and private mahfils in Pakistan as well as abroad. While the Sabri

Brothers' glory days are over, the Faisalabad-based brothers **Mehr Ali** and **Sher Ali** maintain a real spiritual power in their performances, both in Pakistan and on their international tours.

From Nusrat's lineage, the **Rizwan-Muazzam Qawwali Group** are among the best-known younger performers of qawwali. As nephews of Nusrat, Rizwan and Muazzam Mujahid Ali Khan have a peerless family heritage, but also an impossible act to follow. They are a young, exciting qawwali group in the best tradition and have been frequent performers at WOMAD. Another of Nusrat's nephews, his star pupil **Rahat Fateh Ali Khan** (who sat with and sang alongside his uncle from a very young age) has gone on to gather a following of his own, as many fans believe him to be Nusrat's rightful musical heir. **Faiz Ali Faiz**, an impressive live performer from Lahore, has also taken Nusrat as his model, and has gained an international following thanks to his recordings for the French label Accords Croisés.

Qawwali Fusion

While the traditional strains of qawwali continue to flourish, there are modern secular forms in Bollywood and Lahore films (the only public arena in which you'll hear women's qawwali) and, of course, the world-music fusions which have raised its profile in the West. Two of the most successful, commercially and artistically, were *Mustt Mustt* and *Night Song*, the two albums on which Nusrat Fateh Ali Khan collaborated with the Canadian producer Michael Brook for the Real World label. The title track, "Mustt Mustt" became known internationally, first through Massive Attack's remix, and then when Nusrat's original became the soundtrack for a Coca-Cola advert shown in India and around the world during the cricket World Cup.

To outsiders, it may seem startling that Nusrat, purveyor-in-chief of one of the world's most passionate spiritual traditions, should have allowed his music to be used to promote what is perhaps the archetypal Western consumer product. But many qawwals believe that an essential part of their role is to reach as many people as possible – they may, after all, be drawn into a spiritual path even via the unlikely route of a soft-drink commercial. On his Japanese tour, indeed, Nusrat spent the evening before his first concert studying the music of Japanese TV adverts. Concluding that this must be the way to reach people, Nusrat incorporated subtle elements from the ads in his concerts.

The nature of qawwali music, with its basic eight-beat cycles and Western-friendly chord sequences, makes it highly suitable for dance remixes. Real World commissioned several second-generation British Asian outfits to remix the Michael Brook/Nusrat releases for *Star Rise*, which, when it was released shortly after Nusrat's death in 1997, became something of a tribute album to his pioneering qawwali fusion. The inventive dance mixes included the likes of Talvin Singh, Black Star Liner, Asian Dub Foundation and Joi, although perhaps the most effective is Nitin Sawhney's drum-and-bass-style collage.

One of the most successful of qawwali fusions has been the *Qawwali Flamenco* collaboration of Faiz Ali Faiz and flamenco singers Miguel Poveda and Duquende with guitarist Chicuelo. Despite a vague Gypsy connection, there's no real reason why this should work, but it does, both on disc and on stage. Israeli musician Shye Ben-Tzur came up with a completely different kind of qawwali fusion when he worked with the qawwals of the Ajmer shrine in India to create an album, *Heeyam*, as well as concert performances at the Jaipur Festival. It's perhaps a testimony to the all-embracing pluralism of Sufi music that Israeli Jews and Indian Muslims can work together with no problems.

Cross-cultural fusions can have their difficulties, however. Michael Brook found that a couple of edits on the *Mustt Mustt* album had mangled the Sufi lyrics – although on that release the problem was minimized as most of the vocals were tarana syllables with no specific meaning. This was not the case with *Night Song*, however, so Brook transcribed the lyrics phonetically to ensure that he didn't cut in the middle of a line.

It's worth noting that qawwali lyrics are typically in a mixture of Punjabi, Urdu and Farsi, often in various dialects, and that even audiences in Pakistan may not understand all the words. The test of a good qawwali session, however, is that it can weave a spell over an audience regardless of language. The new audiences dancing to qawwali fusion, while condemned by purists, are seen by others as simply extending the tradition. In 2007, Italian producer and remixer Gaudi re-worked some Nusrat tracks from the 1970s to the 1990s for the album *Dub Qawwali*, which brought another new audience to the maestro's music to mark the tenth anniversary of his death.

Other Sufi Music

Sufi shrines are an integral part of life in Pakistan and, in addition to qawwali, there are many other styles of Sufi music associated with them.

Across the country wandering minstrels still visit shrines to perform. One of the most notable is **Sain Zahoor**, who is seen at the Mian Meer shrine in Lahore in the documentary *Sufi Soul*, and regularly performs at the shrine of Bulleh Shah in Kasur. A colourful figure with bells on his ankles and cooing the words "Allah-hoo" into the belly of his three-stringed *ektara* dangling with tassels, he has become a popular figure at festivals and picked up a BBC Award for World Music in 2006. "I am a messenger", he says, "spreading the words of the saints as widely as possible amongst the people."

The southern province of Sindh is justifiably called the "land of the Sufis" as there are more Sufi shrines here than anywhere else in the country. The most notable are those of **Lal Shahbaz Qalandar** in Sehwan, with its strong drumming tradition and *damal* dance, and of **Shah Abdul Latif** in Bhitshah. Abdul Latif was a poet and musician who founded a music school and created an instrument called the *danbur* (said to be developed from an Egyptian original) with five strings, a large belly and a long neck. Musicians have performed at his shrine every night since

Simon Broughton

Sain Zahoor at the Mian Meer shrine in Lahore

713

Abdul Latif died in 1752, intoning his poetry in an intense falsetto as they beat and pluck the danbur. "This is the only music in which there has been no change", claims Khan Mohammad Fakir, the leader of the group at Bhitshah. "All others in the world have changed over time, but not this."

The folk music of **Baluchistan**, the southwesterly province of Pakistan, is also dominated by Sufi and trance music, although the Baluchis are also to be found in neighbouring Iran and Pakistan. Their main instruments are the *sorud* (a strange skull-shaped fiddle), *tanburang* (lute), *benju* (zither) and *doneli* (double flute) with dholak drum. Leading exponents – or at least those who have been recorded – include Yaru Maliri, Rasulbakhsh Zangeshahi, Abdorahman Surizehi and the Baluchi Ensemble of Karachi, with female singer Rahima.

By far the most popular Sufi singer in South Asia today is **Abida Parveen** (see box below). Born of a musical father in Larkana, Sindh, she has made her way in what is traditionally a male profession to become a performer like no other, with an extraordinary vocal power underlined by dramatic head-shakes and arm movements. She sings kafi songs and the Sufiana Kalam (Sayings of the Sufis), essentially ballads of human or divine love (as well as *ghazals*) in Sindhi, Punjabi, Seraiki and Urdu, usually accompanied by harmonium, sitar, and tabla and dholak percussion.

Abida Parveen

A few questions put to Abida Parveen after a long night-time performance at the urs of Shah Abdul Latif in Sindh.

Where do you get the inspiration or power for your performance?

When someone listens to this music, it is in fact his or her heart and soul that is listening. It creates a spiritual atmosphere due to the presence of the saints. God's light is spotlighting the saint, and when the poetry is being sung it becomes like a medication for humanity. There is no need to explain it, it can be in any language. For instance, the poetry of Rumi is in Persian yet it has gained prominence the world over, the same for Abdul Latif. The languages are different but the message is the same. It is all because of the power of God's light that this happens.

What does Sufism mean to you?

We have two physical eyes, but these eyes may not be seeing the complete picture. There is another eye in the heart. It sees that which is unseen, the holy radiations. If through the poetry or through Sufi music these holy radiations manage to penetrate someone, then that is Sufism. This is spirituality. But how can you describe what you are experiencing inside? The fire of love, this burning love cannot be put into words.

Why are there so few women performers in this field?

My father was a big singer. It was in that environment in which musical notes filled my ears. I was educated by my father, and the shrines were around me. If you go there, you will see that each one has its own colour as far as the music is concerned, as here at Shah Abdul Latif. Sufism is not a gender issue. I have been given a mission. I have this work and work cannot be divided – this for a women and this for man. This is a continuity perpetuated by God and the Lord is making it happen.

Simon Broughton

Abida Parveen

⊙ Hommage à Nusrat Fateh Ali Khan
Network, Germany

An excellent two-CD compilation of fourteen performances dedicated to the memory of Nusrat Fateh Ali Khan by an impressive and wide-ranging line-up of Sufi musicians – from Azerbaijan to Senegal – including some outstanding Pakistani classical performers, notably Salamat Ali Khan and Shafqat Ali Khan. An impressive tribute reflecting Nusrat's spiritual influence round the world.

⊙ Land of the Sufis: Soul Music from the Indus Valley
Shanachie, US

A collection by Peter Pannke, who has been an energetic recorder of Sufi music in Pakistan. These studio recordings focus on Sindh, Baluchistan and Punjab and include a rare recording of a qawwali tarana by Nasiruddin Saami, accompanied by one of the last great sarangi players, Allah Rakha Khan, who also gets a solo track. The brother qawwals Bahauddin and Qutbuddin from Karachi also feature, and there are several rustic, trance-like Qalandar pieces.

⊙ Mystic Fiddle of the Proto-Gypsies
Shanachie, US

Excellent performances by Yaru Maliri on the bowed *sorud*, the four-string Baluchi fiddle carved from a single block of wood, with sympathetic strings amplifying the sound. Wild, passionate performances with flying harmonics, accompanied by tamburag lute. Sufi poems provide the lyrical numbers. Wonderful.

★ Sufi Soul
Network, Germany

This two-CD compilation covers the whole range of Sufi music, from Moroccan Gnawa and Turkish Mevlevi to Iranian and Central Asian singers, with several excellent Pakistani musicians along the way, including Nusrat and the Sabri Brothers. There are excellent contributions from the southern province of Sindh: a poem by Shah Abdul Latif, mystic qalandar dance music and a track from Baluchi sorud (fiddle) player Yar Mohammad.

DVD Sufi Soul: The Mystic Music of Islam
World Music Network, UK

A very accessible documentary about Sufi music presented by William Dalrymple. Filmed in Syria, Turkey and Morocco as well as Pakistan and India, it includes great qawwali sequences as well as Sain Zahoor and Abida Parveen. Directed by Simon Broughton.

★ Troubadours of Allah
Schott/Wergo, Germany

A great two-CD collection from the Indus valley by Peter Pannke to accompany a lavishly illustrated book of the same title (in German). It represents an unrivalled collection of Pakistani Sufi music, with 21 performers and ensembles recorded mainly at shrines in Sindh.

Bakhshi Javed Salamat Ali

Based in the village of Liran, near Faisalabad in Pakistan, the Javed Salamat Brothers are the resident qawwals at a Sufi shrine and specialize in Punjabi qawwali.

⊙ Musiques du Pendjab: Vol. 3 – Le Qawwali
Arion, France

This is one of the finest examples of qawwali in its rightful context, performed at the shrine of a Sufi saint. The main emphasis is on the poetry of the Punjabi mystics, notably Baba Bulleh Shah.

Baluchi Ensemble of Karachi

The Baluch are a stateless people settled mainly in Pakistan (but also in Afghanistan and Iran), and famed for their music. This ensemble, with their singer Rahima, is based in the Baluchi quarter of Karachi.

⊙ Love Songs and Trance Hymns
Shanachie, US

Festive songs for weddings and circumcision ceremonies, plus trance songs and lullabies, including one for the Sufi saint Qalandar, whose tomb is likened to a child's cradle. Instruments include the sorud and the dholak drum.

Faiz Ali Faiz

Born in 1962 and based in Lahore, Punjab, Faiz Ali Faiz is one of the high-profile qawwali singers on the international circuit. Alongside his international debut on World Village and the Nusrat tribute disc above, he's also been involved in fusions with flamenco and gospel singers.

Faiz Ali Faiz

⊙ Your Love Makes Me Dance
Accords Croisés, France

Faiz Ali Faiz hasn't been shy of facing up to the huge shadow that Nusrat has cast over subsequent singers. He's been criticized for imitating him too closely, but there's no denying he's stunning to hear and see in concert. This collection of titles made famous by Nusrat takes its title from a poem by Bulleh Shah.

⊙ Qawwali Flamenco
Accords Croisés, France

An inspired collaboration between Faiz Ali Faiz and his qawwali party with flamenco singers Miguel Poveda and Duquende with the guitarist Chicuelo. Qawwali favourites like "Allah-Hoo" and "Dam Mast Qalandar" are here, but given a fizzing new twist.

Faqirs of Sindh

The six-strong group of Shah-Jo fakir musicians that regularly perform at the shrine of Shah Abdul Latif in Bhitshah.

⊙ Faqirs of Sindh
Ocora, France

With its high falsetto vocals and other-worldly harmonies, this is not easy listening, but it's an authentic and remarkable musical tradition with the percussive twang of the plucked danbur. Recorded in Paris when the group was on tour.

Nusrat Fateh Ali Khan

Born in Faisalabad, Pakistan, into a family which has produced qawwali singers for six centuries – his father was also a celebrated classical musician and qawwal – Nusrat Fateh Ali Khan was the world's best-known qawwal. In addition to the devotional repertoire, he made a number of dance-oriented recordings and tracks for films including *Natural Born Killers*, *Dead Man Walking*, *The Last Temptation of Christ* and *Bandit Queen*.

⊙ Nusrat Fateh Ali Khan in Concert
DEL, Netherlands

Only released in 2007, this is the best posthumous release in a decade. Recorded in Birmingham in 1993, this three-CD set is beautifully atmospheric and serves as a timely reminder of Nusrat's musical prowess as he performs one favourite after another.

⊙ Nusrat Fateh Ali Khan en concert à Paris
Ocora, France

A milestone in qawwali recordings – on five discs, available separately – recorded during Nusrat's peak year in 1989. An essential set for every serious collection, this moves with great ease between a multitude of languages and verses both modern and ancient. The Persian poetry of Amir Khusrau is rendered with hypnotic energy, while the exquisite Punjabi verses of Baba Bulleh Shah acquire a new dimension when heard through this technically flawless recording. Start with Vol. 2, which contains ghazals by Rumi and Baba Bulleh Shah. Very helpful notes and textual translations in three languages.

★ The Last Prophet
Real World, UK

One of several excellent Real World recordings, this particular disc stands out as an ideal compromise between traditional and modern qawwali and is probably the best place for the beginner to start.

⊙ Mustt Mustt
Real World, UK

Nusrat's most successful fusion album. The title track (Mustt means "intoxicated" or "high") is also re-mixed by trip-hop band Massive Attack.

⊙ Shahen-Shah
Real World, UK

Lighter qawwali songs in modern Urdu and Punjabi. Easy lyrics and beautiful melodies make them more accessible to a younger generation.

⊙ Traditional Sufi Qawwalis: Live in London
Navras, UK

Four CDs, available separately, of sama-style qawwali at its very best, recorded in front of an enthusiastic and knowledgeable audience. Nusrat himself considered it one of his greatest performances. Most of the tracks are authentic, traditional numbers that would rarely be sung at larger public concerts, making it a must for beginners and connoisseurs alike. Vol. 2 is a particularly good place to start, with a qawwali ghazal and qawwali sung in classical Indian ragas, while Vol. 3 includes Nusrat's most exceptional "Rang" on disc.

Abida Parveen

Born in Larkana, Sindh, in 1954, she received her musical training from her father Ghulam Haider and then Ustad Salamat Ali Khan. She started singing professionally on Pakistani radio in 1973 and is the most popular Sufi singer in South Asia today, performing around the world and regularly at the urs of Shah Abdul Latif.

★ Songs of the Mystics
Navras, UK

Abida Parveen is at her best in live performance, when the spirit of the occasion grabs her. A double CD of impressive ghazal and kafi performances in front of a live audience in 1989, although there are some nasty fades on applause.

⊙ Baba Bulleh Shah
Times Music, India

The nearest Abida has come to a fusion album, singing the words of the mystic poet Bulleh Shah to the accompaniment of sarangi, mandolin, mandola, keyboard and bass guitar. One of the albums that won her a wide following in India.

⊙ Ishq
Accords Croisés, France

A high-quality production of Abida's devotional music.

Rizwan-Muazzam Qawwali Group

By far the best group of young qawwals to emerge in Pakistan for over a decade. The two lead singers, Rizwan Mujahid Ali Khan and Muazzam Mujahid Ali Khan, both in their early twenties, are nephews of the late Nusrat Fateh Ali Khan.

★ Sacrifice to Love
Real World, UK

One of the best qawwali recordings since the death of Nusrat. On their second international release, Rizwan-Muazzam live up to their impeccable pedigree. Tracks in Hindi and Farsi, the original languages of the genre, as well as Urdu, mark this out from other young Pakistani groups. At its best this album is highly charged, spiritual and trance-inducing.

The Sabri Brothers

Haji Ghulam Farid Sabri and his younger brother Maqbool Ahmed created a duo of Pakistan's best-loved qawwals, their musical lineage stretching back through many generations of great musicians. The brothers did much to popularise qawwali outside Pakistan.

Jami
Piranha, Germany

The Sabris at their esoteric best. The mystical poetry of fifteenth-century Persian poet Jami, coupled with the Sabris' musical sensitivity and percussive expertise is an earth-moving event. The album is dedicated to Haji Ghulam Farid Sabri, who finally fulfilled his life-long wish to record the poetry of Jami. Although it turned out to be his finest performance ever, he did not live to see its release.

The Sindhi Music Ensemble

Vocalists Sohrab Kafir (male) and Husna Naz (female) are backed by a small instrumental ensemble of flute, bowed fiddle, harmonium and percussion.

⊙ Sufi Music from Sindh
Welt Musik/Schott Wergo, Germany

If anywhere can claim to be the cradle of Sufism, it is the province of Sindh in the south of Pakistan. The region is strewn with the graves of holy men and this disc features the music heard at their shrines. Swinging trance music.

Sikh Devotional Music

Nusrat Fateh Ali Khan

The great Sufi qawwali singer was also something of a raagi in his own right, often inserting Sikh holy verses into the main body of his songs, before going on to record an entire disc of shabads.

⊙ Ustad Nusrat Fateh Ali Khan Qawwal Party Vol. 13
OSA, Pakistan

Featuring the poetry of Sikh gurus, for many non-Sikh fans, this remarkable Khan recording served as an introduction to shabad, albeit sung in the qawwali style.

Bhai Avtar Singh Raagi

The late Avtar Singh – Bhai is an honorific title, meaning "brother" – represented the eleventh generation of a distinguished family of raagis dating back to the time of the third Sikh guru, Guru Amar Das (1479–1574).

⊙ Anmol Reetan
T-Series, India

A four-disc set available as two separate double CDs, this is by far the most outstanding collection of traditional *reetan* (compositions) of shabads, with a truly antiquated feel.

Singh Bandhu (The Singh Brothers)

Child prodigies Tejpal and Surinder Singh began learning shabads while they were still toddlers. They sing in the classical *khayal* vocal style of north India.

⊙ Gavo Sachi Bani
Navras, UK

A superb collection of six typical shabads with excellent liner notes identifying each guru-composer, the raga prescribed for the verse and page references for the Sikh holy book.

Dya Singh

An Australian-based artist who formed his own group to evolve a style of shabad featuring many different musical instruments, drawn from various indigenous musical traditions.

⊙ Australian Sikh Rhythm & Soul
DS, Australia

Debut album featuring Singh at his boldest and best, with a unique sound that blends shabad with Middle Eastern, Mediterranean, blues, jazz and native Australian influences.

Jagjit Singh

Generally better known as a performer in the semi-classical ghazal style of singing Urdu couplets, this Singh also included Hindu, Muslim and Sikh devotional music in his repertoire.

⊙ Mittar Pyare Nu
Sony-BMG, India

Featuring different versions of the famous Guru Govind Singh poem Mittar pyare nu haal mureedan da kehna (Tell my beloved friend about the sorry state of his disciple).

PLAYLIST
Pakistan/North India | Sufi Music

1 **ALLAH HOO Nusrat Fateh Ali Khan** from *In Concert*
This was usually Nusrat's opening number and has become one of his signature pieces.

2 **MUSTT MUSTT Nusrat Fateh Ali Khan** from *Mustt Mustt*
The Massive Attack remix that brought qawwali widespread radio play.

3 **TERE ISHQ NACHAAYA Abida Parveen** from *Songs of the Mystics*
Urgent music from Punjabi poet Bulleh Shah.

4 **AUQUHIAN RAHWAN Sain Zahoor** from *Awards for World Music 2006*
The great Punjabi troubadour sings about the difficult paths of love.

5 **TWO QALANDARI TUNES Yaru Malari** from *The Mystic Fiddle of the Proto-Gypsies*
Great Baluchi trance music sawn out on the sorud fiddle.

6 **SUR SORATH Allah Bachayo Khoso and Ensemble** from *Troubadours of Allah*
Wild *alghosa* double-flute playing and drumming.

7 **SABIR KI JAY HO Rizwan-Muazzam Qawwali** from *Sacrifice to Love*
A song in praise of Sufi saint Baba Farid from this young qawwali group.

The Philippines

filipino fusions

Grace Nono with the Asian Fantasy
Orchestra
John Clewley

That Filipinos excel in making other people's music is well known. Filipino bands
playing covers of Western pop have cornered the hotel-lounge market from Dubai
to Hong Kong, a phenomenon that stretches back at least as far as the 1920s, when
dance bands from Manila such as the Shanghai Swingmasters and the Oriental
Syncopators plied the Pacific hotel and cruise-ship circuit. Occasionally, Filipino
musicians do gain fame for their originality, as in the case of the late jazz pianist
Bobby "The Wildman" Enriquez, but on the whole, when Filipinos choose to make
their own music, the results often don't travel well. This is a shame, because the
Filipino pop music scene is one of Asia's most vibrant, fusing Western pop idioms with
a distinctly Filipino soul. **Eric S. Caruncho** gives the inside story.

The phrase "four hundred years in a convent, fifty years in Hollywood" is often used to sum up the influence of Spanish and American colonialism on the hybrid culture of the Philippines. On the surface, the Philippines may appear to be the most Westernized country in Southeast Asia. It is predominantly Catholic, the most lasting legacy of four centuries of Spanish rule, and a large proportion of the people speak both **Tagalog** (or one of the other major Philippine languages) and English – a hangover from the half-century of domination by the United States. The mass media, especially pop radio and music television, is dominated by Western content.

But Filipinos have a way of adapting foreign influences to their own needs. Its much-vaunted Catholicism, for instance, is in most cases a kind of folk Christianity which has absorbed older animist beliefs. The Filipino *fiesta*, while having roots in Spain, also expresses specific Filipino cultural patterns and behaviours having to do with family and community. Most Filipinos understand English, but actually speak **"Taglish"**, a mixture of Tagalog and English.

The same goes for music. Mainstream Filipino pop music is little distinguishable from Western pop, except for the language. It even follows Western radio formats, whether adult contemporary, R&B, top forty, even hip-hop, and local and foreign hits share chart space.

Until recently, local acts only made up a small proportion of the music sold and played on the radio. But Filipino artists are slowly catching up, and the best of them are claiming a larger proportion of the airwaves and the charts. As audiences mature, they are also demanding more originality from local artists.

Being an archipelago, the Philippines is home to a diverse range of indigenous cultures. There are an estimated **140 indigenous communities**, from the hill tribes of the Northern Cordillera through the aboriginal Aetas of the Central Plain to the Islamized tribes of Mindanao, each with its own distinctive style of music. Most indigenous music is connected to the tribe's rituals, and there is a wide variety of native instruments ranging from bamboo flutes to boat lutes to brass gongs. The **kulintang music of Southern Mindanao** is reminiscent of Indonesian gamelan, making use of instruments such as the **kulintang** (tuned gongs), the **gabbang** (bamboo xylophone), and the **agong** (brass gong) which are analogous to Indonesian gamelan instruments. The **non-Muslim tribes of northern and central Mindanao**, on the other hand, prefer the **kudlong** or **hegalong** (a two-stringed boat lute), the **kubing** (bamboo Jew's harp) and various flutes. The mountain tribes of the Cordillera, on the other hand, use brass gongs in a very different way to accompany ritual chants.

Boris Lelong

The Lemhadong folk musicians of Lake Sebu in the southern Philippines

Unfortunately, very little of this indigenous tribal music has been recorded, and even less released. In recent years, however, there have been moves to record the music of indigenous musicians, spearheaded by artists who have been influenced by them. These include Joey Ayala and Grace Nono, who has released works by contemporary masters such as the Maguindanao kulintang master **Aga Butocan** and the Maranao singer and instrumentalist **Sindao Banisil** on her own label, Tao Music.

Colonization

Under **Spanish rule**, Filipino musicians quickly adapted the musical forms and instruments of their colonizers. The **guitar**, a quintessentially Spanish instrument, was widely adopted as the instrument of choice for vocal accompaniment, and to this day, many amateur groups keep the **rondalla** alive. This is a string ensemble that came from Spain via Mexico during the days of the galleon trade, with instruments similar to those of the Mexican mariachi, minus the brass: guitar, string bass, the mandolin-like *laud*, *bandurria* and *octavina*.

The Spanish operetta or **zarzuela** was introduced in the nineteenth century. It was quickly adapted by Filipino composers, who penned their own Tagalog lyrics to these popular works, even turning them against their masters before and during the Philippine revolution, when numerous subversive pieces were performed.

This tradition continued into the **American colonial period** after Spain ceded the Philippines to the US as part of the Treaty of Paris of 1898 that ended the Spanish-American War. But the new colonizers introduced their own popular music to the islands, resulting in new hybrids. Musical historians have theorized that **jazz** might have been introduced to the Philippines by black American soldiers deserting to the Filipino side during the Filipino-American War. In any case, Filipinos soon developed a taste for American popular music. Within the space of a few years, **Filipino jazz big-bands** were performing in local *vodavil* (vaudeville) theatres and cabarets, as well as the more up-market nightclubs. A number of these bands, such as the **Oriental Syncopators** and the **Shanghai Swingmasters**, even managed to get bookings from Hong Kong, Tokyo and the Shanghai Bund (this was, perhaps, the beginnings of the Filipino hotel-lounge band phenomenon). Eventually, vaudeville performers such as **Katy de la Cruz** began to perform show tunes with Tagalog lyrics.

The preferred popular-song form until the 1950s, however, was the **kundiman** or **Tagalog love ballad**, a form that, curiously, had its origins in nationalist art songs during the nineteenth century. Kundiman crooners such as **Ruben Tagalog** and **Sylvia la Torre** were bona fide radio and recording stars, at least until the onslaught of Western pop on the radio in the late 1950s wooed younger listeners away. But to this day, echoes of the plaintive kundiman can be detected in modern popular songs.

Pinoy Rock'n'Roll

Almost from the beginning, Filipino popular music tended to mimic Western trends. When rock'n'roll and rhythm and blues revolutionized Western pop in the 1950s, entertainers like **Eddie Mesa**, billed as the "Elvis Presley of the Philippines", emerged. For the most part, however, the artistes concerned merely performed cover versions of hits by the particular pop star they had modelled themselves on. Thus there were performers billed as the "Frank Sinatra of the Philippines", the "Trini Lopez of the Philippines" and even the "Tom Jones of the Philippines". It wasn't until the early 1960s that one of them, **Bobby Gonzales**, thought of combining Tagalog lyrics with rock'n'roll arrangements. His biggest hit was "Hahabul-habol" (Chasing After), a novelty number with a Bill Haley-influenced jump blues arrangement, but presciently, one of the album fillers built around essentially the same instrumental arrangement was titled "Pinoy Rock'n'Roll".

The Sixties saw a genuine Manila band scene emerge from amateur garage-band beginnings. In the early 1960s, guitar-instrumental combos in the Ventures/Shadows mould, such as **RJ and the Riots** and the **Electromaniacs**, became popular, but they were soon swept away by Beatlemania and the subsequent wave of "Filipino Beatles" that followed. One of them, the **Downbeats**, even opened for the actual Beatles in 1966 during their infamous Manila concert, which ended with the Fab Four being chased by President Marcos's goons right into their waiting jet. Bands like the **Bits and Pieces**, **Pink and Purple** the **Moonstrucks** and the **Birth of the Cool** took up residency in the nightclub strip along Roxas Boulevard, with the best of them gigging as far as Japan and Hong Kong.

During the Vietnam War, American military bases like the Subic Naval Base and Clark Air Base in Central Luzon became important "rest and recreation" centres for US troops from the front, spawning a rowdy bar-band scene. Olongapo City especially bred a tougher strain of the Filipino cover band, able to play several sets a night of country and western, rock and soul before a demanding audience. Soon Olongapo bands with names like **Red Fox**, the **Psyclones**, the **Jovials** and the **Soul Jugglers** rivalled their Manila counterparts.

In 1971, the Antipolo Rock Festival brought most of these bands together in what was typically billed as "the Filipino Woodstock". But it wasn't until the following year, after President Marcos had placed the country under martial law, that what became known as **Pinoy rock** really came into its own. During a 1972 concert, **Joey Smith**, drummer and vocalist for the Juan de la Cruz Band, sang a hastily penned Tagalog number called "Himig Natin" (Our Music). This soon became the de facto anthem for Pinoy rock, signalling a major break from the tradition of doing covers towards composing and performing original songs in Tagalog.

A radio programme called *Pinoy Rock and Rhythm* championed the new music, as did the local recording industry, after they assured themselves that the new music would sell. Soon, following Juan de la Cruz's lead, acts such as **Anakbayan**, **Mike Hanopol**, **Maria Cafra** and **Sampaguita** ruled the charts and the airwaves, standing on an equal commercial footing with Western pop for the first time.

The **Juan de la Cruz Band** were the standard-bearers of Pinoy rock. Starting out as a psychedelic combo with their debut *Up In Arms*, they soon trimmed down to a classic power trio, with Smith on drums and vocals, Mike Hanopol on bass and Wally Gonzales on lead guitar. Smith himself was the living embodiment of the music's mongrel origins: the son of an American navy pilot and a Filipino mother, he grew up in Clark Air Base listening to Chuck Berry and Elvis, and took up rock'n'roll at an early age.

Anakbayan (Youth of the Nation, now the name of a radical youth movement) were the Rolling Stones to the Juan de la Cruz Band's Beatles. Fronted by their charismatic drummer Edmond Fortuno, they created a jazzier version of Pinoy rock with songs like "Probinsyana" (Provincial Girl) and "Pagbabalik ng Kuwago" (Return of the Owl). **Mike Hanopol**, the bassist for the Juan de la Cruz Band, proved to be a capable solo performer, combining a trademark blistering lead-guitar style and gravelly voice with a knack for pop hooks. Formerly known as the Psyclones, **Maria Cafra** introduced the hard-edged Olongapo City sound to Filipino audiences, while **Sampaguita** was the

first female Pinoy rocker, both band and singer taking the name from the national flower.

Pinoy rock soon mutated into different genres. Solo performers such as **Florante de Leon** and **Coritha** popularized acoustic Tagalog folk songs, which dwelt on nationalistic themes and harked back to an idealized past. Meanwhile, **Hotdog**, **Cinderella** and the **Apolinario Mabini Hiking Society** spearheaded the so-called "Manila sound", a more commercial format of radio-ready pop songs that was to develop into **"OPM"** (original Pilipino music), the catch-all category for local (as opposed to Western) pop.

In 1978, a relatively unknown folk singer named **Freddie Aguilar** had a monster hit with "Anak" (Child), which eventually went on to sell four million copies in Europe alone and spawn fifty-four cover versions in fourteen languages, making it easily the most successful Filipino recording to date. In their rush to find the "next Freddie Aguilar", his record label came up with a folk-rock trio called **Asin** (Salt), which featured the powerful voice of **Lolita Carbon**. Asin proved to be even more seminal, becoming the first group to sing in Philippine languages other than Tagalog, about topical concerns from armed conflict to environmental degradation to the Filipino diaspora, and one of the first to incorporate indigenous musical instruments such as the kulintang into pop. Even more politicized were

John Clewley

Freddie Aguilar

Heber Bartolome and Banyuhay, whose anthem "Tayo'y Mga Pinoy" (We Are Pinoy) called into question the very colonial values that drove Pinoy pop music in the first place. Mainstream audiences, however, preferred the sweet, innocuous love songs and telegenic pop idols of OPM, and by the beginning of the 1980s, the era of classic Pinoy rock was over.

New Waves

True to form, Filipino musicians soon caught on to the punk movement, and local bands such as the **Jerks**, **Third World Chaos**, the **Deadends**, the **Wuds** and the **Urban Bandits** were soon echoing classic punk themes such as anarchy in their songs. Pinoy punk was a small, insular scene, limited to a handful of Manila clubs and small, DIY record labels, and totally ignored by the mainstream record industry. Pinoy New Wave fared little better, although its standard-bearer, the **Dawn**, went on to a long and successful career despite the grisly murder of their lead guitarist. Contemporaries like the **Ethnic Faces**, **Identity Crisis** and **Violent Playground**, however, soon sank into obscurity.

Meanwhile, a different sort of underground music scene was bubbling under the surface. Individual musicians had absorbed the lessons of the first generation of Pinoy rock artists and were creating and recording their own music. The most distinctive of these was **Joey Ayala**. The son of 1950s bohemians, Ayala had been a poet and short-story writer before turning his talents to music. He spent his formative years in Mindanao, where he combined the influence of topical folk-rockers such as Asin with the music and nature mysticism of the *lumad*, the indigenous tribes of the region. He called his band **Bagong Lumad** (New Natives) and to the standard guitars and drums added kulintang gongs, kubing and hegalong lute, creating a fusion of Pinoy folk-rock and ethnic music. Although he made his first, home-recorded cassette album – *Panganay ng Umaga* (Firstborn of the Morning) – in 1982, it took a dozen years for the rest of the country to catch on.

Grace Nono, a native of Mindanao and a veteran of the local new-wave scene, also turned to the lumad for inspiration. Adapting the melismatic scales of tribal music to her vocal style, and relying on intricate arrangements making extensive use of indigenous instrumentation, Nono recorded a series of albums on her label Tao Music, often collaborating with her jazz-guitarist husband Bob Aves.

Ayala and Nono spawned a minor trend towards "ethnic" music, although few of their followers matched their lyrical gifts. One exception was the percussion ensemble **Pinikpikan**, which evolved its own style of ethnic party music to become the country's leading roots band.

Meanwhile, the total lack of music-industry interest in local music (outside the most blatantly commercial pop) proved salutary, since bands and musicians, under no pressure to "sell out", were free to experiment. Incubated in a handful of small clubs, the "alternative" music scene in 1990s Manila soon gave birth to dozens of bands playing anything from hardcore punk to thrash metal to ska and reggae.

All this changed when the **Eraserheads**, formed as a college band five years earlier, landed a major-label deal in 1993. Though barely proficient with their instruments, their debut album, *Ultraelectromagneticpop!*, revealed a flair for melodic hooks as well as lyrics that captured contemporary reality from the viewpoint of young middle-class Filipinos. The Eraserheads became bona fide pop stars, going from strength to strength with each succeeding album, and their collected work is a testament to what it was like to be a young Filipino growing up in the 1990s.

The Eraserheads' multi-platinum success paved the way for other bands such as **Rivermaya**, **Yano**, **Color it Red**, **Wolfgang**, **Tropical Depression**, **Put3Ska** and scores more. Although the so-called "alternative music" boom soon peaked, and the music industry shifted its interest to more commercial, if less original, pop acts, a space had been created for contemporary Filipino pop music to flourish.

Today, despite worldwide recession in the music industry, contemporary Filipino pop music is more diverse than ever, with bands finding new audiences through non-traditional means, such as mobile phone ringtones, the Internet, advertising and television. Their music has also become more truly bilingual, as younger musicians no longer find it necessary to compose in Tagalog to affirm their identity (although radio singles are still invariably in Tagalog). Many bands have links to an earlier generation of musicians: **Sandwich**, **Cambio** and **Pupil**, for instance, are spin-offs of the Eraserheads, while **Bamboo** emerged from Rivermaya. The independent music scene is even more diverse, with bands experimenting with electronic music, Brazilian beats, hip-hop, jazz and rhythm and blues, adapting foreign idioms like their forebears to express Filipino realities.

A useful website for information about Filipino music is *philmusic.com*, and for buying CDs, *www.liyra.com*.

Traditional

⊙ Philippines: Women Artists of Lake Sebu
Buda, France

The eighty-thousand-strong T'boli people live in a mountainous region of southwestern Mindanao, their land threatened by the advance of large corporations. This disc is a marvellous evocation of people in tune with their environment; beautiful performances from a female collective on local fiddles, lutes, pipes and gongs by the lake in south Mindanao.

★ Utom: Summoning the Spirit. Music in the T'boli Heartland
Rykodisc, US

Amid the noises of birds, insects and trees, a lute player evokes the sounds of a cicada and woodpecker, a woman strums a hypnotic bamboo zither and a shaman plays his flute; also features ceremonial gongs, dances and drums. One of the best evocations of traditional indigenous life recorded anywhere.

Sindao Banisil

Singer/instrumentalist Sindao Banisil is one of the last performers of Maranao oral traditions (the Maranao, or "people of the lake" are from the western highlands of Mindanao).

⊙ Pakaradia-an
Tao Music, Philippines

The title ("entertainment") is reflected in this collection of lullabies, instrumentals, children's and religious songs. Some songs are connected with the epic tale, "Darangan", which Banisil sings in special vocal styles that feature classical language and texts from the Koran.

Aga Mayo Butocan

A contemporary master of the Maguindanao style of the kulintang, or tuned brass gongs, Butocan is also an ethnomusicologist and a teacher, and has devised a system of notation for her instrument.

⊙ Maguindanao Kulintang
Tao Music, Philippines

This recording showcases Butocan's performing on solo kulintang, although the instrument is more often used as part of an ensemble in actual performance.

Pinoy Rock, Pop, Folk and Fusion

⊙ Pagbabalik: Pinoy Folk Rock
Vicor Music, Philippines

A useful compilation of the early hits of Freddie Aguilar, Asin, Coritha and Florante, including Aguilar's "Anak" and "Bayan Ko".

⊙ Pinoy Rock: 40th Anniversary Collection
Vicor Music, Philippines

Hits from the first era of Pinoy Rock, including "Himig Natin" by Juan de la Cruz, and songs by Anakbayan, Maria Cafra and Mike Hanopol.

Freddie Aguilar

Aguilar (b. 1953) is synonymous with Pinoy rock. Armed with a guitar and a winning formula of Western folk-rock married to Filipino melodies, he has been hugely influential at home and across Asia.

★ Greatest Hits
Ugat/Vicor Music, Philippines

Impassioned vocals and simple lyrics, backed by Aguilar's trademark guitar sound. Includes "Anak", the biggest-selling Filipino record of all time and one of the most covered Asian songs ever.

Asin

Asin form a vital link between the first generation of Pinoy rockers and subsequent artists such as Joey Ayala. They were the first to deal with topical concerns such as the environment and armed conflict in Mindanao, the first to incorporate indigenous musical instruments in their songs, and among the first to challenge Manila's hegemony by singing in languages other than Tagalog.

⊙ Masdan Mo Ang Kapaligiran
Vicor Music, Philippines

A compilation of their essential hits.

Bob Aves

Aves is Grace Nono's husband and a Berklee-schooled jazz guitarist and arranger.

⊙ Translating the Gongs
Tao Music, Philippines

Aves adapts the intricate scales and modes of traditional Maguindanao music to jazz guitar, a fusion that succeeds admirably.

Joey Ayala

Former writer Ayala pioneered the fusion of ethnic music and Pinoy folk-rock in the early 1980s with his self-recorded first album.

⊙ Magkabilaan
Universal Records, Philippines

Ayala's second album, rerecorded in 1991, shows his vision fully formed. The title track outlines his environmental philosophy, and other songs such as "Manong Pawikan" (Brother Sea Turtle) zero in on more specific concerns. The album also includes arguably his most popular love song, "Walang Hanggang Paalam" (Never Ending Farewell), at one time adopted as a wedding song by Filipino activists.

Bamboo

Bamboo Mañalac was lead vocalist for Rivermaya before leaving the band to go solo.

⊙ As the Music Plays
EMI, Philippines
He scored an immediate hit with "Noypi", a hard rocking number that harks back to early Pinoy rock's defiant declarations of Filipino identity. The band's current popularity rivals that of his old band.

Eraserheads

The most critically and commercially successful band to come out of the Filipino alternative music scene.

⊙ Anthology
BMG, Philippines
This two-disc collection offers a useful overview. Front man Ely Buendia has a lyrical gift for capturing vignettes of Filipino life that ring true, and a knack for framing them in hooky, melodic power-pop.

Florante

Late 1970s troubadour.

⊙ The Best of Florante
Universal Records, Philippines
Gentle acoustic folk in a nationalist vein. Includes "Ako'y Pinoy" (I am Pinoy), "Pinay" and "Handog".

Mike Hanopol

Gravel-voiced guitar-slinger, previously a bassist with the Juan de la Cruz Band (see below).

⊙ Laki Sa Layaw
Ivory Music, Philippines
A greatest-hits compilation that includes "Laki sa Layaw", "Mr Kenkoy", "Tulungan Natin" and "Upos na Lang", among others.

Juan de la Cruz Band

Pinoy-rock pioneers, featuring Mike Hanopol on bass and Joey Smith on drums and vocals.

⊙ The Best of the Juan de la Cruz Band
Vicor Music, Philippines
Compiles all the hits from the band's Pinoy-rock period, mostly in a heavy blues-rock vein.

⊙ Up In Arms
Shadoks Music, Germany
A rare glimpse of the band in their pre-Pinoy-rock, psychedelic phase. Much sought-after by fans of the genre.

Jun Lopito

Generally regarded as the best guitarist in Manila, Jun Lopito has played with everyone from Pepe Smith to Grace Nono, and from reggae legends Cocojam to "alternative" rockers the Jerks.

⊙ Bodhisattvas
BMG, Philippines
Eight years in the making, this album compiles various songs from Lopito's career, with help from a who's who of top musicians and stars, a bunch Lopito refers to as bodhisattvas (literally, Buddhist saints). Quality Filipino rock.

Grace Nono

Nono's music has been described as "eco ethnic soul music". A mesmerizing singer and stage performer.

⊙ Opo
Tao Music, Philippines
Nono's art is best showcased by her second album. "Opo" in Tagalog is the respectful way of saying yes, usually to elders. This is Nono's song of life affirmation, driven by dense arrangements that keep a forward momentum to the songs.

Pinikpikan

Named after a local chicken dish, in which the chicken is prepared with a "rhythm stick" before it is cooked, the eleven-strong Pinikpikan was the Philippines' most likely candidate for success on the world music scene. Their sound was driven by traditional drums, gongs and other percussion instruments, with a rock and funk sensibility. They performed their last gig in 2008, but promised a new project, called Kalayo.

Atas
Tao Music, Philippines/Tropical Music, Germany
Pinikpikan's second album, released in 1999, is the only one available internationally and is a good introduction to their energetic and vibrant style. "Atas" (Mission) features singer Grace Nono and guitarist Bob Aves as guest musicians.

Rivermaya

The Eraserheads' only rival in the melodic pop sweepstakes, Rivermaya's hooks derive from front man Rico Blanco's fondness for the anthemic guitar grandeur of 1980s new wave.

⊙ Greatest Hits
BMG, Philippines
Hits compilation gathering their early works during the band's first period.

⊙ Isang Ugat, Isang Dugo
Viva Records, Philippines
An oddity in the band's discography, this album of covers finds the band essaying versions of early Filipino punk and new wave, including the Jerks' "Romantic Kill", the Wuds' "Inosente Lang ang Nagtataka" and Violent Playground's "Tupperware Party".

Sampaguita

Pinoy rock's first female star.

⊙ Greatest Hits
Ivory Music, Philippines
Catchy pop-rock. Includes "Bonggahan", "Nosi Balasi" and "Easy Lang Pare".

Yano

This agit-punk outfit came out of the University of the Philippines in 1994. Singer Dong Abay and guitarist Eric Gancio expressed the resentment felt by the Filipino underclass towards the country's ruling elite.

⊙ **Yano**
BMG, Philippines
"Kumusta Na?" (How Are You?) criticizes the 1986 Edsa Revolt's failure to improve the lot of the country's poor, while other songs take aim at such targets as traditional politicians ("Trapo") and religious hypocrites ("Banal na Aso, Santong Kabayo").

PLAYLIST
The Philippines

1 **BEEP BEEP** Juan de la Cruz Band from *The Best of the Juan de la Cruz Band*
"Himig Natin" is Pinoy rock's anthem, but this number, a tribute to the distinctively Filipino mode of transport known as the jeepney, is more representative of the band's blues-rock roots.

2 **ANAK** Freddie Aguilar from *Greatest Hits*
The biggest-selling and most-covered Filipino song, with a hypnotic groove and keening delivery that cuts across cultural barriers.

3 **PAGBABALIK** Asin from *Masdan Mo Ang Kapaligiran*
The spine-tingling delivery by Lolita Carbon underscores the homesickness felt by Filipino expats throughout the world.

4 **MINDANAO** Joey Ayala from *Magkabilaan*
Ayala sings in Cebuano here, evoking both the landscape and the distinct culture of his adopted home by using indigenous scales and rhythms.

5 **YAYEYAN** Grace Nono from *Opo*
Mesmerizing vocals and a dense, intricate arrangement showcase Nono's aspirations to a truly world music with Philippine roots.

6 **ANG HULING EL BIMBO** Eraserheads from *Anthology*
Ely Buendia somehow takes a long-forgotten novelty dance-craze and builds a song about the shattered dreams of youth around it.

7 **TSINELAS** Yano from *Yano*
"Tsinelas" are flip-flops, the preferred footwear of the Filipino poor, and Yano uses the image to express the class anger bubbling beneath the apparently tranquil surface of Philippine society.

8 **NOYPI** Bamboo from *As the Music Plays*
A defiant hard-rock anthem of Filipino pride.

9 **KALIPAY** Pinikpikan from *Atas*
A song about finding happiness through dancing, with exuberant vocals, wild electric guitar, local gongs and bamboo.

Polynesia

many islands, one voice

The Tahitian Gospel Choir
Michael Chansin/Triloka Records

You might not think so from the bland grass-skirt compilations generally available both internationally and in local markets, but authentic Polynesian folk traditions are alive and the level of community participation is high. Common threads can be seen and heard in the performing arts of island cultures separated by thousands of kilometres of ocean, reflecting ancient lines of migration and cultural exchange. Ethnomusicologist Richard Moyle provides an expert introduction to the "real music of paradise".

olynesia is generally reckoned to be that vast area of the Pacific Ocean forming an approximate triangle between Easter Island in the east, Hawaii in the north and New Zealand in the south (see separate chapters for the latter two). Colonization is believed to have occurred from Melanesia to the distant west, beginning more than three thousand years ago.

Cultural and linguistic similarities among adjacent island groups have prompted anthropologists to divide the region into two broad areas, East and West Polynesia. To these similarities can be added music, because even before the first European explorers, travel among islands for trade was common, as was the sharing of songs and dances. Today, the islands of Samoa and Tonga, along with the smaller islands of Tokelau, Niue, Uvea and Futuna, have dances with the same names, and many of these trace their origin to Samoa.

Much modern Polynesian music has a Western sound to it, but the presence of foreign elements is not a new phenomenon. The so-called "borrowing" of particular musical effects and dance movements was already in operation among neighbouring island groups at the time of European contact. Western styles and instruments have simply provided composers and arrangers with yet another source of material. To a visitor's ear, the musical results may sound somewhat contrived and inauthentic, but to Polynesian performers and audiences, the origin of the music is less important than the reason for using it. Visitors may focus on the sound, but Polynesians focus on the poetic content, a contrast of means and end.

Traditional Instruments

Most Polynesian music is centred on the human voice (see box overleaf) and the act of singing exists mainly to enhance the uttered word. Dancing adds a visual dimension, and any accompanying instruments help to synchronize the sounds and actions of singers and dancers. Group singing dominates all parts of Polynesia, and songs typically express the views of a village, school, church or other organization.

Songs intended for solo singing tend to relate to the activities of individuals such as priests (in former times) and healers, because singing opened a line of communication with the supernatural world in a way that the spoken word could not. Vestiges of such indigenous belief may account for the ongoing esteem that composers and conductors continue to enjoy in both secular and Christian contexts.

The primary focus on singing also accounts for the **few melodic instruments**. The **nose-flute**, once used widely in Polynesia for personal entertainment, has been replaced by Western instruments and recorded music (although Tonga's government radio-station call sign is a flute solo performed some forty years ago by the late **Ve'ehala**, the country's former spokesman on culture). Wherever bamboo grew naturally, flutes were made from its wood. With one thumb blocking one nostril and holding the closer end of the instrument, the other hand operated the finger-holes to produce melodies of three or four notes as the player blew through the other nostril. Although simple to construct and play, the nose-flute is an artefact of a bygone era, sometimes made in cultural classes in schools or manufactured for tourists, but no longer part of the living musical tradition.

Most Polynesian instruments are **idiophones**, which are thumped on the ground or struck directly with hand or stick. Wooden **sounding-boards** have long gone from Samoa and Tokelau, and bamboo **stamping-tubes** have disappeared from most parts of Polynesia. Hawaii has retained a variety of such instruments, including lengths of split bamboo struck against the body, a double gourd which is struck against the ground and hit with the hand, pairs of stones clicked in the hand like castanets, and pairs of sticks struck together. What makes these instruments unusual is not their shape or materials, but the fact that it is the dancers who use them while they perform. The same person can simultaneously be singer, dancer and instrumentalist.

Polynesians in general and Samoans in particular use the world's oldest musical instrument, **the human body**. The Samoan *fa'ataupati* dance features fast, wordless and synchronized actions by men who rhythmically slap their sides, chests and feet to the unchanging rhythm of a beaten tin. Handclapping is also used to accompany singing. Samoans make greatest use of clapping in dance songs, holding cupped hands at right angles to produce a *po* sound, and also flat and parallel for a *pati* sound. Using exaggerated movements, a group leader signals to the singers the moments when each type of clap is to be used. For Samoa, **ad hoc instruments** include a floor mat, rolled up and held in place by a leg while the seated player strikes it with light sticks. An empty bottle placed inside the roll amplifies the sound. Similarly, Rotuman groups may beat a pile of folded mats.

The earliest **brass bands** entered Polynesia in the late nineteenth century, as gifts given to

Brass band accompanying Samoan dances, Apia, Western Samoa

Polynesian Hymns

The influence of missionaries in nineteenth-century Polynesia was extensive and rapid. Villages and even entire islands converted to Christianity within a short time, and the foreign influence extended beyond religious belief itself and into local society. Most wooden or bone images of local gods or ancestors were seized and destroyed, but the few that were spared underwent a dramatic transformation over the following century: from objects of religious ritual to tokens of missionary conquest to cultural treasures. Virtually everywhere, missionaries successfully preached that traditional dancing was evil, and whole categories of dance now exist only in the published accounts of eighteenth-century explorers and traders. Some categories, such as Samoa's *poula* night-dances and Hawaii's *hula*, went underground. But although missionaries offered no substitute dances of their own for those they banned, they did introduce a new musical idiom – the four-part hymn.

The earliest **Polynesian hymns** simply translated verses from British or American hymns into the local languages, but before long, local composers were creating their own music and words. In Tonga, this resulted in the creation of **hiva usu**, sung unaccompanied in four or more parts, often departing from standard European harmony, featuring a solo or duet and always sung as loud as possible. **Loudness** was and still is an unforgettable feature of locally composed hymns in French Polynesia and the Cook Islands, where they are called **himene** (or a local variant such as *imene*). These compositions are probably Polynesia's most complex vocal works, with up to twelve solo and group parts. Solo parts are permitted some flexibility of melody and words, so that no two performances or even verses are necessarily identical. A Cook Island himene is considered *reka* ("sweet") if the solo parts include one or both of two vocal techniques, each one different from the one-note-per-syllable singing of the group parts. One technique is to sing a series of rapid notes to the syllable "*he*" as a kind of vocal decoration. The other is to sing a similarly rapid series of notes, usually very high-pitched, to the same vowel (much like a coloratura soprano). When sung inside a nineteenth-century coral cement church – and many are still in use – the bare walls reflect the sound to the point of pain and the overall effect is of a solid wall of sound.

The himene of **Rapaiti**, a small French territory a thousand miles south of Tahiti, are instantly recognizable even though they use the same combinations of group and solo singing parts as the Cook Islands and the rest of French Polynesia. In these other regions, each verse ends with a long drawn-out cadence, and while this is being sung, a female soloist will start the next verse and eventually the whole group joins in. But on Rapaiti, the pitch of the long notes in the cadence – the notes that everyone is singing – drops a semitone, as if the batteries in the playback machine had suddenly died. However, this feature is quite deliberate: it's repeated

prominent chiefs by British or German political leaders hoping to win trade concessions. Ownership of a set of instruments quickly became a status symbol quite separate from the quality of music that local musicians were able to produce. Samoan songs of the early 1900s even imitated the sounds of these bands, particularly the sections where the melody was carried by the bass instruments. Only a few Tongan and Samoan bands are still owned by villages, most being the property of the police and used for formal government events. A growing trend is for the band to play an arrangement of a local song, but to include a section where members down their instruments and sing a verse before picking them up again for an instrumental finish.

String bands provide the stereotypical Polynesian instrumental sound. Tongan **hiva kakala** (topical songs) typify these bands, with groups of men accompanied by guitars and perhaps also a banjo. Unique to these songs, however, is the practice of some men singing in falsetto above other male voice-parts. The melody in these and other multi-part Tongan songs is positioned in the second-lowest part, not the highest. String bands in Tahiti and the Cook Islands have a distinctive sound because they contain a rapidly strummed ukulele as lead instrument pitched far above the other instruments.

Action Songs, Drum Dances

When Polynesian performers moved their bodies as they sang, early European visitors to the Pacific were unsure whether they were watching songs or dances, and the term "**action song**" is now applied to a variety of performances in New Zealand and the Cook Islands. The actions combine narrative depictions and more abstract movements, even when the dancers are seated. As with most Polynesian dances, the body is divided horizontally at the waist: the legs act as time-markers to the sing-

at the end of each verse and the overall pitch of the song slides down and down. The CD *The Tahitian Choir* has striking examples.

Another feature of himene is the rhythmic grunting which men perform at certain parts of each verse, giving rise to names such as *himene tuki* in the Cook Islands, where "*tuki*" means "grunt". The grunting of syllables such as *he* or *hi* gives these songs a powerful pulse, propelling the music forward.

The singing of **European choral works** finds its grandest form in Tonga, where British anthems and entire oratorios are memorized and sung unaccompanied by some choirs. The Maopa Free Wesleyan Church choir of Nuku'alofa even performs Handel's *Messiah*, accompanied by a police band, and local-language arrangements of choral works by Bach and Mozart are as popular now as they were a generation ago.

For more than a century, the singing of European hymns suffered from the penetrating nasal sound of choir sopranos, but this had more to do with culture than the voices themselves. Four-part hymns (soprano, alto, tenor, bass) represented a novelty, but one with an obvious hierarchy of importance. The melody was thought to be the most important part, and so was assigned to the most important women singers, who happened to be the senior choir members whose voices had started to fall with age. Younger singers of lower rank were assigned the alto part. Such etiquette had the unfortunate effect of forcing the older women to reach notes so high that they caused discomfort. Only in recent years has this system changed, and most singers now are assigned parts according to their vocal range rather than social status. However, the old practice remains in force in some Cook Island choirs, where the very high solo female parts are sung by more experienced, and therefore, older women, and it's common to see these people pressing a finger or hard object against their temple while they sing, as a distraction from the physical pain of reaching notes well above their comfortable range.

The high public profile of such church music reflects the cultural significance of Christianity in Polynesia. In many islands, nineteenth-century lyrics, some composed by missionaries themselves, still form part of regular church services, and nineteenth-century standards of dress are the norm. Sunday activities are dominated by the church and village life virtually comes to a halt, the air turning blue with smoke from wood fires preparing communal meals. In Samoa, the deep booms from the giant slit drums called **logo** and in Samoa and Tonga the persistent beating of pairs of smaller **lali** slit drums call the fearful and faithful to worship. Although some congregations still sing unaccompanied, most use some form of keyboard, ranging from the small pedal-harmonium to bells-and-whistles electronic organs; the latter are now favoured by charismatic churches.

ing and the torso and arms interpret the lyrics of the song. The old saying "Keep your eyes on the hands" does have some truth in it.

However, not all Polynesian dances accompany singing, as the visually spectacular **drum dances** of French Polynesia and the Cook Islands demonstrate. The drum orchestra consists of several wood slit drums tuned to a different pitch, a free-standing "bongo" drum, and a large double-headed skin drum. All of the slit drums beat the same rhythm, which continues for about half a minute before instantly changing to another rhythm, and the changes continue like this for the rest of the dance. Women rapidly rotate their hips as they dance, their grass skirts emphasizing the movement as they hold their arms above their heads. Men rapidly open and close their legs in a scissor-like movement, with arms outstretched on either side. When a woman moves right up close to a male dancer and performs in this manner, the sexual connotations are clear and are approved while on the dancefloor.

A Polynesian audience doesn't sit quietly throughout a song or dance and applaud after an item. An **active audience** is integral to a successful performance. Singers – and especially dancers – react when they hear appreciative shouts and calls, and when the audience responds and applauds even more strongly in turn, this back-and-forth movement of energy raises the performance to a near-mystical level. Audience members demonstrate their appreciation of particular dancers by getting up and placing money on the dancer's body or wrapping a valuable piece of cotton or bark cloth around their feet, or even briefly joining in the dancing. At fundraising dances, basins are strategically placed in front of the stage, and money-counters are on hand to assess and later publicly announce the extent of local generosity. To be a valued member of Polynesian society, one has to show conspicuous generosity.

The competitive part of Samoan society is openly displayed when two groups of performers meet in a formal context such as after a large-scale work project involving both local residents and guests. On such occasions, a **fiafia** entertainment evening results, with host and visitors alternating in a period of dancing. Behind the smiling faces and graceful movements flows an undercurrent of serious competition, as each group tries to outdo the other in skill and innovation, demonstrating social superiority through artistic superiority. And it's only a small step from this to a formal performance competition such as Samoa's **Teuila Festival**.

Most Polynesian regions have their own national festivals, such as Tonga's Heilala, Tahiti's Heiva and the Cook Islands' Maeva Nui. These events attract competing groups from around the country and are also marketed as tourist attractions. Both traditional and more creative items are incorporated, and it has become something of a custom for non-winning teams to accuse the judges of bias.

Samoa

Although divided politically into American Samoa and Samoa (formerly Western Samoa), the two nations share a musical heritage. The **ma'ulu'ulu** is the most common group dance, featuring lines of seated or kneeling women, sometimes together with men, performing synchronized actions as they sing. It's used for specific important events, with specially composed music and lyrics.

The **sasa**, also performed seated by a mixed group, normally has no lyrics and relies for audience appeal on the precision and high speed of the movements. Performed while seated cross-legged, dancers include a blend of abstract movements, along with imitation of domestic tasks such as grating coconut, making kava, paddling a canoe and cutting grass with a machete. Accompaniment comes from a single repetitive rhythm beaten on an empty cabin-bread tin. In recent years, sasa created in New Zealand have been more adventurous, incorporating elements of go-go and break dancing into the routines, while performances in Samoa itself have remained more conservative.

Group dances make up the bulk of a Samoan concert, but the final dance features one individual. This **taualuga** ("roof") dance is socially significant, because it is when the interplay between the two classes of family heads or matai (*ali'i* "chiefs" and tulafale "orators") takes a visual form. At a formal meeting, an orator speaks on behalf of his chief and praises him as much as possible, so that the chief will receive a goodly portion of any valuables being distributed. The chief will keep his orator happy and loyal by giving back to him a generous portion of those same valuables. Working independently, each kind of matai is relatively ineffective, but acting as a complementary pair, they form a powerful social force. The most senior matai titleholder, or his son or daughter, will dance centre-stage and demonstrate through dance the characteristics of someone of ali'i rank – an expressionless face, small and dignified movements. Everyone else on the stage dances around the edge and these people are *tulafale* (real or hon-

Rapanui (Easter Island)

Easter Island, known locally as **Rapanui**, is one of the most isolated inhabited places on Earth. Its prehistoric settlement by Polynesian voyagers reflects their impressive navigational skill, and the descendants of these settlers continue to inhabit the island today. While well-known for its iconic *moai aringa ora* statues, the cultural heritage of pre-contact Rapanui is also preserved in the island's traditional music.

Culture-bearers and research expeditions throughout the twentieth century have ensured that knowledge of **ancient song-forms** such as *riu* (traditional songs), *ute* (commemorative songs), *patautau* (chants), *kai kai* (string figure chants), and *hakakio* (songs of thanksgiving) has been preserved, and these song-forms are used in modern-day celebrations.

As elsewhere in Polynesia, music once served important functions in Rapanui ceremonial life, with genres such as *hui tupuna* (lineage chants) and *riu tuai* (ancestral songs) providing common ground for inter-clan diplomacy. According to oral tradition, songs were also used in battle, as incantations for witchcraft and as the basis for communicating with the spirit world. Traditionally, all Rapanui music revolved around the **human voice**, accompanied only by unique **stone percussion instruments** such as the *pukeho* (slate sounding board) and *maea poro* (hand-held stone percussion).

Ad and Lucia Linkels

Upaupa (accordions), played during Carnaval Rapanui on Easter Island

In 1888, Rapanui was annexed by the Republic of Chile and remains a **Chilean protectorate** to this day. This colonial period resulted in significant changes to Rapanui performance culture, including the abandonment of some performance practices and the adoption of local forms of **Latin American popular music genres** such as *corrido* and tango, which are otherwise uncommon in Polynesia. In some cases, imported genres such as **himene** (hymn singing) provided a new medium for the maintenance of indigenous performance practices. Imported instruments including the accordion, guitar, ukulele and the unusual **kauaha** (horse-jaw rattle) are all now regarded as traditional and used to accompany performances of traditional music.

Since the 1970s, contact with other Polynesian island groups through cultural exchanges and festivals has led to the adoption (and adaption) of pan-Pacific string-band music and **aparima** action songs. Contemporary Rapanui ensembles such as **Kari Kari** and **Matato'a** employ these alongside indigenous traditions to assert a sense of their unique cultural identity within Chilean and Polynesian contexts and at international festivals. Visitors to contemporary Rapanui would be likely to encounter Latin dance-music, reggae and rock alongside pan-Pacific pop and local traditions in the island's vibrant live music scene.

Dan Bendrups

orary for the purposes of this dance). The tulafale dance movements are the opposite of those of the ali'i – broad, fast and sometimes noisy. The object is to create as big a contrast as possible between their own actions and those of the ali'i and so to highlight his own dignity and superiority, just as in real life the tulafale and ali'i behave differently on formal occasions.

Men dressed as warrior escorts and twirling large bush knives or axes have traditionally been part of large-scale presentations of valuables to visiting dignitaries. In 1966 the knives were replaced by sticks with flaming pads at each end and twirled skilfully as part of a nightclub act. Thus was born the *ailao afi* ("**fire dance**"), now a standard part of both hotel entertainment and the Teuila national competitions. More recently, it has been imitated by other Polynesian island groups.

Tonga

Tonga's nineteenth-century Catholic-Protestant missionary rivalry resulted in Wesleyan (now Methodist) missionaries banning **local dances**, but Catholic priests allowing them. Until only a few

Micronesia

Micronesia is a group of numerous small islands and island groups east of the Philippines and north of Melanesia; among the better known are Kiribati, the Marshall Islands, the Federated States of Micronesia, Guam, Nauru and the northern Marianas. Culturally, Micronesia has a lot in common with Polynesia. **Vocal music** is much more important than the instrumental variety and lyrics are the most important element of a song. There is both heightened speech-singing as well as polyphonic choral music and hymn singing, and song and dance are almost inseparable, just as in Polynesia.

Particularly interesting are the **ancient stick dances**, performed standing and sitting. Performers recount the history of their people, genealogies and the pattern of the stars. Some of the most remarkable **chants** in Micronesia recount historical or legendary voyages, often with specific navigational details. The songs, however, are in mostly forgotten languages and people only understand a few words of them. Generally speaking, Micronesian dance movements do not illustrate or interpret poetry as in Polynesia, but decorate it.

There are even fewer musical instruments in Micronesia than in Polynesia. The Micronesians use **body percussion** and whatever nature offers them – shells, conches, coconut wood and leaves – to make simple flutes and a Jew's harp. On some of the atolls there are no instruments at all, but since contact with Europeans, guitars, harmonicas and ukuleles have become widespread.

Ad Linkels

David Fanshawe

Satawal stick dancers doing one of their sitting numbers

generations ago, dancers had to be descendants of people living in Catholic-controlled areas, but such rules are now relaxed and schools routinely feature *ula, faha'ula, me'etu'epaki* and *'otuhaka* dances in their concerts and festivals. Tonga boasts Polynesia's largest groups for its most significant contemporary dance, the **lakalaka.** Arising in the late nineteenth century, perhaps as a reaction to missionary bans, the lakalaka features rows of women on the left and men on the right, with their own different sets of movements performed in tight synchrony as they sing. Behind the dancers stands a group of singers to boost the sound. The dance groups can be huge, occasionally exceeding a thousand people, with no need for electronic amplification.

Festivals of Polynesia

Festivals are the most convenient way to see and hear the songs and dance of Polynesian nations at their highest levels of performance. National festivals are held annually and are usually competitive. Samoa's **Teuila Festival**, held in the first week of September, combines musical performances with sports matches and a beauty pageant, as does American Samoa's **Flag Day** in mid-April. Singing and dancing are integral to Tonga's **agricultural shows**, held in five regional locations during September and October, with the king in attendance. The largest annual performance event in the Cook Islands is the **Constitution Festival** in July, and includes sports, historical and cultural displays, singing and dancing. The **Maire Maiva** festival each June is more for local residents, featuring inter-island performing arts competitions. Tahiti's **Heiva i Tahiti**, which runs from the end of June to Bastille Day (July 14), features elaborate processions, competitive singing and dancing, various races on land and sea, archery, fire walking, tattooing and traditional games. **Niue** celebrates its independence in mid-October with a day of displays and performances, and Easter Island's **Tapati Rapa Nui** festival is in late January. **Tuvalu Independence** celebrations on 1 October are likewise comprehensive.

The international **Pacific Arts Festival** is held every four years, and the tenth was held in American Samoa in 2008. Most Polynesian nations select a representative team to attend this non-competitive display of song, dance and drama, a week-long celebration of both local innovative developments and traditional regional links. Although not intended as a tourist attraction, large numbers of visitors attend. New Zealand's **Polyfest** gathering of Auckland secondary-schools teams is arguably the largest of its kind in the entire Pacific region. Over three days in mid-March in a large open-air setting, some 160 groups of Maori, Samoan, Tongan, Niuean and Tokelauan performers – more than 9000 in all – compete for prizes and status, cheered on by a total audience of over 200,000. Auckland City itself hosts the annual **Pasifika** festival, featuring a wide variety of Polynesian performers and several hundred stalls. The free two-day event attracts over 100,000 people.

Cook Islands

The Cook Islands and French Polynesia have a long history of contact stretching into the pre-colonial era. Today, parties of singers and dancers from one region tour the other with a programme of new and exciting creations, so there are broad similarities in the performing arts as ideas are noted, memorized and incorporated into local compositions.

The **ute** is sung by a group of men and women and composed to honour or comment on a contemporary situation or event, with either praise or criticism. Many ute divide their poetic lines into eight beats, the men devoting the final four beats to rhythmic grunting as the women continue to sing. The grunting may even be divided into two parts.

Few Polynesian sounds can match the sheer excitement of the **drum dances** for which French Polynesia and the Cook Islands are justly famous. The Tahitian *'ote'a* and the Cook Islands *ura pau* feature wooden slit drums and skin drums beaten in tight synchrony as groups of men and women dance. The drummers begin one at a time, then the whole ensemble plays for around thirty seconds before abruptly changing speed and rhythm for another short burst.

Tuvalu

The islands of Tuvalu (formerly the Ellice Islands) were thoroughly "missionized" by nineteenth-century Samoan converts to Christianity who ruthlessly banned most local dances. The **fatele** dance, however, was allowed to continue, apparently because the singing could incorporate Christian themes. Rows of standing women danced a series of movements as men behind them sang a short song. With each repetition of the song, the tempo increased and general excitement rose, to the point where it became almost impossible to perform movements or sing words. Some of the singers also beat a large box with the hands, the sound keeping all participants in time. Today, the fatele represents the most common form of dance in both Tuvalu and its small neighbour, Tokelau.

Taku

Polynesian Outliers are a string of small, isolated islands, mostly atolls, stretching in a northwest-southeast line through Melanesia and into Micronesia. They are inhabited by Polynesian-speaking peoples believed to have arrived there in a reverse migration after the Polynesian Triangle was colonized, and they continue to exist in relative isolation. Lying east of Bougainville in Papua New Guinea, Taku is a case in point. Having banned missionaries and churches in the 1960s, the community continues a largely traditional lifestyle and uniquely practises indigenous religion. Many of the thousand-plus songs in the active repertoire of this village of 180 adults express religious beliefs. Song types include *tuki*, *sau* and *llu*, the slow, sweeping melodies of which are unique in Polynesia.

In this egalitarian society there are no song or dance leaders. Singing is in unison and anyone present may start a song. Dance movements likewise are in synchrony and anyone can be the first to stand and begin dancing.

Purotu are male performance-specialists responsible for creating and teaching new songs and dances and leading the singing at public gatherings on the *marae* ritual arena. There, singers and dancers wear protective emblems and take care to avoid any errors, because of the constant presence of unseen spirits who demand perfection and will punish mistakes with sickness or death. This behaviour appears to have been common throughout Polynesia in pre-missionary times. Rapidly rising sea levels may force the relocation of Taku's population in the near future.

New Zealand

Because of historical links, Tokelauans, Niueans and Cook Islanders are New Zealand citizens as a birthright, and there are many more in New Zealand than in their respective island nations. Modern communications all make for easy and fast publicity and imitation of new performance styles. For popular music relating to this diaspora, see the separate chapter on New Zealand/Aotearoa.

DISCOGRAPHY Polynesia

POLYNESIA

⊙ Exotic Voices and Rhythms of the South Seas
ARC, UK
The cover and title make this disc look like a collection of bland tourist pap. It's actually a very well-chosen and accessible collection of David Fanshawe's recordings from several Polynesian islands, as well as music from Melanesia and Micronesia.

⊙ Fiafia: Dances from the South Pacific for Children and Adults
Pan, Netherlands
A wide-ranging compilation of songs from Tuvalu, French Polynesia, Samoa, Tonga, Hawaii and the Cook Islands.

⊙ Music of the South Pacific
ARC, UK
A collection of excellent recordings by David Fanshawe covering several Polynesian islands. Includes polyphonic hymn singing from the Cook Islands, a Tongan kava-drinking song, lakalaka dance and nose-flute, and Samoan dancing.

★ Spirit of Polynesia
Saydisc, UK
An excellent collection of recordings by David Fanshawe from almost all Polynesian countries. Includes the Tahitian choir from Rapa Iti, a Tongan faikava song, atmospheric recordings from Easter Island, spectacular drum dances from the Cook Islands, the Marquesas Pig Dance, a Fijian meke dance and Honourable Ve'ehala, the celebrated flautist from Tonga.

Western Polynesia

★ Afo 'o e 'ofa – Strings of Love: Tongan String-band Music
Pan, Netherlands
The best and most authentic example of modern Polynesian music, trying to find a balance between the old Tongan way of life and imported elements from overseas. Recordings from kava parties, village balls, hotel floorshows and pop bands. Lovely harmonies.

⊙ Fa'a-Samoa: The Samoan Way ... Between Conch Shell and Disco
Pan, Netherlands
A musical portrait of Western Samoa at the end of the twentieth century. Massive choirs, action songs and ma'ulu'ulu, plus string bands and police brass bands.

⊙ Faikava: The Tongan Kava Circle
Pan, Netherlands
Like kava itself, it's worth acquiring the taste for this. Intimate and genuine performances of strangely beautiful singing as you might hear it on an exceptional night down the kava club. Mostly acapella, but a few tracks have string-band accompaniment.

▦ Festival Music from Niue
Kiwi Pacific, New Zealand
Action and other songs recorded in Rotorua, New Zealand in 1985. The mixed choir uses the wooden *palau* (or *nafa*) drum and occasional acoustic guitar to keep time, but no other instruments.

⊙ Ifi Palasa: Tongan Brass
Pan, Netherlands
A wide variety of Tongan bands plus some indigenous wind instruments – conches and nose-flutes. Includes Tchaikovsky's *1812 Overture* played by a college band, with live fireworks and church bells.

⊙ Ko E Temipale Tapu: The Holy Temple
Pan, Netherlands
The beating of lali (wooden slit drums) introduces a wonderful collection of church choirs. Ancient Tongan hymns performed in the old style as well as Wesleyan-style church hymns, some with a brass band.

⊙ Malie! Beautiful! Dance Music of Tonga
Pan, Netherlands
Probably the best available compilation of Tongan dance songs, including me'etu'upaki, 'otuhaka, *tau'olunga*, ma'ulu'ulu and lakalaka dances. Ranges from pre-Christian to contemporary material. Mostly voices and percussion with occasional guitars and banjo.

⊙ Songs from the Second Float
Ode, New Zealand
Live recordings of group songs and dances at both ritual and informal events on Taku, made over a ten-year period. Contains an informative sixteen-page booklet.

⊙ Tuvalu: A Polynesian Atoll Society
Pan, Netherlands
A microcosm of Polynesian music from Tuvalu. Ancient music, church music, fatele, and a couple of contemporary songs, including one about AIDS.

Eastern Polynesia

⊙ Heiva i Tahiti, Festival of Life
ARC, UK
David Fanshawe's atmospheric live recordings from the Tahiti July festivals in 1982 and 1986. 'Ote'a, drum dances, aparima action songs and religious and secular himene are featured, but they work better live than on disc.

⊙ Himene: Polynesian Polyphonies
Buda/Musique du Monde, France
Protestant church choirs singing himene – the peculiarly Polynesian fusion of ancient chant and European hymns. Recorded in Tahiti and several eastern Polynesian island groups, it's good for comparing different styles, although the recordings are not as vivid as the Triloka and Shanachie CDs below.

⊙ Imene Tapu and Other Choral Music of the Cook Islands
Pan, Netherlands
Traditional church choirs contrasted with contemporary secular choral music.

★ Pacific Chants – Traditional Music of Eastern Polynesia Recorded by David Fanshawe (1978–88)
ARC, UK
A fascinating mix of Polynesian choral music from the enormous recording archives of David Fanshawe. The himene of Tahiti, the neighbouring Society Islands and the Cook Islands, punctuated by some Otea log drumming, conch-shell blasts, and the atmospheric sound of the Pacific Ocean itself. Authoritative liner notes.

⊙ Te Kuki 'Airani – The Cook Islands: Songs, Rhythms and Dances
Pan, Netherlands
A must for drumming fans. Spectacular drum dances, action songs, chants and choral music, plus string band and brass band tracks. Recorded on the islands of Rarotonga and Atiu.

⊙ Te Pito O Te Henua – End of the World: Easter Island Songs and Dances
Pan, Netherlands
A great collection, opening with the atmospheric sound of conch shells by the ocean. It includes songs accompanied by clapped stones, a rain-inducing song accompanied by a downpour, church songs, upaupa accordion music, a Rapanui tango and more.

Cook Islands National Arts Theatre

Established in 1969, this large arts group has represented the Cook Islands internationally, showcasing a wide range of styles.

⊙ Drums, Songs and Chants of the Cook Islands
Ode, New Zealand
Does what it says on the (cabin-bread) tin, with chants, songs, action songs and drumming from most parts of the archipelago.

Gilbert and Ellice Islands Festival Company

A cultural group from what are now Kiribati and Tuvalu, who demonstrate the contrast between Micronesian and mostly Polynesian styles respectively.

▦ Music of Gilbert and Ellice Islands
Kiwi Pacific, New Zealand
These 1972 recordings from the South Pacific Festival of Arts in Fiji include sitting dances (with and without sticks), standing dances and examples of the fatele dance.

Matato'a

Rapanui's most high-profile and influential band are led by Keva Atan and have an international reputation.

★ Ma'ohi
Tupuna Productions, Chile
A representative sample of the group's output, which mixes traditional and contemporary songs, performed on a combination of rock and traditional instruments. It includes songs that have made them famous in Chile and Polynesia, and two video clips. For purchases and further information see *www.matatoa.com*.

The Tahitian Choir

The first Polynesian world music success; discovered on the island of Rapa Iti in 1992.

★ The Tahitian Choir: Rapa Iti
Triloka, US
Very successful recordings by Pascal Nabet-Meyer of the uniquely haunting sounds of this extraordinary pitch-sliding choir.

Tubai Choir

Another talented choral group from the relatively unspoilt island of Tubai.

⊙ **Tubai Choir: Polynesian Odyssey**
Shanachie, US
An album of (mostly) Christian choral music, again recorded by Pascal Nabet-Meyer.

The Western Samoa Festival Performers

A fifty-strong group recorded at the South Pacific Festival of Arts in 1976, when they were led by Perefoti Tamati.

⊙ **Festival Music from Western Samoa**
Kiwi Pacific, New Zealand
Live recordings of a fiafia, which include an action song, kava ceremony song, octopus song and a closing *taualaga*.

PLAYLIST
Polynesia

1 HIMENE TARAVA POINT VENUS Tahiti Nui Residents from *Pacific Chants*
Recorded in 1979 to celebrate the 182nd anniversary of missionaries in Tahiti, massed choirs create a pulsing, hypnotic chant.

2 TUKI SONG Local Men at a Party from *Songs from the Second Float*
A tuki song commemorating the 1843 bombardment of the island by an American ship. This perennial party favourite uses a form of energetic vocal accentuation unique to Taku.

3 FAKATAPU Kanokupolu Village from *Malie! Beautiful! Dance Music of Tonga*
Tonga's specialism in large-scale performance groups is typified in this magnificent lakalaka dance by a large group from Kanokupolu village. Composed in 1953 for Queen Elizabeth II's visit to Tonga.

4 IMENE TUKI Mangaia Island from *Music of the South Pacific*
Cook Island "grunting songs" are among the Pacific's most complex vocal creations, and this one celebrates an early Polynesian missionary.

5 OPARU EOPARU E Local Choir from *The Tahitian Choir: Rapa Iti*
An imene song recounting a historic event divides the choir into both group and solo voices, with a distinctive local treatment through its steadily descending phrase-endings.

6 TE VAKA VAU I ALOFI/KO FAINGA LA OTE FAIVA Gilbert and Ellice Islands Festival Company from *Music of Gilbert and Ellice Islands*
Two Ellice (Tuvalu) fatele songs/dances about working in the bush and catching flying fish – both with typically accelerating tempos.

7 TANGIMAUSIA Beulah College Brass Band from *Ifi Palasa: Tongan Brass*
A rousing brass-band number with crashing cymbals, originally a Fijian tune.

8 RORE Cook Islands National Arts Theatre from *Drums, Songs and Chants of the Cook Islands*
Fiery stop-start tattoos on this log-drum dance from Aitutaki island.

9 TAUALAGA The Western Samoa Festival Performers from *Festival Music from Western Samoa*
Powered by drumming and hand claps, a soaring mixed choir celebrate the culmination of an evening's entertainment.

10 IA ORANA, KA NOHO Marcos Rapu Tuki and Christobal Pakarati from *Te Pito O Te Henua*
Short but sweet, this surprisingly jaunty guitar-based song of farewell mixes Spanish and Rapanui in a heart-warming way.

Sri Lanka

serendipitous sounds

Sri Lankan Cultural Troupe playing with
African musicians
John Clewley

The beautiful, jewel-like island of Sri Lanka, which lies just off the southern tip of India, is probably best known for three things – tea, the Tamil Tigers separatist movement and the tsunami that washed over its shores on Boxing Day 2004. Fortunately, although the threat of civil war continues, the destruction caused by the waves is becoming a thing of the past. **Lalith Ganhewa** and **Afdhel Aziz** tell the musical history of the island formerly known as Ceylon (and by Arabs and Persians as Serendib) and look at its emerging talent.

Sri Lanka – known as Ceylon during the years of Portuguese, Dutch and British colonization – has a population of around eighteen million. Some 70 percent of the inhabitants are Buddhist **Sinhalese**, but in the north, where a guerilla war for independence has been waged since the 1980s, there is a substantial proportion of Hindu and Christian **Tamils**. There are also significant groups of **Muslims**, many of whom speak Tamil, and small numbers of **Burghers** (descendants of Dutch and Portuguese settlers). In addition, it was only in the 1920s that the island absorbed the last of its forest-dwelling aboriginal people, the **Veddas**, whose animistic religion led them to pray to mountains, trees and even thunderstorms, using drum rituals to placate the spirits. All across the island there is ritual music to be heard, played by Buddhists, Christians, Hindus and Muslims alike.

Roots and Baila

Sri Lanka's colonial history, its mix of peoples and its position on trade routes between Asia and the Arab world have ensured diversity in its music and culture. By far the most significant influence, however, has been **Buddhism**. The Lord Buddha visited the island in 300 BC and Buddhism took deep root among its inhabitants, a fact that has helped them to maintain an identity quite independent from south India. Buddhism also, of course, informs the sacred and ritual music of much of the island. On a more **folk** level, the music is essentially agricultural – songs for day-to-day work, for harvesting rice in the paddy fields or for transporting goods on bullock carts.

An enduring outside influence on the music came from the **Portuguese**, who colonized the island in the sixteenth century, bringing with them a tradition of ballads – **cantigas** – along with instruments such as the guitar and **banderinha** (ukelele). They also brought African slaves, introducing an African element to the island's musical mix. The songs of the Portuguese workers and slaves were known as **kaffirinha**, and over time they gradually developed into a Ceylonese dance music called **baila**, acquiring Sinhalese words along the way.

Four centuries on, baila remains very much at the heart of Sri Lankan popular music, although the old acoustic forms (often no more than voice, guitar and handclaps or improvised percussion) have largely given way to combos with electric guitars, drums and synthesizers. Still, no party, wedding or other function would be complete without

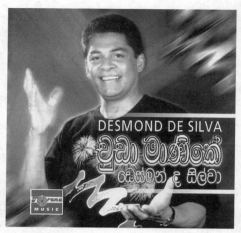

Desmond de Silva

the band breaking into a baila such as "Hai Hui Babi Achchi", "Biuva Neda Wadakaha Sudiya" or "Chuda Maanikee". And baila has provided Sri Lanka with many of its leading music stars of the late twentieth century – singers such as the late **Voli Bastian**, **Anton Jones**, **M.S. Fernando**, **Paul Fernando** and **Walter Fernando**, and the acknowledged "King of Baila" over the past three decades, **Desmond de Silva**.

Stage Sounds

Theatrical music is another important strand. Buddhist Sri Lanka had a traditional, open-air song and drama culture – known as **Kolam** or **Sokari** or **Nadagam** – and until quite recently, even in the towns, theatre was the only real entertainment medium.

The local theatre seems to have begun drawing on South Indian themes and music in the eighteenth century. In the nineteenth century, after the ancient kingdom of Kandy fell into the hands of the British, trade between India and Ceylon took off, bringing Hindustani music from north India to the island. Around 1870 a prominent drama group called **Elphinstone**, led by **K.M. Balivala**, came to Ceylon and performed in the capital, Colombo. They were hugely popular and theatre music became predominantly Hindustani in style thereafter, becoming known as **Nurthi**.

Important figures in this movement included **C. Don Bastian Jayaweera Bandara**, who used Indian music in his stage plays, and the producers **Charles Dias** and **John de Silva**. De Silva produced a number of Ceylonese folk stories at the Tower Hall theatre, hiring the Hindustani musician **Vishvanath Laugi** to compose the music.

This mix of Hindustani music and Sinhalese songs became very popular, and "Danno Budunge" from De Silva's play *Sirisangabo* remains the best-known standard in Sri Lankan popular music.

Gramophones reached Ceylon in 1901 and by 1903 records were produced in Sinhalese – the first, appropriately, being a stage song called "Nurthi". In these early years of recording, a number of Sinhalese singers became established stars, recording songs largely from the Tower Hall productions. They reached even more people after the establishment of Radio Ceylon in 1925, a state-run station which was to enjoy a monopoly until private radio stations were set up in the 1990s.

Songwriter Club

With the emergence of Indian cinema, **Hindi film music** began to make big waves in Sri Lanka. Indian melodies were often rearranged, adding Sinhalese lyrics. By the beginning of the 1960s, Hindi film music had pretty much conquered the island and was a staple of Radio Ceylon (which developed a larger audience in India than at home and sold airtime to Indian producers).

In Sri Lanka, however, Sinhalese singers like **Sunil Shantha**, **Surya Shankar Molligoda** and **Ananda Samarakoon** developed just as much of a following and set a new trend with narrative songs of everyday life. This started a trend, in which lyrics played the chief role, known as "songwriter club", the giant of which was the writer **Mahagama Sekara**. All his songs had very simple ideas, but were infused with a profoundly Sinhalese poetry. The singers Ananda Samarakoon and Sunil Shantha also composed their own music, the former later composing Sri Lanka's national anthem – allegedly in two days flat, after a Ceylonese athlete unexpectedly won a medal in the first Olympics after independence.

Sri Lanka also produced its own movies and film music. Initially, these were little different from their Indian counterparts, except for the language, but in the 1950s the composer **Mohammed Gauss** began creating uniquely Sri Lankan compositions. His lead was followed by a number of composers, most notably **Premasiri Kemadasa**, a self-taught musician who made a conscious effort to create an indigenous style of music, and the giant of today's Sri Lankan music scene, **W.D. Amaradeva**, who began his career as a violinist in Gauss's orchestra and is often credited with creating the modern Sri Lankan sound by combining folk music with Indian raga music.

The Swinging Sixties and The Moonstones

In the mid-1960s, dozens of groups were formed around the island, playing guitar and other acoustic instruments, and singing **calypso-style baila**. Oddly, they often took Mexican-style names – the result, apparently, of a Mexican group brought over to play in a resort hotel – and they even played a few Mexican songs.

Early groups included **Las Bambas**, **Los Muchachos** and the **Humming Birds**. Their soft baila songs became so popular that Radio Ceylon (or Sri Lanka Broadcasting Company – SLBC – as it became after the island was renamed in 1972) devoted special programmes to it. More groups soon followed, notably **The Moonstones** (later the Golden Chimes and Super Golden Chimes), led by **Clarence Wijewardane** and **Annesley Malewana**. If Sri Lanka can be said to have had a Lennon and McCartney, these were the men, shaping a generation of pop music.

Inspired by Wijewardane and Malawana, Sri Lankan groups had quite a blossoming in the late 1960s and early 1970s, with a string of successful releases on the Sooriya Records label. But with the explosion of the South Indian movie industry and music scene in the late 1970s, Sri Lanka became flooded with Hindi records, and local pop took a back seat.

To its credit, the SLBC took action in order to preserve the Sri Lankan music industry. The new chairman, Ridgway Thilakarathne, issued guidelines which gave preference to songs of *Deshabimane Gee* (national feeling) by "graded artists". This system had the effect of encouraging arrangers to become more ethnically oriented, which led to a revival of folk instruments as well as local singers and record labels. The cream of today's musicians – names such as W.D. Amaradeva, **Sanath Nandasiri**, **T.M. Jayarathne**, **Neela Wickramasinghe**, **Nanda Malini** and **Victor Ratnayake** – came to prominence in these "Ridgway Years". More recently, Malini has become known for her social and political protest songs, with lyrics by **Sunil Ariyarathne**, while Ratnayake has become famous for performing a seemingly never-ending succession of solo concerts featuring his own compositions.

Another achievement of the SLBC in this period came through the more or less single-handed efforts of the ethnomusicologist **Cyril de Silva Kulatillake**, who researched and recorded the traditional folk cultures of Sri Lanka's various ethnic groups.

Western-style Pop, Radio and TV

Alongside Hindi and Sinhalese pop, Sri Lanka's sophisticated population has long listened to – and played – Western music, including classical, light classical (a strong local tradition) and pop. The country has had Western-style pop groups since the mid-1960s, when the charts were often headed by outfits like **Minon and the Jet Liners** and **Gabo and the Breakaways**.

The explosion in western-style pop and semi-classical music, however, came when Sri Lanka opened its doors to a market economy in 1977. This led to the formation of two influential record companies – **Tharanga**, run by former journalist Vijaya Ramanayake, and **Singlanka**, run by Ananda Ganegoda. Ramanayake introduced tape cassettes to Sri Lanka and within no time these dominated a greatly enlarged music market. He also produced a number of outstanding local artists, including **Vijaya Kumarathunge** (the late husband of the nation's former president, Chandrika Kumarathunge), **Milton Perera** and **Neela Wickramasinghe**. Singlanka, meantime, nurtured artists such as the much-respected Sanath Nandasiri and crooner **Milton Mallawarachchi**.

In the 1990s Sri Lanka opened up further to both Indian and Western music, depriving SLBC of its monopoly and licensing private radio and TV stations. By the end of the decade there were over a dozen stations in operation, and as broadcasting quality increased, so too did the quality of studio recordings, with **Torana Records** especially meeting the challenge from foreign competition in style.

The Western-oriented pop radio stations have inevitably changed the style of local pop, fuelling the demand for acts which combine traditional instruments, lyrics and melodies with new production techniques and more daring approaches. Stations like the Sinhalese-language Sires FM (*sirasa. com*) and Tamil-language Shakthi FM (*shakthifm. com*) kick-started the revolution, alongside a plethora of music-focused TV variety shows on channels including the state-owned Rupavahini and the independent MTV (which has nothing to do with the Viacom-owned music channel).

The New Generation

A new generation of artists has recently emerged on the club scene, working in Sinhalese, Tamil and English and plugged into the audience in the Sri Lankan diaspora. These include Ranidu and Iraj,

the Sri Lankan equivalent of Pharrell and Snoop Dog – friends who are also multi-talented producers, rappers and singers, with a knack for blending engaging hooks with polished production values. Ranidu's song "Ahankare Nagare", from the album *Divyapura/All My Life* was remixed by Iraj to become a global hit. Bathiya and Santhush are more like Boyz II Men. Classically trained singer and pianist Bathiya is the son of a military general, while the quieter Santhush is the emotional pulse of the duo. Since their inception in 1998, they have achieved fourteen entries in the Sri Lankan music charts, along with seven number-one singles. Their 2005 album *Neththara* became one of the highest-selling releases in Sri Lanka. With influences ranging from Sri Lankan musicians like W.D. Amaradeva and Rookantha Goonatillake to Ray Charles and Eric Clapton, the duo have advanced Sinhalese pop music with a sound that is infectiously joyous. All of these artists have been helped by DJ Nihal Arthanayake, the BBC Radio 1 DJ born in Sri Lanka but raised in Britain, who has been an influential ambassador for contemporary Sri Lankan music.

Finally, the British-born Tamil artist **M.I.A.** (Maya Arulpragasam) is bound to be seen as controversial. After all, as the daughter of a Tamil militant and as one who has been known to espouse

M.I.A.

sympathy to the Eelam cause, she doesn't exactly endear herself to the vast majority of the Sri Lankan population. Yet there is no denying the impact that she has had on the global world-music scene and she is probably the most successful international artist the country has ever had. Her music draws on a wide range of roots, not just Sri Lankan – from the baile funk of the South American *favelas* to the intricate, structured beats of US producer Timbaland (who has worked with her on several tracks). Her lyrics are provocative, militant, feminist and fiery – and her two albums *Arular* (after her father) and *Kala* (after her mother), recorded in Chennai and the Caribbean among other places, have earned her a global following that no other Sri Lankan artist has ever had.

DISCOGRAPHY Sri Lanka

⊙ Best 16 Calypso Hits of Sri Lanka
Torana Music, Sri Lanka
An enjoyable collection of calypso-style baila songs from the 1960s and 1970s, rerecorded in 1999 by Stanley Peris with both new and original artists.

⊙ Sanara Gee 16 – Tharu Arundathi
Torana Music, Sri Lanka
Sixteen beautiful light-classical Sinhalese songs from a roll call of top artists – W.D. Amaradeva, Victor Ratnyake, Sanath Nandasiri, Edward Jayakody, Nirosha Virajini and Dayarathne Ranathunge. The second song on the album "Thala Mala Peedii" is a dual-language song in Sinhalese and Tamil, sung by Ratnyake and Virajini, of a tale of two lovers facing the racial problem of Sri Lanka.

⊙ Sri Lanka: Cantigas do Ceilão
Tradisom, Portugal
Field recordings of cantigas – the prototype of bailas – from the Portuguese Burgher community of Batticaloa. Perhaps a bit specialist for most tastes.

⊙ Sri Lanka: Musiques rituelles et religieuses
Ocora, France
There aren't many international recordings of traditional Sri Lankan music and these date from 1979. The highlight here is a Shiva temple ritual with *nagaswaram* oboe and drumming, but there are also Buddhist chants and a song from a Christian passion, testifying to Sri Lanka's religious diversity.

W.D. Amaradeva

Born Albert Perera in 1927, Amaradeva began his career as a violin player in Mohammed Gauss's orchestra, but soon made his mark as a singer and composer. He is still a towering figure of Sri Lankan light music and has made more than three thousand recordings.

⊙ Pandith Amaradeva Vol. 2: Mindada Heesare
Singlanka Racords, Sri Lanka
Sixteen classic Sri Lankan songs, performed by the master. All have poetic lyrics, to which Amaradeva gives soft light-orchestral arrangements.

Bathiya and Santhush

Currently Sri Lanka's most successful pop outfit, the duo of Bathiya Jayakody and Santhush Weeraman met at music school in Colombo. Since 1998, they have released half a dozen albums and won a huge audience at home and abroad with their contemporary sound and lyrics in Sinhalese and English.

⊙ Vasanthaye
Torana Records, Sri Lanka
Their first album from 1998 which changed the face of Sinhalese pop. Literally meaning "A New Beginning", this album was one of the first to blaze a trail in exploring the mix of contemporary Sinhalese and Western music, with an exuberant, youthful spirit and glossy pop production.

Herbert Dayaseela

Herbert Dayaseela is a fourth-generation folk musician, and an orchestra member of the SLBC. He holds international workshops on Sri Lankan drumming and folk music.

★ Sihala Gee – Folk Songs of Sri Lanka
Local cassette, Sri Lanka
This private release is usually available in Sri Lankan cassette bars and provides a good overview of Sri Lankan folk-song traditions.

Sunil Edirisinghe

Sunil Edirisinghe, born in 1949 into a prominent family on the local arts scene, forged his musical career singing the theme song "Sandakada Pahanaka" from the film *Mathara Aachchii*, directed by his brother Sathischandra. He has since released eight bestselling albums.

⊙ Rosa Kusuma
Singlanka, Sri Lanka
This is probably the best of Edirisinghe's CD releases, with meaningful songs, richly arranged and performed.

Diliup Gabadamudalige

Composer, pianist and vocalist Gabadamudalige came to prominence in the 1970s and has been compared by local critics to Elton John. His compositions are an interesting fusion of Sri Lankan melodies and Western forms. After the tsunami he wrote a song called "We're Calling the World", which was very widely played.

⊙ New Frontier
Sound Lanka International Records, Germany
Gabadamudalige's debut album fuses Western pop, jazz, classical and Eastern music, blending traditional Sri Lankan melodies with Western classical arrangements.

Rookantha Gunathilake

The prince of Sri Lankan pop, Rookantha rose to fame as a film singer, debuting with the hit song "Bambara Pahase" in the film *Sapthakanya*. He is now based in the US.

⊙ **Charuka**
Torana Music, Sri Lanka
This 1997 album shows Gunathilake clearly assimilating American influences before he moved there to live. It was a huge seller in Sri Lanka, notching up sales (as have all of his titles) of more than 100,000 cassettes.

Premasiri Khemadasa

Born in 1937, Khemadasa is best known for his film scores and operatic pieces, which often draw on Sinhalese folk forms.

★ **Landmarks in the History of Singhala Film Music**
Musings, Sri Lanka
An excellent compilation of Khemadasa's genuinely ground-breaking film soundtracks, which are widely considered masterpieces in Sri Lanka.

Nanda Malini

Born in 1949, Malini started out as a film singer, record-ing the duet "Galana Gangaki Jeevithee" with Narada Disasekara for Sri Lanka's first colour film. Her best work, however, has been with lyricist Sunil Ariyarathne, one of Sri Lanka's great talents and a living library of Sinhalese poetry. Together they have forged a reputation for protest songs, and Malini was also the first Sinhalese singer to release an album in Tamil.

⊙ **Nilabare**
Singlanka Records, Sri Lanka
This late-1990s album shows Nanda keeping up with trends, using a group of young composers and even trying a Sinhalese song in ragga style.

M.I.A.

Born in Hounslow, West London, in 1977, Mathangi "Maya" Arulpragasam is the daughter of a Tamil militant and activist. Her family returned to Sri Lanka when she was six months old, although her father was often in hiding and the family had to spend time in exile in Tamil Nadu. She returned to London aged 11 and started listening to rap and hip-hop. As M.I.A. (Missing in Acton/Action) she com-posed "Galang", which became an underground hit and signed to XL Records, releasing her debut *Arular* in 2005. She currently lives in New York.

⊙ **Kala**
XL Records, UK
Named after her mother, this 2007 release is extremely eclec-tic, mixing influences from India, Trinidad, Jamaica and the US with very contemporary production. A global artist with Sri Lankan roots.

The Moonstones

Clarence Wijewardane and Annesley Malewana formed The Moonstones in 1966, naming the group after the main export of their home town, Ratnapura. Only together for four years, they were the local equivalent of the Beatles, pioneering the use of the electric guitar in Sri Lankan music. Wijewardane (d. 1996) went on to form Golden Chimes and then Super Golden Chimes, once again with Malewana.

⊙ **Unforgettable Memories of Clarence**
⊙ **Annesley Malawana**
Torana Music, Sri Lanka
These two CDs contain the best-known songs of both artists. Although originally they sang many of them together, all of the tracks were rerecorded to make individual albums.

Sanath Nandasiri

Nandasiri is a classical singer and tabla player and received his musical education in India. He is Dean of the Music Faculty at the University of Colombo.

⊙ **Ma Hada Asapuwa**
Singlanka, Sri Lanka
A good CD compilation of Nandasiri's songs, which has sold more than 80,000 copies on cassette.

Ranidu

A multi-talented producer and musician, Ranidu Lankage is at the heart of the rise of Sri Lankan hip-hop and R&B music. With airplay on BBC and MTV, he has many fans in the diasporic audience.

⊙ **Diviyapura/All My Life**
Ransilu, Sri Lanka
With its classic pop melodies and gorgeously catchy vocals, this 2003 album gained much critical acclaim, drawing on R&B influences to create a seamless synthesis of soul and Sri Lankan pop.

Victor Ratnayake

In 1973, Ratnayake became the first singer in Sri Lanka to hold a one-man concert – a set of mainly love songs which he called "Sa" (Sinhalese for the first note of a scale) and which has been hugely popular in performance since the 1980s.

⊙ **Sa**
Sooriya Records, Sri Lanka
A live recording of Ratnayake's legendary song-cycle, featur-ing his finest compositions.

PLAYLIST
Sri Lanka

1 **THALA MALA PEEDII Victor Ratnyake and Nirosha Virajini** from *Sanara Gee 16 – Tharu Arundathi*
A popular bilingual song of two star-crossed lovers across the racial divide, sung in Sinhalese and Tamil.

2 **MINDADA HEESARE W.D. Amaradeva** from *Mindada Heesare*
A perfect example of Amaradeva's fluid, resonant voice, coupled with his soft, subtle violin.

3 **MALATA BAMBARAKU SE Clarence Wijewardane** from *Unforgettable Memories of Clarence*

Translating as "Like a Bee to a Flower", this is a trademark melody built around an electric guitar.

4 **AHANKARA NAGARE Ranidu** from *Diviyapura*
With a mesmerizing Sinhalese chorus, Ranidu's biggest international hit to date has been included on many compilations.

5 **JIMMY M.I.A.** from *Kala*
Slinky, sexy take on Bollywood, featuring lush strings and exotic vocals.

Taiwan

return to innocence

Stars of the "Return to Innocence" lawsuit
Guo Yingnan and his wife Guo Xiuzhu
Oppenheimer, Wolfe & Donnelly

When sixteenth-century Portuguese mariners reached the island of what is now known as Taiwan, its mountains, gorges and sub-tropical forests led them to call it Formosa ("beautiful"). The island was subsequently colonized by a variety of other countries, most notably China, with whom Taiwan shares many musical traditions. More recently, however, there has been a revival of interest in Taiwan's distinct national identity, including the culture of its aboriginal tribes. Writing from Taipei, **Wang Ying-fen** explores the many facets of this multi-ethnic island's music.

Formerly known as Formosa, Taiwan is a mountainous island off the southeastern shore of the Asian continent. Originally inhabited by aboriginal peoples of Malay-Polynesian origin, the island went through periods of colonization by the Dutch and the Spanish (1624–62), the Chinese (1662–1895), the Japanese (1895–1945) and the Chinese again (1945–present), with each period bringing in new immigrants and new cultural elements. Currently the **aboriginal** groups make up less than two percent of the population, while the overwhelming majority of the population are Han Chinese migrants, who have come from many regions of China over the centuries. The **Hoklo** (about two thirds of the population), whose language is referred to as Taiwanese, are descendants of southern Fujianese who migrated to Taiwan from the seventeenth century; the **Hakka** (about seventeen percent) migrated from eastern Guangdong province a little later than the Fujianese; and the "**Mainlanders**" (about twelve percent) followed Chiang Kai-shek and the Nationalist government to Taiwan around 1949. The music of the mainlanders is covered in the article on Chinese Han Traditional music, on p.495.

During the first period of Chinese rule and the Japanese colonial period, the Hoklo, Hakka and aboriginal peoples were more or less able to maintain the languages, dialects and musical culture of their ancestors, despite the rapid modernization and the influx of Western music and mass media brought by the Japanese. After the Nationalist government came to Taiwan in 1949, however, martial law was implemented to defend Taiwan from invasion by mainland Chinese Communists. Mandarin was strongly promoted as Taiwan's official language and local languages were suppressed. Moreover, Peking Opera and Chinese orchestral music (a new genre modelled on Western orchestral music) were officially upheld as National Opera and National Music. As a result, many non-mainlanders grew up unable to speak their mother tongues fluently. This, of course, hugely affected the transmission of the traditional culture of each ethnic group, not least its music.

Since the lifting of martial law in 1987, the people of Taiwan have become highly conscious of their own ethnic identity as well as of the island's cultural and political outlook. Many efforts have been made to revive traditional music and to make it fit into modern Taiwanese society. Meanwhile, contemporary popular music has become an important means to make political statements, to bridge ethnic boundaries, and to enhance "Taiwan consciousness".

Hoklo Traditional Music

The Hoklo have inherited a wide variety of the musical styles that their Fujianese ancestors brought to Taiwan, including folk songs, instrumental music and operas. Folk songs are learnt informally, while the instrumental and operatic genres have been transmitted in amateur music clubs known as **quguan**. Such music clubs are voluntary associations where villagers or urban community members gather to learn, and their main function is to provide music troupes to perform for temple festivals or for weddings and funerals. Even today, in cities or villages, temple festivals remain the best showcases of traditional music and opera.

On the southernmost tip of Taiwan, on the isolated **Hengchun Peninsula**, one can still hear folk singers, often accompanied by **moon guitar** (*yueqin*), a simple plucked lute with only two strings. There are just five tunes in the Hengchun yueqin repertoire, but they are varied to fit the seven linguistic tones of the Taiwanese dialect, thus creating an endless number of songs. The most famous singer is the legendary **Chen Da** (1905–81), whose recordings have touched many hearts. In other parts of Taiwan, ballad singers such as the acclaimed **Yang Xiuqing** (a blind female singer) use different tunes from those of the Hengchun singers.

Among the instrumental styles, *nanguan* and *beiguan* are the most important. **Nanguan** is a vocal and instrumental ensemble form that originated in Quanzhou area in Fujian province (China). An ensemble generally consists of four silk-and-bamboo instruments (see p.502) and one wooden clapper. Plucked lutes (the *pipa* and *sanxian*) play a skeletal melody, while the flute (*dongxiao*), fiddle (*erxian*) and the singer perform ornamented versions of it. Quiet, elegant and meditative, the music has an unmistakably ancient feeling. The songs are in Quanzhou dialect, with each word carefully enunciated and sung to a melismatic melody. The doyen of the art of nanguan singing is **Tsai Hsiao-Yüeh**.

Recently some new clubs have been conducting innovative experiments in bringing nanguan closer to a modern audience. Successful examples include the group **Hantang Yuefu**, which has made several tours abroad since the late 1980s, and the new **Gang-a-tsui** nanguan troupe.

Nanguan singer Tsai Hsiao Yueh with ensemble

In contrast to nanguan, a **beiguan** instrumental ensemble is loud and noisy, with several double-reed *suona* playing together with percussion instruments. Even today in Taipei, you can often hear the wailing sounds of the suonas as they are played in parades for temple festivals or funerals.

Two operatic genres remain active and popular: the **budaixi hand-puppet theatre** and the *gezaixi* opera (known as *gua-a-hi* in Taiwanese). Several traditional budaixi troupes still survive, such as **Yiwanran** and **Xiao Xiyuan**, but the so-called **jinguang** (literally "gold-light") hand-puppet theatre troupes are gaining popularity, with their larger puppets, flashy staging, special effects and hybrid accompaniment which combines traditional music with popular songs, both native and Western. In the 1970s the first jinguang hand-puppet theatre, created by the innovative Huang Junxiong, was broadcast as a television series and became an instant success, creating several hand-puppet superstars. Now a cable television station named **Pili** is totally devoted to such shows, and their plots have even become hot topics on Internet discussion groups.

Gezaixi opera is commonly held to be the only genre that is truly native to Taiwan. Still relatively young, gezaixi is constantly absorbing new elements in order to adapt itself to the rapidly changing Taiwanese society. Nowadays, it can be seen on

television, on makeshift outdoor stages in front of temples and even on modern concert stages.

Each context requires something different. TV gezaixi is more like soap opera, and has produced several superstars, such as **Yang Lihua**. Makeshift outdoor stages often feature the so-called **o-pe-ra-hi** (inherited from the Japanese colonial period), in which popular songs, modern costumes and Japanese *chambala*-style fighting are mingled with traditional-style performance. Keyboards and drum kit are added to the traditional accompaniment of percussion, string and wind instruments. Modern concert stages feature the so-called "refined" gezaixi, in which scripts are set rather than improvised, and large Chinese orchestras added. **Ming Hua Yuan** has been the most successful gezaixi troupe in recent years. With five sub-troupes performing all over Taiwan and an opera school of its own, it continues to demonstrate how a family business can become a major cultural enterprise.

Hakka Traditional Music

Gezaixi is not only popular among the Taiwanese but also among the Hakka. This explains why the Hakka **tea-picking opera** has now become gezaixi-like, although the music contains Hakka tunes. Besides the opera, the Hakka people are best known for their **shan'ge** or mountain songs.

Similar to the Hengchun folk songs, the Hakka use only three tunes to fit the six linguistic tones of the Hakka dialect. Experienced singers are good at improvising song texts – often as a means to test each other's wits. Nowadays, mountain songs are taught in many places, and contests are often held.

Hakka instrumental music known as **bayin** (eight sounds) is still practised in some music clubs, and often features the double-reed suona. The **Chen Family Bayin Troupe** of Miaoli County, led by Zheng Rongxing, is currently the best-known ensemble of this genre.

Taiwanese Aborigines

The aborigines in Taiwan are generally classified into plains tribes and mountain tribes, each with its own languages and culture. The plains tribes have long been assimilated by the Han Chinese, while the mountain tribes, although also facing assimilation, still retain many of their traditions. Of the dozen mountain tribes, the Amis, Bunun, Tsou, Paiwan and Rukai are particularly famed for their **polyphonic singing**.

Aboriginal music is primarily vocal, and each group has its own distinctive style, which soon becomes apparent even to an untrained ear. The **Amis**, with a population of around 170,000 in the eastern part of the island, are the largest indigenous group: their songs have beautiful, wide-ranging, yodelling-like melodies, with the northern group singing in call and response and the southern subgroup in free counterpoint. There are about 50,000 **Bunun** in the central mountains, and their music is richly chordal. The 6000 **Sedeq**, who also live in the central mountains, are well known for their three-part canonic singing. Famed for their art and crafts, the **Paiwan** and **Rukai**, numbering around 84,000 and 11,500 respectively, live in the south and southeastern part of the island; Paiwan's northern subgroup and Rukai sing with a strong drone, while Paiwan's southern subgroup use a Ryukyu scale (*do mi fa sol si do*). Singing accompanies almost every aspect of tribal life, from daily chores to rituals. Among the more famous rituals are the annual Harvest Festival of the Amis tribe, held around July and August on the eastern coast, and the three-day Pastaai ceremony (Ceremony of the Dwarfs) of the **Saisiat** tribe, held every other year in the tenth lunar month. Instruments such as the Jew's harp, musical bows and nose-flutes were mainly used for courtship.

In recent years, efforts have been made by the aborigines, as well as by the Han people and the government, to preserve and revive aboriginal cultures. One important development was the formation of the **Formosa Aboriginal Dance Troupe** in 1991, which consists of young members from various tribes. They study closely with elderly tribe members, and aim to represent aboriginal music and dance as authentically as possible. The group has performed widely and successfully both at home and abroad.

Despite all these efforts, however, what really made aboriginal music famous in Taiwan was the use of the song "Return to Innocence" as the theme of the 1996 Olympic Games. Recorded by the German pop group Enigma, the track samples a song sung by an old Amis couple (**Guo Yingnan** – aboriginal name Difang Duana, and his wife **Guo Xiuzhu**) without proper acknowledgement, resulting in a lawsuit which aroused much international and domestic attention. The publicity surrounding "Return to Innocence" was probably one of the things which sparked off a revival of interest in indigenous Taiwanese music. In 2004, meanwhile, a rare international project led to a group of Bunun singers collaborating with the American cellist David Darling on a recording, Mudanin Kata, and a series of concerts.

Pop and Rock

The first Taiwanese pop songs were recorded in the late 1920s and early 1930s for Columbia Records. Several of them, such as "Wang Chunfeng" (Longing for the Spring Breeze) or "Yuyehua" (Flowers in Rainy Nights), became widely popular and are now considered classics. After Taiwan was ceded to China in 1945, however, **Mandarin pop** – brought in by mainlanders and helped along by the government's promotion of Mandarin as the official language – had a broader appeal, while post-war Taiwanese pop songs, which adopted Japanese *enka*-style singing and melodies, were downgraded and became popular mainly among the working class and the older generation.

Among **Mandarin** singers, Taiwan-born **Teresa Teng** (1953–95) was a star throughout the Chinese world. Her father arrived from the mainland with the Nationalist troops around 1949, and she began to sing at a young age to help her struggling family. For many, Teng's singing style and voice quality – modelled on Shanghai pop singers of the 1920s and 1930s – represent the quintessential Chinese singing style. Teng believed passionately in the idea of "Big China", in which all Chinese form one culture, no matter where they live, which is perhaps why she had so many fans all over the world.

Mandarin singing star Teresa Teng

Even today, many mainland Chinese pop singers openly acknowledge her as their inspiration.

Despite the popularity of Teresa Teng and other Mandarin pop singers, intellectuals in post-war Taiwan considered Mandarin pop songs as vulgar and shallow and preferred listening to Western folk-song artists of the 1960s. After a series of setbacks in Taiwan's foreign relations in the 1970s, however, these intellectuals grew conscious of their own over-dependence on the West and started to search for their roots in Chinese culture. As a result, some college students began to compose "Chinese modern folk songs". Soon this became a widespread "folk-song movement" among college students in the late 1970s and produced quite a number of student singer-songwriters, many of whom have played important roles in Taiwan's pop music scene up to the present day.

The lifting of martial law in 1987 marked another turning point in Taiwan's pop-music scene. It enabled the majority Hoklo population to finally embrace their own identity and their own Taiwanese dialect, a development which brought major changes to the content and the social status of **Taiwanese pop songs**. In 1989, Rock Records, the most important Mandarin record company, issued an experimental Taiwanese album entitled *Song of Madness* by a group of musicians named **Blacklist Studio**. Instead of singing about love and homesickness – the age-old themes of traditional Taiwanese songs – the album focused on the lives of ordinary people: on politics, the craziness and hardship of life, taxi drivers and festivals. Combining rap, rock, lyrical ballads and some Taiwanese traditional music, the project anticipated several major styles that followed. In 1990, Rock issued a Tai-

wanese album by **Lin Qiang**, who combines rock with Taiwanese lyrics to sing about ordinary Taiwanese life. This album was an instant hit and marked the beginning of so-called **New Taiwanese Song**, a blend of rock, rap and ballad styles, which quickly became part of the mainstream market. In addition, Hakka dialect also began to appear in the songs of the hit group, **New Formosa Band**, led by Chen Sheng (Bobby Chen) and Huang Lianyu (who is himself a Hakka).

Among the New Taiwanese Song musicians, **Wu Bai** (literally Five Hundred) is an excellent rock guitarist and has also been a leading figure in mainstream Taiwanese rock. But the most interesting figure is surely **Jutoupi**, who has created a unique style of his own. His three *Funny Rap* albums skilfully mingle Taiwanese dialect with Mandarin (spoken with different accents reflecting the various ethnic groups in Taiwan) to make sarcastic comments on many sensitive issues such as politics, sex, the ambiguity of Taiwan's identity as a nation and so on. Musically, these albums sample a wide variety of the styles that exist (or once existed) on the island, ranging from traditional folk songs to Western pop and rock.

Jutoupi's fourth album, released in 1996, was even more radical. *Hexie de Yewan O A A* was a dance album created entirely from samplings of aboriginal songs and music, with each song featuring a different tribe. This was the first time aboriginal music had appeared on a mainstream record – albeit rather transformed. In the same year, **Zhang Huimei**, an aboriginal girl of the Puyuma tribe, became an overnight superstar. Although she sings Mandarin pop songs, one of her songs, "Sister", clearly states her aboriginal identity through its use of Amis language and melody.

Starting in the late 1990s, both aboriginal and Hakka performers have been gaining increasing popularity. Promoted mainly by independent labels such as TCM, Trees, Wildfire and Wind, these musicians blend traditional elements with the new, and are creating Taiwan's own brand of world music. In the meantime, **Shan Ling** (a.k.a. **Chthonic**) – a symphonic black metal band who mix Chinese musical instruments and classical poetry with Taiwanese history and aboriginal mythology – have been active on the international rock circuit. With the rise of these non-Mandarin pop and rock singers, Taiwan's multi-ethnic society is now being reflected in its popular music.

Taiwanese traditional music

Chen Da

Chen Da (1905–81) was the best-known singer of the Hengchun peninsula. He was discovered by folk-song collectors in 1967 and became a legend. His straightforward vocals and improvised lyrics are deeply moving and have inspired a whole host of subsequent musicians.

⊙ **Hengchun Bandao Juexiang – Youchang Shiren Chen Da de Ge (Final Calls from Hengchun Peninsula – Songs of Chen Da the Minstrel)**
National Center for Traditional Arts, Taiwan
Accompanied by a monograph, this two-CD set collects invaluable historical recordings of Hengchun folk songs sung by Chen Da and other representative singers in 1967 and 1971.

Qiu Huorong, Pan Yujiao and Sanchung Nanyishe Beiguan Club

Qiu Huorong and Pan Yujiao are the two most active exponents of beiguan music and opera, winning several awards and teaching many young students. Sanchung Nanyishe Beiguan Club is one of the few traditional beiguan music clubs that has remained active.

⊙ **Tianguan Sifu (Heavenly Officials Bestowing Good Fortune)**
Crystal Records, Taiwan
In this album, most of track 1 and the whole of track 7 are good examples of the music of the beiguan ensemble, with the double-reed suona playing the lead melody. This music is often heard during temple festivals in Taiwan. Other parts include samples of ritual operas, presented at the beginning of a performance to bring good fortune.

Tsai Hsiao-Yüeh and Tainan Nanshengshe Nanguan Club

Tsai Hsiao-Yüeh began studying nanguan at the age of fourteen and recorded two LPs at the age of sixteen. Celebrated for the quality of her voice, she is a member of the Tainan Nanshengshe Nanguan Club. One of the oldest in Taiwan, it was the first group from the country to tour Europe (in 1982).

★ **Nan-kouan: Musique et Chant Courtois de la Chine du Sud Vols 1–6**
Ocora, France
Six CDs covering Tsai's entire repertoire, recorded in France in the 1980s when her voice was still at its best. They demonstrate her singing style, full of subtle nuances and ornaments. Producer Kristofer Schipper supplies excellent liner notes.

Hakka and Aboriginal music

⊙ **The Inner Voices of the Hakkas in Taiwan**
Wind Records, Taiwan
This four-CD set features the music of the southernmost of the two groups of Hakkas. There are two CDs of mountain songs and two CDs of bayin instrumental ensemble. Wind

Records also publish an extensive catalogue of aboriginal recordings.

⊙ **Polyphonies Vocales des Aborigènes de Taiwan**
Inédit, France
Featuring music from the Amis, Bunun, Paiwan and Rukai tribes, this is a good introduction to aboriginal singing. Includes archive recordings from the 1960s and a concert recorded in Paris in 1988. Enigma obviously enjoyed it: "Return to Innocence" samples the first track.

⊙ **Music of the Hakka: Mountain Songs and Bayin Instrumental Music**
Inédit, France
A four-piece group who perform at Taiwanese temple fairs, weddings and funerals, recorded in Paris in 2005. It's dynamic music featuring shawm (*hakke*), gongs, drums and woodblocks, plus occasional flute and gliding fiddle.

★ **Taiwan: Music of the Aboriginal Tribes**
Jecklin Discs, Switzerland
These late-1980s field recordings by Swiss scholar Wolfgang Laade provide the best sample of the various musical styles of seven mountain tribes and even one plains tribe (most plains tribes have been almost completely assimilated by the Han people). Excellent eighty-page booklet.

★ **Sounds from Wartime Taiwan (1943): Kurosawa and Masu's Recordings of Taiwan Aboriginal and Han Chinese Music**
National Taiwan University Press, Taiwan
More field recordings, this time from the first comprehensive survey of Taiwan music, carried out – incredibly – in the middle of World War II. The trilingual notes to this three-CD set are valuable historical documents in themselves.

★ **David Darling and the Wulu Bunun: Mudanin Kata**
Riverboat, UK
This 2004 collaboration of the American cellist with singers from the village of Wulu does a good job of framing and showcasing their extraordinary music. A soft song over simple chordal cello gives way to a beautiful interlude of soft pizzicato against a shimmering background of forest creatures.

Pop Music

⊙ **Het Eyland Formosa**
Rock Records/Magic Stone, Taiwan
A compilation of modern arrangements of traditional or composed songs sung by leading aboriginal singers, including Kimbo, Samingad and many others.

Blacklist Studio

Blacklist Studio were a group of musicians who came together to record this CD of "Taiwan consciousness" in 1989. Of particular note is Chen Minzhang, who takes Chen Da as his model and is the only popular musician to make a special effort to incorporate elements of traditional Taiwanese music (beiguan, gezaixi tunes) into his own.

⊙ **Song of Madness**
Rock Records, Taiwan
The first attempt by popular musicians to use the Taiwanese language and to comment on Taiwanese society. Combines

749

rock and rap, with some lyrical songs accompanied by a single guitar. These three forms became the main styles of New Taiwanese Song.

Jutoupi

Zhu Yuexin began as the "Bob Dylan of Taiwan", but then changed his style completely, adopting the confrontational name Jutoupi (Pigheadskin) and producing an intriguing punk/rap/rock mix, blended with a whole range of Taiwanese and Western styles. After a trio of albums in this vein, he changed direction yet again, drawing on aboriginal music for inspiration.

⊙Funny Rap 3: ROC on Taiwan
Rock Records/Mandala Works, Taiwan
The third and last of Jutoupi's *Funny Rap* albums: the first was memorably titled *You Sick Suck Nutz Psycho Mania Crazy Taipei City*, the second more simply *Happy New Year*. All are remarkable for addressing political issues, sex and other difficult topics in a mixture of Mandarin, Taiwanese, English and various dialects, encapsulating Taiwanese society and its ethnic diversity.

⊙ Hexie de Yewan O A A
Rock Records/Magic Stone, Taiwan
A big stylistic jump for Jutoupi, from rap to house, and a change in theme from Taiwanese society to the aborigines. Each song features samples of the music of one tribe over dance music. The notes carefully document the sources of the music sampled and acknowledge the artists involved. The first mainstream album in Taiwan to feature aboriginal music.

Lin Qiang (Lim Giong)

When Lin Qiang's song "Marching Forward" swept Taiwan in 1990, he became an instant role-model, not only because he created a new style of Taiwanese pop songs, but also because he presented the image of a typical Taiwanese guy that young people could identify with. Unhappy with superstardom, however, he subsequently followed a more experimental path and recently he has been producing electronic and film music.

⊙ Marching Forward
Rock Records, Taiwan
An important landmark in Taiwan's pop history. In contrast with the old enka-style pop songs enjoyed by the previous generation, New Taiwanese Songs combine rock with Taiwanese dialect and have a youthful appeal. The album's hugely successful title-track generates an optimism seldom found in the old Taiwanese pop songs.

Samingad (Chi Hsiao-Chün)

Born to a musical family of the Puyuma tribe, Samingad is one of the first aboriginal singers to make a name singing traditional songs in their native language, but with modern arrangements. She has moved many hearts, both at home and abroad, with her powerful voice and her reinterpretation of traditional songs which she learned from her grandmother, as well as featuring newly composed songs.

⊙ Voice of Puyuma
⊙ Wild Fire, Spring Wind
Rock Records/Magic Stone, Taiwan
Samingad's first two albums feature traditional Puyuma songs, but also include some new material composed by Balikawes (Lu Sen-bao) and contemporary Puyuma musicians.

PLAYLIST
Taiwan

1 **SIXIANGQI (I REMEMBER) Chen Da** from *Hengchun Bandao Juexiang*
A Hoklo folk song classic that has inspired not only musicians, but also dancers, not to mention listeners.

2 **YOUYUAN QIANLI (UNITED BY DESTINY) Tsai Hsiao-Yüeh** from *Nan-kouan: Musique et Chant Courtois de la Chine du Sud Vols 2–3*
A good illustration of Tsai Hsiao-Yüeh's singing style, with accompaniment by a nanguan ensemble.

3 **MALKAKIV MALVANIS David Darling and Wulu Bunun** from *Mudanin Kata*
A charming trio of cello, Bunun singers and birdsong.

4 **MARCHING FORWARD Lin Qiang** from *Marching Forward*
The first Taiwanese song to become a mainstream hit (in 1990).

5 **OLDIES JUST WANNA HAVE FUN Jutoupi** from *Funny Rap 3*
A typical example of Jutoupi's clever pastiche of traditional and imported elements in Taiwan's music history.

Thailand

hot and spicy from the thai blender

Racy star of pop-oriented luk thung
Arpaporn Nakornsawan
John Clewley

Thailand – Southeast Asia's top tourist destination – is well-known for its temples, festivals, fine food and beaches. Tourists pack Bangkok's shiny shopping malls, but few pick up on the incredibly diverse music that pulses round the kingdom. If you travel locally, whether by bus, train or tuk tuk (motorized rickshaw), you'll be assailed by patriotic songs, protest folk-rock, Thai country music and pop, or the rap-style vocals of Central Thai folk music and Laotian traditional music from the northeast. Go to a temple and the monks will be chanting. **John Clewley**, resident in Bangkok, delves into one of the liveliest music scenes in Southeast Asia.

Thailand, a nation of over sixty million people, is placed at the confluence of Asia's two major cultural forces – India and China. Thais retain discernible influences from both civilizations but, canny assimilators that they are, traits from other neighbouring groups have been absorbed as well, including Burmese, Indonesian (Javanese), Khmer, Lao and Malay. Everything gets put through the Thai blender, including Western influences (although Thailand was one of the few countries in Asia never to be colonized by Europeans).

Music is a fundamental part of Thai life. It features in Buddhist and Brahmin ceremonies, animist rituals and court and dance dramas. Every province has its own style of dance, rooted in the local ethnic mix and rural life. There is also a wide range of popular song styles. Thai country music (**luk thung**) vies with **string** (Thai pop) as the nation's most popular, although tourists are steered towards classical ensembles, the strange and eerie sounds made by *pii klong* musicians at Thai boxing matches and the popular jazz compositions of the country's saxophone-playing monarch **King Bumiphol Aduladej**.

Consider the ethnic diversity of Thailand – there are some eighty languages and dialects (nine different Chinese dialects alone) at the last count –

and you'll understand why there is so much music. And given that it was only in the second half of the twentieth century that road transport opened up the country, you can see why the four main regions – central, north, northeast and the south – developed their own distinctive musical styles.

In the north can be found the graceful *fon lep* (fingernail) paired dances, *saw* vocal styles and the eerie and unique sound of the **pin pia** (chest-resonating stick zither); in the central region, mixed-sex rap-like jousting of **lam tad**, **pleng i-saw** and **pleng choi**; in the northeast, the thrilling vocals and verbal tricks of **lam** and the bubbling rhythms of **pong lang**; and in the south, the Malay/Arabic influenced ensembles playing for **rong ngang** dancers, wailing **dikir** chanting and the music that accompanies shadow plays, **nang taloong**.

Other ethnic groups – collectively known in Thai as **chao khao** (mountain people) – inhabit the mountainous regions, and they still celebrate their own New Year festivities and other important events with dance and music (see box on p.760).

Historical Roots

Indian musical instruments had been in use in Thailand since the seventh century, but a more specifically Thai identity emerged when the first

John Clewley

Hang Krueang (chorus line) at a luk thung event

Thai Classical and Court Music

Thai **classical and court music** sounds strange and entrancing at first hearing, with metal gongs, eerie pipes, fiddles and zithers improvising around the slow, floating, melancholic melodies. The earliest type of ensemble, the **piphat**, dates back seven hundred years to the Sukhothai period, and historians believe the first ensembles had one woodwind and four percussion instruments, which suggests the music was rhythmic in character, and initially developed to accompany classical dance-drama (*khon* or *lakorn*) and shadow puppet theatre (*nang*).

Classical **instruments** – mainly Chinese and Indian in origin – can be divided into four categories: woodwind (the oboe-like **pi** and the **klui**, a bamboo flute), stringed (zithers like the **jakay**), melodic percussion (for example, the **ranat**, a boat-shaped wooden xylophone, and gong circles like the **khlong wong yai**) and rhythmic percussion (drums like the **tapone** and **ching** temple bells). There are three kinds of **ensemble**: the piphat consists of woodwind (especially the pi) plus melodic and rhythmic percussion; the **khrung sai** has strings, woodwind (klui) and rhythmic percussion; and the **mahori** combines all four categories of instruments.

If the sound seems strange to Western ears, perhaps it's because it uses a different tuning system in which the octave is divided into seven equal notes rather than the mixture of tones and semitones used in the West. The result is that four out of the seven notes are quite "out of tune" with anything in Western music. In many pieces, one or two of the notes are omitted, or only touched on in passing, which gives the music a pentatonic feel. All the instruments improvise around the lead melody, which is usually performed by the gong circle. The **ranat ek** (xylophone) may split each beat with some trilling and rolling, while the **pi nai** will embellish the melody with variations. Other instruments will insert slurs, glissando and syncopation at the same time.

Classical musicians have absorbed influences from other cultures, especially Cambodian traditions. A feature of some songs is the playing of Lao, Mon, Cambodian or Laotian styles in an impressionistic way. "Khamien Sai-Yok", composed in 1877, was based on a Cambodian lullaby, and describes musically the sound of a waterfall, birds singing and so on. In other borrowings, each part is given a Lao or Cambodian lilt, instantly understood as such by Thai listeners.

In the early part of the twentieth century, classical music could be heard on the streets of Bangkok as musicians practised around Phra Arthit road, just across from the Khao San road travellers' area. Sadly, the street musicians are long gone but the country's oldest classical band, **Duriyapraneet**, can still be found in the same area. The band celebrated its centenary in 1998, and family members continue to perform.

The 2004 movie *Hom Rong* (The Overture), a biopic on the last great classical maestro, *ranat* player **Luang Pradit Pairoh** (1881–1954, real name: Sorn Silapabanieng), has done a great deal to dispel the notion among Thais that classical music is dull, rekindling interest in the genre. The movie covers Sorn's life from the golden age of classical music in Rama V's reign to its near-extinction when absolute monarchy was abolished in 1932. The thrilling duels between ranat players, rather like jazz musicians "cutting" each other in concert, are a highlight of the movie and an excellent entry point into the music.

Classical music is widely taught in schools and at universities and as a result, many Thais can play one or two instruments. A revival has been underway for some time, aided by royal patronage from the classical-playing Crown Princess Maha Chakri Srindhorn.

Modern classical bands like Fong Naam and Kangsadan, have tried to modernize the tradition by combining the music with Western forms like jazz and rock. **Fong Naam**, led by American Bruce Gaston and ranat player Boonyong Ketkhong, have been the pioneers over the past twenty years, recording both reinterpretations of classics and new compositions. Although the band is best-known abroad for its classical repertoire, it has a more experimental reputation at home. **Kangsadan** and **Boy Thai**, which combine classical instruments with a modern percussion combo, have followed Fong Naam's footsteps, with Boy Thai adopting reggae and samba styles and attracting a teen audience. In 1995, Kangsadan leader **Chaiyoot Tosa-ngan**, a ranat master, successfully performed his "Ranat Ek Concerto" with a Western symphony orchestra, while more recently his brother **Narong-rit (Khun-In)** has taken a more pop/jazz route with his band **Off Beat Siam**.

Thai kingdom of **Sukhothai** was created in 1257. The Thai alphabet was created around this time and court documents suggest that music was a key part of life: Sukhothai Thais played wind, string and percussion instruments and enjoyed singing. Of the more than fifty instruments used in classical and folk music from this time, many are of Chinese and Indian (via Java) origin. By the start of the **Ayuthaya** period (1354–76), the **classical** Thai ensembles – *piphat*, *khrung sai* and *mahori* – were in evidence, and dance-dramas popular. Apparently, music-making got so out of hand that the playing of music on rivers – Ayuthaya was a city built on water – or near royal buildings was banned.

Following the establishment of a new capital in Bangkok in 1782, **court music** was again encouraged, and during the reigns of King Rama II (1809–24) and Rama IV (1851–68) many new styles and compositions were introduced. This was a time of great social change as education became more widespread and new technology arrived, in the form of the phonograph, cinema, radio and electrification.

Western **military bands** first played in Thailand during this period, introducing Western marching music; classical and choral music followed. Thais adapted their traditional music to the new forms, and Thai royals were sent to study in Europe. As a result, during the reigns of both Rama V (1868–1910) and Rama VI (1910–25), court and classical styles were influenced by ideas from the West.

The Modern Era

By the time constitutional monarchy was introduced in 1932, changes that would have far-reaching consequences for Thai popular music were already underway. Court musicians were transferred to the Fine Arts Department and Western sounds were all the rage. Led by the father of contemporary Thai music, **Phra Jenduriyang**, who wrote the national anthem, Thai musicians began to play Western classical and film music, jazz and tango.

Violinist "Khru Euah" (Teacher Euah) Sunthornsanan established Thailand's first jazz band in the 1930s, and later set up the hugely influential **Suntharaporn** band. The music that he helped to create was known as **pleng Thai sakorn**, the Thai take on Western music, and incorporated Thai melodies and airs (*pleng* is the central Thai word for song); this later developed into the schmaltzy **luk grung**. Khru Euah left a legacy of ballads and compositions like "Khaun Don", "Khuan-

chai Chula", and "Sawasdee Pimai", which are still played today. Interestingly, he later started to blend his jazz style with music from the classical band **Duriyapraneet**, thereby creating Thai traditional music with a Western flavour, a forerunner of the cross-cultural sound of classical fusion bands like **Boy Thai**, **Fong Naam**, and **Khun-In** and **Off Beat Siam**.

New influences from the West dragged Thai music into the rock'n'roll era during the 1950s and 60s (Elvis remains enormously popular). The popularity of Western stars like Cliff Richard and the Shadows encouraged Thais to mimic the new sounds, and a new term was coined, **wong shadow** ("wong" means group, while "shadow" comes from Cliff's band). The term would shift again in the 1980s, when Thai forms of Western pop were labelled "string". In the early 1970s, musicians like the late Rewat Buddhinan, a former member of Thailand's most revered pop band, **The Impossibles**, and one of the founders of the Thai entertainment giant GMM Grammy, started to develop Thai-language rock. Protest rock also took off, reflecting increasing activism for democracy.

From Songs for Life to Reggae

Starting as a form of progressive protest rock in the early 1970s, **pleng phua cheewit** (songs for life) came about as dramatic social changes were taking place in Thai society (the first democratic government was elected in 1973, lasting three years before a military coup). **Caravan** was the pioneering band, blending Thai folk songs with Western folk-rock, and its members were at the forefront of resistance to the then military rulers.

On 6 October 1976, right-wing activists, police and soldiers brutally suppressed students at Thammasat University, leaving many dead. Caravan, like many others, escaped to the jungle, joining clandestine Communist groups and underground radio. The band continued to perform for farmers, creating memorable songs like "Nok See Luang" (Yellow Bird), "Berp Khow" (Every Handful of Rice) and the most famous Caravan song of all, "Khon Gap Kwai" (Man and Buffalo). The term "songs for life" comes from a poem by Thailand's best-known Marxist intellectual, the late Jit Poumisak, who was the lyricist behind several of Caravan's most popular songs. An amnesty eventually returned student activists to mainstream society. Caravan disbanded but all its individual members have successful solo careers.

Carabou 25th anniversary tribute album

In the 1980s, **Carabou** emerged on the back of nationalistic hits like the million-selling "Made in Thailand" and "Ameri-Koi". Led by outspoken Ad Carabou (Yuenyong Ophakul), the band was one of the first rock outfits to tour nationally. Before splitting, Carabou recorded fifteen albums; the band recently reformed for its 25th anniversary.

The street protests of 2006 brought many of the old protest rockers such as Caravan out of semi-retirement as they turned up to entertain the protesters. Currently, the top singer in the genre is the ever-earnest **Pongsit Kamphee**, a former roadie with Caravan. But much of the style, while still enormously popular with working-class males, remains rooted in Western folk-rock music from the seventies. Recently, however, several musicians, such as southerner **Job** of the **Job 2 Do** band, have begun to mix songs-for-life vocal styles with reggae. The best of the reggae bands that play in the classic Marley style (with Thai lyrics) are the **Srirajah Rockers**.

Luk Thung – Thai Country Music

The luk grung (literally "child of the city") which developed from pleng Thai sakorn is associated with Bangkok's ruling elite, and deals with romantic, idealistic and nationalistic themes. The lyrics of **luk thung** ("child of the fields"), on the other hand, deal with the harsh realities of life for poor struggling migrant workers. DJ and luk thung historian Jenpope Jobkrabunwan says that the music was initially folk-oriented, based on vocal styles of Central folk styles like pleng i-saw, pleng choi and lam tad, but this changed in the 1950s due to external influences as diverse as Malay strings, Hollywood movie music and "yodelling" country-and-western vocal styles from Gene Autry and Hank Williams – even Latin brass and rhythms (Asian tours by Latin bandleader Xavier Cugat influenced many Asian pop styles).

Meanwhile local entertainment styles like *likay* not only influenced singing styles, but also brought skits and comedy breaks to a typical luk thung show. Go to a temple fair (see box on p.757), either in Bangkok or in the provinces, and you'll be guaranteed to hear one of Asia's great popular musics. Luk thung shows are glitzy affairs, with large orchestras, a chorus of up to fifty dancers (who change costumes constantly – from drunken farmers to Marie Antoinette, from Superman to giant watermelons), a string of support singers, comedians and, naturally, the star.

The term "luk thung" – popularly abreviated to LT – was first publicly used in 1964, by television producer Jamnong Rangsitkuhn for a TV programme on regional music, although the first recorded LT song was probably "Oh, the Vegetable Grower's Wife" in 1937. **Kamrot Samboonanon** emerged in the 1940s and **Toon Tongjai** shortly after, and both sang what were called *pleng talat* (market songs) or *pleng cheewit* (life songs), which blended folk music (*pleng phua bahn*), Thai classical music and popular folk-based dances like the *ramwong*. **Chai Muangsing** sang a style partly derived from likay (travelling popular theatre), called *pleng lae* and he mixed this with Western popular music, creating a new sound in the process. All these styles coalesced into luk thung during the 1950s.

After World War II, the restrictive policies of the Pibul Songkram administration – which had banned popular music like lam tad – were abandoned. Migrants began to flock to Bangkok looking for work, and Thai jazz and swing bands began to proliferate with the huge influx of foreign music. By the time the late **Suraphon Sombatjalern** made his debut with "Nam Da Sow Vienne" (Tears of the Laotian Girl) in 1952, the social conditions and the entertainment business were in place for him to develop the sound. Suraphon was at his peak in the 1960s, singing and composing hundreds of hits, many of which remain popular today. With female singer **Ponsri Woranut**, he developed the LT style into a mature form until his untimely death in 1968.

In the early seventies, many luk thung films were produced – *Mon Rak Luk Thung* (Love Country Style) was the most successful Thai musical film ever – and as a national road network was constructed and rural development accelerated, the stars took their massive travelling shows to all corners of the country. These were golden years for the genre, before political troubles temporarily pushed the form into the background.

The emotional singing style of luk thung developed from regional accents (initially from the central region and particularly from Suphanburi) and heavy vocal ornamentation via *luk khor* (or heavy vibrato) and *auen* (sustaining notes, rather like bending "blue" notes in blues and jazz vocalization). Both these techniques are similar to the *kobushi* technique found in Japanese *enka* music.

Luk thung megastar **Pumpuang Duangjan** once said that because the music is so emotional, the singer must be able to create a strongly charged atmosphere. Pumpuang got her start with **Waipot Petsupan** band. Waipot has been very influential in the development of luk thung (he knows and sings all the central folk styles) and inspired and taught many stars like **Yodrak Salakjai** (the most recorded LT artist of all time); he and **Ploen Promdeng** became big stars after Suraphon died, before the emergence in the 1970s of Yodrak and **Sayan Sanya**.

Like Pumpuang, many luk thung singers came from the central region town of Suphanburi, and they added their own unique accent to the style. Sayan Sanya was a rice farmer and pump jockey, and Pumpuang herself was an illiterate flower-seller and the daughter of a farm labourer. Because their rural peasant background mirrored those of many of their fans, they could identify directly with the themes and stories that their audiences related to.

Typical luk thung songs narrate mini-novellas, and feature truck drivers, peasant lads or girls, poor farmers, maids, migrant workers and prostitutes; themes centre around leaving home and going to the big city, dreaming of becoming an LT star, infidelity, grief, tragedy and sexual pleasure. The song titles tell it like it is: "Namta Siplor" (Tears of the Truck Driver); "Namta Sao Serp" (Tears of the Waitress); "Mai Tai Klap Ma Taeng" (If I Survive I'll Return and Marry You); "Klin Khlone Sap Khwai" (The Smell of Mud and Buffaloes); "Men Sap Khon Jon" (The Poor Are Smelly). Risqué lyrics are banned, but a sexual charge can be carried by the singing and presentation alone – some commentators have suggested that they are one of the few public spaces where sexual pleasure can be presented.

As Pumpuang's career carried on into the economic boom of the 1980s, luk thung faced a stiff challenge from "string" combos and international pop. But Pumpuang's songwriter/teacher Lop Birat developed a more dancefloor-oriented sound which she called **electronic luk thung** (the group **Grand X** had mixed both songs for life and disco with luk thung in the 1980s). Prior to this, the *hang khruang* (chorus) just hung around on the stage, but with Pumpuang they danced and pepped up the show. Moreover, very few singers had the vocal range to follow her and her fame increased enormously. She even became the first LT singer to perform at a *hi-so* (high society) concert and she designed her own costumes.

Bangkokians often look down their noses at luk thung as music for country bumpkins. This conflict between the city and the village, a direct result of rapid industrialization, was neatly contrasted in Pumpuang's song "Sao AM" (AM Girl), which contrasted a village girl and her AM-band radio with a rich city boy and his FM radio. More recent songs have centred more around modernity and consumption and less about rural issues – foreign products, Pepsi, mobile phones, foreign phrases and idioms are increasingly being used in LT lyrics as migrants in the city seek to be "modern" like everyone else in the city.

When Pumpuang Duangjan died in 1992, aged just 31, many thought it was the end of the line for the genre. Her cremation, in her home town of Suphanburi, was attended by thousands, ranging from royalty to her legions of supporters among the rural and urban poor. Fast forward to July 2008, however, and thousands of fans gathered again, this time to attend the funeral rites of singer Yodrak Salakjai. Whatever the gloomy predications, luk thung remains hugely popular across the kingdom.

Since Pumpuang's death, the top luk thung slot has been occupied by **"Got" Chakrapand Arbkornburi**, whose switch from pop to full-time LT has brought many younger listeners to the style; perky **Arpaporn Nakornsawan** and smoky-voiced **Siriporn Ampaiwong** top the female lists. Gruff-voiced **Mike Piromporn**, originally a *mor lam* performer, is Got's main challenger. A new generation of singers has also emerged, with artists like Rung Suriya, Dao Mayuri, Monsit Kamsoi, Koong Suthiraj, Yingyong Yodbuangarm, Yui Yardyuh, Tai Orathai, Fon Thanasunthorn and **Ekachai Srivichai** (the south's number-one LT artist). There is some truth, however, in the criticism that many new luk thung stars are being artificially manufactured just like their pop and rock counterparts,

Fifty years ago, **Ngan Wat**, the Thai temple fair, was a focal point for the community. Today, some of these colourful events have been displaced by competing forms of entertainment, but if you visit Thailand at the right time, you'll find a temple fair somewhere. Look for the end of Buddhist Lent ("Awk Pansa"), or New Years (choose any from Western, Thai, Chinese and hill-tribe). Also look out for kite, mask, rain, fruit and other festivals, which are held across the country and always include concerts.

A typical fair lasts between seven and ten days, before everyone packs up and moves on to the next temple. A huge, brightly-lit Ferris wheel dominates the scene, towering over the shooting galleries, water-dip lotteries and little car races, and even drawing the crowds away from the fortune tellers and strange freak shows offering the sight of a "two-headed woman" or "wolf-boy". Smaller stalls sell cheap toys, clothes, books and tasty, hard-to-find speciality foods. But the main reason to visit is the entertainment at the temple site itself: an evening luk thung or mor lam show. In the old days, one of the famous Bangkok temple fairs like the **Wat Samut Chedi** (Golden Mount Temple) fair would be the place where a luk thung singer made their debut; these days it's more likely to be a talent show.

The fair at **Wat Plapachai**, in Chinatown, usually held every January, is typical. Working people, many of them migrant workers from the north and northeast, flock to the fair, and as there is also a Chinese temple in the grounds, a *ngiuew* Chinese theatre performance is thrown in every night. A luk thung or mor lam star performs in the temple school grounds, and a gig costs just 50 baht – just over a dollar. A modern development is the town fair, usually held in the grounds in front of the offices of the municipal authorities. All the rides and food from a temple fair are there, but because the site is much bigger, there's more of everything. Each town will have its own special features. The **Buriram** fair in February, for example, has two main music sites: one for major luk thung and mor lam stars; the other the venue for a *kantrum* battle-of-the-bands. In a country which is undergoing rapid modernization, the temple fair is one of the few places where you can still experience what is left of Thailand's traditional popular culture.

and that there's a tendency to rate a pretty face over vocal expertise.

For many years, luk thung was typically sung by performers from the Suphanburi area in the central plains, but more regional voices are being heard in the genre now, with northeasterners prominent (a recent poll of the top twenty LT singers in the seventies revealed not one star from the northeast, but that has now changed almost completely). A slightly faster rhythm, *luk thung Isan*, has developed, created initially by "Khru" Salah Khunavudh in the 1980s and initially sung by, among others, **Pimpa Pornsiri**. Mike Piromporn and Siriporn are two outstanding examples of this trend.

Mor Lam and the Mor Lam Sing revolution

Ask a Thai in Bangkok about **Isan** (the Thai name for the Lao-dominated northeastern region) and they'll come up with the usual images: it's poor, hot and arid, the people eat *som tam* (fiery hot, green papaya salad) and they speak Laotian. They might add that there are fine boxers and great comedians, and, if they like luk thung, they may even mention

mor lam, the traditional music of the Laotians, dominated by the sound of the bamboo mouth-organ, the **khaen**.

Folk forms usually fade as pop music gains in popularity – and as a developing country shifts from a rural to an urban society – but in Isan the traditional forms of mor lam continue to coexist with the modern ones. The big shows by major stars like **Jintara Poonlarp**, **Pong Lang Sa-Orn**, **Pornsak Songsaeng** and **Nok Noi Ulaiporn** (perhaps the best big mor lam show in the business) are very similar in style to luk thung events, and most mor lam singers can sing in both styles. The subject matter of the two styles is similar, and there are some musical similarities in terms of presentation. But the rhythms of mor lam are funkier, the melodies a little different and the rapid-fire, rap-like vocals are delivered in Laotian. While luk thung is a syncretic form, created from a range of modern and folk styles, contemporary mor lam is a direct descendant of the ancient folk music of the Laotians.

At its most basic, mor lam is formed around the mor lam (master of singing) and a *mor khaen* (khaen player). Singers narrate stories and epics, rush into courting jousts or tell the news, varying their delivery from sad to joyous, while wailing, whooping and compelling the audience to listen and dance. All the while, the music is driven by the punchy tones of the khaen (complete with drone), as the mor khaen vamps around the singer or sets off on a solo. The effect is mesmerizing and a performance can last all night.

Pattana Kitiarsa identifies seven forms of mor lam from the northeast: *lam phun* (narrative lam), *lam glawn/lam lon* (poetry, repartee lam), *lam phaya yoi* (courting poetry lam), *lam sing* (a racy, modern take on lam glawn), *lam mu* (large theatrical group lam), *lam ploen* (a theatrical, modernized version of lam glawn) and *lam pramo Thai* (lam for shadow puppet theatre). Some critics also include *lam phi fa* (healing lam) but this style of lam is purely for healing and not entertainment.

In the mid-1980s, a new turbo-charged, electrified version of mor lam glawn developed, called **mor lam sing** or just **lam sing**. Pioneering singers like bandleader **Ratri Sriwilai**, **Sunthorn Chairunggrueang**, **Prasan Wiangsima** and **Chamthong Siangesane**, all veteran lam glawn singers, appear to have independently begun to modernize lam glawn during the early to mid-1980s in response to competition from clubs, discos, TV soaps, karaoke, pleng luk thung, pleng phua cheewit, string and even international pop. The younger generation in Isan also sought this racy style as a form of identity and modernity, to be hip and different.

As a result, lam bands became smaller, used more Western instruments, upped the tempo and beat of the music and abandoned some of the more formal aspects of a typical lam glawn gig. Small, exciting gigs by groups from the urban centres of Khon Kaen and Ubon Ratchathani take place all over Isan. Sing has revolutionized the genre and even affected how some luk thung songs are produced. A notable development from lam sing is the rock-oriented sound of bands like **Rock Salaeng** and **Rock Sadert**.

Traditional mor lam performer Chaweewan is disgusted by what she calls the vulgarization of mor lam. She says the young performers aren't trained properly and have no understanding of the mor lam's role. Videos of pretty, scantily-clad mor lam singers are available and there are even how-to videos available for would-be stars. Ken Dalao is more philosophical, however. "It won't last, it's just a fashion. Mor lam glawn has been going for hundreds of years; it'll still be going in a hundred years, too."

Both have a point. Mor lam has survived because it is adaptable and is still a relevant part of people's lives, in both its traditional and modern forms. When central-Thai likay started to make inroads into Isan, the Isan counterpart **mor lam mu**

John Clewley

Jintara Poonlarp

developed to challenge the Siamese invader. And when luk thung did the same, mor lam changed again to *lam ploen* (the basic large show format for troupes of mor lam), incorporating elements of both styles, but in a Laotian context. The point is that much mor lam sing is fun and exciting. It still features the khaen and not the synthesizer, and it is what the younger generation wants.

One of the most interesting new bands from the northeast is **Pong Lang Sa-Orn** ("Sa-Orn" means "enjoy" in Laotian), who have risen to great fame over the past few years for their glitzy, comic shows. A **pong lang** is a wooden xylophone that is attached to a tree and played almost vertically, and the funky instrumental music played in ponglang music – based on ponglang, *pin* (Laotian lute), ching, *chap* and khaen – is actually ancient, predating Indian-based music. Originally the instrument that was played, the *kroh lor*, was used to scare away birds while farmers watched their crops or went hunting and the name is derived from a tune, "Lai Pong-Lang". The style was researched and developed in the 1970s by the late National artist **Pleung Chairaassamee** and

A Mor Lam Trio in Performance

Until the untimely death of **Bunpheng Faiphewchai** in 2008, she and her husband, mor lam **Khen Dalao**, would perform together as a trio with **Chaweewan Damnoen**; all three are "national artists", a title awarded annually by the Office of the National Cultural Commission. Unlike mor khaen, who are largely self-taught, Dalao studied with his uncle for a year, mainly learning texts, and started singing at sixteen. He has been at it for over fifty years: "You must be literate to learn texts about history, religion and folk tales; you must know *dhamma* (Buddhist teachings) and the arts generally. After all that, you can start learning to sing and how to be a mor lam performer."

A performance by this trio was scintillating. Before they began, the mor lam would perform a *wai khru* ritual, praising the teacher. In a quiet room, Dalao would make a *wai* (pray) on his knees to a tray that contained *kai* (articles of worship), usually from the mor lam's teacher: five pairs of candles and flowers in banana leaves, a pair of large candles, a bottle of rice wine, a comb, some hair and a one baht coin. He did this before every performance. The other mor lam would perform a similar ritual for their own teachers.

On a simple stage with a couple of hanging microphones, the three mor lam and a mor khaen would kick off with a loud **"Oh la naw!"** (Oh Fortune!) and each singer in turn would run through a few words of respect for their teachers, a greeting to the assembled villagers and a description of the event being celebrated, which could be a funeral or the completion of a new house. Then the real music began as the mor lams took turns in verbal jousting. They would sing, then move off to dance while another took the mic, before returning to savage the others with their wit and virtuosity. They would move through the slow mor lam rhythm (*lam tan san*) and on to the choppy rhythms of *lam tan yao* before hitting the danceable *lam toei*. The gig would end at daybreak with a plaintive conclusion (*sarup*). This type of verbal jousting seems to exists in many cultures across Southeast Asia and the central Thais, the Siamese, have their own version of lam – *pleng*; the Cambodians have *lakhon ayai*.

John Clewley

Chaweewan Damnoen, Khen Dalao and Bunpheng Faiphewchai (left to right)

has gone from being found only in Central Isan provinces like Kalasin to being performed all over the region; he also developed the *woad*, a set of barrel-shaped bamboo pan pipes. Cute girls playing the *pin hai* (rubber-band jar bass) were added in the late 1970s.

Kantrum

Most visitors to the lower northeastern towns of Surin and Buriram are attracted by the elephant races in Surin or the kite festival in Buriram. Others go for the majestic Khmer temple ruins of

759

Hill-tribe Music

They travelled from remote mountains, from restricted border areas, from miles away, using bicycles, pick-ups, buses and boats. Some had come from neighbouring countries, especially Burma and Laos. Nothing, absolutely nothing could have kept twenty musicians and five thousand hill-tribe fans from the second UNESCO-sponsored international pop concert by Mekong tribe musicians, held at the Chiang Mai University auditorium on 3 November 2007. They came to listen to their own music and deal with the issues that affected them: statelessness, restrictions on movement, human trafficking, HIV-AIDS, prostitution, drug use, negative images in the media and lack of access to mainstream society (some 37% of hill-tribers have no identity cards and are therefore denied the same rights as Thais).

In the mountains of the northwest there are six main ethnic groups (plus the **Shan**) living at high altitudes: the **Karen**, **Hmong**, **Lahu**, **Mien**, **Akha** and **Lisu**. Each tribe has its own cultural and musical traditions and many have been living in the area for 150 years. The Shan (or Tai Yai as the Thais call them) aren't really hill dwellers, but are included in this group because they are the largest migrant community in Chiang Mai, numbering more than 200,000. Living among the hill tribes in Burma, they have their own funky and highly active pop scene (what happens in Thailand tends to be mirrored in both Laos and Burma).

Traditionally, the rapidly disappearing music of the hill tribes is part of social life, and it is still used for rituals like weddings, New Year festivities (all the groups have New Year dates that differ from the Thai or Western New Year) and they enthusiastically try to keep these key events going. Some groups ban tourists to preserve authenticity and identity. However, the traditional sung courting poetry found in some groups is slowly disappearing as human trafficking and prostitution deplete the numbers of young people, a problem which is compounded by the fact that many youngsters want to move to the city.

Instruments are traditionally hand-made using local materials like bamboo and gourds, so zithers, flutes and percussion instruments feature strongly. Many tribes also have a simplified version of the Laotian khaen, smaller and with fewer pipes. Aged brass gongs retain pride of place in many villages and are used in important ceremonies.

While it is true that skilled instrument-making craftsmen and quality traditional players are getting harder to find, a new generation has started to modernize its tribal identity by creating pop music in their own languages, using the imagery and iconography of rock to create their own anthems. Karen and Shan musicians, both of which had lively "jungle rock" scenes in the sixties and seventies, have led the way.

"Delicious", a song performed at the concert by Karen musician **Chi Suwichan** highlighted the importance of preserving forest and water resources, while Lisu singer **Yuseuk Laoyipa** highlighted the frustrations of statelessness in "Citizenship" and Akha artist **Sae Vaver Jeupor** sang "Don't Forget Your Own Culture".

Suwichan is also one of a number of musicians keen to explore and share ideas with other tribal groups. His work with the Chiang Mai-based **Rasi Dip** band and the outstanding veteran Khmer musician from Surin, **Lung Deep** (Uncle Deep), mixes the music of the mountains and the valleys, pointing the way to a brighter future for the hill tribes.

Khao Phanom Rung and Muang Tam. Many miss out on lower Isan's best kept secret – **kantrum**.

While mor lam is the music of the Laotians in Isan, kantrum is the music of the Thai-Cambodians who live near the Cambodian border. This fast-action dance style developed alongside local forms of traditional Cambodian music like *jariang* (folk narratives) and *ruem-trosh* (old New Year dances). **Cho-kantrum**, the traditional ensemble, incorporates a pair of singers, two kantrum drums, **ching** (temple bells), **krab** (wooden sticks), **sko** (a pair of conga-like drums called *klawn kantrum* in Thai), and the **tro**, a two-string fiddle. The fiddle operates like the khaen in mor lam, supporting and vamping lines around the singers. During the

1980s, musicians in Surin started to electrify the sound, adding an electric bass, drum kit, electric **phin** (a lute with between two and four strings) and a chorus of cute dancers. Modern kantrum was born.

Until his untimely death at 35 several years ago, **Darkie** was the undisputed king of kantrum. He exploded onto the scene in the late 1980s with his classic "Kantrum Rock" series, made a few movies and then, in 1997, scored a nationwide hit with the first kantrum crossover album to have success in the mainstream pop market: *Darkie Rock II: Buk Jah*. Darkie put the wailing fiddle centre-stage, cranked up the rhythms (kantrum has a harder beat than even mor lam) and set off with his deep, distinctive voice. Since his sad demise, Khong Khoi, Oh-Yot, Samanchai and Ai Num Muang Surin have carried the torch; perhaps the most promising of the newcomerrs is **Songseang Lungluangchai**, who has recorded several excellent albums of Darkie covers – if you can't find any Darkie albums, look out for Songsaeng.

Thai Pop Today

The Asian pop scene is booming, led by East Asia – Japan, Korea and Taiwan – and Thai pop and the entertainment industry in general have recovered since the Asian economic meltdown of the late 1990s. Up until then, the music industry had developed exponentially on the back of the economic miracle. But Thailand remains the second biggest market in Southeast Asia after Indonesia.

The growth of **string bands** (small pop combos) during the 1980s was spurred by the rapid development of the Thai media industries. Styles range from the internationally-recognized pop of **Tata Young** (music videos in Bollywood, cult following in Japan), the mainstream pop of megastar **Thongchai "Bird" Macintyre**, to easy listening standards (pleng sakorn), dance, boy bands, girl bands, rock, indie rock, heavy metal, reggae, ska, Thai rap and so on. Pop, rock and dance from the US and Britain remain popular with Thais, but increasingly Asian pop – particularly from Japan and increasingly South Korea – is proving to be just as popular and influential.

Perhaps the most talented and original of all the rock outfits of the past 25 years are the brothers **Asanee and Wasan**, who are popular enough to have reunited in 2008 for a world tour of the Thai diaspora.

The brightest pop development has been with so-called **alternative music**, initially inspired by

John Clewley

Pod, lead singer of Modern Dog

British bands like Oasis and the Manic Street Preachers. The top rock outfit, **Modern Dog**, emerged from this movement in 1992. But since then, **Loso**, **Pru**, **Big Ass**, **Flure**, **Apartment Khun Pa** and **Bodyslam** have grabbed the limelight. US-born rappers **Thaitanic** have displaced **Joey Boy** as rapper kings, while electro-clash band **Futon**, now making a name internationally with their Thai-Japanese-Western background, point the way to future hybridization. Ska arrived belatedly in Thailand, but there are now at least half a dozen active ska bands, led by **Teddy Ska** and **Skalaxy**.

DISCOGRAPHY Thailand

The list below includes a number of Western and Japanese-label CDs because they are readily available. But to really get into Thai music, you need to buy from local stores in Thailand or online (avoid Western sites that hawk cheap compilation CDs for astronomical prices). Most department stores/hypermarkets/malls have general music stores, some of which sell luk thung and mor lam. It's best to seek out small stores located in or near markets – evening markets are great for music vendors.

Bangkok Music Company stores do fabulous reissues of Thai pop (especially early luk thung) on the Mere Mai Mere Pleng label, with hand-painted black and white covers – see the ground floor of MBK or Pantip Plaza. For classical music, luk thung and folk music, branches of the government-run Suksapan books and stationery chain are also worth a look: the store on Ratchdamnoen Avenue in Bangkok, just around the corner from Khao San Road, is particularly good.

DVDs

DVD Hom Rong (The Overture)
Sahamongkol, Thailand
A beautifully filmed 2004 biopic on the life of Thailand's greatest classical musician, Luang Pradit Pairoh (Sorn Silapabanleng) and his rise to fame as the genre moved from a golden era under King Rama V to an oppressive environment at the end of absolute monarchy. Told in flashback, the film climaxes with a thrilling ranat ek duel.

DVD Mon Rak Luk Thung
Krungthai, Thailand
Directed by Rungsri Tannapuk in 1970, this spawned a host of "Mon Rak ..." titles. Golden-era luk thung with a host of stars offering fourteen great songs on rural life for movie stars Mit Chaibancha and Petchara Chaowarat to whisper sweet nothings to. Legal copies are available dirt-cheap in Chinatown.

DVD Mon Rak Transistor
Mongol, Thailand
A touching and tragi-comic tribute to luk thung king Surapon Sombatjalern: a rags to riches (and back to rags) saga of a poor country boy who seeks fame as a luk thung star, leaving his girl behind in the village. Running through the film as a refrain is a killer cover version of Surapon's hit "Mai Lerm" (Don't Forget). Unmissable.

Classical

⊙ Music of Chiang Mai
Auvidis/Unesco, France
Three well-recorded tracks from different ensembles. A piphat orchestra playing music for the likay theatre; Chinese-influenced ritual music with lutes, two-string fiddle, flute, drum and percussion; and an "old Thai instrumental ensemble" with two-string fiddles, zither, flute and drum.

⊙ The Spirit of Lanna: Music From the North of Thailand
AMI Records, Thailand
Top-quality recording from the Lai Muang Ensemble, featuring multi-instrumentalist Somboon "Khru Boy" Kawichai, whose peejum (bamboo pipes), salwa and pin pia playing is exceptional.

Fong Naam

Led by Bruce Gaston and virtuoso ranat player Boonyong Ketkhong, this is one of the most interesting classical ensembles playing traditional and contemporary music.

⊙ Ancient Contemporary Music from Thailand
Celestial Harmonies, US
A double album showing off a wide range of Fong Naam's artistry, from schmaltzy lounge numbers to Laotian folk and spectacular classical pieces for piphat and string ensembles. Comes with detailed notes on the structure of Thai music and how to listen.

⊙ The Hang Hong Suite
Nimbus, UK
This excellent disc features spectacular and uplifting funeral music as well as parodies of the music of neighbouring cultures. Another album, The Sleeping Angel (Nimbus, UK) includes piphat and mahori music, as well as a splendid ranat solo. Outstanding sound quality.

⊙ Siamese Classical Music Vols 1–5
Marco Polo, Hong Kong
For those with a particular interest in the development of Thai classical music, these albums introduce the main historical styles and different ensembles. Vol. 1: The Piphat Ensemble before 1400 AD; Vol. 2: The Piphat Ensemble 1351–1767; Vol. 3: The String Ensemble (two-stringed fiddles, zither and percussion); Vol. 4: The Piphat Sepha (music from the last two centuries); Vol. 5: The Mahori Orchestra (including flute, strings, tuned and untuned percussion).

Kangsadan

A band set up in the late 1980s to develop new interpretations of Thai classical music. Initially, the group depended on masters like the late flute player Khru Jamnien and jazz saxophonist Tewan Sapsanyakorn. Also included were youngsters like the Tosa-nga brothers, who have since made a name for themselves in their own right.

⊙ The Golden Jubilee Overture
Pisces Music, Thailand
In 1995, ranat expert Chaiyut Tosa-nga composed the Golden Jubilee Overture, performed here with other pieces for King Bhumibol Adulyadej's fiftieth year on the throne.

The Prasit Thawon Ensemble

A leading classical ensemble, founded in 1958. Based in Bangkok, they take their name from the celebrated late musician and composer Master Prasit Thawon, who was the last student of the great maestro Luang Pradit Pairoh (1881–1954).

★ Thai Classical Music
Nimbus, UK
Brilliant playing from some of Thailand's best performers, mainly in the piphat style. Includes the overture "Homrong Sornthong" and, on the track "Cherd Chin", some scintillating dialogues between different instruments. The best example of piphat on CD.

Narongrit Tosa-nga

Brother of Boy Thai's leader Chaiyut, who now goes by the name of the sinister ranat ek master Khun-In, from the movie Hom Rong.

⊙ Off Beat Siam
AMI Records, Thailand
Off Beat Siam is an ambitious fusion of Thai classical and contemporary music, with styles ranging from traditional to hip-hop, jazz, jazz-funk and salsa. Khun-In's classical ranat features throughout, whether taking the lead, accompanying or just cascading in the background.

Modern Music (Pleng Thai Sakorn)

Euah Sunthornsanan

Violinist, composer and bandleader "Khru" (Guru) Euah may be no more, but his band is still going strong.

⊙ Chabab Derm (Old Songs) Vols 1–6, 7–10
Bangkok Cassette, Thailand
Euah popularized Modern Thai music. Some of the most popular Thai songs ever recorded were performed by his Suntaraporn Band and a bevy of singers.

Tribal Music

⊙ Karenni: Music from the Border Areas of Thailand and Burma
Pan, Netherlands
The Karen are the largest of the Thai hill tribes, and this is the most accessible of the recordings listed here. Exciting

gong music, drums, and a whole range of instruments – xylophone, zithers, flutes and percussion – from the Karen's bamboo world.

⊙ Lanna Thai: Instrumental Music of Northwest Thailand
Pan, Netherlands
An excellent collection of music from the various hill tribes – Hmong, Lahu, Lisu, Kayah and ethnic Chinese. Some of the music is rather hard-going, but there are some fine ensembles, processions and a great recording of a Kayah tubular zither accompanied by clucking chickens – and people trying to hush them.

Siriporn Ampaiwong

Originally a mor lam singer, Siriporn has developed into a top luk thung singer, smoothing out her voice for ballads.

⊙ Bor Rak Si Dam
PGM, Thailand
The upbeat title track of this album (also available on a "best hits" collection) has become something of an Isan anthem.

Got Chakrapand Arbkornburi

The rumour goes that the late Grammy label co-founder and former Impossibles member Rewat Buddhinan, observing Got's middling rock career, told the singer to try his hand at luk thung. That was more than ten years ago, and Got is now the biggest name in the business. His clean looks and spectacular shows make him a firm favourite with all ages, even bringing youngsters back to luk thung.

⊙ 12 years of Grammy Gold
Grammy, Thailand
Packed full of sad love ballads, this one is for the ladies.

Pumpuang Duangjan

When Pumpuang died in 1994, 200,000 people attended her royal-sponsored cremation at Wat Thep Kradan in Suphanburi, and a nation mourned the loss of its greatest popular singer. No one could sing luk thung with her range and emotional power. Her career stretched from the end of the golden period, when she sang with Sayan Sanya, to the development of dancefloor-oriented electronic luk thung.

★ Pumpuang Li Bor Sor (Pumpuang – Many Years)
Topline, Thailand
An essential two-CD or cassette set (available separately) that covers most of Pumpuang's greatest hits. The classics on Vol. 1, *Pleng Wan* (Sweet Songs), like "Chao Na Sang Friend" (Rice Farmer without a Partner) and "Kwam Rak Mun Ya Comb" (Love is Like a Bitter Medicine) have never been bettered. Vol. 2, *Pleng Man* (Exciting Songs), collects up-tempo dance tracks like "Uh Uh Raw, Jang" (Hmm, He's Really Handsome).

Luk Thung

For current LT stars, go for the compilations that are regularly released by the big two record labels – GMM Grammy and RS Promotion – and then look for individual albums by the singers you like. Don't pay the same price as an international release.

⊙ Mon Rak Luk Thung (Love Country Style)
Bangkok Cassette, Thailand
This is the original soundtrack album from the classic film, with a host of big names and fourteen golden-era songs. Well worth looking out for.

Arpaporn Nakornsawan

One of the most successful of the new wave of stars who sing a more pop-oriented LT style, with flashy costumes, racy shows and lots of chat. Look out for her double-CD "best hits" compilations on Grammy.

⊙ Lerk Leow, Kha (We've Split Up, Thanks)
Boxing Sound, Thailand
When Arpaporn put the song "Laerk leow, kha" on everyone's lips in 1997, she started a craze: many other singers, including Boontone Khon-num, replied to her hookline with "Long Lerk Du Si" (Just Split Up and See What Happens). The humorous, street-savvy side of luk thung.

Mike Piromporn

A mor lam singer who specializes in haunting ballads and luk thung isan.

⊙ Mike Piromporn – 12 Years of Grammy Gold
Grammy, Thailand
Piromporn's image as a blue-collar boy can be seen from the blurb on the album cover: "12 years at the heart of the workforce".

Sayan Sanya

A poor rice farmer from the central heartland around Suphanburi with a big nose and long jaw, Sayan paid his dues singing wherever he could before he rose to stardom in the 1970s. He has the most mellifluous voice in the business and recorded with Pumpuang Duangjan.

⊙ Sayan: Dao Thong (Sayan: Golden Star)
Bangkok Cassette, Thailand
The sad solo trumpet on the opening track sets the moody tone for the modern master to reveal his honeyed voice on this superb greatest hits collection. This is classic 1970s luk thung from the era of big shows, massive chorus lines and real brass instruments. As Yodrak once said, "Women cry when he sings."

Vintage Suraphon Sombatjalern album

Suraphon Sombatjalern

Born and bred in Supanburi, the genre's heartland, Suraphon was consistently the best luk thung singer in the business. Indeed, the style grew up with his career, from his first hit in 1952 to his last one, "Sixteen Years" (the most requested LT song on Thai radio).

Luam Pleng (Mixed Songs) Vols 1-4
Bangkok Cassette, Thailand
The greatest of all the luk thung singers/composers: great voice, great songs, great backing. Includes songs that really set the style's future direction, "Na Da Sao Vienne" (Tears of the Laotian Girl) and "Sip-hok Pi Hen Kwam Lang" (Sixteen years of Memories) and many others. Siamese soul.

Mor Lam and Laotian Music

⊙ **Instrumental Music of Northeast Thailand**
King, Japan
One of the best collections of traditional Laotian instrumental styles on CD. Many styles are played: *soeng* (group mor lam), southern Laotian tunes and styles, khaen solos and some particularly fine *bong lang*. The khaen playing by master Thongkham Thaika is outstanding.

⊙ **Mo Lam Singing of Northeast Thailand**
King, Japan
Chaweewan Damnoen headlines this fine collection of many lam (singing) styles, including *wai khru* (paying respects to teacher), lam glawn, lam ploen and songs from Laos. Includes rarely heard *lam phi fah*, for a musical ceremony to drive out bad spirits from someone possessed. Thongkham Thaika is the excellent khaen player.

Isan Slété

A six-piece group put together by academic and multi-instrumentalist Dr Jareonchai Chonpairot and led by Saman Hongsa. Saman's wife, Sri-ubon Hongsa, is the female vocalist and the khaen player is Thawee Sridamanee.

★ **Songs and Music from Northeast Thailand**
Globestyle, UK
A wide cross-section of Laotian mor lam styles, from the verbal jousting of "Lam Toei Thammada" to all-action lam ploen. Also featured are the ancient instrumental style pong lang, named after a wooden xylophone tied to a tree, and the woad, a set of bamboo panpipes.

Pong Lang Sa-Orn

Led by the mercurial Sompong "Aed" Kunaprathom and flanked by the livewire pin hai-plucking pair Lula and Lala, the band's shows are not only musically excellent, they're also very, very funny.

⊙ **The Music**
RS Promotion, Thailand
Debut album that catapulted the pong lang ensemble to fame, selling half a million copies.

Jintara Poonlarp

Jintara is the heir to Banyen Rakken's throne as the Queen of Mor Lam. Born in the northeast, she is one of the most popular and prolific of all mor lam artists, with more than forty albums to her credit. Her rough-edged, smoky voice is perfect for the rap-style vocals of the genre.

★ **Luam Hit 19 Pii Tawng Chut**
Master Tape, Thailand
Nineteen glorious years in two volumes. Vol. 1 features slow, plaintive mor lam, the closest Thailand has to the blues, with a few luk thung songs. Vol 2 showcases mor lam dance songs with the hits "Pi Ja Jeap Dong Nai?" (Where Do You Hurt?) and "Chao Bao Hai" (The Groom's Gone).

Chalard Songserm

National artist mor lam singer Chalard Songserm, an old student of Saman Hongsa (see Isan Slété above), is joined by his singing missus Mukda and a host of the Isan region's best musicians, including the virtuoso khaen master Sombat Simlar on this new high-quality recording, produced by classical guitarist Hucky Eichelmann.

⊙ **Rhythms of I-Sarn, Vols 1 & 2**
AMI Records, Thailand
Covering a wide range of Laotian styles from across the northeast region, there are some excellent tracks on this two-CD set, including Simlar's amazing train-sounding khaen solo and several songs and tunes from Thai-Cambodians in the lower northeast.

Kantrum

⊙ **Kantrum Aya Done Ta, Vols 1 & 2**
PK Sound, Thailand
Features some of the current crop of kantrum stars: Jane Saijai, Mor Wam, Songsaeng and Samanchai. The latter sings terrific Khmer/Thai mixed luk thung songs, with excellent covers of the late Pumpuang's songs in kantrum style.

Darkie

For more than a decade, Darkie lit up the kantrum scene of the lower northeast region with his fast-paced Thai-Cambodian dance music. Driven by drums and funky fiddle and drums, kantrum is now popular throughout Thailand.

★ **Darkie, Rock II: Buk Jah**
Movie Music, Thailand
The first ever kantrum crossover: a hit album nationwide. Kantrum features alongside mor lam and luk thung sung in Cambodian. Darkie's booming voice moves from rap-like delivery to sobs and wails, shadowed closely by the fiddle and some funky rhythms. Unmissable.

⊙ **Kantrum Rocks I & II**
M&M, Thailand
These seminal late 1980s recordings marked the start of Darkie's rise to fame and are still available. Raw-edged and full of hard beats.

String and Songs for Life

⊙ **12 Khon, 12 Baep (Twelve People, Twelve Styles)**
KC, Thailand
A good compilation including most of the big names of the songs for life movement: Caravan, Pongsit Kampee and Carabou. Released for the 25th anniversary celebrations of the Democracy Movement in October 1998.

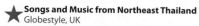

Carabou

Ad Carabou (Yuenyong Ophakul) spent part of his youth in Manila, where he avidly watched Freddie Aguilar's shows. His six-member outfit debuted in 1981 and over the next fifteen albums went on to massive fame. Influential lyrics about social problems made them very popular as supporters of underdogs, but sadly, the music became mired in rock clichés and Dylanesque acoustics.

⊙ Made in Thailand
Krabue, Thailand
Dating from the height of their popularity in the mid-1980s, Carabou's fifth album was right in tune with the times and targeted social problems like consumerism, the sex trade and a failing education system.

⊙ Mon Pleng Carabou 25
Warner Music, Thailand
Tribute album celebrating Carabou's 25th anniversary by major stars from different styles like "Songs for Life" icon Nga Caravan, luk thung singers Sunaree Ratchasima and Sayan Sanya, and rockers like Pod (Modern Dog) and Billy Ogan. The best cover is of "Refugee" by Pongsit Kamphee and Kanakham Abhiradee.

Modern Dog

Four students from Chulalongkorn University who won a talent contest and signed with up-and-coming indie label Bakery Music. Single-handedly responsible for kicking off the alternative-rock craze of the 1990s.

⊙ Modern Dog
Bakery Music, Bangkok
An important release for Thai rock music. Modern Dog turned the rock world upside down with this album of self-penned alternative songs. The catchy love song, "Korn" (Before), stayed at the top of local charts for weeks due to singer Pod's unique singing style and witty lyrics.

PLAYLIST
Thailand

1 **LAM KLON: WAI KHRU (Paying Respect to My Teacher) Chaweewan Damnoen** from *Mo Lam Singing of Northeast Thailand*
Soulful r-e-s-p-e-c-t from the National artist in a ceremony that opens every concert.

2 **MAI LERM (DON'T FORGET) LT King Surapon Sombatchareon** from *Luam Pleng*
Ultimate tear-jerking ballad from the master; also check out the cover version, used as a song and refrain in the movie Mon Rak Transistor.

3 **BOR RAK SI DAM Siriporn Ampaiwong** from *Bor Rak Si Dam*
Play this funky, upbeat song anywhere in the northeast and people go nuts. The anthem of Isan.

4 **MADE IN THAILAND Carabou** from *Made in Thailand*
It's 25 years since this song launched the buffalo-horned band to fame, but Slap bass and Ad Carabou's distinctive voice still sound fresh.

Tibet and Bhutan

raising the roof

Tibetan singer in exile Yungchen Lhamo
Steve Pyke

Tibet, the "roof of the world" has long exerted a fascination on the outside world. After the formation of the People's Republic of China in 1949, the Chinese sent in troops, eventually granting the Tibetans autonomy, but not independence. After an uprising in Lhasa in 1959, however, Tibet's spiritual leader, the Dalai Lama, went into exile, while his followers suffered a severe onslaught on their religious life during the Cultural Revolution. Although the thousands who followed the Dalai Lama into exile have had to struggle to preserve their rich cultural and religious heritage abroad, they've successfully modernized their traditions and increasingly engaged with audiences worldwide. Mark Trewin reports from inside and outside Tibet.

Tibetan civilization came close to complete destruction following the invasion by Communist China in 1950. In the darkest days of the Cultural Revolution (roughly 1966–76), all but a few of Tibet's six thousand monasteries – the main centres of culture and learning – were destroyed. Since the 1980s, however, political reforms in China have led to a controlled revival: selected monastic centres have been reopened, and the cultural noose has been loosened to the extent that traditional classical and folk songs are played by the state-run broadcasting organizations in Lhasa. There are occasional anti-Chinese protests, notably in the run-up to the 2008 Beijing Olympics. There are large Tibetan populations outside the so-called "Tibet Autonomous Region" (TAR): in Kham (the Chinese provinces of Sichuan and Yunnan) and Amdo (Qinghai and Gansu). The wider area of "ethnic Tibet" extends across the Himalayan region, consisting of the countries of Bhutan and Nepal, and the Himalayan districts of India, including the former kingdoms of Sikkim and Ladakh. Most of these remote border areas have also been opened up after decades of isolation, and have themselves undergone rapid changes. There is a large exile community of Tibetan monks in southern India and many Tibetan exiles have settled throughout the world.

Music of the Monasteries

The ritual music of Tibet's historic **Buddhist monastic traditions** is undeniably the country's most important and distinctive contribution to the world's musical heritage. Just as Tibetan Buddhism was a unique development of the Mahayana form of Buddhism originating in India, so its vocal and instrumental traditions have become distinctly Tibetan in character, fostering extraordinary musical phenomena quite unknown in any other part of the world.

Several of the well-known Tibetan monasteries like **Sera** (in Lhasa) and **Tashi Lhunpo** (the seat of the Panchen Lama, the second most important religious leader in Tibetan Buddhism, in Shigatse) have newer exile monasteries in Bylakuppe in Karnataka state, South India. There they claim they can lead a purer, more spiritual life and preserve their chants, dances and traditions better. The Tashi Lhunpo monastery, for instance, has beautiful old manuscripts brought out of Tibet with an arcane chant notation now known by only a few prayer leaders.

Behind the stereotyped image of rows of seated monks chanting in the diffuse glow of butter-lamps lies a complex realm of sensory experience in which man-made sounds play an essential role. In general, music is used by monks as a vehicle for the recitation of sacred texts: the *sutras* (basic teachings of the Buddha) and the *tantras* (secret commentaries). The exact form the music takes, however, varies considerably according to the function and importance of the ritual, with the more impressive and dramatic musical forces employed to heighten and emphasize particular parts of the liturgy, especially on certain occasions in the ritual calendar.

Tashi Lhunpo Monastery

Chant notation in a manuscript from the Tashi Lhunpo monastery

Tashi Lhunpo monks playing trumpets in 1986

All monks learn the fundamental **chant** styles which accompany daily worship, including unaccompanied recitations of prayers and **mantras**, and beautiful choral hymns used to deliver special poetic verses. Often these chants are quietly accompanied by the principal musical instruments – the **cymbals** (*bübchal*) and large **frame-drums** (*nga*) – which outline the metrical structure of the chant melodies prescribed for each text. By contrast, in a more specialized, profound chanting style known as **yang**, all sense of time disappears as the booming resonances of every drum-stroke mark the initiation of individually intoned syllables, each of which is sustained in a low register, and subjected to subtle tonal inflections and embellishments.

These other-worldly chant styles are a special feature of the more esoteric **Tantric rituals**, in which the practitioners come into ecstatic contact with the nature of the invoked deities. Such higher-status rituals usually call for the use of special instruments, many of indigenous shamanistic origin, to appeal to the deities in question; these are chosen according to their rich symbolic properties as well as their specific sound qualities. The cymbals and drums lead the ensemble in exclusively instrumental passages which present

a dramatic, almost overwhelming contrast to the chanted sections of a ritual performance. These instruments are now played in different ways, and much more powerfully: the drum-strokes are thunderous, while the cymbals prove to be a particularly versatile instrument, rendering a wide range of sonorities from loud resonant clashes to tightly controlled rolls. Additional instruments – all percussion and winds – include the haunting calls of the **conch-shell trumpet** (*dungkar*) or **human thighbone trumpet** (*kangling*), the incisive rattle of the **pellet-drum** (*damaru*, made from a human skull or wood) and the brilliant jangle of the **hand-bell** (*drilbu*). Most spectacularly, pairs of **long metal trumpets** (*dungchen*) occasionally contribute rousing blasts in a deep growl. The only truly melodic instrument, also played in pairs, is the **oboe** (*gyaling*). Its penetrating nasal sound, sustained by circular breathing, projects a soaring melody above the rich, sonorous textures of the rest of the ensemble. The effect is a powerful, majestic and scintillating wall of sound. Although these instruments are best appreciated in their true ritual context, where they are sparingly deployed, they are frequently featured on recordings.

The range of recordings available today exhibits a variety of musical styles and techniques, which

Tibetan Monastic Festivals

Attracting hordes of pilgrims (and increasingly tourists), festivals are traditionally held by the more important monasteries over a period of days, often in winter. Several were revived in Tibet in the 1980s, while many have flourished continuously in Himalayan areas, most accessibly in Ladakh. They feature **cham**, colourful masked tantric dances performed by the monks and accompanied by the monastery's orchestra. Depicting various deities, spirits and demons, they ritually re-enact the conquest of evil. Their climax may include one or more of various elements: the appearance of possession-oracles, the exhibition of huge **thangkas** (Buddhist images), or large-scale exorcisms using fire, swords or even firearms. The symbolism often draws on local folk traditions and some performances involve lay ritual specialists and lay musicians as guardians of exceptional, localized genres. In Ladakh, **lharnga** ("god-drumming"), consisting of vigorous kettle-drums (*daman*) and penetrating oboes (*surna*), assists in the possessions and exorcisms, and accompanies ceremonial functions such as the escorting of lamas, royalty and nobility. A probably related genre in Central Tibet, using similar instruments, is the recently revived **gar** repertory of outdoor ceremonial music, formerly maintained in Lhasa and Tashilhunpo (traditional seat of the Panchen Lama). In the eastern region of Amdo (Gansu province), some monasteries, notably Labrang, maintained a highly unusual ceremonial repertory known as Dhodar, which borrowed the instruments of Han Chinese temples: *guan* (oboes), *sheng* (mouth organs) *di* (flutes) and *yunluo* (set of gongs). This was revived in 1980 for the visit of the then Panchen Lama.

Tibet
A giant thangka is displayed annually in the summer, with an attendant festival, in Drepung Monastery (Lhasa) and twice a year (winter and summer) in Drepung (Central Tibet). Thangka displays or cham festivals and dances also take place in Shigatse, Tsurphu, Reting, Mindroling, Samye, Sakya and Shalu, all major monastic centres in Tibet.

Ladakh
The main monastic festivals are Hemis (around late June) and Phyiang (end July/early August). Stok and Matho follow one another in early March. The Ladakh Festival, which lasts two weeks from the beginning of September, is tourist-oriented but includes plenty of music and dancing. For exact dates, phone the tourist office in Leh ((91) 1982 52094).

Bhutan
The festivals in Paro and Thimphu are the most famous, but they get so overcrowded that it's worth trying out others, especially off-season, to get a better traditional atmosphere. Check *www.bhutan.gov.bt* for locations and dates.

in part are distinguished by the four orthodox monastic schools – the Nyingmapa, Sakyapa, Kagyupa and Gelugpa – and the Bönpo tradition (which is closest to Tibet's shamanistic roots). Differences are also to be found between their various sub-divisions, and even individual monasteries, since many aspects of the performing style are transmitted orally, despite the use of musical notation, while the larger monasteries developed more specialized musical instruction. Much of this variation has been patterned geographically: although the Gelugpa tradition dominated Central Tibet under the ruling Dalai Lamas, other schools are strongly represented in the Himalayan regions, notably the Nyingmapa (the oldest and closest to Indian Tantrism) and, especially in Bhutan and Ladakh, the Kagyupa.

In terms of stylistic differences, the clearest contrast is between the **Nyingmapa**, which may be described as "romantic" in style, and the **Gelugpa**, which is more "classical". The former is rhythmically more dramatic and melodically elaborate, and tends to make more of a feature of special instrumental styles. The latter is more restrained, even austere, and instruments are used less extensively, yet it exhibits a more profound development of vocal techniques.

These include a particular type of yang chanting known as **gyü-ke** (tantric voice), which is produced by forcing the voice into an exceptionally low register unusually rich in overtones. This produces a diphonic – or chordal – texture where the subtle modifications of the vowel-sounds in the secret text, itself now disguised, produce ethereal resonances floating in the upper register – a sort of overtone singing which probably indicates ancient cultural practices shared with other parts of Central Asia such as Mongolia. Gyü-ke still

Bhutan: the Last Shangri-La?

Until recently it was almost as if the only detectable influence of the outside world on this remote Himalayan kingdom was its unerring ability to live up to the image of James Hilton's *Lost Horizon*. Its policy of isolationism since the Chinese occupation of neighbouring Tibet was such that when in 1971 John Levy, by virtue of a personal contact with its royal ruler, was admitted to the country's unique fortress-monasteries (*dzong*) to make recordings there – still the only documents of its monastic traditions to have been released – he discovered a wealth of musical traditions in a strictly preserved time-capsule.

Besides the music of the state religion, the Drukpa Kagyupa branch of Tibetan Buddhism, the country's main folk genres are of two types, both essentially Bhutanese in character: *zhungdra* are refined court songs with typically long decorative phrases extended over simple rhythmic accompaniments; *bödra* songs, of a lighter nature, are thought to be of Tibetan origin. Both are often accompanied by the dramnyen lute, which although widely distributed throughout the Himalayas, has the status of a national instrument in Bhutan.

Turning to parliamentary democracy in 2008, Bhutan has witnessed a controlled development full of distinctive twists and disturbing changes. Although it remains one of the poorest countries in the world, this is in part because it officially pursues a goal of "Gross National Happiness" rather than economic growth. Here cultural expression plays an essential role, and not only because the country has become a notable (albeit exclusive) tourist destination. In reality, however, a mass rejection of traditional music has erupted with alarming speed and extent: at a state-organized competitive festival in 1995, according to the government newspaper *Kuensel*, traditional performers were booed off the stage, in preference to the new genre of *rigsar*. A blend of popular Indian and Western elements, using electronic keyboards, these songs emerged during the 1980s with the spread of cassette technology, and the development of modern influences has been accelerated by the arrival of television in 1999 and the subsequent growth of Internet usage.

Nevertheless there are signs that Bhutan's wider engagement with the outside world may rekindle interest in its unique musical traditions. The two pioneering international Tibetan-language feature films of Bhutanese lama filmmaker **Khyentse Norbu** – *The Cup* (1999) and *Travellers and Magicians* (2003) – have given some traditional musicians a higher profile. Traditional artists from the Royal Academy of Performing Arts have also toured abroad since the late 1990s, and one of the Academy's principal performers, **Jigme Drukpa**, has achieved international acclaim as the country's leading performer and cultural ambassador.

Grappa

Jigme Drukpa

survives in Central Tibet and is well maintained to the extent that the chanting masters of exiled monasteries like Shechen in Kathmandu are recent arrivals from Tibet. This extraordinary style is particularly associated with the two Tantric colleges of **Gyümé** (which favours the fifth interval, representing Yama, God of Death) and **Gyütö** (which emphasizes the tenth harmonic). The Gyütö tradition is among the most remarkable of the sacred Tibetan styles, and being maintained in exile in India, has achieved much attention in the West through recordings and concert performances.

Moreover, the Gyütö monks have been at the forefront of adapting ritual practices to Western performance models, and many other monastic choirs have followed suit in more recent years, including groups from Tibet itself. Although ritual practice takes precedence over musical performance, the monks clearly take delight and pride in the purely musical dimensions of their discipline, and are capable of (and comfortable with) adjusting to Western tastes and expectations. As a result, there are an increasing variety of fine, accessible recordings available today.

Another important category of monastic music is that associated with monastic **festivals**. Rarely represented on sound recordings, these are in any case, of course, best observed *in situ* (see box).

Secular Music

Although best known for its distinctive ritual styles, Tibet also has a rich and varied secular heritage which is under-represented in recordings and remains largely unknown outside the region and the Tibetan diaspora. Whereas only wind and percussion instruments are used in sacred music, in the secular tradition strings are common. Singing is the most prevalent form of music, often acapella or accompanied by the **dramnyen lute**, the principal and most distinctive traditional instrument of the Tibetan region.

In Tibet itself, secular music has fared rather better under Chinese rule than monastic music, and since the 1980s, the official Lhasa-based Song and Dance Ensemble has played an active role in maintaining and reviving key traditional forms, and has even toured in the West. Its equivalent guardian body outside Tibet is the **Tibetan Institute of Performing Arts (TIPA)**, based in Dharamsala (India), the seat of the Dalai Lama's government-in-exile. Established by the Dalai Lama shortly after he fled to India in 1959, it has played a key role not only in preserving traditional music, but also in training musicians, some of whom have become solo artists in several countries. Despite these two organizations' different objectives and approaches, they share an Asian adaptation of Western performance models, focusing on the three key "classic" genres of **lhamo**, **nangma** and **gar**.

TIPA in fact started principally as a troupe of musicians, singers and actors specializing in **lhamo** (or *ache-lhamo*), a kind of opera from Central Tibet accompanied by cymbals and drum. Based on classical narratives with Buddhist themes, these music dramas are nevertheless secular in orientation and were designed – rather like medieval mystery plays – to educate people in and attract people to Buddhist belief. The sung texts are interspersed with improvised and typically comical episodes, as well as dramatic instrumental effects. This enchanting and lively genre provides a fascinating insight into the nature of Buddhist experience in Tibetan culture. A new phenomenon in Tibet itself is modernized lhamo, with added Tibetan, Chinese and Western instruments. The Amdo variety of the genre in particular, known as **namthar**, has developed into a highly popular modern form which includes *ali* (a plucked lute), bowed fiddles and dulcimer (*gyümang*, equivalent to the Chinese *yangchin*).

Once patronized by Tibet's wealthier families as entertainment, **nangma** and the related genre of **töshe** (supposedly of western Tibetan origin) not only form part of the core repertoire of official arts bodies, but have also enjoyed a popular revival in karaoke-style clubs in Lhasa. Consisting of suites of songs, they begin in a slow tempo and speed up to a rousing finish. The songs are performed in an elegant style, accompanied by the restrained sounds of the Tibetan lute, dulcimer, two-string fiddle (*piwang*) and flute (*lingbu*), and are followed by a lively dance where foot-stamping adds a percussive, syncopated element. The singing, dancing and instrumental sections all follow different rhythmic patterns, and considerable skill and virtuosity is expected of the lute player in leading the ensemble.

Nangma and töshe overlap in style with court songs in the **gar** repertoire, a body of music associated with musicians formerly maintained at the palaces of the Dalai and Panchen Lamas. Besides purely instrumental pieces for kettledrums (*daman*), oboes (*surna*) and gong-chimes (*kharnga chupa*) which accompanied the Lamas' public and festive appearances, a distinctive, enlarged nangma ensemble – including special lutes apparently of Central Asian origin called *tambura* and *gandza* – provided light music for state entertainments.

Besides these main genres, there is an enormous variety of **folk song** styles associated with everyday life – work songs, courtship songs, wedding songs, pilgrimage songs, songs of social and political comment, and even thieves' songs. Particularly celebrated are the long, unaccompanied songs, sung in free rhythm in a high voice with glottal embellishments. Their difficult and archaic technique makes them much appreciated when performed by buskers in Lhasa's main square or in government-sponsored concerts.

Alongside singing, dance forms abound, particularly at weddings, New Year, spring and harvest festivals, and as part of other popular entertainment forms such as horse-races, polo and archery competitions. Besides the universal use of the dramnyen lute, other instruments to be heard in Himalayan regions such as Ladakh are ensembles of kettledrums and oboes, used to accompany social dances and other public events.

Another important element of Tibet's musical legacy is the sung epic of **Gesar**, Tibet's hero protector and avenger, which harks back to the mighty empire of the eighth century. The bards, alternating narration and singing, often claim to be directly inspired by Gesar in a trance, although there are few epic bards left in Tibet today.

Plateau Pop

Whereas officially sanctioned groups, whether in Tibet itself or in exile, present a solid pan-Tibetan identity through the preservation of traditional culture, modern musical expressions have developed in other, ever-widening contexts. Besides the obvious political barrier which largely separates developments within the TAR from those elsewhere, language barriers have also fundamentally shaped new developments in Tibetan music (in the broadest sense). Thus songs in the Tibetan language which are aimed at Tibetan-speaking audiences tend to value lyrics with unmistakable (if indirect) political significance above musical style.

Modernization of traditional Tibetan music is not, however, a recent phenomenon. The seeds of change were already taking place in pre-Communist Tibet where, by the 1940s, recordings of popular music from India, China and the West were freely, if not widely, available – including, according to Heinrich Harrer (of *Seven Years in Tibet* fame), the latest hits of Bing Crosby. In the 1950s, by contrast, many traditional Tibetan songs were subjected to modernization in Chinese popular idioms for the purpose of spreading Communist ideology, setting the tone for later developments.

After the dark years of the suppression of the Tibetan uprising in 1959 and the Cultural Revolution, a fragile easing of restrictions has taken place since the 1980s, leading to the emergence of two new forms of Tibetan popular music, each of them having to negotiate censorship in a climate of great tension and sporadic unrest. It is forbidden, for example, to refer to religion and lamas (especially the Dalai Lama), but some songs, like "Chörten Karpo", get round this by using metaphorical language: *chörten karpo*, the "white stupa [a type of Buddhist monument] that we will always carry in our hearts", is taken as alluding to the Buddhist faith, or even the Dalai Lama himself.

One very popular strand of new music, **Tibetan pop**, is heavily influenced by the most banal Chinese equivalent (synthesized accompaniments and easy melodies). This music is played all over Tibet in public places and in the innumerable karaoke bars in urban centres (most of which play mainly Chinese pop). One of the leading figures of the late 1980s and 1990s was **Jampa Tsering** (died 1997), who studied music in Shanghai and was a member of the Tibet Song and Dance Ensemble, from which he was expelled when he began to gain a popular following in karaoke bars. The content of much of his material (such as *Songs from the Holy Land*) tested the limits of political freedom and were restricted by the Chinese authorities. Other leading singers since that period have been the Kham singer **Yadong** and – prior to her exile in the US – **Dadön (Dawadolma)**. More recently the Shigatse singer **Han Hong** (the Chinese stage name of Ingdzin Droma), has drawn strongly on Chinese folk and pop idioms, as well as jazz, rock and blues, although her vocal style retains some Tibetan characteristics. Although many of her songs express a pride in Tibetan identity and culture, their perspective comes from Beijing, where she now lives: her song "Heaven's Road" (2006), celebrating the completion of the Qingzang Railway between Tibet and China, was a big hit throughout China. At the same time, some Chinese pop stars such as **Dadawa** and **Sa Ding Ding** have shown a curiosity in Tibetan music and language. On the other hand, the rise of stars such as **Agyang Tshering** (the Tibetan name of a Han Chinese singer from a Tibetan area of Sichuan) represents a further disconnection between ethnicity and musical identity which is deeply disturbing for many Tibetans under Chinese rule.

However, another kind of new Tibetan music grafts new lyrics, often with moralistic, if not covertly political, undertones, onto traditional melodic and instrumental themes. It is accompanied by the dramnyen lute in the Central Tibetan style, or by the mandolin in the Amdo (northeast Tibet)

Universal Music China

Sa Ding Ding

style. There is a wealth of new musicians, most of them peasants who busk round the country during the winter months. As they are neither rich nor part of any established infrastructure there are very few tapes available, but most Lhasans are able to sing the most famous of these songs.

Another important feature of Lhasa's musical life is the traditional **nangma music bar**, a sort of Tibetan version of the karaoke bar, where customers jump up on stage to sing and dance classical nangma and töshe songs. Opened for the first time in 1998, they are currently seriously threatened by the government, partly because they challenge the Chinese businesses of karaoke bars, and partly because they advocate, by their very existence, a traditional music heritage instead of a modern one.

Music in Exile

Outside the TAR, young refugees newly arriving in the Himalayan regions since the 1960s quickly started to embrace new musical styles and opportunities. However, they did not identify greatly with locally emerging popular styles, even those among indigenous Tibetan-speaking groups.

Although Tibetan-speakers in the Himalayas have been exposed to South Asian forms of popular cinema for several decades, the remote mountainous terrain has inhibited access to new music technologies and other styles. In Ladakh, **Indian film music** has been the major influence on modern music, locally broadcast on radio since the 1970s. In the 1980s, local studio recording facilities and cassette distribution enabled local stars such as **Phunsok Ladakhi** to shadow the musical fashions of Bollywood, successfully blending modern Indian and Western influences with indigenous styles. Elsewhere, many Himalayan areas had to wait for the arrival of satellite and digital technologies for the mass media to have any significant impact, so that even in isolated Bhutan, local versions of Indian popular music very rapidly became the predominant popular form among young people during the 1990s (see box).

Tibetan exiles, on the other hand, being fiercely anti-Chinese, and remaining un-integrated in India or Nepal, largely rejected musical influences from these countries, turning instead to the West for both musical and political inspiration and support. They did, however, quickly exploit the possibilities of cheap cassette technology becoming available in North India during the 1980s, and soon demonstrated a creative versatility and eclecticism which may surprise Western traditionalists as much as it shocks their own elders. The short-

lived but influential band **Rangzen Shönu** (Freedom Youths) pioneered a new form of Tibetan popular music, drawing strongly on US country and rock styles (using acoustic guitars and bass rather than traditional instruments), which provided a way of expressing the political hopes and frustrations of young exiles. Their album *Modern Tibetan Folk Songs* (1988) proved immensely popular among exile communities, and even, by way of smuggled cassettes, in Tibet itself. Several Tibetan-language rock bands have since emerged (**R59, Buddha Boys, JJI Exile Brothers**) and have a popular following through recordings and at concerts and festivals throughout the Indian subcontinent. Today there is a well-organized music scene linking exile communities in South Asia, with Tibetan-run production companies, recording studios and (since 2003) the Tibet Music Awards. Being based largely upon Internet votes, the latter attracts a following in Tibet, and Tibetan artists in TAR such as **Yadong** and **Kunga Phunsog** have been among the award-winners.

The content of this music scene, though, is far from limited to Tibetan rock or pop from either side of the Himalayas. Traditional forms, represented by TIPA, still dominate most musical activity, and many of the most widely appreciated artists, such as Delhi-based **Pasang Dolma**, come from traditional musical backgrounds with a TIPA training. Their conservative innovation occupies the middle ground of a broad spectrum of musical responses to life in exile.

With significant numbers of Tibetans living in Western countries, increasingly born outside Tibet, similar varieties of modern styles have proliferated across the world. Besides TIPA-related traditional song and dance groups such as **Chaksampa** (US) and **Gang Chenpa** (Netherlands), there are a growing number of Tibetan-language rock bands and popular solo artists – **Sonam Palkyi** (Switzerland), **Trinkhor** (Germany) and **Phurbu T. Namgyal** (US), for example. Several singers, notably the exiled Tibetan pop star **Dadön**, have succeeded in reaching Western audiences through their commitment to fund raising events and campaign work, but mostly they remain dependent upon wide distribution of their recordings among Tibetan exile audiences, especially in South Asia.

Tibet and the West

A very different musical strand has emerged in the West. Aimed at non-Tibetan-speaking listeners largely unfamiliar with the original ritual performance contexts, this has focused on the amazing

Tibetan Buddhist nun Choying Drolma

sounds and musical techniques offered by Tibetan traditions, while many collaborative projects have served to generate support for Tibetan social and political causes.

Long before the arrival of Tibetans in the Western world, there was a fascination with the rich and mysterious sonorities of Tibetan ritual music, especially among students of Tibetan Buddhism and "serious" composers, among whom a tradition of **experimental composition** can be traced to the pioneering creations of the American composer Henry Eichheim in the 1920s, through Karlheinz Stockhausen to minimalist composer Philip Glass.

Western interest in the more peaceful and meditational aspects of Tibetan music is similarly evident in the evocative soundscapes of **New Age music** of the 1970s and its subsequent offshoots. American Buddhists **Henry Wolff** and **Nancy Hennings** were pioneers in this field with their first album of *Tibetan Bells* in 1971. In 1981, French musician **Alain Presencer** produced *The Singing Bowls of Tibet* (Saydisc), a remarkable album of compositions and arrangements based on the enchantingly ethereal sounds of these unusual bowl-shaped bells used – though apparently not in Tibet itself – for meditational and other religious purposes. The growth of dharma centres in the West, serving Western Buddhist converts as well as an increasing number of Tibetan exiles, has created a growing market for meditational music intended primarily as aids to religious practice. There are now a number of CDs featuring individual Tibetan practitioners, such as Belgian resident teacher **Lama Karta** and Montana-based nun **Ani Tsering Wangmo**. The peace songs of **Dechen Shak Dagsay** (Switzerland), meanwhile, have had wider exposure through Bernardo Bertolucci's film *Little Buddha* (1993).

Other Tibetan-themed films in a run of successes in recent years – including the pioneering Tibetan-language feature films of Bhutanese lama filmmaker **Khyentse Norbu** (see box) – created high-profile opportunities for several Tibetan musicians. Chaksampa co-founder **Sonam Tashi** (stage name Acho Danny) was assistant director of *Seven Years in Tibet* (1997) and has since enjoyed a successful solo career developing an appealing rock-oriented dramnyen style. The film also gave birth to **Gang Chenpa**, whose lead singer **Namgyal Lhamo** has since also ventured solo. Philip Glass's soundtrack for *Kundun* (1997) gave wide exposure to the stunning chanting of the **Gyütö Monks**, with whom Glass had previously collaborated in Mickey Hart's *Freedom Chants* project alongside Japanese-American music-guru **Kitaro**.

With the help of Richard Gere, Kitaro also collaborated with Tibetan musician **Nawang Khechog** (based in Australia, then the US), enabling him to become one of the first Tibetan artists to achieve widespread solo acclaim in the West. Another apparently incongruous but successful collaboration has been between the Tibetan Buddhist nun **Choying Drolma** (in Nepal) and the American progressive guitarist **Steve Tibbetts**, demonstrating a fresh dynamic in East–West partnerships.

In the last decade or so, many other traditional Tibetan artists across the world have independently succeeded in bringing Tibetan musical traditions to new audiences. They include **Tenzin Gonpo** and **Tsering Wangdu** (France), **Loten Namling** (Switzerland), **Tenzin Choegyal** (Australia) and **Soname** (UK). Many have demonstrated extreme courage as well as artistic dedication: after university training in the US, **Ngawang Choephel** returned to Tibet for a documentary field trip but was imprisoned by the Chinese authorities for six years before a major campaign secured his release. **Gompo Kyab** returned to Amdo to set up a recording studio, and in collaboration with Canadian exile **Jamyang Yeshi**'s "Shining Spirit" project, reunited – musically at least – members of a family of musicians divided between Tibet and North America.

Yungchen Lhamo: Divine Songstress

It was a truly visionary moment when a holy man gave the name **Yungchen Lhamo** (the Tibetan Buddhist name of Sarasvati, the Hindu goddess of music and song) to a girl born in a Chinese labour camp near Lhasa: since fleeing Tibet in 1989, she has forged a career for herself as one of Tibet's most powerful voices in exile. "I am determined to make a path as a solo vocalist", she says. "My childhood was one of such despair and poverty. Since I escaped, by foot over the Himalayas like so many other Tibetans, I have been able to find freedom in the West. Part of the Chinese rationale for the occupation of Tibet is that the Tibetan people are backward and inferior. By forging a path for Tibetan artists, I am showing what we really can do if we have freedom. Tibet has many young, courageous and talented people working to keep our culture dynamic and alive. Tibetan culture will not die, nor remain static. We will grow as part of the modern world as long as we have a chance of freedom – something most Tibetans unfortunately do not have."

The most remarkable international success, however, has been that of the singer **Yungchen Lhamo** (see box) who since 1994 has performed regularly at WOMAD festivals and benefit concerts across the world, and has recorded three acclaimed albums on the Real World label. Famous for the transformative power of her live solo performances, she is equally adept at winning new listeners by exploring studio-based forms. She seems to be equally comfortable on stage and working with electronic sounds – or as she once described them, "the invisible orchestra which just fell from the sky". Above all she holds out a lifeline which every Tibetan exile awaiting their return can identify with: "Even though I lost everything, I didn't lose my voice."

With thanks to Isabelle Henrion and Stephen Jones

DISCOGRAPHY Tibet and Bhutan

Despite the unfavourable conditions for recording traditional Tibetan music, much of which presents many technical and listening challenges, there is now a wealth of fine, accessible recordings which have emerged from exile communities since the 1960s. Recordings of modern artists listed here are limited to those widely distributed in the West. Good up-to-date sources of information on popular artists in Tibet itself and among exile communities are *www.tibetlink.com* and *www.musictibet.com*. The first three compilations listed below are pioneering collections of field recordings which remain absolute classics. Although their sound quality is in some cases limited, they are chosen for their historical and cultural value.

Traditional

⊙ The Music of Tibetan Buddhism
Rounder, US
Three discs covering the four main Tibetan monastic orders recorded by Peter Crossley-Holland in 1961. There are impressive instrumental extracts, and some extraordinary chant and overtone singing from the Gelugpa monks. With informative notes, this is a good introduction to ritual music.

⊙ Tibet Anthology
Wind Records, Taiwan
The only current survey of music in Tibet itself, recorded in 1993–94 by Chinese scholar Mao Jizeng on six CDs. Sacred music is rather under-represented with just one disc, but there is excellent coverage of lesser-known forms of court music, ballads, folk songs and dance. Vol. 1: *The Opera Music of Tibet*; Vol. 2: *The Religious Music of Tibet*; Vol. 3: *Tibetan Song and Dance Music*; Vol. 4: *Tibetan Folk Songs*; Vol. 5: *Tibetan Court Music and Instrumental Music*; Vol. 6: *Tibetan Ballad Singing and Minorities' Music in Tibet*.

⊙ Tibetan Buddhist Rites from the Monasteries of Bhutan Vols 1–4
Lyrichord, US
A unique four-volume collection of field recordings from Bhutan made by John Levy in 1973. Trumpets blast and cymbals crash with a real sense of presence. The excellent recordings feature monastic rituals of the Drukpa Kargyupa (dominant in Bhutan), but the Nyingmapa tradition is also represented. The fourth volume is a rare and fascinating compilation of Tibetan and Bhutanese folk music, featuring the enchanting music of the dramnyen lute.

⊙ Achelhamo/Celestial Female: Parts from Tibetan Opera
Pan, Netherlands
Featuring Achelhamo and Amdo operatic styles, this disc is for confirmed devotees of Tibetan opera, but is worth listing as one of the few recordings featuring music from inside Tibet itself. Recorded by Chinese scholar Tian Liantao in Lhasa and Gansu.

⊙ Amdo: The Tibetan Monastery of Labrang
Ocora, France
The Labrang monastery has been a major centre for the painful reconstruction of Buddhism in the Tibetan region of Amdo. Apart from the haunting vocal liturgy punctuated by cymbals

and trumpets, this disc also features the monks' unique adaptation of Chinese temple music, as well as lively Amdo opera.

⊙The Diamond Path: Rituals of Tibetan Buddhism
Shanachie, US
A vivid and colourful 1994 recording by David Lewiston of the Yamantaka Trochu rite from Khampagar Monastery, in the foothills of India's Western Himalayas. With a magnificent-sounding ritual orchestra including some thunderous dungchen trumpets, the ceremony gives "the energy to dispel fear and to manifest infinite compassion". It comes in one continuous track lasting over an hour.

⊙ Ladakh: Musique de Monastère et de Village
Chant du Monde, France
An appealingly-balanced package of field recordings of Ladakh's ritual and secular musical heritage. Part of a monastic service from Phyiang (Dregung Kagyupa) monastery exhibits contrasting chant styles, including the sustained yang style, and impressive instrumental interludes. The village folk music comes with lively oboes and kettledrums. Good notes, with some extraordinary chant notation.

⊙ Tibet: Heart of Dharma
Ellipsis Arts, US
Recent field recordings of high quality by veteran David Lewiston, featuring ritual music from two contrasting traditions maintained in India: the Loseling college of Drepung monastery (Gelugpa), which specializes in the extraordinary multiphonic chant style more usually associated with the Gyütö college; and Khampagar monastery (Drukpa Kagyupa), which features dramatic instrumental styles. The 64-page booklet provides an excellent introduction.

⊙ Tibet: Musique Sacrée
Ocora, France
Very listenable and atmospheric recordings made in monasteries in Nepal. Illustrates the contrasting styles of the Nyingmapa order (Tengboche monastery), with powerful instrumental episodes, and the more restrained chants (notably the sustained yang style) of the Gelugpa order (Thami monastery).

⊙ Tibet: The Monastery of Gyütö – Voice of the Tantra
Ocora, France
Superbly recorded by Radio France engineers in 1975, this two-CD reissue comes from one of the first performances in the West by these monks, at a time when most of them were great masters who had lived in Tibet before being exiled in India. It's a fabulous example of their extraordinary chanting style, with thrilling instrumental passages too. Powerful listening supported by expertly written, detailed notes.

⊙ Tibetan Nuns
Sunset, France
Fine and rare example of nuns' chanting from Nangi nunnery in Nepal. The unaccompanied chants, in honour of the Buddhist order's founder, are beautifully pure and well blended. Despite deplorable notes, the clear, intimate and atmospheric recording makes for delightful, accessible listening.

Gang Chenpa

This independent song-and-dance ensemble based in the Netherlands got together during the making of the film *Seven Years in Tibet*. Their lead singer Namgyal Lhamo has since also made solo albums featuring her sweet, lyrical voice.

⊙ Voices from Tibet
Music & Words, Holland
Pleasing selection of traditional styles including lively syncopated dance-songs (nangma), dramnyen lute and dulcimer, and some great acrobatic unaccompanied folk songs.

Gyütö Monks

Originally a Tantric college in Lhasa, the Gyütö monastery, now relocated in India, trains monks in a unique style of yang chanting made famous in the West through concert tours since the mid-1970s, and latterly as a feature of Philip Glass's soundtrack to the film *Kundun*.

⊙ Freedom Chants
Rykodisc, US
Produced by Mickey Hart, this album was recorded during their US tour in 1988, and exhibits their extraordinary chanting style.

Jigme Drukpa

A lone figure in recording terms, Jigme Drukpa is the only native traditional artist from Bhutan to have recorded a CD of his country's folk music in the West.

⊙ Endless Songs from Bhutan
Grappa, Norway
An idyllic and unique treasury of Bhutanese and Tibetan-style folk songs, also featuring the Bhutanese bamboo flute, *yangchin* (hammer dulcimer) and dranyen (lute). Recorded in Norway when Jigme was on tour in 1998; song translations and synopses included.

Tashi Lhunpo Monks

One of the most important monasteries in Central Tibet, and traditional seat of the Panchen Lama, Tashi Lhunpo has maintained its prestigious musical traditions from its exile base in southern India, and in recent years has toured in the West and made recordings.

★ Dawn Till Dusk
30 IPS, UK
After featuring on compilations issued by the Tibet Foundation in the UK, this is the monks' first complete album. The large choir offers powerful, rich chanting, beautifully captured on this majestic, atmospheric recording, with some awesome orchestral forces (the long trumpets, in particular, are stunning). Well-presented and accessible listening, with good notes, this is a great "ear-opener" for new listeners.

Tibetan Institute of Performing Arts (TIPA)

The cultural flagship of the Dalai Lama's government in exile for the last five decades, based in Dharamsala, India.

★ Dama Suna
Erato/Detour, France
An unusually broad selection of mostly secular Tibetan music, and a useful and informative first-time buy. Contains nineteen tracks, including regional folk songs, nangma, gar, lhamo, as well as three atmospheric examples of ritual chant by the Gyütö monks. Good notes and lyric translations.

Contemporary

Choying Drolma and Steve Tibbetts

Choying Drolma, born in Kathmandu in 1971 to Tibetan exiles, is a Buddhist nun from the Nagi Gompa nunnery in Boudhanath, Nepal. Her "discovery" by US guitarist Steve Tibbetts led to their unlikely-sounding, but highly successful collaboration.

Chö
Rykodisc, US
Beautifully combining yogic meditational songs with mainly acoustic Western instruments, their first album achieves a lightness and clarity of sound texture which transcends descriptive labels as well as cultural boundaries.

 Selwa
Six Degrees, US
Their second, award-winning album is enriched with broader instrumentation including electronic sounds and percussion, but the blend is mainly as organic and transcendent as ever. Fresh, delicate instrumental gestures shade Choying's mesmerizing chants.

Nawang Khechog

After many years spent in India as a Buddhist monk, Tibetan flautist Nawang Khechog took up the didgeridoo while living in Australia, where he produced three albums before moving to the US.

Karuna
Domo, US
Although Nawang has produced a number of albums since moving to the US, his first, produced by New Age/spiritual musician Kitaro, is probably the best showcase of Khechog's own imaginative style of experimental music, blending ambient sounds with the primal sounds of ancient cultures, including echoes of his native Eastern Tibet.

Soname Yangchen

Soname escaped from Tibet as a child and grew up in India before moving to England. In her autobiography, she describes singing as "my passion, my great release from bondage": "My people were gagged, but I could sing for them."

Unforgettable Land
Fortunate Recordings, UK
A creative blend of traditional and original songs, including unaccompanied folk songs from her childhood, gentle acoustic layers and experimental mixes. Soname's debut album reveals a naturally versatile voice – soulful, exuberant, acrobatic – with further potential tapped on her second album, *Plateau*, released on World Village.

Yungchen Lhamo

The aptly named "Divine Songstress", from Tibet via Australia, has captivated live audiences worldwide with her haunting vocal style, and currently reigns supreme in the world of contemporary Tibetan music.

Coming Home
Real World, UK
Whereas her first album for Real World, *Tibet, Tibet*, concentrated on simple unaccompanied songs, the second, produced by Hector Zazou, appeals to a wider audience by using Western instruments, electronic sounds and multi-tracking techniques. Although verging on a New Age sensibility, the accompaniments are generally inspiring and sensitive, and the communicative power and sublime beauty of her ever-soulful voice holds listeners spellbound.

Ama
Real World, UK
Yungchen's fourth album exhibits new studio-based adventures in melody, rhythm, instrumentation and texture. Incorporates world grooves ranging from Middle-Eastern-tinged percussion to African vocal polyphony, and explores new quasi-improvisational approaches and lyric paths (in English and Tibetan), supported by Annie Lennox. Together with traditional vocal echoes, this new range and richness of expression – at times intense, deep, provocative, enthralling – represents the mature development of her artistic and spiritual vision.

PLAYLIST
Tibet and Bhutan

1 **OM MANI PADME HUNG Yungchen Lhamo** from *Ama*
Rousing rallying-call and inspirational mix from the world's most successful Tibetan singer.

2 **KYANDRO SEMKYE Choying Drolma and Steve Tibbetts** from *Cho*
Beautiful, intimately accompanied chanting from one of the most successful East–West collaborations.

3 **NAGPO CHENPO (The Great Dark One) Gyütö Monks** from *Voice of the Tantra*
Stunning deep chanting in a powerful performance which transports the listener into the esoteric sound-world of these famous monks.

4 **DOLMA PUJA (Tara Prayer) Tashi Lhunpo Monks** from *Dawn till Dusk*
Exhilarating multi-layered rhythmic recitation of chants: a shimmering monument of polyphonic sonority.

5 **LMENE TENDEL (Food Offering) Nangi Nuns** from *Tibetan Nuns*
Atmospheric showcase of mesmerizing acapella chanting.

6 **GAR (Instrumental Offering) Tibetan Institute of Performing Arts** from *Dama Suna*
Rare example of impressive drums and plaintive oboes. Magnificent.

7 **LHODRAK MARPAI ZHAB Jigme Drukpa** from *Endless Songs from Bhutan*
Delicate performance of zhungdra from a lone traditional voice of Bhutan.

8 **SOMEDAY Yungchen Lhamo** from *Ama*
Sublime, soulful song of yearning from the great songstress of Tibet.

Vietnam

music on the move

The Ca Tru Thai Ha Ensemble
Barley Norton

For far too long, Vietnam was thought of as a war rather than a country. But its image is at last changing, and since the 1990s it has been on a course of rapid economic and cultural change and has become a popular travel destination. Little known internationally, Vietnamese music is rich, diverse and dynamic. From the gong music of ethnic minority groups living in the remote central highlands, to ancient court music of the imperial capital of Hue, to the protest and love songs of Trinh Cong Son, Vietnamese music has a lot to offer. Barley Norton and Philip Blackburn explore Vietnam's fascinating sounds.

Vietnam, a long, thin country winding along the shores of the South China Sea, boasts distinctive music cultures in the north, centre and south. The Red River Delta in the north, which has been populated by the Viet people for several thousand years, is the source of numerous musical traditions including water puppetry, folk music-theatre, refined art songs and the regional folk song of **quan ho**. The central and southern regions became part of Vietnam through a long period of expansion from the north between the tenth and eighteenth centuries. The main musical traditions in the central regions are imperial court music, a haunting style of Hue singing and a distinctive style of opera, whereas the south is famous for the melancholic songs of reformed music theatre and delicate chamber music played on traditional instruments. The mountainous regions in the north and centre of the country are also home to ethnic minority groups such as the Hmong, Thai, Bahnar and E-De, who each have their own languages, traditions and music, adding yet another dimension to Vietnam's diverse soundscape.

The development of indigenous musical traditions has been influenced by China (Vietnam was under Chinese rule from 111 BC to AD 939) and to a lesser extent by India, but foreign influence has been most pronounced through contact with the West and the enduring legacy of French colonialism, the American war and Communism. As Vietnam moves rapidly down the path of modernization and towards a liberalized market economy, the effects of globalization on musical practices are increasing, yet at the same time there is a return to tradition and many pre-revolutionary musical forms are being revitalized.

Theatrical Music

Vietnam's traditional theatre, with its strong Chinese influence, is akin to opera, though it includes heightened speech. Despite being used as a vehicle for propaganda in the war years, the plots and characters performed today are traditional, and musical accompaniment – including a well-known repertoire of songs – forms an integral part of the performance. Performances of the classical opera *tuong* are hard to come by these days, and *cheo* and *cai luong*, although still regularly performed, have suffered declining audiences and are losing out to television and the Internet. Other traditional arts have seen something of a revival, however, most notably water puppetry and folk-song performances. The stimulus came largely from tourism,

but renewed interest in the ritual music of *chau van* and the complexities of *ca tru* and *nhac tai tu* chamber music have been more home-grown.

Cheo, or folk opera, is based on popular legends and stories of everyday events, often with a biting satirical edge. Most of the music, as with other forms of traditional Vietnamese theatre, is not composed for each play, but drawn from a common fund of music which has evolved over the years.

The cheo orchestra generally consists of flute, plucked and bowed strings, gongs and drums. Although the movements have become highly stylized over the centuries, cheo's free form allows the actors considerable room for interpretation. Although cheo was used to promote the aims of the Communist Party and the war effort from the 1950s to the 1970s, traditionally cheo has the reputation of being anti-establishment, especially in its clown character, who comments freely on the action and current events. So incensed were the kings of the fifteenth-century Le dynasty that cheo was banned from the court, while artists and their descendants were excluded from public office. The state-supported cheo ensembles in contemporary Vietnam continue to innovate and put on performances, although audiences have declined and these days, people prefer a medley of short, popular extracts rather than listening to long folk-plays in their entirety.

Tuong (known in southern Vietnam as *hat boi*) evolved from classical Chinese opera. It was originally performed for royal entertainment, before being adopted by travelling troupes. Its storylines are usually historical epics dealing with such Confucian principles as filial piety and relations between the monarch and his subjects. Tuong, like cheo, is governed by rigorous rules in which the characters are rendered instantly recognizable by their make-up and costume. Setting and atmosphere are conjured not by props and scenery, but through nuances of gesture and musical conventions.

Cai luong, or "reformed theatre", originated in southern Vietnam in the early twentieth century. As it developed, the music, plots, costumes and sets of cai luong drew on diverse influences, including various types of Vietnamese music and performance styles as well as Chinese, French and other foreign sources. The action of cai luong plays is often a mix of historical drama and contemporary themes from everyday life. Its music is a similar blend: chamber music played on amplified traditional instruments for the set pieces; electric guitar, keyboards and drums during the scene changes. Cai luong's use of contemporary

Cai luong theatre

vernacular has made it highly adaptable and enabled it to keep pace with Vietnam's social changes.

The traditional music accompanying cai luong theatre draws on the closely related **ca Hue** (see box on Vietnamese classical music) and **nhac tai tu** repertoires. Nhac tai tu, or "skilled amateur chamber music" is played as pure chamber music, sometimes without the voice. This is one of the most delightful and tricky of all Vietnamese genres: there is a fundamental melodic framework, but the players have a great degree of improvisational latitude. They must think and respond quickly, as in a game, and the resulting modal inflections are exquisite. Although modern conservatoire training fails to prepare students for this most satisfying of all styles, there is now a resurgence of interest by young players in learning the demands of tai tu.

Water puppetry (*roi nuoc*) is an art unique to Vietnam. The **Thang Long National Puppet Theatre**, with its singers and instrumentalists from Hanoi, has taken its colourful show around the world. Roi nuoc's origins are obscure, beyond that it developed in the murky rice paddies of the Red River Delta and usually took place in spring, when there was less farm work to be done. The earliest record of a performance dates from 1121, which suggests that by this date water puppetry was already a feature of the royal court.

Obscured behind a split-bamboo screen, puppeteers standing waist-deep in water manipulate the wooden puppets, some of which weigh over 10kg, using long poles hidden beneath the surface. Dragons, ducks, lions, unicorns, phoenixes and frogs spout fire and smoke, throw balls and generally cavort – miraculously avoiding tangling the poles. Brief scenes of rural life, such as water-buffalo fights, fishing or rice-planting take place alongside lion and dragon dances, legendary exploits and a watery promenade of fairy-like immortals. Even fireworks emerge to dance upon the water, which itself takes on different characters, from soft-focus shimmering red and gold to seething and furious during naval battles.

After a period of decline, Vietnam's water-puppet troupes have played to great acclaim internationally and at home since the 1980s and teaching projects supported by international donors have further revitalized the genre. The newly carved puppets, revamped programme and elaborate staging can be seen nightly in Hanoi and Ho Chi Minh City. Where before **gongs and drums** alone were used for scene-setting and building atmosphere, today's national troupes often maintain a larger ensemble, similar to cheo, including **zithers and flutes**. The songs are also borrowed from the cheo repertoire, particularly declamatory styles and popular folk tunes, and the shows often include a short recital of traditional music before the puppets emerge.

Vietnamese Classical: the Imperial Music of Hue

The city of Hue, situated on the Hue river delta in the centre of the country, was the last capital of the old Vietnamese kingdom from 1802 to 1945. The remains of the palace were devastated in the 1968 Tet offensive, but UNESCO declared the complex to be a World Heritage Site in 1993, since when a restoration process has been under way.

The city has a long heritage of dance and ceremonial music. From the early seventeenth century, 120 courtly dancers and musicians were trained at special conservatoires associated with the palace. The emperors required dignified instrumental music for their rituals and audiences, as well as the intimate chamber music (**ca Hue**) enjoyed by their refined people. These styles of ritual and chamber music are at the heart of Vietnam's classical music tradition.

From the fall of the Republic of Vietnam in 1975 until 1993, court music, **nhac cung dinh**, was rarely performed, but it is now being revived. Elderly musicians have begun to teach the tradition to the younger generation and a court band is now employed at the palace to play when visitors appear. For a fee, visitors can even dress up in royal clothes and ascend the throne as the emperor once did, while being serenaded by the court band.

Folk, Ritual and Chamber music

One of the most famous folk-song traditions is **quan ho**, an antiphonal song form which originates from the northern Bac Ninh province. Quan ho was traditionally an intimate social practice involving alternate singing between pairs of men and women from different villages in the province. Each pair would improvise lyrics and melodies in response to the other and through this practice strong bonds of friendship and love were developed between singers. Traditionally, quan ho was part of the fabric of rural life and it was performed at village festivals in honour of local deities. Since the mid-1960s, quan ho has been strongly promoted by the Vietnamese government as a national folk song tradition and it was recently acknowledged by UNESCO as "intangible cultural heritage". At large festivals each lunar spring professional troupes can now be heard performing standardized versions of quan ho songs on the stage, more for the television cameras than for local villagers.

Chau van is a sacred ritual music used to invoke the spirits during spirit possession ceremonies. The places of worship are spirit temples adorned with statues of goddesses and male spirits belonging to the pantheon of an indigenous religious system known as the Mother Religion or Four Palace Religion. During the performance of vibrant song by a male spirit-priest with **moon-lute and percussion** accompaniment, a medium is possessed by a series of deities from the pantheon. Because of the anti-superstition stance of

the Vietnamese government until 1986, the style was practised in secret for many years, although some pieces were adapted to praise the state and revolutionary Communism. **Pham Van Ty** is one of the leading musicians of this style. Chau van is currently being revived by older practitioners in its original religious context, where ritualizing is a vehicle for coming to terms with personal difficulties and dramatic social change. At the same time, the re-enactment of spirit possession has found a new place on the cheo stage in folklorized performances that officially celebrate ritual as national tradition in a government-led bid to promote Vietnamese cultural identity.

Jerker Andersson

Guitar legend Kim Sinh on the moon lute

The song tradition known as **ca tru**, or *hat a dao*, probably dates back to the fifteenth century, when it was performed by a large ensemble at village festivals in honour of the guardian spirits of the village. Over the centuries, the ca tru ensemble and performance contexts evolved. In the nineteenth century, ca tru became a refined form of chamber music appreciated by scholars and poets, and in the early twentieth century it was very popular as a form of entertainment in "singing bars". The contemporary ensemble consists of a female singer, who accompanies herself with complex rhythms on bamboo clappers (*phach*), and two instrumentalists, one who plays the three-string *dan day* lute and another who plays a small "praise drum" (*trong chau*). Ca tru singers are famous for using a special, highly ornamented vocal technique, and lutenists are skilled at improvising a subtle accompaniment to the voice. The drummer's role is to mark the end of phrases with codified patterns and to praise (or criticize) the performance as it progresses.

In the latter part of the twentieth century, ca tru was little performed. It was not encouraged by the Communist government because of its past associations with the elite classes and, when it was performed in singing bars, with prostitution. In the last decade, however, there has been a revival of interest, and the Hanoi-based **Ca Tru Thai Ha Ensemble**, led by Nguyen Van Mui, have promoted ca tru at home and abroad. The ca tru tradition is mostly restricted to the north. In the centre around the city of Hue, the refined chamber music of **ca Hue** is now performed for tourists on sampans on the Perfume River.

Traditional Instruments

A visiting US politician, Hubert H. Humphrey, once stepped off a plane with the intention of smoothing relations by attempting a little Vietnamese – a tonal language. But instead of "I am honoured to be here", listeners heard "the sunburnt duck lies sleeping". The voice and its inherent melodic information are at the root of Vietnamese music, and most instruments, to some extent, imitate the inflections of the voice: delicate pitch bends, ornaments and subtle slides.

According to classical Confucian theory, instruments fall into **eight categories of sound**: silk, stone, skin, clay, metal, air, wood and bamboo. Quite a few Vietnamese instruments are related to similar instruments in China and other parts of East Asia, but there are also instruments that are unique to Vietnam.

Many instruments whose strings are now made of steel, gut or nylon originally had silk strings, but silk is now out of fashion, more for acoustic than ecological reasons. The most famous of these instruments, and unique to Vietnam, is the single-stringed **dan bau** (or *dan doc huyen*), an ingenious invention perfectly suited to its job of mimicking vocal inflections. Its one string, originally silk, is stretched over a long amplified sounding-box, fixed at one end. The other end is attached to a buffalo-horn tremolo arm or "whammy bar", which can be flexed to stretch or relax the string's tension. Meanwhile, the string is plucked with a plectrum at its harmonic nodes to produce overtones that swoop and glide and quiver over a range of three octaves. Nowadays, the instrument is often used with a small electric amplifier so that its delicate but extraordinary sound can be heard alongside other instruments.

Other important **"silk" instruments** include the *dan nguyet* (moon lute), which is frequently used in traditional singing and theatre and has a beautiful circular body from which it gets its name; the dan day, a three-stringed lute with a long fingerboard used in ca tru and unique to Vietnam; the *dan ty ba*, a four-stringed lute like a Chinese *pipa*; the *dan tranh*, a sixteen-string zither; the *dan nhi*, a two-string fiddle of Chinese origin with the bow running between the strings; and the *dan luc huyen cam*, a regular guitar with a fingerboard scalloped to allow for wider pitch-bends.

In the **stone** category, a pile of rocks lies in the corner of the Research Institute in Ho Chi Minh City. This six-thousand-year-old lithophone called the **dan da** is the world's second-oldest musical instrument, the oldest being an identical set now in Paris. Played with heavy wooden mallets, it sounds just as it sounded long ago, with six ringing tones (roughly D-F-G-A-C-D) – a pentatonic scale. The instrument originated from a particular slate quarry in the central highlands where the stones, formed from petrified wood, sing like nowhere else.

Among the **skins**, various kinds of drums (*trong*) are used, played with acrobatic use of the sticks in the air and on the sides. Some originated in China, while others were introduced from India via the Cham people. One example is the double-headed "rice drum" (*trong com*), which was developed from the Indian *mridangam*; the name derives from thin patches of cooked rice-paste stuck on each membrane.

Representing **clay**, four thimble-size teacups are held in the fingers and often played as percussion instruments for Hue chamber music. Representing **metal**, the *sinh tien*, coin clappers, are another invention unique to Vietnam, combining in one unit a rasping scraper, wooden clapper and a sistrum rattle made from old coins. Bronze gongs are occasionally found in minority music (such as that of the E-De tribe of the central highlands), but Vietnam is the only country in Southeast Asia where tuned gamelan-type gong-chimes are not used.

Air, **wood** and **bamboo** furnish a whole range of wind instruments, such as the many side- and end-blown flutes used for folk songs and to accompany poetry recitals. The *ken*, a double-reed oboe, is played in funeral processions and other outdoor ceremonies. Five thin bones often dangle from the ken player's mouthpiece to suggest the delicate fingers of a young woman, while disguising the hideous grin necessary to play the instrument. The *song lang* is a slit drum, played by the foot, used to count the measures in tai tu chamber music, while the *k'longput*, a rack of horizontal **tuned bamboo pipes**, is the only percussion instrument you don't actually touch: instead, players clap their hands to produce deep resonances. It is native to the Bahnar people of the central highlands, who are said to have created it after hearing the wind blowing into the openings of bamboo in the forest. Similarly, the *t'rung* is a suspended ladder of tuned bamboo pipes sounding rather like a high xylophone and popular for its ability to imitate the sound of water.

Neo-traditional Music

Turn on the television during the Tet Lunar New Year festivities and you can't miss the public face of Vietnamese traditional music: ethnic-costumed dancers, musicians and singers smilingly portraying the happy life of the worker. Great arrangements of well-known tunes from all over the country, including some token minorities' music, are spiced up with fancy hats and bamboo pianos. This choreographed entertainment, known as nhac *dan toc hien dai* or modern national music, has only been "traditional" since 1956, when the Hanoi Conservatoire of Music was founded and the teaching of folk music was deliberately "improved".

For the first time, music was learned from written Western notation (leading to the neglect of improvisational skills while opening the way for huge orchestras), and conductors were employed. Tunings were tempered to accommodate Western-style harmonies, while new instruments were invented to play bass and to fill out chords in the enlarged bands. Music schools and conservatoires,

with the mandate of preserving and developing traditional music, took over from the families and professional apprenticeships which had formerly passed on the oral tradition. Trained conservatoire graduates have spread throughout the country, promoted through competitions and state-sponsored ensembles on TV, radio, and even in the lobbies of classier hotels.

The new corpus of neo-traditional music has become an emblem of national pride and scientific improvement, which, much to the chagrin of traditional musicians outside the system, is still strongly supported by the state. Vietnamese and Chinese folk tunes, melodies from the ethnic minorities, European classical symphonies and popular film tunes are all ripe fodder for the arranger's pen. Of the current group of neo-traditional bands **Thang Long**, **Phu Dong**, and **Gia Dinh "Ba Pho"** are among the most imaginative and skilled.

Pop, Rock and Fusion

The pop music scene has grown and diversified since the 1990s, as Vietnamese have become more influenced by international musical styles and trends. Sentimental ballads about love and loss dominate mainstream performances in cafes and karaoke bars, but many younger musicians are being inspired by international styles like rock, jazz, R&B and rap and are experimenting with fusions between pop and traditional musics.

The world of commercial pop is overflowing with young, glamorous (mostly female) singers vying to become the next big star. In Ho Chi Minh City, the entertainment capital, you can see singers dressed up in glitzy outfits on the back of motorbikes or diving into taxis, rushing from gig to gig. One by one they come on stage to sing one or two pop standards with the resident band before hopping down the road to repeat the routine. Many of these shows feature old favourites by the most celebrated songwriters of the previous generation like the late **Van Cao** (d. 1995), who wrote numerous love songs and also composed the national anthem, and **Trinh Cong Son** (d. 2001), the undisputed number one Vietnamese songwriter.

Trinh Cong Son first gained notoriety in the 1960s and 70s for his anti-war songs, which led to him being dubbed by Joan Baez as "the Vietnamese Bob Dylan", a label that stuck. His song "Ngu di Con" (Lullaby) about a mother mourning her soldier son, was a huge hit and sold over two million copies in Japan in 1972. At the end of the Vietnam War in 1975, he refused to escape to the US and the new Communist government forced him to work on agricultural and labour projects to help rebuild the country after the war. He returned to live in Ho Chi Minh City in 1979 and continued composing apolitical love songs and songs inspired by his love for his country until his death. Although Trinh Cong Son's songs were not permitted to be performed live until the mid-1990s, he remains Vietnam's most influential songwriter, with more than six hundred songs to his credit and many young singers have recorded new arrangements of his songs.

Of the numerous pop divas, **Hong Nhung** (Trinh Cong Son's protégée), Thanh Lam, My Linh, Tran Thu Ha and **My Tam** are some of the most famous. While the singing style of these divas is strongly influenced by Western pop, many have also drawn on traditional styles. **Thanh Lam**, who also plays the pear-shaped lute the *ty ba*, uses traditional vocal colours and techniques in her collaborations with Quoc Trung and Le Minh Son, two of the leading young composers who draw on traditional music in their songs. **My Linh**'s recordings of songs by Pho Duc Phuong, a pioneer of East-West fusions, are influenced by the highly ornamented style of ca tru, and **Tran Thu Ha** became famous for her distinctive style of singing and for the use of daring, sexy lyrics on **Ngoc Dai**'s controversial album *Nhat Thuc* (Solar Eclipse). Alongside moves to make pop songs sound more Vietnamese, some young divas, notably **Thanh Thao**, have been modernizing pop by using hip-hop beats and working with rappers. **Rap** is a new trend in Vietnam, and artists including Phong Dat, Tien Dat, Lil' Knight and Young Uno have a growing underground following.

Since the late 1990s there has been a **Vietnamese rock** revolution, largely supported by forward-looking Vietnamese youth hungry for an alternative to mainstream love songs. The most successful rock bands are **Buc Tuong** (The Wall), **Anh Sang** (The Light), **Gat Tan Day** (Full Ashtray) and **Da Vang** (Yellow Skin). These bands sing in both Vietnamese and English, and although their music is quite derivative of classic Western rock and heavy-metal groups like Pink Floyd and Metallica, it also has a distinctive Vietnamese twist. On Buc Tuong's best-selling album *Vo Hinh* (Invisible), for instance, riffs on the two-stringed moon-lute and rhythms on traditional drums can be heard alongside electric-guitar power-chords, while the lyrics combine folk legends with commentary on the rapid social changes and consumerism that are affecting Vietnamese society.

Popular music inside Vietnam is being influenced by the cultural flow between Vietnam and the **Vietnamese diaspora**, particularly the large communities living in the US and France. The first pop star to return to Vietnam was the US-based crooner **Jimmy J.C. Nguyen**, who caused a flurry of interest when he toured in the mid-1990s, and since then numerous pop and rap artists from California have performed in Vietnam. In France, the jazz guitarist **Nguyên Lê**, who works with the singer **Huong Thanh**, has been at the forefront of Vietnamese-influenced world music with albums combining traditional songs with jazz and other sounds from around the world.

Guitarist Nguyên Lê and singer Huong Thanh

⭐ **Mother Mountain and Father Sea**
White Cliffs Media, US

An excellent six-disc box-set that introduces a wide selection of Vietnamese music. The set is organized geographically, with five of the CDs focusing on the distinctive musical traditions from different regions, and the sixth covers religious and ritual music from across the country. A superb 48-page booklet gives an informative description of the forms and styles.

⊙ **Music from Vietnam Vols 1, 2, 3, and 5**
Caprice, Sweden

Volume 1 makes a good introduction (in conservatoire style) to traditional music, also featuring *quan ho* folksongs, cai luong and cheo theatre, chau van possession ritual and new folk. On Volume 2, three local instrumental and vocal groups give the enticing flavour of the city of Hue, featuring Nguyen Manh Cam, former drummer to the emperor. Volumes 3 and 5 focus on the astonishing musical traditions of the minority cultures residing in the centre and north. Volume 3 includes music of the E-de, Nung, Muong and Hmong, with wonderful pipes, flutes, mouth-organs and songs. The fifth volume features music from the central highlands and coast, including music of gong chime ensembles of the Bahnar and Giarai, and the drum and oboe music of the Cham people. The fourth volume, listed below, features the music of Kim Sinh.

⊙ **The Music of Vietnam**
Rounder, US

Double CD in Rounder's reissued Anthology of World Music series. The first disc covers court theatrical and ritual music, while the second really hots up with drumming and chamber music – a welcome antidote to today's conservatoire-dominated style. While more recent releases outdo this set in terms of sound quality, these early 1970s recordings preserve the subtlest nuances of phrasing.

⭐ **Musiques des Montagnards**
Chant du Monde, France

Two CDs of extraordinary archival and modern recordings from the central and northern highlands. Fourteen ethnic groups are covered and excellently described in the copious booklet.

⊙ **Stilling Time: Traditional Musics of Vietnam**
Innova, US

A sampler of field recordings from all over Vietnam, including songs and gong music of the ethnic minorities, as well as nhac tai tu and the only Phu Dong recordings to be found on CD. An introduction to the many surprises in store for the musical traveller.

⊙ **Vocal Music from the Northern Plains**
VDE /Gallo, Switzerland

A fresh recording of several ca tru, cheo and quan ho songs, notable for the enchanting cheo singing by Huong Thanh and performances by young ca tru singers.

Theatrical Music

⊙ **Court Theatre Music: Hat Boi**
Audivis/Unesco, France

Hat boi (known as hat tuong in northern Vietnam) shares many conventions with Chinese opera, especially vocal styles, costumes and gestures. But the essence of Vietnam can be heard in the details: spirited ken (oboe) wailing and invigorating use of the trong chien battle drum. Much is lost by not seeing a performance, but the music, the thorough liner notes, and the general air of antiquity help the imagination along.

⊙ **Vietnamese Folk Theatre: Hat Cheo**
King, Japan

A generous quantity of cheo theatre, expertly played by the Quy Bon family and recorded in Hanoi. Features a chau van performance of music from possession ritual and the famous story of the cross-dressing Thi Mau going to a temple.

Ritual, Folk and Chamber Music

⊙ **Ca Tru and Quan Ho**
Audivis/Unesco, France

Unique and fascinating recordings of the chamber-music genre ca tru and the quan ho folk-songs made by the eminent scholar Tran Van Khe in Hanoi in 1976, shortly after the end of the Vietnam War.

⊙ **Ca Tru: The Music of North Vietnam**
Nimbus, UK

A recording by the best exponents of ca tru today, the Ca Tru Thai Ha Ensemble. The disc features exhilarating, highly ornamented singing by Nguyen Thuy Hoa and Thanh Hoai, with sensitive accompaniments by Nguyen Manh Tien on the three-stringed lute (dan day) and Nguyen Van Mui on the "praise drum" (trong chau).

⊙ **Vietnam: Buddhist Music from Hue**
Inédit, France

An atmospheric recording, full of ceremonial presence. It begins with sonorous drums and bells before two oboes come in for music marking the ascent to the "Esplanade of Heaven". Features the complete ceremony of Khai Kinh, "Opening the Sacred Texts", recorded in the Kim Tien Pagoda in Hue. This sort of religious music does not make for easy listening on CD, but is nevertheless impressive, with rich vocals, drums, bells and strings.

⊙ **Vietnam: Traditions of the South**
Audivis/Unesco, France

Southern ritual music from the eclectic Cao Dai, Buddhist, and indigenous spirit-possession religions, as well as a good helping of traditional cai luong theatre music.

Kim Sinh

Kim Sinh (b. 1930) is a blind singer and guitarist, with something of a cult international following (including Ry Cooder). Based in Hanoi, he has performed and taught in Vietnam for many years and came to international attention in the 1990s with his virtuosic displays of many styles from cai luong to Hawaiian guitar.

⊙ **The Art of Kim Sinh**
King, Japan

Released in 1993, this disc influenced a whole generation of young Californian guitarists and one struggles not to draw

VIETNAM

comparisons with the blues. The Vietnamese guitar has the fret board hollowed out to enable the pitch bends and slides that are so integral to Vietnamese music.

⭐ Music from Vietnam Vol. 4: The Artistry of Kim Sinh
Caprice, Sweden

This features studio performances recorded in 2001 on the Vietnamese guitar, Hawaiian guitar and moon lute, with accompaniment provided by his son, Kim Tanh.

Le Tuan Hung

Australian-based Le Tuan Hung is an expert dan tranh zither musician rooted in the nhac tai tu tradition, who has been pushing the boundaries with his output of contemporary compositions and multi-cultural collaborations combining Vietnamese instruments with Balinese flutes, Japanese bells and electronics.

⭐ Echoes of Ancestral Voices: Traditional Music of Vietnam
Move, Australia

No flashy displays here, in performances with his wife Dang Kim Hien, just a fragile, uncompromising intensity. Hien's unearthly lullabies and elegant nhac tai tu duos using delicious microtones make this one of the most worthwhile discs of the traditional repertoire.

Nguyen Vinh Bao

Nguyen Vinh Bao (b. 1917) is recognised as a master musician, arguably the greatest living exponent of nhac tai tu, who has dedicated his life to refining his playing of the zither (dan tranh) and other strings. He taught at the Saigon National Conservatory from 1955 to 1964 and during a year's residence at an American University in the 1970s made a significant contribution to scholarly work on modal theory.

⊙ Nguyen Vinh Bao Ensemble
Ocora, France

This showcases the master's authoritative artistry in pure form, undiluted by gimmicks.

Tran Van Khe

Born in 1921 in southern Vietnam into a family of traditional musicians, Tran Van Khe studied musicology in Paris and was director of research at the Centre National de la Recherche Scientifique (CNRS) for many years. He has published numerous books and articles on Vietnamese music and is a distinguished performer of southern chamber music.

⊙ Vietnam: Improvisations
Ocora, France

Tran Van Khe teams up with his son Tran Quang Hai with modern interpretations and improvisations using traditional modes.

⊙ Vietnam: Poésies et Chants
Ocora, France

Tran Van Khe and friends chant poetry and ravish the zither and moon lute in the nhac tai tu repertory. Intimate performances backed up by excellent notes and translations.

Neo-traditional Music

Gia Dinh "Ba Pho"

The acclaimed multi-instrumentalist Ba Pho honed his musical skills at the Central Music and Dance Troupe in Hanoi. In the 1990s he formed his own group, the "Ba Pho Family", with Mai Lien, his wife, Ba Nha, his son, and the bamboo flute specialist Le Tuan Tu, all of whom were trained in neo-traditional music at the Hanoi Music Conservatoire.

⊙ Homeland (Que Huong)
Dunya, Italy

This international release from the talented Ba Pho "family" is a well-executed compilation of neo-traditional and folk music (with a Trinh Cong Son song thrown in for good measure).

Khac Chi Ensemble

Ho Khac Chi (b. 1950) is a virtuoso of the dan bau. Educated in the Hanoi Music Conservatoire, he started the Khac Chi Ensemble in 1982 and moved to Canada ten years later. The group now includes his wife Hoang Ngoc Bich, Le To Quyen (vocals) and Nguyen Hoai Chau (percussion).

⊙ Moonlight in Vietnam
Rounder/Henry Street, US

Accomplished performances of neo-traditional music on the monochord (dan bau) and on instruments adopted from ethnic minority groups such as the k'longput, t'rung and a stick fiddle with a resonating disc held in the player's mouth.

Pop, Rock and Fusion

⭐ Hò! Roady Music from Vietnam
Trikont, Germany

A brilliant idea – crass, funky street music from Vietnam taken from popular cassettes and recorded in situ with mopeds and car horns as part of the soundscape. It opens in cracking style with a plucked dan bau playing "Riders in the Sky" with what sounds like fireworks as backing. There's a wild funeral brass band (a touch of India here) and all sorts of surprises.

Buc Tuong (The Wall)

Graduates from a Hanoi construction college, Buc Tuong started performing professionally in 1998 and have become the most famous Vietnamese rock group. Their success has been masterminded by their songwriter and vocalist Tran Lap who has a knack of capturing the spirit of the moment with songs about social issues, love and national tragedy.

⊙ Vo Hinh (Invisible)
Dihavina, Vietnam

Check this out if you want to know what Vietnamese youth are getting excited about. Highlights include "Bai Ca Song Hong" (Red River Song), which begins with a moon-lute solo before the power chords take over.

Ngoc Dai

Ngoc Dai is a Hanoi-based pianist, composer and producer. He is a leading light of the contemporary popular music scene and his songwriting style combines interests in technology, jazz, rock and traditional musics.

⊙ Nhat Thuc (Solar Eclipse)
Phuong Nam Phim, Vietnam

This disc caused a storm of controversy on its release in 2001, due to its challenging mix of electronic and traditionally-inflected pop songs performed by diva Tran Thu Ha and off-stage wrangling over the use and crediting of risqué poems by Vi Thuy Linh as lyrics.

Nguyên Lê

The jazz guitarist Nguyên Lê's quest to unite Vietnamese traditional song with the global musicians of his Paris milieu has resulted in half a dozen albums fronted by the singer Huong Thanh. His projects draw liberally on different cultural influences, reflecting his philosophical approach to world music. "Let us redefine world music", he says, "as the new identity the children of the diaspora are building between the streams of today and the search for the deepest tradition."

WITH HUONG THANH

 Fragile Beauty
ACT, France

This inspiring 2008 album, which blends Vietnamese traditional song with jazz harmonies, draws inspiration from Buddhist-influenced images often found in Vietnamese poetry.

⊙ Moon and Wind
ACT, France

Huong Thanh sets out her store with an album of classic traditional songs set to jazz- and world-influenced arrangements.

Quoc Trung

Quoc Trung made a name for himself in the 1990s as one of the leading producers in Vietnam, especially for his work with the band Phuong Dong (The Orient) featuring the diva Thanh Lam. Since then he has developed his musical style by mixing electronic and dance music with traditional influences.

⊙ The Road to Infinity (Duong Xa Van Dam)
APE, Vietnam

In this innovative 2005 release, Quoc Trung creates a sonorous soundscape through a fusion of electronic beats and traditional melodies performed by excellent musicians such as the singer Thanh Hoai and the multi-instrumentalist Xuan Dieu.

Thu Hien

Along with ca Hue singer Ai Hue, Thu Hien is never far away from any visitor in Hue who shows an interest in local music – and she offers performances in your hotel or on a boat trip.

⊙ Ai Ra Xu Hue
Hue, Vietnam

The perfumed voice of Thu Hien singing the mellowest Hue pop music.

PLAYLIST
Vietnam

1 **LY CONG TRANG (LY TU DIA) AND VONG CO Kim Sinh** from *Music from Vietnam 4: The Artistry of Kim Sinh*
A dazzling display of classic nhac tai tu by the legendary lutenist and guitarist Kim Sinh.

2 **FRAGILE BEAUTY Nguyên Lê and Huong Thanh** from *Fragile Beauty*
A sensitive jazz- and world-influenced arrangement of a Vietnamese song, which deftly encapsulates Buddhist-inspired sentiments.

3 **TREN DINH PHU VAN My Linh** from *Huyen Thoai Ho Nui Coc*
Ca tru-inspired vocalizing by diva My Linh of a classic song by Pho Duc Phuong.

4 **CANNON FIRE LULLS THE NIGHT Tran Duy Tinh** from *A Tribute to Trinh Cong Son*
Unplugged vocal and acoustic-guitar rendition of an anti-war song by Trinh Cong Son.

5 **MUOU AND HAT NOI Quach Thi Ho** from *Ca Tru and Quan Ho*
The sound of the past in this seminal 1970s recording of the unforgettable Quach Thi Ho, the late queen of ca tru singing.

6 **ALTERNATING SONG Ly Ta May, Cha Ta May and Li Se Co** from *Music of the Montagnards of Northern Vietnam*
Haunting, fragile polyphony and dexterous verbal exchange about longing and love by Hani singers from the northern Lao Cai province.

7 **VC'S BLUES V.C. Hooker** from *Hò! Roady Music from Vietnam*
A raw street-recording of distorted, amplified guitar and vocals performed by an itinerant blind musician. A form of Vietnamese blues.

8 **LITHOPHONE FROM NDUT LIENG KRAK Jean Schwarz** from *Mnong Gar Music from Vietnam*
A new piece performed on an ancient stone instrument, the lithophone, discovered in the central highlands and now in the Musée de l'Homme in Paris. The oldest rock music in the world.

INTRIGUED, INSPIRED, BEMUSED... BY WORLD MUSIC?

"Songlines is a cracking way into the wide world of music"
Andy Kershaw

YOU NEED SONGLINES MAGAZINE

SONGLINES MUSIC TRAVEL

Introducing *Songlines Music Travel* – from the experts behind the UK's best magazine covering music from around the world.

'I had expected good sounds, but what I had not predicted was that we were about to get a privileged insight into a country and its culture, one that only music can provide'
Kevin Rushby in *The Guardian*
Songlines Music Travel trip to Mali, January 2009

CONTACT Visit www.songlines.co.uk/musictravel or call +44 (0)20 8505 2582 for further details

Packed full of artist interviews, CD, DVD & world cinema reviews, concert listings, travel adventures, city and beginner's guides and frontline reports, *Songlines* is *the* magazine that looks at the world through its music.

Edited by Simon Broughton, co-editor of *The Rough Guide to World Music*, each issue comes with a free, exclusive compilation CD, which features tracks from the ten best album releases, as well as a guest playlist. These have included comedian Alexei Sayle, filmmaker Wim Wenders, author Louis de Bernières and musicians Nigel Kennedy, Peter Gabriel and Kate Bush.

Music is about people, politics and places – *Songlines* is your reliable guide to it all.

NEW TO SONGLINES? Check out the free interactive sampler at www.songlines.co.uk/interactive or download our podcast through iTunes
CONTACT US To purchase the current issue or to subscribe, please visit www.songlines.co.uk or call +44 (0)20 7371 2777

A WORLD OF MUSIC FROM NONESUCH RECORDS

NESUCH

Sérgio & Odair Assad
Jardim Abandonado

Isabel Bayrakdarian
Gomidas Songs

Paolo Conte
The Best Of Paolo Conte

Ry Cooder
Chávez Ravine

Ry Cooder & Manuel Galbán
Mambo Sinuendo

Kronos Quartet
Pieces Of Africa

Kronos Quartet
Floodplain

Kronos Quartet & Asha Bhosle
You've Stolen My Heart: Songs From R.D. Burman's Bollywood

Youssou N'Dour
Egypt

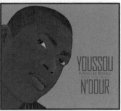

Youssou N'Dour
Rokku Mi Rokka

Fernando Otero
Pagina De Buenos Aires

Astor Piazzolla
Tango: Zero Hour

Rokia Traoré
Tchamantché

Nonesuch Explorer Series
Shakuhachi: The Japanese Flute

Plus many more **Explorer Series** titles
from Africa, America, Europe & Asia

WWW.NONESUCH.COM

NONESUCH

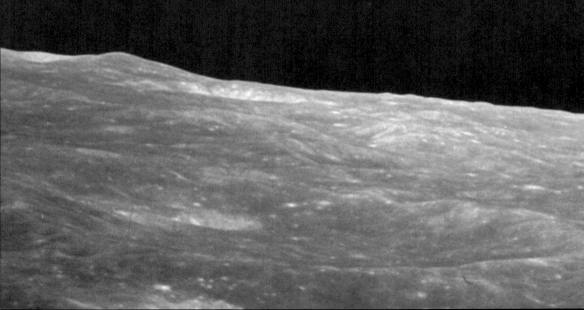

BEAUTIFUL TO LOOK AT

REAL W

WONDERFUL TO HEAR

REALWORLD RECORDS
THE SOUNDS OUR PLANET MAKES

WWW.REALWORLDRECORDS.COM

Travel

Andorra The Pyrenees, Pyrenees & Andorra Map, Spain

Antigua Antigua & Barbuda DIR, The Caribbean

Argentina Argentina, Argentina Map, Buenos Aires, South America on a Budget

Aruba The Caribbean

Australia Australia, Australia Map, East Coast Australia, Melbourne, Sydney, Tasmania

Austria Austria, Europe on a Budget, Vienna

Bahamas The Bahamas, The Caribbean

Barbados Barbados DIR, The Caribbean

Belgium Belgium & Luxembourg, Bruges DIR, Brussels, Brussels Map, Europe on a Budget

Belize Belize, Central America on a Budget, Guatemala & Belize Map

Benin West Africa

Bolivia Bolivia, South America on a Budget

Brazil Brazil, Rio, South America on a Budget

British Virgin Islands The Caribbean

Brunei Malaysia, Singapore & Brunei [1 title], Southeast Asia on a Budget

Bulgaria Bulgaria, Europe on a Budget

Burkina Faso West Africa

Cambodia Cambodia, Southeast Asia on a Budget, Vietnam, Laos & Cambodia Map [1 Map]

Cameroon West Africa

Canada Canada, Montréal, Pacific Northwest, Toronto, Toronto Map, Vancouver

Cape Verde West Africa

Cayman Islands The Caribbean

Chile Chile, Chile Map, South America on a Budget

China Beijing, China, Hong Kong & Macau, Hong Kong & Macau DIR, Shanghai

Colombia South America on a Budget

Costa Rica Central America on a Budget, Costa Rica, Costa Rica & Panama Map

Croatia Croatia, Croatia Map, Europe on a Budget

Cuba Cuba, Cuba Map, The Caribbean, Havana

Cyprus Cyprus, Cyprus Map

Czech Republic The Czech Republic, Czech & Slovak Republics, Europe on a Budget, Prague, Prague DIR, Prague Map

Denmark Copenhagen, Denmark, Europe on a Budget, Scandinavia

Dominica The Caribbean

Dominican Republic Dominican Republic, The Caribbean

Ecuador Ecuador, South America on a Budget

Egypt Egypt, Egypt Map

El Salvador Central America on a Budget

England Britain, Camping in Britain, Devon & Cornwall, Dorset, Hampshire and The Isle of Wight [1 title], England, Europe on a Budget, The Lake District, London, London DIR, London Map, London Mini Guide, Walks In London & Southeast England

Estonia The Baltic States, Europe on a Budget

Fiji Fiji

Finland Europe on a Budget, Finland, Scandinavia

France Brittany & Normandy, Corsica, Corsica Map, The Dordogne & the Lot, Europe on a Budget, France, France Map, Languedoc & Roussillon, The Loire Valley, Paris, Paris DIR, Paris Map, Paris Mini Guide, Provence & the Côte d'Azur, The Pyrenees, Pyrenees & Andorra Map

French Guiana South America on a Budget

Gambia The Gambia, West Africa

Germany Berlin, Berlin Map, Europe on a Budget, Germany, Germany Map

Ghana West Africa

Gibraltar Spain

Greece Athens DIR, Athens Map, Crete, Crete Map, Europe on a Budget, Greece, Greece Map, Greek Islands, Ionian Islands

Guadeloupe The Caribbean

Guatemala Central America on a Budget, Guatemala, Guatemala & Belize Map

Guinea West Africa

Guinea-Bissau West Africa

Guyana South America on a Budget

Holland see Netherlands

Honduras Central America on a Budget

Hungary Budapest, Europe on a Budget, Hungary

Iceland Iceland, Iceland Map

India Goa, India, India Map, Kerala, Rajasthan, Delhi & Agra [1 title], South India, South India Map

Indonesia Bali & Lombok, Southeast Asia on a Budget

Ireland Dublin DIR, Dublin Map, Europe on a Budget, Ireland, Ireland Map

Israel Jerusalem

Italy Europe on a Budget, Florence DIR, Florence & Siena Map, Florence & the best of Tuscany, Italy, The Italian Lakes, Naples & the Amalfi Coast, Rome, Rome DIR, Rome Map, Sardinia, Sicily, Sicily Map, Tuscany & Umbria, Tuscany Map, Venice, Venice DIR, Venice Map

Jamaica Jamaica, The Caribbean

Japan Japan, Tokyo

Jordan Jordan

Kenya Kenya, Kenya Map

Korea Korea

Laos Laos, Southeast Asia on a Budget, Vietnam, Laos & Cambodia Map [1 Map]

Latvia The Baltic States, Europe on a Budget

Lithuania The Baltic States, Europe on a Budget

Luxembourg Belgium & Luxembourg, Europe on a Budget

Malaysia Malaysia Map, Malaysia, Singapore & Brunei [1 title], Southeast Asia on a Budget

Mali West Africa

Malta Malta & Gozo DIR

Martinique The Caribbean

Mauritania West Africa

Mexico Baja California, Baja California, Cancún & Cozumel DIR, Mexico, Mexico Map, Yucatán, Yucatán Peninsula Map

Monaco France, Provence & the Côte d'Azur

Montenegro Montenegro

Morocco Europe on a Budget, Marrakesh DIR, Marrakesh Map, Morocco, Morocco Map,

Nepal Nepal

Netherlands Amsterdam, Amsterdam DIR, Amsterdam Map, Europe on a Budget, The Netherlands

Netherlands Antilles The Caribbean

DIR: Rough Guide **DIRECTIONS** for short breaks

Available from all good bookstores

Rough Guides don't just travel

For more information go to www.roughguides.com

ROUGH GUIDES

Listen Up!

"By far the most stimulating and imaginative book on the subject currently on the market . . . This is a terrific book"
Classic FM Magazine reviewing The Rough Guide to Opera

"Mind-expanding and irresistible"
Mark Ellen, The Word

THE ROUGH GUIDE book of
Playlists

5000 SONGS YOU MUST DOWNLOAD

Covers iPod touch, iPod nano,
iPod classic and iPod shuffle

MENU

THE ROUGH GUIDE to
iPods & iTunes

6TH EDITION   THE GLOBAL BESTSELLER

THE ROUGH GUIDE to
Opera

Matthew Boyden

The songs • the singers • the stories • the soul

THE ROUGH GUIDE to
Soul and R&B

Peter Shapiro

Rough Guide Music Titles

The Beatles • The Best Music You've Never Heard • Blues • Bob Dylan
Classical Music • Heavy Metal • Jimi Hendrix • iPods & iTunes
Led Zeppelin • Nirvana • Opera • Pink Floyd • Book of Playlists
The Rolling Stones • Soul and R&B • Velvet Underground • World Music

Lost classics • Hidden gems • Amazing stories

THE BEST MUSIC YOU'VE NEVER HEARD

Musical splendours off the beaten track

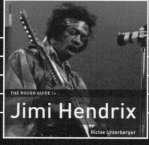

THE ROUGH GUIDE to
Jimi Hendrix

Richie Unterberger

THE ROUGH GUIDE to
Nirvana

Gillian Gaar

ROUGH GUIDES

www.roughguides.com
MAKE THE MOST OF YOUR TIME ON EARTH

Index

Aramirè 267
arbaj 690
arbeidssongar 292
Arbete och Fritid 418
Arbkornburi, "Got" Chakra-
     pand 756, 763
Arcady 237
Archie 364
Ardealul Ensemble 329
Ardijah 696
Argentina, La 392
Ari Thunda 294
Arirang 662
Ariyarathne, Sunil 739
Arkè String Quartet 593
Arkhangelsk Jazz
     Group 341
Armandinho 313
Armeanca, Dan 326
Armenulić, Silvana 43
Armstrong, Tommy 98
Arnaudov, Goce 272
Arnauth, Mafalda 314
Arnberg, Matts 418
Árni Magnússon Insti-
     tute 228
Arpeggiata, L' 267
Arsenal 341
Artemis 176
Arunachalam, Karukurichi
     P. 553
Arvanitaki, Eleftheria 180,
     186
Asakusa Jinta 643
Asanee-Wasan 761
Asano, Syo 640
Asanovi 274
Asavari, Ragini 536
Asazaki, Ikue 648, 654
Aseana Percussion Unit 678
Asher, James 120
Ashkabad 491, 493
Asian All Stars 591
Asian Dub Foundation 97,
     107, 116, 120, 590
Asian Equation/Sister
     India 117
Asian Underground 590
Asin 721, 723
askomandoúra 173
asli 672
Atalyja 31
atan 450
Atanasov, Nikolai 50
Atanasovski, Pece 271
Atari, Kohsuke 648
Atkins, Mark 456, 464
Atlan, Françoise 144, 147
Atlas, Natacha 116
Atomik harmonik 384
At-Tambur 319
Attensam Quartett 20
Attwenger 14, 15
Atxaga, Bernardo 405
Audemard, Laurent 143

Audio Active 642
Aufwind 163, 170
Aung, Dennis Mun 477
Aurelia 35
Auserón, Santiago 407
Australia 454
Austria 18
Aute, Luís Eduardo 407
Auvo Quartet 128
Avadå Band 420
Avertere 128
Aves, Bob 723
Avitabile, Enzo 264
Avleddha 257
Avsenik brothers 384
avtentichen folklor 50
Awie 677
Axelsson, Marie 418
ayai 482
Ayala, Joey 722, 723
ayaya 192
Ayivor, Kofi 282
Ayub, Mohammed 113
Azaad 113
Azala 405
Azis 54, 56, 58, 202
Azzola, Marcel 140

B

B21 117
Ba Cissoko 144
Ba Dain, Peter 476
Baalbek Festival 208
Babakhanov, Ari 492
Babić, Milovan 378
Babu, Nidhu 470
Back of the Moon 366
Bäckström, Ola 415
Bad Taste 228
bada khyal 561
Badakhshan Ensemble 492
Badev, Nikola 272
Badger, George Percy 278
Badmarsh and Shri 116
Bær, Johan Anders 352,
     354
bagad 136
Bagad Kemper 136, 147
Bagad Men Ha Tan 139
Baggili, Karim 37
Bagong Lumad 722
bagpipes 87, 139, 173,
     363, 416
Bahu, Sultan 709
baila 738
Bailardo, Ricardo 206
Bain, Aly 362, 370
Bairashev, Bolot 632
Baisha xiyue 511
Bajrami, Selma 42
Bajramović, Šaban 45, 202,
     210, 326, 376, 377, 381
Bajuk, Lidija 71, 72

Bakhshi Javed Salamat
     Ali 715
Bakić, Bakija 378
bal musette 140, 152
Bala, Adnan 6
Balachander, S. 553, 556
balada 676
Balakrishna, Khalil 591
balalaika 340
Balamuralikrishna, M. 562,
     563, 567
Balaraman 555
Balashov, Yuri 343
Balasubramaniam, S.P. 579
Baldacchino, Frans "Il-
     budaj" 278, 279
Baldrian 87
Bålgari 52
Bali Arts Festival 609
bali-balian 606
Balivala, K.M. 738
Balkan Horses 55
Balkana 52
Balkanika 380
Balkanska, Valya 51
Balkanton 54
balladar 292
ballu tundu 267
Balogh, Kálmán 223
balss 26
Baltic Crossing 88
Baltic States 22
Baltinget 88
Baluchi 199
Baluchi Ensemble of Kara-
     chi 715
balungan 599
Bambas, Las 739
Bamboche, La 139
Bamboo 722, 724
bamboo band style 681
bamboo music 683
band baajaa 689
Band de Seilhac 140
Banda 81
Banda d'En Vinaixa, La 406
Banda tis Florinas 183
Bandara, C. Don Bastian
     Jayaweera 738
banderinha 738
Banditaliana 253
bandolim 318
bandoneon 129
bandonion orchestra 160
BandonionFreunde Es-
     sen 160, 165
bandura 427, 428
bandurria 720
Bandyopadhyay, San-
     geeta 564
Banerjee, Nikhil 540, 546
Banerjee, Shubankar 182
bang dhut 618

Bangladesh 467
bani 565
Banisil, Sindao 720, 723
banjo 239
Bann, Getano 461
Bano, Iqbal 564, 703
banse 543
bånsuller 292
bansuri 540, 543, 553, 567,
     689
Bao, Nguyen Vinh 786
Bapa, Alexander 631
Bapa, Sayan 631
Baraban 259, 265
Baras, Sara 392
Barbara 153, 155
Barbería del Sur, La 398
Barbès City Limits 141
Baris 607
Bariu, Laver 7, 9
Barnes, Jim and Sylvia 365
Baro Drom 81
Barong 607
Barons, Krišjānis 26
Barouh, Pierre 154
Barovero, Fabio 254
Bärtavela 262
Bartoš, František 76
Bartoš, Július Šuka 80
Basco 88
Basnet, Kumar 691
bassu 63
Bastars Hag e Vab 139
Bastian, Voli 738
Batagov, Anton 342
Batak-house 616
Bathiya and Santhush 741
Batis 176
Batista family 385
batt kine 476
Battlefield Band 362, 363,
     365, 369
Baul, Parvathy 472
Bauls 470, 560
Baumgartner, Dallas 207
Baumgartner, Lousson 207
Bauweraerts, Jorunn 34
bayan 543
bayin 747
Bazar Blå 422
Bazurov, Boris 340, 344
Beam 95
Beamer, Mahi 528
Bécaud, Gilbert 153
Becker, Roland 136, 139,
     147
Bee, Kenny 514
beenu 700
Begin 647
Begley, Brendan and Séa-
     mus 238, 243
beguine 144
Beier, Ludovic 140
beiguan 745, 746
bel canto 152

INDEX

815